Lecture Notes in Computer Science   12362

More information about this series at http://www.springer.com/series/7412

Andrea Vedaldi · Horst Bischof ·
Thomas Brox · Jan-Michael Frahm (Eds.)

Computer Vision – ECCV 2020

16th European Conference
Glasgow, UK, August 23–28, 2020
Proceedings, Part XVII

Springer

Editors
Andrea Vedaldi 🆔
University of Oxford
Oxford, UK

Horst Bischof 🆔
Graz University of Technology
Graz, Austria

Thomas Brox 🆔
University of Freiburg
Freiburg im Breisgau, Germany

Jan-Michael Frahm
University of North Carolina at Chapel Hill
Chapel Hill, NC, USA

ISSN 0302-9743   ISSN 1611-3349   (electronic)
Lecture Notes in Computer Science
ISBN 978-3-030-58519-8   ISBN 978-3-030-58520-4   (eBook)
https://doi.org/10.1007/978-3-030-58520-4

LNCS Sublibrary: SL6 – Image Processing, Computer Vision, Pattern Recognition, and Graphics

This Springer imprint is published by the registered company Springer Nature Switzerland AG
The registered company address is: Gewerbestrasse 11, 6330 Cham, Switzerland

Foreword

Hosting the European Conference on Computer Vision (ECCV 2020) was certainly an exciting journey. From the 2016 plan to hold it at the Edinburgh International Conference Centre (hosting 1,800 delegates) to the 2018 plan to hold it at Glasgow's Scottish Exhibition Centre (up to 6,000 delegates), we finally ended with moving online because of the COVID-19 outbreak. While possibly having fewer delegates than expected because of the online format, ECCV 2020 still had over 3,100 registered participants.

Although online, the conference delivered most of the activities expected at a face-to-face conference: peer-reviewed papers, industrial exhibitors, demonstrations, and messaging between delegates. In addition to the main technical sessions, the conference included a strong program of satellite events with 16 tutorials and 44 workshops.

Furthermore, the online conference format enabled new conference features. Every paper had an associated teaser video and a longer full presentation video. Along with the papers and slides from the videos, all these materials were available the week before the conference. This allowed delegates to become familiar with the paper content and be ready for the live interaction with the authors during the conference week. The live event consisted of brief presentations by the oral and spotlight authors and industrial sponsors. Question and answer sessions for all papers were timed to occur twice so delegates from around the world had convenient access to the authors.

As with ECCV 2018, authors' draft versions of the papers appeared online with open access, now on both the Computer Vision Foundation (CVF) and the European Computer Vision Association (ECVA) websites. An archival publication arrangement was put in place with the cooperation of Springer. SpringerLink hosts the final version of the papers with further improvements, such as activating reference links and supplementary materials. These two approaches benefit all potential readers: a version available freely for all researchers, and an authoritative and citable version with additional benefits for SpringerLink subscribers. We thank Alfred Hofmann and Aliaksandr Birukou from Springer for helping to negotiate this agreement, which we expect will continue for future versions of ECCV.

August 2020

Vittorio Ferrari
Bob Fisher
Cordelia Schmid
Emanuele Trucco

Preface

Welcome to the proceedings of the European Conference on Computer Vision (ECCV 2020). This is a unique edition of ECCV in many ways. Due to the COVID-19 pandemic, this is the first time the conference was held online, in a virtual format. This was also the first time the conference relied exclusively on the Open Review platform to manage the review process. Despite these challenges ECCV is thriving. The conference received 5,150 valid paper submissions, of which 1,360 were accepted for publication (27%) and, of those, 160 were presented as spotlights (3%) and 104 as orals (2%). This amounts to more than twice the number of submissions to ECCV 2018 (2,439). Furthermore, CVPR, the largest conference on computer vision, received 5,850 submissions this year, meaning that ECCV is now 87% the size of CVPR in terms of submissions. By comparison, in 2018 the size of ECCV was only 73% of CVPR.

The review model was similar to previous editions of ECCV; in particular, it was double blind in the sense that the authors did not know the name of the reviewers and vice versa. Furthermore, each conference submission was held confidentially, and was only publicly revealed if and once accepted for publication. Each paper received at least three reviews, totalling more than 15,000 reviews. Handling the review process at this scale was a significant challenge. In order to ensure that each submission received as fair and high-quality reviews as possible, we recruited 2,830 reviewers (a 130% increase with reference to 2018) and 207 area chairs (a 60% increase). The area chairs were selected based on their technical expertise and reputation, largely among people that served as area chair in previous top computer vision and machine learning conferences (ECCV, ICCV, CVPR, NeurIPS, etc.). Reviewers were similarly invited from previous conferences. We also encouraged experienced area chairs to suggest additional chairs and reviewers in the initial phase of recruiting.

Despite doubling the number of submissions, the reviewer load was slightly reduced from 2018, from a maximum of 8 papers down to 7 (with some reviewers offering to handle 6 papers plus an emergency review). The area chair load increased slightly, from 18 papers on average to 22 papers on average.

Conflicts of interest between authors, area chairs, and reviewers were handled largely automatically by the Open Review platform via their curated list of user profiles. Many authors submitting to ECCV already had a profile in Open Review. We set a paper registration deadline one week before the paper submission deadline in order to encourage all missing authors to register and create their Open Review profiles well on time (in practice, we allowed authors to create/change papers arbitrarily until the submission deadline). Except for minor issues with users creating duplicate profiles, this allowed us to easily and quickly identify institutional conflicts, and avoid them, while matching papers to area chairs and reviewers.

Papers were matched to area chairs based on: an affinity score computed by the Open Review platform, which is based on paper titles and abstracts, and an affinity

score computed by the Toronto Paper Matching System (TPMS), which is based on the paper's full text, the area chair bids for individual papers, load balancing, and conflict avoidance. Open Review provides the program chairs a convenient web interface to experiment with different configurations of the matching algorithm. The chosen configuration resulted in about 50% of the assigned papers to be highly ranked by the area chair bids, and 50% to be ranked in the middle, with very few low bids assigned.

Assignments to reviewers were similar, with two differences. First, there was a maximum of 7 papers assigned to each reviewer. Second, area chairs recommended up to seven reviewers per paper, providing another highly-weighed term to the affinity scores used for matching.

The assignment of papers to area chairs was smooth. However, it was more difficult to find suitable reviewers for all papers. Having a ratio of 5.6 papers per reviewer with a maximum load of 7 (due to emergency reviewer commitment), which did not allow for much wiggle room in order to also satisfy conflict and expertise constraints. We received some complaints from reviewers who did not feel qualified to review specific papers and we reassigned them wherever possible. However, the large scale of the conference, the many constraints, and the fact that a large fraction of such complaints arrived very late in the review process made this process very difficult and not all complaints could be addressed.

Reviewers had six weeks to complete their assignments. Possibly due to COVID-19 or the fact that the NeurIPS deadline was moved closer to the review deadline, a record 30% of the reviews were still missing after the deadline. By comparison, ECCV 2018 experienced only 10% missing reviews at this stage of the process. In the subsequent week, area chairs chased the missing reviews intensely, found replacement reviewers in their own team, and managed to reach 10% missing reviews. Eventually, we could provide almost all reviews (more than 99.9%) with a delay of only a couple of days on the initial schedule by a significant use of emergency reviews. If this trend is confirmed, it might be a major challenge to run a smooth review process in future editions of ECCV. The community must reconsider prioritization of the time spent on paper writing (the number of submissions increased a lot despite COVID-19) and time spent on paper reviewing (the number of reviews delivered in time decreased a lot presumably due to COVID-19 or NeurIPS deadline). With this imbalance the peer-review system that ensures the quality of our top conferences may break soon.

Reviewers submitted their reviews independently. In the reviews, they had the opportunity to ask questions to the authors to be addressed in the rebuttal. However, reviewers were told not to request any significant new experiment. Using the Open Review interface, authors could provide an answer to each individual review, but were also allowed to cross-reference reviews and responses in their answers. Rather than PDF files, we allowed the use of formatted text for the rebuttal. The rebuttal and initial reviews were then made visible to all reviewers and the primary area chair for a given paper. The area chair encouraged and moderated the reviewer discussion. During the discussions, reviewers were invited to reach a consensus and possibly adjust their ratings as a result of the discussion and of the evidence in the rebuttal.

After the discussion period ended, most reviewers entered a final rating and recommendation, although in many cases this did not differ from their initial recommendation. Based on the updated reviews and discussion, the primary area chair then

made a preliminary decision to accept or reject the paper and wrote a justification for it (meta-review). Except for cases where the outcome of this process was absolutely clear (as indicated by the three reviewers and primary area chairs all recommending clear rejection), the decision was then examined and potentially challenged by a secondary area chair. This led to further discussion and overturning a small number of preliminary decisions. Needless to say, there was no in-person area chair meeting, which would have been impossible due to COVID-19.

Area chairs were invited to observe the consensus of the reviewers whenever possible and use extreme caution in overturning a clear consensus to accept or reject a paper. If an area chair still decided to do so, she/he was asked to clearly justify it in the meta-review and to explicitly obtain the agreement of the secondary area chair. In practice, very few papers were rejected after being confidently accepted by the reviewers.

This was the first time Open Review was used as the main platform to run ECCV. In 2018, the program chairs used CMT3 for the user-facing interface and Open Review internally, for matching and conflict resolution. Since it is clearly preferable to only use a single platform, this year we switched to using Open Review in full. The experience was largely positive. The platform is highly-configurable, scalable, and open source. Being written in Python, it is easy to write scripts to extract data programmatically. The paper matching and conflict resolution algorithms and interfaces are top-notch, also due to the excellent author profiles in the platform. Naturally, there were a few kinks along the way due to the fact that the ECCV Open Review configuration was created from scratch for this event and it differs in substantial ways from many other Open Review conferences. However, the Open Review development and support team did a fantastic job in helping us to get the configuration right and to address issues in a timely manner as they unavoidably occurred. We cannot thank them enough for the tremendous effort they put into this project.

Finally, we would like to thank everyone involved in making ECCV 2020 possible in these very strange and difficult times. This starts with our authors, followed by the area chairs and reviewers, who ran the review process at an unprecedented scale. The whole Open Review team (and in particular Melisa Bok, Mohit Unyal, Carlos Mondragon Chapa, and Celeste Martinez Gomez) worked incredibly hard for the entire duration of the process. We would also like to thank René Vidal for contributing to the adoption of Open Review. Our thanks also go to Laurent Charling for TPMS and to the program chairs of ICML, ICLR, and NeurIPS for cross checking double submissions. We thank the website chair, Giovanni Farinella, and the CPI team (in particular Ashley Cook, Miriam Verdon, Nicola McGrane, and Sharon Kerr) for promptly adding material to the website as needed in the various phases of the process. Finally, we thank the publication chairs, Albert Ali Salah, Hamdi Dibeklioglu, Metehan Doyran, Henry Howard-Jenkins, Victor Prisacariu, Siyu Tang, and Gul Varol, who managed to compile these substantial proceedings in an exceedingly compressed schedule. We express our thanks to the ECVA team, in particular Kristina Scherbaum for allowing open access of the proceedings. We thank Alfred Hofmann from Springer who again

serve as the publisher. Finally, we thank the other chairs of ECCV 2020, including in particular the general chairs for very useful feedback with the handling of the program.

August 2020   Andrea Vedaldi
                                                                      Horst Bischof
                                                                     Thomas Brox
                                                               Jan-Michael Frahm

Organization

General Chairs

Vittorio Ferrari	Google Research, Switzerland
Bob Fisher	University of Edinburgh, UK
Cordelia Schmid	Google and Inria, France
Emanuele Trucco	University of Dundee, UK

Program Chairs

Andrea Vedaldi	University of Oxford, UK
Horst Bischof	Graz University of Technology, Austria
Thomas Brox	University of Freiburg, Germany
Jan-Michael Frahm	University of North Carolina, USA

Industrial Liaison Chairs

Jim Ashe	University of Edinburgh, UK
Helmut Grabner	Zurich University of Applied Sciences, Switzerland
Diane Larlus	NAVER LABS Europe, France
Cristian Novotny	University of Edinburgh, UK

Local Arrangement Chairs

Yvan Petillot	Heriot-Watt University, UK
Paul Siebert	University of Glasgow, UK

Academic Demonstration Chair

Thomas Mensink	Google Research and University of Amsterdam, The Netherlands

Poster Chair

Stephen Mckenna	University of Dundee, UK

Technology Chair

Gerardo Aragon Camarasa	University of Glasgow, UK

Tutorial Chairs

Carlo Colombo	University of Florence, Italy
Sotirios Tsaftaris	University of Edinburgh, UK

Publication Chairs

Albert Ali Salah	Utrecht University, The Netherlands
Hamdi Dibeklioglu	Bilkent University, Turkey
Metehan Doyran	Utrecht University, The Netherlands
Henry Howard-Jenkins	University of Oxford, UK
Victor Adrian Prisacariu	University of Oxford, UK
Siyu Tang	ETH Zurich, Switzerland
Gul Varol	University of Oxford, UK

Website Chair

Giovanni Maria Farinella	University of Catania, Italy

Workshops Chairs

Adrien Bartoli	University of Clermont Auvergne, France
Andrea Fusiello	University of Udine, Italy

Area Chairs

Lourdes Agapito	University College London, UK
Zeynep Akata	University of Tübingen, Germany
Karteek Alahari	Inria, France
Antonis Argyros	University of Crete, Greece
Hossein Azizpour	KTH Royal Institute of Technology, Sweden
Joao P. Barreto	Universidade de Coimbra, Portugal
Alexander C. Berg	University of North Carolina at Chapel Hill, USA
Matthew B. Blaschko	KU Leuven, Belgium
Lubomir D. Bourdev	WaveOne, Inc., USA
Edmond Boyer	Inria, France
Yuri Boykov	University of Waterloo, Canada
Gabriel Brostow	University College London, UK
Michael S. Brown	National University of Singapore, Singapore
Jianfei Cai	Monash University, Australia
Barbara Caputo	Politecnico di Torino, Italy
Ayan Chakrabarti	Washington University, St. Louis, USA
Tat-Jen Cham	Nanyang Technological University, Singapore
Manmohan Chandraker	University of California, San Diego, USA
Rama Chellappa	Johns Hopkins University, USA
Liang-Chieh Chen	Google, USA

Timothy Hospedales	University of Edinburgh and Samsung, UK
Gang Hua	Wormpex AI Research, USA
Slobodan Ilic	Siemens AG, Germany
Hiroshi Ishikawa	Waseda University, Japan
Jiaya Jia	The Chinese University of Hong Kong, SAR China
Hailin Jin	Adobe Research, USA
Justin Johnson	University of Michigan, USA
Frederic Jurie	University of Caen Normandie, France
Fredrik Kahl	Chalmers University, Sweden
Sing Bing Kang	Zillow, USA
Gunhee Kim	Seoul National University, South Korea
Junmo Kim	Korea Advanced Institute of Science and Technology, South Korea
Tae-Kyun Kim	Imperial College London, UK
Ron Kimmel	Technion-Israel Institute of Technology, Israel
Alexander Kirillov	Facebook AI Research, USA
Kris Kitani	Carnegie Mellon University, USA
Iasonas Kokkinos	Ariel AI, UK
Vladlen Koltun	Intel Labs, USA
Nikos Komodakis	Ecole des Ponts ParisTech, France
Piotr Koniusz	Australian National University, Australia
M. Pawan Kumar	University of Oxford, UK
Kyros Kutulakos	University of Toronto, Canada
Christoph Lampert	IST Austria, Austria
Ivan Laptev	Inria, France
Diane Larlus	NAVER LABS Europe, France
Laura Leal-Taixe	Technical University Munich, Germany
Honglak Lee	Google and University of Michigan, USA
Joon-Young Lee	Adobe Research, USA
Kyoung Mu Lee	Seoul National University, South Korea
Seungyong Lee	POSTECH, South Korea
Yong Jae Lee	University of California, Davis, USA
Bastian Leibe	RWTH Aachen University, Germany
Victor Lempitsky	Samsung, Russia
Ales Leonardis	University of Birmingham, UK
Marius Leordeanu	Institute of Mathematics of the Romanian Academy, Romania
Vincent Lepetit	ENPC ParisTech, France
Hongdong Li	The Australian National University, Australia
Xi Li	Zhejiang University, China
Yin Li	University of Wisconsin-Madison, USA
Zicheng Liao	Zhejiang University, China
Jongwoo Lim	Hanyang University, South Korea
Stephen Lin	Microsoft Research Asia, China
Yen-Yu Lin	National Chiao Tung University, Taiwan, China
Zhe Lin	Adobe Research, USA

Haibin Ling	Stony Brooks, State University of New York, USA
Jiaying Liu	Peking University, China
Ming-Yu Liu	NVIDIA, USA
Si Liu	Beihang University, China
Xiaoming Liu	Michigan State University, USA
Huchuan Lu	Dalian University of Technology, China
Simon Lucey	Carnegie Mellon University, USA
Jiebo Luo	University of Rochester, USA
Julien Mairal	Inria, France
Michael Maire	University of Chicago, USA
Subhransu Maji	University of Massachusetts, Amherst, USA
Yasushi Makihara	Osaka University, Japan
Jiri Matas	Czech Technical University in Prague, Czech Republic
Yasuyuki Matsushita	Osaka University, Japan
Philippos Mordohai	Stevens Institute of Technology, USA
Vittorio Murino	University of Verona, Italy
Naila Murray	NAVER LABS Europe, France
Hajime Nagahara	Osaka University, Japan
P. J. Narayanan	International Institute of Information Technology (IIIT), Hyderabad, India
Nassir Navab	Technical University of Munich, Germany
Natalia Neverova	Facebook AI Research, France
Matthias Niessner	Technical University of Munich, Germany
Jean-Marc Odobez	Idiap Research Institute and Swiss Federal Institute of Technology Lausanne, Switzerland
Francesca Odone	Università di Genova, Italy
Takeshi Oishi	The University of Tokyo, Tokyo Institute of Technology, Japan
Vicente Ordonez	University of Virginia, USA
Manohar Paluri	Facebook AI Research, USA
Maja Pantic	Imperial College London, UK
In Kyu Park	Inha University, South Korea
Ioannis Patras	Queen Mary University of London, UK
Patrick Perez	Valeo, France
Bryan A. Plummer	Boston University, USA
Thomas Pock	Graz University of Technology, Austria
Marc Pollefeys	ETH Zurich and Microsoft MR & AI Zurich Lab, Switzerland
Jean Ponce	Inria, France
Gerard Pons-Moll	MPII, Saarland Informatics Campus, Germany
Jordi Pont-Tuset	Google, Switzerland
James Matthew Rehg	Georgia Institute of Technology, USA
Ian Reid	University of Adelaide, Australia
Olaf Ronneberger	DeepMind London, UK
Stefan Roth	TU Darmstadt, Germany
Bryan Russell	Adobe Research, USA

Mathieu Salzmann	EPFL, Switzerland
Dimitris Samaras	Stony Brook University, USA
Imari Sato	National Institute of Informatics (NII), Japan
Yoichi Sato	The University of Tokyo, Japan
Torsten Sattler	Czech Technical University in Prague, Czech Republic
Daniel Scharstein	Middlebury College, USA
Bernt Schiele	MPII, Saarland Informatics Campus, Germany
Julia A. Schnabel	King's College London, UK
Nicu Sebe	University of Trento, Italy
Greg Shakhnarovich	Toyota Technological Institute at Chicago, USA
Humphrey Shi	University of Oregon, USA
Jianbo Shi	University of Pennsylvania, USA
Jianping Shi	SenseTime, China
Leonid Sigal	University of British Columbia, Canada
Cees Snoek	University of Amsterdam, The Netherlands
Richard Souvenir	Temple University, USA
Hao Su	University of California, San Diego, USA
Akihiro Sugimoto	National Institute of Informatics (NII), Japan
Jian Sun	Megvii Technology, China
Jian Sun	Xi'an Jiaotong University, China
Chris Sweeney	Facebook Reality Labs, USA
Yu-wing Tai	Kuaishou Technology, China
Chi-Keung Tang	The Hong Kong University of Science and Technology, SAR China
Radu Timofte	ETH Zurich, Switzerland
Sinisa Todorovic	Oregon State University, USA
Giorgos Tolias	Czech Technical University in Prague, Czech Republic
Carlo Tomasi	Duke University, USA
Tatiana Tommasi	Politecnico di Torino, Italy
Lorenzo Torresani	Facebook AI Research and Dartmouth College, USA
Alexander Toshev	Google, USA
Zhuowen Tu	University of California, San Diego, USA
Tinne Tuytelaars	KU Leuven, Belgium
Jasper Uijlings	Google, Switzerland
Nuno Vasconcelos	University of California, San Diego, USA
Olga Veksler	University of Waterloo, Canada
Rene Vidal	Johns Hopkins University, USA
Gang Wang	Alibaba Group, China
Jingdong Wang	Microsoft Research Asia, China
Yizhou Wang	Peking University, China
Lior Wolf	Facebook AI Research and Tel Aviv University, Israel
Jianxin Wu	Nanjing University, China
Tao Xiang	University of Surrey, UK
Saining Xie	Facebook AI Research, USA
Ming-Hsuan Yang	University of California at Merced and Google, USA
Ruigang Yang	University of Kentucky, USA

Kwang Moo Yi	University of Victoria, Canada	
Zhaozheng Yin	Stony Brook, State University of New York, USA	
Chang D. Yoo	Korea Advanced Institute of Science and Technology, South Korea	
Shaodi You	University of Amsterdam, The Netherlands	
Jingyi Yu	ShanghaiTech University, China	
Stella Yu	University of California, Berkeley, and ICSI, USA	
Stefanos Zafeiriou	Imperial College London, UK	
Hongbin Zha	Peking University, China	
Tianzhu Zhang	University of Science and Technology of China, China	
Liang Zheng	Australian National University, Australia	
Todd E. Zickler	Harvard University, USA	
Andrew Zisserman	University of Oxford, UK	

Technical Program Committee

Sathyanarayanan N. Aakur	Samuel Albanie	Pablo Arbelaez
Wael Abd Almgaeed	Shadi Albarqouni	Shervin Ardeshir
Abdelrahman Abdelhamed	Cenek Albl	Sercan O. Arik
Abdullah Abuolaim	Hassan Abu Alhaija	Anil Armagan
Supreeth Achar	Daniel Aliaga	Anurag Arnab
Hanno Ackermann	Mohammad S. Aliakbarian	Chetan Arora
Ehsan Adeli	Rahaf Aljundi	Federica Arrigoni
Triantafyllos Afouras	Thiemo Alldieck	Mathieu Aubry
Sameer Agarwal	Jon Almazan	Shai Avidan
Aishwarya Agrawal	Jose M. Alvarez	Angelica I. Aviles-Rivero
Harsh Agrawal	Senjian An	Yannis Avrithis
Pulkit Agrawal	Saket Anand	Ismail Ben Ayed
Antonio Agudo	Codruta Ancuti	Shekoofeh Azizi
Eirikur Agustsson	Cosmin Ancuti	Ioan Andrei Bârsan
Karim Ahmed	Peter Anderson	Artem Babenko
Byeongjoo Ahn	Juan Andrade-Cetto	Deepak Babu Sam
Unaiza Ahsan	Alexander Andreopoulos	Seung-Hwan Baek
Thalaiyasingam Ajanthan	Misha Andriluka	Seungryul Baek
Kenan E. Ak	Dragomir Anguelov	Andrew D. Bagdanov
Emre Akbas	Rushil Anirudh	Shai Bagon
Naveed Akhtar	Michel Antunes	Yuval Bahat
Derya Akkaynak	Oisin Mac Aodha	Junjie Bai
Yagiz Aksoy	Srikar Appalaraju	Song Bai
Ziad Al-Halah	Relja Arandjelovic	Xiang Bai
Xavier Alameda-Pineda	Nikita Araslanov	Yalong Bai
Jean-Baptiste Alayrac	Andre Araujo	Yancheng Bai
	Helder Araujo	Peter Bajcsy
		Slawomir Bak

Mahsa Baktashmotlagh
Kavita Bala
Yogesh Balaji
Guha Balakrishnan
V. N. Balasubramanian
Federico Baldassarre
Vassileios Balntas
Shurjo Banerjee
Aayush Bansal
Ankan Bansal
Jianmin Bao
Linchao Bao
Wenbo Bao
Yingze Bao
Akash Bapat
Md Jawadul Hasan Bappy
Fabien Baradel
Lorenzo Baraldi
Daniel Barath
Adrian Barbu
Kobus Barnard
Nick Barnes
Francisco Barranco
Jonathan T. Barron
Arslan Basharat
Chaim Baskin
Anil S. Baslamisli
Jorge Batista
Kayhan Batmanghelich
Konstantinos Batsos
David Bau
Luis Baumela
Christoph Baur
Eduardo
    Bayro-Corrochano
Paul Beardsley
Jan Bednavr'ik
Oscar Beijbom
Philippe Bekaert
Esube Bekele
Vasileios Belagiannis
Ohad Ben-Shahar
Abhijit Bendale
Róger Bermúdez-Chacón
Maxim Berman
Jesus Bermudez-cameo

Florian Bernard
Stefano Berretti
Marcelo Bertalmio
Gedas Bertasius
Cigdem Beyan
Lucas Beyer
Vijayakumar Bhagavatula
Arjun Nitin Bhagoji
Apratim Bhattacharyya
Binod Bhattarai
Sai Bi
Jia-Wang Bian
Simone Bianco
Adel Bibi
Tolga Birdal
Tom Bishop
Soma Biswas
Mårten Björkman
Volker Blanz
Vishnu Boddeti
Navaneeth Bodla
Simion-Vlad Bogolin
Xavier Boix
Piotr Bojanowski
Timo Bolkart
Guido Borghi
Larbi Boubchir
Guillaume Bourmaud
Adrien Bousseau
Thierry Bouwmans
Richard Bowden
Hakan Boyraz
Mathieu Brédif
Samarth Brahmbhatt
Steve Branson
Nikolas Brasch
Biagio Brattoli
Ernesto Brau
Toby P. Breckon
Francois Bremond
Jesus Briales
Sofia Broomé
Marcus A. Brubaker
Luc Brun
Silvia Bucci
Shyamal Buch

Pradeep Buddharaju
Uta Buechler
Mai Bui
Tu Bui
Adrian Bulat
Giedrius T. Burachas
Elena Burceanu
Xavier P. Burgos-Artizzu
Kaylee Burns
Andrei Bursuc
Benjamin Busam
Wonmin Byeon
Zoya Bylinskii
Sergi Caelles
Jianrui Cai
Minjie Cai
Yujun Cai
Zhaowei Cai
Zhipeng Cai
Juan C. Caicedo
Simone Calderara
Necati Cihan Camgoz
Dylan Campbell
Octavia Camps
Jiale Cao
Kaidi Cao
Liangliang Cao
Xiangyong Cao
Xiaochun Cao
Yang Cao
Yu Cao
Yue Cao
Zhangjie Cao
Luca Carlone
Mathilde Caron
Dan Casas
Thomas J. Cashman
Umberto Castellani
Lluis Castrejon
Jacopo Cavazza
Fabio Cermelli
Hakan Cevikalp
Menglei Chai
Ishani Chakraborty
Rudrasis Chakraborty
Antoni B. Chan

Kwok-Ping Chan
Siddhartha Chandra
Sharat Chandran
Arjun Chandrasekaran
Angel X. Chang
Che-Han Chang
Hong Chang
Hyun Sung Chang
Hyung Jin Chang
Jianlong Chang
Ju Yong Chang
Ming-Ching Chang
Simyung Chang
Xiaojun Chang
Yu-Wei Chao
Devendra S. Chaplot
Arslan Chaudhry
Rizwan A. Chaudhry
Can Chen
Chang Chen
Chao Chen
Chen Chen
Chu-Song Chen
Dapeng Chen
Dong Chen
Dongdong Chen
Guanying Chen
Hongge Chen
Hsin-yi Chen
Huaijin Chen
Hwann-Tzong Chen
Jianbo Chen
Jianhui Chen
Jiansheng Chen
Jiaxin Chen
Jie Chen
Jun-Cheng Chen
Kan Chen
Kevin Chen
Lin Chen
Long Chen
Min-Hung Chen
Qifeng Chen
Shi Chen
Shixing Chen
Tianshui Chen

Weifeng Chen
Weikai Chen
Xi Chen
Xiaohan Chen
Xiaozhi Chen
Xilin Chen
Xingyu Chen
Xinlei Chen
Xinyun Chen
Yi-Ting Chen
Yilun Chen
Ying-Cong Chen
Yinpeng Chen
Yiran Chen
Yu Chen
Yu-Sheng Chen
Yuhua Chen
Yun-Chun Chen
Yunpeng Chen
Yuntao Chen
Zhuoyuan Chen
Zitian Chen
Anchieh Cheng
Bowen Cheng
Erkang Cheng
Gong Cheng
Guangliang Cheng
Jingchun Cheng
Jun Cheng
Li Cheng
Ming-Ming Cheng
Yu Cheng
Ziang Cheng
Anoop Cherian
Dmitry Chetverikov
Ngai-man Cheung
William Cheung
Ajad Chhatkuli
Naoki Chiba
Benjamin Chidester
Han-pang Chiu
Mang Tik Chiu
Wei-Chen Chiu
Donghyeon Cho
Hojin Cho
Minsu Cho

Nam Ik Cho
Tim Cho
Tae Eun Choe
Chiho Choi
Edward Choi
Inchang Choi
Jinsoo Choi
Jonghyun Choi
Jongwon Choi
Yukyung Choi
Hisham Cholakkal
Eunji Chong
Jaegul Choo
Christopher Choy
Hang Chu
Peng Chu
Wen-Sheng Chu
Albert Chung
Joon Son Chung
Hai Ci
Safa Cicek
Ramazan G. Cinbis
Arridhana Ciptadi
Javier Civera
James J. Clark
Ronald Clark
Felipe Codevilla
Michael Cogswell
Andrea Cohen
Maxwell D. Collins
Carlo Colombo
Yang Cong
Adria R. Continente
Marcella Cornia
John Richard Corring
Darren Cosker
Dragos Costea
Garrison W. Cottrell
Florent Couzinie-Devy
Marco Cristani
Ioana Croitoru
James L. Crowley
Jiequan Cui
Zhaopeng Cui
Ross Cutler
Antonio D'Innocente

Rozenn Dahyot
Bo Dai
Dengxin Dai
Hang Dai
Longquan Dai
Shuyang Dai
Xiyang Dai
Yuchao Dai
Adrian V. Dalca
Dima Damen
Bharath B. Damodaran
Kristin Dana
Martin Danelljan
Zheng Dang
Zachary Alan Daniels
Donald G. Dansereau
Abhishek Das
Samyak Datta
Achal Dave
Titas De
Rodrigo de Bem
Teo de Campos
Raoul de Charette
Shalini De Mello
Joseph DeGol
Herve Delingette
Haowen Deng
Jiankang Deng
Weijian Deng
Zhiwei Deng
Joachim Denzler
Konstantinos G. Derpanis
Aditya Deshpande
Frederic Devernay
Somdip Dey
Arturo Deza
Abhinav Dhall
Helisa Dhamo
Vikas Dhiman
Fillipe Dias Moreira
   de Souza
Ali Diba
Ferran Diego
Guiguang Ding
Henghui Ding
Jian Ding

Mingyu Ding
Xinghao Ding
Zhengming Ding
Robert DiPietro
Cosimo Distante
Ajay Divakaran
Mandar Dixit
Abdelaziz Djelouah
Thanh-Toan Do
Jose Dolz
Bo Dong
Chao Dong
Jiangxin Dong
Weiming Dong
Weisheng Dong
Xingping Dong
Xuanyi Dong
Yinpeng Dong
Gianfranco Doretto
Hazel Doughty
Hassen Drira
Bertram Drost
Dawei Du
Ye Duan
Yueqi Duan
Abhimanyu Dubey
Anastasia Dubrovina
Stefan Duffner
Chi Nhan Duong
Thibaut Durand
Zoran Duric
Iulia Duta
Debidatta Dwibedi
Benjamin Eckart
Marc Eder
Marzieh Edraki
Alexei A. Efros
Kiana Ehsani
Hazm Kemal Ekenel
James H. Elder
Mohamed Elgharib
Shireen Elhabian
Ehsan Elhamifar
Mohamed Elhoseiny
Ian Endres
N. Benjamin Erichson

Jan Ernst
Sergio Escalera
Francisco Escolano
Victor Escorcia
Carlos Esteves
Francisco J. Estrada
Bin Fan
Chenyou Fan
Deng-Ping Fan
Haoqi Fan
Hehe Fan
Heng Fan
Kai Fan
Lijie Fan
Linxi Fan
Quanfu Fan
Shaojing Fan
Xiaochuan Fan
Xin Fan
Yuchen Fan
Sean Fanello
Hao-Shu Fang
Haoyang Fang
Kuan Fang
Yi Fang
Yuming Fang
Azade Farshad
Alireza Fathi
Raanan Fattal
Joao Fayad
Xiaohan Fei
Christoph Feichtenhofer
Michael Felsberg
Chen Feng
Jiashi Feng
Junyi Feng
Mengyang Feng
Qianli Feng
Zhenhua Feng
Michele Fenzi
Andras Ferencz
Martin Fergie
Basura Fernando
Ethan Fetaya
Michael Firman
John W. Fisher

Matthew Fisher
Boris Flach
Corneliu Florea
Wolfgang Foerstner
David Fofi
Gian Luca Foresti
Per-Erik Forssen
David Fouhey
Katerina Fragkiadaki
Victor Fragoso
Jean-Sébastien Franco
Ohad Fried
Iuri Frosio
Cheng-Yang Fu
Huazhu Fu
Jianlong Fu
Jingjing Fu
Xueyang Fu
Yanwei Fu
Ying Fu
Yun Fu
Olac Fuentes
Kent Fujiwara
Takuya Funatomi
Christopher Funk
Thomas Funkhouser
Antonino Furnari
Ryo Furukawa
Erik Gärtner
Raghudeep Gadde
Matheus Gadelha
Vandit Gajjar
Trevor Gale
Juergen Gall
Mathias Gallardo
Guillermo Gallego
Orazio Gallo
Chuang Gan
Zhe Gan
Madan Ravi Ganesh
Aditya Ganeshan
Siddha Ganju
Bin-Bin Gao
Changxin Gao
Feng Gao
Hongchang Gao

Jin Gao
Jiyang Gao
Junbin Gao
Katelyn Gao
Lin Gao
Mingfei Gao
Ruiqi Gao
Ruohan Gao
Shenghua Gao
Yuan Gao
Yue Gao
Noa Garcia
Alberto Garcia-Garcia
Guillermo
   Garcia-Hernando
Jacob R. Gardner
Animesh Garg
Kshitiz Garg
Rahul Garg
Ravi Garg
Philip N. Garner
Kirill Gavrilyuk
Paul Gay
Shiming Ge
Weifeng Ge
Baris Gecer
Xin Geng
Kyle Genova
Stamatios Georgoulis
Bernard Ghanem
Michael Gharbi
Kamran Ghasedi
Golnaz Ghiasi
Arnab Ghosh
Partha Ghosh
Silvio Giancola
Andrew Gilbert
Rohit Girdhar
Xavier Giro-i-Nieto
Thomas Gittings
Ioannis Gkioulekas
Clement Godard
Vaibhava Goel
Bastian Goldluecke
Lluis Gomez
Nuno Gonçalves

Dong Gong
Ke Gong
Mingming Gong
Abel Gonzalez-Garcia
Ariel Gordon
Daniel Gordon
Paulo Gotardo
Venu Madhav Govindu
Ankit Goyal
Priya Goyal
Raghav Goyal
Benjamin Graham
Douglas Gray
Brent A. Griffin
Etienne Grossmann
David Gu
Jiayuan Gu
Jiuxiang Gu
Lin Gu
Qiao Gu
Shuhang Gu
Jose J. Guerrero
Paul Guerrero
Jie Gui
Jean-Yves Guillemaut
Riza Alp Guler
Erhan Gundogdu
Fatma Guney
Guodong Guo
Kaiwen Guo
Qi Guo
Sheng Guo
Shi Guo
Tiantong Guo
Xiaojie Guo
Yijie Guo
Yiluan Guo
Yuanfang Guo
Yulan Guo
Agrim Gupta
Ankush Gupta
Mohit Gupta
Saurabh Gupta
Tanmay Gupta
Danna Gurari
Abner Guzman-Rivera

JunYoung Gwak
Michael Gygli
Jung-Woo Ha
Simon Hadfield
Isma Hadji
Bjoern Haefner
Taeyoung Hahn
Levente Hajder
Peter Hall
Emanuela Haller
Stefan Haller
Bumsub Ham
Abdullah Hamdi
Dongyoon Han
Hu Han
Jungong Han
Junwei Han
Kai Han
Tian Han
Xiaoguang Han
Xintong Han
Yahong Han
Ankur Handa
Zekun Hao
Albert Haque
Tatsuya Harada
Mehrtash Harandi
Adam W. Harley
Mahmudul Hasan
Atsushi Hashimoto
Ali Hatamizadeh
Munawar Hayat
Dongliang He
Jingrui He
Junfeng He
Kaiming He
Kun He
Lei He
Pan He
Ran He
Shengfeng He
Tong He
Weipeng He
Xuming He
Yang He
Yihui He

Zhihai He
Chinmay Hegde
Janne Heikkila
Mattias P. Heinrich
Stéphane Herbin
Alexander Hermans
Luis Herranz
John R. Hershey
Aaron Hertzmann
Roei Herzig
Anders Heyden
Steven Hickson
Otmar Hilliges
Tomas Hodan
Judy Hoffman
Michael Hofmann
Yannick Hold-Geoffroy
Namdar Homayounfar
Sina Honari
Richang Hong
Seunghoon Hong
Xiaopeng Hong
Yi Hong
Hidekata Hontani
Anthony Hoogs
Yedid Hoshen
Mir Rayat Imtiaz Hossain
Junhui Hou
Le Hou
Lu Hou
Tingbo Hou
Wei-Lin Hsiao
Cheng-Chun Hsu
Gee-Sern Jison Hsu
Kuang-jui Hsu
Changbo Hu
Di Hu
Guosheng Hu
Han Hu
Hao Hu
Hexiang Hu
Hou-Ning Hu
Jie Hu
Junlin Hu
Nan Hu
Ping Hu

Ronghang Hu
Xiaowei Hu
Yinlin Hu
Yuan-Ting Hu
Zhe Hu
Binh-Son Hua
Yang Hua
Bingyao Huang
Di Huang
Dong Huang
Fay Huang
Haibin Huang
Haozhi Huang
Heng Huang
Huaibo Huang
Jia-Bin Huang
Jing Huang
Jingwei Huang
Kaizhu Huang
Lei Huang
Qiangui Huang
Qiaoying Huang
Qingqiu Huang
Qixing Huang
Shaoli Huang
Sheng Huang
Siyuan Huang
Weilin Huang
Wenbing Huang
Xiangru Huang
Xun Huang
Yan Huang
Yifei Huang
Yue Huang
Zhiwu Huang
Zilong Huang
Minyoung Huh
Zhuo Hui
Matthias B. Hullin
Martin Humenberger
Wei-Chih Hung
Zhouyuan Huo
Junhwa Hur
Noureldien Hussein
Jyh-Jing Hwang
Seong Jae Hwang

Sung Ju Hwang
Ichiro Ide
Ivo Ihrke
Daiki Ikami
Satoshi Ikehata
Nazli Ikizler-Cinbis
Sunghoon Im
Yani Ioannou
Radu Tudor Ionescu
Umar Iqbal
Go Irie
Ahmet Iscen
Md Amirul Islam
Vamsi Ithapu
Nathan Jacobs
Arpit Jain
Himalaya Jain
Suyog Jain
Stuart James
Won-Dong Jang
Yunseok Jang
Ronnachai Jaroensri
Dinesh Jayaraman
Sadeep Jayasumana
Suren Jayasuriya
Herve Jegou
Simon Jenni
Hae-Gon Jeon
Yunho Jeon
Koteswar R. Jerripothula
Hueihan Jhuang
I-hong Jhuo
Dinghuang Ji
Hui Ji
Jingwei Ji
Pan Ji
Yanli Ji
Baoxiong Jia
Kui Jia
Xu Jia
Chiyu Max Jiang
Haiyong Jiang
Hao Jiang
Huaizu Jiang
Huajie Jiang
Ke Jiang

Lai Jiang
Li Jiang
Lu Jiang
Ming Jiang
Peng Jiang
Shuqiang Jiang
Wei Jiang
Xudong Jiang
Zhuolin Jiang
Jianbo Jiao
Zequn Jie
Dakai Jin
Kyong Hwan Jin
Lianwen Jin
SouYoung Jin
Xiaojie Jin
Xin Jin
Nebojsa Jojic
Alexis Joly
Michael Jeffrey Jones
Hanbyul Joo
Jungseock Joo
Kyungdon Joo
Ajjen Joshi
Shantanu H. Joshi
Da-Cheng Juan
Marco Körner
Kevin Köser
Asim Kadav
Christine Kaeser-Chen
Kushal Kafle
Dagmar Kainmueller
Ioannis A. Kakadiaris
Zdenek Kalal
Nima Kalantari
Yannis Kalantidis
Mahdi M. Kalayeh
Anmol Kalia
Sinan Kalkan
Vicky Kalogeiton
Ashwin Kalyan
Joni-kristian Kamarainen
Gerda Kamberova
Chandra Kambhamettu
Martin Kampel
Meina Kan

Christopher Kanan
Kenichi Kanatani
Angjoo Kanazawa
Atsushi Kanehira
Takuhiro Kaneko
Asako Kanezaki
Bingyi Kang
Di Kang
Sunghun Kang
Zhao Kang
Vadim Kantorov
Abhishek Kar
Amlan Kar
Theofanis Karaletsos
Leonid Karlinsky
Kevin Karsch
Angelos Katharopoulos
Isinsu Katircioglu
Hiroharu Kato
Zoltan Kato
Dotan Kaufman
Jan Kautz
Rei Kawakami
Qiuhong Ke
Wadim Kehl
Petr Kellnhofer
Aniruddha Kembhavi
Cem Keskin
Margret Keuper
Daniel Keysers
Ashkan Khakzar
Fahad Khan
Naeemullah Khan
Salman Khan
Siddhesh Khandelwal
Rawal Khirodkar
Anna Khoreva
Tejas Khot
Parmeshwar Khurd
Hadi Kiapour
Joe Kileel
Chanho Kim
Dahun Kim
Edward Kim
Eunwoo Kim
Han-ul Kim

Gil Levi	Sheng Li	Renjie Liao
Evgeny Levinkov	Shiwei Li	Shengcai Liao
Aviad Levis	Shuang Li	Shuai Liao
Jose Lezama	Siyang Li	Yiyi Liao
Ang Li	Stan Z. Li	Ser-Nam Lim
Bin Li	Tianye Li	Chen-Hsuan Lin
Bing Li	Wei Li	Chung-Ching Lin
Boyi Li	Weixin Li	Dahua Lin
Changsheng Li	Wen Li	Ji Lin
Chao Li	Wenbo Li	Kevin Lin
Chen Li	Xiaomeng Li	Tianwei Lin
Cheng Li	Xin Li	Tsung-Yi Lin
Chenglong Li	Xiu Li	Tsung-Yu Lin
Chi Li	Xuelong Li	Wei-An Lin
Chun-Guang Li	Xueting Li	Weiyao Lin
Chun-Liang Li	Yan Li	Yen-Chen Lin
Chunyuan Li	Yandong Li	Yuewei Lin
Dong Li	Yanghao Li	David B. Lindell
Guanbin Li	Yehao Li	Drew Linsley
Hao Li	Yi Li	Krzysztof Lis
Haoxiang Li	Yijun Li	Roee Litman
Hongsheng Li	Yikang LI	Jim Little
Hongyang Li	Yining Li	An-An Liu
Houqiang Li	Yongjie Li	Bo Liu
Huibin Li	Yu Li	Buyu Liu
Jia Li	Yu-Jhe Li	Chao Liu
Jianan Li	Yunpeng Li	Chen Liu
Jianguo Li	Yunsheng Li	Cheng-lin Liu
Junnan Li	Yunzhu Li	Chenxi Liu
Junxuan Li	Zhe Li	Dong Liu
Kai Li	Zhen Li	Feng Liu
Ke Li	Zhengqi Li	Guilin Liu
Kejie Li	Zhenyang Li	Haomiao Liu
Kunpeng Li	Zhuwen Li	Heshan Liu
Lerenhan Li	Dongze Lian	Hong Liu
Li Erran Li	Xiaochen Lian	Ji Liu
Mengtian Li	Zhouhui Lian	Jingen Liu
Mu Li	Chen Liang	Jun Liu
Peihua Li	Jie Liang	Lanlan Liu
Peiyi Li	Ming Liang	Li Liu
Ping Li	Paul Pu Liang	Liu Liu
Qi Li	Pengpeng Liang	Mengyuan Liu
Qing Li	Shu Liang	Miaomiao Liu
Ruiyu Li	Wei Liang	Nian Liu
Ruoteng Li	Jing Liao	Ping Liu
Shaozi Li	Minghui Liao	Risheng Liu

Sheng Liu
Shu Liu
Shuaicheng Liu
Sifei Liu
Siqi Liu
Siying Liu
Songtao Liu
Ting Liu
Tongliang Liu
Tyng-Luh Liu
Wanquan Liu
Wei Liu
Weiyang Liu
Weizhe Liu
Wenyu Liu
Wu Liu
Xialei Liu
Xianglong Liu
Xiaodong Liu
Xiaofeng Liu
Xihui Liu
Xingyu Liu
Xinwang Liu
Xuanqing Liu
Xuebo Liu
Yang Liu
Yaojie Liu
Yebin Liu
Yen-Cheng Liu
Yiming Liu
Yu Liu
Yu-Shen Liu
Yufan Liu
Yun Liu
Zheng Liu
Zhijian Liu
Zhuang Liu
Zichuan Liu
Ziwei Liu
Zongyi Liu
Stephan Liwicki
Liliana Lo Presti
Chengjiang Long
Fuchen Long
Mingsheng Long
Xiang Long

Yang Long
Charles T. Loop
Antonio Lopez
Roberto J. Lopez-Sastre
Javier Lorenzo-Navarro
Manolis Lourakis
Boyu Lu
Canyi Lu
Feng Lu
Guoyu Lu
Hongtao Lu
Jiajun Lu
Jiasen Lu
Jiwen Lu
Kaiyue Lu
Le Lu
Shao-Ping Lu
Shijian Lu
Xiankai Lu
Xin Lu
Yao Lu
Yiping Lu
Yongxi Lu
Yongyi Lu
Zhiwu Lu
Fujun Luan
Benjamin E. Lundell
Hao Luo
Jian-Hao Luo
Ruotian Luo
Weixin Luo
Wenhan Luo
Wenjie Luo
Yan Luo
Zelun Luo
Zixin Luo
Khoa Luu
Zhaoyang Lv
Pengyuan Lyu
Thomas Möllenhoff
Matthias Müller
Bingpeng Ma
Chih-Yao Ma
Chongyang Ma
Huimin Ma
Jiayi Ma

K. T. Ma
Ke Ma
Lin Ma
Liqian Ma
Shugao Ma
Wei-Chiu Ma
Xiaojian Ma
Xingjun Ma
Zhanyu Ma
Zheng Ma
Radek Jakob Mackowiak
Ludovic Magerand
Shweta Mahajan
Siddharth Mahendran
Long Mai
Ameesh Makadia
Oscar Mendez Maldonado
Mateusz Malinowski
Yury Malkov
Arun Mallya
Dipu Manandhar
Massimiliano Mancini
Fabian Manhardt
Kevis-kokitsi Maninis
Varun Manjunatha
Junhua Mao
Xudong Mao
Alina Marcu
Edgar Margffoy-Tuay
Dmitrii Marin
Manuel J. Marin-Jimenez
Kenneth Marino
Niki Martinel
Julieta Martinez
Jonathan Masci
Tomohiro Mashita
Iacopo Masi
David Masip
Daniela Massiceti
Stefan Mathe
Yusuke Matsui
Tetsu Matsukawa
Iain A. Matthews
Kevin James Matzen
Bruce Allen Maxwell
Stephen Maybank

Helmut Mayer
Amir Mazaheri
David McAllester
Steven McDonagh
Stephen J. Mckenna
Roey Mechrez
Prakhar Mehrotra
Christopher Mei
Xue Mei
Paulo R. S. Mendonca
Lili Meng
Zibo Meng
Thomas Mensink
Bjoern Menze
Michele Merler
Kourosh Meshgi
Pascal Mettes
Christopher Metzler
Liang Mi
Qiguang Miao
Xin Miao
Tomer Michaeli
Frank Michel
Antoine Miech
Krystian Mikolajczyk
Peyman Milanfar
Ben Mildenhall
Gregor Miller
Fausto Milletari
Dongbo Min
Kyle Min
Pedro Miraldo
Dmytro Mishkin
Anand Mishra
Ashish Mishra
Ishan Misra
Niluthpol C. Mithun
Kaushik Mitra
Niloy Mitra
Anton Mitrokhin
Ikuhisa Mitsugami
Anurag Mittal
Kaichun Mo
Zhipeng Mo
Davide Modolo
Michael Moeller

Pritish Mohapatra
Pavlo Molchanov
Davide Moltisanti
Pascal Monasse
Mathew Monfort
Aron Monszpart
Sean Moran
Vlad I. Morariu
Francesc Moreno-Noguer
Pietro Morerio
Stylianos Moschoglou
Yael Moses
Roozbeh Mottaghi
Pierre Moulon
Arsalan Mousavian
Yadong Mu
Yasuhiro Mukaigawa
Lopamudra Mukherjee
Yusuke Mukuta
Ravi Teja Mullapudi
Mario Enrique Munich
Zachary Murez
Ana C. Murillo
J. Krishna Murthy
Damien Muselet
Armin Mustafa
Siva Karthik Mustikovela
Carlo Dal Mutto
Moin Nabi
Varun K. Nagaraja
Tushar Nagarajan
Arsha Nagrani
Seungjun Nah
Nikhil Naik
Yoshikatsu Nakajima
Yuta Nakashima
Atsushi Nakazawa
Seonghyeon Nam
Vinay P. Namboodiri
Medhini Narasimhan
Srinivasa Narasimhan
Sanath Narayan
Erickson Rangel
    Nascimento
Jacinto Nascimento
Tayyab Naseer

Lakshmanan Nataraj
Neda Nategh
Nelson Isao Nauata
Fernando Navarro
Shah Nawaz
Lukas Neumann
Ram Nevatia
Alejandro Newell
Shawn Newsam
Joe Yue-Hei Ng
Trung Thanh Ngo
Duc Thanh Nguyen
Lam M. Nguyen
Phuc Xuan Nguyen
Thuong Nguyen Canh
Mihalis Nicolaou
Andrei Liviu Nicolicioiu
Xuecheng Nie
Michael Niemeyer
Simon Niklaus
Christophoros Nikou
David Nilsson
Jifeng Ning
Yuval Nirkin
Li Niu
Yuzhen Niu
Zhenxing Niu
Shohei Nobuhara
Nicoletta Noceti
Hyeonwoo Noh
Junhyug Noh
Mehdi Noroozi
Sotiris Nousias
Valsamis Ntouskos
Matthew O'Toole
Peter Ochs
Ferda Ofli
Seong Joon Oh
Seoung Wug Oh
Iason Oikonomidis
Utkarsh Ojha
Takahiro Okabe
Takayuki Okatani
Fumio Okura
Aude Oliva
Kyle Olszewski

Björn Ommer
Mohamed Omran
Elisabeta Oneata
Michael Opitz
Jose Oramas
Tribhuvanesh Orekondy
Shaul Oron
Sergio Orts-Escolano
Ivan Oseledets
Aljosa Osep
Magnus Oskarsson
Anton Osokin
Martin R. Oswald
Wanli Ouyang
Andrew Owens
Mete Ozay
Mustafa Ozuysal
Eduardo Pérez-Pellitero
Gautam Pai
Dipan Kumar Pal
P. H. Pamplona Savarese
Jinshan Pan
Junting Pan
Xingang Pan
Yingwei Pan
Yannis Panagakis
Rameswar Panda
Guan Pang
Jiahao Pang
Jiangmiao Pang
Tianyu Pang
Sharath Pankanti
Nicolas Papadakis
Dim Papadopoulos
George Papandreou
Toufiq Parag
Shaifali Parashar
Sarah Parisot
Eunhyeok Park
Hyun Soo Park
Jaesik Park
Min-Gyu Park
Taesung Park
Alvaro Parra
C. Alejandro Parraga
Despoina Paschalidou

Nikolaos Passalis
Vishal Patel
Viorica Patraucean
Badri Narayana Patro
Danda Pani Paudel
Sujoy Paul
Georgios Pavlakos
Ioannis Pavlidis
Vladimir Pavlovic
Nick Pears
Kim Steenstrup Pedersen
Selen Pehlivan
Shmuel Peleg
Chao Peng
Houwen Peng
Wen-Hsiao Peng
Xi Peng
Xiaojiang Peng
Xingchao Peng
Yuxin Peng
Federico Perazzi
Juan Camilo Perez
Vishwanath Peri
Federico Pernici
Luca Del Pero
Florent Perronnin
Stavros Petridis
Henning Petzka
Patrick Peursum
Michael Pfeiffer
Hanspeter Pfister
Roman Pflugfelder
Minh Tri Pham
Yongri Piao
David Picard
Tomasz Pieciak
A. J. Piergiovanni
Andrea Pilzer
Pedro O. Pinheiro
Silvia Laura Pintea
Lerrel Pinto
Axel Pinz
Robinson Piramuthu
Fiora Pirri
Leonid Pishchulin
Francesco Pittaluga

Daniel Pizarro
Tobias Plötz
Mirco Planamente
Matteo Poggi
Moacir A. Ponti
Parita Pooj
Fatih Porikli
Horst Possegger
Omid Poursaeed
Ameya Prabhu
Viraj Uday Prabhu
Dilip Prasad
Brian L. Price
True Price
Maria Priisalu
Veronique Prinet
Victor Adrian Prisacariu
Jan Prokaj
Sergey Prokudin
Nicolas Pugeault
Xavier Puig
Albert Pumarola
Pulak Purkait
Senthil Purushwalkam
Charles R. Qi
Hang Qi
Haozhi Qi
Lu Qi
Mengshi Qi
Siyuan Qi
Xiaojuan Qi
Yuankai Qi
Shengju Qian
Xuelin Qian
Siyuan Qiao
Yu Qiao
Jie Qin
Qiang Qiu
Weichao Qiu
Zhaofan Qiu
Kha Gia Quach
Yuhui Quan
Yvain Queau
Julian Quiroga
Faisal Qureshi
Mahdi Rad

Filip Radenovic
Petia Radeva
Venkatesh
    B. Radhakrishnan
Ilija Radosavovic
Noha Radwan
Rahul Raguram
Tanzila Rahman
Amit Raj
Ajit Rajwade
Kandan Ramakrishnan
Santhosh
    K. Ramakrishnan
Srikumar Ramalingam
Ravi Ramamoorthi
Vasili Ramanishka
Ramprasaath R. Selvaraju
Francois Rameau
Visvanathan Ramesh
Santu Rana
Rene Ranftl
Anand Rangarajan
Anurag Ranjan
Viresh Ranjan
Yongming Rao
Carolina Raposo
Vivek Rathod
Sathya N. Ravi
Avinash Ravichandran
Tammy Riklin Raviv
Daniel Rebain
Sylvestre-Alvise Rebuffi
N. Dinesh Reddy
Timo Rehfeld
Paolo Remagnino
Konstantinos Rematas
Edoardo Remelli
Dongwei Ren
Haibing Ren
Jian Ren
Jimmy Ren
Mengye Ren
Weihong Ren
Wenqi Ren
Zhile Ren
Zhongzheng Ren

Zhou Ren
Vijay Rengarajan
Md A. Reza
Farzaneh Rezaeianaran
Hamed R. Tavakoli
Nicholas Rhinehart
Helge Rhodin
Elisa Ricci
Alexander Richard
Eitan Richardson
Elad Richardson
Christian Richardt
Stephan Richter
Gernot Riegler
Daniel Ritchie
Tobias Ritschel
Samuel Rivera
Yong Man Ro
Richard Roberts
Joseph Robinson
Ignacio Rocco
Mrigank Rochan
Emanuele Rodolà
Mikel D. Rodriguez
Giorgio Roffo
Grégory Rogez
Gemma Roig
Javier Romero
Xuejian Rong
Yu Rong
Amir Rosenfeld
Bodo Rosenhahn
Guy Rosman
Arun Ross
Paolo Rota
Peter M. Roth
Anastasios Roussos
Anirban Roy
Sebastien Roy
Aruni RoyChowdhury
Artem Rozantsev
Ognjen Rudovic
Daniel Rueckert
Adria Ruiz
Javier Ruiz-del-solar
Christian Rupprecht

Chris Russell
Dan Ruta
Jongbin Ryu
Ömer Sümer
Alexandre Sablayrolles
Faraz Saeedan
Ryusuke Sagawa
Christos Sagonas
Tonmoy Saikia
Hideo Saito
Kuniaki Saito
Shunsuke Saito
Shunta Saito
Ken Sakurada
Joaquin Salas
Fatemeh Sadat Saleh
Mahdi Saleh
Pouya Samangouei
Leo Sampaio
    Ferraz Ribeiro
Artsiom Olegovich
    Sanakoyeu
Enrique Sanchez
Patsorn Sangkloy
Anush Sankaran
Aswin Sankaranarayanan
Swami Sankaranarayanan
Rodrigo Santa Cruz
Amartya Sanyal
Archana Sapkota
Nikolaos Sarafianos
Jun Sato
Shin'ichi Satoh
Hosnieh Sattar
Arman Savran
Manolis Savva
Alexander Sax
Hanno Scharr
Simone Schaub-Meyer
Konrad Schindler
Dmitrij Schlesinger
Uwe Schmidt
Dirk Schnieders
Björn Schuller
Samuel Schulter
Idan Schwartz

William Robson Schwartz
Alex Schwing
Sinisa Segvic
Lorenzo Seidenari
Pradeep Sen
Ozan Sener
Soumyadip Sengupta
Arda Senocak
Mojtaba Seyedhosseini
Shishir Shah
Shital Shah
Sohil Atul Shah
Tamar Rott Shaham
Huasong Shan
Qi Shan
Shiguang Shan
Jing Shao
Roman Shapovalov
Gaurav Sharma
Vivek Sharma
Viktoriia Sharmanska
Dongyu She
Sumit Shekhar
Evan Shelhamer
Chengyao Shen
Chunhua Shen
Falong Shen
Jie Shen
Li Shen
Liyue Shen
Shuhan Shen
Tianwei Shen
Wei Shen
William B. Shen
Yantao Shen
Ying Shen
Yiru Shen
Yujun Shen
Yuming Shen
Zhiqiang Shen
Ziyi Shen
Lu Sheng
Yu Sheng
Rakshith Shetty
Baoguang Shi
Guangming Shi

Hailin Shi
Miaojing Shi
Yemin Shi
Zhenmei Shi
Zhiyuan Shi
Kevin Jonathan Shih
Shiliang Shiliang
Hyunjung Shim
Atsushi Shimada
Nobutaka Shimada
Daeyun Shin
Young Min Shin
Koichi Shinoda
Konstantin Shmelkov
Michael Zheng Shou
Abhinav Shrivastava
Tianmin Shu
Zhixin Shu
Hong-Han Shuai
Pushkar Shukla
Christian Siagian
Mennatullah M. Siam
Kaleem Siddiqi
Karan Sikka
Jae-Young Sim
Christian Simon
Martin Simonovsky
Dheeraj Singaraju
Bharat Singh
Gurkirt Singh
Krishna Kumar Singh
Maneesh Kumar Singh
Richa Singh
Saurabh Singh
Suriya Singh
Vikas Singh
Sudipta N. Sinha
Vincent Sitzmann
Josef Sivic
Gregory Slabaugh
Miroslava Slavcheva
Ron Slossberg
Brandon Smith
Kevin Smith
Vladimir Smutny
Noah Snavely

Roger
  D. Soberanis-Mukul
Kihyuk Sohn
Francesco Solera
Eric Sommerlade
Sanghyun Son
Byung Cheol Song
Chunfeng Song
Dongjin Song
Jiaming Song
Jie Song
Jifei Song
Jingkuan Song
Mingli Song
Shiyu Song
Shuran Song
Xiao Song
Yafei Song
Yale Song
Yang Song
Yi-Zhe Song
Yibing Song
Humberto Sossa
Cesar de Souza
Adrian Spurr
Srinath Sridhar
Suraj Srinivas
Pratul P. Srinivasan
Anuj Srivastava
Tania Stathaki
Christopher Stauffer
Simon Stent
Rainer Stiefelhagen
Pierre Stock
Julian Straub
Jonathan C. Stroud
Joerg Stueckler
Jan Stuehmer
David Stutz
Chi Su
Hang Su
Jong-Chyi Su
Shuochen Su
Yu-Chuan Su
Ramanathan Subramanian
Yusuke Sugano

Masanori Suganuma
Yumin Suh
Mohammed Suhail
Yao Sui
Heung-Il Suk
Josephine Sullivan
Baochen Sun
Chen Sun
Chong Sun
Deqing Sun
Jin Sun
Liang Sun
Lin Sun
Qianru Sun
Shao-Hua Sun
Shuyang Sun
Weiwei Sun
Wenxiu Sun
Xiaoshuai Sun
Xiaoxiao Sun
Xingyuan Sun
Yifan Sun
Zhun Sun
Sabine Susstrunk
David Suter
Supasorn Suwajanakorn
Tomas Svoboda
Eran Swears
Paul Swoboda
Attila Szabo
Richard Szeliski
Duy-Nguyen Ta
Andrea Tagliasacchi
Yuichi Taguchi
Ying Tai
Keita Takahashi
Kouske Takahashi
Jun Takamatsu
Hugues Talbot
Toru Tamaki
Chaowei Tan
Fuwen Tan
Mingkui Tan
Mingxing Tan
Qingyang Tan
Robby T. Tan

Xiaoyang Tan
Kenichiro Tanaka
Masayuki Tanaka
Chang Tang
Chengzhou Tang
Danhang Tang
Ming Tang
Peng Tang
Qingming Tang
Wei Tang
Xu Tang
Yansong Tang
Youbao Tang
Yuxing Tang
Zhiqiang Tang
Tatsunori Taniai
Junli Tao
Xin Tao
Makarand Tapaswi
Jean-Philippe Tarel
Lyne Tchapmi
Zachary Teed
Bugra Tekin
Damien Teney
Ayush Tewari
Christian Theobalt
Christopher Thomas
Diego Thomas
Jim Thomas
Rajat Mani Thomas
Xinmei Tian
Yapeng Tian
Yingli Tian
Yonglong Tian
Zhi Tian
Zhuotao Tian
Kinh Tieu
Joseph Tighe
Massimo Tistarelli
Matthew Toews
Carl Toft
Pavel Tokmakov
Federico Tombari
Chetan Tonde
Yan Tong
Alessio Tonioni

Andrea Torsello
Fabio Tosi
Du Tran
Luan Tran
Ngoc-Trung Tran
Quan Hung Tran
Truyen Tran
Rudolph Triebel
Martin Trimmel
Shashank Tripathi
Subarna Tripathi
Leonardo Trujillo
Eduard Trulls
Tomasz Trzcinski
Sam Tsai
Yi-Hsuan Tsai
Hung-Yu Tseng
Stavros Tsogkas
Aggeliki Tsoli
Devis Tuia
Shubham Tulsiani
Sergey Tulyakov
Frederick Tung
Tony Tung
Daniyar Turmukhambetov
Ambrish Tyagi
Radim Tylecek
Christos Tzelepis
Georgios Tzimiropoulos
Dimitrios Tzionas
Seiichi Uchida
Norimichi Ukita
Dmitry Ulyanov
Martin Urschler
Yoshitaka Ushiku
Ben Usman
Alexander Vakhitov
Julien P. C. Valentin
Jack Valmadre
Ernest Valveny
Joost van de Weijer
Jan van Gemert
Koen Van Leemput
Gul Varol
Sebastiano Vascon
M. Alex O. Vasilescu

Subeesh Vasu
Mayank Vatsa
David Vazquez
Javier Vazquez-Corral
Ashok Veeraraghavan
Erik Velasco-Salido
Raviteja Vemulapalli
Jonathan Ventura
Manisha Verma
Roberto Vezzani
Ruben Villegas
Minh Vo
MinhDuc Vo
Nam Vo
Michele Volpi
Riccardo Volpi
Carl Vondrick
Konstantinos Vougioukas
Tuan-Hung Vu
Sven Wachsmuth
Neal Wadhwa
Catherine Wah
Jacob C. Walker
Thomas S. A. Wallis
Chengde Wan
Jun Wan
Liang Wan
Renjie Wan
Baoyuan Wang
Boyu Wang
Cheng Wang
Chu Wang
Chuan Wang
Chunyu Wang
Dequan Wang
Di Wang
Dilin Wang
Dong Wang
Fang Wang
Guanzhi Wang
Guoyin Wang
Hanzi Wang
Hao Wang
He Wang
Heng Wang
Hongcheng Wang

Hongxing Wang
Hua Wang
Jian Wang
Jingbo Wang
Jinglu Wang
Jingya Wang
Jinjun Wang
Jinqiao Wang
Jue Wang
Ke Wang
Keze Wang
Le Wang
Lei Wang
Lezi Wang
Li Wang
Liang Wang
Lijun Wang
Limin Wang
Linwei Wang
Lizhi Wang
Mengjiao Wang
Mingzhe Wang
Minsi Wang
Naiyan Wang
Nannan Wang
Ning Wang
Oliver Wang
Pei Wang
Peng Wang
Pichao Wang
Qi Wang
Qian Wang
Qiaosong Wang
Qifei Wang
Qilong Wang
Qing Wang
Qingzhong Wang
Quan Wang
Rui Wang
Ruiping Wang
Ruixing Wang
Shangfei Wang
Shenlong Wang
Shiyao Wang
Shuhui Wang
Song Wang

Tao Wang
Tianlu Wang
Tiantian Wang
Ting-chun Wang
Tingwu Wang
Wei Wang
Weiyue Wang
Wenguan Wang
Wenlin Wang
Wenqi Wang
Xiang Wang
Xiaobo Wang
Xiaofang Wang
Xiaoling Wang
Xiaolong Wang
Xiaosong Wang
Xiaoyu Wang
Xin Eric Wang
Xinchao Wang
Xinggang Wang
Xintao Wang
Yali Wang
Yan Wang
Yang Wang
Yangang Wang
Yaxing Wang
Yi Wang
Yida Wang
Yilin Wang
Yiming Wang
Yisen Wang
Yongtao Wang
Yu-Xiong Wang
Yue Wang
Yujiang Wang
Yunbo Wang
Yunhe Wang
Zengmao Wang
Zhangyang Wang
Zhaowen Wang
Zhe Wang
Zhecan Wang
Zheng Wang
Zhixiang Wang
Zilei Wang
Jianqiao Wangni

Anne S. Wannenwetsch
Jan Dirk Wegner
Scott Wehrwein
Donglai Wei
Kaixuan Wei
Longhui Wei
Pengxu Wei
Ping Wei
Qi Wei
Shih-En Wei
Xing Wei
Yunchao Wei
Zijun Wei
Jerod Weinman
Michael Weinmann
Philippe Weinzaepfel
Yair Weiss
Bihan Wen
Longyin Wen
Wei Wen
Junwu Weng
Tsui-Wei Weng
Xinshuo Weng
Eric Wengrowski
Tomas Werner
Gordon Wetzstein
Tobias Weyand
Patrick Wieschollek
Maggie Wigness
Erik Wijmans
Richard Wildes
Olivia Wiles
Chris Williams
Williem Williem
Kyle Wilson
Calden Wloka
Nicolai Wojke
Christian Wolf
Yongkang Wong
Sanghyun Woo
Scott Workman
Baoyuan Wu
Bichen Wu
Chao-Yuan Wu
Huikai Wu
Jiajun Wu

Jialin Wu
Jiaxiang Wu
Jiqing Wu
Jonathan Wu
Lifang Wu
Qi Wu
Qiang Wu
Ruizheng Wu
Shangzhe Wu
Shun-Cheng Wu
Tianfu Wu
Wayne Wu
Wenxuan Wu
Xiao Wu
Xiaohe Wu
Xinxiao Wu
Yang Wu
Yi Wu
Yiming Wu
Ying Nian Wu
Yue Wu
Zheng Wu
Zhenyu Wu
Zhirong Wu
Zuxuan Wu
Stefanie Wuhrer
Jonas Wulff
Changqun Xia
Fangting Xia
Fei Xia
Gui-Song Xia
Lu Xia
Xide Xia
Yin Xia
Yingce Xia
Yongqin Xian
Lei Xiang
Shiming Xiang
Bin Xiao
Fanyi Xiao
Guobao Xiao
Huaxin Xiao
Taihong Xiao
Tete Xiao
Tong Xiao
Wang Xiao

Yang Xiao
Cihang Xie
Guosen Xie
Jianwen Xie
Lingxi Xie
Sirui Xie
Weidi Xie
Wenxuan Xie
Xiaohua Xie
Fuyong Xing
Jun Xing
Junliang Xing
Bo Xiong
Peixi Xiong
Yu Xiong
Yuanjun Xiong
Zhiwei Xiong
Chang Xu
Chenliang Xu
Dan Xu
Danfei Xu
Hang Xu
Hongteng Xu
Huijuan Xu
Jingwei Xu
Jun Xu
Kai Xu
Mengmeng Xu
Mingze Xu
Qianqian Xu
Ran Xu
Weijian Xu
Xiangyu Xu
Xiaogang Xu
Xing Xu
Xun Xu
Yanyu Xu
Yichao Xu
Yong Xu
Yongchao Xu
Yuanlu Xu
Zenglin Xu
Zheng Xu
Chuhui Xue
Jia Xue
Nan Xue

Tianfan Xue
Xiangyang Xue
Abhay Yadav
Yasushi Yagi
I. Zeki Yalniz
Kota Yamaguchi
Toshihiko Yamasaki
Takayoshi Yamashita
Junchi Yan
Ke Yan
Qingan Yan
Sijie Yan
Xinchen Yan
Yan Yan
Yichao Yan
Zhicheng Yan
Keiji Yanai
Bin Yang
Ceyuan Yang
Dawei Yang
Dong Yang
Fan Yang
Guandao Yang
Guorun Yang
Haichuan Yang
Hao Yang
Jianwei Yang
Jiaolong Yang
Jie Yang
Jing Yang
Kaiyu Yang
Linjie Yang
Meng Yang
Michael Ying Yang
Nan Yang
Shuai Yang
Shuo Yang
Tianyu Yang
Tien-Ju Yang
Tsun-Yi Yang
Wei Yang
Wenhan Yang
Xiao Yang
Xiaodong Yang
Xin Yang
Yan Yang

Yanchao Yang
Yee Hong Yang
Yezhou Yang
Zhenheng Yang
Anbang Yao
Angela Yao
Cong Yao
Jian Yao
Li Yao
Ting Yao
Yao Yao
Zhewei Yao
Chengxi Ye
Jianbo Ye
Keren Ye
Linwei Ye
Mang Ye
Mao Ye
Qi Ye
Qixiang Ye
Mei-Chen Yeh
Raymond Yeh
Yu-Ying Yeh
Sai-Kit Yeung
Serena Yeung
Kwang Moo Yi
Li Yi
Renjiao Yi
Alper Yilmaz
Junho Yim
Lijun Yin
Weidong Yin
Xi Yin
Zhichao Yin
Tatsuya Yokota
Ryo Yonetani
Donggeun Yoo
Jae Shin Yoon
Ju Hong Yoon
Sung-eui Yoon
Laurent Younes
Changqian Yu
Fisher Yu
Gang Yu
Jiahui Yu
Kaicheng Yu

Ke Yu
Lequan Yu
Ning Yu
Qian Yu
Ronald Yu
Ruichi Yu
Shoou-I Yu
Tao Yu
Tianshu Yu
Xiang Yu
Xin Yu
Xiyu Yu
Youngjae Yu
Yu Yu
Zhiding Yu
Chunfeng Yuan
Ganzhao Yuan
Jinwei Yuan
Lu Yuan
Quan Yuan
Shanxin Yuan
Tongtong Yuan
Wenjia Yuan
Ye Yuan
Yuan Yuan
Yuhui Yuan
Huanjing Yue
Xiangyu Yue
Ersin Yumer
Sergey Zagoruyko
Egor Zakharov
Amir Zamir
Andrei Zanfir
Mihai Zanfir
Pablo Zegers
Bernhard Zeisl
John S. Zelek
Niclas Zeller
Huayi Zeng
Jiabei Zeng
Wenjun Zeng
Yu Zeng
Xiaohua Zhai
Fangneng Zhan
Huangying Zhan
Kun Zhan

Xiaohang Zhan
Baochang Zhang
Bowen Zhang
Cecilia Zhang
Changqing Zhang
Chao Zhang
Chengquan Zhang
Chi Zhang
Chongyang Zhang
Dingwen Zhang
Dong Zhang
Feihu Zhang
Hang Zhang
Hanwang Zhang
Hao Zhang
He Zhang
Hongguang Zhang
Hua Zhang
Ji Zhang
Jianguo Zhang
Jianming Zhang
Jiawei Zhang
Jie Zhang
Jing Zhang
Juyong Zhang
Kai Zhang
Kaipeng Zhang
Ke Zhang
Le Zhang
Lei Zhang
Li Zhang
Lihe Zhang
Linguang Zhang
Lu Zhang
Mi Zhang
Mingda Zhang
Peng Zhang
Pingping Zhang
Qian Zhang
Qilin Zhang
Quanshi Zhang
Richard Zhang
Rui Zhang
Runze Zhang
Shengping Zhang
Shifeng Zhang

Shuai Zhang
Songyang Zhang
Tao Zhang
Ting Zhang
Tong Zhang
Wayne Zhang
Wei Zhang
Weizhong Zhang
Wenwei Zhang
Xiangyu Zhang
Xiaolin Zhang
Xiaopeng Zhang
Xiaoqin Zhang
Xiuming Zhang
Ya Zhang
Yang Zhang
Yimin Zhang
Yinda Zhang
Ying Zhang
Yongfei Zhang
Yu Zhang
Yulun Zhang
Yunhua Zhang
Yuting Zhang
Zhanpeng Zhang
Zhao Zhang
Zhaoxiang Zhang
Zhen Zhang
Zheng Zhang
Zhifei Zhang
Zhijin Zhang
Zhishuai Zhang
Ziming Zhang
Bo Zhao
Chen Zhao
Fang Zhao
Haiyu Zhao
Han Zhao
Hang Zhao
Hengshuang Zhao
Jian Zhao
Kai Zhao
Liang Zhao
Long Zhao
Qian Zhao
Qibin Zhao

Qijun Zhao
Rui Zhao
Shenglin Zhao
Sicheng Zhao
Tianyi Zhao
Wenda Zhao
Xiangyun Zhao
Xin Zhao
Yang Zhao
Yue Zhao
Zhichen Zhao
Zijing Zhao
Xiantong Zhen
Chuanxia Zheng
Feng Zheng
Haiyong Zheng
Jia Zheng
Kang Zheng
Shuai Kyle Zheng
Wei-Shi Zheng
Yinqiang Zheng
Zerong Zheng
Zhedong Zheng
Zilong Zheng
Bineng Zhong
Fangwei Zhong
Guangyu Zhong
Yiran Zhong
Yujie Zhong
Zhun Zhong
Chunluan Zhou
Huiyu Zhou
Jiahuan Zhou
Jun Zhou
Lei Zhou
Luowei Zhou
Luping Zhou
Mo Zhou
Ning Zhou
Pan Zhou
Peng Zhou
Qianyi Zhou
S. Kevin Zhou
Sanping Zhou
Wengang Zhou
Xingyi Zhou

Additional Reviewers

Hanxiao Liu
Hongyu Liu
Huidong Liu
Miao Liu
Xinxin Liu
Yongfei Liu
Yu-Lun Liu
Amir Livne
Tiange Luo
Wei Ma
Xiaoxuan Ma
Ioannis Marras
Georg Martius
Effrosyni Mavroudi
Tim Meinhardt
Givi Meishvili
Meng Meng
Zihang Meng
Zhongqi Miao
Gyeongsik Moon
Khoi Nguyen
Yung-Kyun Noh
Antonio Norelli
Jaeyoo Park
Alexander Pashevich
Mandela Patrick
Mary Phuong
Bingqiao Qian
Yu Qiao
Zhen Qiao
Sai Saketh Rambhatla
Aniket Roy
Amelie Royer
Parikshit Vishwas
   Sakurikar
Mark Sandler
Mert Bülent Sarıyıldız
Tanner Schmidt
Anshul B. Shah

Ketul Shah
Rajvi Shah
Hengcan Shi
Xiangxi Shi
Yujiao Shi
William A. P. Smith
Guoxian Song
Robin Strudel
Abby Stylianou
Xinwei Sun
Reuben Tan
Qingyi Tao
Kedar S. Tatwawadi
Anh Tuan Tran
Son Dinh Tran
Eleni Triantafillou
Aristeidis Tsitiridis
Md Zasim Uddin
Andrea Vedaldi
Evangelos Ververas
Vidit Vidit
Paul Voigtlaender
Bo Wan
Huanyu Wang
Huiyu Wang
Junqiu Wang
Pengxiao Wang
Tai Wang
Xinyao Wang
Tomoki Watanabe
Mark Weber
Xi Wei
Botong Wu
James Wu
Jiamin Wu
Rujie Wu
Yu Wu
Rongchang Xie
Wei Xiong

Yunyang Xiong
An Xu
Chi Xu
Yinghao Xu
Fei Xue
Tingyun Yan
Zike Yan
Chao Yang
Heran Yang
Ren Yang
Wenfei Yang
Xu Yang
Rajeev Yasarla
Shaokai Ye
Yufei Ye
Kun Yi
Haichao Yu
Hanchao Yu
Ruixuan Yu
Liangzhe Yuan
Chen-Lin Zhang
Fandong Zhang
Tianyi Zhang
Yang Zhang
Yiyi Zhang
Yongshun Zhang
Yu Zhang
Zhiwei Zhang
Jiaojiao Zhao
Yipu Zhao
Xingjian Zhen
Haizhong Zheng
Tiancheng Zhi
Chengju Zhou
Hao Zhou
Hao Zhu
Alexander Zimin

Contents – Part XVII

Class-Wise Dynamic Graph Convolution for Semantic Segmentation 1
  Hanzhe Hu, Deyi Ji, Weihao Gan, Shuai Bai, Wei Wu, and Junjie Yan

Character-Preserving Coherent Story Visualization 18
  *Yun-Zhu Song, Zhi Rui Tam, Hung-Jen Chen, Huiao-Han Lu,
  and Hong-Han Shuai*

GINet: Graph Interaction Network for Scene Parsing 34
  *Tianyi Wu, Yu Lu, Yu Zhu, Chuang Zhang, Ming Wu, Zhanyu Ma,
  and Guodong Guo*

Tensor Low-Rank Reconstruction for Semantic Segmentation 52
  *Wanli Chen, Xinge Zhu, Ruoqi Sun, Junjun He, Ruiyu Li,
  Xiaoyong Shen, and Bei Yu*

Attentive Normalization 70
  Xilai Li, Wei Sun, and Tianfu Wu

Count- and Similarity-Aware R-CNN for Pedestrian Detection 88
  *Jin Xie, Hisham Cholakkal, Rao Muhammad Anwer,
  Fahad Shahbaz Khan, Yanwei Pang, Ling Shao, and Mubarak Shah*

TRADI: Tracking Deep Neural Network Weight Distributions 105
  *Gianni Franchi, Andrei Bursuc, Emanuel Aldea, Séverine Dubuisson,
  and Isabelle Bloch*

Spatiotemporal Attacks for Embodied Agents 122
  *Aishan Liu, Tairan Huang, Xianglong Liu, Yitao Xu, Yuqing Ma,
  Xinyun Chen, Stephen J. Maybank, and Dacheng Tao*

Caption-Supervised Face Recognition: Training a State-of-the-Art Face
Model Without Manual Annotation 139
  Qingqiu Huang, Lei Yang, Huaiyi Huang, Tong Wu, and Dahua Lin

Unselfie: Translating Selfies to Neutral-Pose Portraits in the Wild 156
  Liqian Ma, Zhe Lin, Connelly Barnes, Alexei A. Efros, and Jingwan Lu

Design and Interpretation of Universal Adversarial Patches
in Face Detection 174
  *Xiao Yang, Fangyun Wei, Hongyang Zhang,
  and Jun Zhu*

Few-Shot Object Detection and Viewpoint Estimation for Objects
in the Wild.   192
   Yang Xiao and Renaud Marlet

Weakly Supervised 3D Hand Pose Estimation via Biomechanical
Constraints.   211
   Adrian Spurr, Umar Iqbal, Pavlo Molchanov, Otmar Hilliges,
   and Jan Kautz

Dynamic Dual-Attentive Aggregation Learning for Visible-Infrared Person
Re-identification   229
   Mang Ye, Jianbing Shen, David J. Crandall, Ling Shao, and Jiebo Luo

Contextual Heterogeneous Graph Network for Human-Object
Interaction Detection   248
   Hai Wang, Wei-shi Zheng, and Ling Yingbiao

Zero-Shot Image Super-Resolution with Depth Guided Internal
Degradation Learning   265
   Xi Cheng, Zhenyong Fu, and Jian Yang

A Closest Point Proposal for MCMC-based Probabilistic
Surface Registration   281
   Dennis Madsen, Andreas Morel-Forster, Patrick Kahr, Dana Rahbani,
   Thomas Vetter, and Marcel Lüthi

Interactive Video Object Segmentation Using Global and Local
Transfer Modules   297
   Yuk Heo, Yeong Jun Koh, and Chang-Su Kim

End-to-end Interpretable Learning of Non-blind Image Deblurring.   314
   Thomas Eboli, Jian Sun, and Jean Ponce

Employing Multi-estimations for Weakly-Supervised
Semantic Segmentation   332
   Junsong Fan, Zhaoxiang Zhang, and Tieniu Tan

Learning Noise-Aware Encoder-Decoder from Noisy Labels by Alternating
Back-Propagation for Saliency Detection   349
   Jing Zhang, Jianwen Xie, and Nick Barnes

Rethinking Image Deraining via Rain Streaks and Vapors   367
   Yinglong Wang, Yibing Song, Chao Ma, and Bing Zeng

Finding Non-uniform Quantization Schemes Using Multi-task
Gaussian Processes   383
   Marcelo Gennari do Nascimento, Theo W. Costain,
   and Victor Adrian Prisacariu

Is Sharing of Egocentric Video Giving Away Your Biometric Signature?.   399
  Daksh Thapar, Chetan Arora, and Aditya Nigam

Captioning Images Taken by People Who Are Blind.   417
  Danna Gurari, Yinan Zhao, Meng Zhang, and Nilavra Bhattacharya

Improving Semantic Segmentation via Decoupled Body
and Edge Supervision   435
  *Xiangtai Li, Xia Li, Li Zhang, Guangliang Cheng, Jianping Shi,
  Zhouchen Lin, Shaohua Tan, and Yunhai Tong*

Conditional Entropy Coding for Efficient Video Compression   453
  *Jerry Liu, Shenlong Wang, Wei-Chiu Ma, Meet Shah, Rui Hu,
  Pranaab Dhawan, and Raquel Urtasun*

Differentiable Feature Aggregation Search for Knowledge Distillation   469
  *Yushuo Guan, Pengyu Zhao, Bingxuan Wang, Yuanxing Zhang,
  Cong Yao, Kaigui Bian, and Jian Tang*

Attention Guided Anomaly Localization in Images   485
  *Shashanka Venkataramanan, Kuan-Chuan Peng, Rajat Vikram Singh,
  and Abhijit Mahalanobis*

Self-supervised Video Representation Learning by Pace Prediction   504
  Jiangliu Wang, Jianbo Jiao, and Yun-Hui Liu

Full-Body Awareness from Partial Observations   522
  Chris Rockwell and David F. Fouhey

Reinforced Axial Refinement Network for Monocular
3D Object Detection   540
  Lijie Liu, Chufan Wu, Jiwen Lu, Lingxi Xie, Jie Zhou, and Qi Tian

Self-supervised Multi-task Procedure Learning from Instructional Videos   557
  Ehsan Elhamifar and Dat Huynh

CosyPose: Consistent Multi-view Multi-object 6D Pose Estimation   574
  Yann Labbé, Justin Carpentier, Mathieu Aubry, and Josef Sivic

In-Domain GAN Inversion for Real Image Editing   592
  Jiapeng Zhu, Yujun Shen, Deli Zhao, and Bolei Zhou

Key Frame Proposal Network for Efficient Pose Estimation in Videos.   609
  Yuexi Zhang, Yin Wang, Octavia Camps, and Mario Sznaier

Exchangeable Deep Neural Networks for Set-to-Set Matching
and Learning   626
  Yuki Saito, Takuma Nakamura, Hirotaka Hachiya, and Kenji Fukumizu

Making Sense of CNNs: Interpreting Deep Representations
and Their Invariances with INNs.................................... 647
   Robin Rombach, Patrick Esser, and Björn Ommer

Cross-Modal Weighting Network for RGB-D Salient Object Detection 665
   Gongyang Li, Zhi Liu, Linwei Ye, Yang Wang, and Haibin Ling

Open-Set Adversarial Defense 682
   Rui Shao, Pramuditha Perera, Pong C. Yuen, and Vishal M. Patel

Deep Image Compression Using Decoder Side Information 699
   Sharon Ayzik and Shai Avidan

Meta-Sim2: Unsupervised Learning of Scene Structure for Synthetic
Data Generation 715
   Jeevan Devaranjan, Amlan Kar, and Sanja Fidler

A Generic Visualization Approach for Convolutional Neural Networks 734
   Ahmed Taha, Xitong Yang, Abhinav Shrivastava, and Larry Davis

Interactive Annotation of 3D Object Geometry Using 2D Scribbles........ 751
   Tianchang Shen, Jun Gao, Amlan Kar, and Sanja Fidler

Hierarchical Kinematic Human Mesh Recovery 768
   Georgios Georgakis, Ren Li, Srikrishna Karanam, Terrence Chen,
   Jana Košecká, and Ziyan Wu

Multi-loss Rebalancing Algorithm for Monocular Depth Estimation........ 785
   Jae-Han Lee and Chang-Su Kim

Author Index 803

Class-Wise Dynamic Graph Convolution
for Semantic Segmentation

Hanzhe Hu[1]([✉])[iD], Deyi Ji[2][iD], Weihao Gan[2], Shuai Bai[3], Wei Wu[2],
and Junjie Yan[2]

[1] Peking University, Beijing, China
huhz@pku.edu.cn
[2] SenseTime Group Limited, Beijing, China
{jideyi,ganweihao,wuwei,yanjunjie}@sensetime.com
[3] Beijing University of Posts and Telecommunications, Beijing, China
baishuai@bupt.edu.cn

Abstract. Recent works have made great progress in semantic segmentation by exploiting contextual information in a local or global manner with dilated convolutions, pyramid pooling or self-attention mechanism. In order to avoid potential misleading contextual information aggregation in previous works, we propose a class-wise dynamic graph convolution (CDGC) module to adaptively propagate information. The graph reasoning is performed among pixels in the same class. Based on the proposed CDGC module, we further introduce the Class-wise Dynamic Graph Convolution Network (CDGCNet), which consists of two main parts including the CDGC module and a basic segmentation network, formi2ng a coarse-to-fine paradigm. Specifically, the CDGC module takes the coarse segmentation result as class mask to extract node features for graph construction and performs dynamic graph convolutions on the constructed graph to learn the feature aggregation and weight allocation. Then the refined feature and the original feature are fused to get the final prediction. We conduct extensive experiments on three popular semantic segmentation benchmarks including Cityscapes, PASCAL VOC 2012 and COCO Stuff, and achieve state-of-the-art performance on all three benchmarks.

Keywords: Semantic segmentation · Graph convolution · Coarse-to-fine framework

1 Introduction

Semantic Segmentation is a fundamental and challenging problem in computer vision, which aims to assign a category label to each pixel in an image. It has

H. Hu—This work is done when Hanzhe Hu is an intern at SenseTime Group Limited.

Electronic supplementary material The online version of this chapter (https:// doi.org/10.1007/978-3-030-58520-4_1) contains supplementary material, which is available to authorized users.

© Springer Nature Switzerland AG 2020
A. Vedaldi et al. (Eds.): ECCV 2020, LNCS 12362, pp. 1–17, 2020.
https://doi.org/10.1007/978-3-030-58520-4_1

been widely applied to many scenarios, such as autonomous driving, scene understanding and image editing.

Recent state-of-the-art semantic segmentation methods based on the fully
convolutional network (FCN) [23] have made great progress. To capture the
long-range contextual information, the atrous spatial pyramid pooling (ASPP)
module in DeepLabv3 [6] aggregates spatial regularly sampled pixels at different dilated rates and the pyramid pooling module in PSPNet [42] partitions
the feature maps into multiple regions before pooling. More comprehensively,
PSANet [43] was proposed to generate dense and pixel-wise contextual information, which learns to aggregate information via a predicted attention map.
Non-local Network [31] adopts self-attention mechanism, which enables every
pixel to receive information from every other pixels in the image, resulting in a
much complete pixel-wise representation (Fig. 1).

Fig. 1. Viusal example from left to right, top to bottom is : original image, groundtruth,
deeplabv3 result, the proposed CDGCNet result. From the two indicated regions, our
method preserves more contextual details and accurate prediction along boundaries.

However, the ways of utilizing the contextual information in existing
approaches are still problematic. From one point of view, larger receptive field
in deeper network is necessary for semantic prediction. Also, dilated based or
the pooling based methods take even larger contextual information into consideration. These two operations are neither adaptive nor friendly to pixel-wised
segmentation prediction problem. Another view of self-attention based methods (PSANet [43], Non-local Network [31], and etc. [12,15,18,38]) is that, pixels
from long-range non-local regions have different feature representations, which
results in major issues on two aspects when optimizing the convolution neural
network. First, contextual information is learned from previous network layers
by considering the local and non-local cues. Considering the large variations and
uncorrelations in contextual representations, weighted convoluting all the regions
together results in difficulties of learning discriminative pixel-level features. For
example, feature of a sky location with neighborhood tree region should be different from the one of a sky location with building region, which should not
be learned together. Second, contextual information is also class-specific. That

means, feature of a tree region is not proper to contribute to the learning of a sky region. The target is to directly distinguish whether the region is a sky region or not.

Aiming to address the above issues, we propose the Class-wise Dynamic Graph Convolution Network (CDGCNet), which can efficiently utilize the long-range contextual dependencies and aggregate the useful information for better pixel label prediction. Since graph convolution is remarkable at leveraging relations between nodes and can serve as a suitable reasoning method. It is worth noting that self-attention method is actually to build a fully-connected graph, so we further improve the structure of plain GCN for better performance. First, we adopt the class-wise strategy to construct the graph (node and edge) for each class, so that the useful information for each class can be independently learned. Second, for the graph of each class, not all the context regions are included during graph reasoning. Specifically, the hard positive and negative regions are dynamically identified into the graph transform. With these two designs in graph, the most important contextual information can be exploited for pixel level semantic prediction.

The overall framework of the proposed CDGCNet method is shown in Fig. 2, which follows the coarse-to-fine paradigm. The first part is a simple but complete semantic segmentation network, called basic network, which can generate coarse prediction map and it can be any of state-of-the-art semantic segmentation architectures. The second part is the CDGC module. Firstly, the CDGC module takes coarse prediction map and feature map from the basic network as inputs, and transforms the prediction map into class mask to extract node features from different classes for graph construction. After that, for each class, dynamic graph convolution is performed on the constructed graph to learn the feature aggregation and weight allocation. Finally, the refined feature and the original feature are fused to get the final prediction.

The main contributions of this paper are summarized as follows:

- The proposed CDGCNet utilizes a class-wise learning strategy so that semantically related features are considered for contextual learning.
- During the graph construction on each class, hard positive and hard negative information are dynamically sampled from the coarse segmentation result, which avoids heavy graph connections and benefits the feature learning.
- We conduct extensive experiments on several public datasets, and obtain state-of-the-art performances on the Cityscapes [9], PASCAL VOC 2012 [11] and COCO Stuff [2] datasets.

2 Related Work

Semantic Segmentation. Benefiting from the success of deep neural networks [14,17,29], semantic segmentation has achieved great progress. FCN [23] is the first approach to adopt fully convolutional network for semantic segmentation. Later, many FCN-baed works are proposed, such as UNet [26], Seg-Net [1], RefineNet [22], PSPNet [42], DeepLab series [4–7]. Chen *et al.* [5] and

Yu *et al.* [37] removed the last two downsample layers to obtain a dense prediction and utilized dilated convolutions to enlarge the receptive field. In our model, we also adopt the above paradigm to get a better feature map and hence, improve the performance of the model.

Context. Context plays a critical role in various vision tasks including semantic segmentation. Many works are proposed to generate better feature representations by exploiting better contextual information. From the spatial perspective, DeepLab v3 [6] employs multiple atrous convolutions with different dilation rates to capture contextual information, while PSPNet [42] employs pyramid pooling over sub-regions of four pyramid scales to harvest information. These methods, however, are all focusing on enlarging receptive fields in a local perspective and hence lose global context information. While from the attention perspective, Wang *et al.* [31] extend the idea of self-attention from transformer [30] into the vision field and proposed the non-local module to generate the attention map by calculating the correlation matrix between each spatial point in the feature map, and then the attention map guides the dense contextual information aggregation. Later, DANet [12] applied both spatial and channel attention to gather information around the feature maps. Unlike works mentioned above, our proposed module separately allocates attention to pixels belonging to the same category, effectively avoiding wrong contextual information aggregation.

Graph Reasoning. Graph-based methods have been very popular these days and shown to be an efficient way of relation reasoning. CRF [3] is proposed based on the graph model for image segmentation and works as an effective postprocessing method in DeepLab [5]. Recently, Graph Convolution Networks (GCN) [16] are proposed for semi-supervised classification, and Wang *et al.* [32] use GCN to capture relations between objects in video recognition tasks. Later, a few works based on GCN have been proposed onto the semantic segmentation problem, including [8,19,20], which all similarly model the relations between regions of the image rather than individual pixels. Concretely, clusters of pixels are defined as the vertices of the graph, hence graph reasoning is performed in the intermediate space projected from the original feature space to reduce computation cost . Different from these recent GCN-based methods, we perform graph convolution in a class-wise manner, where GCNs are employed only to the nodes in the same category, leading to a better feature learning. The refined features thus can provide a better prediction result in semantic segmentation task.

3   Approach

In this section, we will describe the proposed class-wise dynamic graph convolution (CDGC) module in detail. Firstly, we will revisit the basic knowledge of graph convolutional network. Then we will present a general framework of our network and introduce class-wise dynamic graph convolution module which separately performs graph reasoning on the pixels within the same category, hence

producing a refined prediction map for semantic segmentation. Finally, we will bring out the supervision manner of the proposed model.

3.1 Preliminaries

Graph Convolution. Given an input feature $X \in \mathbb{R}^{N \times D}$, where N is the number of nodes in the feature map and D is the feature dimension, we can build a feature graph G from this input feature. Specifically, the graph G can be formulated as $G = \{V, \varepsilon, A\}$ with V as its nodes, ε as its edges and A as its adjacency matrix. Normally, the adjacency matrix A is a binary matrix, in practice, we try many ways to construct the graph, including top-k binary matrix or dynamic learnable matrix, and further design a novel dynamic sampling method to construct the graph and perform extensive experiments to verify its validity. Intuitively, unlike standard convolutions which operates on a local regular grid, the graph enables us to compute the response of a node based on its neighbors defined in the adjacency matrix, hence receiving a much wider receptive field than regular convolutions. Formally, the graph convolution is defined as,

$$Z = \sigma(AXW), \tag{1}$$

where $\sigma(\cdot)$ denotes the non-linear activation function, $A \in \mathbb{R}^{N \times N}$ is the adjacency matrix measuring the relations of nodes in the graph and $W \in \mathbb{R}^{D \times D}$ is the weight matrix. In our experiments, we use ReLU as activation function and perform experiments with different graph construction methods.

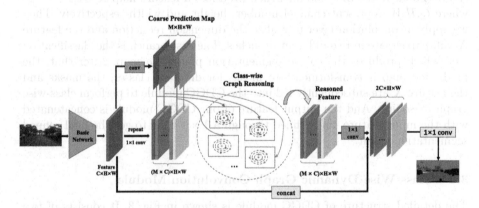

Fig. 2. An Overview of the Class-wise Dynamic Graph Convolution Network. Given an input image, we first feed it into the basic segmentation network to get the high-level feature map and the corresponding coarse segmentation result. Then the CDGC module is applied to preform graph reasoning along nodes of the feature map, producing a refined feature which is subsequently fused with the original feature to get the final refined segmentation result. Specially, in the class-wise graph reasoning part, different colors of lines and dots denote different classes of pixels, under the guidance of coarse prediction map, most positive pixels are sampled while also harvesting few hard pixels in different colors from the target color.

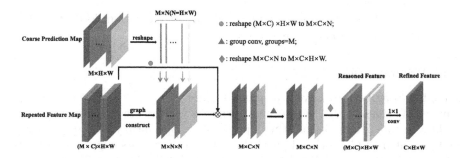

Fig. 3. The details of Class-wise Dynamic Graph Convolution Module.

3.2   Overall Framework

As illustrated in Fig. 2, we present the Class-wise Dynamic Graph Convolution Network to adaptively capture long-range contextual information. We use the ResNet-101 pretrained on the ImageNet dataset as the backbone, replace the last two down-sampling operations and employ dilation convolutions in the subsequent convolutional layers, hence enlarging the resolution and receptive field of the feature map, so the output stride becomes 8 instead of 16.

Our model consists of two parts: basic network and CDGC module. Specifically, we adopt ResNet-101 together with atrous spatial pyramid pooling (ASPP) as the basic complete segmentation network. An input image is passed through the backbone and ASPP module, then produces a feature map $X \in \mathbb{R}^{C \times H \times W}$, where C,H,W represent channel number, height and width respectively. Then we apply a convolution layer to realize the dimension reduction and the feature X will participate in two different branches. The first branch is the classification step which produces the coarse segmentation prediction map. After that, the prediction map is transformed into masks for different classes, the masks and the feature X are subsequently fed into the CDGC module to perform class-wise graph reasoning. And the output feature of our CDGC module is concatenated with the input feature, and refined through a 1×1 conv to get the final refined segmentation result.

3.3   Class-Wise Dynamic Graph Convolution Module

The detailed structure of CDGC module is shown in Fig. 3. It consists of two subsequent processes, including graph construction and reasoning. The proposed module is based on a coarse-to-fine framework, where the input is the feature map X, coarse prediction map and the output is the refined feature map.

Class-wise Learning Strategy. Different from previous works [8,19,20] where graph construction is performed on all the nodes of different classes in the feature map, we adopt a class-wise learning strategy. There are several advantages. First, contextual information from different classes is considered separately so that the irrelevant region can be excluded to avoid the difficulty of learning. Second, it

is easy to hard-mine the important information for a binary task (determine whether it is the target class or not) compared to the multi-class task learning.

Specifically, in the training process, a coarse-to-fine framework is adopted. The coarse prediction can be generated from a basic network. Each coarse predicted category is utilized to filter out the corresponding category and perform a graph construction based on the filtering operation. Hence, graph reasoning and information transmission only occur inside the chosen category, protecting the process of context aggregation from the interference of features in other categories.

Graph Construction. (1) Similarity Graph. Intuitively, we can build the graph (which is adjacency matrix in our formulation) based on the similarity between different nodes, for two node features x_i, x_j, the pairwise similarity between two nodes is defined as,

$$F(x_i, x_j) = \phi(x_i)^T \phi'(x_j), \tag{2}$$

where ϕ, ϕ' denote two different transformations of the original features. In practice, we adopt linear transformations, hence $\phi(x) = wx$ and $\phi'(x) = w'x$. The parameters w and w' are both $D \times D$ dimensions weights which can be learned via back propagation, forming a dynamically learned graph construction method. After computing the similarity matrix, we perform normalization on each row of the matrix so that the sum of all the edge values connected to one node i will be 1. In practice, we choose softmax as normalization function, so the output adjacency matrix will be,

$$A_{ij} = \frac{exp(F(x_i, x_j))}{\sum_{j=1}^{N} exp(F(x_i, x_j))} \tag{3}$$

(2) Dynamic Sampling. The original sampling method adopts a fully-connected fashion for pixels in the same category. However, since the prediction mask is obtained from a coarse segmentation result, it is possible that the sampled pixels are not actually belong to the same category, which makes the sampled set include 'easy positive' part and 'hard negative' part. In order to allocate enough attention to these hard-to-classify pixels, we develop a dynamic sampling method which focuses on selecting out these hard pixels. As shown in Fig. 4, in the training process, we take coarse segmentation mask and groundtruth mask as input, and compute the intersection set between them, which is pure 'easy positive' part. Formally, we denote the coarse segmentation mask, groundtruth mask set as C and G respectively, hence the intersection set can be denoted as $C \cap G$. Then with coarse segmentation mask subtracting the intersection set, the rest part is pure 'hard negative' denoted as $C - C \cap G$. Similarly, with groundtruth mask getting rid of the intersection set, the rest part is pure 'hard positive', denoted as $G - C \cap G$. Besides, some ratio of 'easy positive' samples are needed to guide the learning of these hard pixels, so we randomly choose some ratio of

pixels from the intersection set which consists of pure 'easy positive' samples, so we finally get the sampled set denoted as,

$$Sampled = C - C \cap G + G - C \cap G + ratio \cdot C \cap G$$
$$= C \cup G - (1 - ratio) \cdot C \cap G \tag{4}$$

Therefore, with this dynamic sampling method, our graph construction process can pay enough attention to these hard pixels.

Specifically, dynamic sampling is only used at the training stage but not the inference stage. At the training stage, we use both coarse prediction mask and groundtruth mask to mine hard positive and negative samples in a class-wise manner. Besides, some easy positive samples are also selected to guide the hard samples learning. All these samples compose the graph nodes for the training stage. At the inference stage, pixels in the same category according to the coarse prediction mask are sampled to construct the graph.

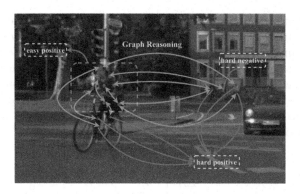

Fig. 4. Illustration of dynamic sampling method. For one category 'rider' in this image, green and red points denote easy and hard samples, respectively. Hard positive samples consist of distant objects and boundaries. And hard negative samples denote the illegible object (person) in this image, which is likely to be recognized as rider.

Graph Reasoning. Discriminative pixel-level feature representations are essential for semantic segmentation, which could be obtained by the proposed graph convolution based module in a class-wise manner. By exploiting the relations between pixels sampled by category, the intra-class consistency can be preserved and moreover, inter-class discrepancy can also be enhanced with our dynamic sampling method.

The detailed structure of CDGC module is shown in Fig. 3. The module takes the repeated feature map $X \in \mathbb{R}^{(M \times C) \times H \times W}$ and coarse prediction map $P \in \mathbb{R}^{M \times H \times W}$ as input, where M, C, H, W denote the number of classes in the dataset, dimension of the feature map, height and width, respectively. Inspired by point cloud segmentation [25,33], we treat nodes in the feature map as the vertexes in the graph. Therefore, we transform the feature map to the

graph representation: $X \in \mathbb{R}^{M \times C \times N}$, where $N = H \times W$ denotes the number of nodes in the feature map. Similarly, we transform the coarse prediction map into $P \in \mathbb{R}^{M \times N}$. Applying the graph construction methods discussed above, we can obtain the adjacency matrix of the feature map for each category, treating each graph feature $x \in \mathbb{R}^{C \times N}$ separately (M in total), thus producing M adjacency matrices integrated as $A \in \mathbb{R}^{M \times N \times N}$.

Following the paradigm of graph convolution, we multiply the adjacency matrix and the transposed feature map to get the sampled feature map $X \in \mathbb{R}^{M \times C \times N}$. Subsequently, group graph convolution is performed, resulting in a feature $X \in \mathbb{R}^{M \times C \times N}$ which will be reshaped back to the original grid form: $X \in \mathbb{R}^{M \times C \times H \times W}$. Then a 1×1 conv is performed to learn the weights of adaptively aggregrating feature maps for M classes, producing a refined feature $X \in \mathbb{R}^{C \times H \times W}$. Once obtaining the refined feature map, we combine this feature map with the input feature map to get the final output. Specifically, the combine method is concatenation or summation. Finally ,the output feature is passed through the conventional 1×1 convolution layer to get the final segmentation prediction map.

3.4 Loss Function

Both coarse and refined output are supervised with the semantic labels. Moreover, following normal practice in previous state-of-the-art works [39,42,44], we add the auxiliary supervision for improving the performance, as well as making the network easier to optimize. Specifically, the output of the third stage of our backbone ResNet-101 is further fed into a auxiliary layer to produce a auxiliary prediction, which is supervised with the auxiliary loss. As for the main path, coarse segmentation result and refined segmentation result are produced and hence require proper supervision. We apply standard cross entropy loss to supervise the auxiliary output and the coarse prediction map, and employ OHEM loss [27] for the refined prediction map. In a word, the loss can be formulated as follows,

$$L = \alpha \cdot l_c + \beta \cdot l_f + \gamma \cdot l_a \tag{5}$$

where α, β, γ are used to balance the coarse prediction loss l_c, refined prediction loss l_f and auxiliary loss l_a.

4 Experiments

To evaluate the performance of our proposed CDGC module, we carry out extensive experiments on benchmark datasets including Cityscapes [9], PASCAL VOC 2012 [11] and COCO Stuff [2]. Experimental results demonstrate that the proposed method can effectively boost the performance of the state-of-the-art methods. In the following section, we will introduce the datasets and implementation details, and then perform ablation study on Cityscapes dataset. Finally, we report the results on PASCAL VOC 2012 dataset and COCO Stuff dataset.

4.1   Datasets and Evaluation Metrics

Cityscapes. The Cityscapes dataset [9] is tasked for urban scene understanding, which contains 30 classes and only 19 classes of them are used for scene parsing evaluation. The dataset contains 5000 finely annotated images and 20000 coarsely annotated images. The finely annotated 5000 images are divided into 2975/500/1525 images for training, validation and testing.

PASCAL VOC 2012. The PASCAL VOC 2012 dataset [11] is one of the most competitive semantic segmentation dataset which contains 20 foreground object classes and 1 background class. The dataset is split into 1464/1449/1556 images for training, validation and testing. [13] has augmented this dataset with annotations ,resulting in 10582 train-aug images.

COCO Stuff. The COCO Stuff dataset [2] is a challenging scene parsing dataset containing 59 semantic classes and 1 background class. The training and test set consist of 9K and 1K images respectively.

In our experiments, the mean of class-wise Intersection over Union (mIoU) is used as the evaluation metric.

4.2   Implementation Details

We choose the ImageNet pretrained ResNet-101 as our backbone and remove the last two down-sampling operations, and employ dilated convolutions in the subsequent convolution layers, making the output stride equal to 8. For training, we use the stochastic gradient descent (SGD) optimizer with initial learning rate 0.01, weight decay 0.0005 and momentum 0.9 for Cityscapes dataset. Moreover, we adopt the 'poly' learning rate policy, where the initial learning rate is multiplied by $(1 - \frac{iter}{max\_iter})^{power}$ with power=0.9. For Cityscapes dataset, we adopt the crop size as 769×769, batch size as 8 and training iterations as 30K. For PASCAL VOC 2012 dataset, we set the initial learning rate as 0.001, weight decay as 0.0001, crop size as 513×513, batch size as 16 and training iterations as 30K. For COCO Stuff dataset, we set initial learning rate as 0.001, weight decay as 0.0001, crop size as 520×520, batch size as 16, and training iterations as 60K. Moreover, the loss weights α, β, γ are set to be 0.6, 0.7 and 0.4 respectively.

4.3   Ablation Study

In this subsection, we conduct extensive ablation experiments on the validation set of Cityscapes with different settings for our proposed CDGCNet.

The Impact of Class-Wise Learning Strategy. We use the dilated ResNet-101 as the baseline network, and final segmentation result is obtained by directly upsampling the output. To evaluate the effectiveness of the proposed class-wise learning strategy, we carry out the experiments where plain GCN and class-wise GCN are adopted separately. Concretely, plain GCN is realized by simply performing graph construction operation on the feature map obtained from the

Table 1. Performance comparisons of our proposed class-wise GCN and plain-GCN on Cityscapes validation set.

Method	mIOU (%)
ResNet-101 Baseline	76.3
ResNet-101 + plain-GCN	78.2
ResNet-101 + class-GCN	79.4

Table 2. Detailed performance comparisons of our proposed Class-wise Dynamic Graph Convolution module on Cityscapes validation set.

Method	mIOU (%)
ResNet-101 Baseline	76.3
ResNet-101 + ASPP	78.4
ResNet-101 + CDGC(concat)	79.4
ResNet-101 + CDGC(sum)	79.2
ResNet-101 + ASPP+CDGC(sum)	79.9
ResNet-101 + ASPP + CDGC(concat)	80.0

backbone, while class-wise GCN is realized in a class-wise manner. Their graph construction methods are similar. As shown in Table 1, the proposed class-wise GCN reasoning performs better than the plain GCN. Since plain-CGN adopts fully connected fashion onto the input feature map, it serves similarly as self-attention based method, which is likely to mislead the contextual information aggregation with features from pixels of other categories, while our method, on the other hand, is capable of avoiding this kind of problem.

The Impact of CDGC Module. Based on the dilated ResNet-101 backbone, we subsequently add ASPP module and the proposed module to evaluate the performance, as shown in Table 2. The graph is constructed based on dynamic similarity. The result of solely adding ASPP module is 78.4%, which is about 1% lower than solely adding CDGC module. Furthermore, we perform experiments on the feature aggregation manners which include concatenation and summation. As results shown in Table 2, the CDGC module can significantly improve the performance over the baseline network by 3% in mIOU and concatenation method is slightly better than the summation one, so we will use concatenation aggregation method in later comparisons. Finally, we choose ResNet-101 plus ASPP module as our basic segmentation network and use CDGC module to get the final refined prediction map, achieving 1.6% gain in mIOU, which demonstrates that CDGC module can be easily plugged into any state-of-the-art segmentation network to further boost the performance. The effect of CDGC module can be visualized in Fig. 5. Some details and boundaries are refined compared to the coarse map predicted by the basic network. These results prove that our proposed CDGC module can significantly capture long-range contextual information together with local cue and also preserve intra-class consistency, which can effectively boost the performance of segmentation.

Comparisons of Different Graph Construction Methods. In this subsection, we evaluate the performance of our module using two different graph construction methods mentioned before. Specifically, we use ResNet-101+ASPP as basic segmentation network and the original feature is concatenated with refined feature to get the final prediction map. Table 3 indicates the

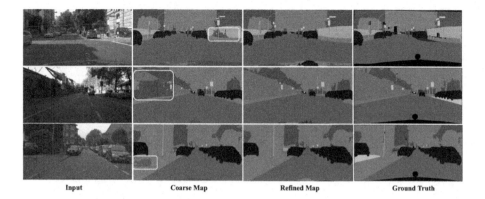

| Input | Coarse Map | Refined Map | Ground Truth |

Fig. 5. Visualization results on Cityscapes validation set.

Table 3. Performance comparisons of graph construction method on Cityscapes validation set.

Method	mIOU (%)
ResNet-101 + ASPP	78.4
ResNet-101 + ASPP + CDGC(sim)	80.0
ResNet-101 + ASPP + CDGC(ds 0.2)	79.8
ResNet-101 + ASPP + CDGC(ds 0.4)	80.3
ResNet-101 + ASPP + CDGC(ds 0.6)	80.8
ResNet-101 + ASPP + CDGC(ds 0.8)	80.9
ResNet-101 + ASPP + CDGC(ds 1.0)	81.1

Table 4. Performance influences with different evaluation strategies on Cityscapes validation set.

Method	MS	Flip	mIOU (%)
CDGCNet			81.1
CDGCNet	✓		81.6
CDGCNet		✓	81.4
CDGCNet	✓	✓	**81.9**

performance on Cityscapes validation set by adopting different graph construction method, where 'sim' denotes the similarity graph method and 'ds' denotes the dynamic sampling method and the easy positive sampling ratio is set as [0.2, 0.4, 0.6, 0.8]. As can be seen in Table 3, as the easy positive sampling ratio grows, the performance becomes better since the easy positive samples serve as the guiding criterion for learning the reasonable weights for hard samples. From the result shown in Table 3, when sampling ratio is above 0.4, the dynamic sampling method can outperform the similarity graph method since it gives more attention to hard samples including hard positive ones and hard negative ones while similarity graph adaptively learn the parameters of the construction weights, which may not be efficiently learned in similarity graph method.

The Impact of Hard Samples. We further perform experiments to evaluate the impact of hard samples utilized in dynamic sampling method. At the training stage, we construct the graph with dynamic sampling method while keeping the ratio of easy positive samples as 1.0. From the result shown in Table 5, utilizing hard samples can improve the performance since extra attention can be paid to hard pixels, hence performing a better feature learning process.

Table 5. Performance comparisons of different samples used in dynamic sampling method on Cityscapes validation set.

Sample	mIOU(%)
Easy Positive	79.9
Easy Positive + Hard Positive	80.5
Easy Positive + Hard Negative	80.0
Easy Positive + Hard Positive + Hard Negative	81.1

The Impact of Evaluation Strategies. Based on details discussed above, we propose Class-wise Dynamic Graph Convolution Network (CDGCNet) with ResNet-101+ASPP as basic network and dynamic sampling method to construct the graph. Like previous work [12,15,34,38,42], we also adopt the left-right flipping and multi-scale [0.75, 1.0, 1.25, 1.5, 1.75, 2.0] evaluation strategies. From Table 4, MS/Flip improves the performance by 0.8% on validation set.

Visualizations of Class-Wise Features. Qualitative results are provided in Figure 6 to compare the difference of class-wise features before and after CDGC module. We use white squares to mark the challenging regions which compose of hard samples. As shown in the figure, after class-wise dynamic graph convoluton, hard pixels can be effectively resolved. In particular, in the first and third lines, hard pixels are specified to hard negative pixels and can be successfully distinguished. While in the second line, hard pixels are specified to hard positive pixels, as shown in the visualization, ambiguity is well taken care of. Moreover, with dynamic sampling method mining hard samples, boundary information is preserved and enhanced, hence producing better results.

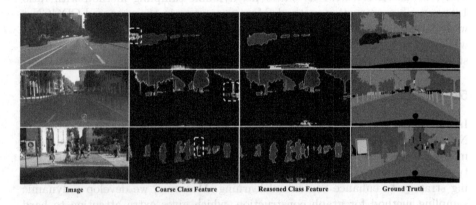

Fig. 6. Visualizations of class-wise features before and after graph convolution on Cityscapes validation set. From left to right: input image, class-wise feature before CDGC module, class-wise feature after CDGC module, ground truth. From top to bottom, the visualized category is car, vegetation and person.

Table 6. Comparisons with State-of-the-art methods on three benchmark datatsets.

Methods	Backbone	Cityscapes mIOU(%)	PASCAL VOC 2012 mIOU(%)	COCO Stuff mIOU(%)
FCN [23]	VGG-16	-	62.2	22.7
DeepLab-CRF [5]	VGG-16	-	71.6	-
DAG-RNN [28]	VGG-16	-	-	31.2
RefineNet [22]	ResNet-101	73.6	-	33.6
GCN [24]	ResNet-101	76.9	-	-
SAC [41]	ResNet-101	78.1	-	-
CCL [10]	ResNet-101	-	-	35.7
PSPNet [42]	ResNet-101	78.4	82.6	-
BiSeNet [35]	ResNet-101	78.9	-	-
DFN [36]	ResNet-101	79.3	82.7	-
DSSPN [21]	ResNet-101	-	-	37.3
SGR [20]	ResNet-101	-	-	39.1
PSANet [43]	ResNet-101	80.1	-	-
DenseASPP [34]	DenseNet-161	80.6	-	-
GloRe [8]	ResNet-101	80.9	-	-
EncNet [40]	ResNet-101	-	82.9	-
DANet [12]	ResNet-101	81.5	82.6	39.7
CDGCNet(Ours)	ResNet-101	**82.0**	**83.9**	**40.7**

4.4   Comparisons with State-of-the-Arts

Furthermore, we evaluate our method on the test set of three benchmark datasets: Cityscapes, PASCAL VOC 2012 and COCO Stuff datasets. Specifically, we use ResNet-101 as backbone, dynamic sampling method with ratio 1.0 as graph construction method. Moreover, we train the proposed CDGCNet with both training and validation set and use the multi-scale and flip strategies while testing. From Table 6, it can be observed that our CDGCNet achieves state-of-the-art performance on all three benchmark datasets.

5   Conclusions

In this paper, we have presented the Class-wise Dynamic Graph Convolution Network (CDGCNet) which can adaptively capture long-range contextual information, hence performing a reliable graph reasoning along nodes for better feature aggregation and weight allocation. Specifically, we utilize a class-wise learning strategy to enhance contextual learning. Moreover, we develop a dynamic sampling method for graph construction, which gives extra attention to hard samples, thus benefiting the feature learning. The ablation experiments demonstrate the effectiveness of CDGC module. Our CDGCNet achieves outstanding performance on three benchmark datasets, *i.e.* Cityscapes, PASCAL VOC 2012 and COCO Stuff.

References

1. Badrinarayanan, V., Kendall, A., Cipolla, R.: Segnet: a deep convolutional encoder-decoder architecture for image segmentation. IEEE Trans. Pattern Analysis Machine Intell. **39**(12), 2481–2495 (2017)
2. Caesar, H., Uijlings, J., Ferrari, V.: Coco-stuff: thing and stuff classes in context. In: Proceedings of the IEEE Conference on Computer Vision and Pattern Recognition, pp. 1209–1218 (2018)
3. Chandra, S., Usunier, N., Kokkinos, I.: Dense and low-rank gaussian CRFs using deep embeddings. In: Proceedings of the IEEE International Conference on Computer Vision, pp. 5103–5112 (2017)
4. Chen, L.C., Papandreou, G., Kokkinos, I., Murphy, K., Yuille, A.L.: Semantic image segmentation with deep convolutional nets and fully connected CRFs. arXiv preprint arXiv:1412.7062 (2014)
5. Chen, L.C., Papandreou, G., Kokkinos, I., Murphy, K., Yuille, A.L.: Deeplab: semantic image segmentation with deep convolutional nets, atrous convolution, and fully connected crfs. IEEE Trans. Pattern Anal. Mach. Intell. **40**(4), 834–848 (2017)
6. Chen, L.C., Papandreou, G., Schroff, F., Adam, H.: Rethinking atrous convolution for semantic image segmentation. arXiv preprint arXiv:1706.05587 (2017)
7. Chen, L.C., Zhu, Y., Papandreou, G., Schroff, F., Adam, H.: Encoder-decoder with atrous separable convolution for semantic image segmentation. In: Proceedings of the European Conference on Computer Vision (ECCV), pp. 801–818 (2018)
8. Chen, Y., Rohrbach, M., Yan, Z., Shuicheng, Y., Feng, J., Kalantidis, Y.: Graph-based global reasoning networks. In: Proceedings of the IEEE Conference on Computer Vision and Pattern Recognition, pp. 433–442 (2019)
9. Cordts, M., et al.: The cityscapes dataset for semantic urban scene understanding. In: Proceedings of the IEEE Conference on Computer Vision and Pattern Recognition, pp. 3213–3223 (2016)
10. Ding, H., Jiang, X., Shuai, B., Qun Liu, A., Wang, G.: Context contrasted feature and gated multi-scale aggregation for scene segmentation. In: Proceedings of the IEEE Conference on Computer Vision and Pattern Recognition, pp. 2393–2402 (2018)
11. Everingham, M., Van Gool, L., Williams, C.K., Winn, J., Zisserman, A.: The pascal visual object classes (VOC) challenge. Int. J. Comput. Vis. **88**(2), 303–338 (2010). https://doi.org/10.1007/s11263-009-0275-4
12. Fu, J., et al.: Dual attention network for scene segmentation. In: Proceedings of the IEEE Conference on Computer Vision and Pattern Recognition, pp. 3146–3154 (2019)
13. Hariharan, B., Arbeláez, P., Bourdev, L., Maji, S., Malik, J.: Semantic contours from inverse detectors. In: 2011 International Conference on Computer Vision, pp. 991–998. IEEE (2011)
14. He, K., Zhang, X., Ren, S., Sun, J.: Deep residual learning for image recognition. In: Proceedings of the IEEE Conference on Computer Vision and Pattern Recognition, pp. 770–778 (2016)
15. Huang, Z., Wang, X., Huang, L., Huang, C., Wei, Y., Liu, W.: Ccnet: Criss-cross attention for semantic segmentation. arXiv preprint arXiv:1811.11721 (2018)
16. Kipf, T.N., Welling, M.: Semi-supervised classification with graph convolutional networks. arXiv preprint arXiv:1609.02907 (2016)

17. Krizhevsky, A., Sutskever, I., Hinton, G.E.: Imagenet classification with deep convolutional neural networks. In: Advances in Neural Information Processing Systems, pp. 1097–1105 (2012)
18. Li, X., Zhong, Z., Wu, J., Yang, Y., Lin, Z., Liu, H.: Expectation-maximization attention networks for semantic segmentation. In: The IEEE International Conference on Computer Vision (ICCV), October 2019
19. Li, Y., Gupta, A.: Beyond grids: learning graph representations for visual recognition. In: Advances in Neural Information Processing Systems. pp. 9225–9235 (2018)
20. Liang, X., Hu, Z., Zhang, H., Lin, L., Xing, E.P.: Symbolic graph reasoning meets convolutions. In: Advances in Neural Information Processing Systems, pp. 1853–1863 (2018)
21. Liang, X., Zhou, H., Xing, E.: Dynamic-structured semantic propagation network. In: Proceedings of the IEEE Conference on Computer Vision and Pattern Recognition, pp. 752–761 (2018)
22. Lin, G., Milan, A., Shen, C., Reid, I.: Refinenet: multi-path refinement networks for high-resolution semantic segmentation. In: Proceedings of the IEEE Conference on Computer Vision and Pattern Recognition, pp. 1925–1934 (2017)
23. Long, J., Shelhamer, E., Darrell, T.: Fully convolutional networks for semantic segmentation. In: Proceedings of the IEEE Conference on Computer Vision and Pattern Recognition, pp. 3431–3440 (2015)
24. Peng, C., Zhang, X., Yu, G., Luo, G., Sun, J.: Large kernel matters-improve semantic segmentation by global convolutional network. In: Proceedings of the IEEE Conference on Computer Vision and Pattern Recognition, pp. 4353–4361 (2017)
25. Qi, C.R., Su, H., Mo, K., Guibas, L.J.: Pointnet: deep learning on point sets for 3D classification and segmentation. In: Proceedings of the IEEE Conference on Computer Vision and Pattern Recognition, pp. 652–660 (2017)
26. Ronneberger, O., Fischer, P., Brox, T.: U-Net: convolutional networks for biomedical image segmentation. In: Navab, N., Hornegger, J., Wells, W.M., Frangi, A.F. (eds.) MICCAI 2015, Part III. LNCS, vol. 9351, pp. 234–241. Springer, Cham (2015). https://doi.org/10.1007/978-3-319-24574-4_28
27. Shrivastava, A., Gupta, A., Girshick, R.: Training region-based object detectors with online hard example mining. In: Proceedings of the IEEE Conference on Computer Vision and Pattern Recognition, pp. 761–769 (2016)
28. Shuai, B., Zuo, Z., Wang, B., Wang, G.: Scene segmentation with DAG-recurrent neural networks. IEEE Trans. Pattern Anal. Mach. Intel. **40**(6), 1480–1493 (2017)
29. Simonyan, K., Zisserman, A.: Very deep convolutional networks for large-scale image recognition. arXiv preprint arXiv:1409.1556 (2014)
30. Vaswani, A., et al.: Attention is all you need. In: Advances in Neural Information Processing Systems, pp. 5998–6008 (2017)
31. Wang, X., Girshick, R., Gupta, A., He, K.: Non-local neural networks. In: Proceedings of the IEEE Conference on Computer Vision and Pattern Recognition, pp. 7794–7803 (2018)
32. Wang, X., Gupta, A.: Videos as space-time region graphs. In: Ferrari, V., Hebert, M., Sminchisescu, C., Weiss, Y. (eds.) ECCV 2018. LNCS, vol. 11209, pp. 413–431. Springer, Cham (2018). https://doi.org/10.1007/978-3-030-01228-1_25
33. Wang, Y., Sun, Y., Liu, Z., Sarma, S.E., Bronstein, M.M., Solomon, J.M.: Dynamic graph CNN for learning on point clouds. ACM Trans. Graph. (TOG) **38**(5), 146 (2019)

34. Yang, M., Yu, K., Zhang, C., Li, Z., Yang, K.: Denseaspp for semantic segmentation in street scenes. In: Proceedings of the IEEE Conference on Computer Vision and Pattern Recognition. pp. 3684–3692 (2018)
35. Yu, C., Wang, J., Peng, C., Gao, C., Yu, G., Sang, N.: BiSeNet: bilateral segmentation network for real-time semantic segmentationBiSeNet: bilateral segmentation network for real-time semantic segmentation. In: Ferrari, V., Hebert, M., Sminchisescu, C., Weiss, Y. (eds.) ECCV 2018. LNCS, vol. 11217, pp. 334–349. Springer, Cham (2018). https://doi.org/10.1007/978-3-030-01261-8_20
36. Yu, C., Wang, J., Peng, C., Gao, C., Yu, G., Sang, N.: Learning a discriminative feature network for semantic segmentation. In: Proceedings of the IEEE Conference on Computer Vision and Pattern Recognition, pp. 1857–1866 (2018)
37. Yu, F., Koltun, V.: Multi-scale context aggregation by dilated convolutions. arXiv preprint arXiv:1511.07122 (2015)
38. Yuan, Y., Wang, J.: Ocnet: Object context network for scene parsing. arXiv preprint arXiv:1809.00916 (2018)
39. Zhang, F., et al.: Acfnet: attentional class feature network for semantic segmentation. In: Proceedings of the IEEE International Conference on Computer Vision, pp. 6798–6807 (2019)
40. Zhang, H., et al.: Context encoding for semantic segmentation. In: Proceedings of the IEEE Conference on Computer Vision and Pattern Recognition, pp. 7151–7160 (2018)
41. Zhang, R., Tang, S., Zhang, Y., Li, J., Yan, S.: Scale-adaptive convolutions for scene parsing. In: Proceedings of the IEEE International Conference on Computer Vision, pp. 2031–2039 (2017)
42. Zhao, H., Shi, J., Qi, X., Wang, X., Jia, J.: Pyramid scene parsing network. In: Proceedings of the IEEE Conference on Computer Vision and Pattern Recognition, pp. 2881–2890 (2017)
43. Zhao, H., et al.: PSANet: point-wise spatial attention network for scene parsing. In: Ferrari, V., Hebert, M., Sminchisescu, C., Weiss, Y. (eds.) ECCV 2018. LNCS, vol. 11213, pp. 270–286. Springer, Cham (2018). https://doi.org/10.1007/978-3-030-01240-3_17
44. Zhu, Z., Xu, M., Bai, S., Huang, T., Bai, X.: Asymmetric non-local neural networks for semantic segmentation. In: Proceedings of the IEEE International Conference on Computer Vision, pp. 593–602 (2019)

Character-Preserving Coherent Story Visualization

Yun-Zhu Song$^{(\boxtimes)}$ ⓘ, Zhi Rui Tam ⓘ, Hung-Jen Chen ⓘ, Huiao-Han Lu ⓘ, and Hong-Han Shuai ⓘ

National Chiao Tung University, Hsinchu, Taiwan
{yunzhusong.eed07g,ray.eed08g,hjc.eed07g,hsiaohan.eed05g, hhshuai}@nctu.edu.tw

Abstract. Story visualization aims at generating a sequence of images to narrate each sentence in a multi-sentence story. Different from video generation that focuses on maintaining the continuity of generated images (frames), story visualization emphasizes preserving the global consistency of characters and scenes across different story pictures, which is very challenging since story sentences only provide sparse signals for generating images. Therefore, we propose a new framework named Character-Preserving Coherent Story Visualization (CP-CSV) to tackle the challenges. CP-CSV effectively learns to visualize the story by three critical modules: story and context encoder (story and sentence representation learning), figure-ground segmentation (auxiliary task to provide information for preserving character and story consistency), and figure-ground aware generation (image sequence generation by incorporating figure-ground information). Moreover, we propose a metric named Fréchet Story Distance (FSD) to evaluate the performance of story visualization. Extensive experiments demonstrate that CP-CSV maintains the details of character information and achieves high consistency among different frames, while FSD better measures the performance of story visualization.

Keywords: Story visualization · Evaluation metric · Foreground segmentation

1 Introduction

"Objects in pictures should so be arranged as by their very position to tell their own story."

— Johann Wolfgang von Goethe *(1749–1832)*

Story Visualization task aims to generate meaningful and coherent sequences of images according to the story text [18], which is challenging since it requires

---

Electronic supplementary material The online version of this chapter (https://doi.org/10.1007/978-3-030-58520-4_2) contains supplementary material, which is available to authorized users.

© Springer Nature Switzerland AG 2020
A. Vedaldi et al. (Eds.): ECCV 2020, LNCS 12362, pp. 18–33, 2020.
https://doi.org/10.1007/978-3-030-58520-4_2

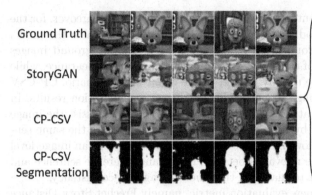

Ground Truth

StoryGAN

CP-CSV

CP-CSV
Segmentation

Eddy raises his ears and gathers his hands on his chest. Eddy talks while gathering his hands on his chest. Eddy becomes a sullen face. Pororo talks while sitting at the table. Pororo says something and smiles. Eddy smiles and raises his ears and stands up.

Fig. 1. Story Visualization task prompts to generate image sequences given story descriptions. Our proposed CP-CSV can generate image sequences closely related to the synthesized segmentation result.

an understanding of both natural language and images. Specifically, *Story Visualization* generates a sequence of images to narrate a given story written in a multi-sentence paragraph. Figure 1 shows an illustrative example of *Story Visualization*. As the saying goes, "A picture is worth a thousand words," and a good visualization puts the color inside of the story world and assists the comprehension quickly.

Nevertheless, it remains a challenging task due to the following three challenges. 1) <u>Sequence Coherence.</u> Building transformation between sentences and images requires the ability to tackle cross-domain representation learning, which is highly similar to the text-to-image tasks. However, the major difference between *Story Visualization* and *Text-to-Image* is that *Story Visualization* generates an image sequence based on the whole story comprehension whereas *Text-to-Image* is only based on a single sentence information. In other words, directly applying *Text-to-Image* for story visualization may result in an incoherent image sequences, i.e., images with different contexts. 2) <u>High Variety by Character Dominance.</u> Since the story characters usually occupy a large proportion of pictures (dominance), the pictures change dramatically when different characters appear (variety). The high variety between frames makes the learning of sequence coherence difficult. 3) <u>Implicit Objectives.</u> The goal of the task is to generate high-quality and coherent image sequences that can depict the whole story. However, the subjective and obscure concepts are not standardized into a learning objective function.

Based on the observations, in this paper, we propose a novel framework, namely, *Character-Preserving Coherent Story Visualization (CP-CSV)*, to visualize a story with distinctive characters and a highly-coherent storyline. Specifically, to address the first challenge, two text encoders are used to process the sentence-level and story-level input text. The context encoder focuses on a single sentence and extracts the character information to enhance the character generation, while a story encoder embraces the whole paragraph and utilizes two

GRU layers to filter the context information at each time step. Moreover, for the second challenge, we introduce figure-ground information to enable the model to be aware of the foreground and background. Since the foreground images often represent the point of the story, especially the character appearance, while the background images are usually related to the whole story scenario, CP-CSV generates not only the image sequences but also their segmentation results. In detail, the intermediate features of the segmentation generator assist the image sequence generation layer by layer, and the two generators share the same sentence encoder. Second, following the previous work [18], we adopt an image-level discriminator to assure the relevance between image and reference sentence and a story-level discriminator to maintain the whole paragraph consistency.

Finally, we propose a new evaluation metric, namely Fréchet Story Distance (FSD), to measure the quality of the generated story sequence, which is built on the principle of Fréchet Inception Distance (FID). The FID is a commonly used evaluation metric to quantify the generated image quality by the feature distance between generated images and the reference images. However, the FID takes one image at a time, therefore, it can not capture the temporal series features. On the other hand, Fréchet Video Distance (FVD) adopts the pre-trained Inflated 3D Convnet (I3D, [30]) as a backbone to extract the temporal-aware data distribution. Despite the FVD can evaluate the quality of generated videos, it is not suitable for the Visual Story task because of the limitation of the backbone network. Specifically, the minimum length requirement in I3D is seven, however, most story visualization datasets, e.g. Pororo-SV and VIST, take five sentence-image pairs to form a story. Consequently, we replace the I3D network with a different backbone model R(2+1)D [29] to form a novel story-consistency evaluation metric FSD. The spatial-temporal feature extractions in R(2+1)D are decomposed, therefore, eliminate the input length limitation naturally. We study the FSD behaviors under different consistency perturbations.

For model performance comparison, in addition to objective evaluations, we conduct a user study for comparing the proposed CP-CSV with state-of-the-art methods. Moreover, we illustrate the connection between segmentation results and the generated images. The experimental results manifest that our model can improve the image quality as well as the image sequence coherence.

The contributions are summarized as follows.

- We introduce the segmentation images during training to enhance the model being aware of the figure-ground components and propose a feasible architecture to incorporate the information. The illustration of the synthesized visual story indicates the effectiveness of the segmentation images.
- We build a consistency-evaluation metric FSD for *Story Visualization* task and study the metric behavior under different perturbations.
- Both quantitative and qualitative experimental results manifest that CP-CSV achieves the state-of-the-art for image quality and story consistency.

2   Related Work

2.1   GAN-based Text-to-Image Synthesis

Automatically synthesizing realistic images from text by Generative Adversarial Networks (GANs) [9] has been widely-studied recently. To improve the quality of text-to-image generation, a variety of models have been proposed and can be categorized into three types: 1) semantic relevance enhancement, 2) resolution enhancement and 3) image diversification. Specifically, semantic relevance enhancement focuses on improving the correlation between ground truth text and generated images. For example, given the base image and text attributes on a desired location, multi-conditional GAN (MC-GAN) [22] is proposed to control both the object and background information jointly for generating a realistic object with the given background. Moreover, since diverse linguistic expressions pose difficulties in extracting consistent semantics, SD-GAN [31] is proposed to implicitly disentangle semantics to attain both high- and low-level semantic knowledge for refined synthesis. Because texts usually contain unimportant words, SEGAN [27] suppresses the word-level attention weights of unimportant words to improve the semantic consistency between the synthesized image and its corresponding ground truth image. MirrorGAN [23] employs a mirror structure, which reversely learns from generated images to output texts for validating whether generated images are consistent with the input texts.

On the other hand, to enhancing the image resolution, different mechanisms are incorporated into GAN. For example, a two-stage stackGAN [34] is proposed to generate low-resolution images and refine the resolution by reading the text description again. To further improve the quality of generated images, StackGAN++ [33] is proposed to use multi-stage GANs to generate multi-scale images. AttnGAN [28] uses attention mechanism to integrate the word-level and sentence-level information into GANs, while DM-GAN [35] uses dynamic memory to refine blurry image contents generated from the GAN network. The third type of methods aims at improving the diversity of generated images and avoiding mode collapse. For example, the discriminator in AC-GAN [21] predicts not only the authenticity of the images but also the label of the images, promoting the diversity of the generated images. Building on the AC-GAN, TAC-GAN [7] synthesizes the image conditioned on corresponding text descriptions instead of on a class label, which helps disentangle the content of images from their styles and makes model generate diverse images based on different content. Text-SeGAN [2] follows the similar idea and revises the discriminator in TAC-GAN by measuring the semantic relevance between the image and text instead of class label prediction to diversify generated results.

To enhance both semantic relevance and resolution, several works take the layout or segmentation as intermediate structures and show the improvement on image quality of text-to-image generation. For example, Hong et al. [14] propose to construct a semantic layout based on the text, and generate image consequently. Obj-GAN [17] applies the same two-stage structure as above while using an object-driven attention mechanism for extracting fine-grained

information. However, although the above approaches improve the quality of text-to-image generation, story visualization imposes different challenges that are not well-addressed as mentioned in the introduction. Specifically, the challenge of story visualization is to ensure the consistency across the generated sequence. For example, StoryGAN [18] preserves global consistency by using a story-level discriminator. Several topics are also related to the consistency maintenance, e.g., text-to-video generation [10,19], dialogue-to-image [4,25], instruction-to-image generation [8], storyboard creation [3]. CP-CSV is different from previous works since 1) the consistency of video generation emphasizes the continuity between consecutive frames, and 2) CP-CSV further utilizes the figure-ground auxiliary information to preserve the characters and disentangle the background for a better consistency.

2.2 Evaluation Metrics of Image Generation

Evaluation methods of generated images are vital for assessing model performance. Traditional evaluation metrics of image generation, including IS (Inception Score) [24] and FID (Fréchet Inception Distance) [11], focus on scoring the image quality and diversity by comparing the generated images to real images in the distribution. Due to the rise of the text-to-image generation, the semantic relationship between text and generated images should be considered. Therefore, R-precision [28] is proposed to measure the correlation between a generated image and its corresponding text. SOA (Semantic Object Accuracy) [13] measures semantic connection by checking if a generated image contains objects that are specifically mentioned in the image caption. FVD (Fréchet Video Distance) [30] extends FID to calculate the distance between videos. However, it is limited to a long image sequence that contains over seven images. Our proposed FSD (Fréchet Story Distance) eliminates the length limitation and thus is better for evaluating the quality of short story.

3 Character-Preserving Coherent Story Visualization

3.1 Overview

Story Visualization aims at generating a sequence of images from an input story $S = [s_1, \cdots, s_t, \cdots, s_T]$, where s_t denotes the t-th sentence in S and T is the number of sentences in the story. The ground truth image sequence is denoted as $X = [x_1, \cdots, x_t, \cdots, x_T]$, while the generated image sequence is denoted as $\hat{X} = [\hat{x}_1, \cdots, \hat{x}_t, \cdots, \hat{x}_T]$. To address the challenges mentioned in the introduction, we propose Character-Preserving Coherent Story Visualization (CP-CSV), of which the model architecture is shown in Fig. 2. In our model, the input story S is first encoded into a vector h_s with a story encoder proposed by [18]. Afterward, to make the generated images consistent with each other, the context encoder takes h_s as the initial state and sequentially encodes each sentence in S into the sentence representations $O = [o_1, \cdots, o_t, \cdots, o_T]$. Different from the video generation task, of which two consecutive frames are similar, two consecutive pictures

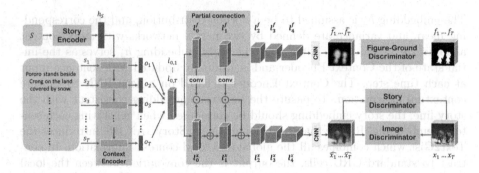

Fig. 2. System framework of CP-SCV. Story/context encoder extracts story/sentence level information. Figure-ground/story/image discriminator learns to distinguish whether the figure-ground/image sequence-story pair/image-sentence pair is true. Our proposed partial connection network is applied to the first and the second level features.

may change significantly in *Story Visualization*. Therefore, CP-CSV is designed to construct a sequence of distinct but coherent images. Since similar background pictures are usually shared in the same story, whereas foregrounds might change dramatically due to the different character appearances from frames to frames as shown in Fig. 1. Therefore, in the training stage, we introduce an auxiliary task, i.e., figure-ground segmentation, to assist CP-CSV for recognizing the figure-ground positions. When the model is capable of locating the foreground and background-position, it is easier to preserve the character formation while maintaining the scene coherence of the backgrounds.

Meanwhile, to automatically evaluate the performance of story visualization, the evaluation metric should take both the image quality and the sequence coherency into consideration. One possible way is to exploit the metrics for video generation. For example, the Fréchet Video Distance (FVD) [30] tackles the video quality evaluation problem by calculating the 2-Wasserstein distance between the synthesized video data distribution and the reference video data distribution. However, the feature extraction model of FVD, I3D [1], requires a long image sequence to calculate the distance. Therefore, FVD may not be suitable for evaluating the quality of story visualization. The sequence length of a story is usually short and does not reach the minimum frame length requirement in I3D. Therefore, we build a novel evaluation metric called Fréchet Story Distance (FSD), which can extract the features of image sequences with arbitrary length. Moreover, the proposed FSD is consistent, even with the noise intensity.

3.2 Story and Context Encoder

For the story encoder and the context encoder, we follow the design of Story-GAN [18]. Specifically, the story encoder aims at learning a mapping function for encoding the whole story S to an embedding h_s representing the whole story.

The embedding h_s is assumed to be a normal distribution, and the corresponding mean and variance are defined by two neural networks with story content as input, $\mu(S)$ and $\sigma(S)$. After that, the story embedding h_s serves as the initial state of the Context Encoder and is gradually updated with sentence input at each time step. The Context Encoder is based on a deep RNN to capture contextual information. To ensure the sentence embedding consistent with the story line, the story embedding should be considered when generating each sentence embedding. Rather than traditional RNNs, StoryGAN [18] introduces the Text2Gist which combines all the global and local context information. In contrast to standard GRU cells, the output is the convolution between the local hidden vectors and a filter with global information. As such, the convolution operation strikes to filter the crucial part from the whole story at each time step and forms a story-aware sentence embedding o_t. For the whole paragraph, the embedding is denoted as $O = [o_1, \cdots, o_t \cdots, o_T]$.

3.3   Figure-Ground Aware Generation

In story visualization, foreground items usually narrate the characters' actions and foreground visual scenes, while the clarity and spatial location of foreground items play an important role on the visualization quality. Equipped with figure-ground information, it is easier to preserve the characters and maintain the background consistency. Therefore, in order to learn such information, we introduce a foreground segmentation generation module to improve the quality of the generated images. Since the ground truth of the foreground segmentation is unavailable in story visualization datasets, we exploit a pre-trained salient object detection model [26] and manually label the foreground segmentation on 1,600 images from the Pororo-SV dataset for finetuning the model.[1]

To simultaneously incorporate the foreground segmentation into the image generation process and exploit the foreground segmentation as the auxiliary task, we design two generators: an image generator visualizing the story and a foreground map generator predicting the foreground regions. By sharing the representations between these two related tasks, we can enable CP-CSV to generalize the original generator better. Specifically, base on the previous StoryGAN generator, we add another generator parallel to the existing image generator to synthesize foreground segmentation maps conditioned on the same foreground area sentences latent vectors O as the image generator. The purpose of this segment generator is to generate the low-level foreground latent feature, which can enhance the quality of generated images. In other words, the image generator could follow the location information of the foreground area (e.g., characters) and synthesize the corresponding characters with much better quality, especially at the boundary of characters.

One possible approach to incorporate foreground features into image features is to exploit the Gated network, which has been proven to aggregate different

---

[1] The details of the foreground segmentation model will be presented in the implementation details in Sect. 4.1. The results are shown in Fig. 3. The segmentation images we used are released at https://github.com/yunzhusong/ECCV2020_CPCSV.

information effectively. However, the Gated network is usually applied to the deep layers to fuse the high-level information, which may not be suitable for incorporating the figure-ground information. Therefore, we propose to exploit the Partial Connection Network for integrating the features of foreground segmentation, which can be viewed as an affine transformation based on segment features. Specifically, the segment features from the k-th layer denoted as l_k^f are first projected to the latent space of image features l_k^x through a convolution layer F_f, then multiplying the image features to highlight the scene.

$$p_k^f = \mathcal{F}_f(l_k^f) \tag{1}$$

$$l_k^x = p_k^f * l_k^x + l_k^x \tag{2}$$

For learning segment features, a figure-ground discriminator D_{fg} is needed to ensure the learning of foreground segment generation. Similar to the image discriminator, the figure-ground discriminator learns whether the generated segmentation $\hat{f}_t$ matches the given sentence and story latent feature by discriminating between ground truth segmentation f_t.

3.4   Loss Function

Let W_g, W_i, W_s and W_f be the parameters representing generator, image, story and figure ground discriminator, respectively. The final objective function for CP-CSV is similar to loss function proposed in GANs:

$$\min_{W_g} \max_{W_i, W_s, W_f} \lambda_1 \mathcal{L}_{image} + \lambda_2 \mathcal{L}_{fg} + \lambda_3 \mathcal{L}_{story}, \tag{3}$$

where λ_1, λ_2, λ_3 are weighting terms to balance the model learning. The conditional loss function for foreground learning $\mathcal{L}_{fg}$ is defined as

$$\begin{aligned} \mathcal{L}_{fg,D} &= \sum_{t=1}^{T} -\mathbb{E}[\log(D_{fg}(f_t, s_t, h_s))] - \mathbb{E}_{\hat{f}_t \sim p_g}[\log(1 - D_{fg}(\hat{f}_t, s_t, h_s)], \\ \mathcal{L}_{fg,G} &= \mathbb{E}_{z \sim p_z}[\log(1 - D_{fg}(G_{fg}(s_t, z, h_s), s_t, h_s)] + \lambda_4 \mathcal{L}_{KL}, \end{aligned} \tag{4}$$

where $\mathcal{L}_{KL}$ is a regularization term for smoothing the semantic latent space and increasing the input variety for the sake of relieving the issue of mode collapse. Specifically, the KL regularization term is obtained as follows:

$$\mathcal{L}_{KL} = KL(N(\mu(S), diag(\sigma^2(S)))\|N(0, \mathbf{I})), \tag{5}$$

where $diag(\cdot)$ is used to restrict $\sigma^2(S)$ as a diagonal matrix for computational tractability, $\mu(.)$ and $\sigma(.)$ are two neural networks and take story S as input to predict a mean and variance for a normal distribution respectively.

The loss functions for image L_{image} and story L_{story} remain unchanged from the original StoryGAN.

$$\begin{aligned} \mathcal{L}_{image,D} &= \sum_{t=1}^{T} -\mathbb{E}[\log(D_{image}(x_t, s_t, h_s))] - \mathbb{E}_{\hat{x}_t \sim p_g}[\log(1 - D_{image}(\hat{x}_t, s_t, h_s))], \\ \mathcal{L}_{image,G} &= \mathbb{E}_{z \sim p_z} \log(1 - D_{image}(G(s_t, z, h_s), s_t, h_s) + \lambda_4 \mathcal{L}_{KL} \end{aligned} \tag{6}$$

$$\mathcal{L}_{story,D} = -\mathbb{E}[log(D_{story}(X,S))] - \mathbb{E}_{\hat{X}\sim p_g}[log(1 - D_{story}(\hat{X},S))],$$
$$\mathcal{L}_{story,G} = \mathbb{E}_{z\sim p_z} log(1 - D_{story}([G_{image}(s_t,z,h_s)]_{t=1}^T),S) + \lambda_4 \mathcal{L}_{KL} \quad (7)$$

Our objective function is updated using Adam with a learning rate of 0.0001 and 0.0004 for generators and discriminators. We find out that reducing the learning rate by half at epoch 20, 40, 80 helps stabilize the learning process. The values for λ_1, λ_2, λ_3, λ_4 are 5, 1, 1, 1 respectively.

3.5   Fréchet Story Distance

Previous work usually exploits the metric of image quality evaluation for story visualization. In this case, FID is the commonly-used metric to measure the image quality by calculating the 2-Wasserstein distance between the generated images and the reference images. However, for story visualization, the evaluation metric should take not only the image quality but also the consistency between frames into consideration,not included in the FID. In the field of *Video Generation*, FVD [30] is commonly used to evaluate a sequence of generated images [5,6], which adopts Inflated 3D ConvNet (I3D) to extract the video latent representation.

However, the inherent limitation of the I3D prevents FVD from operating directly to our task, since the minimum required frame number is seven. Simultaneously, the length of the image sequence in *Story Visualization Task* is usually smaller than the requirement. Indeed, we could modify the task description to achieve the frame length requirement, e.g., by considering more sentences as a story or generating multi-images from a sentence. One obvious shortcoming of expending story length is losing the comparability since the image generation is based on the whole story, differnet sentence length may alter the story line. On the other hand, generating multi-images from a sentence may confuse the model and even weaken the relevance between text and image.

To tackle the third challenge of *Story Visualization Task*, i.e., the lack of standard evaluation metric, we propose Fréchet Story Distance (FSD) as a new evaluation metric for *Story Visualization Task*, which is built on the principle of FID and FVD but with different backbone model, R(2+1)D [29]. The R(2+1)D network factorizes the 3D convolution filters into 2D spatial convolution and 1D temporal convolution, and the details are omitted here. The considerations of adopting R(2+1)D are the flexibility of sequence length and the strong ability to capture temporal consistency.

Given image sequence with arbitrary length, the last average pooling layer's output is taken as the sequence representation. With the representations of generated data P_G and reference data P_R, the distance between the two data representations is defined by 2-Wasserstein distance and calculated by:

$$d(P_R, P_G) = |\mu_R - \mu_G|^2 + Tr(\Sigma_R + \Sigma_G - 2(\Sigma_R\Sigma_G)^{1/2}),$$

where μ_R and μ_G are the means, and Σ_R and Σ_G are the covariance matrices. Finally, we observe the behaviors of FSD under different noise attacks. The detail experimental setting and results are discussed in Sect. 4.7.

Fig. 3. Illustrate the images and segmentation images. The upper rows indicate the ground truth (GT), while the lower rows are from our model. Results show a high correlation between generated images and generated segmentations.

4   Experimental Results

4.1   Implementation Details

For CP-CSV implementation, two techniques are applied to stabilize the training of GAN. First, Spectral Normalization [20] is performed to discriminators. Second, Two Time-scale Update Rule (TTUR) is applied for selecting different learning rates for the generator and discriminators [12]. Using these techniques, CP-CSV can produce better images and lower variance scores between different training sessions.

We conduct extensive experiments on the Pororo-SV dataset. Since the Pororo-SV dataset does not include the figure-ground information, we train a model in a semi-supervised manner. Specifically, we utilize a pre-trained state-of-the-art salient object detection model [26] to obtain the segmentation images. The detection model is fine-tuned on the Pororo-SV dataset by 1,600 manually-labeled samples. The second row of Fig. 3 demonstrates the examples of the segmentation results generated from the pre-trained model. We also release the segmentation images for the Pororo-SV dataset and Clever dataset.

4.2   Dataset

The following datasets are for training CP-CSV or for analyzing the FSD.

Pororo-SV: The Pororo-SV dataset [18] introduced by StoryGAN is modified from the Pororo dataset [16] to fit the story visualization task. It contains 13,000 training pairs and 2,334 testing pairs. Following the task formulated in StoryGAN, we also consider every five consecutive images as a story. There are several descriptions for one image, and one description is randomly selected during the training and testing phases.

VIST: The VIST dataset [15] originally used for sequential vision-to-language tasks contains 50,136 stories. Each story consists of five images and five matched captions. Different from the visual storytelling task, we take captions as input and generate the corresponding images to form a story. In this paper, the VIST dataset is only applied to analyze FSD behavior.

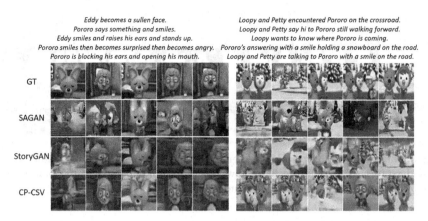

Fig. 4. Illustrate the synthesized image sequences. GT refers to Ground Truth.

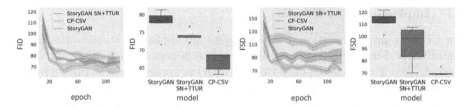

Fig. 5. FID and FSD average results using five different random seeds. CP-CSV drops faster in terms of FID and FSD scores compared to StoryGAN and StoryGAN with Spectral Normalization and TTUR.

4.3   Baselines

To the best of our knowledge, in story visualization task, there is only one state-of-the-art, i.e., StoryGAN [18]. To better know our model performance, we also compare CP-CSV with two other text-to-image models.

SAGAN: Based on the self-attention generative network proposed by Zhang *et al.* [32], we reimplement the SAGAN by taking the encoded sentence in the story S, character labels, and a noise term as input. Each image within the same story is generated independently.

StoryGAN: StoryGAN follows the Li *et al.* [18].

4.4   Qualitative Comparison

To get a more evident concept about the performance, Fig. 4 shows the comparison between synthesized image sequences of baseline models and CP-CSV. In contrast to SAGAN, which does not take the whole story as input, StoryGAN and CP-CSV exhibit better ability to maintain scene consistency. Besides, with the figure-ground information, CP-CSV can preserve the character details and shapes better, since it is easier to locate the position of characters. From the

Table 1. Quantitative evaluation results. ↓ denotes the lower is better.

	FID↓	FVD↓	FSD↓
SAGAN [32]	84.70	324.86	101.11
StoryGAN [18]	77.67	274.59	111.09
CP-CSV	**67.76**	**190.59**	**71.51**

Table 2. Human evaluation results of visual image quality, sequence consistency and text-image relevance. "Ours/SAGAN" represents the A/B test of CP-CSV and SAGAN. "Ours/StoryGAN" represents the A/B test of CP-CSV and StoryGAN. The values are shown in percentage.

	Quality		Consistency		Relevance	
	our	baseline	our	baseline	our	baseline
Ours/SAGAN	**0.72**	0.28	**0.82**	0.18	**0.63**	0.37
Ours/StoryGAN	**0.71**	0.29	**0.54**	0.46	**0.53**	0.47

lower rows of Fig. 3, they show the two output results of our model. We can find that the connection between segmentation images and generated images is evident and apparent, suggesting that our architecture can effectively utilize the figure-ground information. More examples are shown in Supplementary.

4.5 Quantitative Comparison

Table 1 shows the story evaluation results, measured by FID, FVD, and the proposed FSD. The FID takes one image at a time to perform the evaluation. In contrast, FVD takes the whole story, noting that the input images are self duplicated before feeding to FVD due to the limitation describing in Sect. 3.5. Besides, we conduct a human survey for the synthesized visual story, and there are three modalities. Given three sequences of images and the corresponding paragraphs, users rank the sequences according to 1) the visual image quality, 2) consistency between images, and 3) the relevance between image and sentence. The pairwise comparison results in Table 2 are extracted from the ranking results. Our model is ranked higher than all baselines on three modalities. The performance on image quality is especially disparity, demonstrating the effectiveness of the proposed figure-ground aware generation.

4.6 Architecture Search

To better understand the effectiveness of the proposed model and its variants, we conducted several comparative experiments by calculating FID, FVD, and FSD values. The generation flow is firstly discussed, i.e., the **cascade** generation and the **parallel** generation. In our experimental settings, the **cascade** generates the segmentation before the image. Once obtaining the segmentation,

Table 3. The evaluation results of different architectures for combining the figure-ground information.

	FID↓	FVD↓	FSD↓
baseline	74.60	189.46	98.61
baseline + SEG (Cascade)	73.46	182.52	86.80
baseline + SEG (Parallel, k = 1, 2, 3, 4)	84.41	194.9	81.46
baseline + SEG (Parallel, k = 3, 4)	80.54	179.42	99.66
Ours (baseline + SEG (Parallel, k = 1, 2))	**69.55**	**177.27**	**72.60**

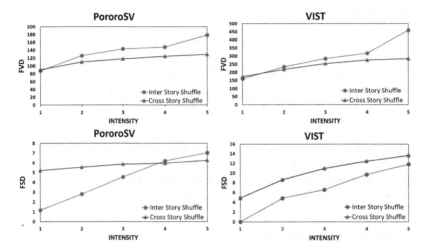

Fig. 6. FVD and FSD analysis of two kinds of perturbations.

it takes the down-sample to extract the figure-ground features. The features are then combine into the image generator to form the final result. On the other hand, the **parallel** generates the segmentation and image simultaneously, and takes the latent features to combine into the image generator. The variants of **parallel** are introducing the figure-ground information at different layers. Our experimental results shown in Table 3 suggest that the figure-ground information should be incorporated at early stage, the possible reason is that the information of segmentation is close to high-level concept, i.e., the character position, however, the last few layers tackle more detail formation. As for the inferior of **cascade** may from the process of down-sampling the generated segmentation, which highly relies on the segmentation quality.

4.7 FSD Analysis

The FSD is proposed to evaluate the sequence coherency of the visual story. To identify whether FSD is sensitive to the sequence consistency, we apply two

Table 4. Pearson correlation coefficient of metric measurements and perturbation intensity.

	Pororo-SV		VIST	
	Inter-S	Cross-S	Inter-S	Cross-S
FVD	0.9671	0.9583	0.9697	0.9685
FSD	0.9984	0.9957	0.9876	0.9724

different types of perturbations to the real image sequences: 1) Inter-Story Shuffle: Swapping the sequence order within a story, and the intensity is increasing with the needed steps to reorder the sequence. 2) Cross-Story Shuffle: Exchange the images with the images from other stories, and the intensity is increasing with the number of outside images. We test these noises under two datasets, i.e., Pororo-SV and VIST. To compare with the behavior of FVD, we also analyze the deviation of the FVD under these settings. Note that to maintain consistency with the FVD evaluation for the models, the input sequence length would be duplicated to reach the minimum length requirement of the I3D network instead of considering more sentences as a story. The line charts in Fig. 6 show how the metrics react to the inter-story shuffle and the cross-story shuffle perturbations. The generated images with different FSD scores are shown in Supplementary.

5   Conclusions

In this paper, we introduce the figure-ground segmentation images to address the Story Visualization task, based on the observation of different changing rate between foreground and background, and propose a novel framework called Character-Preserving Coherent Story Visualization (CP-CSV) to incorporate the segmentation information layer by layer. Qualitative and quantitative experiments suggest CP-CSV outperforms the state-of-the-art story visualization model. Moreover, to give an automatic evaluation metric of Story Visualization for consistency, Fréchet Story Distance (FSD) is built on the principle of FID and FVD. The perturbation studies show that FSD is highly sensitive to the story consistency. We provide more examples in the supplementary.

Acknowledgements. We are grateful to the National Center for High-performance Computing for computer time and facilities. This work was supported in part by the Ministry of Science and Technology of Taiwan under Grants MOST-108-2221-E-009-088, MOST-109-2221-E-009-114-MY3, MOST-109-2634-F-009-018, MOST-109-2218-E-009-016 and MOST-108-2218-E-009-056.

References

1. Carreira, J., Zisserman, A.: Quo vadis, action recognition? A new model and the kinetics dataset. In: proceedings of the IEEE Conference on Computer Vision and Pattern Recognition, pp. 6299–6308 (2017)

2. Cha, M., Gwon, Y.L., Kung, H.: Adversarial learning of semantic relevance in text to image synthesis. Proceedings of the AAAI Conference on Artificial Intelligence. **33**, 3272–3279 (2019)
3. Chen, S., et al.: Neural storyboard artist: Visualizing stories with coherent image sequences. In: Proceedings of the 27th ACM International Conference on Multimedia, pp. 2236–2244 (2019)
4. Cheng, Y., Gan, Z., Li, Y., Liu, J., Gao, J.: Sequential attention gan for interactive image editing via dialogue. arXiv preprint arXiv:1812.08352 (2018)
5. Clark, A., Donahue, J., Simonyan, K.: Adversarial video generation on complex datasets. (2019)
6. Dandi, Y., Das, A., Singhal, S., Namboodiri, V., Rai, P.: Jointly trained image and video generation using residual vectors. In: The IEEE Winter Conference on Applications of Computer Vision, pp. 3028–3042 (2020)
7. Dash, A., Gamboa, J.C.B., Ahmed, S., Liwicki, M., Afzal, M.Z.: Tac-gan-text conditioned auxiliary classifier generative adversarial network. arXiv preprint arXiv:1703.06412 (2017)
8. El-Nouby, A., et al.: Tell, draw, and repeat: generating and modifying images based on continual linguistic instruction. In: Proceedings of the IEEE International Conference on Computer Vision, pp. 10304–10312 (2019)
9. Goodfellow, I., et al.: Generative adversarial nets. In: Advances in Neural Information Processing Systems, pp. 2672–2680 (2014)
10. He, J., Lehrmann, A., Marino, J., Mori, G., Sigal, L.: Probabilistic video generation using holistic attribute control. In: Ferrari, V., Hebert, M., Sminchisescu, C., Weiss, Y. (eds.) ECCV 2018. LNCS, vol. 11209, pp. 466–483. Springer, Cham (2018). https://doi.org/10.1007/978-3-030-01228-1_28
11. Heusel, M., Ramsauer, H., Unterthiner, T., Nessler, B., Hochreiter, S.: Gans trained by a two time-scale update rule converge to a local nash equilibrium. In: Advances in Neural Information Processing Systems, pp. 6626–6637 (2017)
12. Heusel, M., Ramsauer, H., Unterthiner, T., Nessler, B., Hochreiter, S.: GANs trained by a two time-scale update rule converge to a local nash equilibrium. In: NIPS (2017)
13. Hinz, T., Heinrich, S., Wermter, S.: Semantic object accuracy for generative text-to-image synthesis. arXiv preprint arXiv:1910.13321 (2019)
14. Hong, S., Yang, D., Choi, J., Lee, H.: Inferring semantic layout for hierarchical text-to-image synthesis. In: Proceedings of the IEEE Conference on Computer Vision and Pattern Recognition, pp. 7986–7994 (2018)
15. Huang, T.H., et al.: Visual storytelling. In: HLT-NAACL (2016)
16. Kim, K.M., Heo, M.O., Choi, S.H., Zhang, B.T.: Deepstory: Video story qa by deep embedded memory networks. arXiv preprint arXiv:1707.00836 (2017)
17. Li, W., et al.: Object-driven text-to-image synthesis via adversarial training. In: Proceedings of the IEEE Conference on Computer Vision and Pattern Recognition, pp. 12174–12182 (2019)
18. Li, Y., et al.: Storygan: a sequential conditional GAN for story visualization. In: CVPR (2019)
19. Li, Y., Min, M.R., Shen, D., Carlson, D., Carin, L.: Video generation from text. In: Thirty-Second AAAI Conference on Artificial Intelligence (2018)
20. Miyato, T., Kataoka, T., Koyama, M., Yoshida, Y.: Spectral normalization for generative adversarial networks. ArXiv abs/1802.05957 (2018)
21. Odena, A., Olah, C., Shlens, J.: Conditional image synthesis with auxiliary classifier GANs. In: Proceedings of the 34th International Conference on Machine Learning-Volume 70, pp. 2642–2651. JMLR. org (2017)

22. Park, H., Yoo, Y., Kwak, N.: MC-GAN: multi-conditional generative adversarial network for image synthesis. In: The British MachineVision Conference (BMVC) (2018)

23. Qiao, T., Zhang, J., Xu, D., Tao, D.: Mirrorgan: learning text-to-image generation by redescription. Proceedings of the IEEE Conference on Computer Vision and Pattern Recognition (2019)

24. Salimans, T., Goodfellow, I., Zaremba, W., Cheung, V., Radford, A., Chen, X.: Improved techniques for training GANs. In: Advances in Neural Information Processing Systems, pp. 2234–2242 (2016)

25. Sharma, S., Suhubdy, D., Michalski, V., Kahou, S.E., Bengio, Y.: Chatpainter: Improving text to image generation using dialogue. arXiv preprint arXiv:1802.08216 (2018)

26. Sun, K., Xiao, B., Liu, D., Wang, J.: Deep high-resolution representation learning for human pose estimation. In: CVPR (2019)

27. Tan, H., Liu, X., Li, X., Zhang, Y., Yin, B.: Semantics-enhanced adversarial nets for text-to-image synthesis. In: Proceedings of the IEEE International Conference on Computer Vision, pp. 10501–10510 (2019)

28. Xu, T., et al.: Attngan: Fine-grained text to image generation with attentional generative adversarial networks (2018)

29. Tran, D., Wang, H., Torresani, L., Ray, J., LeCun, Y., Paluri, M.: A closer look at spatiotemporal convolutions for action recognition. In: Proceedings of the IEEE Conference on Computer Vision and Pattern Recognition, pp. 6450–6459 (2018)

30. Unterthiner, T., van Steenkiste, S., Kurach, K., Marinier, R., Michalski, M., Gelly, S.: Towards accurate generative models of video: A new metric & challenges. arXiv preprint arXiv:1812.01717 (2018)

31. Yin, G., Liu, B., Sheng, L., Yu, N., Wang, X., Shao, J.: Semantics disentangling for text-to-image generation. 2019 IEEE/CVF Conference on Computer Vision and Pattern Recognition (CVPR), pp. 2322–2331 (2019)

32. Zhang, H., Goodfellow, I., Metaxas, D., Odena, A.: Self-attention generative adversarial networks. arXiv preprint arXiv:1805.08318 (2018)

33. Zhang, H., et al.: Stackgan++: Realistic image synthesis with stacked generative adversarial networks. arXiv: 1710.10916 (2017)

34. Zhang, H., et al.: Stackgan: ext to photo-realistic image synthesis with stacked generative adversarial networks. In: ICCV (2017)

35. Zhu, M., Pan, P., Chen, W., Yang, Y.: DM-GAN: dynamic memory generative adversarial networks for text-to-image synthesis. In: Proceedings of the IEEE Conference on Computer Vision and Pattern Recognition, pp. 5802–5810 (2019)

GINet: Graph Interaction Network for Scene Parsing

Tianyi Wu[1,2], Yu Lu[3], Yu Zhu[1,2], Chuang Zhang[3], Ming Wu[3], Zhanyu Ma[3], and Guodong Guo[1,2(✉)]

[1] Institute of Deep Learning, Baidu Research, Beijing, China
{wutianyi01,zhuyu05,guoguodong01}@baidu.com
[2] National Engineering Laboratory for Deep Learning Technology and Application, Beijing, China
[3] Beijing University of Posts and Telecommunications, Beijing, China
{aniki,zhangchuang,wuming,mazhanyu}@bupt.edu.cn

Abstract. Recently, context reasoning using image regions beyond local convolution has shown great potential for scene parsing. In this work, we explore how to incorperate the linguistic knowledge to promote context reasoning over image regions by proposing a Graph Interaction unit (GI unit) and a Semantic Context Loss (SC-loss). The GI unit is capable of enhancing feature representations of convolution networks over high-level semantics and learning the semantic coherency adaptively to each sample. Specifically, the dataset-based linguistic knowledge is first incorporated in the GI unit to promote context reasoning over the visual graph, then the evolved representations of the visual graph are mapped to each local representation to enhance the discriminated capability for scene parsing. GI unit is further improved by the SC-loss to enhance the semantic representations over the exemplar-based semantic graph. We perform full ablation studies to demonstrate the effectiveness of each component in our approach. Particularly, the proposed GINet outperforms the state-of-the-art approaches on the popular benchmarks, including Pascal-Context and COCO Stuff.

Keywords: Scene parsing · Context reasoning · Graph interaction

1 Introduction

Scene parsing is a fundamental and challenging task with great potential values in various applications, such as robotic sensing and image editing. It aims at classifying each pixel in an image to a specified semantic category, including

---

T. Wu and Y. Lu—Equal contribution.

Electronic supplementary material The online version of this chapter (https://doi.org/10.1007/978-3-030-58520-4_3) contains supplementary material, which is available to authorized users.

A. Vedaldi et al. (Eds.): ECCV 2020, LNCS 12362, pp. 34–51, 2020.
https://doi.org/10.1007/978-3-030-58520-4_3

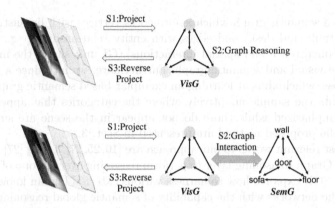

Fig. 1. Comparison of different contextual reasoning frameworks. *Top*: Contextual reasoning over the visual graph. *Bottom*: Our proposed Graph Interaction Network(GINet). Note: *VisG*: visual graph. *SemG*: semantic graph.

objects (*e.g.*, bicycle, car, people) and stuff (*e.g.*, road, bench, sky). Modeling context information is essential for scene understanding [2,3,41]. Since the work by Long [31] with fully convolutional networks (FCN), it has attracted more and more attention for context modeling in semantic segmentation or scene parsing.

Early works are some approaches that lie in the stack of local convolutions to capture the context information. Several works employed dilation convolution [6–9,47,48,51], kronecker convolution [47] and pooling operations [30,57] to obtain a wider context information. Recent works [15,53,55] introduced non-local operations [45] to integrate the local feature with their contextual dependencies adaptively to capture richer contextual information. Later, several approaches [21,24,61] were proposed to reduce the computation of non-local operations. More recently, using image regions for context reasoning [10,25,27,56] has shown great potential for scene parsing. These methods were proposed to learn a graph representation from visual features, where the vertices in the graph define clusters of pixels ("region"), and edges indicate the similarity or relation between these regions in the feature space. In this way, contextual reasoning can be performed in the interaction graph space, then the evolved graph is projected back to the original space to enhance the local representations for scene parsing.

In this paper, instead of solely performing context reasoning over the visual graph representation for 2D input images or visual features (as shown in the top of Fig. 1), we seek to incorporate linguistic knowledge, such as linguistic correlation and label dependency, to share the external semantic information across locations that can promote context reasoning over the visual graph. Specifically, we propose a Graph Interaction unit (GI unit), which first incorporates the dataset-based linguistic knowledge into feature representation over the visual graph, and re-projects the evolved representations of the visual graph back into each location representation for enhancing the discriminative capability (as shown in the bottom of Fig. 1). Intuitively, the external knowledge is

modeled as a semantic graph which is formed as vertices with linguistic entities (e.g., cup, table and desk) and edges with entity relationships (e.g., semantic hierarchy, concurrence and spatial interactions). GI unit shows the interaction between the visual and semantic graph. Furthermore, we introduce a Semantic Context Loss, which aims at learning an exemplar-based semantic graph to better represents the sample adaptively, where the categories that appear in the scene are emphasized while those do not appear in the scene are suppressed. Details of the proposed method are presented in Sect. 3.

The most relevant works to our approach are [10,25,27]. Liang [27] proposed a Symbolic Graph Reasoning layer to perform reasoning over a group of symbolic nodes. The SGR explores how to harness various external human knowledge for endowing the networks with the capability of semantic global reasoning. In contrast, our method explores how to incorporate a dataset-based linguistic knowledge to promote context reasoning over image regions. Li [25] proposed a Graph Convolutional Unit to project a 2D feature map into a sample-dependent graph structure by assigning pixels to the vertices of the graph and learning a primitive grouping of scene components. Chen [10] introduced the Global Reasoning unit for reasoning globally, which projects information from the coordinate space to nodes in an interactive space graph to directly reason over globally-aware discriminative features. Different from these approaches, we propose to reason over the visual graph and the prior semantic graph. The semantic graph is employed to promote contextual reasoning and lead the generation of the exemplar-based semantic graph from the visual graph.

We conduct extensive experiments on different challenging datasets to validate the advantages of the proposed GI unit and SC-loss for scene parsing. Meanwhile, ablation studies are performed to demonstrate the effectiveness of each component in our approach. Experimental results are shown in Sect. 4.

The main contributions of this work include:

- A novel Graph Interaction unit (GI unit) is proposed for contextual modeling, which incorporates the dataset-based linguistic knowledge for promoting context reasoning over the visual graph. Moreover, it learns an exemplar-based semantic graph as well.
- A Semantic Context Loss (SC-loss) is proposed to regularize the training procedure in our approach, which emphasizes the categories that appear in the scene and suppresses those do not appear in the scene.
- A Graph Interaction Network (GINet) is developed, based on the proposed GI unit and SC-loss for scene parsing; It provides significant gains in performance over the state-of-the-art approaches on Pascal-Context [33] and COCO Stuff [4], and achieves a competitive performance on ADE20K dataset [59].

2   Related Work

In this section, we briefly overview the recent progress in contextual modeling for scene parsing. They can be mainly divided into two categories based on whether graph reasoning is considered.

There are several model variants of FCN [31] proposed to exploit the contextual information. Some methods [7,8,14,29,42–44,52,53,57] were proposed to learn the multi-scale contextual information. DeepLabv2 [7] and DeepLabv3 [8] utilized an atrous spatial pyramid pooling to capture contextual information, which consists of parallel dilation convolutions with different dilation rates. TKCN [47] introduced a tree-structured feature aggregation module for encoding hierarchical contextual information. The pyramid pooling module is proposed by PSPNet [57] to collect the effective contextual prior, containing information on different scales. Moreover, the encoder-decoder structures [1,5,34,36,60] based on UNet [37] fuse the high-level and mid-level features to obtain context information. DeepLabV3+ [9] combines the properties of the above two methods that add a decoder upon DeepLabV3 to help model obtain multi-level contextual information and preserve spatial information. Differently, CGNet [49] proposed a Context Guided block for learning the joint representation of both local features and surrounding context. In addition, inspired by ParseNet [30], a global scene context was utilized in some methods [50,58] by introducing a global context branch in the network. EncNet [54] introduced Encoding Module to capture the global semantic context and predict scaling factors to selectively highlight feature maps. Recently, there were many efforts [15,53,55] to break the local limitations of the convolution operators by introducing the Non-local block [45] into the feature representation learning to capture spatial context information. Furthermore, some methods [21,24,61] proposed to reduce the computational complexity of Non-Local operations. More recently, SPGNet [11] proposed a Semantic Prediction Guidance module which learns to re-weight the local features through the guidance from pixel-wise semantic prediction.

Some other methods introduced a graph propagation mechanism into the CNN network to capture a more extensive range of information. GCU [25] got inspiration from region-based recognition and presented a graph-based representation on semantic segmentation and object detection tasks. GloRe [10] and LatenGNN [56] performed a global relation reasoning by aggregating features with similar semantics to an interactive space. SGR [27] extracted the representation nodes of each category from the features and use external knowledge structures to reason about the relationship between categories. These methods have typical projection, reasoning, and back projection steps. Based on these steps, our approach further promotes graph reasoning by incorporating semantic knowledge. Finally, Graphonomy and GraphML [17,18] proposed to propogate graph features of different datasets to unify the human parsing task. However, our approach explores the correlation between visual and semantic graph to facilitates the context modeling capabilities of the model.

3   Approach

In this section, we first introduce the framework of the proposed Graph Interaction Network (GINet). Then we present the design of the Graph Interaction unit (GI unit) in details. Finally, we give a detailed description of the proposed Semantic Context loss (SC-loss) for the GINet.

3.1 Framework of Graph Interaction Network (GINet)

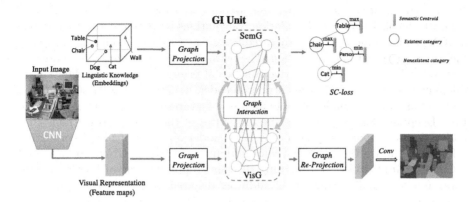

Fig. 2. The overall framework of the proposed Graph Interaction Network (GINet). (Color figure online)

Different from previous methods that only perform contextual reasoning over the visual graph built on visual features [10,25], our GINet facilitates the graph reasoning by incorporating semantic knowledge to enhance the visual representations. The proposed framework is illustrated in Fig. 2. Firstly, we adopted a pre-trained ResNet [20] as the backbone network, where visual features can be extracted given an input 2D image. Meanwhile, the dataset-based linguistic knowledge can be extracted in the form of categorical entities (classes), which is fed into word embedding (e.g., GloVe [35]) to achieve semantic representations. Secondly, visual features and semantic embedding representations are passed by the graph projection operations in the proposed GI unit to construct two graphs, respectively. A detailed definitions of graph projection operations are presented in Sect. 3.2. Accordingly, one graph that encodes dependencies between visual areas is built over visual features, where nodes indicate visual regions and edges represent the similarity or relation between those regions. The other graph is built over the dataset-dependent categories (represented by word embeddings), which encodes the linguistic correlation and label dependency. Next, a graph interaction operation is processed in the GI unit, where the semantic graph is employed to promote contextual reasoning over the visual graph and guide the generation of the exemplar-based semantic graph extracted from the visual graph. Then, the evolved visual graph generated by the GI unit is passed by Graph Re-projection operation for enhancing the discriminative ability for each local visual representation, while the semantic graph is updated and constrained by the Semantic Context loss during the training phase. Finally, we employ an 1×1 Conv followed by a simple bilinear upsampling to obtain the parsing results.

3.2   Graph Interaction Unit

The goal of the proposed GI unit is to incorporate dataset-based linguistic knowledge for promoting the local representations. First, the GI unit takes visual and semantic representations as inputs, conduct contextual reasoning by generating a visual graph and a semantic graph. Second, a graph interaction is performed between the two graphs to evolve node features by the guidance of similarity of visual nodes and semantic nodes.

Graph Construction: The first step is to define the projection that maps the original visual and semantic features to an interaction space. Formally, given the visual feature maps $X \in \mathbb{R}^{L \times C}$, where $L = H \times W$, H and W indicate the height and width of the feature map, and C is the channel dimensions. We aim to construct a visual graph representation $P \in \mathbb{R}^{N \times D}$, where N is the number of nodes in the visual graph and D is the desired feature dimension for each node. Inspired by the works [17,26], we introduce a transformation matrix $Z \in \mathbb{R}^{N \times L}$ that projects the local presentation X to a high-level graph representation P, which can be computed as follows:

$$P = ZXW, \tag{1}$$

where $W \in \mathbb{R}^{C \times D}$ is introduced as trainable parameters to convert the feature dimension from C to D, and Z adaptively aggregates local features to a node in the visual graph.

Next, we define a dataset-dependent semantic graph. Particularly, we aim to build a semantic graph presentation $S \in \mathbb{R}^{M \times D}$ over the object categories of a specific dataset, to encode the linguistic correlation and label dependency. M denotes the number of nodes, which is equal to the number of categorical entities (classes) in the dataset. D is the feature dimension for each node in the semantic graph. Specifically, we first use the off-the-shelf word vectors [35] to get semantic representation $l_i \in \mathbb{R}^K$ for each category $i \in \{0, 1, .., M - 1\}$, $K = 300$. Then, a MLP layer is employed to adjust the linguistic embedding to suit the reasoning with the visual graph. This transformation process can be formulated as follow:

$$S_i = MLP(l_i), i \in \{0, 1, .., M - 1\}, \tag{2}$$

where S_i represents node features for each category.

Graph Interaction: Next, we present how our GI unit incorporates dataset-based linguistic knowledge for promoting context reasoning and extracting the exemplar-based semantic graph from the visual graph. For simplicity, we abbreviate the visual graph and semantic graph as VisG and SemG, respectively. We first evolve both graphs separately and then perform the interaction between graphs. Then SemG and VisG attentively propagate information interatively, including 1) Semantic to Visual (S2V), and 2) Visual to Semantic (V2S).

Specifically, we first perform graph convolution [23] on the VisG to get evolved graph representation $\widetilde{P}$ that is suitable for interacting with the SemG. This process can be formulated as follows:

$$\widetilde{P} = f((A_v + I)PW_v), \tag{3}$$

where the adjacency matrix $A_v \in \mathbb{R}^{N \times N}$ is randomly initialized and updated by the gradient descent; I is an identity matrix; $W_v \in \mathbb{R}^{D \times D}$ are trainable parameters; and f is a nonlinear activation function. Through reasoning over the VisG, we can update node representation to capture more visual context information and to interact with SemG. Next we perform similar graph convolution [23] on the SemG for adjusting the representation of SemG, according to:

$$\widetilde{S} = f((A_s + I)SW_s), \tag{4}$$

where $\widetilde{S}$ indicates an updated the graph representation of SemG; $A_s \in \mathbb{R}^{M \times M}$ is a learnable adjacency matrix or co-occurrence matrix that represents connections between semantic correlation or label dependency; $W_s \in \mathbb{R}^{D \times D}$ are trainable parameters. By performing a propagation of feature information from neighboring nodes, we can improve the representation of each semantic node.

In S2V step: we utilize the evolved SemG to promote contextual reasoning over the VisG $\widetilde{P}$. Specifically, to explore the relationship between two nodes from VisG and SemG, we compute their feature similarity as a guidance matrix $G^{s2v} \in \mathbb{R}^{N \times M}$. For one node $\widetilde{p}_i \in \mathbb{R}^D$ in the VisG $\widetilde{P}$ and one node $\widetilde{s}_j \in \mathbb{R}^D$ in the SemG, we can compute the guide information $G^{s2v}_{i,j}$ that represents the assignment weight of the node $\widetilde{s}_j$ in SemG to the node $\widetilde{p}_i$ in VisG as follows:

$$G^{s2v}_{i,j} = \frac{\exp\left(W_p\widetilde{p}_i \cdot W_s\widetilde{s}_j\right)}{\sum_{m=1}^{M} \exp\left(W_p\widetilde{p}_i \cdot W_s\widetilde{s_m}\right)}, \tag{5}$$

where $i \in \{1, ..., N\}, j \in \{1, ..., M\}$ and $W_p \in \mathbb{R}^{D/2 \times D}$ and $W_s \in \mathbb{R}^{D/2 \times D}$ are a learnable matrix to further reduce the feature dimension. After obtaining the guidance matrix G^{s2v}, we can distill information from SemG to enhance the representation of VisG, according to :

$$P_o = \widetilde{P} + \beta_{s2v}G^{s2v}\widetilde{S}W_{s2v}, \tag{6}$$

where $W_{s2v} \in \mathbb{R}^{D \times D}$ is a trainable weight matrix, $\beta_{s2v} \in \mathbb{R}^N$ is a learnable vector with zero initialization and can be updated by a standard gradient decent. We use a simple sum to melt information from graphs, which may be alternatively replaced by other commutative operators such as mean, max, or concatenate. With the help of the guidance matrix G_{s2v}, we effectively constructed the correlation between visual regions and semantic concepts, and incorporate corresponding semantic features into the visual node representation.

In V2S step: we adopt a similar method elaborated in Eq. (5) to obtain the guidance matrix $G_{v2s} \in \mathbb{R}^{M \times N}$. Formally, the guide information $G^{v2s}_{i,j}$ that can be calculated as follows:

$$G^{v2s}_{i,j} = \frac{\exp\left(W_s\widetilde{s}_i \cdot W_p\widetilde{p}_j\right)}{\sum_{n=1}^{N} \exp\left(W_s\widetilde{s}_i \cdot W_p\widetilde{p_n}\right)}, \tag{7}$$

where $i \in \{1, ..., M\}, j \in \{1, ..., N\}$. After getting the guidance matrix G^{v2s}, we update the graph representation of the SemG for generating the exemplar-based SemG according to:

$$S_o = \beta_{v2s}\widetilde{S} + G^{v2s}\widetilde{P}W_{v2s}, \tag{8}$$

where $W_{v2s} \in \mathbb{R}^{D \times D}$ is a trainable weight matrix, $\beta_{v2s} \in \mathbb{R}^M$ is a learnable vector and initialized by zeros. We extract the exemplar-based semantic graph from VisG with the guidance matrix G_{v2s}. By combining the S2V and V2S steps, the proposed GI unit enables the whole model to learn more discriminative features for performing fine pixel-wise classification and generate a semantic graph for each input image.

Unit Outputs: The GI unit has two outputs, one is the exemplar-based SemG, which are described in detail in Sect. 3.3, and the other is the VisG enhanced by semantic information. The evolved node representation of VisG can be used to enhance the discriminative ability of each pixel feature further. As previous methods [25, 26], we reuse projection matrix Z to reverse project the P_o to 2D pixel features. Formally, Given node features $P_o \in \mathbb{R}^{N \times D}$ of the VisG, the reverse projection (or Graph Re-Projection) can be formulated as follows:

$$\widetilde{X} = Z^T P_o W_o + X, \qquad (9)$$

where $W_o \in \mathbb{R}^{D \times C}$ is a trainable weight matrix that transform the node representation from $\mathbb{R}^D$ to $\mathbb{R}^C$, $Z^T \in \mathbb{R}^{L \times N}$ means the transposed matrix of Z, and we employ a residual connection [20] to promote the gradient propagation during training.

3.3 Semantic Context Loss

We propose a Semantic Context Loss or simply SC-loss to constrain the generation of exemplar-based SemG. It emphasizes the categories that appear in the scene and suppresses those do not appear in the scene, which makes the GINet a capable of enhancing the external semantic knowledge adaptively to each sample. Specifically, we first define a learnable semantic centroid $c_i \in \mathbb{R}^D$ for each category. Then, for each semantic node $\widetilde{s}_i \in \mathbb{R}^D$ in a SemG $\widetilde{S}_o$, we compute a score v_i by performing a simple dot product with a sigmoid activation upon $\widetilde{s}_i$ and c_i. The v_i ranges from 0 to 1 and is trained with the BCE loss. The SC-loss minimizes the similarity between the node feature in the semantic graph and the semantic centroid of nonexistent categories, and maximizes the similarity to existent classes. If v_i is closer to 1, the corresponding category exists in the current sample; Otherwise, it does not exist. The SC-loss can be formulated as follows:

$$Loss_{sc} = -\frac{1}{M} \sum_{i=1}^{M} (y_i \cdot \log v_i) + (1 - y_i) \log(1 - v_i), \qquad (10)$$

where $y_i \in \{0, 1\}$ represents the presence of each category in ground truth. The proposed SC-loss is different from SE-loss in EncNet [54]. It built an additional fully connected layer on top of the Encoding Layer [54] to make individual predictions and was employed to improve the parsing of small objects. However, our SC-loss is employed to improve the generation of exemplar-based SemG.

We also add a full convolution segmentation head attached to Res4 of the backbone to obtain the segmentation result. Therefore, the objective of the

GINet consists of a SC-loss, an auxiliary loss, and a cross-entropy loss, which can be formulated as:

$$Loss = \lambda Loss_{sc} + \alpha Loss_{aux} + Loss_{ce}, \tag{11}$$

where λ and α are hyper-parameters, the selection of λ is discussed in the experiment section, and α for auxiliary loss is set to 0.4 similar some previous methods [15,46,54,55].

4   Experiments

In this section, we perform a series of experiment to evaluate the effectiveness of our proposed Graph Interaction unit and SC-loss. Firstly, we give an introduction of the datasets that are used for scene parsing, i.e., Pascal-Context [33], COCO Stuff [4], and ADE20K [59]. Next, we conduct extensive evaluations with ablation studies of our proposed method on these datasets.

4.1   Datasets

Pascal-Context [33] is a classic set of annotations for PASCAL VOC2010, which has 10,103 images. In the training set, there are 4,998 images. The remaining 5,105 images form the validation set. Following previous works [54,55,59], we use the same 59 most frequent categories along with one background category(60 in total) in our experiments.

COCO Stuff [4] has a total number of 10,000 images with 183 classes including an'unlabeled' class, where 9,000 images are used for training while 1,000 images for validation. We follow the same settings as in [15,24], the results are reported on the data contains 171 categories (80 objects and 91 stuff) annotated for each pixel.

ADE20K [59] is a large scale dataset for scene parsing with 25,000 images and 151 categories. The dataset is split into the training set, validation set and test set with 20,000, 2,000, and 3,000 images, respectively. Following the standard benchmark [59], we validate our method on 150 categories, where the background class is not included.

4.2   Implementation Details

During training, we use ResNet-101 [20] (pre-trained on ImageNet) as our backbone. For retaining the resolution of the feature map, we use the Joint Pyramid Upsampling Module [46] instead of the dilation convolution for saving the training time, resulting in stride-8 models. We empirically set the number of nodes in VisG as 64, and node dimensions as 256. Similar to prior works [8,54], we employ a poly learning rate policy [7] where the initial learning rate is updated by $lr = base\_lr * (1 - \frac{iter}{total\_iter})^{0.9}$ after each iteration. The SGD [39] optimizer is applied with 0.9 momentum and 1e-4 weight decay. The input size for all

Table 1. Ablation study on PASCAL-Context dataset. "GI" indicates Graph Interaction Unit. "SCm-loss" represents Semantic Context Loss. "VisG" means that context reasoning is only performed on visual graph.

Method	Backbone	GI	SC-loss	mIoU
baseline	Res50			48.5
+VisG	Res50			50.2
GINet	Res50	✓		51.0
GINet	Res50	✓	✓	51.7
baseline	Res101			51.4
+VisG	Res101			53.0
GINet	Res101	✓		53.9
GINet	Res101	✓	✓	54.6

Table 2. Comparisons of accuracy and efficiency with other methods. All experiments are based on ResNet50. "Para" represents the extra parameters relative to the backbone. "FPS" indicates the inference speed of models.

Methods	mIoU	Para (M)	FPS
baseline	48.5	9.5	48.6
+GCU [25]	50.4	11.9	40.3
+GloRe [26]	50.2	11.2	45.3
+PSP [57]	50.4	23.1	37.5
+ASPP [8]	49.4	16.1	28.2
GINet(ours)	51.7	10.2	46.0

datasets is set to 520 × 520. For data augmentation, we apply random flip, random crop, and random scale (0.5 to 2) using the zero-padding if needed. The batch size is set to 16 for all datasets. We set the initial learning rate to 0.005 on ADE20K dataset and 0.001 for others. The networks are trained for 30k, 150k, 100k iterations on Pascal-Context [33], ADE20K [59], COCO Stuff dataset [4], respectively.

During the validation phase, we follow [46,54,55] to average the multi-scale {0.5, 0.75, 1.0, 1.25, 1.5, 1.75} predictions of network. The performance is measured by the standard mean intersection of union (mIoU) in all experiments.

4.3 Experiments on Pascal-Context

We first conduct experiments on the Pascal-Context dataset with different settings and compare our GINet with other popular context modeling methods. Then we show and analyze the visualization results of our GINet. Finally, we compare with state-of-the-art to validate the efficiency and effectiveness of our method.

Ablation Study. First, we show the effectiveness of the proposed GI unit and SC-loss. Then, we compare our method with other popular context modeling methods and study the influence of SC-loss in terms of weight. Finally, different word embedding approaches are tested to show the robustness of our proposed method.

Effectiveness of GI unit and SC-loss We design a detailed ablation study to verify the effect of our GI unit and SC-loss. Specifically, FCN with Joint Pyramid Upsampling Module [46] is chosen as our baseline model. As shown in Table 1,

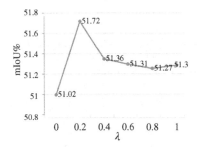
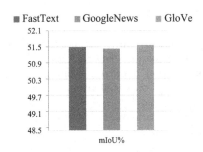

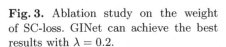

Fig. 3. Ablation study on the weight of SC-loss. GINet can achieve the best results with $\lambda = 0.2$.

Fig. 4. Ablation study on different word embedding methods. (Color figure online)

the baseline model achieves 48.5% mIoU. By performing reasoning over the VisG (row2), there is an improvement in performance by 1.7% (50.2 v.s. 48.5). Instead, by adopting our GI unit upon the baseline model to capture context information from both visual regions and linguistic knowledge, one can see from Table 1 (row 3), there is a significant increase in performance by 2.5% (51.0 v.s. 48.5), which demonstrates the effectiveness of the GI unit and our context modeling method. Furthermore, by constraining the global information of semantic concepts, SC-loss can further improve the model performance to 51.7% mean IoU. Deeper pre-trained backbone provides better feature representations. GINet configured with ResNet-101 can obtain 54.6% mIoU, which outperforms the baseline mode by 3.2% in terms of mIoU.

Comparisons with Context Modeling Methods. Firstly, we compare the GINet with VisG-based context reasoning methods i.e., GCU [25], GloRe [10]. GloRe, GCU uses the typical projection, reasoning, and back-projection methods to model spatial context information. To ensure the fairness, we reproduce these methods. We report the model performances in terms of mIoU. As shown in Table 2, Compared to GCU's 50.4% and GloRe's 50.2%, our GINet achieves the highest score of 51.7% mIoU. This proves the effectiveness of introducing linguistic knowledge and label dependency upon the visual image region reasoning. PSPNet [57] and DeepLab [8] are classic methods for constructing visual context information, and their performance is lower than our GINet. To further analyze the efficiency of these context modeling methods, we list the inference speed (frame per second, denoted as FPS) of these models. FPS is measured on a Tesla-V100 GPU with input size 512 × 512. As shown in Table 2, our model achieves 46.0 FPS, which outperforms all other context modeling methods.

Importance of the Weights of the SC-loss. In order to study the necessity and effectiveness of the SC-loss, we train our GINet using different weights for the SC-loss, e.g., $\lambda = \{0.2, 0.4, 0.6, 0.8, 1.0\}$. It is worth noting that $\lambda = 0$ means that the SC-loss is not applied. As shown in Fig. 3, SC-loss can effectively improve the model performance when $\lambda = 0.2$. In our experiments, higher weights don't bring more performance increase.

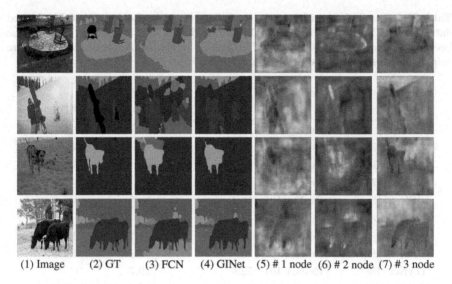

(1) Image   (2) GT   (3) FCN   (4) GINet   (5) # 1 node   (6) # 2 node   (7) # 3 node

Fig. 5. Visualization of results and weights of projection matrices, all examples are from the Pascal-Context validation dataset.(*Best viewed in color.*)

GINet with Different Word Embedding. By default, we use GloVe [35] as the initial representation of SemG. To verify the robustness of our method and see the influence of using different word embedding representations, we conduct experiments by applying three popular word embedding methods, *e.g.*, FastText [22], GoogleNews [32] and GloVe [35]. As shown in Fig. 4, there is no significant performance fluctuation using different word embedding representations. This observation suggests that our method is quite general. No mather what word mebedding methods are used, the proposed approach can capture the semantic information effectively.

Visualization and Analysis. In this section, we provide a visualization of scene parsing results and projection matrix. Then we analyze the qualitative results delivered by the proposed method.

The scene parsing results are shown in Fig. 5. Specifically, the first and second columns list the RGB input images and the ground truth scene parsing images, respectively. We compare baseline FCN [31] with our method in column 3 and column 4. One can see from the predicted parsing results images that our method shows considerable improvements. Particularly, it can be seen from rows 2 and 3, where the snow scene changes significantly in texture and color due to the illumination variation in the second and the fourth examples. By incorporating the semantic graph to promote the reasoning over the visual graph, our method successfully obtained more accurate parsing results. In the fourth row, it is fairly difficult to distinguish the green and yellow grass in the image only by the spatial

Table 3. Comparison with the state-of-the-art approaches on PASCAL-Context dataset, COCO stuff test set, and ADE20K validation set. "†" means the model has been pre-trained on COCO Stuff. "-" means no public results available. "*" means employing online hard example mining (OHEM[38]).

Method	Backbone	mIoU%		
		PASCAL-Context	COCO Stuff	ADE20K
CCL [13]	ResNet-101	51.6	35.7	-
PSPNet [57]	ResNet-101	47.8	-	43.29
EncNet [54]	ResNet-101	51.7	-	44.65
TKCN [47]	ResNet-101	51.7	-	-
CFNet [48]	ResNet-101	52.4	36.6	-
DUpsampling [40]	Xception-71	52.5	-	-
SGR† [27]	ResNet-101	52.5	39.1	44.32
DSSPN [28]	ResNet-101	-	37.3	43.68
DANet [15]	ResNet-101	52.6	39.7	-
ANN* [61]	ResNet-101	52.8	-	45.24
FastFCN [46]	ResNet-101	53.1	-	44.34
GCU [25]	ResNet-101	-	-	44.81
EMANet [24]	ResNet-101	53.1	39.9	-
SVCNet [12]	ResNet-101	53.2	39.6	-
CCNet* [21]	ResNet-101	-	-	45.22
DMNet [19]	ResNet-101	54.4	-	45.50
ACNet* [16]	ResNet-101	54.1	40.1	**45.90**
GINet (Ours)	ResNet-101	**54.9**	**40.6**	45.54

context, while our method still identified the object correctly by incorporating semantic information, where the color changes mislead the FCN method.

Moreover, we can show that our method aggregates similar features from the visual feature map into a node in the visual graph. The graph nodes learn rich representations of different regions, and reasoning on these nodes can effectively capture relationships of image regions. We select three nodes (marked as #1, #2 and, #3) and show their corresponding projection weights in columns 5, 6, and 7, respectively. It can be observed that different nodes correspond to relevant regions in the image (the brighter areas in the image means high response). It can be seen from the 2nd row in Fig. 5, node #1 aggregates and corresponds more with the background areas, while node #2 highlights the main objects in the images and node #3 shows more responses to the sky area in this example.

Comparisons with State-of-the-Art Methods. We report 60 categories performance (including background) to compare with the state-of-the-art methods. As shown in Table 3, our GINet achieves the best performance and out-

performs the SOTA DMNet[19] by 0.5%, which shows that our method is truly competitive. DMNet incorporates multiple Dynamic Convolutional Modules to adaptively exploit multi-scale filters to handle the scale variation of objects. In addition, the ACNet [16] obtains 54.1% mIoU, which captured the pixel-aware contexts by a competitive fusion of global context and local context according to different per-pixel demands. However, our method extracts the semantic representation from the visual features under the guidance of the general semantic graph, and construct a semantic centroid to get the similarity score for each category.

4.4   Experiments on COCO Stuff

To further demonstrate the generalization of our GINet, we also conduct experiments on the COCO Stuff dataset [4]. Comparisons with state-of-the-art methods are shown in Table 3. Remarkably, the proposed model achieves 40.6% in terms of mIoU, which outperforms the best methods by a large margin. Among the current state-of-the-art methods, ACNet [16] introduced a data-driven gating mechanism to capture global context and local context according to pixel-aware context demand, DANet [15] deployed the self-attention module to capture long-range contextual information, and EMANet [24] proposesd the EMA Unit to formulate the attention mechanism into an expectation-maximization manner. In contrast to these methods, our GINet considers the operation of capturing long-range dependencies as the way of graph reasoning, and additionally introduces the semantic context to enhance the discriminant property for the features.

4.5   Experiments on ADE20K

Finally, we compare our method and conduct experiments on the ADE20K dataset [59]. Table 3 compares the GINet performance against state-of-the-art methods. Our GINet outperforms the prior works and sets the new state-of-the-art mIoU to 45.54%. It is noting that our result is obtained by a regular training strategy in contrast to ANN [61], CCNet [21] and ACNet [16] where OHEM [38] is applied to help cope with difficult training cases. The ANN proposes an asymmetric fusion of non-local blocks to explore the long-range spatial relevance among features of different levels. The CCNet used a recurrent crisscross attention module that aggregates contextual information from all pixels. We emphasize that achieving such an improvement on the ADE20K dataset is hard due to the complexity of this dataset.

5   Conclusion

We have presented a graph interaction unit to promote contextual reasoning over the visual graph by incorporating the semantic knowledge. We have also developed a Semantic Context loss upon the semantic graph output of graph

interaction unit to emphasize the categories that appear in the scene and suppress those do not appear in the scene. Based on the proposed graph interaction unit and Semantic Context loss, we have developed a novel framework called Graph Interaction Network (GINet). The proposed approach based on the new framework outperforms state-of-the-art methods by a significant gain in performance on two challenging scene parsing benchmarks, e.g., Pascal-Context and COCO Stuff, and achieves a competitive performance on ADE20K dataset.

References

1. Badrinarayanan, V., Kendall, A., Cipolla, R.: Segnet: a deep convolutional encoder-decoder architecture for image segmentation. IEEE Trans. Pattern Anal. Mach. Intell. **39**(12), 2481–2495 (2017)
2. Belongie, S., Malik, J., Puzicha, J.: Shape matching and object recognition using shape contexts. IEEE Trans. Pattern Anal. Mach. Intell. **24**(4), 509–522 (2002)
3. Biederman, I., Mezzanotte, R.J., Rabinowitz, J.C.: Scene perception: detecting and judging objects undergoing relational violations. Cogn. Pychol. **14**(2), 143–177 (1982)
4. Caesar, H., Uijlings, J., Ferrari, V.: Coco-stuff: thing and stuff classes in context. In: CVPR (2018)
5. Chaurasia, A., Culurciello, E.: Linknet: exploiting encoder representations for efficient semantic segmentation. In: 2017 IEEE Visual Communications and Image Processing (VCIP) (2017)
6. Chen, L.C., Papandreou, G., Kokkinos, I., Murphy, K., Yuille, A.L.: Semantic image segmentation with deep convolutional nets and fully connected crfs. arXiv preprint arXiv:1412.7062 (2014)
7. Chen, L.C., Papandreou, G., Kokkinos, I., Murphy, K., Yuille, A.L.: Deeplab: semantic image segmentation with deep convolutional nets, atrous convolution, and fully connected crfs. IEEE Trans. Pattern Anal. Mach. Intell. **40**(4), 834–848 (2017)
8. Chen, L.C., Papandreou, G., Schroff, F., Adam, H.: Rethinking atrous convolution for semantic image segmentation. arXiv preprint arXiv:1706.05587 (2017)
9. Chen, L.C., Zhu, Y., Papandreou, G., Schroff, F., Adam, H.: Encoder-decoder with atrous separable convolution for semantic image segmentation. In: Ferrari, V., Hebert, M., Sminchisescu, C., Weiss, Y. (eds.) ECCV 2018. LNCS, vol. 11211, pp. 833–851. Springer, Cham (2018). https://doi.org/10.1007/978-3-030-01234-2_49
10. Chen, Y., Rohrbach, M., Yan, Z., Shuicheng, Y., Feng, J., Kalantidis, Y.: Graph-based global reasoning networks. In: CVPR (2019)
11. Cheng, B., et al.: Spgnet: semantic prediction guidance for scene parsing. In: ICCV (2019)
12. Ding, H., Jiang, X., Shuai, B., Liu, A.Q., Wang, G.: Semantic correlation promoted shape-variant context for segmentation. In: Proceedings of the IEEE Conference on Computer Vision and Pattern Recognition, pp. 8885–8894 (2019)
13. Ding, H., Jiang, X., Shuai, B., Qun Liu, A., Wang, G.: Context contrasted feature and gated multi-scale aggregation for scene segmentation. In: CVPR (2018)
14. Eigen, D., Fergus, R.: Predicting depth, surface normals and semantic labels with a common multi-scale convolutional architecture. In: ICCV (2015)
15. Fu, J., et al.: Dual attention network for scene segmentation. In: CVPR (2019)

16. Fu, J., et al.: Adaptive context network for scene parsing. In: Proceedings of the IEEE International Conference on Computer Vision, pp. 6748–6757 (2019)
17. Gong, K., Gao, Y., Liang, X., Shen, X., Wang, M., Lin, L.: Graphonomy: Universal Human Parsing Via Graph Transfer Learning. In: CVPR (2019)
18. He, H., Zhang, J., Zhang, Q., Tao, D.: Grapy-ml: Graph pyramid mutual learning for cross-dataset human parsing. CoRR abs/1911.12053 (2019). http://arxiv.org/abs/1911.12053
19. He, J., Deng, Z., Qiao, Y.: Dynamic multi-scale filters for semantic segmentation. In: The IEEE International Conference on Computer Vision (ICCV), October 2019
20. He, K., Zhang, X., Ren, S., Sun, J.: Deep residual learning for image recognition. In: CVPR (2016)
21. Huang, Z., Wang, X., Huang, L., Huang, C., Wei, Y., Liu, W.: Ccnet: Criss-cross attention for semantic segmentation. arXiv preprint arXiv:1811.11721 (2018)
22. Joulin, A., Grave, E., Bojanowski, P., Douze, M., Jégou, H., Mikolov, T.: Fasttext. zip: Compressing text classification models. arXiv preprint arXiv:1612.03651 (2016)
23. Kipf, T.N., Welling, M.: Semi-supervised classification with graph convolutional networks (2016)
24. Li, X., Zhong, Z., Wu, J., Yang, Y., Lin, Z., Liu, H.: Expectation-maximization attention networks for semantic segmentation. In: Proceedings of the IEEE International Conference on Computer Vision, pp. 9167–9176 (2019)
25. Li, Y., Gupta, A.: Beyond grids: learning graph representations for visual recognition. In: Advances in Neural Information Processing Systems, pp. 9225–9235 (2018)
26. Li, Y., Gu, C., Dullien, T., Vinyals, O., Kohli, P.: Graph matching networks for learning the similarity of graph structured objects. arXiv preprint arXiv:1904.12787 (2019)
27. Liang, X., Hu, Z., Zhang, H., Lin, L., Xing, E.P.: Symbolic graph reasoning meets convolutions. In: Advances in Neural Information Processing Systems (2018)
28. Liang, X., Zhou, H., Xing, E.: Dynamic-structured semantic propagation network. In: CVPR (2018)
29. Lin, G., Shen, C., Van Den Hengel, A., Reid, I.: Efficient piecewise training of deep structured models for semantic segmentation. In: CVPR (2016)
30. Liu, W., Rabinovich, A., Berg, A.C.: Parsenet: Looking wider to see better. arXiv preprint arXiv:1506.04579 (2015)
31. Long, J., Shelhamer, E., Darrell, T.: Fully convolutional networks for semantic segmentation. In: CVPR (2015)
32. Mikolov, T., Chen, K., Corrado, G., Dean, J.: Efficient estimation of word representations in vector space. arXiv preprint arXiv:1301.3781 (2013)
33. Mottaghi, R., et al.: The role of context for object detection and semantic segmentation in the wild. In: CVPR (2014)
34. Peng, C., Zhang, X., Yu, G., Luo, G., Sun, J.: Large kernel matters-improve semantic segmentation by global convolutional network. In: CVPR (2017)
35. Pennington, J., Socher, R., Manning, C.: Glove: Global vectors for word representation. In: Proceedings of the 2014 Conference on Empirical Methods in Natural Language Processing (EMNLP) (2014)
36. Pohlen, T., Hermans, A., Mathias, M., Leibe, B.: Full-resolution residual networks for semantic segmentation in street scenes. In: CVPR (2017)
37. Ronneberger, O., Fischer, P., Brox, T.: U-net: convolutional networks for biomedical image segmentation. In: International Conference on Medical Image Computing and Computer-assisted Intervention (2015)

38. Shrivastava, A., Gupta, A., Girshick, R.: Training region-based object detectors with online hard example mining. In: The IEEE Conference on Computer Vision and Pattern Recognition (CVPR), June 2016
39. Sutskever, I., Martens, J., Dahl, G., Hinton, G.: On the importance of initialization and momentum in deep learning. In: International Conference on Machine Learning (2013)
40. Tian, Z., He, T., Shen, C., Yan, Y.: Decoders matter for semantic segmentation: data-dependent decoding enables flexible feature aggregation. In: CVPR (2019)
41. Tu, Z., Chen, X., Yuille, A.L., Zhu, S.C.: Image parsing: unifying segmentation,detection, and recognition. Int. J. Comput. Vis. **63**, 113–140 (2005)
42. Wang, Q., Guo, G.: LS-CNN: characterizing local patches at multiple scales for face recognition. IEEE Trans. Inf. Forensics Secur. **15**, 1640–1653 (2019)
43. Wang, Q., Wu, T., Zheng, H., Guo, G.: Hierarchical pyramid diverse attention networks for face recognition. In: Proceedings of the IEEE/CVF Conference on Computer Vision and Pattern Recognition (CVPR), June 2020
44. Wang, Q., Zheng, Y., Yang, G., Jin, W., Chen, X., Yin, Y.: Multiscale rotation-invariant convolutional neural networks for lung texture classification. IEEE J. Biomed. Health Inf. **22**(1), 184–195 (2018)
45. Wang, X., Girshick, R., Gupta, A., He, K.: Non-local neural networks (2017)
46. Wu, H., Zhang, J., Huang, K., Liang, K., Yu, Y.: Fastfcn: Rethinking dilated convolution in the backbone for semantic segmentation. arXiv preprint arXiv:1903.11816 (2019)
47. Wu, T., Tang, S., Zhang, R., Cao, J., Li, J.: Tree-structured kronecker convolutional network for semantic segmentation. In: ICME (2019)
48. Wu, T., Tang, S., Zhang, R., Guo, G., Zhang, Y.: Consensus feature network for scene parsing. arXiv preprint arXiv:1907.12411 (2019)
49. Wu, T., Tang, S., Zhang, R., Zhang, Y.: Cgnet: A light-weight context guided network for semantic segmentation. arXiv preprint arXiv:1811.08201 (2018)
50. Yu, C., Wang, J., Peng, C., Gao, C., Yu, G., Sang, N.: Learning a discriminative feature network for semantic segmentation. In: CVPR (2018)
51. Yu, F., Koltun, V.: Multi-scale context aggregation by dilated convolutions. arXiv preprint arXiv:1511.07122 (2015)
52. Yuan, Y., Chen, X., Wang, J.: Object-contextual representations for semantic segmentation. arXiv preprint arXiv:1909.11065 (2019)
53. Yuan, Y., Wang, J.: Ocnet: Object context network for scene parsing. arXiv preprint arXiv:1809.00916 (2018)
54. Zhang, H., et al.: Context encoding for semantic segmentation. In: CVPR (2018)
55. Zhang, H., Zhang, H., Wang, C., Xie, J.: Co-occurrent features in semantic segmentation. In: CVPR (2019)
56. Zhang, S., Yan, S., He, X.: Latentgnn: Learning efficient non-local relations for visual recognition. arXiv preprint arXiv:1905.11634 (2019)
57. Zhao, H., Shi, J., Qi, X., Wang, X., Jia, J.: Pyramid scene parsing network. In: CVPR (2017)
58. Zhao, H., et al.: PSANet: point-wise spatial attention network for scene parsing. In: Ferrari, V., Hebert, M., Sminchisescu, C., Weiss, Y. (eds.) ECCV 2018. LNCS, vol. 11213, pp. 270–286. SpringerSpringer, Cham (2018). https://doi.org/10.1007/978-3-030-01240-3_17
59. Zhou, B., Zhao, H., Puig, X., Fidler, S., Barriuso, A., Torralba, A.: Scene parsing through ade20k dataset. In: CVPR (2017)

60. Zhou, L., Zhang, C., Wu, M.: D-linknet: linknet with pretrained encoder and dilated convolution for high resolution satellite imagery road extraction. In: CVPR Workshops (2018)
61. Zhu, Z., Xu, M., Bai, S., Huang, T., Bai, X.: Asymmetric non-local neural networks for semantic segmentation. In: Proceedings of the IEEE International Conference on Computer Vision, pp, 593–602 (2019)

Tensor Low-Rank Reconstruction
for Semantic Segmentation

Wanli Chen[1]($\boxtimes$), Xinge Zhu[1], Ruoqi Sun[2], Junjun He[2,3], Ruiyu Li[4],
Xiaoyong Shen[4], and Bei Yu[1]

[1] The Chinese University of Hong Kong, New Territories, Hong Kong
{wlchen,byu}@cse.cuhk.edu.hk, zx018@ie.cuhk.edu.hk
[2] Shanghai Jiao Tong University, Shanghai, China
{ruoqisun7,hejunjun}@sjtu.edu.cn
[3] ShenZhen Key Lab of Computer Vision and Pattern Recognition,
SIAT-SenseTime Joint Lab, Shenzhen Institutes of Advanced Technology,
Chinese Academy of Sciences, Beijing, China
[4] SmartMore, Shenzhen, China
{ryli,xiaoyong}@smartmore.com

Abstract. Context information plays an indispensable role in the success of semantic segmentation. Recently, non-local self-attention based methods are proved to be effective for context information collection. Since the desired context consists of spatial-wise and channel-wise attentions, 3D representation is an appropriate formulation. However, these non-local methods describe 3D context information based on a 2D similarity matrix, where space compression may lead to channel-wise attention missing. An alternative is to model the contextual information directly without compression. However, this effort confronts a fundamental difficulty, namely the high-rank property of context information. In this paper, we propose a new approach to model the 3D context representations, which not only avoids the space compression but also tackles the high-rank difficulty. Here, inspired by tensor canonical-polyadic decomposition theory (*i.e*, a high-rank tensor can be expressed as a combination of rank-1 tensors.), we design a low-rank-to-high-rank context reconstruction framework (*i.e*, RecoNet). Specifically, we first introduce the tensor generation module (TGM), which generates a number of rank-1 tensors to capture fragments of context feature. Then we use these rank-1 tensors to recover the high-rank context features through our proposed tensor reconstruction module (TRM). Extensive experiments show that our method achieves state-of-the-art on various public datasets. Additionally, our proposed method has more than 100 times less computational cost compared with conventional non-local-based methods.

Keywords: Semantic segmentation · Low-rank reconstruction · Tensor decomposition

Electronic supplementary material The online version of this chapter (https://doi.org/10.1007/978-3-030-58520-4_4) contains supplementary material, which is available to authorized users.

© Springer Nature Switzerland AG 2020
A. Vedaldi et al. (Eds.): ECCV 2020, LNCS 12362, pp. 52–69, 2020.
https://doi.org/10.1007/978-3-030-58520-4_4

1   Introduction

Semantic segmentation aims to assign the pixel-wise predictions for the given image, which is a challenging task requiring fine-grained shape, texture and category recognition. The pioneering work, fully convolutional networks (FCN) [30], explores the effectiveness of deep convolutional networks in segmentation task. Recently, more work achieves great progress from exploring the contextual information [1,4,5,24,32,48], in which non-local based methods are the recent mainstream [15,46,49].

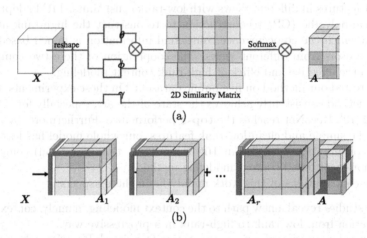

(a)

(b)

Fig. 1. (a) Non-local vs. (b) our proposed RecoNet, which is based on tensor low-rank reconstruction. Note that 2D similarity matrix exists in non-local based methods and our RecoNet is formed with all 3D tensors.

These methods model the context representation by rating the element-wise importance for contextual tensors. However, the context features obtained from this line lack of channel-wise attention, which is a key component of context. Specifically, for a typical non-local block, the 2D similarity map $A \in \mathbb{R}^{HW \times HW}$ is generated by the matrix multiplication of two inputs with dimension of $H \times W \times C$ and $C \times H \times W$, respectively. It is noted that the channel dimension C is eliminated during the multiplication, which implies that only the spatial-wise attention is represented while the channel-wise attention is compressed. Therefore, these non-local based methods could collect fine-grained spatial context features but may sacrifice channel-wise context attention.

An intuitive idea tackling this issue is to construct the context directly instead of using the 2D similarity map. Unfortunately, this approach confronts a fundamental difficulty because of the high-rank property of context features [46]. That is, the context tensor should be high-rank to have enough capacity since contexts vary from image to image and this large diversity cannot be well-represented by very limited parameters.

Inspired by tensor canonical-polyadic decomposition theory [19], *i.e.*, a high-rank tensor can be expressed as a combination of rank-1 tensors, we propose a new approach of modeling high-rank contextual information in a progressive manner without channel-wise space compression. We show the workflow of non-local networks and RecoNet in Fig. 1. The basic idea is to first use a series of low-rank tensors to collect fragments of context features and then build them up to reconstruct fine-grained context features. Specifically, our proposed framework consists of two key components, rank-1 tensor generation module (TGM) and high-rank tensor reconstruction module (TRM). Here, TGM aims to generate the rank-1 tensors in channel, height and width directions, which explore the context features in different views with low-rank constraints. TRM adopts tensor canonical-polyadic (CP) reconstruction to reconstruct the high-rank attention map, in which the co-occurrence contextual information is mined based on the rank-1 tensors from different views. The cooperation of these two components leads to the effective and efficient high-rank context modeling.

We tested our method on five public datasets. On these experiments, the proposed method consistently achieves the state-of-the-art, especially for PASCAL-VOC12 [12], RecoNet reaches the **top-1** performance. Furthermore, by incorporating the simple and clean low-rank features, our whole model has less computation consumption (more than **100** times lower than non-local) compared to other non-local based context modeling methods.

The contributions of this work mainly lie in three aspects:

- Our studies reveal a new path to the context modeling, namely, context reconstruction from low-rank to high-rank in a progressive way.
- We develop a new semantic segmentation framework RecoNet, which explores the contextual information through tensor CP reconstruction. It not only keeps both spatial-wise and channel-wise attentions, but also deals with high-rank difficulty.
- We conduct extensive experiments to compare the proposed methods with others on various public datasets, where it yields notable performance gains. Furthermore, RecoNet al.so has less computation cost, *i.e*, more than **100** times smaller than non-local based methods.

2   Related Work

Tensor Low-rank Representation. According to tensor decomposition theory [19], a tensor can be represented by the linear combination of series of low-rank tensors. The reconstruction results of these low-rank tensors are the principal components of original tensor. Therefore, tensor low-rank representation is widely used in computer vision task such as convolution speed-up [20] and model compression [44]. There are two tensor decomposition methods: Tuker decomposition and CP decompostion [19]. For the Tuker decomposition, the tensor is decomposed into a set of matrices and one core tensor. If the core tensor is diagonal, then Tuker decomposition degrades to CP decomposition. For the CP decomposition, the tensor is represented by a set of rank-1 tensors (vectors).

In this paper, we apply this theory for *reconstruction*, namely reconstructing high-rank contextual tensor from a set of rank-1 context fragments.

Self-attention in Computer Vision. Self attention is firstly proposed in natural language processing (NLP) [8,9,36,42]. It serves as a global encoding method that can merge long distance features. This property is also important to computer vision tasks. Hu *et al.*. propose SE-Net [17], exploiting channel information for better image classification through channel wise attention. Woo *et al.*. propose CBAM [38] that combines channel-wise attention and spatial-wise attention to capture rich feature in CNN. Wang *et al.*. propose non-local neural network [37]. It catches long-range dependencies of a featuremap, which breaks the receptive field limitation of convolution kernel.

Context Aggregation in Semantic Segmentation. Context information is so important for semantic segmentation and many researchers pay their attention to explore the context aggregation. The initial context harvesting method is to increase receptive fields such as FCN [30], which merges feature of different scales. Then feature pyramid methods [4,5,48] are proposed for better context collection. Although feature pyramid collects rich context information, the contexts are not gathered adaptively. In other words, the importance of each element in contextual tensor is not discriminated. Self-attention-based methods are thus proposed to overcome this problem, such as EncNet [45], PSANet [49], APC-Net [15], and CFNet [46]. Researchers also propose some efficient self-attention methods such as EMANet [21], CCNet [18], A^2Net [6], which have lower computation consumption and GPU memory occupation. However, most of these methods suffer from channel-wise space compression due to the 2D similarity map. Compared to these works, our method differs essentially in that it uses the 3D low-rank tensor reconstruction to catch long-range dependencies without sacrificing channel-wise attention.

3   Methodology

3.1   Overview

The semantic information prediction from an image is closely related to the context information. Due to the large varieties of context, a high-rank tensor is required for the context feature representation. However, under this constraint, modeling the context features directly means a huge cost. Inspired by the CP decomposition theory, although the context prediction is a high-rank problem, we can separate it into a series of low-rank problems and these low-rank problems are easier to deal with. Specifically, we do not predict context feature directly, instead, we generate its fragments. Then we build up a complete context feature using these fragments. The low-rank to high-rank reconstruction strategy not only maintains 3D representation (for both channel-wise and spatial-wise), but also tackles with the high-rank difficulty.

The pipeline of our model is shown in Fig. 2, which consists of low-rank tensor generation module (TGM), high-rank tensor reconstruction module (TRM), and

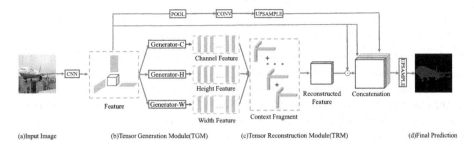

(a)Input Image   (b)Tensor Generation Module(TGM)   (c)Tensor Reconstruction Module(TRM)   (d)Final Prediction

Fig. 2. The pipeline of our framework. Two major components are involved, *i.e*, Tensor Generation Module (TGM) and Tensor Reconstruction Module (TRM). TGM peroforms the low-rank tensor generation while TRM achieves the high-rank tensor reconstruction via CP construction theory.

global pooling module (GPM) to harvest global context in both spatial and channel dimensions. We upsample the model output using bilinear interpolation before semantic label prediction.

In our implementation, multiple low-rank perceptrons are used to deal with the high-rank problem, by which we learn parts of context information (*i.e*, context fragments). We then build the high-rank tensor via tensor reconstruction theory [19].

Formulation: Assuming we have $3r$ vectors in C/H/W directions $\boldsymbol{v}_{ci} \in \mathbb{R}^{C \times 1 \times 1}$, $\boldsymbol{v}_{hi} \in \mathbb{R}^{1 \times H \times 1}$ and $\boldsymbol{v}_{wi} \in \mathbb{R}^{1 \times 1 \times W}$, where $i \in r$ and r is the tensor rank. These vectors are the CP decomposed fragments of $\boldsymbol{A} \in \mathbb{R}^{C \times H \times W}$, then tensor CP rank-$r$ reconstruction is defined as:

$$\boldsymbol{A} = \sum_{i=1}^{r} \lambda_i \boldsymbol{v}_{ci} \otimes \boldsymbol{v}_{hi} \otimes \boldsymbol{v}_{wi}, \tag{1}$$

where λ_i is a scaling factor.

3.2   Tensor Generation Module

In this section, we first provide some basic definitions and then show how to derive the low-rank tensors from the proposed module.

Context Fragments. We define context fragments as the outputs of the tensor generation module, which indicates some rank-1 vectors $\boldsymbol{v}_{ci}$, $\boldsymbol{v}_{hi}$ and $\boldsymbol{v}_{wi}$ (as defined in previous part) in the channel, the height and the width directions. Every context fragment contains a part of context information.

Feature Generator. We define three feature generators: Channel Generator, Height Generator and Width Generator. Each generator is composed of Pool-Conv-Sigmoid sequence. Global pooling is widely used in previous works [28,48] as the global context harvesting method. Similarly, here we use global average

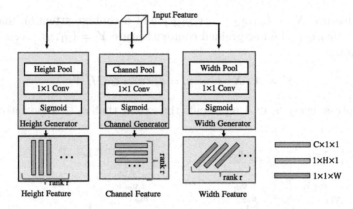

Fig. 3. Tensor Generation Module. Channel Pool, Height Pool and Width Pool are all global average pooling.

pooling in feature generators, obtaining the global context representation in C/H/W directions.

Context Fragments Generation. In order to learn fragments of context information across the three directions, we apply channel, height and width generator on the top of input feature. We repeat this process r times obtaining $3r$ learnable vectors $\boldsymbol{v}_{ci} \in \mathbb{R}^{C \times 1 \times 1}$, $\boldsymbol{v}_{hi} \in \mathbb{R}^{1 \times H \times 1}$ and $\boldsymbol{v}_{wi} \in \mathbb{R}^{1 \times 1 \times W}$, where $i \in r$. All vectors are generated using independent convolution kernels. Each of them learns a part of context information and outputs as context fragment. The TGM is shown in Fig. 3.

Non-linearity in TGM. Recalling that TGM generates $3r$ rank-1 tensors and these tensors are activated by Sigmoid function, which re-scales the values in context fragments to $[0, 1]$. We add the non-linearity for two reasons. Firstly, each re-scaled element can be regarded as the weight of a certain kind of context feature, which satisfy the definition of attention. Secondly, all the context fragments shall not be linear dependent so that each of them can represent different information.

3.3 Tensor Reconstruction Module

In this part, we introduce the context feature reconstruction and aggregation procedure. The entire reconstruction process is clean and simple, which is based on Eq. (1). For a better interpretation, we first introduce the context aggregation process.

Context Aggregation. Different from previous works that only collect spatial or channel attention [45,49], we collect attention distribution in both directions simultaneously. The goal of TRM is to obtain the 3D attention map $\boldsymbol{A} \in \mathbb{R}^{C \times H \times W}$ which keeps response in both spatial and channel attention. After that, context feature is obtained by element-wise product. Specifically, given

an input feature $\boldsymbol{X} = \{x_1, x_2, \ldots, x_{CHW}\}$ and a context attention map $\boldsymbol{A} = \{a_1, a_2, \ldots, a_{CHW}\}$, the fine-grained context feature $\boldsymbol{Y} = \{y_1, y_2, \ldots, y_{CHW}\}$ is then given by:

$$\boldsymbol{Y} = \boldsymbol{A} \cdot \boldsymbol{X} \iff y_i = a_i \cdot x_i, i \in CHW. \tag{2}$$

In this process, every $a_i \in \boldsymbol{A}$ represents the extent that $x_i \in \boldsymbol{X}$ be activated.

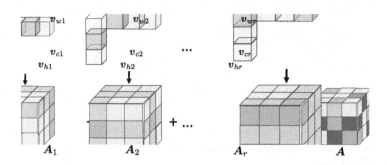

Fig. 4. Tensor Reconstruction Module (TRM). The pipeline of TRM consists of two main steps, *i.e*, sub-attention map generation and global context reconstruction. The processing from top to bottom (see ↓) indicates the sub-attention map generation from three dimensions (channel/height/width). The processing from left to right (see $\boldsymbol{A}_1 + \boldsymbol{A}_2 + \cdots + \boldsymbol{A}_r = \boldsymbol{A}$) denotes the global context reconstruction from low-rank to high-rank.

Low-rank Reconstruction. The tensor reconstruction module (TRM) tackles the high-rank property of context feature. The full workflow of TRM is shown in Fig. 4, which consists of two steps, *i.e*, sub-attention map aggregation and global context feature reconstruction. Firstly, three context fragments $\boldsymbol{v}_{c1} \in \mathbb{R}^{C \times 1 \times 1}$, $\boldsymbol{v}_{h1} \in \mathbb{R}^{1 \times H \times 1}$ and $\boldsymbol{v}_{w1} \in \mathbb{R}^{1 \times 1 \times W}$ are synthesized into a rank-1 sub-attention map $\boldsymbol{A}_1$. This sub-attention map represents a part of 3D context feature, and we will show the visualization of some $\boldsymbol{A}_i, i \in [1, r]$ in experimental result part. Then, other context fragments are reconstructed following the same process. After that we aggregate these sub-attention maps using weighted mean:

$$\boldsymbol{A} = \sum_{i=1}^{r} \lambda_i \boldsymbol{A}_i. \tag{3}$$

Here $\lambda_i \in (0, 1)$ is a learnable normalize factor. Although each sub-attention map represents low-rank context information, the combination of them becomes a high-rank tensor. The fine-grained context features in both spatial and channel dimensions are obtained after Eq. (3) and Eq. (2).

3.4   Global Pooling Module

Global pooling module (GPM) is commonly used in previous work [46, 48]. It is composed of a global average pooling operation followed with a 1 × 1 convolution. It harvests global context in both spatial and channel dimensions. In our proposed model, we apply GPM for the further boost of network performance.

3.5   Network Details

We use ResNet [16] as our backbone and apply dilation strategy to the output of Res-4 and Res-5 of it. Then, the output stride of our proposed network is 8. The output feature of Res-5 block is marked as X. TGM+TRM and GPM are then added on the top of X. Following previous works [45, 48], we also use auxiliary loss after Res-4 block. We set the weight α to 0.2. The total loss $\mathcal{L}$ is formulated as follows:

$$\mathcal{L} = \mathcal{L}_{main} + \alpha \mathcal{L}_{aux}. \tag{4}$$

Finally, we concatenate X with the context featuremap generated by TGM+TRM and the global context generated by GPM to make the final prediction.

3.6   Relation to Previous Approaches

Compared with non-local and its variants that explore the pairwise relationship between pixels, the proposed method is essentially unary attention. Unary attention has been widely used in image classification such as SENet [17] and CBAM [38]. It is also broadly adopted in semantic segmentation such as DFN [43] and EncNet [45]. Apparently, SENet is the simplest formation of RecoNet. The 3D attention map of SENet $\boldsymbol{A}_{SE} \in \mathbb{R}^{C \times H \times W}$ is as Formula (5):

$$\begin{aligned}
\boldsymbol{A}_{SE} &= \boldsymbol{v}_c \otimes \boldsymbol{v}_h \otimes \boldsymbol{v}_w, \\
\boldsymbol{v}_h &= \boldsymbol{e}, \\
\boldsymbol{v}_w &= \boldsymbol{e}^\top, \\
\boldsymbol{e} &= \{1, 1, 1, \ldots 1\}.
\end{aligned} \tag{5}$$

RecoNet degenerates to SENet by setting tensor rank $r = 1$. Meanwhile, $\boldsymbol{v}_h = \boldsymbol{e}$ and $\boldsymbol{v}_w = \boldsymbol{e}^\top$. From Formula (5), it is observed that the weights in H and W directions are the same, which implies that SENet only harvests channel attention while sets the same weights in spatial domain. EncNet [45] is the updated version of SENet, which also uses the same spatial weights. Different spatial weights are introduced in CBAM, which extends Formula (5) to Eq. (6).

$$\boldsymbol{A}_{CBAM} = \boldsymbol{v}_c \otimes \boldsymbol{v}_{h,w}, \boldsymbol{v}_{h,w} \in \mathbb{R}^{1 \times H \times W}. \tag{6}$$

Here $\boldsymbol{A}_{CBAM} \in \mathbb{R}^{C \times H \times W}$ is the 3D attention map of CBAM. The spatial attention is considered in CBAM. However, single rank-1 tensor $\boldsymbol{A}_{CBAM}$ can not

represent complicated context information. Considering an extreme case, the spatial attention is CP-decomposed into 2 rank-1 tensors $v_h \in \mathbb{R}^{1 \times H \times 1}$ and $v_w \in \mathbb{R}^{1 \times 1 \times W}$. Then, A_{CBAM} becomes a sub-attention map of RecoNet.

Simple but effective is the advantage of unary attentions, but they are also criticized for not being able to represent complicated features or for being able to represent features only in one direction (spatial/channel). RecoNet not only takes the advantage of simplicity and effectiveness from unary attention, but also delivers comprehensive feature representations from multi-view (*i.e*, spatial and channel dimension).

4   Experiments

Many experiments are carried out in this section. We use five datasets: PASCAL-VOC12, PASCAL-Context, COCO-Stuff, ADE20K and SIFT-FLOW to test the performance of RecoNet.

4.1   Implementation Details

RecoNet is implemented using Pytorch [31]. Following previous works [13,45], synchronized batch normalization is applied. The learning rate scheduler is $lr = base\_lr \times (1 - \dfrac{iter}{total\_iters})^{power}$. We set $base\_lr$ to 0.001 for PASCAL-VOC12, PASCAL-Context and COCO-Stuff datasets. The $base\_lr$ for ADE20K and SIFT-FLOW is 0.01 and 0.0025. Here we set $power$ to 0.9. SGD optimizer is applied with weight decay 0.0001 and momentum 0.9. We train ADE20K and COCO-Stuff for 120 epochs and 180 epochs respectively. For other datasets, we train 80 epochs. The batch size we set for all datasets is 16 and all input images are randomly cropped into 512×512 before putting into neural network. The data augmentation method we use is the same with previous works [45,48]. Specifically, we randomly flip and scale the input images (0.5 to 2).

We use multi-scale and flip evaluation with input scales [0.75, 1, 1.25, 1.5, 1.75, 2.0] times of original scale. The evaluation metrics we use is mean Intersection-over-Union (mIoU).

4.2   Results on Different Datasets

PASCAL-VOC12. We first test RecoNet using PASCAL-VOC12 [12] dataset, a golden benchmark of semantic segmentation, which includes 20 object categories and one background class. The dataset contains 10582, 1449, 1456 images for training, validation and testing. Our training set contains images from PASCAL augmentation dataset. The results are shown in Table 1. RecoNet reaches 85.6% mIoU, surpassing current best algorithm using ResNet-101 by 1.2%, which is a large margin.

Table 1. Results on PASCAL-VOC12 w/o COCO-pretrained model

	FCN [30]	PSPNet [48]	EncNet [45]	APCNet [15]	CFNet [46]	DMNet [14]	RecoNet
Aero	76.8	91.8	94.1	95.8	95.7	**96.1**	93.7
Bike	34.2	71.9	69.2	75.8	71.9	**77.3**	66.3
Bird	68.9	94.7	**96.3**	84.5	95.0	94.1	95.6
Boat	49.4	71.2	**76.7**	76.0	76.3	72.8	72.8
Bottle	60.3	75.8	86.2	80.6	82.8	78.1	**87.4**
Bus	75.3	95.2	96.3	96.9	94.8	**97.1**	94.5
Car	74.7	89.9	90.7	90.0	90.0	**92.7**	92.6
Cat	77.6	95.9	94.2	96.0	95.9	96.4	**96.5**
Chair	21.4	39.3	38.8	42.0	37.1	39.8	**48.4**
Cow	62.5	90.7	90.7	93.7	92.6	91.4	**94.5**
Table	46.8	71.7	73.3	75.4	73.0	75.5	**76.6**
Dog	71.8	90.5	90.0	91.6	93.4	92.7	**94.4**
Horse	63.9	94.5	92.5	95.0	94.6	95.8	**95.9**
mbike	76.5	88.8	88.8	90.5	89.6	91.0	**93.8**
Person	73.9	89.6	87.9	89.3	88.4	90.3	**90.4**
Plant	45.2	72.8	68.7	75.8	74.9	76.6	**78.1**
Sheep	72.4	89.6	92.6	92.8	**95.2**	94.1	93.6
Sofa	37.4	**64**	59.0	61.9	63.2	62.1	63.4
Train	70.9	85.1	86.4	88.9	**89.7**	85.5	88.6
Tv	55.1	76.3	73.4	79.6	78.2	77.6	**83.1**
mIoU	62.2	82.6	82.9	84.2	84.2	84.4	**85.6**

Following previous work [13–15, 45, 46], we use COCO-pertained model during training. We first train our model on MS-COCO [26] dataset for 30 epochs, where the initial learning rate is set to 0.004. Then the model is fine-tuned on PASCAL augmentation training set for another 80 epochs. Finally, we fine-tune our model on original VOC12 train+val set for extra 50 epochs and the initial lr is set to 1e-5. The results in Table 2 show that RecoNet-101 outperforms current state-of-the-art algorithms with the same backbone. Moreover, RecoNet al.so exceeds state-of-the-art methods that use better backbone such as Xception [7]. By applying ResNet-152 backbone, RecoNet reaches 89.0% mIoU without adding extra data. The result is now in the **1st** place of the PASCAL-VOC12 challenge[1].

PASCAL-Context. [41] is a densely labeled scene parsing dataset includes 59 object and stuff classes plus one background class. It contains 4998 images for training and 5105 images for testing. Following previous works [15, 45, 46], we evaluate the dataset with background class (60 classes in total). The results are shown in Table 3. RecoNet performs better than all previous approaches that use non-local block such as CFNet and DANet, which implies that our proposed context modeling method is better than non-local block.

COCO-Stuff. [2] is a challenging dataset which includes 171 object and stuff categories. The dataset provides 9000 images for training and 1000 images for

---

[1] http://host.robots.ox.ac.uk:8080/anonymous/PXWAVA.html.

Table 2. Results on PASCAL-VOC w. COCO-pretrained model

Method	Backbone	mIoU
CRF-RNN [50]		74.7
DPN [29]		77.5
Piecewise [25]		78.0
ResNet38 [40]		84.9
PSPNet [48]	ResNet-101	85.4
DeepLabv3 [4]	ResNet-101	85.7
EncNet [45]	ResNet-101	85.9
DFN [43]	ResNet-101	86.2
CFNet [46]	ResNet-101	87.2
EMANet [21]	ResNet-101	87.7
DeeplabV3+ [5]	Xception	87.8
DeeplabV3+ [5]	Xception+JFT	89.0
RecoNet	ResNet-101	**88.5**
RecoNet	ResNet-152	**89.0**

Table 3. Results on PASCAL-Context test set with background (60 classes)

Method	Backbone	mIoU
FCN-8s [30]		37.8
ParseNet [28]		40.4
Piecewise [25]		43.3
VeryDeep [39]		44.5
DeepLab-v2 [3]	ResNet-101	45.7
RefineNet [24]	ResNet-152	47.3
PSPNet [48]	ResNet-101	47.8
MSCI [23]	ResNet-152	50.3
Ding et al. [11]	ResNet-101	51.6
EncNet [45]	ResNet-101	51.7
DANet [13]	ResNet-101	52.6
SVCNet [10]	ResNet-101	53.2
CFNet [46]	ResNet-101	54.0
DMNet [14]	ResNet-101	54.4
RecoNet	ResNet-101	**54.8**

Table 4. Results on COCO-Stuff test set (171 classes)

Method	Backbone	mIoU
FCN-8s [30]		22.7
DeepLab-v2 [3]	ResNet-101	26.9
RefineNet [24]	ResNet-101	33.6
Ding et al. [11]	ResNet-101	35.7
SVCNet [10]	ResNet-101	39.6
DANet [13]	ResNet-101	39.7
EMANet [21]	ResNet-101	39.9
RecoNet	ResNet-101	**41.5**

Table 5. Results on SIFT-Flow test set

Method	pixel acc.	mIoU
Sharma et al. [34]	79.6	-
Yang et al. [41]	79.8	-
FCN-8s [30]	85.9	41.2
DAG-RNN+CRF [35]	87.8	44.8
Piecewise [25]	88.1	44.9
SVCNet [10]	89.1	46.3
RecoNet	**89.6**	**46.8**

Table 6. Results on ADE20K *val* set

Method	Backbone	mIoU
RefineNet [24]	ResNet-152	40.70
PSPNet [48]	ResNet-101	43.29
DSSPN [22]	ResNet-101	43.68
SAC [33]	ResNet-101	44.30
EncNet [45]	ResNet-101	44.65
CFNet [46]	ResNet-50	42.87
CFNet [46]	ResNet-101	44.89
CCNet [18]	ResNet-101	45.22
RecoNet	ResNet-50	**43.40**
RecoNet	ResNet-101	**45.54**

testing. The outstanding performance of RecoNet (as shown in Table 4) illustrates that the context tensor we modeled has enough capacity to represent complicated context features.

SIFT-Flow. [27] is a dataset that focuses on urban scene, which consists of 2488 images in training set and 500 images for testing. The resolution of images is 256×256 and 33 semantic classes are annotated with pixel-level labels. The result in Table 5 shows that the proposed RecoNet outperforms previous state-of-the-art methods.

ADE20K. [51] is a large scale scene parsing dataset which contains 25K images annotated with 150 semantic categories. There are 20K training images, 2K validation images and 3K test images. The experimental results are shown in Table 6. RecoNet shows better performance than non-local based methods such as CCNet [18]. The superiority on result means RecoNet can collect richer context information.

4.3 Ablation Study

In this section, we perform the thorough ablation experiments to investigate the effect of different components in our method and the effect of different rank number. These experiments provide more insights of our proposed method. The experiments are conducted on PASCAL-VOC12 *validation* set and more ablation studies can be found in supplementary material.

Different Components. In this part, we design several variants of our model to validate the contributions of different components. The experimental settings are the same with previous part. Here we have three main components, including global pooling module (GPM) and tensor low-rank reconstruction module inducing TGM and TRM. For fairness, we fix the tensor rank $r = 64$. The influence of each module is shown in Table 7. According to our experiment results, tensor low-rank reconstruction module contributes 9.9% mIoU gain in network performance and the pooling module also improves mIoU by 0.6%. Then we use the auxiliary loss after Res-4 block. We finally get 81.4% mIoU by using GPM and TGM+TRM together. The result shows that the tensor low-rank reconstruction module dominants the entire performance.

Tensor Rank. Tensor rank r determines the information capacity of our reconstructed attention map. In this experiment, we use ResNet101 as the backbone. We sample r from 16 to 128 to investigate the effect of tensor rank. An intuitive thought is that the performance would be better with the increase of r. However, our experiment results on Table 8 illustrates that the larger r does not always lead to a better performance. Because we apply TGM+TRM on the input feature $X \in \mathbb{R}^{512 \times 64 \times 64}$, which has maximum tensor rank 64. An enormous r may increase redundancy and lead to over-fitting, which harms the network performance. Therefore, we choose $r = 64$ in our experiments.

Comparison with Previous Approaches. In this paper, we use deep-base ResNet as our backbone. Specifically, we replace the first 7×7 convolution in ResNet with three consequent 3×3 convolutions. This design is widely adopted in semantic segmentation and serves as the backbone network of many prior works [18,21,45,46,48]. Since the implementation details and backbones vary in

Table 7. Ablation study on different components. The experiments are implemented using PASCAL-VOC12 validation dataset. FT represents fine-tune on PASCAL-VOC12 original training set

Method	TGM+TRM	GPM	Aux-loss	MS/Flip	FT	mIoU %
ResNet-50						68.7
ResNet-50	√					78.6
ResNet-50	√	√				79.2
ResNet-50	√	√	√			79.8
ResNet-101	√	√	√			81.4
ResNet-101	√	√	√	√		82.1
ResNet-101	√	√	√	√	√	82.9

Table 8. Ablation study on tensor rank. The results are obtained by using ResNet101 backbone and multi-scale evaluation

Method	Tensor Rank	mIoU %
RecoNet	16	81.2
RecoNet	32	81.8
RecoNet	48	81.4
RecoNet	**64**	**82.1**
RecoNet	80	81.6
RecoNet	96	81.0
RecoNet	128	80.7

Table 9. Results on PASCAL-VOC12 *val* set. RecoNet achieves the best performance with relatively small cost

Method	SS	MS/Flip	FLOPs
ResNet-101	-	-	190.6G
DeepLabV3+ [5]	79.45	80.59	+84.1G
PSPNet [48]	79.20	80.36	+77.5G
DANet [13]	79.64	80.78	+117.3G
PSANet [49]	78.71	79.92	+56.3G
CCNet [18]	79.51	80.77	+65.3G
EMANet [21]	80.09	81.38	+43.1G
RecoNet	**81.40**	**82.13**	**+41.9G**

different algorithms. In order to compare our method with previous approaches in absolutely fair manner, we implemented several state-of-the-art algorithms (listed in Table 9) based on our ResNet101 backbone and training setting. The results are shown in Table 9. We compare our method with feature pyramid approaches such as PSPNet [48] and DeepLabV3+ [5]. The evaluation results show that our algorithm not only surpass these method in mIoU but also in FLOPs. Also, we compare our method with non-local attention based algorithms such as DANet [13] and PSANet [49]. It is noticed that our single-scale result outperforms their multi-scale results, which implies the superiority of our method. Additionally, we compare RecoNet with other low-cost non-local methods such as CCNet [18] and EMANet [21], where RecoNet achieves the best performance with relatively small cost.

Table 10. Computational cost and GPU occupation of TGM+TRM. FLOPs (FLoating point Operations). We use tensor rank $r = 64$ for evaluation

Method	Channel	FLOPs	GPU Memory
Non-Local [37]	512	19.33G	88.00MB
APCNet [15]	512	8.98G	193.10MB
RCCA [18]	512	5.37G	41.33MB
A^2Net [6]	512	4.30G	25.00MB
AFNB [52]	512	2.62G	25.93MB
LatentGNN [47]	512	2.58G	44.69MB
EMAUnit [21]	512	2.42G	24.12MB
TGM+TRM	512	**0.0215G**	**8.31MB**

Fig. 5. Visualization of sub-attention map. From left to right are Image, Ground Truth, $A_i \cdot X$, $A_j \cdot X$, $A_k \cdot X$, and $A_l \cdot X$. It can be found that sub-attention maps mainly focus on the different parts of image.

4.4 Further Discussion

We further design several experiments to show computational complexity of the proposed method, and visualize some sub-attention maps from the reconstructed context features.

Computational Complexity Analysis. Our proposed method is based on the low-rank tensors, thus having large advantage on computational consumption. Recalling that non-local block has computational complexity of $\mathcal{O}(CH^2W^2)$. On the TGM stage, we generates a series of learnable vectors using 1×1 convolutions. The computational complexity is $\mathcal{O}(C^2 + H^2 + W^2)$ while on the TRM stage, we reconstruct the high-rank tensor from these vectors and the complex-

ity is $\mathcal{O}(CHW)$ for each rank-1 tensor. Since $CHW >> C^2 > H^2 = W^2$, the total complexity is $\mathcal{O}(rCHW)$, which is much smaller than non-local block. Here r is the tensor rank. Table 10 shows the FLOPs and GPU occupation of TGM+TRM. From the table we can see that the cost of TGM+TRM is neglegible compared with other non-local based methods. Our proposed method has about **900** times less FLOPs and more than **100** times less FLOPs compared with non-local block and other non-local-based methods, such as A^2Net [6] and LatentGNN [47]. Besides of these methods, we calculate the FLOPs and GPU occupation of RCCA, AFNB and EMAUnit, which is core component of CCNet [18], AsymmetricNL [52] and EMANet [21]. It can be found that TGM+TRM has the lowest computational overhead.

Visualization. In our proposed method, context features are constructed by the linear combination of sub-attention maps, *i.e*, $A_i \cdot X$. Therefore, we visualize their heat maps to check the part of features they activate. We randomly select four sub-attention maps $A_i \cdot X$, $A_j \cdot X$, $A_k \cdot X$, $A_l \cdot X$, as shown in Fig. 5. We can see that different sub-attention maps activate different parts of the image. For instance, for the last case, the four attention maps focus on the foreground, the horse, the person, and the background, respectively, which implies that the low-rank attention captures the context fragments and RecoNet can catch long-range dependencies.

5   Conclusion

In this paper, we propose a tensor low-rank reconstruction for context features prediction, which overcomes the feature compression problem that occurred in previous works. We collect high-rank context information by using low-rank context fragments that generated by our proposed tensor generation module. Then we use CP reconstruction to build up high-rank context features. We embed the fine-grained context features into our proposed RecoNet. The state-of-the-arts performance on different datasets and the superiority on computational consumption show the success of our context collection method.

References

1. Badrinarayanan, V., Kendall, A., Cipolla, R.: SegNet: a deep convolutional encoder-decoder architecture for image segmentation. IEEE TPAMI **39**(12), 2481–2495 (2017)
2. Caesar, H., Uijlings, J., Ferrari, V.: COCO-Stuff: thing and stuff classes in context. In: Proceedings of the CVPR, pp. 1209–1218 (2018)
3. Chen, L.C., Papandreou, G., Kokkinos, I., Murphy, K., Yuille, A.L.: DeepLab: semantic image segmentation with deep convolutional nets, atrous convolution, and fully connected CRFs. IEEE TPAMI **40**(4), 834–848 (2018)
4. Chen, L.C., Papandreou, G., Schroff, F., Adam, H.: Rethinking atrous convolution for semantic image segmentation. arXiv preprint arXiv:1706.05587 (2017)

5. Chen, L.-C., Zhu, Y., Papandreou, G., Schroff, F., Adam, H.: Encoder-decoder with atrous separable convolution for semantic image segmentation. In: Ferrari, V., Hebert, M., Sminchisescu, C., Weiss, Y. (eds.) ECCV 2018, Part VII. LNCS, vol. 11211, pp. 833–851. Springer, Cham (2018). https://doi.org/10.1007/978-3-030-01234-2_49

6. Chen, Y., Kalantidis, Y., Li, J., Yan, S., Feng, J.: A 2-nets: double attention networks. In: Proceedings of the NIPS, pp. 352–361 (2018)

7. Chollet, F.: Xception: deep learning with depthwise separable convolutions. In: Proceedings of the CVPR, pp. 1251–1258 (2017)

8. Chorowski, J.K., Bahdanau, D., Serdyuk, D., Cho, K., Bengio, Y.: Attention-based models for speech recognition. In: Proceedings of the NIPS, pp. 577–585 (2015)

9. Cui, Y., Chen, Z., Wei, S., Wang, S., Liu, T., Hu, G.: Attention-over-attention neural networks for reading comprehension. In: Proceedings of the ACL (2017)

10. Ding, H., Jiang, X., Shuai, B., Liu, A.Q., Wang, G.: Semantic correlation promoted shape-variant context for segmentation. In: Proceedings of the CVPR, pp. 8885–8894 (2019)

11. Ding, H., Jiang, X., Shuai, B., Qun Liu, A., Wang, G.: Context contrasted feature and gated multi-scale aggregation for scene segmentation. In: Proceedings of the CVPR, pp. 2393–2402 (2018)

12. Everingham, M., Van Gool, L., Williams, C.K., Winn, J., Zisserman, A.: The pascal visual object classes (VOC) challenge. Int. J. Comput. Vis. **88**(2), 303–338 (2010)

13. Fu, J., Liu, J., Tian, H., Fang, Z., Lu, H.: Dual attention network for scene segmentation. arXiv preprint arXiv:1809.02983 (2018)

14. He, J., Deng, Z., Qiao, Y.: Dynamic multi-scale filters for semantic segmentation. In: Proceedings of the ICCV, pp. 3562–3572 (2019)

15. He, J., Deng, Z., Zhou, L., Wang, Y., Qiao, Y.: Adaptive pyramid context network for semantic segmentation. In: Proceedings of the CVPR, pp. 7519–7528 (2019)

16. He, K., Zhang, X., Ren, S., Sun, J.: Deep residual learning for image recognition. In: Proceedings of the CVPR, pp. 770–778 (2016)

17. Hu, J., Shen, L., Sun, G.: Squeeze-and-excitation networks. In: Proceedings of the CVPR, pp. 7132–7141 (2018)

18. Huang, Z., Wang, X., Huang, L., Huang, C., Wei, Y., Liu, W.: CCNet: criss-cross attention for semantic segmentation. In: Proceedings of the ICCV, pp. 603–612 (2019)

19. Kolda, T.G., Bader, B.W.: Tensor decompositions and applications. SIAM Rev. (SIREV) **51**, 3 (2009)

20. Lebedev, V., Ganin, Y., Rakhuba, M., Oseledets, I., Lempitsky, V.: Speeding-up convolutional neural networks using fine-tuned CP-decomposition. In: Proceedings of the ICLR (2015)

21. Li, X., Zhong, Z., Wu, J., Yang, Y., Lin, Z., Liu, H.: Expectation-maximization attention networks for semantic segmentation. In: Proceedings of the ICCV, pp. 9167–9176 (2019)

22. Liang, X., Xing, E., Zhou, H.: Dynamic-structured semantic propagation network. In: Proceedings of the CVPR, pp. 752–761 (2018)

23. Lin, D., Ji, Y., Lischinski, D., Cohen-Or, D., Huang, H.: Multi-scale context intertwining for semantic segmentation. In: Ferrari, V., Hebert, M., Sminchisescu, C., Weiss, Y. (eds.) ECCV 2018, Part III. LNCS, vol. 11207, pp. 622–638. Springer, Cham (2018). https://doi.org/10.1007/978-3-030-01219-9_37

24. Lin, G., Milan, A., Shen, C., Reid, I.: RefineNet: multi-path refinement networks for high-resolution semantic segmentation. In: Proceedings of the CVPR, pp. 1925–1934 (2017)

25. Lin, G., Shen, C., Van Den Hengel, A., Reid, I.: Efficient piecewise training of deep structured models for semantic segmentation. In: Proceedings of the CVPR, pp. 3194–3203 (2016)
26. Lin, T.Y., et al.: Microsoft COCO: common objects in context. In: Fleet, D., Pajdla, T., Schiele, B., Tuytelaars, T. (eds.) ECCV 2014, Part V. LNCS, vol. 8693, pp. 740–755. Springer, Cham (2014). https://doi.org/10.1007/978-3-319-10602-1_48
27. Liu, C., Yuen, J., Torralba, A.: SIFT flow: dense correspondence across scenes and its applications. IEEE TPAMI **33**(5), 978–994 (2011)
28. Liu, W., Rabinovich, A., Berg, A.C.: ParseNet: Looking wider to see better. arXiv preprint arXiv:1506.04579 (2015)
29. Liu, Z., Li, X., Luo, P., Loy, C.C., Tang, X.: Semantic image segmentation via deep parsing network. In: Proceedings of the ICCV, pp. 1377–1385 (2015)
30. Long, J., Shelhamer, E., Darrell, T.: Fully convolutional networks for semantic segmentation. In: Proceedings of the CVPR, pp. 3431–3440 (2015)
31. Paszke, A., et al.: Automatic differentiation in PyTorch. In: NIPS Workshop (2017)
32. Ronneberger, O., Fischer, P., Brox, T.: U-net: convolutional networks for biomedical image segmentation. In: Navab, N., Hornegger, J., Wells, W.M., Frangi, A.F. (eds.) MICCAI 2015, Part III. LNCS, vol. 9351, pp. 234–241. Springer, Cham (2015). https://doi.org/10.1007/978-3-319-24574-4_28
33. Rui, Z., Sheng, T., Zhang, Y., Li, J., Yan, S.: Scale-adaptive convolutions for scene parsing. In: Proceedings of the ICCV, pp. 2031–2039 (2017)
34. Sharma, A., Tuzel, O., Liu, M.Y.: Recursive context propagation network for semantic scene labeling. In: Proceedings of the NIPS (2014)
35. Shuai, B., Zup, Z., Wang, B., Wang, G.: Scene segmentation with DAG-recurrent neural networks. IEEE TPAMI **40**(6), 1480–1493 (2018)
36. Vaswani, A., et al.: Attention is all you need. In: Proceedings of the NIPS, pp. 5998–6008 (2017)
37. Wang, X., Girshick, R., Gupta, A., He, K.: Non-local neural networks. In: Proceedings of the CVPR, pp. 7794–7803 (2018)
38. Woo, S., Park, J., Lee, J.-Y., Kweon, I.S.: CBAM: convolutional block attention module. In: Ferrari, V., Hebert, M., Sminchisescu, C., Weiss, Y. (eds.) ECCV 2018, Part VII. LNCS, vol. 11211, pp. 3–19. Springer, Cham (2018). https://doi.org/10.1007/978-3-030-01234-2_1
39. Wu, Z., Shen, C., Hengel, A.v.d.: Bridging category-level and instance-level semantic image segmentation. arXiv preprint arXiv:1605.06885 (2016)
40. Wu, Z., Shen, C., Van Den Hengel, A.: Wider or deeper: revisiting the resnet model for visual recognition. Pattern Recogn. **90**, 119–133 (2019)
41. Yang, J., Price, B., Cohen, S., Yang, M.H.: Context driven scene parsing with attention to rare classes. In: Proceedings of the CVPR, pp. 3294–3301 (2014)
42. Yang, Z., Yang, D., Dyer, C., He, X., Smola, A., Hovy, E.: Hierarchical attention networks for document classification. In: Proceedings of the NAACL, pp. 1480–1489 (2016)
43. Yu, C., Wang, J., Peng, C., Gao, C., Yu, G., Sang, N.: Learning a discriminative feature network for semantic segmentation. In: Proceedings of the CVPR, pp. 1857–1866 (2018)
44. Yu, X., Liu, T., Wang, X., Tao, D.: On compressing deep models by low rank and sparse decomposition. In: Proceedings of the CVPR, pp. 7370–7379 (2017)
45. Zhang, H., et al.: Context encoding for semantic segmentation. In: Proceedings of the CVPR, pp. 7151–7160 (2018)

46. Zhang, H., Zhang, H., Wang, C., Xie, J.: Co-occurrent features in semantic segmentation. In: Proceedings of the CVPR, pp. 548–557 (2019)
47. Zhang, S., He, X., Yan, S.: LatentGNN: learning efficient non-local relations for visual recognition. In: Proceedings of the ICML, pp. 7374–7383 (2019)
48. Zhao, H., Shi, J., Qi, X., Wang, X., Jia, J.: Pyramid scene parsing network. In: Proceedings of the CVPR, pp. 2881–2890 (2017)
49. Zhao, H., et al.: PSANet: point-wise spatial attention network for acene parsing. In: Ferrari, V., Hebert, M., Sminchisescu, C., Weiss, Y. (eds.) ECCV 2018, Part IX. LNCS, vol. 11213, pp. 270–286. Springer, Cham (2018). https://doi.org/10.1007/978-3-030-01240-3_17
50. Zheng, S., et al.: Conditional random fields as recurrent neural networks. In: Proceedings of the ICCV, pp. 1529–1537 (2015)
51. Zhou, B., Zhao, H., Puig, X., Fidler, S., Barriuso, A., Torralba, A.: Scene parsing through ADE20K dataset. In: Proceedings of the CVPR, pp. 633–641 (2017)
52. Zhu, Z., Xu, M., Bai, S., Huang, T., Bai, X.: Asymmetric non-local neural networks for semantic segmentation. In: Proceedings of the ICCV, pp. 593–602 (2019)

Attentive Normalization

Xilai Li, Wei Sun, and Tianfu Wu$^{(\boxtimes)}$

Department of Electrical and Computer Engineering,
NC State University,
Raleigh, USA
{xli47,wsun12,tianfu_wu}@ncsu.edu

Abstract. In state-of-the-art deep neural networks, both feature normalization and feature attention have become ubiquitous. They are usually studied as separate modules, however. In this paper, we propose a light-weight integration between the two schema and present Attentive Normalization (AN). Instead of learning a single affine transformation, AN learns a mixture of affine transformations and utilizes their weighted-sum as the final affine transformation applied to re-calibrate features in an instance-specific way. The weights are learned by leveraging channel-wise feature attention. In experiments, we test the proposed AN using four representative neural architectures in the ImageNet-1000 classification benchmark and the MS-COCO 2017 object detection and instance segmentation benchmark. AN obtains consistent performance improvement for different neural architectures in both benchmarks with absolute increase of top-1 accuracy in ImageNet-1000 between 0.5% and 2.7%, and absolute increase up to 1.8% and 2.2% for bounding box and mask AP in MS-COCO respectively. We observe that the proposed AN provides a strong alternative to the widely used Squeeze-and-Excitation (SE) module. The source codes are publicly available at the ImageNet Classification Repo and the MS-COCO Detection and Segmentation Repo.

1 Introduction

Pioneered by Batch Normalization (BN) [19], feature normalization has become ubiquitous in the development of deep learning. Feature normalization consists of two components: *feature standardization* and *channel-wise affine transformation*. The latter is introduced to provide the capability of undoing the standardization (by design), and can be treated as *feature re-calibration* in general. Many variants of BN have been proposed for practical deployment in terms of variations of training and testing settings with remarkable progress obtained. They can be roughly divided into two categories:

i) Generalizing feature standardization. Different methods are proposed for computing the mean and standard deviation or for modeling/whitening the data

Electronic supplementary material The online version of this chapter (https://doi.org/10.1007/978-3-030-58520-4_5) contains supplementary material, which is available to authorized users.

A. Vedaldi et al. (Eds.): ECCV 2020, LNCS 12362, pp. 70–87, 2020.
https://doi.org/10.1007/978-3-030-58520-4_5

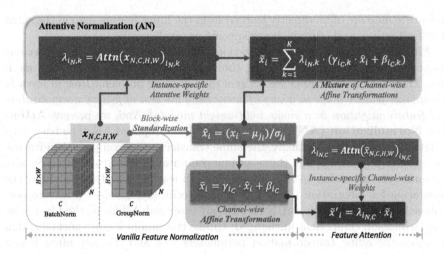

Fig. 1. Illustration of the proposed Attentive Normalization (AN). AN aims to harness the best of a base feature normalization (e.g., BN or GN) and channel-wise feature attention in a single light-weight module. See text for details.

distribution in general, within a min-batch. They include Batch Renormalization [18], Decorrelated BN [16], Layer Normalization (LN) [1], Instance Normalization (IN) [42], Instance-level Meta Normalization [20], Group Normalization (GN) [47], Mixture Normalization [21] and Mode Normalization [5]. Switchable Normalization (SN) [28] and its sparse variant (SSN) [39] learn to switch between different vanilla schema. These methods adopt the vanilla channel-wise affine transformation after standardization, and are often proposed for discriminative learning tasks.

ii) Generalizing feature re-calibration. Instead of treating the affine transformation parameters directly as model parameters, different types of task-induced conditions (*e.g.*, class labels in conditional image synthesis using generative adversarial networks) are leveraged and encoded as latent vectors, which are then used to learn the affine transformation parameters, including different conditional BNs [2,6,29,33,43], style-adaptive IN [22] or layout-adaptive IN [31,40]. These methods have been mainly proposed in generative learning tasks, except for the recently proposed Instance-level Meta Normalization [20] in discriminative learning tasks.

In the meanwhile, *feature attention* has also become an indispensable mechanism for improving task performance in deep learning. For computer vision, spatial attention is inherently captured by convolution operations within short-range context, and by non-local extensions [17,45] for long-range context. Channel-wise attention is relatively less exploited. The squeeze-and-excitation (SE) unit [13] is one of the most popular designs, which learn instance-specific channel-wise attention weights to re-calibrate an input feature map. Unlike the affine transformation parameters in feature normalization, the attention weights for re-calibrating

an feature map are often directly learned from the input feature map in the spirit of self-attention, and often instance-specific or pixel-specific.

Although both feature normalization and feature attention have become ubiquitous in state-of-the-art DNNs, they are usually studied as separate modules. Therefore, in this paper we address the following problem: *How to learn to re-calibrate feature maps in a way of harnessing the best of feature normalization and feature attention in a single light-weight module?* And, we present **Attentive Normalization (AN)**: Fig. 1 illustrates the proposed AN. The basic idea is straightforward. Conceptually, the affine transformation component in feature normalization (Sect. 3.1) and the re-scaling computation in feature attention play the same role in learning-to-re-calibrate an input feature map, thus providing the foundation for integration (Sect. 3.2). More specifically, consider a feature normalization backbone such as BN or GN, our proposed AN keeps the block-wise standardization component unchanged. Unlike the vanilla feature normalization in which the affine transformation parameters (γ's and β's) are often frozen in testing, we want the affine transformation parameters to be adaptive and dynamic in both training and testing, controlled directly by the input feature map. The intuition behind doing so is that it will be more flexible in accounting for different statistical discrepancies between training and testing in general, and between different sub-populations caused by underlying inter-/intra-class variations in the data.

To achieve the dynamic and adaptive control of affine transformation parameters, the proposed AN utilizes a simple design (Sect. 3). It learns a mixture of K affine transformations and exploits feature attention mechanism to learn the instance-specific weights for the K components. The final affine transformation used to re-calibrate an input feature map is the weighted sum of the learned K affine transformations. We propose a general formulation for the proposed AN and study how to learn the weights in an efficient and effective way (Sect. 3.3).

2 Related Work

Feature Normalization. There are two types of normalization schema, feature normalization (including raw data) [1,5,18,19,21,28,39,42,47] and weight normalization [15,36]. Unlike the former, the latter is to normalize model parameters to decouple the magnitudes of parameter vectors from their directions. We focus on feature normalization in this paper.

Different feature normalization schema differ in how the mean and variance are computed. BN [19] computes the channel-wise mean and variance in the entire min-batch which is driven by improving training efficiency and model generalizability. BN has been deeply analyzed in terms of how it helps optimization [38]. DecorBN [16] utilizes a whitening operation (ZCA) to go beyond the centering and scaling in the vanilla BN. BatchReNorm [18] introduces extra parameters to control the pooled mean and variance to reduce BN's dependency on the batch size. IN [42] focuses on channel-wise and instance-specific statistics which stems from the task of artistic image style transfer. LN [1] computes

the instance-specific mean and variance from all channels which is designed to help optimization in recurrent neural networks (RNNs). GN [47] stands in the sweet spot between LN and IN focusing on instance-specific and channel-group-wise statistics, especially when only small batches are applicable in practice. In practice, synchronized BN [32] across multiple GPUs becomes increasingly favorable against GN in some applications. SN [28] leaves the design choices of feature normalization schema to the learning system itself by computing weighted sum integration of BN, LN, IN and/or GN via softmax, showing more flexible applicability, followed by SSN [39] which learns to make exclusive selection. Instead of computing one mode (mean and variance), MixtureNorm [21] introduces a mixture of Gaussian densities to approximate the data distribution in a mini-batch. ModeNorm [5] utilizes a general form of multiple-mode computation. Unlike those methods, the proposed AN focuses on generalizing the affine transformation component. Related to our work, Instance-level Meta normalization(ILM) [20] first utilizes an encoder-decoder sub-network to learn affine transformation parameters and then add them together to the model's affine transformation parameters. Unlike ILM, the proposed AN utilizes a mixture of affine transformations and leverages feature attention to learn the instance-specific attention weights.

On the other hand, conditional feature normalization schema [2,6,22,31,33, 40,43] have been developed and shown remarkable progress in conditional and unconditional image synthesis. Conditional BN learns condition-specific affine transformations in terms of conditions such as class labels, image style, label maps and geometric layouts. Unlike those methods, the proposed AN learns self-attention data-driven weights for mixture components of affine transformations.

Feature Attention. Similar to feature normalization, feature attention is also an important building block in the development of deep learning. Residual Attention Network [44] uses a trunk-and-mask joint spatial and channel attention module in an encoder-decoder style for improving performance. To reduce the computational cost, channel and spatial attention are separately applied in [46]. The SE module [13] further simplifies the attention mechanism by developing a light-weight channel-wise attention method. The proposed AN leverages the idea of SE in learning attention weights, but formulates the idea in a novel way.

Our Contributions. This paper makes three main contributions: (i) It presents Attentive Normalization which harnesses the best of feature normalization and feature attention (channel-wise). To our knowledge, AN is the first work that studies self-attention based conditional and adaptive feature normalization in visual recognition tasks. (ii) It presents a lightweight integration method for deploying AN in different widely used building blocks of ResNets, DenseNets, MobileNetsV2 and AOGNets. (iii) It obtains consistently better results than the vanilla feature normalization backbones by a large margin across different neural architectures in two large-scale benchmarks, ImageNet-1000 and MS-COCO.

3   The Proposed Attentive Normalization

In this section, we present details of the proposed attentive normalization. Consider a DNN for 2D images, denote by $\mathbf{x}$ a feature map with axes in the convention order of (N, C, H, W) (i.e., batch, channel, height and width). $\mathbf{x}$ is represented by a 4D tensor. Let $i = (i_N, i_C, i_H, i_W)$ be the address index in the 4D tensor. $\mathbf{x}_i$ represents the feature response at a position i.

3.1   Background on Feature Normalization

Existing feature normalization schema often consist of two components (Fig. 1):

   i) Block-wise Standardization. Denote by B_j a block (slice) in a given 4-D tensor $\mathbf{x}$. For example, for BN, we have $j = 1, \cdots, C$ and $B_j = \{\mathbf{x}_i | \forall i, i_C = j\}$. We first compute the empirical mean and standard deviation in B_j, denoted by μ_j and σ_j respectively: $\mu_j = \frac{1}{M} \sum_{x \in B_j} x$, $\sigma_j = \sqrt{\frac{1}{M} \sum_{x \in B_j} (x - \mu_j)^2 + \epsilon}$, where $M = |B_j|$ and ϵ is a small positive constant to ensure $\sigma_j > 0$ for the sake of numeric stability. Then, let j_i be the index of the block that the position i belongs to, and we standardize the feature response by,

$$\hat{\mathbf{x}}_i = \frac{1}{\sigma_{j_i}} (\mathbf{x}_i - \mu_{j_i}) \tag{1}$$

   ii) Channel-wise Affine Transformation. Denote by γ_c and β_c the scalar coefficient (re-scaling) and offset (re-shifting) parameter respectively for the c-th channel. The re-calibrated feature response at a position i is then computed by,

$$\tilde{\mathbf{x}}_i = \gamma_{i_C} \cdot \hat{\mathbf{x}}_i + \beta_{i_C}, \tag{2}$$

where γ_c's and β_c's are shared by all the instances in a min-batch across the spatial domain. They are usually frozen in testing and fine-tuning.

3.2   Background on Feature Attention

We focus on channel-wise attention and briefly review the Squeeze-Excitation (SE) module [13]. SE usually takes the feature normalization result (Eq. 2) as its input (the bottom-right of Fig. 1), and learns channel-wise attention weights:

   i) The squeeze module encodes the inter-dependencies between feature channels in a low dimensional latent space with the reduction rate r (e.g., $r = 16$),

$$S(\tilde{\mathbf{x}}; \theta_S) = v, \, v \in \mathbb{R}^{N \times \frac{C}{r} \times 1 \times 1}, \tag{3}$$

which is implemented by a sub-network consisting of a global average pooling layer (AvgPool), a fully-connected (FC) layer and rectified linear unit (ReLU) [23]. θ_S collects all the model parameters.

   ii) The excitation module computes the channel-wise attention weights, denoted by λ, by decoding the learned latent representations v,

$$E(v; \theta_E) = \lambda, \, \lambda \in \mathbb{R}^{N \times C \times 1 \times 1}, \tag{4}$$

which is implemented by a sub-network consisting of a FC layer and a sigmoid layer. θ_E collects all model parameters.

Then, the input, $\tilde{\mathbf{x}}$ is re-calibrated by,

$$\tilde{\mathbf{x}}_i^{SE} = \lambda_{i_N,i_C} \cdot \hat{\mathbf{x}}_i = (\lambda_{i_N,i_C} \cdot \gamma_{i_C}) \cdot \hat{\mathbf{x}}_i + \lambda_{i_N,i_C} \cdot \beta_{i_C}, \tag{5}$$

where the second step is obtained by plugging in Eq. 2. **It is thus straightforward to see the foundation facilitating the integration between feature normalization and channel-wise feature attention.** However, the SE module often entails a significant number of extra parameters (e.g., ~2.5M extra parameters for ResNet50 [10] which originally consists of ~25M parameters, resulting in 10% increase). We aim to design more parsimonious integration that can further improve performance.

3.3 Attentive Normalization

Our goal is to generalize Eq. 2 in re-calibrating feature responses to enable dynamic and adaptive control in both training and testing. On the other hand, our goal is to simplify Eq. 5 into a single light-weight module, rather than, for example, the two-module setup using BN+SE. In general, we have,

$$\tilde{\mathbf{x}}_i^{AN} = \Gamma(\mathbf{x}; \theta_\Gamma)_i \cdot \hat{\mathbf{x}}_i + \mathbb{B}(\mathbf{x}; \theta_\mathbb{B})_i, \tag{6}$$

where both $\Gamma(\mathbf{x}; \theta_\Gamma)$ and $\mathbb{B}(\mathbf{x}; \theta_\mathbb{B})$ are functions of the entire input feature map (without standardization[1]) with parameters θ_Γ and $\theta_\mathbb{B}$ respectively. They both compute 4D tensors of the size same as the input feature map and can be parameterized by some attention guided light-weight DNNs. The subscript in $\Gamma(\mathbf{x}; \theta_\Gamma)_i$ and $\mathbb{B}(\mathbf{x}; \theta_\mathbb{B})_i$ represents the learned re-calibration weights at a position i.

In this paper, we focus on learning instance-specific channel-wise affine transformations. To that end, we have three components as follows.

i) Learning a Mixture of K Channel-wise Affine Transformations. Denote by $\gamma_{k,c}$ and $\beta_{k,c}$ the re-scaling and re-shifting (scalar) parameters respectively for the c-th channel in the k-th mixture component. They are model parameters learned end-to-end via back-propagation.

ii) Learning Attention Weights for the K Mixture Components. Denote by $\lambda_{n,k}$ the instance-specific mixture component weight ($n \in [1, N]$ and $k \in [1, K]$), and by λ the $N \times K$ weight matrix. λ is learned via some attention-guided function from the entire input feature map,

$$\lambda = A(\mathbf{x}; \theta_\lambda), \tag{7}$$

where θ_λ collects all the parameters.

iii) Computing the Final Affine Transformation. With the learned $\gamma_{k,c}$, $\beta_{k,c}$ and λ, the re-calibrated feature response is computed by,

$$\tilde{\mathbf{x}}_i^{AN} = \sum_{k=1}^{K} \lambda_{i_N,k} [\gamma_{k,i_C} \cdot \hat{\mathbf{x}}_i + \beta_{k,i_C}], \tag{8}$$

---

[1] We tried the variant of learning $\Gamma()$ and $\mathbb{B}()$ from the standardized features and observed it works worse, so we ignore it in our experiments.

where $\lambda_{i_N,k}$ is shared by the re-scaling parameter and the re-shifting parameter for simplicity. Since the attention weights λ are adaptive and dynamic in both training and testing, the proposed AN realizes adaptive and dynamic feature re-calibration. Compared to the general form (Eq. 6), we have,

$$\Gamma(\mathbf{x})_i = \sum_{k=1}^{K} \lambda_{i_N,k} \cdot \gamma_{k,i_C}, \quad \mathbb{B}(\mathbf{x})_i = \sum_{k=1}^{K} \lambda_{i_N,k} \cdot \beta_{k,i_C}. \tag{9}$$

Based on the formulation, there are **a few advantages of the proposed AN in training, fine-tuning and testing** a DNN:

- The channel-wise affine transformation parameters, γ_{k,i_C}'s and β_{k,i_C}'s, are shared across spatial dimensions and by data instances, which can learn population-level knowledge in a more fine-grained manner than a single affine transformation in the vanilla feature normalization.
- $\lambda_{i_N,k}$'s are instance specific and learned from features that are not standardized. Combining them with γ_{k,i_C}'s and β_{k,i_C}'s (Eq. 8) enables AN paying attention to both the population (what the common and useful information are) and the individuals (what the specific yet critical information are). The latter is particularly useful for testing samples slightly "drifted" from training population, that is to improve generalizability. Their weighted sum encodes more direct and "actionable" information for re-calibrating standardized features (Eq. 8) without being delayed until back-propagation updates as done in the vanilla feature normalization.
- In fine-tuning, especially between different tasks (*e.g.*, from image classification to object detection), γ_{k,i_C}'s and β_{k,i_C}'s are usually frozen as done in the vanilla feature normalization. They carry information from a source task. But, θ_λ (Eq. 7) are allowed to be fine-tuned, thus potentially better realizing transfer learning for a target task. This is a desirable property since we can decouple training correlation between tasks. For example, when GN [47] is applied in object detection in MS-COCO, it is fine-tuned from a feature backbone with GN trained in ImageNet, instead of the one with BN that usually has better performance in ImageNet. As we shall show in experiments, the proposed AN facilitates a smoother transition. We can use the proposed AN (with BN) as the normalization backbone in pre-training in ImageNet, and then use AN (with GN) as the normalization backbone for the head classifiers in MS-COCO with significant improvement.

Details of Learning Attention Weights. We present a simple method for computing the attention weights $A(\mathbf{x}; \theta_\lambda)$ (Eq. 7). Our goal is to learn a weight coefficient for each component from each individual instance in a mini-batch (i.e, a $N \times K$ matrix). The question of interest is how to characterize the underlying importance of a channel c from its realization across the spatial dimensions (H, W) in an instance, such that we will learn a more informative instance-specific weight coefficient for a channel c in re-calibrating the feature map $\mathbf{x}$.

In realizing Eq. 7, the proposed method is similar in spirit to the squeeze module in SENets [13] to maintain light-weight implementation. To show the difference, let's first rewrite the vanilla squeeze module (Eq. 3),

$$v = S(\mathbf{x}; \theta_S) = ReLU(fc(AvgPool(\mathbf{x}); \theta_S)), \tag{10}$$

where the mean of a channel c (via global average pooling, $AvgPool(\cdot)$) is used to characterize its underlying importance. We generalize this assumption by taking into account both mean and standard deviation empirically computed for a channel c, denoted by μ_c and σ_c respectively. More specifically, we compare three different designs using:

i) The mean μ_c only as done in SENets.
ii) The concatenation of the mean and standard deviation, (μ_c, σ_c).
iii) The coefficient of variation or the relative standard deviation (RSD), $\frac{\sigma_c}{\mu_c}$. RSD measures the dispersion of an underlying distribution (i.e., the extent to which the distribution is stretched or squeezed) which intuitively conveys more information in learning attention weights for re-calibration.

RSD is indeed observed to work better in our experiments[2]. Equation 7 is then expanded with two choices,

$$Choice\ 1:\ A_1(\mathbf{x}; \theta_\lambda) = Act(fc(RSD(\mathbf{x}); \theta_\lambda)),$$
$$Choice\ 2:\ A_2(\mathbf{x}; \theta_\lambda) = Act(BN(fc(RSD(\mathbf{x}); \theta_{fc}); \theta_{BN})), \tag{11}$$

where $Act(\cdot)$ represents a non-linear activation function for which we compare three designs:

i) The vanilla $ReLU(\cdot)$ as used in the squeeze module of SENets.
ii) The vanilla $sigmoid(\cdot)$ as used in the excitation module of SENets.
iii) The channel-wise $softmax(\cdot)$.
iv) The piece-wise linear hard analog of the sigmoid function, so-called $hsigmoid$ function [12], $hsigmoid(a) = \min(\max(a + 3.0, 0), 6.0)/6.0$.

The $hsigmoid(\cdot)$ is observed to work better in our experiments. In the Choice 2 (Eq. 11), we apply the vanilla BN [19] after the FC layer, which normalizes the learned attention weights across all the instances in a mini-batch with the hope of balancing the instance-specific attention weights better. The Choice 2 improves performance in our experiments in ImageNet.

In AN, we have another hyper-parameter, K. For stage-wise building block based neural architectures such as the four neural architectures tested in our experiments, we use different K's for different stages with smaller values for early stages. For example, for the 4-stage setting, we typically use $K = 10, 10, 20, 20$ for the four stages respectively based on our ablation study. The underlying assumption is that early stages often learn low-to-middle level features which are considered to be shared more between different categories, while later stages learn more category-specific features which may entail larger mixtures.

---

[2] In implementation, we use the reverse $\frac{\mu_c}{\sigma_c + \epsilon}$ for numeric stability, which is equivalent to the original formulation when combing with the fc layer.

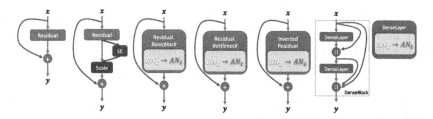

Fig. 2. Illustration of integrating the proposed AN in different building blocks. The first two show the vanilla residual block and the SE-residual block. The remaining four are: the Basicblock and Bottleneck design of a residual block, the inverted residual block (used in MobileNetV2), and the DenseBlock. For the residual block and its variants, the proposed AN is used to replace the vanilla BN(s) followed the last 3×3 convolution in different blocks. This potentially enables jointly integrating local spatial attention (conveyed by the 3×3 convolution) in learning the instance-specific attention weights, which is also observed helpful in [30] and is shown beneficial for the SE module itself in our experiments (Table 3). For the dense block, we replace the second vanilla BN (after the 1×1 convolution applied to the concatenated features) with our AN.

4   Experiments

In this section, we first show the ablation study verifying the design choices in the proposed AN. Then, we present detailed comparisons and analyses.

Data and Evaluation Metric. We use two benchmarks, the ImageNet-1000 classification benchmark (ILSVRC2012) [35] and the MS-COCO object detection and instance segmentation benchmark [26]. The ImageNet-1000 benchmark consists of about 1.28 million images for training, and 50,000 for validation, from 1,000 classes. We apply a single-crop with size 224×224 in evaluation. Following the common protocol, we report the top-1 and top-5 classification error rates tested using a single model on the validation set. For the MS-COCO benchmark, there are 80 categories of objects. We use `train2017` in training and evaluate the trained models using `val2107`. We report the standard COCO metrics of Average Precision (AP) at different intersection-over-union (IoU) thresholds, e.g., AP_{50} and AP_{75}, for bounding box detection (AP^{bb}_{IoU}) and instance segmentation (AP^{m}_{IoU}), and the mean AP over IoU=0.5 : 0.05 : 0.75, AP^{bb} and AP^m for bounding box detection and instance segmentation respectively.

Neural Architectures and Vanilla Feature Normalization Backbones. We use four representative neural architectures: (i) *ResNets* [10] (ResNet50 and ResNet101), which are the most widely used architectures in practice, (ii) *DenseNets* [14], which are popular alternatives to ResNets, (iii) *MobileNetV2* [37]. MobileNets are popular architectures under mobile settings and MobileNetV2 uses inverted residuals and linear Bottlenecks, and (iv) *AOGNets* [24], which are grammar-guided networks and represent an interesting direction of network architecture engineering with better performance than

ResNets and DenseNets. So, the improvement by our AN will be both broadly useful for existing ResNets, DenseNets and MobileNets based deployment in practice and potentially insightful for on-going and future development of more advanced and more powerful DNNs in the community.

In classification, we use BN [19] as the feature normalization backbone for our proposed AN, denoted by **AN (w/ BN)**. We compare with the vanilla BN, GN [47] and SN [28]. In object detection and instance segmentation, we use the Mask-RCNN framework [8] and its cascade variant [3] in the MMDetection code platform [4]. We fine-tune feature backbones pretrained on the ImageNet-1000 dataset. We also test the proposed AN using GN as the feature normalization backbone, denoted by **AN (w/ GN)** in the head classifier of Mask-RCNN.

Where to Apply AN? Figure 2 illustrates the integration of our proposed AN in different building blocks. At the first thought, it is straightforward to replace all vanilla feature normalization modules (*e.g.*, BN) in a DNN. It may not be necessary to do so, similar in spirit to the SE-residual block which re-calibrates the residual part once in a building block. As we shall see, our ablation study supports the design choice shown in Fig. 2.

Initialization of our AN. The initialization of $\gamma_{k,c}$'s and $\beta_{k,c}$'s (Eq. 8) is based on, $\gamma_{k,c} = 1.0 + \mathcal{N}(0,1) \times 0.1$ and $\beta_{k,c} = \mathcal{N}(0,1) \times 0.1$, where $\mathcal{N}(0,1)$ represents the standard Gaussian distribution. This type of initialization is also adopted for conditional BN used in the BigGAN [2].

4.1 Ablation Study

We compare different design choices in our proposed AN using ResNet50 in ImageNet-1000. Table 1 summarizes the results. There are four categories of design choices: The first three are related to the realization of learning the attention weights (Eq. 7): three types of inputs, two architectural choices and four activation function choices. The last one refers to the number K of components in the mixture of affine transformation which is used for each of the four stages in ResNet50

Table 1. Ablation study on different design choices in AN with BN as feature normalization backbone using ResNet50+Bottleneck in ImageNet-1000. * means AN is applied to all the BNs of the network.

Design Choices in AN (w/ BN)	#Params	FLOPS	top-1	top-5
mean + $A_2(\cdot)$ + hsigmoid + $K = \left(\begin{smallmatrix}10\\20\\20\end{smallmatrix}\right)$	25.76M	4.09G	21.85	5.92
(mean,std) + $A_2(\cdot)$ + hsigmoid + $K = \left(\begin{smallmatrix}10\\20\\20\end{smallmatrix}\right)$	25.82M	4.09G	21.73	5.85
RSD + $\mathbf{A_1}(\cdot)$ + hsigmoid + $K = \left(\begin{smallmatrix}10\\20\\10\end{smallmatrix}\right)$	25.76M	4.09G	21.76	6.05
RSD + $A_2(\cdot)$ + **softmax** + $K = \left(\begin{smallmatrix}10\\20\\20\end{smallmatrix}\right)$	25.76M	4.09G	21.72	5.90
RSD + $A_2(\cdot)$ + **relu** + $K = \left(\begin{smallmatrix}10\\20\\10\end{smallmatrix}\right)$	25.96M	4.09G	21.89	6.04
RSD + $A_2(\cdot)$ + **sigmoid** + $K = \left(\begin{smallmatrix}10\\20\\20\end{smallmatrix}\right)$	25.76M	4.09G	21.96	5.91
RSD + $A_2(\cdot)$ + hsigmoid + $\mathbf{K} = \left(\begin{smallmatrix}5\\10\\10\end{smallmatrix}\right)$	25.76M	4.09G	21.92	5.93
RSD + $A_2(\cdot)$ + hsigmoid + $\mathbf{K} = \left(\begin{smallmatrix}20\\40\\20\end{smallmatrix}\right)$	25.96M	4.09G	21.62	5.63
RSD + $A_2(\cdot)$ + hsigmoid + $K = \left(\begin{smallmatrix}10\\20\\20\end{smallmatrix}\right)$	25.76M	4.09G	**21.59**	**5.58**
* RSD + $A_2(\cdot)$ + hsigmoid + $K = \left(\begin{smallmatrix}10\\20\\20\end{smallmatrix}\right)$	26.96M	4.10G	22.15	6.24

and we empirically select three options for simplicity. All the models are trained using the same settings (the vanilla setup in Sect. 4.2).

The best combination is RSD $+$ $A_2(\cdot)$ $+$ hsigmoid $+$ $K = \left(\begin{smallmatrix} 10 & 10 \\ 20 & 20 \end{smallmatrix}\right)$. During our development, we first observed the best combination based on our intuitive reasoning and small experiments (a few epochs) in the process, and then design this ablation study to verify the design choices. Based on the observed best combination, we further verify that *replacing all vanilla BNs is not helpful* (the last row in Table 1). One explanation is that we may not need to re-calibrate the features using our AN (as well as other channel-wise feature attention methods) for both before and after a 1×1 convolution, since channel-wise re-calibration can be tackled by the 1×1 convolution kernel and the vanilla feature normalization themselves in training. The ablation study is in support of the intuitions and design choices discussed in Sect. 3.3.

4.2   Image Classification in ImageNet-1000

Common Training Settings. We use 8 GPUs (NVIDIA V100) to train models using the same settings for apple-to-apple comparisons. The method proposed in [9] is used to initialize all convolutions for all models. The batch size is 128 per GPU. With FP16 optimization used in training to reduce the training time. The mean and standard deviation for block-wise standardization are computed *within* each GPU. The initial learning rate is 0.4, and the cosine learning rate scheduler [27] is used with 5 warm-up epochs and weight decay 1×10^{-4} and momentum 0.9. For AN, the best practice observed in our ablation study (Table 1) is used. AN is not used in the stem layer in all the models. In addition to the common settings, we have two different setups in experimental comparisons:

i) The Vanilla Setup. We adopt the basic data augmentation scheme (random crop and horizontal flip) in training as done in [10]. We

Table 2. Comparisons between BN and our AN (w/ BN) in terms of the top-1 and top-5 error rates (%) in the ImageNet-1000 validation set using *the vanilla setup* and *the state-of-the-art setup.* † means the model is not trained by us. All other models are trained from scratch under the same settings.

The vanilla setup				
Method	#Params	FLOPS	top-1	top-5
ResNet34+BN	21.80M	3.68G	$25.58_{\downarrow(1.15)}$	$8.19_{\downarrow(0.76)}$
ResNet34+AN	21.92M	3.68G	**24.43**	**7.43**
ResNet50-BN	25.56M	4.09G	$23.01_{\downarrow(1.42)}$	$6.68_{\downarrow(0.80)}$
†ResNet50-GN [47]	25.56M	4.09G	$23.52_{\downarrow(1.93)}$	$6.85_{\downarrow(0.97)}$
†ResNet50-SN [28]	25.56M	–	$22.43_{\downarrow(0.83)}$	$6.35_{\downarrow(0.47)}$
†ResNet50-SE [13]	28.09M	4.12G	$22.37_{\downarrow(0.78)}$	$6.36_{\downarrow(0.48)}$
ResNet50-SE	28.09M	4.12G	$22.35_{\downarrow(0.76)}$	$6.09_{\downarrow(0.21)}$
ResNet50-AN	25.76M	4.09G	**21.59**	**5.88**
ResNet101-BN	44.57M	8.12G	$21.33_{\downarrow(0.72)}$	$5.85_{\downarrow(0.44)}$
ResNet101-AN	45.00M	8.12G	**20.61**	**5.41**
DenseNet121-BN	7.98M	2.86G	$25.35_{\downarrow(2.73)}$	$7.83_{\downarrow(1.41)}$
DenseNet121-AN	8.34M	2.86G	**22.62**	**6.42**
MobileNetV2-BN	3.50M	0.34G	$28.69_{\downarrow(2.02)}$	$9.33_{\downarrow(0.77)}$
MobileNetV2-AN	3.56M	0.34G	**26.67**	**8.56**
AOGNet12M-BN	12.26M	2.19G	$22.22_{\downarrow(0.94)}$	$6.06_{\downarrow(0.30)}$
AOGNet12M-AN	12.37M	2.19G	**21.28**	**5.76**
AOGNet40M-BN	40.15M	7.51G	$19.84_{\downarrow(0.51)}$	$4.94_{\downarrow(0.22)}$
AOGNet40M-AN	40.39M	7.51G	**19.33**	**4.72**
The state-of-the-art setup				
Method	#Params	FLOPS	top-1	top-5
ResNet50-BN	25.56M	4.09G	$21.08_{\downarrow(1.16)}$	$5.56_{\downarrow(0.52)}$
ResNet50-AN	25.76M	4.09G	**19.92**	**5.04**
ResNet101-BN	44.57M	8.12G	$19.71_{\downarrow(0.86)}$	$4.89_{\downarrow(0.26)}$
ResNet101-AN	45.00M	8.12G	**18.85**	**4.63**
AOGNet12M-BN	12.26M	2.19G	$21.63_{\downarrow(1.06)}$	$5.60_{\downarrow(0.22)}$
AOGNet12M-AN	12.37M	2.19G	**20.57**	**5.38**
AOGNet40M-BN	40.15M	7.51G	$18.70_{\downarrow(0.57)}$	$4.47_{\downarrow(0.21)}$
AOGNet40M-AN	40.39M	7.51G	**18.13**	**4.26**

tation scheme (random crop and horizontal flip) in training as done in [10]. We

train the models for 120 epochs. All ResNets [10] use the vanilla stem layer with 7×7 convolution. The MobileNetsV2 uses 3×3 convolution in the stem layer. The AOGNets use two consecutive 3×3 convolution in the stem layer. All the γ and β parameters of the feature normalization backbones are initialized to 1 and 0 respectively.

ii) The State-of-the-Art Setup. There are different aspects in the vanilla setup which have better variants developed with better performance shown [11]. *We want to address whether the improvement by our proposed AN are truly fundamental or will disappear with more advanced tips and tricks added in training ConvNets.* First, on top of the basic data augmentation, we also use label smoothing [41] (with rate 0.1) and the mixup (with rate 0.2) [48]. We increase the total number of epochs to 200. We use the same stem layer with two consecutive 3×3 convolution for all models. For ResNets, we add the zero γ initialization trick, which uses 0 to initialize the last normalization layer to make the initial state of a residual block to be identity.

Results Summary. Table 2 shows the comparison results for the two setups respectively. **Our proposed AN consistently obtains the best top-1 and top-5 accuracy results with more than 0.5% absolute top-1 accuracy increase (up to 2.7%) in all models without bells and whistles.** *The improvement is often obtained with negligible extra parameters* (e.g., 0.06M parameter increase in MobileNetV2 for 2.02% absolute top-1 accuracy increase, and 0.2M parameter increase in ResNet50 with 1.42% absolute top-1 accuracy increase) *at almost no extra computational cost* (up to the precision used in measuring FLOPs). With ResNet50, our AN also outperforms GN [47] and SN [28] by 1.93% and 0.83% in top-1 accuracy respectively. For GN, it is known that it works (slightly) worse than BN under the normal (big) mini-batch setting [47]. For SN, our result shows that it is more beneficial to improve the re-calibration component than to learn-to-switch between different feature normalization schema. We observe that the proposed AN is more effective for small ConvNets in terms of performance gain. Intuitively, this makes sense. Small ConvNets usually learn less expressive features. With the mixture of affine transformations and the instance-specific channel-wise feature re-calibration, the proposed AN offers the flexibility of clustering intra-class data better while separating inter-class data better in training.

Table 3. Comparisons between SE and our AN (w/ BN) in terms of the top-1 and top-5 error rates (%) in the ImageNet-1000 validation set using *the vanilla setup*. By "(All)", it means SE or AN is used for all the three BNs in a bottleneck block.

Method	#Params	FLOPS	top-1	top-5
ResNet50-SE (BN₃)	28.09M	4.12G	$22.35_{\downarrow(0.76)}$	$6.09_{\downarrow(0.21)}$
ResNet50-SE (BN₂)	26.19M	4.12G	$22.10_{\downarrow(0.55)}$	$6.02_{\downarrow(0.14)}$
ResNet50-SE (All)	29.33M	4.13G	$22.13_{\downarrow(0.52)}$	$5.96_{\downarrow(0.08)}$
ResNet50-AN (w/BN₃)	26.35M	4.11G	$21.78_{\downarrow(0.19)}$	$5.98_{\downarrow(0.1)}$
ResNet50-AN (w/BN₂)	**25.76M**	**4.09G**	**21.59**	**5.88**
ResNet50-AN (All)	25.92M	4.10G	$21.85_{\downarrow(0.26)}$	$6.06_{\downarrow(0.18)}$

Comparisons with the SE Module. Our proposed AN provides a strong alternative to the widely used SE module. Table 3 shows the comparisons. We

Table 4. Detection and segmentation results in MS-COCO `val2017` [26]. All models use 2× lr scheduling (180k iterations). $\overline{BN}$ means BN is frozen in fine-tuning for object detection. † means that models are not trained by us. All other models are trained from scratch under the same settings. The numbers show sequential improvement in the two AOGNet models indicating the importance of adding our AN in the backbone and the head respectively.

Architecture	Backbone	Head	#Params	AP^{bb}	AP^{bb}_{50}	AP^{bb}_{75}	AP^{m}	AP^{m}_{50}	AP^{m}_{75}
MobileNetV2	$\overline{BN}$	-	22.72M	$34.2_{\downarrow(1.8)}$	$54.6_{\downarrow(2.4)}$	$37.1_{\downarrow(1.8)}$	$30.9_{\downarrow(1.6)}$	$51.1_{\downarrow(2.7)}$	$32.6_{\downarrow(1.9)}$
	AN (w/ BN)	-	22.78M	**36.0**	**57.0**	**38.9**	**32.5**	**53.8**	**34.5**
ResNet50	$\overline{BN}$	-	45.71M	$39.2_{\downarrow(1.6)}$	$60.0_{\downarrow(2.1)}$	$43.1_{\downarrow(1.4)}$	$35.2_{\downarrow(1.2)}$	$56.7_{\downarrow(2.2)}$	$37.6_{\downarrow(1.1)}$
	$\overline{BN} + SE(BN_3)$	-	48.23M	$40.1_{\downarrow(0.7)}$	$61.2_{\downarrow(0.9)}$	$43.8_{\downarrow(0.7)}$	$35.9_{\downarrow(0.5)}$	$57.9_{\downarrow(1.0)}$	$38.1_{\downarrow(0.6)}$
	$\overline{BN} + SE(BN_2)$	-	46.34M	$40.1_{\downarrow(0.7)}$	$61.2_{\downarrow(0.9)}$	$43.8_{\downarrow(0.7)}$	$35.9_{\downarrow(0.5)}$	$57.9_{\downarrow(1.0)}$	$38.4_{\downarrow(0.3)}$
	AN (w/ BN)	-	45.91M	**40.8**	**62.1**	**44.5**	**36.4**	**58.9**	**38.7**
	†GN	GN [47]	45.72M	$40.3_{\downarrow(1.3)}$	$61.0_{\downarrow(1.0)}$	$44.0_{\downarrow(1.7)}$	$35.7_{\downarrow(1.7)}$	$57.9_{\downarrow(1.6)}$	$37.7_{\downarrow(2.2)}$
	†SN	SN [28]	-	$41.0_{\downarrow(0.6)}$	$62.3_{\downarrow(-0.3)}$	$45.1_{\downarrow(0.6)}$	$36.5_{\downarrow(0.9)}$	$58.9_{\downarrow(0.6)}$	$38.7_{\downarrow(1.2)}$
	AN (w/ BN)	AN (w/ GN)	45.96M	**41.6**	62.0	**45.7**	**37.4**	**59.5**	**39.9**
ResNet101	$\overline{BN}$	-	64.70M	$41.4_{\downarrow(1.7)}$	$62.0_{\downarrow(2.1)}$	$45.5_{\downarrow(1.8)}$	$36.8_{\downarrow(1.4)}$	$59.0_{\downarrow(2.0)}$	$39.1_{\downarrow(1.6)}$
	AN (w/ BN)	-	65.15M	**43.1**	**64.1**	**47.3**	**38.2**	**61.0**	**40.7**
	†GN	GN [47]	64.71M	$41.8_{\downarrow(1.4)}$	$62.5_{\downarrow(1.5)}$	$45.4_{\downarrow(1.9)}$	$36.8_{\downarrow(1.2)}$	$59.2_{\downarrow(2.1)}$	$39.0_{\downarrow(2.6)}$
	AN (w/ BN)	AN (w/ GN)	65.20M	**43.2**	64.0	47.3	**38.8**	**61.3**	**41.6**
AOGNet12M	$\overline{BN}$	-	33.09M	$40.7_{\downarrow(1.3)}$	$61.4_{\downarrow(1.6)}$	$44.6_{\downarrow(1.5)}$	$36.4_{\downarrow(1.4)}$	$58.4_{\downarrow(1.7)}$	$38.8_{\downarrow(1.6)}$
	AN (w/ BN)	-	33.21M	$42.0_{\downarrow(1.0)}$	$63.1_{\downarrow(1.1)}$	$46.1_{\downarrow(0.7)}$	$37.8_{\downarrow(0.9)}$	$60.1_{\downarrow(1.0)}$	$40.4_{\downarrow(1.3)}$
	AN (w/ BN)	AN (w/ GN)	33.26M	**43.0**	**64.2**	**46.8**	**38.7**	**61.1**	**41.7**
AOGNet40M	$\overline{BN}$	-	60.73M	$43.4_{\downarrow(0.7)}$	$64.2_{\downarrow(0.9)}$	$47.5_{\downarrow(0.7)}$	$38.5_{\downarrow(0.5)}$	$61.0_{\downarrow(1.0)}$	$41.4_{\downarrow(0.4)}$
	AN (w/ BN)	-	60.97M	$44.1_{\downarrow(0.8)}$	$65.1_{\downarrow(1.1)}$	$48.2_{\downarrow(0.9)}$	$39.0_{\downarrow(1.2)}$	$62.0_{\downarrow(1.2)}$	$41.8_{\downarrow(1.5)}$
	AN (w/ BN)	AN (w/ GN)	61.02M	**44.9**	**66.2**	**49.1**	**40.2**	**63.2**	**43.3**

observe that applying SE after the second BN in the bottleneck in ResNet50 is also beneficial with better performance and smaller number of extra parameters.

4.3   Object Detection and Segmentation in COCO

In object detection and segmentation, high-resolution input images are beneficial and often entailed for detecting medium to small objects, but limit the batch-size in training (often 1 or 2 images per GPU). GN [47] and SN [28] have shown significant progress in handling the applicability discrepancies of feature normalization schema from ImageNet to MS-COCO. We test our AN in MS-COCO following the standard protocol, as done in GN [47]. We build on the MMDetection code platform [4]. We observe further performance improvement.

We first summarize the details of implementation. Following the terminologies used in MMDetection [4], there are four modular components in the R-CNN detection framework [7,8,34]: *i) Feature Backbones*. We use the pre-trained networks in Table 2 (with the vanilla setup) for fair comparisons in detection, since we compare with some models which are not trained by us from scratch and use the feature backbones pre-trained in a way similar to our vanilla setup and with on par top-1 accuracy. In fine-tuning a network with AN (w/ BN) pre-trained in ImageNet such as ResNet50+AN (w/ BN) in Table 2, we freeze the stem layer and the first stage as commonly done in practice. For the remaining stages, we freeze the standardization component only (the learned mixture of affine transformations and the learned running mean and standard deviation), but allow the attention weight sub-network to be fine-tuned. *ii) Neck Backbones*: We test

Table 5. Results in MS-COCO using the cascade variant [3] of Mask R-CNN.

Architecture	Backbone	Head	#Params	AP^{bb}	AP^{bb}_{50}	AP^{bb}_{75}	AP^m	AP^m_{50}	AP^m_{75}
ResNet101	BN	–	96.32M	$44.4_{\downarrow(1.4)}$	$62.5_{\downarrow(1.8)}$	$48.4_{\downarrow(1.4)}$	$38.2_{\downarrow(1.4)}$	$59.7_{\downarrow(2.0)}$	$41.3_{\downarrow(1.4)}$
	AN (w/ BN)	–	96.77M	**45.8**	**64.3**	**49.8**	**39.6**	**61.7**	**42.7**
AOGNet40M	BN	–	92.35M	$45.6_{\downarrow(0.9)}$	$63.9_{\downarrow(1.1)}$	$49.7_{\downarrow(1.1)}$	$39.3_{\downarrow(0.7)}$	$61.2_{\downarrow(1.1)}$	$42.7_{\downarrow(0.4)}$
	AN (w/ BN)	–	92.58M	**46.5**	**65.0**	**50.8**	**40.0**	**62.3**	**43.1**

the feature pyramid network (FPN) [25] which is widely used in practice. *iii) Head Classifiers.* We test two setups: *(a) The vanilla setup* as done in GN [47] and SN [28]. In this setup, we further have two settings: with vs without feature normalization in the bounding box head classifier. The former is denoted by "-" in Table 4, and the latter is denoted by the corresponding type of feature normalization scheme in Table 4 (*e.g.*, GN, SN and AN (w/ GN)). We experiment on using AN (w/ GN) in the bounding box head classifier and keeping GN in the mask head unchanged for simplicity. Adding AN (w/ GN) in the mask head classifier may further help improve the performance. When adding AN (w/ GN) in the bounding box head, we adopt the same design choices except for "Choice 1, $A_1(\cdot)$" (Eq. 11) used in learning attention weights. *(b) The state-of-the-art setup* which is based on the cascade generalization of head classifiers [3] and does not include feature normalization scheme, also denoted by "–" in Table 5. *iv) RoI Operations.* We test the RoIAlign operation [8].

Result Summary. The results are summarized in Table 4 and Table 5. Compared with the vanilla BN that are frozen in fine-tuning, our AN (w/ BN) improves performance by a large margin in terms of both bounding box AP and mask AP (*1.8% & 1.6%* for MobileNetV2, *1.6% & 1.2%* for ResNet50, *1.7% & 1.4%* for ResNet101, *1.3% & 1.4%* for AOGNet12M and *0.7% & 0.5%* for AOGNet40M). It shows the advantages of the self-attention based dynamic and adaptive control of the mixture of affine transformations (although they themselves are frozen) in fine-tuning.

With the AN further integrated in the bounding box head classifier of Mask-RCNN and trained from scratch, we also obtain better performance than GN and SN. Compared with the vanilla GN [47], our AN (w/ GN) improves bounding box and mask AP by 1.3% and 1.7% for ResNet50, and 1.4% and 2.2% for ResNet101. Compared with SN [28] which outperforms the vanilla GN in ResNet50, our AN (w/ GN) is also better by 0.6% bounding box AP and 0.9% mask AP increase respectively. Slightly less improvements are observed with AOGNets. Similar in spirit to the ImageNet experiments, we want to verify whether the advantages of our AN will disappear if we use state-of-the-art designs for head classifiers of R-CNN such as the widely used cascade R-CNN [3]. Table 5 shows that similar improvements are obtained with ResNet101 and AOGNet40M.

5   Conclusion

This paper presents Attentive Normalization (AN) that aims to harness the best of feature normalization and feature attention in a single lightweight module. AN learns a mixture of affine transformations and uses the weighted sum via a self-attention module for re-calibrating standardized features in a dynamic and adaptive way. AN provides a strong alternative to the Squeeze-and-Excitation (SE) module. In experiments, AN is tested with BN and GN as the feature normalization backbones. AN is tested in both ImageNet-1000 and MS-COCO using four representative networks (ResNets, DenseNets, MobileNetsV2 and AOGNets). It consistently obtains better performance, often by a large margin, than the vanilla feature normalization schema and some state-of-the-art variants.

Acknowledgement. This work is supported in part by NSF IIS-1909644, ARO Grant W911NF1810295, NSF IIS-1822477 and NSF IUSE-2013451. The views presented in this paper are those of the authors and should not be interpreted as representing any funding agencies.

References

1. Ba, L.J., Kiros, R., Hinton, G.E.: Layer normalization. CoRR abs/1607.06450 (2016). http://arxiv.org/abs/1607.06450
2. Brock, A., Donahue, J., Simonyan, K.: Large scale gan training for high fidelity natural image synthesis. arXiv preprint arXiv:1809.11096 (2018)
3. Cai, Z., Vasconcelos, N.: Cascade R-CNN: delving into high quality object detection. In: 2018 IEEE Conference on Computer Vision and Pattern Recognition, CVPR 2018, Salt Lake City, UT, USA, 18–22 June 2018, pp. 6154–6162 (2018). https://doi.org/10.1109/CVPR.2018.00644, http://openaccess.thecvf.com/content_cvpr_2018/html/Cai_Cascade_R-CNN_Delving_CVPR_2018_paper.html
4. Chen, K., et al.: MMDetection: Open mmlab detection toolbox and benchmark. arXiv preprint arXiv:1906.07155 (2019)
5. Deecke, L., Murray, I., Bilen, H.: Mode normalization. In: 7th International Conference on Learning Representations, ICLR 2019, New Orleans, LA, USA, 6–9 May 2019 (2019). https://openreview.net/forum?id=HyN-M2Rctm
6. Dumoulin, V., et al.: Adversarially learned inference. CoRR abs/1606.00704 (2016). http://arxiv.org/abs/1606.00704
7. Girshick, R.: Fast R-CNN. In: Proceedings of the International Conference on Computer Vision (ICCV) (2015)
8. He, K., Gkioxari, G., Dollár, P., Girshick, R.B.: Mask R-CNN. In: IEEE International Conference on Computer Vision, ICCV 2017, Venice, Italy, 22–29 October 2017, pp. 2980–2988 (2017). https://doi.org/10.1109/ICCV.2017.322
9. He, K., Zhang, X., Ren, S., Sun, J.: Delving deep into rectifiers: surpassing human-level performance on imagenet classification. In: 2015 IEEE International Conference on Computer Vision, ICCV 2015, Santiago, Chile, 7–13 December 2015, pp. 1026–1034 (2015). https://doi.org/10.1109/ICCV.2015.123
10. He, K., Zhang, X., Ren, S., Sun, J.: Deep residual learning for image recognition. In: IEEE Conference on Computer Vision and Pattern Recognition (CVPR) (2016)

11. He, T., Zhang, Z., Zhang, H., Zhang, Z., Xie, J., Li, M.: Bag of tricks for image classification with convolutional neural networks. CoRR abs/1812.01187 (2018). http://arxiv.org/abs/1812.01187
12. Howard, A., et al.: Searching for mobilenetv3. CoRR abs/1905.02244 (2019). http://arxiv.org/abs/1905.02244
13. Hu, J., Shen, L., Sun, G.: Squeeze-and-excitation networks. CoRR abs/1709.01507 (2017). http://arxiv.org/abs/1709.01507
14. Huang, G., Liu, Z., van der Maaten, L., Weinberger, K.Q.: Densely connected convolutional networks. In: Proceedings of the IEEE Conference on Computer Vision and Pattern Recognition (2017)
15. Huang, L., Liu, X., Lang, B., Yu, A.W., Wang, Y., Li, B.: Orthogonal weight normalization: solution to optimization over multiple dependent stiefel manifolds in deep neural networks. In: Proceedings of the Thirty-Second AAAI Conference on Artificial Intelligence, (AAAI-18), The 30th Innovative Applications of Artificial Intelligence (IAAI-18), and the 8th AAAI Symposium on Educational Advances in Artificial Intelligence (EAAI-18), New Orleans, Louisiana, USA, 2–7 February 2018, pp. 3271–3278 (2018). https://www.aaai.org/ocs/index.php/AAAI/AAAI18/paper/view/17072
16. Huang, L., Yang, D., Lang, B., Deng, J.: Decorrelated batch normalization. In: 2018 IEEE Conference on Computer Vision and Pattern Recognition, CVPR 2018, Salt Lake City, UT, USA, 18–22 June 2018, pp. 791–800 (2018)
17. Huang, Z., Wang, X., Huang, L., Huang, C., Wei, Y., Liu, W.: Ccnet: Criss-cross attention for semantic segmentation. CoRR abs/1811.11721 (2018). http://arxiv.org/abs/1811.11721
18. Ioffe, S.: Batch renormalization: towards reducing minibatch dependence in batch-normalized models. In: Advances in Neural Information Processing Systems 30: Annual Conference on Neural Information Processing Systems 2017, Long Beach, CA, USA, 4–9 December 2017, pp. 1945–1953 (2017)
19. Ioffe, S., Szegedy, C.: Batch normalization: accelerating deep network training by reducing internal covariate shift. In: Blei, D., Bach, F. (eds.) Proceedings of the 32nd International Conference on Machine Learning (ICML-15), pp. 448–456. JMLR Workshop and Conference Proceedings (2015). http://jmlr.org/proceedings/papers/v37/ioffe15.pdf
20. Jia, S., Chen, D., Chen, H.: Instance-level meta normalization. In: IEEE Conference on Computer Vision and Pattern Recognition, CVPR 2019, Long Beach, CA, USA, 16–20 June 2019, pp. 4865–4873 (2019), http://openaccess.thecvf.com/content_CVPR_2019/html/Jia_Instance-Level_Meta_Normalization_CVPR_2019_paper.html
21. Kalayeh, M.M., Shah, M.: Training faster by separating modes of variation in batch-normalized models. IEEE Trans. Pattern Anal. Mach. Intell. 42, 1–1 (2019). https://doi.org/10.1109/TPAMI.2019.2895781
22. Karras, T., Laine, S., Aila, T.: A style-based generator architecture for generative adversarial networks. arXiv preprint arXiv:1812.04948 (2018)
23. Krizhevsky, A., Sutskever, I., Hinton, G.E.: Imagenet classification with deep convolutional neural networks. In: Neural Information Processing Systems (NIPS), pp. 1106–1114 (2012)
24. Li, X., Song, X., Wu, T.: Aognets: compositional grammatical architectures for deep learning. In: IEEE Conference on Computer Vision and Pattern Recognition, CVPR 2019, Long Beach, CA, USA, 16–20 June 2019, pp. 6220–6230 (2019)

25. Lin, T., Dollár, P., Girshick, R.B., He, K., Hariharan, B., Belongie, S.J.: Feature pyramid networks for object detection. In: 2017 IEEE Conference on Computer Vision and Pattern Recognition, CVPR 2017, Honolulu, HI, USA, 21–26 July 2017, pp. 936–944 (2017). https://doi.org/10.1109/CVPR.2017.106
26. Lin, T., et al.: Microsoft COCO: common objects in context. CoRR abs/1405.0312 (2014). http://arxiv.org/abs/1405.0312
27. Loshchilov, I., Hutter, F.: SGDR: stochastic gradient descent with restarts. CoRR abs/1608.03983 (2016). http://arxiv.org/abs/1608.03983
28. Luo, P., Ren, J., Peng, Z.: Differentiable learning-to-normalize via switchable normalization. CoRR abs/1806.10779 (2018). http://arxiv.org/abs/1806.10779
29. Miyato, T., Koyama, M.: CGANS with projection discriminator. arXiv preprint arXiv:1802.05637 (2018)
30. Pan, X., Zhan, X., Shi, J., Tang, X., Luo, P.: Switchable whitening for deep representation learning. In: 2019 IEEE/CVF International Conference on Computer Vision, ICCV 2019, Seoul, Korea (South), 27 October–2 November 2019, pp. 1863–1871. IEEE (2019). https://doi.org/10.1109/ICCV.2019.00195
31. Park, T., Liu, M., Wang, T., Zhu, J.: Semantic image synthesis with spatially-adaptive normalization. In: IEEE Conference on Computer Vision and Pattern Recognition, CVPR 2019, Long Beach, CA, USA, 16–20 June 2019, pp. 2337–2346 (2019)
32. Peng, C., et al.: Megdet: a large mini-batch object detector. In: 2018 IEEE Conference on Computer Vision and Pattern Recognition, CVPR 2018, Salt Lake City, UT, USA, 18–22 June 2018, pp. 6181–6189 (2018)
33. Perez, E., de Vries, H., Strub, F., Dumoulin, V., Courville, A.C.: Learning visual reasoning without strong priors. CoRR abs/1707.03017 (2017). http://arxiv.org/abs/1707.03017
34. Ren, S., He, K., Girshick, R., Sun, J.: Faster R-CNN: towards real-time object detection with region proposal networks. In: Neural Information Processing Systems (NIPS) (2015)
35. Russakovsky, O., et al.: ImageNet large scale visual recognition challenge. Int. J. Comput. Vis. **115**(3), 211–252 (2015). https://doi.org/10.1007/s11263-015-0816-y
36. Salimans, T., Kingma, D.P.: Weight normalization: a simple reparameterization to accelerate training of deep neural networks. In: Advances in Neural Information Processing Systems 29: Annual Conference on Neural Information Processing Systems 2016, Barcelona, Spain, 5–10 December 2016, p. 901 (2016)
37. Sandler, M., Howard, A., Zhu, M., Zhmoginov, A., Chen, L.C.: Mobilenetv 2: inverted residuals and linear bottlenecks. In: Proceedings of the IEEE Conference on Computer Vision and Pattern Recognition, pp. 4510–4520 (2018)
38. Santurkar, S., Tsipras, D., Ilyas, A., Madry, A.: How does batch normalization help optimization? In: Advances in Neural Information Processing Systems 31: Annual Conference on Neural Information Processing Systems 2018, NeurIPS 2018, Montréal, Canada, 3–8 December 2018, pp. 2488–2498 (2018), http://papers.nips.cc/paper/7515-how-does-batch-normalization-help-optimization
39. Shao, W., et al.: SSN: learning sparse switchable normalization via sparsestmax. CoRR abs/1903.03793 (2019). http://arxiv.org/abs/1903.03793
40. Sun, W., Wu, T.: Image synthesis from reconfigurable layout and style. In: International Conference on Computer Vision, ICCV (2019)
41. Szegedy, C., Vanhoucke, V., Ioffe, S., Shlens, J., Wojna, Z.: Rethinking the inception architecture for computer vision. CoRR abs/1512.00567 (2015). http://arxiv.org/abs/1512.00567

42. Ulyanov, D., Vedaldi, A., Lempitsky, V.S.: Instance normalization: The missing ingredient for fast stylization. CoRR abs/1607.08022 (2016). http://arxiv.org/abs/1607.08022
43. de Vries, H., Strub, F., Mary, J., Larochelle, H., Pietquin, O., Courville, A.C.: Modulating early visual processing by language. In: Advances in Neural Information Processing Systems 30: Annual Conference on Neural Information Processing Systems 2017, Long Beach, CA, USA, 4–9 December 2017, pp. 6597–6607 (2017). http://papers.nips.cc/paper/7237-modulating-early-visual-processing-by-language
44. Wang, F., et al.: Residual attention network for image classification. In: 2017 IEEE Conference on Computer Vision and Pattern Recognition, CVPR 2017, Honolulu, HI, USA, 21–26 July 2017, pp. 6450–6458 (2017). https://doi.org/10.1109/CVPR.2017.683
45. Wang, X., Girshick, R.B., Gupta, A., He, K.: Non-local neural networks. In: 2018 IEEE Conference on Computer Vision and Pattern Recognition, CVPR 2018, Salt Lake City, UT, USA, 18–22 June 2018, pp. 7794–7803 (2018). https://doi.org/10.1109/CVPR.2018.00813, http://openaccess.thecvf.com/content_cvpr_2018/html/Wang_Non-Local_Neural_Networks_CVPR_2018_paper.html
46. Woo, S., Park, J., Lee, J., Kweon, I.S.: CBAM: convolutional block attention module. In: Computer Vision - ECCV 2018–15th European Conference, Proceedings, Part VII, Munich, Germany, 8–14 September 2018, pp. 3–19 (2018). https://doi.org/10.1007/978-3-030-01234-2_1
47. Wu, Y., He, K.: Group normalization. In: Ferrari, V., Hebert, M., Sminchisescu, C., Weiss, Y. (eds.) ECCV 2018. LNCS, vol. 11217, pp. 3–19. Springer, Cham (2018). https://doi.org/10.1007/978-3-030-01261-8_1
48. Zhang, H., Cissé, M., Dauphin, Y.N., Lopez-Paz, D.: mixup: beyond empirical risk minimization. In: 6th International Conference on Learning Representations, ICLR 2018, Vancouver, BC, Canada, 30 April–3 May 2018, Conference Track Proceedings (2018). https://openreview.net/forum?id=r1Ddp1-Rb

Count- and Similarity-Aware R-CNN for Pedestrian Detection

Jin Xie[1], Hisham Cholakkal[2,3], Rao Muhammad Anwer[2,3],
Fahad Shahbaz Khan[2,3], Yanwei Pang[1(✉)], Ling Shao[2,3], and Mubarak Shah[4]

[1] Tianjin Key Laboratory of Brain-Inspired Artificial Intelligence, School of
Electrical and Information Engineering, Tianjin University, Tianjin, China
{jinxie,pyw}@tju.edu.cn
[2] Mohamed bin Zayed University of Artificial Intelligence, Abu Dhabi, UAE
{hisham.cholakkal,rao.anwer,fahad.khan,ling.shao}@mbzuai.ac.ae
[3] Inception Institute of Artificial Intelligence, Abu Dhabi, UAE
[4] University of Central Florida, Orlando, USA
shah@crcv.ucf.edu

Abstract. Recent pedestrian detection methods generally rely on additional supervision, such as visible bounding-box annotations, to handle heavy occlusions. We propose an approach that leverages pedestrian count and proposal similarity information within a two-stage pedestrian detection framework. Both pedestrian count and proposal similarity are derived from standard full-body annotations commonly used to train pedestrian detectors. We introduce a count-weighted detection loss function that assigns higher weights to the detection errors occurring at highly overlapping pedestrians. The proposed loss function is utilized at both stages of the two-stage detector. We further introduce a count-and-similarity branch within the two-stage detection framework, which predicts pedestrian count as well as proposal similarity. Lastly, we introduce a count and similarity-aware NMS strategy to identify distinct proposals. Our approach requires neither part information nor visible bounding-box annotations. Experiments are performed on the CityPersons and CrowdHuman datasets. Our method sets a new state-of-the-art on both datasets. Further, it achieves an absolute gain of 2.4% over the current state-of-the-art, in terms of log-average miss rate, on the heavily occluded (**HO**) set of CityPersons test set. Finally, we demonstrate the applicability of our approach for the problem of human instance segmentation. Code and models are available at: https://github.com/Leotju/CaSe.

Keywords: Pedestrian detection · Human instance segmentation

J. Xie and H. Cholakkal—Contribute equally to this work.

Electronic supplementary material The online version of this chapter (https://doi.org/10.1007/978-3-030-58520-4_6) contains supplementary material, which is available to authorized users.

A. Vedaldi et al. (Eds.): ECCV 2020, LNCS 12362, pp. 88–104, 2020.
https://doi.org/10.1007/978-3-030-58520-4_6

1   Introduction

Pedestrian detection is a challenging computer vision problem and serves as an important component in many vision systems. Despite recent progress, detecting heavily occluded pedestrians remains a key challenge in real-world applications due to the frequent occurrence of occlusions. The most common type of occlusion in pedestrian detection is *crowd occlusion* caused by other pedestrians. This is evident in recent benchmarks, such as CityPersons [30], where crowd occlusion alone accounts for around 49%. In this work, we tackle the problem of heavily occluded pedestrian detection.

Most existing pedestrian detection approaches either rely on part information [25,36] or exploit visible bounding-box annotations [20,31,37] to handle occlusions. Typically, part-based approaches are computationally expensive and require a large number of part detectors. Recent approaches relying on visible bounding-box supervision, in addition to standard full-body annotations, have shown superior performance for occluded pedestrian detection. However, this reliance on visible bounding-box annotations introduces another level of supervision. In this work, we propose an approach for occluded pedestrian detection that requires neither part information nor visible bounding-box supervision.

State-of-the-art pedestrian detectors [2,3,5,6,16,20,27] are mostly based on two-stage detection framework. One of the most commonly used two-stage object detection frameworks is that of Faster R-CNN [21], later adapted for pedestrian detection [30]. Here [21,30], a region proposal network (RPN) is employed in the first stage to generate pedestrian proposals. The second stage, also known as Fast R-CNN, consists of an RoI (region-of-interest) feature extraction from each proposal followed by classification confidence prediction and bounding-box regression. During inference, a post-processing strategy, such as non-maximum suppression (NMS), is used to remove duplicate bounding-box predictions.

While promising results have been achieved when adapting Faster R-CNN for standard pedestrian detection [30], its performance on heavily occluded pedestrians is far from satisfactory. This is likely due to the fact that the number of overlapping pedestrian instances in an RoI pooled region are not explicitly taken into account, during either training or inference. In this work, we argue that pedestrian count and proposal similarities are useful cues for tackling crowd occlusion with no additional annotation cost. Pedestrian count information within an RoI is readily available with full-body annotations that are typically used in pedestrian detection training. During training, a higher pedestrian count within an RoI indicates a high level of crowd occlusion. In such crowd occlusion scenarios, multiple highly overlapping pedestrians need to be detected from a large number of spatially adjacent duplicate proposals. A proposal similarity embedding is desired to identify distinct proposals from multiple duplicate proposals for each pedestrian. Count and similarity predictions at inference are expected to aid accurate detection of highly overlapping pedestrians (crowd occlusion).

Contributions: To the best of knowledge, we are the first to leverage pedestrian count *and* proposal similarity information in a two-stage framework for occluded

pedestrian detection. Our contributions are: **(i)** a count-weighted detection loss is introduced for the classification and regression parts of both the RPN and Fast R-CNN modules, during training. As a result, a higher weight is assigned to proposals with a large number of overlapping pedestrians, improving the performance during heavy-occlusion. **(ii)** We introduce a count-and-similarity branch to accurately predict both pedestrian count and proposal similarity, leading to a novel multi-task setting in Faster R-CNN. **(iii)** Both the predicted count and proposal similarity embedding are utilized in our count and similarity-aware NMS strategy (CAS-NMS), to identify distinct proposals in a crowded scene. **(iv)** Extensive experiments are performed on CityPersons [30] and CrowdHuman [22]. Our count- and similarity-aware, R-CNN based pedestrian detection approach, dubbed as *CaSe*, achieves state-of-the-art results on both datasets. On heavily occluded (**HO**) set of the CityPersons test set, our detector improves the state-of-the-art results [20], reducing the log-average miss rate from 41.0% to 38.6%. Note that [20] requires both full-body and visible bounding-box annotations. In contrast, our approach only utilizes full-body annotations. **(v)** Additionally, we validate our proposed components by integrating them into Mask R-CNN framework for person instance segmentation, achieving consistent improvement in performance on OCHuman [33].

2 Related Work

Several pedestrian detectors apply a part-based approach [17,19,25,35,36], where a set of part detectors is learned with each one designed for handling a specific occlusion pattern. Different from these approaches, more recent works aim at exploiting additional visible bounding-box (VBB) supervision to either output visible part regions [37] or provide support for learning occlusion scenarios [20]. Here, we look into an alternative approach that neither uses part information nor requires additional VBB annotation for occluded pedestrian detection.

Generally, object detectors [18,21] employ non-maximum suppression (NMS) as a post processing strategy. Several previous works have investigated improving NMS for the generic object detection [1,11,12,26]. Despite being extensively investigated for generic object detection, less attention has been paid to improve NMS in the context of occluded pedestrian detection [10,13]. The work of [13] proposes an approach that learns to predict the threshold according to the instance-specific density. The work of [10] introduces an approach based on the joint processing of detections and penalization for double detections. Improving NMS for occluded pedestrian detection is an open problem, as most existing pedestrian detectors [14,20,27] still employ traditional post-processing strategy.

Recent works have investigated problem of improving bounding-box regression for crowd occlusion [27,32]. The work of [27] introduces repulsion losses that penalize predicted boxes from shifting towards other ground-truth objects, requiring each predicted box to be away from those with different ground-truths. The work of [32] proposes an approach that learns to adapt the predicted

boxes closer to the corresponding ground-truths. Both of these approaches are employed on the regression part of the pedestrian detector. Instead, our proposed count-weighted detection loss is designed for both classification and regression parts of the two-stage Faster R-CNN detector. In addition to the count-weighted detection loss, we introduce a parallel count-and-similarity branch within the Fast R-CNN module of Faster R-CNN to accurately predict both pedestrian count and proposal similarity. Further, we use both predicted count and proposal similarity embedding for distinct proposal identification during inference.

3   Baseline Two-Stage Detection Framework

In this work, we base our approach on the popular Faster R-CNN framework [21] that is adopted in several two-stage pedestrian detectors [20, 28, 30] as their base architecture. Faster R-CNN employs a region proposal network (RPN), during the first stage, to generate class-agnostic proposals and their confidence scores, respectively. In the second stage, also known as Fast R-CNN, RoI (region-of-interest) features are extracted from each proposal, followed by a detection branch that generates classification score (*e.g.*, probability of a proposal being a pedestrian) and regressed bounding-box coordinates for each proposal.

The detection problem can be formulated as a joint minimization of the classification and regression losses, in both the RPN and Fast R-CNN modules [21], where $L_{det} = L_{rpn} + L_{frc}$. Here, both L_{rpn} and L_{frc} are computed as an accumulation of the average classification and regression loss L_c and L_r, in their respective modules. L_c and L_r are given by:

$$L_c = \frac{1}{N_{cls}} \sum_i L_{cls}(p_i, p_i^*) \quad L_r = \lambda \frac{1}{N_{reg}} \sum_i L_{reg}(l_i, l_i^*), \qquad (1)$$

where i represents index of a proposal in a mini-batch, p_i represents the predicted probability of proposal i being a pedestrian, and p_i^* is the ground-truth label of the proposal. The predicted location of a positive proposal i is denoted by l_i and l_i^* denotes the associated ground-truth location. N_{cls} and N_{reg} are the total number of proposals during classification and regression, respectively. λ is the parameter to balance the two loss terms. The classification loss (L_{cls}), is a cross-entropy loss for RPN and Fast R-CNN modules. The regression loss (L_{reg}), for both RPN and Fast R-CNN modules, is Smooth-L1 loss function.

4   Our Approach

Motivation: The above-mentioned two-stage Faster R-CNN baseline is trained using full-body pedestrian annotations. In recent methods [20, 31, 32, 34, 37], this two-stage standard pedestrian detection framework, or Faster R-CNN, has been extended to incorporate additional visible bounding-box annotations. Here, we propose an approach that does not rely on additional visible bounding-box supervision and instead utilizes pedestrian count information within an RoI, which is readily available with standard full-body annotations.

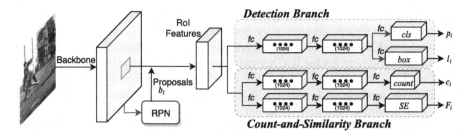

Fig. 1. Overall architecture of the proposed count- and similarity-aware pedestrian detector (CaSe). Our CaSe consists of a Detection Branch (Sect. 4.1) and a Count-and-Similarity branch (Sect. 4.2). We introduce a count-weighted detection loss that employ a count-weighting in regression and classification losses of both the RPN and Fast R-CNN stages of Faster R-CNN. The detection branch predicts the pedestrian location (l_i) and its probability (p_i). The count-and-similarity branch introduced in our CaSe consists of two outputs: the count prediction (c_i) and similarity embedding (F_i). The count-prediction estimates the number of ground-truth instances in a given RoI, whereas the similarity embedding measures the similarity between all overlapping proposals. Both these outputs are further used for distinct proposal identification during inference.

Overall Architecture: Figure 1 shows the overall network architecture. It consists of a detection branch and a count-and-similarity branch. Both these branches take the RoI feature of a proposal as input. Our approach leverages count information within the baseline pedestrian detection framework at two different stages. First, our count-weighted detection loss integrate a count weighting into the classification and regression losses of both modules (RPN and Fast R-CNN). Second, a parallel network, which we call the count-and-similarity branch, is introduced to improve bounding-box prediction by estimating the number of pedestrian instances for a given pedestrian proposal and its similarity with overlapping proposals. Further, we use both predicted count and proposal similarity embedding to identify distinct proposals during inference, by introducing a novel post-processing strategy. Both the detection and count-and-similarity branches in our network are jointly trained with the loss function $L = L'_{det} + L_{cas}$. Here, L_{cas} is the training loss for the count-and-similarity branch and L'_{det} is the proposed count-weighted detection loss, employed in *both* the RPN and Fast R-CNN modules. Next, we describe the detection branch and the associated count-weighted detection loss. Then, the proposed count-and-similarity branch is presented in Sect. 4.2. Finally, inference of the proposed framework and our novel post-processing strategy are described in Sect. 4.3.

4.1 Detection Branch

As described earlier (Sect. 3), our framework is based on two-stage Faster R-CNN, employed in several pedestrian detection methods [20,30]. Next, we introduce a novel count-weighted detection loss to improve both the localization

and classification performance of the Faster R-CNN under heavy occlusion. Our count-weighted detection loss is integrated in both RPN and Fast R-CNN modules.

Count-Weighted Detection Loss: Different to detecting isolated pedestrians in a sparse scene, pedestrian detection in crowded scenes is a more challenging problem due to the presence of multiple highly overlapping pedestrians. To counter this issue, we introduce a weight w_i proportional to the ground-truth count of a proposal in the classification and regression loss terms in Eq. 1. This implies that a higher weight is assigned to detection errors occurring at highly overlapping pedestrians (crowd occlusions). Our count-weighted detection loss function L'_{det} (CW-loss) has the following terms:

$$L'_c = \frac{1}{N_{cls}} \sum_i w_i L_{cls}(p_i, p_i^*) \quad L'_r = \lambda \frac{1}{N_{reg}} \sum_i w_i L_{reg}(l_i, l_i^*), \qquad (2)$$

where w_i is the loss weight that assigns a higher weightage to a proposal overlapping with a large number of ground-truth boxes. The weight w_i of each proposal box b_i can be obtained from its ground-truth count c_i^* as

$$w_i = 1 + \alpha \cdot \mathbf{max}(c_i^* - 1, 0), \qquad (3)$$

where α is a balancing factor, empirically set to 0.5. It can be observed that, if a positive proposal b_i overlaps with multiple ground-truth bounding-boxes, a higher weight w_i will be assigned to that sample. This implies that the proposals at crowded image regions will be assigned with a higher weightage *during training*, compared to the proposals from less crowded regions. Next, we explain how to compute the ground-truth count using the full-body bounding-box annotations which are readily available during training.

Ground-truth Count of a Proposal: The ground-truth count c_i^* of a proposal b_i depends on the number of overlapping full-body (ground-truth) bounding-boxes. First, we compute the intersection-over-union (IoU) between b_i and all its overlapping ground-truth bounding boxes. Then, c_i^* is computed as the number of ground-truth bounding boxes with an $IoU \geq th$. Here, th is empirically set to 0.5. During training, the ground-truth count c_i^* of a proposal is used to compute the loss weight (Eq. 3). Further, it is used as a ground-truth count to train our count-and-similarity branch.

4.2 Count-and-Similarity Branch

Combined Use of Count and Similarity: In the presence of crowd occlusion, many highly overlapping duplicate proposals are generated and assigned a higher classification score by the detector. This is problematic when using a fixed overlap threshold to remove duplicate proposals. Figure 2 shows an example with

two highly overlapping pedestrians (crowd occlusion). In such a case, a count prediction for an RoI can be used to obtain the number of overlapping pedestrians. This count prediction can be utilized to adapt the overlap threshold, thereby removing duplicate proposals based on their classification scores. However, count alone is sub-optimal for identifying distinct proposals in crowd occlusion scenarios since several proposals with higher classification scores may belong to the same pedestrian instance. Therefore, it is desired to identify distinct proposals belonging to different (overlapping) pedestrians. To this end, we utilize a similarity embedding that projects RoI features into a low-dimensional representation, where the euclidean distance is inversely proportional to similarity between proposals (see Fig. 2). Instead of calculating the euclidean distance for all pairs of overlapping proposals (above a certain threshold), we use count prediction as an indicator to compute the distance for only a subset of pairs having a predicted count more than one. This leads to speed-up during inference, compared to exhaustively computing the distance for all pairs of overlapping proposals.

Our count-and-similarity branch is shown in Fig. 1. It has two parallel sub-branches, where, the first predicts the number of pedestrians present within a proposal (RoI), and the second outputs a similarity embedding for estimating the proposal similarity. During training, we define the loss L_{cas} on each RoI as $L_{cas} = L_{cp} + L_{se}$. Here L_{cp} denotes the counting loss for the first sub-branch and L_{se} denotes the similarity embedding loss for the second sub-branch.

Proposal Count: The pedestrian count of a given proposal b_i is predicted by a sub-branch that consists of three fully-connected (fc) layers, where the last layer outputs the pedestrian count c_i. The three fc layers are separated by a ReLU layer. The count loss L_{cp} is a mean-squared error (MSE) loss that penalize the deviation of the predicted count from its ground truth. *i.e.*, $L_{cp} = \frac{1}{N_{cp}} \sum_{i=1}^{N_{cp}} \|c_i - c_i^*\|_2^2$, where N_{cp} denotes number of proposals used when training with the count loss, and c_i^* represents the ground-truth count of a proposal, described in Sect. 4.1.

Proposal Similarity: As mentioned earlier, the predicted count alone is sub-optimal to identify distinct proposals in a crowded scene. To address this issue, we introduce a similarity embedding sub-branch that projects RoI feature of a proposal b_i to a low-dimensional feature embedding F_i. The similarity embedding sub-branch has a structure similar to its parallel (count) sub-branch, except its final fc layer outputs a 64-dimensional feature embedding F_i. The euclidean distance between the feature embedding of two proposals is proportional to their dissimilarity. Proposals with no pedestrians can be removed based on their predicted count. Hence, the euclidean distance between two overlapping proposals only needs to be computed if both proposals contain at least one pedestrian.

For a given proposal b_i, we first select its overlapping proposals with an $IoU \geq 0.5$. Let b_j be one of the selected proposals that has a ground-truth count $c_j^* \geq 1$, and a feature embedding F_j. We train the similarity embedding sub-branch with proposals having a ground-truth count of at least one, using the contrastive loss:

Fig. 2. An illustrative example showing operations during inference of our CaSe detector. On left: Predictions from the detection and count-and-similarity branches. On right: final output of our CaSe framework including a count and similarity-aware post-processing step. The red box (b_H) indicates the proposal with highest classification confidence score, and all its overlapping proposals (b_j) are shown with dotted boxes. Although the yellow box b_2 has a large count prediction ($c_2 = 1.7$), it is highly similar to b_H, as indicated by the distance $d_{2H} = 0.01$, and is thus removed by our count and similarity-aware post-processing step. Similarly, cyan box is removed due to low count prediction $c_3 = 0.4$. The green box belonging to another pedestrian is predicted with a high count ($c_1 = 1.6$) and a higher distance $d_{1H} = 1.6$, hence not removed. (Color figure online)

$$L_{se} = \frac{\sum_{ij}(y_{ij}d_{ij}^2 + (1 - y_{ij})\,\mathbf{max}(\delta - d_{ij}, 0)^2)}{N_{se}} \tag{4}$$

where $d_{ij} = \|F_i - F_j\|_2$ indicates the distance between the feature embeddings F_i and F_j. The binary label y_{ij} indicates the ground-truth similarity, where proposals of the same ground-truth bounding box are labelled as similar, *i.e.*, $y_{ij} = 1$. N_{se} is the number of proposals used when training with the similarity embedding loss. The margin δ is set to 2. Training of our similarity embedding sub-branch using contrastive loss (L_{se} helps in projecting RoI features to a low-dimensional feature embedding, where the distance between proposals of two distinct overlapping instances is large.) Next, we describe the procedure to identify distinct proposals, during inference.

4.3 Inference

During inference, our approach predicts both the count and similarity embedding in addition to pedestrian classification and regression. This is followed by a count and similarity-aware post-processing step for removing duplicate proposals. In crowded scenes, there are multiple ground-truth boxes with a very high overlap. Hence, the detected proposals are also expected to be highly overlapped. Traditional post-processing involves an NMS strategy where a fixed overlap threshold is employed to eliminate overlapping bounding-box predictions. This often results in a loss of correct target bounding-boxes. To counter this issue, we

introduce a post-processing step, named count and similarity-aware NMS (CAS-NMS), that considers both the count and similarity between proposals.

Figure 2 shows the procedure involved in our CAS-NMS. We first sort the proposals based on their classification confidence scores. Let b_H be the proposal with the highest classification score. Similar to traditional NMS, all the proposals overlapping with b_H are selected as possible duplicate proposals (*i.e.*, $IoU \geq$ 0.5). Let b_j be one such selected proposal that has $IoU \geq$ 0.5 with b_H. In scenarios where b_j corresponds to a distinct pedestrian (*i.e.*, different to the one localized by b_H), it is common that (i) there are more than one pedestrians in b_H, (ii) there is at least one pedestrian in b_j, and (iii) both b_H and b_j are dissimilar. Our CAS-NMS uses predicted count and similarity embedding of both b_H and b_j, and categorizes b_j as a duplicate proposal, when any of the three criteria mentioned above are not fulfilled. *i.e.*, If predicted counts c_H, c_j of the proposals are below thresholds t_2, t_1, or the distance $d_{jH} = \|F_j - F_H\|_2$ between the similarity embeddings of both proposals is below a threshold N_{st}. Since, the distance between proposals is required only in the third criterion, d_{jH} is computed only for proposals satisfying the first two criteria. Our CAS-NMS removes duplicate proposals and preserves only distinct proposals containing at least one pedestrian. More details are available at https://github.com/Leotju/CaSe.

5   Experiments

5.1   Datasets and Evaluation Metrics

Datasets: We perform experiments on two challenging datasets: CityPersons [30] and CrowdHuman [22]. CityPersons contains 2975 training, 500 validation, and 1525 test images. It is suitable to evaluate performance on occluded pedestrians, as around 70% of the pedestrians in the dataset depict various levels of occlusions [30]. CrowdHuman contains crowded scenes and is therefore also suitable to evaluate performance on crowd occlusions. It consists of 15000, 4370, and 5000 images in the training, validation and test sets, respectively. Further, it contains more 470K human instances in the training and validation sets, with many images containing more than 20 person instances.

Evaluation Metrics: For both datasets, we report pedestrian detection performance using average-log miss rate (MR), computed over the false positive per image (FPPI) range of $[10^{-2}, 10^0]$ [8]. We select MR^{-2} to report the results and its lower value to mirror better detection performance. On CityPersons dataset, following [20,30], we report results on two different degrees of occlusions: Reasonable (**R**), and Heavy Occlusion (**HO**) to evaluate our approach. In the **R** set, the visibility ratio is larger than 65%, whereas the visibility ratio in the **HO** set ranges from 20% to 65%. And the height of pedestrians over 50 pixels is taken for detection evaluation, as in [20,31]. On CrowdHuman dataset, we follow the same evaluation protocol as in [22].

5.2 Implementation Details

Our framework utilizes an ImageNet pre-trained backbone (*e.g.* VGG-16 [23]). On CityPersons datasets, we follow the same experimental protocol as in [20]. On CrowdHuman datasets, we follow the same experimental protocol as in [22]. In case of CityPersons, the ($\times 1$) input scale is 1024×2048 and $\times 1.3$ input scale is 1344×2688. For CrowdHuman, the scale of input images is resized such that the shorter side is at 800 pixels while the longer side does not exceed more than 1400 pixels. In our experiments, the hyper-parameters $t_2 = 1.5$, $t_1 = 1$ and $N_{st} = 1.5$ are fixed for all datasets. Further, for the similarity sub-branch, the number of dissimilar and similar pairs are set to 16 and 32, respectively, for all the experiments. Our network is trained on NVIDIA GPUs and a mini-batch comprises 2 images per GPU.

5.3 CityPersons Dataset

State-of-the-Art Comparison: We compare our CaSe detector with the recent state-of-the-art methods, namely Repulsion Loss [27], F.RCNN+ATT-vbb [31], F.RCNN+ATT-part [31], OR-CNN [32], TLL [24], Bi-Box [37], Adaptive-NMS [13], FRCN+A+DT [34], and MGAN [20] on the CityPersons validation set. Table 1 shows the state-of-the-art comparison on the validation set. Note that different set of ground-truth pedestrian examples are used for training by existing state-of-the-art pedestrian detection methods. For fair comparison, we therefore select the same set of ground-truth pedestrian examples that are at least 50 pixels tall with different visibility (mentioned in 'Training Setting' column of Table 1) and an input scale, when comparing with each existing method.

Among recently introduced pedestrian detectors, ATT-vbb [31], OR-CNN [32], Bi-Box [37], FRCN+A+DT [34], and MGAN [20] utilize full-body and additional visible bounding-box (VBB) supervision. Our CaSe outperforms all these approaches on both the **R** and **HO** sets, *without* using VBB supervision. When using an input scale of $\times 1$, Repulsion Loss [27] achieves a log-average miss rate of 13.2% and 56.9% on the **R** and **HO** sets, respectively. Our CaSe provides superior detection performance compared to [27] with a log-average miss rate of 11.0% and 50.3% on the **R** and **HO** sets, respectively. Similarly, a consistent improvement in performance is obtained over [27], when using an input scale of $\times 1.3$ and the same training settings.

On the validation set, the best reported result for the **HO** subset is 39.4%, in terms of a log-average miss rate, obtained by the recently introduced MGAN [20] with an input scale of $\times 1.3$. Our CaSe sets a new state-of-the-art on the **HO** set with a log-average miss rate of 37.4%. Our detector also outperforms existing methods on the **R** set. Additionally, we present the results on the test set in Table 2. Note that the test set is withheld and the results are obtained by

Table 1. State-of-the-art comparisons (in terms of log-average miss rate) on the CityPersons validation set. Best results are boldfaced in each case. For fair comparison, we select the same set of ground-truth pedestrian examples and input scale when comparing our CaSe with each existing method. We also compare with existing methods using additional visible bounding-box (VBB) supervision. Our CaSe detector sets a new-state-of-the-art on both sets. Under heavy occlusions (**HO** set), our CaSe outperforms the state-of-the-art MGAN [20], reducing the error from 39.4% to 37.4%, without using additional VBB supervision.

Method	VBB	Training setting		R	HO
		Visibility	Input scale		
TLL [24]	×	–	×1	14.4	52.0
F.RCNN+ATT-vbb [31]	✓	≥65%	×1	16.4	57.3
F.RCNN+ATT-part [31]	×		×1	16.0	56.7
Repulsion Loss [27]	×		×1	13.2	56.9
Adaptive-NMS [13]	×		×1	11.9	55.2
MGAN [20]	✓		×1	11.5	51.7
CaSe (Ours)	×		×1	**11.0**	**50.3**
OR-CNN [32]	✓	≥50%	×1	12.8	55.7
MGAN [20]	✓		×1	10.8	46.7
CaSe (Ours)	×		×1	**10.1**	**45.2**
ALFNet [14]	×	≥0%	×1	12.0	51.9
CSP [15]	×		×1	11.0	49.3
MGAN [20]	✓		×1	11.3	42.0
CaSe (Ours)	×		×1	**10.5**	**40.5**
Repulsion Loss [27]	×	≥65%	×1.3	11.6	55.3
Adaptive-NMS [13]	×		×1.3	10.8	54.0
MGAN [20]	✓		×1.3	10.3	49.6
CaSe (Ours)	×		×1.3	**9.6**	**48.2**
OR-CNN [32]	✓	≥50%	×1.3	11.0	51.3
MGAN [20]	✓		×1.3	9.9	45.4
CaSe (Ours)	×		×1.3	**9.1**	**43.6**
Bi-box [37]	✓	≥30%	×1.3	11.2	44.2
FRCN +A +DT [34]	✓		×1.3	11.1	44.3
MGAN [20]	✓		×1.3	10.5	39.4
CaSe (Ours)	×		×1.3	**9.8**	**37.4**

Table 2. State-of-the-art comparison (in terms of log-average miss rate) on the CityPersons test set. Note that the test set is withheld. The results are obtained by sending our detection predictions to the authors of CityPersons [30] for evaluation. Our approach achieves state-of-the-art results on both the **R** and **HO** sets. On the **HO** set, our approach significantly outperforms the recently introduced MGAN [20], reducing the error from 41.0% to 38.6%.

Method	R	HO
Adaptive Faster RCNN [30]	13.0	50.5
MS-CNN [4]	13.3	51.9
Rep. Loss [27]	11.5	52.6
OR-CNN [32]	11.3	51.4
Cascade MS-CNN [4]	11.6	47.1
Adaptive-NMS [13]	11.4	–
MGAN [20]	9.3	41.0
CaSe (Ours)	**9.2**	**38.6**

sending our detector predictions to the authors of CityPersons [30]. Our detector outperforms all reported methods on both sets of the test set. Figure 3 shows the qualitative detection comparisons between Repulsion Loss approach [27] and our CaSe. Note that similar to our approach, Repulsion Loss method [27] also specifically targets at handling occlusions.

Comparison with PedHunter and APD: Other than methods exploiting additional VBB information, the work of [7], termed as PedHunter, utilizes extra head annotations. PedHunter [7] integrates three novel training strategies to the pedestrian detector training stage, achieving promising results. We integrate the PedHunter training strategies by re-implementing them in our framework and observe this to further improve the performance[1]. Through the integration of PedHunter modules, our CaSe can achieve a log-average miss rate of 8.0% and 41.2% on **R** and **HO** subsets of CityPersons validation set. APD [29] uses a stronger backbone (DLA-34), instead of VGG-16. For a fair comparison with APD, we re-train our model using DLA-34 backbone. Our method outperforms APD on both **R** and **HO** sets of CityPersons validation set and achieves log-average miss rates of 8.3% and 43.2%, respectively.

Ablation Study: Here, we analyze our CaSe approach on the CityPersons benchmark by demonstrating impact of progressively integrating our contributions: count-weighted detection loss (CW-loss), count-and-similarity branch

---

[1] Thanks to the PedHunter [7] authors for sharing head annotation on CityPersons validation set through email correspondence.

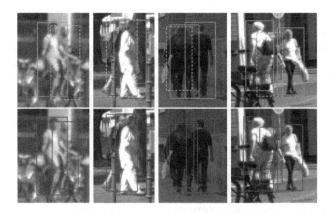

Fig. 3. Qualitative detection results on CityPersons validation set using Repulsion loss [27] (top) and our proposed CaSe (bottom). Detection results from the Repulsion loss and our CaSe are shown in green and red bounding-boxes, respectively. False negative detection results are shown with dashed orange bounding-boxes. (Color figure online)

Table 3. Comparison (in log-average miss rate) of our CaSe with the baseline on the CityPersons validation set. We report results using two training settings: visibility ≥65% with ×1.3 and ×1.0 input scales. In both settings, we observe a consistent improvement in performance due to progressively integrating one contribution at a time. Note that Baseline + CW-loss + CSB just shows the impact of joint training the detection branch (using CW-loss) and the count-and-similarity branch (CSB). The predictions from CSB are further utilized in CAS-NMS, resulting in a significant improvement in our overall results (CaSe: Baseline + CW-loss + CSB + CAS-NMS).

Input scale	Baseline	CW-Loss	CSB	CAS-NMS	R	HO
×1.3	✓				12.2	53.5
	✓	✓			11.3	51.5
	✓	✓	✓		10.8	49.3
	✓	✓	✓	✓	**9.6**	**48.2**
×1.0	✓				13.8	57.0
	✓	✓	✓	✓	**11.0**	**50.3**

(CSB), and count and similarity-aware NMS (CAS-NMS). Table 3 shows the results. For an extensive comparison, we report results using two standard settings. We use pedestrians with a height larger than 50 and visibility larger than 65% as training data and an input image scale of 1.3× and 1.0×. Note that we use same network backbone (VGG) for all the experiments in Table 3. Our approach yields a significant improvement in performance over the baseline.)

Table 4. Comparison (in log-average miss rate) with other loss function on CityPersons Val. set. Our CW-loss outperforms other approaches on both **R** and **HO**.

	Scale	Visiblity	R	HO
Agg. Loss [32]	×1.3	≥50%	11.4	52.6
CW Loss (Ours)	×1.3	≥50%	10.8	47.1
Rep. Loss [27]	×1.3	≥65%	11.6	55.3
CW Loss (Ours)	×1.3	≥65%	11.3	51.5

Table 5. Comparison (in log-average miss-rate) with state-of-the-art methods [13] that improves NMS on CityPersons validation sets.

	Scale	R	HO
Adaptive NMS [13]	×1.0	11.9	55.2
Our CaSe	×1.0	11.0	50.3
Adaptive NMS [13]	×1.3	10.8	54.0
Our CaSe	×1.3	9.6	48.2

We further compare our CW-loss with other loss function [27,32] on CityPersons validation sets. For fair comparison, we use the same set of ground-truth pedestrian examples (visibility) and input scale for training our CaSe when comparing with each method. Table 4 shows that our CW-loss outperforms both the Rep. Loss [27] and Agg. loss [32], on **R** and **HO** sets. The results in Table 5 demonstrate the effectiveness of our method compared to the Adaptive-NMS[13] using *same* ground-truth pedestrian examples, input scale and backbone.

As described in Sect. 4.2, both the count prediction and similarity embedding are crucial for our CAS-NMS. To validate the impact of the similarity embedding, we perform an experiment by removing the similarity prediction from our CAS-NMS. This leads to inferior results (53.1), likely due to multiple false positive detections, compared to using both count prediction and similarity embedding (50.3) on the **HO** set. Removing the count prediction in our CAS-NMS leads to lower inference speed, highlighting the importance of count[2].

Inference Time: For a 1024 × 2048 input, baseline and our CaSe operates at an inference time of 305, 330 ms, respectively. There is only a slight increase in inference time of our CaSe compared to baseline, thanks to the combined utilization of predicted count and similarity embedding in our CAS-NMS. For a fair comparison, both methods are evaluated on a single Titan X GPU.

5.4   CrowdHuman Dataset

Table 6 shows the state-of-the-art comparison on the recently introduced Crowd-Human dataset. We use the same protocol to report the results as used in the original dataset [22]. Note that all the methods in Table 6 employ the same backbone (ResNet50 + FPN). The Adaptive-NMS [13] and MGAN methods [20] obtain a log-average miss rate of 49.7% and 49.3%, respectively. Our approach sets a new state-of-the-art on this dataset by outperforming both Adaptive-NMS and MGAN methods with a log-average miss rate of 47.9%.

---

[2] More results are available at https://github.com/Leotju/CaSe.

Table 6. State-of-the-art comparison (in log-average miss rate) on the CrowdHuman dataset. Note that all methods employ the same network backbone (ResNet50 + FPN). Best results are boldfaced. Our detector significantly outperforms the state-of-the-art MGAN, achieving a log-average miss rate of 47.9%.

Method	FPN [22]	Adaptive NMS [13]	MGAN [20]	CaSe (Ours)
MR^{-2}	50.4	49.7	49.3	**47.9**

Table 7. Comparison on OCHuman for person instance segmentation. Here, AP_M indicates accuracy (AP) on moderately overlapped ground-truths (IoU with other ground-truths are between 0.5 and 0.75), while AP_H indicates accuracy on heavily overlapped ground-truths (IoU with other ground-truths are larger than 0.75). Our CaSe achieves consistent improvements, on both *val* and *test* sets, over Mask R-CNN.

Method	*val* sets			*test* sets		
	AP	AP_M	AP_H	AP	AP_M	AP_H
Mask RCNN [9,33]	16.3	19.4	11.3	16.9	18.9	12.8
CaSe (Ours)	17.5	20.2	13.0	18.0	20.1	13.9

5.5   Results on Person Instance Segmentation

Finally, we also evaluate our approach for the person instance segmentation task. We integrate our novel components (CW-loss, CSB and CAS-NMS) into Mask-RCNN [9]. We report the results on OCHuman [33], following the same protocol as in [33]. Note that the state-of-the-art [33] for person instance segmentation relies on additional human pose annotation. Table 7 shows the comparison of our approach with the baseline Mask RCNN on OCHuman. The results for the baseline and our approach are shown without using human pose information. Our approach outperforms the baseline, in terms of mask AP.

6   Conclusion

We propose an approach by leveraging pedestrian count and proposal similarity information within a two-stage pedestrian detection framework. We introduce a count-weighted detection loss for both the RPN and Fast R-CNN modules of two stage Faster R-CNN. Further, we propose a count-and-similarity branch that predicts both pedestrian count and proposal similarity. Lastly, we introduce a count and similarity-aware NMS strategy to remove duplicate proposals in crowded scenes. Experiments are performed on CityPersons and CrowdHuman datasets. Our results clearly show the effectiveness of our pedestrian detection approach towards handling heavy occlusions. Additionally, we demonstrate the applicability of our components for the problem of human instance segmentation.

Acknowledgment. The work is supported by the National Key R&D Program of China (Grant # 2018AAA0102800 and 2018AAA0102802) and National Natural Science Foundation of China (Grant # 61632018).

References

1. Bodla, N., Singh, B., Chellappa, R., Davis, L.S.: Soft-NMS - improving object detection with one line of code. In: ICCV (2017)
2. Brazil, G., Yin, X., Liu, X.: Illuminating pedestrians via simultaneous detection & segmentation. In: ICCV (2017)
3. Cai, Z., Fan, Q., Feris, R.S., Vasconcelos, N.: A unified multi-scale deep convolutional neural network for fast object detection. In: Leibe, B., Matas, J., Sebe, N., Welling, M. (eds.) ECCV 2016. LNCS, vol. 9908, pp. 354–370. Springer, Cham (2016). https://doi.org/10.1007/978-3-319-46493-0_22
4. Cai, Z., Vasconcelos, N.: Cascade r-cnn: High quality object detection and instance segmentation. arXiv preprint arXiv:1906.09756 (2019)
5. Cao, J., Pang, Y., Han, J., Gao, B., Li, X.: Taking a look at small-scale pedestrians and occluded pedestrians. IEEE Trans. Image Process. **29**, 3143–3152 (2020)
6. Cao, J., Pang, Y., Zhao, S., Li, X.: High-level semantic networks for multi-scale object detection. IEEE Trans. Circ. Syst. Video Technol. **30**, 3372–3386 (2019)
7. Chi, C., Zhang, S., Xing, J., Lei, Z., Li, S.Z.X.Z.: Pedhunter: occlusion robust pedestrian detector in crowded scenes. In: AAAI (2020)
8. Dollar, P., Wojek, C., Schiele, B., Perona, P.: Pedestrian detection: an evaluation of the state of the art. TPAMI **34**, 743–761 (2012)
9. He, K., Gkioxari, G., Dollár, P., Girshick, R.: Mask R-CNN. In: ICCV (2017)
10. Hosang, J., Benenson, R., Schiele, B.: Learning non-maximum suppression. In: CVPR (2017)
11. Hu, H., Gu, J., Zhang, Z., Dai, J., Wei, Y.: Relation networks for object detection. In: CVPR (2018)
12. Jiang, B., Luo, R., Mao, J., Xiao, T., Jiang, Y.: Acquisition of localization confidence for accurate object detection. In: ECCV (2018)
13. Liu, S., Huang, D., Wang, Y.: Adaptive NMS: refining pedestrian detection in a crowd. In: CVPR (2019)
14. Liu, W., Liao, S., Hu, W., Liang, X., Chen, X.: Learning efficient single-stage pedestrian detectors by asymptotic localization fitting. In: ECCV (2018)
15. Liu, W., Liao, S., Ren, W., Hu, W., Yu, Y.: High-level semantic feature detection: a new perspective for pedestrian detection. In: CVPR (2019)
16. Mao, J., Xiao, T., Jiang, Y., Cao, Z.: What can help pedestrian detection? In: CVPR (2017)
17. Mathias, M., Benenson, R., Timofte, R., Gool, L.V.: Handling occlusions with franken-classifiers. In: ICCV (2013)
18. Nie, J., Anwer, R.M., Cholakkal, H., Khan, F.S., Pang, Y., Shao, L.: Enriched feature guided refinement network for object detection. In: ICCV (2019)
19. Ouyang, W., Wang, X.: Joint deep learning for pedestrian detection. In: ICCV (2013)
20. Pang, Y., Xie, J., Khan, M.H., Anwer, R.M., Khan, F.S., Shao, L.: Mask-Guided attention network for occluded pedestrian detection. In: ICCV (2019)
21. Ren, S., He, K., Girshick, R., Sun, J.: Faster R-CNN: towards real-time object detection with region proposal networks. In: NIPS (2015)

22. Shao, S., et al.: Crowdhuman: A benchmark for detecting human in a crowd. arXiv preprint arXiv:1805.00123 (2018)
23. Simonyan, K., Zisserman, A.: Very deep convolutional networks for large-scale image recognition. arXiv preprint arXiv:1409.1556 (2014)
24. Song, T., Sun, L., Xie, D., Sun, H., Pu, S.: Small-scale pedestrian detection based on topological line localization and temporal feature aggregation. In: ECCV (2018)
25. Tian, Y., Luo, P., Wang, X., Tang, X.: Deep learning strong parts for pedestrian detection. In: ICCV (2015)
26. Tychsen-Smith, L., Petersson, L.: Improving object localization with fitness nms and bounded IOU loss. In: CVPR (2018)
27. Wang, X., Xiao, T., Jiang, Y., Shao, S., Sun, J., Shen, C.: Repulsion loss: detecting pedestrians in a crowd. In: CVPR (2018)
28. Xie, J., Pang, Y., Cholakkal, H., Anwer, R.M., Khan, F.S., Shao, L.: PSC-net: learning part spatial co-occurrence for occluded pedestrian detection. arXiv preprint arXiv:2001.09252 (2020)
29. Zhang, J., et al.: Attribute-aware pedestrian detection in a crowd. arXiv preprint arXiv:1910.09188 (2019)
30. Zhang, S., Benenson, R., Schiele, B.: Citypersons: a diverse dataset for pedestrian detection. In: CVPR (2017)
31. Zhang, S., Yang, J., Schiele, B.: Occluded pedestrian detection through guided attention in CNNs. In: CVPR (2018)
32. Zhang, S., Wen, L., Bian, X., Lei, Z., Li, S.Z.: Occlusion-aware R-CNN: detecting pedestrians in a crowd. In: ECCV (2018)
33. Zhang, S.H., et al.: Pose2seg: detection free human instance segmentation. In: CVPR (2019)
34. Zhou, C., Yang, M., Yuan, J.: Discriminative feature transformation for occluded pedestrian detection. In: ICCV (2019)
35. Zhou, C., Yuan, J.: Non-rectangular part discovery for object detection. In: BMVC (2014)
36. Zhou, C., Yuan, J.: Multi-label learning of part detectors for heavily occluded pedestrian detection. In: ICCV (2017)
37. Zhou, C., Yuan, J.: Bi-box regression for pedestrian detection and occlusion estimation. In: ECCV (2018)

TRADI: Tracking Deep Neural Network Weight Distributions

Gianni Franchi[1,2(✉)], Andrei Bursuc[3], Emanuel Aldea[2], Séverine Dubuisson[4], and Isabelle Bloch[5]

[1] ENSTA Paris, Institut Polytechnique de Paris, Palaiseau, France
gianni.franchi@ensta-paris.fr
[2] SATIE, Université Paris-Sud, Université Paris-Saclay, Gif-sur-Yvette, France
[3] valeo.ai, Paris, France
[4] CNRS, LIS, Aix Marseille University, Marseille, France
[5] LTCI, Télécom Paris, Institut Polytechnique de Paris, Palaiseau, France

Abstract. During training, the weights of a Deep Neural Network (DNN) are optimized from a random initialization towards a nearly optimum value minimizing a loss function. Only this final state of the weights is typically kept for testing, while the wealth of information on the geometry of the weight space, accumulated over the descent towards the minimum is discarded. In this work we propose to make use of this knowledge and leverage it for computing the distributions of the weights of the DNN. This can be further used for estimating the epistemic uncertainty of the DNN by aggregating predictions from an ensemble of networks sampled from these distributions. To this end we introduce a method for tracking the trajectory of the weights during optimization, that does neither require any change in the architecture, nor in the training procedure. We evaluate our method, TRADI, on standard classification and regression benchmarks, and on out-of-distribution detection for classification and semantic segmentation. We achieve competitive results, while preserving computational efficiency in comparison to ensemble approaches.

Keywords: Deep Neural Networks · Weight distribution · Uncertainty · Ensembles · Out-of-distribution detection

1 Introduction

In recent years, Deep Neural Networks (DNNs) have gained prominence in various computer vision tasks and practical applications. This progress has been

This work was supported by ANR Project MOHICANS (ANR-15-CE39-0005). We would like to thank Saclay-IA cluster and CNRS Jean-Zay supercomputer.

Electronic supplementary material The online version of this chapter (https://doi.org/10.1007/978-3-030-58520-4_7) contains supplementary material, which is available to authorized users.

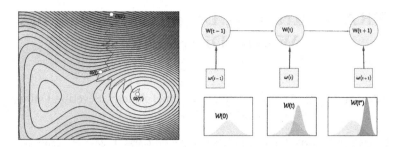

Fig. 1. Our algorithm uses Kalman filtering for tracking the distribution $\mathcal{W}$ of all DNN weights across training steps from a generic prior $\mathcal{W}(0)$ to the final estimate $\mathcal{W}(t^*)$. We also estimate the covariance matrix of all the trainable network parameters. Popular alternative approaches rely typically either on ensembles of models trained independently [31] with a significant computational cost, approximate ensembles [10] or on averaging weights collected from different local minima [23].

in part accelerated by multiple innovations in key parts of DNN pipelines, *e.g.*, architecture design [18,30,47,49], optimization [27], initialization [12,17], regularization [22,48], *etc.*, along with a pool of effective heuristics identified by practitioners. Modern DNNs achieve now strong accuracy across tasks and domains, leading to their potential utilization as key blocks in real-world applications.

However, DNNs have also been shown to be making mostly over-confident predictions [15], a side-effect of the heuristics used in modern DNNs. This means that for ambiguous instances bordering two classes (*e.g.*, human wearing a cat costume), or on unrelated instances (*e.g.*, plastic bag not "seen" during training and classified with high probability as rock), DNNs are likely to fail silently, which is a critical drawback for decision making systems. This has motivated several works to address the predictive uncertainty of DNNs [6,10,31], usually taking inspiration from Bayesian approaches. Knowledge about the distribution of the network weights during training opens the way for studying the evolution of the underlying covariance matrix, and the uncertainty of the model parameters, referred to as the epistemic uncertainty [26]. In this work we propose a method for estimating the distribution of the weights by tracking their trajectory during training. This enables us to sample an ensemble of networks and estimate more reliably the epistemic uncertainty and detect out-of-distribution samples.

The common practice in training DNNs is to first initialize its weights using an appropriate random initialization strategy and then slowly adjust the weights through optimization according to the correctness of the network predictions on many mini-batches of training data. Once the stopping criterion is met, the final state of the weights is kept for evaluation. We argue that the trajectory of weights towards the (local) optimum reveals abundant information about the structure of the weight space that we could exploit, instead of discarding it and looking

only at the final point values of the weights. Popular DNN weight initialization techniques [12,17] consist of an effective layer-wise scaling of random weight values sampled from a Normal distribution. Assuming that weights follow a Gaussian distribution at time $t = 0$, owing to the central limit theorem weights will also converge towards a Gaussian distribution. The final state is reached here through a noisy process, where the stochasticity is induced by the weight initialization, the order and configuration of the mini-batches, *etc.* We find it thus reasonable to see optimization as a random walk leading to a (local) minimum, in which case "tracking" the distribution makes sense (Fig. 1). To this end, Kalman filtering (KF) [14] is an appropriate strategy for tractability reasons, as well as for the guaranteed optimality as long as the underlying assumptions are valid (linear dynamic system with Gaussian assumption in the predict and update steps)[1]. To the best of our knowledge, our work is the first attempt to use such a technique to track the DNN weight distributions, and subsequently to estimate its epistemic uncertainty.

Contributions. The keypoints of our contribution are: **(a)** this is the first work which filters in a tractable manner the trajectory of the entire set of trainable parameters of a DNN during the training process; **(b)** we propose a tractable approximation for estimating the covariance matrix of the network parameters; **(c)** we achieve competitive or state of the art results on most regression datasets, and on out-of-distribution experiments our method is better calibrated on three segmentation datasets (CamVid [7] , StreetHazards [20], and BDD Anomaly [20]); **(d)** our approach strikes an appealing trade-off in terms of performance and computational time (training + prediction).

2   TRAcking of the Weight DIstribution (TRADI)

In this section, we detail our approach to first estimate the distribution of the weights of a DNN at each training step, and then generate an ensemble of networks by sampling from the computed distributions at training conclusion.

2.1   Notations and Hypotheses

- X and Y are two random variables, with $X \sim \mathcal{P}_X$ and $Y \sim \mathcal{P}_Y$. Without loss of generality we consider the observed samples $\{\mathbf{x}_i\}_{i=1}^n$ as vectors and the corresponding labels $\{y_i\}_{i=1}^n$ as scalars (class index for classification, real value for regression). From this set of observations, we derive a training set of n_l elements and a testing set of n_τ elements: $n = n_l + n_\tau$.
- Training/Testing sets are denoted respectively by $\mathcal{D}_l = (\mathbf{x}_i, y_i)_{i=1}^{n_l}$, $\mathcal{D}_\tau = (\mathbf{x}_i, y_i)_{i=1}^{n_\tau}$. Data in $\mathcal{D}_l$ and $\mathcal{D}_\tau$ are assumed to be i.i.d. distributed according to their respective unknown joint distribution $\mathcal{P}_l$ and $\mathcal{P}_\tau$.

---

[1] Recent theoretical works [40] show connections between optimization and KF, enforcing the validity of our approach.

- The DNN is defined by a vector containing the K trainable weights $\boldsymbol{\omega} = \{\omega_k\}_{k=1}^K$. During training, $\boldsymbol{\omega}$ is iteratively updated for each mini-batch and we denote by $\boldsymbol{\omega}(t)$ the state of the DNN at iteration t of the optimization algorithm, realization of the random variable $W(t)$. Let g denote the architecture of the DNN associated with these weights and $g_{\boldsymbol{\omega}(t)}(x_i)$ its output at t. The initial set of weights $\boldsymbol{\omega}(0) = \{\omega_k(0)\}_{k=1}^K$ follows $\mathcal{N}(0, \sigma_k^2)$, where the values σ_k^2 are fixed as in [17].
- $\mathcal{L}(\boldsymbol{\omega}(t), y_i)$ is the loss function used to measure the dissimilarity between the output $g_{\boldsymbol{\omega}(t)}(\mathbf{x}_i)$ of the DNN and the expected output y_i. Different loss functions can be considered depending on the type of task.
- Weights on different layers are assumed to be independent of each another at all times. This assumption is not necessary from a theoretical point of view, yet we need it to limit the complexity of the computation. Many works in the related literature rely on such assumptions [13], and some take the assumptions even further, *e.g.* [5], one of the most popular modern BNNs, supposes that all weights are independent (even from the same layer). Each weight $\omega_k(t)$, $k = 1, \ldots, K$, follows a non-stationary Normal distribution (i.e. $W_k(t) \sim \mathcal{N}(\mu_k(t), \sigma_k^2(t))$) whose two parameters are tracked.

2.2 TRAcking of the DIstribution (TRADI) of Weights of a DNN

Tracking the Mean and Variance of the Weights. DNN optimization typically starts from a set of randomly initialized weights $\boldsymbol{\omega}(0)$. Then, at each training step t, several SGD updates are performed from randomly chosen mini-batches towards minimizing the loss. This makes the trajectory of the weights vary or oscillate, but not necessarily in the good direction each time [33]. Since gradients are averaged over mini-batches, we can consider that weight trajectories are averaged over each mini-batch. After a certain number of epochs, the DNN converges, *i.e.* it reaches a local optimum with a specific configuration of weights that will then be used for testing. However, this general approach for training does not consider the evolution of the distribution of the weights, which may be estimated from the training trajectory and from the dynamics of the weights over time. In our work, we argue that the history of the weight evolution up to their final state is an effective tool for estimating the epistemic uncertainty.

More specifically, our goal is to estimate, for all weights $\omega_k(t)$ of the DNN and at each training step t, $\mu_k(t)$ and $\sigma_k^2(t)$, the parameters of their normal distribution. Furthermore, for small networks we can also estimate the covariance $\text{cov}(W_k(t), W_{k'}(t))$ for any pair of weights $(\omega_k(t), \omega_k'(t))$ at t in the DNN (see material for details). To this end, we leverage mini-batch SGD in order to optimize the loss between two weight realizations. The loss derivative with respect to a given weight $\omega_k(t)$ over a mini-batch $B(t)$ is given by:

$$\nabla \mathcal{L}_{\omega_k(t)} = \frac{1}{|B(t)|} \sum_{(\mathbf{x}_i, y_i) \in B(t)} \frac{\partial \mathcal{L}(\boldsymbol{\omega}(t-1), y_i)}{\partial \omega_k(t-1)} \tag{1}$$

Weights $\omega_k(t)$ are then updated as follows:

$$\omega_k(t) = \omega_k(t-1) - \eta \nabla \mathcal{L}_{\omega_k(t)} \tag{2}$$

with η the learning rate.

The weights of DNNs are randomly initialized at $t = 0$ by sampling $W_k(0) \sim \mathcal{N}(\mu_k(0), \sigma_k^2(0))$, where the parameters of the distribution are set empirically on a per-layer basis [17]. By computing the expectation of $\omega_k(t)$ in Eq. (2), and using its linearity property, we get:

$$\mu_k(t) = \mu_k(t-1) - \mathbb{E}\left[\eta \nabla \mathcal{L}_{\omega_k(t)}\right] \tag{3}$$

We can see that $\mu_k(t)$ depends on $\mu_k(t-1)$ and on another function at time $(t-1)$: this shows that the means of the weights follow a Markov process.

As in [2,53] we assume that during back-propagation and forward pass weights to be independent. We then get:

$$\sigma_k^2(t) = \sigma_k^2(t-1) + \eta^2 \mathbb{E}\left[(\nabla \mathcal{L}_{\omega_k(t)})^2\right] - \eta^2 \mathbb{E}^2\left[\nabla \mathcal{L}_{\omega_k(t)}\right] \tag{4}$$

This leads to the following state and measurement equations for $\mu_k(t)$:

$$\begin{cases} \mu_k(t) = \mu_k(t-1) - \eta \nabla \mathcal{L}_{\omega_k(t)} + \varepsilon_\mu \\ \omega_k(t) = \mu_k(t) + \tilde{\varepsilon}_\mu \end{cases} \tag{5}$$

with ε_μ being the state noise, and $\tilde{\varepsilon}_\mu$ being the observation noise, as realizations of $\mathcal{N}(0, \sigma_\mu^2)$ and $\mathcal{N}(0, \tilde{\sigma}_\mu^2)$ respectively. The state and measurement equations for the variance σ_k are given by:

$$\begin{cases} \sigma_k^2(t) = \sigma_k^2(t-1) + \left(\eta \nabla \mathcal{L}_{\omega_k(t)}\right)^2 + \varepsilon_\sigma \\ z_k(t) = \sigma_k^2(t) - \mu_k(t)^2 + \tilde{\varepsilon}_\sigma \\ \text{with } z_k(t) = \omega_k(t)^2 \end{cases} \tag{6}$$

with ε_σ being the state noise, and $\tilde{\varepsilon}_\sigma$ being the observation noise, as realizations of $\mathcal{N}(0, \sigma_\sigma^2)$ and $\mathcal{N}(0, \tilde{\sigma}_\sigma^2)$, respectively. We ignore the square empirical mean of the gradient on the equation as in practice its value is below the state noise.

Approximating the Covariance. Using the measurement and state transition in Eq. (5–6), we can apply a Kalman filter to track the state of each trainable parameter. As the computational cost for tracking the covariance matrix is significant, we propose to track instead only the variance of the distribution. For that, we approximate the covariance by employing a model inspired from Gaussian Processes [52]. We consider the Gaussian model due to its simplicity and good results. Let $\Sigma(t)$ denote the covariance of $W(t)$, and let $\mathbf{v}(t) = (\sigma_0(t), \sigma_1(t), \sigma_2(t), \ldots, \sigma_K(t))$ be a vector of size K composed of the standard deviations of all weights at time t. The covariance matrix is approximated by $\hat{\Sigma}(t) = (\mathbf{v}(t)\mathbf{v}(t)^T) \odot \mathcal{K}(t)$, where $\odot$ is the Hadamard product, and $\mathcal{K}(t)$ is the kernel corresponding to the $K \times K$ Gram matrix of the weights of the DNN,

with the coefficient (k, k') given by $\mathcal{K}(\omega_k(t), \omega_{k'}(t)) = \exp\left(-\frac{\|\omega_k(t) - \omega_{k'}(t)\|^2}{2\sigma_{\text{rbf}}^2}\right)$. The computational cost for storing and processing the kernel $\mathcal{K}(t)$ is however prohibitive in practice as its complexity is quadratic in terms of the number of weights (e.g., $K \approx 10^9$ in recent DNNs).

Rahimi and Recht [45] alleviate this problem by approximating non-linear kernels, e.g. Gaussian RBF, in an unbiased way using random feature representations. Then, for any translation-invariant positive definite kernel $\mathcal{K}(t)$, for all $(\omega_k(t), \omega_{k'}(t))$, $\mathcal{K}(\omega_k(t), \omega_{k'}(t))$ depends only on $\omega_k(t) - \omega_{k'}(t)$. We can then approximate the matrix by:

$$\mathcal{K}(\omega_k(t), \omega_{k'}(t)) \equiv \mathbb{E}\left[\cos(\Theta\omega_k(t) + \Phi)\cos(\Theta\omega_{k'}(t) + \Phi)\right]$$

where $\Theta \sim \mathcal{N}(0, \sigma_{\text{rbf}}^2)$ (this distribution is the Fourier transform of the kernel distribution) and $\Phi \sim \mathcal{U}_{[0,2\pi]}$. In detail, we approximate the high-dimensional feature space by projecting over the following N-dimensional feature vector:

$$\mathbf{z}(\omega_k(t)) \equiv \sqrt{\frac{2}{N}}\left[\cos(\theta_1\omega_k(t) + \phi_1), \dots, \cos(\theta_N\omega_k(t) + \phi_N))\right]^\top \tag{7}$$

where the $\theta_1, \dots, \theta_N$ are i.i.d. from $\mathcal{N}(0, \sigma_{rbf}^2)$ and $\phi_1, \dots, \phi_N$ are i.i.d. from $\mathcal{U}_{[0,2\pi]}$. In this new feature space we can approximate kernel $\mathcal{K}(t)$ by $\hat{\mathcal{K}}(t)$ defined by:

$$\hat{\mathcal{K}}(\omega_k(t), \omega_{k'}(t)) = \mathbf{z}(\omega_k(t))^\top \mathbf{z}(\omega_{k'}(t)) \tag{8}$$

Furthermore, it was proved in [45] that the probability of having an error of approximation greater than $\epsilon \in \mathbb{R}^+$ depends on $\exp(-N\epsilon^2)/\epsilon^2$. To avoid the Hadamard product of matrices of size $K \times K$, we evaluate $r(\omega_k(t)) = \sigma_k(t)\mathbf{z}(\omega_k(t))$, and the value at index (k, k') of the approximate covariance matrix $\hat{\Sigma}(t)$ is given by:

$$\hat{\Sigma}(t)(k, k') = r(\omega_k(t))^\top r(\omega_k(t)). \tag{9}$$

2.3   Training the DNNs

In our approach, for classification we use the cross-entropy loss to get the log-likelihood similarly to [31]. For regression tasks, we train over two losses sequentially and modify $g_{\omega(t)}(\boldsymbol{x}_i)$ to have two output heads: the classical regression output $\mu_{pred}(\boldsymbol{x}_i)$ and the predicted variance of the output σ_{pred}^2. This modification is inspired by [31]. The first loss is the MSE $\mathcal{L}_1(\boldsymbol{\omega}(t), \boldsymbol{y}_i) = \|g_{\omega(t)}(\boldsymbol{x}_i) - \boldsymbol{y}_i\|_2^2$ as used in the traditional regression tasks. The second loss is the negative log-likelihood (NLL) [31] which reads:

$$\mathcal{L}_2(\boldsymbol{\omega}(t), y_i) = \frac{1}{2\sigma_{\text{pred}}(\mathbf{x}_i)^2}\|\mu_{\text{pred}}(\mathbf{x}_i) - y_i\|^2 + \frac{1}{2}\log\sigma_{\text{pred}}(\mathbf{x}_i)^2 \tag{10}$$

We first train with loss $\mathcal{L}_1(\boldsymbol{\omega}(t), y_i)$ until reaching a satisfying $\boldsymbol{\omega}(t)$. In the second stage we add the variance prediction head and start fine-tuning from $\boldsymbol{\omega}(t)$ with loss $\mathcal{L}_2(\boldsymbol{\omega}(t), y_i)$. In our experiments we observed that this sequential training is more stable as it allows the network to first learn features for the target task and then to predict its own variance, rather than doing both in the same time (which is particularly unstable in the first steps).

2.4 TRADI Training Algorithm Overview

We detail the TRADI steps during training in Appendix, Sect. 1.3. For tracking purposes we must store $\mu_k(t)$ and $\sigma_k(t)$ for all the weights of the network. Hence, the method computationally lighter than Deep Ensembles, which has a training complexity scaling with the number of networks composing the ensemble. In addition, TRADI can be applied to any DNN without any modification of the architecture, in contrast to MC Dropout that requires adding dropout layers to the underlying DNN. For clarity we define $\mathcal{L}(\boldsymbol{\omega}(t), B(t)) = \frac{1}{|B(t)|} \sum_{(x_i,y_i) \in B(t)} \mathcal{L}(\boldsymbol{\omega}(t), y_i)$. Here $\mathbf{P}_\mu$, $\mathbf{P}_\sigma$ are the noise covariance matrices of the mean and variance respectively and $\mathbf{Q}_\mu$, $\mathbf{Q}_\sigma$ are the optimal gain matrices of the mean and variance respectively. These matrices are used during Kalman filtering [24].

2.5 TRADI Uncertainty During Testing

After having trained a DNN, we can evaluate its uncertainty by sampling new realizations of the weights from to the tracked distribution. We call $\tilde{\boldsymbol{\omega}}(t) = \{\tilde{\omega}_k(t)\}_{k=1}^K$ the vector of size K containing these realizations. Note that this vector is different from $\boldsymbol{\omega}(t)$ since it is sampled from the distribution computed with TRADI, that does not correspond exactly to the DNN weight distribution. In addition, we note $\boldsymbol{\mu}(t)$ the vector of size K containing the mean of all weights at time t.

Then, two cases can occur. In the first case, we have access to the covariance matrix of the weights (by tracking or by an alternative approach) that we denote $\boldsymbol{\Sigma}(t)$, and we simply sample new realizations of $W(t)$ using the following formula:

$$\tilde{\boldsymbol{\omega}}(t) = \boldsymbol{\mu}(t) + \boldsymbol{\Sigma}^{1/2}(t) \times \boldsymbol{m}_1 \tag{11}$$

in which $\boldsymbol{m}_1$ is drawn from the multivariate Gaussian $\mathcal{N}(\mathbf{0}_K, \boldsymbol{I}_K)$, where $\mathbf{0}_K, \boldsymbol{I}_K$ are respectively the K-size zero vector and the $K \times K$ size identity matrix.

When we deal with a DNN (the considered case in this paper), we are constrained for tractability reasons to approximate the covariance matrix following the random projection trick proposed in the previous section, and we generate new realizations of $W(t)$ as follows:

$$\tilde{\boldsymbol{\omega}}(t) = \boldsymbol{\mu}(t) + \boldsymbol{R}(\boldsymbol{\omega}(t)) \times \boldsymbol{m}_2 \tag{12}$$

where $\boldsymbol{R}(\boldsymbol{\omega}(t))$ is a matrix of size $K \times N$ whose rows $k \in [1, K]$ contain the $\boldsymbol{r}(\omega_k(t))^\top$ defined in Sect. 2.2. $\boldsymbol{R}(\boldsymbol{\omega}(t))$ depends on $(\theta_1, \ldots, \theta_N)$ and on $(\phi_1, \ldots, \phi_N)$ defined in Eq. (7). $\boldsymbol{m}_2$ is drawn from the multivariate Gaussian $\mathcal{N}(\mathbf{0}_N, \boldsymbol{I}_N)$, where $\mathbf{0}_N, \boldsymbol{I}_N$ are respectively the zero vector of size N and the identity matrix of size $N \times N$. Note that since $N \ll K$, computations are significantly accelerated.

Then similarly to works in [26,37], given input data $(\mathbf{x}^*, y^*) \in \mathcal{D}_\tau$ from the testing set, we estimate the marginal likelihood as Monte Carlo integration. First, a sequence $\{\tilde{\boldsymbol{\omega}}^j(t)\}_{j=1}^{N_{\text{model}}}$ of N_{model} realizations of $W(t)$ is drawn (typically, $N_{\text{model}} = 20$). Then, the marginal likelihood of y^* over $W(t)$ is approximated by:

$$\mathcal{P}(y^*|x^*) = \frac{1}{N_{\text{model}}} \sum_{j=1}^{N_{\text{model}}} \mathcal{P}(y^*|\tilde{\boldsymbol{\omega}}^j(t), \mathbf{x}^*) \tag{13}$$

For regression, we use the strategy from [31] to compute the log-likelihood of the regression and consider that the outputs of the DNN applied on $\mathbf{x}^*$ are the

parameters $\{\mu^j_{\text{pred}}(\mathbf{x}^*), (\sigma^j_{\text{pred}}(\mathbf{x}^*))^2\}^{N_{\text{model}}}_{j=1}$ of a Gaussian distribution (see Sect. 2.3). Hence, the final output is the result of a mixture of N_{model} Gaussian distributions $\mathcal{N}(\mu^j_{\text{pred}}(\mathbf{x}^*), (\sigma^j_{\text{pred}}(\mathbf{x}^*))^2)$. During testing, if the DNN has BatchNorm layers, we first update BatchNorm statistics of each of the sampled $\tilde{\omega}^j(t)$ models, where $j \in [1, N_{\text{model}}]$ [23].

3   Related Work

Uncertainty estimation is an important aspect for any machine learning model and it has been thoroughly studied across years in statistical learning areas. In the context of DNNs a renewed interest has surged in dealing with uncertainty, In the following we briefly review methods related to our approach.

Bayesian Methods. Bayesian approaches deal with uncertainty by identifying a distribution of the parameters of the model. The posterior distribution is computed from a prior distribution assumed over the parameters and the likelihood of the model for the current data. The posterior distribution is iteratively updated across training samples. The predictive distribution is then computed through Bayesian model averaging by sampling models from the posterior distribution. This simple formalism is at the core of many machine learning models, including neural networks. Early approaches from Neal [39] leveraged Markov chain Monte Carlo variants for inference on Bayesian Neural Networks. However for modern DNNs with millions of parameters, such methods are intractable for computing the posterior distribution, leaving the lead to gradient based methods.

Modern Bayesian Neural Networks (BNNs). Progress in variational inference [28] has enabled a recent revival of BNNs. Blundell *et al.* [6] learn distributions over neurons via a Gaussian mixture prior. While such models are easy to reason along, they are limited to rather medium-sized networks. Gal and Ghahramani [10] suggest that Dropout [48] can be used to mimic a BNN by sampling different subsets of neurons at each forward pass during test time and use them as ensembles. MC Dropout is currently the most popular instance of BNNs due to its speed and simplicity, with multiple recent extensions [11,32,50]. However, the benefits of Dropout are more limited for convolutional layers, where specific architectural design choices must be made [25,38]. A potential drawback of MC Dropout concerns the fact that its uncertainty is not reducing with more training steps [41,42]. TRADI is compatible with both fully-connected and convolutional layers, while uncertainty estimates are expected to improve with training as it relies on the Kalman filter formalism.

Ensemble Methods. Ensemble methods are arguably the top performers for measuring epistemic uncertainty, and are largely applied to various areas, *e.g.* active learning [3]. Lakshminarayan *et al.* [31] propose training an ensemble of DNNs with different initialization seeds. The major drawback of this method is its computational cost since one has to train multiple DNNs, a cost which is particularly high for computer vision architectures, *e.g.*, semantic segmentation, object detection. Alternatives to ensembles use a network with multiple prediction heads [35], collect weight checkpoints from local minima and average them [23] or fit a distribution over them and sample networks [37].

Although the latter approaches are faster to train than ensembles, their limitation is that the observations from these local minima are relatively sparse for such a high dimensional space and are less likely to capture the true distributions of the space around these weights. With TRADI we are mitigating these points as we collect weight statistics at each step of the SGD optimization. Furthermore, our algorithm has a lighter computational cost than [31] during training.

Kalman Filtering (KF). The KF [24] is a recursive estimator that constructs an inference of unknown variables given measurements over time. With the advent of DNNs, researchers have tried integrating ideas from KF in DNN training: for SLAM using RNNs [8,16], optimization [51], DNN fusion [36]. In our approach, we employ KF for keeping track of the statistics of the network during training such that at "convergence" we have a better coverage of the distribution around each parameter of a multi-million parameter DNN. The KF provides a clean and relatively easy to deploy formalism to this effect.

Weight Initialization and Optimization. Most DNN initialization techniques [12,17] start from weights sampled from a Normal distribution, and further scale them according to the number of units and the activation function. BatchNorm [22] stabilizes training by enforcing a Normal distribution of intermediate activations at each layer. WeightNorm [46] has a similar effect over the weights, making sure they are sticking to the initial distributions. From a Bayesian perspective the L_2 regularization, known as weight decay, is equivalent to putting a Gaussian prior over the weights [4]. We also consider a Gaussian prior over the weights, similar to previous works [6,23] for its numerous properties, ease of use and natural compatibility with KF. Note that we use it only in the filtering in order to reduce any major drift in the estimation of distributions of the weights across training, while mitigating potential instabilities in SGD steps.

4   Experiments

We evaluate TRADI on a range of tasks and datasets. For regression , in line with prior works [10,31], we consider a toy dataset and the regression benchmark [21]. For classification we evaluate on MNIST [34] and CIFAR-10 [29]. Finally, we address the Out-of-Distribution task for classification, on MNIST/notMNIST [31], and for semantic segmentation, on CamVid-OOD, StreetHazards [19], and BDD-Anomaly [19]. Unless otherwise specified, we use mini-batches of size 128 and Adam optimizer with fixed learning rate of 0.1 in all our experiments.

4.1   Toy Experiments

Experimental Setup. As evaluation metric we use mainly the NLL uncertainty. In addition for classification we consider the accuracy, while for regression we use the root mean squared error (RMSE). For the out- of-distribution experiments we use the AUC, AUPR, FPR-95%-TPR as in [20], and the Expected Calibration Error (ECE) as in [15]. For our implementations we use PyTorch [44]. Unless otherwise specified, we use mini-batches of size 128 and Adam optimizer with fixed learning rate of 0.1 in all our experiments. We provide other implementation details on per-experiment basis.

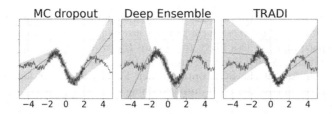

Fig. 2. Results on a synthetic regression task comparing MC dropout, Deep Ensembles, and TRADI. x-axis: spatial coordinate of the Gaussian process. Black lines: ground truth curve. Blue points: training points. Orange areas: estimated variance. (Color figure online)

First we perform a qualitative evaluation on a one-dimensional synthetic dataset generated with a Gaussian Process of zero mean vector and as covariance function an RBF kernel $\mathcal{K}$ with $\sigma^2 = 1$, denoted $GP(\mathbf{0}, \mathcal{K})$. We add to this process a zero mean Gaussian noise of variance 0.3. We train a neural network composed of one hidden layer and 200 neurons. In Fig. 2 we plot the regression estimation provided by TRADI, MC Dropout [10] and Deep Ensembles [31]. Although $GP(\mathbf{0}, \mathcal{K})$ is one of the simplest stochastic processes, results show clearly that the compared approaches do not handle robustly the variance estimation, while TRADI neither overestimates nor underestimates the uncertainty.

4.2   Regression Experiments

For the regression task, we consider the experimental protocol and the data sets from [21], and also used in related works [10,31]. Here, we consider a neural network with one hidden layer, composed of 50 hidden units trained for 40 epochs. For each dataset, we do 20-fold cross-validation. For all datasets, we set the dropout rate to 0.1 except for *Yacht Hydrodynamics* and *Boston Housing* for which it is set to 0.001 and 0.005, respectively. We compare against MC Dropout [10] and Deep Ensembles [31] and report results in Table 1. TRADI outperforms both methods, in terms of both RMSE and NLL. Aside from the proposed approach to tracking the weight distribution, we assume that an additional reason for which our technique outperforms the alternative methods resides in the sequential training (MSE and NLL) proposed in Sect. 2.3.

Table 1. Comparative results on regression benchmarks

Datasets	RMSE			NLL		
	MC dropout	Deep ensembles	TRADI	MC dropout	Deep ensembles	TRADI
Boston housing	2.97 ± 0.85	3.28 ± 1.00	$\mathbf{2.84 \pm 0.77}$	2.46 ± 0.25	2.41 ± 0.25	$\mathbf{2.36 \pm 0.17}$
Concrete strength	5.23 ± 0.53	6.03 ± 0.58	$\mathbf{5.20 \pm 0.45}$	3.04 ± 0.09	3.06 ± 0.18	$\mathbf{3.03 \pm 0.08}$
Energy efficiency	1.66 ± 0.16	2.09 ± 0.29	$\mathbf{1.20 \pm 0.27}$	1.99 ± 0.09	$\mathbf{1.38 \pm 0.22}$	1.40 ± 0.16
Kin8nm	0.10 ± 0.00	0.09 ± 0.00	$\mathbf{0.09 \pm 0.00}$	-0.95 ± 0.03	$\mathbf{-1.2 \pm 0.02}$	-0.98 ± 0.06
Naval propulsion	0.01 ± 0.00	0.00 ± 0.00	$\mathbf{0.00 \pm 0.00}$	-3.80 ± 0.05	$\mathbf{-5.63 \pm 0.05}$	-2.83 ± 0.24
Power plant	4.02 ± 0.18	4.11 ± 0.17	$\mathbf{4.02 \pm 0.14}$	2.80 ± 0.05	$\mathbf{2.79 \pm 0.04}$	2.82 ± 0.04
Protein structure	4.36 ± 0.04	4.71 ± 0.06	$\mathbf{4.35 \pm 0.03}$	2.89 ± 0.01	2.83 ± 0.02	$\mathbf{2.80 \pm 0.02}$
Wine quality red	0.62 ± 0.04	0.64 ± 0.04	$\mathbf{0.62 \pm 0.03}$	0.93 ± 0.06	0.94 ± 0.12	$\mathbf{0.93 \pm 0.05}$
Yacht hydrodynamics	1.11 ± 0.38	1.58 ± 0.48	$\mathbf{1.05 \pm 0.25}$	1.55 ± 0.12	1.18 ± 0.21	$\mathbf{1.18 \pm 0.39}$

4.3   Classification Experiments

For the classification task, we conduct experiments on two datasets. The first one is the MNIST dataset [34], which is composed of a training set containing 60k images and a testing set of 10k images, all of size 28×28. Here, we use a neural network with 3 hidden layers, each one containing 200 neurons, followed by ReLU non-linearities and BatchNorm, and fixed the learning rate $\eta = 10^{-2}$. We share our results in Table 2. For the MNIST dataset, we generate $N_{model} = 20$ models, in order to ensure a fair comparison with Deep Ensembles. The evaluation underlines that in terms of performance TRADI is positioned between Deep Ensembles and MC Dropout. However, in contrast to Deep Ensembles our algorithm is significantly lighter because only a single model needs to be trained, while Deep Ensembles approximates the weight distribution by a very costly step of independent training procedures (in this case 20).

We conduct the second experiment on CIFAR-10 [29], with WideResnet 28×10 [55] as DNN. The chosen optimization algorithm is SGD, $\eta = 0.1$ and the dropout rate was fixed to 0.3. Due to the long time necessary for Deep Ensembles to train the DNNs we set $N_{model} = 15$. Comparative results on this dataset, presented in Table 2, allow us to make similar conclusions with experiments on the MNIST dataset.

Table 2. Comparative results on image classification

Method	MNIST		CIFAR-10	
	NLL	ACCU	NLL	ACCU
Deep ensembles	**0.035**	**98.88**	0.173	95.67
MC Dropout	0.065	98.19	0.205	95.27
SWAG	0.041	98.78	**0.110**	**96.41**
TRADI (ours)	0.044	98.63	0.205	95.29

4.4   Uncertainty Evaluation for Out-of-Distribution (OOD) Test Samples

In these experiments, we evaluate uncertainty on OOD classes. We consider four datasets, and the objective of these experiments is to evaluate to what extent the trained DNNs are overconfident on instances belonging to classes which are not present in the training set. We report results in Table 3.

Baselines. We compare against Deep Ensembles and MC Dropout, and propose two additional baselines. The first is the Maximum Classifier Prediction (MCP) which uses the maximum softmax value as prediction confidence and has shown competitive performance [19,20]. Second, we propose a baseline to emphasize the ability of TRADI to capture the distribution of the weights. We take a *trained* network and randomly perturb its weights with noise sampled from a Normal distribution. In this way we generate an ensemble of networks, each with different noise perturbations – we practically sample networks from the vicinity of the local minimum. We refer to it as *Gaussian perturbation ensemble*.

First we consider MNIST trained DNNs and use them on a test set composed of 10k MNIST images and 19k images from NotMNIST [1], a dataset of instances of ten classes of letters. Standard DNNs will assign letter instances of NotMNIST to a class number with high confidence as shown in [1]. For these OOD instances, our approach is able to decrease the confidence as illustrated in Fig. 3a, in which we represent the *accuracy vs confidence* curves as in [31].

Table 3. Distinguishing in- and out-of-distribution data for semantic segmentation (CamVid, StreetHazards, BDD Anomaly) and image classification (MNIST/notMNIST)

Dataset	OOD technique	AUC	AUPR	FPR-95%-TPR	ECE	Train time
MNIST/notMNIST	Baseline (MCP)	94.0	96.0	24.6	**0.305**	2 m
3 hidden layers	Gauss. perturbation ensemble	94.8	96.4	19.2	0.500	2 m
	MC Dropout	91.8	94.9	35.6	0.494	2m
	Deep Ensemble	**97.2**	**98.0**	**9.2**	0.462	31 m
	SWAG	90.9	94.4	31.9	0.529	
	TRADI (ours)	96.7	97.6	11.0	0.407	2 m
CamVid-OOD	Baseline (MCP)	75.4	10.0	65.1	0.146	30 m
ENET	Gauss. perturbation ensemble	76.2	10.9	62.6	0.133	30 m
	MC Dropout	75.4	10.7	63.2	0.168	30 m
	Deep Ensemble	**79.7**	**13.0**	**55.3**	0.112	5 h
	SWAG	75.6	12.1	65.8	0.133	
	TRADI (ours)	79.3	**12.8**	57.7	**0.110**	41 m
StreetHazards	Baseline (MCP)	88.7	6.9	26.9	0.055	13 h 14 m
PSPNet	Gauss. perturbation ensemble	57.08	2.4	71.0	0.185	13 h 14 m
	MC Dropout	69.9	6.0	32.0	0.092	13 h 14 m
	Deep Ensemble	**90.0**	7.2	25.4	0.051	132 h 19 m
	TRADI (ours)	89.2	**7.2**	**25.3**	**0.049**	15 h 36 m
BDD Anomaly	Baseline (MCP)	86.0	5.4	27.7	0.159	18 h 08 m
PSPNet	Gauss. perturbation ensemble	86.0	4.8	27.7	0.158	18 h 08 m
	MC Dropout	85.2	5.0	29.3	0.181	18 h 08 m
	Deep Ensemble	87.0	6.0	**25.0**	0.170	189 h 40 m
	TRADI (ours)	86.1	5.6	26.9	**0.157**	21 h 48 m

The *accuracy vs confidence* curve is constructed by considering, for different confidence thresholds, all the test data for which the classifier reports a confidence above the threshold, and then by evaluating the accuracy on this data. The confidence of a DNN is defined as the maximum prediction score. We also evaluate the OOD uncertainty using AUC, AUPR and FPR-95%-TPR metrics, introduced in [20] and the ECE metrics introduced in [15]. These criteria characterize the quality of the prediction that a testing sample is OOD with respect to the training dataset. We also measured the computational training times of all algorithms implemented in PyTorch on a PC equipped with Intel Core i9-9820X and one GeForce RTX 2080 Ti and report them in Table 3. We note that TRADI DNN with 20 models provides incorrect predictions on such OOD samples with lower confidence than Deep Ensembles and MC Dropout.

In the second experiment, we train a Enet DNN [43] for semantic segmentation on CamVid dataset [7]. During training, we delete three classes (pedestrian, bicycle, and car), by marking the corresponding pixels as unlabeled. Subsequently, we test with data containing the classes represented during training, as well as the deleted ones. The goal of this experiment is to evaluate the DNN behavior on the deleted classes which represent thus OOD classes. We refer to this setup as CamVid-OOD. In this experiment we use $N_{model} = 10$ models trained for 90 epochs with SGD and using a learning rate $\eta = 5 \times 10^{-4}$. In Fig. 3b and 3c we illustrate the *accuracy vs confidence* curves and the *calibration* curves [15] for the CamVid experiment. The calibration curve as explained in [15] consists in dividing the test set into bins of equal size according to the confidence, and in computing the accuracy over each bin. Both the calibration and the *accuracy vs confidence* curves highlight whether the DNN predictions are good for

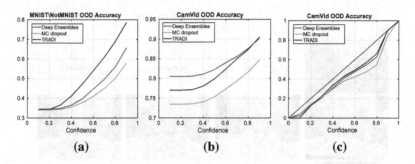

Fig. 3. (a) and (b) Accuracy vs confidence plot on the MNIST \notMNIST and CamVid experiments, respectively. (c) Calibration plot for the CamVid experiment.

different levels of confidence. However, the calibration provides a better understanding of what happens for different scores.

Finally, we conducted experiments on the recent OOD benchmarks for semantic segmentation StreetHazards [19] and BDD Anomaly [19]. The former consists of 5,125/1,031/1,500 (train/test-in-distribution/test-OOD) synthetic images [9] with annotations for 12 classes for training and a 13th OOD class found only in the test-OOD set. The latter is a subset of BDD [54] and is composed of 6,688/951/361 images, with the classes *motorcycle* and *train* as anomalous objects. We follow the experimental setup from [19], *i.e.*, PSPNet [56] with ResNet50 [18] backbone. On StreetHazards, TRADI outperforms Deep Ensembles and on BDD Anomaly Deep Ensembles has best results close to the one of TRADI.

Results show that TRADI outperforms the alternative methods in terms of calibration, and that it may provide more reliable confidence scores. Regarding *accuracy vs confidence*, the most significant results for a high level of confidence, typically above 0.7, show how overconfident the network tends to behave; in this range, our results are similar to those of Deep Ensembles. Lastly, in all experiments TRADI obtains performances close to the best AUPR and AUC, while having a computational time /training time significantly smaller than Deep Ensembles.

Qualitative Discussion. In Fig. 4 we give as example a scene featuring the three OOD instances of interest (*bike, car, pedestrian*). Overall, MC Dropout outputs a noisy uncertainty map, but fails to highlight the OOD samples. By contrast, Deep Ensembles is overconfident, with higher uncertainty values mostly around the borders of the objects. TRADI uncertainty is higher on borders and also on pixels belonging to the actual OOD instances, as shown in the zoomed-in crop of the pedestrian in Fig. 4 (row 3).

(a) Input + GT   (b) MC Dropout   (c) Deep Ensembles   (d) TRADI

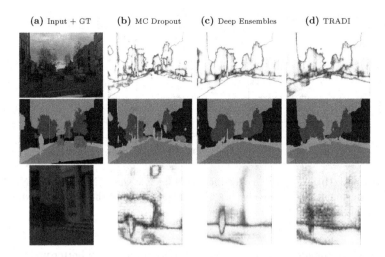

Fig. 4. Qualitative results on CamVid-OOD. Columns: (a) input image and ground truth; (b)-(d) predictions and confidence scores by MC Dropout, Deep Ensembles, and TRADI. Rows: (1) input and confidence maps; (2) class predictions; (3) zoomed-in area on input and confidence maps

5 Conclusion

In this work we propose a novel technique for computing the epistemic uncertainty of a DNN. TRADI is conceptually simple and easy to plug to the optimization of any DNN architecture. We show the effectiveness of TRADI over extensive studies and compare against the popular MC Dropoutand the state of the art Deep Ensembles. Our method exhibits an excellent performance on evaluation metrics for uncertainty quantification, and in contrast to Deep Ensembles, for which the training time depends on the number of models, our algorithm does not add any significant cost over conventional training times.

Future works involve extending this strategy to new tasks, *e.g.*, object detection, or new settings, *e.g.*, active learning. Another line of future research concerns transfer learning. So far TRADI is starting from randomly initialized weights sampled from a given Normal distribution. In transfer learning, we start from a pre-trained network where weights are expected to follow a different distribution. If we have access to the distribution of the DNN weights we can improve the effectiveness of transfer learning with TRADI.

References

1. Notmnist dataset. http://yaroslavvb.blogspot.com/2011/09/notmnist-dataset. html
2. Andrychowicz, M., et al.: Learning to learn by gradient descent by gradient descent. In: Advances in Neural Information Processing Systems, pp. 3981–3989 (2016)
3. Beluch, W.H., Genewein, T., Nürnberger, A., Köhler, J.M.: The power of ensembles for active learning in image classification. In: Proceedings of the IEEE Conference on Computer Vision and Pattern Recognition, pp. 9368–9377 (2018)

4. Bishop, C.M.: Pattern Recognition and Machine Learning. Springer, Heidelberg (2006)

5. Blundell, C., Cornebise, J., Kavukcuoglu, K., Wierstra, D.: Weight uncertainty in neural network. In: Bach, F., Blei, D. (eds.) Proceedings of the 32nd International Conference on Machine Learning. Proceedings of Machine Learning Research, 07–09 July 2015, vol. 37, pp. 1613–1622. PMLR, Lille, France (2015) http://proceedings.mlr.press/v37/blundell15.html

6. Blundell, C., Cornebise, J., Kavukcuoglu, K., Wierstra, D.: Weight uncertainty in neural networks. arXiv preprint arXiv:1505.05424 (2015)

7. Brostow, G.J., Shotton, J., Fauqueur, J., Cipolla, R.: Segmentation and recognition using structure from motion point clouds. In: Forsyth, D., Torr, P., Zisserman, A. (eds.) ECCV 2008. LNCS, vol. 5302, pp. 44–57. Springer, Heidelberg (2008). https://doi.org/10.1007/978-3-540-88682-2_5

8. Chen, C., Lu, C.X., Markham, A., Trigoni, N.: Ionet: learning to cure the curse of drift in inertial odometry. In: The Thirty-Second AAAI Conference on Artificial Intelligence (AAAI-18) (2018)

9. Dosovitskiy, A., Ros, G., Codevilla, F., Lopez, A., Koltun, V.: CARLA: an open urban driving simulator. In: Proceedings of the 1st Annual Conference on Robot Learning, pp. 1–16 (2017)

10. Gal, Y., Ghahramani, Z.: Dropout as a bayesian approximation: representing model uncertainty in deep learning. In: International Conference on Machine Learning, pp. 1050–1059 (2016)

11. Gal, Y., Hron, J., Kendall, A.: Concrete dropout. In: NIPS (2017)

12. Glorot, X., Bengio, Y.: Understanding the difficulty of training deep feedforward neural networks. In: Proceedings of the Thirteenth International Conference on Artificial Intelligence and Statistics, pp. 249–256 (2010)

13. Graves, A.: Practical variational inference for neural networks. In: Advances in Neural Information Processing Systems, pp. 2348–2356 (2011)

14. Grewal, M.S.: Kalman Filtering. Springer, Heidelberg (2011). https://doi.org/10.1007/978-3-642-04898-2_321

15. Guo, C., Pleiss, G., Sun, Y., Weinberger, K.Q.: On calibration of modern neural networks. In: Proceedings of the 34th International Conference on Machine Learning, vol. 70, pp. 1321–1330. JMLR. org (2017)

16. Haarnoja, T., Ajay, A., Levine, S., Abbeel, P.: Backprop kf: learning discriminative deterministic state estimators. In: Advances in Neural Information Processing Systems, pp. 4376–4384 (2016)

17. He, K., Zhang, X., Ren, S., Sun, J.: Delving deep into rectifiers: surpassing human-level performance on imagenet classification. In: Proceedings of the IEEE International Conference on Computer Vision, pp. 1026–1034 (2015)

18. He, K., Zhang, X., Ren, S., Sun, J.: Deep residual learning for image recognition. In: Proceedings of the IEEE Conference on Computer Vision and Pattern Recognition, pp. 770–778 (2016)

19. Hendrycks, D., Basart, S., Mazeika, M., Mostajabi, M., Steinhardt, J., Song, D.: A benchmark for anomaly segmentation. arXiv preprint arXiv:1911.11132 (2019)

20. Hendrycks, D., Gimpel, K.: A baseline for detecting misclassified and out-of-distribution examples in neural networks. arXiv preprint arXiv:1610.02136 (2016)

21. Hernández-Lobato, J.M., Adams, R.: Probabilistic backpropagation for scalable learning of bayesian neural networks. In: International Conference on Machine Learning, pp. 1861–1869 (2015)

22. Ioffe, S., Szegedy, C.: Batch normalization: Accelerating deep network training by reducing internal covariate shift. arXiv preprint arXiv:1502.03167 (2015)

23. Izmailov, P., Podoprikhin, D., Garipov, T., Vetrov, D., Wilson, A.G.: Averaging weights leads to wider optima and better generalization. arXiv preprint arXiv:1803.05407 (2018)
24. Kalman, R.E.: A new approach to linear filtering and prediction problems. J. Basic Eng. **82**(1), 35–45 (1960)
25. Kendall, A., Badrinarayanan, V., Cipolla, R.: Bayesian segnet: model uncertainty in deep convolutional encoder-decoder architectures for scene understanding. arXiv preprint arXiv:1511.02680 (2015)
26. Kendall, A., Gal, Y.: What uncertainties do we need in bayesian deep learning for computer vision? In: Advances in Neural Information Processing Systems, pp. 5574–5584 (2017)
27. Kingma, D.P., Ba, J.: Adam: A method for stochastic optimization. arXiv preprint arXiv:1412.6980 (2014)
28. Kingma, D.P., Welling, M.: Auto-encoding variational bayes. In: 2nd International Conference on Learning Representations, ICLR 2014, Banff, AB, Canada, 14–16 April 2014, Conference Track Proceedings (2014)
29. Krizhevsky, A., Hinton, G., et al.: Learning multiple layers of features from tiny images. Tecnical report, Citeseer (2009)
30. Krizhevsky, A., Sutskever, I., Hinton, G.E.: Imagenet classification with deep convolutional neural networks. In: Advances in Neural Information Processing Systems, pp. 1097–1105 (2012)
31. Lakshminarayanan, B., Pritzel, A., Blundell, C.: Simple and scalable predictive uncertainty estimation using deep ensembles. In: Advances in Neural Information Processing Systems, pp. 6402–6413 (2017)
32. Lambert, J., Sener, O., Savarese, S.: Deep learning under privileged information using heteroscedastic dropout. In: 2018 IEEE/CVF Conference on Computer Vision and Pattern Recognition, pp. 8886–8895 (2018)
33. Lan, J., Liu, R., Zhou, H., Yosinski, J.: LCA: loss change allocation for neural network training. In: Advances in Neural Information Processing Systems, pp. 3614–3624 (2019)
34. LeCun, Y., Bottou, L., Bengio, Y., Haffner, P., et al.: Gradient-based learning applied to document recognition. Proc. IEEE **86**(11), 2278–2324 (1998)
35. Lee, S., Purushwalkam, S., Cogswell, M., Crandall, D., Batra, D.: Why m heads are better than one: Training a diverse ensemble of deep networks. arXiv preprint arXiv:1511.06314 (2015)
36. Liu, C., Gu, J., Kim, K., Narasimhan, S.G., Kautz, J.: Neural rgb (r) d sensing: depth and uncertainty from a video camera. In: Proceedings of the IEEE Conference on Computer Vision and Pattern Recognition, pp. 10986–10995 (2019)
37. Maddox, W., Garipov, T., Izmailov, P., Vetrov, D., Wilson, A.G.: A simple baseline for bayesian uncertainty in deep learning. arXiv preprint arXiv:1902.02476 (2019)
38. Mukhoti, J., Gal, Y.: Evaluating bayesian deep learning methods for semantic segmentation. CoRR abs/1811.12709 (2018). http://arxiv.org/abs/1811.12709
39. Neal, R.M.: Bayesian Learning for Neural Networks. Springer, Heidelberg (1996). https://doi.org/10.1007/978-1-4612-0745-0
40. Ollivier, Y.: The extended kalman filter is a natural gradient descent in trajectory space. arXiv preprint arXiv:1901.00696 (2019)
41. Osband, I.: Risk versus uncertainty in deep learning: Bayes, bootstrap and the dangers of dropout (2016)
42. Osband, I., Aslanides, J., Cassirer, A.: Randomized prior functions for deep reinforcement learning. In: NeurIPS (2018)

43. Paszke, A., Chaurasia, A., Kim, S., Culurciello, E.: Enet: a deep neural network architecture for real-time semantic segmentation. arXiv preprint arXiv:1606.02147 (2016)
44. Paszke, A., et al.: Pytorch: An imperative style, high-performance deep learning library. In: Advances in Neural Information Processing Systems, pp. 8024–8035 (2019)
45. Rahimi, A., Recht, B.: Random features for large-scale kernel machines. In: Advances in Neural Information Processing Systems, pp. 1177–1184 (2007)
46. Salimans, T., Kingma, D.P.: Weight normalization: a simple reparameterization to accelerate training of deep neural networks. In: Advances in Neural Information Processing Systems, pp. 901–909 (2016)
47. Simonyan, K., Zisserman, A.: Very deep convolutional networks for large-scale image recognition. arXiv preprint arXiv:1409.1556 (2014)
48. Srivastava, N., Hinton, G., Krizhevsky, A., Sutskever, I., Salakhutdinov, R.: Dropout: a simple way to prevent neural networks from overfitting. J. Mach. Learn. Res. **15**(1), 1929–1958 (2014), http://dl.acm.org/citation.cfm?id=2627435.2670313
49. Szegedy, C., et al.: Going deeper with convolutions. arxiv 2014. arXiv preprint arXiv:1409.4842 1409 (2014)
50. Teye, M., Azizpour, H., Smith, K.: Bayesian uncertainty estimation for batch normalized deep networks. In: ICML (2018)
51. Wang, G., Peng, J., Luo, P., Wang, X., Lin, L.: Batch kalman normalization: Towards training deep neural networks with micro-batches. arXiv preprint arXiv:1802.03133 (2018)
52. Williams, C.K., Rasmussen, C.E.: Gaussian Processes for Machine Learning, vol. 2. MIT press, Cambridge (2006)
53. Yang, G.: Scaling limits of wide neural networks with weight sharing: Gaussian process behavior, gradient independence, and neural tangent kernel derivation. arXiv preprint arXiv:1902.04760 (2019)
54. Yu, F., et al.: Bdd100k: A diverse driving video database with scalable annotation tooling. arXiv preprint arXiv:1805.04687 (2018)
55. Zagoruyko, S., Komodakis, N.: Wide residual networks. arXiv preprint arXiv:1605.07146 (2016)
56. Zhao, H., Shi, J., Qi, X., Wang, X., Jia, J.: Pyramid scene parsing network. In: Proceedings of the IEEE Conference on Computer Vision and Pattern Recognition, pp. 2881–2890 (2017)

Spatiotemporal Attacks for Embodied Agents

Aishan Liu[1], Tairan Huang[1], Xianglong Liu[1,2(✉)], Yitao Xu[1], Yuqing Ma[1],
Xinyun Chen[3], Stephen J. Maybank[4], and Dacheng Tao[5]

[1] State Key Laboratory of Software Development Environment, Beihang University,
Beijing, China
xlliu@nlsde.buaa.edu.cn
[2] Beijing Advanced Innovation Center for Big Data-Based Precision Medicine,
Beihang University, Beijing, China
[3] UC Berkeley, London, USA
[4] Birkbeck, University of London, London, UK
[5] UBTECH Sydney AI Centre, School of Computer Science, Faculty of Engineering,
The University of Sydney, Sydney, Australia

Abstract. Adversarial attacks are valuable for providing insights into
the blind-spots of deep learning models and help improve their robustness. Existing work on adversarial attacks have mainly focused on static
scenes; however, it remains unclear whether such attacks are effective
against embodied agents, which could navigate and interact with a
dynamic environment. In this work, we take the first step to study adversarial attacks for embodied agents. In particular, we generate spatiotemporal perturbations to form 3D adversarial examples, which exploit the
interaction history in both the temporal and spatial dimensions. Regarding the temporal dimension, since agents make predictions based on historical observations, we develop a trajectory attention module to explore
scene view contributions, which further help localize 3D objects appeared
with highest stimuli. By conciliating with clues from the temporal dimension, along the spatial dimension, we adversarially perturb the physical
properties (*e.g.*, texture and 3D shape) of the contextual objects that
appeared in the most important scene views. Extensive experiments on
the EQA-v1 dataset for several embodied tasks in both the white-box
and black-box settings have been conducted, which demonstrate that our
perturbations have strong attack and generalization abilities (Our code
can be found at https://github.com/liuaishan/SpatiotemporalAttack).

Keywords: Embodied agents · Spatiotemporal perturbations · 3D
adversarial examples

Electronic supplementary material The online version of this chapter (https://
doi.org/10.1007/978-3-030-58520-4_8) contains supplementary material, which is available to authorized users.

© Springer Nature Switzerland AG 2020
A. Vedaldi et al. (Eds.): ECCV 2020, LNCS 12362, pp. 122–138, 2020.
https://doi.org/10.1007/978-3-030-58520-4_8

1   Introduction

Deep learning has demonstrated remarkable performance in a wide spectrum of areas [22,28,34], but it is vulnerable to adversarial examples [7,14,35]. The small perturbations are imperceptible to human but easily misleading deep neural networks (DNNs), thereby bringing potential security threats to deep learning applications [24,25,30]. Though challenging deep learning, adversarial examples are valuable for understanding the behaviors of DNNs, which could provide insights into the weakness and help improve the robustness [43]. Over the last few years, significant efforts have been made to explore model robustness to the adversarial noises using *adversarial attacks* in the static and non-interactive domain, *e.g.*, 2D images [2,11,14] or static 3D scenes [26,38,42].

With great breakthroughs in multimodal techniques and virtual environments, embodied task has been introduced to further foster and measure the agent perceptual ability. An agent must intelligently navigate a simulated environment to achieve specific goals through egocentric vision [8,9,15,41]. For example, an agent is spawned in a random location within an environment to answer questions such as *"What is the color of the car?"*. Das *et al.* [8] first introduced the embodied question answering (EQA) problem and proposed a model consisting of a hierarchical navigation module and a question answering module. Concurrently, Gordon *et al.* [15] studied the EQA task in an interactive environment named AI2-THOR [20]. Recently, several studies have been proposed to improve agent performance using different frameworks [9] and point cloud perception [37]. Similar to EQA, embodied vision recognition (EVR) [40] is an embodied task, in which an agent instantiated close to an occluded target object to perform visual object recognition.

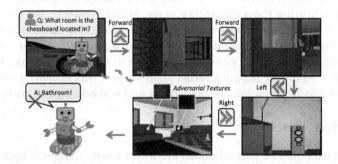

Fig. 1. Embodied agents must navigate the environment through egocentric views to answer given questions. By adversarially perturbing the physical properties of 3D objects using our spatiotemporal perturbations, the agent gives the wrong answer (the correct answer is "living room") to the question. The contextual objects perturbed are: sofa and laptop.

In contrast to static tasks, embodied agents are free to move to different locations and interact with the dynamic environment. Rather than solely using

a one-shot image, embodied agents observe 3D objects from different views and make predictions based on historical observations (trajectory). Current adversarial attacks mainly focused on the static scenes and ignored the information from the temporal dimension. However, since agents utilize contextual information to make decisions (*i.e.*, answer questions), only considering a single image or an object appeared in one scene view may not be sufficient to generate strong adversarial attacks for the embodied agent.

In this work, we provide the first study of adversarial attacks for embodied agents in dynamic environments, as demonstrated in Fig. 1. By exploiting the interaction history in both the temporal and spatial dimensions, our adversarial attacks generate 3D spatiotemporal perturbations. Regarding the temporal dimension, since agents make predictions based on historical observations, we develop a trajectory attention module to explore scene view contributions, which could help to localize 3D objects that appeared with highest stimuli for agents' predictions. Coupled with clues from the temporal dimension, along the spatial dimension, we adversarially perturb the physical properties (*e.g.*, 3D shape, and texture) of the contextual objects that appeared in the most important scene views. Currently, most embodied agents input 2D images transformed and processed from 3D scenes by undifferentiable renderers. To apply the attack using a gradient-based strategy, we replace the undifferentiable renderer with a differentiable one by introducing a neural renderer [19].

To evaluate the effectiveness of our spatiotemporal attacks, we conduct extensive experiments in both the white-box and black-box settings using different models. We first demonstrate that our generated 3D adversarial examples are able to attack the state-of-the-art embodied agent models and significantly outperform other 3D adversarial attack methods. Also, our adversarial perturbations can be transferred to attack the black-box renderer using non-differentiable operations, indicating the applicability of our attack strategy, and the potential of extending it to the physical world. We also provide a discussion of adversarial training using our generated attacks, and a perceptual study indicating that contrary to the human vision system, current embodied agents are mostly more sensitive to object textures rather than shapes, which sheds some light on bridging the gap between human perception and embodied perception.

2   Related Work

Adversarial examples or perturbations are intentionally designed inputs to mislead deep neural networks [35]. Most existing studies address the static scene including 2D images and static 3D scenes.

In the 2D image domain, Szegedy *et al.* [35] first introduced adversarial examples and used the L-BFGS method to generate them. By leveraging the gradients of the target model, Goodfellow *et al.* [14] proposed the Fast Gradient Sign Method (FGSM) which could generate adversarial examples quickly. In addition, Mopuri *et al.* [29] proposed a novel approach to generate universal perturbations for DNNs for object recognition tasks. These methods add perturbations on 2D image pixels rather than 3D objects and fail to attack the embodied agents.

Some recent work study adversarial attacks in the static 3D domain. A line of work [26,38,42] used differentiable renderers to replace the undifferentiable one, and perform attacks through gradient-based strategies. They mainly manipulated object shapes and textures in 3D visual recognition tasks. On the other hand, Zhang *et al.* [44] learned a camouflage pattern to hide vehicles from being detected by detectors using an approximation function. Adversarial patches [5,24] have been studied to perform real-world 3D adversarial attacks. In particular, Liu *et al.* [24] proposed the PS-GAN framework to generate scrawl-like adversarial patches to fool autonomous-driving systems. However, all these attacks mainly considered the static scenes and ignored the temporal information. Our evaluation demonstrates that by incorporating both spatial and temporal information, our spatiotemporal attacks are more effective for embodied tasks.

Another line of work studies adversarial attacks against reinforcement learning agents [13,18,21,23,31]. These works mainly consider adversarial attacks against reinforcement learning models trained for standard game environments, where the model input only includes the visual observation. For example, most of existing work focuses on single-agent tasks such as Atari [4], while Gleave *et al.* [13] studied adversarial attacks in multi-agent environments. Different from prior work, we focus on tasks related to embodied agents (i.e., EQA and EVR), with richer input features including both vision and language components.

3 Adversarial Attacks for the Embodiment

The embodiment hypothesis is the idea that intelligence emerges in the interaction of an agent with an environment and as a result of sensorimotor activity [8,33]. To achieve specific goals, embodied agents are required to navigate and interact with the dynamic environment through egocentric vision. For example, in the EQA task, an agent is spawned at a random location in a 3D dynamic environment to answer given questions through navigation and interaction.

3.1 Motivations

Though showing promising results in the virtual environment, the agent robustness is challenged by the emergence of adversarial examples. Most of the agents are built upon deep learning models which have been proved to be weak in the adversarial setting [14,35]. By performing adversarial attacks to the embodiment, an adversary could manipulate the embodied agents and force them to execute unexpected actions. Obviously, it would pose potential security threats to agents in both the digital and physical world.

From another point of view, adversarial attacks for the embodiment are also beneficial to understand agents' behaviors. As black-box models, most deep-learning-based agents are difficult to interpret. Thus, adversarial attacks provide us with a new way to explore model weakness and blind-spots, which are valuable to understand their behaviors in the adversarial setting. Further, we can improve model robustness and build stronger agents against noises.

3.2   Problem Definition

In this paper, we use 3D adversarial perturbations (adversarial examples) to attack embodied agents in a dynamic environment.

In a **static scenario**, given a deep neural network $\mathbb{F}_\theta$ and an input image **I** with ground truth label y, an adversarial example $\mathbf{I}^{adv}$ is the input that makes the model conducted the wrong label

$$\mathbb{F}_\theta(\mathbf{I}^{adv}) \neq y \quad s.t. \quad \|\mathbf{I} - \mathbf{I}^{adv}\| < \epsilon,$$

where $\| \cdot \|$ is a distance metric to quantify the distance between the two inputs **I** and $\mathbf{I}^{adv}$ sufficiently small.

For the **embodiment**, an agent navigates the environment to fulfil goals and observe 3D objects in different time steps t. The input image $\mathbf{I}_t$ at time step t for an agent is the rendered result of a 3D object from a renderer $\mathcal{R}$ by $\mathbf{I}_t = \mathcal{R}(\mathbf{x}, \mathbf{c}_t)$. **x** is the corresponding 3D object and $\mathbf{c}_t$ denotes conditions at t (*e.g.*, camera views, illumination, *etc.*). To attack the embodiment, we need to consider the agent trajectory in temporal dimension and choose objects to perturb in the 3D spatial space. In other words, we generate adversarial 3D object $\mathbf{x}^{adv}$ by perturbing its physical properties at multiple time steps. The rendered image set $\{\mathbf{I}_1, ..., \mathbf{I}_N\}$ is able to fool the agent $\mathbb{F}_\theta$:

$$\mathbb{F}_\theta(\mathcal{R}(\mathbf{x}_t^{adv}, \mathbf{c}_t)) \neq y \quad s.t. \quad \|\mathbf{x}_t - \mathbf{x}_t^{adv}\| < \epsilon,$$

where t belongs to a time step set we considered.

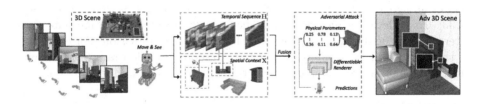

Fig. 2. Our framework exploits interaction histories from both the temporal and the spatial dimension. In the temporal dimension, we develop a trajectory attention module to explore scene view contributions. Thus, important scene views are extracted to help localize 3D objects that appeared with highest stimuli for agents predictions. By conciliating with clues from the temporal dimension, along the spatial dimension, we adversarially perturb the 3D properties (*e.g.*, 3D shape, and texture) of the contextual objects appeared in the most important scene views.

4   Spatiotemporal Attack Framework

In this section, we illustrate our framework to generate 3D adversarial perturbations for embodied agents in the dynamic environment. In Fig. 2, we present an

overview of our attack approach, which incorporates history interactions from both the temporal and spatial dimensions.

Motivated by the fact that agents make predictions based on historical scene views (trajectory), we attack the 3D objects appeared in scene views containing the highest stimuli to the agent's prediction. In the temporal dimension, we develop a trajectory attention module $\mathcal{A}$ to explore scene view contributions, which directly calculates the contribution weight for each time step scene view $\{\mathbf{I}_1, ..., \mathbf{I}_N\}$ to the agent prediction $\mathbb{F}_\theta$. Given a N-step trajectory, the K most important historical scene views $\mathbf{S}$ are selected by $\mathcal{A}$ to help localize 3D objects that appeared with highest stimuli.

Meanwhile, rather than solely depending on single objects, humans always collect discriminative contextual information when making predictions. By conciliating with clues from the temporal dimension, along the spatial dimension, we adversarially perturb the physical properties ϕ of multiple 3D contextual objects $\mathbf{X}$ appeared in the most important scene views. Moreover, to attack physical properties (i.e., 3D shapes and textures), we also employ a differentiable renderer $\mathbb{R}_\delta$ to use the gradient-based attacks.

Thus, by coupling both temporal and spatial information, our framework generates spatiotemporal perturbations to form 3D adversarial examples, which could perform adversarial attacks for the embodiment.

4.1 Temporal Attention Stimulus

To achieve specific goals, embodied agents are required to navigate the environment and make decisions based on the historical observations. Conventional vision tasks, e.g., classification, mainly base on one-shot observation in static images. In contrast, we should consider historical information (trajectory) such as last N historical scene views observed by the agent $\mathbf{H} = \{\mathbf{I}_{t-N}, \mathbf{I}_{t-N+1}, ..., \mathbf{I}_{t-1}\}$, and adversarially perturb the 3D objects that appeared in them. Thus, we can formulate the attack loss:

$$\mathcal{L}_{adv}(\mathbf{H}, y; \mathbb{F}_\theta) = \mathrm{P}(y|\mathbf{H}), \tag{1}$$

where $\mathrm{P}(\cdot|\cdot)$ denotes the prediction probability of the model, and y indicates the ground truth label (i.e., correct answer, object class or action w.r.t. question answering, visual recognition and navigation, respectively). To attack agents, the equation above aims to decrease the confidence of the correct class.

There is extensive biological evidence that efficient perception requires both specialized visual sensing and a mechanism to prioritize stimuli, i.e., visual attention. Agents move their eyes towards a specific location or focus on relevant locations to make predictions by prioritizing different scene views [6]. To improve attack abilities, we must design a visual attention module that selects a suitable set of visual features (historical scene views) to perform attack. Inspired by [32], given scene views $\mathbf{H}$, we first compute the gradient of target class y w.r.t. normalized feature maps $\mathbf{Z}$ of a specified layer. These gradients flowing back are global average pooled to obtain weight $\mathbf{w}_t$ for the t-th scene view:

$$\mathbf{w}_t = \max(0, \sum_{n=1}^{r} \frac{1}{u \times v} \sum_{j=1}^{v} \sum_{i=1}^{u} \frac{\partial \mathrm{P}(y|\mathbf{H})}{\partial \mathbf{Z}_{i,j}^n}), \tag{2}$$

where $u \times v$ represents the size of the feature map, and r indicates total feature map numbers in a specified layer. Then, We normalize each weight according to their mean vector $\boldsymbol{\mu}$ and variance vector $\boldsymbol{\sigma}$:

$$\overline{\mathbf{w}}_t = \frac{\mathbf{w}_t - \boldsymbol{\mu}}{\boldsymbol{\sigma}^2 + \epsilon}, \tag{3}$$

Thus, our trajectory attention module calculates the contribution of each scene view in the trajectory $\mathbf{H}$ towards the model decision for class y:

$$\mathcal{A}(\mathbf{H}, y; \mathbb{F}_\theta) = \langle \overline{\mathbf{w}}_1, ..., \overline{\mathbf{w}}_N \rangle. \tag{4}$$

The weights directly reflect the contribution of observed views at different time steps in the trajectory. Thus, we can further adversarially perturb the 3D objects that appeared in those scene views containing higher weights to execute a stronger attack.

4.2 Spatially Contextual Perturbations

Adversarial attacks in the static scene usually manipulate pixel values in the static image or different frames. In contrast, adversarial attacks for the embodiment require us to perturb the physical properties of 3D objects. Simply, we could randomly choose an object appeared in the most important scene views based on the attention weights to perform attacks. However, when humans look at an object, they always collect a discriminative context for that object [12]. In other words, we concentrate on that object while simultaneously being aware of its surroundings and context. The contextual information enables us to perform much stronger adversarial attacks. As shown in Fig. 1, when asking "*What room is the chessboard located in?*", it is better to perturb contextual objects rather than only the target object "chessboard". To answer the question, agent relied on contextual objects (*e.g.*, sofa, laptop, *etc*), that convey critical factors and key features about the answer "living room".

Coupled with the clues from the temporal dimension, we further perturb the 3D contextual objects appeared in the K most important views. Specifically, given K most important scene views selected by our trajectory attention module $\mathbf{S} = \{\mathbf{S}_1, ..., \mathbf{S}_K\}$, we perturb M 3D objects $\mathbf{X} = \{\mathbf{x}_1, ..., \mathbf{x}_M\}$ appeared in $\mathbf{S}$. Thus, the adversarial attack loss can be formalized as:

$$\mathcal{L}_{adv}(\mathbf{X}, y; \mathbb{F}_\theta, \mathbb{R}_\delta) = \mathrm{P}(y|\mathbf{S}, \mathbb{R}_\delta(\mathbf{X}, \mathbf{c})). \tag{5}$$

Let $\boldsymbol{\phi}_m$ be the 3D physical parameters of object $\mathbf{x}_m$ (*e.g.*, texture, shape, *etc*). With the contribution weight $\overline{\mathbf{w}}$ for the K most important scene views, we add the following perturbation to $\boldsymbol{\phi}_m$:

$$\Delta\phi_m = \sum_{k=1}^{K} \mathbb{1}(\mathbf{x}_m \in \Phi(\mathbf{S}_k)) \cdot \overline{\mathbf{w}}_k \cdot$$

$$\nabla_{\phi_m} \mathcal{L}_{adv}(\mathbf{x}_m, y; \mathbb{F}_\theta, \mathbb{R}_\delta),$$

(6)

where $\Phi(\cdot)$ extracts the objects appeared in scene views.

4.3   Optimization Formulations

Based on the above discussion, we generate 3D adversarial perturbations using the optimization formulation:

$$\mathcal{L}(\mathbf{X}; \mathbb{F}_\theta, \mathbb{R}_\delta) = \mathrm{E}_{\mathbf{c}\sim\mathbf{C}} \Bigg[\mathcal{L}_{adv}(\mathbf{X}, y; \mathbb{F}_\theta, \mathbb{R}_\delta, \mathbf{c}) + \\ \lambda \cdot \mathcal{L}_{per}(\mathbf{X}, \mathbf{X}^{adv}; \mathbb{R}_\delta, \mathbf{c}) \Bigg],$$

(7)

where we append the adversarial attack loss with a perceptual loss:

$$\mathcal{L}_{per}(\mathbf{x}, \mathbf{x}_{adv}; \mathbb{R}_\delta, \mathbf{c}) = ||\mathbb{R}_\delta(\mathbf{x}, \mathbf{c}) - \mathbb{R}_\delta(\mathbf{x}_{adv}, \mathbf{c})||,$$

(8)

which constrains the magnitude of the total noises added to produce a visually imperceptible perturbation. $\mathbf{C}$ represents different conditions (*e.g.*, camera views, illumination, *etc.*) and λ balances the contribution of each part.

Recent studies have highlighted that adversarial perturbations are ineffective to different transformations and environmental conditions (*e.g.*, illuminations, rotations, *etc*). In the dynamic environment, the viewing angles and environmental conditions change frequently. Thus, we further introduce the idea of *expectation of transformations* [3] to enhance the attack success rate of our perturbations as shown in the expectation of different conditions $\mathbf{C}$ in Eq. (7). Specifically, for each object to attack, we select five positional views one meter away with an azimuth angle uniformly ranging from $[0°, 180°]$ to optimize the overall loss.

It is intuitive to directly place constraints on physical parameters such as the contour or color range of object surfaces. However, one potential disadvantage is that different physical parameters have different units and ranges. Therefore, we constrain the RGB intensity changes in the 2D image space after the rendering process to keep the consistency of the change of different parameters (*i.e.*, shape or texture).

5   Experiments

In this section, we evaluate the effectiveness of our 3D spatiotemporal adversarial attacks against agents in different settings for different embodied tasks. We also provide a discussion of defense with adversarial training, and an ablation study of how different design choices affect the attack performance.

5.1 Experimental Setting

For both EQA and EVR tasks, we use the EQA-v1 dataset [8], a visual question answering dataset grounded in the simulated environment. It contains 648 environments with 7,190 questions for training, 68 environments with 862 questions for validation, and 58 environments with 933 questions for testing. It divides the task into T_{-10}, T_{-30}, T_{-50} by steps from the starting point to the target. We restrict the adversarial perturbations to be bounded by 32-pixel values per frame of size 224×224, in terms of ℓ_∞ norm.

5.2 Evaluation Metrics

To measure agent performance, we use evaluation metrics as in [8,9,37]:

- top-1 accuracy: whether the agent's prediction matches ground truth ($\uparrow$ is better);
- d_T: the distance to the target object at navigation termination ($\downarrow$ is better);
- d_Δ: change in distance to target from initial to the final position ($\uparrow$ is better);
- d_{min}: the smallest distance to the target at any point in the episode ($\downarrow$ is better);

Note that the goal of adversarial attacks is compromising the performance of the embodied agents, *i.e.*, making worse values of the evaluation metrics above.

5.3 Implementation Details

We use the SGD optimizer for adversarial perturbation generation, with momentum 0.9, weight decay 10^{-4}, and a maximum of 60 iterations. For the hyperparameters of our framework, we set λ to 1, K to 3, and M as the numbers of all contextual objects observed in these frames. For EQA, we generate adversarial perturbations using PACMAN-RL+Q [8] as the target model (we use "PACMAN" for simplicity), and we use Embodied Mask R-CNN [40] as the target model for EVR. In our evaluation, we will demonstrate that the attacks generated against one model could transfer to different models.

For both EQA and EVR, unless otherwise specified, we generate adversarial perturbations on texture only, *i.e.*, in Eq. 6, we only update the parameters corresponding to texture, because it is more suitable for future extension to physical attacks in the real 3D environment. In the supplementary material, we also provide a comparison of adversarial perturbations on shapes, where we demonstrate that with the same constraint of perturbation magnitude, texture attacks achieve a higher attack success rate.

5.4 Attack via a Differentiable Renderer

we first provide the quantitative and qualitative results of our 3D adversarial perturbations on EQA and EVR through our differentiable renderer. For EQA,

besides PACMAN, we also evaluate the transferability of our attacks using the following models: (1) NAV-GRU, an agent using GRU instead of LSTM in navigation [37]; (2) NAV-React, an agent without memory and fails to use historical information [8]; and (3) VIS-VGG, an agent using VGG to encode visual information [9]. For EVR, we evaluate the white-box attacks on Embodied Mask R-CNN. As most of the embodied tasks can be directly divided into navigation and problem-solving stages, i.e., question answering or visual recognition, we attack each of these stages. We compare our spatiotemporal attacks to MeshAdv [38] and Zeng et al. [42], both of which are designed for the static 3D environment, and thus do not leverage the temporal information.

For **question answering** and **visual recognition**, we generate 3D adversarial perturbations using our proposed method on the test set and evaluate

Table 1. Quantitative evaluation of agent performance on EQA task using different models in clean and adversarial settings (ours, MeshAdv [38] and Zeng et al. [42]). Note that the goal of attacks is to achieve a worse performance. We observe that our spatiotemporal attacks outperform the static 3D attack algorithms, achieving higher d_T and d_{min} as well as lower d_Δ and accuracy.

		Navigation									QA		
		d_T (↓ is better)			d_Δ (↑ is better)			d_{min} (↓ is better)			accuracy (↑ is better)		
		T_{-10}	T_{-30}	T_{-50}	T_{-10}	T_{-30}	T_{-50}	T_{-10}	T_{-30}	T_{-50}	T_{-10}	T_{-30}	T_{-50}
PACMAN	Clean	1.05	2.43	3.82	0.10	0.45	1.86	0.26	0.97	1.99	50.23%	44.19%	39.94%
	MeshAdv	1.06	2.44	3.90	0.09	0.44	1.78	0.31	1.17	2.33	16.07%	15.34%	13.11%
	Zeng et al.	**1.07**	2.46	3.88	**0.08**	0.42	1.80	0.42	1.37	2.43	17.15%	16.38%	14.32%
	Ours	1.06	**3.19**	**5.58**	0.09	**−0.39**	**0.10**	**0.90**	**2.47**	**5.33**	**6.17%**	**4.26%**	**3.42%**
NAV-GRU	Clean	1.03	2.47	3.92	0.12	0.41	1.76	0.34	1.02	2.07	48.97%	43.72%	38.26%
	MeshAdv	1.07	2.50	3.92	0.08	0.38	1.76	0.38	1.28	2.48	17.22%	17.01%	14.25%
	Zeng et al.	1.09	2.47	3.87	0.06	0.41	1.81	0.36	1.38	2.51	17.14%	16.56%	15.11%
	Ours	**1.13**	**2.96**	**5.42**	**0.02**	**−0.08**	**0.26**	**0.96**	**2.58**	**4.98**	**8.41%**	**6.23%**	**5.15%**
NAV-React	Clean	**1.37**	2.75	4.17	**−0.22**	0.13	1.51	0.31	0.99	2.08	48.19%	43.73%	37.62%
	MeshAdv	1.05	2.79	4.25	0.10	0.09	1.43	0.32	1.29	2.47	15.36%	14.78%	11.29%
	Zeng et al.	1.10	2.79	4.21	0.05	0.09	1.47	0.36	1.59	2.32	15.21%	14.13%	13.29%
	Ours	1.22	**2.85**	**5.70**	−0.07	**0.03**	**−0.02**	**1.06**	**2.59**	**5.47**	**8.26%**	**5.25%**	**5.39%**
VIS-VGG	Clean	1.02	2.38	3.67	0.13	0.50	2.01	0.38	1.05	2.26	50.16%	45.81%	37.84%
	MeshAdv	1.06	2.41	3.67	0.09	0.47	2.01	0.40	1.11	2.52	16.69%	15.24%	15.21%
	Zeng et al.	1.06	2.43	3.70	0.09	0.45	1.98	0.44	1.41	2.44	15.13%	14.84%	14.21%
	Ours	**1.18**	**2.83**	**5.62**	**−0.03**	**0.05**	**0.06**	**1.04**	**2.01**	**5.12**	**6.33%**	**4.84%**	**4.29%**

(a) Clean Scene   (b) Adversarial Scene

Fig. 3. Given the question *"What is next to the fruit bowl in the living room?"*, we show the last 5 views of the agent for EQA in the same scene with and without adversarial perturbations. The contextual objects perturbed including table, chairs and fruit bowel. The agent gives wrong answers "television" to the question (ground truth: chair) after seeing adversarial textures in subfigure (b). Yellow boxes show the perturbed texture (Color figure online).

agent performance throughout the entire process, *i.e.*, the agent is randomly placed and navigate to answer a question or recognize an object. As shown in Table 1, for white-box attacks, there is a significant drop in question answering accuracy from 50.23%, 44.19% and 39.94% to 6.17%, 4.26% and 3.42% for tasks with 10, 30, and 50 steps, respectively. Further, the visual recognition accuracy drastically decreases from 89.91% to 18.32%. The black-box attacks also result in a large drop in accuracy. The visualization of the last five steps before the agent's decision for EQA is shown in Fig. 3. Our perturbations are unambiguous for human prediction but misleading to the agent.

For **navigation**, we generate 3D adversarial perturbations that intentionally stop the agent, *i.e.*, make the agent predict *Stop* during the navigation process. As shown in Table 1, for both white-box and black-box attacks, the values of d_T and d_{min} significantly increase compared to the clean environment when adding our perturbations, especially for long-distance tasks, *i.e.*, T_{-50}. Further, the values of d_Δ decreases to around 0 after attack, which reveals that agents make a small number of movements to the destination. Also, some d_Δ even become negative, showing that the agent is moving away from the target.

To understand the transferability of attacks, we study attention similarities between models. The results can be found in the Supplementary Material.

In a word, our generated 3D adversarial perturbations achieve strong attack performance in both the white-box and black-box settings for navigation and problem-solving in the embodied environment.

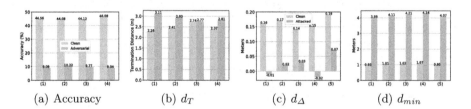

| (a) Accuracy | (b) d_T | (c) d_Δ | (d) d_{min} |

Fig. 4. Method (1) to (4) represents PACMAN, NAV-GRU, NAV-React and VIS-VGG, respectively. Our framework generates adversarial perturbations with strong transferabilities to non-differentiable renderers.

5.5   Transfer Attack onto a Non-differentiable Renderer

Our proposed framework aims to adversarially attack $\mathbb{F}_\theta(\mathbb{R}_\delta(\mathbf{x}_1, \mathbf{x}_2, ..., \mathbf{x}_n))$ by end-to-end gradient-based optimization. In this section, we further examine the potential of our framework in practice, where no assumptions about the non-differentiable renderer are given. By enabling interreflection and rich illumination, non-differentiable renderers can render images at high computational cost, so that the rendered 2D image is more likely to be an estimate of real-world physics. Thus, these experiments are effective to illustrate the transferability of generated adversarial perturbations and their potential in practical scenarios.

Specifically, we use the original non-differentiable renderer $\mathcal{R}$ for EQA-V1, which is implemented on OpenGL with unknown parameters, as the black-box renderer. We first generate 3D adversarial perturbations using our neural renderer $\mathbb{R}_\delta$, then save the perturbed scenes. We evaluate agent performance through the non-differentiable renderer $\mathcal{R}$ on those perturbed scenes to test the transferability of our adversarial perturbations.

As shown in Fig. 4, our spatiotemporal attacks can easily be transferred to a black-box renderer. However, our generated adversarial perturbations are less effective at attacking the non-differentiable renderer compared to the neural renderer. Many recent studies have reported that attacking the 3D space is much more difficult than attacking the image space [38,42]. Further, we believe there are three other reasons for this phenomenon: (1) To generate attacks for the non-differentiable renderer, we first generate 3D adversarial perturbations using a differentiable renderer, then save the perturbed scenes into OBJ, MTL, and JPG files (the required files of the non-differentiable renderer to render a 3D scene) and feed them to the renderer. The information loss comes from the JPG compression process, which may decrease the attack success rate. (2) The parameter difference between $\mathbb{R}_\delta$ and $\mathcal{R}$ may causes some minute rendering differences for the same scenarios. As adversarial examples are very sensitive to image transformations [16,39], the attacking ability is impaired; (3) The adversarial perturbation generated by optimization-based or gradient-based methods fails to obtain strong transferability due to either overfitting or underfitting [10].

5.6   Generalization Ability of the Attack

In this section, we further investigate the generalization ability of our generated adversarial perturbations. Given questions and trajectories, we first perturb the objects and save the scene. Then, loading the same perturbed scene, we ask agents different questions and change their start points to test their performance.

We first use the same perturbations on **different questions** (denoted as "Q"). We fix the object in questions during perturbation generation and test to be the same. For example, we generate the perturbations based on question *"What is the color of the table in the living-room?"* and test the success rate on question *"What is next to the table in the living-room?"*. Moreover, we use the same perturbations to test agents from **different starting points** (*i.e.*, different

Table 2. Generalization ability experiments. Our 3D perturbations generalize well in settings using different questions and starting points.

	QA accuracy		
	T_{10}	T_{30}	T_{50}
Clean	51.42%	42.68%	39.15%
Attack	6.05%	3.98%	3.52%
Q	10.17%	8.13%	7.98%
T	8.19%	7.26%	7.14%

trajectories, denoted as "T"). We first generate the perturbations and then test them by randomly spawning agents at different starting points (*i.e.*, random rooms and locations) under the same questions. As shown in Table 2, the attacking ability drops a little compared to the baseline attack (generate perturbation and test at the scene with the same questions and starting point, denoted as

"Attack") in both setting with higher QA accuracy but still very strong, which indicates the strong generalization ability of our spatiotemporal perturbations.

5.7   Improving Agent Robustness with Adversarial Training

Given the vulnerability of existing embodied agents with the presence of adversarial attacks, we study defense strategies to improve the agent robustness. In particular, we base our defense on adversarial training [14,27,36], where we integrate our generated adversarial examples for model training.

Training. We train 2 PACMAN models augmented with adversarial examples (*i.e.*, we generate 3D adversarial perturbations on object textures, denoted as *AT*) or Gaussian noises (denoted as *GT*), respectively. We apply the common adversarial training strategy that adds a fixed number of adversarial examples in each epoch [1,14], and we defer more details in the supplementary material.

Testing. We create a test set of 110 questions in 5 houses. Following [14, 17], we add different common noises including adversarial perturbations and Gaussian noises. To conduct fair comparisons, adversarial perturbations are generated in the white-box setting (*e.g.*, for our adversarially trained model, we generate adversarial perturbations

Table 3. Agent robustness in scenes with different noises. Adversarial training provides the most robust agent.

	QA		Navigation	
	Adv	Gaussian	Adv	Gaussian
Vanilla	5.67%	22.14%	1.39	1.20
GT	8.49%	32.90%	1.32	1.09
AT	**23.56%**	**38.87%**	**1.17**	**1.01**

against it). The results in Table 3 support the fact that training on our adversarial perturbations can improve the agent robustness towards some types of noises (*i.e.*, higher QA accuracy, and lower d_T).

5.8   Ablation Study

Next, we present a set of ablation studies to further demonstrate the effectiveness of our proposed strategy through different hyper-parameters K and M, *i.e.*, different numbers of historical scene views and contextual objects considered. All experiments in this section are conducted on T_{-30}.

Historical Scene Views Numbers. As for K, we set $K = 1, 2, 3, 4, 5$, with a maximum value of $M = 5$. For a fair comparison, we set the overall magnitude of perturbations to 32/255. As shown in Fig. 5 (a), for navigation, we nearly obtain the optimal attack success rate when $K = 3$. The results are similar to the question answering. However, the attack ability does not

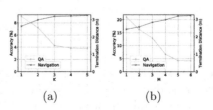

(a)   (b)

Fig. 5. Ablation study with different K and M values in (a) and (b).

increase as significantly as that for navigation when increasing K. Obviously,

(a)   (b)

Fig. 6. Visualization of last 5 views and corresponding attention maps. (a) denotes the locational and compositional question, and (b) denotes the color-related question.

the agent mainly depends on the target object and contextual objects to answer the questions. The contextual objects to be perturbed are quite similar to the increasing number of historical scene views considered.

Contextual Objects Numbers. As for M, we set $M = 1, 2, 3, 4, 5, 6$ and $K = 3$ to evaluate the contribution of the context to adversarial attacks. Similarly, we set the overall magnitude of adversarial perturbations to $32/255$ for adversarial attacks with different M values, *i.e.*, perturbations are added onto a single object or distributed to several contextual objects. As shown in Fig. 5(b), the attack success rate increases significantly with the increasing of M and converges at around 5. The reason is the maximum number of objects observable in 3 frames is around 5 or 6. Further, by considering the type of questions, we could obtain a deeper understanding about how an agent makes predictions. For questions about location and composition, *e.g.*, "*What room is the $<OBJ>$ located in?*" and "*What is on the $<OBJ>$ in the $<ROOM>$?*", the attack success rate using context outperforms single object attack significantly with 4.67% and 28.51%, respectively. However, attacks on color-related questions are only 3.56% and 9.88% after contextual attack and single object attack, respectively. Intuitively, agents rely on different information to solve different types of questions. According to the attention visualization study shown in Fig. 6, agents generally utilize clues from contextual objects to answer locational and compositional questions while mainly focus on target objects when predicting their colors.

6   Conclusion

In this paper, we generate spatiotemporal perturbations to form 3D adversarial examples, which could attack the embodiment. Regarding the temporal dimension, we develop a trajectory attention module to explore scene view contributions, which further help localize 3D objects appeared with highest stimuli. By conciliating with clues from the temporal dimension, along the spatial dimension, we adversarially perturb the physical properties (*e.g.*, texture) of the contextual objects that appeared in the most important scene views. Extensive experiments on the EQA-v1 dataset for several embodied tasks in both the white-box and black-box settings are conducted, which demonstrate that our framework has strong attack and generalization abilities.

Currently, most embodied tasks could only be evaluated in the simulated environment. In the future, we are interested in performing spatiotemporal attacks in real-world scenarios. Using projection or 3D printing, we could bring our perturbations into the real-world to attack a real agent.

Acknowledgement. This work was supported by National Natural Science Foundation of China (61872021, 61690202), Beijing Nova Program of Science and Technology(Z191100001119050), Fundamental Research Funds for Central Universities (YWF-20-BJ-J-646), and ARC FL-170100117.

References

1. Alexey, K., Ian, G., Samy, B.: Adversarial machine learning at scale. In: International Conference on Learning Representations (2017)
2. Athalye, A., Carlini, N., Wagner, D.: Obfuscated gradients give a false sense of security: Circumventing defenses to adversarial examples. arXiv preprint arXiv:1802.00420 (2018)
3. Athalye, A., Engstrom, L., Ilyas, A., Kwok, K.: Synthesizing robust adversarial examples. arXiv preprint arXiv:1707.07397 (2017)
4. Bellemare, M.G., Naddaf, Y., Veness, J., Bowling, M.: The arcade learning environment: An evaluation platform for general agents. J. Artif. Intell. Res. **47**, 253–279 (2013)
5. Brown, T.B., Mané, D., Roy, A., Abadi, M., Gilmer, J.: Adversarial patch. arXiv preprint arXiv:1712.09665 (2017)
6. Carlone, L., Karaman, S.: Attention and anticipation in fast visual-inertial navigation. IEEE Trans. Robot. **35**, 1–20 (2018)
7. Chen, W., Zhang, Z., Hu, X., Wu, B.: Boosting decision-based black-box adversarial attacks with random sign flip. In: Proceedings of the European Conference on Computer Vision (2020)
8. Das, A., Datta, S., Gkioxari, G., Lee, S., Parikh, D., Batra, D.: Embodied question answering. In: IEEE Conference on Computer Vision and Pattern Recognition (2018)
9. Das, A., Gkioxari, G., Lee, S., Parikh, D., Batra, D.: Neural modular control for embodied question answering. arXiv preprint arXiv:1810.11181 (2018)
10. Dong, Y., Liao, F., Pang, T., Su, H.: Boosting adversarial attacks with momentum. In: IEEE Conference on Computer Vision and Pattern Recognition (2018)
11. Gao, L., Zhang, Q., Song, J., Liu, X., Shen, H.: Patch-wise attack for fooling deep neural network. In: European Conference on Computer Vision (2020)
12. Garland-Thomson, R.: Staring: how we look. Oxford University Press, Oxford
13. Gleave, A., Dennis, M., Kant, N., Wild, C., Levine, S., Russell, S.A.: Adversarial policies: Attacking deep reinforcement learning. In: International Conference on Learning Representations (2020)
14. Goodfellow, I.J., Shlens, J., Szegedy, C.: Explaining and harnessing adversarial examples (2014). arXiv preprint arXiv:1412.6572 (2014)
15. Gordon, D., Kembhavi, A., Rastegari, M., Redmon, J., Fox, D., Farhadi, A.: IQA: visual question answering in interactive environments. In: IEEE Conference on Computer Vision and Pattern Recognition (2018)
16. Guo, C., Rana, M., Cisse, M., Van Der Maaten, L.: Countering adversarial images using input transformations. arXiv preprint arXiv:1711.00117 (2017)

17. Hendrycks, D., Dietterich, T.: Benchmarking neural network robustness to common corruptions and perturbations. In: International Conference on Learning Representations (2019)
18. Huang, S.H., Papernot, N., Goodfellow, I.J., Duan, Y., Abbeel, P.: Adversarial attacks on neural network policies. arXiv preprint arXiv: 1702.02284 (2017)
19. Kato, H., Ushiku, Y., Harada, T.: Neural 3D mesh renderer. In: IEEE Conference on Computer Vision and Pattern Recognition (2018)
20. Kolve, E., et al.: AI2-THOR: An interactive 3D environment for visual AI. arXiv preprint arXiv:1712.05474 (2017)
21. Kos, J., Song, D.X.: Delving into adversarial attacks on deep policies. arXiv preprint arXiv: 1705.06452 (2017)
22. Krizhevsky, A., Sutskever, I., Hinton, G.E.: Imagenet classification with deep convolutional neural networks. In: International Conference on Neural Information Processing Systems (2012)
23. Lin, Y.C., Hong, Z.W., Liao, Y.H., Shih, M.L., Liu, M.Y., Sun, M.: Tactics of adversarial attack on deep reinforcement learning agents. In: IJCAI (2017)
24. Liu, A., et al.: Perceptual-sensitive GAN for generating adversarial patches. In: 33rd AAAI Conference on Artificial Intelligence (2019)
25. Liu, A., Wang, J., Liu, X., Cao, b., Zhang, C., Yu, H.: Bias-based universal adversarial patch attack for automatic check-out. In: European Conference on Computer Vision (2020)
26. Liu, H.T.D., Tao, M., Li, C.L., Nowrouzezahrai, D., Jacobson, A.: Beyond pixel norm-balls: Parametric adversaries using an analytically differentiable renderer (2019)
27. Madry, A., Makelov, A., Schmidt, L., Tsipras, D., Vladu, A.: Towards deep learning models resistant to adversarial attacks. arXiv preprint arXiv:1706.06083 (2017)
28. Mohamed, A.R., Dahl, G.E., Hinton, G.: Acoustic modeling using deep belief networks. IEEE Trans. Audio Speech Lang. Process. 20, 14–22 (2011)
29. Mopuri, K.R., Ganeshan, A., Radhakrishnan, V.B.: Generalizable data-free objective for crafting universal adversarial perturbations. IEEE Trans. Pattern Anal. Mach. Intel. 41, 2452–2465 (2018)
30. Papernot, N., McDaniel, P., Goodfellow, I., Jha, S., Celik, Z.B., Swami, A.: Practical black-box attacks against deep learning systems using adversarial examples. arXiv preprint (2016)
31. Pattanaik, A., Tang, Z., Liu, S., Bommannan, G., Chowdhary, G.: Robust deep reinforcement learning with adversarial attacks. In: AAMAS (2018)
32. Selvaraju, R.R., Cogswell, M., Das, A., Vedantam, R., Parikh, D., Batra, D.: Gradcam: Visual explanations from deep networks via gradient-based localization. In: IEEE International Conference on Computer Vision (2017)
33. Smith, L., Gasser, M.: The development of embodied cognition: six lessons from babies. Artif. Life 11(1–2), 13–29 (2005)
34. Sutskever, I., Vinyals, O., Le, Q.: Sequence to sequence learning with neural networks. In: NeurIPS (2014)
35. Szegedy, C., et al.: Intriguing properties of neural networks. arXiv preprint arXiv:1312.6199 (2013)
36. Tu, Z., Zhang, J., Tao, D.: Theoretical analysis of adversarial learning: a minimax approach. In: Advances in Neural Information Processing Systems (2019)
37. Wijmans, E., et al.: Embodied question answering in photorealistic environments with point cloud perception. In: IEEE Conference on Computer Vision and Pattern Recognition (2019)

38. Xiao, C., Yang, D., Li, B., Deng, J., Liu, M.: Meshadv: adversarial meshes for visual recognition. In: IEEE Conference on Computer Vision and Pattern Recognition (2019)
39. Xie, C., Wang, J., Zhang, Z., Ren, Z., Yuille, A.: Mitigating adversarial effects through randomization. arXiv preprint arXiv:1711.01991 (2017)
40. Yang, J., et al.: Embodied visual recognition. In: IEEE International Conference on Computer Vision (2019)
41. Yu, L., Chen, X., Gkioxari, G., Bansal, M., Berg, T.L., Batra, D.: Multi-target embodied question answering. In: IEEE Conference on Computer Vision and Pattern Recognition (2019)
42. Zeng, X., et al.: Adversarial attacks beyond the image space. In: IEEE Conference on Computer Vision and Pattern Recognition (2019)
43. Zhang, T., Zhu, Z.: Interpreting adversarially trained convolutional neural networks. arXiv preprint arXiv:1905.09797 (2019)
44. Zhang, Y., Foroosh, H., David, P., Gong, B.: Camou: earning physical vehicle camouflages to adversarially attack detectors in the wild. In: International Conference on Learning Representations (2019)

Caption-Supervised Face Recognition: Training a State-of-the-Art Face Model Without Manual Annotation

Qingqiu Huang[1]([✉]) [iD], Lei Yang[1] [iD], Huaiyi Huang[1] [iD], Tong Wu[2] [iD], and Dahua Lin[1] [iD]

[1] The Chinese University of Hong Kong, Hong Kong, China
{hq016,yl016,hh016,dhlin}@ie.cuhk.edu.hk
[2] Tsinghua Univerisity, Beijing, China
wutong16.thu@gmail.com

Abstract. The advances over the past several years have pushed the performance of face recognition to an amazing level. This great success, to a large extent, is built on top of millions of annotated samples. However, as we endeavor to take the performance to the next level, the reliance on annotated data becomes a major obstacle. We desire to explore an alternative approach, namely using captioned images for training, as an attempt to mitigate this difficulty. Captioned images are widely available on the web, while the captions often contain the names of the subjects in the images. Hence, an effective method to leverage such data would significantly reduce the need of human annotations. However, an important challenge along this way needs to be tackled: the names in the captions are often noisy and ambiguous, especially when there are multiple names in the captions or multiple people in the photos. In this work, we propose a simple yet effective method, which trains a face recognition model by progressively expanding the labeled set via both selective propagation and caption-driven expansion. We build a large-scale dataset of captioned images, which contain $6.3M$ faces from $305K$ subjects. Our experiments show that using the proposed method, we can **train a state-of-the-art face recognition model without manual annotation** (99.65% in LFW). This shows the great potential of caption-supervised face recognition.

1 Introduction

Recent years have seen remarkable advances in face recognition [7,39,42,47,49, 51]. However, state-of-the-art face recognition models are primarily trained on large-scale annotated datasets [5,12,23], which is becoming a major problem as we pursue further improvement. Obtaining massive amount of accurately annotated data has never been a trivial task. As the scale increases, the cost of annotation, the difficulty in quality control, and the ambiguities faced by the annotators gradually approaches a prohibitive level.

© Springer Nature Switzerland AG 2020
A. Vedaldi et al. (Eds.): ECCV 2020, LNCS 12362, pp. 139–155, 2020.
https://doi.org/10.1007/978-3-030-58520-4_9

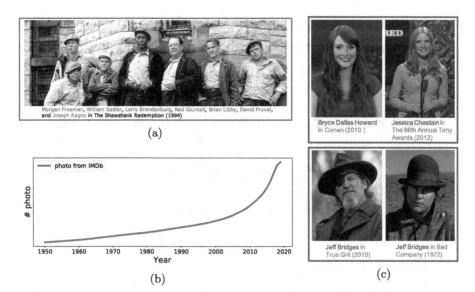

Fig. 1. Captions are often provided by those people who are familiar with the subjects in the photos. The first row shows that captions are often accurate even for difficult cases, *e.g.* different subjects that look similar or an subject that looks differently. The second row shows a key challenge of caption-supervised learning, namely multi-to-multi associations.

An effective way to mitigate this heavy reliance on manual annotations has therefore become a common quest of the community. Semi-automatic schemes have been explored in the development of some large-scale datasets, *e.g.* using search engines [5,12] and clustering with a trained model [23]. However, it has been observed that the noises and bias introduced by these schemes significantly hurt the performance [38].

In this paper, we explore an alternative approach to addressing this problem, namely, to exploit the tremendous amount of captioned images available on the web. This is motivated by the observation that the captions of the photos with people often contain the names of the subjects. These names can provide valuable supervisory signals for training face recognition models. It is also worth noting that in addition to the large quantity, captioned images have another important advantage – the names in the captions are often very accurate even for images that are very difficult to be distinguished visually, as illustrated in Fig. 1. This is partly ascribed to the fact that the captions are usually provided by "experts", *i.e.* those people who are familiar with the subjects in the photos or the underlying stories.

While it sounds appealing, training a face recognition model based on caption images is indeed a very challenging task. The key challenge lies in *inexact labels*, *i.e.* a label may be corresponding to one of the several instances in a photo or none of them. Inexact labels would arise when a photo contains more than

one faces or a caption contains more than one names. As we are exploring the setting without manual annotation, the associations between faces and names need to be resolved in a certain way, explicitly or implicitly. On the other hand, it is also noteworthy that this is not the same as a multi-instance learning (MIL) problem [30,40,43], as for a considerable portion of the cases, we have exactly one face in the photo and one name in the caption. Figure 2 how caption-supervised face recognition differs from other widely studied learning paradigms.

To tackle the challenges caused by inexact labels while fully exploiting the portion of samples with one-to-one correspondence, we propose a simple method that combines selective propagation with caption-driven expansion. Specifically, our method begins with those samples with one-to-one correspondence as initial labeled seeds, and iteratively expand the labeled set by propagating the labels to neighbors with selective criteria and reasoning about co-existing associations based on captions. We found that by leveraging both the learned feature space and the caption-based supervision, the labeled set can significantly grow while maintaining high accuracy in the inferred labels.

To facilitate this study, we construct a large-scale dataset named *MovieFace* by collecting movie photos and their captions. This dataset contains $6.3M$ faces with $305K$ identities, and the faces exhibit large variations in scale, pose, lighting, and are often subject to partial occlusion. Our model trained on this dataset **without any manual annotation** achieves competitive performance on MS1M [12], a widely used testbed for face recognition techniques. For example, a network with the ResNet-50 backbone [13] trained thereon achieves the accuracy of 99.65% in LFW [14].

Our contributions consist in three aspects: (1) We explore a new paradigm to train face recognition model without manual annotation, namely, caption-supervied training. (2) We develop a simple yet effective method for this, which exploits both the learned feature space and the caption-based supervision in an iterative label expansion process. (3) We construct a large dataset *MovieFaces* without manual annotation to support this study, and manage to train a state-of-the-art model thereon. Overall, this work demonstrates the great potential of caption-supervised face recognition and provides a promising way towards it.

2   Related Work

Semi-supervised Face Recognition. Some of the researchers are also concerned about the unaffordable annotation cost in face recognition and try to alleviate the challenges with the help of semi-supervised learning [33,48,51]. Roli *et al.* [33] employed a self-training strategy with multiple PCA-based classifiers, where the labels of unlabeled samples were inferred with an initial classifier and then added to augment the labeled set. Zhao *et al.* [53] took LDA [2] as the classifier under a similar self-training scheme. Gao *et al.* [10] developed a semi-supervised sparse representation-based approach by modeling both linear and non-linear variation between the labeled and unlabeled samples. Zhan *et al.* [51] proposed a consensus-driven propagation algorithm to assign pseudo labels with

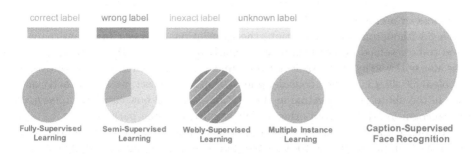

Fig. 2. Comparison of different learning problems and our Caption-Supervised Face Recognition (CSFR). In CSFR, photos contain only one face and one mentioned name can be taken as samples with correct labels and others are with inexact labels.

the help of a constructed relational graph. Although some of these methods are claimed to achieve great performance with only a few labeled samples [51], they are usually tested on some artificial benchmarks modified from fully-labeled datasets, the distribution of which is not natural. The caption-supervised face recognition proposed in this work is much more practical and effective, which would be shown in Sect. 5.

Webly-Supervised Face Recognition. Webly-Supervised Learning(WSL) leverages raw data from the Internet and needs no human annotation [11,21]. While the scale of training sources can be easily expanded in this case, massive data noise has become the bottleneck to the classification performance [45]. Efforts have been devoted to addressing the problem from different angles. Some proposed robust algorithms to learn directly against noisy data, as Patrini *et al.* [29] proposed a robust loss correction procedure and Rolnick *et al.* [34] explored the robustness of the DNN itself when enough examples are available. Others aimed to remove or correct mislabeled data as [3,21,36], while they suffer from distinguishing mislabelled examples from hard training examples. In the specific scenario of face recognition, where noise exists in nearly all the existing large-scale databases [38], a widely accepted solution is to adopt a cleaning procedure to improve the quality of large-scale face datasets [29] Gallo *et al.* [9] proposed a pipeline to improve face recognition systems based on Center loss. Jin *et al.* [22] proposed a graph-based cleaning method that employed the community detection algorithm to delete mislabeled images. Similar to us, Chen *et al.* [6] also made use of web sources and avoided human annotation, but they focused more on dealing with data noise by distinguishing the misclassifications with modification signal. In comparison to most WSL methods, our caption-supervised setting takes full advantage of the web data by transferring the issue of data noise to a multiple instance problem, leading to a breathtaking performance even with a simple approach.

Multiple Instance Learning. Multiple Instance Learning (MIL) has an especial yet practical setting that the instances and labels are provided in groups, respectively. It provides more information than semi-supervised manner yet lacks a accurate one-to-one mapping compared with fully-supervised manner. It was originally proposed for drug activity prediction [8] and are now widely applied to many domains [1]. Since a complete survey of MIL is out of the scope of this paper, here we only introduced some recent works based on deep networks. Most of the MIL works focus on how to aggregate the scores or the features of multiple instances [20,30,40,43]. Wu *et al.* [43] proposed to use max pooling for score aggregation, which aimed to find the positive instances or patches for image classification. Pinheiro *et al.* [30] used log-sum-exp pooling in a CNN for weakly supervised semantic segmentation. Wang *et al.* [40] summarized the aggregation module of previous works as MIL Pooling on instance scores. It then proposed MI-Net, which applied MIL Pooling to instance features with a deeply-supervised fashion. Instead of pooling, Ilse *et al.* [20] proposed an attention-based MIL Network, which used learnable weights for feature aggregation. Suffering from the same drawback that the information of the web data is provided by users, directly adopting MIL methods to data with an unstable quality would achieve much worse results compared to our approach, which would be shown in Sect. 5.

3   Methodology

To take full advantage of the caption supervision, we propose a framework named caption-supervised face recognition by progressively expanding the labeled samples. Specifically, we maintain a labeled set containing samples with correct labels and an unlabeled set with inexact samples during training. The labeled set would be iteratively enlarged by selective propagation and caption-driven expansion. The former aims to enlarge the number of instances with the help of a trained model. The latter would increase both identities and instances with by means of the caption supervision. Specifically, our framework consists of three stages, namely labeled set initialization, selective propagation and caption-driven expansion, as shown in Fig. 3. The last two stages would be run iteratively until converge, *i.e.* no extra samples can be added to the labeled set.

I. Labeled Set Initialization. Suppose that there are n faces $\{f_1, \cdots, f_n\}$ and m identites mentioned in the caption $\{y_1, \cdots, y_m\}$ in the a photo. Here $y_i \in \{1, \cdots, N\}, i \in \{1, \cdots, m\}$ and N is the total number of identities in the dataset. As we mentioned before, some photos contain just one face and one mentioned identity in its caption, which we name as "one2one" samples. Considering the high quality of the captions, we take the faces in "one2one" photos as labeled samples, namely

$$\mathcal{I}(f_n) = y_m, \quad \text{if } n = 1, m = 1$$

These samples would be used to initialize the labeled set.

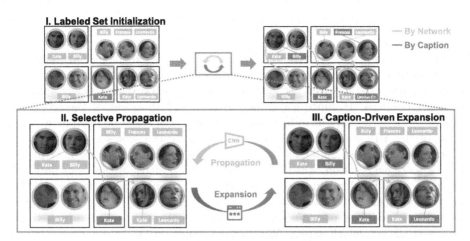

Fig. 3. Our framework for caption-supervised face recognition. It consists of three stages: (I). Initialize a labeled set with those samples containing just one face detected and one identity mentioned in the caption. (II). Then a network is trained on the labeled set and applied to the unlabeled samples. Samples (in orange) would be selected and added to the labeled set following such criterions: (1) with a high prediction score, and (2) the predicted identity is mentioned in the caption (III). We get more labels with the help of caption (in blue), *i.e.* we assign the identity to the face if only one face left in the photo and one identity left in the caption. By running stage II and III iteratively, we would finally propagate the labels to almost all the samples. (Colour figure online)

II. Selective Propagation. With the labeled set, we train a neural network in a fully-supervised manner, which would then be applied to the unlabeled faces. Here we denote the predition score of an unlabeled face f_i as $\mathbf{p}_i \in \mathcal{R}^{\bar{N}}$, where $\bar{N}$ is the number of identities in the labeled set and $\bar{N} \leq N$. At the propagation stage, a face would be labeled under the following criterions: (1) the predicted identity is mentioned in the caption, and (2) the prediction score is higher than a threshold τ, as shown in Eq. 1

$$\mathcal{I}(f_i) = k, \quad \text{if} \begin{cases} \text{argmax}(\mathbf{p}_i) = k \\ k \in \{y_1, \cdots, y_m\} \\ p_{ik} > \tau \end{cases} \tag{1}$$

Since the trained model is incapable of predicting unseen persons, only the number of samples in the labeled set would be increased in a selective manner while the number of identities would remain constant at this stage.

III. Caption-driven Expansion. Here we make a reasonable assumption that if there are only one unlabeled face and one unassigned identity in a photo, then the label of the face should be the left identity. After some of the faces are labeled at stage II, there would be some photos with only one unlabeled face and one mentioned identity left. Base on the assumption, the face would be labeled, as

shown in Eq. 2, where $\mathcal{U}$ denotes the filter to get the unlabeled ones from a face or identity set.

$$\mathcal{I}(f_i) = y_j, \quad \text{if} \begin{cases} \mathcal{U}(\{f_1, \cdots, f_n\}) = f_i \\ \mathcal{U}(\{y_1, \cdots, y_n\}) = y_j \end{cases} \tag{2}$$

At this stage, the number of the identities as well as the number of the samples in the labeled set would increase, and the driving force comes from the information extracted from caption. After new identities are added, i.e. the labeled set is enlarged, we would finetune the model with the whole labeled set, which contains both old samples and newly added identities.

The proposed framework is so simple that can be reimplemented easily. More importantly, it works well surprisingly on the caption-supervised datasets, even outperforming a model trained on a fully-supervised dataset like MS1M [12], the results of which would be demonstrated in Sect. 5. However, there are also some imperfections with the proposed framework, which would also be discussed in Sect. 5 to benefit the further explorations.

4   Dataset

Table 1. Comparison between datasets for face recognition.

Dataset	# ID	# face	# annotation
LFW [14]	5K	13K	Automatic
CelebFaces [37]	10K	202K	Manually
IMDb-Face [38]	59K	1.7M	Manually
CASIA [50]	10K	500K	Semi-automatic
VGGFace2 [5]	9K	3.3M	Semi-automatic
MS1Mv2 [7,12]	85K	5.8M	Semi-automatic
MegaFace [23]	670K	4.7M	Automatic
MovieFace	305K	6.3M	Caption

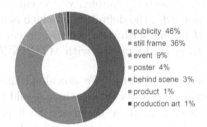

- publicity 46%
- still frame 36%
- event 9%
- poster 4%
- behind scene 3%
- product 1%
- production art 1%

Fig. 4.   Different types of photo in MovieFace.

Datasets play an important role in most of the researches in computer vision [4, 15,25]. Since there is no large-scale dataset to support caption-supervised face recognition, we build a dataset, namely MovieFace, in this paper. A comparison of some popular datasets for face recognition is shown in Table 1, from which we can see that our proposed dataset is competitive to the existing largest datasets, for both identities and faces. But our datasets would continuously grow without any manual efforts as shown in Fig. 1. More details of MovieFace would be introduced below. And note that MovieFace is a part of MovieNet [18], which is a holistic dataset that support various of research topics in person recogntion [16, 17,27,44,44], video analysis [19,31,32] and story understanding [35,46].

Leonardo DiCaprio and Kate Winslet in Titanic (1997)   Kate Winslet in Titanic (1997)   Leonardo DiCaprio, Kate Winslet, Billy Zane, and Frances Fisher in Titanic (1997)   James Cameron and Linda Hamilton at an event for Titanic (1997)   James Cameron, Leonardo DiCaprio, and Kate Winslet in Titanic (1997)

Fig. 5. Here we show some samples from MovieFace

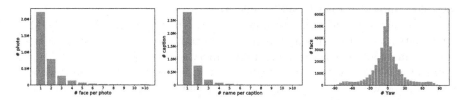

Fig. 6. Here we show some statistics of MovieFace including (a) number of faces per photo, (b) number of name entities per caption, and (c) the yaw distribution of faces.

Face Processing. We get different types of photos from IMDb[1] including "still frame", "poster", "publicity", "event", "behind the scenes", "product" and "production art", the definition of which can be seen in the description page[2]. Totally $3.9M$ photos with name entities in caption are downloaded. Then we detect all the faces in the photos with MTCNN [52], resulting in $6.3M$ faces detected.

Identity Processing. We download the caption of each photo. For each name mentioned in the caption, there would be a hyperlink to the person's homepage, which is created by the users. So it is easy for us to get the identities of the mentioned persons by the hyperlinks. There are $5.8M$ name entities appeared in the captions, belonging to $305K$ unique identities.

Dataset Statistic. We show the percentage of each type of photos in Fig. 4. Different types of photos would capture faces of a person under different situations, which would highly raise the diversity of the dataset. Some photos and captions from *Titanic* are shown in Fig. 5, from which we can also see the high quality and diversity of MovieFace. We further calculate the yaw of each face, the distributions of which are shown in Fig. 6. And one of the most critical factors for the caption-supervised setting is probably the number of faces per photo and the number of names per caption. If all the photos contain just one face and one mentioned name, then the caption-supervised problem would degenerate into a simple fully-supervised one. The less the faces per photo, the easier for us to train a powerful model. The distributions of the number of faces and the number of names are shown in Fig. 6. We can see that more than 50% of the photos

---

[1] https://www.imdb.com/.

[2] https://help.imdb.com/article/contribution/images-videos/imdb-image-faqs/ G64MGN2G43F42PES#.

contain just one face and more than 60% of the captions contain just one name, which would highly benefit the training process.

5 Experiments

5.1 Experiment Setting

We test our method on three benchmarks on face recognition/verification, which is the application that motivates this work. We not only compare it with various methods, but also investigate important design choices via a series of ablation studies.

Training Set. Following the convention in face recognition, we train networks on large training sets that are *completely disjoint* from the testing sets, namely the identities (*i.e.* classes) used for testing are excluded from the training set. Specifically, six large datasets below are used for training: **(1) MS-Celeb-1M** [12]. This dataset consists of $100K$ identities, each with about 100 facial images on average. In total, the dataset contains $10M$ images. As the original identity labels were extracted *automatically* from webpages and thus are very noisy. We clean up the annotations according to [7], resulting in a subset that contains $5.8M$ images from $86K$ classes. **(2) Megaface2** [23]. It contains $4.7M$ images from $672K$ identities. This dataset is automatically collected from the Internet and the distribution is very long-tail. **(3) IMDb-Face** [38], collects large-scale images for the IMDb website. It develops an effective way to clean the dataset and produces a noise-controlled dataset with $1.7M$ images from $59K$ identities. **(4) CASIA** [50]. This dataset uses the same source as IMDb-Face for data collection. In addition to images, it also collects tags for semi-automatic clean. Applying tag-constrained similarity clustering, it cleans the collected image prudently and result in a dataset contains $494,414$ images of $10,575$ subjects. **(5) MovieFace**. To facilitate the study in caption supervised face recognition, we also collect a large-scale face dataset from IMDb website. This dataset comprises $3.9M$ photos with corresponding captions. We detect $6.3M$ face images from photos and extract $305K$ identities from captions. Note that our collected dataset does not involve any manual annotations.

Testing Set. The trained networks are then evaluated on three testing sets: **(1) LFW** [14], the *de facto* standard testing set for face verification under unconstrained conditions, which contains $13,233$ face images from $5,749$ identities. **(2) IJB-A** [24], which contains $5,712$ face images from 500 identities. It partitions all pairs of face images into 10 disjoint sets, and the final result is the average of those obtained from individual partitions. **(3) Megaface & Facescrub**, the largest and most challenging public benchmark for face recognition, which combines the gallery sets from both Megaface [23] (with $1M$ images from $690K$ identities), and Facescrub [28] (with $100K$ images from 530 identities). Specifically, the evaluation is done as follows. In each testing, one image from each celebrity in Facescrub will be mixed into the Megaface gallery to form an augmented gallery set, while the remaining images will be used as queries. The

task is to identify the ones from the corresponding classes that were mixed into the gallery, among a large number of distractors from Megaface.

Metrics. We assess the performance on two tasks, namely *face identification* and *face verification*. Face identification is to select top k images from the gallery, where the performance is measured by the top-k hit rate, *i.e.* , the fraction of predictions where the true identity occurs in the top-k list. Face verification is to determine whether two given face images are from the same identity. We use a widely adopted metric [23,24] namely the true positive rate under the condition that the false positive rate is fixed to be 0.001.

Networks. We conducted two series of experiments, with different network architectures. First, to experiment over different training sets and loss functions within a reasonable budget, we use a modified ResNet-50 [13] with input size reduced to 112×112. To further study how different methods work with very deep networks, we conducted another series of experiments for selected methods using R-100 and ArcLoss [7], which achieves the state-of-the-art in face recognition benchmarks. For all settings, the networks are trained using SGD with momentum. The mini-batch sizes are set to 2,048 and 1,024 respectively for ResNet-50 and R-100.

5.2   Comparison to Fully Supervised Training

Table 2. Comparion of the Performance between Webly-Supervised and Fully-Supervised Face Recognition

Dataset	Softmax loss			Cosine loss			ArcFace		
	LFW	IJBA	MegaFace	LFW	IJBA	MegaFace	LFW	IJBA	MegaFace
MS1M	**99.52**	**88.24**	**84.44**	99.63	**91.93**	94.33	99.85	96.82	97.92
MegaFace2	98.35	55.48	53.47	98.75	79.94	66.81	99.28	86.60	84.75
IMDb-Face	98.70	73.21	73.02	99.37	84.17	79.99	99.65	94.25	94.81
CASIA	98.08	55.05	58.63	98.28	60.79	71.33	99.00	72.05	78.90
MovieFace	99.10	77.75	83.34	**99.65**	88.95	**95.44**	99.83	**96.96**	96.96

The results are shown in Table 2. MovieFace is trained by supervision of captions, which can be automatically collected from the web; While other datasets are trained under the supervision of labels, which are usually obtained by massive human annotations. Comparing the performance of models under different settings, we observe that: (1) The model trained on MovieFace yields comparable identification/verification accuracies with trained MS1M, for different loss functions and the ArcFace method; (2) Under all different settings, it consistently outperforms models trained on other three datasets, namely MegaFace2, IMDb-Face, and CASIA, by a large margin; (3) By applying the state-of-the-art method ArcFace on IJBA, it can further produce performance gain over MS1M

by 0.14 percent, despite the fact that no explicit annotation is offered when learned caption-supervised.

5.3 Comparison to SSL and MIL Methods

SSL Methods. We collect images that only have one face and one name item in their captions to form a training set S_1/One2One, where the face is labeled with the name item. To employ semi-supervised methods in our setting, we first regard the S_1 data as labeled data and use it to train a feature extractor. With the trained feature extractor, we extract features for all unlabeled images except S_1 and apply it in our scenario. To avoid the overlap between S_1 labels and pseudo labels, we adopt a multitask scheme for training, *i.e.* , there are two classifiers on top of the network for S_1 labels and pseudo labels respectively.

As unlabeled face images are likely to belong to an unseen identity, clustering are widely adopted to exploit unlabeled face data [41,49,51]. We study two clustering methods in our settings, namely K-means [26] and LTC [49]. K-means is the most widely used unsupervised clustering methods, while the recent proposed LTC introduces supervised clustering and shows its effectiveness in exploiting unlabeled face images. For K-means, we set the number of clusters to the total number of identities extracted from captions. For LTC [49], we use S_1 as the labeled set to train the clustering models.

The results in Table 3 shows that: (1) Compared with the model trained on S_1, K-means achieves comparable performance over three benchmarks. Relying on simple assumptions that all samples are distributed around a center, K-means may fail to handle the complex distribution in large-scale dataset in real-world setting, especially when the number of clusters is inaccurate. (2) LTC outperforms the model trained on S_1 consistently. Although it is more effective than K-means in exploiting large-scale unlabeled data, the improvement is limited. As a supervised method, LTC assumes the distribution between training set and testing set is similar. In our scenario, we take S_1 as the labeled data for training, but there is no guarantee that the remained unlabeled data has a similar distribution to S_1.

MIL Methods. Multiple Instance Learning (MIL) aims to train a model with samples annotated by a bag-level label. Comparing to fully-supervised learning where every instance is labeled with its category, a bag of instances is annotated with just one category in MIL, which means that at least one of the instance in the bag belongs the labeled category. A bag of faces are fed to a network and their features are aggregated in the last but one layer with MIL pooling. Existing method for MIL using neural network can be formulated as different kinds of MIL pooling [40]. We try 3 kinds of MIL pooling in this paper, namely average pooling, max pooling, and log-exp-sum pooling.

In addition to methods designed specifically for multiple instance learning, we also compare with an intuitive baseline. For an image with K labels, each instance on the image is assigned a soft label over the K classes, with the ground-

truth probability on each instance setting to $\frac{1}{K}$. It is similar to mean-pooling but do not require instances on an image appear in a batch during training.

As shown in Table 3, max-pooling achieves the best results. As the training proceeds, the features are more discriminative and thus the max-pooling may select the most prominent feature for supervision. As for mean-pooling, it eliminates the variance between different instances on an image, weakening the discriminative powers of features. Compared with SSL methods, the inferior performance of MIL-based approach indicates the importance of correctly predicting the unknown labels, especially in a fine-grained feature learning scenario like face recognition.

Table 3. (a). Comparison on the performance between our framework and some poplar methods in SSL and MIL in MovieFace. S_1 represents data of One2One. S_4 represents data with inexact labels. (b). Ablation of Different Stages in our Framework. $S_1/S_2/S_3$ repersents training data of One2One/Propogation/Expansion, respectively.

	method	LFW	IJBA	MegaFace
SSL	S_1	99.05	68.67	79.81
	K-means	99.01	67.57	79.9
	LTC	99.07	71.34	80.55
MIL	$S_1 + S_4$	97.83	45.31	70.2
	mean-pooling	97.85	45.22	69.62
	max-pooling	98.32	49.06	73.11
	LES-pooling	98.17	48.25	72.06
CSFR	ours	99.10	77.50	83.34

(a)

Data/Method	LFW	IJBA	MegaFace
S_1	99.05	68.67	79.81
$S_1 + S_2$	99.07	75.06	82.41
$S_1 + S_2 + S_3$	99.10	77.50	83.34
$S_2 + S_3$	98.57	69.99	69.52

(b)

5.4 Ablation Study and Discussion

The Quality of Data Propogation and Expansion. As illustrated in Table 3b, by adding propagation data where more faces for existing identities are labeled (*i.e.* $S_1 + S_2$), the model brings a performance gain from 79.81 to 82.41 in MegaFace; by further considering expansion data where faces of new identities are tagged (*i.e.* $S_1 + S_2 + S_3$), the model receives further performance gain. As shown in Fig. 7b, the annotated data increases from 51% to 90% with one round of label propagation and label expansion. To evaluate the performance of annotated data, we only use the annotated data to train a face recognition model. As Table 3b illustrates, the annotated data itself (*i.e.* $S_2 + S_3$) achieves comparable result as S_1.

Relation Between Face Recognition Model and the Year. We investigate the relation between the performance of face recognition model and the year. The key variant is the number of collected images. As shown in Fig. 1, this data source continuously growing every year, the performance of face recognition benefits

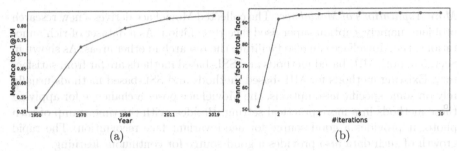

(a)   (b)

Fig. 7. (a). MegaFace top-1 Identification@1M. vs. year. As the increase of photos with captions, the performance face recognition has been remarkably boosted. (b). Ratio of annotated face images vs. iterations. After the second round of iteration, around 90% of face has been assigned a label, indicating the effectiveness of our label expansion algorithm.

Tom Hanks **and** Michael Clarke Duncan **in The Green Mile (1999)**   Joaquin Phoenix **in Joker (2019)**

Fig. 8. Some noisy cases in caption-supervised face recognition.

from the increase of the images. With the proposed method, we effectively leverage the photos with captions and greatly boost the performance of the face recognition model. Figure 1 illustrates the data source showing an exponential growth in recent years, indicating the potential improvement space of the proposed method.

Noisy Cases. Since the caption supervision is not specially designed for face recognition, it may sometimes introduce noise. Some noisy cases of MovieFace are shown in Fig. 8. 1) Usually, a website user would only mention the persons that he pays attention to. For example, the policeman in the background is ignored in this photo. What's worse, the prisoner is annotated even though his face is invisible. Therefore, it is easy for our model to wrongly associate the prisoner's name with the policeman in the background. 2) Since the user writing the caption with a strong context, they can correctly annotate some extremely hard cases, *e.g.* a face with heavy makeup. However, forcing the model to learn from such noisy cases may impair the performance.

More Applications of MovieFace. The collected MovieFace derives a new research problem, namely, caption supervised face recognition. As a dataset of rich annotations, the MovieFace can also facilitate the research in other areas. As shown in Sect. 5.3, both MIL-based methods and SSL-based methods are far from satisfactory. Existing methods for MIL-based methods and SSL-based methods usually rely on some specific assumptions, the MovieFace poses a challenge for applying these methods in a more practical setting. Besides, with the time stamp of each photo, it provides a good source for age-invariant face recognition. The rapid growth of such data also provides a good source for continuous learning.

6   Conclusion

In this paper, we address a meaningful research topic named caption-supervised face recognition. It aims to train a face recognizer with the millions of web images with captions, which are free and continuously growing. We build a large-scale dataset named MovieFace, containing more than $6.3M$ faces from $305K$ identities, to support this research topic. With the proposed dataset, we demonstrate that we can train a state-of-the-art face model without any manual annotation by a simple approach, which shows the immeasurable potential of this topic. Also, extensive experiments and analyses are executed to promote further researches on caption-supervised face recognition.

Acknowledgment. This work is partially supported by the SenseTime Collaborative Grant on Large-scale Multi-modality Analysis (CUHK Agreement No. TS1610626 & No. TS1712093), the General Research Fund (GRF) of Hong Kong (No. 14203518 & No. 14205719), and Innovation and Technology Support Program (ITSP) Tier 2, ITS/431/18F.

References

1. Amores, J.: Multiple instance classification: review, taxonomy and comparative study. Artif. Intell. **201**, 81–105 (2013)
2. Blei, D.M., Ng, A.Y., Jordan, M.I.: Latent dirichlet allocation. J. Mach. Learn. Res. **3**, 993–1022 (2003)
3. Brodley, C.E., Friedl, M.A.: Identifying mislabeled training data. CoRR (2011)
4. Caba Heilbron, F., Escorcia, V., Ghanem, B., Carlos Niebles, J.: Activitynet: a large-scale video benchmark for human activity understanding. In: Proceedings of the IEEE Conference on Computer Vision and Pattern Recognition, pp. 61–970 (2015)
5. Cao, Q., Shen, L., Xie, W., Parkhi, O.M., Zisserman, A.: Vggface2: A dataset for recognising faces across pose and age. In: IEEE International Conference on Automatic Face & Gesture Recognition (FG 2018) (2018)
6. Chen, B., Deng, W.: Weakly-supervised deep self-learning for face recognition. In: IEEE International Conference on Multimedia and Expo, ICME (2016)
7. Deng, J., Guo, J., Xue, N., Zafeiriou, S.: Arcface: Additive angular margin loss for deep face recognition. In: Proceedings of IEEE Conference on Computer Vision and Pattern Recognition (CVPR) (2019)

8. Dietterich, T.G., Lathrop, R.H., Lozano-Pérez, T.: Solving the multiple instance problem with axis-parallel rectangles. Artif. Intell. **89**, 1–2 (1997)

9. Gallo, I., Nawaz, S., Calefati, A., Piccoli, G.: A pipeline to improve face recognition datasets and applications. In: International Conference on Image and Vision Computing New Zealand, IVCNZ (2018)

10. Gao, Y., Ma, J., Yuille, A.L.: Semi-supervised sparse representation based classification for face recognition with insufficient labeled samples. IEEE Trans. Image Process. **26**, 2545–2560 (2017)

11. Guo, S., et al.: Curriculumnet: Weakly supervised learning from large-scale web images. Lecture Notes in Computer Science (2018)

12. Guo, Y., Zhang, L., Hu, Y., He, X., Gao, J.: MS-Celeb-1M: a dataset and benchmark for large-scale face recognition. In: Leibe, B., Matas, J., Sebe, N., Welling, M. (eds.) ECCV 2016, Part III. LNCS, vol. 9907, pp. 87–102. Springer, Cham (2016). https://doi.org/10.1007/978-3-319-46487-9_6

13. He, K., Zhang, X., Ren, S., Sun, J.: Deep residual learning for image recognition. In: Proceedings of IEEE Conference on Computer Vision and Pattern Recognition (CVPR) (2016)

14. Huang, G.B., Mattar, M., Berg, T., Learned-Miller, E.: Labeled faces in the wild: A database for studying face recognition in unconstrained environments (2008)

15. Huang, H., Zhang, Y., Huang, Q., Guo, Z., Liu, Z., Lin, D.: Placepedia: comprehensive place understanding with multi-faceted annotations. In: Proceedings of the European Conference on Computer Vision (ECCV) (2020)

16. Bosetti, G., Firmenich, S., Rossi, G., Winckler, M., Barbieri, T.: Web objects ambient: an integrated platform supporting new kinds of personal web experiences. In: Bozzon, A., Cudre-Maroux, P., Pautasso, C. (eds.) ICWE 2016. LNCS, vol. 9671, pp. 563–566. Springer, Cham (2016). https://doi.org/10.1007/978-3-319-38791-8_49

17. Huang, Q., Xiong, Y., Lin, D.: Unifying identification and context learning for person recognition. In: The IEEE Conference on Computer Vision and Pattern Recognition (CVPR) (2018)

18. Huang, Q., Xiong, Y., Rao, A., Wang, J., Lin, D.: Movienet: A holistic dataset for movie understanding. In: Proceedings of the European Conference on Computer Vision (ECCV) (2020)

19. Huang, Q., Xiong, Y., Xiong, Y., Zhang, Y., Lin, D.: From trailers to storylines: An efficient way to learn from movies. arXiv preprint arXiv:1806.05341 (2018)

20. Ilse, M., Tomczak, J.M., Welling, M.: Attention-based deep multiple instance learning. arXiv preprint arXiv:1802.04712 (2018)

21. Jiang, L., Zhou, Z., Leung, T., Li, L., Fei-Fei, L.: Mentornet: Regularizing very deep neural networks on corrupted labels. CoRR (2017)

22. Jin, C., Jin, R., Chen, K., Dou, Y.: A community detection approach to cleaning extremely large face database. Comp. Int. Neurosc. **4**, 24 (2018)

23. Kemelmacher-Shlizerman, I., Seitz, S.M., Miller, D., Brossard, E.: The megaface benchmark: 1 million faces for recognition at scale. In: Proceedings of the IEEE Conference on Computer Vision and Pattern Recognition (CVPR) (2016)

24. Klare, B.F., et al.: Pushing the frontiers of unconstrained face detection and recognition: Iarpa janus benchmark a. In: Proceedings of IEEE Conference on Computer Vision and Pattern Recognition (CVPR) (2015)

25. Krizhevsky, A., Sutskever, I., Hinton, G.E.: Imagenet classification with deep convolutional neural networks. In: Advances in Neural Information Processing Systems, pp. 1097–1105 (2012)

26. Lloyd, S.: Least squares quantization in PCM. IEEE Trans. Inf. Theory **28**, 129–137 (1982)
27. Loy, C.C., et al.: Wider face and pedestrian challenge 2018: Methods and results. arXiv preprint arXiv:1902.06854 (2019)
28. Ng, H.W., Winkler, S.: A data-driven approach to cleaning large face datasets. In: ICIP (2014)
29. Patrini, G., Rozza, A., Menon, A.K., Nock, R., Qu, L.: Making deep neural networks robust to label noise: a loss correction approach. In: Proceedings of the IEEE Conference on Computer Vision and Pattern Recognition (CVPR) (2017)
30. Pinheiro, P.O., Collobert, R.: From image-level to pixel-level labeling with convolutional networks. In: Proceedings of the IEEE Conference on Computer Vision and Pattern Recognition (CVPR) (2015)
31. Rao, A., et al.: A unified framework for shot type classification based on subject centric lens. In: Proceedings of the European Conference on Computer Vision (ECCV) (2020)
32. Rao, A., et al.: A local-to-global approach to multi-modal movie scene segmentation. In: Proceedings of the IEEE/CVF Conference on Computer Vision and Pattern Recognition (2020)
33. Roli, F., Marcialis, G.L.: Semi-supervised PCA-based face recognition using self-training. In: Yeung, D.-Y., Kwok, J.T., Fred, A., Roli, F., de Ridder, D. (eds.) SSPR /SPR 2006. LNCS, vol. 4109, pp. 560–568. Springer, Heidelberg (2006). https://doi.org/10.1007/11815921_61
34. Rolnick, D., Veit, A., Belongie, S.J., Shavit, N.: Deep learning is robust to massive label noise. CoRR (2017)
35. Shao, D., Xiong, Yu., Zhao, Y., Huang, Q., Qiao, Yu., Lin, D.: Find and focus: retrieve and localize video events with natural language queries. In: Ferrari, V., Hebert, M., Sminchisescu, C., Weiss, Y. (eds.) ECCV 2018, Part IX. LNCS, vol. 11213, pp. 202–218. Springer, Cham (2018). https://doi.org/10.1007/978-3-030-01240-3_13
36. Sukhbaatar, S., Fergus, R.: Learning from noisy labels with deep neural networks. In: International Conference on Learning Representations (ICLR) Workshop (2015)
37. Sun, Y., Wang, X., Tang, X.: Deep learning face representation from predicting 10,000 classes. In: Proceedings of the IEEE conference on computer vision and pattern recognition (CVPR) (2014)
38. Wang, F., et al.: The devil of face recognition is in the noise. In: Ferrari, V., Hebert, M., Sminchisescu, C., Weiss, Y. (eds.) ECCV 2018, Part IX. LNCS, vol. 11213, pp. 780–795. Springer, Cham (2018). https://doi.org/10.1007/978-3-030-01240-3_47
39. Wang, H., et al.: Cosface: Large margin cosine loss for deep face recognition. In: Proceedings of the IEEE Conference on Computer Vision and Pattern Recognition (2018)
40. Wang, X., Yan, Y., Tang, P., Bai, X., Liu, W.: Revisiting multiple instance neural networks. Pattern Recognit. **74**, 15–24 (2018)
41. Wang, Z., Zheng, L., Li, Y., Wang, S.: Linkage based face clustering via graph convolution network. In: Proceedings of the IEEE Conference on Computer Vision and Pattern Recognition (CVPR) (2019)
42. Wen, Y., Zhang, K., Li, Z., Qiao, Yu.: A discriminative feature learning approach for deep face recognition. In: Leibe, B., Matas, J., Sebe, N., Welling, M. (eds.) ECCV 2016, Part VII. LNCS, vol. 9911, pp. 499–515. Springer, Cham (2016). https://doi.org/10.1007/978-3-319-46478-7_31

43. Wu, J., Yu, Y., Huang, C., Yu, K.: Deep multiple instance learning for image classification and auto-annotation. In: Proceedings of the IEEE Conference on Computer Vision and Pattern Recognition (CVPR) (2015)

44. Xia, J., Rao, A., Huang, Q., Xu, L., Wen, J., Lin, D.: Online multi-modal person search in videos. In: Vedaldi, A., Bischof, H., Brox, T., Frahm, J.-M. (eds.) ECCV 2020, Part XII. LNCS, vol. 12357, pp. 174–190. Springer, Cham (2020). https://doi.org/10.1007/978-3-030-58610-2_11

45. Xiao, T., Xia, T., Yang, Y., Huang, C., Wang, X.: Learning from massive noisy labeled data for image classification. In: Proceedings of the IEEE conference on computer vision and pattern recognition (CVPR) (2015)

46. Xiong, Y., Huang, Q., Guo, L., Zhou, H., Zhou, B., Lin, D.: A graph-based framework to bridge movies and synopses. In: The IEEE International Conference on Computer Vision (ICCV) (2019)

47. Yang, L., Chen, D., Zhan, X., Zhao, R., Loy, C.C., Lin, D.: Learning to cluster faces via confidence and connectivity estimation. In: Proceedings of the IEEE/CVF Conference on Computer Vision and Pattern Recognition (2020)

48. Yang, L., Huang, Q., Huang, H., Xu, L., Lin, D.: Learn to propagate reliably on noisy affinity graphs. In: Proceedings of the European Conference on Computer Vision (ECCV) (2020)

49. Yang, L., Zhan, X., Chen, D., Yan, J., Loy, C.C., Lin, D.: Learning to cluster faces on an affinity graph. In: Proceedings of the IEEE Conference on Computer Vision and Pattern Recognition (CVPR) (2019)

50. Yi, D., Lei, Z., Liao, S., Li, S.Z.: Learning face representation from scratch. arXiv preprint arXiv:1411.7923 (2014)

51. Zhan, X., Liu, Z., Yan, J., Lin, D., Loy, C.C.: Consensus-driven propagation in massive unlabeled data for face recognition. In: Ferrari, V., Hebert, M., Sminchisescu, C., Weiss, Y. (eds.) ECCV 2018. LNCS, vol. 11213, pp. 576–592. Springer, Cham (2018). https://doi.org/10.1007/978-3-030-01240-3_35

52. Zhang, K., Zhang, Z., Li, Z., Qiao, Y.: Joint face detection and alignment using multitask cascaded convolutional networks. IEEE Signal Process. Lett. **23**, 1499–1503 (2016)

53. Zhao, X., Evans, N., Dugelay, J.L.: Semi-supervised face recognition with lda self-training. In: IEEE International Conference on Image Processing (2011)

Unselfie: Translating Selfies to Neutral-Pose Portraits in the Wild

Liqian Ma[1]([✉]), Zhe Lin[2], Connelly Barnes[2], Alexei A. Efros[2,3], and Jingwan Lu[2]

[1] KU Leuven, Leuven, Belgium
liqian.ma@esat.kueuvan.be
[2] Adobe Research, Antwerp, Belgium
[3] UC Berkeley, Berkeley, USA

Abstract. Due to the ubiquity of smartphones, it is popular to take photos of one's self, or "selfies." Such photos are convenient to take, because they do not require specialized equipment or a third-party photographer. However, in selfies, constraints such as human arm length often make the body pose look unnatural. To address this issue, we introduce *unselfie*, a novel photographic transformation that automatically translates a selfie into a neutral-pose portrait. To achieve this, we first collect an unpaired dataset, and introduce a way to synthesize paired training data for self-supervised learning. Then, to *unselfie* a photo, we propose a new three-stage pipeline, where we first find a target neutral pose, inpaint the body texture, and finally refine and composite the person on the background. To obtain a suitable target neutral pose, we propose a novel nearest pose search module that makes the reposing task easier and enables the generation of multiple neutral-pose results among which users can choose the best one they like. Qualitative and quantitative evaluations show the superiority of our pipeline over alternatives.

Keywords: Image editing · Selfie · Human pose transfer

1 Introduction

Smartphone cameras have democratized photography by allowing casual users to take high-quality photos. However, there still remains a tension between the ease of capture and the photograph's quality. This is particularly apparent in the case of personal portraits. On one hand, it is easy to take a photo of oneself (a selfie) by using the front camera of a smartphone. On the other hand, one can usually take a much higher-quality photograph by relying on an extra photographer, or equipment such as a tripod or selfie stick. While less convenient, these avoid the compositional problem that tends to occur in selfies: an unnatural body pose.

Electronic supplementary material The online version of this chapter (https://doi.org/10.1007/978-3-030-58520-4_10) contains supplementary material, which is available to authorized users.

A. Vedaldi et al. (Eds.): ECCV 2020, LNCS 12362, pp. 156–173, 2020.
https://doi.org/10.1007/978-3-030-58520-4_10

| Input | Result | Input | Result |

Fig. 1. We automatically *unselfie* selfie photos into neutral-pose portraits.

In this paper, we introduce a new photographic transformation that we call *unselfie*. This transformation aims to make selfie photos look like a well-composed portrait, captured by a third party photographer, showing a neutral body pose with relaxed arms, shoulders and torso. We call this desired result a "neutral-pose portrait." The unselfie transform moves any raised arms downward, adjusts the pose of the shoulder and torso, tweaks the details of the clothing and then fills in any exposed background regions (see Fig. 1).

There are three main challenges that we need to tackle in order to be able to *unselfie* photos: (1) Paired (selfie, neutral-pose portrait) training data do not exist, so we need to train a model without such data; (2) The same selfie pose can reasonably correspond to multiple plausible neutral poses, so we need to be able to handle this multiplicity; (3) Changing the pose creates holes in the background, so we need to fill in the holes while maintaining a smooth transition between the background and the human body.

We first tried out several previous methods to see if they could address challenge (1). We collected separate sets of selfie and neutral-pose portraits and used the unsupervised approach CycleGAN [62] for unpaired translation. Cycle-GAN excels at appearance-level translation that modifies textures and colors, but cannot perform large geometric transformations which are often needed for reposing the complex human body. It also produces unnatural poses with artifacts that result in more noticeable artifacts later in our pipeline. We also tried unsupervised person generation approaches [10,32]. Though better than Cycle-GAN, these are not designed for our Unselfie task and produce lower quality results than seen in their papers. As shown in our experiments, these methods result in noticeable artifacts on the generated person images, and texture details are missing because appearance information is compressed heavily.

Due to these reasons, we instead propose to synthesize (selfie, neutral-pose portrait) pairs and use a self-supervised learning approach. In particular, we propose a way to synthesize paired selfie images from neutral-pose portraits by using a non-parametric nearest pose search module to retrieve the nearest selfie pose given a neutral-pose portrait, and then synthesize a corresponding self i.e. We also adopt a nearest pose search module during inference. Given an

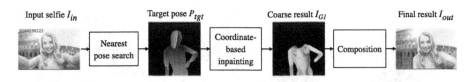

Fig. 2. Our three-stage pipeline. Based on the input selfie I_{in}, we extract its pose information using DensePose [1]. We perform nearest neighbour search on the pose representation to find the target neutral pose P_{tgt} that has the most similar pose configuration in the upper torso region. Using DensePose, we map the pixels in the input selfie to the visible regions of the target pose and then use coordinate-based inpainting [14] to synthesize a coarse human body. We then use a composition step to refine the coarse result by adding more details and composite it into the original background.

input selfie pose, we retrieve the best matching neutral poses, which we use to synthesize the final portraits. This addresses challenge (2) by enabling diverse outputs to be synthesized and allowing users to choose among them.

The synthesized paired data mentioned above can be directly used to train a supervised person image generation network like [33,50,63], but there still exist noticeable artifacts in the results as shown in our experiments. These methods are sensitive to the pixel-level domain gap between our synthetic paired training data and the real selfies testing data (see Fig. 3). Inspired by [14], we use the coordinate-based inpainting method to inpaint the body texture in UV space. This space is mostly invariant to the original body pose, and is therefore more robust to imperfections in the synthesized data. Additionally, the coordinate-based inpainting method can reuse visible pixels and thus give sharper results.

To address challenge (3), we adopt a gated convolutional layer [58] based composition network to jointly refine the body appearance, fill the background holes, and maintain smooth transitions between the human body and background.

Overall, to address the unselfie task, we propose a three-stage pipeline shown in Fig. 2: we first search for a nearest neutral pose in a database, then perform coordinate-based inpainting of the body texture, and finally use a composition module to refine the result and composite it on the background. We conducted several experiments and compared our method with alternatives to demonstrate the effectiveness of our pipeline.

To the best of our knowledge, this work is the first to target the problem of selfie to neutral-pose portrait translation, which could be a useful and popular application among casual photographers. Our contributions include: 1) We collect a new dataset of unpaired selfies and neutral-pose portraits and introduce a way to synthesize paired training data for self-supervised learning; 2) We introduce a three-stage pipeline to translate selfies into neutral-pose portraits; 3) We propose a novel nearest pose search module to obtain suitable multi-modal target neutral poses; 4) We design an all-in-one composition module to refine the foreground, complete the background, and compose them together seamlessly.

2   Related Work

Image Generation and Translation. Generative models, such as VAEs [22] and GANs [2,5,13,21,34,45] can synthesize realistic-looking images from noise. To allow more control during the generation process, much research has been devoted to conditional image generation, with class labels [37], attributes [7], text [48,60], key-points [32,47] and images [20,62] as conditioning signals. Image-to-image translation networks are conditioned on images, such as semantic segmentation maps, edge maps and RGB images [20]. To alleviate the need of collecting paired data, researchers have introduced unsupervised methods based on the ideas of cycle-consistency [62] and shared latent space [28]. Subsequent works [19,24,31] further extended the unsupervised approach to solve multi-modal image-to-image translation problems by disentangling content and style representations. These methods mainly focus on appearance manipulation. Recently, research efforts have also been extended to modify the underlying geometry in image translation tasks [44,53]. In general, unsupervised image manipulation is quite challenging [26], especially if the goal is to modify the underlying geometry.

Image Completion. The goal of image completion is to fill in missing regions of an image. Applications of image completion include image inpainting and image out-painting. Traditional patch-based texture synthesis approaches [3,8,18,55] work well for images containing simple and repetitive structures, but may fail to handle images of complex scenes. To tackle this problem, modern approaches apply deep learning for image completion due to its ability to gain semantic understanding of the image content [39,41,56–58]. One of the first deep learning methods for image inpainting is context encoder [41], which uses an encoder-decoder architecture. In order to achieve better results, some prior works apply the PatchMatch idea [3] at the feature level, such as Contextual Attention [57] and ShiftNet [56]. Recently, Yu et al. [58] introduce a gated convolutional layer, which learns a dynamic feature gating mechanism for each channel and each spatial location. In our framework, we also use the gated convolutional layer [58] in both the coordinate-based inpainting network and the composition network to fill in holes in the UV map and the background.

Person Image Generation. Person image generation is a challenging task, as human bodies have complex non-rigid structures with many degrees of freedom [38], Previous works in this space usually generate person images by conditioning on these structures. Ma et al. [33] propose to condition on image and pose keypoints to transfer the human pose. [23] and [9] generate clothed person by conditioning on fine-grained body and clothing segmentation. Recent works [36,52] also extend the conditions to attributes. To model the correspondences between two human poses explicitly, recent works introduce flow-based techniques which improve the appearance transfer result quality significantly [14,15,29,40,49,50,63]. Siarohin et al. [50] propose deformable skip-connections to warp the feature maps with affine transformations. Grigorev et al. [14] propose to inpaint the body texture in the UV space which is mostly invariant

to the pose in the image space. Although these methods achieve good results, they need paired training data, *i.e.* two images containing the same individual in two different body poses, which may be difficult to collect in many applications. To address this, several unpaired methods have been proposed [10,32,42]. [32] and [10] propose to decompose a person image into different factors which are then used to reconstruct the original image. Other works also adopt human parsing algorithms to help out on the difficult unpaired setting [46,51]. Raj *et al.* [46] generate training pairs from a single image via data augmentation. Inspired by [46], we synthesize selfie data from neutral-pose portrait data to construct paired training data. These human synthesis approaches focus on generating realistic human appearance in a relatively simple background environment (*i.e.* fashion or surveillance datasets) given a target pose. Our work on the other hand handles selfie photos captured in the wild that contain a wide variety of backgrounds, lighting conditions, identities and poses. Compared to fashion photos, the background pixels in selfies are of greater importance.

3   Our Method

Our goal is to convert a selfie I_{in} into a neutral-pose portrait I_{out} as shown in Fig. 2. We collect separate sets of selfie and portrait photos and synthesize paired training data for self-supervised learning (Sect. 3.1). Due to the complexity of the problem, we solve it in three stages. In the first stage, we use a non-parametric nearest pose search module (Sect. 3.2) to find the target neutral pose P_{tgt} that closely matches the pose in the upper torso region of the self i.e. We then map the pixels in the selfie to regions of the target pose based on the correspondences between the two pose representations. This design makes the remaining problem easier, since most of the pixels can be directly borrowed from the input selfie and thus fewer pixels need to be modified by the remaining steps. In the second stage, inspired by the previous work [14], we train a coordinate-based inpainting model to synthesize the coarse appearance of the human body (Sect. 3.3). In the final stage, we train a composition model to synthesize details and fix artifacts in the body region caused by pose changes, fill in holes in the background, and seamlessly compose the synthesized body onto the original photo (Sect. 3.4).

We use DensePose [1] in all three stages of our *unselfie* pipeline. Unlike keypoint based representations [6], which predict a limited amount of pose information described by sparse keypoints, DensePose provides a dense UV-map for the entire visible human body. The UV-map is an ideal pose representation for our purposes, because it provides body shape and orientation information, which are useful for the pose search module. Color values in UV space are also relatively invariant to the person's pose, so this also enables the coordinate-based inpainting step to produce sharp results.

Ground truth   Portrait pose   Nearest selfie pose P_{src} Synthesized selfie
portrait image I_{tgt} P_{tgt} From $\{P_{selfie}^{i}\}$ image I_{src}

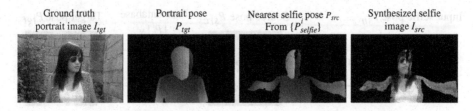

Fig. 3. Synthesized (portrait, selfie) pairs in image space. Given a neutral-pose portrait I_{tgt}, we use DensePose to extract its pose P_{tgt}. We perform nearest neighbour search to find the closest pose from the selfie pose database. The selfie image I_{src} is synthesized from pixels in I_{tgt} by the correspondence between P_{tgt} and P_{src}. The displayed I_{tgt} and P_{tgt} are cropped due to alignment (Sect. 3.2)

Ground truth portrait   Synthesized selfie   Synthesized selfie
texture-map T_{tgt} coordinate-map C_{src} texture-map T_{src}

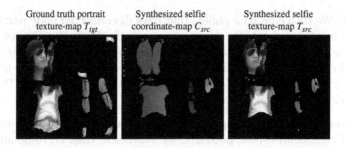

Fig. 4. Synthesized (portrait, selfie) pairs in UV space to train our coordinate-based inpainting network.

3.1 Datasets

We are not aware of any datasets that contain selfie photos and their corresponding portrait photos taken at the exact same place and time. However, there are many unpaired selfies and neutral-pose portraits online.

Unpaired Selfies and Neutral-Pose Portraits. We collect 23169 photos of people in frontal and neutral poses from the following public datasets: DeepFashion [30], DeepFashion2 [11], and ATR [25]. We apply the DensePose algorithm to extract the pose information from all the images. The extracted DensePose representations form a neutral pose database $\{P_{neutral}^{i}\}$. Because many images in DeepFashion dataset have clean backgrounds, they are not diverse enough for our composition network to learn proper background inpainting. Therefore, we apply a state-of-the-art matting technique [54] to extract the foreground humans and paste them into random background images to increase the data diversity.

We collect 4614 selfie photos from the Internet using the following strategy. We first search with keywords like "selfie girl," "selfie boy," etc. Many photos returned by the search engines contain cellphones. These are not the selfies we desire but are third-person view photos of someone taking selfies. Since Mask R-CNN [16] is pretrained on the COCO dataset [27], which contains person and cell phone classes, we use it to select photos that contain a single person without any

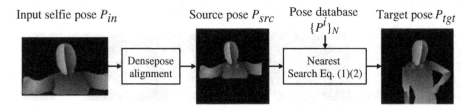

Fig. 5. Nearest pose search module. The detected selfie DensePose P_{in} is first aligned so that the two shoulder points are centered in the image P_{src}. Then we perform nearest neighbour search to find a target pose P_{tgt} from the neutral pose database that closely matches the input selfie pose in the upper torso region.

cell phones. We then eliminate photos that have disconnected body parts or have any of the frontal upper body parts missing in the DensePose representation. We also use this strategy to create the neutral-pose portrait dataset. Finally, we manually clean up the remaining data in case any of the previous filters fail. We create a 4114/500 split for training and testing. We denote the DensePose representation of selfie photos as $\{P^i_{selfie}\}$.

Synthesized Paired Training Data. To allow self-supervised training, based on the collected neutral-pose portraits, we synthesize their corresponding selfie data using DensePose. As shown in Fig. 3, given a neutral pose P_{tgt}, we first search for a selfie pose P_{src} from $\{P^i_{selfie}\}$ that matches the input neutral pose the best in the upper torso region. Through DensePose correspondences, we map the portrait image pixels to the nearest selfie pose (see Sect. 3.2 for more details). Due to the pose change and self-occlusion, the synthesized selfie might contain holes caused by mistakes of DensePose or by pixels visible in the selfie but not visible in the original portrait such as the armpits or the backside of arms. Though not perfect, these paired images can be used to train supervised human synthesis models like [33,50,63]. However, the results have noticeable artifacts as shown in our experiments in Sect. 4.1.

Instead of using the synthetic paired images to synthesize pixels directly, we convert them into the UV space (see Fig. 4) and perform texture inpainting in the UV coordinate space by building on [14]. In particular, we first obtain ground truth portrait texture map T_{tgt} from I_{tgt} with DensePose mapping. Then, we obtain the selfie coordinate map C_{src} from the nearest selfie pose P_{src} masked by the visible region of T_{tgt}. Finally from C_{src}, we sample the pixels from T_{tgt} to synthesize the selfie texture map T_{src}. C_{src} and T_{src} are used as input to train the coordinate-based inpainting model (see Sect. 3.3).

3.2   Nearest Pose Search

Because our goal is to turn a selfie into a neutral-pose portrait, it is important to define what we desire for the target neutral pose. Motivated by the success of retrieval-based image synthesis [43], we propose a retrieval-based approach

where given a selfie pose at testing time, we perform non-parametric nearest pose search to find the neutral poses in the $\{P^i_{neutral}\}$ database that match the input selfie pose the best. Compared to pixel-level pose translation using approaches like CycleGAN [62], our approach has several advantages: (1) It is simpler and more explainable since no training is needed; (2) the retrieved target poses are guaranteed to be natural since they come from real photos; (3) we can generate multiple unselfie results by choosing the top-K most similar poses as the target poses and we can allow users to choose their favorite result; (4) the retrieved poses are similar to the input pose which makes pose correction easier since fewer pixels need to be modified.

During inference, given an input selfie, we search for the k-nearest target neutral poses. At training time, we reverse the search direction: given a target neutral pose, we search for a matching self i.e. This allows us to synthesize synthetic data, which are used to self-supervise the inpainting and composition networks. The procedure is otherwise the same at both training and inference time.

In the remainder of this subsection, we describe the details of our pose search module. As shown in Fig. 5, we first align the input selfie pose P_{in} by putting two selected shoulder points in the center of the image to obtain the source pose P_{src}. All neutral poses are also aligned in the same way. We calculate the pose similarity in the frontal torso region excluding the head, since the later stages of our pipeline keep the head region intact and only correct the body pose. The DensePose representation P is an IUV map which contains three channels. The P^I channel contains indices of body parts to which pixels belong, and the P^{UV} channels contain the UV coordinates.

Based on P^I and P^{UV}, we propose a two-step search strategy to calculate pose similarity. First, we search for suitable target poses based on global information such as body shape and position. To determine the global similarity between two poses, we use the following equation:

$$d^I(P_1, P_2) = \sum_{x \in R_1 \cup R_2} \mathbb{1}(P_1^I(x) \neq P_2^I(x)), \tag{1}$$

where R refers to the front torso regions of the body. We iterate over all pixels in both torso regions and count the number of pixels that belong to different body parts in the two poses. If there is large body part index mismatch in the torso regions, the two poses are dissimilar at a global level.

Among the top-K pose candidates selected based on d_I, we further improve the ranking by leveraging local pose information given by the UV coordinates. In particular, for pixels belonging to torso regions in both poses, we calculate the sum of the distances of their UV coordinates:

$$d^{UV}(P_1, P_2) = \sum_{x \in R_1 \cap R_2} \|P_1^{UV}(x) - P_2^{UV}(x)\|_2. \tag{2}$$

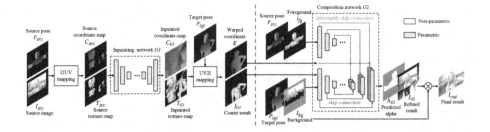

Fig. 6. Left: coordinate-based inpainting stage. Right: composition stage.

3.3 Coordinate-Based Inpainting

Inspired by self-supervised image inpainting work [41,58] and human synthesis work [14], we learn to reuse the visible body pixels to fill in the invisible body parts. As illustrated in Fig. 6 left, we first use an Image-to-UV (I2UV) mapping to translate pose P_{src} and the color image I_{src} from the image domain to the UV domain. Defined in the UV domain, C_{src} stores the associated $\{x, y\}$ coordinates of pixels in the original image space. Likewise in the UV domain, T_{src} contains the RGB colors of the associated pixels in the original image I_{src}: these are looked up by using bilinear sampling via $T_{src} = I_{src}(C_{src})$.

After the I2UV mapping, we use an inpainting neural network G_1 to inpaint the coordinate-map C_{src}. We concatenate C_{src} and T_{src} as input to the network. The network outputs the inpainted coordinate-map $C_{G_1} = G_1(C_{src}, T_{src})$. We then perform bilinear sampling to obtain the inpainted texture-map $T_{G_1} = I_{src}(C_{G_1})$.

Finally, we map C_{G_1} and T_{G_1} back to the image space with UV-to-Image (UV2I) mapping using the bilinear sampling operations $E = C_{G_1}(P_{tgt})$, $I_{G_1} = T_{G_1}(P_{tgt})$. To train G_1, we use three loss functions, identity loss $L_{idt}^{G_1}$, reconstruction loss $L_1^{G_1}$ and perceptual loss $L_P^{G_1}$ [61] as follows,

$$L_{idt}^{G_1} = \mathbb{E}\big[\|C_{G_1} - C_{src}\|_2^2 V_{src}\big], \tag{3}$$

$$L_1^{G_1} = \mathbb{E}\big[\|T_{G_1} - T_{tgt}\|_1 V_{tgt}\big], \tag{4}$$

$$L_P^{G_1} = \mathbb{E}\big[\|\phi(T_{G_1}) - \phi(T_{tgt})\|_2^2 V_{tgt}\big], \tag{5}$$

V_{src} and V_{tgt} are binary masks that select the non-empty regions in the coordinate map C_{src} and T_{tgt}, respectively. T_{tgt} is the ground truth texture mapped from image domain to UV domain (Fig. 4 left), that is, $T_{tgt} = I2UV(I_{tgt})$. The identity loss encourages the existing coordinates to stay unchanged while the network synthesizes coordinates elsewhere. The reconstruction loss and perceptual loss are performed in the pixel space instead of the coordinate space and use the ground truth image for supervision. The overall loss for G_1 is

$$\min_{G_1} L^{G_1} = L_1^{G_1} + \lambda_1 L_P^{G_1} + \lambda_2 L_{idt}^{G_1}, \tag{6}$$

3.4   Composition

The advantage of doing inpainting in the coordinate space is that the network can copy and paste original pixels to fill in missing regions based on body symmetry and therefore the synthesized pixels tend to look sharp. However, in some cases, a small number of visible pixels get copied into a much larger region resulting in flat and unrealistic appearance. In addition, when arms are moved down, holes will appear in the background due to dis-occlusion.

To address these problems, we use an all-in-one composition network to add details and fix artifacts in the body region and fill in the gaps between the body and the background by synthesizing a natural transition. As illustrated in Fig. 6 right, we use a U-net architecture equipped with gated convolutional layers [58] for G_2. The U-net architecture helps preserve the high resolution features through skip-connections. The gated convolutional layer improves the inpainting result quality when dealing with holes of arbitrary shape. To keep the body appearance more consistent, we also use deformable skip connections [14, 50] to propagate the appearance information from the source image I_{src} to the result despite large changes in poses. The network synthesizes missing foreground pixels, fills in background holes and also produces an alpha mask A_{G_2}. A_{G_2} is used to blend the synthesized pixels I_{G_2} into the background image I_{bg}, i.e. $I_{out} = I_{G_2}A_{G_2} + I_{bg}(1 - A_{G_2})$. We add the original head and neck regions into I_{bg} so that after blending the head regions will remain untouched.

To train G_2, we apply reconstruction loss $L_1^{G_2}$, perceptual loss $L_P^{G_2}$ [61], alpha loss $L_A^{G_2}$ and adversarial loss $L_{adv}^{G_2,D}$,

$$L_1^{G_2} = \mathbb{E}\big[\|I_{out} - I_{tgt}\|_1(1 + H)\big], \tag{7}$$

$$L_P^{G_2} = \mathbb{E}\big[\|\phi(I_{out}) - \phi(I_{tgt})\|_2^2(1 + H)\big], \tag{8}$$

$$L_A^{G_2} = \mathbb{E}\big[\|A_{G_2} - H\|_1\big], \tag{9}$$

$$\min_{G_2}\max_{D} L_{adv}^{G_2,D} = \mathbb{E}\big[(D(I_{tgt}))^2(1 + H)\big]$$
$$+ \mathbb{E}\big[(D(I_{out}) - 1)^2(1 + H)\big], \tag{10}$$

where I_{tgt} denotes the ground truth neutral-pose portrait. $H \in [0,1]$ is a binary spatial mask to encourage the network to focus more on synthesizing foreground and filling dis-occluded holes and the details are explained later. When applied to different spatial size, H will be resized to the corresponding spatial size by nearest-neighbor scaling accordingly. As to the adversarial learning, we use the same residual discriminator as that of [63]. The overall loss for G_2 is

$$\min_{G_2}\max_{D} L^{G_2} = \lambda_3 L_1^{G_2} + \lambda_4 L_P^{G_2} + \lambda_5 L_{adv}^{G_2,D} + L_A^{G_2}. \tag{11}$$

There is a big domain gap between the training and testing data. During testing, arms in real selfies are moved downward revealing a large hole in the background. During training, we also mimic the dis-occluded background holes. In particular, we calculate a binary mask $H = H_{selfie} \cup H_{neutral}$, which is

also used in Eq. 7 to 10. H_{selfie} and $H_{neutral}$, which are estimated using an off-the-shelf DeepMatting model [54] and binarized with threshold 0.1, denote the body regions from the selfie and the neutral-pose portrait, respectively. The synthesized hole mask H is then applied to I_{bg} to mimic dis-occluded background holes.

4   Experiments

We compare our approach with several prior work through a qualitative evaluation, a user study and a quantitative evaluation[1]. Note that none of the previous approaches address exactly our unselfie problem, so we cannot compare our approach with previous work using their datasets and result quality for previous work on our dataset is worse than the result quality in those papers. We present ablation studies to validate the effectiveness of different algorithm choices. Finally, we discuss the limitations and future work. If not otherwise specified, we use the top-1 retrieved neutral pose as target pose. Note that there may be JPEG compression artifacts in the input selfies.

4.1   Comparisons with Existing Methods

Since we defined a brand new unselfie application, there is no prior work to compare to that addresses the exact same problem. Nevertheless, we introduce some modifications to two state-of-the-art human synthesis methods, DPIG [32] and PATN [63], so that we can compare to them directly in our new application setting. Note that these methods synthesize pixels based on a pre-specified target pose. To make their approaches work, we need to perform our proposed nearest pose search module to calculate P_{tgt} and then use their approaches to synthesize the final pixels. DPIG is a key-points based unsupervised approach. For fair comparison, we replace their key-points with the DensePose representation. We also made various other improvements for it to produce comparable results to ours (see supplementary material). PATN is a key-points based supervised method, so we use our synthesized paired images for self-supervised training by using DensePose IUV map as the input pose representation and feeding I_{src}, I_{bg} as input to their model. In the supplementary material, we also compare our approach with another keypoint-based unsupervised approach VUNET [10]. Due to low result quality and space limitations, we do not show those results here.

Qualitative Evaluation. Figure 7 shows that our method synthesizes more photo-realistic body and background appearance compared to prior art. We manually picked the best target pose out of results using our top-5 retrieved poses. The multi-modal results are reported in the material. In the top row, the short-sleeved clothing style is better preserved. In the second row, the stripe

---

[1] More results and implementation details are reported in the supplementary materials.

Input selfie	DPIG [32]	PATN [63]	Ours

Fig. 7. Comparisons with state-of-the-art methods. Please zoom in to see details.

pattern is better preserved, and the synthesized arms are sharper. In the bottom two rows, our method synthesizes better clothing and background details and produces more natural transitions between foreground and background. The reasons that our method outperforms the baselines are: 1) unsupervised methods, like DPIG, encode images into heavily compressed features, which results in loss of details and texture inconsistency between the generated output and the input. They perform well in more constrained settings (clean backgrounds and simple texture), while our task involves complex images in the wild; 2) these baseline methods are more sensitive to the domain gap between training and testing data since they directly synthesize image pixels. Our method performs foreground inpainting in the coordinate space and then uses a composition module to refine details and fill in background holes and thus is less sensitive to the

Table 1. User study and, FID/KID scores.

Model	Human prefers ours	FID↓	KID↓
DPIG [32]	0.798	88.27	0.026
VUNET [10]	0.851	135.90	0.077
PATN [63]	0.822	104.74	0.041
Ours	N/A	**71.93**	**0.014**

Table 2. Ablation study.

Model	FID↓	KID↓
Ours w/o L_P^{G2}	82.09	0.019
Ours w/o Deform	73.87	0.017
Ours w/o Gated	72.89	**0.014**
Ours	**71.93**	**0.014**

Input selfie	d_I	d_{UV}	Ours

Fig. 8. Ablation study results for nearest pose search.

Input selfie	w/o $L_P^{G_2}$	w/o Deform	w/o Gated	Ours

Fig. 9. Ablation study for composition network.

domain gap between imperfect synthesized selfies at training and perfect selfies at testing.

User Study. For a useful real-world application, we believe qualitative perceptual evaluation is more important. Thus, we perform a user study on Amazon Mechanical Turk (AMT). Similar to previous works [19,24], given the input selfie and a pair of results generated by our approach and one of the baseline approaches, users are asked to pick one that looks better than the other. Within each Human Intelligence Task (HIT), we compare our method with the same baseline method. We randomly generate 200 result pairs including 10 sanity pairs where the answers are obvious. After filtering out careless users based on their answers on the sanity pairs, we calculate the user study statistics using the remaining 190 questions. We have three HITs for three baseline methods. Each HIT is done by 20 users. As shown in Table 1, our method is preferred over others. We assume a null hypothesis that on average, half the users prefer ours for a given paired comparison. We use a one-sample permutation t-test [12] to measure p using 10^6 permutations and find $p < 10^{-6}$ for the 3 baselines.

Quantitative Evaluation. Since we do not have the ground truth neutral portraits corresponding to input selfies, we cannot use metrics like SSIM. To quantitatively compare our result quality with other baselines, we report Frechet Inception Distance (FID) [17] and Kernel Inception Distance (KID) [4] as shown in Table 1. We aim to translate the body into a neutral pose while keeping the rest of the image intact. Therefore, a good translation method should have low FID and KID values when compared to both the portraits and the selfie domains. As suggested by [35], we combine both real selfie and real portrait images into the real domain, and compute the FID and KID values between our synthesized results (*i.e.* fake domain) and the real domain. The mean FID and KID values are averaged over 10 different splits of size 50 randomly sampled

Fig. 10. Failure cases. Left: input, result. Right: input, foreground mask, result.

Input selfie   BG I_{bg} Inpainted BG I_{ibg} Result with I_{bg} Result with I_{ibg}

Fig. 11. Results of using inpaited background.

from each domain. The trend of FID and KID is consistent with the user study result, and our method outperforms others significantly.

4.2   Ablation Study

Analysis of the Pose Search Module. We compare three ablation settings: 1) using body index distance only (*i.e.* d_I); 2) using UV distance only (*i.e.* d_{UV}); 3) using our two-step strategy. As shown in Fig. 8, the neutral poses retrieved by d_I have a reasonable body shape and size but the local coordinates mismatch resulting in the cloth regions being distorted (see the elongated buttons). For the neutral poses retrieved by d_{UV}, the body shape and size are not compatible with the head region. The retrieved body part is too small. Our two-step strategy combines the benefits of d_I and d_{UV} and retrieves better poses.

Analysis of the Compositing Network. We compare three ablation settings. **w/o** $L_P^{G_2}$: removing perception loss $L_P^{G_2}$. **w/o Deform:** removing deformable skip-connection. **w/o Gated:** use normal conv layer instead of gated conv layer [58]. As shown in Fig. 9, removing any of the components will result in noticeable result degradation. Our full setting synthesizes more details in the foreground, smoother transition between the foreground and the background and also better fills the large background holes. The quantitative results reported in Table 2 are consistent with the above observations.

4.3   Limitations

Our approach has several limitations. First, as shown in Fig. 10 left, for challenging non-frontal selfie poses/viewpoints, our nearest pose search module might struggle with finding compatible neutral poses, which results in the synthesized result containing arms or shoulders that are too slim or wide compared to the head region. This problem happens less than 10% of the time in our top-1 result,

and users can usually find a good compatible pose from our top-5 results. Second, this example also reveals the limitation of our background synthesis. We also show one example obtained by inpainting the background with an extra off-the-shelf model [59] in Fig. 11 to demonstrate the benefits from the image inpainting model trained on large-scale datasets. Finally, our system is prone to errors in DensePose detection. Figure 10 right, DensePose failed to detect her left arm as foreground. Therefore the composition module retained her left arm in the result.

5 Conclusion

In this work, we introduce a novel "unselfie" task that translates a selfie into a portrait with a neutral pose. We collect an unpaired dataset and introduce a way to synthesize paired training data for self-supervised learning. We design a three-stage framework to first retrieve a target neutral pose to perform warping, then inpaint the body texture, and finally fill in the background holes and seamlessly compose the foreground into the background. Qualitative and quantitative evaluations demonstrate the superiority of our framework over other alternatives.

Acknowledgements. This work was partially funded by Adobe Research. We thank He Zhang for helping mask estimation. Selfie photo owners: #139639837-Baikal360, #224341474-Drobot Dean, #153081973-MaximBeykov, #67229337-Oleg Shelomentsev, #194139222-Syda Productions, #212727509-Photocatcher, #168103021-sosiukin, #162277318-rh2010, #225137362-BublikHaus, #120915150-wollertz, #133457041-ilovemayorova, #109067715-Tupungato, #121680430-Mego-studio, #206713499-Paolese – stock.adobe.com.

References

1. Alp Güler, R., Neverova, N., Kokkinos, I.: Densepose: dense human pose estimation in the wild. In: CVPR (2018)
2. Arjovsky, M., Chintala, S., Bottou, L.: Wasserstein gan. In: ICLR (2017)
3. Barnes, C., Shechtman, E., Finkelstein, A., Goldman, D.B.: PatchMatch: a randomized correspondence algorithm for structural image editing. ACM Trans. Graph. (TOG) **28**(3), 24 (2009)
4. Bińkowski, M., Sutherland, D.J., Arbel, M., Gretton, A.: Demystifying MMD GANs. In: ICLR (2018)
5. Brock, A., Donahue, J., Simonyan, K.: Large scale GAN training for high fidelity natural image synthesis. In: ICLR (2019)
6. Cao, Z., Hidalgo, G., Simon, T., Wei, S.E., Sheikh, Y.: OpenPose: realtime multi-person 2D pose estimation using Part Affinity Fields. In: arXiv preprint arXiv:1812.08008 (2018)
7. Choi, Y., Choi, M., Kim, M., Ha, J.W., Kim, S., Choo, J.: Stargan: unified generative adversarial networks for multi-domain image-to-image translation. In: CVPR (2018)

8. Darabi, S., Shechtman, E., Barnes, C., Goldman, D.B., Sen, P.: Image melding: combining inconsistent images using patch-based synthesis. ACM Trans. Graph. (TOG) **31**(4), 82:1–82:10 (2012)

9. Dong, H., Liang, X., Gong, K., Lai, H., Zhu, J., Yin, J.: Soft-gated warping-gan for pose-guided person image synthesis. In: NeurIPS (2018)

10. Esser, P., Sutter, E., Ommer, B.: A variational U-net for conditional appearance and shape generation. In: CVPR (2018)

11. Ge, Y., Zhang, R., Wu, L., Wang, X., Tang, X., Luo, P.: A versatile benchmark for detection, pose estimation, segmentation and re-identification of clothing images (2019)

12. Good, P.: Permutation tests: a practical guide to resampling methods for testing hypotheses. Springer Science & Business Media (2000)

13. Goodfellow, I., et al.: Generative adversarial nets. In: NIPS (2014)

14. Grigorev, A., Sevastopolsky, A., Vakhitov, A., Lempitsky, V.: Coordinate-based texture inpainting for pose-guided image generation. In: CVPR (2019)

15. Han, X., Hu, X., Huang, W., Scott, M.R.: Clothflow: A flow-based model for clothed person generation. In: ICCV (2019)

16. He, K., Gkioxari, G., Dollár, P., Girshick, R.: Mask R-CNN. In: ICCV (2017)

17. Heusel, M., Ramsauer, H., Unterthiner, T., Nessler, B., Hochreiter, S.: Gans trained by a two time-scale update rule converge to a local nash equilibrium. In: NIPS (2017)

18. Huang, J.B., Kang, S.B., Ahuja, N., Kopf, J.: Image completion using planar structure guidance. ACM Trans. Graph. (TOG) **33**(4), 129 (2014)

19. Huang, X., Liu, M.-Y., Belongie, S., Kautz, J.: Multimodal unsupervised image-to-image translation. In: Ferrari, V., Hebert, M., Sminchisescu, C., Weiss, Y. (eds.) ECCV 2018. LNCS, vol. 11207, pp. 179–196. Springer, Cham (2018). https://doi.org/10.1007/978-3-030-01219-9_11

20. Isola, P., Zhu, J., Zhou, T., Efros, A.A.: Image-to-image translation with conditional adversarial networks. In: CVPR (2017)

21. Karras, T., Laine, S., Aila, T.: A style-based generator architecture for generative adversarial networks. In: CVPR (2019)

22. Kingma, D.P., Welling, M.: Auto-encoding variational bayes. In: ICLR (2014)

23. Lassner, C., Pons-Moll, G., Gehler, P.V.: A generative model of people in clothing. In: ICCV (2017)

24. Lee, H.-Y., Tseng, H.-Y., Huang, J.-B., Singh, M., Yang, M.-H.: Diverse image-to-image translation via disentangled representations. In: Ferrari, V., Hebert, M., Sminchisescu, C., Weiss, Y. (eds.) ECCV 2018. LNCS, vol. 11205, pp. 36–52. Springer, Cham (2018). https://doi.org/10.1007/978-3-030-01246-5_3

25. Liang, X., et al.: Deep human parsing with active template regression. IEEE Trans. Pattern Anal. Mach. Intell. (TPAMI) **37**(12), 2402–2414 (2015)

26. Liang, X., Zhang, H., Lin, L., Xing, E.: Generative semantic manipulation with mask-contrasting GAN. In: Ferrari, V., Hebert, M., Sminchisescu, C., Weiss, Y. (eds.) ECCV 2018. LNCS, vol. 11217, pp. 574–590. Springer, Cham (2018). https://doi.org/10.1007/978-3-030-01261-8_34

27. Lin, T.-Y., et al.: Microsoft COCO: common objects in context. In: Fleet, D., Pajdla, T., Schiele, B., Tuytelaars, T. (eds.) ECCV 2014. LNCS, vol. 8693, pp. 740–755. Springer, Cham (2014). https://doi.org/10.1007/978-3-319-10602-1_48

28. Liu, M.Y., Breuel, T., Kautz, J.: Unsupervised image-to-image translation networks. In: NIPS (2017)

29. Liu, W., Piao, Z., Min, J., Luo, W., Ma, L., Gao, S.: Liquid warping gan: a unified framework for human motion imitation, appearance transfer and novel view synthesis. In: ICCV (2019)
30. Liu, Z., Luo, P., Qiu, S., Wang, X., Tang, X.: DeepFashion: powering robust clothes recognition and retrieval with rich annotations. In: CVPR (2016)
31. Ma, L., Jia, X., Georgoulis, S., Tuytelaars, T., Van Gool, L.: Exemplar guided unsupervised image-to-image translation with semantic consistency. In: ICLR (2019)
32. Ma, L., Sun, Q., Georgoulis, S., Van Gool, L., Schiele, B., Fritz, M.: Disentangled person image generation. In: CVPR (2018)
33. Ma, L., Xu, J., Sun, Q., Schiele, B., Tuytelaars, T., Van Gool, L.: Pose guided person image generation. In: NIPS (2017)
34. Mao, X., Li, Q., Xie, H., Lau, R.Y., Wang, Z., Paul Smolley, S.: Least squares generative adversarial networks. In: ICCV (2017)
35. Mejjati, Y.A., Richardt, C., Tompkin, J., Cosker, D., Kim, K.I.: Unsupervised attention-guided image-to-image translation. In: NeurIPS (2018)
36. Men, Y., Mao, Y., Jiang, Y., Ma, W.Y., Lian, Z.: Controllable person image synthesis with attribute-decomposed GAN. In: CVPR (2020)
37. Mirza, M., Osindero, S.: Conditional generative adversarial nets. arXiv preprint arXiv:1411.1784 (2014)
38. Moeslund, T.B., Hilton, A., Krüger, V.: A survey of advances in vision-based human motion capture and analysis. Comput. Vis. Image Underst. (CVIU) 104(2), 90–126 (2006)
39. Nazeri, K., Ng, E., Joseph, T., Qureshi, F., Ebrahimi, M.: EdgeConnect: structure guided image inpainting using edge prediction. In: ICCV Workshops (2019)
40. Neverova, N., Alp Güler, R., Kokkinos, I.: Dense pose transfer. In: Ferrari, V., Hebert, M., Sminchisescu, C., Weiss, Y. (eds.) ECCV 2018. LNCS, vol. 11207, pp. 128–143. Springer, Cham (2018). https://doi.org/10.1007/978-3-030-01219-9_8
41. Pathak, D., Krahenbuhl, P., Donahue, J., Darrell, T., Efros, A.A.: Context encoders: feature learning by inpainting. In: CVPR (2016)
42. Pumarola, A., Agudo, A., Sanfeliu, A., Moreno-Noguer, F.: Unsupervised person image synthesis in arbitrary poses. In: CVPR (2018)
43. Qi, X., Chen, Q., Jia, J., Koltun, V.: Semi-parametric image synthesis. In: CVPR (2018)
44. Qian, S., et al.: Make a face: towards arbitrary high fidelity face manipulation. In: ICCV (2019)
45. Radford, A., Metz, L., Chintala, S.: Unsupervised representation learning with deep convolutional generative adversarial networks. In: ICLR (2016)
46. Raj, A., Sangkloy, P., Chang, H., Hays, J., Ceylan, D., Lu, J.: SwapNet: image based garment transfer. In: Ferrari, V., Hebert, M., Sminchisescu, C., Weiss, Y. (eds.) ECCV 2018. LNCS, vol. 11216, pp. 679–695. Springer, Cham (2018). https://doi.org/10.1007/978-3-030-01258-8_41
47. Reed, S.E., Akata, Z., Mohan, S., Tenka, S., Schiele, B., Lee, H.: Learning what and where to draw. In: NIPS (2016)
48. Reed, S.E., Akata, Z., Yan, X., Logeswaran, L., Schiele, B., Lee, H.: Generative adversarial text to image synthesis. In: ICML (2016)
49. Ren, Y., Yu, X., Chen, J., Li, T.H., Li, G.: Deep image spatial transformation for person image generation. In: CVPR (2020)
50. Siarohin, A., Sangineto, E., Lathuilière, S., Sebe, N.: Deformable gans for pose-based human image generation. In: CVPR (2018)
51. Song, S., Zhang, W., Liu, J., Mei, T.: Unsupervised person image generation with semantic parsing transformation. In: CVPR (2019)

52. Weng, S., Li, W., Li, D., Jin, H., Shi, B.: Misc: Multi-condition injection and spatially-adaptive compositing for conditional person image synthesis. In: CVPR (2020)
53. Wu, W., Cao, K., Li, C., Qian, C., Loy, C.C.: Transgaga: Geometry-aware unsupervised image-to-image translation. In: CVPR (2019)
54. Xu, N., Price, B., Cohen, S., Huang, T.: Deep image matting. In: CVPR (2017)
55. Xu, Z., Sun, J.: Image inpainting by patch propagation using patch sparsity. IEEE Trans. Image Process. (TIP) 19(5), 1153–1165 (2010)
56. Yan, Z., Li, X., Li, M., Zuo, W., Shan, S.: Shift-net: image inpainting via deep feature rearrangement. In: Ferrari, V., Hebert, M., Sminchisescu, C., Weiss, Y. (eds.) Computer Vision – ECCV 2018. LNCS, vol. 11218, pp. 3–19. Springer, Cham (2018). https://doi.org/10.1007/978-3-030-01264-9_1
57. Yu, J., Lin, Z., Yang, J., Shen, X., Lu, X., Huang, T.S.: Generative image inpainting with contextual attention. In: CVPR (2018)
58. Yu, J., Lin, Z., Yang, J., Shen, X., Lu, X., Huang, T.S.: Free-form image inpainting with gated convolution. In: ICCV (2019)
59. Zeng, Y., Lin, Z., Yang, J., Zhang, J., Shechtman, E., Lu, H.: High-resolution image inpainting with iterative confidence feedback and guided upsampling. In: ECCV (2020)
60. Zhang, H., et al.: Stackgan: Text to photo-realistic image synthesis with stacked generative adversarial networks. In: ICCV (2017)
61. Zhang, R., Isola, P., Efros, A.A., Shechtman, E., Wang, O.: The unreasonable effectiveness of deep features as a perceptual metric. In: CVPR (2018)
62. Zhu, J.Y., Park, T., Isola, P., Efros, A.A.: Unpaired image-to-image translation using cycle-consistent adversarial networks. In: ICCV (2017)
63. Zhu, Z., Huang, T., Shi, B., Yu, M., Wang, B., Bai, X.: Progressive pose attention transfer for person image generation. In: CVPR (2019)

Design and Interpretation of Universal Adversarial Patches in Face Detection

Xiao Yang[1], Fangyun Wei[2], Hongyang Zhang[3], and Jun Zhu[1(✉)]

[1] Department of Computer Science and Technology, BNRist Center,
Institute for AI, Tsinghua University, Beijing, China
yangxiao19@mails.tsinghua.edu.cn, dcszj@mail.tsinghua.edu.cn
[2] Microsoft Research Asia, Beijing, China
fawe@microsoft.com
[3] TTIC, Chicago, USA
hongyanz@ttic.edu

Abstract. We consider universal adversarial patches for faces—small visual elements whose addition to a face image reliably destroys the performance of face detectors. Unlike previous work that mostly focused on the algorithmic design of adversarial examples in terms of improving the success rate as an attacker, in this work we show an *interpretation* of such patches that can prevent the state-of-the-art face detectors from detecting the real faces. We investigate a phenomenon: patches designed to suppress real face detection appear face-like. This phenomenon holds generally across different initialization, locations, scales of patches, backbones and face detection frameworks. We propose new optimization-based approaches to automatic design of universal adversarial patches for varying goals of the attack, including scenarios in which true positives are suppressed without introducing false positives. Our proposed algorithms perform well on real-world datasets, deceiving state-of-the-art face detectors in terms of multiple precision/recall metrics and transferability.

1 Introduction

Adversarial examples still remain knotty in computer vision [4,8,36], machine learning [25,43], security [28], and other domains [16] despite the huge success of deep neural networks [35,40,41]. In computer vision and machine learning, study of adversarial examples serves as evidences of substantial discrepancy between the human vision system and machine perception mechanism [2,12,27,32]. In security, adversarial examples have raised major concerns on the vulnerability of machine learning systems to malicious attacks. The problem can be stated

---

X. Yang, F. Wei and H. Zhang—Equal contribution.

Electronic supplementary material The online version of this chapter (https://doi.org/10.1007/978-3-030-58520-4_11) contains supplementary material, which is available to authorized users.

© Springer Nature Switzerland AG 2020
A. Vedaldi et al. (Eds.): ECCV 2020, LNCS 12362, pp. 174–191, 2020.
https://doi.org/10.1007/978-3-030-58520-4_11

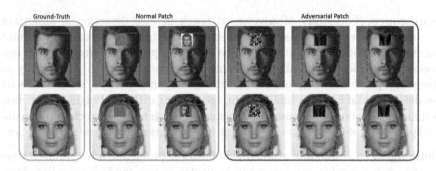

Fig. 1. Properties and effect of different patches. In each image we show true positive (solid blue lines), false positive (red) and missed detection (dashed blue lines). **Left (green) box:** the clean input images. **Middle (orange) box:** pasting an un-optimized noise patch or a downsized face patch on the image does not affect the detectors. **Right (purple) box:** universal adversarial patches produced by different methods successfully suppress true positives, From the fourth to sixth column: The Baseline method *Patch-IoU* appears person-like and induces false positives; our *Patch-Score-Focal* and *Patch-Combination* avoid the false positives. The patches are not necessarily pasted at forehead as demonstrated in Sect. 3. (Color figure online)

as modifying an image, subject to some constraints, so that learning system's response is drastically altered, e.g., changing the classifier or detector output from correct to incorrect. The constraints either come in the *human-imperceptible* form such as bounded ℓ_p perturbations [3,39,43], or in the *human-perceptible* form such as small patches [10,33]. The focus of this work is the latter setting.

While image classification has been repeatedly shown to be broadly vulnerable to adversarial attacks [32], it is less clear whether object detection is similarly vulnerable [13,21–23,29]. State-of-the-art detectors propose thousands of candidate bounding boxes and the adversarial examples are required to fool all of them simultaneously. Nonetheless, for selected object categories the attacks and defenses have been studied extensively. They include objects like stop signs or pedestrians [10,24,33], but few attempts have been made on generating adversarial examples for faces. This is in spite of face detection as a task enjoying significant attention in recent years, due to its practical significance on its own and as a building block for applications such as face alignment, recognition, attribute analysis, and tracking. Publicly available face detectors [19,26,44,45] can achieve performance on par with humans, e.g., on FDDB [15] and WIDER FACE dataset [38], and are insensitive to the variability in occlusions, scales, poses and lighting. However, much remains unknown concerning the behaviors of face detectors on adversarial patches. Our work sheds new light on this question and shows that a simple approach of pasting a single universal patch onto a face image can dramatically harm the accuracy of state-of-the-art face detectors. We propose multiple approaches for building adversarial patches, that address different desired precision/recall characteristics of the resulting performance. In addition to empirical performance, we are interested in understanding the nature of adversarial patch on face detection.

Significance. The study of adversarial patch in face detection is important in multiple aspects: a) In security, adversarial patch serves as one of the most common forms of physical attacks in the detection problems, among which face detection has received significant attention in recent years. b) The study of adversarial patch may help understand the discrepancy between state-of-the-art face detectors and human visual system, towards algorithmic designs of detection mechanism as robust as humans. c) Adversarial patch to face detectors is human-perceptible and demonstrates significant interpretation as shown in this paper.

Challenges. In commonly studied classification problems, adversarial perturbations are inscrutable and appear to be unstructured, random noise-like. Even when structure is perceptible, it tends to bear no resemblance to the categories involved. Many observations and techniques for classification break down when we consider more sophisticated face detection tasks. Compared with other detection tasks, generating adversarial examples for face detection is more challenging, because the state-of-the-art face detectors are able to detect very small faces (e.g., 6×6 pixels [26]) by applying the multi-scale training and testing data augmentation. While there is a large literature on the algorithmic designs of adversarial examples in terms of improving the success rate as an attacker, in this work we focus on the *interpretation* of learning a small, universal adversarial patch which, once being attached to human faces, can prevent the state-of-the-art face detectors from detecting the real faces.

Our Results. The gist of our findings is summarized in Fig. 1. We consider state-of-the-art face detectors, that perform very accurately on natural face images. We optimize a universal adversarial patch, to be pasted on input face images, with the goal of suppressing scores of true positive detection on training data. This is in sharp contrast to most of existing works on adversarial examples for faces in the form of sample-specific, imperceptible perturbations, but a *universal* (independent of the input image) and *interpretable* (semantically meaningful) patch that reliably destroys the performance of face detectors is rarely studied in the literature. Our patch yields the following observations.

- It succeeds in drastically suppressing true positives in test data. The attack also transfers between different face detection frameworks, that is, a patch which is trained on one detection framework deceives another detection framework with a high success rate.
- It looks face-like to humans, as well as to the detectors. Thus, in addition to reducing recall, it reduces precision by inducing false positives.
- Despite superficial face-likeness of the learned adversarial patch, it cannot be simply replaced by a real face patch, nor by a random noise pattern; affixing these to real faces does not fool the detectors.
- Surprisingly, these observations hold generally across different detection frameworks, patch initialization, locations and scales of pasted patch, etc. For example, even while initializing the patch with an image of a non-face object or a complex scene, after 100 epochs the resulting adversarial patch comes to resemble a face (see Fig. 2).

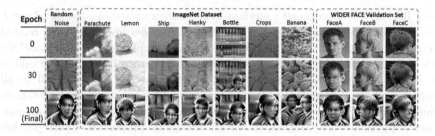

Fig. 2. Adversarial patches from different *initialization* by *Patch-IoU*. The first row is the initial patches, and the second and the third row represent the intermediate and final patches. All of the final patches here are detected as faces by face detectors.

In some scenarios the attacker may want to suppress correct detection without creating false positives (e.g., to hide the presence of any face). We propose modified approaches that produce patches with this property. Intuitively, the approaches minimize the confidence scores of bounding boxes as long as they are larger than a threshold. Experiments verify the effectiveness of the proposed approaches (see the last two columns in Fig. 1).

Summary of Contributions. Our work explores the choices in design of universal adversarial patches for face detection.

- We show how such patches can be optimized to harm performance of existing face detectors. We also show that when the objective is purely to suppress true detection, the resulting patches are interpretable as face-like and can be detected by baseline detectors, with this property holding true across different experimental settings.
- In response to some security-focused scenarios where the adversary may want to suppress correct detection without creating false positives, we describe methods to produce equally successful universal adversarial patches that do not look like faces to either humans nor the face detectors, thus reducing detection rate without increasing false positives. Our proposed algorithms deceive the state-of-the-art face detectors [26] on real-world datasets in terms of multiple precision/recall metrics and transferability.

2 Related Work

Adversarial Examples on Object Detection. Adversarial examples on general object detection have been extensively studied in the recent years [18,42]. A commonly explored domain for adversarial examples in detection is stop sign detection [6,9–11]. Inspired by an observation that both segmentation and detection are based on classifying multiple targets on an image, [36] extended the methodology of generating adversarial examples to the general object detection

tasks. Recently, [33] proposed a method to generate a universal adversarial patch to fool YOLO detectors on pedestrian data set. Another line of research related to our work is the perturbation-based adversarial examples for face detectors [20]. This line of works adds sample-specific, human-imperceptible perturbations to the images globally. In contrast, our adversarial patches are universal to all samples, and our patches are visible to humans and show strong interpretation. While optimizing a patch to fool detectors has previously been used as a simulation of physical-world attacks, to our knowledge no properties of such patches to human visual system have been shown.

Adversarial Examples in Face Recognition. To fool a face recognition system in the physical world, prior work has relied on active explorations via various forms of physical attacks [1,5,17]. For example, [30,31,37] designed a pair of eyeglass frames which allows a face to evade being recognized or to impersonate another individual. However, these adversarial examples did not afford any semantic interpretation. Though scaled adversarial perturbations of robustly trained classifiers might have semantic meaning to humans [43], those adversarially trained classifiers are not widely used due to an intrinsic trade-off between robustness and accuracy [34,43].

Face Detection. Face detection is typically less sensitive to the variation of face scales, angles, and other external factors such as occlusions and image qualities. Modern face detection algorithms [19,26,44,45] take advantage of anchor[1] based object detection methods, such as SSD [23] and RetinaNet [22], Faster R-CNN [29] and Mask R-CNN [13], and can achieve performance on par with humans on many public face detection benchmarks, such as FDDB and WIDER FACE dataset. They can detect faces as small as 6 pixels by applying multi-scale training and testing data augmentation, which serves as one of the primary differences with general object detection.

3   Interpretation of Adversarial Patch as Face

In this section, we present our main experimental results on the interpretation of adversarial patch. We show that, on one hand, the adversarial patch optimized by the proposed *Patch-IoU* method looks like a face. The patch can be detected by the baseline face detection model, even in the absence of extra constraints to encourage the patch to be face-like. On the other hand, attaching a face picture to a real face does not fool the detector (see Fig. 1). The phenomenon holds generally across different setups.

---

[1] Anchors are a set of predefined and well-designed initial rectangles with different scales and ratios. They are densely tiled on feature maps for object classification and bounding box regression.

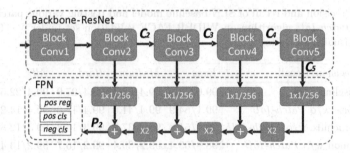

Fig. 3. SLN framework in our face detection baseline model, where $\times 2$ represents the bilinear upsampling, $+$ represents the element-wise summation, and $1 \times 1/256$ represents the 1×1 convolution with 256 output channels. The feature map P_2 is used as the only detection layer where all anchors are tiled with stride 4 pixels. The positive classification loss is our main attacking target.

3.1 Preliminaries on Face Detection

Dataset. We use WIDER FACE [38] training dataset to learn both the face detector and the adversarial patch. The WIDER FACE dataset contains 32,203 images and 393,703 annotated face bounding boxes with high degree of variability in scales, poses, occlusions, expression, makeup, and illumination. According to the detection rate of EdgeBox [46], WIDER FACE dataset is split into 3 subsets: Easy, Medium and Hard. The face detector and adversarial patch are evaluated on the validation set. The set of ground-truth bounding boxes for an image is defined as $\{B_i\}$, where $B_i = (x^i, y^i, w^i, h^i)$, (x^i, y^i) is the center of the box, and w^i and h^i are the width and height of the bounding box, respectively.

Face Detection Framework. We use the state-of-the-art face detection framework [26] as the baseline model, and we name it as Single Level Network (SLN). Figure 3 illustrates the network structure. We use ResNet [14] as backbone, with a bottom-up feature refusion procedure in Feature Pyramid Network (FPN) [21]. We obtain a high-resolution and informative feature map P_2 (stride equals to 4 pixels). Anchors with scales $\{16, 32, 64, 128\}$ and aspect ratio 1 are tiled on P_2 uniformly. We denote by $\{A_i\}$ the set of all anchors. We apply IoU regression loss, anchor matching criterion, and group sampling strategy in [26] to train our baseline model. Formally, let $\text{IoU}(A_i, B_j)$ denote the IoU between the i-th anchor and the j-th ground-truth bounding box. Anchors with $\text{IoU}(A_i, B_j) > 0.6$ and $\text{IoU}(A_i, B_j) < 0.4$ will be set as positive and negative samples. Finally, we define a multi-task loss $\mathcal{L} = \mathcal{L}_{cls}^p + \mathcal{L}_{cls}^n + \mathcal{L}_{reg}$, where $\mathcal{L}_{cls}^p$ and $\mathcal{L}_{cls}^n$ denote the standard cross entropy loss for positive and negative samples, respectively, and $\mathcal{L}_{reg} = \frac{1}{N_{reg}} \sum_{(A_i, B_j)} \|1 - \text{IoU}(A_i, B_j)\|_2^2$ represents the IoU least square regression loss. If not specified, we use ResNet-18 as our defaulted backbone.

Training Details of Face Detector. We use random horizontal flip and scale jittering as data augmentation during training. For scale jittering, each image is resized by a factor of $0.25 \times n$, where n is randomly chosen from [1, 8]. We set

Table 1. Precision and recall of SLN baseline model and pasting various patches with (without) *Patch-IoU* algorithm on WIDER FACE validation set under $\delta = 0.99$ (see Fig. 2 for visualized results).

Precision/Recall	*Easy*	*Medium*	*Hard*	*All*
Baseline-SLN	99.0/73.4	99.4/62.4	99.4/27.9	99.4/22.5
Noise w/o *Patch-IoU*	99.1/54.9	99.4/41.5	99.4/17.6	99.4/14.2
Parachute w/o *Patch-IoU*	99.1/51.8	99.3/37.2	99.3/15.8	99.3/12.8
Lemon w/o *Patch-IoU*	98.9/53.4	99.2/39.4	99.2/16.7	99.2/13.4
Bottle w/o *Patch-IoU*	99.1/53.5	99.4/41.1	99.4/17.3	99.4/13.9
Banana w/o *Patch-IoU*	99.1/55.2	99.4/41.4	99.4/17.5	99.4/14.1
FaceA w/o *Patch-IoU*	51.8/30.2	61.4/24.2	61.8/10.3	61.8/8.3
FaceB w/o *Patch-IoU*	77.8/39.5	83.5/30.1	83.6/12.9	83.6/10.4
FaceC w/o *Patch-IoU*	98.4/38.3	98.9/29.8	98.9/12.7	98.9/10.2
Noise w/*Patch-IoU*	2.7/2.7	6.5/3.7	7.3/1.8	7.3/1.4
Parachute w/*Patch-IoU*	2.1/0.5	4.8/0.7	5.9/0.4	5.9/0.3
Lemon w/*Patch-IoU*	0.2/0.1	0.9/0.3	1.0/0.2	1.0/0.1
Bottle w/*Patch-IoU*	1.1/1.1	2.2/1.2	2.5/0.6	2.6/0.5
Banana w/*Patch-IoU*	10.2/5.0	19.0/5.6	20.3/2.5	20.3/2.0
FaceA w/*Patch-IoU*	0.0/0.0	0.0/0.0	0.0/0.0	0.0/0.0
FaceB w/*Patch-IoU*	0.1/0.0	2.3/0.2	2.6/0.1	2.6/0.1
FaceC w/*Patch-IoU*	0.1/0.1	0.2/0.1	0.3/0.0	0.3/0.0

the initial learning rate as 0.01 and decay the learning rate by a factor of 0.1 on the 60-th and the 80-th epochs. We use Non-Maximum Suppression (NMS) as post-processing. The first line in Table 1 shows the precision and recall of the baseline model. *Easy*, *Medium*, *Hard*, and *All*[2] represent the results from easy subset, medium subset, hard subset and the whole validation set, respectively.

3.2   Design of Adversarial Patch

Details of Adversarial Patch. In our work we need craft a universal adversarial patch that can be pasted at input faces, with the objective of fooling face detectors. For detection, as opposed to balanced classification problems, there are two types of errors: the false-positive error and the false-negative error. In response to an intrinsic trade-off between precision and recall in the face detection tasks, existing works set a score threshold δ to keep high precision: output proposals with confidence scores higher than δ are treated as faces. The goal of adversary is to decrease the confidence scores to be lower than δ by pasting a

---

[2] Official WIDER FACE testing script (http://shuoyang1213.me/WIDERFACE/) only gives results of *Easy*, *Medium* and *Hard* subsets. We reimplement the test script to support testing on the whole validation set.

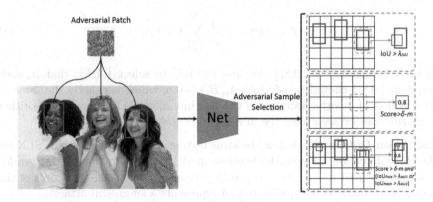

Fig. 4. Different optimization methods for generating adversarial patches. The core difference is to involve different samples in the optimization of adversarial patch. From top to bottom: *Patch-IoU*, *Patch-Score-Focal* and *Patch-Combination*, respectively.

carefully-calculated, universal patch to human faces. We show that the adversarial patch can make the real faces invisible to various detectors. Formally, we define the patch P as a rectangle which is denoted by (x^P, y^P, w^P, h^P), where (x^P, y^P) is the center of the patch relative to the ground-truth bounding box B_i, and w^P and h^P represent its width and height, respectively. In our experiments, we set both w^P and h^P as 128 since the largest anchor size is 128 in the SLN face detection framework. For each of the ground-truth bounding box $B_i = (x^i, y^i, w^i, h^i)$ in the given training image, the patch P is resized to $\alpha\sqrt{w^i h^i}$ $(0 < \alpha < 1)$ and then placed on B_i with its center position (x^P, y^P). We randomly initialize the patch, and set $\alpha = 0.5$ and $(x^P, y^P) = (w^i/2, \alpha\sqrt{w^i h^i}/2)$, unless otherwise specified. All of the training settings, including the training dataset and the hyper-parameter tuning, are the same as the SLN (or other face detection framework) baseline model.

Optimization. Previous adversarial attacks on object detectors [24] have shown some progress through inverse optimization for the loss function of the detectors, and the-state-of-art method in [33] also generates adversarial patches by minimizing the object score of the detector. Inspired by this, we focus on adversarial face patches to design a baseline method named *Patch-IoU*. Specifically, we firstly define *Adversarial Sample Set* $\{AS_i\}$ as the set of selected samples which are involved in the training optimization of the adversarial patch. Each *Adversarial Sample* $AS_i = (A_i, B_i, S_i, P)$ contains four elements: the anchor A_i, the ground-truth bounding box B_i, the face confidence score S_i which represents the output of the classification layer with the softmax operation, and the adversarial patch P^3, respectively. We freeze all weights of the face detector; the patch P is the only variable to be optimized by gradient ascent algorithm. Our goal is to maximize the following loss function:

---

[3] All AS_i's share an identical adversarial patch P.

$$\mathcal{L}_{Adv}(P) = -\frac{1}{N}\sum_{i=1}^{N}\log(S_i), \tag{1}$$

where N is the size of $\{AS_i\}$. We use the IoU to select $\{AS_i\}$, that is, each sample in $\{AS_i\}$ should satisfy $\text{IoU}(A_i, B_i) > 0.6$, which is exactly the same as the selection of positive samples in the baseline model. Our baseline algorithm *Patch-IoU* can be seen from the first row of Fig. 4.

Evaluation Details. We follow the same testing settings as that of the SLN (or other face detection framework) baseline model. Similar to the existing works, we set a threshold $\delta = 0.99$ to keep high precision: decreasing the scores of the ground-truth faces to be smaller than δ represents a successful attack.

We show our visualized results in Fig. 1 and the first column of Fig. 2, i.e., the evolution of the adversarial patch with random initialization. Table 1 (see Baseline, Noise w/o *Patch-IoU* and Noise w/*Patch-IoU* three lines) presents the corresponding numerical results on precision and recall with (without) *Patch-IoU* optimization. We have three main observations:

- The drop of recall implies that the detector fails to detect the real faces in the presence of the adversarial patch, i.e., Score(RealFace) $< \delta$.
- The patch with 100-epoch training appears face-like. The drop of precision implies that the detector *falsely recognizes* the adversarial patch as a human face, i.e., Score(AdversarialPatch) $> \delta$.
- Attaching an additional face photo to the real faces with the same size and location as the adversarial patch indeed affects precision more than other setups, but we do not obverse significant drop of recall.

3.3 Generality

The interpretation of adversarial patch is not a unique property of the setup in Sect. 3.2. Instead, we show that it is a general phenomenon which holds across different initialization, patch locations and scales, backbones, and detection frameworks.

Initialization. We randomly select seven images from ImageNet [7], three faces from WIDER FACE validation set, and one random image as our initialization. Figure 2 shows the evolution of patches across different training epochs. We observe that the patches come to resemble human faces, even while initializing the patches with non-face objects or a complex scene.

Patch Locations and Scales. To examine whether the interpretation holds across different locations and scales, we run the algorithm with different patch *scales*: $\alpha \in \{0.3, 0.35, 0.4\}$ and *locations*: top $(x^P, y^P) = (w^i/2, \alpha\sqrt{w^i h^i}/2)$, center $(x^P, y^P) = (w^i/2, h^i/2)$, and bottom $(x^P, y^P) = (w^i/2, h^i - \alpha\sqrt{w^i h^i}/2)$. We observe a similar phenomenon for all these setups, as shown in Fig. 5.

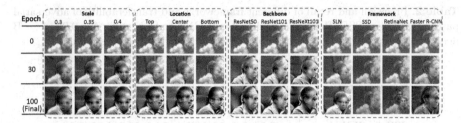

Fig. 5. Optimization results by *Patch-IoU* across different scales, locations, backbones and detection frameworks. *Patch-IoU* generates face-like adversarial patch which is falsely detected by various detectors.

Backbones. We see in Fig. 5 that the adversarial patches look like human faces for different backbones, including ResNet-50, ResNet-101 and ResNext-101.

Detection Frameworks. Besides the face detection framework SLN, we also test three popular detection frameworks: SSD [23], RetinaNet [22] and Faster R-CNN [29]. For Faster R-CNN, we use the SLN as our region proposal network, and the RoIAlign [13] is applied on each proposal to refine face classification and bounding box regression. Except for the detection architecture, all of the experimental setups for the baseline model and the adversarial patch training are the same. Similarly, we observe that the adversarial patches come to resemble human faces (see Fig. 5).

Numerical Results. We also report the numerical results of the algorithm. We set $\delta = 0.99$ and show the precision and recall of using various patches to attack the SLN face detector on the WIDER FACE validation set. Table 1 illustrates the effect of eight representative kinds of initialization with (without) *Patch-IoU* optimization. We do not report the numerical results about different patch locations and scales, backbones and detection frameworks, since the results and phenomenon are identical as the initialization. It can be seen that pasting a patch (even initialized as face) without any optimization will cause the recall to drop, but not so drastically. In contrast, the *Patch-IoU* can cause the recall to decrease dramatically across different initialization, leading to a successful attack. However, the adversarial patches also reduce the precision because the face-like patches are falsely detected and the scores of the patches are even higher than those of the true faces. We defer more discussions about evaluation metrics and the issue of precision drop in *Patch-IoU* method to Sect. 4.

Transferability Between Different Frameworks. We also study the transferability of adversarial patch between different frameworks. Formally, we attach patches optimized from SSD, RetinaNet and Faster R-CNN, respectively, on each ground-truth bounding box in WIDER FACE validation set, and test their attacking performance on SLN baseline detector. Table 2 shows the numerical results. The patch trained on the Faster R-CNN framework enjoys higher success rate as an attacker on the SLN than the SSD and RetinaNet.

Table 2. Precision and recall of different frameworks and transferability of adversarial patch attack from SSD, RetinaNet and Faster R-CNN to SLN under $\delta = 0.99$. A $\rightarrow$ B denotes that the adversarial patch is optimized by detector A and tested on B.

Precision/Recall	*Easy*	*Medium*	*Hard*	*All*
Baseline-SLN	99.0/73.4	99.4/62.4	99.4/27.9	99.4/22.5
Patch-IoU-SLN	2.7/2.7	6.5/3.7	7.3/1.8	7.3/1.4
SSD $\rightarrow$ SLN	42.5/29.9	53.4/25.1	54.1/10.7	54.1/8.6
RetinaNet $\rightarrow$ SLN	37.4/28.7	48.5/24.5	49.2/10.5	49.2/8.5
Faster R-CNN $\rightarrow$ SLN	32.9/3.8	44.9/3.4	46.3/1.5	46.3/1.2

Besides, we examine generality across training datasets. The final patches are face-like and can be falsely detected by baseline face detector. To examine the attacking performance of only part of the adversarial patch that is optimized by *Patch-IoU*, we remove a half and one third area of the whole patch and test the performance of the remaining part of the patch on the WIDER FACE validation dataset. Due to limited space, we show these results in Appendix A.

3.4   Interpretation of Adversarial Patch

Anchor mechanism with different scales based face detectors provides plenty of facial candidate proposals. This essentially belongs to an ensemble defense strategy compared to classification tasks when adversarial patches strive to lower the classification score of each proposal. Therefore, the adversarial patch will be optimized towards reducing the scores of more proposals. The previous method *Patch-IoU* only optimizes proposals over a certain range of *IoU*, not including its own adversarial patch. Unconstrained optimization for patches can reduce classification scores of most proposals, yet appearing face-like phenomenon in the face detection task. That makes us rethink what is an effective patch optimization method for deceiving face detectors.

4   Improved Optimization of Adversarial Patch

Current baseline optimization method *Patch-IoU* appear face-like phenomenon on the adversarial patch. In this section, we first introduce an evaluation criterion of what kind of patch belongs to a better optimization. Then we propose two improved optimization methods, *Patch-Score-Focal* and *Patch-Combination*, based on above analysis. We demonstrate the effectiveness of the proposed approaches by visualized and numerical results.

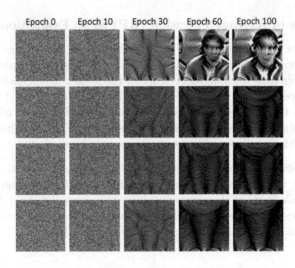

Fig. 6. From top to bottom, the four rows represent the adversarial patches of *Patch-IoU*, *Patch-Score*, *Patch-Score-Focal* and *Patch-Combination*, respectively.

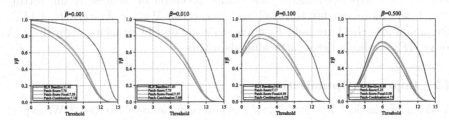

Fig. 7. Threshold-F_β curve and AF_β under $\beta = [0.001, 0.01, 0.1, 0.5]$. *Patch-Combination* benefits from the confidence scores and location information of ground-truth and the patch and outperforms other methods.

4.1 Evaluation Metric

Attacking Criteria. We set a confidence score threshold δ to keep high precision (> 0.99) in order to reduce the possibility of raising false positives. Note that the adversarial patch by *Patch-IoU* can be detected as faces (see Sect. 3.2). To successfully attack a face detector under the policy that none of the bounding boxes in the images should be detected as faces, we define our criteria as follows:

- **Criterion 1:** Reducing the confidence scores of true faces to be lower than δ;
- **Criterion 2:** Preventing the confidence score of adversarial patch from being higher than δ.

Shortcomings of Average Precision (AP) as an Evaluation Metric

- Reducing the confidence scores of true faces does not change the relative rankings among positive (faces) and negative (backgrounds) proposals. As a result, AP remains unchanged even when the attack is successful.
- The fake faces appearing on the adversarial patch are treated as false positives. Thus the AP becomes small due to large amounts of false positives. However, this should be considered an unsuccessful attack when the goal is to prevent false positives while suppressing true predictions.

We introduce some examples to illustrate the above arguments in Appendix D.

We see that a successful attacking algorithm should reduce the recall of the test images while keeping the precision above the given threshold δ. The observation motivates us to use the recall conditioning on the high precision and the F_β score to evaluate the algorithms. F_β score is defined as:

$$F_\beta = \frac{1 + \beta^2}{\beta^2 \text{Precision}^{-1} + \text{Recall}^{-1}},$$

where β is a hyper-parameter that trades precision off against recall; setting $\beta < 1$ sets more weights to recall and vice versa. We use Average F_β (AF_β), the area under the Threshold-F_β curve, to evaluate the attacking algorithms. A lower AF_β implies a better attacking algorithm.

4.2 Improved Optimization

As described in Sect. 3.2, *Patch-IoU* method may violate *Criterion 2*. We expect the optimized patch to meet two criterions. Therefore, we first introduce a score-based optimization method named *Patch-Score*. Specifically, we set the adversarial sample set $\{AS_i = (A_i, B_i, S_i, P)\}$ as those samples with $S_i > \delta - m$, where m is a hyper-parameter on the relaxation of the constraint. This procedure for adversarial sample set selection forces the scores of both adversarial patch and true faces to be lower than predefined threshold δ. We set $\delta - m = 0.5$ as default.

Although *Patch-Score* satisfies *Criterion 1* and *Criterion 2* simultaneously, we show that some high-score negative samples may also be selected as adversarial samples AS_i, which may degrade the performance as an attacker. In response to this issue, we propose two solutions, namely, *Patch-Score-Focal* and *Patch-Combination*.

***Patch-Score-Focal* Optimization.** Focal loss [22] aims at solving the extreme imbalance issue between foreground and background proposals in the object detection. The core idea is to assign small weights to the vast majority of easily-classified negatives and prevent them from dominating the classification loss. Our method is inspired from the Focal loss and adapts to the adversarial patch training. Formally, we replace the loss in *Patch-Score* by

$$\mathcal{L}_{Adv}(P) = -\frac{1}{N} \sum_{i=1}^{N} S_i^\gamma \log(S_i), \tag{2}$$

Table 3. Precision and recall comparisons of Baseline-SLN, *Patch-Score*, *Patch-Score-Focal* and *Patch-Combination* with $\delta = 0.99$.

Precision/Recall	*Easy*	*Medium*	*Hard*	*All*
Baseline-SLN	99.0/73.4	99.4/62.4	99.4/27.9	99.4/22.5
Patch-Score	98.5/25.5	98.9/19.7	99.0/8.3	99.0/6.7
Patch-Score-Focal	98.4/23.1	98.9/17.9	98.9/7.6	98.9/6.1
Patch-Combination	98.2/**20.6**	98.7/**15.6**	98.7/**6.6**	98.7/**5.4**

where γ is a hyper-parameter and S_i^γ represents the modulating factor which sets different weights for different samples. In contrast to the Focal loss which assigns smaller weights to the easily-classified samples, our goal is to filter out negative proposals whose score are higher than $\delta - m$ and set bigger weights to those negative samples with higher scores. We name this optimization method as *Patch-Score-Focal* (see the second row in Fig. 4). We set $\delta - m = 0.5$ and $\gamma = 2$ as suggested in [22].

***Patch-Combination* Optimization.** On one hand, *Patch-IoU* aims to select adversarial samples according to the higher IoUs of the ground-truth faces, without any score-related constraints in the adversarial patch optimization. On the other hand, *Patch-Score* is to select those samples with confidence scores higher than $\delta - m$, and thus the selected samples may include many negative proposals in the absence of information from the ground-truth faces. We combine the advantages of both methods and propose a new optimization method named *Patch-Combination*. Formally, we restrict each adversarial sample $AS_i = (A_i, B_i, S_i, P)$ to satisfy the following conditions: 1) $S_i > \delta - m$; 2) $IoU(A_i, B_i) > \lambda_1$ or $IoU(A_i, P) > \lambda_2$. The third row of Fig. 4 illustrates the methodology. We set $\delta - m = 0.5$, $\lambda_1 = 0.3$ and $\lambda_2 = 0.3$ as default.

4.3 Experimental Results

We use WIDER FACE training set and SLN baseline model for adversarial patch training; except for the adversarial sample set selection procedure, the same optimization setups for *Patch-IoU* training are applied to the *Patch-Score*, *Patch-Score-Focal* and *Patch-Combination* methods. Visualized results are illustrated in the second to the fourth rows of Fig. 6. In contrast to *Patch-IoU* method, no faces can be detected by our improved optimization algorithms since they all satisfy *Criterion 1* and *Criterion 2*.

Besides the visualized results, we also show numerical results. Figure 7 shows four Threshold-F_β[4] curves and AF_β (lower AF_β means a better attack) under different $\beta = [0.001, 0.01, 0.1, 0.5]$. Table 3 also shows the comparisons of precision and recall with $\delta = 0.99$. Moreover, we also reduce the adversarial patch to

---

[4] Define s_p and s_n as positive and negative logits. We compute $s = s_p - s_n$ as the confidence score when plotting Threshold-F_β curve for better visualization.

different proportions and paste the patch on different positions for comparisons in Appendix B. In Appendix C, we examine the transferability of the adversarial patch between different models. *Patch-Combination* and *Patch-Score-Focal* achieve better performance than *Patch-Score* on extensive experiments, with better optimization design of adversarial sample set. This is because *Patch-Combination* benefits from the interpretation that attacking an ensemble defense (*e.g.* plenty of proposals in face detection) should fully consider the full use of global information in the optimization.

5 Conclusions

In this paper, we perform a comprehensive interpretation of adversarial patches to state-of-the-art anchor based face detectors. Firstly we show a face-like phenomenon of the generated adversarial patches by previous method *Patch-IoU*, which makes the detectors falsely recognize the patches as human faces across different settings. That is very instructive for the understanding of universal adversarial samples from an optimization perspective. Besides, we propose *Patch-Score-Focal* and *Patch-Combination* methods to obtain more effective adversarial patches. Extensive experiments verify the effectiveness and transferability of the proposed methods. We also believe that these promising insights and methods will inspire further studies for the community.

Acknowledgement. We thank Gregory Shakhnarovich for helping to improve the writing of this paper and valuable suggestions on the experimental designs. X. Yang and J. Zhu were supported by the National Key Research and Development Program of China (No. 2017YFA0700904), NSFC Projects (Nos. 61620106010, U19B2034, U181146), Beijing Academy of Artificial Intelligence, Tsinghua-Huawei Joint Research Program, Tiangong Institute for Intelligent Computing, and NVIDIA NVAIL Program with GPU/DGX Acceleration. H. Zhang was supported in part by the Defense Advanced Research Projects Agency under cooperative agreement HR00112020003.

References

1. Athalye, A., Engstrom, L., Ilyas, A., Kwok, K.: Synthesizing robust adversarial examples. arXiv preprint arXiv:1707.07397 (2017)
2. Biggio, B., et al.: Evasion attacks against machine learning at test time. In: Joint European Conference on Machine Learning and Knowledge Discovery in Databases, pp. 387–402 (2013)
3. Blum, A., Dick, T., Manoj, N., Zhang, H.: Random smoothing might be unable to certify ℓ_∞ robustness for high-dimensional images. arXiv preprint arXiv:2002.03517 2(2) (2020)
4. Brendel, W., et al.: Adversarial vision challenge. In: The NeurIPS'18 Competition, pp. 129–153 (2020)
5. Brown, T.B., Mané, D., Roy, A., Abadi, M., Gilmer, J.: Adversarial patch. arXiv preprint arXiv:1712.09665 (2017)

6. Chen, S.-T., Cornelius, C., Martin, J., Chau, D.H.P.: ShapeShifter: robust physical adversarial attack on faster R-CNN object detector. In: Berlingerio, M., Bonchi, F., Gärtner, T., Hurley, N., Ifrim, G. (eds.) ECML PKDD 2018. LNCS (LNAI), vol. 11051, pp. 52–68. Springer, Cham (2019). https://doi.org/10.1007/978-3-030-10925-7_4

7. Deng, J., Dong, W., Socher, R., Li, L.J., Li, K., Fei-Fei, L.: ImageNet: a large-scale hierarchical image database. In: CVPR 2009 (2009)

8. Dong, Y., et al.: Benchmarking adversarial robustness on image classification. In: Proceedings of the IEEE/CVF Conference on Computer Vision and Pattern Recognition (CVPR), pp. 321–331 (2020)

9. Eykholt, K., et al.: Physical adversarial examples for object detectors. arXiv preprint arXiv:1807.07769 (2018)

10. Eykholt, K., et al.: Robust physical-world attacks on deep learning visual classification. In: IEEE Conference on Computer Vision and Pattern Recognition, pp. 1625–1634 (2018)

11. Eykholt, K., et al.: Note on attacking object detectors with adversarial stickers. arXiv preprint arXiv:1712.08062 (2017)

12. Goodfellow, I.J., Shlens, J., Szegedy, C.: Explaining and harnessing adversarial examples. In: International Conference on Learning Representations (ICLR) (2015)

13. He, K., Gkioxari, G., Dollár, P., Girshick, R.: Mask R-CNN. In: Proceedings of the IEEE International Conference on Computer Vision, pp. 2961–2969 (2017)

14. He, K., Zhang, X., Ren, S., Sun, J.: Deep residual learning for image recognition. In: Proceedings of the IEEE Conference on Computer Vision and Pattern Recognition, pp. 770–778 (2016)

15. Jain, V., Learned-Miller, E.: FDDB: a benchmark for face detection in unconstrained settings (2010)

16. Jia, R., Liang, P.: Adversarial examples for evaluating reading comprehension systems. arXiv preprint arXiv:1707.07328 (2017)

17. Kurakin, A., Goodfellow, I., Bengio, S.: Adversarial examples in the physical world. In: International Conference on Learning Representations (ICLR) Workshops (2017)

18. Lee, M., Kolter, Z.: On physical adversarial patches for object detection. arXiv preprint arXiv:1906.11897 (2019)

19. Li, J., et al.: DSFD: dual shot face detector. In: Proceedings of the IEEE Conference on Computer Vision and Pattern Recognition, pp. 5060–5069 (2019)

20. Li, Y., Yang, X., Wu, B., Lyu, S.: Hiding faces in plain sight: Disrupting ai face synthesis with adversarial perturbations. arXiv preprint arXiv:1906.09288 (2019)

21. Lin, T.Y., Dollár, P., Girshick, R., He, K., Hariharan, B., Belongie, S.: Feature pyramid networks for object detection. In: Proceedings of the IEEE Conference on Computer Vision and Pattern Recognition, pp. 2117–2125 (2017)

22. Lin, T.Y., Goyal, P., Girshick, R., He, K., Dollár, P.: Focal loss for dense object detection. In: Proceedings of the IEEE International Conference on Computer Vision, pp. 2980–2988 (2017)

23. Liu, W., et al.: SSD: single shot MultiBox detector. In: Leibe, B., Matas, J., Sebe, N., Welling, M. (eds.) ECCV 2016. LNCS, vol. 9905, pp. 21–37. Springer, Cham (2016). https://doi.org/10.1007/978-3-319-46448-0_2

24. Liu, X., Yang, H., Liu, Z., Song, L., Li, H., Chen, Y.: Dpatch: an adversarial patch attack on object detectors. arXiv preprint arXiv:1806.02299 (2018)

25. Madry, A., Makelov, A., Schmidt, L., Tsipras, D., Vladu, A.: Towards deep learning models resistant to adversarial attacks. In: International Conference on Learning Representations (ICLR) (2018)

26. Ming, X., Wei, F., Zhang, T., Chen, D., Wen, F.: Group sampling for scale invariant face detection. In: Proceedings of the IEEE Conference on Computer Vision and Pattern Recognition, pp. 3446–3456 (2019)
27. Nguyen, A., Yosinski, J., Clune, J.: Deep neural networks are easily fooled: High confidence predictions for unrecognizable images. In: The IEEE Conference on Computer Vision and Pattern Recognition (CVPR), pp. 427–436 (2015)
28. Papernot, N., McDaniel, P., Wu, X., Jha, S., Swami, A.: Distillation as a defense to adversarial perturbations against deep neural networks. In: IEEE Symposium on Security and Privacy (2016)
29. Ren, S., He, K., Girshick, R., Sun, J.: Faster R-CNN: towards real-time object detection with region proposal networks. In: Advances in Neural Information Processing Systems, pp. 91–99 (2015)
30. Sharif, M., Bhagavatula, S., Bauer, L., Reiter, M.K.: Accessorize to a crime: real and stealthy attacks on state-of-the-art face recognition. In: Proceedings of the 2016 ACM SIGSAC Conference on Computer and Communications Security, pp. 1528–1540 (2016)
31. Sharif, M., Bhagavatula, S., Bauer, L., Reiter, M.K.: A general framework for adversarial examples with objectives. ACM Trans. Privacy Secur. (TOPS) **22**(3), 16 (2019)
32. Szegedy, C., et al.: Intriguing properties of neural networks. In: International Conference on Learning Representations (ICLR) (2014)
33. Thys, S., Van Ranst, W., Goedemé, T.: Fooling automated surveillance cameras: adversarial patches to attack person detection. In: Proceedings of the IEEE Conference on Computer Vision and Pattern Recognition Workshops (2019)
34. Tsipras, D., Santurkar, S., Engstrom, L., Turner, A., Madry, A.: Robustness may be at odds with accuracy. arXiv preprint arXiv:1805.12152 (2018)
35. Wei, F., Sun, X., Li, H., Wang, J., Lin, S.: Point-set anchors for object detection, instance segmentation and pose estimation. arXiv preprint arXiv:2007.02846 (2020)
36. Xie, C., Wang, J., Zhang, Z., Zhou, Y., Xie, L., Yuille, A.: Adversarial examples for semantic segmentation and object detection. In: IEEE International Conference on Computer Vision, pp. 1369–1378 (2017)
37. Yamada, T., Gohshi, S., Echizen, I.: Privacy visor: method for preventing face image detection by using differences in human and device sensitivity. In: IFIP International Conference on Communications and Multimedia Security, pp. 152–161 (2013)
38. Yang, S., Luo, P., Loy, C.C., Tang, X.: Wider face: a face detection benchmark. In: IEEE Conference on Computer Vision and Pattern Recognition (CVPR) (2016)
39. Yang, Y.Y., Rashtchian, C., Zhang, H., Salakhutdinov, R., Chaudhuri, K.: Adversarial robustness through local lipschitzness. arXiv preprint arXiv:2003.02460 (2020)
40. You, S., Huang, T., Yang, M., Wang, F., Qian, C., Zhang, C.: Greedynas: towards fast one-shot NAS with greedy supernet. In: Proceedings of the IEEE/CVF Conference on Computer Vision and Pattern Recognition, pp. 1999–2008 (2020)
41. You, S., Xu, C., Xu, C., Tao, D.: Learning from multiple teacher networks. In: Proceedings of the 23rd ACM SIGKDD International Conference on Knowledge Discovery and Data Mining, pp. 1285–1294 (2017)
42. Zhang, H., Wang, J.: Towards adversarially robust object detection. In: IEEE International Conference on Computer Vision, pp. 421–430 (2019)

43. Zhang, H., Yu, Y., Jiao, J., Xing, E.P., Ghaoui, L.E., Jordan, M.I.: Theoretically principled trade-off between robustness and accuracy. In: International Conference on Machine Learning (ICML) (2019)
44. Zhang, S., Wen, L., Shi, H., Lei, Z., Lyu, S., Li, S.Z.: Single-shot scale-aware network for real-time face detection. Int. J. Comput. Vision **127**(6–7), 537–559 (2019)
45. Zhu, C., Tao, R., Luu, K., Savvides, M.: Seeing small faces from robust anchor's perspective. In: Proceedings of the IEEE Conference on Computer Vision and Pattern Recognition, pp. 5127–5136 (2018)
46. Zitnick, C.L., Dollár, P.: Edge boxes: locating object proposals from edges. In: Fleet, D., Pajdla, T., Schiele, B., Tuytelaars, T. (eds.) ECCV 2014. LNCS, vol. 8693, pp. 391–405. Springer, Cham (2014). https://doi.org/10.1007/978-3-319-10602-1_26

Few-Shot Object Detection and Viewpoint Estimation for Objects in the Wild

Yang Xiao[1]([✉]) and Renaud Marlet[1,2]

[1] LIGM, Ecole des Ponts, Univ Gustave Eiffel, CNRS, Marne-la-Vallée, France
yang.xiao@enpc.fr
[2] valeo.ai, Paris, France

Abstract. Detecting objects and estimating their viewpoint in images are key tasks of 3D scene understanding. Recent approaches have achieved excellent results on very large benchmarks for object detection and viewpoint estimation. However, performances are still lagging behind for novel object categories with few samples. In this paper, we tackle the problems of few-shot object detection and few-shot viewpoint estimation. We propose a meta-learning framework that can be applied to both tasks, possibly including 3D data. Our models improve the results on objects of novel classes by leveraging on rich feature information originating from base classes with many samples. A simple joint feature embedding module is proposed to make the most of this feature sharing. Despite its simplicity, our method outperforms state-of-the-art methods by a large margin on a range of datasets, including PASCAL VOC and MS COCO for few-shot object detection, and Pascal3D+ and ObjectNet3D for few-shot viewpoint estimation. And for the first time, we tackle the combination of both few-shot tasks, on ObjectNet3D, showing promising results.

Keywords: Few-shot learning · Meta learning · Object detection · Viewpoint estimation

1 Introduction

Detecting objects in 2D images and estimate their 3D pose, as shown in Fig. 1, is extremely useful for tasks such as 3D scene understanding, augmented reality and robot manipulation. With the emergence of large databases annotated with object bounding boxes and viewpoints, deep-learning-based methods have achieved very good results on both tasks. However these methods, that rely on rich labeled data, usually fail to generalize to *novel* object categories when only a few annotated samples are available. Transferring the knowledge learned from large base categories with abundant annotated images to novel categories with scarce annotated samples is a *few-shot learning* problem.

To address few-shot detection, some approaches simultaneously tackle few-shot classification and few-shot localization by disentangling the learning of

© Springer Nature Switzerland AG 2020
A. Vedaldi et al. (Eds.): ECCV 2020, LNCS 12362, pp. 192–210, 2020.
https://doi.org/10.1007/978-3-030-58520-4_12

Training

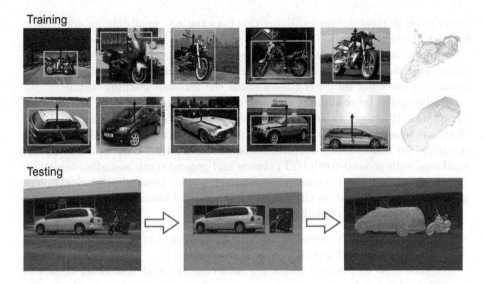

Testing

Fig. 1. Few-shot object detection and viewpoint estimation. Starting with images labeled with bounding boxes and viewpoints of objects from base classes, and given only a few similarly labeled images for new categories (top), we predict in a query image the 2D location of objects of new categories, as well as their 3D poses, leveraging on just a few arbitrary 3D class models (bottom).

category-agnostic and category-specific network parameters [59]. Others attach a reweighting module to existing object detection networks [23,64]. Though these methods have made significant progress, current few-shot detection evaluation protocols suffer from statistical unreliability and the prediction depends heavily on the choice of support data, which makes direct comparison difficult [57].

In parallel to the endeavours made in few-shot object detection, recent work proposes to perform category-agnostic viewpoint estimation that can be directly applied to novel object categories without retraining [63,65]. However, these methods either require the testing categories to be similar to the training ones [65], or assume the exact CAD model to be provided for each object during inference [63]. Differently, the meta-learning-based method MetaView [53] introduces the category-level few-shot viewpoint estimation problem and addresses it by learning to estimate category-specific keypoints, requiring extra annotations. In any case, precisely annotating the 3D pose of objects in images is far more tedious than annotating their 2D bounding boxes, which makes few-shot viewpoint estimation a non-trivial yet largely under-explored problem.

In this work, we propose a consistent framework to tackle both problems of few-shot object detection and few-shot viewpoint estimation. For this, we exploit, in a meta-learning setting, task-specific class information present in existing datasets, i.e., images with bounding boxes for object detection and, for viewpoint estimation, 3D poses in images as well as a few 3D models for the different classes. Considering that these few 3D shapes are available is a realistic

assumption in most scenarios. Using this information, we obtain an embedding for each class and condition the network prediction on both the class-informative embeddings and instance-wise query image embeddings through a feature aggregation module. Despite its simplicity, this approach leads to a significant performance improvement on novel classes under the few-shot learning regime.

Additionally, by combining our few-shot object detection with our few-shot viewpoint estimation, we address the realistic joint problem of learning to detect objects in images and to estimate their viewpoints from only a few shots. Indeed, compared to other viewpoint estimation methods, that only evaluate in the ideal case with ground-truth (GT) classes and ground-truth bounding boxes, we demonstrate that our few-shot viewpoint estimation method can achieve very good results even based on the predicted classes and bounding boxes.

To summarize, our contributions are:

- We define a simple yet effective unifying framework that tackles both few-shot object detection and few-shot viewpoint estimation.
- We show how to leverage just a few arbitrary 3D models of novel classes to guide and boost few-shot viewpoint estimation.
- Our approach achieves state-of-the-art performance on various benchmarks.
- We propose a few-shot learning evaluation of the new joint task of object detection and view-point estimation, and provide promising results.

2   Related Work

Since there is a vast amount of literature on both object detection and viewpoint estimation, we focus here on recent works that target these tasks in the case of limited annotated samples.

Few-Shot Learning. Few-shot learning refers to learning from a few labeled training samples per class, which is an important yet unsolved problem in computer vision [16,28,56]. One popular solution to this problem is meta-learning [2,4,14,21,22,25,27,41,48,56,58], where a meta-learner is designed to parameterize the optimization algorithm or predict the network parameters by "learning to learn". Instead of just focusing on the performance improvement on novel classes, some other work has been proposed for providing good results on both base and novel classes [10,16,38]. While most existing methods tackle the problem of few-shot image classification, we find that other few-shot learning tasks such as object detection and viewpoint estimation are under-explored.

Object Detection. The general deep-learning models for object detection can be divided into two groups: proposal-based methods and direct methods without proposals. While the R-CNN series [11,12,17,18,45] and FPN [29] fall into the former line of work, the YOLO series [42–44] and SSD [31] belong to the latter. All these methods mainly focus on learning from abundant data to improve detection regarding accuracy and speed. Yet, there are also some attempts to

solve the problem with limited labeled data. Chen *et al.* [15] proposes to transfer a pre-trained detector to the few-shot task, while Karlinsky *et al.* [46] exploits distance metric learning to model a multi-modal distribution of each object class.

More recently, Wang *et al.* [59] propose specialized meta-strategies to disentangle the learning of category-agnostic and category-specific components in a detection model. Other approaches based on meta-learning learn a class-attentive vector for each class and use these vectors to reweight full-image features [23] or region-of-interest (RoI) features [64]. Object detection with limited labeled samples is also addressed by approaches targeting weak supervision [5,6,47,49] and zero-shot learning [3,40,66], but these settings are different from ours.

Viewpoint Estimation. Deep-learning methods for viewpoint estimation follow roughly three different paths: direct estimation of Euler angles [24,33,50,55, 62,63], template-based matching [20,32,51], and keypoint detection relying on 3D bounding box corners [13,34,36,39,52] or semantic keypoints [35,65].

Most of the existing viewpoint estimation methods are designed for known object categories or instances; very little work reports performance on unseen classes [36,53,54,63,65]. Zhou et al. [65] propose a category-agnostic method to learn general keypoints for both seen and unseen objects, while Xiao et al. [63] show that better results can be obtained when exact 3D models of the objects are additionally provided. In contrast to these category-agnostic methods, Tseng et al. [53] specifically address the few-shot scenario by training a category-specific viewpoint estimation network for novel classes with limited samples.

Instead of using exact 3D object models as [63], we propose a meta-learning approach to extract a class-informative canonical shape feature vector for each novel class from a few labeled samples, with random object models. Besides, our network can be applied to both base and novel classes without changing the network architecture, while [53] requires a separate meta-training procedure for each class and needs keypoint annotations in addition to the viewpoint.

3 Approach

In this section, we first introduce the setup for few-shot object detection and few-shot viewpoint estimation (Sect. 3.1). Then we describe our common network architecture for these two tasks (Sect. 3.2) and the learning procedure (Sect. 3.3).

3.1 Few-Shot Learning Setup

We have training samples $(x, y) \in (\mathcal{X}, \mathcal{Y})$ for our two tasks, and a few 3D shapes.

- For object detection, x is an image, $y = \{(\mathsf{cls}_i, \mathsf{box}_i) \mid i \in \mathsf{Obj}_x\}$ indicates the class label cls_i and bounding box box_i of each object i in the image.
- For viewpoint estimation, $x = (\mathsf{cls}, \mathsf{box}, \mathsf{img})$ represents an object of class $\mathsf{cls}(x)$ pictured in bounding box $\mathsf{box}(x)$ of an image $\mathsf{img}(x)$, $y = \mathsf{ang} = (\mathsf{azi}, \mathsf{ele}, \mathsf{inp})$ is the 3D pose (viewpoint) of the object, given by Euler angles.

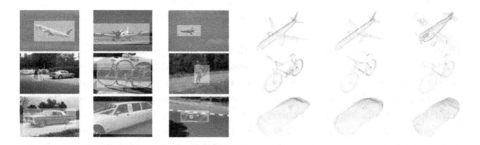

Fig. 2. Example of class data for object detection (left) & viewpoint estimation (right).

For each class $c \in C = \{\mathsf{cls}_i \mid x \in \mathcal{X}, i \in \mathsf{Obj}_x\}$, we consider a set Z_c of *class data* (see Fig. 2) to learn from using meta-learning:

- For object detection, $Z_c = \{(x, \mathsf{mask}_i) \mid x \in \mathcal{X}, i \in \mathsf{Obj}_x\}$ is made of images x plus an extra channel with a binary mask for bounding box box_i of $i \in \mathsf{Obj}_x$.
- For viewpoint estimation, Z_c is an additional set of 3D models of class c.

At each training iteration, class data z_c is randomly sampled in Z_c for each $c \in C$.

In the few-shot setting, we have a partition of the classes $C = C_{\mathrm{base}} \cup C_{\mathrm{novel}}$ with many samples for base classes in C_{base} and only a few samples (including shapes) for novel classes in C_{novel}. The goal is to transfer the knowledge learned on base classes with abundant samples to little-represented novel classes.

3.2   Network Description

Our general approach has three steps that are visualized in Fig. 3. First, query data x and class-informative data z_c pass respectively through the query encoder $\mathcal{F}^{\mathrm{qry}}$ and the class encoder $\mathcal{F}^{\mathrm{cls}}$ to generate corresponding feature vectors. Next, a feature aggregation module $\mathcal{A}$ combines the query features with the class features. Finally, the output of the network is obtained by passing the aggregated features through a task-specific predictor $\mathcal{P}$:

- For object detection, the predictor estimates a classification score and an object location for each region of interest (RoI) and each class.
- For viewpoint estimation, the predictor selects quantized angles by classification, that are refined using regressed angular offsets.

Few-Shot Object Detection. We adopt the widely-used Faster R-CNN [45] approach in our few-shot object detection network (see Fig. 3(a)). The query encoder $\mathcal{F}^{\mathrm{qry}}$ includes the backbone, the region proposal network (RPN) and the proposal-level feature alignment module. In parallel, the class encoder $\mathcal{F}^{\mathrm{cls}}$ is here simply the backbone sharing the same weights as $\mathcal{F}^{\mathrm{qry}}$, that extracts the

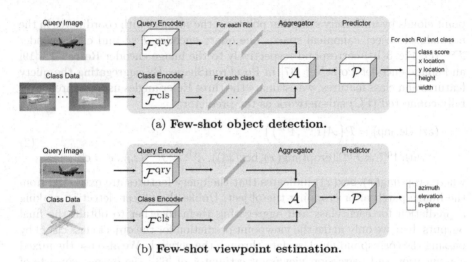

(a) **Few-shot object detection.**

(b) **Few-shot viewpoint estimation.**

Fig. 3. Method overview. (a) For object detection, we sample for each class c one image x in the training set containing an object j of class c, to which we add an extra channel for the binary mask mask_j of the ground-truth bounding box box_j of object j. Each corresponding vector of class features $\mathsf{f}_c^{\mathrm{cls}}$ (red) is then combined with each vector of query features $\mathsf{f}_i^{\mathrm{qry}}$ (blue) associated to one of the region of interest i in the query image, via an aggregation module. Finally, the aggregated features $\mathsf{f}_{i,c}^{\mathrm{agg}}$ pass through a predictor that estimates a class probability $\mathsf{cls}_{i,c}$ and regresses a bounding box $\mathsf{box}_{i,c}$. (b) For few-shot viewpoint estimation, class information is extracted from a few point clouds with coordinates in normalized object canonical space, and the output of the network is the 3D pose represented by three Euler angles. (Color figure online)

class features from RGB images sampled in each class, with an extra channel for a binary mask of the object bounding box [23,64]. Each extracted vector of query features is aggregated with each extracted vector of class features before being processed for class classification and bounding box regression:

$$(\mathsf{cls}_{i,c}, \mathsf{box}_{i,c}) = \mathcal{P}\Big(\mathcal{A}\big(\mathsf{f}_i^{\mathrm{qry}}, \mathsf{f}_c^{\mathrm{cls}}\big)\Big)$$
$$\text{for } \mathsf{f}_i^{\mathrm{qry}} \in \mathcal{F}^{\mathrm{qry}}(x), \ \mathsf{f}_c^{\mathrm{cls}} = \mathcal{F}^{\mathrm{cls}}(z_c), \ c \in C_{\mathrm{train}} \tag{1}$$

where C_{train} is the set of all training classes, and where $\mathsf{cls}_{i,c}$ and $\mathsf{box}_{i,c}$ are the predicted classification scores and object locations for the ith RoI in query image x and for class c. The prediction branch in Faster R-CNN is class-specific: the network outputs $N_{\mathrm{train}} = |C_{\mathrm{train}}|$ classification scores and N_{train} box regressions for each RoI. The final predictions are obtained by concatenating all the class-wise network outputs.

Few-Shot Viewpoint Estimation. For few-shot viewpoint estimation, we rely on the recently proposed PoseFromShape [63] architecture to implement our network. To create class data z_c, we transform the 3D models in the dataset into

point clouds by uniformly sampling points on the surface, with coordinates in the normalized object canonical space. The query encoder $\mathcal{F}^{qry}$ and class encoder $\mathcal{F}^{cls}$ (cf. Fig. 3(b)) correspond respectively to the image encoder ResNet-18 [19] and shape encoder PointNet [37] in PoseFromShape. By aggregating the query features and class features, we estimate the three Euler angles using a three-layer fully-connected (FC) sub-network as the predictor:

$$(\mathsf{azi}, \mathsf{ele}, \mathsf{inp}) = \mathcal{P}\Big(\mathcal{A}\big(\mathsf{f}^{qry}, \mathsf{f}^{cls}\big)\Big)$$

$$\text{with } \mathsf{f}^{qry} = \mathcal{F}^{qry}(\mathsf{crop}(\mathsf{img}(x), \mathsf{box}(x))), \ \mathsf{f}^{cls} = \mathcal{F}^{cls}(z_c), \ c = \mathsf{cls}(x) \qquad (2)$$

where $\mathsf{crop}(\mathsf{img}(x), \mathsf{box}(x))$ indicates that the query features are extracted from the image patch after cropping the object. Unlike the object detection making a prediction for each class and aggregating them together to obtain the final outputs, here we only make the viewpoint prediction for the object class $\mathsf{cls}(x)$ by passing the corresponding class data through the network. We also use the mixed classification-and-regression viewpoint estimator of [63]: the output consists of angular bin classification scores and within-bin offsets for three Euler angles: azimuth (azi), elevation (ele), and in-plane rotation (inp).

Feature Aggregation. In recent few-shot object detection methods such as MetaYOLO [23] and Meta R-CNN [64], feature are aggregated by reweighting the query features f^{qry} according to the output f^{cls} of the class encoder $\mathcal{F}^{cls}$:

$$\mathcal{A}(\mathsf{f}^{qry}, \mathsf{f}^{cls}) = \mathsf{f}^{qry} \otimes \mathsf{f}^{cls} \qquad (3)$$

where $\otimes$ represents channel-wise multiplication and f^{qry} has the same number of channels as f^{cls}. By jointly training the query encoder $\mathcal{F}^{qry}$ and the class encoder $\mathcal{F}^{cls}$ with this reweighting module, it is possible to learn to generate meaningful reweighting vectors f^{cls}. ($\mathcal{F}^{qry}$ and $\mathcal{F}^{cls}$ actually share their weights, except the first layer [64].)

We choose to rely on a slightly more complex aggregation scheme. The fact is that feature subtraction is a different but also effective way to measure similarity between image features [1,26]. The image embedding f^{qry} itself, without any reweighting, contains relevant information too. Our aggregation thus concatenates the three forms of the query feature:

$$\mathcal{A}(\mathsf{f}^{qry}, \mathsf{f}^{cls}) = [\mathsf{f}^{qry} \otimes \mathsf{f}^{cls}, \mathsf{f}^{qry} - \mathsf{f}^{cls}, \mathsf{f}^{qry}] \qquad (4)$$

where $[\cdot, \cdot, \cdot]$ represents channel-wise concatenation. The last part of the aggregated features in Eq. (4) is independent of the class data. As observed experimentally (Sect. 4.1), this partial disentanglement does not only improve few-shot detection performance, it also reduces the variation introduced by the randomness of support samples.

3.3   Learning Procedure

The learning consists of two phases: *base-class training* on many samples from base classes ($C_{\mathrm{train}} = C_{\mathrm{base}}$), followed by *few-shot fine-tuning* on a balanced

small set of samples from both base and novel classes ($C_{\text{train}} = C_{\text{base}} \cup C_{\text{novel}}$). In both phases, we optimize the network using the same loss function.

Detection Loss Function. Following Meta R-CNN [64], we optimize our few-shot object detection network using the same loss function:

$$\mathcal{L} = \mathcal{L}_{\text{rpn}} + \mathcal{L}_{\text{cls}} + \mathcal{L}_{\text{loc}} + \mathcal{L}_{\text{meta}} \tag{5}$$

where $\mathcal{L}_{\text{rpn}}$ is applied to the output of the RPN to distinguish foreground from background and refine the proposals, $\mathcal{L}_{\text{cls}}$ is a cross-entropy loss for box classifier, $\mathcal{L}_{\text{loc}}$ is a smoothed-L1 loss for box regression, and $\mathcal{L}_{\text{meta}}$ is a cross-entropy loss encouraging class features to be diverse for different classes [64].

Viewpoint Loss Function. For the task of viewpoint estimation, we discretize each Euler angle with a bin size of 15 degrees and use the same loss function as PoseFromShape [63] to train the network:

$$\mathcal{L} = \sum_{\theta \in \{\text{azi,ele,inp}\}} \mathcal{L}_{\text{cls}}^{\theta} + \mathcal{L}_{\text{reg}}^{\theta} \tag{6}$$

where $\mathcal{L}_{\text{cls}}^{\theta}$ is a cross-entropy loss for angle bin classification of Euler angle θ, and $\mathcal{L}_{\text{reg}}^{\theta}$ is a smoothed-L1 loss for the regression of offsets relatively to bin centers. Here we remove the meta loss $\mathcal{L}_{\text{meta}}$ used in object detection since we want the network to learn useful inter-class similarities for viewpoint estimation, instead of the inter-class differences for box classification in object detection.

Class Data Construction. For viewpoint estimation, we make use of all the 3D models available for each class (typically less than 10) during both training stages. By contrast, the class data used in object detection requires the label of object class and location, which is limited by the number of annotated samples for novel classes. Therefore, we use large number of class data for base classes in the base training stage (typically $|Z_c| = 200$, as in Meta R-CNN [64]) and limit its size to the number of shots for both base and novel classes in the K-shot fine-tuning stage ($|Z_c| = K$).

For inference, after learning is finished, we construct once and for all class features, instead of randomly sampling class data from the dataset, as done during training. For each class c, we average all corresponding class features used in the few-shot fine-tuning stage:

$$\text{f}_c^{\text{cls}} = \frac{1}{|Z_c|} \sum_{z_c \in Z_c} \mathcal{F}^{\text{cls}}(z_c). \tag{7}$$

This corresponds to the offline computation of all red feature vectors in Fig. 3(a).

Table 1. Few-shot object detection evaluation on PASCAL VOC. We report the mAP with IoU threshold 0.5 (AP50) under 3 different splits for 5 novel classes with a small number of shots. *Results averaged over multiple random runs.

Method\Shots	Novel set 1					Novel set 2					Novel set 3				
	1	2	3	5	10	1	2	3	5	10	1	2	3	5	10
LSTD [15]	8.2	1.0	12.4	29.1	38.5	11.4	3.8	5.0	15.7	31.0	12.6	8.5	15.0	27.3	36.3
MetaYOLO [23]	14.8	15.5	26.7	33.9	47.2	15.7	15.2	22.7	30.1	40.5	**21.3**	25.6	28.4	42.8	45.9
MetaDet* [59]	18.9	20.6	30.2	36.8	49.6	**21.8**	23.1	27.8	31.7	43.0	20.6	23.9	29.4	43.9	44.1
Meta R-CNN* [64]	19.9	25.5	35.0	45.7	51.5	10.4	19.4	29.6	34.8	45.4	14.3	18.2	27.5	41.2	48.1
TFA* w/fc [57]	22.9	34.5	40.4	46.7	52.0	16.9	26.4	30.5	34.6	39.7	15.7	27.2	34.7	40.8	44.6
TFA* w/cos [57]	**25.3**	**36.4**	42.1	47.9	52.8	18.3	**27.5**	30.9	34.1	39.5	17.9	27.2	34.3	40.8	45.6
Ours*	24.2	35.3	**42.2**	**49.1**	**57.4**	21.6	24.6	**31.9**	**37.0**	**45.7**	21.2	**30.0**	**37.2**	**43.8**	**49.6**

Table 2. Few-shot object detection evaluation on MS-COCO. We report the mean Averaged Precision and mean Averaged Recall on the 20 novel classes of COCO. *Results averaged over multiple random runs.

Shots	Method	Average precision						Average recall					
		0.5:0.95	0.5	0.75	S	M	L	1	10	100	S	M	L
10	LSTD [15]	3.2	8.1	2.1	0.9	2.0	6.5	7.8	10.4	10.4	1.1	5.6	19.6
	MetaYOLO [23]	5.6	12.3	4.6	0.9	3.5	10.5	10.1	14.3	14.4	1.5	8.4	28.2
	MetaDet* [59]	7.1	14.6	6.1	1.0	4.1	12.2	11.9	15.1	15.5	1.7	9.7	30.1
	Meta R-CNN* [64]	8.7	19.1	6.6	2.3	7.7	14.0	12.6	17.8	17.9	**7.8**	15.6	27.2
	TFA* w/fc [57]	9.1	17.3	8.5	–	–	–	–	–	–	–	–	–
	TFA* w/cos [57]	9.1	17.1	8.8	–	–	–	–	–	–	–	–	–
	Ours*	**12.5**	**27.3**	**9.8**	**2.5**	**13.8**	**19.9**	**20.0**	**25.5**	**25.7**	7.5	**27.6**	**38.9**
30	LSTD [15]	6.7	15.8	5.1	0.4	2.9	12.3	10.9	14.3	14.3	0.9	7.1	27.0
	MetaYOLO [23]	9.1	19.0	7.6	0.8	4.9	16.8	13.2	17.7	17.8	1.5	10.4	33.5
	MetaDet* [59]	11.3	21.7	8.1	1.1	6.2	17.3	14.5	18.9	19.2	1.8	11.1	34.4
	Meta R-CNN* [64]	12.4	25.3	10.8	2.8	11.6	19.0	15.0	21.4	21.7	**8.6**	20.0	32.1
	TFA* w/fc [57]	12.0	22.2	11.8	–	–	–	–	–	–	–	–	–
	TFA* w/cos [57]	12.1	22.0	12.0	–	–	–	–	–	–	–	–	–
	Ours*	**14.7**	**30.6**	**12.2**	3.2	**15.2**	**23.8**	**22.0**	**28.2**	**28.4**	8.3	**30.3**	**42.1**

4   Experiments

In this section, we evaluate our approach and compare it with state-of-the-art methods on various benchmarks for few-shot object detection and few-shot viewpoint estimation. For a fair comparison, we use the same splits between base and novel classes [23,53]. For all the experiments, we run 10 trials with random support data and report the average performance.

4.1   Few-Shot Object Detection

We adopt a well-established evaluation protocol for few-shot object detection [23,59,64] and report performance on PASCAL VOC [7,8] and MS-COCO [30].

Table 3. Ablation study on the feature aggregation scheme. Using the same class splits of PASCAL VOC as in Table 1, we measure the performance of few-shot object detection on the novel classes. We report the average and standard deviation of the AP50 metric over 10 runs. f^{qry} is the query features and f^{cls} is the class features.

Method \ Shots	Novel set 1		Novel set 2		Novel set 3	
	3	10	3	10	3	10
$[f^{qry} \otimes f^{cls}]$	35.0 ± 3.6	51.5 ± 5.8	29.6 ± 3.5	45.4 ± 5.5	27.5 ± 5.2	48.1 ± 5.9
$[f^{qry} \otimes f^{cls}, f^{qry}]$	36.6 ± 7.1	49.6 ± 4.3	27.5 ± 5.7	41.6 ± 3.7	28.7 ± 5.9	44.0 ± 2.7
$[f^{qry} \otimes f^{cls}, f^{qry}, f^{cls}]$	37.6 ± 7.2	54.2 ± 4.9	30.0 ± 2.9	41.0 ± 5.3	33.6 ± 5.0	47.5 ± 2.3
$[f^{qry} \otimes f^{cls}, f^{qry} - f^{cls}]$	39.2 ± 4.5	55.5 ± 3.9	31.7 ± 6.2	45.2 ± 3.3	35.6 ± 5.6	48.9 ± 3.3
$[f^{qry} \otimes f^{cls}, f^{qry} - f^{cls}, f^{qry}]$	$\mathbf{42.2 \pm 2.1}$	$\mathbf{57.4 \pm 2.7}$	$\mathbf{31.9 \pm 2.7}$	$\mathbf{45.7 \pm 1.8}$	$\mathbf{37.2 \pm 3.5}$	$\mathbf{49.6 \pm 2.2}$

Experimental Setup. PASCAL VOC 2007 and 2012 consist of 16.5k train-val images and 5k test images covering 20 categories. Consistent with the few-shot learning setup in [23,59,64], we use VOC 07 and 12 train-val sets for training and VOC 07 test set for testing. 15 classes are considered as base classes, and the remaining 5 classes as novel classes. For a fair comparison, we consider the same 3 splits as in [23,57,59,64], and for each run we only draw K random shots from each novel class where $K \in \{1, 2, 3, 5, 10\}$. We report the mean Average Precision (mAP) with intersection over union (IoU) threshold at 0.5 (AP50). For MS-COCO, we set the 20 PASCAL VOC categories as novel classes and the remaining 60 categories as base classes. Following [31,45], we report standard COCO evaluation metrics on this dataset with $K \in \{10, 30\}$.

Training Details. We use the same learning scheme as [64], which uses the SGD optimizer with an initial learning rate of 10^{-3} and a batch size of 4. In the first training stage, we train for 20 epochs and divide the learning rate by 10 after each 5 epochs. In the second stage, we train for 5 epochs with learning rate of 10^{-3} and another 4 epochs with a learning rate of 10^{-4}.

Quantitative Results. The results are summarized in Table 1 and 2. Our method outperforms state-of-the-art methods in most cases for the 3 different dataset splits of PASCAL VOC, and it achieves the best results on the 20 novel classes of MS-COCO, which validates the efficacy and generality of our approach. Moreover, our improvements on the difficult COCO dataset (around 3 points in mAP) is much larger than the gap among previous methods. This demonstrates that our approach can generalize well to novel classes even in complex scenarios with ambiguities and occluded objects. By comparing results on objects of different sizes contained in COCO, we find that our approach obtains a much better improvement on medium and large objects while it struggles on small objects.

Different Feature Aggregations. We analyze the impact of different feature aggregation schemes. For this purpose, we evaluate K-shot object detection on

Table 4. Intra-dataset 10-shot viewpoint estimation evaluation. We report Acc30(↑) / MedErr(↓) on the same 20 novel classes of ObjectNet3D for each method, while 80 used as base classes. All models are trained and evaluated on ObjectNet3D.

Method	bed	bookshelf	calculator	cellphone	computer	door	f_cabinet
StarMap+F [65]	0.32 / 47.2	0.61 / 21.0	0.26 / 50.6	0.56 / 26.8	0.59 / 24.4	- / -	0.76 / 17.1
StarMap+M [65]	0.32 / 42.2	0.76 / 15.7	0.58 / 26.8	0.59 / 22.2	0.69 / 19.2	- / -	0.76 / 15.5
MetaView [53]	0.36 / 37.5	0.76 / 17.2	**0.92** / 12.3	0.58 / 25.1	0.70 / 22.2	- / -	0.66 / 22.9
Ours	**0.64** / **14.7**	**0.89** / **8.3**	0.90 / **8.3**	**0.63** / **12.7**	**0.84** / **10.5**	**0.90** / **0.9**	**0.84** / **10.5**

Method	guitar	iron	knife	microwave	pen	pot	rifle
StarMap+F [65]	0.54 / 27.9	0.00 / 128	0.05 / 120	0.82 / 19.0	- / -	0.51 / 29.9	0.02 / 100
StarMap+M [65]	0.59 / 21.5	0.00 / 136	0.08 / 117	0.82 / 17.3	- / -	0.51 / 28.2	0.01 / 100
MetaView [53]	0.63 / 24.0	0.20 / 76.9	0.05 / **97.9**	0.77 / 17.9	- / -	0.49 / 31.6	0.21 / **80.9**
Ours	**0.72** / **17.1**	**0.37** / **57.7**	**0.26** / 139	**0.94** / **7.3**	**0.45** / **44.0**	**0.74** / **12.3**	**0.29** / 88.4

Method	shoe	slipper	stove	toilet	tub	wheelchair	TOTAL
StarMap+F [65]	- / -	0.08 / 128	0.80 / 16.1	0.38 / 36.8	0.35 / 39.8	0.18 / 80.4	0.41 / 41.0
StarMap+M [65]	- / -	0.15 / 128	0.83 / 15.6	0.39 / 35.5	0.41 / 38.5	0.24 / 71.5	0.46 / 33.9
MetaView [53]	- / -	0.07 / 115	0.74 / 21.7	0.50 / 32.0	0.29 / 46.5	0.27 / 55.8	0.48 / 31.5
Ours	**0.51** / **29.4**	**0.25** / **96.4**	**0.92** / **9.4**	**0.69** / **17.4**	**0.66** / **15.1**	**0.36** / **64.3**	**0.64** / **15.6**

PASCAL VOC with $K \in \{3, 10\}$. The results are reported in Table 3. We can see that our feature aggregation scheme $[f^{qry} \otimes f^{cls}, f^{qry} - f^{cls}, f^{qry}]$ yields the best precision. In particular, although the difference $[f^{qry} - f^{cls}]$ could in theory be learned from the individual feature vectors $[f^{qry}, f^{cls}]$, the network performs better when explicitly provided with their subtraction. Moreover, our aggregation scheme significantly reduces the variance introduced by the random sampling of few-shot support data, which is one of the main issues in few-shot learning.

4.2 Few-Shot Viewpoint Estimation

Following the few-shot viewpoint estimation protocol proposed in [53], we evaluate our method under two settings: *intra*-dataset on ObjectNet3D [60] (reported in Table 4) and *inter*-dataset between ObjectNet3D and Pascal3D+ [61] (reported in Table 5). In both datasets, the number of available 3D models for each class vary from 2 to 16. We use the most common metrics for evaluation: Acc30, which is the percentage of estimations with a rotational error smaller than 30°, and MedErr, which computes the median rotational error measured in degrees. Complying with previous work [53,65], we only use the non-occluded and non-truncated objects for evaluation and assume in this subsection that the ground truth classes and bounding boxes are provided at test time.

Training Details. The model is trained using the Adam optimizer with a batch size of 16. During the base-class training stage, we train for 150 epochs with a learning rate of 10^{-4}. For few-shot fine-tuning, we train for 50 epochs with learning rate of 10^{-4} and another 50 epochs with a learning rate of 10^{-5}.

Table 5. Inter-dataset 10-shot viewpoint estimation evaluation. We report Acc30($\uparrow$) / MedErr($\downarrow$) on the 12 novel classes of Pascal3D+, while the 88 base classes are in ObjectNet3D. All models are trained on ObjectNet3D and tested on Pascal3D+.

Method	aero	bike	boat	bottle	bus	car	chair
StarMap+F [65]	0.03/102	0.05/98.8	0.07/98.9	0.48/31.9	0.46/33.0	0.18/80.8	0.22/74.6
StarMap+M [65]	0.03/99.2	0.08/88.4	0.11/92.2	0.55/28.0	0.49/31.0	0.21/81.4	0.21/80.2
MetaView [53]	0.12/104	0.08/91.3	0.09/108	0.71/24.0	0.64/22.8	0.22/73.3	0.20/89.1
Ours	**0.24/65.0**	**0.34/52.4**	**0.27/77.3**	**0.88/12.6**	**0.78/8.2**	**0.49/34.0**	**0.33/77.4**

Method	table	mbike	sofa	train	tv	TOTAL	
StarMap+F [65]	0.46/31.4	0.09/91.6	0.32/44.7	0.36/41.7	0.52/29.1	0.25/64.7	
StarMap+M [65]	0.29/36.8	0.11/83.5	0.44/42.9	0.42/33.9	0.64/25.3	0.28/60.5	
MetaView [53]	0.39/36.0	0.14/74.7	0.29/46.2	0.61/23.8	0.58/26.3	0.33/51.3	
Ours	**0.60/21.2**	**0.41/45.2**	**0.58/21.3**	**0.71/12.6**	**0.78/19.1**	**0.52/28.3**	

Compared Methods. For few-shot viewpoint estimation, we compare our method to MetaView [53] and to two adaptations of StarMap [65]. More precisely, the authors of MetaView [53] re-implemented StarMap with one stage of ResNet-18 as the backbone, and trained the network with MAML [9] for a fair comparison in the few-shot regime (entries StarMap+M in Table 4 and 5). They also provided StarMap results by just fine-tuning it on the novel classes using the scarce labeled data (entries StarMap+F in Table 4 and 5).

Intra-dataset Evaluation. We follow the protocol of [53,63] and split the 100 categories of ObjectNet3D into 80 base classes and 20 novel classes. As shown in Table 4, our model outperforms the recently proposed meta-learning-based method MetaView [53] by a very large margin in overall performance: +16 points in Acc30 and half MedErr (from 31.5° down to 15.6°). Besides, keypoint annotations are not available for some object categories such as door, pen and shoe in ObjectNet3D. This limits the generalization of keypoint-based approaches [53,65] as they require a set of manually labeled keypoints for network training. By contrast, our model can be trained and evaluated on all object classes of ObjectNet3D as we only rely on the shape pose. More importantly, our model can be directly deployed on different classes using the same architecture, while MetaView learns a set of separate category-specific semantic keypoint detectors for each class. This flexibility suggests that our approach is likely to exploit the similarities between different categories (e.g.., bicycle and motorbike) and has more potentials for applications to robotics and augmented reality.

Inter-dataset Evaluation. To further evaluate our method in a more practical scenario, we use a source dataset for base classes and another target dataset for novel (disjoint) classes. Using the same split as MetaView [53], we use all 12 categories of Pascal3D+ as novel categories and the remaining 88 categories of ObjectNet3D as base categories. Distinct from the previous intra-dataset

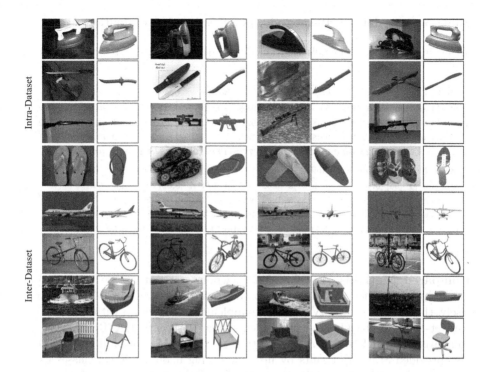

Fig. 4. Qualitative results of few-shot viewpoint estimation. We visualize results on ObjectNet3D and Pascal3D+. For each category, we show three success cases (the first six columns) and one failure case (the last two columns). CAD models are shown here only for the purpose of illustrating the estimated viewpoint.

experiment that focuses more on the cross-category generalization capacity, this inter-dataset setup also reveals the cross-domain generalization ability.

As shown in Table 5, our approach again significantly outperforms StarMap and MetaView. Our overall improvement in inter-dataset evaluation is even larger than in intra-dataset evaluation: we gain +19 points in Acc30 and again divide MedErr by about 2 (from 51.3° down to 28.3°). This indicates that our approach, by leveraging viewpoint-relevant 3D information, not only helps the network generalize to novel classes from the same domain, but also addresses the domain shift issues when trained and evaluated on different datasets.

Visual Results. We provide in Fig. 4 visualizations of viewpoint estimation for novel objects on ObjectNet3D and Pascal3D+. We show both success (green boxes) and failure cases (red boxes) to help analyze possible error types. We visualize four categories giving the largest median errors: iron, knife, rifle and slipper for ObjectNet3D, and aeroplane, bicycle, boat and chair for Pascal3D+. The most common failure cases come from objects with similar appearances in ambiguous poses, e.g., iron and knife in ObjectNet3D, aeroplane and boat in

Table 6. Evaluation of joint few-shot detection and viewpoint estimation. We report the percentage of correct predictions on novel classes of ObjectNet3D, first using the ground-truth classes and bounding boxes, then the estimated classes and bounding boxes given by our object detector. Predicted bounding boxes are considered correct with a IoU threshold at 0.5 and estimated viewpoints are considered correct with a rotation error less than 30°. Ours (all-shot) is learned on all training data of the novel classes.

Method	bed	bshelf	calc	cphone	comp	door	fcabin	guit	iron	knife	micro	pen	pot	rifle	shoe	slipper	stove	toilet	tub	wchair	mean
Evaluated using ground-truth classes and bounding boxes (viewpoint estimation)																					
StarMap+M[65]	32	76	58	59	69	–	76	59	0	8	82	–	51	1	–	15	83	39	41	24	46
MetaView[53]	36	76	92	58	70	–	66	63	20	5	77	–	49	21	–	7	74	50	29	27	48
Ours (10-shot)	64	89	90	63	84	90	84	72	37	26	94	45	74	29	51	25	92	69	66	36	64
Ours (all-shot)	81	92	96	65	91	93	89	83	58	28	95	51	81	48	63	53	94	86	77	70	75
Evaluated using predicted classes and bounding boxes (detection + viewpoint estimation)																					
Ours (10-shot)	55	76	74	52	57	69	63	70	44	8	57	22	55	12	6	19	80	65	56	21	48
Ours (all-shot)	65	80	82	56	62	70	66	75	48	9	60	27	61	20	8	32	83	71	67	38	54

Pascal3D+. Other failure cases include the heavy clutter cases (bicycle) and large shape variations between training objects and testing objects (chair).

4.3   Evaluation of Joint Detection and Viewpoint Estimation

To further show the generality of our approach in real-world scenarios, we consider the joint problem of detecting objects from novel classes in images and estimating their viewpoints. The fact is that evaluating a viewpoint estimator on ground-truth classes and bounding boxes is a toy setting, not representative of actual needs. On the contrary, estimating viewpoints based on predicted detections is much more realistic and challenging.

To experiment with this scenario, we split ObjectNet3D into 80 base classes and 20 novel classes as in Sect. 4.2, and train the object detector and viewpoint estimator based on the abundant annotated samples for base classes and scarce labeled samples for novel classes. Unfortunately, the codes of StarMap+F/M and MetaView are not available. The only available information is the results on perfect, ground-truth classes and bounding boxes available in publications. We thus have to reason relatively in terms of baselines. Concretely, we compare these results obtained on ideal input to the case where we use predicted classes and bounding boxes, in the 10-shot scenario. As an upper bound, we also consider the "all-shot" case where all training data of the novel classes are used.

As recalled in Table 6, our few-shot viewpoint estimation outperforms other methods by a large margin when evaluated using ground-truth classes and bounding boxes in the 10-shot setting. When using predicted classes and bounding boxes, accuracy drops for most categories. One explanation is that viewpoint estimation becomes difficult when the objects are truncated by imperfect predicted bounding boxes, especially for tiny objects (e.g., shoes) and ambiguous

objects with similar appearances in different poses (e.g., knifes, rifles). Yet, by comparing the performance gap between our method when tested using predicted classes and boxes and MetaView when tested using ground-truth classes and boxes, we find that our approach is able to reach the same viewpoint accuracy of 48%, which is a considerable achievement.

5   Conclusion

In this work, we presented an approach to few-shot object detection and viewpoint estimation that can tackle both tasks in a coherent and efficient framework. We demonstrated the benefits of this approach in terms of accuracy, and significantly improved the state of the art on several standard benchmarks for few-shot object detection and few-shot viewpoint estimation. Moreover, we showed that our few-shot viewpoint estimation model can achieve promising results on the novel objects detected by our few-shot detection model, compared to the existing methods tested with ground-truth bounding boxes.

Acknowledgements. We thank Vincent Lepetit and Yuming Du for helpful discussions.

References

1. Ammirato, P., Fu, C.Y., Shvets, M., Kosecka, J., Berg, A.C.: Target driven instance detection (2018). arXiv preprint arXiv:1803.04610
2. Andrychowicz, M., et al.: Learning to learn by gradient descent by gradient descent. In: International Conference on Neural Information Processing Systems (NeurIPS) (2016)
3. Bansal, A., Sikka, K., Sharma, G., Chellappa, R., Divakaran, A.: Zero-shot object detection. In: Ferrari, V., Hebert, M., Sminchisescu, C., Weiss, Y. (eds.) ECCV 2018. LNCS, vol. 11205, pp. 397–414. Springer, Cham (2018). https://doi.org/10.1007/978-3-030-01246-5_24
4. Bertinetto, L., Henriques, J.F., Valmadre, J., Torr, P.H.S., Vedaldi, A.: Learning feed-forward one-shot learners. In: International Conference on Neural Information Processing Systems (NeurIPS) (2016)
5. Bilen, H., Vedaldi, A.: Weakly supervised deep detection networks. In: IEEE Conference on Computer Vision and Pattern Recognition (CVPR), pp. 2846–2854 (2016)
6. Diba, A., Sharma, V., Pazandeh, A.M., Pirsiavash, H., Gool, L.V.: Weakly supervised cascaded convolutional networks. In: IEEE Conference on Computer Vision and Pattern Recognition (CVPR), pp. 5131–5139 (2017)
7. Everingham, M., Eslami, S.M.A., Van Gool, L., Williams, C.K.I., Winn, J., Zisserman, A.: The PASCAL visual object classes challenge: a retrospective. Int. J. Comput. Vis. 111(1), 98–136 (2015). https://doi.org/10.1007/s11263-014-0733-5
8. Everingham, M., Van Gool, L., Williams, C.K.I., Winn, J., Zisserman, A.: The PASCAL visual object classes (VOC) challenge. Int. J. Comput. Vis. (IJCV) 88, 303–338 (2010). https://doi.org/10.1007/s11263-009-0275-4

9. Finn, C., Abbeel, P., Levine, S.: Model-agnostic meta-learning for fast adaptation of deep networks. In: International Conference on Machine Learning (ICML) (2017)

10. Gidaris, S., Komodakis, N.: Dynamic few-shot visual learning without forgetting. In: IEEE Conference on Computer Vision and Pattern Recognition (CVPR), pp. 4367–4375 (2018)

11. Girshick, R.: Fast R-CNN. In: IEEE International Conference on Computer Vision (ICCV) (2015)

12. Girshick, R., Donahue, J., Darrell, T., Malik, J.: Rich feature hierarchies for accurate object detection and semantic segmentation. In: IEEE Conference on Computer Vision and Pattern Recognition (CVPR) (2014)

13. Grabner, A., Roth, P.M., Lepetit, V.: 3D pose estimation and 3D model retrieval for objects in the wild. In: IEEE Conference on Computer Vision and Pattern Recognition (CVPR), pp. 3022–3031 (2018)

14. Ha, D., Dai, A., Le, Q.V.: HyperNetworks. In: International Conference on Learning Representations (ICLR) (2017)

15. Hao, C., Yali, W., Guoyou, W., Yu, Q.: LSTD: a low-shot transfer detector for object detection. In: AAAI Conference on Artificial Intelligence (AAAI) (2018)

16. Hariharan, B., Girshick, R.B.: Low-shot visual recognition by shrinking and hallucinating features. In: IEEE International Conference on Computer Vision (ICCV) (2017)

17. He, K., Gkioxari, G., Dollár, P., Girshick, R.B.: Mask R-CNN. In: IEEE International Conference on Computer Vision (ICCV), pp. 2980–2988 (2017)

18. He, K., Zhang, X., Ren, S., Sun, J.: Spatial pyramid pooling in deep convolutional networks for visual recognition. IEEE Trans. Pattern Anal. Mach. Intell. (PAMI) **37**, 1904–1916 (2015)

19. He, K., Zhang, X., Ren, S., Sun, J.: Deep residual learning for image recognition. In: IEEE Conference on Computer Vision and Pattern Recognition (CVPR), pp. 770–778 (2016)

20. Hinterstoisser, S., et al.: Model based training, detection and pose estimation of texture-less 3D objects in heavily cluttered scenes. In: Lee, K.M., Matsushita, Y., Rehg, J.M., Hu, Z. (eds.) ACCV 2012. LNCS, vol. 7724, pp. 548–562. Springer, Heidelberg (2013). https://doi.org/10.1007/978-3-642-37331-2_42

21. Hu, H., Gu, J., Zhang, Z., Dai, J., Wei, Y.: Relation networks for object detection. In: IEEE Conference on Computer Vision and Pattern Recognition (CVPR), pp. 3588–3597 (2018)

22. Hu, S.X., et al.: Empirical Bayes transductive meta-learning with synthetic gradients. In: International Conference on Learning Representations (ICLR) (2020)

23. Kang, B., Liu, Z., Wang, X., Yu, F., Feng, J., Darrell, T.: Few-shot object detection via feature reweighting. In: IEEE International Conference on Computer Vision (ICCV) (2019)

24. Kehl, W., Manhardt, F., Tombari, F., Ilic, S., Navab, N.: SSD-6D: making RGB-based 3D detection and 6D pose estimation great again. In: IEEE International Conference on Computer Vision (ICCV), pp. 1530–1538 (2017)

25. Koch, G., Zemel, R., Salakhutdinov, R.: Siamese neural networks for one-shot image recognition. In: ICML workshops (2015)

26. Kuo, W., Angelova, A., Malik, J., Lin, T.Y.: ShapeMask: learning to segment novel objects by refining shape priors. In: IEEE International Conference on Computer Vision (ICCV), pp. 9206–9215 (2019)

27. Lee, K., Maji, S., Ravichandran, A., Soatto, S.: Meta-learning with differentiable convex optimization. In: IEEE Conference on Computer Vision and Pattern Recognition (CVPR) (2019)

28. Li, F.F., Fergus, R., Perona, P.: One-shot learning of object categories. IEEE Trans. Pattern Anal. Mach. Intell. (PAMI) **28**, 594–611 (2006)
29. Lin, T.Y., Dollár, P., Girshick, R.B., He, K., Hariharan, B., Belongie, S.J.: Feature pyramid networks for object detection. In: IEEE Conference on Computer Vision and Pattern Recognition (CVPR), pp. 936–944 (2017)
30. Lin, T.-Y., et al.: Microsoft COCO: common objects in context. In: Fleet, D., Pajdla, T., Schiele, B., Tuytelaars, T. (eds.) ECCV 2014. LNCS, vol. 8693, pp. 740–755. Springer, Cham (2014). https://doi.org/10.1007/978-3-319-10602-1_48
31. Liu, W., et al.: SSD: single shot MultiBox detector. In: Leibe, B., Matas, J., Sebe, N., Welling, M. (eds.) ECCV 2016. LNCS, vol. 9905, pp. 21–37. Springer, Cham (2016). https://doi.org/10.1007/978-3-319-46448-0_2
32. Massa, F., Russell, B.C., Aubry, M.: Deep exemplar 2D–3D detection by adapting from real to rendered views. In: IEEE Conference on Computer Vision and Pattern Recognition (CVPR), pp. 6024–6033 (2016)
33. Mousavian, A., Anguelov, D., Flynn, J., Kosecka, J.: 3D bounding box estimation using deep learning and geometry. In: IEEE Conference on Computer Vision and Pattern Recognition (CVPR), pp. 5632–5640 (2017)
34. Oberweger, M., Rad, M., Lepetit, V.: Making deep heatmaps robust to partial occlusions for 3D object pose estimation. In: Ferrari, V., Hebert, M., Sminchisescu, C., Weiss, Y. (eds.) ECCV 2018. LNCS, vol. 11219, pp. 125–141. Springer, Cham (2018). https://doi.org/10.1007/978-3-030-01267-0_8
35. Pavlakos, G., Zhou, X., Chan, A., Derpanis, K.G., Daniilidis, K.: 6-DoF object pose from semantic keypoints. In: IEEE International Conference on Robotics and Automation (ICRA), pp. 2011–2018 (2017)
36. Pitteri, G., Ilic, S., Lepetit, V.: CorNet: generic 3D corners for 6D pose estimation of new objects without retraining. In: IEEE International Conference on Computer Vision Workshops (ICCVw) (2019)
37. Qi, C.R., Su, H., Mo, K., Guibas, L.J.: PointNet: deep learning on point sets for 3D classification and segmentation. In: IEEE Conference on Computer Vision and Pattern Recognition (CVPR), pp. 77–85 (2017)
38. Qi, H., Brown, M., Lowe, D.G.: Low-shot learning with imprinted weights. In: IEEE Conference on Computer Vision and Pattern Recognition (CVPR), pp. 5822–5830 (2017)
39. Rad, M., Lepetit, V.: BB8: a scalable, accurate, robust to partial occlusion method for predicting the 3D poses of challenging objects without using depth. In: IEEE International Conference on Computer Vision (ICCV), pp. 3848–3856 (2017)
40. Rahman, S., Khan, S., Porikli, F.: Zero-shot object detection: learning to simultaneously recognize and localize novel concepts. In: Jawahar, C.V., Li, H., Mori, G., Schindler, K. (eds.) ACCV 2018. LNCS, vol. 11361, pp. 547–563. Springer, Cham (2019). https://doi.org/10.1007/978-3-030-20887-5_34
41. Ravi, S., Larochelle, H.: Optimization as a model for few-shot learning. In: International Conference on Learning Representations (ICLR) (2017)
42. Redmon, J., Divvala, S.K., Girshick, R.B., Farhadi, A.: You only look once: unified, real-time object detection. In: IEEE Conference on Computer Vision and Pattern Recognition (CVPR), pp. 779–788 (2016)
43. Redmon, J., Farhadi, A.: YOLO9000: better, faster, stronger. In: IEEE Conference on Computer Vision and Pattern Recognition (CVPR), pp. 6517–6525 (2017)
44. Redmon, J., Farhadi, A.: YOLOV3: an incremental improvement (2018). arXiv preprint arXiv:1804.02767

45. Ren, S., He, K., Girshick, R., Sun, J.: Faster R-CNN: towards real-time object detection with region proposal networks. In: International Conference on Neural Information Processing Systems (NeuIPS) (2015)
46. Schwartz, E., et al.: RepMet: representative-based metric learning for classification and few-shot object detection. In: IEEE Conference on Computer Vision and Pattern Recognition (CVPR), pp. 5192–5201 (2019)
47. Shen, X., Efros, A.A., Aubry, M.: Discovering visual patterns in art collections with spatially-consistent feature learning. In: IEEE Conference on Computer Vision and Pattern Recognition (CVPR) (2019)
48. Snell, J., Swersky, K., Zemel, R.S.: Prototypical networks for few-shot learning. In: International Conference on Neural Information Processing Systems (NeurIPS) (2017)
49. Song, H.O., Lee, Y.J., Jegelka, S., Darrell, T.: Weakly-supervised discovery of visual pattern configurations. In: International Conference on Neural Information Processing Systems (NeurIPS) (2014)
50. Su, H., Qi, C.R., Li, Y., Guibas, L.J.: Render for CNN: viewpoint estimation in images using CNNs trained with rendered 3D model views. In: IEEE International Conference on Computer Vision (ICCV), pp. 2686–2694 (2015)
51. Sundermeyer, M., Marton, Z.-C., Durner, M., Brucker, M., Triebel, R.: Implicit 3D orientation learning for 6D object detection from RGB images. In: Ferrari, V., Hebert, M., Sminchisescu, C., Weiss, Y. (eds.) ECCV 2018. LNCS, vol. 11210, pp. 712–729. Springer, Cham (2018). https://doi.org/10.1007/978-3-030-01231-1_43
52. Tekin, B., Sinha, S.N., Fua, P.: Real-time seamless single shot 6D object pose prediction. In: IEEE Conference on Computer Vision and Pattern Recognition (CVPR), pp. 292–301 (2018)
53. Tseng, H.Y., et al.: Few-shot viewpoint estimation. In: British Machine Vision Conference (BMVC) (2019)
54. Tulsiani, S., Carreira, J., Malik, J.: Pose induction for novel object categories. In: IEEE International Conference on Computer Vision (ICCV), pp. 64–72 (2015)
55. Tulsiani, S., Malik, J.: Viewpoints and keypoints. In: IEEE Conference on Computer Vision and Pattern Recognition (CVPR) (2015)
56. Vinyals, O., Blundell, C., Lillicrap, T.P., Kavukcuoglu, K., Wierstra, D.: Matching networks for one shot learning. In: International Conference on Neural Information Processing Systems (NeurIPS) (2016)
57. Wang, X., Huang, T.E., Darrell, T., Gonzalez, J.E., Yu, F.: Frustratingly simple few-shot object detection. In: International Conference on Machine Learning (ICML), July 2020
58. Wang, Y.-X., Hebert, M.: Learning to learn: model regression networks for easy small sample learning. In: Leibe, B., Matas, J., Sebe, N., Welling, M. (eds.) ECCV 2016. LNCS, vol. 9910, pp. 616–634. Springer, Cham (2016). https://doi.org/10.1007/978-3-319-46466-4_37
59. Wang, Y.X., Ramanan, D., Hebert, M.: Meta-learning to detect rare objects. In: IEEE International Conference on Computer Vision (ICCV), October 2019
60. Xiang, Yu., et al.: ObjectNet3D: a large scale database for 3D object recognition. In: Leibe, B., Matas, J., Sebe, N., Welling, M. (eds.) ECCV 2016. LNCS, vol. 9912, pp. 160–176. Springer, Cham (2016). https://doi.org/10.1007/978-3-319-46484-8_10
61. Xiang, Y., Mottaghi, R., Savarese, S.: Beyond PASCAL: a benchmark for 3D object detection in the wild. In: IEEE Winter Conference on Applications of Computer Vision (WACV) (2014)

62. Xiang, Y., Schmidt, T., Narayanan, V., Fox, D.: PoseCNN: a convolutional neural network for 6D object pose estimation in cluttered scenes. In: Robotics: Science and Systems (RSS) (2018)
63. Xiao, Y., Qiu, X., Langlois, P., Aubry, M., Marlet, R.: Pose from shape: deep pose estimation for arbitrary 3D objects. In: British Machine Vision Conference (BMVC) (2019)
64. Yan, X., Chen, Z., Xu, A., Wang, X., Liang, X., Lin, L.: Meta R-CNN : towards general solver for instance-level low-shot learning. In: IEEE International Conference on Computer Vision (ICCV) (2019)
65. Zhou, X., Karpur, A., Luo, L., Huang, Q.: StarMap for category-agnostic keypoint and viewpoint estimation. In: Ferrari, V., Hebert, M., Sminchisescu, C., Weiss, Y. (eds.) ECCV 2018. LNCS, vol. 11205, pp. 328–345. Springer, Cham (2018). https://doi.org/10.1007/978-3-030-01246-5_20
66. Zhu, P., Wang, H., Saligrama, V.: Zero shot detection. IEEE Trans. Circ. Syst. Video Technol. (TCSVT) **30**, 998–1010 (2019)

Weakly Supervised 3D Hand Pose Estimation via Biomechanical Constraints

Adrian Spurr[1,2]([⊠]), Umar Iqbal[2], Pavlo Molchanov[2], Otmar Hilliges[1], and Jan Kautz[2]

[1] Advanced Interactive Technologies, ETH Zurich, Zürich, Switzerland
{adrian.spurr,otmar.hilliges}@inf.ethz.ch
[2] NVIDIA, Santa Clara, USA
{uiqbal,pmolchanov,jkautz}@nvidia.com

Abstract. Estimating 3D hand pose from 2D images is a difficult, inverse problem due to the inherent scale and depth ambiguities. Current state-of-the-art methods train fully supervised deep neural networks with 3D ground-truth data. However, acquiring 3D annotations is expensive, typically requiring calibrated multi-view setups or labour intensive manual annotations. While annotations of 2D keypoints are much easier to obtain, how to efficiently leverage such *weakly-supervised* data to improve the task of 3D hand pose prediction remains an important open question. The key difficulty stems from the fact that direct application of additional 2D supervision mostly benefits the 2D proxy objective but does little to alleviate the depth and scale ambiguities. Embracing this challenge we propose a set of novel losses that constrain the prediction of a neural network to lie within the range of biomechanically feasible 3D hand configurations. We show by extensive experiments that our proposed constraints significantly reduce the depth ambiguity and allow the network to more effectively leverage additional 2D annotated images. For example, on the challenging freiHAND dataset, using additional 2D annotation without our proposed biomechanical constraints reduces the depth error by only 15%, whereas the error is reduced significantly by 50% when the proposed biomechanical constraints are used.

Keywords: 3D hand pose · Weakly-supervised · Biomechanical constraints

1 Introduction

Vision-based reconstruction of the 3D pose of human hands is a difficult problem that has applications in many domains. Given that RGB sensors are ubiquitous,

---

A. Spurr—This work was done during an internship at NVIDIA.

Electronic supplementary material The online version of this chapter (https://doi.org/10.1007/978-3-030-58520-4_13) contains supplementary material, which is available to authorized users.

A. Vedaldi et al. (Eds.): ECCV 2020, LNCS 12362, pp. 211–228, 2020.
https://doi.org/10.1007/978-3-030-58520-4_13

recent work has focused on estimating the full 3D pose [6,18,25,34,44] and dense surface [5,13,15] of human hands from 2D imagery alone. This task is challenging due to the dexterity of the human hand, self-occlusions, varying lighting conditions and interactions with objects. Moreover, any given 2D point in the image plane can correspond to multiple 3D points in world space, all of which project onto that same 2D point. This makes 3D hand pose estimation from monocular imagery an ill-posed inverse problem in which depth and the resulting scale ambiguity pose a significant difficulty.

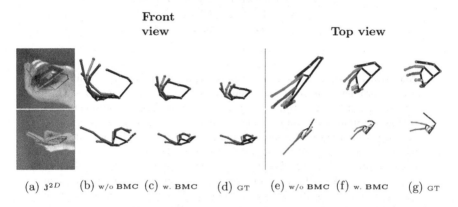

(a) J^{2D} (b) w/o BMC   (c) w. BMC   (d) GT   (e) w/o BMC   (f) w. BMC   (g) GT

Fig. 1. Impact of the proposed biomechanical constraints (BMC). (b,e) Supplementing fully supervised data with 2D annotated data yields 3D poses with correct 2D projections, yet they are anatomically implausible. (c,f) Adding our biomechanical constraints significantly improves the pose prediction quantitatively and qualitatively. The resulting 3D poses are anatomically valid and display more accurate depth/scale even under severe self- and object occlusions, thus are closer to the ground-truth (d,g).

Most of the recent methods use deep neural networks for hand pose estimation and rely on a combination of fully labeled real and synthetic training data (e.g., [4,6,15,15,18,25,34,46,48]). However, acquiring full 3D annotations for real images is very difficult as it requires complex multi-view setups and labour intensive manual annotations of 2D keypoints in all views [14,45,49]. On the other hand, synthetic data does not generalize well to realistic scenarios due to domain discrepancies. Some works attempt to alleviate this by leveraging additional 2D annotated images [5,18]. Such kind of *weakly-supervised* data is far easier to acquire for real images as compared to full 3D annotations. These methods use these annotations in a straightforward way in the form of a reprojection loss [5] or supervision for the 2D component only [18]. However, we find that the improvements stemming from including the weakly-supervised data in such a manner are mainly a result of 3D poses that agree with the 2D projection. Yet, the uncertainties arising due to depth ambiguities remain largely unaddressed and the resulting 3D poses can still be implausible. Therefore, these methods still rely on large amounts of fully annotated training data to reduce these ambiguities. In contrast, our goal is to *minimize* the requirement of 3D

annotated data as much as possible and *maximize* the utility of weakly-labeled real data.

To this end, we propose a set of biomechanically inspired constraints (**BMC**) which can be integrated in the training of neural networks to enable anatomically plausible 3D hand poses even for data with 2D supervision only. Our key insight is that the human hand is subject to a set of limitations imposed by its biomechanics. We model these limitations in a differentiable manner as a set of *soft constraints*. Note that this is a challenging problem. While the bone length constraints have been used successfully [37,47], capturing other biomechanical aspects is more difficult. Instead of fitting a hand model to the predictions, we *extract* the quantities in question directly from the predictions to impose our constraints. As such, the method of extraction has to be carefully designed to work under noisy and malformed 3D joint predictions while simultaneously being fully differentiable under any pose. We propose to encode these constraints into a set of losses that are fully differentiable, interpretable and which can be incorporated into the training of any deep learning architecture that predicts 3D joint configurations. Due to this integration, we do not require a post-refinement step during test time. More specifically, our set of soft constraints consists of three equations that define i) the range of valid bone lengths, ii) the range of valid palm structure, and iii) the range of valid joint angles of the thumb and fingers. The main advantage of our set of constraints is that all parameters are interpretable and can either be set manually, opening up the possibility of personalization, or be obtained from a small set of data points for which 3D labels are available. As backbone model, we use the 2.5D representation proposed by Iqbal *et al.* [18] due to its superior performance. We identify an issue in absolute depth calculation and remedy it via a novel refinement network. In summary, we contribute:

- A novel set of differentiable soft constraints inspired by the biomechanical structure of the human hand.
- Quantitative and qualitative evidence that demonstrates that our proposed set of constraints improves 3D prediction accuracy in *weakly supervised settings*, resulting in an improvement of 55% as opposed to 32% as yielded by straightforward use of weakly-supervised data.
- A neural network architecture that extends [18] with a refinement step.
- Achieving state-of-the-art performance on Dexter+Object using only synthetic and weakly-supervised real data, indicating cross-data generalizability.

The proposed constraints require no special data nor are they specific to a particular backbone architecture.

2   Related Work

Hand pose estimation from monocular RGB has gained traction in recent years due numerous possible applications. Generally there are two trains of thought.

Model-based methods ensure plausible poses by fitting a hand model to the observation via optimization. As they are not learning-based, they are sensitive to initial conditions, rely on temporal information [17,26–28] or do not

take the image into consideration during optimization [28]. Whereas some make use of geometric primitives [26–28], other simply model the joint angles directly [8,11,20,22,31,41], learn a lower dimensional embedding of the joints [23], pose [17] or go a step further and model muscles of the hand [1]. Different to these methods, we propose to incorporate these constraints *directly* into the training procedure of a neural network in a fully differentiable manner. As such, we do not fit a hand model to the prediction, but *extract* and constrain the biomechanical quantities from them directly. The resulting network predicts biomechanically-plausible poses and does not suffer from the same disadvantages.

Learning-based methods utilize neural networks that either directly regress the 3D positions of the hand keypoints [18,25,34,38,44,48] or predict the parameters of a deformable hand model [4,5,15,42,46]. Zimmermann *et al.* [48] are the first to use deep neural network for root-relative 3D hand pose estimation from RGB images via a multi-staged approach. Spurr *et al.* [34] learn a unified latent space that projects multiple modalities into the same space, learning a lower level embedding of the hands. Similarly, Yang *et al.* [44] learn a latent space that disentangles background, camera and hand pose. However, all these methods require large numbers of fully labeled training data. Cai *et al.* [6] try to alleviate this problem by introducing an approach that utilizes paired RGB-D images to regularize the depth predictions. Mueller *et al.* [25] attempt to improve the quality of synthetic training data by learning a GAN model that minimizes the discrepancies between real and synthetic images. Iqbal *et al.* [18] decompose the task into learning 2D and root-relative depth components. This decomposition allows to use weakly-labeled real images with only 2D pose annotations which are cheap to acquire. While these methods demonstrate better generalization by adding a large number weakly-labeled training samples, the main drawback of this approach is that the depth ambiguities remain unaddressed. As such, training using only 2D pose annotations does not impact the depth predictions. This may result in 3D poses with accurate 2D projections, but due to depth ambiguities the 3D poses can still be implausible. In contrast, in this work, we propose a set of biomechanical constraints that ensures that the predicted 3D poses are always anatomically plausible during training (see Fig. 1). We formulate these constraints in form of a fully-differentiable loss functions which can be incorporated into any deep learning architecture that predicts 3D joint configurations. We use a variant of Iqbal *et al.* [18] as a baseline and demonstrate that the requirement of fully labeled real images can be significantly minimized while still maintaining performance on par with fully-supervised methods.

Other recent methods directly predict the parameters of a deformable hand model, *e.g.*, MANO [32], from RGB images [5,15,29,42,46]. The predicted parameters consist of the shape and pose deformations wrt. a mean shape and pose that are learned using large amounts of 3D scans of the hand. Alternatively, [13,21] circumvent the need for a parametric hand model by directly predicting the mesh vertices from RGB images. These methods require both shape and pose annotations for training, therefore obtaining such kind of training data is even harder. Hence, most methods rely on synthetic training data. Some

methods [4,5,46] alleviate this by introducing re-projection losses that measure the discrepancy between the projection of 3D mesh with labeled 2D poses [5] or silhouettes [4,46]. Even though they utilize strong hand priors in form of a mean hand shape and by operating on a low-dimensional PCA space, using re-projection losses with weakly-labeled data still does not guarantee that the resulting 3D poses will be anatomically plausible. Therefore, all these methods rely on a large number of fully labeled training data. In body pose estimation, such methods generally resort to adversarial losses to ensure plausibility [19].

Biomechanical constraints have also been used in the literature to encourage plausible 3D poses by imposing biomechanical limits on the structure of the hands [9,10,12,24,33,36,39,40,43] or via a learned refinement model[7]. Most methods [2,9,10,24,33,36,39,43] impose these limits via inverse kinematic in a post-processing step, therefore the possibility of integrating them for neural network training remains unanswered. Our proposed soft-constraints are fully integrated into the network, which does not require a post-refinement step during test time. Similar to our method, [12,40] also penalize invalid bone lengths. However, we additionally model the joint limits and palmar structure.

3   Method

Our method is summarized in Fig. 2. Our key contribution is a set of novel constraints that constitute a biomechanical model of the human hand and capture the bone lengths, joint angles and shape of the palm. We emphasize that we do not fit a kinematic model to the predictions, but instead extract the quantities in question directly from the predictions in order to constrain them. Therefore the method of extraction is carefully designed to work under noisy and malformed 3D joint predictions while simultaneously being fully differentiable in any configuration. These biomechanical constraints provide an inductive bias to the neural network. Specifically, the network is guided to predict anatomically plausible hand poses for weakly-supervised data (*i.e.* 2D only), which in turn increases generalizability. The model can be combined with any backbone architecture that predicts 3D keypoints. We first introduce the notations used in this paper followed by the details of the proposed biomechanical losses. Finally, we discuss the integration with a variant of [18].

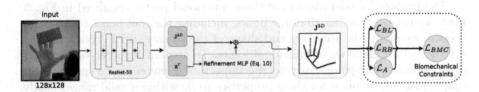

Fig. 2. Method overview. A model takes an RGB image and predicts the 3D joints on which we apply our proposed BMC. These guide the model to predict plausible poses.

Notation. We use bold capital font for matrices, bold lowercase for vector and roman font for scalars. We assume a right hand. The joints $[\mathbf{j}_1^{3D}, \ldots, \mathbf{j}_{21}^{3D}] = \mathbf{J}^{3D} \in \mathbb{R}^{21 \times 3}$ define a kinematic chain of the hand starting from the root joint $\mathbf{j}_1^{3D}$ and ending in the fingertips. For the sake of simplicity, the joints of the hands are grouped by the fingers, denoted as the respective set $F1, \ldots, F5$, visualized in Fig. 3a. Each $\mathbf{j}_i^{3D}$, except the root joint (CMC), has a parent, denoted as $p(i)$. We define a bone $\mathbf{b}_i = \mathbf{j}_{i+1}^{3D} - \mathbf{j}_{p(i+1)}^{3D}$ as the vector pointing from the parent joint to its child joint. Hence $[\mathbf{b}_1, \ldots, \mathbf{b}_{20}] = \mathbf{B} \in \mathbb{R}^{20 \times 3}$. The bones are named according to the child joint. For example, the bone connecting MCP to PIP is called PIP bone. We define the five root bones as the MCP bones, where one endpoint is the root $\mathbf{j}_1^{3D}$. Intuitively, the root bones are those that lie within and define the palm. We define the bones $\mathbf{b}_i$ with $i = 1, \ldots, 5$ to correspond to the root bones of fingers $F1, \ldots, F5$. We denote the angle $\alpha(v_1, v_2) = \arccos\left(\frac{\mathbf{v}_1^T \mathbf{v}_2}{\|\mathbf{v}_1\|_2 \|\mathbf{v}_2\|_2}\right)$ between the vectors $\mathbf{v}_1, \mathbf{v}_2$. The interval loss is defined as $\mathcal{I}(x; a, b) = \max(a - x, 0) + \max(x - b, 0)$. The normalized vector is defined as $\text{norm}(\mathbf{x}) = \frac{\mathbf{x}}{\|\mathbf{x}\|_2}$. Lastly, $\mathrm{P_{xy}}(\mathbf{v})$ is the orthogonal projection operator, projecting $\mathbf{v}$ orthogonally onto the **x**-**y** plane where **x**,**y** are vectors.

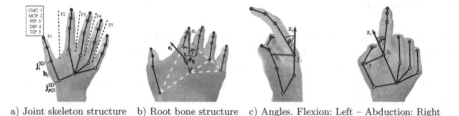

a) Joint skeleton structure   b) Root bone structure   c) Angles. Flexion: Left – Abduction: Right

Fig. 3. Illustration of our proposed biomechanical structure.

3.1   Biomechanical Constraints

Our goal is to integrate our biomechanical soft constraints (BMC) into the training procedure that encourages the network to predict feasible hand poses. We seek to avoid iterative optimization approaches such as inverse kinematics in order to avert significant increases in training time.

The proposed model consists of three functional parts, visualized in Fig. 3. First, we consider the length of the bones, including the root bones of the palm. Second, we model the structure and shape of the palmar region, consisting of a rigid structure made up of individual joints. To account for inter-subject variability of bones and palm structure, it is important to not enforce a specific mean shape. Instead, we allow for these properties to lie within a valid range. Lastly, the model describes the articulation of the individual fingers. The finger motion is described via modeling of the flexion and abduction of individual bones. As their limits are interdependent, they need to be modeled jointly. As such, we propose a novel constraint that takes this interdependence into account.

The limits for each constraint can be attained manually from measurements, from the literature (e.g. [9,33]), or acquired in a data-driven way from 3D annotations, should they be available.

Bone Length. For each bone i, we define an interval $[b_i^{\min}, b_i^{\max}]$ of valid bone length and penalize if the length $||\mathbf{b}_i||_2$ lies outside of this interval:

$$\mathcal{L}_{\mathrm{BL}}(\mathbf{J}^{3D}) = \frac{1}{20} \sum_{i=1}^{20} \mathcal{I}(||\mathbf{b}_i||_2; b_i^{\min}, b_i^{\max})$$

This loss encourages keypoint predictions that yield valid bone lengths. Figure 3a shows the length of a bone in blue.

Root Bones. To attain valid palmar structures we first interpret the root bones as spanning a mesh and compute its curvature by following [30]:

$$c_i = \frac{(\mathbf{e}_{i+1} - \mathbf{e}_i)^T (\mathbf{b}_{i+1} - \mathbf{b}_i)}{||\mathbf{b}_{i+1} - \mathbf{b}_i||^2}, \text{ for } i \in \{1, 2, 3, 4\} \tag{1}$$

Where $\mathbf{e}_i$ is the edge normal at bone $\mathbf{b}_i$:

$$\mathbf{n}_i = \mathrm{norm}(\mathbf{b}_{i+1} \times \mathbf{b}_i), \text{ for } i \in \{1, 2, 3, 4\}$$

$$\mathbf{e}_i = \begin{cases} \mathbf{n}_1, & \text{if } i = 1 \\ \mathrm{norm}(\mathbf{n}_i + \mathbf{n}_{i-1}), & \text{if } i \in \{2, 3, 4\} \\ \mathbf{n}_4, & \text{if } i = 5 \end{cases} \tag{2}$$

Positive values of c_i denote an arched hand, for example when pinky and thumb touch. A flat hand has no curvature. Figure 3b visualizes the mesh in dashed yellow and the triangle over which the curvature is computed in dashed purple.

We ensure that the root bones fall within correct angular ranges by defining the angular distance between neighbouring $\mathbf{b}_i, \mathbf{b}_{i+1}$ across the plane they span:

$$\phi_i = \alpha(\mathbf{b}_i, \mathbf{b}_{i+1}) \tag{3}$$

We constrain both the curvature c_i and angular distance ϕ_i to lie within a valid range $[c_i^{\min}, c_i^{\max}]$ and $[\phi_i^{\min}, \phi_i^{\max}]$:

$$\mathcal{L}_{\mathrm{RB}}(\mathbf{J}^{3D}) = \frac{1}{4} \sum_{i=1}^{4} \left(\mathcal{I}(c_i; c_i^{\min}, c_i^{\max}) + \mathcal{I}(\phi_i; \phi_i^{\min}, \phi_i^{\max}) \right)$$

$\mathcal{L}_{\mathrm{RB}}$ ensures that the predicted joints of the palm define a valid structure, which is crucial since the kinematic chains of the fingers originate from this region.

Joint Angles. To compute the joint angles, we first need to define a consistent frame $\mathbf{F}_i$ of a local coordinate system for each finger bone $\mathbf{b}_i$. $\mathbf{F}_i$ must be consistent with respect to the movements of the finger. In other words, if one constructs $\mathbf{F}_i$ given a pose $\mathbf{J}_1^{3D}$, then moves the fingers and corresponding $\mathbf{F}_i$

into pose $\mathbf{J}_2^{3D}$, the resulting $\mathbf{F}_i$ should be the same as if constructed from $\mathbf{J}_2^{3D}$ directly.

We assume right-handed coordinate systems. To construct $\mathbf{F}_i$, we define two out of three axes based on the palm. We start with the first layer of fingers bones (PIP bones). We define their respective z-component of $\mathbf{F}_i$ as the normalized bone of their respective parent bone (in this case, the root bones): $\mathbf{z}_i = \text{norm}(\mathbf{b}_{p(i)})$. Next, we define the x-axis, based on the plane normals spanned by two neighbouring root bones:

$$\mathbf{x}_i = \begin{cases} -\mathbf{n}_{p(i)}, & \text{if } p(i) \in \{1,2\} \\ -\text{norm}(\mathbf{n}_{p(i)} + \mathbf{n}_{p(i)-1}), & \text{if } p(i) \in \{3,4\} \\ -\mathbf{n}_4, & \text{if } p(i) = 5 \end{cases} \tag{4}$$

Where $\mathbf{n}_i$ is defined as in Eq. 2. Lastly, we compute the last axis $\mathbf{y}_i = \text{norm}(\mathbf{z}_i \times \mathbf{x}_i)$. Given $\mathbf{F}_i$, we can now define the flexion and abduction angles. Each of these angles are given with respect to the local z-axis of $\mathbf{F}_i$. Given $\mathbf{b}_i$ in its local coordinates $\mathbf{b}_i^{\mathbf{F}_i}$ wrt. $\mathbf{F}_i$, we define the flexion and abduction angles as:

$$\begin{aligned} \theta_i^{\text{f}} &= \alpha(\text{P}_{xz}(\mathbf{b}_i^{\mathbf{F}_i}), \mathbf{z}_i) \\ \theta_i^{\text{a}} &= \alpha(\text{P}_{xz}(\mathbf{b}_i^{\mathbf{F}_i}), \mathbf{b}_i^{\mathbf{F}_i}) \end{aligned} \tag{5}$$

Figure 3c visualizes $\mathbf{F}_i$ and the resulting angles. Note that this formulation leads to ambiguities, where different bone orientations can map to the same $(\theta_i^{\text{f}}, \theta_i^{\text{a}})$-point. We resolve this via an octant lookup, which leads to angles in the intervals $\theta_i^{\text{f}} \in [-\pi, \pi]$ and $\theta_i^{\text{a}} \in [-\pi/2, \pi/2]$ respectively. See appendix for more details.

Given the angles of the first set of finger bones, we can then construct the remaining two rows of finger bones. Let $\mathbf{R}^{\theta_i}$ denote the rotation matrix that rotates by θ_i^{f} and θ_i^{a} such that $\mathbf{R}^{\theta_i}\mathbf{z}_i = \mathbf{b}_i^{\mathbf{F}_i}$, then we iteratively construct the remaining frames along the kinematic chain of the fingers:

$$\mathbf{F}_i = \mathbf{R}^{\theta_i}\mathbf{F}_{p(i)} \tag{6}$$

This method of frame construction via rotating by θ_i^{f} and θ_i^{a} ensures consistency across poses. The remaining angles can be acquired as described in Eq. 5.

Lastly, the angles need to be constrained. One way to do this is to consider each angle independently and penalize them if they lie outside an interval. This corresponds to constraining them within a box in a 2D space, where the endpoints are the min/max of the limits. However, finger angles have interdependency, therefore we propose an alternative approach to account for this. Given points $\theta_i = (\theta_i^{\text{f}}, \theta_i^{\text{a}})$ that define a range of motion, we approximate their convex hull on the $(\theta^{\text{f}}, \theta^{\text{a}})$-plane with a fixed set of points $\mathcal{H}_i$. The angles are constrained to lie within this structure by minimizing their distance to it:

$$\mathcal{L}_A(\mathbf{J}^{3D}) = \frac{1}{15}\sum_{i=1}^{15} D_H(\theta_i, \mathcal{H}_i) \tag{7}$$

Where D_H is the distance of point θ_i to the hull $\mathcal{H}_i$. Details on the convex hull approximation and implementation can be found in the appendix.

3.2 Z^{root} Refinement

The 2.5D joint representation allows us to recover the value of the absolute pose Z^{root} up to a scaling factor. This is done by solving a quadratic equation dependent on the 2D projection $\mathbf{J}^{2D}$ and relative depth values $\mathbf{z}^r$, as proposed in [18]. In practice, small errors in $\mathbf{J}^{2D}$ or $\mathbf{z}^r$ can result in large deviations of Z^{root}. This leads to big fluctuations in the translation and scale of the predicted pose, which is undesirable. To alleviate these issues, we employ an MLP to refine and smooth the calculated $\hat{Z}^{root}$:

$$\hat{Z}_{ref}^{root} = \hat{Z}^{root} + M_{MLP}(\mathbf{z}^r, \mathbf{K}^{-1}\mathbf{J}^{2D}, \hat{Z}^{root}; \omega) \tag{8}$$

Where M_{MLP} is a multilayered perceptron with parameters ω that takes the predicted and calculated values $\mathbf{z}^r \in \mathbb{R}^{21}$, $\mathbf{K}^{-1}\mathbf{J}^{2D} \in \mathbb{R}^{21\times3}$, $Z^{root} \in \mathbb{R}$ and outputs a residual term. Alternatively, one could predict Z^{root} directly using an MLP with the same input. However, as the exact relationship between the predicted variables and Z^{root} is known, we resort to the refinement approach instead of requiring a model to learn what is already known.

3.3   Final Loss

The biomechanical soft constraints is constructed as follows:

$$\mathcal{L}_{BMC} = \lambda_{BL}\mathcal{L}_{BL} + \lambda_{RB}\mathcal{L}_{RB} + \lambda_A\mathcal{L}_A \tag{9}$$

Our final model is trained on the following loss function:

$$\mathcal{L} = \lambda_{J2D}\mathcal{L}_{J2D} + \lambda_{\mathbf{z}^r}\mathcal{L}_{\mathbf{z}^r} + \lambda_{Z_{ref}^{root}}\mathcal{L}_{Z^{root}} + \mathcal{L}_{BMC} \tag{10}$$

where $\mathcal{L}_{J2D}$, $\mathcal{L}_{\mathbf{z}^r}$ and $\mathcal{L}_{Z^{root}}$ are the L1 loss on any available $\mathbf{J}^{2D}$, $\mathbf{z}^r$ and Z^{root} labels respectively. The weights λ_i balance the individual loss terms.

4   Implementation

We use a ResNet-50 backbone [16]. The input to our model is a 128×128 RGB image from which the 2.5D representation is directly regressed. The model and its refinement step is trained on fully supervised and weakly-supervised data. The network was trained for 70 epochs using SGD with a learning rate of $5e\text{-}3$ and a step-wise learning rate decay of 0.1 after every 30 epochs. We apply the biomechanical constraints directly on the predicted 3D keypoints $\mathbf{J}^{3D}$.

5   Evaluation

Here we introduce the datasets used, show the performance of our proposed $\mathcal{L}_{BMC}$ and compare in extensive settings. Specifically, we study the effect of adding weakly supervised data to complement fully supervised training. All

experiments are conducted in a setting where we assume access to a fully supervised dataset, as well as a supplementary weakly supervised real dataset. Therefore we have access to 2D ground-truth annotations and the computed constraint limits. We study two cases of 3D supervision sources:

Synthetic Data. We choose RHD. Acquiring fully labeled synthetic data is substantially easier as compared to real data. Section 5.3–5.5 consider this setting.

Partially Labeled Real Data. In Sect. 5.6 we gradually increase the number of real 3D labeled samples to study how the proposed approach works under different ratio of fully to weakly supervised data.

To make clear what kind of supervision is used we denote $3D_A$ if 3D annotation is used from dataset A. We indicate usage of 2D from dataset A as $2D_A$. Section 5.3 and 5.4 are evaluated on FH.

5.1   Datasets

Each dataset that provides 3D labels comes with the camera intrinsics. Hence the 2D pose can be easily acquired from the 3D pose. Table 1 provides an overview of datasets used. The test set of HO-3D and FH are available only via a submission system with limited number of total submissions. Therefore for the ablation study (Sect. 5.4) and inspecting the effect of weak-supervision (Sect. 5.3), we divide the training set into a training and validation split. For these sections, we choose to evaluate on FH due to its large number of samples and variability in both hand pose and shape.

Table 1. Overview of datasets used for evaluation.

Name	Type	joints #	train/test #
Rendered Hand Pose (RHD) [48]	Synth	21	42k/2.7k
FreiHAND (FH) [49]	Real	21	33k/4.0k
Dexter+Object (D+O) [35]	Real	5	-/3.1k
Hand-Object 3D (HO-3D) [14]	Real	21	11k/6.6k

5.2   Evaluation Metric

HO-3D. The error given by the submission system is the mean joint error in mm. The INTERP is the error on test frames sampled from training sequences that are not present in the training set. The EXTRAP is the error on test samples that have neither hand shapes nor objects present in the training set. We used the version of the dataset that was available at the time [3].

FH. The error given by the submission system is the mean joint error in mm. Additionally, the area under the curve (AUC) of the percentage of correct keypoints (PCK) plot is reported. The PCK values lie in an interval 0 mm 50 mm with 100 equally spaced thresholds. Both the aligned (using procrustes analysis) and unaligned scores are given. We report the aligned score. The unaligned score can be found in the appendix.

Table 2. The effect of weak-supervision on the **validation** split of FH. Training on synthetic data (RHD) leads to poor accuracy on real data (FH). Adding real 2D labeled data reduces 3D prediction error due to better alignment with the 2D projection. Adding our proposed $\mathcal{L}_{BMC}$ significantly reduces the 3D error due to more accurate **Z**.

Effect of weak-supervision	Description	Mean Error ↓		
		2D (px)	Z (mm)	3D (mm)
3D$_{RHD}$ + **3D**$_{FH}$	Fully supervised, synthetic+real	3.72	5.69	8.78
+ $\mathcal{L}_{BMC}$ (**ours**)	+BMC	**3.70**	**5.44**	**8.60**
3D$_{RHD}$	Fully supervised, synthetic only	12.35	20.02	30.82
+ **2D**$_{FH}$	+ Weakly supervised, real	3.80	17.02	20.92
+ $\mathcal{L}_{BMC}$ (**ours**)	+BMC	**3.79**	**9.97**	**13.78**

D+O. We report the AUC for the PCK thresholds of 20 to 50 mm comparable with prior work [5,46,49]. For [18,25,34,48] we report the numbers as presented in [46] as they consolidate all AUC of related work in a consistent manner using the same PCK thresholds. For [4], we recomputed the AUC for the same interval based on the values provided by the authors.

5.3   Effect of Weak-Supervision

We first inspect how weak-supervision affects the performance of the model. We decompose the 3D prediction error on the validation set of FH in terms of its 2D ($\mathbf{J}^{2D}$) and depth component ($\mathbf{Z}$) via the pinhole camera model $\mathbf{Z}^{-1}\mathbf{K}\mathbf{J}^{3D} = \mathbf{J}^{2D}$ and evaluate their individual error.

We train four models using different data sources. 1) Full 3D supervision on both synthetic RHD and real FH ($\mathbf{3D}_{RHD}$ + $\mathbf{3D}_{FH}$), which serves as an upper bound for when all 3D labels are available 2) Fully supervised on RHD which constitutes our lower bound on accuracy ($\mathbf{3D}_{RHD}$) 3) Fully supervised on RHD with naive application of weakly-supervised FH ($+\mathbf{2D}_{FH}$) 4) Like setting 3) but adding our proposed constraints ($+\mathcal{L}_{BMC}$).

Table 2 shows the results. The model trained with full 3D supervision from real and synthetic data reflects the best setting. Adding $\mathcal{L}_{BMC}$ during training slightly reduces 3D error (8.78 mm to 8.6 mm) primarily due to a regularization effect. When the model is trained only on synthetic data ($\mathbf{3D}_{RHD}$) we observe a significant rise (8.78mm to 30.82 mm) in 3D error due to the poor generalization from synthetic data. When weak-supervision is provided from the real data ($+\mathbf{2D}_{FH}$), the error is reduced (30.82 mm to 20.92 mm). However, inspecting this more closely we observe that the improvement comes mainly from 2D error reduction (12.35px to 3.8px), whereas the depth component is improved marginally (20.02 mm to 17.02 mm). Observing these samples qualitatively (Fig. 1), we see that many do not adhere to biomechanical limits of the human hand. By penalizing such violations via our proposed losses $\mathcal{L}_{BMC}$ to the weakly supervised setting we see a significant improvement in 3D error (20.92mm to 13.78mm)

which is due to improved depth accuracy (20.02mm to 9.97mm). Inspecting (*e.g.* Fig. 1) closer, we see that the model predicts the correct 3D pose in challenging settings such as heavy self- and object occlusion, despite having never seen such samples in 3D. Since $\mathcal{L}_{\mathbf{BMC}}$ describes a valid range, rather than a specific pose, slight deviations from the ground truth 3D pose have to be expected which explains the small remaining quantitative gap from the fully supervised model.

5.4   Ablation Study

We quantify the individual contributions of our proposals on the validation set of FH and reproduce these results on HO-3D in supplementary. Each error metric is computed for the root-relative 3D pose.

Refinement Network. Table 3 shows the impact of Z^{root} refinement (Sect. 3.2). We train two models that include (w. refinement) or omit (w/o refinement) the refinement step, using full supervision on FH ($\mathbf{3D_{FH}}$). Using refinement, the mean

Table 3. Effect of Z^{root} refinement

Ablation Study	EPE (mm)		AUC ↑
	mean ↓	median ↓	
w/o refinement	11.20	8.62	0.95
w. refinement (**ours**)	**9.76**	**8.14**	**0.97**

error is reduced by 1.44mm which indicates that refining effectively reduces outliers.

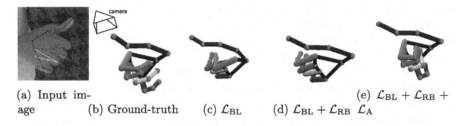

(a) Input image   (b) Ground-truth   (c) $\mathcal{L}_{\mathbf{BL}}$ (d) $\mathcal{L}_{\mathbf{BL}} + \mathcal{L}_{\mathbf{RB}}$ (e) $\mathcal{L}_{\mathbf{BL}} + \mathcal{L}_{\mathbf{RB}} + \mathcal{L}_{\mathbf{A}}$

Fig. 4. Impact of our proposed losses. (a) All predicted 3D poses project to the same 2D pose. (b) Ground-truth pose. (c) $\mathcal{L}_{\mathbf{BL}}$ results in poses that have correct bone lengths, but may have invalid angles and palm structure. (d) Including $\mathcal{L}_{\mathbf{RB}}$ imposes a correct palm, but the fingers are still articulated wrong. (e) Adding $\mathcal{L}_{\mathbf{A}}$ leads to the finger bones having correct angles. The resulting hand is plausible and close to the ground-truth.

Components of BMC. In Table 4, we perform a series of experiments where we incrementally add each of the proposed constraints. For 3D guidance, we use the synthetic RHD and *only* use the 2D labels of FH. We first run the baseline model trained only on this data ($3D_{RHD} + 2D_{FH}$). Next, we add the bone length loss $\mathcal{L}_{BL}$, followed by the root bone loss $\mathcal{L}_{RB}$

Table 4. Effect of BMC components.

Ablation Study	EPE (mm)		AUC ↑
	mean ↓	median ↓	
$3D_{RHD} + 2D_{FH}$	20.92	16.93	0.81
$+ \mathcal{L}_{BL}$ (ours)	17.58	14.81	0.88
$+ \mathcal{L}_{RB}$ (ours)	15.48	13.49	0.91
$+ \mathcal{L}_{A}$ (ours)	**13.78**	**11.61**	**0.92**
$3D_{RHD} + 3D_{FH}$	8.78	7.25	0.98

and the angle loss $\mathcal{L}_A$. An upper bound is given by our model trained fully supervised on both datasets ($3D_{RHD} + 3D_{FH}$). Each component contributes positively towards the final performance, totalling a decrease of 6.24mm in mean error as compared to our weakly-supervised baseline, significantly closing the gap to the fully supervised upper bound. A qualitative assessment of the individual losses can be seen in Fig. 4.

Co-dependency of Angles. In Table 5, we show the importance of modeling the dependencies between the flexion and abduction angle limits (Sect. 3), instead of regarding them independently. Co-dependent angle limits yield a decrease in mean error of 1.40 mm.

Table 5. Effect of angle constraints

Ablation Study	EPE (mm)		AUC ↑
	mean ↓	median ↓	
Independent	15.57	13.45	0.91
Dependent	13.78	11.61	0.92

Constraint Limits. In Table 6, we investigate the effect of the used limits on the final performance, as one may have to resort to approximations. For this, we instead take the hand parameters from RHD and perform the same weakly-supervised experiment as before ($+\mathcal{L}_{BMC}$). Approximating the limits from another dataset slightly increases the error, but still clearly outperforms the 2D baseline.

5.5   Bootstrapping with Synthetic Data

We validate $\mathcal{L}_{BMC}$ on the **test set** of FH and HO-3D. We train the same four models like in Sect. 5.3 using fully supervised RHD and weakly-supervised real data $R \in [FH, HO-3D]$.

Table 6. Effect of limits

Ablation Study	EPE (mm)		AUC ↑
	mean ↓	median ↓	
Approximated	16.14	13.93	0.90
Computed	13.78	11.61	0.92

For all results here we perform training on the *full* dataset and evaluate on the official test split via the online submission system. Additionally, we evaluate the cross-dataset performance on D+O dataset to show how our proposed constraints improves generalizability and compare with prior work [4,5,18,25,46].

FH. The second column of Table 7 shows the dataset performance for R = FH. Training solely on RHD ($3D_{RHD}$) performs the worst. Adding real data ($+2D_{FH}$) with 2D labels reduces the error, as we reduce the real/synthetic domain gap. Including the proposed $\mathcal{L}_{BMC}$ results in an accuracy boost.

Table 7. Results on the respective **test** split, evaluated by the *submission systems*. Training on RHD leads to poor accuracy on both FH and HO-3D. Adding weakly-supervised data improves results, as expected. By including our proposed $\mathcal{L}_{BMC}$, our model incurs a significant boost in accuracy, especially evident for the INTERP score.

	Description	R=FH		R=HO-3D	
		mean ↓	AUC ↑	EXTRAP ↓	INTERP ↓
$3D_{RHD} + 3D_R$	Fully sup. upper bound	0.90	0.82	18.22	5.02
$3D_{RHD}$	Fully sup. lower bound	1.60	0.69	20.84	33.57
$+2D_R$	+ Weakly sup	1.26	0.75	19.57	25.16
$+ \mathcal{L}_{BMC}$ (**ours**)	+ BMC	**1.13**	**0.78**	**18.42**	**10.31**

Table 8. Datasets used by prior work for evaluation on D+O. With solely fully-supervised synthetic and weakly-supervised real data, we outperform recent works and perform on par with [46]. All other works rely on full supervision from real and synthetic data. *These works report unaligned results.

D+O	Annotations used			
	Synth	Real	Scans	AUC ↑
Ours (weakly sup.)	3D	**2D only**		**0.82**
Zhang (2019) [46]	3D	3D	3D	0.82
Boukhayma (2019) [5]	3D	3D	3D	0.76
Iqbal (2018)* [18]	3D	3D		0.67
Baek (2019)* [4]	3D	3D	3D	0.61
Zimmermann (2018)[48]	3D	3D		0.57
Spurr (2018) [34]	3D	3D		0.51
Mueller (2018)* [25]	3D	Unlabeled		0.48

HO-3D. The third column of Table 7 shows a similar trend for R = HO-3D. Most notably, our constraints yield a decrease of 14.85 mm for INTERP. This is significantly larger than the relative decrease the 2D data adds (-8.41mm). For EXTRAP, BMC yields an improvement of 1.15mm, which is close to the 1.27mm gained from 2D data. This demonstrates that $\mathcal{L}_{BMC}$ is beneficial in leveraging 2D data more effectively in unseen scenarios.

D+O. In Table 8 we demonstrate the cross-data performance on D+O for R = FH. Most recent works have made use of MANO [4,5,46], leveraging a low-dimensional embedding of highly detailed hand scans and require custom synthetic data [4,5] to fit the shape. Using only fully supervised *synthetic data* and *weakly-supervised* real data in conjunction with $\mathcal{L}_{BMC}$, we reach state-of-the-art.

5.6 Bootstrapping with Real Data

We study the impact of our biomechanical constrains on reducing the number of labeled samples required in scenarios where few real 3D labeled samples are available. We train a model in a setting where a fraction of the data contains the full 3D labels and the remainder contains only 2D supervision.

Here we choose $R = FH$, use the entire training set and evaluate on the test set. For each fraction of fully labelled data we evaluate two models. The first is trained on both the fully and weakly labeled samples. The second is trained with the addition of our proposed constraints. We show the results in Fig. 5. For a given AUC, we plot the number of labeled samples required to reach it. We observe that for lower labeling percentages, the amount of labeled data required is approximately *half* using $\mathcal{L}_{\mathbf{BMC}}$. This showcases its effectiveness in low label settings and demonstrates the decrease in requirement for fully annotated training data.

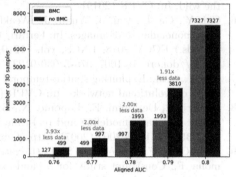

Fig. 5. Number of 3D samples required to reach a certain aligned AUC on FH.

6 Conclusion

We propose a set of fully differentiable biomechanical losses to more effectively leverage weakly supervised data. Our method consists of a novel procedure to encourage anatomically correct predictions of a backbone network via a set of novel losses that penalize invalid bone length, joint angles as well as palmar structures. Furthermore, we have experimentally shown that our constraints can more effectively leverage weakly-supervised data, which show improvement on both within- and cross-dataset performance. Our method reaches state-of-the-art performance on the aligned D+O objective using 3D synthetic and 2D real data and reduces the need of training data by half in low label settings on FH.

Acknowledgments. We are grateful to Christoph Gebhardt and Shoaib Ahmed Siddiqui for the aid in figure creation and Abhishek Badki for helpful discussions.

References

1. Albrecht, I., Haber, J., Seidel, H.P.: Construction and animation of anatomically based human hand models. In: SIGGRAPH (2003)
2. Aristidou, A.: Hand tracking with physiological constraints. Vis. Comput. **34**(2), 213–228 (2018). https://doi.org/10.1007/s00371-016-1327-8

3. Armagan, A., et al.: Measuring generalisation to unseen viewpoints, articulations, shapes and objects for 3D hand pose estimation under hand-object interaction. In: ECCV (2020)
4. Baek, S., Kim, K.I., Kim, T.K.: Pushing the envelope for RGB-based dense 3D hand pose estimation via neural rendering. In: CVPR (2019)
5. Boukhayma, A., de Bem, R., Torr, P.H.: 3D hand shape and pose from images in the wild. In: CVPR (2019)
6. Cai, Y., Ge, L., Cai, J., Yuan, J.: Weakly-supervised 3D hand pose estimation from monocular RGB images. In: Ferrari, V., Hebert, M., Sminchisescu, C., Weiss, Y. (eds.) ECCV 2018. LNCS, vol. 11210, pp. 678–694. Springer, Cham (2018). https://doi.org/10.1007/978-3-030-01231-1_41
7. Cai, Y., et al.: Exploiting spatial-temporal relationships for 3D pose estimation via graph convolutional networks. In: CVPR (2019)
8. Cerveri, P., De Momi, E., Lopomo, N., Baud-Bovy, G., Barros, R., Ferrigno, G.: Finger kinematic modeling and real-time hand motion estimation. Ann. Biomed. Eng. **35**(11), 1989–2002 (2007). https://doi.org/10.1007/s10439-007-9364-0
9. Chen Chen, F., Appendino, S., Battezzato, A., Favetto, A., Mousavi, M., Pescarmona, F.: Constraint study for a hand exoskeleton: human hand kinematics and dynamics. J. Robot. (2013)
10. Cobos, S., Ferre, M., Uran, M.S., Ortego, J., Pena, C.: Efficient human hand kinematics for manipulation tasks. In: IROS (2008)
11. Cordella, F., Zollo, L., Guglielmelli, E., Siciliano, B.: A bio-inspired grasp optimization algorithm for an anthropomorphic robotic hand. Int. J. Interact. Des. Manuf. **6**(2), 113–122 (2012). https://doi.org/10.1007/s12008-012-0149-9
12. Dibra, E., Wolf, T., Oztireli, C., Gross, M.: How to refine 3D hand pose estimation from unlabelled depth data? In: 3DV (2017)
13. Ge, L., et al.: 3D hand shape and pose estimation from a single RGB image. In: CVPR (2019)
14. Hampali, S., Rad, M., Oberweger, M., Lepetit, V.: HOnnotate: a method for 3D annotation of hand and object poses. In: CVPR (2020)
15. Hasson, Y.,et al.: Learning joint reconstruction of hands and manipulated objects. In: CVPR (2019)
16. He, K., Zhang, X., Ren, S., Sun, J.: Deep residual learning for image recognition. In: CVPR (2016)
17. Heap, T., Hogg, D.: Towards 3D hand tracking using a deformable model. In: FG (1996)
18. Iqbal, U., Molchanov, P., Breuel, T., Gall, J., Kautz, J.: Hand pose estimation via latent 2.5D heatmap regression. In: Ferrari, V., Hebert, M., Sminchisescu, C., Weiss, Y. (eds.) ECCV 2018. LNCS, vol. 11215, pp. 125–143. Springer, Cham (2018). https://doi.org/10.1007/978-3-030-01252-6_8
19. Kanazawa, A., Black, M.J., Jacobs, D.W., Malik, J.: End-to-end recovery of human shape and pose. In: CVPR (2018)
20. Kuch, J.J., Huang, T.S.: Vision based hand modeling and tracking for virtual teleconferencing and telecollaboration. In: CVPR (1995)
21. Kulon, D., Wang, H., Güler, R.A., Bronstein, M., Zafeiriou, S.: Single image 3D hand reconstruction with mesh convolutions. In: BMVC (2019)
22. Lee, J., Kunii, T.L.: Model-based analysis of hand posture. IEEE Comput. Graph. Appl. **15**(5), 77–86 (1995)
23. Lin, J., Wu, Y., Huang, T.S.: Modeling the constraints of human hand motion. In: IEEE Workshop on Human Motion (2000)

24. Melax, S., Keselman, L., Orsten, S.: Dynamics based 3D skeletal hand tracking. In: ACM SIGGRAPH Symposium on Interactive 3D Graphics and Games (2013)
25. Mueller, F., et al.: GANerated hands for real-time 3D hand tracking from monocular RGB. In: CVPR (2018)
26. Oikonomidis, I., Kyriazis, N., Argyros, A.A.: Full DOF tracking of a hand interacting with an object by modeling occlusions and physical constraints. In: ICCV (2011)
27. Oikonomidis, I., Kyriazis, N., Argyros, A.A.: Efficient model-based 3D tracking of hand articulations using kinect. In: BMVC (2011)
28. Panteleris, P., Oikonomidis, I., Argyros, A.: Using a single RGB frame for real time 3D hand pose estimation in the wild. In: WACV (2017)
29. Pavlakos, G., et al.: Expressive body capture: 3D hands, face, and body from a single image. In: CVPR (2019)
30. Reed, N.: What is the simplest way to compute principal curvature for a mesh triangle? (2019). https://computergraphics.stackexchange.com/questions/1718/what-is-the-simplest-way-to-compute-principal-curvature-for-a-mesh-triangle
31. Rhee, T., Neumann, U., Lewis, J.P.: Human hand modeling from surface anatomy. In: ACM SIGGRAPH Symposium on Interactive 3D Graphics and Games (2006)
32. Romero, J., Tzionas, D., Black, M.J.: Embodied hands: modeling and capturing hands and bodies together. In: SIGGRAPH-Asia (2017)
33. Ryf, C., Weymann, A.: The neutral zero method–a principle of measuring joint function. Injury **26**, 1–11 (1995)
34. Spurr, A., Song, J., Park, S., Hilliges, O.: Cross-modal deep variational hand pose estimation. In: CVPR (2018)
35. Sridhar, S., Mueller, F., Zollhöfer, M., Casas, D., Oulasvirta, A., Theobalt, C.: Real-time joint tracking of a hand manipulating an object from RGB-D input. In: Leibe, B., Matas, J., Sebe, N., Welling, M. (eds.) ECCV 2016. LNCS, vol. 9906, pp. 294–310. Springer, Cham (2016). https://doi.org/10.1007/978-3-319-46475-6_19
36. Sridhar, S., Oulasvirta, A., Theobalt, C.: Interactive markerless articulated hand motion tracking using RGB and depth data. In: ICCV (2013)
37. Sun, X., Shang, J., Liang, S., Wei, Y.: Compositional human pose regression. In: ICCV (2017)
38. Tekin, B., Bogo, F., Pollefeys, M.: H+o: unified egocentric recognition of 3D hand-object poses and interactions. In: CVPR (2019)
39. Tompson, J., Stein, M., Lecun, Y., Perlin, K.: Real-time continuous pose recovery of human hands using convolutional networks. ACM Trans. Graph. (ToG) **33**(5), 1–10 (2014)
40. Wan, C., Probst, T., Gool, L.V., Yao, A.: Self-supervised 3D hand pose estimation through training by fitting. In: CVPR (2019)
41. Wu, Y., Huang, T.S.: Capturing articulated human hand motion: a divide-and-conquer approach. In: ICCV (1999)
42. Xiang, D., Joo, H., Sheikh, Y.: Monocular total capture: posing face, body, and hands in the wild. In: CVPR (2019)
43. Xu, C., Cheng, L.: Efficient hand pose estimation from a single depth image. In: ICCV (2013)
44. Yang, L., Yao, A.: Disentangling latent hands for image synthesis and pose estimation. In: CVPR (2019)
45. Zhang, J., Jiao, J., Chen, M., Qu, L., Xu, X., Yang, Q.: 3D hand pose tracking and estimation using stereo matching. arXiv:1610.07214 (2016)
46. Zhang, X., Li, Q., Mo, H., Zhang, W., Zheng, W.: End-to-end hand mesh recovery from a monocular RGB image. In: ICCV (2019)

47. Zhou, X., Huang, Q., Sun, X., Xue, X., Wei, Y.: Towards 3D human pose estimation in the wild: a weakly-supervised approach. In: ICCV (2017)
48. Zimmermann, C., Brox, T.: Learning to estimate 3D hand pose from single RGB images. In: ICCV (2017)
49. Zimmermann, C., Ceylan, D., Yang, J., Russell, B., Argus, M., Brox, T.: Frei-HAND: a dataset for markerless capture of hand pose and shape from single RGB images. In: ICCV (2019)

Dynamic Dual-Attentive Aggregation Learning for Visible-Infrared Person Re-identification

Mang Ye[1], Jianbing Shen[1(✉)], David J. Crandall[2], Ling Shao[1,4],
and Jiebo Luo[3]

[1] Inception Institute of Artificial Intelligence, Abu Dhabi, UAE
shenjianbingcg@gmail.com
[2] Indiana University, Bloomington, USA
[3] University of Rochester, Rochester, USA
[4] Mohamed bin Zayed University of Artificial Intelligence, Abu Dhabi, UAE
https://github.com/mangye16/DDAG

Abstract. Visible-infrared person re-identification (VI-ReID) is a challenging cross-modality pedestrian retrieval problem. Due to the large intra-class variations and cross-modality discrepancy with large amount of sample noise, it is difficult to learn discriminative part features. Existing VI-ReID methods instead tend to learn global representations, which have limited discriminability and weak robustness to noisy images. In this paper, we propose a novel dynamic dual-attentive aggregation (DDAG) learning method by mining both intra-modality part-level and cross-modality graph-level contextual cues for VI-ReID. We propose an intra-modality weighted-part attention module to extract discriminative part-aggregated features, by imposing the domain knowledge on the part relationship mining. To enhance robustness against noisy samples, we introduce cross-modality graph structured attention to reinforce the representation with the contextual relations across the two modalities. We also develop a parameter-free dynamic dual aggregation learning strategy to adaptively integrate the two components in a progressive joint training manner. Extensive experiments demonstrate that DDAG outperforms the state-of-the-art methods under various settings.

Keywords: Person re-identification · Graph attention · Cross-modality

1 Introduction

Person re-identification (Re-ID) techniques [59,68] have achieved human-level performance with part-level deep feature learning [4,40,67]. However, most of these techniques consider images of people collected by visible-spectrum cameras in the daytime, and thus are not applicable to night-time applications. Infrared cameras can be used to collect imagery in low light conditions [50], but matching this imagery to visible-spectrum images is a significant challenge.

© Springer Nature Switzerland AG 2020
A. Vedaldi et al. (Eds.): ECCV 2020, LNCS 12362, pp. 229–247, 2020.
https://doi.org/10.1007/978-3-030-58520-4_14

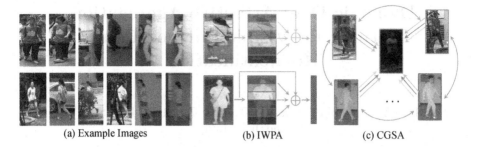

(a) Example Images   (b) IWPA   (c) CGSA

Fig. 1. Idea Illustration: (a) Example images from SYSU-MM01 dataset [50] with high sample noise due to data annotation/collection difficulty. Main components: (b) intra-modality weighted-part aggregation (IWPA), it learns discriminative part-aggregated features by mining the contextual part information within each modality. (c) cross-modality graph structured attention (CGSA), it enhances the representation by incorporating the neighborhood information from the two modalities.

Cross-modality visible-infrared person re-identification (VI-ReID) [50,58] aims to solve this problem by matching images of people captured by visible and infrared (including near- [50] and far-infrared (thermal) [29]) cameras. VI-ReID is challenging due to large visual differences between the two modalities and changing camera environments, leading to large intra- and cross-modality variations. Moreover, due to difficulties in data collection and annotation, VI-ReID usually suffers from high sample noise caused by inaccurate person detection results, *eg* extreme background clutter, as shown in Fig. 1(a). Related cross-modality matching studies have been extensively conducted in visible near-infrared (VIS-NIR) face recognition [28,52]. However, the visual differences between images of people are much greater than those between face images, so those methods are not applicable for VI-ReID [50].

These challenges make it difficult to reliably learn discriminative part-level features using state-of-the-art single-modality Re-ID systems [40,45,55,67]. As a compromise, existing VI-ReID methods mainly focus on learning multi-modal sharable global features, either via one- [7,49,50] or two-stream networks [9,58]. Some work also integrates modality discriminant supervision [7,9] or GAN generated images [44,49] to handle the modality discrepancy. However, global feature learning methods are sensitive to background clutter and can not explicitly handle the modality discrepancy. In addition, part-based feature-learning methods [40,45,66,67] for single-modality Re-ID are typically incapable of capturing reliable part features under a large cross-domain gap [50]. Moreover, the learning is easily contaminated by noisy samples and destabilized when the appearance discrepancy is large across the two modalities. All of these challenges result in less discriminative cross-modality features and unstable training.

To address the above limitations, we propose a novel dynamic dual-attentive aggregation (DDAG) learning method with a two-stream network. DDAG includes two main components, as shown in Fig. 1: an intra-modality weighted-part aggregation (IWPA) and a cross-modality graph structured attention (CGSA)

(CGSA). Our main idea is to mine contextual cues at both an intra-modality part-level and cross-modality graph-level, to enhance feature representation learning. IWPA aims to learn discriminative part-aggregated features by simultaneously mining the contextual relations among the body parts within each modality and imposing the domain knowledge to handle the modality discrepancy. Our design is computationally efficient because we learn the modality-specific part-level attention rather than pixel-level attention [47,65], and it also results in stronger robustness against background clutter. We further develop a residual BatchNorm connection with weighted-part aggregation to reduce the impact of noisy body parts, and adpatively handle the part discrepancy in the aggregated features.

CGSA focuses on learning an enhanced node feature representation by incorporating the relationship between the person images across the two modalities. We eliminate the negative impact of samples with large variations by exploiting the contextual information in the cross-modality graph, assigning adaptive weights to both intra- and cross-modality neighbors with a mutli-head attentive graph scheme [42]. This strategy also reduces the modality discrepancy and smooths the training process. In addition, we introduce a parameter-free dynamic dual aggregation learning strategy to dynamically aggregate the two attentive modules in a mutli-task end-to-end learning manner, which enables complex dual-attentive network to converge stably, while simultaneously reinforcing each attentive component. Our main contributions are as follows:

- We propose a novel dynamic dual-attentive aggregation learning method to mine contextual information at both intra-modality part and cross-modality graph levels to facilitate feature learning for VI-ReID.
- We design an intra-modality weighted-part attention module to learn discriminative part-aggregated representation, adaptively assigning the weights of different body parts.
- We introduce a cross-modality graph structured attention scheme to enhance feature representations by mining the graphical relations between the person images across the two modalities, which smooths the training process and reduces the modality gap.
- We establish a new baseline on two VI-ReID datasets, outperforming the state-of-the-art by a large margin.

2 Related Work

Single-Modality Person Re-ID aims to match person images from visible cameras [18]. Existing works have achieved human-level performance on the widely-used datasets with end-to-end deep learning [1,14,15,17,39,54], either by global [17,64] or part-level feature learning [39,40,67]. However, these approaches are usually unable to handle the ambiguous modality discrepancy in VI-ReID [50], which limits their applicability in night-time surveillance scenarios.

Cross-modality Person Re-ID addresses person re-identification across different types of images, such as between visible-spectrum and infrared [49,50,57], varying illuminations [62] or even between images and non-visual data like text descriptions [5,21]. For visible-Infrared-ReID (VI-ReID), Wu *et al.* [50] introduced a zero-padding strategy with a one-stream network for cross-modality feature representation learning. A two-stream network with dual-constrained top-ranking loss was proposed in [58] to handle both the intra- and cross-modality variations. In addition, Dai *et al.* [7] proposed an adversarial training framework with the triplet loss to jointly discriminate the identity and modality. Recently, Wang *et al.* [49] presented a dual-level discrepancy method with GAN to handle the modality difference at various levels. Similar technique was also adopted in [44]. Two modality-specific [9] and modality-aware learning [56] methods were proposed to handle the modality discrepancy at the classifier level. Meanwhile, other papers have investigated a better loss function [2,23] to handle the modality gap. However, these methods usually focus on learning global feature representations, which ignore the underlying relationship between different body parts and neighborhoods across two modalities.

Contemporaneously, some recent methods investigate the modality-aware collaborative ensemble learning [56] or grayscale augmented tri-modal learning [60]. An intermediate X-modality is designed in [19] to address the modality discrepancy. A powerful baseline with non-local attention is presented in [59].

Visible Near-Infrared Face Recognition addresses the cross-modality face recognition problem, which is also closely related to VI-ReID [13,28,30,32,46, 52]. Early research mainly focused on learning modality-aware metrics [31] or dictionaries [16]. With the emergence of deep neural networks, most methods now focus on learning multi-modal sharable features [52], cross-modality matching models [34] or disentangled representations [51]. However, the modality difference of VI-ReID is much greater than that of face recognition due to the different camera environments and large visual appearances change, which limits the applicability of their methods to the VI-ReID [48,57].

Attention Mechanisms have been widely used in various applications to enhance the feature representation [3,37,42,53]. For person Re-ID, attention is used to combine the spatial-temporal information from different video frames [8,10,20,24]. Some work [22,26,41] has also investigated using multi-scale or different convolutional channels to capture the pixel-level/small-region-level attentions [35,36]. However, they are usually unstable for optimization in VI-ReID due to the large cross-modality discrepancy and noise.

Our part-attention module is also closely related to non-local networks [47, 65]. However, the pixel-level design of these models is sensitive and inefficient for handling the noise encountered in VI-ReID task. In comparison, we design a learnable weighted part-level attention with a BatchNorm residual connection.

3 Proposed Method

Figure 2 provides an overview of our proposed dynamic dual-attentive aggregation learning (DDAG) method. DDAG is developed on top of a two-stream network (Sect. 3.1), and contains an intra-modality weighted-part attention for discriminative part-aggregated features learning (Sect. 3.2) and a cross-modality graph structured attention for shared global feature learning (Sect. 3.3). Finally, we propose a parameter-free dynamic dual aggregation learning strategy to adaptively aggregate the two components for end-to-end joint training (Sect. 3.4).

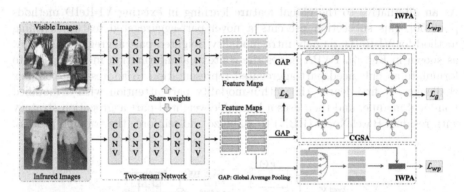

Fig. 2. The proposed DDAG learning framework for VI-ReID. **IWPA**: Intra-modality Weighted-Part Aggregation for discriminative part-aggregated features learning by mining the contextual part relations within each modality. **CGSA**: Cross-modality Graph Structured Attention for global feature learning by utilizing the neighborhood structural relations across two modalities. We further introduce a parameter-free dynamic dual aggregation learning strategy to adaptively aggregate two components.

3.1 Baseline Cross-modality Re-ID

We first present our baseline cross-modality Re-ID model with a two-stream network for incorporating two different modalities. To handle the different properties of the two modalities, the network parameters of the first convolutional block[1] in each stream are different in order to capture modality-specific low-level feature patterns. Meanwhile, the network parameters of the deep convolutional blocks are shared for two modalities in order to learn modality-sharable middle-level feature representations. After the convolutional layers with adaptive pooling, a shared batch normalization layer is added to learn the shared feature embedding. Compared with the two-stream structures in [11,25,56,58], our design captures more discriminative features by mining sharable information in middle-level convolutional blocks rather than high-level embedding layers.

---

[1] We adopt ResNet50 as the backbone network, following [44,49,58].

To learn discriminative features, we combine the identity loss $\mathcal{L}_{id}$ and online hard-mining triplet loss $\mathcal{L}_{tri}$ [61] as our baseline learning objective $\mathcal{L}_b$,

$$\mathcal{L}_b = \mathcal{L}_{id} + \mathcal{L}_{tri}. \tag{1}$$

The identity loss $\mathcal{L}_{id}$ encourages an identity-invariant feature representation. The triplet loss $\mathcal{L}_{tri}$ optimizes the triplet-wise relationships among different person images across the two modalities.

3.2   Intra-modality Weighted-Part Aggregation

As an alternative to the global feature learning in existing VI-ReID methods [7,49,50], this subsection presents a novel part-agggregated feature learning method for VI-ReID, namely intra-modality weighted-part aggregation (IWPA, as shown in Fig. 3). IWPA mines the contextual information in local parts to formulate an enhanced part-aggregated representation to address the complex challenges. It first learns the within-modality part attention with a modified non-local module, and then uses a learnable weighted-part aggregation strategy with residual BatchNorm (RBN) to stabilize and reinforce the training process.

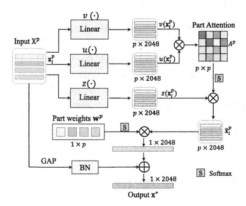

Fig. 3. Illustration of the proposed IWPA module, which mines the part-level relationships to learn the weighted-part aggregation with a residual BatchNorm connection.

Part Attention. The input of our IWPA module is the extracted feature maps from the last residual block of the network, from which we extract the attention-enhanced part features. We denote the output feature maps of the last convolutional block as $\{X = \mathbf{x}_k \in \mathbb{R}^{C \times H \times W}\}_{k=1}^{K}$, where C represents the channel dimension ($C = 2048$ in our experiments), H and W represent the feature map size, and K represents the batch size. To obtain the part features, the feature maps are directly divided into p non-overlapping parts with a region pooling strategy. The part features of each input image are then represented by $X^p = \{\mathbf{x}_i^p \in \mathbb{R}^{C \times 1}\}_{i=1}^{p}$. Similar to [47], we feed each part into three 1×1

convolutional layers $u(\cdot)$, $v(\cdot)$ and $z(\cdot)$. The intra-modality part-based non-local attention $\alpha_{i,j}^p \in [0,1]^{p \times p}$ is then

$$\alpha_{i,j}^p = \frac{f(\mathbf{x}_i^p, \mathbf{x}_j^p)}{\sum_{\forall j} f(\mathbf{x}_i^p, \mathbf{x}_j^p)}, \tag{2}$$

where $f(\mathbf{x}_i^p, \mathbf{x}_j^p)$ represents the pairwise similarity between two part features. To enhance the discriminability, an exponential function is added to magnify the relationship, which enlarges the part attention discrepancy [63]. It is formulated by

$$f(\mathbf{x}_i^p, \mathbf{x}_j^p) = \exp(u(\mathbf{x}_i^p)^T v(\mathbf{x}_j^p)), \tag{3}$$

where $u(\mathbf{x}_i^p) = W_u \mathbf{x}_i^p$ and $v(\mathbf{x}_j^p) = W_v \mathbf{x}_j^p$ are two embeddings with convolutional operations $u(\cdot)$ and $v(\cdot)$. W_u and W_v are the corresponding weight parameters in u and v. With the exponential function, our attention calculation can be treated as a normalization with a softmax function. Note that our attention map is $p \times p$ to capture the part relationships, which is much smaller than that of pixel-level attention $HW \times HW$ in [47,65], making it more efficient. Meanwhile, the part relation is robust against noisy regions and local clutters in the person images.

With the learned part attention, attention-enhanced part features are then represented by the inner product of the embedded part features $z(\mathbf{x}_i^p)$ and the calculated attention A^p, which is formulated by

$$\bar{\mathbf{x}}_i^p = \mathbf{a}_i^p * z(\mathbf{x}_i^p), \tag{4}$$

where $\mathbf{a}_i^p \in A^p = \{\alpha_{i,j}^p\}^{p \times p}$ is the calculated part attention map. Therefore, the refined part features consider the relationship between different body parts. However, the simple average pooling or concatenation of part features is not powerful enough for fine-grained person Re-ID task, and may cause noisy parts accumulation. Meanwhile, it is inefficient to train multiple part-level classifiers, as in [40,56]. To address these issues, we design a residual BatchNorm (RBN) weighted-part aggregation strategy.

Residual BatchNorm Weighted-Part Aggregation. This idea consists of two main parts: First, we use a residual BatchNorm connection of the original input feature map $\mathbf{x}^o$ after average pooling, and the residual learning strategy enables very deep neural networks to be trained and stabilizes the training process. Second, we use a learnable weighted combination of attention-enhanced part features to formulate a discriminative part-aggregated feature representation. In summary, it is formulated by

$$\mathbf{x}^* = \text{BN}(\mathbf{x}^o) + \sum_{i=1}^p w_i^p \bar{\mathbf{x}}_i^p, \tag{5}$$

where $\mathbf{x}^o \in \mathbb{R}^{C \times 1}$ represents the global adaptive pooling output of the input feature map X^p. BN indicates the batch normalization operation, and $\mathbf{w}^p = \{w_i^p\}_{i=1}^p$ represents a learnable weight vector of different parts to handle the

modality discrepancy. Our design has three primary advantages: (1) it avoids multiple part-level classifier learning [40], making it computationally efficient for both training and testing, and it is more robust to background clutter compared to the pixel-level attention techniques [22,47]; (2) it enhances the discrimination power by adaptively aggregating attentive part features in the final feature representation; and (3) the residual BatchNorm (RBN) connection performs much better than the widely-used general residual connection with identity mapping [12,65] (as verified in Sect. 4.2), stabilizing the training process and enhancing the representational power for the cross-modality Re-ID under abundant noise. We use $\mathbf{x}^*$ as the representation of an input sample in the testing phase.

3.3   Cross-modality Graph Structured Attention

Another major challenge is that VI-ReID datasets often contain many incorrectly annotated images or image pairs with large visual differences across the two modalities (as shown in Fig. 1), making it difficult to mine the discriminative local part features and damaging the optimization process. In this subsection, we present our cross-modality graph structured attention, which incorporates the structural relations across two modalities to reinforce the feature representations. The main idea is that the feature representations of person images belonging to the same identity across the two modalities are mutually beneficial.

Graph Construction. At each training step, we adopt an identity-balanced sampling strategy for training [58]. Specifically, for each of n different randomly-selected identities, m visible and m infrared images are randomly sampled, resulting in $K = 2mn$ images in each training batch. We formulate an undirected graph $\mathcal{G}$ with a normalized adjacency matrix,

$$A^g = A_0^g + \mathbb{I}_K, \tag{6}$$

where $A_0^g(i,j) = l_i * l_j$ (l_i and l_j are the corresponding one-hot labels of two graph nodes). $\mathbb{I}_K$ is an identity matrix, indicating that each node is connected to itself. The graph construction is efficiently computed by matrix multiplication between the one-hot labels in each training batch.

Graph Attention. This measures the importance of a node i to another node j within the graph, across two modalities. We denote the input node features by $X^o = \{\mathbf{x}_k^o \in \mathbb{R}^{C \times 1}\}_{k=1}^{K}$, which are outputs of the pooling layer. The graph attention coefficients $\alpha_{i,j}^g \in [0,1]^{K \times K}$ are then computed by

$$\alpha_{i,j}^g = \frac{\exp(\Gamma(\lceil h(\mathbf{x}_i^o), h(\mathbf{x}_j^o) \rfloor \cdot \mathbf{w}^g))}{\sum_{\forall A^g(i,k)>0} \exp(\Gamma(\lceil h(\mathbf{x}_i^o), h(\mathbf{x}_k^o) \rfloor \cdot \mathbf{w}^g))}, \tag{7}$$

where $\Gamma(\cdot)$ represents the LeakyRelu operation. $\lceil , \rfloor$ is the concatenation operation. $h(\cdot)$ is a transformation matrix to reduce the input node feature dimension

C to d, and d is set to 256 in our experiments. $\mathbf{w}^g \in \mathbb{R}^{2d \times 1}$ represents a learnable weighting vector that measures the importance of different feature dimensions in the concatenated features, similar to [43]. Note that our design fully utilizes relations between all the images across two modalities, reinforcing the representation using context information of the same identity.

To enhance the discriminability and stabilize the graph attention learning, we employ a multi-head attention technique [38] by learning multiple $h^l(\cdot)$ and $\mathbf{w}^{l,g}$ ($l = 1, 2 \cdots, L$, L is the total number of heads) with the same structure and optimizing them separately. After concatenating the outputs of multiple heads, the graph structured attention-enhanced feature is then represented by

$$\mathbf{x}_i^g = \phi \Big\lceil \sum\nolimits_{\forall A^g(i,k)>0} \alpha_{i,j}^{g,l} \cdot h^l(\mathbf{x}_j^o) \Big\rfloor_{l=1}^{L}, \tag{8}$$

and $\mathbf{x}_i^g$ is then robust to outlier samples, where ϕ is the ELU activation function. To guide the cross-modality graph structured attention learning, we introduce another graph attention layer with a one-head structure, where the final output node features are represented by $X^{g'} = \{\mathbf{x}_i^{g'}\}_{k=1}^{K}$. We adopt the negative log-likelihood (NLL) loss function for the graph attention learning, formulated by

$$\mathcal{L}_g = - \sum\nolimits_i^K \log(\mathrm{softmax}(\mathbf{x}_i^{g'})). \tag{9}$$

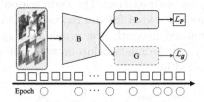

Fig. 4. Illustration of parameter-free dynamic dual aggregation learning. We decompose the overall training framework into two parts: instance-level part-aggregated feature learning $\mathcal{L}_P$ and graph-level global feature learning $\mathcal{L}_g$. We treat $\mathcal{L}_P$ as the dominant loss and progressively add $\mathcal{L}_g$ in the overall training process.

3.4   Dynamic Dual Aggregation Learning

Incorporating the above proposed intra-modality weighted-part attention and cross-modality graph-structured attention into an end-to-end joint learning framework is highly challenging. This is primarily because the two components focus on different learning objectives with very deep network structures, and directly combining them easily will result in *gradient explosion* problem after several steps. Moreover, the features from the same identity across two modalities are quite different in VI-ReID due to the large cross-modality variations,

as demonstrated in Fig. 1. Therefore, the graph-structured attention would be unstable due to the large feature difference across the two modalities at the early stage.

To address the above issues, we introduce a dynamic dual aggregation learning strategy to adaptively integrate the above introduced two components. Specifically, we decompose the overall framework into two different tasks, instance-level part-aggregated feature learning $\mathcal{L}_P$ and graph-level global feature learning $\mathcal{L}_g$. The instance-level part-aggregated feature learning $\mathcal{L}_P$ is a combination of the baseline learning objective $\mathcal{L}_b$ and the intra-modality weighted-part attention loss $\mathcal{L}_{wp}$, represented by

$$\mathcal{L}_P = \mathcal{L}_b \underbrace{- \frac{1}{K} \sum\nolimits_{i=1}^{K} y_i \log(p(y_i|\mathbf{x}_i^*))}_{part\ attention\ loss\ \mathcal{L}_{wp}}, \tag{10}$$

where $p(y_i|\mathbf{x}_i^*)$ represents the probability of $\mathbf{x}_i^*$ being correctly classified into the groundtruth label y_i. The second term represents the instance-level part-aggregated feature learning with weighted-part attention within each modality. It is formulated by the identity loss on top of the aggregated part feature $\mathbf{x}^*$.

Dynamic Dual Aggregation Learning. Motivated by multi-task learning [6], our basic idea is that the instance-level part-aggregated feature learning $\mathcal{L}_P$ acts as the dominant loss, and then we progressively add the graph-level global feature learning loss $\mathcal{L}_g$ for optimization. The main reason for doing this is that it is easier to learn an instance-level feature representation with $\mathcal{L}_P$ at an early stage. With a better learned network, the graph-level global feature learning optimizes the features using the relationship between the person images across the two modalities, denoted by

$$\mathcal{L}^t = \mathcal{L}_P^t + \frac{1}{1 + \mathbb{E}(\mathcal{L}_P^{t-1})} \mathcal{L}_g^t, \tag{11}$$

where t is the epoch number, and $\mathbb{E}(\mathcal{L}_P^{t-1})$ represents the average loss value in the previous epoch. In this dynamic updating framework (as shown in Fig. 4), the graph-level global loss $\mathcal{L}_g$ is progressively added into the overall learning process. This strategy shares a similar spirit to the gradient normalization in multi-task learning [6], but it does not introduce any additional hyper-parameter tuning.

When we optimize $\mathcal{L}_P$, the parameters of the identity classifier in the weighted-part attention loss $\mathcal{L}_{wp}$ are the same as those for the identity classifier in $\mathcal{L}_b$. Our motivation here is that this setting can guarantee that instance-level part-aggregated feature learning is directly performed on the part-aggregated features rather than additional classifiers, ensuring the discriminability of the learned features. Meanwhile, it avoids additional network parameters training.

4 Experimental Results

4.1 Experimental Settings

We use two publicly available VI-ReID datasets (SYSU-MM01 [50] and RegDB [29]) for the experiments. The rank-k matching accuracy and mean Average Precision (mAP) are used as evaluation metrics, following [50].

SYSU-MM01 [50] is a large-scale dataset collected by four RGB and two near-infrared cameras. The major challenge is that person images are captured in both indoor and outdoor environments. In total, the training set contains 22,258 visible and 11,909 near-infrared images of 395 identities. It contains two different testing settings, *all-search* and *indoor-search* mode. The query set contains 3,803 images of 96 identities captured from near-infrared cameras. The gallery set contains the images captured by all four RGB cameras in the *all-search* mode, while the *indoor-search* mode contains images of two indoor RGB cameras. Details on the experimental settings can be found in [50].

RegDB [29] is collected by a dual-camera system, including one visible and one far-infrared camera. In total, this dataset contains 412 person identities, each of which has 10 visible and 10 far-infrared images. Following [57], we randomly select 206 identities for training and the remaining 206 identities for testing. Thus the testing set contains 2,060 visible and 2,060 far-infrared images. We evaluate both visible-to-infrared and infrared-to-visible query settings. The performance is averaged over ten trials on random training/testing splits [49,57].

Implementation Details. Our proposed method is implemented in PyTorch. Following existing VI-ReID works, ResNet50 [12] is adopted as our backbone network for fair comparison, following [59]. The first residual block is specific for each modality while the other four blocks are shared. The stride of the last convolutional block is set to 1, in order to obtain a fine-grained feature map. We initialize the convolutional blocks with the pre-trained ImageNet parameters, as done in [58]. All the input images are firstly resized to 288×144. We adopt random cropping with zero-padding and horizontal flipping for data augmentation. SGD optimizer is adopted for optimization, and the momentum parameter is set to 0.9. We set the initial learning rate to 0.1 with a warm-up strategy [27]. The learning rate decays by 0.1 at the 30th epoch and 0.01 at the 50th epoch, with a total of 80 training epochs. By default, we randomly select 8 identities, and then randomly select 4 visible and 4 infrared images to formulate a training batch. We set $p = 3$ in Eq. 5, $L = 4$ in Eq. 8.

4.2 Ablation Study

Evaluation of Each Component. This subsection evaluates the effectiveness of each component on the SYSU-MM01 dataset under both *all-search* and *indoor search* modes. Specifically, "B" represents the baseline results with a two-stream network trained by $\mathcal{L}_b$. "P" denotes the intra-modality weighted-part aggregation. "G" indicates the cross-modality graph structured attention.

Table 1. Evaluation of each component on the large-scale SYSU-MM01 dataset. "*B*" represents the baseline results with a two-stream network trained by $\mathcal{L}_b$. "*P*" denotes the intra-modality weighted-part attention. "*G*" indicates the cross-modality graph structured attention. Dynamic dual-learning is adopted when aggregating two components. Rank at r accuracy(%) and mAP (%) are reported.

Datasets	All search					Indoor search				
Methods	$r = 1$	$r = 5$	$r = 10$	$r = 20$	mAP	$r = 1$	$r = 5$	$r = 10$	$r = 20$	mAP
B	48.18	75.81	85.73	93.52	47.64	49.52	78.86	88.70	95.27	58.12
$B + P$	53.69	81.16	88.38	94.56	51.37	58.08	84.91	92.37	97.26	65.07
$B + G$	50.75	78.43	86.71	93.62	49.73	52.90	83.50	92.65	97.75	62.26
$B + P + G$	54.75	82.31	90.39	95.81	53.02	61.02	87.13	94.06	98.41	67.98

We make several observations through the results shown in Table 1. *1) Effectiveness of baseline*: Using shared convolutional blocks, we achieve better performance than the two-stream network in [9,25,56,58]. Meanwhile, some training tricks taken from single-modality Re-ID [67] also contributes to this super baseline. *2) Effectiveness of P*: the intra-modality weighted-part aggregation significantly improves the performance. This experiment demonstrates that learning part-level weighted-attention features is beneficial for cross-modality Re-ID. *3) Effectiveness of G*: When we include the cross-modality graph structured attention ($B + G$), performance is improved by using the relationship between the person images across two modalities to reduce the modality discrepancy. *4) Effectiveness of dual-aggregation*: When aggregating two attention modules with the dynamic dual aggregation strategy, the performance is further improved, demonstrating that these two attentions are mutually beneficial to each other.

Why Weighted Part Attention with RBN? We next compare different part attention designs on the SYSU-MM01 dataset under the *all-search* mode. The results are shown in Table 2 and we make several observations. (1) *Effectiveness of weighted scheme*. We compare the *weighted* part features with average/concatenation schemes (termed as *weighted, avg* and *concat* in Table 2).

Table 2. Evaluation of re-weighted part attention with different designs on the SYSU-MM01 dataset (*all-search mode*). Rank at r accuracy (%) and mAP (%) are reported. (*Setting: Baseline + Part attention.*)

Method	Res	$r = 1$	$r = 10$	$r = 20$	mAP
B	N/A	48.18	85.73	93.52	47.64
avg	Res	48.34	86.03	93.72	48.43
concat	Res	50.34	86.43	94.19	49.77
weight	Res	51.06	86.78	94.39	49.92
weight	RBN	53.69	88.38	94.56	51.37

Table 3. Evaluation of graph attention on the SYSU-MM01 dataset (*all-search mode*). N_g represents the number of images selected for graph construction. Rank at r accuracy (%) and mAP (%) are reported. (*Setting: Baseline + Graph attention.*)

N_g	0	1	2	4	8
Rank-1	48.18	49.26	49.85	50.45	50.75
mAP	47.64	48.42	49.12	49.46	49.73

We observe that the proposed learnable weighted-part scheme performs consistently better than its two counterparts. Another benefit of the weighted aggregation is that the feature dimension of final representation is much smaller than the concatenation strategy in [40], which is more suitable for real applications with resource-demanding scenarios. (2) *Effectiveness of residual BN (RBN) scheme.* We compare the general residual connection with the residual BN connection. Results demonstrate that RBN performs significantly better than the general residual connection. This suggests that the BN operation enhances the predictive and stable behavior of the training process [33], which is more suitable for VI-ReID with abundant noise. Note that the performance significantly drops without the residual connection.

Why Graph Structured Attention? We now evaluate the effect of different numbers (N_g) of selected images for graph attention calculation. The results are shown in Table 3. A larger N_g means that more neighbor images from the same identity are considered and the relationship is more reliable. Thus the accuracy is consistently improved with increasing N_g, demonstrating that the graph structured attention can largely reduce the modality discrepancy. Moreover, the infrared images capture less information than the visible images, but with much more noise. Mining the relation across two modalities, especially from the visible images, is thus beneficial for the cross-modality feature learning. The graph attention might also be applied in single-modality person re-identification.

Parameter Analysis. We evaluate the effect of different body parts p and different numbers of graph attention heads L on the large-scale SYSU-MM01 dataset, under the challenging *all-search* mode. The results are shown in Fig. 5.

(1) As shown in the left figure, a larger p captures more fine-grained part features and improves the performance. However, when p is too large, the performance drops since small body parts cannot contain sufficient information for part attention learning. (2) As demonstrated in the right figure, a large L provides more reliable relationship mining, and thus consistently improves the performance. However, it also greatly increases the difficulty of optimization, which results in a slightly decreased performance with a too large L. Thus, we select $p = 3$ and $L = 4$ in all our experiments.

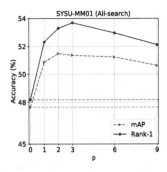 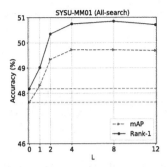

Fig. 5. Evaluation of different body parts p in Eq. 4 (left) and different numbers of graph attention heads L in Eq. 8 (right) on SYSU-MM01 dataset, under the challenging *all-search* mode. Rank-1 matching accuracy (%) and mAP (%) are reported.

Table 4. Comparison with the state-of-the-arts on SYSU-MM01 dataset on two different settings. Rank at r accuracy (%) and mAP (%) are reported.

Settings		All search				Indoor search			
Method	Venue	$r = 1$	$r = 10$	$r = 20$	mAP	$r = 1$	$r = 10$	$r = 20$	mAP
One-stream [50]	ICCV17	12.04	49.68	66.74	13.67	16.94	63.55	82.10	22.95
Two-stream [50]	ICCV17	11.65	47.99	65.50	12.85	15.60	61.18	81.02	21.49
Zero-Pad [50]	ICCV17	14.80	54.12	71.33	15.95	20.58	68.38	85.79	26.92
TONE [57]	AAAI18	12.52	50.72	68.60	14.42	20.82	68.86	84.46	26.38
HCML [57]	AAAI18	14.32	53.16	69.17	16.16	24.52	73.25	86.73	30.08
cmGAN [7]	IJCAI18	26.97	67.51	80.56	31.49	31.63	77.23	89.18	42.19
BDTR [58]	IJCAI18	27.32	66.96	81.07	27.32	31.92	77.18	89.28	41.86
eBDTR [58]	TIFS19	27.82	67.34	81.34	28.42	32.46	77.42	89.62	42.46
HSME [11]	AAAI19	20.68	32.74	77.95	23.12	–	–	–	–
D^{2}RL [49]	CVPR19	28.9	70.6	82.4	29.2	–	–	–	–
MAC [56]	MM19	33.26	79.04	90.09	36.22	36.43	62.36	71.63	37.03
MSR [9]	TIP19	37.35	83.40	93.34	38.11	39.64	89.29	97.66	50.88
AlignGAN [44]	ICCV19	42.4	85.0	93.7	40.7	45.9	87.6	94.4	54.3
HPILN [23]	arXiv19	41.36	84.78	94.31	42.95	45.77	91.82	**98.46**	56.52
LZM [2]	arXiv19	45.00	89.06	–	45.94	49.66	92.47	–	59.81
AGW [59]	arXiv20	47.50	84.39	92.14	47.65	54.17	91.14	95.98	62.97
Xmodal [19]	AAAI20	49.92	89.79	**95.96**	50.73	–	–	–	–
DDAG (Ours)	–	**54.75**	**90.39**	95.81	**53.02**	**61.02**	**94.06**	98.41	**67.98**

4.3   Comparison with State-of-the-Art Methods

This subsection presents a comparison with the current state-of-the-arts on two different datasets. The comparison includes eBDTR [58], D^{2}RL [49], MAC [56], MSR [9], AlignGAN [44] and Xmodal [19]. Note that AlignGAN [44] represents the state-of-the-art by aligning the features in both the feature level and pixel level with generated images. Xmodal generates an intermediate modality

to bridge the gap. We also compare with several arXiv papers, including EDFL [25], HPILN [23], LZM [2] and AGW [59]. The results on two public datasets are shown in Tables 4 and 5.

Table 5. Comparison with the state-of-the-art methods on RegDB dataset on visible-infrared and infrared-visible settings. Rank at r accuracy (%) and mAP (%) are reported.

Setting	Visible to infrared				Infrared to visible			
Method	$r = 1$	$r = 10$	$r = 20$	mAP	$r = 1$	$r = 10$	$r = 20$	mAP
HCML [57]	24.44	47.53	56.78	20.08	21.70	45.02	55.58	22.24
Zero-Pad [50]	17.75	34.21	44.35	18.90	16.63	34.68	44.25	17.82
BDTR [58]	33.56	58.61	67.43	32.76	32.92	58.46	68.43	31.96
eBDTR [58]	34.62	58.96	68.72	33.46	34.21	58.74	68.64	32.49
HSME [11]	50.85	73.36	81.66	47.00	50.15	72.40	81.07	46.16
D^2RL [49]	43.4	66.1	76.3	44.1	–	–	–	–
MAC [56]	36.43	62.36	71.63	37.03	36.20	61.68	70.99	36.63
MSR [9]	48.43	70.32	79.95	48.67	–	–	–	–
EDFL [25]	52.58	72.10	81.47	52.98	51.89	72.09	81.04	52.13
AlignGAN [44]	57.9	–	–	53.6	56.3	–	–	53.4
Xmodal [19]	62.21	83.13	91.72	60.18	–	–	–	–
DDAG (Ours)	**69.34**	**86.19**	**91.49**	**63.46**	**68.06**	**85.15**	**90.31**	**61.80**

The following observations can be made: 1) Methods with two-stream networks (*EDFL* [25], *MSR* [9], *LZM* [2] and our proposed *DDAG*) generally perform better than the one-stream network methods (*cmGAN* [7], *D^{2}RL* [49] and *Zero-Pad* [50]). We conjecture that the main reason is that two-stream networks can simultaneously learn modality-specific and modality-sharable features, which are more suitable for VI-ReID. 2) Our proposed DDAG significantly outperforms the current state-of-the-art AlignGAN [44] by a large margin on both datasets. Note that AlignGAN generates cross-modality image pairs to reduce the modality gap in both feature level and pixel level. In comparison, we do not require the time-consuming and resource-demanding image generation [44,49], and our training process is quite efficient without the adversarial training [7], or the additional modality generation [19].

Another experiment on the RegDB dataset (Table 5) shows that DDAG is robust to different query settings. We achieve much better performance under both *visible-to-infrared* and *infrared-to-visible* query settings, suggesting that DDAG can learn better modality-sharable features by utilizing the part relationship within each modality and graph-structured relations across two modalities.

5   Conclusion

We present a dynamic dual-attentive aggregation learning (DDAG) framework for VI-ReID. DDAG is innovative in two aspects: its IWPA component utilizes the part relationship within each modality to enhance the feature representation by simultaneously considering the part differences and relations; the CGSA module incorporates the neighborhood information across the two modalities to reduce the modality gap. We further design a dynamic dual aggregation learning strategy to seamlessly aggregate the two components. DDAG outperforms the state-of-the-art models on various settings, usually by a large margin. We believe the findings can also be applied in general single-modality person re-identification by mining the relation across multiple body parts, contextual images.

References

1. Bai, S., Tang, P., Torr, P.H., Latecki, L.J.: Re-ranking via metric fusion for object retrieval and person re-identification. In: CVPR, pp. 740–749 (2019)
2. Basaran, E., Gokmen, M., Kamasak, M.E.: An efficient framework for visible-infrared cross modality person re-identification. arXiv preprint arXiv:1907.06498 (2019)
3. Cao, J., Pang, Y., Han, J., Li, X.: Hierarchical shot detector. In: ICCV, pp. 9705–9714 (2019)
4. Chen, B., Deng, W., Hu, J.: Mixed high-order attention network for person re-identification. In: ICCV, pp. 371–381 (2019)
5. Chen, D., et al.: Improving deep visual representation for person re-identification by global and local image-language association. In: Ferrari, V., Hebert, M., Sminchisescu, C., Weiss, Y. (eds.) ECCV 2018. LNCS, vol. 11220, pp. 56–73. Springer, Cham (2018). https://doi.org/10.1007/978-3-030-01270-0_4
6. Chen, Z., Badrinarayanan, V., Lee, C.Y., Rabinovich, A.: GradNorm: gradient normalization for adaptive loss balancing in deep multitask networks. In: ICML, pp. 793–802 (2018)
7. Dai, P., Ji, R., Wang, H., Wu, Q., Huang, Y.: Cross-modality person re-identification with generative adversarial training. In: IJCAI, pp. 677–683 (2018)
8. Fang, P., Zhou, J., Roy, S.K., Petersson, L., Harandi, M.: Bilinear attention networks for person retrieval. In: ICCV, pp. 8030–8039 (2019)
9. Feng, Z., Lai, J., Xie, X.: Learning modality-specific representations for visible-infrared person re-identification. IEEE TIP **29**, 579–590 (2020)
10. Gong, Y., Zhang, Y., Poellabauer, C., et al.: Second-order non-local attention networks for person re-identification. In: ICCV, pp. 3760–3769 (2019)
11. Hao, Y., Wang, N., Li, J., Gao, X.: HSME: hypersphere manifold embedding for visible thermal person re-identification. In: AAAI, pp. 8385–8392 (2019)
12. He, K., Zhang, X., Ren, S., Sun, J.: Deep residual learning for image recognition. In: CVPR, pp. 770–778 (2016)
13. He, R., Wu, X., Sun, Z., Tan, T.: Learning invariant deep representation for NIR-VIS face recognition. In: AAAI, pp. 2000–2006 (2017)
14. Hou, R., Ma, B., Chang, H., Gu, X., Shan, S., Chen, X.: Interaction-and-aggregation network for person re-identification. In: CVPR, pp. 9317–9326 (2019)

15. Hou, R., Ma, B., Chang, H., Gu, X., Shan, S., Chen, X.: VRSTC: occlusion-free video person re-identification. In: CVPR, pp. 7183–7192 (2019)
16. Huang, D.A., Frank Wang, Y.C.: Coupled dictionary and feature space learning with applications to cross-domain image synthesis and recognition. In: ICCV, pp. 2496–2503 (2013)
17. Jingya, W., Xiatian, Z., Shaogang, G., Wei, L.: Transferable joint attribute-identity deep learning for unsupervised person re-identification. In: CVPR, pp. 2275–2284 (2018)
18. Leng, Q., Ye, M., Tian, Q.: A survey of open-world person re-identification. IEEE TCSVT 30(4), 1092–1108 (2019)
19. Li, D., Wei, X., Hong, X., Gong, Y.: Infrared-visible cross-modal person re-identification with an X modality. In: AAAI, pp. 4610–4617 (2020)
20. Li, S., Bak, S., Carr, P., Wang, X.: Diversity regularized spatiotemporal attention for video-based person re-identification. In: CVPR, pp. 369–378 (2018)
21. Li, S., Xiao, T., Li, H., Yang, W., Wang, X.: Identity-aware textual-visual matching with latent co-attention. In: ICCV, pp. 1890–1899 (2017)
22. Li, W., Zhu, X., Gong, S.: Harmonious attention network for person re-identification. In: CVPR, pp. 2285–2294 (2018)
23. Lin, J.W., Li, H.: HPILN: a feature learning framework for cross-modality person re-identification. arXiv preprint arXiv:1906.03142 (2019)
24. Liu, C.T., Wu, C.W., Wang, Y.C.F., Chien, S.Y.: Spatially and temporally efficient non-local attention network for video-based person re-identification. In: BMVC (2019)
25. Liu, H., Cheng, J.: Enhancing the discriminative feature learning for visible-thermal cross-modality person re-identification. arXiv preprint arXiv:1907.09659 (2019)
26. Liu, X., et al.: HydraPlus-Net: attentive deep features for pedestrian analysis. In: ICCV, pp. 350–359 (2017)
27. Luo, H., et al.: A strong baseline and batch normalization neck for deep person re-identification. arXiv preprint arXiv:1906.08332 (2019)
28. Mudunuri, S.P., Venkataramanan, S., Biswas, S.: Dictionary alignment with re-ranking for low-resolution NIR-VIS face recognition. IEEE TIFS 14(4), 886–896 (2019)
29. Nguyen, D.T., Hong, H.G., Kim, K.W., Park, K.R.: Person recognition system based on a combination of body images from visible light and thermal cameras. Sensors 17(3), 605 (2017)
30. Pang, M., Cheung, Y.M., Shi, Q., Li, M.: Iterative dynamic generic learning for face recognition from a contaminated single-sample per person. IEEE TNNLS (2020)
31. Pang, M., Cheung, Y.M., Wang, B., Lou, J.: Synergistic generic learning for face recognition from a contaminated single sample per person. IEEE TIFS 15, 195–209 (2019)
32. Peng, C., Wang, N., Li, J., Gao, X.: Re-ranking high-dimensional deep local representation for NIR-VIS face recognition. IEEE TIP 28, 4553–4565 (2019)
33. Santurkar, S., Tsipras, D., Ilyas, A., Madry, A.: How does batch normalization help optimization? In: NeurIPS, pp. 2483–2493 (2018)
34. Sarfraz, M.S., Stiefelhagen, R.: Deep perceptual mapping for cross-modal face recognition. Int. J. Comput. Vision 122(3), 426–438 (2017)
35. Shao, R., Lan, X., Li, J., Yuen, P.C.: Multi-adversarial discriminative deep domain generalization for face presentation attack detection. In: CVPR, pp. 10023–10031 (2019)

36. Shao, R., Lan, X., Yuen, P.C.: Joint discriminative learning of deep dynamic textures for 3D mask face anti-spoofing. IEEE TIFS **14**(4), 923–938 (2018)
37. Si, J., et al.: Dual attention matching network for context-aware feature sequence based person re-identification. In: CVPR, pp. 5363–5372 (2018)
38. Song, G., Chai, W.: Collaborative learning for deep neural networks. In: NeurIPS, pp. 1837–1846 (2018)
39. Sun, Y., et al.: Perceive where to focus: learning visibility-aware part-level features for partial person re-identification. In: CVPR, pp. 393–402 (2019)
40. Sun, Y., Zheng, L., Yang, Y., Tian, Q., Wang, S.: Beyond part models: person retrieval with refined part pooling (and a strong convolutional baseline). In: Ferrari, V., Hebert, M., Sminchisescu, C., Weiss, Y. (eds.) ECCV 2018. LNCS, vol. 11208, pp. 501–518. Springer, Cham (2018). https://doi.org/10.1007/978-3-030-01225-0_30
41. Tay, C.P., Roy, S., Yap, K.H.: AANet: attribute attention network for person re-identifications. In: CVPR, pp. 7134–7143 (2019)
42. Vaswani, A., et al.: Attention is all you need. In: NeurIPS, pp. 5998–6008 (2017)
43. Veličković, P., Cucurull, G., Casanova, A., Romero, A., Lio, P., Bengio, Y.: Graph attention networks. In: ICLR (2018)
44. Wang, G., Zhang, T., Cheng, J., Liu, S., Yang, Y., Hou, Z.: RGB-infrared cross-modality person re-identification via joint pixel and feature alignment. In: ICCV, pp. 3623–3632 (2019)
45. Wang, G., Yuan, Y., Chen, X., Li, J., Zhou, X.: Learning discriminative features with multiple granularities for person re-identification. In: ACM MM, pp. 274–282. ACM (2018)
46. Wang, N., Gao, X., Sun, L., Li, J.: Bayesian face sketch synthesis. IEEE TIP **26**(3), 1264–1274 (2017)
47. Wang, X., Girshick, R., Gupta, A., He, K.: Non-local neural networks. In: CVPR, pp. 7794–7803 (2018)
48. Wang, Z., Wang, Z., Zheng, Y., Wu, Y., Zeng, W., Satoh, S.: Beyond intra-modality: a survey of heterogeneous person re-identification. In: IJCAI (2020)
49. Wang, Z., Wang, Z., Zheng, Y., Chuang, Y.Y., Satoh, S.: Learning to reduce dual-level discrepancy for infrared-visible person re-identification. In: CVPR, pp. 618–626 (2019)
50. Wu, A., Zheng, W.s., Yu, H.X., Gong, S., Lai, J.: RGB-infrared cross-modality person re-identification. In: ICCV, pp. 5380–5389 (2017)
51. Wu, X., Huang, H., Patel, V.M., He, R., Sun, Z.: Disentangled variational representation for heterogeneous face recognition. In: AAAI, pp. 9005–9012 (2019)
52. Wu, X., Song, L., He, R., Tan, T.: Coupled deep learning for heterogeneous face recognition. In: AAAI, pp. 1679–1686 (2018)
53. Xu, K., et al.: Show, attend and tell: neural image caption generation with visual attention. In: ICML, pp. 2048–2057 (2015)
54. Yang, W., Huang, H., Zhang, Z., Chen, X., Huang, K., Zhang, S.: Towards rich feature discovery with class activation maps augmentation for person re-identification. In: CVPR, pp. 1389–1398 (2019)
55. Yao, H., Zhang, S., Hong, R., Zhang, Y., Xu, C., Tian, Q.: Deep representation learning with part loss for person re-identification. IEEE TIP **28**(6), 2860–2871 (2019)
56. Ye, M., Lan, X., Leng, Q., Shen, J.: Cross-modality person re-identification via modality-aware collaborative ensemble learning. IEEE Trans. Image Process. (TIP) **29**, 9387–9399 (2020)

57. Ye, M., Lan, X., Li, J., Yuen, P.C.: Hierarchical discriminative learning for visible thermal person re-identification. In: AAAI, pp. 7501–7508 (2018)
58. Ye, M., Lan, X., Wang, Z., Yuen, P.C.: Bi-directional center-constrained top-ranking for visible thermal person re-identification. IEEE TIFS **15**, 407–419 (2020)
59. Ye, M., Shen, J., Lin, G., Xiang, T., Shao, L., Hoi, S.C.H.: Deep learning for person re-identification: a survey and outlook. arXiv preprint arXiv:2001.04193 (2020)
60. Ye, M., Shen, J., Shao, L.: Visible-infrared person re-identification via homogeneous augmented tri-modal learning. IEEE TIFS **16**, 728–739 (2020)
61. Ye, M., Shen, J., Zhang, X., Yuen, P.C., Chang, S.F.: Augmentation invariant and instance spreading feature for softmax embedding. IEEE TPAMI (2020)
62. Zeng, Z., Wang, Z., Wang, Z., Zheng, Y., Chuang, Y.Y., Satoh, S.: Illumination-adaptive person re-identification. IEEE TMM (2020)
63. Zhang, X., Yu, F.X., Karaman, S., Zhang, W., Chang, S.F.: Heated-up softmax embedding. arXiv preprint arXiv:1809.04157 (2018)
64. Zhang, X., et al.: AlignedReID: surpassing human-level performance in person re-identification. arXiv preprint arXiv:1711.08184 (2017)
65. Zhang, Y., Li, K., Li, K., Zhong, B., Fu, Y.: Residual non-local attention networks for image restoration. In: ICLR (2019)
66. Zhao, L., Li, X., Zhuang, Y., Wang, J.: Deeply-learned part-aligned representations for person re-identification. In: ICCV, pp. 3219–3228 (2017)
67. Zheng, F., et al.: Pyramidal person re-identification via multi-loss dynamic training. In: CVPR, pp. 8514–8522 (2019)
68. Zheng, L., Shen, L., Tian, L., Wang, S., Wang, J., Tian, Q.: Scalable person re-identification: a benchmark. In: ICCV, pp. 1116–1124 (2015)

Contextual Heterogeneous Graph Network for Human-Object Interaction Detection

Hai Wang[1,2], Wei-shi Zheng[1,2,3(✉)], and Ling Yingbiao[1]

[1] School of Data and Computer Science, Sun Yat-sen University, Guangzhou, China
wangh577@mail2.sysu.edu.cn, wszheng@ieee.org, isslyb@mail.sysu.edu.cn
[2] Key Laboratory of Machine Intelligence and Advanced Computing,
Ministry of Education, Guangzhou, China
[3] Peng Cheng Laboratory, Shenzhen 518005, China

Abstract. Human-object interaction (HOI) detection is an important task for understanding human activity. Graph structure is appropriate to denote the HOIs in the scene. Since there is an subordination between human and object—human play subjective role and object play objective role in HOI, the relations between homogeneous entities and heterogeneous entities in the scene should also not be equally the same. However, previous graph models regard human and object as the same kind of nodes and do not consider that the messages are not equally the same between different entities. In this work, we address such a problem for HOI task by proposing a heterogeneous graph network that models humans and objects as different kinds of nodes and incorporates intra-class messages between homogeneous nodes and inter-class messages between heterogeneous nodes. In addition, a graph attention mechanism based on the intra-class context and inter-class context is exploited to improve the learning. Extensive experiments on the benchmark datasets V-COCO and HICO-DET verify the effectiveness of our method and demonstrate the importance to extract intra-class and inter-class messages which are not equally the same in HOI detection.

Keywords: Human-object interaction · Heterogeneous graph · Neural network

1 Introduction

Given a still image, human-object interaction (HOI) detection requires detecting the positions of people and objects and reasoning about their interactions, such as "eating pizza" and "drinking water". HOI is crucial for understanding the

---

Electronic supplementary material The online version of this chapter (https://doi.org/10.1007/978-3-030-58520-4_15) contains supplementary material, which is available to authorized users.

A. Vedaldi et al. (Eds.): ECCV 2020, LNCS 12362, pp. 248–264, 2020.
https://doi.org/10.1007/978-3-030-58520-4_15

visual relationships [18,24] between entities in human activity and has attracted increasing interest. Over the past few years, tasks of recognizing individual visual objects, *e.g.*, object detection [10,22] and pose estimation [1,4], have witnessed impressive progress thanks to the development of deep learning. Inspired by this progress, a few deep learning methods have been proposed to address HOI detection tasks.

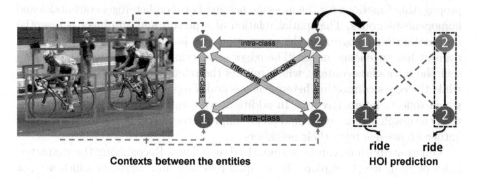

Contexts between the entities   **HOI prediction**

Fig. 1. In the picture on the left, we can see that the two people are subjective in the interaction of "riding" with their bicycles which are objective. The intra-class context between two riders or bicycles is the similarities in some aspects reflecting HOI and the inter-class context between the rider and bicycle is the interactiveness (whether they have interaction). The contexts can be explored to improve HOI recognition in the picture on the right.

HOI recognition considers not only the human, object instances, but also the relations of the entities. Many works [26,32,33,36,37] have studied the interaction of the human-object pair utilizing spatial context or fine-grained features. Generally, an activity scene includes a number of humans and objects. However, most works only focused on recognizing the interaction(s) of one human-object pair and neglect scene understanding. Since multiple relations potentially exist in the complicated scene, the relationship reasoning is important for a more comprehensive understanding of human activity. [27] employed a graph model to infer the relationships, while the authors modeled the people and objects as the same kind of nodes and all the relations as the same edges in the graph which equally treats all the relations in activity scene as interactions. However, human and object play different roles (subject and object) in HOI. There are inter-class context between heterogeneous entities (subject and object) and intra-class context between homogeneous entities (subject-subject, object-object) in activity scene, which means the relations are not equally the same. For example, in Fig. 1, the inter-class context between the rider and bicycle is interactiveness which means whether they are interacting with each other, and the intra-class context between riders (bicycles) can be the similarities in the aspects related to HOI, like appearance, pose or spatial configurations, which are different with inter-class context. Therefore, processing all the relations in a same way is defective.

If we further explore messages from the unequal contexts in the scene to better process the relationships, HOI detection can be improved.

Since it is convenient to represent the entities as nodes and the relations as the edges connecting them, the graph structure is appropriate for modeling HOI. In this paper, we propose our contextual heterogeneous graph network to deeper explore the relations between humans and objects. We discriminatively represent human and object entities as heterogeneous nodes and elaborate different propagating functions for the message passing between heterogeneous nodes and homogeneous nodes. The spatial relation of a person and an object is essential information for recognizing the interaction and is encoded into the edges that connect heterogeneous nodes. The edges connecting homogeneous nodes represent the intra-class context, which reflects the relevance of homogeneous nodes, while the edges connecting heterogeneous nodes represent the inter-class context which reflects interactiveness. In addition, we combine the contextual learning with the graph attention method [31] to improve the effectiveness when the nodes gather knowledge from their neighbors.

Our contributions can be summarized as follows. Recognizing the characteristics of HOI, we (1) explore the unequal relations and messages which are not studied before between humans and objects (subjective and objective roles) in activity scenes and (2) propose a graph-structure framework with heterogeneous nodes and attention mechanism to learn the intra-class and inter-class messages. (3) We evaluate our method on two evaluation datasets, V-COCO and HICO-DET, and we find that our heterogeneous node graph model is effective and outperforms state-of-the-art methods.

2   Related Work

Human-Object Interaction Detection is important for understanding human activity in social scenes. Studies performed before the advent of deep learning produced some interesting conclusions. [12] used the Bayesian model to study interactions. Given the localization of a human and object, [26] learned the probability distribution of their spatial relationship. A representation for inferring the spatial relationship from the visual appearance reference point was proposed by [36]. Traditional methods also include utilizing atomic pose exemplars [16], learning a compositional model [6], and exploiting relationship of body parts and objects [5,37].

Several HOI datasets, such as V-COCO [13] and HICO [3], have been reported over the years. With the assistance of DNN, the methods proposed over the years have achieved significant progresses. Some zero-shot learning methods have gained great progresses. [30] addressed the issue by predicting verbs in images and [25] recognized the interactions by the analogies between the pairwise relations. [2] utilized a multistream network to learn human and object features and the corresponding spatial relations separately. In [11], a network that utilizes human action to estimate the object localization density map was proposed. [8] proposed an instance attention module to highlight the instance

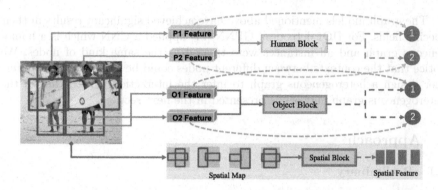

Fig. 2. An overview of the feature extraction module. The spatial map is introduced in Sect. 3.3. The human block and object block further extract the nodes' initial states from the proposal region features. After extraction, the people in the image are denoted as circles in deep orange, and the objects (surfboards) are similarly denoted as the circles in light blue. (Color figure online)

region. Pose information was exploited in works like the turbo learning framework [7] and the fine-grained multi-level feature network [33], which have made impressive results. Fine-grained methods also include RPNN [39] which designed the bodypart graphs to improve localization of related objects and action recognition. In [21], the authors focused on suppressing noninteracting HOI pairs in images before recognition by a two-stage model. [33] used an attention module to select instance-centric context information. We further infer the HOI relationships by learning the unequal messages between different entities and propose a graph network which denotes the subjective entities and objective entities as heterogeneous nodes.

Graph Neural Networks (GNNs) combine a graphical model and a neural network. A GNN learns potential features for nodes by iteratively propagating messages from neighboring nodes and updating hidden states by embedded functions. [29] provided a formal definition of early GNN approaches and demonstrated the approximation properties and computational capabilities of GNNs. [17] constructed a graph convolution network (GCN) to learn a scalable graph-structure context. In [9], the MPNN framework was proposed as a general model that abstracts the commonalities of several well-known graph networks. [31] combined the attention mechanism with a GNN and demonstrated their graph attention network (GAT). GraphSAGE [15] aggregates neighbor nodes, propagates to the far nodes layer by layer, and generates embeddings for unseen nodes by iterative propagations. Visual classification was processed by constructing knowledge graph [19,34] and skeleton-based action learning task was also improved by more comprehensive pose information learned by graph structure [20]. Heterogeneous graph has ever been exploited in [38] to address VQA task, while their graph infers a global category and ours infers the relationships of heterogeneous nodes.

The graph models mentioned above have achieved significant results in their specific fields. For HOI detection, GPNN [27] applied a GNN which is a homogeneous graph and all instances were treated as the same kind of nodes. We notice that the contexts between different nodes could be unequal; thus, we further design a heterogeneous graph to infer the interaction. The details of the heterogeneous graph network is presented in the next section.

3 Approach

3.1 Preliminary

Given an image, the HOI task is to first detect the people and objects and then predict the interaction label of every human-object pair. We denote the people who play subjective roles as subject nodes $p_1, p_2, \cdots, p_N$, and objects as object nodes $o_1, o_2, \cdots, o_M$ in our graph. The hidden embedding of the subject node is denoted as $\mathbf{h}_p$ and the object node as $\mathbf{h}_o$. In the following subsections, we introduce the pipeline of our heterogeneous graph network, the intra-class and inter-class context learning functions and adopted graph attention method, prediction function, sequentially.

3.2 Pipeline

Figure 2 shows an overview of the feature extraction module. After detection, we extract the human and object features, as well as the spatial configurations of the human-object pairs by the multistream extraction module with the bounding boxes produced by the object detector [28]. HOI representation can be denoted as a graph $\mathcal{G}(\mathcal{V}, \mathcal{E})$, where human and object entities are represented as nodes in node set $\mathcal{V}$ and the relations among the entities are denoted as edges in edge set $\mathcal{E}$. Our heterogeneous graph is a fully connected graph consisting of two types of nodes, subject nodes and object nodes, which belong to two subsets, $\mathcal{V}_p$ and $\mathcal{V}_o$, respectively. The initial states of the nodes are the extracted features of the entities. The characteristics of the relations among homogeneous entities and heterogeneous entities are not equally the same: the former represents the similarity in some aspects which relate to HOI between homogeneous entities, while the latter represents the interactiveness of a subject and an object. We regard them as intra-class context and inter-class context respectively, and are denoted as two kinds of edges in the heterogeneous graph.

The relationship reasoning procedure is illustrated in Fig. 3. Our learning strategy is to iteratively propagate messages between nodes to gather information from other nodes and update the node hidden embeddings. The first stage of the relationship reasoning procedure is the message passing stage, which consists of two steps: intra-class message passing between homogeneous nodes and inter-class message passing between heterogeneous nodes. For each node $v \in \mathcal{V}$, the intra-class message aggregation method can simply be formulated as follows:

$$\mathbf{M}_v^{intra} = \mathrm{Agg}_1(\{\mathcal{F}_1(\mathbf{h}_u, \ \mathbf{e}_{vu}), \quad \forall u \in \mathcal{N}_v^{intra}\}), \tag{1}$$

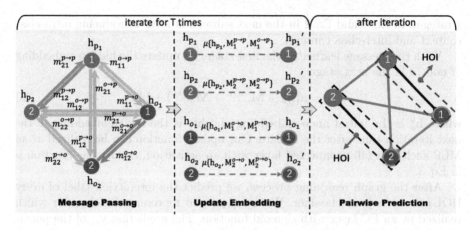

Fig. 3. An illustration of the reasoning procedure of our graph neural network. Each node gathers messages from homogeneous neighborhoods ($m^{p \to p}$ or $m^{o \to o}$) and heterogeneous neighborhoods ($m^{p \to o}$ or $m^{o \to p}$) in a fully connected graph. The messages from homogeneous nodes contain intra-class information that strengthens the expression, and the messages from heterogeneous nodes contain inter-class information about what interactions they have and who they interact with. Each node updates the hidden state with the previous state and the gathered messages by update function $\mu(\cdot)$. Finally the model predicts the label of each HOI pair.

where $\mathbf{M}_v^{intra}$ (includes $m^{p \to p}$ for subject nodes and $m^{o \to o}$ for object nodes in Fig. 3) is the intra-class message that v gathers from its homogeneous neighborhood $\mathcal{N}_v^{intra}$ and $\mathbf{e}_{vu}$ is the edge that connects v and neighbor node u, thus representing the intra-class context among them. The aggregation function $\mathrm{Agg}_1(\cdot)$ and message passing function $\mathcal{F}_1(\cdot)$ in Eq. 1 will be clearly presented in Subsect. 3.3. The intuition behind Eq. 1 can be interpreted as follows: an entity can learn the information about the interaction from relevant entities that have the same or similar interaction by the graph deep reasoning. Similarly, the inter-class message aggregation can be denoted by the following:

$$\mathbf{M}_v^{inter} = \mathrm{Agg}_2(\{\mathcal{F}_2(\mathbf{h}_u, \mathbf{e}_{vu}), \quad \forall u \in \mathcal{N}_v^{inter}\}), \tag{2}$$

where $\mathbf{M}_v^{inter}$ (includes $m^{o \to p}$ for subject nodes and $m^{p \to o}$ for object nodes in Fig. 3) represents the inter-class message propagated from heterogeneous neighborhood of v. The idea of Eq. 2 can be interpreted as follows: the features of two heterogeneous entities which interact with each other should have some consistency with respect to the semantic knowledge of interaction after some learning processes. For example, we know that a tennis racket is used to play tennis and that a man waving his arm forward above his head is likely to bat and thus both the racket and the man are related to "play tennis" to some extent. From this perspective, they are consistent in "playing tennis" and supposed to learn from each other, by which they could "know each other better" and strengthen their interaction relation. We demonstrate the explicit information aggregation

strategies in Eq. 1 and Eq. 2 in the next subsection after introducing intra-class context and inter-class context.

With the message learned in the first stage, we update the hidden embedding of node v in the next stage:

$$\mathbf{h'}_v = \mu(\mathbf{h}_v + \mathbf{M}_v^{intra} + \mathbf{M}_v^{inter}) + \mathbf{h}_v^0, \tag{3}$$

where $\mathbf{h}_v^0$ is the initial node embedding and $\mathbf{h'}_v$ is the node embedding in the next iteration time after the update. Our update function can be realized as an MLP such as a fully connected layer with an activation, denoted as function μ in Eq. 3.

After the graph reasoning process, we predict the interaction label of every HOI pair by a joint classifier. We use $f_{cls}(\cdot)$ to represent the classifier which realized by an FC layer with sigmoid function. The prediction $\mathbf{y}_{ij}$ of the pair is computed as follow:

$$\mathbf{y}_{ij} = f_{cls}(\mathbf{h}_{p_i} + \mathbf{h}_{o_j} + \mathbf{e}_{p_i o_j}). \tag{4}$$

3.3   Contextual Learning

Intra-class Learning. Generally, human activity scene is a complicated scene which involves multiple entities, so contextual learning is important to infer the relationships between humans and objects. In our heterogeneous graph, the intra-class context is the similarity between homogeneous nodes with respect to the interactions. It is intuitive that if many people are interacting with the same or similar object(s), e.g., a group of people are rowing a boat, they are very likely performing the same or relevant actions. In order to explore the intra-class context, for each node we compute a vector $\mathbf{r}$, which will be used to compute intra-class context. We denote $f(\cdot)$ as the function realized by an FC layer with ReLU. The computation of vector $\mathbf{r_i}$ of node p_i is formulated as follows:

$$\mathbf{r}_i = \max\{f(\mathbf{h}_{p_i} + \mathbf{h}_{o_j} + \mathbf{s}_{p_i o_j}), \quad \forall o_j \in \mathcal{N}_{p_i}^{inter}\}, \tag{5}$$

where $\mathbf{s}_{p_i o_j}$ is the encoded spatial configuration feature between p_i and o_j. To extract the spatial feature, we construct a 2-channel spatial map consisting of a human map and an object map for a human-object pair. Each map has one channel with a value of 1 in the area of the human(object) position and 0 in others. Finally, we resize the scale to 64×64. A spatial location encoder which consists of CNN layers and FC layers will be used to extract the spatial feature from the map. Here, $\mathbf{r}_i$ can reflect the knowledge about the interactions p_i have in this scene, since $\mathbf{h}_{p_i}$ contains information about the appearance of p_i, and the combination of $\mathbf{h}_{p_i}$, $\mathbf{h}_{o_j}$ and $\mathbf{s}_{p_i o_j}$ contains the information for inferring the interaction between p_i and o_j.

The contextual learning are utilized with graph attention in message passing layers. For nodes p_i and p_j, we first compute the cosine similarity of $\mathbf{r}_i$ and $\mathbf{r}_j$ to represent the intra-class context between them:

$$\epsilon_{ij} = \frac{\overrightarrow{\mathbf{r}_i} \cdot \overrightarrow{\mathbf{r}_j}}{\left\|\overrightarrow{\mathbf{r}_i}\right\| \left\|\overrightarrow{\mathbf{r}_j}\right\|}, \tag{6}$$

The attention weight in the process of gathering homogeneous nodes' messages is their normalization after the softmax function:

$$\alpha_{ij} = \frac{\exp(\epsilon_{ij})}{\sum_{k=1}^{M} \exp(\epsilon_{ik})}. \tag{7}$$

In summary, to node p_i, Eq. 1 can be clearly rewritten as the following:

$$\mathbf{M}_{p_i}^{intra} = \text{mean}(\sum_{p_j \in \mathcal{N}_{p_i}^{intra}} \alpha_{ij} \cdot f(\mathbf{h}_{p_j})). \tag{8}$$

The computation of $\mathbf{r}$ for object nodes is similar, and the graph attention of object nodes is exploited in the same way. By learning with the intra-class context, the nodes will be able to tell which homogeneous nodes are relevant and gather more messages from them, while the irrelevant nodes will be eliminated during the reasoning.

Inter-class Learning. The inter-class context is the interactiveness that reflects prior interactive knowledge in HOI. We introduces a interactiveness weight $\mathbf{w}$ to represent the inter-class context. Inspired by GPNN [27], the inter-activeness weight of subject node p_i and object node o_j is computed by an FC layer with activation:

$$\mathbf{w}_{ij} = f(\mathbf{h}_{p_i} + \mathbf{h}_{o_j} + \mathbf{s}_{p_i o_j}), \qquad w_{ij} \in \mathbb{R}. \tag{9}$$

During training, we minimize the binary classification cross-entropy loss $\mathcal{L}_w$ to optimize $\mathbf{w}$:

$$\mathcal{L}_w = -\frac{1}{NM} \sum_i^N \sum_j^M (\mathbf{1}_{ij} \cdot log(\hat{\mathbf{w}}_{ij}) \\ + (1 - \mathbf{1}_{ij}) \cdot log(1 - \hat{\mathbf{w}}_{ij})), \tag{10}$$

where the label is 1 if the human and object are interacting with each other and 0 otherwise. N and M are the numbers of people and objects. The loss function is used to learn whether the subject node p_i is interacting with the object node o_j.

The inter-class message that p_i gets from o_j is a combined knowledge of the hidden embedding $\mathbf{h}_{o_j}$ and the spatial configuration $\mathbf{s}_{p_i o_j}$ because they are both necessary for recognizing the pairwise interaction. Adopting graph attention mechanism, to node p_i Eq. 2 can similarly be rewritten as:

$$\mathbf{M}_{p_i}^{inter} = \max\{\frac{\exp(\mathbf{w}_{ij})}{\sum_{k=1}^{M} \exp(\mathbf{w}_{ik})} \cdot f(\mathbf{s}_{p_i o_j} \oplus \mathbf{h}_{o_j}), \quad \forall o_j \in \mathcal{N}_{p_i}^{inter}\}, \tag{11}$$

where $\oplus$ means concatenation. Since inter-class context is expected to tell whether the entities have interaction or not, the maximization can help the inter-class message focus on those interactive heterogeneous nodes and neglect many non-interactive nodes. The inter-class learning strengthens the relations between heterogeneous nodes which are interactive.

3.4   HOI Prediction

After the reasoning of the graph, the model predicts the interaction of each HOI pair by a joint classifier. Our prediction is computed as follows:

$$\mathbf{y}_{ij} = f(\mathbf{h}_{p_i} + \mathbf{h}_{o_j} + \mathbf{s}_{p_i o_j}). \tag{12}$$

During training, We minimize the binary classification cross-entropy loss $\mathcal{L}_{ho}$ for prediction. In summary, the objective function is the weighted sum of the interaction classification loss $\mathcal{L}_{ho}$ and interactiveness loss $\mathcal{L}_w$:

$$\mathcal{L} = \lambda \cdot \mathcal{L}_{ho} + \mathcal{L}_w. \tag{13}$$

During inference, we compute the HOI detection score s of h and o with the prediction score $\mathbf{y}$:

$$s = \mathbf{y} \cdot s_h \cdot s_o, \tag{14}$$

where s_h, s_o are the object detection confidences of h and o.

4   Experiments

4.1   Datasets and Metrics

Datasets. We evaluate our model on two HOI datasets: V-COCO and HICO-DET. **V-COCO** [13] is a subset of COCO2014 [23] that includes 5,400 images, 8431 people instances in trainval set and 4946 images, 7768 people instances in test set. The instance-level annotations are for the classification of 29 action categories (5 of them are only for humans). In addition, there are two roles of interaction targets in the annotations: instrument and direct object, which should be classified in recognition.

HICO-DET [2] includes the image-level classes' annotations of HICO and further provides instance-level bounding boxes for instances and pair-wise class labels. There are 38,118 images and 117,871 instances in the training subset, with 9,658 images, and 33,405 instances in the testing subset. The annotations consist of 600 HOI categories and 117 action categories.

Metric. We adopt the mean average precision (mAP), which is generally used in detection tasks, for our evaluation. We regard a prediction as a true positive when both the human and object bounding boxes have IoUs with ground truth boxes larger than 0.5 and the predicted label is accurate.

4.2 Implementation Details

We employ a faster R-CNN [28] with the ResNet-50-FPN [22] backbone pre-trained on MS-COCO as the object detector. A pretrained feature extractor with the ResNet-50 backbone is adopted to extract image features. Both the human and object streams contains a residual convolution block and 2 FC layers. These feature extraction blocks are used to further extract instance-level features from image features according to the proposed boxes produced by the detector. The spatial stream consists of 3 convolutional layers and a max-pooling layer.

During training, we keep the ResNet-50 backbone frozen and employ SGD optimizer. We set minibatch size as 4, an initial learning rate as 0.001 and decay by 0.6 every 10 epochs. We regard each HOI pair as positive sample if it is labeled with ground truth interaction(s), and as a negative sample otherwise. The iteration time is set to 2 since we didn't find obvious improvement when we increased it, and λ is set to 6. We train our model for 40 epochs. Our experiments are conducted on a single Nvidia Titan X GPU.

4.3 Ablation Studies

We conduct the mAP evaluation following the official setting of each dataset. For V-COCO, we evaluate the AP_{role} for 24 HOI actions with the role setting. For HICO-DET, we conduct two modes, Default mode and Known Object mode. More details can be seen in [13] and [2]. In this subsection, we analyze the significance of the heterogeneous nodes graph, the intra-class and inter-class message, and contextual graph attention. Table 1, 2 and 3 show the detailed results of our ablation studies.

Heterogeneous Graph Structure. The heterogeneous graph model is the key structure for aggregating the messages which are not all equally the same in HOI and deeper inferring the relationships. To show the impact of our method, we conduct experiment on a baseline model consisting of the object detector, the feature extraction backbone and the multistream module, which are completely the same as the proposed model has except for the absence of the most important heterogeneous graph with the learned intra-class, inter-class knowledge. We further separately evaluate the effectiveness of the aggregated knowledge of intra-class message and inter-class message by only computing $\mathbf{M}^{intra}$ and $\mathbf{M}^{inter}$ in the reasoning procedure, respectively.

Table 1 clearly shows that both the aggregations of intra-class and inter-class messages bring considerable improvements. With the messages, the performances increase 5.3 mAP in V-COCO and nearly 4 mAP in HICO-DET with both the two setting. This result verifies that both the two kinds of contextual knowledge are very valuable in improving the expression of the features for HOI.

Table 1. Ablation study results on V-COCO and HICO-DET((%)

Method	V-COCO	HICO-DET	
	AP_{role}	Default (Full)	Known object (Full)
baseline	47.4	13.73	16.92
baseline + $\mathbf{M}^{intra}$	52.0	16.70	20.07
baseline + $\mathbf{M}^{inter}$	51.4	16.13	19.34
baseline + $\mathbf{M}^{intra}$ + $\mathbf{M}^{inter}$ (proposed)	52.7	17.57	21.00
w/o graph attention	49.5	15.34	19.86
w/o intra-class context	51.2	16.60	20.08
w/o interactiveness weight	51.9	16.49	19.95

Graph Attention. The graph attention employed in message passing layers enhances the efficiency of nodes gathering useful information from neighbors with which they have significant relations. To verify the effectiveness of the graph attention method, we conduct experiments on the graph model that without computing the intra-class context (Eq. (7)) and the interactiveness weight $\mathbf{w}$. In this condition, the nodes gather messages indiscriminately from the neighborhood without any guidance of the context. Table 1 illustrates that compared with the proposed model, the mAP clearly decreases when we do not adopt the contextual graph attention, dropping approximately 3 mAP in V-COCO and 2 mAP in HICO-DET. The reason behind this result is likely that without the guidance of graph contextual attention, nodes cannot selectively learn valuable information and from neighbors that resemble or have strong relevance with them and instead gather more useless messages from those unrelated nodes.

We further evaluate the importance of intra-class context weight and interactiveness weight, respectively. Employing any of them, the performances clearly improve. By analyzing the results, we can see that it is important to realize the subordination and discriminate the messages that are not equally the same.

Comparison of Heterogeneous Graph and Homogeneous Graph. To further verify the importance of heterogeneous structure, we design our homogeneous graph which denotes people and objects as the same nodes. In the homogeneous graph, the message passing process shares the same layer and formula. We separately set the message formulation as the same with intra-class function (Eq. (8)) and inter-class function (Eq. (11)) in heterogeneous graph. We report the results in Table 2, and show that the heterogeneous structure performs clearly better than the homogeneous. The result verifies that with heterogeneous structure, our model can learn HOIs better.

Analysis in Scenes with Different Complexities. Since our graph learns the intra-class message which is considered between instances that play the same role in HOI, the effectiveness is related to the complexity of the scenes. To analyze the affect of scenes complexity, we divide the dataset into two subsets: the

Table 2. Performance comparison of heterogeneous graph and homogeneous graph(%)

Method	V-COCO	HICO-DET	
	$\mathbf{AP}_{role}$	Default (Full)	Known object (Full)
Homogeneous (intra-class)	49.3	13.5	16.8
Homogeneous (inter-class)	48.9	12.6	16.1
Heterogeneous	52.7	17.5	21.0

Table 3. The performance in different scenes on V-COCO and HICO-DET(%). "C" and "S" represent complex scene and simple scene respectively

Dataset	V-COCO		HICO-DET	
Subset	C	S	C	S
Baseline	50.4	41.2	14.7	12.5
Proposed (w/o $\mathbf{M}^{intra}$)	53.5	44.1	16.4	15.7
Proposed (w/o $\mathbf{M}^{inter}$)	54.7	42.4	17.5	14.0
Proposed	55.1	44.1	18.3	15.7

complex scenes that have many entities and multiple interactions, and the simple scenes that only have one person and one object. According to the labels, We count about 4k complex scenes and about 600 simple scenes in V-COCO test set, and about 7k complex scenes and 2.5k simple scenes in HICO-DET test set. We evaluate the heterogeneous graph on the two subsets and make comparisons with the baseline model to reveal the effectiveness. Furthermore, we also evaluate the intra-class message and the inter-class message. Table 3 illustrates the comparison results, which show that our model makes great progress in both complex and simple scenes. The intra-class messages explicitly improve the result in complex scenes, which reveals that by reasoning among different nodes with intra-class context, our model can tell which homogeneous entities are relevant and learn more from relevant entities, while eliminate irrelevant entities. Therefore, the model can selectively propagate useful messages between homogeneous nodes and improve the recognition. The mAP increases with the inter-class messages, which shows that the inter-class messages can lead to better understanding between subject and object.

4.4   Performance and Comparison

This section we compare the performances of the heterogeneous graph model with previous deep methods. For HICO-DET we further evaluate the results with the Full, Rare and Non-Rare settings, which consider 600, 138, and 462 HOI actions, respectively. Table 4 and Table 5 illustrate the performances on V-COCO and HICO-DET.

Table 4. Performance comparison on the V-COCO

Method	$AP_{role}(\%)$
Gupta.S [13]	31.8
InteractNet [11]	40.0
GPNN [27]	44.0
iCAN [8]	45.3
Feng *et al.* [7]	42.0
XU *et al.* [35]	45.9
Wang *et al.* [33]	47.3
Prior [21]	47.8
RPNN [39]	47.5
PMFNet [32]	52.0
Proposed	**52.7**

For **V-COCO**, the proposed model outperforms state-of-the-art methods and improves the mAP by 0.7. We outperform previous graph network GPNN by 8.7 mAP, demonstrating the effectiveness of the heterogeneous graph and the importance to discriminate intra-class message and inter-class message.

For **HICO-DET**, the results also demonstrate the significance of our method. We achieve state-of-the-art performance in both Default mode and Known Object mode. Compared with GPNN, our method boosts the performance 34% in Default mode.

Table 5. Performance comparison on the HICO-DET

Method	Default (%)			Known object (%)		
	Full	Rare	Non-rare	Full	Rare	Non-rare
HO-RCNN [2]	7.81	5.37	8.54	10.41	8.94	10.85
InteractNet [11]	9.94	7.16	10.77	–	–	–
GPNN [27]	13.11	9.34	14.23	–	–	–
iCAN [8]	14.84	10.45	16.15	16.26	11.33	17.73
Feng *et al.* [7]	11.4	7.3	12.6	–	–	–
XU *et al.* [35]	14.70	13.26	15.13	–	–	–
Wang *et al.* [33]	16.24	11.16	17.75	17.73	12.78	19.21
Prior [21]	17.03	13.42	**18.11**	19.17	15.51	**20.26**
No-frills [14]	17.18	12.17	18.68	–	–	–
RPNN [39]	17.35	12.78	18.71	–	–	–
PMFNet [32]	17.46	15.65	18.00	20.34	17.47	21.20
Proposed	**17.57**	**16.85**	17.78	**21.00**	**20.74**	**21.08**

Fig. 4. Visual samples of HOI detection in VCOCO. Human and object instances are denoted by purple and blue bounding boxes. The yellow lines represent that the linked instances have interactions with each other. The figures show some more complex cases that with multiple different interactions in the images. (Color figure online)

Figures 4 and 5 illustrate some visualized HOI detection samples tackled by our model in V-COCO and HICO-DET separately. These samples show the effectiveness of our proposed method in detecting HOIs in activity scenes with different complexities varying from the simple kind with only one human-object

Fig. 5. Visual samples of HOI detection in HICO-DET. Human and object instances are denoted by purple and blue bounding boxes. The green lines represent that the linked instances have interactions with each other, while the pink lines mean no interaction within the instances. (Color figure online)

pair to the complicated kind with multiple entities and interactions in the image. The samples also shows that the model works well at recognizing whether the subjects and objects are interactive in different scenes, which reveals the effect of the inter-class context.

5 Conclusions

Since the messages between humans and objects playing the same roles (subjects or objects) and that playing different roles (subject-object) are not equally the same in human-object interactions, in this paper We explore the unequal relations and messages by proposing a heterogeneous graph model. The graph discriminates the messages as intra-class message and inter-class message, and adopt specialized methods and graph attention to aggregate them. We find that the heterogeneous graph further exploring the messages that are not equally the same is effective in reasoning HOI. In V-COCO and HICO-DET datasets, the proposed model gains promised results and outperforms the state-of-the-art method.

Acknowledgements. This work was supported partially by the National Key Research and Development Program of China (2018YFB1004903), NSFC (U1911401, U1811461), Guangdong Province Science and Technology Innovation Leading Talents (2016TX03X157), Guangdong NSF Project (No. 2018B030312002), Guangzhou Research Project (201902010037), and Research Projects of Zhejiang Lab (No. 2019KD0AB03).

References

1. Cao, Z., Simon, T., Wei, S.E., Sheikh, Y.: Realtime multi-person 2D pose estimation using part affinity fields. In: CVPR, pp. 7291–7299 (2017)
2. Chao, Y.W., Liu, Y., Liu, X., Zeng, H., Deng, J.: Learning to detect human-object interactions. In: WACV, pp. 381–389 (2018)
3. Chao, Y.W., Wang, Z., He, Y., Wang, J., Deng, J.: HICO: a benchmark for recognizing human-object interactions in images. In: ICCV, pp. 1017–1025 (2015)
4. Chu, X., Yang, W., Ouyang, W., Ma, C., Yuille, A.L., Wang, X.: Multi-context attention for human pose estimation. In: CVPR, pp. 1831–1840 (2017)
5. Delaitre, V., Sivic, J., Laptev, I.: Learning person-object interactions for action recognition in still images. In: NIPS, pp. 1503–1511 (2011)
6. Desai, C., Ramanan, D., Fowlkes, C.: Discriminative models for static human-object interactions. In: Computer Society Conference on Computer Vision and Pattern Recognition-Workshops, pp. 9–16 (2010)
7. Feng, W., Liu, W., Li, T., Peng, J., Qian, C., Hu, X.: Turbo learning framework for human-object interactions recognition and human pose estimation. arXiv preprint arXiv:1903.06355 (2019)
8. Gao, C., Zou, Y., Huang, J.B.: iCAN: instance-centric attention network for human-object interaction detection. arXiv preprint arXiv:1808.10437 (2018)
9. Gilmer, J., Schoenholz, S.S., Riley, P.F., Vinyals, O., Dahl, G.E.: Neural message passing for quantum chemistry. In: ICML, pp. 1263–1272 (2017)

10. Girshick, R.: Fast R-CNN. In: ICCV, pp. 1440–1448 (2015)
11. Gkioxari, G., Girshick, R., Dollár, P., He, K.: Detecting and recognizing human-object interactions. In: CVPR, pp. 8359–8367 (2018)
12. Gupta, A., Kembhavi, A., Davis, L.S.: Observing human-object interactions: using spatial and functional compatibility for recognition. PAMI **31**(10), 1775–1789 (2009)
13. Gupta, S., Malik, J.: Visual semantic role labeling. arXiv preprint arXiv:1505.04474 (2015)
14. Gupta, T., Schwing, A., Hoiem, D.: No-frills human-object interaction detection: factorization, layout encodings, and training techniques. In: ICCV, pp. 9677–9685 (2019)
15. Hamilton, W., Ying, Z., Leskovec, J.: Inductive representation learning on large graphs. In: NIPS, pp. 1024–1034 (2017)
16. Hu, J.F., Zheng, W.S., Lai, J., Gong, S., Xiang, T.: Recognising human-object interaction via exemplar based modelling. In: ICCV, pp. 3144–3151 (2013)
17. Kipf, T.N., Welling, M.: Semi-supervised classification with graph convolutional networks. arXiv preprint arXiv:1609.02907 (2016)
18. Krishna, R., et al.: Visual genome: connecting language and vision using crowd-sourced dense image annotations. IJCV **123**(1), 32–73 (2017)
19. Lee, C.W., Fang, W., Yeh, C.K., Frank Wang, Y.C.: Multi-label zero-shot learning with structured knowledge graphs. In: CVPR, pp. 1576–1585 (2018)
20. Li, M., Chen, S., Chen, X., Zhang, Y., Wang, Y., Tian, Q.: Actional-structural graph convolutional networks for skeleton-based action recognition. In: CVPR, pp. 3595–3603 (2019)
21. Li, Y.L., Zhou, S., Huang, X., Xu, L., Ma, Z., Fang, H.S., Wang, Y.F., Lu, C.: Transferable interactiveness prior for human-object interaction detection. arXiv preprint arXiv:1811.08264 (2018)
22. Lin, T.Y., Dollár, P., Girshick, R., He, K., Hariharan, B., Belongie, S.: Feature pyramid networks for object detection. In: CVPR, pp. 2117–2125 (2017)
23. Lin, T.-Y., et al.: Microsoft COCO: common objects in context. In: Fleet, D., Pajdla, T., Schiele, B., Tuytelaars, T. (eds.) ECCV 2014. LNCS, vol. 8693, pp. 740–755. Springer, Cham (2014). https://doi.org/10.1007/978-3-319-10602-1_48
24. Lu, C., Krishna, R., Bernstein, M., Fei-Fei, L.: Visual relationship detection with language priors. In: Leibe, B., Matas, J., Sebe, N., Welling, M. (eds.) ECCV 2016. LNCS, vol. 9905, pp. 852–869. Springer, Cham (2016). https://doi.org/10.1007/978-3-319-46448-0_51
25. Peyre, J., Laptev, I., Schmid, C., Sivic, J.: Detecting unseen visual relations using analogies. In: ICCV, pp. 1981–1990 (2019)
26. Prest, A., Schmid, C., Ferrari, V.: Weakly supervised learning of interactions between humans and objects. PAMI **34**(3), 601–614 (2011)
27. Qi, S., Wang, W., Jia, B., Shen, J., Zhu, S.-C.: Learning human-object interactions by graph parsing neural networks. In: Ferrari, V., Hebert, M., Sminchisescu, C., Weiss, Y. (eds.) ECCV 2018. LNCS, vol. 11213, pp. 407–423. Springer, Cham (2018). https://doi.org/10.1007/978-3-030-01240-3_25
28. Ren, S., He, K., Girshick, R., Sun, J.: Faster R-CNN: towards real-time object detection with region proposal networks. In: NIPS, pp. 91–99 (2015)
29. Scarselli, F., Gori, M., Tsoi, A.C., Hagenbuchner, M., Monfardini, G.: Computational capabilities of graph neural networks. TNN **20**(1), 81–102 (2008)
30. Shen, L., Yeung, S., Hoffman, J., Mori, G., Fei-Fei, L.: Scaling human-object interaction recognition through zero-shot learning. In: WACV, pp. 1568–1576 (2018)

31. Veličković, P., Cucurull, G., Casanova, A., Romero, A., Lio, P., Bengio, Y.: Graph attention networks. arXiv preprint arXiv:1710.10903 (2017)
32. Wan, B., Zhou, D., Liu, Y., Li, R., He, X.: Pose-aware multi-level feature network for human object interaction detection. In: ICCV, pp. 9469–9478 (2019)
33. Wang, T., et al.: Deep contextual attention for human-object interaction detection. arXiv preprint arXiv:1910.07721 (2019)
34. Wang, X., Ye, Y., Gupta, A.: Zero-shot recognition via semantic embeddings and knowledge graphs. In: CVPR, pp. 6857–6866 (2018)
35. Xu, B., Wong, Y., Li, J., Zhao, Q., Kankanhalli, M.S.: Learning to detect human-object interactions with knowledge. In: CVPR, June 2019
36. Yao, B., Fei-Fei, L.: Grouplet: a structured image representation for recognizing human and object interactions. In: Computer Society Conference on Computer Vision and Pattern Recognition, pp. 9–16 (2010)
37. Yao, B., Fei-Fei, L.: Modeling mutual context of object and human pose in human-object interaction activities. In: Computer Society Conference on Computer Vision and Pattern Recognition, pp. 17–24 (2010)
38. Yu, W., Zhou, J., Yu, W., Liang, X., Xiao, N.: Heterogeneous graph learning for visual commonsense reasoning. In: NIPS, pp. 2765–2775 (2019)
39. Zhou, P., Chi, M.: Relation parsing neural network for human-object interaction detection. In: ICCV, pp. 843–851 (2019)

Zero-Shot Image Super-Resolution with Depth Guided Internal Degradation Learning

Xi Cheng, Zhenyong Fu[✉], and Jian Yang[✉]

Key Lab of Intelligent Perception and Systems for High-Dimensional Information
of Ministry of Education, Jiangsu Key Lab of Image and Video Understanding
for Social Security, PCA Lab, School of Computer Science and Engineering,
Nanjing University of Science and Technology, Nanjing, China
{chengx,z.fu,csjyang}@njust.edu.cn

Abstract. In the past few years, we have witnessed the great progress
of image super-resolution (SR) thanks to the power of deep learning.
However, a major limitation of the current image SR approaches is that
they assume a pre-determined degradation model or kernel, e.g. *bicubic*,
controls the image degradation process. This makes them easily fail to
generalize in a real-world or non-ideal environment since the degradation model of an unseen image may not obey the pre-determined kernel
used when training the SR model. In this work, we introduce a simple yet effective zero-shot image super-resolution model. Our zero-shot
SR model learns an image-specific super-resolution network (SRN) from
a low-resolution input image alone, without relying on external training sets. To circumvent the difficulty caused by the unknown internal
degradation model of an image, we propose to learn an image-specific
degradation simulation network (DSN) together with our image-specific
SRN. Specifically, we exploit the depth information, naturally indicating
the scales of local image patches, of an image to extract the unpaired
high/low-resolution patch collection to train our networks. According
to the benchmark test on four datasets with depth labels or estimated
depth maps, our proposed depth guided degradation model learning-
based image super-resolution (DGDML-SR) achieves visually pleasing
results and can outperform the state-of-the-arts in perceptual metrics.

Keywords: Image super-resolution · Zero-shot · Depth guidance

1 Introduction

Single image super-resolution (SR) aims to restore a high-resolution (HR) image
from a degraded low-resolution (LR) measurement. Image super-resolution, as

Electronic supplementary material The online version of this chapter (https://
doi.org/10.1007/978-3-030-58520-4_16) contains supplementary material, which is
available to authorized users.

© Springer Nature Switzerland AG 2020
A. Vedaldi et al. (Eds.): ECCV 2020, LNCS 12362, pp. 265–280, 2020.
https://doi.org/10.1007/978-3-030-58520-4_16

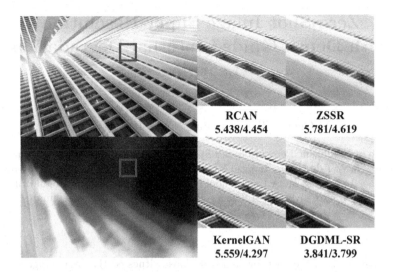

RCAN
5.438/4.454

ZSSR
5.781/4.619

KernelGAN
5.559/4.297

DGDML-SR
3.841/3.799

Fig. 1. Our proposed DGDML-SR can achieve better visual quality than the state of the arts. NIQE and PI scores (lower is better) are shown under each image. (Color figure online)

an inverse procedure of image downscaling, is an ill-posed problem, in which the internal degradation patterns or kernels followed by images are image-specific and unknown. Most modern image super-resolution models, mainly based on supervised learning techniques such as deep convolutional neural networks (CNNs) [11], rely on massive amounts of high-/low-resolution example pairs for training. In reality, collecting a natural pair of high/low-resolution images is difficult; existing SR methods [5,6,14,29,30] resort to manually designed HR/LR image pairs as a surrogate. In these methods, a given high-resolution image is downscaled to generate a low-resolution counterpart using a simple and pre-determined degradation kernel, e.g. a *bicubic* operation, in order to acquire a pair of HR/LR images. In general, current supervised learning-based SR methods generalize poorly due to the simplified degradation model, especially when dealing with the images with details having not been encountered in the training set.

To overcome the above drawbacks, the key is to model the natural degradation in the images. However, degradation kernels are usually complex and differ greatly; they can be affected by many factors such as luminance, sensor noise, motion blur and compression. Thus, to learn a natural degradation and implement a visually pleasing super-resolution, we should treat each image independently, i.e. zero-shot image degradation and super-resolution. Zero-shot image super resolution is more challenging that needs to learn an image-specific SR model from an image alone, without access to external training sets. The main difficulty of zero-shot SR is to acquire HR/LR image patches for training. Recently, Shocher et al. [19] have proposed a zero-shot super-resolution (ZSSR) approach which extracts local patches from an image and then down-

scales them using a pre-determined bicubic operation, analogously to other supervised learning-based SR methods. As such, they construct a patch-level training collection composed of high-/low-resolution pairs of local patches from a single image. However, a natural image is seldom degraded by obeying a simple bicubic rule and an unreasonable assumption about the degradation kernel will impede its inverse super-resolution procedure. Thus, the problem of the unknown degradation model is still far from solved in existing zero-shot SR works.

In this paper, we present a simple yet effective zero-shot SR method without assuming a pre-defined degradation kernel. Instead, we learn the image-specific degradation model in a self-supervised manner. In our method, we sidestep the difficulty of acquiring the patch-level HR/LR training data by leveraging the image depth information. The depth information indicates the distance of each image region relative to the camera. Depth information can be easily computed using a pre-trained depth estimation model [7] or obtained from datasets with depth labels [25,9, 20]. Also, the depth or time-of-flight (TOF) camera is becoming increasingly popular on mobile phones, simplifying the acquisition of depth information. In our method, we view the short-distance local regions as the HR patches, while the distant local regions as the LR patches. After acquiring the HR/LR patch collection, we design two fully-convolutional and image-specific networks: degradation simulation network (DSN), responsible for imitating the unknown degradation kernel of the image, and super-resolution network (SRN), in charge of performing the SR task on the image. Since we have no paired HR/LR local patches but the unpaired HR/LR patch collection, we design a bi-cycle training strategy to learn our degradation simulation network and super-resolution network simultaneously. Guided by the image-specific degradation model internally learned by DSN with the clue of depth information, our zero-shot or image-specific SR network can achieve a satisfactory SR result for a single image, without using any external training set except the image itself. As depicted in Fig. 1, our method can achieve the best NIQE and PI scores, recover more natural and clear textures, and have fewer artifacts.

Our contributions are three-fold: (1) we propose a zero-shot image SR model that does not require the high-resolution labels; (2) our method leverages the depth information of an image and can learn the internal degradation model of the image in a self-supervised manner; and (3) our method can outperform the state-of-the-art in perceptual metrics. Compared with the latest zero-shot and supervised SR methods (e.g. KernelGAN [2]), our approach is average 0.555 better in NIQE [17] and 0.284 better in PI [4] according to the benchmark.

2   Related Work

In the past several years, deep convolutional neural networks (CNN) based image SR models have been proposed [5,6,10,12,30]. Compared with traditional methods [8,23], CNN-based methods are superior in terms of peak signal-to-noise ratio (PSNR). Since the pioneering work of SRCNN [6], CNN-based SR models have been boosted with deeper structures [10,21] by using a progressive upsampling way [12] or a dense structure [22,30]. Although the CNN-based SR methods

can achieve excellent PSNR results, their results are not visually pleasing, since they typically use the Mean Squared Error (MSE) loss, inherently leading to a blurry high-resolution result. To overcome this problem, some new loss functions have been proposed to replace MSE [12,15,16]. Recently, generative adversarial networks (GANs) based SR models [13,24] have been shown to produce more realistic high-resolution results with finer details.

A fundamental limitation of the aforementioned methods is that they unrealistically assume a pre-defined degradation model, e.g. bicubic, to be used in image SR. In reality, the degradation model is unknown and more complex than bicubic, often accompanied by severe distracting factors. Thus, existing supervised SR methods generally fail to obtain a satisfactory SR result in a natural environment outside the training condition. RCAN [30] and SRMD [28] added a variety of conditions (e.g. noise and blur) to the degradation model and can improve the SR result in the natural environment. Xu et al. [26] shot photos on real scenes and used raw images from the digital camera sensors to train an image super-resolution model to fit the natural environment. However, they still fail to address the problem of the unknown degradation model.

To mitigate the deficiency of supervised learning-based SR models in real-world environments, CincGAN [27] learned the degradation model on tasks such as noise reduction in an unsupervised manner, but it still used the bicubic downscaling as an intermediate state. Moreover, CincGAN [27] needs a large external training dataset, which is usually unavailable in real-world environments. Zero-shot image super-resolution [19], aiming to learn an SR model from a single image alone and then apply it to super-resolve the image, has drawn considerable attention recently. Zero-shot super-resolution (ZSSR) [19] used a fixed degradation method such as bicubic as a degradation model for local patches. Bell et al. [2] proposed a novel SR method named KernelGAN that used a deep linear generator to learn the downscaling kernel from a single image. Then, they applied ZSSR to perform the super-resolution on the image with the downscaling kernel learned by KernelGAN. Their method greatly improved ZSSR but cannot model the complex and superposed degradation in reality. Moreover, learning the degradation model via KernelGAN and learning the SR model via ZSSR are separated, thus often resulting in a suboptimal SR result.

3   Approach

A natural image is self-explained in that similar local patches tend to recur across positions and scales within the image [8]. Moreover, similar patches in the original scenery will be rescaled during the imaging process due to the changes of depth. The depth measures the distance of each patch in an image relative to the camera. The image patches near the camera will be enlarged, while the patches with similar appearance but away from the camera will be shrunk. In other words, the distant patches captured in an image are more blurred and smaller in appearance than the short-distance patches. We call it depth guided self-similarity prior in images. Figure 2 gives an example of this prior, in which

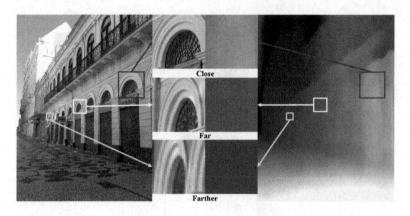

Fig. 2. An example of the image self-similarity and its relation with depth information. We select different patches with different levels of depth (Close, Far, Farther). These patches shares similar textures and the close patch is clearer than the farther patch.

the relative distance of an image patch can be continuously measured by the depth; the image patches with similar textures become more blurred when their depths are deeper. In this work, we exploit the depth guided information in single image super-resolution.

3.1 Depth Guided Training Data Generation

To learn the internal degradation model in an image, we use the depth information to construct a training set from the image. In a nutshell, we treat the distant patches as the low-resolution image patches and the short-distance patches as the high-resolution image patches. Note that we do not use a given degradation kernel as in ZSSR [19], where the image patches need to be downscaled first using a pre-determined degradation operation, i.e., the bicubic. Instead, we only extract the image patches with different depths, hoping to learn a more realistic degradation model from these image patches. Thus, our method could be flexible.

Formally, for a given low-resolution image I, we first convert it from the RGB color space into the YCbCr color space and take the Y, i.e. luminance, channel to calculate the contrast of each patch. Contrast information, reflecting the texture details contained in an image, plays an important clue for building our HR and LR sample patches. Patches with low contrast often contain few image details and thus are useless for training our model. We process the contrast measurement as follows:

$$C = \frac{Y_{max} - Y_{min}}{255}, \tag{1}$$

where C is the range of luminance (i.e. contrast), Y_{max} and Y_{min} denote the 99% and 1% value of the Y channel, respectively. In our work, we set the threshold for C as 0.05; if the range of brightness spans less than the threshold, we define the patch as low contrast and will eliminate it from our training data.

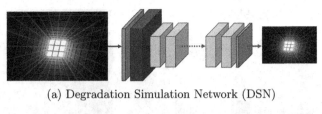

(a) Degradation Simulation Network (DSN)

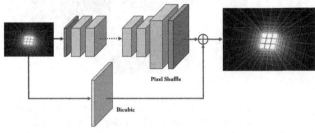

(b) Super-Resolution Network (SRN)

Fig. 3. The proposed structure of the generators in degradation simulation network (DSN) and super-resolution network (SRN).

Then, we calculate the global mean depth value $\bar{d}$ over the entire depth map as follows:

$$\bar{d} = \frac{1}{HW} \sum_{i=1}^{H} \sum_{j=1}^{W} D_{ij}, \qquad (2)$$

where H and W denote the height and width of the depth map. Next, we choose a larger image patch (e.g. 64×64 pixels) with a mean depth smaller than $\bar{d}$ as a high-resolution image patch; similarly, we choose a smaller image patch (e.g. 32×32 pixels) with a mean depth bigger than $\bar{d}$ as a low-resolution image patch. As such, we will get a patch-level training collection, (I_{HR}, I_{LR}), from the test image, in which $I_{HR} = \{x_i^h\}$ consists of the high-resolution image patches and $I_{LR} = \{y_i^l\}$ consists of the low-resolution image patches. Notably, (I_{HR}, I_{LR}) are *unpaired* since for each HR patch in I_{HR}, we have no corresponding LR patch in I_{LR}, and vice versa.

3.2   Network Structure

With the depth guided training data (I_{HR}, I_{LR}) extracted from the low-resolution test image I, we train a lightweight and image-specific Super-Resolution Network (SRN), denoted as G^H, for I from scratch. G^H is fully-convolutional and can super-resolve I to $I \uparrow s = G^H(I)$ of arbitrary size, where s is the desired SR scale factor. However, learning G^H from the unpaired data (I_{HR}, I_{LR}) is challenging as the training objective will be highly under-constrained. As suggested in [31], we pair the super-resolution network G^H with another image-specific Degradation Simulation Network (DSN), denoted as G^L,

aiming to learn the internal degradation model—how the high-resolution patches are degraded to low-resolution patches during the imaging process—of a specific image I. We will detail the structures of these two networks in the following.

Degradation Simulation Network (DSN). The degradation simulation network G^L is lightweight and fully-convolutional, containing five convolutional layers. The structure of G^L is shown in Fig. 3. G^L maps a high-resolution image patch to a low-resolution counterpart. The degradation simulation network G^L in our method indeed learns a specific degradation kernel encoded inside the image, specifying how the imaging process changes the resolutions of patches in the image. Our proposed method will degenerate to models like ZSSR [19] if we use a handcrafted degradation kernel (e.g. a bicubic downscaling) to replace our DSN—a data-driven degradation model. A comparative experiment on this aspect will be detailed in Sect. 5.5. Specifically, G^L is defined as:

$$\tilde{x}_i^l = G^L(x_i^h) = F^{out}((F_5 \cdots F_1(F^{in}(x_i^h))) \downarrow), \tag{3}$$

where x_i^h means a high-resolution image patch, $\tilde{x}_i^l$ is the generated low-resolution patch from x_i^h, and F denotes the convolution layers in the degradation simulation network. F^{in} and F^{out} denote the convolution layers mapping the channels to the desired sizes.

Super-Resolution Network (SRN). The super-resolution network G^H also uses a lightweight design, in which we stack ten convolutional layers for feature extraction. We apply sub-pixel convolution [18] to upsample the extracted features and predict the high-frequency details. To reduce the computational cost and the number of model parameters, we use the bicubic interpolation for upsampling low-resolution features to generate the low-frequency and blurred HR images. Finally, we apply a global residual learning to merge two branches together to synthesize a visually pleasing high-resolution image as follows:

$$\tilde{y}_i^h = G^H(y_i^l) = F^{out}((F_{10} \cdots F_1(F^{in}(y_i^l))) \uparrow^p) + y_i^l \uparrow^b, \tag{4}$$

where $\tilde{y}_i^h$ is the high-resolution image patch generated by SRN, $\uparrow^p$ and $\uparrow^b$ denote the subpixel shuffle and bicubic interpolation, respectively. Figure 3 shows the details of the network structure of SRN.

3.3   Bi-cycle Training

To learn the degradation simulation network (DSN) and the super-resolution network (SRN) for producing realistic LR and HR image patches respectively, we further equip these two networks with two discriminator networks: D^L for DSN and D^H for SRN. Since the local patches in our depth guided training collection are unpaired, we propose a bi-cycle training strategy to learn these four lightweight networks (G^L, D^L, G^H and D^H) for an image. The concrete learning process contains four steps: (1) our SRN maps the LR patches to the fake HR patches, learning to super-resolve the images; (2) the synthesized HR

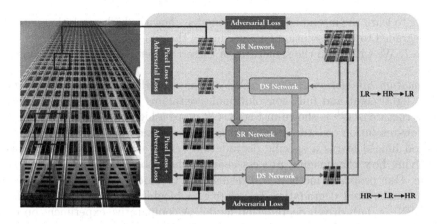

Fig. 4. The proposed structure of bi-cycle training. The first cycle maps LR to HR then back to LR and the second cycle maps HR to LR then back to HR.

patches are remapped back to their LR patches through DSN; (3) we map the HR image patches to the fake LR counterparts using DSN, simulating the image degradation during the imaging process; and (4) the simulated LR patches is then regenerated back to their HR patches through SRN (Fig. 4).

Our bi-cycle training consists of two closed processing cycles: in the first cycle, step (1) and (2), we map the real LR patches to fake HR patches and then remap the synthesized fake HR patches back to LR patches; and in the second cycle, step (3) and (4), we map the real HR patches to fake LR patches and then remap the generated fake LR patches back to HR patches. In each cycle in our model, we consider the adversarial loss to penalize the distribution mismatching and the pixel-wise reconstruction loss of patches as our learning objectives. More concretely, the step (1) optimizes the following Wasserstein GAN [1] objective:

$$L_{GAN}^{SRN} = \mathbb{E}_{y^l}[D^H(G^H(y^l))] - \mathbb{E}_{x^h}[D^H(x^h)], \tag{5}$$

where $y^l \sim I_{LR}$ is the sampled low-resolution image patch and $x^h \sim I_{HR}$ is the sampled high-resolution image patch. In the step (2), we jointly optimize the Wasserstein GAN objective and the cycle-consistent loss based L-1 norm as below:

$$L_{cycle}^{SRN} = \mathbb{E}_{y^l}[D^L(G^L(G^H(y^l)))] - \mathbb{E}_{y^l}[D^L(y^l)] + \mathbb{E}_{y^l}[\|G^L(G^H(y^l)) - y^l\|_1]. \tag{6}$$

Similarly, in step (3) and (4), we optimize the following two objectives, respectively:

$$L_{GAN}^{DSN} = \mathbb{E}_{x^h}[D^L(G^L(x^h))] - \mathbb{E}_{y^l}[D^L(y^l)]. \tag{7}$$

and

$$L_{cycle}^{DSN} = \mathbb{E}_{x^h}[D^H(G^H(G^L(x^h)))] - \mathbb{E}_{x^h}[D^H(x^h)] + \mathbb{E}_{x^h}[\|G^H(G^L(x^h)) - x^h\|_1]. \tag{8}$$

After completing the training, we input the entire low-resolution image I into the super-resolution network (SRN) to produce a high-resolution image $G^H(I)$.

4   Discussion

Difference to SelfExSR. SelfExSR [8] is a searching based method while our DGDML-SR is learning-based. Although both two methods leverage the internal self-similarity of images, their exact manners are different. SelfExSR searches for similar patches within the image and applies the clear patches to recover the similar but blurred ones. Our DGDML-SR uses the internal patches extracted according to the image depth information to learn the image-specific degradation model and super-resolution model, simultaneously.

Difference to ZSSR. Both of ZSSR [19] and our DGDML-SR are zero-shot image super-resolution methods. ZSSR selects patches from the image randomly and uses the bicubic or other pre-determined degradation kernels to downscale the patches. After that ZSSR learns the SR model using the downscaled patches and the original patches; the learned SR model is subsequently used to super-resolve the entire image. Our DGDML-SR does not rely on a pre-determined degradation model; instead we learn the degradation model using a neural network. Thus, our method will not suffer from the deficiency of using a pre-determined degradation kernel. More importantly, even though in the same experimental environment (i.e. similar hyperparameters and paired data generated with bicubic downsampling), our method is still better than ZSSR. For example, on Set5 [3], the PSNR score of our method is 0.21 dB higher than ZSSR.

Difference to KernelGAN. KernelGAN [2] learns the degradation kernel using a deep linear network. However, their degradation kernel learning is independent of the SR model they used; in other words, KernelGAN is not an end-to-end SR model. KernelGAN needs to learn the degradation kernel first and then use this kernel to generate the HR/LR patches for training a ZSSR network as the final SR model. In comparison, our DGDML-SR is an end-to-end model that could simultaneously learn the degradation kernel and the super-resolution network, using the unpaired image patches from the test image alone.

5   Experiment

In this section, we conduct experiments to evaluate the performance of the proposed zero-shot SR method based on depth guided internal degradation learning. Section 5.1 introduces the datasets used in our experiment and also the experimental setup. Then we show the quantitative and qualitative comparisons with the state of the arts in Sect. 5.2 and Sect. 5.3, respectively. In Sect. 5.4, we present two examples of zero-shot super-resolution using the estimated depth information. In the ablation study in Sect. 5.5, we evaluate the performance of our proposed method with and without learning the degradation model.

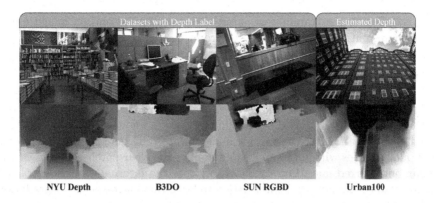

Fig. 5. Examples of images and depth maps from NYU Depth [20], B3DO [9], SUN-RGBD [25] and Urban100 [8].

5.1 Dataset and Training Setup

In the experiments, we select images from NYU depth V2 [20], B3DO [9], Xtion of SUN RGBD [25] and Urban100 [8] dataset. The first three datasets consist of only low-resolution RGB images and low-resolution depth images, while their high-resolution counterparts remain unknown. Among these datasets, NYU has the best image quality and the complete depth information. The image quality of B3DO and SUN RGBD is worse than NYU. In addition to the lower-resolution images and depth maps, they have JPEG compression with an unknown level and more sensor noise. Moreover, their depth information is often incomplete and even incorrect, making these two datasets more challenging. The last dataset only has RGB images without depth labels and we estimate the depth with a pre-trained monocular depth estimation model [7]. On all four datasets, we convert the images from RGB to YCbCr color space and the Y channel is taken out for training and testing. We set the HR (with the bigger region) and LR (with the smaller region) sliding windows on each of the images as mentioned in Sect. 3.1. We use the 64×64 (HR) and 32×32 (LR) sliding windows to extract the image patches for $\times 2$ scaling. For scaling $\times 4$, we use 128×128 (HR) and 32×32 (LR) patch sizes. We then rotate and flip the image patches to augment these patches, so that the number of patches is increased by eight times.

We implement the networks proposed in this paper using PyTorch1.2. We conduct all experiments on one Nvidia RTX2080Ti GPU card. We use RMSprop as the optimizer; the initial learning rate is 0.0001; the batch size is 64; and the learning rate is reduced by 10 times after each iteration of 60 epoch, for a total of 150 epochs. In our environment, it takes less than 10 s to train a lightweight super-resolution network in each epoch.

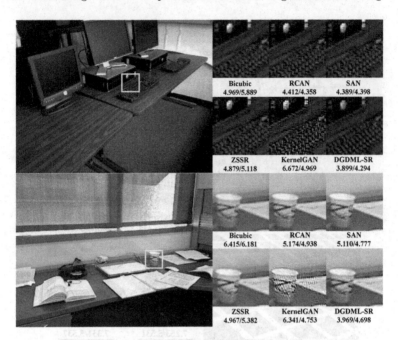

Fig. 6. We compare the visual quality of the super-resolved images from our proposed DGDML-SR with Bicubic, RCAN [30], SAN [5], ZSSR [19], KernelGAN [2]. The NIQE and PI score for these results are shown under each image.

5.2 Comparison with the State of the Arts

In this section, we compare our method with the state of the arts. In this task we do not have high-resolution labels, thus we use non-reference image quality assessment methods, including NIQE [17] and PI [4] as the comparison metrics. Lower PI and NIQE scores mean better visual quality. In Table 1, we compare our proposed DGDML-SR with the state of the art zero-shot methods as well as supervised methods including Bicubic, ZSSR [19], RCAN [30], SAN [5] and KernelGAN [2]. The best result is highlighted.

As shown in Table 1, the recent proposed deep learning based zero-shot methods show great advantages against the supervised methods according to NIQE on the NYU depth dataset. On the other two datasets with worse quality and unknown JPEG compressions, KernelGAN usually generates over-sharped results and amplifies the distracting artifacts. The supervised methods, including RCAN and SAN, overly smooth the details and cannot cope with the compression artifacts either. Among the above methods, our proposed DGDML-SR can achieve almost the best NIQE and PI scores.

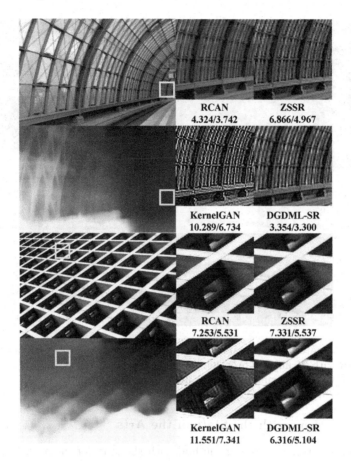

Fig. 7. Quality comparison of RCAN [29], ZSSR [19], KernelGAN [2] and our DGDML-SR on img_002 and img_043 from Urban100 [8] with estimated depth map. NIQE and PI scores are shown under each image.

5.3   Visual Comparison

In this section, we compare the visual quality of the high-resolution images generated by our method with those generated by early developed methods, including Bicubic, ZSSR [19], RCAN [30], SAN [5] and KernelGAN [2]. Figure 6 shows the zoomed results. Two examples we choose are the img_044 from NYU Depth V2 and the img_0089 from B3DO. The red squares indicate where the patches are taken out. The method name and its NIQE score are shown under the image patch. Similar to the results shown in Sect. 5.2, zero-shot methods can generally generate more details. Due to the linear degradation structure in KernelGAN [2], it cannot handle the multiple degradations and usually generates poor results for the image from B3DO. Among the above methods, our proposed DGDML-SR could generate sharper edges and more high-frequent details with no extra high-resolution training datasets, which shows great advantages compared with the state of the arts.

Table 1. Performance comparison of our proposed DGDML-SR with the state of the art zero-shot methods including bicubic, ZSSR [19], KernelGAN [2] and supervised methods including RCAN [29] and SAN [5] in terms of NIQE (lower is better) and PI (lower is better).

	Methods	Scale	NYU	B3DO	SUN
			NIQE/PI	NIQE/PI	NIQE/PI
Zero-Shot	Bicubic	×2	6.378/6.570	5.786/6.203	5.284/5.931
		×4	8.876/8.086	7.885/6.526	7.542/6.006
	ZSSR [19]	×2	5.753/6.139	5.041/5.360	4.362/5.327
		×4	—/—	—/—	—/—
	KernelGAN [2]	×2	5.620/**4.896**	6.859/**4.751**	6.613/4.847
		×4	6.888/6.591	6.500/5.899	6.457/6.012
	Our DGDML-SR	×2	**4.824**/5.454	**4.281**/4.884	**4.008**/**4.734**
		×4	**6.712**/**6.280**	**5.996**/**5.779**	**5.473**/**5.590**
Supervised	RCAN [29]	×2	5.868/6.126	5.108/4.955	4.813/4.911
		×4	8.387/7.972	6.524/6.404	6.458/6.571
	SAN [5]	×2	6.141/6.258	5.163/5.073	4.713/4.908
		×4	8.399/7.975	6.544/6.516	6.248/6.482

5.4 Super-Resolving Image with Estimated Depth

In this section, we use a pre-trained depth estimation model [7] to calculate the depth information for an image without the ground-truth depth label map. Figure 7 shows the zoom-in details of the high-resolution images (img_002 and img_043 from Urban100 [8]) generated by RCAN [30], ZSSR [19], KernelGAN [2] and our method. The NIQE and PI indexes of each method are shown under the zoom-in image patches. In Fig. 7, the results of RCAN are over-smoothed, losing the high-frequent details. KernelGAN's results are over-sharped while ZSSR's results are blurred at the dense textures. Among these methods, our proposed DGDML-SR can recover sharper edges and more high-frequent details of the image and can also achieve the highest score under the quantitative index.

5.5 Ablation Study

In this section, we first evaluate our depth guided (DG) strategy for collecting the training HR/LR patches. DG generates the unpaired data with the guidance of depth information that helps the network learn a more natural degradation kernel and meanwhile reduce the number of training patches. Without DG, we have to adopt a trivial manner to select the unpaired HR/LR training patches: we randomly select a large region as an HR patch and a small region as an LR patch. By ignoring the depth or scale information, this trivial strategy will be highly prone to select a short-distance region as an LR patch and a distant region as an HR patch. Another important aim of DG is to filter out the low-quality local

Table 2. Performance comparison with and without the depth guided internal degradation learning (DG) and bi-cycle training (BCN) in terms of NIQE (lower is better).

Methods	NYU	B3DO	SUN
None	5.929	5.193	4.926
DG	5.809	4.676	4.687
BCN	5.499	4.328	4.253
DG+BCN	**4.824**	**4.281**	**4.008**

patches such that we can decrease the computational burden significantly. The second important aspect of our method we also evaluate is the bi-cycle training strategy, denoted as BCN. No-BCN means we remove the cycle-consistent loss from our training objectives. BCN, the bi-cycle training strategy, ensures that our training process will be well-constrained. We conduct ablation study on DG and BCN, and show the results in Table 2. From top to the bottom are the model without DG and BCN, models containing one of the two strategies and the model contains both of them. The results show that the method with DG+BCN has a lower NIQE score, indicating better perceptual quality.

6   Conclusion

In this work, we have proposed a novel zero-shot image super-resolution method, in which we have designed a degradation simulation network (DSN) to learn the internal degradation model from a single image. With the help of DSN, our image-specific super-resolution network can produce satisfactory zero-shot SR results. More specifically, to extract the effective unpaired HR/LR patches from the image, we exploit the depth information to extract the natural HR/LR patches. Our zero-shot SR model can decrease the NIQE score at least 0.912 among the evaluation datasets. Compared with those recently proposed methods with pre-determined degradation kernels, our work can learn a more natural degradation model without relying on extra high-resolution training images and achieve better performance not only in quantitative comparison but also in visual quality on NYU Depth, B3DO, SUN and Urban100 datasets.

Acknowledgement. This work was supported by the NSFC (No. U1713208 and 61876085), Program for Changjiang Scholars and CPSF (No. 2017M621748 and 2019T120430).

References

1. Arjovsky, M., Chintala, S., Bottou, L.: Wasserstein generative adversarial networks. In: International Conference on Machine Learning, pp. 214–223 (2017)

2. Bell-Kligler, S., Shocher, A., Irani, M.: Blind super-resolution kernel estimation using an internal-GAN. arXiv preprint arXiv:1909.06581 (2019)
3. Bevilacqua, M., Roumy, A., Guillemot, C., Alberi-Morel, M.L.: Low-complexity single-image super-resolution based on nonnegative neighbor embedding (2012)
4. Blau, Y., Mechrez, R., Timofte, R., Michaeli, T., Zelnik-Manor, L.: The 2018 PIRM challenge on perceptual image super-resolution. In: Leal-Taixé, L., Roth, S. (eds.) ECCV 2018. LNCS, vol. 11133, pp. 334–355. Springer, Cham (2019). https://doi.org/10.1007/978-3-030-11021-5_21
5. Dai, T., Cai, J., Zhang, Y., Xia, S.T., Zhang, L.: Second-order attention network for single image super-resolution. In: Proceedings of the IEEE Conference on Computer Vision and Pattern Recognition, pp. 11065–11074 (2019)
6. Dong, C., Loy, C.C., He, K., Tang, X.: Image super-resolution using deep convolutional networks. IEEE Trans. Pattern Anal. Mach. Intell. **38**(2), 295–307 (2015)
7. Godard, C., Aodha, O.M., Firman, M., Brostow, G.J.: Digging into self-supervised monocular depth estimation. In: Proceedings of the IEEE International Conference on Computer Vision, pp. 3828–3838 (2019)
8. Huang, J.B., Singh, A., Ahuja, N.: Single image super-resolution from transformed self-exemplars. In: Proceedings of the IEEE Conference on Computer Vision and Pattern Recognition, pp. 5197–5206 (2015)
9. Janoch, A., et al.: A category-level 3D object dataset: putting the kinect to work. In: Fossati, A., Gall, J., Grabner, H., Ren, X., Konolige, K. (eds.) Consumer Depth Cameras for Computer Vision. Advances in Computer Vision and Pattern Recognition, pp. 141–165. Springer, London (2013). https://doi.org/10.1007/978-1-4471-4640-7_8
10. Kim, J., Kwon Lee, J., Mu Lee, K.: Accurate image super-resolution using very deep convolutional networks. In: Proceedings of the IEEE Conference on Computer Vision and Pattern Recognition, pp. 1646–1654 (2016)
11. Krizhevsky, A., Sutskever, I., Hinton, G.E.: ImageNet classification with deep convolutional neural networks. In: Advances in Neural Information Processing Systems, pp. 1097–1105 (2012)
12. Lai, W.S., Huang, J.B., Ahuja, N., Yang, M.H.: Deep Laplacian pyramid networks for fast and accurate super-resolution. In: Proceedings of the IEEE Conference on Computer Vision and Pattern Recognition, pp. 624–632 (2017)
13. Ledig, C., et al.: Photo-realistic single image super-resolution using a generative adversarial network. In: Proceedings of the IEEE Conference on Computer Vision and Pattern Recognition, pp. 4681–4690 (2017)
14. Lim, B., Son, S., Kim, H., Nah, S., Mu Lee, K.: Enhanced deep residual networks for single image super-resolution. In: Proceedings of the IEEE Conference on Computer Vision and Pattern Recognition Workshops, pp. 136–144 (2017)
15. Mechrez, R., Talmi, I., Shama, F., Zelnik-Manor, L.: Maintaining natural image statistics with the contextual loss. In: Jawahar, C.V., Li, H., Mori, G., Schindler, K. (eds.) ACCV 2018. LNCS, vol. 11363, pp. 427–443. Springer, Cham (2019). https://doi.org/10.1007/978-3-030-20893-6_27
16. Mechrez, R., Talmi, I., Zelnik-Manor, L.: The contextual loss for image transformation with non-aligned data. In: Ferrari, V., Hebert, M., Sminchisescu, C., Weiss, Y. (eds.) Computer Vision – ECCV 2018. LNCS, vol. 11218, pp. 800–815. Springer, Cham (2018). https://doi.org/10.1007/978-3-030-01264-9_47
17. Mittal, A., Soundararajan, R., Bovik, A.C.: Making a "completely blind" image quality analyzer. IEEE Signal Process. Lett. **20**(3), 209–212 (2012)

18. Shi, W., et al.: Real-time single image and video super-resolution using an efficient sub-pixel convolutional neural network. In: Proceedings of the IEEE Conference on Computer Vision and Pattern Recognition, pp. 1874–1883 (2016)
19. Shocher, A., Cohen, N., Irani, M.: "zero-shot" super-resolution using deep internal learning. In: Proceedings of the IEEE Conference on Computer Vision and Pattern Recognition, pp. 3118–3126 (2018)
20. Silberman, N., Hoiem, D., Kohli, P., Fergus, R.: Indoor segmentation and support inference from RGBD images. In: Fitzgibbon, A., Lazebnik, S., Perona, P., Sato, Y., Schmid, C. (eds.) ECCV 2012. LNCS, vol. 7576, pp. 746–760. Springer, Heidelberg (2012). https://doi.org/10.1007/978-3-642-33715-4_54
21. Tai, Y., Yang, J., Liu, X.: Image super-resolution via deep recursive residual network. In: Proceedings of the IEEE Conference on Computer Vision and Pattern Recognition, pp. 3147–3155 (2017)
22. Tai, Y., Yang, J., Liu, X., Xu, C.: MemNet: a persistent memory network for image restoration. In: Proceedings of the IEEE International Conference on Computer Vision, pp. 4539–4547 (2017)
23. Timofte, R., De Smet, V., Van Gool, L.: A+: adjusted anchored neighborhood regression for fast super-resolution. In: Cremers, D., Reid, I., Saito, H., Yang, M.-H. (eds.) ACCV 2014. LNCS, vol. 9006, pp. 111–126. Springer, Cham (2015). https://doi.org/10.1007/978-3-319-16817-3_8
24. Wang, X., et al.: ESRGAN: enhanced super-resolution generative adversarial networks. In: Leal-Taixé, L., Roth, S. (eds.) ECCV 2018. LNCS, vol. 11133, pp. 63–79. Springer, Cham (2019). https://doi.org/10.1007/978-3-030-11021-5_5
25. Xiao, J., Owens, A., Torralba, A.: SUN3D: a database of big spaces reconstructed using SfM and object labels. In: Proceedings of the IEEE International Conference on Computer Vision, pp. 1625–1632 (2013)
26. Xu, X., Ma, Y., Sun, W.: Towards real scene super-resolution with raw images. In: Proceedings of the IEEE Conference on Computer Vision and Pattern Recognition, pp. 1723–1731 (2019)
27. Yuan, Y., Liu, S., Zhang, J., Zhang, Y., Dong, C., Lin, L.: Unsupervised image super-resolution using cycle-in-cycle generative adversarial networks. In: Proceedings of the IEEE Conference on Computer Vision and Pattern Recognition Workshops, pp. 701–710 (2018)
28. Zhang, K., Zuo, W., Zhang, L.: Learning a single convolutional super-resolution network for multiple degradations. In: Proceedings of the IEEE Conference on Computer Vision and Pattern Recognition, pp. 3262–3271 (2018)
29. Zhang, Y., Li, K., Li, K., Wang, L., Zhong, B., Fu, Y.: Image super-resolution using very deep residual channel attention networks. In: Ferrari, V., Hebert, M., Sminchisescu, C., Weiss, Y. (eds.) ECCV 2018. LNCS, vol. 11211, pp. 294–310. Springer, Cham (2018). https://doi.org/10.1007/978-3-030-01234-2_18
30. Zhang, Y., Tian, Y., Kong, Y., Zhong, B., Fu, Y.: Residual dense network for image super-resolution. In: Proceedings of the IEEE Conference on Computer Vision and Pattern Recognition, pp. 2472–2481 (2018)
31. Zhu, J.Y., Park, T., Isola, P., Efros, A.A.: Unpaired image-to-image translation using cycle-consistent adversarial networks. In: Proceedings of the IEEE International Conference on Computer Vision, pp. 2223–2232 (2017)

A Closest Point Proposal
for MCMC-based Probabilistic Surface
Registration

Dennis Madsen[✉], Andreas Morel-Forster, Patrick Kahr, Dana Rahbani,
Thomas Vetter, and Marcel Lüthi

Department of Mathematics and Computer Science, University of Basel,
Basel, Switzerland
{dennis.madsen,andreas.forster,patrick.kahr,dana.rahbani,
thomas.vetter,marcel.luethi}@unibas.ch

Abstract. We propose to view non-rigid surface registration as a probabilistic inference problem. Given a target surface, we estimate the posterior distribution of surface registrations. We demonstrate how the posterior distribution can be used to build shape models that generalize better
and show how to visualize the uncertainty in the established correspondence. Furthermore, in a reconstruction task, we show how to estimate
the posterior distribution of missing data without assuming a fixed point-
to-point correspondence. We introduce the closest-point proposal for the
Metropolis-Hastings algorithm. Our proposal overcomes the limitation of
slow convergence compared to a random-walk strategy. As the algorithm
decouples inference from modeling the posterior using a propose-and-
verify scheme, we show how to choose different distance measures for
the likelihood model. All presented results are fully reproducible using
publicly available data and our open-source implementation of the registration framework.

Keywords: Probabilistic registration · Gaussian Process Morphable
Model · Metropolis-hastings proposal · Point distribution model

1   Introduction

The ability to quantify the uncertainty of a surface registration is important in
many areas of shape analysis. It is especially useful for the reconstruction of partial data, or for the analysis of data where the exact correspondence is unclear,
such as smooth surfaces. Within the medical area, the uncertainty of a partial
data reconstruction is needed to make informed surgical decisions [27]. Uncertainty estimates can also be used to build better generalizing Point Distribution
Models (PDMs) by assigning an uncertainty measure to each landmark [12,20].

D. Madsen and A. Morel-Forster—Joint first authors. Code available at https://github.
com/unibas-gravis/icp-proposal.

© Springer Nature Switzerland AG 2020
A. Vedaldi et al. (Eds.): ECCV 2020, LNCS 12362, pp. 281–296, 2020.
https://doi.org/10.1007/978-3-030-58520-4_17

In this paper, we propose an efficient, fully probabilistic method for surface registration based on Metropolis-Hastings (MH) sampling. Efficiency is gained by introducing a specialized proposal based on finding the closest points between a template and a target mesh. With this, we benefit from the geometry-aware proposal, while at the same time obtaining an uncertainty estimate for the registration result. We formulate the non-rigid surface registration problem as an approximation of the posterior distribution over all possible instances of point-to-point correspondences, given a target surface. With this approach, the registration uncertainty is the remaining variance in the posterior distribution. We use the MH algorithm to sample surface registrations from the posterior distribution. Our method can escape local optima and aims to capture the full posterior distribution of registrations.

Our method improves on previous works in the literature in different ways. In [17,28], the MH algorithm is used to estimate the uncertainty in non-rigid registration. These papers are working on the image domain, and are not transferable to the surface registration setting. MH has also been used in [21] to fit an Active Shape Model to images and in [30] to fit a Morphable Face Model to an image, both of which only make use of the framework to avoid local optima and to easily integrate different likelihood terms. The main problem with the MH algorithm is the commonly used random-walk approach, which suffers from very long convergence times when working in high-dimensional parameter spaces. To overcome this problem, informed proposal distributions can be designed to perform directed sample updates. In [16], a Bayesian Neural Network is learned to produce informed samples for the MH framework in the case of 3D face reconstruction from a 2D image. This, however, requires training a neural network for each class of shapes to be registered. In [14], local random-walk is combined with an image-dependent global proposal distribution. This image dependent distribution is, however, not directly transferable to the problem of surface registration. We perform registration by warping a single template mesh to a target surface. No training data is required with our method, whereas most state-of-the-art neural-network-based non-rigid registration methods require thousands of meshes in correspondence for training [6,10]. These methods work well for newer non-rigid registration challenges such as the FAUST dataset [4], where the focus is to learn shape articulation from a training dataset. This is not something we would advocate using our method for. Our method targets settings with no, or limited, available training data and adds to existing methods by providing an uncertainty measure, which is especially important within the medical domain.

Even though newer registration methods exist, Iterative Closest Point (ICP) and Coherent Point Drift (CPD) are still most commonly used for surface registration scenarios without available training data.[1] The ICP algorithm was originally developed for rigid alignment of point sets [3,5]. ICP iteratively estimates the point-to-point correspondences between two surfaces and then computes a

---

[1] In this paper, we focus on non-rigid registration. We, therefore, refer to their non-rigid versions whenever ICP or CPD is mentioned.

transformation based on the established correspondence. Finally, this transformation is applied to the reference surface. The algorithm has later been modified for non-rigid surface registration [7]. In general, standard ICP is very efficient and produces good results. However, a bad initialization may lead the algorithm to local optima from which it is unable to recover. Moreover, it is impossible to estimate the correspondence uncertainty of the registration result. Multiple extensions have been proposed to make the algorithm more robust in scenarios such as missing data or large articulation deformation differences [1,13,25]. In [18], the ICP method is improved using Simulated Annealing and MCMC. Their method is a robust version of the ICP algorithm, which can find the global optimal rigid registration of point clouds. They do not, however, measure the registration uncertainty, nor are they able to perform non-rigid registrations. An extensive review of different ICP methods can be found in [26]. The CPD method [22,23] is a probabilistic alternative to ICP. Yet, it does not provide an uncertainty estimate for the registration result.

As it is common in non-rigid registration, we do not infer the rigid alignment. Fortunately, MH allows for easy integration of proposal distributions of parameters other than the shape. The proposal distribution can therefore easily be extended to include translation, rotation, scaling as shown in [21], or texture, illumination, and camera position as in [30].

In this paper, we show how closest-point information can be incorporated into the MH algorithm to take geometric information into account. We introduce a novel closest-point-proposal (CP-proposal) to use within the MH algorithm. Our proposal can make informed updates while maintaining the theoretical convergence properties of the MH algorithm. To propose probabilistic surface deformations, we make use of a Gaussian Process Morphable Model (GPMM) as our prior model. In [8], GPMMs are applied to face surface registration. However, the authors formulate the registration problem as a parametric registration problem, which does not provide an uncertainty measure for the established correspondence. Several alternatives already exist to the random-walk proposal, such as MALA [9], Hamiltonian [24] or NUTS [11]. While the mentioned proposals work well in lower-dimensional spaces and for smoother posteriors, we experienced that they get computationally demanding in high dimensional spaces and have problems when the posterior is far from smooth.

In our experiments, we register femur bones, where the biggest challenge is establishing correspondence along the long smooth surface of the femur shaft. In another experiment, we use our method to reconstruct missing data. To that end, we compute the posterior distribution of registrations for faces where the nose has been removed. Unlike ICP or CPD, we can give an uncertainty estimate for each point in the surface reconstruction. Furthermore, we show how the standard non-rigid ICP algorithm can end up in local optima, while our method consistently provides good registrations and can also quantify the correspondence uncertainty. The three main contributions of this paper are:

– We introduce a theoretically sound, informed closest-point-proposal for the MH framework, with a well-defined transition ratio, Sect. 3.2.

- We show the usefulness of the posterior distribution of registrations for completing partial shapes and for building better generalizing PDMs, Sect. 4.2.
- We demonstrate that the MH algorithm with our proposal leads to better and more robust registration results than the standard non-rigid ICP and CPD algorithms, Sect. 4.3.

2   Background

In this section, we formally introduce the GPMM as presented in [19], and we show how the analytic posterior, which we use in our CP-proposal, is computed.

2.1   Gaussian Process Morphable Model (GPMM)

GPMMs are a generalization of the classical point distribution models (PDMs) [19]. The idea is to model the deformations, which relate a given reference shape to the other shapes within a given shape family, using a Gaussian process. More formally, let $\Gamma_R \subset \mathbb{R}^3$ be a reference surface. We obtain a probabilistic model of possible target surfaces Γ by setting

$$\Gamma = \{x + u(x)|x \in \Gamma_R\} \tag{1}$$

where the deformation field u is distributed according to a Gaussian process $u \sim GP(\mu, k)$ with mean function μ and covariance function $k : \Gamma_R \times \Gamma_R \to \mathbb{R}^{3\times3}$. Let $\Gamma_1, \ldots, \Gamma_n$ be a set of surfaces for which correspondence to the reference surface Γ_R is known. From this, it follows that we can express any surface Γ_i as:

$$\Gamma_i = \{x + u_i(x)|x \in \Gamma_R\}. \tag{2}$$

Classical PDMs define the mean and covariance function as:

$$\mu_{\text{PDM}}(x) = \frac{1}{n} \sum_{i=1}^{n} u_i(x)$$

$$k_{\text{PDM}}(x, x') = \frac{1}{n-1} \sum_{i=1}^{n} (u_i(x) - \mu_{\text{PDM}}(x))(u_i(x') - \mu_{\text{PDM}}(x'))^T. \tag{3}$$

However, GPMMs also allow us to define the mean and covariance function analytically. Different choices of covariance functions lead to different well-known deformation models, such as radial basis functions, b-splines, or thin-plate-splines. To model smooth deformations, we choose a zero-mean Gaussian process with the following covariance function:

$$k(x, x') = g(x, x') * I_3, \tag{4}$$

$$g(x, x') = s \cdot \exp(\frac{-\|x - x'\|^2}{\sigma^2}), \tag{5}$$

where I_3 is the identity matrix and $g(x, x')$ is a Gaussian kernel.

The model, as stated above, is a possibly infinite-dimensional non-parametric model. In [19], they propose to use the truncated Karhunen-Loéve expansion to

obtain a low-rank approximation of the Gaussian process. In this representation, the Gaussian process $GP(\mu, k)$ is approximated as:

$$u[\boldsymbol{\alpha}](x) = \mu(x) + \sum_{i=1}^{r} \alpha_i \sqrt{\lambda_i} \phi_i(x), \ \alpha_i \sim \mathcal{N}(0, 1) \quad (6)$$

where r is the number of basis functions used in the approximation and λ_i, ϕ_i are the i-th eigenvalue and eigenfunction of the covariance operator associated with the covariance function k. Consequently, any deformation u is uniquely determined by a coefficient vector $\boldsymbol{\alpha} = (\alpha_1, \dots, \alpha_r)$. Hence, we can easily express any surface Γ as:

$$\Gamma[\boldsymbol{\alpha}] = \{x + \mu(x) + \sum_{i=1}^{r} \alpha_i \sqrt{\lambda_i} \phi_i(x) | x \in \Gamma_R\} \quad (7)$$

with associated probability

$$p(\Gamma[\boldsymbol{\alpha}]) = p(\boldsymbol{\alpha}) = (2\pi)^{-\frac{r}{2}} \exp(-\|\boldsymbol{\alpha}\|)^2. \quad (8)$$

2.2   Analytical Posterior Model

GPMMs make it simple and efficient to constrain a model to match known correspondences, such as user annotations or the estimated correspondence from taking the closest point. Indeed, the corresponding *posterior model* is again a Gaussian process, whose parameters are known in closed form.

Let $u \sim GP(\mu, k)$ be a GPMM and $\epsilon \sim \mathcal{N}(0, \Sigma)$, $\Sigma = \sigma_{noise} I_3$ be the certainty of each known landmark. Every landmark l_R on the reference surface can then be matched with its corresponding landmark l_T on the target. The set L consists of the n reference landmarks and its expected deformation to match the target

$$L = \{(l_R^1, l_T^1 - l_R^1), \dots, (l_R^n, l_T^n - l_R^n)\} = \{(l_R^1, \hat{u}^1), \dots, (l_R^n, \hat{u}^n)\}, \quad (9)$$

with $\hat{u}$ being subject to Gaussian noise ϵ. Using Gaussian process regression, we obtain the posterior model $u_p \sim GP(\mu_p, k_p)$, which models the possible surface deformations that are consistent with the given landmarks. Its mean and covariance function are given by:

$$\mu_p(x) = \mu(x) + K_X(x)^T (K_{XX} + \epsilon)^{-1} \hat{U}$$
$$k_p(x, x') = k(x, x') + K_X(x)^T (K_{XX} + \epsilon)^{-1} K_X(x'). \quad (10)$$

Here we defined $K_X(x) = \left(k(l_R^i, x) \right)_{i=1,\dots,n}$, a vector of the target deformation as $\hat{U} = (l_T^i - l_R^i)_{i=1,\dots,n}$ and the kernel matrix $K_{XX} = \left(k(l_R^i, l_R^j) \right)_{i,j=1,\dots,n}$.

3   Method

We formulate the registration problem as Bayesian inference, where we obtain the posterior distribution of parameters $\boldsymbol{\alpha}$ given the target surface as:

$$P(\boldsymbol{\alpha}|\Gamma_T) = \frac{P(\Gamma_T|\boldsymbol{\alpha})P(\boldsymbol{\alpha})}{\int P(\Gamma_T|\boldsymbol{\alpha})P(\boldsymbol{\alpha})d\boldsymbol{\alpha}}. \quad (11)$$

The prior probability, computed with Eq. (8), pushes the solution towards a more likely shape given the GPMM space, by penalizing unlikely shape deformations. The likelihood term can easily be customized with different distance measures and probability functions, depending on the application goal at hand. We are usually interested in modeling the L2 distance between two surfaces (d_{l2}), for which we can use the independent point evaluator likelihood:

$$P(\Gamma_T|\alpha) = \prod_{i=1}^{n} \mathcal{N}(d_{l2}(\Gamma_T^i, \Gamma[\alpha]^i); 0, \sigma_{l2}^2), \tag{12}$$

as also used in [21]. The L2 distance between the i-th point $\Gamma[\alpha]^i \in R^3$ and its closest point on the surface Γ_T is rated using a zero-mean normal distribution with the expected standard deviation for a good registration. The variance σ_{l2}^2 is the observation noise of the points of our target surface. We can register for a better Hausdorff distance [2] by changing the likelihood to:

$$P(\Gamma_T|\alpha) = Exp(d_H(\Gamma_T, \Gamma[\alpha]); \lambda_H) \tag{13}$$

with d_H being the Hausdorff distance between the two meshes and Exp being the exponential distribution with pdf $p(d) = \lambda_H e^{-\lambda_H d}$.

3.1   Approximating the Posterior Distribution

The posterior distribution defined in Eq. (11) can unfortunately not be obtained analytically. Yet, we can compute the unnormalized density value for any shape described by α. This allows us to use the Metropolis-Hastings algorithm [29] to generate samples from the posterior distribution in the form of a Markov-chain. The MH algorithm is summarized in Algorithm 1.

A general way to explore the parameter space is to use a random-walk proposal, i.e. a Gaussian update distribution in the parameter space

$$Q(\alpha'|\alpha) \sim \mathcal{N}(\alpha, \sigma_l). \tag{14}$$

We usually combine differently scaled distributions, each with a specified σ_l, to allow for both local and global exploration of the posterior distribution. For each proposal, one distribution is chosen at random.

Algorithm 1. Metropolis-Hastings sampling

1: $\alpha_0 \leftarrow$ arbitrary initialization
2: **for** $i = 0$ to S **do**
3:     $\alpha' \leftarrow$ sample from $Q(\alpha'|\alpha_i)$
4:     $t \leftarrow \dfrac{q(\alpha_i|\alpha')p(\Gamma_T|\alpha')p(\alpha')}{q(\alpha'|\alpha_i)p(\Gamma_T|\alpha_i)p(\alpha_i)}$. {acceptance threshold}
5:     $r \leftarrow$ sample from $\mathcal{U}(0,1)$
6:     **if** $t > r$ **then**
7:         $\alpha_{i+1} \leftarrow \alpha'$
8:     **else**
9:         $\alpha_{i+1} \leftarrow \alpha_i$

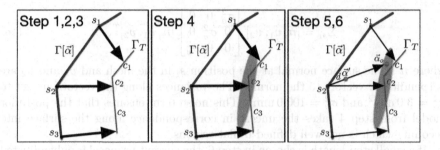

Fig. 1. Visualization of the CP-Proposal with the current instance (blue) from the model, and the target surface (red). The grey ellipse in the centre window shows the landmark noise for s_2. The right window shows how an update for s_2 is generated based on the posterior sample α_o and the step size d. (Color figure online)

3.2   CP-proposal

A random-walk in the parameter space of the prior GPMM model $\mathcal{M}$ is time-consuming as it usually is high-dimensional. Instead, we propose to accelerate convergence by using an informed proposal. For the proposal to reach a unique stationary distribution, we have to be able to compute the transition probability, which requires the proposal to be stochastic. We propose the CP-proposal, which takes the geometry of the model and the target into account to guide the proposed change. Internally, we use a posterior model $\mathcal{M}_\alpha$ based on estimated correspondences to propose randomized informed samples. From a current state α, we propose an update α' by executing the following steps (visualized in Fig. 1):

1. Sample m points $\{s_i\}$ on the current model instance $\Gamma[\alpha]$.
2. For every point s_i, $i \in [0 \dots m]$ find the closest point c_i on the target Γ_T.
3. Construct the set of observations L based on corresponding landmark pairs (s_i, c_i) according to Eq. (9) and define the noise $\epsilon_i \sim \mathcal{N}(0, \Sigma_{s_i})$ using Eq. (16).
4. Compute the analytic posterior $\mathcal{M}_\alpha$ (Eq. (10)) with L and $\{\Sigma_{s_i}\}$.
5. Get α_o by first drawing a random shape[2] from the posterior model $\mathcal{M}_\alpha$ and then projecting it into the prior model $\mathcal{M}$.
6. We generate

$$\alpha' = \alpha + d(\alpha_o - \alpha) \tag{15}$$

with $d \in [0.0 \dots 1.0]$ being a step-length.

The noise ϵ in step 3 is modeled with low variance along the normal direction and high variance along the surface. The variance at each point s_i in $\Gamma[\alpha]$ is computed by:

---

[2] Sampling all α_i independently from $\mathcal{N}(0, 1)$ and constructing the shape with Eq. (7).

$$\Sigma_{s_i} = [n, v_1, v_2] \begin{bmatrix} \sigma_n^2 & 0 & 0 \\ 0 & \sigma_v^2 & 0 \\ 0 & 0 & \sigma_v^2 \end{bmatrix} [n, v_1, v_2]^T, \tag{16}$$

where n is the surface normal at the position s_i in the mesh and v_1 and v_2 are perpendicular vectors to the normal. The variances along the vectors are set to $\sigma_n^2 = 3.0\,\mathrm{mm}^2$ and $\sigma_v^2 = 100.0\,\mathrm{mm}^2$. This noise term ensures that the posterior model from step 4 takes the uncertain correspondence along the surface into account, which is not well defined in flat regions.

If a small step-length is chosen in step 6, the current proposal is only adjusted slightly in the direction of the target surface, resulting in a locally restricted step. With a step size of 1.0, the proposed sample is an independent sample from the posterior in Eq. (10).

In practice, closest-point based updates often find wrong correspondences if the sizes of Γ and Γ_T greatly differ. This is especially problematic in the case of elongated thin structures. It is, therefore, useful also to establish the correspondence from Γ_T to Γ from time to time.

Computing the Transition Probability. For each new proposal α' from the CP-proposal distribution, we need to compute the transition probability as part of the acceptance threshold (see Algorithm 1 step 4). The transition probability $q(\alpha'|\alpha)$ is equal to the probability of sampling the shape corresponding to α_o from the posterior model $\mathcal{M}_\alpha$, computed in step 4 of the CP-proposal. For $q(\alpha|\alpha')$, the transition probability is computed in the same way. We solve Eq. (15) for α'_o after swapping α and α' and evaluate the corresponding shape likelihood under the posterior distribution $\mathcal{M}_{\alpha'}$.

4   Experiments

In the following, we perform registration experiments on surfaces of femur bones as well as a reconstruction experiment of missing data on face scans. For the face experiment, the face template and the face GPMM from [8] are used together with 10 available face scans. For the femur experiments, we use 50 healthy femur meshes extracted from computed tomography (CT) images[3]. Each surface is complete, i.e. no holes or artifacts. This setting is optimal for the standard ICP algorithm and therefore serves as a fair comparison to the CPD algorithm and our probabilistic implementation. The CPD experiments are performed with the MATLAB code from [22] and all other experiments with the Scalismo[4] library.

4.1   Convergence Comparison

We compare the convergence properties of our CP-proposal and random-walk. The CP-proposal configuration is mentioned together with its definition in

---

[3] Available via the SICAS Medical Image Repository [15].
[4] https://scalismo.org.

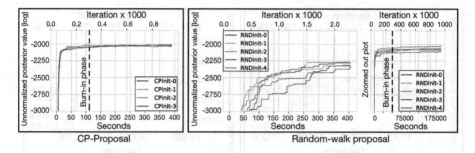

Fig. 2. Convergence plots for the femur GPMM registrations with 50 components. Our CP-proposal is shown to the left and the random-walk (including a zoomed out plot) to the right. The CP-proposal needs 300 iterations, while the random-walk needs more than 200k samples for the burn-in phase without reaching the same registration quality even after 1M iterations. Run-time in seconds is shown on the lower x-axis and number of MH iterations on the upper.

Sect. 3.2. For the random-walk, we use a mixture of the proposals defined in Eq. (14), with σ_l being set to six different levels, from 1.0 mm to 0.01 µm, and all six proposal distributions equally likely to be sampled from.

In Fig. 2, the convergence time of the standard random-walk and the CP-proposal is shown. The experiment is performed with a GPMM with a low-rank approximation of 50 components, see Sect. 2.1. We randomly initialize the model parameters and start 5 registrations in parallel. As expected, our proposal leads to much faster convergence. In Fig. 3 we see a posterior plot comparison of the two proposals. Notice how less likely samples are often accepted, which makes it different from deterministic methods such as ICP and CPD.

4.2   Posterior Estimation of Missing Data

We use a face GPMM to estimate the posterior distribution of noses from partial face data, where the nose has been removed. In Fig. 4, we see that there is no perfect overlap between the face model and the scan.

Therefore, we need to change our likelihood function to adjust for a possible changing number of correspondence points during the registration. To obtain a close fit on average, while also penalizing far away points, we use the collective average likelihood introduced in [30] and extend it with the Hausdorff likelihood,

$$P(\Gamma_T|\boldsymbol{\alpha}) \propto \mathcal{N}(d_{CL}(\Gamma_T, \Gamma[\boldsymbol{\alpha}]); 0, \sigma_{CL}^2) \cdot Exp(d_H(\Gamma_T, \Gamma[\boldsymbol{\alpha}]); \lambda_H), \qquad (17)$$

where

$$d_{CL} = \frac{1}{N} \sum_{i=1}^{N} \|\Gamma_R^i - \Gamma_T^i\|^2. \qquad (18)$$

Here the closest point of Γ_R^i on the target is Γ_T^i and N is the number of landmarks in the reference mesh Γ_R.

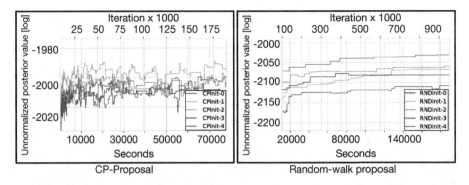

Fig. 3. Posterior plot comparison of the CP-proposal and random-walk. Even with a very small update step for the random-walk, it has difficulties to explore the posterior in the high-dimensional setting. The CP-proposal, on the other hand, can more efficiently explore the high-dimensional space.

On a technical note, using ICP to predict correspondence in a missing data scenario maps all points from the reference, which are not observed in the target to the closest border. To counter this effect, we filtered away all predicted correspondences, where the predicted target point is part of the target surface's boundary. This is also done in e.g. [1].

In Fig. 4, we show the correspondence uncertainty from the posterior registration distribution. Our method infers a larger correspondence uncertainty in the outer region. However, as the surface is observed, the uncertainty is low in the direction of the face surface normals but high within the surface. This is because there is no anatomical distinctive feature to predict the correspondence more precisely. High uncertainty is also inferred on the nose, where data is missing. In contrast to the outer region, the uncertainty in the direction of the normal of the reconstructed nose surface is large. This shows that uncertainty visualization can be used to detect missing areas or to build better PDMs by incorporating the uncertainty of the registration process as demonstrated next.

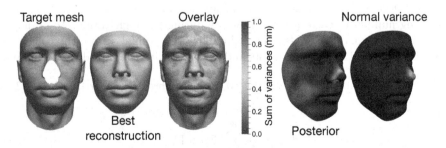

Fig. 4. Nose reconstruction with the face GPMM. No uncertainty in the outer region of the face along the normal indicates that only the correspondence is uncertain compared to the nose.

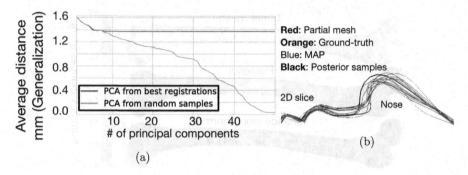

(a)

(b)

Fig. 5. (a) shows the better generalization of a PDM using 100 random samples from the posterior distributions of each of the 10 targets, compared to only using the most likely samples. The blue line flattens out as no more than 9 principal components are computed with 10 meshes. (b) 2D slice view of posterior face samples. The MAP solution does not explain the ground-truth shape, whereas the random samples cover the ground-truth shape. (Color figure online)

PDMs from Posterior Distributions. In this experiment, we show how to benefit from probabilistic registration when building new PDMs from a small dataset with partially missing data, which is common in medical imaging. If much more data is available, the influence of using the posterior is reduced as the variability gained from the probabilistic framework can be gained by including a lot more data. In Sect. 4.2, we registered the 10 available face scans by computing the posterior distribution of reconstructions for each target. In Fig. 5b we show samples from the posterior distribution of nose reconstructions.

In Fig. 5a, we compare two different PDMs' generalization abilities, i.e. the capability to represent unseen data [31]. One PDM is built following the classical approach of only using the most likely registrations. The other PDM is built from 100 random samples from each of the 10 posterior distributions. We compute the average generalization of all 10 PDMs built using a leave-one-out scheme. The plot shows that the PDM built from the posteriors generalizes better.

4.3   Registration Accuracy - ICP vs CPD vs CP-proposal

In this experiment, we compare the best sample, also known as Maximum a posteriori (MAP) from our probabilistic method, with the ICP and CPD methods. We use a femur GPMM approximated with 200 basis functions. From the model, we sample 100 random meshes as starting points for the registration. We, therefore, end up with 100 registrations for each target. In Fig. 7 we show the summary of all 5000 registrations (All) and some individual representative target meshes.

The naming scheme combines the registration method (ICP, CPD, or MH with CP) with the likelihood function which was used (L2). The box plot shows the variation of the average L2 surface distances from all 100 registrations of each target. As the ICP and CPD methods converge at maximum 100 iterations, we

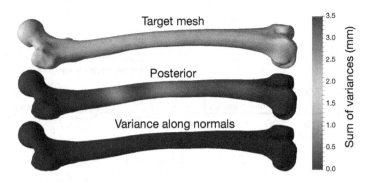

Fig. 6. Femur registration with uncertainty. The registration uncertainty is visualized with the point-wise sum of variances. As expected, the higher uncertainty of the established correspondence coincides with the shaft region with the least characteristic shape. No variance is observed along the normals, so the uncertainty is only in the correspondence along the surface.

also restrict our sampling method to 100 samples. The chain usually converges within 100–300 samples as shown in Fig. 2.

The CP-proposal is consistently better than the ICP and CPD registrations, and at the same time provides much less fluctuation in the quality. The few outliers for our method are cases where the chain has not converged. In Fig. 6, we show the uncertainty of the established correspondence of a registration from 1000 samples (300 samples for the burn-in phase). Depicted is the uncertainty of individual points from the posterior distribution from a single registration. Note the high uncertainty values along the shaft, which indicate that the established correspondence is less reliable in that region. No variance along the normals indicates that the uncertainty is purely correspondence shift within the surface.

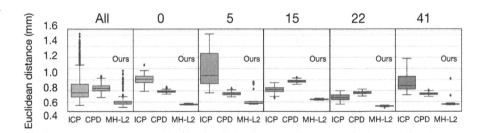

Fig. 7. Distances between the final registrations and their target meshes. For each target mesh, we randomly initialize 100 registrations. The MAP sample from our CP-proposal is superior to ICP and CPD. The femur target id (0 to 49) is shown on top of each plot.

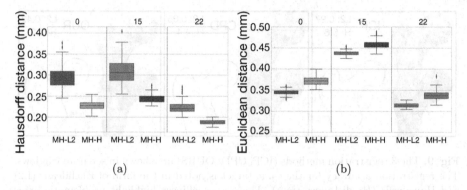

(a)   (b)

Fig. 8. Registration result comparison using either the Hausdorff or the Euclidean distance likelihood. (a) Euclidean distance and (b) Hausdorff distance between the MAP samples and the target meshes. The plots show that the average L2 surface distance is only slightly worse when the Hausdorff (H) likelihood is used.

Alternative Hausdorff Distance Likelihood. In Fig. 8a, we compare the registration results based on their Hausdorff distance, and we compare results from sampling using the L2 likelihood, Eq. (12), and the Hausdorff likelihood, Eq. (13). As expected, we can focus the registration to avoid large Hausdorff distances. The equivalent L2 likelihood experiment is shown in Fig. 8b and shows that while optimizing for the Hausdorff distance, the average L2 surface distance is increasing only slightly. This demonstrates the capability to change the likelihood in our framework based on the application's needs.

Drawbacks of Deterministic Methods. The main problem with ICP and CPD is that they cannot recover from local optima. If the algorithm finds the closest point on the wrong part of the target, we end up with a bad registration. In Fig. 9, we show a registration result of the 3 registration methods. The ICP method can get the overall length of the bone correct but ends up with a registration, where the structure is folding around itself. The CPD approach is more robust than ICP as it preserves the topological structure of the point sets. Our method additionally provides an uncertainty map.

Run-Time Comparison. The number of components in the low-rank approximation can be seen as regularization of the deformations. More complex local deformations can be obtained using more components. The algorithm run-time scales linearly in the number of components, with the run-time being 2.5 times slower for each time the model rank doubles. For models with rank 50, 100 and 200, the CP-proposal takes: 46 s, 110 s and 275 s. In comparison, the ICP implementation takes 30 s, 69 s and 155 s. The CPD implementation does not make use of the GPMM model and takes 75 s for 100 samples with our setup. While our method is slower than the two others, we still get reasonable run-times while inferring more accurate results and estimate the full posterior instead of a single estimate.

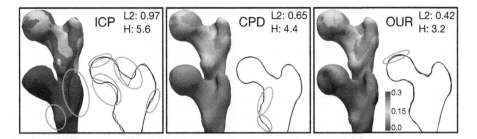

Fig. 9. The 3 registration methods (ICP, CPD, OURS) are shown in separate windows. The registration accuracy for the same target is noted in the form of Euclidean- (L2) and Hausdorff- (H) distances (mm). The orange ellipses highlight problematic areas of the registration for each method. For each method, we show the target with the registration overlaid, the 3D-registration, and a 2D slice of the registration (colored) and the target (black). Notice how our method (in comparison to ICP and CPD) shows the correspondence uncertainty (summed point variances (mm^2) for each landmark). (Color figure online)

5   Conclusion

In this paper, we presented a probabilistic registration framework. Our main contribution is the informed proposal for the MH algorithm, which makes it possible to work in a high-dimensional model space that would be difficult to explore with pure random-walk. Our informed proposal integrates geometry awareness in the update step, which results in faster convergence. In the case of missing data, our method provides an estimate of the posterior over possible reconstructions. Thus our framework can provide uncertainty measures for critical tasks such as surface reconstruction in the medical domain, as required for surgical decision making. Using our framework, different likelihood terms can be combined and used, while the choice is restricted to the L2 norm in standard ICP and CPD. Finally, we showed how to build PDMs that generalize better using the posterior distribution of registrations.

Acknowledgements.. This research is sponsored by the Gebert Rüf Foundation under the project GRS-029/17.

References

1. Amberg, B., Romdhani, S., Vetter, T.: Optimal step nonrigid ICP algorithms for surface registration. In: 2007 IEEE Conference on Computer Vision and Pattern Recognition, pp. 1–8. IEEE (2007)
2. Aspert, N., Santa-Cruz, D., Ebrahimi, T.: MESH: measuring errors between surfaces using the Hausdorff distance. In: Proceedings. IEEE International Conference on Multimedia and Expo, vol. 1, pp. 705–708. IEEE (2002)
3. Besl, P.J., McKay, N.D.: Method for registration of 3-D shapes. In: Sensor Fusion IV: Control Paradigms and Data Structures, vol. 1611, pp. 586–607. International Society for Optics and Photonics (1992)

4. Bogo, F., Romero, J., Loper, M., Black, M.J.: Faust: dataset and evaluation for 3D mesh registration. In: Proceedings of the IEEE Conference on Computer Vision and Pattern Recognition, pp. 3794–3801 (2014)
5. Chen, Y., Medioni, G.: Object modelling by registration of multiple range images. Image Vis. Comput. **10**(3), 145–155 (1992)
6. Deprelle, T., Groueix, T., Fisher, M., Kim, V., Russell, B., Aubry, M.: Learning elementary structures for 3D shape generation and matching. In: Advances in Neural Information Processing Systems, pp. 7433–7443 (2019)
7. Feldmar, J., Ayache, N.: Rigid, affine and locally affine registration of free-form surfaces. Int. J. Comput. Vis. **18**(2), 99–119 (1996). https://doi.org/10.1007/BF00054998
8. Gerig, T., et al.: Morphable face models-an open framework. In: 2018 13th IEEE International Conference on Automatic Face & Gesture Recognition (FG 2018), pp. 75–82. IEEE (2018)
9. Grenander, U., Miller, M.I.: Representations of knowledge in complex systems. J. Roy. Stat. Soc. Ser. B (Methodol.) **56**(4), 549–581 (1994)
10. Groueix, T., Fisher, M., Kim, V.G., Russell, B.C., Aubry, M.: 3D-CODED: 3D correspondences by deep deformation. In: Ferrari, V., Hebert, M., Sminchisescu, C., Weiss, Y. (eds.) ECCV 2018. LNCS, vol. 11206, pp. 235–251. Springer, Cham (2018). https://doi.org/10.1007/978-3-030-01216-8_15
11. Hoffman, M.D., Gelman, A.: The No-U-Turn sampler: adaptively setting path lengths in Hamiltonian Monte Carlo. J. Mach. Learn. Res. **15**(1), 1593–1623 (2014)
12. Hufnagel, H., Pennec, X., Ehrhardt, J., Ayache, N., Handels, H.: Generation of a statistical shape model with probabilistic point correspondences and the expectation maximization-iterative closest point algorithm. Int. J. Comput. Assist. Radiol. Surg. **2**(5), 265–273 (2008). https://doi.org/10.1007/s11548-007-0138-9
13. Hufnagel, H., Pennec, X., Ehrhardt, J., Handels, H., Ayache, N.: Point-based statistical shape models with probabilistic correspondences and affine EM-ICP. In: Horsch, A., Deserno, T.M., Handels, H., Meinzer, H.P., Tolxdorff, T. (eds.) Bildverarbeitung für die Medizin 2007. Informatik aktuell, pp. 434–438. Springer, Berlin (2007). https://doi.org/10.1007/978-3-540-71091-2_87
14. Jampani, V., Nowozin, S., Loper, M., Gehler, P.V.: The informed sampler: a discriminative approach to Bayesian inference in generative computer vision models. Comput. Vis. Image Underst. **136**, 32–44 (2015)
15. Kistler, M., Bonaretti, S., Pfahrer, M., Niklaus, R., Büchler, P.: The virtual skeleton database: an open access repository for biomedical research and collaboration. J. Med. Internet Res. **15**(11), e245 (2013)
16. Kortylewski, A., et al.: Informed MCMC with Bayesian neural networks for facial image analysis. arXiv preprint arXiv:1811.07969 (2018)
17. Le Folgoc, L., Delingette, H., Criminisi, A., Ayache, N.: Quantifying registration uncertainty with sparse Bayesian modelling. IEEE Trans. Med. Imaging **36**(2), 607–617 (2016)
18. Liu, H., Liu, T., Li, Y., Xi, M., Li, T., Wang, Y.: Point cloud registration based on MCMC-SA ICP algorithm. IEEE Access **7**, 73637–73648 (2019)
19. Lüthi, M., Gerig, T., Jud, C., Vetter, T.: Gaussian process morphable models. IEEE Trans. Pattern Anal. Mach. Intell. **40**, 1860–1873 (2018)
20. Ma, J., Lin, F., Honsdorf, J., Lentzen, K., Wesarg, S., Erdt, M.: Weighted robust PCA for statistical shape modeling. In: Zheng, G., Liao, H., Jannin, P., Cattin, P., Lee, S.-L. (eds.) MIAR 2016. LNCS, vol. 9805, pp. 343–353. Springer, Cham (2016). https://doi.org/10.1007/978-3-319-43775-0_31

21. Morel-Forster, A., Gerig, T., Lüthi, M., Vetter, T.: Probabilistic fitting of active shape models. In: Reuter, M., Wachinger, C., Lombaert, H., Paniagua, B., Lüthi, M., Egger, B. (eds.) ShapeMI 2018. LNCS, vol. 11167, pp. 137–146. Springer, Cham (2018). https://doi.org/10.1007/978-3-030-04747-4_13

22. Myronenko, A., Song, X.: Point set registration: coherent point drift. IEEE Trans. Pattern Anal. Mach. Intell. **32**(12), 2262–2275 (2010)

23. Myronenko, A., Song, X., Carreira-Perpinán, M.A.: Non-rigid point set registration: coherent point drift. In: Advances in Neural Information Processing Systems, pp. 1009–1016 (2007)

24. Neal, R.M., et al.: MCMC using Hamiltonian dynamics. In: Handbook of Markov Chain Monte Carlo, vol. 2, no. 11, p. 2 (2011)

25. Pan, Y., Yang, B., Liang, F., Dong, Z.: Iterative global similarity points: a robust coarse-to-fine integration solution for pairwise 3D point cloud registration. In: 2018 International Conference on 3D Vision (3DV), pp. 180–189. IEEE (2018)

26. Pomerleau, F., Colas, F., Siegwart, R., et al.: A review of point cloud registration algorithms for mobile robotics. Found. Trends® Robot. **4**(1), 1–104 (2015)

27. Risholm, P., Fedorov, A., Pursley, J., Tuncali, K., Cormack, R., Wells, W.M.: Probabilistic non-rigid registration of prostate images: modeling and quantifying uncertainty. In: 2011 IEEE International Symposium on Biomedical Imaging: From Nano to Macro, pp. 553–556. IEEE (2011)

28. Risholm, P., Pieper, S., Samset, E., Wells, W.M.: Summarizing and visualizing uncertainty in non-rigid registration. In: Jiang, T., Navab, N., Pluim, J.P.W., Viergever, M.A. (eds.) MICCAI 2010. LNCS, vol. 6362, pp. 554–561. Springer, Heidelberg (2010). https://doi.org/10.1007/978-3-642-15745-5_68

29. Robert, C., Casella, G.: Monte Carlo Statistical Methods. Springer, Heidelberg (2013)

30. Schönborn, S., Egger, B., Morel-Forster, A., Vetter, T.: Markov chain Monte Carlo for automated face image analysis. Int. J. Comput. Vis. **123**(2), 160–183 (2017). https://doi.org/10.1007/s11263-016-0967-5

31. Styner, M.A., et al.: Evaluation of 3D correspondence methods for model building. In: Taylor, C., Noble, J.A. (eds.) IPMI 2003. LNCS, vol. 2732, pp. 63–75. Springer, Heidelberg (2003). https://doi.org/10.1007/978-3-540-45087-0_6

Interactive Video Object Segmentation Using Global and Local Transfer Modules

Yuk Heo[1], Yeong Jun Koh[2]([✉]), and Chang-Su Kim[1]

[1] School of Electrical Engineering, Korea University, Seoul, Korea
yukheo@mcl.korea.ac.kr, changsukim@korea.ac.kr
[2] Department of Computer Science and Engineering,
Chungnam National University, Daejeon, Korea
yjkoh@cnu.ac.kr

Abstract. An interactive video object segmentation algorithm, which takes scribble annotations on query objects as input, is proposed in this paper. We develop a deep neural network, which consists of the annotation network (A-Net) and the transfer network (T-Net). First, given user scribbles on a frame, A-Net yields a segmentation result based on the encoder-decoder architecture. Second, T-Net transfers the segmentation result bidirectionally to the other frames, by employing the global and local transfer modules. The global transfer module conveys the segmentation information in an annotated frame to a target frame, while the local transfer module propagates the segmentation information in a temporally adjacent frame to the target frame. By applying A-Net and T-Net alternately, a user can obtain desired segmentation results with minimal efforts. We train the entire network in two stages, by emulating user scribbles and employing an auxiliary loss. Experimental results demonstrate that the proposed interactive video object segmentation algorithm outperforms the state-of-the-art conventional algorithms. Codes and models are available at https://github.com/yuk6heo/IVOS-ATNet.

Keywords: Video object segmentation · Interactive segmentation · Deep learning

1 Introduction

Video object segmentation (VOS) aims at separating objects of interest from the background in a video sequence. It is an essential technique to facilitate many vision tasks, including action recognition, video retrieval, video summarization, and video editing. Many researches have been carried out to perform VOS, and it can be categorized according to the level of automation. Unsupervised VOS segments out objects with no user annotations, but it may fail to detect objects

Electronic supplementary material The online version of this chapter (https://doi.org/10.1007/978-3-030-58520-4_18) contains supplementary material, which is available to authorized users.

(a) Unsupervised   (b) Semi-supervised   (c) Interactive

Fig. 1. Three different levels of supervision in (a) unsupervised VOS, (b) semi-supervised VOS, and (c) interactive VOS. Unsupervised VOS demands no user interaction. Semi-supervised VOS needs pixel-level annotations of an object. Interactive VOS uses quick scribbles and allows interactions with a user repeatedly.

of interest or separate multiple objects. Semi-supervised VOS extracts target objects, which are manually annotated by a user in the first frame or only a few frames in a video sequence. However, semi-supervised approaches require time-consuming pixel-level annotations (at least 79 s per instance as revealed in [5]) to delineate objects of interest.

Therefore, as an alternative approach, we consider interactive VOS, which allows users to interact with segmentation results repeatedly using simple annotations, *e.g.* scribbles, point clicks, or bounding boxes. In this regard, the objective of interactive VOS is to provide reliable segmentation results with minimal user efforts. A work-flow to achieve this objective was presented in the 2018 DAVIS Challenge [5]. This work-flow employs scribble annotations as supervision, since it takes only about 3 s to draw a scribble on an object instance. In this scenario, a user provides scribbles on query objects in a selected frame and the VOS algorithm yields segment tracks for the objects in all frames. We refer to this turn of user-algorithm interaction as a segmentation round. Then, we repeat segmentation rounds to refine the segmentation results until satisfactory results are obtained as illustrated in Fig. 1(c).

In this paper, we propose a novel approach to achieve interactive VOS using scribble annotations with the work-flow in [5]. First, we develop the annotation network (A-Net), which produces a segmentation mask for an annotated frame using scribble annotations for query objects. Next, we propose the transfer network (T-Net) to transfer the segmentation result to other target frames subsequently to obtain segment tracks for the query objects. We design the global transfer module and the local transfer module in T-Net to convey segmentation information reliably and accurately. We train A-Net and T-Net in two stages by mimicking scribbles and employing an auxiliary loss. Experimental results verify that the proposed algorithm outperforms the state-of-the-art interactive VOS algorithms on the DAVIS2017 [35]. Also, we perform a user study to demonstrate the effectiveness of the proposed algorithm in real-world applications.

This paper has three main contributions:

1. Architecture of A-Net and T-Net with the global and local transfer modules.
2. Training strategy with the scribble imitation and the auxiliary loss to activate the local transfer module and make it effective in T-Net.
3. Remarkable performance on the DAVIS dataset in various conditions.

2   Related Work

Unsupervised VOS: Unsupervised VOS is a task to segment out primary objects [22] in a video without any manual annotations. Before the advance of deep learning, diverse information, including motion, object proposals, and saliency, was employed to solve this problem [21,23,24,32,47]. Recently, many deep learning algorithms with different network architectures have been developed to improve VOS performance using big datasets [35,53]. Tokmakov et al. [43] presented a fully convolutional model to learn motion patterns from videos. Jain et al. [17] merged appearance and motion information to perform unsupervised segmentation. Song et al. [41] proposed an algorithm using LSTM architecture [11] with atrous convolution layers [6]. Wang et al. [48] also adopted LSTM with a visual attention module to simulate human attention.

Semi-supervised VOS: Semi-supervised VOS extracts query objects using accurately annotated masks at the first frames. Early methods for semi-supervised VOS were developed using hand-crafted features based on random walkers, trajectories, or super-pixels [3,16,18]. Recently, deep neural networks have been adopted for semi-supervised VOS. Some deep learning techniques [4,26,45] are based on a time-consuming online learning, which fine-tunes a pre-trained network using query object masks at the first frame. Without the fine-tuning, the algorithms in [9,19,29,33,54] propagate segmentation masks, which are estimated in the previous frame, to the current target frame sequentially for segmenting out query objects. Jang et al. [19] warped segmentation masks in the previous frame to the target frame and refined the warped masks through convolution trident networks. Yang et al. [54] encoded object location information from a previous frame and combined it with visual appearance features to segment out the query object in the target frame. Also, the algorithms in [8,15,31,44] perform matching between the first frame and a target frame in an embedding space to localize query objects. Chen et al. [8] dichotomized each pixel into either object or background using features from the embedding network. Voigtlaender et al. [44] trained their embedding network to perform the global and local matching.

Interactive Image Segmentation: Interactive image segmentation aims at extracting a target object from the background using user annotations. As annotations, bounding boxes were widely adopted in early methods [25,38,42,50]. Recently, point-interfaced techniques have been developed [20,27,40,52]. Maninis et al. [27] used four extreme points as annotations to inform their network

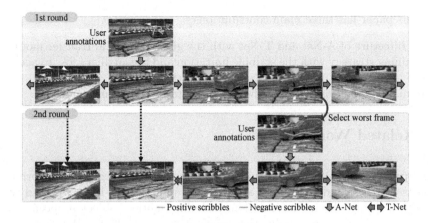

Fig. 2. Overview of the proposed interactive VOS algorithm.

about object boundaries. Jang and Kim [20] corrected mislabeled pixels through the backpropagating refinement scheme.

Interactive VOS: Interactive VOS allows users to interact with segmentation results repeatedly using various input types, *e.g.* points, scribbles, and bounding boxes. Users can refine segmentation results until they are satisfied. Some interactive VOS algorithms [36,39,46] build graph models using the information in user strokes and segment out target objects via optimization. In [1,10], patch matching between target and reference frames is performed to localize query objects. Box interactions can be provided to correct box positions. Benard and Gygli [2] employed two deep learning networks to achieve interactive VOS. They first obtained object masks from point clicks or scribbles using an interactive image segmentation network and then segmented out the objects using a semi-supervised VOS network. Chen *et al.* [8] demanded only a small number of point clicks based on pixel-wise metric learning. Oh *et al.* [30] achieved interactive VOS by following the work-flow in [5]. They used two segmentation networks to obtain segmentation masks from user scribbles and to propagate the segmentation masks to neighboring frames by exploiting regions of interest. However, their networks may fail to extract query objects outside the regions of interest.

3   Proposed Algorithm

We segment out one or more objects in a sequence of video frames through user interactions. To this end, we develop two networks: 1) annotation network (A-Net) and 2) transfer network (T-Net).

Figure 2 is an overview of the proposed algorithm. In the first segmentation round, a user provides annotations (*i.e.* scribbles) for a query object to A-Net, which then yields a segmentation mask for the annotated frame. Then, T-Net transfers the segmentation mask bi-directionally to both ends of the video to compose a segment track for the object. From the second round, the user selects

the poorest segmented frame, and then provides positive and negative scribbles so that A-Net corrects the result. Then, T-Net again propagates the refined segmentation mask to other frames until a previously annotated frame is met. This process is repeated until satisfactory results are obtained.

3.1 Network Architecture

Figure 3 shows the architecture of the proposed algorithm, which is composed of A-Net and T-Net. First, we segment out query objects in an annotated frame I_a via A-Net. Then, to achieve segmentation in a target frame I_t, we develop T-Net, which includes the global and local transfer modules.

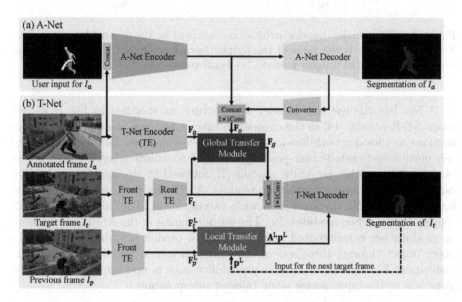

Fig. 3. Architecture of the proposed networks. A target object in an annotated frame I_a is extracted by A-Net in (a), and the result is sequentially propagated to the other frames, called target frames, by T-Net in (b). In this diagram, skip connections are omitted.

A-Net: Through user interactions, A-Net infers segmentation results in an annotated frame I_a. There are two types of interactions according to iteration rounds. In the first round, a user draws scribbles on target objects. In this case, A-Net accepts four-channel input: RGB channels of I_a and one scribble map. In subsequent rounds, the user supplies both positive and negative scribbles after examining the segmentation results in the previous rounds, as illustrated in Fig. 2. Hence, A-Net takes six channels: RGB channels, segmentation mask map in the previous round, and positive and negative scribble maps. We design A-Net to take 6-channel input, but in the first round, fill in the segmentation mask map with 0.5 and the negative scribble map with 0.

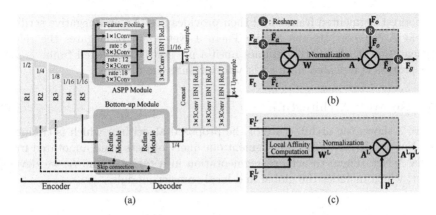

Fig. 4. (a) The encoder-decoder architecture, adopted by the proposed A-Net and T-Net. Each fraction is the ratio of the output feature resolution to the input image resolution. (b) Global transfer module. (c) Local transfer module.

A-Net has the encoder-decoder architecture, as specified in Fig. 4(a). We adopt SE-ResNet50 [14] as the encoder to extract features and employ skip connections to consider both low-level and high-level features. We perform dilated convolution and exclude max-pooling in the R5 convolution layer. Then, we use two parallel modules: an ASPP module [7], followed by up-sampling with bilinear interpolation, and a bottom-up module. ASPP analyzes multi-scale context features using dilated convolution with varying rates. The bottom-up module consists of two refine modules [29]. The output signals of the ASPP and bottom-up modules are concatenated and then used to predict a probability map of a query object through three sets of convolutional layers, ReLU, and batch normalization. Finally, the estimated probability map is up-sampled to be of the same size as the input image using bilinear interpolation.

T-Net: We develop T-Net, which consists of shared encoders, a global transfer module, a local transfer module, and a decoder, as shown in Fig. 3(b). The encoders and decoder in T-Net have the same structures as those of A-Net in Fig. 4(a). The T-Net decoder yields a probability map for query objects in a target frame I_t using the features from the encoder, the global transfer module, and the local transfer module. Let us describe these two transfer modules.

Global Transfer Module: We design the global transfer module to convey the segmentation information of the annotated frame I_a to the target frame I_t. Figure 4(b) shows its structure, which adopts the non-local model in [49]. It takes two feature volumes $\mathbf{F}_t$ and $\mathbf{F}_a$ for I_t and I_a, respectively. Each volume contains C-dimensional feature vectors for $H \times W$ pixels. We then construct an affinity matrix $\mathbf{W}$ between I_t and I_a, by computing the inner products between all possible pairs of feature vectors in $\mathbf{F}_t$ and $\mathbf{F}_a$. Specifically, let $\tilde{\mathbf{F}}_t \in \mathbb{R}^{HW \times C}$ and

$\tilde{\mathbf{F}}_a \in \mathbb{R}^{HW \times C}$ denote the feature volumes reshaped into matrices. We perform the matrix multiplication to obtain the affinity matrix

$$\mathbf{W} = \tilde{\mathbf{F}}_t \times \tilde{\mathbf{F}}_a^T. \tag{1}$$

Its element $\mathbf{W}(i,j)$ represents the affinity of the ith pixel in $\tilde{\mathbf{F}}_t$ to the jth pixel in $\tilde{\mathbf{F}}_a$. Then, we obtain the transition matrix $\mathbf{A}$ by applying the softmax normalization to each column in $\mathbf{W}$.

The transition matrix $\mathbf{A}$ contains matching probabilities from pixels in I_a to those in I_t. Therefore, it can transfer query object probabilities in I_a to I_t. To approximate these probabilities in I_a, we extract a mid-layer feature from the A-Net decoder, down-sample it using the converter, which includes two sets of SE-Resblock [14] and max-pooling layer. Then, its channels are halved by 1 × 1 convolutions after it is concatenated to the output of the A-Net encoder, as shown in Fig. 3. The concatenated feature $\mathbf{F}_o$ is fed into the global transfer module, as shown in Fig. 4(b). Then, it is reshaped into $\tilde{\mathbf{F}}_o$, which represents the query object feature distribution in I_a. Finally, the global transfer module produces the transferred distribution

$$\tilde{\mathbf{F}}_g = \mathbf{A}\tilde{\mathbf{F}}_o, \tag{2}$$

which can be regarded as an inter-image estimate of the query object feature distribution in I_t. Then the distribution is reshaped into $\mathbf{F}_g \in \mathbb{R}^{H \times W \times C}$ to be input to the T-Net decoder.

From the second round, there are N annotated frames, where N is the ordinal index for the round. To obtain reliable segmentation results, we use all information in the N annotated frames. Specifically, we compute the transition matrix $\mathbf{A}^{(i)}$ from the ith annotated frame to I_t and the query object distribution $\mathbf{F}_o^{(i)}$ in the ith annotated frame. Then, we obtain the average of the multiple inter-image estimates of the query object distribution in I_t by

$$\tilde{\mathbf{F}}_g = \frac{1}{N} \sum_{i=1}^{N} \mathbf{A}^{(i)} \tilde{\mathbf{F}}_o^{(i)}. \tag{3}$$

Local Transfer Module: The segmentation information in an annotated frame is propagated bidirectionally throughout the sequence. Thus, during the propagation, when a target frame I_t is to be segmented, there is the previous frame I_p that is already segmented. We design the local transfer module to convey the segmentation information in I_p to I_t.

The local transfer module is similar to the global one, but it performs matching locally since I_t and I_p are temporally adjacent. In other words, object motions between I_t and I_p, which tend to be smaller than those between I_t and I_a, are estimated locally. Furthermore, since I_t and I_p are more highly correlated, motions between them can be estimated more accurately. Therefore, the local module uses higher-resolution features than the global one does. Specifically, the local module takes features from the R2 convolution layer in the encoder

in Fig. 4(a), instead of the R5 layer. $\mathbf{F}_t^L$ and $\mathbf{F}_p^L$, which denote these feature volumes from I_t and I_p, are provided to the local transfer module, as shown in Fig. 4(c). Then, we compute the local affinity matrix $\mathbf{W}^L$, whose (i, j)th element indicates the similarity between the ith pixel I_t and the jth pixel in I_p. Specifically, $\mathbf{W}^L(i, j)$ is defined as

$$\mathbf{W}^L(i, j) = \begin{cases} \mathbf{f}_{t,i}^T \mathbf{f}_{p,j} & j \in \mathcal{N}_i, \\ 0 & \text{otherwise,} \end{cases} \qquad (4)$$

where $\mathbf{f}_{t,i}$ and $\mathbf{f}_{p,j}$ are the feature vectors for the ith pixel in $\mathbf{F}_t^L$ and the jth pixel in $\mathbf{F}_p^L$, respectively. Also, the local region $\mathcal{N}_i$ is the set of pixels, which are sampled from $(2d + 1) \times (2d + 1)$ pixels around pixel i with stride 2 to reduce the computations. In this work, d is set to 4. Then, the affinity is computed for those pixels in the local region only, and set to be zeros for the other pixels.

As in the global module, $\mathbf{W}^L$ is normalized column-by-column to the transition matrix $\mathbf{A}^L$. Also, a segmentation mask map $\mathbf{P}_p$ in the previous frame I_p is down-sampled and vectorized to obtain a probability vector $\mathbf{p}^L$. Then, we obtain $\mathbf{A}^L \mathbf{p}^L$, which is another estimate of the query object distribution in I_t. It has a higher resolution than the estimate in the global module, and thus is added to the corresponding mid-layer in the T-Net decoder, as shown in Fig. 3(b).

Computing global and local similarities in the proposed global and local transfer modules is conceptually similar to [44], but their usage is significantly different. Although [44] also computes global and local distances, it transforms those distances into a single channel by taking the minimum distance at each position. Thus, it loses a substantial amount of distance information. In contrast, the proposed algorithm computes global and local affinity matrices and uses them to transfer object probabilities from annotated and previous frames to a target frame. In Sect. 4.3, we verify that the proposed global and local modules are more effective than the best matching approach in [44].

3.2   Training Phase

We train the proposed interactive VOS networks in two stages, since T-Net should use A-Net output; we first train A-Net and then train T-Net using the trained A-Net.

A-Net Training: To train A-Net, we use the image segmentation dataset in [12] and the video segmentation datasets in [35,53]. Only a small percentage of videos in the DAVIS2017 dataset [35] provide user scribble data. Hence, we emulate user scribbles via two schemes: 1) point generation and 2) scribble generation in [5].

In the first round, A-Net yields a segmentation mask for a query object using positive scribbles only. We perform the point generation to imitate those positive scribbles. We produce a point map by sampling points from the ground-truth mask for the query object. Specifically, we pick one point randomly for every 100–3000 object pixels. We vary the sampling rate to reflect that users provide

scribbles with different densities. Then, we use the generated point map as the positive scribble map.

In each subsequent round, A-Net should refine the segmentation mask in the previous round using both positive and negative scribbles. To mimic an inaccurate segmentation mask, we deform the ground-truth mask using various affine transformations. Then, we extract positive and negative scribbles using the scribble generation scheme in [5], by comparing the deformed mask with the ground-truth. Then, I_a, the deformed mask, and the generated positive and negative scribble maps are fed into A-Net for training.

We adopt the pixel-wise class-balanced cross-entropy loss [51] between A-Net output and the ground-truth. We adopt the Adam optimizer to minimize this loss for 60 epochs with a learning rate of 1.0×10^{-5}. We decrease the learning rate by a factor of 0.2 every 20 epochs. In each epoch, the training is iterated for 7,000 mini-batches, each of which includes 6 pairs of image and ground-truth. For data augmentation, we apply random affine transforms to the pairs.

T-Net Training: For each video, we randomly pick one frame as an annotated frame, and then select seven consecutive frames, adjacent to the annotated frame, in either the forward or backward direction. Among those seven frames, we randomly choose four frames to form a mini-sequence. Thus, there are five frames in a mini-sequence: one annotated frame and four target frames. For each target frame in the mini-sequence, we train T-Net using the features from the trained A-Net, which takes the annotated frame as input.

We compare an estimated segmentation mask with the ground-truth to train T-Net, by employing the loss function

$$\mathcal{L} = \mathcal{L}_c + \lambda \mathcal{L}_{\text{aux}} \tag{5}$$

where $\mathcal{L}_c$ is the pixel-wise class-balanced cross-entropy loss between the T-Net output and the ground-truth. The auxiliary loss $\mathcal{L}_{\text{aux}}$ is the pixel-wise mean square loss between the transferred probability map, which is the output of the local transfer module, and the down-sampled ground-truth. The auxiliary loss $\mathcal{L}_{\text{aux}}$ enforces the front encoders of T-Net in Fig. 3 to generate appropriate features for transferring the previous segmentation mask successfully. Also, λ is a balancing hyper-parameter, which is set to 0.1. We also employ the Adam optimizer to minimize the loss function for 40 epochs with a learning rate of 1.0×10^{-5}, which is decreased by a factor of 0.2 every 20 epochs. The training is iterated 6,000 mini-batches, each of which contains 8 mini-sequences.

3.3   Inference Phase

Suppose that there are multiple target objects. In the first round, for each target object in an annotated frame, A-Net accepts the user scribbles on the object and produces a probability map for the object. To obtain multiple object segmentation results, after zeroing probabilities lower than 0.8, each pixel is assigned to the

target object class, corresponding to the highest probability. Then, T-Net transfers the multiple segmentation masks in the annotated frame bi-directionally to both ends of the sequence. T-Net also compares the multiple probability maps and determines the target object class of each pixel, as done in A-Net. From the second round, the user selects the frame with the poorest segmentation results and then provides additional positive and negative scribbles. The scribbles are then fed into A-Net to refine the segmentation results. Then, we transfer segmentation results bidirectionally with T-Net. In each direction, the transmission is carried out until another annotated frame is found.

During the transfer, we superpose the result of segmentation mask $\mathbf{P}_t^r$ for frame I_t in the current round r with that $\mathbf{P}_t^{r-1}$ in the previous round. Specifically, the updated result $\tilde{\mathbf{P}}_t^r$ in round r is given by

$$\tilde{\mathbf{P}}_t^r = \frac{1}{2}(1 + \frac{t - t_b}{t_r - t_b})\mathbf{P}_t^r + \frac{t_r - t}{2(t_r - t_b)}\mathbf{P}_t^{r-1} \tag{6}$$

where t_r is the annotated frame in round r and t_b is one of the previously annotated frames, which is the closest to t in the direction of the transfer. By employing this superposition scheme, we can reduce drifts due to a long temporal distance between annotated and target frames.

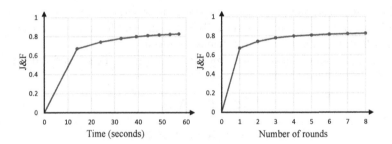

Fig. 5. J&F performances of the proposed algorithm on the validation set in DAVIS2017 according to the time and the number of rounds.

Table 1. Comparison of the proposed algorithm with the conventional algorithms on the DAVIS2017 validation set. The best results are boldfaced.

	AUC-J	J@60s	AUC-J& F	J& F@60s
Najafi et al. [28]	0.702	0.548	–	–
Heo et al. [13]	0.704	0.725	0.734	0.752
Ren et al. [37]	–	–	0.766	0.780
Oh et al. [30]	0.691	0.734	–	–
Proposed	**0.771**	**0.790**	**0.809**	**0.827**

4   Experimental Results

We first compare the proposed interactive VOS algorithm with conventional algorithms. Second, we conduct a user study to assess the proposed algorithm in real-world applications. Finally, we do various ablation studies to analyze the proposed algorithm.

4.1   Comparative Assessment

In this test, we follow the interactive VOS work-flow in [5]. The work-flow first provides a manually generated scribble for each target object in the first round, and then automatically generates additional positive and negative scribbles to refine the worst frames in up to 8 subsequent rounds. There are three different scribbles provided in the first round. In other words, three experiments are performed for each video sequence. The region similarity (J) and contour accuracy (F) metrics are employed to assess VOS algorithms. For the evaluation of interactive VOS, we measure the area under the curve for J score (AUC-J) and for joint J and F scores (AUC-J&F) to observe the overall performance according over the 8 segmentation rounds. Also, we measure the J score at 60 s (J@60s), and the joint J and F score at 60 s (J&F@60s) to evaluate how much performance is achieved within the restricted time.

Fig. 6. Results of the proposed interactive VOS algorithm after 8 rounds.

Figure 5 shows the J&F performances of the proposed algorithm on the validation set in DAVIS2017 [35] according to the time and the number of rounds. The performances increase quickly and saturate at around 40 s or in the third round. Also, we observe that the 8-round experiment is completed within 60 s. Table 1 compares the proposed algorithm with recent state-of-the-art algorithms [13,28,30,37]. The scores of the conventional algorithms are from the respective papers. The proposed algorithm outperforms the conventional

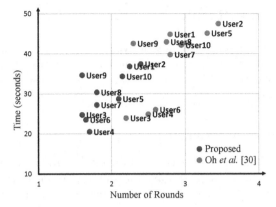

Fig. 7. Comparison of the average times and average round numbers.

Table 2. Summary of the user study results.

	SPV	RPV	J Mean	F Mean
Oh *et al.* [30]	37.9	2.77	0.823	0.817
Proposed	**29.8**	**1.90**	**0.832**	**0.822**

Fig. 8. Examples of scribbles and segmentation results during the user study. Positive and negative scribbles are depicted in green and red, respectively.

algorithms by significant margins in all metrics. Figure 6 presents examples of segmentation results of the proposed algorithm after 8 rounds. We see that multiple primary objects are segmented out faithfully.

4.2   User Study

We conduct a user study, by recruiting 10 off-line volunteers and asking them to provide scribbles repeatedly until they are satisfied. We measure the average time

in seconds per video (SPV), including the interaction time to provide scribbles and the running time of the algorithm, and the average round number in rounds per video (RPV) until the completion. Also, we report the J and F means of all sequences when the interactive process is completed.

We perform the user study for the proposed algorithm and the state-of-the-art interactive VOS algorithm [30]. For this comparison, we use the validation set (20 sequences) in DAVIS2016 [34], in which each video contains only a single query object. This is because the provided source code of [30] works on a single-object case only. Figure 7 plots the average time and the average round number for each user. We observe that all users, except user 3, spend less time and conduct fewer rounds using the proposed algorithm. Table 2 summarizes the user study results. The proposed algorithm is faster than [30] in terms of both SPV and RPV. It is worth pointing out that the proposed algorithm yields better segmentation results within shorter times.

Figure 8 shows examples of segmentation results in the user study. For the "Libby," "Horsejump-High," and "Parkour" sequences, the proposed algorithm deals with occlusions and scale changes of query objects effectively, and completes the segmentation in just a single round. Please see the supplemental video to see how the evaluation works.

Table 3. Ablation study on the local transfer module (J scores on the validation set in DAVIS2017).

Method	Front TE	Rear TE	λ	Round				
				1st	2nd	3rd	4th	5th
I	w/o local transfer module			0.629	0.704	0.741	0.759	0.771
II		✓	0.1	0.653	0.708	0.738	0.751	0.760
III	✓		0.0	0.645	0.706	0.735	0.750	0.761
IV	✓		0.5	0.658	0.721	0.748	0.758	0.772
V	✓		1.0	0.654	0.715	0.742	0.755	0.762
VI (Proposed)	✓		0.1	**0.676**	**0.732**	**0.762**	**0.772**	**0.783**

Table 4. Ablation study to validate the proposed probability transfer approach.

	AUC-J	J@60s	AUC-J& F	J& F@60s
Matching approach [44] (predictions of A-Net)	0.636	0.653	0.654	0.670
Matching approach [44] (scribble annotations)	0.661	0.676	0.674	0.690
Proposed probability transfer approach	**0.771**	**0.790**	**0.809**	**0.827**

4.3 Ablation Studies

We analyze the efficacy of the proposed global and local transfer modules through two ablation studies.

First, we verify that the structure and the training method of the local transfer module are effective. In Table 3, we report the J scores on the validation set in DAVIS2017, by varying the configurations of the local transfer module. In method I, we assess the proposed algorithm without the local transfer module. Note that the J scores in early rounds degrade severely. The local model is hence essential for providing satisfactory results to users quickly in only a few rounds. Method II uses the features of rear TE, instead of those of front TE to compute the affinity matrix of the local transfer module. The features of the front TE are more effective than those of rear TE because of their higher spatial resolution. In method III, without the auxiliary loss $\mathcal{L}_{\mathrm{aux}}$ (*i.e.* $\lambda = 0$ in (5)), the local transfer module becomes ineffective and the performances degrade significantly. Methods IV, V, and VI vary the parameter λ. We see that $\lambda = 0.1$ performs the best by balancing the two losses in (5).

Next, we verify that the proposed global and local transfer modules are more effective for interactive VOS than the global and local matching in [44]. Note that [44] is a semi-supervised VOS algorithm, which estimates matching maps between a target frame and the target object region. We plug its matching modules into the proposed interactive system. More specifically, we compute a global similarity map between a target frame and the target object region in an annotated frame to perform the global matching in [44]. We determine the target object region in two ways: 1) the region predicted by A-Net or 2) the set of scribble-annotated pixels. We then transform the similarity map into a single channel by taking the maximum similarity at each position. Then, we replace $\mathbf{F}_g$, which is the output of the proposed global transfer module, with the single-channel similarity. For the local matching, we obtain a local similarity map between the target frame and the segmentation region in the previous frame to compose another single-channel similarity. We then feed the local matching result, instead of $\mathbf{A}^L \mathbf{p}^L$, to the T-Net decoder. We train these modified networks using the same training set as the proposed networks. The implementation details of the modified networks can be found in the supplemental document. Table 4 compares the performances of the proposed transfer modules with those of the matching modules in [44] on the validation set in DAVIS2017. We observe that the proposed probability transfer approach outperforms the best matching approach [44] significantly.

5   Conclusions

We proposed a novel interactive VOS algorithm using A-Net and T-Net. Based on the encoder-decoder architecture, A-Net processes user scribbles on an annotated frame to generate a segmentation result. Then, using the global and local transfer modules, T-Net conveys the segmentation information to the other frames in the video sequence. These two modules are complementary to each

other. The global module transfers the information from an annotated frame to a target frame reliably, while the local module conveys the information between adjacent frames accurately. In the training process, we introduced the point-generation method to compensate for the lack of scribble-annotated data. Moreover, we incorporated the auxiliary loss to activate the local transfer module and make it effective in T-Net. By employing A-Net and T-Net repeatedly, a user can obtain satisfactory segmentation results. Experimental results showed that the proposed algorithm performs better than the state-of-the-art algorithms, while requiring fewer interaction rounds.

Acknowledgements. This work was supported in part by 'The Cross-Ministry Giga KOREA Project' grant funded by the Korea government (MSIT) (No. GK20P0200, Development of 4D reconstruction and dynamic deformable action model based hyper-realistic service technology), in part by Institute of Information & communications Technology Planning & evaluation (IITP) grant funded by the Korea government (MSIT) (No. 2020-0-01441, Artificial Intelligence Convergence Research Center (Chungnam National University)) and in part by the National Research Foundation of Korea (NRF) through the Korea Government (MSIP) under Grant NRF-2018R1A2B3003896.

References

1. Bai, X., Wang, J., Simons, D., Sapiro, G.: Video SnapCut: robust video object cutout using localized classifiers. ACM Trans. Graph. **28**(3), 70 (2009)
2. Benard, A., Gygli, M.: Interactive video object segmentation in the wild. arXiv:1801.00269 (2017)
3. Brox, T., Malik, J.: Object segmentation by long term analysis of point trajectories. In: Daniilidis, K., Maragos, P., Paragios, N. (eds.) ECCV 2010. LNCS, vol. 6315, pp. 282–295. Springer, Heidelberg (2010). https://doi.org/10.1007/978-3-642-15555-0_21
4. Caelles, S., Maninis, K.K., Pont-Tuset, J., Leal-Taixé, L., Cremers, D., Van Gool, L.: One-shot video object segmentation. In: CVPR (2017)
5. Caelles, S., et al.: The 2018 DAVIS challenge on video object segmentation. arXiv:1803.00557 (2018)
6. Chen, L.C., Papandreou, G., Kokkinos, I., Murphy, K., Yuille, A.L.: Semantic image segmentation with deep convolutional nets and fully connected CRFs. arXiv:1412.7062 (2014)
7. Chen, L.-C., Zhu, Y., Papandreou, G., Schroff, F., Adam, H.: Encoder-decoder with atrous separable convolution for semantic image segmentation. In: Ferrari, V., Hebert, M., Sminchisescu, C., Weiss, Y. (eds.) ECCV 2018. LNCS, vol. 11211, pp. 833–851. Springer, Cham (2018). https://doi.org/10.1007/978-3-030-01234-2_49
8. Chen, Y., Pont-Tuset, J., Montes, A., Van Gool, L.: Blazingly fast video object segmentation with pixel-wise metric learning. In: CVPR (2018)
9. Cheng, J., Tsai, Y.H., Wang, S., Yang, M.H.: SegFlow: joint learning for video object segmentation and optical flow. In: ICCV (2017)
10. Fan, Q., Zhong, F., Lischinski, D., Cohen-Or, D., Chen, B.: JumpCut: non-successive mask transfer and interpolation for video cutout. ACM Trans. Graph. **34**(6), 195:1–195:10 (2015)

11. Gers, F.A., Schmidhuber, J., Cummins, F.: Learning to forget: continual prediction with LSTM. Neural Comput. **12**(10), 2451–2471 (1999)
12. Hariharan, B., Arbelaez, P., Bourdev, L., Maji, S., Malik, J.: Semantic contours from inverse detectors. In: ICCV (2011)
13. Heo, Y., Koh, Y.J., Kim, C.S.: Interactive video object segmentation using sparse-to-dense networks. In: CVPRW (2019)
14. Hu, J., Shen, L., Sun, G.: Squeeze-and-excitation networks. In: CVPR (2018)
15. Hu, Y.-T., Huang, J.-B., Schwing, A.G.: VideoMatch: matching based video object segmentation. In: Ferrari, V., Hebert, M., Sminchisescu, C., Weiss, Y. (eds.) ECCV 2018. LNCS, vol. 11212, pp. 56–73. Springer, Cham (2018). https://doi.org/10.1007/978-3-030-01237-3_4
16. Jain, S.D., Grauman, K.: Supervoxel-consistent foreground propagation in video. In: Fleet, D., Pajdla, T., Schiele, B., Tuytelaars, T. (eds.) ECCV 2014. LNCS, vol. 8692, pp. 656–671. Springer, Cham (2014). https://doi.org/10.1007/978-3-319-10593-2_43
17. Jain, S.D., Xiong, B., Grauman, K.: FusionSeg: learning to combine motion and appearance for fully automatic segmentation of generic objects in videos. In: CVPR (2017)
18. Jang, W.D., Kim, C.S.: Semi-supervised video object segmentation using multiple random walkers. In: BMVC (2016)
19. Jang, W.D., Kim, C.S.: Online video object segmentation via convolutional trident network. In: CVPR (2017)
20. Jang, W.D., Kim, C.S.: Interactive image segmentation via backpropagating refinement scheme. In: CVPR (2019)
21. Jang, W.D., Lee, C., Kim, C.S.: Primary object segmentation in videos via alternate convex optimization of foreground and background distributions. In: CVPR (2016)
22. Koh, Y.J., Jang, W.D., Kim, C.S.: POD: Discovering primary objects in videos based on evolutionary refinement of object recurrence, background, and primary object models. In: CVPR (2016)
23. Koh, Y.J., Kim, C.S.: Primary object segmentation in videos based on region augmentation and reduction. In: CVPR (2017)
24. Koh, Y.J., Lee, Y.-Y., Kim, C.-S.: Sequential clique optimization for video object segmentation. In: Ferrari, V., Hebert, M., Sminchisescu, C., Weiss, Y. (eds.) Computer Vision – ECCV 2018. LNCS, vol. 11218, pp. 537–556. Springer, Cham (2018). https://doi.org/10.1007/978-3-030-01264-9_32
25. Lempitsky, V.S., Kohli, P., Rother, C., Sharp, T.: Image segmentation with a bounding box prior. In: ICCV (2009)
26. Maninis, K.K., et al.: Video object segmentation without temporal information. IEEE Trans. Pattern Anal. Mach. Intell. **41**(6), 1515–1530 (2018)
27. Maninis, K.K., Caelles, S., Pont-Tuset, J., Van Gool, L.: Deep extreme cut: from extreme points to object segmentation. In: CVPR (2018)
28. Najafi, M., Kulharia, V., Ajanthan, T., Torr, P.: Similarity learning for dense label transfer. In: CVPRW (2018)
29. Oh, S.W., Lee, J.Y., Sunkavalli, K., Kim, S.J.: Fast video object segmentation by reference-guided mask propagation. In: CVPR (2018)
30. Oh, S.W., Lee, J.Y., Xu, N., Kim, S.J.: Fast user-guided video object segmentation by interaction-and-propagation networks. In: CVPR (2019)
31. Oh, S.W., Lee, J.Y., Xu, N., Kim, S.J.: Video object segmentation using space-time memory networks. In: ICCV (2019)

32. Papazoglou, A., Ferrari, V.: Fast object segmentation in unconstrained video. In: ICCV (2013)
33. Perazzi, F., Khoreva, A., Benenson, R., Schiele, B., Sorkine-Hornung, A.: Learning video object segmentation from static images. In: CVPR (2017)
34. Perazzi, F., Pont-Tuset, J., McWilliams, B., Van Gool, L., Gross, M., Sorkine-Hornung, A.: A benchmark dataset and evaluation methodology for video object segmentation. In: CVPR (2016)
35. Pont-Tuset, J., Perazzi, F., Caelles, S., Arbeláez, P., Sorkine-Hornung, A., Van Gool, L.: The 2017 DAVIS challenge on video object segmentation. arXiv:1704.00675 (2017)
36. Price, B.L., Morse, B.S., Cohen, S.: LIVEcut: learning-based interactive video segmentation by evaluation of multiple propagated cues. In: ICCV (2009)
37. Ren, H., Yang, Y., Liu, X.: Robust multiple object mask propagation with efficient object tracking. In: CVPRW (2019)
38. Rother, C., Kolmogorov, V., Blake, A.: GrabCut: interactive foreground extraction using iterated graph cuts. ACM Trans. Graph. **23**(3), 309–314 (2004)
39. Shankar Nagaraja, N., Schmidt, F.R., Brox, T.: Video segmentation with just a few strokes. In: ICCV (2015)
40. Song, G., Myeong, H., Lee, K.M.: SeedNet: automatic seed generation with deep reinforcement learning for robust interactive segmentation. In: CVPR (2018)
41. Song, H., Wang, W., Zhao, S., Shen, J., Lam, K.-M.: Pyramid dilated deeper ConvLSTM for video salient object detection. In: Ferrari, V., Hebert, M., Sminchisescu, C., Weiss, Y. (eds.) ECCV 2018. LNCS, vol. 11215, pp. 744–760. Springer, Cham (2018). https://doi.org/10.1007/978-3-030-01252-6_44
42. Tang, M., Gorelick, L., Veksler, O., Boykov, Y.: GrabCut in one cut. In: ICCV (2013)
43. Tokmakov, P., Alahari, K., Schmid, C.: Learning motion patterns in videos. In: CVPR (2017)
44. Voigtlaender, P., Chai, Y., Schroff, F., Adam, H., Leibe, B., Chen, L.C.: FEELVOS: fast end-to-end embedding learning for video object segmentation. In: CVPR (2019)
45. Voigtlaender, P., Leibe, B.: Online adaptation of convolutional neural networks for video object segmentation. In: BMVC (2017)
46. Wang, J., Bhat, P., Colburn, R.A., Agrawala, M., Cohen, M.F.: Interactive video cutout. ACM Trans. Graph. **24**(3), 585–594 (2005)
47. Wang, W., Shen, J., Porikli, F.: Saliency-aware geodesic video object segmentation. In: CVPR (2015)
48. Wang, W., et al.: Learning unsupervised video object segmentation through visual attention. In: CVPR (2019)
49. Wang, X., Girshick, R., Gupta, A., He, K.: Non-local neural networks. In: CVPR (2018)
50. Wu, J., Zhao, Y., Zhu, J.Y., Luo, S., Tu, Z.: MILCut: a sweeping line multiple instance learning paradigm for interactive image segmentation. In: CVPR (2014)
51. Xie, S., Tu, Z.: Holistically-nested edge detection. In: ICCV (2015)
52. Xu, N., Price, B., Cohen, S., Yang, J., Huang, T.S.: Deep interactive object selection. In: CVPR (2016)
53. Xu, N., et al.: YouTube-VOS: a large-scale video object segmentation benchmark. arXiv:1809.03327 (2018)
54. Yang, L., Wang, Y., Xiong, X., Yang, J., Katsaggelos, A.K.: Efficient video object segmentation via network modulation. In: CVPR (2018)

End-to-end Interpretable Learning
of Non-blind Image Deblurring

Thomas Eboli[1]([✉]), Jian Sun[2], and Jean Ponce[1]

[1] Inria, Département d'informatique de l'ENS, ENS, CNRS, PSL University,
Paris, France
{thomas.eboli,jean.ponce}@inria.fr
[2] Xi'an Jiaotong University, Xi'an, China
jiansun@xjtu.edu.cn
https://github.com/teboli/CPCR

Abstract. Non-blind image deblurring is typically formulated as a linear least-squares problem regularized by natural priors on the corresponding sharp picture's gradients, which can be solved, for example, using a half-quadratic splitting method with Richardson fixed-point iterations for its least-squares updates and a proximal operator for the auxiliary variable updates. We propose to precondition the Richardson solver using approximate inverse filters of the (known) blur and natural image prior kernels. Using convolutions instead of a generic linear preconditioner allows extremely efficient parameter sharing across the image, and leads to significant gains in accuracy and/or speed compared to classical FFT and conjugate-gradient methods. More importantly, the proposed architecture is easily adapted to learning both the preconditioner and the proximal operator using CNN embeddings. This yields a simple and efficient algorithm for non-blind image deblurring which is fully interpretable, can be learned end to end, and whose accuracy matches or exceeds the state of the art, quite significantly, in the non-uniform case.

Keywords: Non-blind deblurring · Preconditioned fixed-point method · End-to-end learning

1 Introduction

This presentation addresses the problem of non-blind image deblurring–that is, the recovery of a sharp image given its blurry version and the corresponding uniform or non-uniform motion blur kernel. Applications range from photography [17] to astronomy [34] and microscopy [15]. Classical approaches to this problem include least-squares and Bayesian models, leading to Wiener [40] and Lucy-Richardson [28] deconvolution techniques for example. Since many sharp

Electronic supplementary material The online version of this chapter (https://doi.org/10.1007/978-3-030-58520-4_19) contains supplementary material, which is available to authorized users.

images can lead to the same blurry one, blur removal is an ill-posed problem. To tackle this issue, variational methods [30] inject *a priori* knowledge over the set of solutions using penalized least-squares. Geman and Yang [12] introduce an auxiliary variable to solve this problem by iteratively evaluating a proximal operator [27] and solving a least-squares problem. The rest of this presentation builds on this *half-quadratic splitting* approach. Its proximal part has received a lot of attention through the design of complex model-based [21,36,43,46] or learning-based priors [29]. Far less attention had been paid to the solution of the companion least-squares problem, typically relying on techniques such as conjugate gradient (CG) descent [2] or fast Fourier transform (FFT) [16,42]. CG is relatively slow in this context, and it does not exploit the fact that the linear operator corresponds to a convolution. FFT exploits this property but is only truly valid under periodic conditions at the boundaries, which are never respected by real images.

We propose instead to use Richardson fixed-point iterations [18] to solve the least-squares problem, using approximate inverse filters of the (known) blur and natural image prior kernels as preconditioners. Using convolutions instead of a traditional linear preconditioner allows efficient parameter sharing across the image, which leads to significant gains in accuracy and/or speed over FFT and conjugate-gradient methods. To further improve performance and leverage recent progress in deep learning, several recent approaches to denoising and deblurring unroll a finite number of proximal updates and least-squares minimization steps [1,6,20,22,31]. Compared to traditional convolutional neural networks (CNNs), these algorithms use interpretable components and produce intermediate feature maps that can be directly supervised during training [22,31].

We propose a solver for non-blind deblurring, also based on the splitting scheme of [12] but, in addition to learning the proximal operator as in [44], we also learn parameters in the fixed-point algorithm by embedding the preconditioner into a CNN whose bottom layer's kernels are the approximate filters discussed above. Unlike the algorithm of [44], our algorithm is trainable end to end, and achieves accuracy that matches or exceeds the state of the art. Furthermore, in contrast to other state-of-the-art CNN-based methods [22,44] relying on FFT, it operates in the pixel domain and thus easily extends to non-uniform blurs scenarios.

1.1 Related Work

Uniform Image Deblurring. Classical priors for natural images minimize the magnitude of gradients using the ℓ_2 [30], ℓ_1 [23] and hyper-Laplacian [21] (semi) norms or parametric potentials [36]. Instead of restoring the whole image at once, some works focus on patches by learning their probability distribution [46] or exploiting local properties in blurry images [25]. Handcrafted priors are designed so that the optimization is feasible and easy to carry out but they may ignore the characteristics of the images available. Data-driven priors, on the

other hand, can be learned from a training dataset (*e.g.*, new regularizers). Roth and Black [29] introduce a learnable total variation (TV) prior whose parameters are potential/filter pairs. This idea has been extended in shallow neural networks in [31,32] based on the splitting scheme of [12]. Deeper models based on Roth and Black's learnable prior had been proposed ever since [6,20,22]. The proximal operator can also be replaced by a CNN-based denoiser [24,45] or a CNN specifically trained to mimic a proximal operator [44] or the gradient of the regularized [13]. More generally, CNNs are now used in various image restoration tasks, including non-blind deblurring by refining a low-rank decomposition of a deconvolution filter kernel [41], using a FFT-based solver [33], or to improve the accuracy of splitting techniques [1].

Non-Uniform Image Deblurring. Non-uniform deblurring is more challenging than its uniform counterpart [5,7]. Hirsch et al. [16] consider large overlapping patches and suppose uniform motion on their supports before removing the local blur with an FFT-based uniform deconvolution method. Other works consider pixelwise locally linear motions [3,8,19,35] as simple elements representing complex global motions and solve penalized least-squares problems to restore the image. Finally, geometric non-uniform blur can be used in the case of camera shake to predict motion paths [38,39].

1.2   Main Contributions

Our contributions can be summarized as follows.

- We introduce a convolutional preconditioner for fixed-point iterations that efficiently solves the least-squares problem arising in splitting algorithms to minimize penalized energies. It is faster and/or more accurate than FFT and CG for this task, with theoretical convergence guarantees.
- We propose a new end-to-end trainable algorithm that implements a finite number of stages of half-quadratic splitting [12] and is fully interpretable. It alternates between proximal updates and preconditioned fixed-point iterations. The proximal operator and linear preconditioner are parameterized by CNNs in order to learn these functions from a training set of clean and blurry images.
- We evaluate our approach on several benchmarks with both uniform and non-uniform blur kernels. We demonstrate its robustness to significant levels of noise, and obtain results that are competitive with the state of the art for uniform blur and significantly outperforms it in the non-uniform case.

2   Proposed Method

Let y and k respectively denote a blurry image and a known blur kernel. The *deconvolution* (or *non-blind deblurring*) problem can be formulated as

$$\min_x \frac{1}{2}||y - k \star x||_F^2 + \lambda\Omega(\sum_{i=1}^n k_i \star x), \tag{1}$$

where "$\star$" is the convolution operator, and x is the (unknown) sharp image. The filters k_i $(i = 1, \ldots, n)$ are typically partial derivative operators, and Ω acts as a regularizer on x, enforcing natural image priors. One often takes $\Omega(z) = ||z||_1$ (TV-ℓ_1 model). We propose in this section an end-to-end learnable variant of the method of *half-quadratic splitting* (or *HQS*) [12] to solve Eq. (1). As shown later, a key to the effectiveness of our algorithm is that all linear operations are explicitly represented by convolutions.

Let us first introduce notations that will simplify the presentation. Given some linear filters a_i and b_i $(i = 0, \ldots, n)$ with finite support (square matrices), we borrow the Matlab notation for "stacked" linear operators, and denote by $A = [a_0, \ldots, a_n]$ and $B = [b_0; \ldots; b_n]$ the (convolution) operators respectively obtained by stacking "horizontally" and "vertically" these filters, whose responses are

$$A \star x = [a_0 \star x, \ldots, a_n \star x]; \ B \star x = [(b_0 \star x)^\top, \ldots, (b_n \star x)^\top]^\top; \quad (2)$$

We also define $A \star B = \sum_{i=0}^n a_i \star b_i$ and easily verify that $(A \star B) \star x = A \star (B \star x)$.

2.1 A Convolutional HQS Algorithm

Equation (1) can be rewritten as

$$\min_{x,z} \frac{1}{2} ||y - k \star x||_F^2 + \lambda \Omega(z) \text{ such that } z = F \star x, \quad (3)$$

where $F = [k_1; \ldots; k_n]$. Let us define the energy function

$$E(x, z, \mu) = \frac{1}{2} ||y - k \star x||_F^2 + \lambda \Omega(z) + \frac{\mu}{2} ||z - F \star x||_F^2. \quad (4)$$

Given some initial guess x for the sharp image, (*e.g.* $x = y$) we can now solve our original problem using the *HQS* method [12] with T iterations of the form

$$\begin{aligned} z &\leftarrow \operatorname{argmin}_z E(x, z, \mu); \\ x &\leftarrow \operatorname{argmin}_x E(x, z, \mu); \\ \mu &\leftarrow \mu + \delta t. \end{aligned} \quad (5)$$

The μ update can vary with iterations but must be positive. We could also use the alternating direction method of multipliers (or *ADMM* [27]), for example, but this is left to future work. Note that the update in z has the form

$$z \leftarrow \operatorname{argmin}_z \frac{\mu}{2} ||z - F \star x||_F^2 + \lambda \Omega(z) = \varphi_{\lambda/\mu}(F \star x), \quad (6)$$

where $\varphi_{\lambda/\mu}$ is, by definition, the *proximal operator* [27] associated with Ω (a soft-thresholding function in the case of the ℓ_1 norm [9]) given λ and μ.

The update in x can be written as the solution of a linear least-squares problem:

$$x \leftarrow \operatorname{argmin}_x \frac{1}{2} ||u - L \star x||_F^2, \quad (7)$$

where $u = [y; \sqrt{\mu} z]$ and $L = [k; \sqrt{\mu} F]$.

2.2   Convolutional PCR Iterations

Many methods are of course available for solving Eq. (7). We propose to compute x as the solution of $C \star (u - L \star x) = 0$, where $C = [c_0, \ldots, c_n]$ is composed of $n + 1$ filters and is used in *preconditioned Richardson* (or *PCR*) fixed-point iterations [18].

Briefly, in the generic linear case, PCR is an iterative method for solving a square, nonsingular system of linear equations $Ax = b$. Given some initial estimate $x = x_0$ of the unknown x, it repeatedly applies the iterations

$$x \leftarrow x - C(Ax - b), \qquad (8)$$

where C is a preconditioning square matrix. When C is an *approximate inverse* of A, that is, when the spectral radius η of $\mathrm{Id} - CA$ is smaller than one, preconditioned Richardson iterations converge to the solution of $Ax = b$ with a linear rate proportional to η [18]. When A is an $m \times n$ matrix with $m \geq n$, and x and b are respectively elements of $\mathbb{R}^n$ and $\mathbb{R}^m$, PCR can also be used in Cimmino's algorithm for linear least-squares, where the solution of $\min_x \|Ax - b\|^2$ is found using $C = \rho A^\top$, with $\rho > 0$ sufficiently small, as the solution of $A^\top Ax - A^\top b = 0$, with similar guarantees. Finally, it is also possible to use a different $n \times m$ matrix. When the spectral radius η of the $n \times n$ matrix $\mathrm{Id} - CA$ is smaller than one, the PCR iterations converge once again at a linear rate proportional to η. However, they converge to the (unique in general) solution of $C(Ax - b) = 0$, which may of course be different from the least-squares solution.

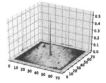

Fig. 1. From left ot right: An example of a blur kernel k from the Levin *et al.* dataset [23]; its approximate inverse kernel c_0; the resulting filter resulting from the convolution of k and c_0 (represented as a surface). It gives an approximate Dirac filter δ.

This method is easily adapted to our context. Since L corresponds to a bank of filters of size $w_k \times w_k$, it is natural to take $C = [c_0, \ldots, c_n]$ to be another bank of $n + 1$ linear filters of size $w_c \times w_c$. Unlike a generic linear preconditioner satisfying $CA \approx \mathrm{Id}$ in matrix form, whose size depends on the square of the image size, C exploits the structure of L and is a linear operator with *much* fewer parameters, *i.e.* $n + 1$ times the size of the c_i's. Thus, C is an approximate inverse filter bank for L, in the sense that

$$\delta \approx L \star C = C \star L = c_0 \star k + \sqrt{\mu} \sum_{i=1}^n c_i \star k_i, \qquad (9)$$

where δ is the Dirac filter. In this setting, C is computed as the solution of

$$C = \operatorname{argmin}_C ||\delta - L \star C||_F^2 + \rho \sum_{i=0}^n ||c_i||_F^2, \qquad (10)$$

The classical solution using the pseudo inverse of L has cost $\mathcal{O}\left((w_k + w_c - 1)^{2 \times 3}\right)$.

$$c_i = \mathcal{F}^{-1}\left(\frac{\tilde{K}_i^*}{\rho J + \sum_{j=0}^n |\tilde{K}_j|^2}\right) \quad \text{for } i = 0 \text{ to } n, \qquad (11)$$

using the fast Fourier transform (FFT) with cost $\mathcal{O}(w_c^2 \log(w_c))$ [11]. $\mathcal{F}^{-1}$ is the inverse Fourier transform, J is a matrix full of ones, $\tilde{K}_i$ is the Fourier transform of k_i (with $k_0 = k$), $\tilde{K}_i^*$ is its complex conjugate and the division in the Fourier domain is entrywise. Note that the use of FFT in this context has nothing to do with its use as a deconvolution tool for solving Eq. (7). Figure 1 shows an example of a blur kernel from [23], its approximate inverse when $n = 0$ and the result of their convolution. Let us define $[A]_\star$ as the linear operator such that $[A]_\star B = A \star B$. Indeed, a *true* inverse filter bank such that equality holds in Eq. (9) does not exist in general (*e.g.*, a Gaussian filter cannot be inverted), but all that matters is that the linear operator associated with $\delta - C \star L$ has a spectral radius smaller than one [18]. We have the following result.

Lemma 1. *The spectral radius of the linear operator* $Id - [L]_\star [C]_\star$, *where C is the optimal solution of* (10) *given by* (11) *is always smaller than 1 when* $[L]_\star$ *has full rank.*

A detailed proof can be found in the supplemental material. We now have our basic non-blind deblurring algorithm, in the form of the Matlab-style CHQS (for *convolutional HQS*, primary) and CPCR (for *convolutional PCR*, auxiliary) functions below.

```
function x = CHQS(y, k, F, μ0)
x = y; μ = μ0;
for t = 0 : T − 1 do
    u = [y; √μφ_{λ/μ}(F ⋆ x)];
    L = [k; √μF];
    C = argmin_C ||δ − C ⋆ L||_F^2 + ρ∑_{i=0}^n ||c_i||_F^2;
    x = CPCR(L, u, C, x);
    μ = μ + δ_t;
end for
end function
```

```
function x = CPCR(A, b, C, x0)
x = x0;
for s = 0 : S − 1 do
    x = x − C ⋆ (A ⋆ x − b);
end for
end function
```

2.3   An End-to-end Trainable CHQS Algorithm

To improve on this method, we propose to learn the proximal operator φ and the preconditioning operator C. The corresponding *learnable* CHQS (LCHQS) algorithm can now be written as a function with two additional parameters θ and ν as follows.

```
function x = LCHQS(y, k, F, μ₀, θ, ν)
x = y; μ = μ₀;
for t = 0 : T − 1 do
    u = [y; √μ φ^θ_{λ/μ}(F ⋆ x)];
    L = [k; √μ F];
    C = argmin_C ||δ − C ⋆ L||²_F + ρ Σ^n_{i=0} ||c_i||²_F;
    x = CPCR(L, u, ψ^ν(C), x);
    μ = μ + δ_t;
end for
end function
```

The function LCHQS has the same structure as CHQS but now uses two parameterized embedding functions φ^θ_τ and ψ^ν for the proximal operator and preconditioner. In practice, these functions are CNNs with learnable parameters θ and ν as detailed in Sect. 3. Note that θ actually determines the regularizer through its proximal operator. The function LCHQS is differentiable with respect to both its θ and ν parameters. Given a set of training triplets $(x^{(i)}, y^{(i)}, k^{(i)})$ (in $i = 1, \ldots, N$), the parameters θ and ν can thus be learned end-to-end by minimizing

$$F(\theta, \nu) = \sum_{i=1}^N ||x^{(i)} - \text{LCHQS}(y^{(i)}, k^{(i)}, F, \theta, \nu)||_1, \tag{12}$$

with respect to these two parameters by "unrolling" the HQS iterations and using backpropagation, as in [6,44] for example. This can be thought of as the "compilation" of a fully interpretable iterative optimization algorithm into a CNN architecture. Empirically, we have found that the ℓ_1 norm gives better results than the ℓ_2 norm in Eq. (12).

Fig. 2. A blurry image from our test set with 2% white noise and the solutions of Eq. (1) with TV-ℓ_1 regularization obtained with different HQS-based methods. From the same optimization problem, HQS-FFT displays boundary artifacts. HQS-CG and CHQS produce images with similar visual quality and PSNR values but HQS-CG is much slower.

3 Implementation and Results

3.1 Implementation Details

Network Architectures. The global architecture of LCHQS shares the same pattern than FCNN [44], *i.e.*, $n = 2$ in Eq. (1) with $k_1 = [1, -1]$ and $k_2 = k_1^\top$, and the model repeats between 1 and 5 stages alternatively solving the proximal problem (6) and the linear least-squares problem (7). The proximal operator φ^θ is the same as the one introduced in [44], and it is composed of 6 convolutional layers with 32 channels and 3×3 kernels, followed by ReLU non-linearities, except for the last one. The first layer has 1 input channel and the last layer has 1 output channel. The network ψ^ν featured in LCHQS is composed of 6 convolutional layers with 32 channels and 3×3 kernels, followed by ReLU non-linearities, except for the last one. The first layer has $n + 1$ input channels (3 in practice with the setting detailed above) corresponding to the filtered versions of x with the c_i's, and the last layer has 1 output channel. The filters c_1 and c_2 are of size 31×31. This size is intentionally made relatively large compared to the sizes of k_1 and k_2 because inverse filters might have infinite support in principle. The size of c_0 is twice the size of the blur kernel k. This choice will be explained in Sect. 3.2. In our implementation, each LCHQS stage has its own θ and ν parameters. The non-learnable CHQS module solves a TV-ℓ_1 problem; the proximal step implements the soft-thresholding operation φ with parameter λ/μ and the least-squares step implements CPCR. The choice of μ will be detailed below.

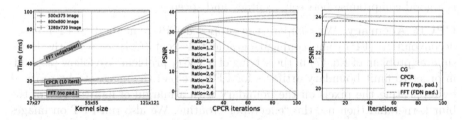

Fig. 3. From left to right: Computation times for CPCR (including computation of C) with FFT applied on images padded with "edgetaper" as recommended in [22] and non-padded images for three image formats; effect of the w_{c_0}/w_k ratio on performance; comparison of CG, FFT and CPCR for solving (7).

Datasets. The training set for uniform blur is made of 3000 patches of size 180×180 taken from BSD500 dataset and as many random 41×41 blur kernels synthesized with the code of [4]. We compute ahead of time the corresponding inverse filters c_i and set the size of c_0 to be 83×83 with Eq. (11) where ρ is set to 0.05, a value we have chosen after cross-validation on a separate test set. We also create a training set for non-uniform motion blur removal made of 3000 180×180 images synthesized with the code of [14] with a locally linear

motion of maximal magnitude of 35 pixels. For both training sets, the validation sets are made of 600 additional samples. In both cases, we add Gaussian noise with standard deviation matching that of the test data. We randomly flip and rotate by 90° the training samples and take 170×170 random crops for data augmentation.

Optimization. Following [22], we train our model in a two-step fashion: First, we supervise the sharp estimate output by each iteration of LCHQS in the manner of [22] with Eq. (12). We use an Adam optimizer with learning rate of 10^{-4} and batch size of 1 for 200 epochs. Second, we further train the network by supervising the final output of LCHQS with Eq. (12) on the same training dataset with an Adam optimizer and learning rate set to 10^{-5} for 100 more epochs *without* the per-layer supervision. We have obtained better results with this setting than using either of the two steps separately.

3.2   Experimental Validation of CPCR and CHQS

In this section, we present an experimental sanity check of CPCR for solving (7) and CHQS for solving (1) in the context of a basic TV-ℓ_1 problem.

Inverse Kernel Size. We test different sizes for the $w_{c_0} \times w_{c_0}$ approximate inverse filter c_0 associated with a $w_k \times w_k$ blur kernel k, in the non-penalized case, with $\lambda = 0$. We use Eq. (11) with ρ set to 0.05. We use 160 images obtained by applying the 8 kernels of [23] to 20 images from the Pascal VOC 2012 dataset. As shown in Fig. 3, the PSNR increases with increasing w_{c_0}/w_k ratios, but saturates when the ratio is larger than 2.2. We use a ratio of 2 which is a good compromise between accuracy and speed.

CPCR Accuracy. We compare the proposed CPCR method to FFT-based deconvolution (FFT) and conjugate gradient descent (CG), to solve the least-squares problem of Eq. (7) in the setting of a TV-ℓ_1 problem. We follow [22] and, in order to limit boundary artifacts for FFT, we pad the images to be restored by replicating the pixels on the boundary with a margin of half the size of the blur kernel and then use the "edgetaper" routine. We also run FFT on images padded with the "replicate" strategy consisting in simply replicating the pixels on the boundary. We solve Eq. (7) with $\mu_0 = 0.008$, $\lambda = 0.003$ and z computed

Table 1. Comparison of different methods optimizing the same TV-ℓ_1 deconvolution model (1) on 160 synthetic blurry images with 2% white noise. We run all the methods on a GPU. The running times are for a 500×375 RGB image.

	ker-1	ker-2	ker-3	ker-4	ker-5	ker-6	ker-7	ker-8	Aver.	Time (s)
HQS-FFT (no pad.)	21.14	20.51	22.31	18.21	23.36	20.01	19.93	19.02	20.69	0.07
HQS-FFT (rep. pad.)	26.45	25.39	**26.27**	22.75	27.64	27.26	24.84	23.54	25.53	0.07
HQS-FFT (FDN pad.)	**26.48**	25.89	**26.27**	23.79	27.66	27.23	25.26	25.02	25.96	0.15
HQS-CG	26.39	25.90	26.24	24.88	27.59	27.31	25.39	25.19	26.12	13
CHQS	26.45	**25.96**	26.26	**25.06**	**27.67**	**27.51**	**25.81**	25.48	**26.27**	0.26

beforehand with Eq. (6). The 160 images previously synthesized are degraded with 2% additional white noise. Figure 3 shows the average PSNR scores for the three algorithms optimizing Eq. (7). After only 5 iterations, CPCR produces an average PSNR higher than the other methods and converges after 10 iterations. The "edgetaper" padding is crucial for FFT to compete with CG and CPCR by reducing the amount of border artifacts in the solution.

CPCR Running Time. CPCR relies on convolutions and thus greatly benefits from GPU acceleration. For instance, for small images of size 500×375 and a blur kernel of size 55×55, 10 iterations of CPCR are in the ballpark of FFT without padding: CPCR runs in 20 ms, FFT runs in 3 ms and FFT with "edgetaper" padding takes 40 ms. For a high-resolution 1280×720 image and the same blur kernel, 10 iterations of CPCR run in 22 ms, FFT without padding runs in 10 ms and "edgetaper" padded FFT in 70 ms. Figure 3 compares the running times of CPCR (run for 10 iterations) with padded/non-padded FFT for three image (resp. kernel) sizes: 500×375, 800×800 and 1280×720 (27×27, 55×55 and 121×121) pixels. Our method is marginally slower than FFT without padding in every configuration (within a margin of 20 ms) but becomes much faster than FFT combined to "edgetaper" padding when the size of the kernel increases. FFT with "replicate" padding runs in about the same time as FFT (no pad) and thus is not shown in Fig. 3. The times have been averaged over 1000 runs.

Running Times for Computing the Inverse Kernels with Eq. (11). Computing the inverse kernels c_i, with an ratio w_c/w_k set to 2, takes 1.0 ± 0.2 ms for a blur kernel k of size 27×27 and 5.4 ± 0.5 ms (results averaged in 1000 runs) for a large 121×121 kernel. Thus, the time for inverting blur kernels is negligible in the overall pipeline.

CHQS Validation. We compare several iterations of HQS using unpadded FFT (HQS-FFT (no pad.)), with "replicate" padding (HQS-FFT (rep. pad)), and the padding strategy proposed in [22] (HQS-FFT (FDN pad.)), CG (HQS-CG), or CPCR (CHQS) for solving the least-squares problem penalized with the TV-ℓ_1 regularized in Eq. (1) and use the same 160 blurry and noisy images than in previous paragraph as test set. We set the number of HQS iterations T to 10, run CPCR for 5 iterations and CG for at most 100 iterations. We use $\lambda = 0.003$ and $\mu_t = 0.008 \times 4^t$ ($t = 0, \ldots, T-1$). Table 1 compares the average PSNR scores obtained with the different HQS algorithms over the test set. As expected, FDN padding greatly improves HQS-FFT results on larger kernels over naive "replicate" padding, $i.e.$ "ker-4" and "ker-8", but overall does not perform as well as CHQS. For kernels 1, 2, 3 and 5, the four methods yield comparable results (within 0.1 dB of each other). FFT-based methods are significantly worse on the other four, whereas our method gives better results than HQS-CG in general, but is 100 times faster. This large speed-up is explained by the convolutional structure of CPCR whereas CG involves large matrix inversions and multiplications. Figure 2 shows a deblurring example from the test set. HQS-FFT (with FDN padding strategy), even with the refined padding technique of [22], produces a solution with boundary artifacts. Both HQS-CG and CHQS restore the

Table 2. PSNR scores for Levin [23] and Sun [37] benchmarks, that respectively feature 0.5% and 1% noise. Best results are shown in bold, second-best underlined. The difference may not always be significant between FDN and LCHQS for the Levin dataset.

	FCNN [44]	EPLL [46]	RGCD [13]	FDN [22]	CHQS	LCHQS$_G$	LCHQS$_F$
Levin [23]	33.08	34.82	33.73	35.09	32.12	35.11 ± 0.05	**35.15 ± 0.04**
Sun [37]	32.24	32.46	31.95	32.67	30.36	32.83 ± 0.01	**32.93 ± 0.01**

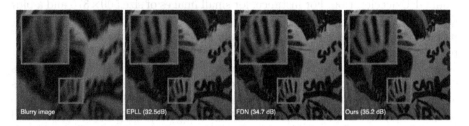

Fig. 4. Comparison of state-of-the-art methods and the proposed LCHQS for one sample of the Levin dataset [23] (better seen on a computer screen). FDN effectively removes the blur but introduces artifacts in flat areas, unlike EPLL and LCHQS.

image with a limited amount of artifacts, but CHQS does it much faster than HQS-CG. This is typical of our experiments in practice.

Discussion. These experiments show that CPCR always gives better results than CG in terms of PSNR, sometimes by a significant margin, and it is about 50 times faster. This suggests that CPCR may, more generally, be preferable to CG for linear least-squares problems when the linear operator is a convolution. CPCR also dramatically benefits from its convolutional implementation on a GPU with speed similar to FFT and is even faster than FFT with FDN padding for large kernels. These experiments also show that CHQS surpasses, in general, HQS-CG and HQS-FFT for deblurring.

Next, we further improve the accuracy of CHQS using supervised learning, as done in previous works blending within a single model variational methods and learning.

3.3   Uniform Deblurring

We compare in this section CHQS and its learnable version LCHQS with the non-blind deblurring state of the art, including optimization-based and CNN-based algorithms.

Comparison on Standard Benchmarks. LCHQS is first trained by using the loss of Eq. (12) to supervise the output of each stage of the proposed model and second trained by only supervising the output of the final layer, in the manner of [22]. The model trained in the first regime is named LCHQS$_G$ and the one further trained with the second regime is named LCHQS$_F$. The other

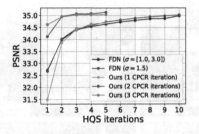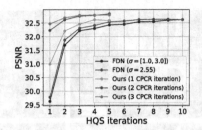

Fig. 5. Performance of FDN [22] and LCHQS on the Levin [23] (left) and Sun [37] (right) datasets.

methods we compare our learnable model to are HQS algorithms solving a TV-ℓ_1 problem: HQS-FFT (with the padding strategy of [22]), HQS-CG and CHQS, an HQS algorithm with a prior over patches (EPLL) [46] and the state-of-the-art CNN-based deblurring methods FCNN [44] and FDN [22]. We use the best model provided by the authors of [22], denoted as FDN_T^{10} in their paper. Table 2 compares our method with these algorithms on two classical benchmarks. We use 5 HQS iterations and 2 CPCR iterations for CHQS and LCHQS. Except for EPLL that takes about 40 seconds to restore an image of the Levin dataset [23], all methods restore a 255×255 black and white image in about 0.2 second. The dataset of Sun *et al.* contains high-resolution images of size around 1000×700 pixels. EPLL removes the blur in 20 min on a CPU while the other methods, including ours, do it in about 1 second on a GPU. In this case, our learnable method gives comparable results to FDN [22], outputs globally much sharper results than EPLL [46] and is much faster. As expected, non-trainable CHQS is well behind its learned competitors (Tab. 2).

Number of Iterations for LCHQS$_G$ and CPCR. We investigate the influence of the number of HQS and CPCR iterations on the performance of LCHQS$_G$ on the benchmarks of Levin *et al.* [23] and Sun *et al.* [37]. FDN implements 10 HQS iterations parameterized with CNNs but operates in the Fourier domain. Here, we compare LCHQS$_G$ to the FDN model trained in a stage-wise manner (denoted as FDN_G^{10} in [22]). Figure 5 plots the mean PSNR values for the datasets of Levin *et al.* and Sun *et al.* [37] after each stage. FDN comes in two versions: one trained on a single noise level (green line) and one trained on noise levels within a given interval (blue line). We use up to 5 iterations of our learnable CHQS scheme, but it essentially converges after only 3 steps. When the number of CPCR iterations is set to 1, FDN and our model achieve similar results for the same number of HQS iterations. For 2/3 CPCR iterations, we do better than FDN for the same number of HQS iterations by a margin of +0.4/0.5dB on both benchmarks. For 3 HQS iterations and more, LCHQS saturates but systematically achieves better results than 10 FDN iterations: +0.15dB for [23] and +0.26dB for [37].

Robustness to Noise. Table 3 compares our methods for various noise levels on the 160 RGB images introduced previously, dubbed from "PASCAL benchmark". FDN corresponds to the model called FDN_T^{10} in [22]. For this experiment,

Fig. 6. Example of image deblurring with an additive noise of 3% (better seen on a computer screen). In this example, we obtain better PSNR scores than competitors and better visual results, for example details around the door or the leaves.

(L)CHQS uses 5 HQS iterations and 2 inner CPCR iterations. We add 1%, 3% and 5% Gaussian noise to these images to obtain three different test sets with gradually stronger noise levels. We train each model to deal with a specific noise level (non-blind setting) but also train a single model to handle multiple noise levels (blind setting) on images with 0.5 to 5% of white noise, as done in [22]. For each level in the non-blind setting, we are marginally above or below FDN results. In terms of average PSNR values, the margins are +0.12dB for 1%, +0.06dB for 3% and -0.05dB for 5% when comparing our models with FDN, but we are above the other competitors by margins between 0.3dB and 2dB. Compared to its noise-dependent version, the network trained in the blind setting yields a loss of 0.2dB for 1% noise, but gains of 0.14 and 0.27dB for 3 and 5% noises, showing its robustness and adaptability to various noises. Figure 6 compares results obtained on a blurry image with 3% noise.

3.4   Non-uniform Motion Blur Removal

Typical non-uniform motion blur models assign to each pixel of a blurry image a local uniform kernel [5]. This is equivalent to replacing the uniform convolution in Eq. (1) by local convolutions for each overlapping patch in an image, as done by Sun *et al.* [35] when they adapt the solver of [46] to the non-uniform case. Note that FDN [22] and FCNN [44] operate in the Fourier domain and thus cannot be easily adapted to non-uniform deblurring, unlike (L)CHQS operating in the spatial domain. We handle non-uniform blur as follows to avoid computing different inverse filters at each pixel. As in [35], we model a non-uniform motion field with *locally* linear motions that can well approximate complex *global* motions such as camera rotations. We discretize the set of the linear motions by

Table 3. Uniform deblurring on 160 test images with 1%, 3% and 5% white noise. Running times are for an 500 × 375 RGB image. The mention "blind" (resp. "non-blind) indicates that a single model handles the three (resp. a specific) noise level(s).

	1% noise	3% noise	5% noise	Time (s)
HQS-FFT	26.48	23.90	22.15	0.2
HQS-CG	26.45	23.91	22.27	13
EPLL [46]	28.83	24.00	22.10	130
FCNN [44]	29.27	25.07	23.53	0.5
FDN [22]	<u>29.42</u>	25.53	23.97	0.6
CHQS	27.08	23.33	22.38	0.3
LCHQS$_G$ (non-blind)	**29.54 ± 0.02**	<u>25.59 ± 0.03</u>	23.87 ± 0.06	0.7
LCHQS$_F$ (non-blind)	**29.53 ± 0.02**	25.56 ± 0.03	23.95 ± 0.05	0.7
LCHQS$_G$ (blind)	29.22 ± 0.02	25.55 ± 0.03	<u>24.05 ± 0.02</u>	0.7
LCHQS$_F$ (blind)	29.35 ± 0.01	**25.71 ± 0.02**	**24.21 ± 0.01**	0.7

Fig. 7. Non-uniform motion deblurring example with 1 % additive Gaussian noise (better seen on a computer screen). The car and the helmet are sharper with our method than in the images produced by our competitors.

considering only those with translations (in pixels) in $\{1, 3 \ldots, 35\}$ and orientations in $\{0°, 6°, \ldots, 174°\}$. In this case, we know in advance all the 511 35 × 35 local blur kernels and compute their approximate inverses ahead of time. During inference, we simply determine which one best matches the local blur kernel and use its approximate inverse in CPCR. This is a parallelizable operation on a GPU. Table 4 compares our approach (in non-blind setting) to existing methods for locally-linear blur removal on a test set of 100 images from PASCAL dataset non-uniformly blurred with the code of [14] and with white noise. For instance for 1% noise, LCHQS$_G$ scores +0.99dB higher than CG-based method, and LCHQS$_F$ pushes the margin up to +1.13dB while being 200 times faster. Figure 7 shows one non-uniform example from the test set.

3.5 Deblurring with Approximated Blur Kernels

In practice one does not have the ground-truth blur kernel but instead an *approximate* version of it, obtained with methods such as [26, 39]. We show that (L)CHQS works well for approximate and/or large filters, different from the

Table 4. Non-uniform deblurring on 100 test images with 1%, 3% and 5% white noise. Running times are for an 500 × 375 RGB image.

	HQS-FFT	HQS-CG	EPLL [46]	CHQS	LCHQS$_G$	LCHQS$_F$
1% noise	23.49	25.84	25.49	25.11	26.83 ± 0.08	**26.98 ± 0.08**
3% noise	23.17	24.18	23.78	23.74	24.91 ± 0.05	**25.06 ± 0.06**
5% noise	22.44	23.10	23.34	22.65	23.97 ± 0.05	**24.14 ± 0.05**
Time (s)	13	212	420	0.8	0.9	0.9

Fig. 8. Real-world blurry images deblurred with an 101 × 101 blur kernel estimated with [26]. We can restore fine details with approximate, large kernels.

ones used in the training set and without any training or fine-tuning. We show in Figure 8 a deblurred image with an approximate kernel obtained with the code of [26] and of support of size 101 × 101 pixels. We obtain with LCHQS$_F$ (blind) of Table 3 a sharper result than FCNN and do not introduce artifacts as FDN, showing the robustness of CPCR and its embedding in HQS to approximate blur kernels. More results are shown in the supplemental material.

4   Conclusion

We have presented a new learnable solver for non-blind deblurring. It is based on the HQS algorithm for solving penalized least-squares problems but uses preconditioned iterative fixed-point iterations for the x-update. Without learning, this approach is superior both in terms of speed and accuracy to classical solvers based on the Fourier transform and conjugate gradient descent. When the preconditioner and the proximal operator are learned, we obtain results that are competitive with or better than the state of the art. Our method is easily extended to non-uniform deblurring, and it outperforms the state of the art by a significant margin in this case. We have also demonstrated its robustness to important amounts of white noise. Explicitly accounting for more realistic noise models [10] and other degradations such as downsampling is left for future work.

Acknowledgments. This works was supported in part by the INRIA/NYU collaboration and the Louis Vuitton/ENS chair on artificial intelligence. In addition, this work was funded in part by the French government under management of Agence Nationale de la Recherche as part of the "Investissements d'avenir" program, reference ANR19-P3IA-0001 (PRAIRIE 3IA Institute). Jian Sun was supported by NSFC under grant numbers 11971373 and U1811461.

References

1. Aljadaany, R., Pal, D.K., Savvides, M.: Douglas-rachford networks: learning both the image prior and data fidelity terms for blind image deconvolution. In: Proceedings of the Conference on Computer Vision and Pattern Recognition, pp. 10235–10244 (2019)
2. Boyd, S.P., Vandenberghe, L.: Convex Optimization. Cambridge University Press, New York (2014)
3. Brooks, T., Barron, J.T.: Learning to synthesize motion blur. In: Proceedings of the Conference on Computer Vision and Pattern Recognition, pp. 6840–6848 (2019)
4. Chakrabarti, A.: A neural approach to blind motion deblurring. In: Leibe, B., Matas, J., Sebe, N., Welling, M. (eds.) ECCV 2016. LNCS, vol. 9907, pp. 221–235. Springer, Cham (2016). https://doi.org/10.1007/978-3-319-46487-9_14
5. Chakrabarti, A., Zickler, T.E., Freeman, W.T.: Analyzing spatially-varying blur. In: Proceedings of the Conference on Computer Vision and Pattern Recognition, pp. 2512–2519 (2010)
6. Chen, Y., Pock, T.: Trainable nonlinear reaction diffusion: a flexible framework for fast and effective image restoration. IEEE Trans. Pattern Anal. Mach. Intell. **39**(6), 1256–1272 (2017)
7. Cho, S., Matsushita, Y., Lee, S.: Removing non-uniform motion blur from images. In: Proceedings of the International Conference on Computer Vision, pp. 1–8 (2007)
8. Couzinie-Devy, F., Sun, J., Alahari, K., Ponce, J.: Learning to estimate and remove non-uniform image blur. In: Proceedings of the Conference on Computer Vision and Pattern Recognition, pp. 1075–1082 (2013)
9. Elad, M.: Sparse and Redundant Representations: From Theory to Applications in Signal and Image Processing. Springer, New York (2010)
10. Foi, A., Trimeche, M., Katkovnik, V., Egiazarian, K.O.: Practical Poissonian-Gaussian noise modeling and fitting for single-image raw-data. IEEE Trans. Image Process. **17**(10), 1737–1754 (2008)
11. Folland, G.B.: Fourier Analysis and its Applications. Wadsworth, Pacific Grove (1992)
12. Geman, D., Yang, C.: Nonlinear image recovery with half-quadratic regularization. IEEE Trans. Image Process. **4**(7), 932–946 (1995)
13. Gong, D., Zhang, Z., Shi, Q., van den Hengel, A., Shen, C., Zhang, Y.: Learning deep gradient descent optimization for image deconvolution. IEEE Transactions on Neural Networks and Learning Systems pp. 1–15 (2020)
14. Gong, D., et al.: From motion blur to motion flow: a deep learning solution for removing heterogeneous motion blur. In: Proceedings of the Conference on Computer Vision and Pattern Recognition, pp. 3806–3815 (2017)
15. Goodman, J.: Introduction to Fourier optics. McGraw-Hill, New York (1996)
16. Hirsch, M., Sra, S., Schölkopf, B., Harmeling, S.: Efficient filter flow for space-variant multiframe blind deconvolution. In: Proceedings of the Conference on Computer Vision and Pattern Recognition, pp. 607–614 (2010)
17. Hu, Z., Yuan, L., Lin, S., Yang, M.: Image deblurring using smartphone inertial sensors. In: Proceedings of the Conference on Computer Vision and Pattern Recognition, pp. 1855–1864 (2016)
18. Kelley, T.: Iterative Methods for Linear and Nonlinear Equations. SIAM (1995)
19. Kim, T.H., Lee, K.M.: Segmentation-free dynamic scene deblurring. In: Proceedings of the Conference on Computer Vision and Pattern Recognition, pp. 2766–2773 (2014)

20. Kobler, E., Klatzer, T., Hammernik, K., Pock, T.: Variational networks: connecting variational methods and deep learning. In: Proceedings of the German Conference on Pattern Recognition, pp. 281–293 (2017)
21. Krishnan, D., Fergus, R.: Fast image deconvolution using hyper-laplacian priors. In: Advances in Neural Information Processing Systems, pp. 1033–1041 (2009)
22. Kruse, J., Rother, C., Schmidt, U.: Learning to push the limits of efficient FFT-based image deconvolution. In: Proceedings of the International Conference on Computer Vision, pp. 4596–4604 (2017)
23. Levin, A., Weiss, Y., Durand, F., Freeman, W.T.: Understanding and evaluating blind deconvolution algorithms. In: Proceedings of the Conference on Computer Vision and Pattern Recognition, pp. 1964–1971 (2009)
24. Meinhardt, T., Möller, M., Hazirbas, C., Cremers, D.: Learning proximal operators: using denoising networks for regularizing inverse imaging problems. In: Proceedings of the International Conference on Computer Vision, pp. 1799–1808 (2017)
25. Michaeli, T., Irani, M.: Blind deblurring using internal patch recurrence. In: Fleet, D., Pajdla, T., Schiele, B., Tuytelaars, T. (eds.) ECCV 2014. LNCS, vol. 8691, pp. 783–798. Springer, Cham (2014). https://doi.org/10.1007/978-3-319-10578-9_51
26. Pan, J., Sun, D., Pfister, H., Yang, M.: Deblurring images via dark channel prior. IEEE Trans. Pattern Anal. Mach. Intell. 40(10), 2315–2328 (2018)
27. Parikh, N., Boyd, S.P.: Proximal algorithms. Found. Trends Optim. 1(3), 127–239 (2014)
28. Richardson, W.H.: Bayesian-based iterative method of image restoration. J. Opt. Soc. Am. 62(1), 55–59 (1972)
29. Roth, S., Black, M.J.: Fields of experts. Int. J. Comput. Vis. 82(2), 205 (2009)
30. Rudin, L.I., Osher, S., Fatemi, E.: Nonlinear total variation based noise removal algorithms. Physica D 60, 259–268 (1992)
31. Schmidt, U., Roth, S.: Shrinkage fields for effective image restoration. In: Proceedings of the Conference on Computer Vision and Pattern Recognition, pp. 2774–2784 (2014)
32. Schmidt, U., Rother, C., Nowozin, S., Jancsary, J., Roth, S.: Discriminative non-blind deblurring. In: Proceedings of the Conference on Computer Vision and Pattern Recognition, pp. 604–611 (2013)
33. Schuler, C.J., Hirsch, M., Harmeling, S., Schölkopf, B.: Learning to deblur. IEEE Trans. Pattern Anal. Mach. Intell. 38(7), 1439–1451 (2016)
34. Starck, J.-L., Murtagh, F.: Multiple resolution in data storage and retrieval. Astronomical Image and Data Analysis. AAL, pp. 267–283. Springer, Heidelberg (2006). https://doi.org/10.1007/978-3-540-33025-7_9
35. Sun, J., Cao, W., Xu, Z., Ponce, J.: Learning a convolutional neural network for non-uniform motion blur removal. In: Proceedings of the Conference on Computer Vision and Pattern Recognition, pp. 769–777 (2015)
36. Sun, J., Xu, Z., Shum, H.: Image super-resolution using gradient profile prior. In: Proceedings of the Conference on Computer Vision and Pattern Recognition, pp. 1–8 (2008)
37. Sun, L., Cho, S., Wang, J., Hays, J.: Edge-based blur kernel estimation using patch priors. In: Proceedings of International Conference on Computational Photography, pp. 1–8 (2013)
38. Tai, Y., Tan, P., Brown, M.S.: Richardson-Lucy deblurring for scenes under a projective motion path. IEEE Trans. Pattern Anal. Mach. Intell. 33(8), 1603–1618 (2011)
39. Whyte, O., Sivic, J., Zisserman, A., Ponce, J.: Non-uniform deblurring for shaken images. Int. J. Comput. Vis. 98(2), 168–186 (2012)

40. Wiener, N.: The Extrapolation, Interpolation, and Smoothing of Stationary Time Series. Wiley, New York (1949)
41. Xu, L., Ren, J.S.J., Liu, C., Jia, J.: Deep convolutional neural network for image deconvolution. In: Advances in Neural Information Processing Systems, pp. 1790–1798 (2014)
42. Xu, L., Tao, X., Jia, J.: Inverse kernels for fast spatial deconvolution. In: Proceedings of the European Conference on Computer Vision, pp. 33–48 (2014)
43. Xu, L., Zheng, S., Jia, J.: Unnatural L0 sparse representation for natural image deblurring. In: Proceedings of the Conference on Computer Vision and Pattern Recognition, pp. 1107–1114 (2013)
44. Zhang, J., Pan, J., Lai, W., Lau, R.W.H., Yang, M.: Learning fully convolutional networks for iterative non-blind deconvolution. In: Proceedings of the Conference on Computer Vision and Pattern Recognition, pp. 6969–6977 (2017)
45. Zhang, K., Zuo, W., Gu, S., Zhang, L.: Learning deep CNN denoiser prior for image restoration. In: Proceedings of the Conference on Computer Vision and Pattern Recognition, pp. 2808–2817 (2017)
46. Zoran, D., Weiss, Y.: From learning models of natural image patches to whole image restoration. In: Proceedings of the International Conference on Computer Vision, pp. 479–486 (2011)

Employing Multi-estimations for Weakly-Supervised Semantic Segmentation

Junsong Fan[1,2], Zhaoxiang Zhang[1,2,3(✉)], and Tieniu Tan[1,2,3]

[1] Center for Research on Intelligent Perception and Computing (CRIPAC),
National Laboratory of Pattern Recognition (NLPR), Institute of Automation,
Chinese Academy of Sciences (CASIA), Beijing, China
{fanjunsong2016,zhaoxiang.zhang}@ia.ac.cn, tnt@nlpr.ia.ac.cn
[2] School of Artificial Intelligence, University of Chinese Academy of Sciences
(UCAS), Beijing, China
[3] Center for Excellence in Brain Science and Intelligence Technology,
CAS, Shanghai, China

Abstract. Image-level label based weakly-supervised semantic segmentation (WSSS) aims to adopt image-level labels to train semantic segmentation models, saving vast human labors for costly pixel-level annotations. A typical pipeline for this problem is first to adopt class activation maps (CAM) with image-level labels to generate pseudo-masks (a.k.a. seeds) and then use them for training segmentation models. The main difficulty is that seeds are usually sparse and incomplete. Related works typically try to alleviate this problem by adopting many bells and whistles to enhance the seeds. Instead of struggling to refine a single seed, we propose a novel approach to alleviate the inaccurate seed problem by leveraging the segmentation model's robustness to learn from multiple seeds. We managed to generate many different seeds for each image, which are different estimates of the underlying ground truth. The segmentation model simultaneously exploits these seeds to learn and automatically decides the confidence of each seed. Extensive experiments on Pascal VOC 2012 demonstrate the advantage of this multi-seeds strategy over previous state-of-the-art.

Keywords: Weakly-supervised learning · Semantic segmentation

1 Introduction

Semantic segmentation has achieved rapid progress with deep learning models [3–5,21]. However, these approaches heavily rely on large-scale pixel-level annotations for training, which is very costly to obtain. To reduce the requirement of precise pixel-level annotations for training, researchers proposed weakly-supervised semantic segmentation (WSSS). WSSS adopts only coarse annotations to train the semantic segmentation models, such as scribbles [20,29], bounding boxes [6,28], and image-level class labels [1,2,13,14,17,23,31]. Among them,

© Springer Nature Switzerland AG 2020
A. Vedaldi et al. (Eds.): ECCV 2020, LNCS 12362, pp. 332–348, 2020.
https://doi.org/10.1007/978-3-030-58520-4_20

the image-level label based WSSS only requires image class labels for training, which are much easier to obtain than other forms of weak annotations. Thus, image label based WSSS got much attention from recent works. In this paper, we focus on the image-level label based WSSS problem.

A common practice to recover targets' spatial information from image-level labels is to adopt the class activation maps (CAM) [39] to generate heat maps for the target objects. These heat maps are utilized to generate pseudo-masks (a.k.a. seeds) to train the desired segmentation models. The CAM is obtained by first training a classification model with the image labels and then applying the last linear classification layer to the feature map columns, which is right before the global average pooling layer. Because the CAM is trained for classification, the highlighted regions are usually only the most discriminative ones. Therefore, only sparse and incomplete seeds can be obtained, and the subsequently trained segmentation models can only predict partial objects.

To alleviate the incomplete seed problem of CAM, researchers adopt multiple dilated convolutions [33], iterative erasing strategy [31], random drop connections [17], region growing algorithms [13], online accumulating activation maps [14], and many other strategies [26] to generate more complete seeds. Though these approaches have achieved significant progress, they usually rely on carefully designed rules and experience-based hyper-parameters to balance the seed's precision and recall, which is hard to generalize.

Instead of struggling for generating a single "perfect" seed for each image by manually designed rules, we propose a novel principled way to employ multiple different seeds simultaneously to train the segmentation models. The different seeds for each image can be seen as the estimates of the common underlying ground truth. We leverage the robustness of the segmentation models to mine useful information from these different seeds automatically. The reasons this strategy works are threefold.

Firstly, different seeds help to reduce the influence of wrong labels. It is generally reasonable to assume that the probability of a pixel obtaining a correct pseudo-label is larger than obtaining a wrong label. Pixels assigned with the same label by all the different seeds are more likely to be right. The contributions of these pixels are not affected, because all the different seeds provide the same label. Meanwhile, pixels with different seed labels provide gradients in different directions; thus, the different gradients can be canceled out to some extent, reducing the risk of optimizing in the wrong direction. *Secondly*, complementary parts may exist in different seeds, making the pseudo-labels more complete as a whole. For example, the mask of a person's body may be absent in one seed, but present in another different seed. *Thirdly*, the segmentation model is robust to noise to some extent. Take the pilot experiments in Table 1 as an example, with 30% of the foreground pixels replaced by noise in the training set, the segmentation model can still achieve about 90% of the performance compared with training with the ground truth. This result may because segmentation models can leverage the knowledge from the whole dataset, thus reducing the

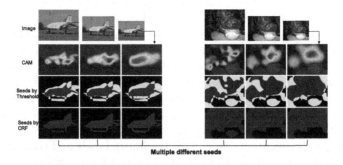

Fig. 1. Examples of the CAM and the generated seeds. The three columns of each group correspond to three different CAM scales. The first row is the image. The second row is the CAM from the VGG16 backbone, and the last two rows show two types of the generated seeds. Our approach simultaneously adopts these different seeds to train the segmentation models.

influence of unsystematic noise. This property helps to mine useful information from multiple seeds.

To further enhance the training process's robustness, we propose a weighted selective training (WST) strategy, which adaptively adjusts the weights among different seeds for each pixel. Compared with previous approaches [14,17,33] that merge multiple CAMs by hand-crafted rules, e.g., average or max fusion, our method can leverage the segmentation model's knowledge to assign weights among different seeds dynamically. We conduct thorough experiments to demonstrate the effectiveness of the proposed approach. On Pascal VOC 2012 dataset, we achieve new state-of-the-art performance with mIoU 67.2% and 66.7% on the validation and the test set, respectively, demonstrating the advantage of our approach. In summary, the main contributions of this paper are as following:

- We propose a new principled approach to alleviate the inaccurate seed problem for WSSS, which simultaneously employs many different seeds to train the segmentation models. A weighted selective training strategy is proposed to mitigate the influence of noise further.
- We conduct thorough experiments to demonstrate the approach's effectiveness and reveal the influence of different kinds of seeds.
- The proposed approach significantly outperforms the single-seed baseline and achieves new state-of-the-art performance on Pascal VOC 2012 dataset with only image-level labels for training.

2   Related Work

2.1   Semantic Segmentation

Recently deep learning based approaches [3–5,21,38] have dominated the semantic segmentation community. These approaches usually adopt fully convolutional

layers and take the semantic segmentation task as a per-pixel classification task. Though these approaches have achieved great progress, they need pixel-level annotations for training, which cost vast human labors to obtain.

2.2 Weakly-Supervised Semantic Segmentation

Weakly-supervised semantic segmentation (WSSS) is proposed to alleviate the annotation burden of segmentation tasks. According to the types of annotations, WSSS approaches can be classified as bounding box based [6,28], scribble based [20,29], and image-level label based [13,14,17,31,33] approaches. In this paper, we focus on the image-level label based WSSS.

Most of the present image-level label based WSSS approaches adopt a two-stage training strategy. It firstly estimates the pseudo-masks (a.k.a. seeds) of target objects from image-level labels and then takes these seeds to train a regular semantic segmentation model. Because of the lack of supervision, the seeds are often incomplete. To alleviate this problem, AE-PSL [31] proposes an iterative erasing strategy that iteratively erases already obtained pseudo-masks in the raw image and re-estimate new regions. MDC [33] proposes to adopt multiple layers with different dilation rates to expand the activated regions. DSRG [13] proposes a seed region growing algorithm to expand the initial seeds gradually. FickleNet [17] uses random connections to generate many different activation maps and assemble them together. OAA [14] accumulates the activation maps along the process of training the CAM to obtain more complete estimates. These approaches apply various hand-crafted rules and carefully adjusted hyper-parameters to generate a single seed for each image. However, it is generally hard to balance the recall and the precision for the underlying target objects. In contrast, we propose to simultaneously adopt many different seeds to train the semantic segmentation models and leverage the segmentation models' robustness to extract useful information from these seeds automatically.

2.3 Learning from Noisy Labels

Some related works also adopt multiple noisy labels to learn [19,36,37]. These approaches rely on noise distribution assumptions that may not hold in the WSSS problem, adopt complicated rules to pre-fuse the labels, or train additional modules to merge them. In contrast, our approach is more computation efficient and can exploit the pseudo-labels dynamically.

3   Pilot Experiments

Before illustrating the detailed approaches, we first conduct pilot experiments to demonstrate that the segmentation model benefits from multiple sets of labels that contain noise. To this end, we manually add noise to the ground truth labels by randomly set partial foreground blocks as background, as shown in Fig. 2. Then we adopt these noisy labels to train the segmentation model. We

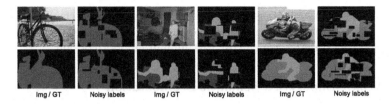

Img / GT   Noisy labels   Img / GT   Noisy labels   Img / GT   Noisy labels

Fig. 2. The hand-crafted noisy labels. Blocks with random sizes are put on the foreground objects. Two different labels with the same noise ratio are shown in the columns.

Table 1. Results on the Pascal VOC 2012 val set by the VGG16-Largefov model. The training data is from the training set with different ratios of hand-crafted noise.

Noise ratio	mIoU (%)	
	One label	Two labels
0 (ground truth)	72.1	-
0.1	70.6	71.0
0.2	68.1	69.0
0.3	64.8	66.2

compare results obtained by only utilizing a single noise label and utilizing two different noisy labels. The results are shown in Table 1. When adopting two sets of different noisy labels, the segmentation model consistently outperforms the single label counterparts under various noise rates.

The intuitive reason for the improvement is because there exists complementary information between the two sets of labels. We discuss a simplified two-class case as an example for illustration. Assume the noise is evenly distributed among all the pixels in the dataset, and the probability of noise is r. When only a single label is available, the signal-to-noise rate is $(1 - r)/r$. When there are two sets of labels, the probability of a pixel obtains two true or two false labels are $(1 - r)^2$ and r^2, respectively. The remaining $2r(1 - r)$ of the pixels receive two contradictory labels, thus do not contribute to the gradients. In this situation, the signal-to-noise rate becomes $(1 - r)^2/r^2$. Generally, r is less than $(1 - r)$, thus simultaneously adopting two different labels helps to reduce the proportion of gradients from wrong noise labels. In other words, those pixels with confusable labels are depreciated. Similar conclusions can be easily generalized to the situation of multiple classes and more sets of different labels.

In the setting of WSSS, seeds are estimated from image-level labels to approach the unknown pixel-level ground truth, and utilized to train the segmentation models. Although different seeds generally are not independent of each other and the noise is not evenly distributed, our experiments empirically demonstrate that there is still some complementary information available from multiple seeds.

Thus, adopting multi-seeds can help the segmentation model recognize more robust estimates and improve the training, as shown in Sect. 5.

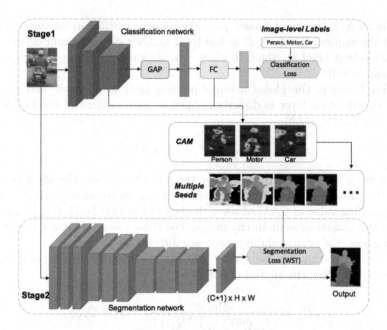

Fig. 3. The framework of our approach. The pipeline for WSSS contains two stages. In the first stage, we train the CAM by the image-level labels and generate multiple seeds via different approaches. In the second stage, we adopt these seeds simultaneously to train the segmentation model. Finally, the segmentation model outputs the semantic segmentation predictions for evaluation.

4   Approach

The whole framework of our approach contains two stages, as shown in Fig. 3. The first stage generates many different seeds from the CAM, and the second stage utilizes all of these seeds to train segmentation models. After training, segmentation results are obtained by inferring the segmentation models.

4.1   The Class Activation Map

The class activation map (CAM) [39] is widely adopted to generate initial estimates (seeds) for WSSS. The first step is to adopt the image-level labels to train a classification network, which contains a global average pooling layer right before the final classification layer. The training loss is simply the multi-class sigmoid loss:

$$L_{cam}(X) = -\sum_{c=1}^{C} y_c \log \sigma(p_c) + (1 - y_c) \log[1 - \sigma(p_c)], \tag{1}$$

Where, X is the input image, p_c is the model's prediction for the c-th class, $\sigma(\cdot)$ is the sigmoid function, C is the total number of foreground classes. y_c is the image-level label for the c-th class, whose value is 1 if the class present in the image else 0.

After training, the global average pooling layer is removed, and the final linear classification layer is directly applied to each column of the last feature map to derive the CAM:

$$M_{i,j}^c = \mathbf{f}_{i,j}^T \mathbf{w}^c, \qquad \{c \in C_{fg}\} \tag{2}$$

Where, $\mathbf{w}^c$ is the weight vector for the c-th class in the classification layer, $\mathbf{f}_{i,j}$ is the feature vector in the feature map at spatial location $\{i, j\}$. $M_{i,j}^c$ is the corresponding value of CAM of the c-th class at location $\{i, j\}$. C_{fg} is the set of foreground classes present in the image. For those classes that are not present in the image, the corresponding maps are directly set to zero.

Before generating the seeds, the CAM is normalized by filtering out negative values and dividing the spatial maximum:

$$\tilde{M}_{i,j}^c = \frac{[M_{i,j}^c]_+}{\max\limits_{i \in 1 \sim H, j \in 1 \sim W} \{[M_{i,j}^c]_+\}}, \qquad \{c \in C_{fg}\} \tag{3}$$

Where, operator $[\cdot]_+$ sets the negative values to 0. H and W are the height and width of the CAM, respectively. The obtained CAM $\tilde{M} \in \mathbb{R}^{C \times H \times W}$ is then bilinearly interpolated to the original image size and utilized to generate the seeds.

4.2   Multi-type Seeds

A common practice to generate seeds is to use the CAM and a hard threshold to estimate foreground regions and adopt saliency models to estimate background regions. CRF is also widely adopted to refine the estimate. In this paper, we adopt two different approaches to generate two types of seeds.

The first approach simply adopts the threshold method to generate seeds. We take pixels with normalized CAM scores large than 0.1 as the foreground. We adopt the same saliency model [11] utilized by previous approaches [14] to estimate the background. Pixels with saliency scores less than 0.06 are taken as background, which follows the same setting in previous approaches. The remaining unassigned pixels and those pixels with conflict assignments are marked as unknown and will be ignored when training the segmentation models.

The second approach concatenates the background scores from the saliency and the foreground scores from the normalized CAM, then adopts the CRF algorithm [16] to refine the scores. Finally, the seeds are obtained by selecting

the class with the largest score for each pixel. With this strategy, every pixel is assigned with a valid pseudo-label, and there are no conflicts and unknowns. Examples of the generated seeds are shown in Fig. 1.

Although the seeds generated by the CRF approach have more details, it may raise additional false positives and false negatives compared with the threshold approach. Therefore, there may exist complementary information in these two types of seeds. As demonstrated in Table 2, even though CRF based seeds perform better than threshold based seeds, there is still a considerable boost by simultaneously adopting both of them for training.

4.3 Multi-scale Seeds

Scale plays an important role in deep convolutional network based approaches. Because the receptive field is fixed, the convolution kernels face quite different input patterns with different scales. The network is forced to handle different scales simultaneously; thus, it generally needs different parameters for different scales. As a result, different patterns may be highlighted by the network in different input scales, and further derives different seeds. To utilize this property, we resize the input image size with different scales and feed them into the network to obtain CAMs under different scales. We adopt these CAMs with different scales to generate multiple seeds.

4.4 Multi-architecture Seeds

Generally, different architectures of the backbone do not produce identically the same predictions. Thus, different architectures can potentially provide different estimates for the underlying ground truth masks. VGG16 [27] and ResNet38 [34] are two widely adopted networks for generating seeds in the WSSS community. We adopt these two different architectures to generate different seeds.

4.5 The Weighted Selective Training

A plain way to adopt different seeds to train the segmentation model is to compute the per-pixel cross-entropy loss with each seed and adopts the average:

$$L_{plain}(X) = \frac{1}{N_k HW} \sum_k \sum_{i,j} \sum_c y_{i,j,c}^{(k)} \log p_{i,j,c}, \qquad (4)$$

Where, X is the input image, $y_{i,j,c}^{(k)}$ is the label for pixel $\{i, j\}$ from the k-th seed, which equals 1 if the label belongs to the c-th class or else 0. $p_{i,j,c}$ is the prediction of the segmentation model at location $\{i, j\}$ for the c-th class, which is normalized by the softmax operator. N_k is the total number of the seeds for the given image. H and W are the height and width of the feature, respectively.

Because of the robustness of the segmentation model and the effect of increasing the signal-to-noise rate by multiple seeds, directly adopting L_{plain} is able to

boost the performance over single-seed baselines. To further improve the robustness over noise labels, we propose to utilize the segmentation model's online predictions to weight different seeds. The training loss becomes:

$$L_{wst}(X) = \frac{1}{HW} \sum_k \sum_{i,j} w_{i,j,k} \sum_c y_{i,j,c}^{(k)} \log p_{i,j,c}, \tag{5}$$

Where, $w_{i,j,k} \in [0,1]$ is the weight for the k-th seed label at location $\{i,j\}$, which is computed by comparing the label with the segmentation model's online prediction:

$$w_{i,j,k} = \exp(s \cdot \tilde{w}_{i,j,k}) / \sum_k \exp(s \cdot \tilde{w}_{i,j,k}), \tag{6}$$

$$\tilde{w}_{i,j,k} = \mathbb{I}[\arg\max_c(p_{i,j,c}) = \arg\max_c(y_{i,j,c})], \tag{7}$$

That is, we take the value as 1 if and only if the segmentation model's prediction matches the pseudo-label, then we adopt the softmax operator to normalize all the values across different seeds to ensure that $\sum_k w_{i,j,k} = 1$. s is a scale factor to control the sharpness of the weight. When s equals 0, the loss is identical to the plain training loss L_{plain}. In practice, we simply set s equals 1. Along the training process, the segmentation model converges and predicts more stable results. As a result, outliers that contradict the prediction will be inhibited, further reducing the influence of the noise.

5   Experiments

5.1   Dataset

Following previous works, we adopt the Pascal VOC 2012 dataset [8] to evaluate our approach. It contains 20 foreground classes and a background class for semantic segmentation. The extended training set [10] contains 10582 images, the validation set contains 1449 images, and the test set contains 1456 images. For training our weakly-supervised models, only the image-level labels are used, i.e., the image class labels of the 20 foreground object classes. The performance is evaluated by the standard mean intersection over union (mIoU) with all the 21 classes.

5.2   Implementation Details

We adopt two popular backbones to generate the seeds, i.e., VGG16 [27] and ResNet38 [34], which are widely adopted in the WSSS community. To obtain larger receptive fields for the details of the objects, we follow the DeepLab's setting to set the last two downsampling layers' strides to 1 and adopt dilated convolutions in the following layers. The total downsampling rate of the feature map is 8. Backbones are pre-trained by the ImageNet classification task [7],

New layers are initialized by Normal distribution with a standard deviation 0.01. The initial learning rate is 0.001 and is poly decayed with power 0.9 every epoch. The learning rate for newly initialized layers is multiplied by 10. We adopt the SGD optimizer and train 20 epochs with the batch size 16. The input images for training are randomly scaled between 0.5 and 1.5, randomly mirrored horizontally with a probability 0.5, and randomly cropped into size 321. After obtaining the seeds, we adopt the proposed approach and follow the standard hyper-parameters to train the DeepLab-v2 segmentation models.

Table 2. Ablation study of the multi-type seeds. Results are obtained by the VGG16-Largefov segmentation model and evaluated on the VOC 12 val set using mIoU (%). The numbers in the parenthesis represent the number of seeds adopted.

CAM-Backbone	Seed-Type		
	Threshold (T.)	CRF (C.)	Both (T.+C.)
VGG16	61.4 (1)	62.9 (1)	**63.8** (2)
RES38	62.3 (1)	62.6 (1)	**63.5** (2)

Table 3. Ablation study of the multi-scale seeds. Results are obtained by the VGG16-Largefov segmentation model and evaluated on the VOC 12 val set using mIoU (%). The numbers in the parenthesis represent the number of seeds adopted.

Seed-Type	Single-Scale	Multi-Scale	Merge-Scale	
			Max	Avg
Threshold (T.)	61.4 (1)	**62.5** (3)	60.2 (1)	61.1 (1)
CRF (C.)	62.9 (1)	**63.5** (3)	62.5 (1)	62.8 (1)
Both (T.+C.)	63.8 (2)	**64.0** (6)	63.7 (2)	63.9 (2)

5.3   The Influence of Multiple Seeds

Multi-type Seeds. We firstly demonstrate that adopting the multi-type seeds helps to train the segmentation network. We generate seeds by both the *threshold* based approach and the *CRF* based approach, as described in Sect. 4.2. The baseline results are obtained by training on these two types of seeds separately, and our approach takes both of them for training. The results are summarized in Table 2. With only a single type of seeds, the best result is achieved by using the CRF based seeds, showing that CRF provides more details based on the low-level RGB cues. However, additional wrong labels may also be incurred by the CRF. Thus by simultaneously adopting these two types of seeds with our approach, there is a further 0.9% improvement, demonstrating that our method can mine useful complementary information from multi-type seeds.

Table 4. Ablation study of the multi-architecture seeds. Results are obtained by the VGG16-Largefov segmentation model and evaluated on the VOC 12 val set using mIoU (%). The numbers in the parenthesis represent the number of seeds adopted.

Seed-Type	CAM-Backbone		
	VGG16	RES38	VGG16+RES38
Threshold (T.)	61.4 (1)	62.3 (1)	**63.5** (2)
CRF (C.)	62.9 (1)	62.6 (1)	**63.1** (2)
Both (T.+C.)	63.8 (2)	63.5 (2)	**64.2** (4)

Table 5. Ablation study of the weighted selective training (WST). Results are obtained by the VGG16-Largefov segmentation model and evaluated on the VOC 12 val set using mIoU (%).

Multi-Type	Multi-Scale	Multi-Architecture	w/o WST	w/ WST
✓			**63.9**	63.8
✓	✓		63.8	**64.0**
✓	✓	✓	63.9	**64.6**

Multi-scale Seeds. To verify the effectiveness of exploiting multi-scale seeds, we generate seeds by inferring CAMs with three different scales, i.e., 1, 0.75, and 0.5. Examples of the multi-scale CAMs and corresponding seeds are shown in Fig. 1. As shown in Table 3, employing multiple seeds of different scales consistently provides improvement over single-scale counterparts. It is also noteworthy that adopting both multi-type seeds and multi-scale seeds simultaneously further improves the performance, demonstrating the effectiveness of our approach. To more concretely demonstrate the advantage of utilizing multiple seeds over single seeds, we also generate a single set of seeds by merging the multi-scale CAMs. Specifically, we merge the CAMs from all the three scales by the max- or the average-fusion. We generate seeds from the merged CAM and adopt them for training. The last two columns in Table 3 shows the results. If we only adopt the merged single-type seeds for training, there is no obvious improvement over the baseline. It may because simply merging multi-scale CAMs introduces some ambiguity and additional noise. In contrast, our approach generates seeds from different CAMs independently and utilizes these different seeds for training, which is more robust to leverage the multi-scale information.

Multi-architecture Seeds. Because of the difference in network depth, receptive field, and connection structures, different networks usually produce different activation maps for the same input. To leverage this character, we adopt different backbones to generate the seeds. In previous works, either VGG16 or ResNet38 is adopted to generate the seeds. Thus we choose these two networks to conduct experiments of the multi-architecture seeds. Results in Table 4 shows

that taking seeds from these two architectures always improves the performance, demonstrating that seeds from different networks can also provide complementary information to the segmentation models.

5.4 The Weighted Selective Training

We conduct ablation studies to demonstrate the effectiveness of the proposed weighted selective training (WST) strategy, as shown in Table 5. The results show that the influence of the WST approach is more apparent when there are more different kinds of seeds. When only adopting the multi-type seeds, there is no noticeable improvement. It may because many ambiguous pixels are set to empty in the threshold-based seeds, which reduces the number of conflict noise labels between the two types of seeds. It is also noteworthy that even without the WST approach, adopting multiple seeds for training improves over the baseline with a clear margin, demonstrating that the segmentation model can effectively learn from multiple seeds, even with noise. Figure 4 is the visualization of the weights among different seeds. It shows that the assigned per-pixel weights can generally inhibit noisy labels.

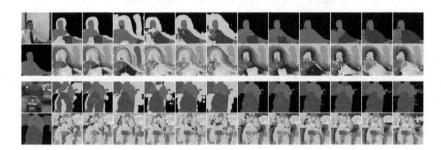

Fig. 4. Visualization of the WST weights among different seeds. The first column shows the input images and online predictions. The rest columns show the seeds and the corresponding weights obtained by the WST approach.

5.5 Comparison with Related Works

We employ all the above approaches to generate many different seeds to train our model to compare with related works. Specifically, two types, three scales, and two architectures are adopted, resulting in 12 different seeds. The VGG16-LargeFov and the ResNet101-LargeFov are two widely used segmentation models for evaluating the WSSS approaches. We report results for both of them, as shown in Table 6 and Table 7, respectively. To the best of our knowledge, previous best results on the VGG16 backbone are achieved by AISI [9] and OAA [14]. Our approach significantly outperforms them by 1.5% and 1.1% mIoU scores on the validation set and the test set, respectively. It is noteworthy that ablation results

Table 6. Comparison with related works. All the results are obtained by the VGG16 backbone and evaluated on the VOC 12 semantic segmentation benchmark.

Method	Publication	mIoU (%)	
		val	test
CCNN [23]	ICCV15	35.3	35.6
EM-Adapt [22]	ICCV15	38.2	39.6
MIL [24]	CVPR15	42.0	40.6
SEC [15]	ECCV16	50.7	51.7
AugFeed [25]	ECCV16	54.3	55.5
STC [32]	PAMI17	49.8	51.2
AE-PSL [31]	CVPR17	55.0	55.7
DCSP [2]	BMVC17	58.6	59.2
AffinityNet [1]	CVPR18	58.4	60.5
GAIN [18]	CVPR18	55.3	56.8
MCOF [30]	CVPR18	56.2	57.6
DSRG [13]	CVPR18	59.0	60.4
MDC [33]	CVPR18	60.4	60.8
AISI [9]	ECCV18	61.9	63.1
SeeNet [12]	NIPS18	61.1	60.7
FickleNet [17]	CVPR19	61.2	61.9
SSNet [35]	ICCV19	57.1	58.6
OAA [14]	ICCV19	63.1	62.8
Ours		**64.6**	**64.2**[a]

[a]http://host.robots.ox.ac.uk:8080/
anonymous/QR5OFW.html

Table 7. Comparison with related works. All the results are obtained by the ResNet101 backbone and evaluated on the VOC 12 semantic segmentation benchmark.

Method	Publication	mIoU (%)	
		val	test
DCSP [2]	BMVC17	60.8	61.9
MCOF [30]	CVPR18	60.3	61.2
DSRG [13]	CVPR18	61.4	63.2
AISI [9]	ECCV18	64.5	65.6
SeeNet [12]	NIPS18	63.1	62.8
FickleNet [17]	CVPR19	64.9	65.3
OAA [14]	ICCV19	65.2	66.4
Ours		**67.2**	**66.7**[b]

[b]http://host.robots.ox.ac.uk:8080/
anonymous/ZHCI9F.html

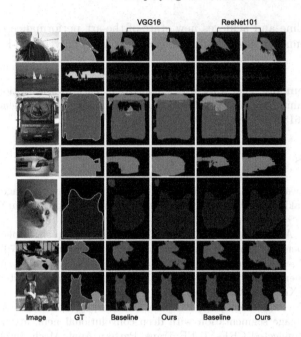

Fig. 5. The prediction results of single-seed baseline and our approach on VOC 2012 val set. The first two columns are images and ground truth (unavailable for training). The third and the fourth columns are obtained by the VGG16 based segmentation model. The last two columns are obtained by the ResNet101 based segmentation model.

in Table 3 reveal that even with only VGG16-CAM based seeds, our approach could achieve mIoU 64.0% on the validation set, which outperforms previous best results by 0.9%, demonstrating the advantage of adopting multiple different seeds. The ResNet101 based segmentation model generally performs better than the VGG16. Our approach also works with this stronger segmentation model, which outperforms previous best results by 2.0% and 0.3% on the validation and the test set, respectively, demonstrating our approach's generalization ability. Figure 5 shows the visualization results of the segmentation models' predictions. Compared with the single seed baseline, our approach generally obtains more complete and robust predictions.

6 Conclusions

Image-level label based weakly-supervised semantic segmentation suffers from incomplete seeds for training. To alleviate this problem, we propose a novel approach to employing multiple different seeds simultaneously to train the segmentation models. We propose a weighted selective training strategy to reduce further the influence of noise in the multiple seeds. Extensive experiments demonstrate that our training framework can effectively mine reliable and complementary information from a group of different seeds. Our approach significantly improves

over the baseline and achieves new state-of-the-art performance on the Pascal VOC 2012 semantic segmentation benchmark with only image-level labels for training.

Acknowledgement. This work was supported in part by the National Key R&D Program of China (No. 2018YFB1402605), the National Natural Science Foundation of China (No. 61836014, No. 61761146004, No. 61773375).

References

1. Ahn, J., Kwak, S.: Learning pixel-level semantic affinity with image-level supervision for weakly supervised semantic segmentation. arXiv preprint arXiv:1803.10464 (2018)
2. Chaudhry, A., Dokania, P.K., Torr, P.H.: Discovering class-specific pixels for weakly-supervised semantic segmentation. arXiv preprint arXiv:1707.05821 (2017)
3. Chen, L.C., Papandreou, G., Kokkinos, I., Murphy, K., Yuille, A.L.: Semantic image segmentation with deep convolutional nets and fully connected CRFs. arXiv preprint arXiv:1412.7062 (2014)
4. Chen, L.C., Papandreou, G., Kokkinos, I., Murphy, K., Yuille, A.L.: DeepLab: semantic image segmentation with deep convolutional nets, atrous convolution, and fully connected CRFs. IEEE Trans. Pattern Anal. Mach. Intell. **40**(4), 834–848 (2018)
5. Chen, L.C., Papandreou, G., Schroff, F., Adam, H.: Rethinking atrous convolution for semantic image segmentation. arXiv preprint arXiv:1706.05587 (2017)
6. Dai, J., He, K., Sun, J.: BoxSup: exploiting bounding boxes to supervise convolutional networks for semantic segmentation. In: Proceedings of the IEEE International Conference on Computer Vision, pp. 1635–1643 (2015)
7. Deng, J., Dong, W., Socher, R., Li, L.J., Li, K., Fei-Fei, L.: ImageNet: a large-scale hierarchical image database. In: IEEE Conference on Computer Vision and Pattern Recognition, CVPR 2009, pp. 248–255. IEEE (2009)
8. Everingham, M., Van Gool, L., Williams, C.K., Winn, J., Zisserman, A.: The Pascal visual object classes (VOC) challenge. Int. J. Comput. Vision **88**(2), 303–338 (2010). https://doi.org/10.1007/s11263-009-0275-4
9. Fan, R., Hou, Q., Cheng, M.M., Yu, G., Martin, R.R., Hu, S.M.: Associating inter-image salient instances for weakly supervised semantic segmentation (2018)
10. Hariharan, B., Arbeláez, P., Bourdev, L., Maji, S., Malik, J.: Semantic contours from inverse detectors (2011)
11. Hou, Q., Cheng, M.M., Hu, X., Borji, A., Tu, Z., Torr, P.H.: Deeply supervised salient object detection with short connections. In: Proceedings of the IEEE Conference on Computer Vision and Pattern Recognition, pp. 3203–3212 (2017)
12. Hou, Q., Jiang, P.T., Wei, Y., Cheng, M.M.: Self-erasing network for integral object attention. arXiv preprint arXiv:1810.09821 (2018)
13. Huang, Z., Wang, X., Wang, J., Liu, W., Wang, J.: Weakly-supervised semantic segmentation network with deep seeded region growing. In: Proceedings of the IEEE Conference on Computer Vision and Pattern Recognition, pp. 7014–7023 (2018)
14. Jiang, P.T., Hou, Q., Cao, Y., Cheng, M.M., Wei, Y., Xiong, H.K.: Integral object mining via online attention accumulation. In: Proceedings of the IEEE International Conference on Computer Vision, pp. 2070–2079 (2019)

15. Kolesnikov, A., Lampert, C.H.: Seed, expand and constrain: three principles for weakly-supervised image segmentation. In: Leibe, B., Matas, J., Sebe, N., Welling, M. (eds.) ECCV 2016. LNCS, vol. 9908, pp. 695–711. Springer, Cham (2016). https://doi.org/10.1007/978-3-319-46493-0_42

16. Krähenbühl, P., Koltun, V.: Efficient inference in fully connected CRFs with Gaussian edge potentials. In: Advances in Neural Information Processing Systems, pp. 109–117 (2011)

17. Lee, J., Kim, E., Lee, S., Lee, J., Yoon, S.: FickleNet: weakly and semi-supervised semantic image segmentation using stochastic inference. In: Proceedings of the IEEE Conference on Computer Vision and Pattern Recognition, pp. 5267–5276 (2019)

18. Li, K., Wu, Z., Peng, K.C., Ernst, J., Fu, Y.: Tell me where to look: guided attention inference network. In: Proceedings of the IEEE Conference on Computer Vision and Pattern Recognition, pp. 9215–9223 (2018)

19. Li, S., et al.: Coupled-view deep classifier learning from multiple noisy annotators. In: AAAI, pp. 4667–4674 (2020)

20. Lin, D., Dai, J., Jia, J., He, K., Sun, J.: ScribbleSup: scribble-supervised convolutional networks for semantic segmentation. In: Proceedings of the IEEE Conference on Computer Vision and Pattern Recognition, pp. 3159–3167 (2016)

21. Long, J., Shelhamer, E., Darrell, T.: Fully convolutional networks for semantic segmentation. In: Proceedings of the IEEE Conference on Computer Vision and Pattern Recognition, pp. 3431–3440 (2015)

22. Papandreou, G., Chen, L.C., Murphy, K., Yuille, A.L.: Weakly- and semi-supervised learning of a DCNN for semantic image segmentation. arXiv preprint arXiv:1502.02734 (2015)

23. Pathak, D., Krähenbühl, P., Darrell, T.: Constrained convolutional neural networks for weakly supervised segmentation. In: Proceedings of the IEEE International Conference on Computer Vision, pp. 1796–1804 (2015)

24. Pinheiro, P.O., Collobert, R.: From image-level to pixel-level labeling with convolutional networks. In: Proceedings of the IEEE Conference on Computer Vision and Pattern Recognition, pp. 1713–1721 (2015)

25. Qi, X., Liu, Z., Shi, J., Zhao, H., Jia, J.: Augmented feedback in semantic segmentation under image level supervision. In: Leibe, B., Matas, J., Sebe, N., Welling, M. (eds.) ECCV 2016. LNCS, vol. 9912, pp. 90–105. Springer, Cham (2016). https://doi.org/10.1007/978-3-319-46484-8_6

26. Shimoda, W., Yanai, K.: Self-supervised difference detection for weakly-supervised semantic segmentation. In: Proceedings of the IEEE International Conference on Computer Vision, pp. 5208–5217 (2019)

27. Simonyan, K., Zisserman, A.: Very deep convolutional networks for large-scale image recognition. arXiv preprint arXiv:1409.1556 (2014)

28. Song, C., Huang, Y., Ouyang, W., Wang, L.: Box-driven class-wise region masking and filling rate guided loss for weakly supervised semantic segmentation. In: Proceedings of the IEEE Conference on Computer Vision and Pattern Recognition, pp. 3136–3145 (2019)

29. Vernaza, P., Chandraker, M.: Learning random-walk label propagation for weakly-supervised semantic segmentation. In: The IEEE Conference on Computer Vision and Pattern Recognition (CVPR), vol. 3, p. 3 (2017)

30. Wang, X., You, S., Li, X., Ma, H.: Weakly-supervised semantic segmentation by iteratively mining common object features. In: Proceedings of the IEEE Conference on Computer Vision and Pattern Recognition, pp. 1354–1362 (2018)

31. Wei, Y., Feng, J., Liang, X., Cheng, M.M., Zhao, Y., Yan, S.: Object region mining with adversarial erasing: a simple classification to semantic segmentation approach. In: IEEE CVPR, vol. 1, p. 3 (2017)

32. Wei, Y., et al.: STC: a simple to complex framework for weakly-supervised semantic segmentation. IEEE Trans. Pattern Anal. Mach. Intell. **39**(11), 2314–2320 (2017)

33. Wei, Y., Xiao, H., Shi, H., Jie, Z., Feng, J., Huang, T.S.: Revisiting dilated convolution: a simple approach for weakly- and semi-supervised semantic segmentation. In: Proceedings of the IEEE Conference on Computer Vision and Pattern Recognition, pp. 7268–7277 (2018)

34. Wu, Z., Shen, C., Van Den Hengel, A.: Wider or deeper: revisiting the ResNet model for visual recognition. Pattern Recogn. **90**, 119–133 (2019)

35. Zeng, Y., Zhuge, Y., Lu, H., Zhang, L.: Joint learning of saliency detection and weakly supervised semantic segmentation. In: Proceedings of the IEEE International Conference on Computer Vision, pp. 7223–7233 (2019)

36. Zhang, D., Han, J., Zhang, Y.: Supervision by fusion: towards unsupervised learning of deep salient object detector. In: Proceedings of the IEEE International Conference on Computer Vision, pp. 4048–4056 (2017)

37. Zhang, J., Zhang, T., Dai, Y., Harandi, M., Hartley, R.: Deep unsupervised saliency detection: a multiple noisy labeling perspective. In: Proceedings of the IEEE Conference on Computer Vision and Pattern Recognition, pp. 9029–9038 (2018)

38. Zheng, S., et al.: Conditional random fields as recurrent neural networks. In: Proceedings of the IEEE International Conference on Computer Vision, pp. 1529–1537 (2015)

39. Zhou, B., Khosla, A., Lapedriza, A., Oliva, A., Torralba, A.: Learning deep features for discriminative localization. In: Proceedings of the IEEE Conference on Computer Vision and Pattern Recognition, pp. 2921–2929 (2016)

Learning Noise-Aware Encoder-Decoder from Noisy Labels by Alternating Back-Propagation for Saliency Detection

Jing Zhang[1,3,4]($\boxtimes$), Jianwen Xie[2], and Nick Barnes[1]

[1] Australian National University, Canberra, Australia
zjnwpu@gmail.com
[2] Cognitive Computing Lab, Baidu Research, Sunnyvale, USA
[3] Australian Centre for Robotic Vision, Brisbane, Australia
[4] Data61, Eveleigh, Australia

Abstract. In this paper, we propose a noise-aware encoder-decoder framework to disentangle a clean saliency predictor from noisy training examples, where the noisy labels are generated by unsupervised hand-crafted feature-based methods. The proposed model consists of two sub-models parameterized by neural networks: (1) a saliency predictor that maps input images to clean saliency maps, and (2) a noise generator, which is a latent variable model that produces noises from Gaussian latent vectors. The whole model that represents noisy labels is a sum of the two sub-models. The goal of training the model is to estimate the parameters of both sub-models, and simultaneously infer the corresponding latent vector of each noisy label. We propose to train the model by using an alternating back-propagation (ABP) algorithm, which alternates the following two steps: (1) learning back-propagation for estimating the parameters of two sub-models by gradient ascent, and (2) inferential back-propagation for inferring the latent vectors of training noisy examples by Langevin Dynamics. To prevent the network from converging to trivial solutions, we utilize an edge-aware smoothness loss to regularize hidden saliency maps to have similar structures as their corresponding images. Experimental results on several benchmark datasets indicate the effectiveness of the proposed model.

Keywords: Noisy saliency · Latent variable model · Langevin dynamics · Alternating back-propagation

1 Introduction

Visual saliency detection aims to locate salient regions that attract human attention. Conventional saliency detection methods [46,59] rely on human designed

---

Jing Zhang—Work was done while Jing Zhang was an intern mentored by Jianwen Xie.

Electronic supplementary material The online version of this chapter (https://doi.org/10.1007/978-3-030-58520-4_21) contains supplementary material, which is available to authorized users.

A. Vedaldi et al. (Eds.): ECCV 2020, LNCS 12362, pp. 349–366, 2020.
https://doi.org/10.1007/978-3-030-58520-4_21

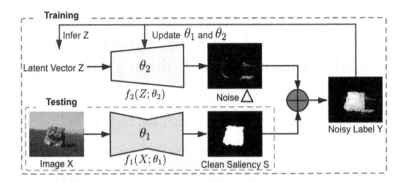

Fig. 1. An illustration of our framework. Representation: Each noisy label Y is represented as a sum of a clean saliency S and a noise map Δ. The clean saliency S is predicted from an image X by an encoder-decoder network f_1, and the noise is produced from a Gaussian noise vector Z by a generator network f_2. Training: given the observed image X and the corresponding noisy label Y, (i) the latent vector Z is inferred by MCMC and (ii) the parameters $\{\theta_1, \theta_2\}$ of the encoder-decoder f_1 and the generator f_2 are updated by the gradient ascent for maximum likelihood. Testing: once the model is learned, the disentangled saliency predictor f_1 is the desired model for saliency prediction. (Color figure online)

features to compute saliency for each pixel or superpixel. The deep learning revolution makes it possible to train end-to-end deep saliency detection models in a data-driven manner [7,19,21,25,30,33–35,38,40,41,51,54,55], outperforming handcrafted feature-based solutions by a wide margin. However, the success of deep models mainly depends on a large amount of accurate human labeling [3,15,31], which is typically expensive and time-consuming.

To relieve the burden of pixel-wise labeling, weakly supervised [17,31,52] and unsupervised saliency detection models [24,50,53] have been proposed. The former direction focuses on learning saliency from cheap but clean annotations, while the latter one studies learning saliency from noisy labels, which are typically obtained by conventional handcrafted feature-based methods. In this paper, we follow the second direction and propose a deep latent variable model that we call the noise-aware encoder-decoder to disentangle a clean saliency predictor from noisy labels. In general, a noisy label can be (1) a coarse saliency label generated by algorithmic pipelines using handcrafted features, (2) an imperfect human-annotated saliency label, or even (3) a clean label, which actually is a special case of noisy label, in which noise is none. Aiming at unsupervised saliency prediction, our paper assumes noisy labels to be produced by unsupervised handcrafted feature-based saliency methods, and places emphasis on disentangled representation of noisy labels by the noise-aware encoder-decoder.

Given a noisy dataset $D = \{(X_i, Y_i)\}_{i=1}^{n}$ of n examples, where X_i and Y_i are image and its corresponding noisy saliency label, we intend to disentangle noise Δ_i and clean saliency S_i from each noisy label Y_i, and learn a clean saliency predictor $f_1 : X_i \rightarrow S_i$. To achieve this, we propose a conditional latent variable

model, which is a disentangled representation of noisy saliency Y_i. See Fig. 1 for an illustration of the proposed model. In the context of the model, each noisy label is assumed to be generated by adding a specific noise or perturbation Δ_i to its clean saliency map S_i that is dependent on its image X_i. Specifically, the model consists of two sub-models: (1) saliency predictor f_1: an encoder-decoder network that maps an input image X_i to a latent clean saliency map S_i, and (2) noise generator f_2: a top-down neural network that produces a noise or error Δ_i from a low-dimensional Gaussian latent vector Z_i.

As a latent variable model, the rigorous maximum likelihood learning (MLE) typically requires to compute an intractable posterior distribution, which is an inference step. To learn the latent variable model, two algorithms can be adopted: variational auto-encoder (VAE) [13] or alternating back-propagation (ABP) [9,44,60]. VAE approximates MLE by minimizing the evidence lower bound with a separate inference model to approximate the true posterior, while ABP directly targets MLE and computes the posterior via Markov chain Monte Carlo (MCMC). In this paper, we generalize the ABP algorithm to learn the proposed model, which alternates the following two steps: (1) learning back-propagation for estimating the parameters of two sub-models, and (2) inferential back-propagation for inferring the latent vectors of training examples. As there may exist infinite combinations of S and Δ such that $S + \Delta$ perfectly matches the provided noisy label Y, we further adopt the edge-aware smoothness loss [37] to serve as a regularization to force each latent saliency map S_i to have a similar structure as its input image X_i. The learned disentangled saliency predictor f_1 is the desired model for testing.

Our solution is different from existing weak or noisy label-based saliency approaches [18,24,50,53] in the following aspects: Firstly, unlike [53], we don't assume the saliency noise distribution is a Gaussian distribution. Our noise generator parameterized by a neural network is flexible enough to approximate any forms of structural noises. Secondly, we design a trainable noise generator to explicitly represent each noise Δ_i as a non-linear transformation of low-dimensional Gaussian noise Z_i, which is a latent variable that need to be inferred during training, while [18,24,50,53] have no noise inference process. Thirdly, we have no constraints on the number of noisy labels generated from each image, while [24,50,53] require multiple noisy labels per image for noise modeling or pseudo label generation. Lastly, our edge-aware smoothness loss serves as a regularization to force the produced latent saliency maps to be well aligned with their input images, which is different from [18], where object edges are used to produce pseudo saliency labels via multi-scale combinatorial grouping (MCG) [1].

Our main contributions can be summarized as follows:

- We propose to learn a clean saliency predictor from noisy labels by a novel latent variable model that we call noise-aware encoder-decoder, in which each noisy label is represented as a sum of the clean saliency generated from the input image and a noise map generated from a latent vector.

- We propose to train the latent variable model by an alternating back-propagation (ABP) algorithm, which rigorously and efficiently maximizes the data likelihood without recruiting any other auxiliary model.
- We propose to use an edge-aware smoothness loss as a regularization to prevent the model from converging to a trivial solution.
- Experimental results on various benchmark datasets show the state-of-the-art performances of our framework in the task of unsupervised saliency detection, and also comparable performances with the existing fully-supervised saliency detection methods.

2 Related Work

Fully supervised saliency detection models [21,25,30,34–36,38,41,57,58] mainly focus on designing networks that utilize image context information, multiscale information, and image structure preservation. [30] introduces feature polishing modules to update each level of features by incorporating all higher levels of context information. [38] presents a cross feature module and a cascaded feedback decoder to effectively fuse different levels of features with a position-aware loss to penalize the boundary as well as pixel dissimilarity between saliency outputs and labels during training. [35] proposes a saliency detection model that integrates both top-down and bottom-up saliency inferences in an iterative and cooperative manner. [34] designs a pyramid attention structure with an edge detection module to perform edge-preserving salient object detection. [25] uses a hybrid loss for boundary-aware saliency detection. [36] proposes to use the stacked pyramid attention, which exploits multi-scale saliency information, along with an edge-related loss for saliency detection.

Learning saliency models without pixel-wise labeling can relieve the burden of costly pixel-level labeling. Those methods train saliency detection models with low-cost labels, such as image-level labels [17,31,48], noisy labels [24,50,53], object contours [18], scribble annotations [52], *etc.* [31] introduces a foreground inference network to produce initial saliency maps with image-level labels, which are further refined and then treated as pseudo labels for iterative training. [50] fuses saliency maps from unsupervised handcrafted feature-based methods with heuristics within a deep learning framework. [53] collaboratively updates a saliency prediction module and a noise module to achieve learning saliency from multiple noisy labels. In [24], the initial noisy labels are refined by a self-supervised learning technique, and then treated as pseudo labels. [18] creates a contour-to-saliency network, where saliency masks are generated by its contour detection branch via MCG [1] and then those generated saliency masks are further used to train its saliency detection branch.

Learning from noisy labels techniques mainly focus on three main directions: (1) developing regularization [26,47]; (2) estimating the noise distribution by assuming that noisy labels are corrupted from clean labels by an unknown noise transition matrix [8,29] and (3) training on selected samples [12,20]. [26] deals with noisy labeling by augmenting the prediction objective with a notion

of perceptual consistency. [47] proposes a framework to solve noisy label problem by updating both model parameters and labels. [29] proposes to simultaneously learn the individual annotator model, which is represented by a confusion matrix, and the underlying true label distribution (*i.e.*, classifier) from noisy observations. [12] proposes to learn an extra network called MentorNet to generate a curriculum, which is a sample weighting scheme, for the base ConvNet called StudentNet. The generated curriculum helps the StudentNet to focus on those samples whose labels are likely to be correct.

3   Proposed Framework

The proposed model consists of two sub-models: (1) a saliency predictor, which is parameterized by an encoder-decoder network that maps the input image X to the clean saliency S; (2) a noise generator, which is parameterized by top-down generator network that produces a noise or error Δ from a Gaussian latent vector Z. The resulting model is a sum of the two sub-models. Given training images with noisy labels, the MLE training of the model leads to an alternating back-propagation algorithm, which will be introduced in details in the following sections. The learned encoder-decoder network, which takes as input the image X and outputs clean saliency S, is our desired model for saliency detection.

3.1   Noise-Aware Encoder-Decoder Network

Let $D = \{(X_i, Y_i)\}_{i=1}^{n}$ be the training dataset, where X_i is the training image, Y_i is the corresponding noisy label, n is the size of the training dataset. Formally, the noise-aware encoder-decoder model can be formulated as follows:

$$S = f_1(X; \theta_1), \tag{1}$$
$$\Delta = f_2(Z; \theta_2), Z \sim \mathcal{N}(0, I_d), \tag{2}$$
$$Y = S + \Delta + \epsilon, \epsilon \sim \mathcal{N}(0, \sigma^2 I_D), \tag{3}$$

where f_1 in Eq. (1) is an encoder-decoder structure parameterized by θ_1 for saliency detection. It takes image X as input and predicts the clean saliency map S. Equation (2) defines a noise generator, where Z is a Gaussian noise vector following $\mathcal{N}(0, I_d)$ (I_d is the d-dimensional identity matrix) and f_2 is a top-down deconvolutional neural network parametrized by θ_2 that generates the noise Δ from Z. In Eq. (3), we assume that the observed noisy label Y is a sum of the clean saliency map S and the noise Δ, plus a Gaussian residual $\epsilon \sim \mathcal{N}(0, \sigma^2 I_D)$, where we assume σ is given and I_D is the D-dimensional identity matrix. Although Z is Gaussian noise, the generated noise Δ is not necessary Gaussian due to the non-linear transformation f_2.

We call our network the noise-aware encoder-decoder network as it explicitly decomposes the noisy labels Y into noise Δ and clean labels S, and simultaneously learns a mapping from image X to clean saliency S via an encoder-decoder network as shown in Fig. 1. Since the resulting model involves latent variables Z,

training the model by maximum likelihood learning needs to learn the parameters θ_1 and θ_2, and also infer the noise latent variable Z_i for each observed data pair (X_i, Y_i). The noise and the saliency information are disentangled once the model is learned. The learned encoder-decoder sub-model $S = f_1(X; \theta_1)$ is the desired saliency detection network.

3.2   Maximum Likelihood via Alternating Back-Propagation

For notation simplicity, let $f = \{f_1, f_2\}$ and $\theta = \{\theta_1, \theta_2\}$. The proposed model is rewritten as a summarized form: $Y = f(X, Z; \theta) + \epsilon$, where $Z \sim \mathcal{N}(0, I_d)$ and ϵ is the observation error. Given a dataset $D = \{(X_i, Y_i)\}_{i=1}^n$, each training example (X_i, Y_i) should have a corresponding Z_i, but all data shares the same model parameter θ. Intuitively, we should infer Z_i and learn θ to minimize the reconstruction error $\sum_{i=1}^n \|Y_i - f(X_i, Z_i; \theta)\|^2$ based on our formulation in Sect. 3.1. More formally, the model seeks to maximize the observed-data log-likelihood: $\mathcal{L}(\theta) = \sum_{i=1}^n \log p_\theta(Y_i|X_i)$. Specifically, let $p(Z)$ be the prior distribution of Z. Let $p_\theta(Y|X, Z) \sim \mathcal{N}(f(X, Z; \theta), \sigma^2 I)$ be the conditional distribution of the noisy labels Y given Z and X. The conditional distribution of Y given X is $p_\theta(Y|X) = \int p(Z)p_\theta(Y|X, Z)dZ$ with the latent variable Z integrated out. The gradient of $\mathcal{L}(\theta)$ can be calculated according to the following identity:

$$
\begin{aligned}
\frac{\partial}{\partial \theta} \log p_\theta(Y|X) &= \frac{1}{p_\theta(Y|X)} \frac{\partial}{\partial \theta} p_\theta(Y|X) \\
&= \mathrm{E}_{p_\theta(Z|Y,X)} \left[\frac{\partial}{\partial \theta} \log p_\theta(Y, Z|X) \right].
\end{aligned}
\tag{4}
$$

The expectation term $\mathrm{E}_{p_\theta(Z|Y,X)}$ is analytically intractable. The conventional way of training such a latent variable model is to approximate the above expectation term with another family of posterior distribution $p_\phi(Z|Y, X)$, such as variational inference. In this paper, we resort to Monte Carlo average through drawing samples from the posterior distribution $p_\theta(Z|Y, X)$. This step corresponds to inferring the latent vector Z of the generator for each training example. Specifically, we use Langevin Dynamics [23] (a gradient-based Monte Carlo method) to sample Z. The Langevin Dynamics for sampling $Z \sim p_\theta(Z|Y, X)$ iterates:

$$
Z_{t+1} = Z_t + \frac{s^2}{2} \left[\frac{\partial}{\partial Z} \log p_\theta(Y, Z_t|X) \right] + s\mathcal{N}(0, I_d),
\tag{5}
$$

with

$$
\frac{\partial}{\partial Z} \log p_\theta(Y, Z|X) = \frac{1}{\sigma^2}(Y - f(X, Z; \theta)) \frac{\partial}{\partial Z} f(X, Z) - Z,
\tag{6}
$$

where t and s are the time step and step size of the Langevin Dynamics respectively. In each training iteration, for a given data pair (X_i, Y_i), we run l steps of Langevin Dynamics to infer Z_i. The Langevin Dynamics is initialized with Gaussian white noise (i.e., cold start) or the result of Z_i obtained from the

previous iteration (*i.e.*, warm start). With the inferred Z_i along with (X_i, Y_i), the gradient used to update the model parameters θ is:

$$\frac{\partial}{\partial\theta}\mathcal{L}(\theta) \approx \sum_{i=1}^{n} \frac{\partial}{\partial\theta} \log p_\theta(Y_i, X_i | Z_i),$$

$$= \sum_{i=1}^{n} \frac{1}{\sigma^2}(Y_i - f(X_i, Z_i; \theta)) \frac{\partial}{\partial\theta} f(X_i, Z_i). \tag{7}$$

Algorithm 1. Alternating back-propagation for noise-aware encoder-decoder

Input: Dataset with noisy labels $D = \{(X_i, Y_i)\}_{i=1}^{n}$, learning epochs K, number of Langevin steps l, Langevin step size s, learning rate γ

Output: Network parameters $\theta = \{\theta_1, \theta_2\}$, and the inferred latent vectors $\{Z_i\}_{i=1}^{n}$

1: Initialize θ_1 with VGG16-Net[27] for image classification, θ_2 with a truncated Gaussian distribution, and Z_i with a standard Gaussian distribution.

2: **for** $k = 1, ..., K$ **do**

3:     **Inferential back-propagation**: For each i, run l steps of Langevin Dynamics with a step size s to sample $Z_i \sim p_\theta(Z_i | Y_i, X_i)$ following Eq. (5), with Z_i initialized as Gaussian white noise or the result from previous iteration.

4:     **Learning back-propagation**: Update model parameters θ by Adam [14] optimizer with a learning rate γ and the gradient $\frac{\partial}{\partial\theta}[\mathcal{L}(\theta) - \lambda l_s(X, S; \theta)]$, where the gradient of $\mathcal{L}(\theta)$ is computed according to Eq. (7).

5: **end for**

To encourage the latent output S of the encoder-decoder f_1 to be a meaningful saliency map, we add a negative edge-aware smoothness loss [37] defined on S to the log-likelihood objective $\mathcal{L}(\theta)$. The smoothness loss serves as a regularization term to avoid a trivial decomposition of S and Δ given Y. Following [37], we use first-order derivatives (*i.e.*, edge information) of both the latent clean saliency map S and image X to compute the smoothness loss

$$l_s(X, S) = \sum_{u,v} \sum_{d \in x,y} \Psi(|\partial_d S_{u,v}| e^{-\alpha|\partial_d X_{u,v}|}), \tag{8}$$

where Ψ is the Charbonnier penalty formula, defined as $\Psi(s) = \sqrt{s^2 + 1e^{-6}}$, (u, v) represents pixel coordinate, and d indexes over the partial derivative in x and y directions. We estimate θ by gradient ascent on $\mathcal{L}(\theta) - \lambda l_s(X, S; \theta)$. In practice, we set $\lambda = 0.7$, and $\alpha = 10$ in Eq. (8).

The whole process of updating both $\{Z_i\}$ and $\theta = \{\theta_1, \theta_2\}$ is summarized in Algorithm 1, which is implemented as alternating back-propagation, because both gradients in Eq. (5) and (7) can be computed via back-propagation.

3.3   Comparison with Variational Inference

The proposed model can also be learned in a variational inference framework, where the intractable $p_\theta(Z|Y, X)$ in Eq. 4 is approximated by a tractable

$q_\phi(Z|Y,X)$, such as $q_\phi(Z|Y,X) \sim \mathcal{N}(\mu_\phi(Y,X), \mathrm{diag}(v_\phi(Y,X)))$, where both μ_ϕ and v_ϕ are bottom-up networks that map (X,Y) to Z, with ϕ standing for all parameters of the bottom-up networks. The objective of variational inference is:

$$\min_\theta \min_\phi \mathrm{KL}(q_{\mathrm{data}}(Y|X)p_\phi(Z|Y,X)\|p_\theta(Z,Y|X))$$
$$= \min_\theta \min_\phi \mathrm{KL}(q_{\mathrm{data}}(Y|X)\|p_\theta(Y|X)) + \mathrm{KL}(p_\phi(Z|Y,X)\|p_\theta(Z|Y,X)). \quad (9)$$

Recall that the maximum likelihood learning in our algorithm is equivalent to minimizing $\mathrm{KL}(q_{\mathrm{data}}(Y|X)\|p_\theta(Y|X))$, where $q_{\mathrm{data}}(Y|X)$ is the conditional training data distribution. The accuracy of variational inference in Eq. 9 depends on the accuracy of an approximation of the true posterior distribution $p_\theta(Z|Y,X)$ by the inference model $p_\phi(Z|Y,X)$. Theoretically, the variational inference is equivalent to the maximum likelihood solution, when $\mathrm{KL}(p_\phi(Z|Y,X)\|p_\theta(Z|Y,X)) = 0$. However, in practice, there is always a gap between them due to the design of the inference model and the optimization difficulty. Therefore, without relying on an extra assisting model, our alternating back-propagation algorithm is more natural, straightforward and computationally efficient than variational inference. We refer readers to [43] for a comprehensive tutorial on latent variable models.

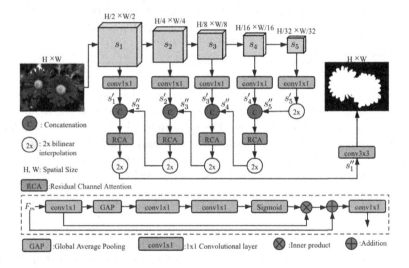

Fig. 2. An illustration of the encoder-decoder-based saliency detection network (Green part in Fig. 1).

3.4   Network Architectural Design

We now introduce the architectural designs of the encoder-decoder network (f_1 in Eq. 1, or the green encoder-decoder in Fig. 1) and the noise generator network (f_2 in Eq. 2, or the yellow decoder in Fig. 1) in this section.

Noise Generator: We construct the noise generator by using four cascaded deconvolutional layers, with a tanh activation function at the end to generate noise map Δ in the range of $[-1, 1]$. Batch normalization and ReLU layers are added between two nearby deconvolutional layers. The dimensionality of the latent variable $d = 8$.

Encoder-Decoder Network: Most existing deep saliency prediction networks are based on widely used backbone networks, including VGG16-Net [27], ResNet [10], etc. Due to stride operations and multiple pooling layers in these deep architectures, the saliency maps that are generated directly using the above backbone networks are low in spatial resolution, causing blurred edges. To overcome this, we propose an encoder-decoder-based framework with VGG16-Net [27] as backbone shown in Fig. 2. We denote the last convolutional layer of each convolutional group of VGG16-Net by $s_1, s_2, ..., s_5$ (corresponding to "relu1_2", "relu2_2", "relu3_3", "relu4_3", and "relu5_3", respectively). To reduce the channel dimension of s_m, 1×1 convolutional layer is used to transform each s_m to a feature map s'_m of channel dimension 32. Then a Residual Channel Attention (RCA) module [56] is adopted to effectively fuse intermediate high- and low-level features as shown in Fig. 2. Specifically, given high- and low-level feature maps s'_m and s'_{m-1}, we first upsample s'_m to s''_m, which has the same spatial size as s'_{m-1}, by bilinear interpolation. Then we concatenate s''_m and s'_{m-1} to form a new feature map F_m. Similar to [56], we feed F_m to the channel attention block to achieve discriminative feature extraction. Inside each channel attention block, we perform "squeeze and excitation" [11] by first "squeezing" the feature map F_m to have half channel size to obtain better nonlinear interactions across channels, and then "exciting" the squeezed feature map to have the original channel size, as shown in Fig. 2. By adding one 3×3 convolutional layer to the lowest level RCA module, we obtain a one-channel saliency map $S_i = f_1(X_i; \theta_1)$.

4   Experiments

4.1   Experimental Setup

Datasets: We evaluate our performance on five saliency benchmark datasets. We used 10,553 images from the DUTS dataset [31] for training, and generate noisy labels from images using handcrafted feature based-methods, such as RBD [59], MR [46] and GS [39] due to their high efficiencies. Testing datasets include DUTS testing set, ECSSD [45], DUT [46], HKU-IS [16] and THUR [4].

Evaluation Metrics: Four evaluation metrics are used to evaluate the performance of ours and competing methods, including two widely used metrics: Mean Absolute Error ($\mathcal{M}$), mean F-measure (F_β), and two newly released structure-aware metrics: mean E-measure (E_ξ) [6] and S-measure (S_α) [5].

Training Details: Each input image is rescaled to 352×352 pixels. The encoder part in Fig. 2 is initialized using the VGG16 weights pretrained for image classification [27]. The weights of other layers are initialized using the "truncated

Gaussian" policy, and the biases are initialized to be zeros. We use the Adam [14] optimizer with a momentum equal to 0.9, and decrease the learning rate by 10% after running 80% of the maximum epochs, which is 20. The learning rate is initialized to be 0.0001. The number of Langevin steps l is 6. The Langevin step size s is 0.3. The σ in Eq. (3) is 0.1. The whole training takes 8 h with a batch size 10 on a PC with an NVIDIA GeForce RTX GPU. We use the PaddlePaddle [2] deep learning platform.

Table 1. Benchmarking performance comparison. Bold numbers represent best performance methods. ↑ & ↓ denote larger and smaller is better, respectively.

	Metric	Fully supervised models							Weakly Sup./Unsup. models					
		DGRL	NLDF	MSNet	CPD	AFNet	SCRN	BASNet	C2S	WSI	WSS	MNL	MSW	Ours
		[32]	[22]	[40]	[41]	[7]	[42]	[25]	[18]	[17]	[31]	[53]	[48]	
DUTS	S_α ↑	.8460	.8162	.8617	.8668	.8671	**.8848**	.8657	.8049	.6966	.7484	.8128	.7588	.8276
	F_β ↑	.7898	.7567	.7917	.8246	.8123	**.8333**	.8226	.7182	.5687	.6330	.7249	.6479	**.7467**
	E_ξ ↑	.8873	.8511	.8829	**.9021**	.8928	.8996	.8955	.8446	.6900	.8061	.8525	.7419	**.8592**
	$\mathcal{M}$ ↓	.0512	.0652	.0490	.0428	.0457	**.0398**	.0476	.0713	.1156	.1000	.0749	.0912	.0601
ECSSD	S_α ↑	.9019	.8697	.9048	.9046	.9074	**.9204**	.9104	-	.8049	.8081	.8456	.8246	.8603
	F_β ↑	.8978	.8714	.8856	.9076	.9008	.9103	**.9128**	-	.7621	.7744	.8098	.7606	.8519
	E_ξ ↑	.9336	.8955	.9218	.9321	.9294	.9333	**.9378**	-	.7921	.8008	.8357	.7876	.8834
	$\mathcal{M}$ ↓	.0447	.0655	.0479	.0434	.0450	.0407	**.0399**	-	.1137	.1055	.0902	.0980	.0712
DUT	S_α ↑	.8097	.7704	.8093	.8177	.8263	**.8365**	.8362	.7731	.7591	.7303	.7332	.7558	.7914
	F_β ↑	.7264	.6825	.7095	.7385	.7425	.7491	**.7668**	.6649	.6408	.5895	.5966	.5970	.7007
	E_ξ ↑	.8446	.7983	.8306	.8450	.8456	.8474	**.8649**	.8100	.7605	.7292	.7124	.7283	.8158
	$\mathcal{M}$ ↓	.0632	.0796	.0636	.0567	.0574	**.0560**	.0565	.0818	.0999	.1102	.1028	.1087	.0703
HKU-IS	S_α ↑	.8968	.8787	.9065	.9039	.9053	**.9158**	.9089	.8690	.8079	.8223	.8602	.8182	.8901
	F_β ↑	.8844	.8711	.8780	.8948	.8877	.8942	**.9025**	.8365	.7625	.7734	.8196	.7337	.8782
	E_ξ ↑	.9388	.9139	.9304	.9402	.9344	.9351	**.9432**	.9103	.7995	.8185	.8579	.7862	.9191
	$\mathcal{M}$ ↓	.0374	.0477	.0387	.0333	.0358	.0337	**.0322**	.0527	.0885	.0787	.0650	.0843	.0428
THUR	S_α ↑	.8162	.8008	.8188	.8311	.8251	**.8445**	.8232	.7922	-	.7751	.8041	-	.8101
	F_β ↑	.7271	.7111	.7177	.7498	.7327	**.7584**	.7366	.6834	-	.6526	6911	-	.7187
	E_ξ ↑	.8378	.8266	.8288	.8514	.8398	**.8575**	.8408	.8107	-	.7747	.8073	-	.8378
	$\mathcal{M}$ ↓	.0774	.0805	.0794	**.0635**	.0724	.0663	.0734	.0890	-	.0966	.0860	-	.0703

4.2 Comparison with the State-of-the-Art Methods

We compare our method with seven fully supervised deep saliency prediction models and five weakly supervised/unsupervised saliency prediction models, and their performances are shown in Table 1 and Fig. 3. Table 1 shows that compared with the weakly supervised/unsupervised models, the proposed method achieves the best performance, especially on DUTS and HKU-IS datasets, where our method achieves an approximately 2% performance improvement for S-measure, and 4% improvement for mean F-measure. Further, the proposed method even achieves comparable performance with some newly released fully supervised models. For example, we achieve comparable performance with NLDF [22] and DGRL [32] on all the five benchmark datasets. Figure 3 shows the 256-dimensional F-measure and E-measure (where the x-axis represents threshold

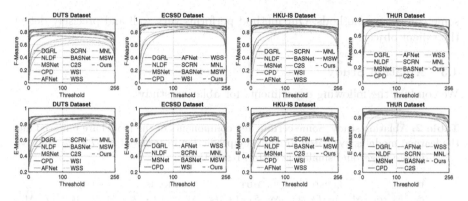

Fig. 3. F-measure and E-measure curves on four datasets (DUTS, ECSSD, HKU-IS, THUR). Best viewed on screen.

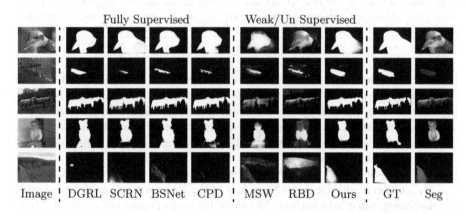

Image | DGRL SCRN BSNet CPD | MSW RBD Ours | GT Seg

Fig. 4. Comparison of saliency predictions, where each row displays an input image, its predicted saliency maps by four fully supervised competing methods (DGRL, SCRN, BASNet, and CPD), one weakly (MSW) and one unsupervised (RBD) methods, our prediction (Ours), the ground truth (GT) saliency map and our segmented foreground image (Seg).

for saliency map binarization) of our method and competing methods on four datasets, where the weakly supervised/unsupervised methods are represented by dotted curves. We can observe that performance of fully supervised models is better than the weakly supervised/unsupervised models. As shown in Fig. 3, our performance shows stability with different thresholds relative to existing methods, indicating the robustness of our proposed solution.

Figure 4 demonstrates a qualitative comparison on several challenging cases. For example, the salient object in the first row is large, and connects to the image border. Most competing methods fail to segment the border-connected region, while our method almost finds the whole salient region. Also, salient object in the second row has a long and narrow shape, which is challenging to

some competing methods. Our method performs very well and precisely detect the salient object.

4.3 Ablation Study

We conduct the following experiments for ablation study.

Table 2. Ablation study. Some certain key components of the model are removed and the learned model is evaluated for saliency prediction in terms of S_α, F_β, E_ξ, and $\mathcal{M}$. ↑ & ↓ denote larger and smaller is better, respectively.

	DUTS				ECSSD				DUT				HKU-IS				THUR			
	S_α	F_β	E_ξ	$\mathcal{M}$	S_α	F_β	E_ξ	$\mathcal{M}$	S_α	F_β	E_ξ	$\mathcal{M}$	S_α	F_β	E_ξ	$\mathcal{M}$	S_α	F_β	E_ξ	$\mathcal{M}$
Model	↑	↑	↑	↓	↑	↑	↑	↓	↑	↑	↑	↓	↑	↑	↑	↓	↑	↑	↑	↓
f_1	.644	.453	.632	.157	.685	.559	.650	.174	.679	.497	.663	.147	.706	.572	.674	.143	.665	.472	.656	.151
$f_1 \& l_s$	.668	.519	.699	.125	.727	.675	.743	.138	.685	.537	.720	.121	.743	.681	.775	.107	.687	.547	.727	.121
$f \& l_c$	.813	.725	.806	.075	.846	.810	.836	.090	.733	.597	.712	.103	.860	.820	.858	.065	.804	.691	.807	.086
Full	.828	.747	.859	.060	.860	.852	.883	.071	.791	.701	.816	.070	.890	.878	.919	.043	.810	.719	.838	.070

(1) **Encoder-decoder f_1 only:** To study the effect of the noise generator, we evaluate the performance of the encoder-decoder (as shown in Fig. 2) directly learned from the noisy labels, without noise modeling. The performance is shown in Table 2 with a label "f_1", which is clearly worse than our results. This result is also consistent with the conclusion that deep neural networks is not robust to noise [49].

(2) **Encoder-decoder f_1 + smoothness loss l_s:** As an extension of method "f_1", one can add the smoothness loss in Eq. (8) as a regularization to better use image prior information. We show its performance with a label "f_1 & l_s" in Table 2. We observe performance improvement compared with "f_1", which indicates the usefulness of the edge-aware smoothness loss.

(3) **Noisy-aware encoder-decoder without edge-aware smoothness loss:** To study the effect of the smoothness regularization, we try to remove the smoothness loss from our model. As a result, we find that it will lead to trivial solutions i.e., $S_i = \mathbf{0}_{H \times W}$ for all training images.

(4) **Alternative smoothness loss:** We also replace our smoothness loss l_s by a cross-entropy loss $l_c(S, X)$ that is also defined on the first-order derivative of the saliency map S and that of the image X. The performance is shown in Table 2 as "$f \& l_c$", which is better than or comparable with the existing weakly supervised/unsupervised methods shown in Table 1. By comparing the performance of "$f \& l_c$" with that of the full model, we observe that the smoothness loss $l_s(S, X)$ in Eq. 8 works better than the cross-entropy loss $l_c(S, X)$. The former puts a soft constraint on their boundaries, while the latter has a strong effect on forcing both boundaries of S and X to be the same. Although saliency boundaries usually are aligned with image boundaries, but they are not exactly the same. A soft and indirect penalty for edge dissimilarity seems to be more useful.

Table 3. Experimental results for model analysis. ↑ & ↓ denote larger and smaller is better, respectively.

Model	DUTS S_α ↑	F_β ↑	E_ξ ↑	$\mathcal{M}$ ↓	ECSSD S_α ↑	F_β ↑	E_ξ ↑	$\mathcal{M}$ ↓	DUT S_α ↑	F_β ↑	E_ξ ↑	$\mathcal{M}$ ↓	HKU-IS S_α ↑	F_β ↑	E_ξ ↑	$\mathcal{M}$ ↓	THUR S_α ↑	F_β ↑	E_ξ ↑	$\mathcal{M}$ ↓
f-BAS	.870	.823	.894	.042	.910	.910	.935	.040	.839	.769	.866	.056	.904	.900	.945	.032	.821	.737	.840	.073
f-RBD	.824	.753	.854	.066	.869	.856	.890	.070	.776	.675	.799	.082	.886	.863	.918	.047	.803	.700	.823	.082
f-MR	.814	.759	.839	.064	.857	.856	.876	.073	.762	.669	.779	.079	.972	.866	.901	.050	.794	.696	.804	.086
f-GS	.787	.740	.811	.071	.826	.836	.843	.087	.737	.652	.753	.083	.837	.843	.865	.062	.804	.723	.840	.071
RBD	.644	.453	.632	.157	.685	.559	.650	.174	.679	.497	.663	.147	.706	.572	.674	.143	.665	.472	.656	.151
MR	.620	.442	.596	.199	.686	.567	.632	.191	.642	.476	.625	.191	.668	.545	.628	.180	.639	.460	.624	.179
GS	.619	.414	.623	.184	.657	.507	.622	.208	.637	.437	.633	.175	.690	.534	.660	.169	.636	.427	.634	.176
f_1*	.840	.769	.868	.054	.893	.883	.915	.054	.783	.676	.802	.073	.894	.871	.926	.040	.815	.720	.834	.077
f*	.861	.803	.887	.045	.906	.899	.927	.046	.815	.721	.836	.060	.905	.887	.933	.036	.831	.743	.849	.070
cVAE	.771	.695	.842	.078	.817	.812	.874	.086	.747	.665	.801	.085	.824	.800	.895	.068	.754	.659	.800	.100
Ours	.828	.747	.859	.060	.860	.852	.883	.071	.791	.701	.816	.070	.890	.878	.919	.043	.810	.719	.838	.070

4.4 Model Analysis

We further explore our proposed model in this section.

(1) **Learn the model from saliency labels generated by fully supervised pre-trained models:** One way to use our method is treating it as a boosting strategy for the current fully-supervised models. To verify this, we first generate saliency maps by using a pre-trained fully-supervised saliency network, *e.g.*, BASNet [25]. We treat the outputs as noisy labels, on which we train our model. The performances are shown in Table 3 as f-BAS. By comparing the performances of f-BAS with those of BASNet in Table 1, we find that f-BAS is comparable with or better than BASNet, which means that our method can further refine the outputs of the state-of-the-art pre-trained fully-supervised models if their performances are still far from perfect.

(2) **Create one single noisy label for each image:** In previous experiments, our noisy labels are generated by handcrafted feature-based saliency methods in the setting of multiple noisy labels per image. Specifically, we produce three noisy labels for each training image by methods RBD [59], MR [46] and GS [39], respectively. As our method has no constraints on the number of noisy labels per image, we conduct experiments to test our models learned in the setting of one noisy label per image. In Table 3, we report the performances of the models learned from noisy labels generated by RBD [59], MR [46] and GS [39], respectively. We use f-RBD, f-MR and f-GS to represent the corresponding results. We observe comparable performances with those using the setting of multiple noisy labels per image, which indicates our method is robust to the number of noisy labels per image and different levels of noisy labels. (RBD ranks the 1st among unsupervised saliency detection models in [3]. RBD, MR and GS can represent different levels of noisy labels). We also show in Table 3 the performances of the above handcrafted feature-based methods, which are denoted by RBD, MR and GS,

respectively. The big gap between RBD/MR/GS and f-RBD/f-MR/f-GS demonstrates the effectiveness of our model.

(3) **Train the model from clean labels:** The proposed noise-aware encoder-decoder can learn from clean labels, because clean labels can be treated as special cases of noisy labels and the noise generator will learn to output zero noise maps in this scenario. We show experiments on training our model from clean labels obtained from the DUTS training dataset. The performances denoted by f^* are shown in Table 3. For comparison purpose, we also train the encoder-decoder component without the noise generator module from clean labels, whose results are displayed in Table 3 with a name f_1^*. We find that (1) our model can still work very well when clean labels are available, and (2) f^* achieves better performance than f_1^*, indicating that even though those clean labels are obtained from training dataset, they are still "noisy" because of imperfect human annotation. Our noise-handling strategy is still beneficial in this situation.

(4) **Train the model by variational inference:** In this paper, we train our model by alternating back-propagation algorithm that maximizes the observed-data log-likelihood, where we adopt Langevin Dynamics to draw samples from the posterior distribution $p_\theta(Z|Y, X)$, and use the empirical average to compute the gradient of the log-likelihood in Eq. (4). One can also train the model in a conditional variational inference framework [28] as shown in Eq. (9). Following cVAE [28], we design an inference network $p_\phi(Z|Y, X)$, which consists of four cascade convolutional layers and a fully connected layer at the end, to map the image X and the noisy label Y to the $d = 8$ dimensional latent space Z. The resulting loss function includes a reconstruction loss $\|Y_i - f(X_i, Z_i, \theta)\|^2$, a KL-divergence loss $\mathrm{KL}(p_\phi(Z|Y, X)\|p_\theta(Z|Y, X))$ and the edge-aware smoothness loss presented in Eq. (8). We present the cVAE results in Table 3. Our results learned by ABP outperforms those by cVAE. The main reason lies in the fact that the gap between the approximate inference model and the true inference model, *i.e.*, $\mathrm{KL}(p_\phi(Z|Y, X)\|p_\theta(Z|Y, X))$, is hard to be zero in practice, especially when the capacity of $p_\phi(Z|Y, X)$ is less than that of $p_\theta(Z|Y, X)$ due to an inappropriate architectural design of $p_\phi(Z|Y, X)$. On the contrary, our Langevin Dynamics-based inference step, which is derived from the model, is more natural and accurate.

5 Conclusion

Although clean pixel-wise annotations can lead to better performance, the expensive and time-consuming labeling process limits the applications of those fully supervised models. Inspired by previous work [24,50,53], we propose a noise-aware encoder-decoder network for disentangled learning of a clean saliency predictor from noisy labels. The model represents each noisy saliency label as an addition of perturbation or noise from an unknown distribution to the clean saliency map predicted from the corresponding image. The clean saliency predictive model is an encoder-decoder framework, while the noise is modeled as a

non-linear transformation of Gaussian latent variables, in which the transformation is parameterized by a neural network. Edge-aware smoothness loss is also utilized to prevent the model from converging to a trivial solution. We propose to train the model by alternating back-propagation algorithm [9,44], which is superior to variational inference. Extensive experiments conducted on different benchmark datasets demonstrate the state-of-the-art performances of our model among the unsupervised saliency detection methods.

Acknowledgments. This research was supported in part by the Australia Research Council Centre of Excellence for Robotics Vision (CE140100016).

References

1. Arbeláez, P., Pont-Tuset, J., Barron, J., Marques, F., Malik, J.: Multiscale combinatorial grouping. In: IEEE Conference on Computer Vision and Pattern Recognition (2014)
2. Baidu: PaddlePaddle. https://www.paddlepaddle.org.cn
3. Borji, A., Cheng, M.M., Jiang, H., Li, J.: Salient object detection: a benchmark. IEEE Trans. Image Process. **24**(12), 5706–5722 (2015)
4. Cheng, M.-M., Mitra, N.J., Huang, X., Hu, S.-M.: SalientShape: group saliency in image collections. Vis. Comput. **30**(4), 443–453 (2013). https://doi.org/10.1007/s00371-013-0867-4
5. Fan, D.P., Cheng, M.M., Liu, Y., Li, T., Borji, A.: Structure-measure: a new way to evaluate foreground maps. In: International Conference on Computer Vision, pp. 4548–4557 (2017)
6. Fan, D.P., Gong, C., Cao, Y., Ren, B., Cheng, M.M., Borji, A.: Enhanced-alignment measure for binary foreground map evaluation. In: International Joint Conference on Artificial Intelligence, pp. 698–704 (2018)
7. Feng, M., Lu, H., Ding, E.: Attentive feedback network for boundary-aware salient object detection. In: IEEE Conference on Computer Vision and Pattern Recognition (2019)
8. Goldberger, J., Ben-Reuven, E.: Training deep neural networks using a noise adaptation layer. In: International Conference on Learning Representations (2017)
9. Han, T., Lu, Y., Zhu, S.C., Wu, Y.N.: Alternating back-propagation for generator network. In: AAAI Conference on Artificial Intelligence (2017)
10. He, K., Zhang, X., Ren, S., Sun, J.: Deep residual learning for image recognition. In: IEEE Conference on Computer Vision and Pattern Recognition, pp. 770–778 (2016)
11. Hu, J., Shen, L., Sun, G.: Squeeze-and-excitation networks. In: IEEE Conference on Computer Vision and Pattern Recognition (2018)
12. Jiang, L., Zhou, Z., Leung, T., Li, L.J., Fei-Fei, L.: MentorNet: learning data-driven curriculum for very deep neural networks on corrupted labels. In: International Conference on Machine Learning (2018)
13. Kingma, D., Welling, M.: Auto-encoding variational bayes. In: International Conference on Learning Representations (2014)
14. Kingma, D.P., Ba, J.: Adam: a method for stochastic optimization. arXiv preprint arXiv:1412.6980 (2014)

15. Li, D., Rodriguez, C., Yu, X., Li, H.: Word-level deep sign language recognition from video: a new large-scale dataset and methods comparison. In: IEEE Winter Conference on Applications of Computer Vision (2020)
16. Li, G., Yu, Y.: Visual saliency based on multiscale deep features. In: IEEE Conference on Computer Vision and Pattern Recognition, pp. 5455–5463 (2015)
17. Li, G., Xie, Y., Lin, L.: Weakly supervised salient object detection using image labels. In: AAAI Conference on Artificial Intelligence (2018)
18. Li, X., Yang, F., Cheng, H., Liu, W., Shen, D.: Contour knowledge transfer for salient object detection. In: European Conference on Computer Vision (2018)
19. Liu, N., Han, J., Yang, M.H.: PicaNet: learning pixel-wise contextual attention for saliency detection. In: IEEE Conference on Computer Vision and Pattern Recognition (2018)
20. Liu, T., Tao, D.: Classification with noisy labels by importance reweighting. IEEE Trans. Pattern Anal. Mach. Intell. **38**(3), 447–461 (2016)
21. Liu, Y., Zhang, Q., Zhang, D., Han, J.: Employing deep part-object relationships for salient object detection. In: International Conference on Computer Vision (2019)
22. Luo, Z., Mishra, A., Achkar, A., Eichel, J., Li, S., Jodoin, P.M.: Non-local deep features for salient object detection. In: IEEE Conference on Computer Vision and Pattern Recognition, pp. 6609–6617 (2017)
23. Neal, R.M.: MCMC using Hamiltonian dynamics. In: Handbook of Markov Chain Monte Carlo, vol. 54, pp. 113–162 (2010)
24. Nguyen, D.T., et al.: DeepUSPS: deep robust unsupervised saliency prediction with self-supervision. In: Advances in Neural Information Processing Systems (2019)
25. Qin, X., Zhang, Z., Huang, C., Gao, C., Dehghan, M., Jagersand, M.: BASNet: boundary-aware salient object detection. In: IEEE Conference on Computer Vision and Pattern Recognition (2019)
26. Reed, S.E., Lee, H., Anguelov, D., Szegedy, C., Erhan, D., Rabinovich, A.: Training deep neural networks on noisy labels with bootstrapping. In: International Conference on Learning Representations (2014)
27. Simonyan, K., Zisserman, A.: Very deep convolutional networks for large-scale image recognition. CoRR abs/1409.1556 (2014)
28. Sohn, K., Lee, H., Yan, X.: Learning structured output representation using deep conditional generative models. In: Advances in Neural Information Processing Systems, pp. 3483–3491 (2015)
29. Tanno, R., Saeedi, A., Sankaranarayanan, S., Alexander, D.C., Silberman, N.: Learning from noisy labels by regularized estimation of annotator confusion. In: IEEE Conference on Computer Vision and Pattern Recognition (2019)
30. Wang, B., Chen, Q., Zhou, M., Zhang, Z., Jin, X., Gai, K.: Progressive feature polishing network for salient object detection. In: AAAI Conference on Artificial Intelligence, pp. 12128–12135 (2020)
31. Wang, L., et al.: Learning to detect salient objects with image-level supervision. In: IEEE Conference on Computer Vision and Pattern Recognition, pp. 136–145 (2017)
32. Wang, T., et al.: Detect globally, refine locally: a novel approach to saliency detection. In: IEEE Conference on Computer Vision and Pattern Recognition (2018)
33. Wang, W., Shen, J., Dong, X., Borji, A.: Salient object detection driven by fixation prediction. In: IEEE Conference on Computer Vision and Pattern Recognition, pp. 1711–1720 (2018)

34. Wang, W., Zhao, S., Shen, J., Hoi, S.C.H., Borji, A.: Salient object detection with pyramid attention and salient edges. In: IEEE Conference on Computer Vision and Pattern Recognition, pp. 1448–1457 (2019)
35. Wang, W., Shen, J., Cheng, M.M., Shao, L.: An iterative and cooperative top-down and bottom-up inference network for salient object detection. In: IEEE Conference on Computer Vision and Pattern Recognition (2019)
36. Wang, W., Zhao, S., Shen, J., Hoi, S.C.H., Borji, A.: Salient object detection with pyramid attention and salient edges. In: IEEE Conference on Computer Vision and Pattern Recognition (2019)
37. Wang, Y., Yang, Y., Yang, Z., Zhao, L., Wang, P., Xu, W.: Occlusion aware unsupervised learning of optical flow. In: IEEE Conference on Computer Vision and Pattern Recognition (2018)
38. Wei, J., Wang, S., Huang, Q.: F3Net: fusion, feedback and focus for salient object detection. In: AAAI Conference on Artificial Intelligence (2020)
39. Wei, Y., Wen, F., Zhu, W., Sun, J.: Geodesic saliency using background priors. In: Fitzgibbon, A., Lazebnik, S., Perona, P., Sato, Y., Schmid, C. (eds.) ECCV 2012. LNCS, vol. 7574, pp. 29–42. Springer, Heidelberg (2012). https://doi.org/10.1007/978-3-642-33712-3_3
40. Wu, R., Feng, M., Guan, W., Wang, D., Lu, H., Ding, E.: A mutual learning method for salient object detection with intertwined multi-supervision. In: IEEE Conference on Computer Vision and Pattern Recognition (2019)
41. Wu, Z., Su, L., Huang, Q.: Cascaded partial decoder for fast and accurate salient object detection. In: IEEE Conference on Computer Vision and Pattern Recognition (2019)
42. Wu, Z., Su, L., Huang, Q.: Stacked cross refinement network for edge-aware salient object detection. In: International Conference on Computer Vision (2019)
43. Xie, J., Gao, R., Nijkamp, E., Zhu, S.C., Wu, Y.N.: Representation learning: a statistical perspective. Annu. Rev. Stat. Appl. 7, 303–335 (2020)
44. Xie, J., Gao, R., Zheng, Z., Zhu, S.C., Wu, Y.N.: Learning dynamic generator model by alternating back-propagation through time. In: AAAI Conference on Artificial Intelligence, vol. 33, pp. 5498–5507 (2019)
45. Yan, Q., Xu, L., Shi, J., Jia, J.: Hierarchical saliency detection. In: IEEE Conference on Computer Vision and Pattern Recognition, pp. 1155–1162 (2013)
46. Yang, C., Zhang, L., Lu, H., Ruan, X., Yang, M.: Saliency detection via graph-based manifold ranking. In: IEEE Conference on Computer Vision and Pattern Recognition, pp. 3166–3173 (2013)
47. Yi, K., Wu, J.: Probabilistic end-to-end noise correction for learning with noisy labels. In: IEEE Conference on Computer Vision and Pattern Recognition (2019)
48. Zeng, Y., Zhuge, Y., Lu, H., Zhang, L., Qian, M., Yu, Y.: Multi-source weak supervision for saliency detection. In: IEEE Conference on Computer Vision and Pattern Recognition (2019)
49. Zhang, C., Bengio, S., Hardt, M., Recht, B., Vinyals, O.: Understanding deep learning requires rethinking generalization. In: International Conference on Learning Representations (2017)
50. Zhang, D., Han, J., Zhang, Y.: Supervision by fusion: towards unsupervised learning of deep salient object detector. In: International Conference on Computer Vision (2017)
51. Zhang, J., Fan, D.P., Dai, Y., Anwar, S., Saleh, F.S., Zhang, T., Barnes, N.: UC-Net: uncertainty inspired RGB-D saliency detection via conditional variational autoencoders. In: IEEE Conference on Computer Vision and Pattern Recognition (2020)

52. Zhang, J., Yu, X., Li, A., Song, P., Liu, B., Dai, Y.: Weakly-supervised salient object detection via scribble annotations. In: IEEE Conference on Computer Vision and Pattern Recognition (2020)
53. Zhang, J., Zhang, T., Dai, Y., Harandi, M., Hartley, R.: Deep unsupervised saliency detection: a multiple noisy labeling perspective. In: IEEE Conference on Computer Vision and Pattern Recognition (2018)
54. Zhang, P., Wang, D., Lu, H., Wang, H., Ruan, X.: Amulet: aggregating multi-level convolutional features for salient object detection. In: International Conference on Computer Vision (2017)
55. Zhang, X., Wang, T., Qi, J., Lu, H., Wang, G.: Progressive attention guided recurrent network for salient object detection. In: IEEE Conference on Computer Vision and Pattern Recognition (2018)
56. Zhang, Y., Li, K., Li, K., Wang, L., Zhong, B., Fu, Y.: Image super-resolution using very deep residual channel attention networks. In: Ferrari, V., Hebert, M., Sminchisescu, C., Weiss, Y. (eds.) ECCV 2018. LNCS, vol. 11211, pp. 294–310. Springer, Cham (2018). https://doi.org/10.1007/978-3-030-01234-2_18
57. Zhao, J.X., Cao, Y., Fan, D.P., Cheng, M.M., Li, X.Y., Zhang, L.: Contrast prior and fluid pyramid integration for RGBD salient object detection. In: IEEE Conference on Computer Vision and Pattern Recognition (2019)
58. Zhao, J.X., Liu, J.J., Fan, D.P., Cao, Y., Yang, J., Cheng, M.M.: EGNet: edge guidance network for salient object detection. In: International Conference on Computer Vision (2019)
59. Zhu, W., Liang, S., Wei, Y., Sun, J.: Saliency optimization from robust background detection. In: IEEE Conference on Computer Vision and Pattern Recognition, pp. 2814–2821 (2014)
60. Zhu, Y., Xie, J., Liu, B., Elgammal, A.: Learning feature-to-feature translator by alternating back-propagation for generative zero-shot learning. In: IEEE Conference on Computer Vision and Pattern Recognition, pp. 9844–9854 (2019)

Rethinking Image Deraining via Rain Streaks and Vapors

Yinglong Wang[1], Yibing Song[2(✉)], Chao Ma[3], and Bing Zeng[1(✉)]

[1] University of Electronic Science and Technology of China, Chengdu, China
ylwanguestc@gmail.com, eezeng@uestc.edu.cn
[2] Tencent AI Lab, Shenzhen, China
yibingsong.cv@gmail.com
[3] MoE Key Lab of Artificial Intelligence, AI Institute,
Shanghai Jiao Tong University, Shanghai, China
chaoma@sjtu.edu.cn

Abstract. Single image deraining regards an input image as a fusion of a background image, a transmission map, rain streaks, and atmosphere light. While advanced models are proposed for image restoration (i.e., background image generation), they regard rain streaks with the same properties as background rather than transmission medium. As vapors (i.e., rain streaks accumulation or fog-like rain) are conveyed in the transmission map to model the veiling effect, the fusion of rain streaks and vapors do not naturally reflect the rain image formation. In this work, we reformulate rain streaks as transmission medium together with vapors to model rain imaging. We propose an encoder-decoder CNN named as SNet to learn the transmission map of rain streaks. As rain streaks appear with various shapes and directions, we use ShuffleNet units within SNet to capture their anisotropic representations. As vapors are brought by rain streaks, we propose a VNet containing spatial pyramid pooling (SSP) to predict the transmission map of vapors in multi-scales based on that of rain streaks. Meanwhile, we use an encoder CNN named ANet to estimate atmosphere light. The SNet, VNet, and ANet are jointly trained to predict transmission maps and atmosphere light for rain image restoration. Extensive experiments on the benchmark datasets demonstrate the effectiveness of the proposed visual model to predict rain streaks and vapors. The proposed deraining method performs favorably against state-of-the-art deraining approaches.

Keyword: Deep image deraining

The results and code are available at https://github.com/yluestc/derain.

Electronic supplementary material The online version of this chapter (https://doi.org/10.1007/978-3-030-58520-4_22) contains supplementary material, which is available to authorized users.

© Springer Nature Switzerland AG 2020
A. Vedaldi et al. (Eds.): ECCV 2020, LNCS 12362, pp. 367–382, 2020.
https://doi.org/10.1007/978-3-030-58520-4_22

1   Introduction

Rain image restoration produces visually pleasing background (i.e., scene content) and benefits recognition systems (e.g., autonomous driving). Attempts [4, 10] of image deraining formulate rain image as the combination of rain streaks and background. These methods limit their restoration performance when the rain is heavy. The limitation occurs because heavy rain consisting of rain streaks and vapors causes severe visual degradation. When the rain streaks are clearly visible, a part of them accumulate to become vapors. The vapors produce the veiling effect which decreases image contrast and causes haze. Figure 1 shows an example. Without considering vapors, existing deraining methods do not perform well to restore heavy rainy images as shown in Fig. 1(b) and Fig. 1(c).

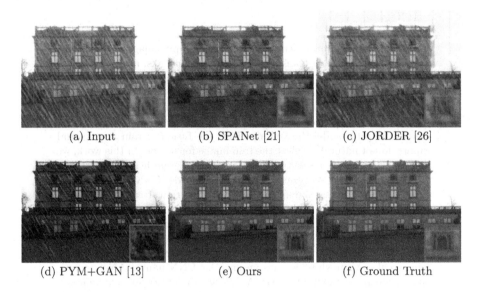

Fig. 1. Rain image restoration results. Input image is shown in (a). Results of SPANet [21], JORDER [26], PYM+GAN [13] are shown in (b)–(d). Ground Truth is shown in (f). The proposed visual model is effective to formulate rain streaks and vapors, which brings high quality deraining result as shown in (e).

Recent study [13] reformulates rain image generation via the following model:

$$\mathbf{I} = \mathbf{T} \odot (\mathbf{J} + \sum_{i=1}^{n} \mathbf{S}_i) + (\mathbb{1} - \mathbf{T}) \odot \mathbf{A} \tag{1}$$

where $\mathbf{I}$ is the rain image, $\mathbf{T}$ is the transmission map, $\mathbf{J}$ is the background to be recovered, $\mathbf{S}_i$ is the rain streak layer, and $\mathbf{A}$ is atmosphere light of the scene. Besides, $\mathbb{1}$ is a matrix whose pixel values are 1 and $\odot$ indicates element-wise multiplication. The transmission map $\mathbf{T}$ encodes influence from vapors to

generate rain images. Based on this model, deraining methods propose various CNNs to predict $\mathbf{T}$, $\mathbf{A}$, and $\mathbf{S}$ to calculate background image $\mathbf{J}$.

Rain streaks and vapors are entangled with each other in practice. Removing them separately is not feasible [13]. Meanwhile, this entanglement makes Eq. (1) difficult to explicitly model both. The limitation raises that the transmission map and rain streaks are not estimated well. The incorrect estimation brings unnatural illumination and color contrasts on the background. Although a generative adversarial network [13] is employed to refine background beyond model constraint, the illumination and color contrasts are not completely corrected as shown in Fig. 1(d).

In this work, we rethink rain image formation by delving rainy model itself. We observe that in Eq. (1), both rain streaks and background are modeled to have the same properties. This is due to the meaning which two terms convey in Eq. (1). The first term $\mathbf{T} \odot (\mathbf{J} + \sum_{i=1}^{n} \mathbf{S}_i)$ indicates that both $\mathbf{S}_i$ and $\mathbf{J}$ are transmitted via $\mathbf{T}$. The rain streaks are regarded as part of the background to be transmitted. The second term $(\mathbb{1} - \mathbf{T}) \odot \mathbf{A}$ shows that rain streaks do not contribute to atmosphere light transmission because only vapors are considered in $\mathbf{T}$. As rain streaks and vapors are entangled with each other, the modeling of rain streaks as background is not accurate. Based on this observation, we propose a visual model which formulates rain streaks as transmission medium. The entanglement of rain streaks and vapors is modeled properly from the transmission medium perspective. We show the proposed model in the following:

$$\mathbf{I} = (\mathbf{T_s} + \mathbf{T_v}) \odot \mathbf{J} + [\mathbb{1} - (\mathbf{T_s} + \mathbf{T_v})] \odot \mathbf{A} \qquad (2)$$

where $\mathbf{T_s}$ and $\mathbf{T_v}$ are the transmission map of rain streaks and vapors, respectively. In our model, all the variables are extended to the same size, so that we utilize element-wise multiplication to describe the relationship of variables.

Rain streaks appear in various shapes and directions. This phenomenon is more obvious in heavy rain. In order to effectively predict $\mathbf{T_s}$, we propose an encoder-decoder CNN with ShuffleNet units [28] named SNet. The group convolutions and channel shuffle improve network robustness upon diverse rain streaks. The learned multiple groups in ShuffleNet units are able to capture anisotropic appearances of rain streaks. Furthermore, we predict transmission map of vapors (i.e., $\mathbf{T_v}$) by using a VNet where there is a spatial pyramid pooling (SPP) structure. VNet takes the concatenation of $\mathbf{I}$ and $\mathbf{T_s}$ as input and use SPP to capture its global and local features in multi-scales for compact representation. On the other hand, we propose an encoder CNN named ANet to predict atmosphere light $\mathbf{A}$. ANet is pretrained by using training data in a simplified low transmission condition, under which we obtain estimated labels of $\mathbf{A}$ from rainy image $\mathbf{I}$. After pretraining ANet, we jointly train SNet, VNet and ANet by measuring the difference between the calculated background $\mathbf{J}$ and the ground truth background. The learned networks well predict $\mathbf{T_s}$, $\mathbf{T_v}$, and $\mathbf{A}$, which are further transformed to generate background images. We evaluate the proposed method on standard benchmark datasets. The proposed visual model is shown effective to model transmission maps of rain streaks and vapors, which are removed in the generated background images.

We summarize the contributions of this work as follows:

- We remodel the rain image formation by formulating rain streaks as transmission medium. The rain streaks and vapor contribute together to transmit both scene content and atmosphere light into input rain images.
- We propose SNet, VNet and ANet to learn rain streaks transmission map, vapor transmission map and atmosphere light. These three CNNs are jointly trained to facilitate the rain image restoration process.
- Experiments on the benchmark datasets show the proposed model is effective to predict rain streaks and vapors. The proposed deraining method performs favorably against state-of-the-art approaches.

2   Related Work

Single image deraining originate from dictionary learning [18] to solve the negative impact of various rain streaks on the background [1,2,8,9,11,16,17,22,23, 29]. Recently, deep learning has obtained better deraining performances compared with the conventional methods. Prevalent deep learning based deraining methods can be categorized as direct mapping method, residual based method and scattering model based methods. Direct mapping based methods directly estimate rain-free background from the observed rainy images via novel CNN networks. It includes the work [21], in which a dataset is first built by incorporating temporal priors and human supervision. Then, a novel SPANet is proposed to solve the random distribution of rain streaks in a local-to-global manner.

A residual rain model is proposed in residual based methods to formulate a rainy image as a summation of the background layer and rain layers. It covers majority of existing deraining methods. For example, Fu et al. train their DerainNet in high-frequency domain instead of the image domain to extract image details to improve deraining visual quality [3]. In the meantime, inspired by the deep residual network (ResNet) [5], a deep detail network which is also trained in high-pass domain was proposed to reduce the mapping range from input to output, to make the learning process easier [4]. Yang et al. create a new model which introduces atmospheric light and transmission to model various rain streaks and veiling effect, but the rainy image is finally decomposed into a rain layer and background layer by their JORDER network. During the training, a binary map is learnt to locate rain streaks to guide the deraining network [25,26]. In [27], the density of rain streaks is classified into three classes and automatically estimated to guide the training of a multi-stream densely connected DID-MDN structure which can better characterize rain streaks with various shape and size. Li et al. regard the rain in rainy images as a summation of multiple rain streak layers, then use a recurrent neural network to remove rain streaks state-wisely [15]. Hu et al. study the visual effect of rain to scene depth, based on which fog is introduced to model the formation of rainy images and the depth feature is learned to guide their end-to-end network to obtain rain layer [7]. In [19], a better and simpler deraining baseline is proposed by considering the network structure, input and output of network, and the loss functions.

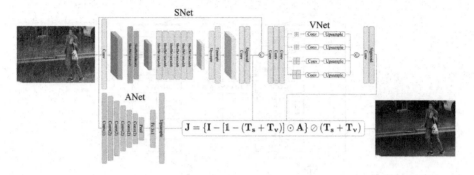

Fig. 2. This figure shows our network structure. The pool denotes adaptive average pooling operation. The Upsample operation after triangle-shaped network extends the atmospheric light **A** to the image size. The notations $\odot$ and $\oslash$ are the pixel-wise multiplication and division, respectively

In the scattering model based methods, atmospheric light and transmission of vapor are rendered and learned to remove rain streaks as well as vapor effect, but rain streaks are treated the same as the background rather than the transmission medium [13]. Different from existing approaches, we reformulate rainy image generation by modeling rain streaks as transmission medium instead of background content, and use two transmission maps to model the influence of rain streaks and vapor on the background. This formulation naturally models the entanglement of rain streaks and vapors and produce more robust results.

3   Proposed Algorithm

We show an overview of the pipeline in Fig. 2. It consists of SNet, VNet and ANet to estimate transmission maps and atmosphere light. The background image can then be computed as follows:

$$\mathbf{J} = \{\mathbf{I} - [\mathbb{1} - (\mathbf{T_s} + \mathbf{T_v})] \odot \mathbf{A}\} \oslash (\mathbf{T_s} + \mathbf{T_v}), \qquad (3)$$

where $\oslash$ is the element-wise division operation. In the following, we first illustrate the network structure of SNet, VNet, and ANet, then we show how we train these three networks in practice and elucidate how these networks function in rain image restoration.

3.1   SNet

We propose a SNet that takes rain image as input and predicts rain streak transmission maps $\mathbf{T_s}$. SNet is an encoder-decoder CNN with ShuffleNet units that consist of group convolutions and shuffling operations. The input CNN features are partially captured by different groups and then shuffled to fuse together. We extend ShuffleNet unit to capture anisotropic representation of rain

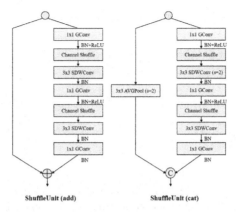

ShuffleUnit (add)   **ShuffleUnit (cat)**

Fig. 3. This figure shows our revised ShuffleNet Units. ShuffleUnit(add) can keep image size unchanged, and ShuffleUnit(cat) downsamples image once. + and C mean addition and concatenation respectively.

streaks as shown in Fig. 2. Our extension is shown in Fig. 3 where we increase the number of group convolutions and deep separable convolution. The features of different groups in single unit will be more discriminative by twice grouping to boost the global feature grouping. Moreover, the depthwise convolution is symmetrically padded (SDWConv) to decrease the influence of padded 0 on the image edges. Finally, we upsample the feature map to original size and convolution layers are followed to fuse multi-group features. The prediction of $\mathbf{T_s}$ on SNet can be written as:

$$\mathbf{T_s} = \mathcal{S}(\mathbf{I}) \tag{4}$$

where $\mathbf{I}$ is the rain image and $\mathcal{S}(\cdot)$ is the SNet inference.

3.2   VNet

We propose a VNet that captures multi-scale features to predict vapor transmission maps $\mathbf{T_v}$. VNet takes the concatenation of rain image $\mathbf{I}$ and $\mathbf{T_s}$ as input where $\mathbf{T_s}$ provides the global intensity information for $\mathbf{T_v}$ and $\mathbf{I}$ supplies the local background information, as different local areas have different vapor intensity. Compared with anisotropic rain streaks, vapor is locally homogeneous and the values of different areas have high correlation. VNet utilizes SPP structure to capture global and local features to provide compact feature representation for $\mathbf{T_v}$ as shown in Fig. 2. The prediction of $\mathbf{T_v}$ on VNet can be written as:

$$\mathbf{T_v} = \mathcal{V}(\text{cat}(\mathbf{I}, \mathbf{T_s})). \tag{5}$$

Algorithm 1. Pretraining ANet

Input: Rainy images $\{\mathbf{I}^{\{t\}}\}$.
1: **for** $i = 1$ to epoch **do**
2:     **for** $j = 1$ to batchnum **do**
3:         Locate rain pixels for $\mathbf{I}^{\{t\}}$ via [25].
4:         Based on Eq. (8), find highest rainy pixel as the ground truth atmospheric light $\mathbf{A}^{\{t\}}$.
5:         Calculate $\mathcal{A}(\mathbf{I}^{\{t\}})$ via Eq. (6).
6:         Updating $\mathcal{A}(\cdot)$ via loss (9).
7:     **end for**
8: **end for**
Output: Learned atmospheric light $\mathbf{A}$.

3.3 ANet

We propose an encoder network ANet to predict atmosphere light. Its structure is shown in Fig. 2. The network inference can be written as:

$$\mathbf{A} = \mathcal{A}(\mathbf{I}), \tag{6}$$

where $\mathcal{A}(\cdot)$ is the ANet inference. As atmosphere light is usually considered constant in the rain image, the output of the encoder is a 3×1 vector. We use an ideal form of our rain model Eq. (2) to create labels of atmospheric light from rain images to pretrain ANet. Then, we integrate ANet into the whole pipeline for joint training. The details are presented in the following.

3.4 Network Training

The pipeline of the whole network consists of a SNet, a VNet, and an ANet to predict $\mathbf{T_s}$, $\mathbf{T_v}$, and $\mathbf{A}$, respectively. Then, we will generate $\mathbf{J}$ according to Eq. (3). We first pretrain ANet using labels from a simplified condition and perform joint training of these three networks.

Pretraining ANet. Sample collection is crucial for pretraining ANet as the ground truth value of atmosphere light is difficult to obtain. Instead of empirically modeling $\mathbf{A}$ as a uniform distribution [13], we generate labels under a simplified condition based on our rain model Eq. (2), where the transmission maps of both rain streaks and vapors are 0. For one pixel x in rain image $\mathbf{I}$, $\mathbf{T_s}(x) + \mathbf{T_v}(\mathbf{x}) = 0$, our visual model of rain image formation can be written as:

$$\mathbf{I}(x) = \mathbf{A}(x) \tag{7}$$

where the pixel value of atmosphere light is equal to that of rain image. In practice, the values of transmission at rain pixel x with high intensity approach 0 (i.e., $\mathbf{T_s}(x) + \mathbf{T_v}(x) \approx 0$). Our model in Eq. 2 can be approximated by:

$$\mathbf{I}(x) = [1 - (\mathbf{T_s}(x) + \mathbf{T_v}(x))] * \mathbf{A}(x) \tag{8}$$

Algorithm 2. Pretraining SNet

Input: Rainy images $\{\mathbf{I}^{\{t\}}\}$ and ground truth background $\{\mathbf{J}^{\{t\}}\}$.
Initialization: $\mathbf{T_v} = 0$ in Eq. (3), $\mathcal{A}(\cdot)$ is initialized with pretrained model in Alg. 1.
1: **for** $i = 1$ to epoch **do**
2:   **for** $j = 1$ to batchnum **do**
3:     Calculate $\mathcal{A}(\mathbf{I}^{\{t\}})$ for $\{\mathbf{I}^{\{t\}}\}$ via Eq. (6).
4:     Calculate $\mathcal{S}(\mathbf{I}^{\{t\}})$ via Eq. (4).
5:     Calculate $\mathcal{J}(\mathbf{I}^{\{t\}})$ via Eq. (3).
6:     Updating $\mathcal{S}(\cdot)$ and fine tuning $\mathcal{A}(\cdot)$ via loss (10).
7:   **end for**
8: **end for**
Output: Learned transmission map $\mathbf{T_s}$ of rain streaks.

---

where the maximum value of $\mathbf{I}(x)$ at rain streak pixels is $\mathbf{A}(x)$. We use [25] to detect rainy pixels in $\mathbf{I}$ and identify the maximum intensity value as ground truth atmospheric light $\mathbf{A}$. In this simplified form, we obtain labels for ANet and train it using the following form:

$$\mathcal{L}_{\mathbf{A}} = \frac{1}{N} \sum_{t=1}^{N} ||\mathcal{A}(\mathbf{I}_t) - \mathbf{A}_t||^2 \qquad (9)$$

where N is the number of training samples. The algorithm is in Algorithm 1.

Pretraining SNet. We pretrain SNet by assuming an ideal case where vapors do not contribute to the transmission (i.e., $\mathbf{T_v} = 0$). We use the input rain image $\mathbf{I}$ and ground truth restoration image $\mathbf{J}$ to train SNet. The objective function can be written as follows:

$$\mathcal{L}_{\mathbf{S}} = \frac{1}{N} \sum_{t=1}^{N} ||\mathcal{J}(\mathbf{I}_t) - \mathbf{J}_t||_F^2 \qquad (10)$$

where $\mathcal{J}(\mathbf{I}_t) = \{\mathbf{I}_t - [\mathbb{1} - \mathcal{S}(\mathbf{I}_t)] \odot \mathcal{A}(\mathbf{I}_t)\} \oslash \mathcal{S}(\mathbf{I}_t)$ derives from Eq. 3. More details are shown in Algorithm 2.

Joint Training. After pretraining ANet and SNet, we perform joint training of the whole network. The overall objective function can be written as:

$$\mathcal{L}_{\text{total}} = \lambda_1 \cdot \frac{1}{N} \sum_{t=1}^{N} ||\nabla \mathcal{J}(\mathbf{I}_t) - \nabla \mathbf{J}_t||_F^2 + \lambda_2 \cdot \frac{1}{N} \sum_{t=1}^{N} ||\mathcal{J}(\mathbf{I}_t) - \mathbf{J}_t||_1 \qquad (11)$$

where ∇ is the gradient operator in both horizontal and vertical directions, λ_1 and λ_2 are constant weights. The value $\mathcal{J}(\mathbf{I}_t)$ is from Eq. (3) consisting of $\mathbf{T_s}$, $\mathbf{T_v}$, and $\mathbf{A}$. These variables are predicted from SNet, VNet, and ANet, respectively. We perform joint training to these networks. As VNet takes the concatenation of $\mathbf{I}$ and $\mathbf{T_s}$ as input, we back propagate the network gradient to SNet via VNet. The details of our joint training is shown in Algorithm 3.

Algorithm 3. Joint training

Input: Rainy images $\{\mathbf{I}^{\{t\}}\}$ and ground truth background $\{\mathbf{J}^{\{t\}}\}$.
Initialization: $\mathcal{A}(\cdot)$ is initialized with fine tuned model in Alg. 2, $\mathcal{S}(\cdot)$ is initialized with pretrained model in Alg. 2.
1: **for** $i = 1$ to epoch **do**
2: **for** $j = 1$ to batchnum **do**
3:   Calculate $\mathcal{A}(\mathbf{I}^{\{t\}})$ for $\{\mathbf{I}^{\{t\}}\}$ via Eq. (6).
4:   Calculate $\mathcal{S}(\mathbf{I}^{\{t\}})$ via Eq. (4).
5:   Calculate $\mathcal{V}(\mathrm{cat}(\mathbf{I}^{\{t\}}, \mathcal{S}(\mathbf{I}^{\{t\}})))$ via Eq. (5).
6:   Calculate $\mathcal{J}(\mathbf{I}^{\{t\}})$ via Eq. (3).
7:   Updating $\mathcal{V}(\cdot)$ and fine tuning $\mathcal{A}(\cdot)$ and $\mathcal{S}(\cdot)$ via loss (11).
8: **end for**
9: **end for**
Output: Learned transmission map $\mathbf{T_s}$ of rain streaks.

3.5 Visualizations

We visualize the intermediate results of our method to verify the effectiveness of our network. In Sect. 3.1, we extract the features of rainy image by 3 separate convolution groups. We show the learned feature maps of different convolution groups in Fig. 4. The (a)–(c) shows that different groups contain different features of rain streaks in various shapes and sizes. The first group extracts slim rain streaks and their shapes are similar, the second group contains wide rain features and the shapes are diversified. The third group captures homogeneous feature representations resembling vapors.

Our rain model allows for the anisotropic transmission map of rain streaks, the homogeneous transmission map of vapor and the atmospheric light of rainy scenes. In Fig. 5, we display the learned transmission map $\mathbf{T_s}$ of rain streaks, the transmission map $\mathbf{T_v}$ of vapor and the atmospheric light $\mathbf{A}$. We can see that $\mathbf{T_s}$ captures the various rain streak information and contains the anisotropy of rainy scenes. While $\mathbf{T_v}$ models the influence of vapor, it possesses the similar values in local areas and different areas are separated by object contours. $\mathbf{A}$ keeps relatively high values, which reflects the fact that atmospheric light possesses high illumination in rainy scenes.

4 Experiments

To assess the performance of our deraining method quantitatively, the commonly used PSNR and SSIM [24] are used as our metrics. In order to evaluate our deraining network more robustly, we measure the quality of deraining results by calculating their Frechet Inception Distance (FID) [6] to the ground truth background. FID is defined via the deep features extracted by Inception-V3 [20], smaller values of FID indicate more similar deraining results to the ground truth. For visual quality evaluation, we show some restored results of real-world and synthetic rainy images. Existing methods [13,15,21,26] are selected to make

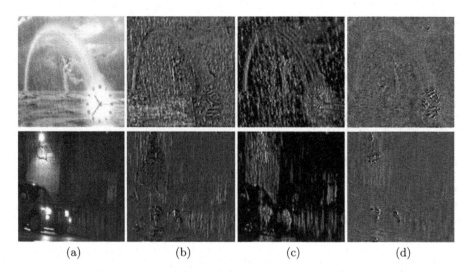

| | (a) | (b) | (c) | (d) |

Fig. 4. Feature maps of different convolution groups. (a) Input rainy images. (b) Features in 1st group. (c) Features in 2nd group. (d) Features in 3rd group. The features of rain streaks in the first group is always slim, the second group extract rain streaks with relatively large size, and the third group contains features of homogeneous vapor.

Table 1. PSNR and SSIM of our ablation studies

Datasets	Rain-I		Rain-II	
Metric	PSNR	SSIM	PSNR	SSIM
C_1	27.15	0.772	25.48	0.793
C_2	27.49	0.806	28.57	0.844
C_3	31.30	0.897	33.86	0.930
Ours	**31.34**	**0.908**	**34.42**	**0.938**

complete comparisons in our paper. The comparisons with another two methods [4,27] are provided in the supplementary file. Except for [13,26,27] which need additional ground truth configuration, these methods are retrained on the same dataset for fair comparisons.

In the training process, we crop 256×256 patches from the training samples, and Adam [12] is used to optimize our network. The learning rate for pretraining ANet is 0.001. While learning $\mathbf{T_s}$, loss $\mathcal{L_S}$ is to train SNet and fine tune ANet in a joint way, the learning rate for SNet is 0.001 and the learning rate for ANet is 10^{-6}. Similarly, in the stage of jointly learning $\mathbf{T_v}$, the learning rate for VNet is 0.001 and the learning rate for SNet and ANet is 10^{-6}. The hyper-parameters λ_1 and λ_2 in Eq. (11) are 0.01 and 1 respectively. Our network is trained on a PC with NVIDIA 1080Ti GPU based on PyTorch framework. The training is converged at the 20-th epoch. Our code will be released publicly.

(a)   (b)   (c)   (d)   (e)   (f)   (g)

Fig. 5. Transmission map of rain streaks and vapor. Input rainy images are shown in (a). Transmission maps $\mathbf{T_s}$ of rain streaks are in (b). Transmission maps $\mathbf{T_v}$ of vapor are in (c). Deraining results with only using $\mathbf{T_s}$ are in (d). Deraining results with $\mathbf{T_v}$ involved are in (e). The Removed rain streaks are shown in (f) and the removed vapors are shown in (g). $\mathbf{T_s}$ is shown to capture anisotropic rain streaks while $\mathbf{T_v}$ models homogeneous vapors.

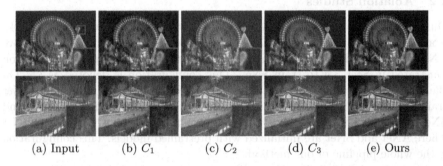

(a) Input   (b) C_1 (c) C_2 (d) C_3 (e) Ours

Fig. 6. Visual results of ablation studies. (a) Input rainy images. (b)–(e) Deraining results under C_1, C_2, C_3 and the whole pipeline, respectively.

4.1 Dataset Constructions

We follow [14] to prepare training dataset where there are 20800 training pairs. The rainy image in each pair is synthesized with ground truth and rendered rainy layer by using screen blend mode. Our evaluation datasets consists of three parts. First, we randomly select 100 images from each dataset in [4,15,25,27], which brings 400 images in total and named as Rain-I. Second, we synthesize 400 images[1] where the synthetic rainy images possess apparent vapor, which is named as Rain-II. Third, we follow the real-world dataset [21] and name it as Rain-III. The real-world rainy images are collected from either existing works or Internet data. The independence between our training and testing datasets ensures the generalization of proposed method.

---

[1] http://www.photoshopessentials.com/photo-effects/rain/.

Table 2. PSNR/SSIM comparisons on our three datasets

Methods	[15]	[26]	[13]	[21]	Ours
Rain-I	27.51/0.897	27.69/0.898	17.96/0.675	28.43/0.848	**31.34/0.908**
Rain-II	26.68/0.830	29.97/0.893	17.99/0.605	30.53/0.905	**34.42/0.938**
Rain-III	34.78/0.943	28.39/0.902	18.48/0.747	35.10/0.948	**35.91/0.951**

Table 3. FID comparisons on our three datasets

Methods	[15]	[26]	[13]	[21]	Ours
Rain-I	62.71	101.74	104.08	81.54	**50.66**
Rain-II	97.30	134.54	118.10	88.15	**67.18**
Rain-III	81.42	89.63	134.34	80.68	**79.86**

4.2 Ablation Studies

Our network consists of SNet, ANet, and VNet. We show how these networks work together to gradually improve image restoration results. We first remove ANet and VNet. The atmosphere light is estimated via the simplified condition illustrated in Sect. 3.4 to train SNet. This configuration is denoted as C_1. On the other side, we incorporate a pretrained ANet and use its output for SNet training, which is denoted as C_2. Also, we perform joint training of ANet and SNet, which is denoted as C_3. Finally, we jointly train ANet, SNet, and VNet where ANet and SNet are initialized with pretrained models. This configuration is the whole pipeline of our method.

Figure 6 and Table 1 show the qualitative and quantitative results. We observe that the results from C_2 are of higher quality than those from C_1. The higher quality indicates that estimating atmosphere light in ideal condition is not stable for effectively image restoration as shown in Fig. 6(b). Compared to C_2, the results from C_3 are more effective to remove rain streaks, which indicates the importance of joint training. However, the vapors are not well removed in the results from C_3. In comparison, by adding VNet to model vapors, we observe haze is further reduced in Fig. 6(e). The numerical evaluations in Table 1 also indicate the effectiveness of joint training and vapor modeling.

4.3 Evaluations with State-of-the-Art

We compare our method with existing deraining methods on three rain datasets (i.e., Rain-I, Rain-II, and Rain-III). The comparisons are categorized as numerical and visual evaluations. The details are presented in the following:

Quantitative Evaluation. Table 2 shows the comparison to existing deraining methods under PSRN and SSIM metrics. Overall, our method achieves favorable results. The PSNR of our method is about 4 dB higher than [21] on Rain-II

dataset. In Table 3, we show the evaluations under the FID metric. This comparison shows that our method achieves lowest FID scores on all three datasets, which indicates that our results resemble most to the ground truth images. The time cost of online inference of comparison methods is shown in Table 4. Our method is able to produce results efficiently.

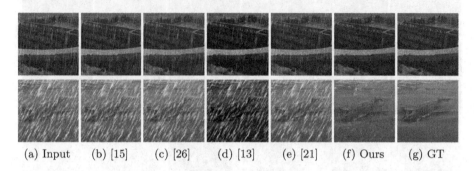

(a) Input   (b) [15]   (c) [26]   (d) [13]   (e) [21]   (f) Ours   (g) GT

Fig. 7. Qualitative comparisons of selected methods and our method on synthetic rainy images. (a) Input rainy images. (b)–(f) Deraining results of RESCAN [15], JORDER [26], PYM+GAN [13], SPANet [21] and our method. (g) Ground truth. These two samples are two failure cases of the state-of-the-art methods.

Table 4. Averaged time cost of comparison methods with a fixed image size of 512×512.

Methods	[15]	[26]	[13]	[21]	Ours
Time	0.47 s	1.39 s	0.45 s	0.66 s	0.03 s

Qualitative Evaluation. We show visual comparison from aspects of synthetic data and real-world data. Figure 7 shows two synthetic rain images where existing methods are able to restore effectively. In comparison, our method is effective to remove both rain streaks and vapors.

Besides synthetic evaluations, we show visual comparisons on real-world images in Fig. 8. When the rain streaks are heavy as shown on the first row of (a), existing methods do not remove these streaks completely. When the rain streaks are mild as shown on the fourth row, all the comparison methods are able to remove their appearance. When the streak edges are blur as shown on the second row, the results of RESCAN and ours are able to faithfully restore while PYM+GAN tends to change the whole color perceptions in Fig. 8(d). Meanwhile, there are artifacts and blocking effects appear on the third row of Fig. 8(d). The limitations also arise in JORDER and SPANET where details are missing shown in Fig. 8(c) and heavy rain streaks remain in Fig. 8(d). Compared to existing methods, our method is able to effectively model both rain streaks and vapors.

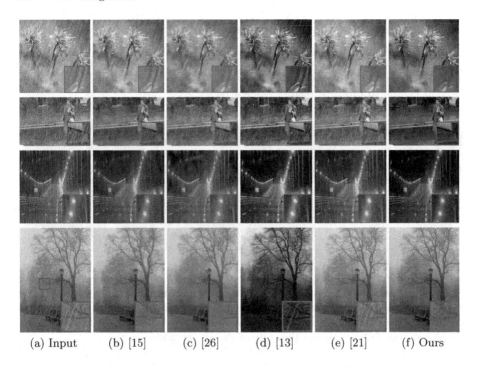

(a) Input   (b) [15]   (c) [26]   (d) [13]   (e) [21]   (f) Ours

Fig. 8. Qualitative comparisons of comparison methods on real-world rainy images. Input images are shown in (a). Deraining results of RESCAN [15], JORDER [26], PYM+GAN [13], SPANet [21] and our method are shown from (b) to (f), respectively.

By jointing training of three subnetworks, the parameters of our visual model is accurately predicted and produces visually pleasing results.

5   Concluding Remarks

"Rain is grace; rain is the sky condescending to the earth; without rain, there would be no life."

—John Updike

Rain nourishes daily life except visual recognition systems. Recent studies on rain image restoration propose models to calculate background images according to rain image formations. A limitation occurs that the appearance of rain consists of rain streaks and vapors, which are entangled with each other in the rain images. We rethink rain image formation by formulating both rain streaks and vapors as transmission medium. We propose two networks to learn transmission maps and atmosphere light that constitute rain image formation. These essential elements in the proposed model are effectively learned via joint network training. Experiments on the benchmark dataset indicate the proposed method performs favorably against state-of-the-art approaches.

Acknowledgement. This work was supported by NSFC (60906119) and Shanghai Pujiang Program.

References

1. Chen, D., Chen, C.-C., Kang, L.: Visual depth guided color image rain streaks removal using sparse coding. IEEE Trans. Circuits Syst. Video Technol. **24**(8), 1430–1455 (2014)
2. Chen, Y.L., Hsu, C.T.: A generalized low-rank appearance model for spatio-temporally correlated rain streaks. In: IEEE International Conference on Computer Vision (ICCV 2013), Sydney, Australia, pp. 1968–1975. IEEE, December 2013
3. Fu, X., Huang, J., Ding, X., Liao, Y., Paisley, J.: Clearing the skies: a deep network architecture for single-image rain removal. IEEE Trans. Image Process. **26**(6), 2944–2956 (2017)
4. Fu, X., Huang, J., Zeng, D., Huang, Y., Ding, X., Paisley, J.: Removing rain from single images via a deep detail network. In: IEEE Conference on Computer Vision and Pattern Recognition (CVPR 2017), Honolulu, HI, USA, pp. 1715–1723. IEEE, July 2017
5. He, K., Zhang, X., Ren, S., Sun, J.: Deep residual learning for image recognition. In: IEEE Conference on Computer Vision and Pattern Recognition (CVPR 2017). IEEE, July 2015
6. Heusel, M., Ramsauer, H., Unterthiner, T., Nessler, B., Hochreiter, S.: GANs trained by a two time-scale update rule converge to a local Nash equilibrium. In: International Conference on Neural Information Processing Systems (NIPS 2017), Long Beach, USA, pp. 6629–6640, December 2017
7. Hu, X., Fu, C.-W., Zhu, L., Heng, P.-A.: Depth-attentional features for single-image rain removal. In: IEEE Conference on Computer Vision and Pattern Recognition (CVPR 2019), Long Beach CA, USA. IEEE, June 2019
8. Huang, D.A., Kang, L.W., Wang, Y.C.F., Lin, C.W.: Self-learning based image decomposition with applications to single image denoising. IEEE Trans. Multimedia **16**(1), 83–93 (2014)
9. Huang, D.A., Kang, L., Yang, M.C., Lin, C.W., Wang, Y.C.F.: Context-aware single image rain removal. In: IEEE International Conference on Multimedia and Expo (ICME 2012), Melbourne, Australia, pp. 164–169. IEEE, July 2012
10. Jiang, T.X., Huang, T.Z., Zhao, X.L., Deng, L.J., Wang, Y.: A novel tensor-based video rain streaks removal approach via utilizing discriminatively intrinsic priors. In: IEEE Conference on Computer Vision and Pattern Recognition (CVPR 2017), Honolulu, HI, USA, pp. 2818–2827. IEEE, July 2017
11. Kang, L., Lin, C.-W., Fu, Y.-H.: Automatic single-image-based rain streaks removal via image decomposition. IEEE Trans. Image Process. **21**(4), 1742–1755 (2012)
12. Kingma, D.P., Ba, J.: Adam: a method for stochastic optimization. In: the 3rd International Conference for Learning Representations (ICLR 2015), San Diego. IEEE (2015)
13. Li, R., Cheong, L.F., Tan, R.T.: Heavy rain image restoration: integrating physics model and conditional adversarial learning. In: IEEE Conference on Computer Vision and Pattern Recognition (CVPR 2019), Long Beach CA, USA. IEEE, June 2019
14. Li, S., Ren, W., Zhang, J., Yu, J., Guo, X.: Fast single image rain removal via a deep decomposition-composition network. Comput. Vis. Image Underst. **186**, 48–57 (2018)

15. Li, X., Wu, J., Lin, Z., Liu, H., Zha, H.: Recurrent squeeze-and-excitation context aggregation net for single image deraining. In: Ferrari, V., Hebert, M., Sminchisescu, C., Weiss, Y. (eds.) ECCV 2018. LNCS, vol. 11211, pp. 262–277. Springer, Cham (2018). https://doi.org/10.1007/978-3-030-01234-2_16

16. Li, Y., Tan, R.T., Guo, X., Lu, J., Brown, M.S.: Rain streak removal using layer priors. In: IEEE Conference on Computer Vision and Pattern Recognition (CVPR 2016), Las Vegas, Nevada, USA, pp. 2736–2744, June 2016

17. Luo, Y., Xu, Y., Ji, H.: Removing rain from a single image via discriminative sparse coding. In: IEEE International Conference on Computer Vision (ICCV 2015), Boston, MA, USA, pp. 3397–3405, December 2015

18. Mairal, J., Bach, F., Ponce, J., Sapiro, G.: Online learning for matrix factorization and sparse coding. J. Mach. Learn. Res. **11**, 19–60 (2010)

19. Ren, D., Zuo, W., Hu, Q., Zhu, P., Meng, D.: Progressive image deraining networks: a better and simpler baseline. In: IEEE Conference on Computer Vision and Pattern Recognition (CVPR 2019), Long Beach CA, USA. IEEE, June 2019

20. Szegedy, C., Vanhoucke, V., Ioffe, S., Shlens, J., Wojna, Z.: Rethinking the inception architecture for computer vision. In: IEEE Conference on Computer Vision and Pattern Recognition (CVPR 2016), pp. 2818–2826, Las Vegas, NV, USA, June 2016

21. Wang, T., Yang, X., Xu, K., Chen, S., Zhang, Q., Lau, R.W.: Spatial attentive single-image deraining with a high quality real rain dataset. In: IEEE Conference on Computer Vision and Pattern Recognition (CVPR 2019), Long Beach CA, USA. IEEE, June 2019

22. Wang, Y., Chen, C., Zhu, S., Zeng, B.: A framework of single-image deraining method based on analysis of rain characteristics. In: IEEE International Conference on Image Processing (ICIP 2013), Phoenix, USA, pp. 4087–4091. IEEE, September 2016

23. Wang, Y., Liu, S., Chen, C., Zeng, B.: A hierarchical approach for rain or snow removing in a single color image. IEEE Trans. Image Process. **26**(8), 3936–3950 (2017)

24. Wang, Z., Bovik, A.C., Sheikh, H.R., Simoncelli, E.P.: Image quality assessment: from error visibility to structural similarity. IEEE Trans. Image Process. **13**(4), 600–612 (2004)

25. Yang, W., Tan, R.T., Feng, J., Liu, J., Guo, Z., Yan, S.: Deep joint rain detection and removal from a single image. In: IEEE Conference on Computer Vision and Pattern Recognition (CVPR 2017), Honolulu, HI, USA, pp. 1685–1694. IEEE, July 2017

26. Yang, W., Tan, R.T., Feng, J., Liu, J., Yan, S., Guo, Z.: Joint rain detection and removal from a single image with contextualized deep networks. IEEE Trans. Pattern Anal. Mach. Intell. **42**(6), 1377–1393 (2019)

27. Zhang, H., Patel, V.M.: Density-aware single image de-raining using a multi-stream dense network. In: IEEE Conference on Computer Vision and Pattern Recognition (CVPR 2018), Salt Lake City, UT, pp. 1685–1694. IEEE, July 2018

28. Zhang, X., Zhou, X., Lin, M., Sun, J.: ShuffleNet: an extremely efficient convolutional neural network for mobile devices. In: Proceedings of the IEEE Conference on Computer Vision and Pattern Recognition, pp. 6848–6856 (2018)

29. Zhang, X., Li, H., Qi, Y., Leow, W.K., Ng, T.K.: Rain removal in video by combining temporal and chromatic properties. In: IEEE International Conference on Multimedia and Expo (ICME 2006), Toronto, Ontario, Canada, vol. 1, pp. 461–464. IEEE, July 2006

Finding Non-uniform Quantization Schemes Using Multi-task Gaussian Processes

Marcelo Gennari do Nascimento🔘, Theo W. Costain$^{(\boxtimes)}$🔘,
and Victor Adrian Prisacariu🔘

Active Vision Lab, University of Oxford, Oxford, UK
{marcelo,costain,victor}@robots.ox.ac.uk
https://code.active.vision

Abstract. We propose a novel method for neural network quantization
that casts the neural architecture search problem as one of hyperparameter search to find non-uniform bit distributions throughout the layers of a
CNN. We perform the search assuming a Multi-Task Gaussian Processes
prior, which splits the problem to multiple tasks, each corresponding to
different number of training epochs, and explore the space by sampling
those configurations that yield maximum information. We then show that
with significantly lower precision in the last layers we achieve a minimal
loss of accuracy with appreciable memory savings. We test our findings
on the CIFAR10 and ImageNet datasets using the VGG, ResNet and
GoogLeNet architectures.

Keywords: Quantization · Bayesian Optimization · Gaussian Process

1 Introduction

The strategy of quantizing neural networks to achieve fast inference has been a
popular method of deploying neural networks in compute constrained environments. Its benefits include significant memory savings, improved computational
speed, and a decreased cost in the energy needed per inference. Many methods
have used this family of strategies, quantizing down to anywhere between 8-bits
and 2-bits, with little loss in accuracy [10,30]. It also bears noting that in most
of these methods, after quantizing to very low precisions (1 to 5 bits), retraining
is necessary to recover accuracy.

Recently, even though the quantization algorithms have significantly
improved, they have almost exclusively *implicitly* assumed that the best strategy is to quantize all the layers uniformly with the same precision. However,
there are two main reasons to believe otherwise: i) we argue that as it has been
interpreted [17] that different layers extract different levels of features, it follows that different layers might require different levels of precision; ii) the idea
of quantization as an approximation to the floating point (FP) version of the

© Springer Nature Switzerland AG 2020
A. Vedaldi et al. (Eds.): ECCV 2020, LNCS 12362, pp. 383–398, 2020.
https://doi.org/10.1007/978-3-030-58520-4_23

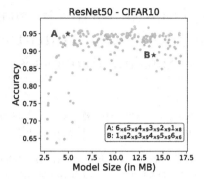

Fig. 1. Gaussian Process prediction for bit distribution in memory vs accuracy plot

network suggests that lower error in the early layers reduces the propagation of errors down the whole network, minimizing any drop in accuracy. We believe that as important as having a good quantization strategy, is to also have a good strategy for the distribution of bits through the network, thereby eliminating any redundant bits. The goal is then to find a configuration in a search space that uses the least amount of bits and achieves the highest accuracy per bit used.

We cast this Neural Architecture Search (NAS) problem into the framework of hyperparameter search, since the bit-width of each layer should ideally be found automatically. As with many NAS approaches, measuring the accuracy of a single configuration can take a considerable amount of time. To mitigate this issue, we propose a two stage approach. First, we map the full search space into a lower dimensional counterpart through a parameterised constraint function, and second, we use a Multi-task Gaussian Process to predict the accuracy at a higher epoch number from lower epoch numbers. This approach allows us to reduce both the complexity of the search space as well as the time required to determine the accuracy of a given configuration. Finally, as our Gaussian Process based approach is suitable for probabalistic inference, we use Bayesian Optimisation (BO) to explore and search the hyperparameter space of variable bit-size configurations.

For the quantization of the network, we use the DSConv method [16]. It achieves high accuracy without significant retraining, meaning the number of epochs needed for full training, and implicitly, the requirement for prediction power, is minimised.

To summarise, our main contributions are as follows:

1. we cast NAS as hyperparameter search, which we apply to the problem of variable bit-size quantization;
2. we reduce the time needed to measure the accuracy of a proposed bit config-uration considerably by using multi-task GPs to infer future accuracy from current estimates;
3. we demonstrate performance across a broad range of configurations, described by Bezier curves and Chebyshev series.

The next sections are as follows: Sect. 2 shows previous work on quantization and hyperparameter search. Section 3 elaborates on the methodology used for search, including the constraint, exploration, and sampling procedures. Section 4 shows the results achieved on the CIFAR10 and ImageNet datasets using the networks listed above. Section 5 draws a conclusion and considers insights from the paper.

2   Related Work

Neural Architecture/Hyperparameter Search. One can consider finding bit distributions as a form of model selection [18], given its complexity and the limit on the parameters that it accepts as a solution. Previous methods have predominantly used Reinforcement Learning (RL) and Evolutionary Algorithms (EA) to model search, which is referred to in the literature as Neural Architecture Search. Examples include NASNet [34], MNasNet [26], ReLeq-Net [6], HAQ [29], among others [1,31] for RL and [13,15,24,33] for EA. Our work overlaps with these papers only on the goal of finding an optimal strategy given a search space.

ReLeQ-Net and HAQ, to the best of our knowledge, are the only methods whose aims are to find the optimal bit distribution through different layers of a network, and are therefore the papers that overlap the most with our work. It is notable that both of them use an RL based approach to search for optimal bit distributions. However, HAQ is more focused on hardware specific optimization, whereas both ours and ReLeQ-Net's methods attempt to be Hardware-Agnostic. Recently some work involving Bayesian Optimization (BO) for model architecture selection has been carried out, with systems such as NASBOT [11]. One of the reasons why BO has not been used for model selection has to do with how unclear it is to find a measure of "distance" between two models, which is the main problem that was addressed by NASBOT.

Alternatively, one can see determining bit distribution as finding hyperparameters to be tuned given a model, *i.e.* not different from finding the optimal learning rates or weight decays. Historically, this has been tackled by BO techniques. In neural networks specifically, this was popularized after the work of [21], and followed by others [2,7,22,27]. As a result BO can be considered a natural method for searching for optimum bit distribution configurations.

Quantization. Quantization strategies can be either trained from scratch or derived from a pretrained network. The methods of [4,10,30,32] initialize their networks from scratch. This ensures that there is no initial bias on the values of the parameters, and they can achieve the minimum difference in accuracy when extremely low bit values are used (1-bit/2-bits) - a notable exception being DoReFa-Net [32], which reportedly had slightly better results when quantizing the network starting from a pretrained network. The methods of [8,14,16,28] quantize the network starting from a pretrained network. These methods start with a bias on the values of the parameters, which can limit how much they recover from the lost accuracy. A benefit of these methods though is that they

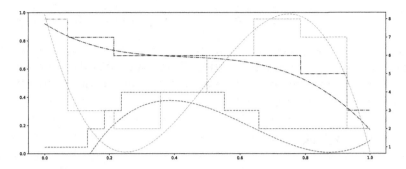

Fig. 2. Three examples of modified Chebyshev functions and their clamped versions. The continuous lines represent the values of the modified Chebyshev functions as function of the layer, which is then converted into bitwidths whose values are represented on the right hand axis. This is for two 8 layer VGG11s and a 20 layer ResNet corresponding to configurations 1) blue: 8,7,6,6,6,6,5,3 2) orange: 8,3,2,4,6,8,7,2 and 3) green: 1,1,1,2,3,4,4,4,4,4,4,3,3,2,2,2,2,2,2,2 (Color figure online)

can be quickly fine-tuned over a few epochs re-achieving state-of-the-art results. These methods are more interesting to us because of their quick deployment cycle. It is worth noting that all of these methods use a uniform distribution of precision, meaning that all layers are quantized to the same number of bits.

3   Method

Our method consists of three parts: constraining, exploring, and sampling the search space. We first constrain the search space by assuming dependence between adjacent bit numbers. We do this by drawing bit distributions from a low-degree Polynomial (in the experiments we use a 2nd degree Bezier curve and a 4th order Chebyshev series). Given a these distributions, we quantize the network using the DSConv [16] method. We explore the space by placing a Gaussian prior over the polynomial parameters, and sampling/retraining a set of hyperparameters that gives the most information about the final payoff function. After exploring, we rank the configurations based on sampling the GP for accuracy, and choose the ones that are the most appropriate for our end-use. Each of these phases will be explained further in this section.

3.1   Constraining the Space

When trying to find the bits, from 1–8, for each layer, the search space will have size of 8^n, where n is the number of layers of the network. For a CNN of 50 layers, the search space will be $2^{150} \approx 10^{45}$, which is a similar size to a game of chess ($\approx 10^{50}$). The size of this space makes an exhaustive search prohibitive.

Our method for constraining the search space relies on the use of parameterised functions. We model a function of degree n with a few parameters, which

describe the search space. We then discretise the function, such that a bit configuration of any layered size network can be sampled from a few parameteres alone.

We use two parameterised functions to illustrate our solution:

- We define the Bezier function $\mathbf{B}(x; \mathbf{w}) = \mathbf{w}^T \phi(x)$ for $x \in \mathbb{R}, \mathbf{w} \in \mathbb{R}^d$, $0 \le x \le 1$, $0 \le w_i \le 1$ $\forall i \in \{i : i \in \mathbb{N}^+, i <= d\}$, where d is the degree of the polynomial. The vector $\phi(x)$ is the feature vector of the Bezier curve *i.e.* for Linear Bezier $\phi(x) = [1-x, \ x]^T$, for Quadratic Bezier $\phi(x) = [(1-x)^2, \ 2(1-x)x, \ x^2]^T$, etc.

- We define the modified Chebysehv function $\mathbf{T}(x; \mathbf{w}) = \frac{(\mathbf{w}-0.5)^T \phi_d(x)+1}{2}$ for $x \in \mathbb{R}, \mathbf{w} \in \mathbb{R}^d$, $-1 \le x \le 1$, $0 \le w_i \le 1$ $\forall i \in \{i : i \in \mathbb{N}^+, i <= d\}$, where d is the degree of the polynomial. The vector $\phi_d(x)$ is defined as $[T_0(x), T_1(x), T_2(x), \ldots, T_{d-1}(x)]^T$ where $T_0(x) = 1, T_1(x) = x$, and $T_{n+1}(x) = 2xT_n(x) - T_{n-1}(x)$

The constraint function, $g(t)$, is then a clamped and rounded version of the chosen polynomial, $p(t)$, such that the bits, b, for each layer generated are between 1 and 8, and $b_i \in \mathbb{N}$. We can define then $g(t) = \lfloor \text{CLAMP}(8p(t)+1), 1, 8) \rceil$, where $\lfloor \cdot \rceil$ is the rounding function, and $\text{CLAMP}(f, a, b) = \min(\max(f, a), b)$.

Figure 2 shows an example of a Chebyshev function and its clamped version. The y-axis in the left indicate the value of the Chebyshev function for different values of x. This is then clamped, rounded, and scaled such that it transforms into a discontinuous line that represents the bit chosen for each layer of a CNN. The bit value is indicated in the y-axis in the right.

By constraining the search space in this way, the minimization problem then shifts as follows:

Naïve Approach	Our Approach

$$\begin{array}{ll} \min_{\mathbf{b}} & \mathcal{L}(t; \mathbf{b}), \mathbf{b} \in \mathbb{N}^n \\ \text{s.t.} & 1 \le b_i \le 8, \ \forall i \in \{1, n\} \end{array} \qquad \begin{array}{ll} \min_{\mathbf{w}} & \mathcal{L}(t; \mathbf{w}), \mathbf{w} \in \mathbb{R}^d \\ \text{s.t.} & b_i = g(\frac{i}{n}), \ \forall i \in \{1, n\} \\ & 0 \le w_j \le 1, \ \forall j \in \{1, d\} \end{array} \qquad (1)$$

where $\mathcal{L}$ is the loss function (to be introduced in Sect. 3.3).

The search then reduces to finding the parameters of the polynomial basis $\mathbf{w}$, which consequently define the bit distributions throughout the layers. The search space is then continuous and compatible with GPs, and significantly reduced to only d dimensions. Using this parameterisation, we are able to easily define a distance metric between configurations to be used when calculating the kernel function and predictive distribution from our Gaussian Process. So, with this setup, the search space can be sufficiently explored in a timely manner.

Quantization Strategy. The method used for quantizing the CNN is DSConv. This is because our aim is to minimize time taken during training, and DSConv has consistently shown good accuracy properties in models, even before retrained.

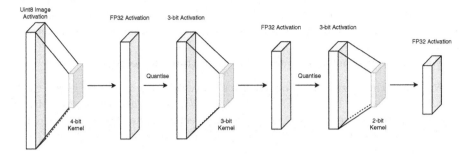

Fig. 3. Quantization given variable bit-widths. Notice that the input is the image, which is a `uint8` tensor (normalization can be dumped into a KDS tensor [16]), so it is not quantized. The quantization of activations is done before the convolution such that the convolution can be done using the same precision.

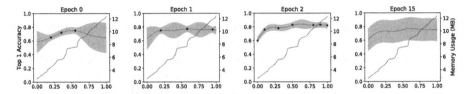

Fig. 4. Multi-task Gaussian Process for inferring accuracy of quantized network. The quantization function is a Bezier Linear with the first parameter set to 0.5 *i.e.* $g(t; w_1) = 0.5 + t(w_1 - 0.5)$. For all figures, the x-axis is the value of w_0, the left y-axis is the accuracy on CIFAR10 of a toy CNN with 10 layers. The right y-axis (red line) shows the model size for a given value of w_0. The epoch correspondences for each task is [0, 1, 2, 15] respectively. After this exploration phase, the decision procedure is run on the predictive distribution of Task 4. (Color figure online)

In this method, both the activations and the weights are quantized, such that fast inference is possible. Each of the weight tensors are divided into blocks of size $B = 32$ depthwise. Each block holds B integers and one FP32 multiplier value. The integers are found by simply scaling each of the block from the original FP32 weight tensor by $\frac{2^{b-1}}{\text{MAX}(w)}$, and then flooring and cropping to range. The FP32 value is calculated by simply minimizing the L2 norm of the block with respect to the original corresponding block: $\xi = \frac{\sum_{i=0}^{B-1} w_i w_{qi}}{\sum_{i=0}^{B-1} w_{qi}^2}$. The activation tensor is quantized similarly, but using Block Floating Point (BFP) format in each of the blocks instead.

In order to take advantage of the low bit multiplication speed, the activation tensor and the weight tensor need to have the same precision. Figure 3 shows how this is done. The activation tensor prior to a convolution layer is set to be quantized to the same bit precision as that layer. The first convolution is not quantized since the input image is already in `uint8` format. Also note that we quantize only the convolutional layers. The Fully Connected layers are all left in the original FP32 precision for training.

3.2   Exploring the Space

Next, we need a way of exploring the space in order to learn the accuracy of the network given a limited set of $\mathbf{w}$ points. We propose a Multi-Task Gaussian Process prior in the neural network, such that each task corresponds to the estimation of the accuracy of the quantized network given $\mathbf{w}$ after a certain number of epochs, e.g. task 1 corresponds to 0 epochs, task 2 to 1 epoch, task 3 to 2 epochs, task 4 to 15 epochs. Let there be m tasks, and a prior on f_l, $l \in \{0, m\}$, such that $f_l \sim \mathcal{GP}(\mu(t), k(t, t'))$. We also place a probability distribution $\mathcal{P}(f_0, f_1, ...f_m)$ over different tasks. Let $y_{(t,l)} = f_l(t) + \epsilon(t)$ be the observation at hyperparameter value t for task l, and let $\epsilon(t) \sim \mathcal{N}(0, \sigma^2; t)$ be the observation noise, which is normally distributed. This defines independent Gaussian Likelihoods $y_{(t,l)} \sim \mathcal{N}(f_l, \sigma^2; t)$. From this model, observations $\mathbf{y}$ are drawn, such that $\mathbf{y} = (y_{11}, ..., y_{s1}..., y_{12}, ..., y_{s2}, ..., y_{1m}, ..., y_{sm})$, where y_{il} is the ith observation of the lth task [23].

We used the Intrinsic Correlation Model (ICM) of [5] and [3] for kernel calculation (in our experiments we made use of the squared exponential kernel). We can then define the mean and the correlation between tasks as:

$$\langle f_l(x) \rangle = \mu_l(x)$$
$$\mathbb{C}(f_l(x), f_{l'}(x')) = k^f(l, l')k^x(x, x') \tag{2}$$

where k^f and k^x are positive semi definite functions, corresponding to the correlation between functions and the correlation between inputs respectively. From this it follows that the covariance is $K = K^f \otimes K^x$, where $\otimes$ is the Kronecker product, K^f is the matrix of correlations between the functions and K^x is the matrix of correlations between the inputs. For a new set of data points x_*, the mean prediction can then be calculated using the normal formula for the predictive distribution:

$$\bar{\mathbf{f}}(x_*) = \mu_l(x_*) + (K^{x_*})^T \Sigma^{-1} \mathbf{y}$$
$$\Sigma = K + D \otimes I \tag{3}$$

where D is an $m \times m$ diagonal matrix where the $(l, l)^{th}$ term is σ_l^2.

Figure 4 shows an example of the Multi-Task setting with a 1D Bezier Curve for ease of visualization. Each plot shows the predictive mean and variance for each epoch after 14 data points have been collected, using the exploration algorithm explained in Sect. 3.2. The idea is to predict what is the distribution of the last task given inputs in earlier tasks.

Exploration Phase. In order to make decisions on what parameters to choose, we need to explore the space to predict the accuracy of the last task. The exploration phase for the multitask Gaussian Process follows the Low-Fidelity Search from [23]. The idea is to find the values of x, l such that it gives us maximal information $\mathbb{I}(y_{(x,l)}; f_m | \mathbf{y}) = \mathbb{H}(y_{(x,l)} | \mathbf{y}) - \mathbb{H}(y_{(x,l)} | \mathbf{y}, f_m)$, where $\mathbf{y}$ is the observation history, and (x, l) is the action to be performed. It is important to weight the information by a measure of the cost that it takes to perform that operation.

So the exploration procedure chooses x, l that maximizes $\mathbb{I}(y_{(x,l)}; f_m \mid \mathbf{y})$ per unit cost. This means that the parameter that has the most information about the payoff function will be picked.

Depending on the dataset and model chosen, the user can favour exploration on one fidelity over the other by decreasing the cost λ of running that particular task. Additionally, we set up a budget on the amount of time in unit cost or number of architectures that we are willing to explore. The Exploration Phase finishes when the Budget has been fully used. After this is finished, the user can run their preferred method of ranking configurations using the posterior of the trained GP.

3.3   Sampling the Space

The naïve goal is to find the highest accuracy per bit possible, which corresponds to finding the minimum of the loss function $\mathcal{L}(t; \mathbf{w}) = -\frac{y_{(t,m)}}{\sum_{i=1}^{n} b_i}$. However, there is a trade-off that must be considered. A model, e.g. ResNet20, using a total of 40 bits and achieving 80% accuracy (ratio of 2%/bit) is arguably worse than a model that uses 43 bits and achieves 85% accuracy (ratio of 1.97%/bit). The goal is instead to find a decision procedure that takes into account the regret of not using more bits based on a set of constraints. This relationship should be linear instead of inversely proportional. A better strategy is to assume that using 4-bits for all layers is the lowest uniform quantization scheme without loss of accuracy. Each bit used less than this should be a reward, and each bit used more than this should be a penalty, this is added (or subtracted) to the accuracy to get an "effective accuracy". We then define the effective accuracy as $\mathcal{E}(a, \mathbf{b}, n) = a - \frac{\sum_{i=1}^{n} b_i - 4n}{k}$, where a is the accuracy of the original network, and k is a constant of penalty per bit. Therefore, for $k = 100$ each bit used in addition to the average of 4-bits incurs a penalty of 1% in the effective accuracy. The reverse incurs a reward of 1% in the effective accuracy. The decision procedure becomes then to minimize the negative effective accuracy, $\mathcal{L} = -\mathcal{E}(a, \mathbf{b}, n)$. Once we have enough information about the GPs, we can rank configurations based on their loss in order to pick the most relevant for us.

4   Experiments and Results

We tested our method in a variety of configurations, using versions of the original VGG, ResNet, and GoogLeNet models, altered in order to take CIFAR10, and ImageNet32 as input. For training CIFAR10 and ImageNet32, we used data augmentation by cropping 32×32 image of the 4-pixel padded original. We used a SGD optimiser with momentum of 0.9, and weight decay of 5×10^{-5}. The learning rate started as 10^{-1}, and was divided by 10 after 150 and 250 epochs.

We ran the exploration procedure on $\sim$65 configurations for each network using the multi-task algorithm outlined above. From these configurations, we could then use the mean of the gaussian to draw estimates of the accuracy

of many different quantization schemes. Using the decision outlined above, we sorted the results by either accuracy, memory, or computational complexity, and selected the points of interest for better visualization and intuition of what the general trend of the found configurations are.

Results on Accuracy Using the CIFAR10 Dataset. Results on CIFAR10 and ablation tests are displayed in Table 1. The configurations are color coded for clarity, with red representing higher bit counts and green representing lower bit counts. These configurations were selected based on the decision procedure outlined above, using the Bezier Linear polynomials.

For comparison, we show 6 configurations of each network: the first and third configurations were picked by our decision procedure; the second and fourth are simply the inverse order of the first and third configurations; the fourth and fifth rows use the traditional uniform distribution of bits for a fair comparison.

It is important to note that the decision to pick these configurations are based on the estimate of the GP rather than on the actual Top-1 results. In order to compare fairly, we also included the Top-1 score and standard deviation from 10 runs after properly training each of them for an additional 30 epochs using the same hyperparameters and optimiser that were used to train their FP32 version. We have also included a delta column which shows the difference between the Top-1 estimate from the GP and the Top-1 after fine-tuning the network. It is remarkable that most of the error in estimation is within 1%, which shows how the GP was able to generalize and interpolate properly as expected.

It can be seen that in general, using more bits in earlier layers yields more accurate, and lighter configurations. The higher accuracy can be explained numerically, since higher bits are used in earlier layers, the error propagation through the network is smaller. The lower memory usage is due to the fact that later layers have a higher number of channels, and therefore using lower precision in those layers yield a massive difference in memory need. For VGG16, the first configuration is both lighter, faster, and more accurate than using 3-bits for all layers. This pattern is repeated for the deeper VGG19 too, where the first configuration yielded superior results to the constant 3-bits for all layers, and also for ResNet18 as well. This "rule of thumb" is somewhat weaker in the GoogLeNet architecture though, even though there is still a clear correlation.

Results on Accuracy Using Chebyshev Series. In order to test robustness of the method in relation to the choice of prior functions, we chose to use a Chebyshev Series of fourth degree, which has a larger search space than the Bezier Linear model. We have tested the model using the CIFAR10 dataset as well, and the results are shown in Table 2.

As it can be seen, the 4th degree introduced more flexibility as to what bit configurations the method is capable of finding. We found that with higher degree of polynomials, the number of architectures to search should also increase. In our experiments, we have searched for ~150 configurations before finding good results. The table shows the expected result that more bits at the beginning compensate for the fewer bits at the end of the network. The ResNet-18 result

Table 1. Results for many configurations on CIFAR10. VGG16 and VGG19 correspond to the architectures introduced in [20]. ResNet18 is the architecture from [9], and the GoogLeNet architecture is from [25]. The Configuration refers to the bit value for each layer of a given model, from earlier layers in the left to later layers in the right. They are color coded for clarity: red for higher bits and green for lower bits. It is important to note that we quantize only the convolutional layers, which means that VGG16 has 13 values, VGG19 has 16 values, ResNet18 has 20 values, and GoogLeNet has 64. Because of its size, the GoogLeNet values were represented by a subscript indicating the number of times that a given bit-width is used. The column "Delta" refers to the difference between the GP estimation of the Top1 accuracy and the actual mean Top1 accuracy ($n = 10$) after properly retraining that particular configuration.

CNN	Configuration (bits per layer)	Top 1 Estimate from GP	Mean Top1	Std	Delta	# Bits	Memory (in MB)
VGG16	32-bit Floating Point	–	93.7%	–	–	–	58.8
	6 555 44 333 22 11	(95.5%)	93.7%	0.2%	−1.8%	50	4.84
	11 22 333 44 555 6	(91.3%)	87.7%	0.2%	−3.6%	50	9.50
	7 66 55 44 33 222 1	(92.1%)	93.7%	0.1%	1.6%	50	5.26
	1 222 33 44 55 66 7	(90.1%)	91.5%	0.4%	1.4%	50	10.75
	4444444444444	(93.3%)	93.8%	0.1%	0.5%	52	8.28
	3333333333333	(92.9%)	93.5%	0.2%	0.6%	39	6.44
VGG19	32-bit Floating Point	–	93.9%	–	–	–	80.1
	6 555 4444 333 222 11	(94.4%)	93.7%	0.1%	−0.7%	54	6.95
	11 222 333 4444 555 6	(91.6%)	89.6%	0.4%	−2.0%	54	12.04
	5 4444 33333 2222 11	(93.9%)	93.5%	0.1%	−0.4%	46	6.14
	11 2222 33333 4444 5	(90.3%)	88.4%	1.2%	−0.9%	46	10.05
	3333333333333333	(92.9%)	93.4%	0.2%	0.5%	48	8.76
	2222222222222222	(92.1%)	92.2%	0.2%	0.1%	32	6.25
ResNet18	32-bit Floating Point	–	95.4%	–	–	–	44.6
	666 5555 4444 3333 2222 1	(96.3%)	95.4%	0.1%	−0.9%	75	3.72
	1 2222 3333 4444 5555 666	(95.9%)	92.9%	0.3%	−3.0%	75	8.00
	44444444 3333333333 22	(95.3%)	95.3%	0.1%	0.0%	60	4.34
	22 3333333333 44444444	(94.5%)	94.2%	0.2%	−0.3%	66	6.08
	33333333333333333333	(94.4%)	95.0%	0.1%	0.6%	60	4.90
	22222222222222222222	(93.1%)	93.3%	0.5%	0.2%	40	3.49
GoogLeNet	32-bit Floating Point	–	95.5%	–	–	–	24.32
	4 ×21 3 ×27 2 ×16	(94.7%)	95.3%	0.1%	0.6%	207	2.35
	2 ×16 3 ×27 4 ×21	(94.6%)	94.2%	0.1%	−0.4%	207	2.98
	6×8 5×13 4×12 3×13 2×13 1×5	(95.8%)	95.3%	0.1%	−0.5%	231	2.65
	1×5 2×13 3×13 4×12 5×14 6×8	(94.7%)	90.5%	0.2%	−4.2%	231	3.73
	3 ×64	(94.7%)	95.1%	0.1%	0.4%	192	2.68
	2 ×64	(93.4%)	93.5%	0.2%	0.1%	127	1.92

resembles the configuration found in Table 4, even though it found a configuration that has more usage of 3-bits, but performs slightly worse. As also expected, when the bit distribution is inverted in the network, it results in both higher memory and lower accuracy.

The same behaviour is found with the VGGs, with the slight difference that as VGG11 is too shallow, it requires more bits to recover the accuracy. VGG16 is considerably deeper, and therefore our algorithm was able to compress it more significantly.

This results shows that our method can be used with a variety of basis. It is worth bearing in mind that the GP processing capability requires the inversion of a matrix, which is proportional to the degree of the polynomial chosen. Therefore our method will only work in a timely manner when using fewer hyperparameters to describe the function.

Table 2. Results of method when using Chebyshev Polynomials of 4th degree.

Method	Network	Bitwidths							Accuracy loss	Memory (as a % of original)
Ours	ResNet18	6	4	33	222	33333333	22		−0.6%	8.0%
		22	33333333	222	33	4	6		−1.2%	11.5%
Ours	VGG11	7	666	7	6	5	4		−0.1%	16.8%
		4	5	6	7	666	7		−0.5%	19.7%
Ours	VGG16	4	3	222	3333	22	11		−0.8%	6.3%
		11	22	3333	222	3	4		−2.4%	8.3%

Results on Network Size. Figure 5 shows the result of the GP-estimated accuracy of different configurations by their model size. The solid purple line links the uniform configurations, starting with all 1s and finishing with all 6s. Therefore, any point that lies above that line is an interesting point, since it gives better accuracy by using the same amount of memory of its uniform counterpart. We have highlighted a number of different interesting configurations with red stars and labelled them from A-M in order to better visualise what each point represent.

As it can be seen in the figure, the choice of bit-usage throughout the network plays an important role in both the accuracy and the memory usage. Even though there is a clear trend that links model size and accuracy, there are a handful of configurations which can perform well on both fronts. It can be seen that, in general, points that are above the purple line are linearly decreasing with bit-usage whereas the ones that are below the purple line are linearly increasing with bit-usage.

The surprising result is that, in the CIFAR10 experiments, even though using uniformly 1-bit for all layers achieves bad results, by just introducing a couple of bits in the first three quarters of the network (such as in points A, C and F), the memory increase is almost negligible, but the accuracy recovery is significant. Adding bits at the end of the network however, achieves the opposite effect. It can also be noticed that points A, C, E, and F, achieve better accuracy than the uniformly 2s configuration whilst using 50% less memory. This is even more evident in point E, in which we used up to 6 bits in the first layers, but still achieved less memory usage due to the usage of 1-bit in the bigger kernels at the end of the network.

In the ImageNet32 experiments, we also see some improvement, albeit less dramatic than the CIFAR10 experiments. The overall massage is still the same, as it can be seen in points H, J and L, for which adding bits in the first layers has achieved good accuracy with small memory increases. It is still noteworthy that even with a dataset as challenging as ImageNet32, due to its substantial decrease of information when compared to the default ImageNet, the GP could find good configurations without needing more datapoints. This shows that this method can be robust to changes in dataset.

Brief Comparison with ReLeQ. One of the other papers that touched in this subject was ReLeQ [6]. As explained in the literature review section, they use a reinforcement learning approach to find optimum bit-distributions over the network. Whilst their quantization methodology varies greatly from that used in this paper, it is worth comparing their results to ours. Their results for the CIFAR10 dataset in two of the networks are shown in Table 3. It can be seen that we achieve similar results for ResNet, though with different mean bits. Since ReLeQ's method does not use the same constraint as our method, it could find more varied solutions. This is a limitation to our method which allows it to find solutions to the network faster whilst using less computational power, but reduces the freedom of choice.

Table 3. Comparison of our accuracy results with ReLeQ's method [6] on CIFAR10. The authors in [6] did not provide their models size in memory, so we estimated using both our and the original author's quantisation scheme to make a fair comparison.

Method	Network	Bitwidths	Accuracy loss	Model size (MB)	
				DSConv	WRPNx1
ReLeQ [6]	ResNet-20	8 22 3 222 3 2 333 222 3 2222 8	0.12%	3.88	3.25
Ours	ResNet-20	666 5555 4444 3333 2222 1	0.1%	3.54	2.91
ReLeQ [6]	VGG-11	8 5 8 5 6666 8	0.17%	6.86	6.61
Ours	VGG-11	777 666 55	0.14%	6.35	5.42
ReLeQ [6]	VGG-16	888 6 8 6 8 6 8 6 8 6 8 6 88	0.1%	13.32	12.54
Ours	VGG16	6 555 44 333 22 11	0.1%	4.62	3.74

Results on ImageNet Using ResNet. For completeness, we have included some of the results found by our algorithm on the more challenging ImageNet dataset [19]. This was trained using an Adam Optimizer [12], with learning rate of 10^{-5}.

Table 4 shows the results. As expected, the same pattern of decreasing precision downstream holds across datasets. Comparing these results with the results from DSConv [16], we can see that a decreasing bit-width throughout the architecture, decreasing from 6 bits to 2, is superior to the "all 4s" and "all 3s".

As with ReLeQ's method, HAQ's method has a weaker constraint on bit distribution, which means it would be able to find configurations that our method would not; However, even with our very strong constraint, we were still able to find configurations that are competitive in memory requirements to those found by HAQ. This shows the strength of the conclusion that later layers require lower precision than earlier layers to maintain the same accuracy.

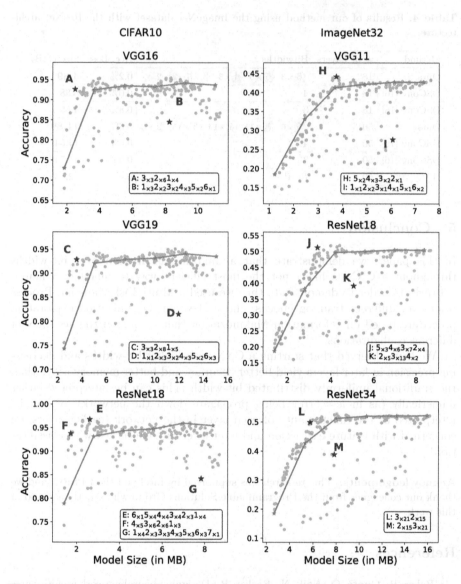

Fig. 5. Scatter plot of the effect on accuracy versus model size of different bit configurations. The left three plots use the CIFAR10 dataset and the right three plots use the ImageNet32 dataset. Note that this is the plot of the estimate as given by the trained GP, and not the actual accuracy given proper training. The solid line refers to the uniform configurations, starting with all 1s and ending with all 6s. Points A-M highlight different configurations as shown in the text boxes. The string of numbers shown refers to the bit size on each layer of the given network. Note that VGG11 has 8 convolutional layers, and therefore points A and B have only 8 numbers. This applies to VGG16 (13 layers), VGG19 (16 layers), ResNet18 (20 layers), and ResNet34 (36 layers) as well.

Table 4. Results of our method using the ImageNet dataset with the ResNet architecture.

Method	# of Layers	Bitwidths	Acc. Loss	Size (MB)
Ours	18	6×3 5×5 4×5 3×5 2×2	0.2%	**4.89**
DSConv [16]	18	4	0.0%	5.88
DSConv [16]	18	3	0.8%	4.55
Ours	50	6×6 5×15 4×14 3×15 2×3	0.6%	**11.89**
DSConv [16]	50	4	0.0%	14.54
DSConv [16]	50	3	0.9%	11.74
HAQ [29]	50	*flexible*	0.0%	12.14

5 Conclusion

In this paper, we demonstrate that a uniform distribution over bit-widths throughout a CNN is likely not the most efficient way to quantize a neural network. In order to demonstrate this, we used a Multi-Task Gaussian Process prior over different training epochs, and a Bayesian Optimization exploration procedure based on Information Maximization that estimated the accuracy of different configurations.

We have observed that starting a CNN with higher bit-widths and decreasing precision in later layers yield better accuracy and better memory usage than the traditional uniformly distributed bit-width. This can be interpreted either numerically (as in less error being propagate down the network), or can be interpreted as the functionality of each layer in the network (earlier layers are concerned with feature extraction and later layers are concerned with classification).

Acknowledgements. This research was supported by Intel and the EPSRC, and we thank our colleagues from the Programmable Solutions Group who greatly assisted in this work.

References

1. Baker, B., Gupta, O., Naik, N., Raskar, R.: Designing neural network architectures using reinforcement learning. arXiv preprint arXiv:1611.02167 (2016)
2. Bergstra, J., Yamins, D., Cox, D.D.: Making a science of model search: hyperparameter optimization in hundreds of dimensions for vision architectures. In: Proceedings of the 30th International Conference on Machine Learning, vol. 28, pp. I–115. JMLR.org (2013)
3. Bonilla, E.V., Chai, K.M., Williams, C.: Multi-task gaussian process prediction. In: Advances in Neural Information Processing Systems, pp. 153–160 (2008)
4. Cai, Z., He, X., Sun, J., Vasconcelos, N.: Deep learning with low precision by half-wave gaussian quantization. In: 2017 IEEE Conference on Computer Vision and Pattern Recognition (CVPR), July 2017. https://doi.org/10.1109/cvpr.2017.574

5. Chai, K.M.: Multi-task learning with Gaussian processes. Ph.D. thesis, The University of Edinburgh (2010)
6. Elthakeb, A.T., Pilligundla, P., Yazdanbakhsh, A., Kinzer, S., Esmaeilzadeh, H.: ReLeQ: a reinforcement learning approach for deep quantization of neural networks. arXiv preprint arXiv:1811.01704 (2018)
7. Feurer, M., Klein, A., Eggensperger, K., Springenberg, J., Blum, M., Hutter, F.: Efficient and robust automated machine learning. In: Advances in Neural Information Processing Systems, vol. 28, pp. 2962–2970 (2015)
8. Han, S., Mao, H., Dally, W.J.: Deep compression: compressing deep neural networks with pruning, trained quantization and Huffman coding. arXiv preprint arXiv:1510.00149 (2015)
9. He, K., Zhang, X., Ren, S., Sun, J.: Deep residual learning for image recognition. In: Proceedings of the IEEE Conference on Computer Vision and Pattern Recognition, pp. 770–778 (2016)
10. Hubara, I., Courbariaux, M., Soudry, D., El-Yaniv, R., Bengio, Y.: Quantized neural networks: training neural networks with low precision weights and activations. J. Mach. Learn. Res. 18(1), 6869–6898 (2017)
11. Kandasamy, K., Neiswanger, W., Schneider, J., Poczos, B., Xing, E.P.: Neural architecture search with Bayesian optimisation and optimal transport. In: Advances in Neural Information Processing Systems, pp. 2016–2025 (2018)
12. Kingma, D.P., Ba, J.: Adam: a method for stochastic optimization. arXiv preprint arXiv:1412.6980 (2014)
13. Kitano, H.: Designing neural networks using genetic algorithms with graph generation system. Complex Syst. 4(4), 461–476 (1990)
14. Lin, X., Zhao, C., Pan, W.: Towards accurate binary convolutional neural network. In: Advances in Neural Information Processing Systems, vol. 30, pp. 345–353 (2017)
15. Liu, H., Simonyan, K., Vinyals, O., Fernando, C., Kavukcuoglu, K.: Hierarchical representations for efficient architecture search. arXiv preprint arXiv:1711.00436 (2017)
16. Nascimento, M.G.D., Fawcett, R., Prisacariu, V.A.: DSConv: efficient convolution operator. In: Proceedings of the IEEE International Conference on Computer Vision, pp. 5148–5157 (2019)
17. Olah, C., Mordvintsev, A., Schubert, L.: Feature visualization. Distill (2017). https://doi.org/10.23915/distill.00007. https://distill.pub/2017/feature-visualization
18. Rasmussen, C.E., Williams, C.K.I.: Gaussian Processes for Machine Learning (Adaptive Computation and Machine Learning). The MIT Press (2005)
19. Russakovsky, O., et al.: ImageNet large scale visual recognition challenge. Int. J. Comput. Vis. (IJCV) 115(3), 211–252 (2015). https://doi.org/10.1007/s11263-015-0816-y
20. Simonyan, K., Zisserman, A.: Very deep convolutional networks for large-scale image recognition. arXiv preprint arXiv:1409.1556 (2014)
21. Snoek, J., Larochelle, H., Adams, R.P.: Practical Bayesian optimization of machine learning algorithms. In: Advances in Neural Information Processing Systems, pp. 2951–2959 (2012)
22. Snoek, J., et al.: Scalable Bayesian optimization using deep neural networks. In: International Conference on Machine Learning, pp. 2171–2180 (2015)
23. Song, J., Chen, Y., Yue, Y.: A general framework for multi-fidelity Bayesian optimization with Gaussian processes. In: The 22nd International Conference on Artificial Intelligence and Statistics, pp. 3158–3167 (2019)

24. Stanley, K.O., Miikkulainen, R.: Evolving neural networks through augmenting topologies. Evol. Comput. **10**(2), 99–127 (2002)
25. Szegedy, C., et al.: Going deeper with convolutions. In: Proceedings of the IEEE Conference on Computer Vision and Pattern Recognition, pp. 1–9 (2015)
26. Tan, M., et al.: MnasNet: platform-aware neural architecture search for mobile. In: Proceedings of the IEEE Conference on Computer Vision and Pattern Recognition, pp. 2820–2828 (2019)
27. Thornton, C., Hutter, F., Hoos, H.H., Leyton-Brown, K.: Auto-WEKA: combined selection and hyperparameter optimization of classification algorithms. In: Proceedings of the 19th ACM SIGKDD International Conference on Knowledge Discovery and Data Mining. KDD 2013, pp. 847–855. ACM, New York (2013). https://doi.org/10.1145/2487575.2487629
28. Vanhoucke, V., Senior, A., Mao, M.Z.: Improving the speed of neural networks on CPUs. In: Deep Learning and Unsupervised Feature Learning Workshop, NIPS. Citeseer (2011)
29. Wang, K., Liu, Z., Lin, Y., Lin, J., Han, S.: HAQ: hardware-aware automated quantization with mixed precision. In: Proceedings of the IEEE Conference on Computer Vision and Pattern Recognition, pp. 8612–8620 (2019)
30. Zhang, D., Yang, J., Ye, D., Hua, G.: LQ-Nets: learned quantization for highly accurate and compact deep neural networks. In: Ferrari, V., Hebert, M., Sminchisescu, C., Weiss, Y. (eds.) ECCV 2018. LNCS, vol. 11212, pp. 373–390. Springer, Cham (2018). https://doi.org/10.1007/978-3-030-01237-3-23
31. Zhong, Z., Yan, J., Wu, W., Shao, J., Liu, C.L.: Practical block-wise neural network architecture generation. In: Proceedings of the IEEE Conference on Computer Vision and Pattern Recognition, pp. 2423–2432 (2018)
32. Zhou, S., Wu, Y., Ni, Z., Zhou, X., Wen, H., Zou, Y.: DoReFa-Net: training low bitwidth convolutional neural networks with low bitwidth gradients. arXiv preprint arXiv:1606.06160 (2016)
33. Zoph, B., Le, Q.V.: Neural architecture search with reinforcement learning. arXiv preprint arXiv:1611.01578 (2016)
34. Zoph, B., Vasudevan, V., Shlens, J., Le, Q.V.: Learning transferable architectures for scalable image recognition. In: Proceedings of the IEEE Conference on Computer Vision and Pattern Recognition, pp. 8697–8710 (2018)

Is Sharing of Egocentric Video Giving Away Your Biometric Signature?

Daksh Thapar[1](✉), Chetan Arora[2], and Aditya Nigam[1]

[1] Indian Institute of Technology Mandi, Mandi, India
d18033@students.iitmandi.ac.in
[2] Indian Institute of Technology Delhi, New Delhi, India
https://egocentricbiometric.github.io/

Abstract. Easy availability of wearable egocentric cameras, and the sense of privacy propagated by the fact that the wearer is never seen in the captured videos, has led to a tremendous rise in public sharing of such videos. Unlike hand-held cameras, egocentric cameras are harnessed on the wearer's head, which makes it possible to track the wearer's head motion by observing optical flow in the egocentric videos. In this work, we create a novel kind of privacy attack by extracting the wearer's gait profile, a well known biometric signature, from such optical flow in the egocentric videos. We demonstrate strong wearer recognition capabilities based on extracted gait features, an unprecedented and critical weakness completely absent in hand-held videos. We demonstrate the following attack scenarios: (1) In a closed-set scenario, we show that it is possible to recognize the wearer of an egocentric video with an accuracy of more than 92.5% on the benchmark video dataset. (2) In an open-set setting, when the system has not seen the camera wearer even once during the training, we show that it is still possible to identify that the two egocentric videos have been captured by the same wearer with an Equal Error Rate (EER) of less than 14.35%. (3) We show that it is possible to extract gait signature even if only sparse optical flow and no other scene information from egocentric video is available. We demonstrate the accuracy of more than 84% for wearer recognition with only global optical flow. (4) While the first person to first person matching does not give us access to the wearer's face, we show that it is possible to match the extracted gait features against the one obtained from a third person view such as a surveillance camera looking at the wearer in a completely different background at a different time. In essence, our work indicates that sharing one's egocentric video should be treated as giving away one's biometric identity and recommend much more oversight before sharing of egocentric videos. The code, trained models, and the datasets and their annotations are available at https://egocentricbiometric.github.io/.

Electronic supplementary material The online version of this chapter (https://doi.org/10.1007/978-3-030-58520-4_24) contains supplementary material, which is available to authorized users.

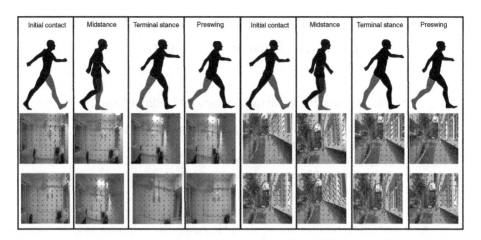

Fig. 1. The figure motivates the presence of the signal to identify a wearer from his/her first person video, even when a wearer is never seen in such videos. Here, we show the relation of optical flow vectors computed from egocentric videos with respect to the gait stance of the camera wearer for two different subjects. The first row shows an indicative third-person stance corresponding to the first person frame. Whereas, the second and third rows show the actual frames captured using the first person camera at the above-specified instance. We synchronized the first-person and third-person videos for purposes of this illustration. We overlay the optical flow vectors for the two different subjects on the respective RGB frames to illustrate the significant difference between the two subjects' optical flow. We draw the reader's attention to the large optical flow observed in the initial contact and pre-swing phases for the first subject (2nd row), whereas for the second subject (3rd row), large optical flow is observed in mid and terminal stance. In this work, we show that it is possible to extract and match the camera wearer's gait features from such optical flow in an open set recognition setting.

1   Introduction

With the reducing cost and increasing comfort level, the use of wearable egocentric cameras is on the rise. Unlike typical point and shoot versions, egocentric cameras are usually harnessed on a wearer's head and allow to capture one's perspective. While the hands-free mode and the first-person perspective make these cameras attractive for adventure sports, and law enforcement, the always-on mode has led to its popularity for life-logging, and geriatric care applications. The broader availability of first-person videos has attracted interest from computer vision community, with specialized techniques proposed for egocentric video summarization, temporal segmentation, and object, action, and activity recognition from first-person viewpoint [1–9] (Fig. 1).

One exciting feature of egocentric videos is that the camera wearer is never visible in them. This has led to many novel applications of egocentric videos, exploiting the unavailability of user identity in such videos. For example, Poleg et al. [10] has observed that since an egocentric camera is mounted on the

wearer's head, the head motion cues are embedded in the observed motion of the captured scene. They have suggested to freely share the observed optical flow in the first-person video to be used as a temporally volatile, authentication signature of the wearer. Their premise is that the optical flow from egocentric videos does not reveal any private identifying information about the wearer. We speculate that the same belief may also be one reason for the wider public sharing of egocentric videos.

In this work, we take position exactly opposite Poleg et al. and posit that the head motion cues contain private information, but they are also highly correlated with the wearer's gait. Human gait is a well known biometric signature [11] and have been traditionally extracted from the third-person view. Hence, through our exploration, we wish to draw the community's attention to a hitherto unknown privacy risk associated with the sharing of egocentric videos, which has never been seen in the videos captured from hand-held cameras. We focus on following specific questions: (1) Given a set of egocentric videos, can we classify a video to its camera wearer? (2) Given two anonymous videos picked from the public video-sharing website, can we say if the same camera wearer captured the two videos without seeing any other video from the wearer earlier? (3) What is the minimum resolution of the optical flow, which may be sufficient to recognize a camera wearer. Specifically, Poleg et al. has suggested the use of global optical flow as privacy safe, temporally volatile signatures. Is it possible to create a wearer's gait profile based on global optical flow? (4) How strong is the gait profile recovered from an egocentric video. Specifically, if there is a corresponding gait profile from a third-person point of view, say from a surveillance camera, is it possible to match the two gait profiles and verify if they belong to the same person? Our findings and specific contributions are as follows:

1. We analyze the biomechanics of a human gait and design a deep neural network, called EgoGaitNet (EGN) to extract the wearer gait from the optical flow in a given egocentric video. In a closed-set setting, when the set of camera wearers are known a-priori, we report an accuracy of 92.5% on the benchmark dataset.
2. We also explore the open-set scenario in which the camera wearers are not known a-priori. For this we train the EGN with ranking loss, and report an Equal Error Ratio (EER) of 14.85% on the benchmark egocentric dataset containing 32% subjects.[1]
3. We tweak the proposed EGN architecture to work with sparse optical flow and show that even with global optical (2 scalars per frame corresponding to the flow in x and y directions), one can identify the camera wearer with a classification accuracy of 77%.
4. While, the three contributions above give a strong capability to recognize a wearer in the closed set setting or identify other egocentric videos from the wearer in a closed set scenario, and they do not reveal the identity/face of the wearer. We propose a novel Hybrid Symmetrical Siamese Network (HSSN),

---

[1] To put the numbers in perspective, for the gait based recognition from third-person views, state of the art EER (on a different third-person dataset) is 4%.

which can extract the gait from third person videos and match it with the gait recovered from EGN. It may be noted that the first-person and third-person videos for this task may have been captured at a completely different time and context/background. Since there is no benchmark dataset available with the corresponding first person and third person videos of the same person, we experiment with dataset generated by us and report an EER of 10.52% for recognizing a wearer across the views.

5. We contribute two new video datasets. The first dataset contains 3.1 h of first-person videos captured from 31 subjects with a variety of physical build in multiple scenarios. The second contains videos captured from 12 subjects for both first-person and third-person setting. We also use the datasets to test the proposed models on the tasks as described above.

2   Related Work

Gait Recognition from Third Person Viewpoint: We note that there has been a significant amount of work on gait recognition from third-person videos that use the trajectory of the limbs [11], joints [12], or silhouette [13–16]. The focus of our work is on extracting gait from egocentric videos. Hence, these works are not directly relevant to the proposed work. However, they serve to support our hypothesis that the motion of the limbs (or the gait in general) also affects the motion of the head, which ultimately gets reflected in the observed optical flow in an egocentric video. Below, we describe only the works related to wearer recognition from first person videos.

Wearer Recognition from Egocentric Videos: Tao et al. [17] have shown that gait features could also be captured from wearable sensors like accelerometer and gyroscope. Finocchiaro et al. [7] estimated the height of the camera from the ground using only the egocentric video. They have extended the original network model proposed in [18] to estimate the height of the wearer, with an Average Mean Error of 14.04 cm over a range of 103 cm of data. They have reported the classification accuracy for relative height (tall, medium, or short) at 93.75%. Jian and Graumann [19], have infered the wearer's pose from the egocentric camera. They have given a learning-based approach that gives the full body 3D joint positions in each frame. The technique uses both the optical flow as well as static scene structures to reveal the viewpoint (e.g., sitting vs. standing).

Hoshen and Poleg [9] have shown that one could identify a camera wearer in a closed set scenario, based on shared optical flow from his/her egocentric camera. They have trained a convolutional neural network using the block-wise optical flow computed from the consecutive egocentric video frames and showed a classification accuracy of 90%. However, their work assumes critical restrictive assumptions relevant to privacy preservation. First, their framework requires many more samples from the same camera wearer to train the classifier for the identification task. The requirement is unrealistic for anonymous videos typically posted on public video sharing websites, with non-cooperating camera wearers.

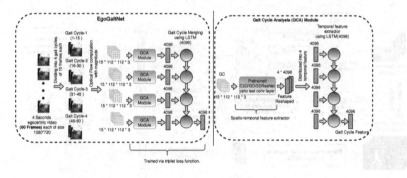

Fig. 2. The network architecture for the proposed first person verification network EgoGaitNet.

Secondly, original head motion signatures suggested by Poleg et al. [10] were computed by averaging the optical flows (resulting in 2 scalars per frame), whereas Hoshen and Poleg have used full-frame optical flows. Thirdly, since the work only matches the first-person to first-person videos, the true identity (or face) of the wearer is never revealed.

Wearer Recognition using Egocentric and Third-Person Videos: There have been techniques that assume the presence of another third-person camera (wearable or static) present simultaneously to the egocentric camera and aim to identify the camera wearer in the third-person view. In [20], authors exploit multiple wearable cameras sharing fields-of-view to measure visual similarity and identify the target subject. Whereas, in [21], the common scene observed by the wearer and a surveillance camera has been used to identify the wearer. Other works compute the location of the wearer directly [22,23] or indirectly (using gaze, social interactions, etc.) [24,25] which is then used to identify the wearer. Unlike our approach, all these techniques assume the presence of the third-person camera view within the same context and time, which though exciting, does not lead to mounting privacy attacks, which is the focus of our work.

3 Proposed Approach

In traditional gait recognition systems, where the subject is visible in the video, the salient features are the limbs' movement. However, in the case of egocentric videos, the subject is not visible, thus ruling out traditional gait recognition methods. Hence for doing so, we look into the biomechanics of gait. A gait cycle consists of multiple gait cycle segments/phases (GCS). Transitioning from these segments causes the overall motion of the body, and hence the correlated motion of the camera harnessed on the head of the camera wearer. Thus, assuming a stationary background, optical flow provides us with information about the GCS transitions.

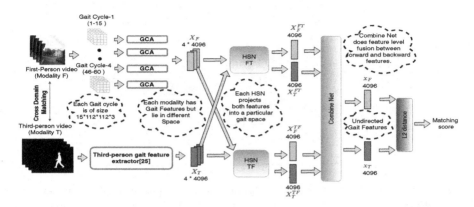

Fig. 3. The network architecture used for the proposed first person to third person Matching Network. The first-person gait feature extractor is taken from the proposed EgoGaitNet. The third-person gait feature extractor is taken from [16].

3.1 Extracting Gait Signatures from Egocentric Videos

In order to extract the gait features from egocentric videos, we propose EgoGait-Net (EGN) model. The architecture of EGN is shown in Fig. 2. We have extracted frames from the videos at 15FPS. We resize each frame to the size of $112 \times 112 \times 3$ and divide each video into clips of 4 s (*i.e.* 60 frames). We compute dense optical flows between each consecutive frame using Gunner Farneback's algorithm [26]. Hence, for each frame, we get $112 \times 112 \times 2$ optical flow matrix, where the channels depict the flow at each point in x and y directions. We compute the magnitude of flow at each point and append the magnitudes with the flow matrix to make it $112 \times 112 \times 3$ optical flow matrix. We hypothesize that each 4-second clip of size $60 \times 112 \times 112 \times 3$ contains the camera wearer's gait information embedded in the optical flow transitions. We further assume that one gait cycle (half step while walking) is 15 frames (1 s) and divides each clip into four parts of 15 frames each. Our choice of gait cycle time (1 s) and the number of gait cycles sufficient to extract gait information (4) is inspired by similar work in third person gait recognition [16].

To extract the gait cycle feature from each of the segmented clips, we propose a Gait Cycle Analysis (GCA) module (as shown in Fig. 2). It consists of a pre-trained spatio-temporal (3D CNN) feature extractor for extracting the intra-gait cycle segment information. We use the features from the last convolutional layer from the 3D CNN and reshape the spatial channels to 1D and obtain a 4×4096 feature vector representation for inputting to the GCA module. Note that the feature vector is obtained from each gait cycle of 15 frames. To further learn features specific to first-person videos, we split the temporal features to make it four vectors of 4096 dimension each. These features are inputted to a temporal feature extractor (LSTM) having 4096 recurrent dimensions (Fig. 2(right side)), and giving us a single 4096 dimensional feature vector representation of a gait cycle. We use four gait cycles to extract the gait signature of a wearer. To learn

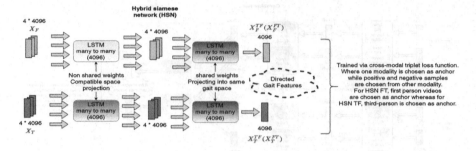

Fig. 4. The network architecture used for the proposed Hybrid Siamese Network (HSN).

inter gait cycle relationships, we pass the 4096 dimensional features corresponding to a gait cycle to a gait cycle merging process, which is an LSTM based architecture with 4096 recurrent dimensions (Fig. 2 (left side)). The output of the LSTM gives us a feature representation of 4096 containing the gait signature of a wearer.

In our experiments, we have done an ablation study to understand the effect of 3D CNN architecture on the performance of EGN. We give the details in the experiment section later as well as in the Supplementary Section.

3.2 Recognizing Wearer from First Person Video

To recognize a wearer from her/his first-person video, we train the EGN network for two scenarios. The first one is closed set recognition, in which the network has already seen the data of every subject during training (classification mode). The second one is the open set scenario in which the testing is done on subjects that have not been seen by the network (metric learning mode).

Closed Set Recognition. For closed set recognition, we train the EGN as a classifier for the camera wearer task. This task is not the prime focus of the work but has been done to compare the performance of the architecture with the current state of the art [9]. A classification layer is added at the end of EGN, and the network is trained using a categorical cross-entropy loss function. To perform the verification task, we have trained our network in a one vs. rest fashion as done by [9] for the fair comparison. We have used ADAM optimizer with a learning rate of 0.0005. We apply dropouts with the dropping probability of 0.5 over the fully connected layer and LSTM except for the classification layer for better regularization. ReLU activation has been used in all the layers except LSTM, where Tanh activation is used. The output of the classification layer is normalized using the softmax activation to convert the output to a pseudo probability vector.

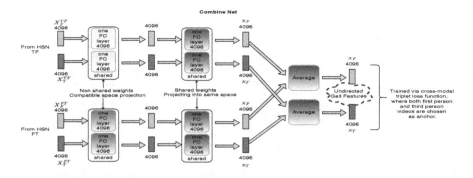

Fig. 5. The network architecture used for the proposed Combine Net.

Open Set Recognition. To perform open set recognition of camera wearer from egocentric videos, we train the EGN network to learn a distance metric between two head motion signatures using triplet loss function. This enables the network to learn a suitable mapping between a sequence of optical flow vectors to a final feature vector (a point in the embedding space defined by the output layer of the network), such that the L_2 distance between the embeddings of the same camera wearer is small and distance between embeddings of different wearers is large. For efficient training of EGN, we apply semi-hard negative mining and dynamic adaptive margin in triplet loss as described by [27]. We use a step-wise modular training procedure to streamline the training of EGN, as described further. First, we train only the 3D CNN, then freeze the 3D CNN and only train the LSTM of GCA module, followed by freezing the GCA and training the gait cycle merging module. Finally, we fine-tune the complete EGN for the first-person recognition task via. triplet loss. Given two video segments i and j, the network must produce an embedding Θ, such that if i and j belong to the same subject, then $L_2(\Theta^i, \Theta^j)$ should tend to 0, otherwise, $L_2(\Theta^i, \Theta^j) \geq \beta$, where β is the margin. The loss has been defined over 3 embeddings: (1) Θ^i: embedding of an anchor video, (2) Θ^{i^+}: embedding of another video from the same wearer, and (3) Θ^{i^-}: embedding of a video from another arbitrary wearer. Formally: $\mathcal{L}(i, i^+, i^-) = \max(0, (\Theta^i - \Theta^{i^+})^2 - (\Theta^i - \Theta^{i^-})^2 + \beta)$ We sum the loss for all possible triples (i, i^+, i^-) to form the cost function J, which is minimized during the training of the proposed architecture: $J = \frac{1}{N} \sum_{i=1}^{N} \mathcal{L}(i, i^+, i^-)$

3.3 Extracting Gait from Sparse Optical Flow

One of the questions that we seek to answer from this work is whether the original head motion signatures proposed by [10], which contain only two scalar values per frame, can reveal wearer's identity? A naive way to do this would be to compute the flow at appropriate spatial resolution and follow the same train and test procedure as done for the dense optical flow. However, given the limited information offered by the global optical flow, we observe severe over-fitting using the naive approach. One possible solution is to use a pre-trained

network. However, here we propose a simple but extremely effective workaround, as described below.

Given a desired optical flow resolution of $x \times y$, we divide each frame into a same-sized grid. We compute the optical flow per cell independently, which is then given as an input to the EGN. However, instead of giving the optical flow of size $x \times y$, we copy the optical flow, coming from each cell to every pixel underlying the cell. This is equivalent to up-sampling the optical flow image using the nearest neighbor technique. We give this up-sampled optical flow as input to the EGN network. Matching the size of the optical flow vector allows us to use a pre-trained network at a much higher resolution and then only fine-tune it on the lower resolution flow as required. As shown in the experimental section, the simple workaround gives us a reasonably good accuracy and allows us to claim the wearer recognition capability even with the frame-level global optical flow. We understand that more sophisticated methods for optical flow up-sampling, including learnable up-sampling, could have used but have not been explored in our experiments.

3.4   Recognizing Wearer from Third Person Video

The main goal of this paper is to match the gait profile extracted from an egocentric video to the gait profile extracted from a third-person video, which allows us to track a camera wearer based on his/her egocentric video alone. To achieve this, we propose two deep neural network architectures called Hybrid Siamese Network (HSN) and Combine Net. The overall pipeline is shown in Fig. 3.

We first extract the third-person gait features using a state-of-the-art third-person gait recognition technique. We have used [16] in our experiments; however, any other similar technique could have been used as well. The input to [16] is 60 RGB frames, divided into four gait cycles as in the case of EGN (which only took optical flow and not RGB). The output of [16] is the gait feature vector of 4×4096 dimension denoted as X_T.

For extracting the gait features from egocentric videos, we use the GCA module described in the EGN and extract a 4096 dimensional feature vector corresponding to each gait cycle segment/phase. Hence for four segments, we get a feature vector of size 4×4096, denoted as X_F in our model. Both X_T and X_F vectors contain the gait information of the camera wearer, but they lie in entirely different spaces as they are coming from very different viewing modalities. To make them compatible, we pass them through the proposed Hybrid Siamese Network (HSN), which is trained to learn a mapping that can project the two vectors into the same gait space.

The HSN is trained using cross-modal triplet loss function (described later below) in which anchors are coming from one modality, and positives and negatives are coming from other modality. This adds a directional attribute to the HSN, causing the metric function learned by HSN to be asymmetric. Hence, we train two HSN networks, one HSN-TF, where the anchor videos are chosen from third-person, and the second HSN-FT, where the anchors are chosen from

egocentric videos. The output embeddings from the two HSN are denotes as X_F^{TF} (X_T^{TF}) and X_F^{FT} (X_T^{FT}) respectively, where subscript T indicates the third person, and F denotes the first-person features.

One way to create an undirectional metric is to merge the matching scores obtained from both HSN TF and HSN FT. Another way is to perform a feature level fusion between the gait features extracted from both the HSN's. The four features (namely $X_F^{\mathrm{TF}}, X_T^{\mathrm{TF}}, X_F^{\mathrm{FT}}, X_T^{\mathrm{FT}}$) transformed by HSN-TF and HSN-FT are not compatible for direct fusion. Hence we propose another neural network *CombineNet* to fuse the features. The details of HSN and Combine Net are given below.

HSN Architecture: As shown in Fig. 4, we first pass both 4×4096 dimensional X_T and X_F vectors through a many-to-many LSTM. The weights of the LSTM for the two vectors are not tied. We follow this up with another many-to-one LSTM network, which transforms the two vectors to a common 4096 dimensional feature space. Both the LSTM layers have a recurrent dimension of 4096. As described earlier, we train two HSNs: HSN-TF, and HSN-FT, with different anchor modalities.

CombineNet Architecture: We combine the asymmetrical features received from the two HSN's using the CombineNet. The Combine Net receives four distinct features of size 4096 (X_F^{TF}, X_T^{TF}, X_F^{FT}, and X_T^{FT}). As shown in Fig. 5, first, a non-shared fully connected layer (FC) is applied over the features. However, since X_F^{TF} and X_T^{TF} are already in the same feature space and so are X_F^{FT} and X_T^{FT}, this FC layer is shared among them. Finally, to transform all the features into the same space, a shared FC layer is applied over the four feature vectors. As the features are now in the same space, both the first-person features and third-person features are averaged for fusion to provide the undirected gait features (X_F, X_T). The training of CombineNet is explained below.

Training Procedure Using Cross-modal Triplet Loss: Both the HSN and CombineNet are trained using cross-modal triplet loss function as described for EGN. However, the selection of triplets is done differently, to learn the desired metrics in both cases. Since the loss function here deals with two modalities, the anchor video is selected from the first modality, whereas the positive and negative videos are selected from the second modality. Despite the different modalities, anchor and positive must belong to the same subject, whereas anchor and negative should belong to different subjects. We train the HSN-FT with cross-modality triplet loss function by selecting the anchors from the first-person videos, whereas for HSN-TF, we select the anchors from third-person videos. We finally freeze the two HSNs and train the CombineNet by selecting both first-person and third-person videos as anchors. For the triplets having first-person videos as the anchor, the positive and negative videos are selected from third-person. Whereas, for triplets having third-person videos as the anchor, the positive and negative videos are selected from the first-person videos.

4   Datasets Used

First Person Social Interactions Dataset (FPSI) [28]: FPSI is a publicly available dataset consisting of video captured by 6 people wearing cameras mounted on their hat, and spending their day at Disney World Resort in Orlando, Florida. We have used only walking sequences from this dataset, where the gait profile of the wearer is reflected in the observed optical flow in the video. *Further, we have tested in the unseen sequence mode where morning videos have been used for training and evening ones for testing.*

Egocentric Video Photographer Recognition Dataset (EVPR) [9]: It consists of videos of 32 subjects taken for egocentric first-person recognition. The data is made using two different cameras. *In our experiments, we use videos captured from one of the cameras for training while the remaining videos have been used for testing.*

Our Dataset for Wearer Recognition in Egocentric Video (IITMD-WFP): We also contribute a new egocentric dataset consisting of 3.1 h of videos captured by 31 different subjects. We introduced variability by taking videos on two different days for each subject. *To maintain testing in unseen sequence settings, we have used the videos from one of the days for training and other for testing.* To introduce further variability in the scene, we have captured in two scenarios: indoor and outdoor, and refer to the respective datasets as DB-01 (indoor), and DB-02 (outdoor). To make sure that the network does not rely on the scene-specific optical flow, we have captured video for each subject in a similar scenario. For both the indoor and outdoor datasets, the path taken by each of the subjects was predefined and fixed, and the videos were captured using the SJCAM 4000 camera. For the biometric applications, it is especially important to show the verification performance over many subjects, since the performance metrics typically degrade quickly with dataset size, due to an exponential increase in the imposter matchings. Hence, we create a combined dataset by merging DB-01, and DB-02, and refer to it as DB-03. We combine EVPR, FPSI, and DB-03 and refer to it as DB-04. After merging, the combined DB-04 dataset contains 69 subjects.

Our Dataset for Wearer Recognition in Third Person Video (IITMD-WTP): To validate our first-person to third-person matching approach, we have collected a dataset containing both third-person and first-person videos of 12 subjects. The third-person videos are captured using Logitech C930 HD camera, whereas the first-person videos from SJCAM 4000 camera. The axis of the third person camera is perpendicular to the walking line of each subject. The total video time of IITMD-WTP dataset is 1 h 3 min having 56,700 frames. For the open-set verification, we use six subjects for training, and remaining unseen subjects for testing. For closed-set analysis, the first five rounds have been used for training and the last five for testing. The representative images and detailed statistics for each dataset have been given in the supplementary material.

5   Experiments and Results

5.1   Hyper-parameters and Ablation Study

Our gait feature extractor module (c.f. Sect. 3.1), uses 3D CNNs for finding spatio-temporal optical flow patterns correlated with wearer's gait. We have performed a rigorous ablation study using different network backbones: C3D [29], I3D [30], and 3D-ResNet [31], which C3D performs the best and has been used for further analysis. We have also compared our architecture with various combination style for merging features from individual gait cycles, and have finally chosen uni-directional LSTM with four gait cycle input. The detailed ablation study is given in the supplementary material.

5.2   Wearer Recognition in Egocentric Videos

Table 1. Comparative analysis of our system with [9] for wearer recognition in egocentric videos. While [9] works only for closed-set scenarios, our system can work both in closed-set as well as open-set scenarios. CA, EER, and DI denote the classification accuracy, Equal Error Rate, and Decidability Index respectively in percentage. Higher CA and lower EER is better.

Dataset	Closed set analysis				Open set analysis		
	[9]		EgoGaitNet		EgoGaitNet		
	CA	EER	CA	EER	EER	CRR	DI
FPSI	76.0	20.34	82.0	19.71	–	–	–
EVPR	90.0	11.3	92.5	9.8	14.35	68.12	1.95
DB-01	95.1	4.38	99.2	2.79	6.43	83.67	2.35
DB-02	93.7	5.03	97.3	3.81	8.23	82.77	2.15
DB-03	94.0	5.72	98.7	4.35	9.39	80.56	2.02
DB-04	85.6	19.64	89.9	15.44	20.61	62.17	0.27

We first analyze our system for recognition capability in egocentric videos. We test in both closed-set (wearers are known and trained for during training) and open-set (wearers are unseen during training) scenarios. Table 1, columns 2–5, compare the performance with [9] for closed-set scenario, in terms of classification accuracy (CA) and Equal Error Rate (EER). The values for EVPR and FPSI datasets have been taken from their paper, whereas for others, we computed the results using the authors' code. It is easy to see that for each dataset, our system improves [9].

For the open-set scenario, we establish the validity of the learned distance by our approach using the decidability index (DI) and rank one correct recognition rate (CRR). Decidability index [32] is a commonly used score in biometrics to evaluate the discrimination between genuine and impostor matching scores in a verification task. The score is defined as: $DI = \frac{|\mu_g - \mu_i|}{\sqrt{(\sigma_g^2 + \sigma_i^2)/2}}$, where $\mu_g(\mu_i)$ is the mean of the genuine (impostor) matching scores, and $\sigma_g(\sigma_i)$ is the standard deviation of the genuine (impostor) matching scores. A large decidability index indicates strong distinguishability characteristics, i.e., high recognition accuracy and robustness. The open-set analysis is not performed over the FPSI dataset as the number of subjects is very small. For the rest of the datasets, half of the subjects from each of the individual datasets were taken for training and rest half for testing. *We believe that open set analysis mimics much more practical*

attack scenarios with uncooperative wearers, which have not been seen at the train time, but we would still like to find other videos captured by them. From Table 1, columns 6–8, it is apparent there is only a minor decrease in the performance of the network compared to the closed-set scenario, which still has a very low error rate. Hence, we can conclude that the proposed model can verify unseen camera wearers also.

The ROC curves for our approach on various datasets are shown in Fig. 6. It can be seen that performance over the EVPR dataset is better than FPSI. This may be due to the fact that the activities performed by the subjects in FPSI are varied, whereas EVPR contains only walking sequences. We

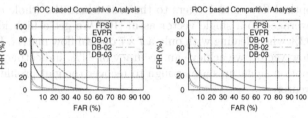

Fig. 6. Left: ROC curves of proposed system on various datasets. Right: The ROC curves for individual datasets when trained and tested on a combined DB-04 dataset. Note that in the combined dataset, an imposter matching increase exponentially and the stable performance of our approach show the technique's strength.

also show the curves for a much larger DB-04 dataset to establish robust recognition performance even with a large number of subjects, indicating significant privacy risk associated with sharing egocentric videos.

Wearer Height Analysis: A doubt regarding our system's good performance can be that it is differentiating based on the wearer's height. We did a limited analysis to verify that there is no such over-fitting in the system. We segregated three subjects of similar height and tested our model on just those 3. For those three subjects of similar height, we got an equal error rate of only 2.03%, showing us that the proposed model can differentiate successfully between the subjects despite having the same height.

Effect of Spatial Resolution of Optical Flow: The experiments so far have been done on dense optical flow. However, one of the questions that we seek to answer is whether the original head motion signatures proposed by [10], which contain only two scalar values per frame, can reveal wearer's identity. As explained in Sect. 3.3, we have created a simple

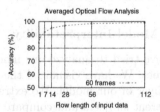

Fig. 7. Performance of our classifier on averaged optical flow, as used in [10].

workaround by simply up-sampling the optical flow given at a lower resolution to the original resolution using the nearest neighbor approach. This allows us to

use a pre-trained network trained with dense optical flow, and fine-tune it with the up-sampled flow. As done in the earlier experiments, we have been careful in separating the unseen wearers at an early stage, which are never shown to the network, either in pre-training or fine-tuning stage. The performance over different sizes of optical flow input is shown in Fig. 7. In the figure, x-axis maps to the number of optical flow values in rows and columns. 112 refers to dense optical flow, and 1 refers to the case where the whole optical flow was globally averaged to a single vector as in [10]. We get a high identification accuracy of 92% when dealing with only a 7×7 optical flow matrix. Even with a single global flow vector, we achieve an accuracy of 84%, indicating that even averaged head motion signatures are enough to recover the gait profile and recognize a camera wearer.

5.3   Wearer Recognition in Third Person Videos

Taking the privacy attack one step further, in this section we show that using HSN proposed in this paper; it is possible to match the gait profile extracted from egocentric videos, even with the one extracted from regular third person videos. For this, we perform experiments on the IITMD-WTP dataset under both closed-set and open-set protocols. For the former, the first five walks of every subject were used for training and the last 5 for testing the system. Whereas in the open-set scenario, only the first six subjects were used for training, and the system has been evaluated on the last six unseen subjects. Table 2 shows the results. We report the scores for both HSN-FT and HSN-TF and the CombineNet, which fuses the features from HSN-FT and HSN-TF.

Table 2. Performance analysis for recognizing a wearer in a third person video. The score fusion approach refers to classifying/verifying a sample by average of HSN-FT and HSN-TF scores.

Model	Closed-set analysis			Open-set analysis		
	EER	CRR	DI	EER	CRR	DI
HSN-FT	11.45	72.46	1.68	15.84	69.27	1.02
HSN-TF	11.02	75.78	1.70	15.36	69.75	1.02
Score Fusion	8.76	76.24	1.72	13.68	71.65	1.05
CombineNet	9.21	79.86	1.71	14.02	73.36	1.06

5.4   Model Interpretability

We have tried to analyze our model to understand if it can learn the wearer's gait cues. We have visualized the activations of 3-D convolutional filters of the first layer of our model. We extract activations from the optical flow input of 2 different subjects and compare the filters having maximum activation corresponding to the two subjects. Figure 8 shows two such filters for subjects 1 and 2. Recall that the first layer in our model is a 3-D CNN layer with the kernel of size $3 \times 3 \times 3$, and input to the network is of the size $15 \times 112 \times 112 \times 3$, where 3 channels correspond to optical flow in x, and y directions, and its magnitude. Recall that we take a gait cycle of 15 frames. The output of the first layer filter

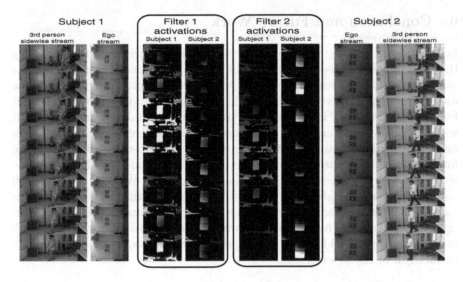

Fig. 8. Filter activations of filter 1 and 2 of first layer for two different subjects with same background and external surroundings. Please refer to the paper text for the details. We speculate on the basis of the visualization that initial layers of the proposed network are temporally segmenting a gait phase. This effectively allows the following layers to learn gait specific features.

is of size $15 \times 112 \times 112$. Figure 8 shows the activations for 10 frames. In the first and last columns, we have shown the 3rd person gait respective to each of the subjects. The second column from the left and right shows the corresponding 1st person video frame. The 3rd and 4th columns show the activations corresponding to each subject's optical flow input from filter 1. The 5th and 6th columns show the activations corresponding to each subject's optical flow input from filter 2. These activations have been overlaid with the input optical flow vectors. Note that the RGB frames are only for illustration purposes, whereas the proposed model only uses the optical flow.

We observe that filter activations are mostly synchronized with the gait phases. For example, filter 1 activations are high when subject 1 moves his/her one leg while the other leg is stationary. We observe that similar movement of subject 2 is captured by filter 2. We speculate that the initial layers of our network are trying to segment the gait and trigger on a specific gait phase, which then is combined into distinguishing features by the later layers. Moreover, it can also be seen that the activations are high in the spatially salient parts of the image. In these parts, one can capture useful features for computing optical flows. Since gait features are present in the transition of optical flows from one frame to another, we believe that the network captures the gait features only and not overfitting over the structure of the input scene.

6   Conclusion and Future Work

In this paper, we have tried to create a new kind of privacy attack by using the head-mounting property of wearable egocentric cameras. Our experiments validate a startling revelation that it is possible to extract gait signatures of the wearer from the observed optical flow in the egocentric videos. Once the gait features are extracted, it is possible to train a deep neural network to match it with the gait features extracted from another egocentric video, or more surprisingly, even with the gait extracted from another third person video. While the former allows us to search other first person videos captured by the wearer, the latter completely exposes the camera wearer's identity. We hope that through our work, we will be able to convince the community that sharing egocentric videos should be treated as sharing one's biometric signatures, and strong oversight may be required before public sharing of such videos. To extend this work in the future, we would like to investigate other body-worn devices' ability to extract gait of the wearer.

References

1. Huang, Y., Cai, M., Li, Z., Sato, Y.: Mutual context network for jointly estimating egocentric gaze and actions. arXiv preprint arXiv:1901.01874 (2019)
2. Xu, J., Mukherjee, L., Li, Y., Warner, J., Rehg, J.M., Singh, V.: Gaze-enabled egocentric video summarization via constrained submodular maximization. In: Proceedings of the IEEE Conference on Computer Vision and Pattern Recognition, pp. 2235–2244 (2015)
3. Kopf, J., Cohen, M.F., Szeliski, R.: First-person hyper-lapse videos. ACM Trans. Graph. (TOG) **33**(4), 78 (2014)
4. Ren, X., Gu, C.: Figure-ground segmentation improves handled object recognition in egocentric video. In: 2010 IEEE Computer Society Conference on Computer Vision and Pattern Recognition, pp. 3137–3144. IEEE (2010)
5. Pirsiavash, H., Ramanan, D.: Detecting activities of daily living in first-person camera views. In: 2012 IEEE Conference on Computer Vision and Pattern Recognition, pp. 2847–2854. IEEE (2012)
6. Kitani, K.M., Okabe, T., Sato, Y., Sugimoto, A.: Fast unsupervised ego-action learning for first-person sports videos. In: CVPR 2011, pp. 3241–3248. IEEE (2011)
7. Finocchiaro, J., Khan, A.U., Borji, A.: Egocentric height estimation. In: 2017 IEEE Winter Conference on Applications of Computer Vision (WACV), pp. 1142–1150. IEEE (2017)
8. Yagi, T., Mangalam, K., Yonetani, R., Sato, Y.: Future person localization in first-person videos. In: Proceedings of the IEEE Conference on Computer Vision and Pattern Recognition, pp. 7593–7602 (2018)
9. Hoshen, Y., Peleg, S.: An egocentric look at video photographer identity. In: Proceedings of the IEEE Conference on Computer Vision and Pattern Recognition, pp. 4284–4292 (2016)
10. Poleg, Y., Arora, C., Peleg, S.: Head motion signatures from egocentric videos. In: Cremers, D., Reid, I., Saito, H., Yang, M.-H. (eds.) ACCV 2014. LNCS, vol. 9005, pp. 315–329. Springer, Cham (2015). https://doi.org/10.1007/978-3-319-16811-1_21

11. Johansson, G.: Visual perception of biological motion and a model for its analysis. Percept. Psychophys. **14**(2), 201–211 (1973)

12. Carter, J.N., Nixon, M.S.: Measuring gait signatures which are invariant to their trajectory. Meas. Control **32**(9), 265–269 (1999)

13. Kale, A., et al.: Identification of humans using gait. IEEE Trans. Image Process. **13**(9), 1163–1173 (2004)

14. Man, J., Bhanu, B.: Individual recognition using gait energy image. IEEE Trans. Pattern Anal. Mach. Intell. **28**(2), 316–322 (2006)

15. Hofmann, M., Rigoll, G.: Exploiting gradient histograms for gait-based person identification. In: 2013 20th IEEE International Conference on Image Processing (ICIP), pp. 4171–4175. IEEE (2013)

16. Thapar, D., Jaswal, G., Nigam, A., Arora, C.: Gait metric learning siamese network exploiting dual of spatio-temporal 3D-CNN intra and LSTM based inter gait-cycle-segment features. Pattern Recogn. Lett. **125**, 646–653 (2019)

17. Tao, W., Liu, T., Zheng, R., Feng, H.: Gait analysis using wearable sensors. Sensors **12**(2), 2255–2283 (2012)

18. Poleg, Y., Ephrat, A., Peleg, S., Arora, C.: Compact CNN for indexing egocentric videos. In: 2016 IEEE Winter Conference on Applications of Computer Vision (WACV), pp. 1–9. IEEE (2016)

19. Jiang, H., Grauman, K.: Seeing invisible poses: estimating 3D body pose from egocentric video. In: 2017 IEEE Conference on Computer Vision and Pattern Recognition (CVPR), pp. 3501–3509. IEEE (2017)

20. Fan, C., et al.: Identifying first-person camera wearers in third-person videos. In: IEEE Conference on Computer Vision and Pattern Recognition (CVPR) (2017)

21. Ardeshir, S., Borji, A.: Ego2Top: matching viewers in egocentric and top-view videos. In: Leibe, B., Matas, J., Sebe, N., Welling, M. (eds.) ECCV 2016. LNCS, vol. 9909, pp. 253–268. Springer, Cham (2016). https://doi.org/10.1007/978-3-319-46454-1_16

22. Hesch, J.A., Roumeliotis, S.I.: Consistency analysis and improvement for single-camera localization. In: 2012 IEEE Computer Society Conference on Computer Vision and Pattern Recognition Workshops, pp. 15–22. IEEE (2012)

23. Murillo, A.C., Gutiérrez-Gómez, D., Rituerto, A., Puig, L., Guerrero, J.J.: Wearable omnidirectional vision system for personal localization and guidance. In: 2012 IEEE Computer Society Conference on Computer Vision and Pattern Recognition Workshops, pp. 8–14. IEEE (2012)

24. Park, H.S., Jain, E., Sheikh, Y.: 3D social saliency from head-mounted cameras. In: Advances in Neural Information Processing Systems, pp. 422–430 (2012)

25. Soo Park, H., Jain, E., Sheikh, Y.: Predicting primary gaze behavior using social saliency fields. In: Proceedings of the IEEE International Conference on Computer Vision, pp. 3503–3510 (2013)

26. Farnebäck, G.: Two-frame motion estimation based on polynomial expansion. In: Bigun, J., Gustavsson, T. (eds.) SCIA 2003. LNCS, vol. 2749, pp. 363–370. Springer, Heidelberg (2003). https://doi.org/10.1007/3-540-45103-X_50

27. Thapar, D., Jaswal, G., Nigam, A., Kanhangad, V.: PVSNet: palm vein authentication siamese network trained using triplet loss and adaptive hard mining by learning enforced domain specific features. arXiv preprint arXiv:1812.06271 (2018)

28. Fathi, A., Hodgins, J.K., Rehg, J.M.: Social interactions: a first-person perspective. In: 2012 IEEE Conference on Computer Vision and Pattern Recognition (CVPR), pp. 1226–1233. IEEE (2012)

29. Tran, D., Bourdev, L., Fergus, R., Torresani, L., Paluri, M.: Learning spatiotemporal features with 3D convolutional networks. In: Proceedings of the IEEE International Conference on Computer Vision, pp. 4489–4497 (2015)
30. Carreira, J., Zisserman, A.: Quo vadis, action recognition? A new model and the kinetics dataset. In: Proceedings of the IEEE Conference on Computer Vision and Pattern Recognition, pp. 6299–6308 (2017)
31. Hara, K., Kataoka, H., Satoh, Y.: Can spatiotemporal 3D CNNs retrace the history of 2D CNNs and ImageNet? In: Proceedings of the IEEE Conference on Computer Vision and Pattern Recognition, pp. 6546–6555 (2018)
32. Ravikanth, C., Kumar, A.: Biometric authentication using finger-back surface. In: 2007 IEEE Conference on Computer Vision and Pattern Recognition, pp. 1–6. IEEE (2007)

Captioning Images Taken by People Who Are Blind

Danna Gurari[(⊠)], Yinan Zhao, Meng Zhang, and Nilavra Bhattacharya

University of Texas at Austin, Austin, USA
danna.gurari@ischool.utexas.edu

Abstract. While an important problem in the vision community is to design algorithms that can automatically caption images, few publicly-available datasets for algorithm development directly address the interests of real users. Observing that people who are blind have relied on (human-based) image captioning services to learn about images they take for nearly a decade, we introduce the first image captioning dataset to represent this real use case. This new dataset, which we call VizWiz-Captions, consists of over 39,000 images originating from people who are blind that are each paired with five captions. We analyze this dataset to (1) characterize the typical captions, (2) characterize the diversity of content found in the images, and (3) compare its content to that found in eight popular vision datasets. We also analyze modern image captioning algorithms to identify what makes this new dataset challenging for the vision community. We publicly-share the dataset with captioning challenge instructions at https://vizwiz.org.

1 Introduction

A popular computer vision goal is to create algorithms that can replicate a human's ability to caption any image [9,29,48]. Presently, we are witnessing an exciting transition where this dream of automated captioning is advancing into a reality, with automated image captioning now a feature available in several popular technology services. For example, companies such as Facebook and Microsoft are providing automated captioning in their social media [4] and productivity (e.g., Power Point) [1] applications to enable people who are blind to make some sense of images they encounter in these digital environments.

While much of the progress has been fueled by the recent creation of large-scale, publicly-available datasets (needed to train and evaluate algorithms), a limitation is that most existing datasets were created in contrived settings. Typically, crowdsourced workers were employed to produce captions for images curated from online, public image databases such as Flickr [6,15,21,26,28,33, 56,57]. Yet, we have observed over the past decade that people have been collecting image captions to meet their real needs. Specifically, people who are

Electronic supplementary material The online version of this chapter (https://doi.org/10.1007/978-3-030-58520-4_25) contains supplementary material, which is available to authorized users.

© Springer Nature Switzerland AG 2020
A. Vedaldi et al. (Eds.): ECCV 2020, LNCS 12362, pp. 417–434, 2020.
https://doi.org/10.1007/978-3-030-58520-4_25

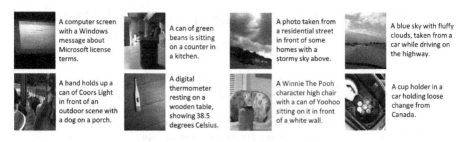

Fig. 1. Examples of captioned images in our new dataset, which we call VizWiz-Captions. These exemplify that images often contain text, exhibit a high variability in image quality, and contain a large diversity of content.

blind have sought descriptions[1] from human-powered services [2, 11, 45, 51, 58] to learn more about pictures they take of their visual surroundings. Unfortunately, images taken by these real users in the wild often exhibit dramatically different conditions than observed in the contrived environments used to design modern algorithms, as we will expand upon in this paper. Examples of some of the unique characteristics of images taken by real users of image captioning services are exemplified in Fig. 1. The consequence is that algorithms tend to perform poorly when deployed on their images.

To address the above problem, we introduce the first publicly-available captioning dataset that consists of images taken by people who are blind. This dataset builds off of prior work which supported real users of a mobile phone application to submit a picture and, optionally, record a spoken question in order to learn about their images [11]. We crowdsourced captions for 39,181 images that were submitted. We also collected metadata for each image that indicates whether text is present and the severity of image quality issues to enable a systematic analysis around these factors. We call this dataset VizWiz-Captions.

We then characterize how our new dataset relates to the momentum of the broader vision community. To do so, we characterize how the captioned content relates/differs to what is contained in eight popular vision datasets that support the image captioning, visual question answering, and image classification tasks. We observe both that VizWiz-Captions shows many distinct visual concepts from those in existing datasets and regularly provides the answers to people's visual questions (Sect. 3.2). We also benchmark modern captioning algorithms, and find that they struggle to caption lower quality images.

We offer this work as a valuable foundation for designing more generalized computer vision algorithms that meet the large diversity of needs for real end users. Our dataset can facilitate and motivate progress for a broader number of scenarios that face similar complexities. For example, wearable lifelogging devices, autonomous vehicles, and robots also can result in varying image quality and many images showing textual information (e.g., street signs, billboards) as important real-world challenges that must be handled to solve downstream tasks.

---

[1] Throughout, we use "caption" and "description" interchangeably.

To facilitate and encourage progress, we organized a dataset challenge and associated workshop to track progress and stimulate discussion about current research and application issues. Details about the dataset, challenge, and workshop can be found at the following link: https://vizwiz.org.

2   Related Work

Captioning Images for People Who are Blind. Given the clear wish from people who are blind to receive descriptions of images [3,10,11,13,37,42,52], many human-in-the-loop [2,3,5,38,45,51] and automated services [1,4] have emerged to do so. A challenge shared across such services is what content to describe. Although there remains a lack of guidance for images taken by people who are blind [49], it is known that many people who are blind report a preference to receive descriptions of images over nothing (even if inaccurate) [23,45,46,53]. Accordingly, to facilitate progress on automated solutions for captioning images taken by this population, we introduce a new dataset to represent this use case. In doing so, we aim to support the design of a cheaper, faster, and more private alternative than is possible with human-based captioning services.

Image Captioning Datasets. Over the past decade, nearly 20 publicly-shared captioning datasets have been created to support the development of automated captioning algorithms [6,14,15,18,19,21,26–28,32,33,43,47,56,57,60]. The trend has been to include a larger number of examples, relying on scraping images from the web (typically Flickr) to support the growth from a few thousand [19,20,43] to hundreds of thousands [15,27,33] of captioned images in such datasets. In doing so, such work has strayed from focusing on real use cases. To help align the vision community to focus on addressing the real interests of people who need image captions, we instead focus on introducing a captioning dataset that emerges from a natural use case.

Accordingly, our work more closely aligns with the earlier datasets that emerged from authentic image captioning scenarios. This includes captioned images in newspaper articles [20] and provided by tour guides about photographs of tourist locations [22]. Unlike these prior works, we focus on a distinct use case (i.e., captioning blind photographers' images) and our new dataset is considerably larger (i.e., contains nearly 40,000 images versus 3,361 [20] and 20,000 [22]).

More generally, to our knowledge, our new captioning dataset is the first that comes with metadata indicating for each image whether text is present and the severity of image quality issues, thereby enabling systematic analysis around these factors. We expect this new dataset will contribute to the design of more robust, general-purpose captioning algorithms.

Content in Vision Datasets. The typical trend for curating images for popular vision datasets is to scrape various web search engines for pre-defined categories/search terms. For example, this is how popular object recognition datasets (e.g., ImageNet [44] and COCO [36]), scene recognition datasets (e.g., SUN [54] and Places205 [59]), and attribute recognition datasets (e.g., SUN-attributes [41]

and COCO-attributes [40]) were created. Observing that automated methods rely on such large-scale datasets to guide what concepts they learn, a question emerges of how well the content in such contrived datasets reflect the interests of real users of image descriptions services. We conduct comparisons between popular vision datasets and our new dataset to provide such insight. This analysis is valuable both for highlighting the value of existing datasets to support a real use case and revealing how vision datasets can be improved.

3   VizWiz-Captions

We now introduce VizWiz-Captions, a dataset that consists of descriptions about images taken by people who are blind. Our work builds upon two existing datasets that contain images taken by real users of a visual description service [24,25]. The images in these datasets originate from users of the mobile phone application VizWiz [11], who each submitted a picture with, optionally, a recorded spoken question in order to receive a description of the image or answer to the question (when one was asked) from remote humans. In total, we used the 39,181 images that are publicly-shared and were not corrupted to obfuscate private content. Of these, 16% (i.e., 6,339) lack a question. We detail below our creation and analysis of this dataset.

3.1   Dataset Creation

Image Captioning System. To collect captions, we designed our captioning task for use in the crowdsourcing platform Amazon Mechanical Turk (AMT). To our knowledge, the only public precedent for crowdsourcing image descriptions from crowdworkers for images taken by people who are blind is the VizWiz mobile phone application [11]. This system offered vague instructions to 'describe the image'. Given this vague precedence, we chose to adapt the more concrete task design from the vision community, as described below.

We employed the basic task interface design used by prior work in the vision community [6,15,28,57]. It displays the image on the left, instructions on the right, and a text entry box below the instructions for entering the description. The instructions specify to include at least eight words as well as what not to do when creating the caption (e.g., do not speculate what people in the image might be saying/thinking or what may have happened in the future/past).

We further augmented the task interface to tailor it to unique characteristics of our captioning problem. These augmentations resulted both from consultation with accessibility experts and iterative refinement over four pilot studies. First, to encourage crowdworkers to address the interests of the target audience, we added the instruction to "Describe all parts of the image that may be important to a person who is blind." Second, to encourage crowdworkers to focus on the content the photographer likely was trying to capture rather than any symptoms of low quality images that inadvertently arise for blind photographers, we instructed crowdworkers "DO NOT describe the image quality issues." However, given that

some images could be insufficient quality for captioning, we provided a button that the crowdworker could click in order to populate the description with pre-canned text that indicates this occurred (i.e., "Quality issues are too severe to recognize visual content."). Next, to discourage crowdworkers from performing the optical character recognition problem when text is present, we added the following instruction: "If text is in the image, and is important, then you can summarize what it says. DO NOT use all the specific phrases that you see in the image as your description of the image." Finally, to enrich our analysis, we asked crowdworkers to provide extra information about each image regarding whether text is present.

Caption Collection and Post-processing. For each of the 39,181 images, we collected redundant results from the crowd. In particular, we employed five AMT crowdworkers to complete our task for every image. We applied a number of quality control methods to mitigate concerns about the quality of the crowd-sourced results, summarized in the Supplementary Materials. In total, we collected 195,905 captions. All this work was completed by 1,623 crowdworkers who contributed a total of 3,736 person-hours. With it being completed over a duration of 101.52 h, this translates to roughly 37 person-hours of work completed every hour. We post-processed each caption by applying a spell-checker to detect and fix misspelled words.

3.2   Dataset Analysis

Quality of Images. We first examined the extent to which the images were deemed to be insufficient quality to caption. This is important to check, since people who are blind cannot verify the quality of the images they take, and it is known their images can be poor quality due to improper lighting (i.e., mostly white or mostly black), focus, and more [12,16,25]. To do so, we tallied how many of the five crowdworkers captioned each image with the pre-canned text indicating insufficient quality for captioning (i.e., "Quality issues are too severe..."). The distribution of images for which none to all 5 crowdworkers used this pre-canned text is as follows: 68.5% for none, 16.7% for 1 person, 5.9% for 2 people, 3.6% for 3 people, 3.1% for 4 people, and 2.2% for all 5 people.

We found that the vast majority of images taken by blind photographers were deemed good enough quality that the content can be recognized. Only 9% of the images were deemed insufficient quality for captioning by the majority of the crowdworkers. A further 22.6% of images were deemed insufficient quality by a minority of the crowdworkers (i.e., 1 or 2). Altogether, these findings highlight a range of difficulty for captioning, based on the extent to which crowdworkers agreed the images are (in)sufficient quality to generate a caption. In Sect. 4, we report the ease/difficulty for algorithms to caption images based on this range of perceived difficulty by humans.

VizWiz-Captions Characterization. Next, we characterized the caption content. For this purpose, we excluded from our analysis all captions that contain the

Table 1. Characterization of our VizWiz-Captions dataset. Shown is the average count per caption as well as the total count of unique words, nouns, verbs, adjectives, and spatial relation words for each dataset with respect to all captions, various subsets to support finer-grained analysis, and MSCOCO-Captions dataset [15] for comparison. (adj = adjectives; spa-rel = spatial relations)

	Average count per image					Unique count for all images				
	words	nouns	verbs	adj	spa-rel	words	nouns	verbs	adj	spa-rel
Ours	13.0	4.4	0.9	1.4	1.9	24,422	16,400	4,040	8,755	275
Ours-WithQues	13.0	4.4	0.9	1.4	1.9	22,261	14,933	3,719	7,882	244
Ours-NoQues	13.0	4.4	0.9	1.5	1.9	10,651	7,249	1,616	3,212	120
Ours-WithText	12.9	4.5	0.9	1.4	1.9	21,161	14,277	3,294	7,263	243
Ours-NoText	13.1	4.2	0.9	1.6	1.9	10,711	7,114	1,933	3,508	127
[15]-All	11.3	3.7	1.0	0.9	1.7	30,122	19,998	6,697	9,651	381
[15]-Sample	11.3	3.7	1.0	0.9	1.7	16,966	11,211	3,822	4,922	197

pre-canned text about insufficient quality images ("Quality issues are too severe...") as well as those that were rejected. This resulted in a total of 168,826 captions.

We first quantified the composition of captions, by examining the typical description length as well as the typical number of objects, descriptors, actions, and relationships. To do so, we computed as a proxy the average number of words as well as the average number of nouns, adjectives, verbs, and spatial relation words per caption. Results are shown in Table 1 (row 1). Our findings reveal that sentences typically consist of roughly 13 words that involve four to five objects (i.e., nouns) in conjunction with one to two descriptors (i.e., adjectives), one action (i.e., verb), and two relationships (i.e., spatial relationship words). Examples of sentences featuring similar compositions include "A hand holding a can of Ravioli over a counter with a glass on it" and "Red car parked next to a black colored SUV in an outside dirt parking lot."

We enriched our analysis by examining the typical caption composition separately for the 16% (i.e., 6,339) of images that originated from a captioning use case and the remaining 84% of images that originated from a VQA use case (meaning the image came paired with a question). Results are shown in Table 1, rows 2–3. We observe that the composition of sentences is almost identical for both use cases. This offers encouraging evidence that the images taken from a VQA setting are useful for large-scale captioning datasets.

We further enriched our analysis by examining how the caption composition changes based on whether the image contains text. We deemed an image as containing text if the majority of the five crowdworkers indicate it does. In our dataset, 63% (24,812) of the images contain text. The caption compositions for both subsets are shown in Table 1, rows 4–5. Our findings reveal that images containing text tend to have more nouns and fewer adjectives than images that lack text. Put differently, the presence of text appears to be more strongly correlated

to the object recognition task. We hypothesize this is in part because crowd-workers commonly employ both a generic object recognition category followed by a specific object category gleaned from reading the text when creating their descriptions; e.g., "a box of Duracell procell batteries" and "a can of Ravioli." It's also possible that text is commonly present in more complex scenes that show a greater number of objects.

We also quantified the diversity of concepts in our dataset. To do so, we report parallel analysis to that above, with a focus on the *absolute number of unique* words, nouns, adjectives, verbs, and spatial relation words across all captions. Results are shown in the right half of Table 1. These results demonstrate that the dataset captures a large diversity of concepts, with over 24,000 unique words. We visualize the most popular words in the Supplementary Materials, and conduct further analysis below to offer insight into how these concepts relate/differ to those found in popular computer vision datasets.

Comparison to Popular Captioning Dataset. We next compared our dataset to the popular MSCOCO-Captions dataset [15], and in particular the complete MSCOCO training set for which the captions are publicly-available.

Paralleling our analysis of VizWiz-Captions, we quantified the average as well as total unique number of words, nouns, adjectives, verbs, and spatial words in MSCOCO-Captions [15]. To enable side-by-side comparison, we not only analyzed the entire MSCOCO-Captions training set but also randomly sampled the same number of images with the identical distribution of number of captions per image as was analyzed for VizWiz-Captions. We call this subset MSCOCO-Sample. Results are shown in Table 1, rows 6–7. The results reveal that VizWiz-Captions tends to have a larger number of words per caption than MSCOCO-Captions; i.e., an average of 13 words versus 11.3 words. This is true both for the full set as well as the sample from MSCOCO-Captions. As shown in Table 1, the greater number of words is due to a greater number of nouns, adjectives, and spatial relation words per caption in VizWiz-Captions. Possible reasons for this include that the images show more complex scenes and that crowdworkers were motivated to provide more descriptive captions when knowing the target audience is people who are blind.

We additionally measured the content overlap between the two datasets. Specifically, we computed the percentage of words that appear both in the most common 3,000 words for VizWiz-Captions and the most common 3,000 words in MSCOCO-Captions. The overlap is 54.4%. This finding underscores a considerable domain shift in the content that blind photographers take pictures of and what artificially constructed datasets represent. We visualize examples of novel concepts not found in MSCOCO-Captions in the Supplementary Materials.

We also assessed the similarity of captions generated by different humans using the specificity score [31] for both our dataset and MSCOCO-Captions. Due to space constraints, we show the resulting distributions of scores in the Supplementary Materials for both datasets. In summary, the scores are similar.

Table 2. Percentage of VQAs for which an image caption contains the answer with respect to both a quantitative ("Quant") and qualitative ("Qual") analysis. Fine-grained quantitative analysis is shown based on the type of answer that is elicited by the visual question (i.e., "yes/no", "#", and "other") as well as based on whether the images contain text. (# = number)

	All images				Images with text				Images without text			
	All	Yes/No	#	Other	All	Yes/No	#	Other	All	Yes/No	#	Other
Quant	33%	1%	8%	34%	35%	1%	10%	36%	30%	1%	3%	31%
Qual	32%	35%	23%	38%	–	–	–	–	–	–	–	–

Comparison to Visual Question Answering Dataset. Given that 84% of the images originate from a VQA use case (i.e., where a question was also submitted about the image), our new dataset offers a valuable test bed to explore the potential for generic image captions to answer users' real visual questions. Accordingly, we explore this for each image in our dataset for which we both have publicly-available answers for the question and the question is deemed to be "answerable" [24,25].

We first evaluate this using a *quantitative measure*. Specifically, for the 24,842 answerable visual questions in the publicly-available training and validation splits, we tally the percentage for which the answer can be found in at least one of the five captions using exact string matching. We set the answer to the most popular answer from the 10 provided with each visual question. We conduct this analysis with respect to all images as well as separately for only those images which are paired with different answer types for the visual questions—i.e., "yes/no" (860 images), "number" (314 images), and "other" (23,668 images). Results are shown in Table 2. Overall, we observe that captions contain the information that people who are blind were seeking for roughly one third of their visual questions. This sets a lower bound, since string matching is an extremely rigid scheme for determining whether text matches.

We perform parallel quantitative analysis based on whether images contain text. For visual questions that contain text (i.e., 15,910 answerable visual questions), we again analyze the visual questions that lead to "yes/no" (447 images), "number" (218 images), and "other" (15,245 images) answers. We also perform this analysis on only the subset of visual questions that lack text (i.e., 8,932 answerable visual questions)—i.e., "yes/no" (413 images), "number" (96 images), and "other" (8,423 images). Results are shown in Table 2. We observe that the answer tends to be contained in the caption more often when the image contains text. This discrepancy is the largest for "number" questions, which we hypothesize is due to images showing currency. People seem to naturally want to characterize how much money is shown for such images, which conveniently is the information sought by those asking the questions.

To also capture when the answer to a visual question is provided implicitly in the captions, we next used a *qualitative approach*. We sampled 300 visual

questions, with 100 for each of the three answer types.[2] Then, one of the authors reviewed each visual question with the answers and five captions to decide whether each visual question was answered by any of the captions about the image. Results are shown in Table 2, row 4. We observe a big jump in percentage for "yes/no" and "number" questions. The greatest boost is observed for "yes/no" visual questions where the percentage jumps from 0% to 35%. We attribute this to the "yes" questions more than the "no" questions–i.e., 22/50 for "yes" and 13/50 for "no"—since content that is asked about may be described when it is present in the image but will almost definitely not be described when it is not. Still, "no" questions often arise because, when the answer can be inferred, the caption typically also answers a valuable follow-up question. For example, a caption that states "A carton of banana flavored milk sits in a clear container with eggs" arguably answers the question "Is this chocolate milk?" (i.e., the answer is "no") while providing additional information (i.e., it is "banana milk").

Altogether, our findings show that at least one third of the visual questions can be answered with image captions. In other words, the captions regularly provide useful information for people who are blind. We attribute this large percentage partly to the fact that many questions for VQA just paraphrase a request to complete the image captioning task; e.g., nearly half of the questions ask a variant of "what is this" or "describe this" [25]. It also may often be obvious to the people providing captions what information the photographer was seeking when submitting the image with a question. Regardless of the reason though, it appears the extra work of devising a question regularly can be unnecessary in practice. A valuable direction for future research is to continue improving our understanding for how to align captions with real end users' interests.

Comparison to Popular Image Classification Datasets. Observing that automated captioning algorithms often build off of pretrained modules that perform more basic tasks such as image classification and object detection (e.g., trend dates back at least to Baby Talk [34] in 2013), we next examine the overlap between concepts in VizWiz-Captions and popular vision datasets that often are used to train such modules. For our analysis, we focus on three visual tasks: recognizing objects, scenes, and attributes.

We began by tallying how many popular concepts from existing vision datasets for the three vision tasks are found in VizWiz-Captions. To do so, we computed matches using extract string matching. When comparing concepts in VizWiz-Captions to the object categories that span both ImageNet [44] and COCO [36], we found that all nine categories that are shared across the two datasets are also found in VizWiz-Captions. Similarly, we found that all scene categories which span both SUN [54] and Places205 [59] (i.e., 70 categories) are

---

[2] For "yes/no" visual questions, we sampled 50 that have the answer "yes" and another 50 with the answer "no." For "number" visual questions, we sampled 50 that begin with the question "How many" and another 50 that begin with "How much." Finally, we randomly sampled another 100 visual questions from the "other" category.

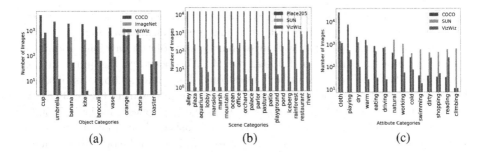

Fig. 2. Histogram showing how many images in our VizWiz-Captions as well as popular vision datasets contain each category for the following vision problems: (a) object recognition, (b) scene classification, and (c) attribute recognition.

captured in VizWiz-Captions. Additionally, all attribute categories that span both COCO-Attributes [41] and SUN-Attributes [40] (i.e., 14 categories) are captured in VizWiz-Captions. Consequently, across all three tasks, all concepts that are shared across the pair of mainstream vision datasets are also present in VizWiz-Captions. This is interesting in part because VizWiz-Captions was not created with any of these tasks in mind. Moreover, it underscores the promise for models trained on existing datasets to generalize well in recognizing some content encountered by people who are blind in their daily lives.

We also tally how many of the images in each dataset contain the popular concepts discussed above. Results are reported with respect to each of three classification tasks in Fig. 2.[3] As shown, the number of examples in VizWiz-Captions is typically considerably fewer than observed for the other two popular datasets per task. This is not entirely surprising given that the absolute number of images in VizWiz-Captions is at least an order of magnitude smaller than most of the datasets (i.e., the object and scene classification datasets). We offer this analysis as a lower bound since *explicitly* asking crowdworkers whether each category is present could reveal a greater prevalence of these concepts. Observing that relying on data from real use cases alone likely provides an insufficient number of examples per category to successfully train algorithms, this finding highlights a potential benefit of contrived datasets in supplementing examples to our real-world dataset. We leave this idea as a valuable area for future work.

We also computed the percentage of all categories from each of the classification datasets that are captured by VizWiz-Captions. Again, we used exact string matching to do so. For object recognition, VizWiz-Captions contains only 1% of the categories in ImageNet and 11% of those in COCO. For scene recognition, VizWiz-Captions contains only 18% of the categories in SUN and 34% of those in Places205. For attribute recognition, VizWiz-Captions contains only 14% of the categories in COCO-Attributes and 7% of those in SUN-Attributes.

---

[3] We show parallel analysis in the Supplementary Materials using the proportions of each dataset rather than absolute numbers. For both sets of results, we only show a subset of the 70 scene categories.

Observing that these vision datasets are reserved to a range of hundreds to at most a thousand categories while we know from Table 1 that VizWiz-Captions contains thousands of unique nouns and adjectives, these datasets appear to provide very little coverage for the diversity of content captured in VizWiz-Captions. Altogether, these findings offer promising evidence that existing contrived image classification datasets provide a considerable mismatch to the concepts encountered by blind users who are trying to learn about their visual surroundings. Our findings serve as an important reminder that much progress is still needed to accommodate the diversity of content found in real-world settings.

4 Algorithm Benchmarking

We next benchmarked state-of-art image captioning algorithms to gauge the difficulty of VizWiz-Captions and what makes it difficult for modern algorithms.

Dataset Splits. Using the same test set as prior work [25], we applied roughly a 70%/10%/20% split for the train/val/test sets respectively, resulting in a 23,431/7,750/8,000 split. To focus algorithms on learning novel captions, we exclude from training and evaluation captions with pre-canned text about insufficient quality images or rejected ones that were deemed spam.

Baselines. We benchmarked nine algorithms based on three modern image captioning algorithms that have been state-of-art methods for the MSCOCO-Captions [15] challenge: Up-Down [8], SGAE [55], and AoANet [30]. Up-Down [8] combines bottom-up and top-down attention mechanisms to consider attention at the level of objects and other salient image regions. SGAE [55] relies on a Scene Graph Auto-Encoder (SGAE) to incorporate language bias into an encoder-decoder framework, towards generating more human-like captions. AoANet [30] employs an Attention on Attention (AoA) module to determine the relevance between attention results and queries. We evaluated all three algorithms, which originally were trained on the MSCOCO-Captions dataset, *as is*. These results are useful in assessing the effectiveness of the MSCOCO training dataset for teaching computers to describe images taken by people who are blind. We also *fine-tuned* each pretrained network to VizWiz-Captions and *trained each network from scratch* on VizWiz-Captions. These algorithms are helpful for assessing the usefulness of each model architecture for describing images taken by people who are blind. For all algorithms, we used the publicly-shared code and default training hyper-parameters reported by the authors. We also benchmarked a commercial text detector[4] on test images containing text.

Evaluation. We evaluated each method with eight metrics that often are used for captioning: BLEU-1-4 [39], METEOR [17], ROUGE-L [35], CIDEr-D [50], and SPICE [7].

---

[4] https://docs.microsoft.com/en-us/azure/cognitive-services/computer-vision/concept-recognizing-text.

Table 3. Performance of top-performing image captioning algorithms on the VizWiz-Captions test set with respect to eight metrics. Results are shown for three variants of the algorithms: when they are pre-trained on MSCOCO-Captions [15], trained only on the VizWiz-Captions dataset, and pre-trained on MSCOCO-Captions followed by fine-tuning to the VizWiz-Captions dataset. (B@ = BLEU-)

		B@1	B@2	B@3	B@4	METEOR	ROUGE	CIDEr	SPICE
[8]	pretrained	52.8	32.8	19.2	11.3	12.6	35.8	18.9	5.8
	from scratch	64.1	44.6	30.0	19.8	18.4	43.2	49.7	12.2
	fine-tuned	62.1	42.3	28.2	18.6	18.0	42.0	48.2	11.6
[55]	pretrained	55.8	36.0	21.8	13.5	13.4	38.1	20.2	5.9
	from scratch	67.3	48.1	33.2	22.8	19.4	46.6	52.4	12.8
	fine-tuned	**68.5**	**49.4**	**34.5**	**23.9**	20.2	**47.3**	**61.2**	13.5
[30]	pretrained	54.9	34.7	21.0	13.2	13.4	37.6	19.4	6.2
	from scratch	66.4	47.9	33.4	23.2	**20.3**	47.1	60.5	**14.0**
	fine-tuned	66.6	47.4	32.9	22.8	19.9	46.6	57.6	13.7

GT1: A public toilet in a stall in a building from above.
GT2: A person is standing next to a white toilet and taking a picture downward.
GT3: A white toilet bowl that is half full of water
GT4: A person stands in front of a toilet.
GT5: A person standing in front of a toilet bowl.
Algorithm: A person standing in front of a toilet
CIDEr-D: 3.20 **METEOR:** 0.92 **ROUGE-L:** 0.93

GT1: The white dog is sitting on a bed.
GT2: A handsome white dog sitting on a bed with a collar
GT3: A small white dog with a black collar sitting on a bed.
GT4: A fluffy white dog on a blue bed sheet
GT5: A white dog sits on a bed looking off in the distance.
Algorithm: A white dog sitting on a bed
CIDEr-D: 2.81 **METEOR:** 0.45 **ROUGE-L:** 0.84

GT1: A white plastic spoon on a wood table surface
GT2: A white plastic spoon sitting on a table
GT3: A white toilet bowl that is half full of water
GT4: White plastic spoon sitting on a wood surface
GT5: White plastic disposable standard spoon, teaspoon for cereal
Algorithm: A spoon sitting on top of a wooden table
CIDEr-D: 2.49 **METEOR:** 0.30 **ROUGE-L:** 0.71

GT1: A book is on a table in front of some wires
GT2: A blue book is sitting right on top of the table
GT3: Blue book with Wyrdest link Terry Pratchett's Discworld quiz book printed on it
GT4: The cover of The Wyrdest Link, a Discworld quizbook by David Langford
GT5: The front cover of a book sitting on a table
Algorithm: A book sitting on top of a table
CIDEr-D: 1.79 **METEOR:** 0.40 **ROUGE-L:** 0.72

GT1: A single bottle of Double Masquerade table wine
GT2: A bottle of table wine called Double Masquerade
GT3: The back of a bottle of table wine
GT4: A bottle of table wine and a person's hand
GT5: A person's hand holds a dark bottle of table wine with a white information label against a light wood surface
Algorithm: A person holding a bottle of wine in front of a table
CIDEr-D: 1.17 **METEOR:** 0.32 **ROUGE-L:** 0.53

GT1: An outdoor car parking lot with cars parked
GT2: A parking lot with several cars is in the foreground while in the background is a wooded area with large trees whose leaves are changing colors.
GT3: Three black and one ash color cars are parked and a vegetation behind them
GT4: Four black cars and a white car parked and some vegetation
GT5: A parking lot by a forest containing several cars.
Algorithm: A group of cars parked in a parking lot
CIDEr-D: 1.23 **METEOR:** 0.29 **ROUGE-L:** 0.37

GT1: A clear plastic bag holds shredded mozzarella inside.
GT2: A bag of mozzarella shredded cheese used in cooking
GT3: A bag of mozzarella cheese is on a white plate
GT4: A bag of Westfield brand shredded mozzarella cheese.
GT5: A bag of medium sized shredded Mozzarella cheese that is mostly full.
Algorithm: A book sitting on top of a table
CIDEr-D: 0.0009 **METEOR:** 0.11 **ROUGE-L:** 0.33

GT1: a type of humidor thermometer reading 74 degrees
GT2: A dial with settings that show the temperature on a wooden panel.
GT3: Photo in the picture is a humidor gauge to give the amount of humidity in the air.
GT4: A humidor or a hygrometer that is at 75 sitting on a wooden surface.
GT5: A humidor hydrometer that is on some wood
Algorithm: a clock sitting on top of a wooden table
CIDEr-D: 0.08 **METEOR:** 0.17 **ROUGE-L:** 0.42

Fig. 3. Examples of a state-of-art image captioning algorithm's successes (top three rows) and failures (bottom row) in generating captions for images taken in a real use case. Results are for SGAE [55] pretrained on MSCOCO-Captions.

Overall Performance. We report the performance of each method in Table 3.

Observing the performance of existing algorithms that are *pretrained* on MSCOCO-Captions [15], we see that they can occasionally accurately predict captions for images coming from blind photographers. This is exciting as it shows that progress on artificially-constructed datasets can translate to successes in real use cases. We attribute the prediction successes to when the images are

both good quality and show objects that are common in MSCOCO-Captions, as exemplified in the top six examples in Fig. 3.

We consistently observe considerable performance improvements from the algorithms when training them on VizWiz-Captions, including when they are trained from scratch and fine-tuned. For instance, we observe roughly a 10% point boost with respect to BLEU-1 and 30% point boost with respect to CIDEr-D across the three algorithms. Still, the scores are considerably lower than what is observed when these same algorithmic frameworks are evaluated on the MSCOCO-Captions test set. For example, we observe the BLEU-1 score is over 20% points lower and the METEOR score is almost 20% points lower, when comparing the performance of the top-performing algorithm for VizWiz-Captions against the top-performing algorithm for MSCOCO-Captions (i.e., AoANet [30]). This finding highlights that VizWiz-Captions currently offers a challenging dataset for the vision community.

When comparing outcomes between algorithms that are trained from scratch on VizWiz-Captions versus fine-tuned to VizWiz-Captions, we do not observe a considerable difference. For instance, we observe better performance when Up-Down [8] and AoANet [30] are trained from scratch on VizWiz-Captions rather than fine-tuned from models pretrained on MSCOCO-Captions, and vice versa for SGAE [55]. We found it surprising there is similar performance, given that VizWiz-Captions is roughly one order of magnitude smaller than MSCOCO-Captions. Valuable areas for future work include investigating the benefit of domain adaptation methods as well as how to successfully leverage larger contrived datasets (e.g., MSCOCO-Captions) to improve the performance of algorithms on VizWiz-Captions.

Fine-Grained Analysis. We enriched our analysis to better understand why algorithms struggle to accurately caption the images. To do so, we evaluated the top-performing algorithms for VizWiz-Captions with respect to two characteristics. First, we characterized performance independently for images in the test set based on whether they are flagged as containing text. We also characterized performance independently for images flagged as different difficulty levels, based on the number of crowdworkers who deemed the images insufficient quality to generate a meaningful caption; i.e., easy is when all five people generated novel captions, medium when 1–2 crowdworkers flagged the images as insufficient quality for captioning, and difficult when 3–4 crowdworkers flagged the images as insufficient quality. Results are shown in Table 4 for the top algorithms from Table 3; i.e., "from scratch" for [8] and [30] and "fine-tuned" for [55].

We observe two trends for the performance of algorithms based on whether text is present. We find the text detector does very poor, underscoring a key challenge for designing algorithms is to figure out how to integrate knowledge about text into captions. In contrast, we find that all captioning algorithms perform better when text is present. Initially, we found this surprising given that none of the benchmarked algorithms were designed to handle text (e.g., by incorporating an optical recognition module). Moreover, images with text cover many more unique concepts than images lacking text, as shown in Table 1. We hypothesize

Table 4. Analysis of the top-performing image captioning algorithms and a text detection algorithm based on whether images contain text and the image "difficulty". (B@ = BLEU-)

		B@1	B@2	B@3	B@4	METEOR	ROUGE	CIDEr	SPICE
[8]	WithText	65.7	46.6	32.3	21.7	19.2	45.1	49.3	12.6
	LackText	60.2	40.0	25.2	15.7	16.9	39.7	46.7	11.4
	Easy	67.8	48.3	33.2	22.2	19.5	45.7	53.2	12.5
	Medium	60.8	40.0	25.4	16.2	17.2	40.4	45.8	11.9
	Difficult	32.1	16.9	9.2	5.4	10.6	26.2	34.7	9.0
[55]	WithText	69.9	51.2	36.6	25.8	21.0	49.3	62.2	14.1
	LackText	65.7	45.9	30.3	20.2	18.7	43.7	55.5	12.5
	Easy	72.2	53.3	38.0	26.7	21.4	50.0	65.8	13.9
	Medium	65.1	44.7	29.3	19.3	18.8	44.3	55.8	13.3
	Difficult	35.6	20.1	11.7	7.4	11.9	28.8	42.7	9.3
[30]	WithText	68.3	50.1	35.8	25.3	21.3	49.2	62.7	14.6
	LackText	63.0	43.7	28.8	18.9	18.5	43.3	52.5	12.9
	Easy	69.8	51.4	36.5	25.6	21.4	49.6	64.3	14.3
	Medium	63.6	44.0	29.2	19.5	19.2	44.5	56.0	14.2
	Difficult	36.0	20.3	11.8	7.6	12.2	29.6	44.3	10.6
Text_API	WithText	14.9	8.8	5.7	3.9	10.4	15.9	24.6	–

the improved performance is because images containing text provide a simpler domain that conforms to a fewer set of templates for the captions. For example, from visual inspection, we observe captions for such images often include "a box/bag of ... on/in ...". The captioning patterns for this simpler domain may be easier to learn for the algorithms. If so, this underscores an inadequacy of current evaluation metrics and a need for new metrics that prioritize the information people who are blind want.

When observing algorithm performance based on the captioning difficulty level, we find it parallels human difficulty with algorithms performing best on the easiest images for humans. While not surprising, this finding underscores the practical difficulty of designing algorithms that can handle low quality images, which we know are somewhat common from real users of image captioning services (i.e., people who are blind).

5   Conclusions

We offer VizWiz-Captions as a valuable foundation for designing image captioning algorithms to support a natural, socially-important use case. More broadly, our analysis reveals important problems that the vision community needs to address in order to deliver more generalized algorithms. Interesting future work

includes holistically improving vision solutions to include consideration of potentially, valuable additional sensors to more effectively meet real users' needs (e.g., GPS, sound waves, infrared).

Acknowledgements. We thank Meredith Ringel Morris, Ed Cutrell, Neel Joshi, Besmira Nushi, and Kenneth R. Fleischmann for their valuable discussions about this work. We thank Peter Anderson and Harsh Agrawal for sharing their code for setting up the EvalAI evaluation server. We thank the anonymous crowdworkers for providing the annotations. This work is supported by National Science Foundation funding (IIS-1755593), gifts from Microsoft, and gifts from Amazon.

References

1. Add alternative text to a shape, picture, chart, SmartArt graphic, or other object. https://support.office.com/en-us/article/add-alternative-text-to-a-shape-picture-chart-smartart-graphic-or-other-object-44989b2a-903c-4d9a-b742-6a75b451c669

2. BeSpecular. https://www.bespecular.com

3. Home - Aira: Aira. https://aira.io/

4. How does automatic alt text work on Facebook? — Facebook Help Center. https://www.facebook.com/help/216219865403298

5. TapTapSee - Blind and Visually Impaired Assistive Technology - powered by the CloudSight.ai Image Recognition API. https://taptapseeapp.com/

6. Agrawal, H., et al.: Nocaps: novel object captioning at scale. arXiv preprint arXiv:1812.08658 (2018)

7. Anderson, P., Fernando, B., Johnson, M., Gould, S.: SPICE: semantic propositional image caption evaluation. In: Leibe, B., Matas, J., Sebe, N., Welling, M. (eds.) ECCV 2016. LNCS, vol. 9909, pp. 382–398. Springer, Cham (2016). https://doi.org/10.1007/978-3-319-46454-1_24

8. Anderson, P., et al.: Bottom-up and top-down attention for image captioning and visual question answering. In: CVPR (2018)

9. Bai, S., An, S.: A survey on automatic image caption generation. Neurocomputing **311**, 291–304 (2018)

10. Bennett, C.L., Mott, M.E., Cutrell, E., Morris, M.R.: How teens with visual impairments take, edit, and share photos on social media. In: Proceedings of the 2018 CHI Conference on Human Factors in Computing Systems, p. 76. ACM (2018)

11. Bigham, J.P., et al.: VizWiz: nearly real-time answers to visual questions. In: Proceedings of the 23rd Annual ACM Symposium on User Interface Software and Technology, pp. 333–342. ACM (2010)

12. Brady, E., Morris, M.R., Zhong, Y., White, S., Bigham, J.P.: Visual challenges in the everyday lives of blind people. In: Proceedings of the SIGCHI Conference on Human Factors in Computing Systems, pp. 2117–2126. ACM (2013)

13. Burton, M.A., Brady, E., Brewer, R., Neylan, C., Bigham, J.P., Hurst, A.: Crowdsourcing subjective fashion advice using VizWiz: challenges and opportunities. In: Proceedings of the 14th International ACM SIGACCESS Conference on Computers and Accessibility, pp. 135–142. ACM (2012)

14. Chen, J., Kuznetsova, P., Warren, D., Choi, Y.: Déja image-captions: a corpus of expressive descriptions in repetition. In: Proceedings of the 2015 Conference of the North American Chapter of the Association for Computational Linguistics: Human Language Technologies, pp. 504–514 (2015)

15. Chen, X., et al.: Microsoft COCO captions: data collection and evaluation server. arXiv preprint arXiv:1504.00325 (2015)
16. Chiu, T.-Y., Zhao, Y., Gurari, D.: Assessing image quality issues for real-world problems. In: Proceedings of the IEEE/CVF Conference on Computer Vision and Pattern Recognition, pp. 3646–3656 (2020)
17. Denkowski, M., Lavie, A.: Meteor universal: language specific translation evaluation for any target language. In: Proceedings of the EACL 2014 Workshop on Statistical Machine Translation (2014)
18. Elliott, D., Keller, F.: Image description using visual dependency representations. In: Proceedings of the 2013 Conference on Empirical Methods in Natural Language Processing, pp. 1292–1302 (2013)
19. Farhadi, A., et al.: Every picture tells a story: generating sentences from images. In: Daniilidis, K., Maragos, P., Paragios, N. (eds.) ECCV 2010. LNCS, vol. 6314, pp. 15–29. Springer, Heidelberg (2010). https://doi.org/10.1007/978-3-642-15561-1_2
20. Feng, Y., Lapata, M.: Automatic image annotation using auxiliary text information. In: Proceedings of ACL 2008: HLT, pp. 272–280 (2008)
21. Gan, C., Gan, Z., He, X., Gao, J., Deng, L.: StyleNet: generating attractive visual captions with styles. In: Proceedings of the IEEE Conference on Computer Vision and Pattern Recognition, pp. 3137–3146 (2017)
22. Grubinger, M., Clough, P., Müller, H., Deselaers, T.: The IAPR TC-12 benchmark: a new evaluation resource for visual information systems. In: International Workshop OntoImage, vol. 5 (2006)
23. Guinness, D., Cutrell, E., Morris, M.R.: Caption crawler: enabling reusable alternative text descriptions using reverse image search. In: Proceedings of the 2018 CHI Conference on Human Factors in Computing Systems, p. 518. ACM (2018)
24. Gurari, D., et al.: VizWiz-Priv: a dataset for recognizing the presence and purpose of private visual information in images taken by blind people. In: Proceedings of the IEEE Conference on Computer Vision and Pattern Recognition, pp. 939–948 (2019)
25. Gurari, D., et al.: VizWiz grand challenge: answering visual questions from blind people. In: Proceedings of the IEEE Conference on Computer Vision and Pattern Recognition, pp. 3608–3617 (2018)
26. Harwath, D., Glass, J.: Deep multimodal semantic embeddings for speech and images. In: 2015 IEEE Workshop on Automatic Speech Recognition and Understanding (ASRU), pp. 237–244. IEEE (2015)
27. Havard, W., Besacier, L., Rosec, O.: SPEECH-COCO: 600k visually grounded spoken captions aligned to MSCOCO data set. arXiv preprint arXiv:1707.08435 (2017)
28. Hodosh, M., Young, P., Hockenmaier, J.: Framing image description as a ranking task: data, models and evaluation metrics. J. Artif. Intell. Res. **47**, 853–899 (2013)
29. Hossain, M.D., Sohel, F., Shiratuddin, M.F., Laga, H.: A comprehensive survey of deep learning for image captioning. ACM Comput. Surv. (CSUR) **51**(6), 118 (2019)
30. Huang, L., Wang, W., Chen, J., Wei, X.-Y.: Attention on attention for image captioning. In: International Conference on Computer Vision (2019)
31. Jas, M., Parikh, D.: Image specificity. In: Proceedings of the IEEE Conference on Computer Vision and Pattern Recognition, pp. 2727–2736 (2015)
32. Kong, C., Lin, D., Bansal, M., Urtasun, R., Fidler, S.: What are you talking about? Text-to-image coreference. In: Proceedings of the IEEE Conference on Computer Vision and Pattern Recognition, pp. 3558–3565 (2014)

33. Krishna, R., et al.: Visual genome: connecting language and vision using crowd-sourced dense image annotations. Int. J. Comput. Vision **123**(1), 32–73 (2017). https://doi.org/10.1007/S11263-016-0981-7

34. Kulkarni, G., et al.: BabyTalk: understanding and generating simple image descriptions. IEEE Trans. Pattern Anal. Mach. Intell. **35**(12), 2891–2903 (2013)

35. Lin, C.-Y.: ROUGE: a package for automatic evaluation of summaries. In: Text Summarization Branches Out, pp. 74–81 (2004)

36. Lin, T.-Y., et al.: Microsoft COCO: common objects in context. In: Fleet, D., Pajdla, T., Schiele, B., Tuytelaars, T. (eds.) ECCV 2014. LNCS, vol. 8693, pp. 740–755. Springer, Cham (2014). https://doi.org/10.1007/978-3-319-10602-1_48

37. MacLeod, H., Bennett, C.L., Morris, M.R., Cutrell, E.: Understanding blind people's experiences with computer-generated captions of social media images. In: Proceedings of the 2017 CHI Conference on Human Factors in Computing Systems, pp. 5988–5999. ACM (2017)

38. Morris, M.R., Johnson, J., Bennett, C.L., Cutrell, E.: Rich representations of visual content for screen reader users. In: Proceedings of the 2018 CHI Conference on Human Factors in Computing Systems, p. 59. ACM (2018)

39. Papineni, K., Roukos, S., Ward, T., Zhu, W.-J.: BLEU: a method for automatic evaluation of machine translation. In: Proceedings of the 40th Annual Meeting on Association for Computational Linguistics, pp. 311–318. Association for Computational Linguistics (2002)

40. Patterson, G., Hays, J.: Sun attribute database: discovering, annotating, and recognizing scene attributes. In: 2012 IEEE Conference on Computer Vision and Pattern Recognition (CVPR), pp. 2751–2758. IEEE (2012)

41. Patterson, G., Hays, J.: COCO attributes: attributes for people, animals, and objects. In: Leibe, B., Matas, J., Sebe, N., Welling, M. (eds.) ECCV 2016. LNCS, vol. 9910, pp. 85–100. Springer, Cham (2016). https://doi.org/10.1007/978-3-319-46466-4_6

42. Petrie, H., Harrison, C., Dev, S.: Describing images on the web: a survey of current practice and prospects for the future. In: Proceedings of Human Computer Interaction International (HCII), no. 71 (2005)

43. Rashtchian, C., Young, P., Hodosh, M., Hockenmaier, J.: Collecting image annotations using Amazon's Mechanical Turk. In: Proceedings of the NAACL HLT 2010 Workshop on Creating Speech and Language Data with Amazon's Mechanical Turk, pp. 139–147. Association for Computational Linguistics (2010)

44. Russakovsky, O., et al.: ImageNet large scale visual recognition challenge. Int. J. Comput. Vision **115**(3), 211–252 (2015). https://doi.org/10.1007/s11263-015-0816-y

45. Salisbury, E., Kamar, E., Morris, M.R.: Toward scalable social alt text: conversational crowdsourcing as a tool for refining vision-to-language technology for the blind. In: Proceedings of HCOMP 2017 (2017)

46. Salisbury, E., Kamar, E., Morris, M.R.: Evaluating and complementing vision-to-language technology for people who are blind with conversational crowdsourcing. In: IJCAI, pp. 5349–5353 (2018)

47. Shuster, K., Humeau, S., Hu, H., Bordes, A., Weston, J.: Engaging image captioning via personality. arXiv preprint arXiv:1810.10665 (2018)

48. Srivastava, G., Srivastava, R.: A survey on automatic image captioning. In: Ghosh, D., Giri, D., Mohapatra, R.N., Savas, E., Sakurai, K., Singh, L.P. (eds.) ICMC 2018. CCIS, vol. 834, pp. 74–83. Springer, Singapore (2018). https://doi.org/10.1007/978-981-13-0023-3_8

49. Stangl, A., Morris, M.R., Gurari, D.: "Person, shoes, tree. Is the person naked?" What people with vision impairments want in image descriptions. In: Proceedings of the 2020 CHI Conference on Human Factors in Computing Systems, pp. 1–13 (2020)
50. Vedantam, R., Lawrence Zitnick, C., Parikh, D.: CIDEr: consensus-based image description evaluation. In: Proceedings of the IEEE Conference on Computer Vision and Pattern Recognition, pp. 4566–4575 (2015)
51. Von Ahn, L., Ginosar, S., Kedia, M., Liu, R., Blum, M.: Improving accessibility of the web with a computer game. In: Proceedings of the SIGCHI Conference on Human Factors in Computing Systems, pp. 79–82. ACM (2006)
52. Voykinska, V., Azenkot, S., Wu, S., Leshed, G.: How blind people interact with visual content on social networking services. In: Proceedings of the 19th ACM Conference on Computer-Supported Cooperative Work & Social Computing, pp. 1584–1595. ACM (2016)
53. Wu, S., Wieland, J., Farivar, O., Schiller, J.: Automatic alt-text: computer-generated image descriptions for blind users on a social network service. In: CSCW, pp. 1180–1192 (2017)
54. Xiao, J., Hays, J., Ehinger, K.A., Oliva, A., Torralba, A.: SUN database: large-scale scene recognition from abbey to zoo. In: 2010 IEEE Conference on Computer Vision and Pattern Recognition (CVPR), pp. 3485–3492. IEEE (2010)
55. Yang, X., Tang, K., Zhang, H., Cai, J.: Auto-encoding scene graphs for image captioning. In: Proceedings of the IEEE Conference on Computer Vision and Pattern Recognition, pp. 10685–10694 (2019)
56. Yoshikawa, Y., Shigeto, Y., Takeuchi, A.: Stair captions: constructing a large-scale Japanese image caption dataset. arXiv preprint arXiv:1705.00823 (2017)
57. Young, P., Lai, A., Hodosh, M., Hockenmaier, J.: From image descriptions to visual denotations: new similarity metrics for semantic inference over event descriptions. Trans. Assoc. Comput. Linguist. **2**, 67–78 (2014)
58. Zhong, Y., Lasecki, W.S., Brady, E., Bigham, J.P.: RegionSpeak: quick comprehensive spatial descriptions of complex images for blind users. In: Proceedings of the 33rd Annual ACM Conference on Human Factors in Computing Systems, pp. 2353–2362. ACM (2015)
59. Zhou, B., Lapedriza, A., Xiao, J., Torralba, A., Oliva, A.: Learning deep features for scene recognition using places database. In: Advances in Neural Information Processing Systems, pp. 487–495 (2014)
60. Zitnick, C.L., Parikh, D., Vanderwende, L.: Learning the visual interpretation of sentences. In: Proceedings of the IEEE International Conference on Computer Vision, pp. 1681–1688 (2013)

Improving Semantic Segmentation via Decoupled Body and Edge Supervision

Xiangtai Li[1], Xia Li[1,2], Li Zhang[3], Guangliang Cheng[4(✉)], Jianping Shi[4], Zhouchen Lin[1], Shaohua Tan[1], and Yunhai Tong[1(✉)]

[1] Key Laboratory of Machine Perception, MOE, School of EECS, Peking University, Beijing, China
{lxtpku,yhtong}@pku.edu.cn
[2] Zhejiang Lab, Hangzhou, China
[3] Department of Engineering Science, University of Oxford, Oxford, England
[4] SenseTime Research, Hong Kong, China
chengguangliang@sensetime.com

Abstract. Existing semantic segmentation approaches either aim to improve the object's inner consistency by modeling the global context, or refine objects detail along their boundaries by multi-scale feature fusion. In this paper, a new paradigm for semantic segmentation is proposed. Our insight is that appealing performance of semantic segmentation requires *explicitly* modeling the object *body* and *edge*, which correspond to the high and low frequency of the image. To do so, we first warp the image feature by learning a flow field to make the object part more consistent. The resulting body feature and the residual edge feature are further optimized under decoupled supervision by explicitly sampling different parts (body or edge) pixels. We show that the proposed framework with various baselines or backbone networks leads to better object inner consistency and object boundaries. Extensive experiments on four major road scene semantic segmentation benchmarks including *Cityscapes*, *CamVid*, *KIITI* and *BDD* show that our proposed approach establishes new state of the art while retaining high efficiency in inference. In particular, we achieve 83.7 mIoU % on Cityscape with only fine-annotated data. Code and models are made available to foster any further research (https://github.com/lxtGH/DecoupleSegNets).

Keywords: Semantic segmentation · Edge supervision · Flow field · Multi-task learning

---

X. Li—Work done while at SenseTime.

Electronic supplementary material The online version of this chapter (https://doi.org/10.1007/978-3-030-58520-4_26) contains supplementary material, which is available to authorized users.

A. Vedaldi et al. (Eds.): ECCV 2020, LNCS 12362, pp. 435–452, 2020.
https://doi.org/10.1007/978-3-030-58520-4_26

1 Introduction

Semantic segmentation is a fundamental task in computer vision that aims to assign an object class label to each pixel in an image. It is a crucial step towards visual scene understanding, and has numerous applications such as autonomous driving [1], image generation [2] and medical diagnosis.

Although the fully convolutional networks (FCNs) [3] have excelled in many major semantic segmentation benchmarks, they still suffer from the following limitations. First, the Receptive Field (RF) of FCNs grows slowly (only linearly) with increasing depth in the network, and such the limited RF is not able to fully model the longer-range relationships between pixels in an image [4,5]. Thus the pixels are difficult to classify as the ambiguity and noise occurs inside the object body. Moreover, the downsampling operations in the FCNs lead to blurred predictions as the fine details disappear within the significantly lower resolution compared to the original image. As a result, the predicted segments tend to be blobby, and the boundary detail is far from satisfactory, which leads to a dramatic performance drop, especially on small objects.

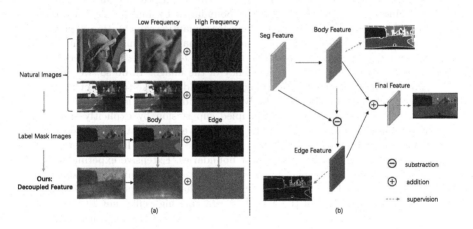

Fig. 1. Illustration of our proposed module and supervision framework. (a). The motivation of our proposed framework. Our methods share the same splits with decoupling natural images into low frequency and high frequency. (b). Illustration of our framework. Our method consists of three steps: First, split segmentation feature into body feature and edge feature. Then both parts are supervised with specifically designed loss. Then merge both refined features for the final prediction.

To tackle the first problem, many approaches [6–8] have been proposed to enlarge the RF, such as dilated convolution, pyramid pooling module [8,9], non-local operators [10–14], graph convolution network (GCN) [15,16] and dynamic graph [17]. For the second problem, prior arts manage to embed the low-level features that contain boundary and edge information into high-level features [18–21]

or directly refine the outputs [22]. However, the interaction between the object body and object edge is ignored. Can we solve both problems simultaneously?

On the other hand, it is natural for humans to distinguish objects by perceiving both object body and edge information. Inspired by this, we explore the relationships between body and edge in an explicit way to obtain the final semantic segmentation result. As shown in the first two rows of Fig. 1(a), a natural image can be decomposed into a low-spatial frequency component which describes the smoothly changing structure, and a high-spatial frequency component that represents the rapidly changing fine details. This is done by first applying mean or Gaussian filter for smoothing, and the remaining high-frequency parts can be obtained by subtraction. With the same philosophy, a segmentation mask can also be decoupled in this manner, where the finely detailed edge part can be obtained by subtraction from the body part. Inspired by this observation, we assume that a feature map for semantic segmentation can also be decoupled into two parts: body feature and edge feature (see Fig. 1(b)). The former contains smooth representation inside the object with low frequency while the latter has sharper details with high frequency.

In this paper, we propose to solve semantic segmentation by explicitly modelling the body consistency and edge preservation in the feature level and then jointly optimizing them in a unified framework. The entire process consists of three steps. First, we propose a novel flow-based method to generate body feature representation by warping each pixel towards object inner parts through a learned offset field to maintain the consistency of body part for each object. Then, we obtain the edge feature by explicitly subtracting the body feature from the input feature. The body feature is supervised by the mask where the edges are ignored during training, while the edge feature is supervised by an edge mask for learning edge prediction. Finally, we merge both optimized features into the final representation for segmentation. As the body generation part is done on a downsampled feature, the edge information is not accurate. We follow the design of [23] to relax the object boundaries during body generation training, which makes both edge and body complementary to each other. Then both parts are merged into a single feature as a reconstructed representation, which is supervised by a commonly used cross-entropy loss. Moreover, the proposed framework is light-weighed and can be plugged into state-of-the-art FCNs [3,6,7,21] based segmentation networks to improve their performance. Our methods achieve top performance on four driving scene semantic segmentation datasets including Cityscapes [24], CamVid [25], KITTI [1] and BDD [26]. In particular, our method achieves 83.7 mIoU on Cityscapes datasets with only fine-annotated data.

The contributions of this paper are as follows,

- We propose a novel framework for the semantic segmentation task by decoupling the body and the edge with different supervisions.
- We propose a lightweight flow-based aggregation module by warping each pixel towards object inner parts through a learned offset field to maintain the consistency of body part for each object.

– Our proposed module can be plugged into state-of-the-art segmentation methods to improve their performance with negligible cost. We carry out extensive experiments on four competitive scene parsing datasets and achieve top performance.

2   Related Work

Semantic Segmentation. Recent approaches for semantic segmentation are predominantly based on FCNs [3]. Some earlier works [27–32] use structured prediction operators such as conditional random fields (CRFs) to refine the output boundaries. Instead of these costly DenseCRF, current state-of-the-art methods [7,8,10,12] boost the segmentation performance by designing sophisticated head networks on dilated backbones [6] to capture contextual information. PSP-Net [7] proposes pyramid pooling module (PPM) to model multi-scale contexts, whilst DeepLab series [8,33,34] uses astrous spatial pyramid pooling (ASPP). In [10–13,35,36], non-local operator [37] and self-attention mechanism [38] are adopted to harvest pixel-wise context from the whole image. Meanwhile, graph convolution networks [15,17,39,40] are used to propagate information over the whole image by projecting features into an interaction space. Different from previous approaches, our method learns a flow field generated by the network itself to warp features towards object inner parts. DCN [41] uses predicted offset to aggregate information in kernel and SPN [42] proposes to propagate information through affinity pairs. Different from both work, our module aims to align pixels towards object inner according to the learned offset field to form body feature which is learned with specific loss supervision. Ding *et al.* [43] models unidirectional acyclic graphs to propagate information within the object guided by the boundary. However, it is not efficient due to the usage of the RNN structure between pixels. Our module is light-weighted and can be plugged into the state-of-the-art methods [7,21] to improve their performance with negligible extra cost, which also proves its efficiency and orthogonality.

Boundary Processing. Several prior works obtain better boundary localization by structure modeling, such as boundary neural fields [22], affinity field [44], random walk [45]. The work [19,20] uses edge information to refine network output by predicting edge maps from intermediate CNN layers. However, these approaches have some drawbacks, such as the potential error propagation from wrong edge estimation since both tasks are not orthogonal. Also overfitting edges brings noise and leads to inferior final segmentation results. Zhu et al. [23] proposes boundary relation loss to utilize coarse predicted segmentation labels for data augmentation. Inspired by the idea of label relaxation [23], we supervise the edge and the body parts respectively. The relaxation body avoids the noise from the edge supervision with the relaxation loss. Experimental results demonstrate both higher model accuracy.

Multi Task Learning. Serveral works have proved the effectiveness of combining networks for complementary tasks learning [46,47]. The works of previous

unified architectures that learn a shared representation using multi-task losses. There are some works [18,48] using learned segmentation and boundary detection network simultaneously and the learned boundaries as an intermediate representation to aid segmentation. GSCNN [18] designs a two-stream network by merging shape information into feature maps explicitly and introduces a dual-task loss to refine both semantic masks and boundary prediction. Different from these works, our goal is to improve the final segmentation results by explicitly optimizing two decoupled feature maps, and we design a specific framework by decoupling semantic body and boundaries into two orthogonal parts with corresponding loss functions and merge them back into final representation for segmentation task.

3   Method

In this section, we will first introduce the entire pipeline of our proposed framework in Sect. 3.1. Then we will describe the detailed description of each component in the Sect. 3.1–3.4. Finally, we present the network architectures equipped with our proposed modules and give some discussion on design in Sect. 3.5.

3.1   Decoupled Segmentation Framework

Given a feature map $F \in \mathbb{R}^{H \times W \times C}$, where C represents the channel dimension and $H \times W$ means spatial resolution, our module outputs the refined feature map $\hat{F}$ with the same size. As stated in the introduction part, F can be decoupled into two terms F_{body} and F_{edge}. In this paper, we assume they meet the additive rule, which means $F: F = F_{body} + F_{edge}$. Our goal is to design components with specific supervision to handle each parts, respectively. We achieve this by first performing body generation and then obtaining the edge part by explicit subtraction where $F_{body} = \alpha(F)$ and $F_{edge} = F - F_{body}$. Then the refined feature $\hat{F}$ can be shown in $\hat{F} = \phi(F) + \varphi(F_{edge}) = F_{body} + \varphi(F - F_{body})$. ϕ is the body generation module, which is designed to aggregate context information inside the object and form a clear body for each object. φ represents the edge preservation module. We will specify the details of ϕ and φ in the following sections.

3.2   Body Generation Module

The body generation module is responsible for generating more consistent feature representations for pixels inside the same object. We observe that pixels inside an object are similar to each other, while those lying along the boundary show discrepancy. We propose to explicitly learn body and edge feature representation. To achieve so, we learn a flow field $\delta \in \mathbb{R}^{H \times W \times 2}$, and use it to warp the original feature map to obtain the explicit body feature representation. This module contains two parts: flow field generation and feature warping.

Flow Field Generation. To generate flows that mainly point towards object centers, it is a reasonable way to highlight the features of object center parts

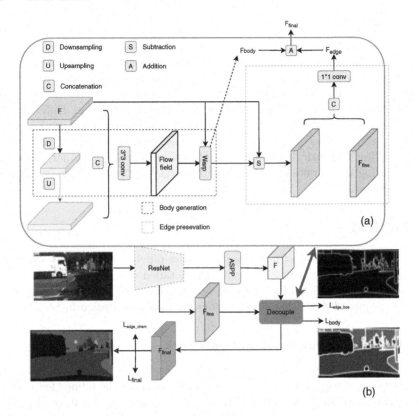

Fig. 2. Illustration of our proposed module and supervision framework. (a) shows the proposed decoupled module with Body Generation and Edge Preservation. (b) gives the examples of deploying our methods into Deeplabv3+ [21].

as explicit guidance. Generally, low-resolution feature maps (or coarse representation) often contain low-frequency terms. Low spatial frequency parts capture the summation of images, and a lower resolution feature map represents the most salient part where we view it as pseudo-center location or the set of seed points. As shown in Fig. 2(a), we adopt encoder-decoder design where the encoder downsamples feature into low-resolution representation with lower spatial frequency parts. We apply strided-convolutions to compress F into the high-frequency map F_{low}. In particular, we adopt three successive 3×3 depthwise convolution to achieve that. For flow field generation, we share the same pipeline as FlowNet-S [49]. In detail, we first upsample F_{low} to the same size as F via bilinear interpolation, then concatenate them together and apply a 3×3 convolution layer to predict the flow map $\delta \in \mathbb{R}^{H \times W \times 2}$. Since our model is based on the dilated backbone network [6], 3×3 kernel is large enough for covering the long distance between pixels in most cases. More empirical improvements analysis on this implementation can be found in Sect. 4.1.

Feature Warping. Each position p_l on standard spatial grid Ω_l is mapped to a new point $\hat{p}$ via $p_l + \delta_l(p_l)$, we then use the differentiable bilinear sampling mechanism to approximate each point p_x in F_{body}. The sampling mechanism, proposed in the spatial transformer networks [50,51], linearly interpolates the values of the four nearest neighbor pixel of p_l. The process is shown in Equation 1.

$$F_{body}(p_x) = \sum_{p \in \mathcal{N}(p_l)} w_p F(p) \tag{1}$$

where w_p, calculated from flow map δ, represents bilinear kernel weights on warped spatial gird. $\mathcal{N}$ represents the involved neighboring pixels.

3.3   Edge Preservation Module

The edge preservation module is designed to deal with high-frequency terms. It also contains two steps: 1) subtracting the body from the original feature F and 2) adding fine-detailed lower-level features as a supplement. First, we subtract the body feature from the original input F. Inspired by recent works on decoder design [21], we add extra low-level feature input as the supplement of missing fine details information to enhance the high-frequency terms in F_{body}. Finally, we concatenate both and adopt a 1×1 convolution layer for fusion. This module can be formulated as Eq. 2, where γ is a convolution layer and $\|$ denotes the concatenation operation.

$$F_{edge} = \gamma((F - F_{body})\|F_{fine}) \tag{2}$$

3.4   Decoupled Body and Edge Supervision

Instead of supervising the final segmentation map only, we jointly supervise all three parts, including F_{body}, F_{edge} and $\hat{F}$, since each part has a specific purpose in our design. In particular, we append auxiliary supervised losses for F_{body} and F_{edge},receptively. For the edge preservation module, we predict a boundary map b during training, which is a binary representation of all the outlines of objects and stuff classes in the images. The total loss L is computed as:

$$L = \lambda_1 L_{body}(s_{body}, \hat{s}) + \lambda_2 L_{edge}(b, s_{final}, \hat{b}, \hat{s}) + \lambda_3 L_{final}(s_{final}, \hat{s}) \tag{3}$$

where $\hat{s}$ represents the ground-truth (GT) semantic labels and $\hat{b}$ is the GT binary masks which is generated by $\hat{s}$. s_{body} and s_{final} denote segmentation map prediction from F_{body} and F_{final} respectively. $\lambda_1, \lambda_2, \lambda_3$ are three hyper-parameters that control the weighting among the three losses and we set them 1 as default. Note that L_{final} is a common cross entropy loss for segmentation task and we detail the first two items as follows.

To make the optimization easier, for the F_{body} part training, we relax the object boundaries during the training. We use the boundaries relaxation loss [23], which only samples part of pixels within the objects for training.

For the edge part, we propose an integrated loss based on the boundaries edge prior which is got from edge prediction part. For semantic segmentation, most of the hardest pixels to classify lie on the boundary between object classes. Moreover, it is not easy to classify the center pixel of a receptive field when potentially half or more of the input context could be a new class. To tackle this problem, we propose to use such edge prior to handling the boundary pixels particularly and perform online hard example mining at a given edge threshold t_b during the training. The total loss contains two terms: L_{bce} is the binary cross-entropy loss for the boundary pixel classification, while L_{ce} represents cross-entropy loss on edges parts in the scene. The formulations are shown in Eq. 4 and Eq. 5.

$$L_{edge}(b, s, \hat{b}, \hat{s}) = \lambda_4 L_{bce}(b, \hat{b}) + \lambda_5 L_{ce}(s, \hat{s}, b) \tag{4}$$

$$L_{ce}(s, \hat{s}, b) = -\frac{1}{K} \sum_{i=1}^{N} w_i \cdot \mathbb{1}[s_{i,\hat{s}_i} < t_K \cap \sigma(b_i) > t_b] \cdot \log s_{i,\hat{s}_i} \tag{5}$$

For L_{edge}, we set $\lambda_4 = 25$ and $\lambda_5 = 1$ to balance the amount of pixels on edges. For L_{ce}, we combine weighted bootstrapped cross-entropy with edge prior from b. We set $K = 0.10 \cdot N$, where N is the total number of pixels in the image and $\hat{s}_i$ is the target class label for pixel i, $s_{i,j}$ is the predicted posterior probability for pixel i and class j, and $\mathbb{1}[x] = 1$ if x is true and 0 otherwise. σ represents the Sigmoid function to indicate whether s is on the boundary. The threshold t_K is set in a way that only the pixels with K highest losses are selected while the threshold t_b is to mask non-boundary pixels. Both loss L_{body} and L_{edge} work complementary with each other by sampling pixels separately from different regions in the image. Such design benefits the final performance shown in the experimental parts.

3.5 Network Architecture

Figure 2 illustrates the whole network architecture, which is based on state-of-the-art model Deeplabv3+ [21]. Here we utilize dilated ResNet as backbone [6,52] only for illustration purpose. In particular, our module is inserted after the ASPP module [21]. The decoupled supervisions are appended at the end of decouple module respectively. Moreover, our module is lightweight and can be deployed upon any FCN architectures such as PSPNet [7] to refine the feature representation. When deployed on the native FCN, it is appended after the final output layer of the backbone. When deployed on the PSPNet, it is appended after the PPM module [7]. F_{fine} shares the same design with Deeplabv3+ for both architectures.

4   Experiment

Experiment Settings and Evaluation Metrics: We first carry out experiments on the Cityscapes dataset, which comprises a large, diverse set of high

resolution (2048 × 1024) images recorded in street scenes. It consists of 5,000 images with high-quality pixel-wise annotations for 19 classes, which is further divided into 2975, 500, and 1525 images for training, validation and testing. To be noted, 20,000 coarsely labeled images provided by this dataset are **not** used. Furthermore, we also evaluate our methods on CamVid [25], KITTI [1] and BDD [26] datasets. For all datasets, we use the standard mean Intersection over Union (mIoU) metric to report segmentation accuracy. For Cityscapes, we also report F-score proposed in [53] by calculating along the boundary of the predicted mask given a small slack in the distance to show the high-quality segmentation boundaries of predicted mask.

Implementation Details: We use PyTorch [54] framework to carry out the following experiments. All networks are trained with the same setting, where stochastic gradient 'xsdescent (SGD) with a batch size of 8 is used as the optimizer, with the momentum of 0.9, the weight decay of $5e - 4$ and the initial learning rate of 0.01. As a common practice, the 'poly' learning rate policy is adopted to decay the initial learning rate by multiplying $(1 - \frac{iter}{total\_iter})^{0.9}$ during training. Data augmentation contains random horizontal flip, random resizing with scales range of [0.75, 2.0], and random cropping with size 832. Specifically, we use ResNet-50, ResNet-101 [52] and Wider-ResNet [55] as the backbones. Additionally, we re-implement the state-of-the-arts [7,21] for fairness. We run the training for 180 epochs for ablation purposes, and we run 300 epochs for the submission to the test server. We first train the base networks without our module as initial weights and then train with our framework with the same epoch for each experiment. All the models are evaluated with the sliding-window manner for a fair comparison.

4.1 Ablation Studies

Improvements over Baseline Model. We first apply our method on naive dilated FCN models [6], where we also include uniform sampling trick [23] to balance classes during training as our strong baselines in Table 1(a). Our naive FCNs achieve 76.6 and 77.8 in mIoU for ResNet-50 and ResNet-101, respectively. After applying our method, we achieve significant improvements over each backbone by 3.5% and 3.0%, respectively. Note that our ResNet-50 based model is 2.2% higher than ResNet-101 baseline, which indicates the performance gain is not from the more convolution layers in Body Generation.

Ablation Studies on Decoupled Supervisions. Then we explore the effectiveness of decoupled supervision in Table 1(b). Directly adding both the body generation and edge preservation module results in a 1.7% improvement, which shows its aligned effect. After appending L_{body}, we get an obvious improvement of 0.5%, and it can avoid uncertain noises on boundaries. L_{bce} has no effect on the final performance since there is no direct supervision to segmentation prediction. Adding L_{ce} will bring about 0.4% improvement, which indicates that our integrated loss can better mine the boundaries based shape prior. Finally, after

Table 1. Experimental results on the Cityscapes validation set with dilated FCN as baselines.

Method	Backbone	mIoU (%)	Δ(%)
FCN naive	ResNet-50	75.4	-
+ US [23](Baseline)	ResNet-50	76.6	-
+ ours	ResNet-50	80.1	3.5↑
+ US [23](Baseline)	ResNet-101	77.8	-
+ ours	ResNet-101	80.8	3.0↑

(a) Ablation study on strong FCN baselines.

Method	L_{body}	L_{bce}	$L_{edge-ohem}$	mIoU (%)	Δ(%)
FCN				76.6	-
+(BG & EP)	-	-	-	78.3	1.7 ↑
	✓	-	-	78.8	0.5↑
	-	✓	-	78.3	-
	-	✓	✓	78.7	0.4↑
	✓	✓	✓	80.1	1.8↑
w/o F_{fine}	✓	✓	✓	79.3	0.8 ↓
w/o ohem	✓	✓	✗	79.0	1.1 ↓

(b) Ablation study on Decoupled Supervision.

Method	mIoU (%)	Δ(%)
FCN + BG & EP (Baseline)	78.3	-
w/o BG warp	76.9	1.4 ↓
w/o BG encoder-decoder	77.3	1.0 ↓
w/o EP	77.9	0.4 ↓

(c) Ablation Study on effect of each component.

Method	mIoU (%)	Δ(%)
FCN (Baseline)	76.6	-
w SPN [42]	77.9	1.3↑
w DCN [41]	78.2	1.6 ↑
+GSCNN [18]	77.8	1.2↑
ours	80.1	3.5↑

(d) Comparison to related methods.

combining all three losses, we get a higher improvement by 1.8%, which demonstrates the orthogonality of our separated supervision design. We also remove the F_{fine} module in Eq. 2, which results in about 0.8% drop in the final performance. This indicates the effectiveness of the edge cue from low-level features. Meanwhile, we also remove the hard pixel mining on $L_{edge-ohem}$, which results in about a 1.1% drop. That shows the effectiveness of our proposed integrated loss on boundaries.

Ablation Study on the Effect of Each Component. Here we carry out more detailed explorations on our component design with no the decoupled supervision setting shown in Table 1. Removing warping in BG achieves 76.9 in mIoU, which is a big decrease while removing the encoder-decoder part of BG results in 77.3% due to the limited receptive field of dilated FCN. Removing EP leads to less performance drop as the main drop of FCN is on large objects shown in Table 2.

Table 2. Experiment results on Cityscapes validation set with more network architectures. Best viewed in color and zoom in.

Method	Backbone	mIoU (%)	Δ(%)	FLOPS
PSPNet [7]	ResNet-50	79.6	-	132.1
+ours	ResNet-50	81.0	1.4↑	+ 9.2 (6.8%)
Deeplabv3+ [21]	ResNet-50	79.7	-	190.1
+ours	ResNet-50	81.5	1.8↑	+9.0 (4.7%)
Deeplabv3+ [12]	Wider-ResNet	81.3	-	664.5
+ours	Wider-ResNet	82.4	1.1↑	+7.5 (1.1%)

(a) Improvements upon different state-of-the-arts. To compute FLOPS, we adopt 512 × 512 images as the input.

Method	mIoU(%)
Deeplabv3+ (ResNet-50)	79.7
+ BG & EP (ResNet-50)	81.5 (1.8↑)
Deeplabv3+ (ResNet-101)	80.7
+ BG & EP (ReseNet-101)	82.6 (1.9↑)
+ BG & EP (ReseNet-101) +MS	83.5

(b) Ablation study on improvement strategy on the validation set.

Comparison with Related Methods. To verify the effectiveness of the BG module, we replace our BG module with DCN and SPN operators. The former

Table 3. Comparison with state-of-the-art on the Cityscapes test set. To be noted, our method **does not use coarse data.**

Method	Backbone	mIoU (%)
AAF [44]	ResNet-101	79.1
PSANet [56]	ResNet-101	80.1
DFN [57]	ResNet-101	79.3
DenseASPP [34]	DenseNet-161	80.6
DAnet [10]	ResNet-101	81.5
CCNet [11]	ResNet-101	81.4
BAFNet [43]	ResNet-101	81.4
ACFNet [58]	ResNet-101	81.9
GFFnet [59]	ResNet-101	82.3
Ours	ResNet-101	**82.8**

(a) Results on Cityscapes test server trained with only fine-data.

Method	Coarse	Backbone	mIoU (%)
PSP [7]	✓	ResNet-101	81.2
Deeplabv3+ [21]	✓	Xception	82.1
DPC [60]	✓	Xception	82.6
Auto-Deeplab [61]	✓	-	82.1
Inplace-ABN [62]	✓	Wider-ResNet	82.0
Video Propagation [23]	✓	Wider-ResNet	83.5
G-SCNN [18]	✗	Wider-ResNet	82.8
Ours	✗	Wider-ResNet	**83.7**

(b) Results on the Cityscapes test server.

is used to aggregate features with learned offset field, while the latter propagate information through learned affinity pair. The first two rows in Table 1(f) demonstrates that our method works better than DCN and SPN, which proves the effectiveness of our BG module design. We also compare with GSCNN [18] in the same setting.

Improvements upon Different Base Models. To further verify the generality of our proposed framework, we test it upon several state-of-the-art models including PSPNet [7] and Deelabv3+ [21] with various backbone network in Table 2(a). It can be seen that our method improves those by around 0.9%–1.5% in mIoU. Note that our baselines are stronger than the original paper. Meanwhile, we also report the FLOPS during the inference stages in the last column of Table 2(a). Our module is extremely lightweight with only 1.1%–6.8% relative FLOPS increment.

Comparison to State-of-the-Arts. For fair comparison, we follow the common procedure of [10,11,18] including stronger backbone (ResNet-101 [52]) and multi-scale inference (MS) to improve the model performance. As shown in Table 2(b), our best model achieves 83.5 mIoU on the validation dataset after applying both techniques. Then we compare our method with state-of-the-arts on the Cityscapes test set in Table 3 using the best model in Table 1. We first report results using ResNet-101 backbone in Table 3(a) and our method achieves **82.8** mIoU which improves by a large margin over all previous works. Moreover, we further apply our methods with a stronger backbone Wider-ResNet [55] pretrained on the Mapillary [63] dataset, which shares the same setting with GSCNN [18]. Our method achieves **83.7** in mIoU and also leads to a significant margin over GSCNN [18]. Table 3(b) shows the previous state-of-arts, which also uses much large coarse video data [23]), while our method achieves much better performance with utilizing only fine-annotated data.

Table 4. Per-category results on the Cityscapes validation set. Note that our method improves all strong baselines in most categories.

Method	mIoU	road	swalk	build.	wall	fence	pole	tlight	sign	veg	terrain	sky	person	rider	car	truck	bus	train	motor	bike
FCN [6]	76.6	98.0	84.5	92.5	50.7	62.7	**67.7**	73.8	81.2	**92.8**	61.2	**94.7**	**83.8**	64.2	95.0	56.4	81.6	60.5	68.2	79.4
Ours	**80.1**	**98.4**	**86.4**	**92.9**	**58.7**	**64.8**	67.0	**74.3**	**82.2**	92.7	**63.0**	94.5	83.6	**66.2**	**95.2**	**78.6**	**91.0**	**83.2**	**69.3**	**79.7**
PSPNet [7]	79.6	98.0	84.5	92.9	54.9	61.9	66.5	72.2	80.9	92.6	**65.6**	**94.8**	83.1	63.5	95.4	83.9	90.6	84.01	67.6	78.5
Ours	**81.0**	**98.2**	**85.8**	**93.4**	**59.5**	**67.0**	**68.7**	**74.6**	**81.6**	**92.8**	65.5	94.3	**83.6**	**65.6**	**95.6**	**86.7**	**92.6**	**87.1**	**68.6**	**79.1**
Deeplabv3+ [21]	79.7	**98.2**	85.3	92.8	58.4	65.4	65.6	70.4	79.2	92.6	65.2	94.8	82.4	63.3	95.3	83.2	90.7	84.1	66.1	77.9
Ours	**81.5**	**98.3**	**86.5**	**93.6**	**60.7**	**66.8**	**70.7**	**73.9**	**81.9**	**93.1**	**66.1**	**95.2**	**84.3**	**67.5**	**95.8**	**86.1**	**92.3**	**85.5**	**72.1**	**80.1**

4.2   Visual Analysis

Improvement Analysis. Here we illustrate a detailed analysis of improvements. First we report mIoU of each category in Table 4. For the FCN model, our method improves a lot on large objects like bus and car in the scene. For Deeplabv3+ and PSPNet models, our method improves mainly on small objects such as traffic light and pole since most large patterns are handled by context aggregation modules like PPM and ASPP. To be more specific, we also evaluate the performance of predicted mask boundaries shown in Fig. 3, where we report the mean F-score of 19 classes at 4-different thresholds. From that figure, we conclude that our methods improve the baseline object boundaries by a significant margin and our method is also slightly better than GSCNN [18] on both different cases with four different thresholds. To be noted, we compared deeplabv3+ ResNet101 backbone in Fig. 3(b) with original paper while GSCNN results in Fig. 3(a) with the ResNet50 backbone implemented by us. Figure 3(c) shows some visual examples of our model prediction with a more precise boundary mask. Figure 4 presents three visual examples over error maps. Our methods can better handle the inconsistency on large objects in FCN and boundaries of small objects in Deeplabv3+, which follows the same observation in Table 4. More visual examples can be found in the supplementary file.

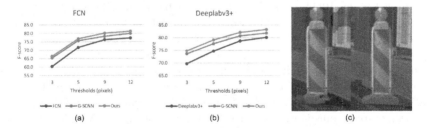

Fig. 3. Improvement analysis on boundaries where F-score is adopted. (a) is the improvement on FCN. (b) is the improvement on Deeplabv3+. (c) is the improvement on mask boundary prediction. Best viewed in color and zoom in.

Visualization on Decoupled Feature Representation and Prediction. We visualize the decoupled feature and prediction masks of our model over

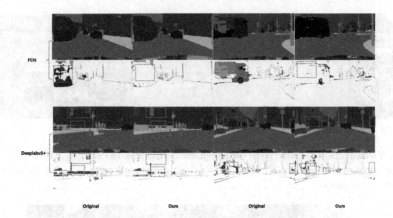

Fig. 4. Comparisons upon on FCN and Deeplabv3+. The first and third rows are prediction masks while the second and last rows are error maps compared with the ground truth mask. The first two rows illustrate the results on FCN and ours, while the last two rows show Deeplabv3+'s and ours'. Our method solves the inner blur problem in large patterns for FCN shown in yellow boxes and fixes missing details and inconsistent results on small objects on Deeplabv3+ shown in red boxes.

Deeplabv3+ in Fig. 4. Figures in (a)–(c) are drawn by doing Principal Component Analysis (PCA) from feature space into RGB space. As shown in Fig. 5, the features in (a) and (b) are complementary to each other, where each pixel in body part shares similar feature representations while pixels on edge varies. The merged feature in (c) have more precise and enhanced boundaries, while the objects in (a) are thinner than (c) due to boundary relaxation. The predicted edge prior in (d) has a more precise location of each object's boundaries. This gives better prior for mining hardest pixels along the boundaries parts. More visualization examples can be found in the supplementary file.

Visualization on Flow Field in BG. We also visualize the learned flow field for FCNs and Deeplabv3+ in Fig. 6. Both cases differ significantly. For the FCN model, we find that the learned flow field point towards the inner part in each object, which is consistent with our goal stated in Sect. 3.2. While for the Deeplabv3+ model, the learned flow is sparse and mainly lies on the object boundaries because enough context has been considered in the ASPP module. This observation is consistent with the results in Table 4: predictions over large objects are mainly improved in FCN (truck, 22%), while those over small objects are mainly improved in Deeplabv3+ (pole, 5%).

4.3   Results on Other Datasets

To further prove the generality of our proposed framework, we also perform more experiments on the other three road sense datasets. Our model is the same as used in Cityscapes datasets, which is based on Deeplabv3+ [21]. Standard

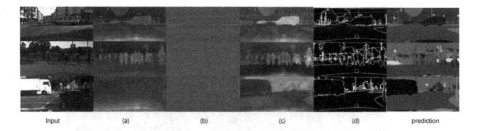

Input   (a)   (b)   (c)   (d)   prediction

Fig. 5. Visualization results based on Deeplabv3+ models. (a) is F_{body}. (b) is $F - F_{body}$. (c) is re-constructed feature $\hat{F}$. (d) is edge prior prediction b with $t_b = 0.8$. Best viewed in color and zoom in.

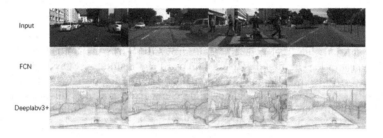

Fig. 6. Flow maps visualization. The second row shows learned flow maps based on FCN, while the last row shows the learned maps based on Deeplabv3+.

settings of each benchmark are used, which are summarized in the supplementary file for the detailed reference.

CamVid: CamVid [25] is another road scene dataset. This dataset involves 367 training images, 101 validation images, and 233 testing images with a resolution of 720 × 960. For a fair comparison, we compare both ImageNet pretrained and Cityscapes pretrained models. As shown in Table 5(a), our methods achieve significant gains over other state-of-the-arts in both cases.

BDD: BDD [26] is a new road scene benchmark consisting 7,000 images for training and 1,000 images for validation. Compared with baseline model [26] which uses dilated backbone (55.2%), our method leads to about **12%** mIoU improvement with single scale inference with the same ResNet-101 backbone and achieves top performance with 66.9% in mIoU.

KITTI: KITTI benchmark [1] has the same data format as Cityscapes, but with a different resolution of 375 × 1242 and more metrics. The dataset consists of 200 training and 200 test images. Since it is a small dataset, we follow the settings from previous work [23,62] by finetuning our best model from the Cityscapes dataset. Our methods rank first on three out of four metrics. It should be noted that method [23] uses both video and coarse data during Cityscapes pretraining process, while we only use the fine-annotated data.

Table 5. Experiments results on other road scene benchmarks.

Method	Backbone	Pretrain	mIoU(%)
DenseDecoder [64]	ResNext-101	ImageNet	70.9
BFP [43]	ResNet-101	ImageNet	74.1
Ours	ResNet-101	ImageNet	**76.5**
VideoGCRF [65]	ResNet-101	Cityscapes	75.2
Video Propagation [23]	Wider-ResNet	Cityscapes	79.8
Ours	ResNet-101	Cityscapes	**81.5**
Ours	Wider-ResNet	Cityscapes	**82.4**

(a) Results on CamVid.

Method	Backbone	mIoU(%)
Dilated [26]	ResNet101	55.2
FasterSeg [66]	-	55.3
Ours	ResNet101	**66.9**

(b) Results on BDD.

Method	IoU class(%)	iIoU class(%)	IoU category(%)	iIoU category(%)
AHiSS [67]	61.2	26.9	81.5	53.4
LDN [68]	63.5	28.3	85.3	59.1
MapillaryAI [62]	69.6	43.2	86.5	68.9
Video Propagation [23]	**72.8**	48.7	**88.9**	75.2
Ours	**72.8**	**49.5**	88.5	**75.5**

(c) Results on KITTI.

5 Conclusions

In this paper, we propose a novel framework to improve the semantic segmentation results by decoupling features into the body and the edge parts to handle inner object consistency and fine-grained boundaries jointly. We propose the body generation module by warping feature towards objects' inner parts then the edge can be obtained by subtraction. Furthermore, we design decoupled loss by sampling pixels from different parts to supervise both modules' training. Both modules are light-weighted and can be deployed into the FCN architecture for end-to-end training. We achieve state-of-the-art results on four road scene parsing datasets, including Cityscapes, CamVid, KITTI and BDD. The superior performance demonstrates the effectiveness of our proposed framework.

References

1. Andreas, G., Philip, L., Raquel, U.: Are we ready for autonomous driving? The KITTI vision benchmark suite. In: CVPR (2012)
2. Wang, T.C., Liu, M.Y., Zhu, J.Y., Tao, A., Kautz, J., Catanzaro, B.: High-resolution image synthesis and semantic manipulation with conditional GANs. In: CVPR (2018)
3. Long, J., Shelhamer, E., Darrell, T.: Fully convolutional networks for semantic segmentation. In: CVPR (2015)
4. Zhou, B., Khosla, A., Lapedriza, A., Oliva, A., Torralba, A.: Object detectors emerge in deep scene CNNs. arXiv preprint (2014)
5. Luo, W., Li, Y., Urtasun, R., Zemel, R.: Understanding the effective receptive field in deep convolutional neural networks. In: NeurIPS (2016)
6. Yu, F., Koltun, V.: Multi-scale context aggregation by dilated convolutions. In: ICLR (2016)
7. Zhao, H., Shi, J., Qi, X., Wang, X., Jia, J.: Pyramid scene parsing network. In: CVPR (2017)

8. Chen, L.C., Papandreou, G., Schroff, F., Adam, H.: Rethinking atrous convolution for semantic image segmentation. arXiv preprint (2017)
9. Hou, Q., Zhang, L., Cheng, M.M., Feng, J.: Strip pooling: rethinking spatial pooling for scene parsing. In: CVPR (2020)
10. Fu, J., Liu, J., Tian, H., Fang, Z., Lu, H.: Dual attention network for scene segmentation. arXiv preprint (2018)
11. Huang, Z., Wang, X., Huang, L., Huang, C., Wei, Y., Liu, W.: CCNet: criss-cross attention for semantic segmentation. In: ICCV (2019)
12. Li, X., Zhong, Z., Wu, J., Yang, Y., Lin, Z., Liu, H.: Expectation-maximization attention networks for semantic segmentation. In: ICCV (2019)
13. He, J., Deng, Z., Qiao, Y.: Dynamic multi-scale filters for semantic segmentation. In: ICCV (2019)
14. Li, X., Zhang, L., You, A., Yang, M., Yang, K., Tong, Y.: Global aggregation then local distribution in fully convolutional networks. In: BMVC (2019)
15. Li, Y., Gupta, A.: Beyond grids: learning graph representations for visual recognition. In: NeurIPS (2018)
16. Zhang, L., Li, X., Arnab, A., Yang, K., Tong, Y., Torr, P.H.: Dual graph convolutional network for semantic segmentation. In: BMVC (2019)
17. Zhang, L., Xu, D., Arnab, A., Torr, P.H.: Dynamic graph message passing networks. In: CVPR (2020)
18. Takikawa, T., Acuna, D., Jampani, V., Fidler, S.: Gated-SCNN: gated shape CNNs for semantic segmentation. In: ICCV (2019)
19. Chen, L.C., Barron, J.T., Papandreou, G., Murphy, K., Yuille, A.L.: Semantic image segmentation with task-specific edge detection using CNNs and a discriminatively trained domain transform. In: CVPR (2016)
20. Gong, K., Liang, X., Li, Y., Chen, Y., Yang, M., Lin, L.: Instance-level human parsing via part grouping network. In: Ferrari, V., Hebert, M., Sminchisescu, C., Weiss, Y. (eds.) ECCV 2018. LNCS, vol. 11208, pp. 805–822. Springer, Cham (2018). https://doi.org/10.1007/978-3-030-01225-0_47
21. Chen, L.-C., Zhu, Y., Papandreou, G., Schroff, F., Adam, H.: Encoder-decoder with atrous separable convolution for semantic image segmentation. In: Ferrari, V., Hebert, M., Sminchisescu, C., Weiss, Y. (eds.) ECCV 2018. LNCS, vol. 11211, pp. 833–851. Springer, Cham (2018). https://doi.org/10.1007/978-3-030-01234-2_49
22. Bertasius, G., Shi, J., Torresani, L.: Semantic segmentation with boundary neural fields. In: CVPR (2016)
23. Zhu, Y., et al.: Improving semantic segmentation via video propagation and label relaxation. In: CVPR (2019)
24. Cordts, M., et al.: The cityscapes dataset for semantic urban scene understanding. In: CVPR (2016)
25. Brostow, G.J., Fauqueur, J., Cipolla, R.: Semantic object classes in video: a high-definition ground truth database. Pattern Recogn. Lett. (2008)
26. Yu, F., et al.: BDD100K: a diverse driving dataset for heterogeneous multitask learning. In: CVPR (2020)
27. Chen, L.C., Papandreou, G., Kokkinos, I., Murphy, K., Yuille, A.L.: Semantic image segmentation with deep convolutional nets and fully connected CRFs. In: ICLR (2015)
28. Lin, G., Shen, C., van den Hengel, A., Reid, I.: Efficient piecewise training of deep structured models for semantic segmentation. In: CVPR (2016)
29. Zheng, S., et al.: Conditional random fields as recurrent neural networks. In: ICCV (2015)

30. Liu, Z., Li, X., Luo, P., Loy, C.C., Tang, X.: Semantic image segmentation via deep parsing network. In: ICCV (2015)
31. He, X., Gould, S.: An exemplar-based CRF for multi-instance object segmentation. In: CVPR (2014)
32. Jampani, V., Kiefel, M., Gehler, P.V.: Learning sparse high dimensional filters: image filtering, dense CRFs and bilateral neural networks. In: CVPR (2016)
33. Chen, L.C., Papandreou, G., Kokkinos, I., Murphy, K., Yuille, A.L.: DeepLab: semantic image segmentation with deep convolutional nets, atrous convolution, and fully connected CRFs. PAMI (2018)
34. Yang, M., Yu, K., Zhang, C., Li, Z., Yang, K.: DenseASPP for semantic segmentation in street scenes. In: CVPR (2018)
35. He, J., Deng, Z., Zhou, L., Wang, Y., Qiao, Y.: Adaptive pyramid context network for semantic segmentation. In: CVPR (2019)
36. Zhu, Z., Xu, M., Bai, S., Huang, T., Bai, X.: Asymmetric non-local neural networks for semantic segmentation. In: ICCV (2019)
37. Wang, X., Girshick, R., Gupta, A., He, K.: Non-local neural networks. In: CVPR (2018)
38. Vaswani, A., et al.: Attention is all you need. In: NeurIPS (2017)
39. Kipf, T.N., Welling, M.: Semi-supervised classification with graph convolutional networks. (2017)
40. Li, X., Yang, Y., Zhao, Q., Shen, T., Lin, Z., Liu, H.: Spatial pyramid based graph reasoning for semantic segmentation. In: CVPR (2020)
41. Dai, J., et al.: Deformable convolutional networks. In: ICCV (2017)
42. Liu, S., De Mello, S., Gu, J., Zhong, G., Yang, M.H., Kautz, J.: Learning affinity via spatial propagation networks. In: NeurIPS (2017)
43. Ding, H., Jiang, X., Liu, A.Q., Thalmann, N.M., Wang, G.: Boundary-aware feature propagation for scene segmentation. In: ICCV (2019)
44. Ke, T.-W., Hwang, J.-J., Liu, Z., Yu, S.X.: Adaptive affinity fields for semantic segmentation. In: Ferrari, V., Hebert, M., Sminchisescu, C., Weiss, Y. (eds.) ECCV 2018. LNCS, vol. 11205, pp. 605–621. Springer, Cham (2018). https://doi.org/10.1007/978-3-030-01246-5_36
45. Bertasius, G., Torresani, L., Yu, S.X., Shi, J.: Convolutional random walk networks for semantic image segmentation. In: CVPR (2017)
46. Misra, I., Shrivastava, A., Gupta, A., Hebert, M.: Cross-stitch networks for multi-task learning. In: CVPR (2016)
47. Kokkinos, I.: UberNet: training a universal convolutional neural network for low-, mid-, and high-level vision using diverse datasets and limited memory. In: CVPR (2017)
48. Xu, D., Ouyang, W., Wang, X., Sebe, N.: PAD-Net: multi-tasks guided prediction-and-distillation network for simultaneous depth estimation and scene parsing. In: CVPR (2018)
49. Dosovitskiy, A., et al.: FlowNet: learning optical flow with convolutional networks. In: CVPR (2015)
50. Jaderberg, M., Simonyan, K., Zisserman, A., Kavukcuoglu, K.: Spatial transformer networks. In: NeurIPS (2015)
51. Zhu, X., Xiong, Y., Dai, J., Yuan, L., Wei, Y.: Deep feature flow for video recognition. In: CVPR (2017)
52. He, K., Zhang, X., Ren, S., Sun, J.: Deep residual learning for image recognition. In: CVPR (2016)

53. Perazzi, F., Pont-Tuset, J., McWilliams, B., Van Gool, L., Gross, M., Sorkine-Hornung, A.: A benchmark dataset and evaluation methodology for video object segmentation. In: CVPR (2016)
54. Paszke, A., et al.: Automatic differentiation in PyTorch. In: NeurIPS Workshop (2017)
55. Zagoruyko, S., Komodakis, N.: Wide residual networks (2016)
56. Zhao, H., et al.: PSANet: point-wise spatial attention network for scene parsing. In: Ferrari, V., Hebert, M., Sminchisescu, C., Weiss, Y. (eds.) ECCV 2018. LNCS, vol. 11213, pp. 270–286. Springer, Cham (2018). https://doi.org/10.1007/978-3-030-01240-3_17
57. Yu, C., Wang, J., Peng, C., Gao, C., Yu, G., Sang, N.: Learning a discriminative feature network for semantic segmentation. In: CVPR (2018)
58. Zhang, F., et al.: ACFNet: attentional class feature network for semantic segmentation. In: ICCV (2019)
59. Li, X., Houlong, Z., Lei, H., Yunhai, T., Kuiyuan, Y.: GFF: gated fully fusion for semantic segmentation. In: AAAI (2020)
60. Chen, L.C., et al.: Searching for efficient multi-scale architectures for dense image prediction. In: Bengio, S., Wallach, H., Larochelle, H., Grauman, K., Cesa-Bianchi, N., Garnett, R. (eds.) NeurIPS (2018)
61. Liu, C., et al.: Auto-DeepLab: Hierarchical neural architecture search for semantic image segmentation. In: CVPR (2019)
62. Rota Bulò, S., Porzi, L., Kontschieder, P.: In-place activated BatchNorm for memory-optimized training of DNNs. In: CVPR (2018)
63. Neuhold, G., Ollmann, T., Rota Bulo, S., Kontschieder, P.: The mapillary vistas dataset for semantic understanding of street scenes. In: ICCV (2017)
64. Bilinski, P., Prisacariu, V.: Dense decoder shortcut connections for single-pass semantic segmentation. In: CVPR (2018)
65. Chandra, S., Couprie, C., Kokkinos, I.: Deep spatio-temporal random fields for efficient video segmentation. In: CVPR (2018)
66. Chen, W., Gong, X., Liu, X., Zhang, Q., Li, Y., Wang, Z.: FasterSeg: searching for faster real-time semantic segmentation. In: ICLR (2020)
67. Meletis, P., Dubbelman, G.: Training of convolutional networks on multiple heterogeneous datasets for street scene semantic segmentation. In: IVS (2018)
68. Krapac, J., Kreso, I., Segvic, S.: Ladder-style DenseNets for semantic segmentation of large natural images. In: ICCV Workshop (2017)

Conditional Entropy Coding for Efficient Video Compression

Jerry Liu[1(✉)], Shenlong Wang[1,2(✉)], Wei-Chiu Ma[1,3(✉)], Meet Shah[1(✉)],
Rui Hu[1(✉)], Pranaab Dhawan[1(✉)], and Raquel Urtasun[1,2(✉)]

[1] Uber ATG, St. Pittsburgh, USA
{jerryl,slwang,weichiu,meet.shah,rui.hu,pdhawan,urtasun}@uber.com
[2] University of Toronto, Toronto, Canada
[3] MIT, Cambridge, USA

Abstract. We propose a very simple and efficient video compression framework that only focuses on modeling the conditional entropy between frames. Unlike prior learning-based approaches, we reduce complexity by not performing any form of explicit transformations between frames and assume each frame is encoded with an independent state-of-the-art deep image compressor. We first show that a simple architecture modeling the entropy between the image latent codes is as competitive as other neural video compression works and video codecs while being much faster and easier to implement. We then propose a novel internal learning extension on top of this architecture that brings an additional ~10% bitrate savings without trading off decoding speed. Importantly, we show that our approach outperforms H.265 and other deep learning baselines in MS-SSIM on higher bitrate UVG video, and against all video codecs on lower framerates, while being thousands of times faster in decoding than deep models utilizing an autoregressive entropy model.

1 Introduction

The efficient storage of video data is vitally important to a large number of settings, from online websites such as Youtube and Facebook to robotics settings such as drones and self-driving cars. This necessitates the use of good video compression algorithms. Both image and video compression are fields that have been extensively researched in the past few decades. Traditional image codecs such as JPEG2000, BPG, and WebP, and traditional video codecs such as HEVC H.265, AVC/H.264 [28,38] are widely used and hand-engineered to work well in a variety of settings. But the lack of learning involved in the algorithm leaves room open for more end-to-end optimized solutions.

Electronic supplementary material The online version of this chapter (https://doi.org/10.1007/978-3-030-58520-4_27) contains supplementary material, which is available to authorized users.

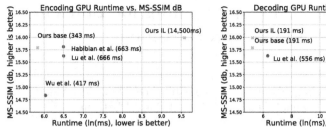

Fig. 1. Plots indicating the GPU runtime vs. MS-SSIM of our model vs. other deep approaches at bitrate 0.2, averaged over a 1920 × 1080 UVG frame. Runtimes are shown independent of the entropy coding implementation. We interpolate to obtain the MS-SSIM estimate at the exact bitrate.

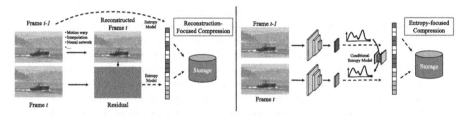

Fig. 2. An illustration of the explicit transformations used in removing redundant information in subsequent frames vs. probabilistic modeling used in entropy coding. A typical lossy compression algorithm will contain elements of both approaches.

Recently, there has been an explosion of deep-learning based image compressors that have been demonstrated to outperform BPG on a variety of evaluation datasets across both MS-SSIM and PSNR as evaluation metrics [9,18,19,23]. This explosion has also recently happened in video compression on a somewhat smaller scale, with the latest advances being able to outperform H.265 on MS-SSIM and PSNR in certain cases [12,14,20,25]. Many of these approaches [12,25,39] involve learning-based generalizations of the traditional video compression techniques of motion-compensation, frame interpolation and residual coding.

While achieving impressive distortion-rate curves, there are several major facts blocking the wide adoption of these approaches for real-world, generic video compression tasks. First, most aforementioned approaches are still slower than standard video codecs at both encoding and decoding stage; moreover, due to the the fact that they explicitly perform interpolation and residual coding between frames, a majority of the computations cannot be parallelized to accelerate coding speed; finally, the domain bias of the training dataset makes it difficult to generalize well to a wide range of different type of videos.

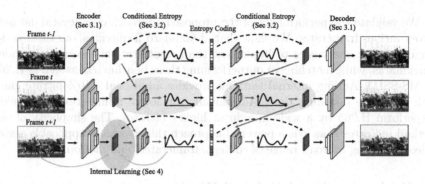

Fig. 3. Overview of the architecture of our approach. We highlight our key contribution, namely the conditional entropy model and internal learning in blue and yellow, respectively. (Color figure online)

In this paper, we address these issues by creating a remarkably simple *entropy-focused* video compression approach that is not only competitive with prior state-of-the-art learned compression, but also *significantly faster* (see Fig. 1), rendering it a practical alternative to existing video codecs. Such an entropy-focused approach focuses on better capturing the correlations between frames during entropy coding rather than performing explicit transformations (e.g. motion compensation). Our contributions are two-fold (illustrated in Fig. 3). First, we propose a base model consisting only of a **conditional entropy model** fitted on top of the latent codes produced by a deep single-image compressor. The intuition for why we don't need explicit transformations can be visualized in Fig. 2: given two video frames, prior works would code the first frame to store the full frame information while coding the second frame to store explicit motion information from frame 1 as well as residual bits. On the other hand, our approach encodes both frames as independent image codes, and reduces the joint bitrate by fitting probability model (an *entropy* model) to maximize the probability of the second image code given the first. We can thus extend this to a full video sequence by still encoding every frame independently, and simply considering every adjacent pair of frames for the probability model. While entropy modeling has been a subcomponent of prior works [14,16,20,25,39], they have tended to be very simple [25], only dependent on the image itself [12,20], or use costly autoregressive models that are intractably expensive during decoding [14,39]; here our conditional entropy model provides a viable means for video compression purely within itself.

Our second contribution is to propose **internal learning** of the latent code during inference. Prior works in video compression operate by using a fixed encoder during the inference/encoding stage. As a result, the latent codes of the video is not optimized towards reconstruction/entropy estimation for the specific test video. We observe as long as the decoder is fixed, we can trade off *encoding runtime* to further optimize the latent codes along the rate-distortion curve, while not affecting *decoding runtime* (Fig. 1, right).

We validate the performance of the proposed approach over several datasets across various framerates. We show that at standard framerates, our base model is much faster and easier to implement than most state-of-the-art deep video benchmarks, while matching or outperforming these benchmarks as well as H.265 on MS-SSIM. Adding internal learning provides additional ~10% bitrate gains with the same decoding time. Additionally, on lower framerates, our models outperform H.265 by a wide margin at higher bitrates. The simplicity of our method indicates that it is a powerful approach that is widely applicable across videos spanning a broad range of content, framerates, and motion.

2   Background and Related Work

2.1   Deep Image Compression

There is an abundance of work on learned, lossy image-compression [8,9,21,23, 24,31–33]. In general, these works follow a general autoencoder architecture minimizing the rate-distortion tradeoff. Typically, an encoder transforms the image into a latent space, quantizes the symbols, and applies entropy coding (typically arithmetic/range coding) on the symbols to output a compressed bitstream. During decoding, the recovered symbols are then fed through a decoder for image reconstruction.

Recent works approximate the rate-distortion tradeoff $\ell(\boldsymbol{x}, \hat{\boldsymbol{x}}) + \beta R(\hat{\boldsymbol{y}})$ in a differentiable manner by replacing the bitrate term R with the cross-entropy between the code distribution and a learned "prior" probability model: $R \approx \mathbb{E}_{x \sim p_{data}}[\log p(E(\boldsymbol{x}); \boldsymbol{\theta})]$. Shannon's source coding theorem [26] indicates that the cross-entropy is an asymptotic lower bound of the bitrate. One way to achieve this optimal bitrate during entropy coding is to use the learned "prior" model as the probability map during arithmetic coding or range coding to code the symbols. Hence, the smaller the cross-entropy term, the more the bitrate can be reduced. This then implies that the more expressive the prior model in modeling the true distribution of latent codes, the smaller the overall bitrate.

Sophisticated prior models have been designed for the quantized representation in order to minimize the cross-entropy with the code distribution. Autoregressive models [21,23,33], hyperprior models [9,23], and factorized models [8,9,31] have been used to model this prior. [23] and [22] suggest that using an autoregressive model is intractably slow in practice, as it requires a pass through the model for every single pixel during decoding. [22] suggests that the hyperprior approach presents a good tradeoff between speed and performance.

A recent model by Liu et al. [17] presents an extension of [23] using residual blocks in the encoder/decoder, outperforming BPG and other deep models on both PSNR and MS-SSIM on Kodak.

2.2   Video Compression

Conceptually, traditional video codecs such as H.264/H.265 exploit temporal correlations between frames by categorizing the frames as follows [28,38]:

- I-frames: compressed as an independent image
- P-frames: predicted from past frames using block-based flow estimate, then encode residual.
- B-frames: similar to P-frames but predicted from both past and future frames.

In order to predict P/B-frames, the motion between frames is predicted via block matching (and the flow is uniformly applied within blocks), and then the resulting difference is separately encoded as the "residual." Generally, if neighboring frames are temporally correlated, encoding the motion and residual vectors requires fewer bits than recording the subsequent frame independently.

Recently, several deep-learning based video compression frameworks [12,15, 18,20,25,39] have been developed. Both Wu et al. [39] and Lu et al. [20] attempt to generalize various parts of the motion-compensation and residual learning framework with neural networks, and get close to H.265 performance (on *very-fast* setting). Rippel et al. [25] achieved state-of-the-art results in MS-SSIM by generalizing flow/residual coding with a global state, spatial multiplexing, and more. Djelouah et al. [12] jointly decode motion and blending coefficients from references frames, and represent residuals in latent space. Habibian et al. [14] utilizes a 3D convolutional architecture to avoid motion compensation, as well as an autoregressive entropy model to outperform [20,39].

These prior works generally require specialized modules and explicit transformations, with the entropy model being an oftentimes intractable autoregressive subcomponent [12,14,39]. A more closely related work is that of Han et al. [15], who propose to model the entropy dependence between codes with an LSTM: $p(\boldsymbol{y}_i|\boldsymbol{y}_{<i})$. In contrast to these prior works, we focus on a *entropy-only* approach, with no explicit transformations across time. More importantly, our base approach carefully exploits the parallel nature of frame encoding/decoding, rendering it orders of magnitude faster than other state-of-the-art while being just as competitive.

2.3   Internal Learning

The concept of internal learning is not new. It is similar to the sample-specific nature of transductive learning [29,35]. "Internal Learning" is a term proposed in [6,13], which exploits the internal recurrence of information within a single-image to train an unsupervised super-resolution algorithm. Many related works have also trained deep networks on a single example, from DIP [34] to GANs [27,30,40]. Also related is Sun et al. [29] who propose "test-time training" on an auxiliary function for each test instance on supervised classification tasks. Concurrently and independently from our work, Campos et al. propose context adaptive optimization in image compression [10], which has demonstrated promising results on finetuning each latent code towards its test image.

In our setting, we leverage the fact that in video compression the ground-truth is simply the video itself, and we apply internal learning in a way that obeys codebook consistency while decreasing the conditional entropy between video frames during decoding. There are unique advantages to using internal learning

in our entropy-only video compression setting: it can optimize for conditional entropy between codes in a way that an independent frame encoder cannot (see Sect. 4).

3 Entropy-Focused Video Compression

Our base model consists of two components: we first encode each frame x_i of a video x with a straightforward, off-the-shelf image compressor consisting of a deep image encoder/decoder (Sect. 3.1) to obtain discrete image codes y_i. Then, we capture the temporal relationships between our y_i's with a conditional entropy model that approximates the joint entropy of the video sequence (Sect. 3.2). The model is trained end-to-end with respect to the rate-distortion loss function (Sect. 3.3).

3.1 Single-Image Encoder/Decoder

We encode every video frame x_i separately with a deep image compressor into a quantized latent code y_i; note that each y_i contains *full* information to reconstruct each frame i and does not depend on previous frames. Our choice of architecture for single-image compression borrows heavily from the state-of-the-art model presented by Liu et al. [17], which has shown to outperform BPG on both MS-SSIM and PSNR. The architecture consists of the image encoder, quantizer, and image decoder. We simplify the model in two ways compared to the original paper: we remove all non-local layers for efficiency/memory reasons, and we remove the autoregressive context estimation due to its decoding intractability ([21,23], also see Fig. 1).

More details about the image encoder/decoder architecture are found in supplementary material. In our video compression model, we use the image encoder/quantizer to produce the quantized code y_i, and the image decoder to produce the reconstruction $\hat{x}_i$. We do not use the existing entropy model (inspired from [9,23]) which are only designed for modeling the intra-image entropy; instead we design our own conditional entropy model, as detailed next.

3.2 Conditional Entropy Model for Video Encoding

Our *entropy model* models the joint entropy of the video frame codes with a deep network in order to reduce the overall bitrate of the video sequence; this is because the cross-entropy between our entropy model and the actual code distribution is a tight lower bound of the bitrate [26]. Our goal is to design our entropy model to capture the temporal correlations as well as possible between the frames such that it can minimize the cross-entropy with the code distribution. Put another way, the bitrate for the entire video sequence code $R(y)$ is tightly approximated by the cross-entropy between the code distribution induced by the encoder $y = E(x), x \sim p_{data}$ and our probability model $p(\cdot|\theta)$: $\mathbb{E}_{x \sim p_{data}}[\log p(y; \theta)]$.

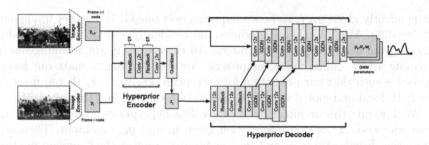

Fig. 4. Diagram of our conditional entropy model, consisting of both a hyperprior encoder (top) and decoder (bottom).

If $y = \{y_1, y_2, ...\}$ represents the sequence of frame codes for the entire video sequence, then a natural factorization of the joint probability $p(y)$ would be to have every subsequent frame depend on the previous frames:

$$R(y) \geq \mathbb{E}_{x \sim p_{data}}[\log p(y; \theta)] = \mathbb{E}_{x \sim p_{data}}[\sum_{i=0}^{n} \log p(y_i | y_{<i}; \theta)] \qquad (1)$$

While other approaches (e.g. B-frames) model dependence in a hierarchical manner, our factorization makes sense in online and low-latency settings, where we want to decode frames sequentially. We further make a 1st-order Markov assumption such that each frame y_i only depends on the previous frame y_{i-1} [1] and a small hyperprior code z_i. Note that z_i counts as side information, inspired from [9], and must also be counted in the bitstream. We encode it with a hyperprior encoder with y_i and y_{i-1} as input (see Fig. 4). We thus have

$$R(y) \geq \mathbb{E}_{x \sim p_x}[\sum_{i=0}^{n} \log p(y_i | y_{i-1}, z_i; \theta) + \log p(z_i; \theta)]$$

We assume that the hyperprior code distribution $p(z_i; \theta)$ is modeled as a factorized distribution, $p(z_i; \theta) = \prod_j p(z_{ij}|\theta_z)$, where j represents each dimension of z_i. Since each z_{ij} is a discrete value, we design each $p(z_{ij}|\theta_z) = c_j(z_{ij} + 0.5; \theta_z) - c_j(z_{ij} - 0.5; \theta_z)$, where each $c_j(\cdot; \theta_z)$ is a cumulative density function (CDF) parametrized as a neural network similar to [9]. In the meantime, we also model each $p(y_i|y_{i-1}, z_i; \theta)$ as a conditional factorized distribution: $\prod_j p(y_{ij}|y_{i-1}, z_i; \theta)$, with $p(y_{ij}|y_{i-1}, z_i; \theta) = g_j(y_{ij} + 0.5|y_{i-1}, z_i; \theta_y) - g_j(y_{ij} - 0.5|y_{i-1}, z_i; \theta_y)$, where g_j is modeled as the CDF of a Gaussian mixture model: $\sum_k w_{jk}\mathcal{N}(\mu_{jk}, \sigma_{jk}^2)$. $w_{jk}, \mu_{jk}, \sigma_{jk}$ are all learned parameters depending on $y_{i-1}, z_i; \theta_y$. Similar to [9,19,23], the GMM parameters are outputs of a deep hyperprior decoder.

Note that our entropy model is *not* autoregressive either at the pixel level or the frame level - mixture parameters for each latent "pixel" y_{ij} are predicted

---

[1] When $i = 0$, y_{i-1} doesn't exist and can be represented as a zeroed-out vector.

independently given y_{i-1}, z_i, hence requiring only one GPU pass per frame during decoding. Also, all y_i's are produced independently with our image encoder, removing the need to specify keyframes. All these aspects are advantageous in designing a fast, online video compressor. Yet we also aim to make our model expressive such that our prediction for each pixel $p(y_{ij}|y_{i-1}, z_i; \theta)$ can incorporate both local and global structure information surrounding that pixel.

We illustrate this architecture in Fig. 4. Our hyperprior encoder encodes our hyperprior code z_i as side information given y_i and y_{i-1} as input. Then, our hyperprior decoder takes z_i and y_{i-1} as input to predict the Gaussian mixture parameters for y_i: σ_i, μ_i, and w_i. We can effectively think of z_i as providing supplemental information to y_{i-1} to better predict y_i. The hyperprior decoder first upsamples z_i to the spatial resolution of y_{i-1} with residual blocks; then, it uses deconvolutions and IGDN nonlinearities [7] to progressively upsample both y_{i-1} and z_i to different resolution feature maps, and fuses the z_i feature to the y_{i-1} at each corresponding upsampled resolution. This helps to incorporate changes between y_{i-1} to y_i, encapsulated by z_i, at multiple resolution levels from more global features at the lower resolution to finer features at higher resolutions. Then, downsampling convolutions and GDN nonlinearities are applied to match the original spatial resolution of the image code and produce the mixture parameters for each pixel of the code.

3.3   Rate-distortion Loss Function

We train our base compression models end-to-end to minimize the rate-distortion tradeoff objective used for lossy compression:

$$L(x) = \underbrace{\mathbb{E}_{x \sim p_{data}}[\sum_{i=0}^{n} ||x_i - \hat{x}_i||^2]}_{\text{Distortion}} + \lambda \underbrace{\mathbb{E}_{x \sim p_{data}}[\sum_{i=0}^{n} \log p(y_i|y_{i-1}, z_i; \theta) + \log p(z_i; \theta)]}_{\text{Rate}} \quad (2)$$

where each $x_i, \hat{x}_i, y_i, z_i$ is a full/reconstructed video frame and code/hyperprior code respectively. The first term describes the reconstruction quality of the decoded video frames, and the second term measures the bitrate as approximated by our conditional entropy model. Each $y_i, \hat{x}_i$ is produced via our image encoder/decoder, while our conditional entropy model captures the dependence of y_i on y_{i-1}, z_i. We can additionally clamp the rate term to enforce a target bitrate R_a: $max(\mathbb{E}_{x \sim p_{data}}[\sum_{i=0}^{n} \log p(y_i|y_{i-1}, z_i; \theta) + \log p(z_i; \theta)], R_a)$.

4   Internal Learning of the Frame Code

We additionally propose an internal learning extension of our base model, which leverages every frame of a test video sequence as its own example for which we can learn a better encoding, helping to provide more gains in rate-distortion performance with our entropy-focused approach.

The goal of a compression algorithm is to find codes that can later be *decoded* according to a codebook that does not change during encoding. This is also intuitively why we can not overfit our entire compression architecture to a single frame in a video sequence; this would imply that every video frame would require a separate decoder to decode. However, we make the observation that in our models, the trained decoder/hyperprior decoder represent our codebook; hence as long as the decoder and hyperprior decoder parameters remain fixed, we can actually optimize the encoder/hyperprior parameters or the latent codes themselves, y_i and z_i, for every frame during inference. In practice we do the latter to reduce the number of parameters to optimize.

One benefit of internal learning in our video compression setting is similar to that suggested by Campos et al. [10]: the test distribution during inference is oftentimes different than the training distribution. This is especially true in videos, where the test distribution may have different artifacts, framerate, etc. Our base conditional entropy model may predict a higher entropy for test videos due to distributional shift - internal learning might help account for the short-comings of out-of-distribution prediction by the encoder/hyperprior encoder.

The second benefit is unique to our video compression setting: we can optimize each frame code to reduce the joint entropy in a way that the base approach cannot. In the base approach, there is a restriction of assuming that y_i is produced by an independent single-image compression model without accounting for past frames as input. Yet there exist configurations of y_i with the same reconstruction quality that are more easily predictive from y_{i-1} in our entropy model $p(y_i|y_{i-1}, z_i)$. Performing internal learning allows us to more effectively search for a more optimal configuration of the frame code and hyperprior code z_i^*, y_i^* such that y_i^* can be more easily predicted by y_{i-1}^*, z_i^* in the entropy model. As a result, internal learning helps open up a wider search space of frame codes that can potentially have a lower joint entropy.

To perform internal learning during inference, we optimize against a similar rate-distortion loss as in Eq. 2:

$$L_{\text{internal}}(x) = \sum_{i=0}^{n} \ell(x_i, \hat{x}_i) + \lambda \left[\sum_{i=0}^{n} \log p(y_i|y_{i-1}, z_i; \theta) + \log p(z_i; \theta) \right] \quad (3)$$

where x denotes the test video sequence that we optimize over, and ℓ represents the reconstruction loss function. We first initialize y_i and z_i as the output from the trained encoder/hyperprior encoder. Then we backpropagate gradients from (Eq. 2) to y_i and z_i for a set number of steps, while keeping all decoder parameters fixed. We can additionally customize λ in Eq. (3) depending on whether we want to tune more for bitrate or reconstruction. If the newly optimized codes are denoted as y_i^* and z_i^*, then we simply store y_i^* and z_i^* during encoding and discard the original y_i and z_i.

We do note that internal learning during inference prevents the ability to perform parallel frame encoding, since y_i^*, z_i^* now depend on y_{i-1}^* as an output of internal learning rather than the image encoder; the gradient steps also increase

the encoding runtime per frame. However, after z_i, y_i are optimized, they are fixed during decoding, and hence decoding runtime does not increase. We analyze the tradeoff of increased computation vs. reduced bitrates in the next section.

5 Experiments

We present a detailed analysis of our video compression approach on numerous datasets, varying factors such as frame-rate and video codec quality.

5.1 Datasets, Metrics, and Video Codecs

Kinetics, CDVL, and UVG, and others: We train on the Kinetics dataset [11]. Then, we benchmark our method against standard video test sets which are commonly used for evaluating video compression algorithms. Specifically, we run evaluations on video sequences from the Consumer Digital Video Library (CDVL) [2] as well as the Ultra Video Group (UVG) [4]. UVG consists of 7 video sequences of 3900 frames total, each 1920 × 1080 and 120fps. Our CDVL dataset consists of 78 video sequences, each 640 × 480 and either 30fps or 60fps. The videos span a wide range of natural image settings as well as motion. For further analysis of our approach, we benchmark on video sequences from MCL-JVC [36] and Video Trace Library (VTL) [5], shown in supplementary material.

NorthAmerica: We collect a video dataset by driving our self-driving fleet in several North American cities and collecting monocular, frontal camera data. The framerate is 10 Hz. Our training set consists of 1160 video sequences of 300 frames each, and our test set consists of 68 video sequences of 300 frames each. All frames are 1920 × 1200 in resolution, and we train on 240 ×150 crops. We focus both on full street driving sequences as well as only on sequences where ego-vehicle is moving (so no red-lights or stop signs).

Metrics: We measure runtime in milliseconds on a per-frame basis for both encoding and decoding. Moreover we plot the rate-distortion curve for multi-scale structural similarity (MS-SSIM) [37], which is a commonly-used perceptual metric that captures the overall structural similarity in the reconstruction. We report the MS-SSIM curve at log-scale similar to [9], where log-scale is defined as $-10 \log_{10}(1 - \text{MS-SSIM})$. Additionally, we report some curves using PSNR: $-10 \log_{10}(\text{MSE})$, where MSE is mean-squared error, and hence measuring the absolute error in the reconstructed image.

Note from Sect. 3.3 that all our base models are trained/optimized with mean-squared error (MSE), and we show that our base models are robust in both MS-SSIM and PSNR. However with internal learning, we demonstrate the flexibility of tuning to different metrics during test-time, so we optimize reconstruction loss towards MS-SSIM and MSE separately (see Sect. 4).

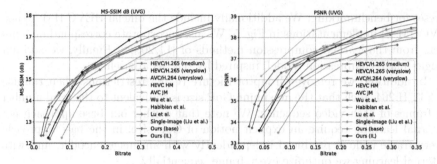

Fig. 5. Rate-distortion plot of our model against competing deep compression works [14,20,39]. Results are on full 1920 × 1080 UVG video.

Video Codecs and Baselines: We benchmark with both libx265 (HEVC/H.265) and libx264 (AVC/H.264). To the best of our knowledge all prior works on learned video compression [12,14,20,25,39] have artificially restricted codec performance either by using a faster setting or by imposing additional limitations on the codecs (such as removing B-frames). In contrast, we benchmark both H.265 and H.264 on the *veryslow* setting in ffmpeg in order to maximize the performance of these codecs. For the sake of illustration (and also to have a consistent comparison in Fig. 5 with other authors) we also plot H.265 with the *medium*

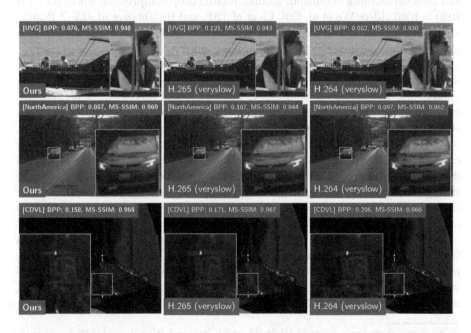

Fig. 6. Demonstration of our approach vs H.265/H.264 on 10 Hz 1920 × 1200 NorthAmerica video, 12 Hz 1920 × 1080 UVG video, and 6 Hz 640 × 480 CDVL video. Even at lower bitrates, our approach demonstrates significant reductions in bitrate and distortion on lower framerate video.

preset for benchmarking. We additionally include the official HEVC HM [3] and AVC JM [1] implementations in Fig. 5. We also incorporate corresponding numbers from the learned compression methods of [14,20,39]. Finally, we add our single-image compression model, inspired by [17], as a baseline.

In addition, we remove Group of Picture (GoP) restrictions when running H.265/H.264, such that the maximum GoP size is equivalent to the total number of frames of each video sequence. We note that neither our base approach nor internal learning require an explicit notion of GoP size: in the base approach, every frame code is produced independently with an image encoder, and with internal learning we optimize every frame sequentially.

Implementation Details: We use a learning rate of $7 \cdot 10^{-5}$ to $2 \cdot 10^{-4}$ for our models at different bitrates, and optimize parameters with Adam. We train with a batch size of 4 on two GPU's. For test/runtime evaluations, we use a single Intel Xeon E5-2687W CPU and 1080Ti GPU. For internal learning we run 10-12 steps of gradient descent per frame. Our range coding implementation is written in C++ interfacing with Python; during encoding/decoding we compute the codes and distributions on GPU, then pass the data over to our C++ implementation.

5.2   Runtime and Rate-distortion on UVG

We showcase runtime vs. MS-SSIM plots of our method (both the base model and internal learning extension) against related deep compression works on UVG 1920×1080 video: Wu et al. [39], Lu et al. [20], and Habibian et al. [14]. [2] Results are shown in Fig. 1, and detail the frame encoding/decoding runtimes on GPU excluding the specific entropy coding implementation.[3]

Overall our base approach is significantly faster than most deep compression works. During decoding, our base approach is *orders of magnitude* faster than approaches that use an autoregressive entropy model (Habibian et al. [14], Wu et al. [39]). We note that closest works in the GPU runtime and MS-SSIM is Lu et al., [20] who reported **666 ms/556 ms** for encoding/decoding. Nevertheless, our GPU-only pass is still faster (**340 ms/ 191 ms** for encoding/decoding). Our entropy coding implementation has room for optimization; the C++ algorithm itself is fast (**140 ms/139 ms** for range encoding/decoding of a 1080p frame) though the Python binding interfacing brings the time up to **1.19/0.65 s** for encoding/decoding. Additionally, we benchmark against prior works' entropy coding runtime as well as codec runtime in supplementary.

While the optional internal learning extension improves the rate-distortion trade-off in all the benchmarks, it brings overhead in encoding runtime. We note that our implementation of internal learning is unoptimized with the backward operator in PyTorch. However, it brings no overhead in decoding runtime, meaning our approach is still faster than all other approaches during decoding.

---

[2] We don't show the results of Djelouah et al. [12] and Rippel et al. [25] because we were unable to get consistent MS-SSIM metrics on the UVG dataset.

[3] We thank the authors for providing us detailed runtime information.

In addition, we evaluate all the competing algorithms' performance and plot the rate-distortion curve on UVG test dataset, as shown in Fig. 5. The results demonstrate that our approach is competitive or even outperforms existing approaches, especially on MS-SSIM.[4] Between bitrate ranges 0.1–0.3, which is where other deep baselines present their numbers, our base approach is as competitive as a motion-compensation approach [20] or one that uses autoregressive entropy models [14]. At higher bitrates, the base approach outperforms H.265 *veryslow* in both MS-SSIM and PSNR. Internal learning further improves upon all bitrates by ~10%.

5.3 Rate-distortion on NorthAmerica

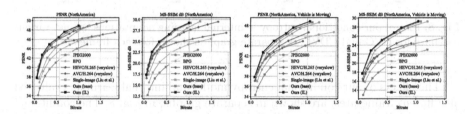

Fig. 7. Plot of our approaches compared against compression baselines for NorthAmerica, both over the entire dataset as well as only when the ego-vehicle has positive velocity.

We show our conditional entropy model and internal learning extension on the NorthAmerica dataset, in Fig. 7. The graph shows that even our single-image Liu model baseline [17] outperforms H.265 on MS-SSIM at higher bitrates and approaches H.265 in PSNR. Our conditional entropy model demonstrates bitrate improvements of 20–50% across bitrates, and internal learning demonstrates an additional 10% improvement.

Figure 7 also shows graphs in which we only analyze video sequences where the autonomous vehicle is in motion, which creates a fairly large gap in H.265 performance. In this setting, both our video compression algorithm as well as the single-image model outperform H.265 by a wide margin on almost all bitrates in MS-SSIM and at higher bitrates in PSNR.

5.4 Varying Framerates on UVG and CDVL

We can additionally control the framerate by dropping frames for CDVL and UVG. We follow a scheme of keeping 1 out of every n frames, denoted as $/n$. We analyze UVG and CDVL video in 1/3, 1/6, and 1/10 settings. Since all UVG videos are 120 Hz, the corresponding framerates are 40 Hz, 20 Hz, 12 Hz.

---

[4] HEVC HM performs much better in PSNR, but as we see in supplementary, HEVC HM/AVC JM are *significantly slower* than ffmpeg codecs and our method.

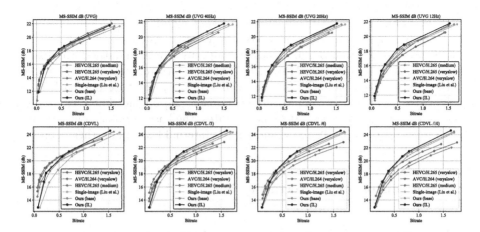

Fig. 8. Plot of our conditional entropy + internal learning adaptations against various baselines for UVG and CDVL. A separate graph is shown for each framerate.

The effects of our conditional entropy model and internal learning, evaluated at different framerates, are shown in separate graphs, in Fig. 8. The conditional entropy model is competitive with H.265 at the original framerate for UVG, and outperforms video codecs at lower framerates. In fact, we found that *single-image compression* matches H.265 *veryslow* on lower framerates! We find a similar effect on CDVL at lower framerates as well, where both single-image compression and our approach far outperform H.265 at lower framerates.

Our base conditional entropy model generally demonstrates a 20%–50% reduction of bitrate compared to the single-image model. The effect of internal learning on each frame code provides an additional 10–20% reduction in bitrate, demonstrating that internal learning of the latent codes during the inference stage provides additional gains.

5.5 Qualitative Results

We showcase qualitative outputs of our model vs H.265 and H.264 *veryslow* in Fig. 6, demonstrating the power of our model on lower framerate video. On 10Hz NorthAmerica, 12Hz UVG video, and 6Hz CDVL video, our model contains big reductions in bitrate compared to video codecs, while producing results that are more even and with fewer artifacts.

6   Conclusion

We propose a novel entropy-focused video compression architecture consisting of a base conditional entropy model as well as an internal learning extension. Rather than explicitly transforming information across frames as in prior work, our model aims to model the correlations between each frame code, as well as

perform internal learning of each frame code during inference to better optimize this entropy model. We show that our lightweight, entropy-focused method is competitive with prior work and video codecs as well as being much faster and conceptually easier to understand. With internal learning, our approach outperforms H.265 in numerous video settings, especially at higher bitrates and lower framerates. Our adaptations are anchored against single-image compression which is robust against varied framerates, whereas video codecs such as H.265/H.264 are not. Hence, we demonstrate that such a video compression approach can have wide applicability in a variety of settings.

References

1. Avc jm reference software. http://iphome.hhi.de/suehring/. Accessed 01 May 2020
2. Consumer digital video library. https://www.cdvl.org/. Accessed 01 Nov 2019
3. Hevc hm reference software. https://vcgit.hhi.fraunhofer.de/jct-vc/HM. Accessed 01 May 2020
4. Ultra video group. http://ultravideo.cs.tut.fi/#testsequences. Accessed 01 Nov 2019
5. Video trace library. http://trace.kom.aau.dk/. Accessed 01 Nov 2019
6. Shocher, A., Cohen, N., Irani, M.: "zero-shot" super-resolution using deep internal learning. In: CVPR (2018)
7. Ballé, J., Laparra, V., Simoncelli, E.P.: Density modeling of images using a generalized normalization transformation. ArXiv (2015)
8. Ballé, J., Laparra, V., Simoncelli, E.P.: End-to-end optimized image compression. In: ICLR (2017)
9. Ballé, J., Minnen, D., Singh, S., Hwang, S.J., Johnston, N.: Variational image compression with a scale hyperprior. In: ICLR (2018)
10. Campos, J., Meierhans, S., Djelouah, A., Schroers, C.: Content adaptive optimization for neural image compression (2019)
11. Carreira, J., Zisserman, A.: Quo vadis, action recognition? A new model and the kinetics dataset (2017)
12. Djelouah, A., Campos, J., Schaub-Meyer, S., Schroers, C.: Neural inter-frame compression for video coding. In: ICCV (2019)
13. Glasner, D., Bagon, S., Irani, M.: Super-resolution from a single image. In: ICCV (2009)
14. Habibian, A., van Rozendaal, T., Tomczak, J.M., Cohen, T.S.: Video compression with rate-distortion autoencoders. In: ICCV (2019)
15. Han, J., Lombardo, S., Schroers, C., Mandt, S.: Deep generative video compression (2019)
16. Lee, J., Cho, S., Beack, S.K.: Context-adaptive entropy model for end-to-end optimized image compression. In: ICLR (2019)
17. Liu, H., Chen, T., Guo, P., Shen, Q., Cao, X., Wang, Y., Ma, Z.: Non-local Attention Optimized Deep Image Compression. ArXiv (2019)
18. Liu, H., Chen, T., Lu, M., Shen, Q., Ma, Z.: Neural Video Compression using Spatio-Temporal Priors. ArXiv (2019)
19. Liu, J., Wang, S., Urtasun, R.: Dsic: deep stereo image compression. In: ICCV (2019)
20. Lu, G., Ouyang, W., Xu, D., Zhang, X., Cai, C., Gao, Z.: Dvc: An end-to-end deep video compression framework. In: CVPR (2019)

21. Mentzer, F., Agustsson, E., Tschannen, M., Timofte, R., Gool, L.V.: Conditional probability models for deep image compression. In: CVPR (2018)
22. Mentzer, F., Agustsson, E., Tschannen, M., Timofte, R., Gool, L.V.: Practical full resolution learned lossless image compression. In: CVPR (2019)
23. Minnen, D., Ballé, J., Toderici, G.: Joint autoregressive and hierarchical priors for learned image compression. In: NIPS (2018)
24. Rippel, O., Bourdev, L.: Real-time adaptive image compression. In: ICML (2017)
25. Rippel, O., Nair, S., Lew, C., Branson, S., Anderson, A.G., Bourdev, L.: Learned video compression. In: ICCV (2019)
26. Shannon, C.E.: A mathematical theory of communication. Bell Syst.Tech. J. **27**, 379–423 (1948)
27. Shocher, A., Bagon, S., Isola, P., Irani, M.: Ingan: capturing and remapping the "DNA" of a natural image. In: ICCV (2019)
28. Sullivan, G.J., Ohm, J.R., Han, W.J., Wiegand, T.: Overview of the high efficiency video coding (HEVC) standard. IEEE Trans Circuits Syst. Video Technol. **22**, 1649–1668 (2012)
29. Sun, Y., Wang, X., Liu, Z., Miller, J., Efros, A.A., Hardt, M.: Test-time training for out-of-distribution generalization (2019)
30. Tamar Rott Shaham, Tali Dekel, T.M.: Singan: Learning a generative model from a single natural image. In: ICCV (2019)
31. Theis, L., Shi, W., Cunningham, A., Huszar, F.: Lossy image compression with compressive autoencoders. In: ICLR (2017)
32. Toderici, G., O'Malley, S.M., Hwang, S.J., Vincent, D.: Variable rate image compression with recurrent neural networks. In: ICLR (2016)
33. Toderici, G., Vincent, D., Johnston, N., Hwang, S.J., Minnen, D., Shor, J., Covell, M.: Full resolution image compression with recurrent neural networks. In: CVPR (2017)
34. Ulyanov, D., Vedaldi, A., Lempitsky, V.S.: Deep image prior. In: CVPR (2018)
35. Vapnik, V.N.: The Nature of Statistical Learning Theory. Springer, Heidelberg (1995). https://doi.org/10.1007/978-1-4757-2440-0
36. Wang, H., et al.: MCL-JCV: a JND-based H.264/AVC video quality assessment dataset. In: ICIP (2016)
37. Wang, Z., Simoncelli, E.P., Bovik, A.C.: Multiscale structural similarity for image quality assessment. In: ACSSC (2003)
38. Wiegand, T., Sullivan, G.J., Bjontegaard, G., Luthra, A.: Overview of the H.264/AVC video coding standard. IEEE Trans. Circuits Syst. Video Technol. **13**, 560–576 (2003)
39. Wu, C.-Y., Singhal, N., Krähenbühl, P.: Video compression through image interpolation. In: Ferrari, V., Hebert, M., Sminchisescu, C., Weiss, Y. (eds.) ECCV 2018, Part VIII. LNCS, vol. 11212, pp. 425–440. Springer, Cham (2018). https://doi.org/10.1007/978-3-030-01237-3_26
40. Zhou, Y., Zhu, Z., Bai, X., Lischinski, D., Cohen-Or, D., Huang, H.: Non-stationary texture synthesis by adversarial expansion. In: SIGGRAPH (2018)

Differentiable Feature Aggregation Search for Knowledge Distillation

Yushuo Guan[1], Pengyu Zhao[1], Bingxuan Wang[1], Yuanxing Zhang[1],
Cong Yao[2], Kaigui Bian[1,3(✉)], and Jian Tang[4]

[1] Peking University, Beijing, China
{david.guan,pengyuzhao,wangbx,longo,bkg}@pku.edu.cn
[2] Megvii (Face++) Technology Inc, Beijing, China
yaocong2010@gmail.com
[3] National Engineering Laboratory for Big Data Analysis and Applications,
Beijing, China
[4] DiDi AI Labs, Beijing, China
tangjian@didiglobal.com

Abstract. Knowledge distillation has become increasingly important
in model compression. It boosts the performance of a miniaturized student network with the supervision of the output distribution and feature
maps from a sophisticated teacher network. Some recent works introduce
multi-teacher distillation to provide more supervision to the student network. However, the effectiveness of multi-teacher distillation methods are
accompanied by costly computation resources. To tackle with both the
efficiency and the effectiveness of knowledge distillation, we introduce the
feature aggregation to imitate the multi-teacher distillation in the single-
teacher distillation framework by extracting informative supervision from
multiple teacher feature maps. Specifically, we introduce DFA, a two-
stage Differentiable Feature Aggregation search method that motivated
by DARTS in neural architecture search, to efficiently find the aggregations. In the first stage, DFA formulates the searching problem as a
bi-level optimization and leverages a novel bridge loss, which consists of
a student-to-teacher path and a teacher-to-student path, to find appropriate feature aggregations. The two paths act as two players against
each other, trying to optimize the unified architecture parameters to the
opposite directions while guaranteeing both expressivity and learnability of the feature aggregation simultaneously. In the second stage, DFA
performs knowledge distillation with the derived feature aggregation.
Experimental results show that DFA outperforms existing distillation
methods on CIFAR-100 and CINIC-10 datasets under various teacher-
student settings, verifying the effectiveness and robustness of the design.

Keywords: Knowledge distillation · Feature aggregation ·
Differentiable architecture search

Y. Guan and P. Zhao: These authors contributed equally to this work.

A. Vedaldi et al. (Eds.): ECCV 2020, LNCS 12362, pp. 469–484, 2020.
https://doi.org/10.1007/978-3-030-58520-4_28

1   Introduction

In recent years, visual recognition tasks have been significantly improved by deeper and larger convolutional networks. However, it is difficult to directly deploy such complicated networks on certain computationally limited platforms such as robotics, self-driving vehicles and most of the mobile devices. Therefore, the community has raised increasing attention on model compression approaches such as model pruning [7,21,34], model quantization [14,19,23] and *knowledge distillation* [13,30,33,37,38].

Knowledge distillation refers to the methods that supervise the training of a small network (*student*) by using the knowledge extracted from one or more well-trained large networks (*teacher*). The key idea of knowledge distillation is to transfer the knowledge from the teacher networks to the student network. The first attempt of the knowledge distillation for deep neural networks leverages both the correct class labels and the soft targets of the teacher network, i.e., the soft probability distribution over classes, to supervise the training of the student network. The recent advances of knowledge distillation can be mainly divided into two categories: *output distillation* [13] and *feature distillation* [30,33,38], as shown in Fig. 1(a–b). More recent works concentrate on multi-teacher distillation with *feature aggregation* [37], where an ensemble of teacher networks provide richer information from the aggregation of output distributions and feature maps. Although an ensemble of teacher networks could provide richer information from the aggregation of output distributions and feature maps, they require much more computation resources than single-teacher distillation.

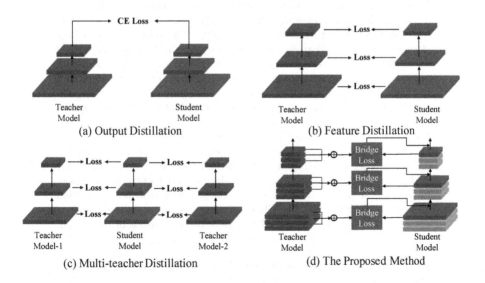

Fig. 1. Illustrations of different knowledge distillation methods. (a) Output distillation. (b) Feature distillation. (c) Multi-teacher distillation. (d) DFA leverages a novel bridge loss for feature distillation, which takes the advantage of NAS and feature aggregation.

To achieve the same effect as the multi-teacher distillation with less computation overheads, we propose DFA, a two-stage Differentiable Feature Aggregation search method in the single-teacher knowledge distillation by coupling features from different layers of a single network as multiple "teachers", and thus avoids the computation expenses on running several large teacher networks. Specifically, DFA first searches for the appropriate feature aggregation, i.e., the weighted sum of the feature maps, for each layer group in the teacher network by finding the best aggregation weights. Then, it conducts the normal feature distillation with the derived aggregations. Inspired by DARTS [24], DFA leverages the differentiable group-wise search in the first stage, which formulates the searching process as a bi-level optimization problem with feature aggregation weights as the upper-level variable and the model parameters as the lower-level variable. Moreover, as the common distillation loss and cross-entropy loss fail to find the appropriate feature aggregations, a novel *bridge loss* is introduced as the objective function in DFA, where (1) a student-to-teacher path is built for searching the layers that match the learning ability of student network, and (2) a teacher-to-student path is established for finding the feature aggregation with rich features and a wealth of knowledge. Experiments on CIFAR-100 [18] and CINIC [6] datasets show that DFA could outperform the state-of-the-art distillation methods, demonstrating the effectiveness of the feature aggregation search.

The main contributions of this paper are as follows:

- We introduce DFA, a Differentiable Feature Aggregation search method to mimic multi-teacher distillation in the single-teacher distillation framework, which first searches for appropriate feature aggregation weights and then conducts the distillation with the derived feature aggregations.
- We propose a novel bridge loss for DFA. The bridge loss consists of a student-to-teacher path and a teacher-to-student path, which simultaneously considers the expressivity and learnability for the feature aggregation.
- Experimental results show that the performance of DFA surpasses the feature aggregations derived by both hand-crafted settings and random search, verifying the strength of the proposed method.

2   Related Work

Knowledge Distillation: Knowledge distillation [2] is firstly introduced in model compression. Despite the classification loss, the student network is optimized by an extra cross-entropy loss with the soft target from the teacher network, i.e. the probability distribution softened by temperature scaling. Hinton et al. [13] employ knowledge distillation in the training of deep neural networks. However, with the huge gap of model capacity among the neural networks, it is hard for the student to learn from the output distribution of a cumbersome teacher directly. Thus, several approaches [16,30,38] exploit feature distillation in the student training, where the student network mimics the feature maps from the teacher network of different layers. Multi-teacher knowledge distillation [37] takes a further step, which takes full advantage of the feature maps and the class

distributions amalgamated from an ensemble of teacher networks. The *feature aggregation* from multiple teachers helps the student learn from different perspectives. However, compared with single-teacher distillation, more computation resources are demanded for extracting useful information from all the teachers.

Neural Architecture Search: With the vigorous development of deep learning, neural architecture search (NAS), an automatic method for designing the structure of neural networks, has been attracting increasing attention recently. The early works mainly sample and evaluate a large number of networks from the search space, and then train the sampled models with reinforcement learning [3,32,41,42] or update the population with the evolutionary algorithm [28,29]. Though achieving state-of-the-art performance, the above works are all computation expensive. Recent works propose the one-shot approaches [1,4,8,24,27,35] in NAS to reduce the computation cost. It models NAS as a single training process for an over-parameterized network covering all candidate sub-networks named supernet, and then selects the network architecture from the trained supernet. Among the one-shot methods, the differentiable architecture search (DARTS) [5,22,24,26,36,40] further relaxes the discrete search space to be continuous and couples the architecture parameters with the model parameters in the supernet. Therefore, the architecture parameters can be jointly optimized in the one-shot training along with the model parameters by gradient descent.

There have been several methods designed for combining NAS with knowledge distillation. DNA [20] searches for the light-weight architecture of the student network from a supernet. KDAS [15] builds up the student network progressively based on an ensemble of independently learned student networks. As opposed to these methods, we try to imitate the multi-teacher distillation in the single teacher distillation framework by finding the appropriate feature aggregations in the teacher network with differentiable search strategy.

3   Method

We propose the two-stage Differentiable Feature aggregation (DFA) method for single-teacher knowledge distillation, as outlined in Algorithm 1. In the first stage (i.e., "AGGREGATION SEARCH"), DFA searches for appropriate feature aggregation weights. In the second stage (i.e., "FEATURE DISTILLATION"), the derived feature aggregations are applied to perform the feature distillation between teacher and student. Details will be described in this section.

3.1   Feature Distillation

DFA is based on feature distillation on G *layer groups*, where a layer group denotes the set of layers with the same spatial size in teacher and student networks. The general design schemes for feature distillation are categorized into

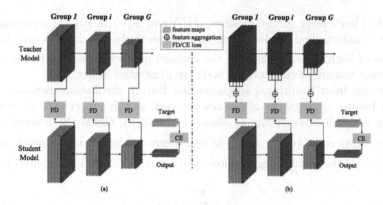

Fig. 2. Comparisons between traditional feature distillation and DFA. (a) Traditional methods implement distillation with the last feature map in each layer group of the teacher network. (b) DFA leverages the feature aggregation of the teacher for distillation, which contains rich features and a wealth of knowledge. "FD" and "CE" represent the feature distillation loss $\mathcal{L}_{\text{fd}}$ and cross entropy loss $\mathcal{L}_{\text{ce}}$ respectively.

Algorithm 1. Algorithm for the two-stage DFA.

1: **function** AGGREGATION SEARCH
2:     Random initialize β, w
3:     **for** group $i = 1, 2, ..., G$ **do**
4:         **for** iteration $k = 1, 2, ..., I_s$ **do**
5:             Optimize β_i by $\mathcal{L}_{\text{val}}(w, \beta)$
6:             Optimize w by $\mathcal{L}_{\text{train}}(w, \beta)$
7:         **end for**
8:     **end for**
9:     Reserve the derived β.
10: **end function**

11: **function** FEATURE DISTILLATION
12:     Get the derived β.
13:     **for** iteration $k = 1, 2, ..., I_v$ **do**
14:         **for** group $i = 1, 2, ..., G$ **do**
15:             Calculate A_i with β_i.
16:         **end for**
17:         Update w by minimizing the
18:         loss defined in Eqn. (4).
19:     **end for**
20: **end function**

---

teacher transform, student transform, distillation position and *distance function* [10]. Teacher transform and student transform extract knowledge from hidden features of the teacher and student networks at the distillation positions respectively. Then, the extracted features are applied to the distance function of distillation. Most approaches [11,33,38] adopt L_2 loss as the distance measurement. Let N_i^T and N_i^S denote the number of layers in the i-th layer group of teacher and student network, the distillation loss is defined as:

$$\mathcal{L}_{\text{fd}} = \sum_{i=1}^{G} L_2(\mathcal{F}_t^i(T_i^{N_i^T}), \mathcal{F}_s^i(S_i^{N_i^S})) \tag{1}$$

where $T_i^{N_i^T}$ and $S_i^{N_i^S}$ denote the feature maps of teacher and student networks drawn from the distillation position of the i-th group. Conforming to the previous work [38], the distillation positions of the teacher and student network lay at

the end of each layer group. Besides, $\mathcal{F}_t^i(\cdot)$ and $\mathcal{F}_s^i(\cdot)$ in Eq. (1) represent the teacher transform and student transform respectively, which map the channel numbers of both $T_i^{N_i^T}$ and $S_i^{N_i^S}$ to the channel number of teacher feature map. Traditional feature distillation methods are illustrated in Fig. 2(a).

Different from traditional single-teacher feature distillation methods, DFA utilizes feature aggregation of teacher network as the supervision for student network for each layer group, as shown in Fig. 2(b). Given the feature aggregation weights $\alpha_i = \{\alpha_i^1, ..., \alpha_i^{N_i^T}\}$ of i-th group in the teacher network, where $\sum_{j=1}^{N_i^T} \alpha_i^j = 1$, the feature aggregation of i-th group A_i can be computed by:

$$A_i = \sum_{j=1}^{N_i^T} \alpha_i^j \, T_i^j. \tag{2}$$

The existing feature distillation methods could be seen as a special case of feature aggregation, where the weight of the last layer for each layer group i of the teacher network, i.e., $\alpha_i^{N_i^T}$, is set to one and the weights of the other layers in the group are set to zero. Given the feature aggregation of different layer groups, the feature distillation loss in Eq. (1) is changed to:

$$\mathcal{L}_{\text{fd}} = \sum_{i=1}^{G} L_2(\mathcal{F}_t^i(A_i), \mathcal{F}_s^i(S_i^{N_i^S}))). \tag{3}$$

Finally, the student network is optimized by a weighted sum of distillation loss $\mathcal{L}_{\text{fd}}$ and classification loss $\mathcal{L}_{\text{ce}}$:

$$\mathcal{L}_{\text{student}} = \mathcal{L}_{\text{ce}} + \gamma_{\text{fd}} * \mathcal{L}_{\text{fd}} \tag{4}$$

where γ_{fd} is the balancing hyperparameter. $\mathcal{L}_{\text{ce}}$ is the standard cross-entropy loss between the ground-truth class label gt and the output distribution of the student $p = \{p^1, ..., p^C\}$:

$$\mathcal{L}_{\text{ce}}(gt, p) = -\sum_{i=1}^{C} \mathbb{I}[i = gt] \log(p^i), \tag{5}$$

where C represents the number of classes and $\mathbb{I}[\cdot]$ is the indicator function.

3.2 Differentiable Group-Wise Search

As the feature aggregation weights are continuous and grow exponentially with the number of layer groups, DFA leverages a differentiable architecture search method to efficiently search for the task-dependent feature aggregation weights for better distillation performance. Inspired by previous attempts that divide the NAS search space into blocks [24,42], DFA implements the feature aggregation search in a group-wise manner, i.e., the weights of other groups keep fixed when

searching for the aggregation weights for layer group i. The group-wise search enables a strong learning capability of the model, leading to only a few epochs to achieve convergence during training. The overall framework of the differentiable group-wise search is shown in Fig. 3.

Search Space: Given the teacher and student networks, DFA aims to find the appropriate feature aggregation weights α_i for each group i. Different from the DARTS-based methods [24], the search space for the feature aggregation is continuous since the combination of different layers could provide richer information than the individual feature map obtained from the discrete search space. Besides, as only one teacher network is utilized in the aggregation search, the training speed and computation overhead are similar to the standard feature distillation. For a stable training process, we represent the feature aggregation weights α as a softmax over a set of architecture parameters β:

$$\alpha_i^j = \frac{\exp(\beta_i^j)}{\sum_{j'=1}^{N_i^T} exp(\beta_i^{j'})}. \tag{6}$$

Optimization of Differentiable Group-Wise Search: The goal of the differentiable group-wise search is to *jointly optimize* the architecture parameters β and the model parameters w of the student network. Specifically, the differentiable search tries to find the β^* that minimizes the validation loss $\mathcal{L}_{val}(w^*(\beta), \beta)$, where the weights of the architecture parameters w^* are obtained by minimizing the training loss $\mathcal{L}_{train}(w, \beta)$ for a certain architecture parameter β. Thus, the joint optimization could be viewed as a bi-level optimization problem with β as the upper-level variable and w as the lower-level variable:

$$\min_{\beta} \quad \mathcal{L}_{val}(w^*(\beta), \beta) + \lambda \mathcal{R}(\beta) \tag{7}$$

$$\text{s.t.} \quad w^*(\beta) = \mathrm{argmin}_w \mathcal{L}_{train}(w, \beta), \tag{8}$$

where $\mathcal{L}_{train}$ and $\mathcal{L}_{val}$ are the training and validation loss respectively. $\mathcal{R}(\cdot)$ denotes the regularization on the architecture parameters β that could slightly boost the performance of DFA. To solve the bi-level optimization problem, β and w are alternately trained in a multi-step way by gradient descent to reach a fixed point of architecture parameters and model parameters.

An intuitive option of training and validation loss is to use $\mathcal{L}_{student}$ in Eq. (4). Though it seems that directly learning from $\mathcal{L}_{student}$ could result in the appropriate architecture parameters for knowledge distillation, actually, training architecture parameters with $\mathcal{L}_{student}$ is equivalent to minimizing the distillation loss between feature aggregation and student feature map:

$$\arg\min_{\beta} \mathcal{L}_{student}(w^*(\beta), \beta) = \arg\min_{\beta} \mathcal{L}_{fd}(w^*(\beta), \beta), \tag{9}$$

as the cross-entropy loss $\mathcal{L}_{ce}$ is irrelevant to the architecture parameters. Since the distillation loss only characterizes the distance between the student feature

maps and the combinations of the teacher feature maps, the architecture parameters tend to be more inclined to choose teachers that are close to the student. In depth, suppose that after training several epochs, the student feature map has learnt some knowledge from the data distribution through cross-entropy loss and teacher network through distillation loss. As the student network is always shallower than the teacher network, the knowledge in the deep layers is hard to learn such that the architecture parameters would prefer the teachers in the shallow layers matching the depth and expressivity of the student, other than selecting deep layers with rich semantics and strong expressivity. Therefore, the feature aggregation learnt from the $\mathcal{L}_{\text{student}}$ deviates from the original target that learning a good teacher for the knowledge distillation. Besides, once the student network finds a matching layer in the teacher group, i.e., the weight of an architecture parameter β_i^j is relative larger than the others, the student transform will learn more about the mapping function from $S_i^{N_i^S}$ to T_i^j. Then, β_i^j will grow much faster than other competitors due to the biased training of transform function, and the corresponding feature map will gradually dominant the feature aggregation under the exclusive competition of the architecture parameters. Notice again that the network is more likely to pick shallow layers in the early training stage. Therefore, the student network would unavoidably suffer from the performance collapse using the search results derived from $\mathcal{L}_{\text{student}}$.

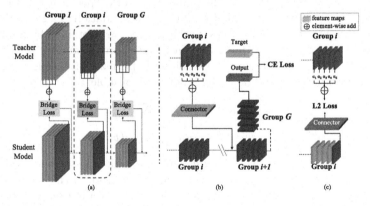

Fig. 3. Differentiable group-wise search of DFA. (a) The differentiable search for group i. (b) The teacher-to-student (TS) path. (c) The student-to-teacher (ST) path. The ST and TS connectors are implemented with 1×1 convolutional layers for matching the channel dimensions between teacher and student.

Bridge Loss for Feature Aggregation Search: To search for an appropriate feature aggregation for the knowledge distillation, we introduce the *bridge loss* to connect the teacher and student networks, where the original information flow of the student network is split into two paths.

In the first teacher-to-student (TS) path as illustrated in Fig. 3(b), DFA takes the feature aggregation of the group i in the teacher network, i.e., A_i, as the input of its $(i + 1)$-th group of the student network, and then computes the teacher-to-student (TS) loss $\mathcal{L}_{TS}$ with standard cross entropy. The TS loss in group i can be expressed as:

$$\mathcal{L}_{TS}^i = \mathcal{L}_{ce}(gt, f_G(...(f_{i+1}(\mathcal{F}_t^i(A_i))))) \tag{10}$$

where gt denotes the ground-truth class label and f_i denotes the convolutional layers of group i in the student network. Different from Eq. (3), the teacher transform $\mathcal{F}_t^i$ is now served as a TS connector that converts the channel dimension of the teacher feature map to the student feature map.

The second student-to-teacher (ST) path has the similar effect as the original $\mathcal{L}_{student}$ in Eq. (4), i.e., exploring the feature aggregation weights that match the learning ability of the student network. As shown in Fig. 3(c), the information flow starts from the student input and ends at the i-th group in the student network. Then, the student network produces $S_i^{N_i^S}$, the last feature map of group i, and compares $S_i^{N_i^S}$ with the feature aggregation A_i by a student-to-teacher (ST) loss $\mathcal{L}_{ST}$:

$$\mathcal{L}_{ST}^i = L_2(\frac{vec(\mathcal{F}_s^i(S_i^{N_i^S}))}{||vec(\mathcal{F}_s^i(S_i^{N_i^S}))||_2}, \frac{vec(A_i)}{||vec(A_i)||_2}) \tag{11}$$

where $vec(\cdot)$ represents the vectorization of the tensor that converts the tensor into a column vector. Same as the distillation loss in Eq. (3), the student transform $\mathcal{F}_s^i$ is served as a ST connector to map the channel numbers from student feature map to teacher feature map, as opposed to $\mathcal{F}_t^i$.

For each group i, the bridge loss $\mathcal{L}_{Bridge}^i$ integrates ST loss $\mathcal{L}_{ST}$ and TS loss $\mathcal{L}_{TS}$ in a single training process for both training loss $\mathcal{L}_{train}$ and validation loss $\mathcal{L}_{val}$:

$$\mathcal{L}_{Bridge}^i = \gamma_{ST}\mathcal{L}_{ST}^i + \gamma_{TS}\mathcal{L}_{TS}^i. \tag{12}$$

where γ_{ST} and γ_{TS} are balancing hyperparameters.

Different from $\mathcal{L}_{student}$, both the model parameters and architecture parameters can be trained towards the ground truth through bridge loss. For the model parameters, the student network before $(i + 1)$-th group tries to imitate the teacher feature aggregation A_i, while the student after $(i + 1)$-th group learns to optimize the cross entropy given A_i. Hence, the joint optimization of ST loss and TS loss for the model weights can be regarded as an approximation of the cross entropy loss of the student network. On the other hand, the architecture parameters are trained by directly optimizing the cross-entropy loss $\mathcal{L}_{TS}$ given the input of the aggregation of teacher feature maps, analogous to the common differentiable architecture search in [24,35]. The deep layers with rich features will be assigned by higher weights in the architecture search, as they contribute to the reduction of the validation loss. In this case, DFA achieves the feature aggregation which helps the student learn a wealth of knowledge from

the teacher. Besides, we still keep ST loss in the architecture training as a regularization. Specifically, though the rich features in the deep layers contribute better performance in the teacher network, they are not always suitable for the student to learn due to the mismatch of expressive power, e.g., it is impractical for a student of three layers to learn from the teacher of ten layers. Introducing ST loss in the validation loss can help the network select the shallow teachers that match the student expressivity, such that the derived feature could provide more knowledge to the student in the early training stage and accelerate the model convergence. In this way, the ST loss and TS loss act as two players against each other, trying to optimize the unified architecture parameters to the opposite directions while guaranteeing both expressivity and learnability of the feature aggregation simultaneously. Hence, the derived feature is more likely to achieve better performance in the final knowledge distillation.

After searching for the architecture parameters with the differentiable groupwise search, DFA trains the student network thoroughly with the derived feature aggregation weights by Eq. (4).

3.3   Time Complexity Analysis

The two-stage design of DFA would not increase the time complexity compared with other feature distillation methods. Let t_T^i, t_S^i denote the computing time of layer group i in the teacher and student network, the differentiable search in the first stage could be calculated by:

$$\mathcal{T}_1 = (\sum_{j=1}^{i}(t_T^j + t_S^j)) + (\sum_{j=1}^{i} t_T^j + \sum_{j=i+1}^{G} t_S^j) = 2\sum_{j=1}^{i} t_T^j + \sum_{j=1}^{G} t_S^j. \quad (13)$$

As the second stage is a usual feature distillation, the overall time complexity of DFA could be derived as:

$$\mathcal{T} = \mathcal{T}_1 + (\sum_{j=1}^{G} t_T^j + \sum_{j=1}^{G} t_S^j) = 2\sum_{j=1}^{i} t_T^j + \sum_{j=1}^{G} t_T^j + 2\sum_{j=1}^{G} t_S^j$$
$$= O(\sum_{j=1}^{G} t_T^j) + O(\sum_{j=1}^{G} t_S^j) \quad (14)$$

which is competitive with other feature distillation methods.

3.4   Implementation Details

The ST connector (student transform) and TS connector (teacher transform) are both implemented with the one-layer convolution networks in order to reconcile the channel dimensions between student and teacher feature maps. The weight of ST loss and TS loss are set to $\gamma_{ST} = 1e - 3$ and $\gamma_{TS} = 1$ in Eq. (12). In both stage of DFA, the pre-ReLU features are extracted in the student and teacher networks for the knowledge distillation, where values no smaller than

−1 are preserved in the feature maps to retain knowledge from both positive values and negative values while avoiding the exploding gradient problem. The model parameters are initialized by He initialization [9]. The feature aggregation weights in each layer group are initialized in the way that only the last feature map has weight 1 and all other feature maps are allocated zero weight.

We follow the same training scheme as DARTS: only the training set are used to update model parameters, and the validation set are leveraged for better feature aggregation parameters. For the update of the architecture parameters, DFA adopts Adam [17] as the optimizer with the momentum of $(0.5, 0.999)$, where the learning rate and weight decay rate are both set to 1e−3.

4 Experiments

4.1 CIFAR-100

CIFAR-100 is a commonly used visual recognition dataset for comparing distillation methods. There are 100 classes in CIFAR-100, and each class contains 500 training images and 100 testing images. To carry out architecture search, the original training images are divided into the training set and validation set with the 7:3 ratio.

We compare our method with eight single-teacher distillation methods: KD [13], FitNets [30], AT [38], Jacobian [31], FT [16], AB [12], SP [33] and Margin [11]. All the experiments are performed on Wide Residual Network [39]. The feature aggregation is searched for 40 epochs at each layer group. We adopt the same training schemes as [39] to train the model parameters in all methods. Specifically, the model is trained by SGD optimizer of 5e−4 weight decay and 0.9 momentum for 200 epochs on both training and validation set. The learning rate is set to 0.1 initially and decayed by 0.2 at 60, 120 and 160 epochs. The batch size is 128. We utilize random crop and random horizontal flip as the data augmentation.

We explore the performance of our method on several teacher-student pairs, which vary in depth (number of layers), width (number of channels), or both, as shown in Table 1. We conduct the experiments on CIFAR-100 over the above teacher-student pairs, and depict the results in Table 2. For the teacher-student pair (1) of different

Table 1. The configuration of teacher and student networks in experiments on CIFAR-100.

	Teacher	Size	Student	Size
(1)	WRN_28_4	5.87M	WRN_16_4	2.77M
(2)	WRN_28_4	5.87M	WRN_28_2	1.47M
(3)	WRN_28_4	5.87M	WRN_16_2	0.7M

widths, DFA has a 1.34% improvement over the output distillation method KD, and also outperforms the other state-of-the-art feature distillation methods. DFA even exhibits a better performance than the teacher network. For the teacher-student pair (2) of different depths, DFA surpasses other feature distillation methods by 0.34%–2.64%. DFA also achieves state-of-the-art results on (3), where the student network compresses both width and depth of the teacher

network. The above experiments verify the effectiveness and robustness of DFA in various scenarios.

Table 2. The experiment results on CIFAR-100. We compare the proposed DFA with eight distillation methods. The best results are illustrated in bold. DFA outperforms other state-of-the-art methods.

	Teacher	Student	KD	FitNets	AT	Jacobian	FT	AB	SP	Margin	DFA
(1)	79.17	77.24	78.4	78.17	77.49	77.84	78.26	78.65	78.7	79.11	**79.74**
(2)	79.17	75.78	76.61	76.14	75.54	76.24	76.51	76.81	77.41	77.84	**78.18**
(3)	79.17	73.42	73.35	73.65	73.3	73.28	74.17	73.9	74.09	75.51	**75.85**

4.2   CINIC-10

CINIC-10 is a large classification dataset containing 270000 images, which are equally split into training, validation and test set with the presence of 10 object categories. The images are collected from CIFAR-10 and ImageNet. Comparing with CIFAR datasets, CINIC-10 could present a more principled perspective of generalisation performance. We explore the performance of DFA and other three state-of-the-art feature distillation methods on CINIC-10. All the experiments are performed on ShuffleNetV2 [25], an efficient network architecture at mobile platforms. We use several variants of ShuffleNetV2 in the experiments, and the basic configuration is shown in Table 3 conforming to [33]. In the model training process, the SGD optimizer is leveraged, with weight decay of 5e-4 and momentum of 0.9. All models are trained with 140 epochs. The learning rate is set to 0.01 initially and decayed by 0.1 at 100, 120 epochs. The batch size is 96. Same as CIFAR dataset, we utilize random crop and random horizontal flip as the data augmentation. We search 5 epochs for each feature group in DFA. The experiment results are shown in Table 4. DFA outperforms the vanilla cross-entropy training as well as the state-of-the-art feature distillation methods.

Ablation Study on Differentiable Search: We study the robustness of DFA by searching the feature aggregation weights from a small dataset and then distillating on a larger dataset. Specifically, we build up a variant of DFA, named as DFA-T, by searching the feature aggregation weights on CIFAR-100 and distillating on CINIC-10. It can be observed that DFA-T is only little inferior to DFA, and still achieves state-of-the-art performance.

4.3   The Effectiveness of Differentiable Search

Comparisons with Other Search Methods: We perform additional experiments on CIFAR-100 to verify the effectiveness of the differentiable feature aggregation search. We compare DFA with the following methods:*"Random"*

Table 3. The configuration of ShuffleNetV2 on CINIC-10 experiments. We leverage standard ShuffleNetV2 blocks in each layer group, where k denotes the kernel size, c and n specify the number of channels and blocks in each layer group. In the end, we add an average pooling layer and a fully connected layer to make final predictions.

Group	Block	k	c	n	Output size
1	Conv-BN-ReLU	3	24	1	32×32
2	ShuffleNetV2 block	3	$116x$	4	16×16
3	ShuffleNetV2 block	3	$232x$	8	8×8
4	ShuffleNetV2 block	3	$464x$	4	4×4
5	ShuffleNetV2 block	3	$1024 * max(1, x)$	1	4×4
6	AvgPool-FC	1	10	1	1×1

Table 4. Experimental results on CINIC-10. The best results are illustrated in bold. "DFA-T" represents the version that searches the feature aggregation weights on CIFAR-100 and implement the feature distillation on CINIC-10.

	Teacher	Size	Acc	Student	Size	Acc	AT	SP	Margin	DFA	DFA-T
(1)	$x = 2.0$	5.37M	86.14	$x = 1.0$	1.27M	83.28	84.71	85.32	85.29	85.38	**85.41**
(2)	$x = 2.0$	5.37M	86.14	$x = 0.5$	0.36M	77.34	79.06	79.15	78.79	**79.51**	79.45
(3)	$x = 1.0$	1.27M	83.28	$x = 0.5$	0.36M	77.34	78.42	79.02	79.69	**79.97**	79.38

represents the method that all feature aggregation weights are randomly selected; "*Average*" indicates that all feature maps in a layer group share the same feature aggregation weight; "*Last*" denotes the method that only the last feature map in each layer group is leveraged for the feature distillation, which is widely used in the knowledge distillation. The results are shown in Table 5.

Obviously, "Random" weights or "Average" weights would degrade the performance, indicating the necessity of a decently designed feature selection strategy. Different from "Last", we observe that DFA would allocate positive weights to the shallow layers in the shallow groups to retrieve knowledge rapidly from the teacher network. The weight assignment in DFA reveals

Table 5. Experimental results of DFA and other search methods on CIFAR-100.

Method	WRN_16_2	WRN_16_4	WRN_28_2
Student	73.42	77.24	75.78
Random	74.25	78.92	77.07
Last	75.51	79.11	77.86
Average	74.11	78.81	76.99
DFA	**75.85**	**79.74**	**78.18**

that feature aggregation contributes to transferring knowledge from the teacher network to the student network, while the differentiable group-wise search helps achieve the optimal feature aggregation weights. Hence, DFA brings about a remarkable improvement on the knowledge distillation task.

Result Analysis: In Fig. 4 *Left*, we display the student network's feature aggregation weights in the configuration (1) of the CIFAR-100 experiment. The feature aggregation weights are initialized with the "Last" scheme and then searched for 40 epochs. It is obvious that the domination of the last feature map in each layer group are weakened as the training continues.

Sensitivity Analysis: We study the impact of regularization on the feature aggregation search mentioned in Sect. 3.2. The right figure in Fig. 4 displays the accuracy of the student models with λ ranging from 0 (no regularization) to 1e−3. Experimental results show that DFA is robust to the regularization in range (0, 1e−3], except a slight decrease without regularization.

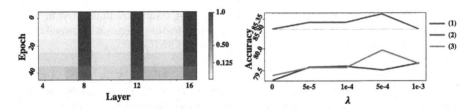

Fig. 4. *Left.* Heatmap of feature aggregation weights in different layers of WRN_16_4. *Right.* The accuracy of the student network on CINIC-10, λ ranges from [0,1e−3]. We select the three teacher and student pairs in the CINIC-10 experiments.

5   Conclusion

In this paper, we propose DFA, a two-stage feature distillation method via differentiable aggregation search. In the first stage, DFA leverages the differentiable architecture search to find appropriate feature aggregation weights. It introduces a bridge loss to connect the teacher and student, where a teacher-to-student loss is built for searching the teacher with rich features and a wealth of knowledge, while a student-to-teacher loss is used to find the aggregation weights that match the learning ability of the student network. In the second stage, DFA performs a standard feature distillation with the derived feature aggregation weights. Experiments show that DFA outperforms several state-of-the-art methods on CIFAR-100 and large-scale CINIC-10 datasets, verifying both the effectiveness and robustness of the design. In-depth analysis also reveals that DFA decently allocates feature aggregation weights on the knowledge distillation task.

Acknowledgment. This work is partially supported by National Key Research and Development Program No. 2017YFB0803302, Beijing Academy of Artificial Intelligence (BAAI), and NSFC 61632017.

References

1. Bender, G., Kindermans, P.J., Zoph, B., Vasudevan, V., Le, Q.: Understanding and simplifying one-shot architecture search. In: ICML, pp. 550–559 (2018)
2. Bucilua, C., Caruana, R., Niculescu-Mizil, A.: Model compression. In: KDD, pp. 535–541. ACM (2006)
3. Cai, H., Yang, J., Zhang, W., Han, S., Yu, Y.: Path-level network transformation for efficient architecture search. In: International Conference on Machine Learning, pp. 678–687 (2018)
4. Cai, H., Zhu, L., Han, S.: ProxylessNAS: direct neural architecture search on target task and hardware. In: ICLR (2019)
5. Chen, X., Xie, L., Wu, J., Tian, Q.: Progressive differentiable architecture search: bridging the depth gap between search and evaluation. In: ICCV (2019)
6. Darlow, L.N., Crowley, E.J., Antoniou, A., Storkey, A.J.: CINIC-10 is not ImageNet or CIFAR-10. arXiv preprint arXiv:1810.03505 (2018)
7. Dong, X., Yang, Y.: Network pruning via transformable architecture search. In: Advances in Neural Information Processing Systems, pp. 759–770 (2019)
8. Dong, X., Yang, Y.: One-shot neural architecture search via self-evaluated template network. In: ICCV, pp. 3681–3690 (2019)
9. He, K., Zhang, X., Ren, S., Sun, J.: Delving deep into rectifiers: surpassing human-level performance on imagenet classification. In: Proceedings of the IEEE International Conference on Computer Vision, pp. 1026–1034 (2015)
10. Heo, B., Kim, J., Yun, S., Park, H., Kwak, N., Choi, J.Y.: A comprehensive overhaul of feature distillation. In: ICCV, October 2019
11. Heo, B., Kim, J., Yun, S., Park, H., Kwak, N., Choi, J.Y.: A comprehensive overhaul of feature distillation. arXiv preprint arXiv:1904.01866 (2019)
12. Heo, B., Lee, M., Yun, S., Choi, J.Y.: Knowledge transfer via distillation of activation boundaries formed by hidden neurons. In: AAAI, vol. 33, pp. 3779–3787 (2019)
13. Hinton, G., Vinyals, O., Dean, J.: Distilling the knowledge in a neural network. arXiv preprint arXiv:1503.02531 (2015)
14. Hubara, I., Courbariaux, M., Soudry, D., El-Yaniv, R., Bengio, Y.: Binarized neural networks. In: Advances in Neural Information Processing Systems, pp. 4107–4115 (2016)
15. Kang, M., Mun, J., Han, B.: Towards oracle knowledge distillation with neural architecture search. arXiv preprint arXiv:1911.13019 (2019)
16. Kim, J., Park, S., Kwak, N.: Paraphrasing complex network: network compression via factor transfer. In: Advances in Neural Information Processing Systems, pp. 2760–2769 (2018)
17. Kingma, D.P., Ba, J.: Adam: a method for stochastic optimization. arXiv preprint arXiv:1412.6980 (2014)
18. Krizhevsky, A., Hinton, G., et al.: Learning multiple layers of features from tiny images (2009)
19. Leng, C., Dou, Z., Li, H., Zhu, S., Jin, R.: Extremely low bit neural network: squeeze the last bit out with ADMM. In: Thirty-Second AAAI Conference on Artificial Intelligence (2018)
20. Li, C., et al.: Blockwisely supervised neural architecture search with knowledge distillation. arXiv preprint arXiv:1911.13053 (2019)
21. Li, H., Kadav, A., Durdanovic, I., Samet, H., Graf, H.P.: Pruning filters for efficient convNets. arXiv preprint arXiv:1608.08710 (2016)

22. Li, W., Gong, S., Zhu, X.: Neural graph embedding for neural architecture search. In: AAAI (2020)
23. Lin, X., Zhao, C., Pan, W.: Towards accurate binary convolutional neural network. In: Advances in Neural Information Processing Systems, pp. 345–353 (2017)
24. Liu, H., Simonyan, K., Yang, Y.: DARTS: differentiable architecture search. In: ICLR (2019)
25. Ma, N., Zhang, X., Zheng, H.T., Sun, J.: ShuffleNet V2: Practical guidelines for efficient CNN architecture design. In: Proceedings of the European Conference on Computer Vision (ECCV), pp. 116–131 (2018)
26. Nayman, N., Noy, A., Ridnik, T., Friedman, I., Jin, R., Zelnik, L.: XNAS: neural architecture search with expert advice. In: Advances in Neural Information Processing Systems, pp. 1975–1985 (2019)
27. Pham, H., Guan, M., Zoph, B., Le, Q., Dean, J.: Efficient neural architecture search via parameter sharing. In: ICML, pp. 4092–4101 (2018)
28. Real, E., Aggarwal, A., Huang, Y., Le, Q.V.: Regularized evolution for image classifier architecture search. In: AAAI, vol. 33, pp. 4780–4789 (2019)
29. Real, E., et al.: Large-scale evolution of image classifiers. In: ICML, pp. 2902–2911 (2017)
30. Romero, A., Ballas, N., Kahou, S.E., Chassang, A., Gatta, C., Bengio, Y.: FitNets: hints for thin deep nets. arXiv preprint arXiv:1412.6550 (2014)
31. Srinivas, S., Fleuret, F.: Knowledge transfer with Jacobian matching. arXiv preprint arXiv:1803.00443 (2018)
32. Tan, M., et al.: MnasNet: platform-aware neural architecture search for mobile. In: CVPR, pp. 2820–2828 (2019)
33. Tung, F., Mori, G.: Similarity-preserving knowledge distillation. In: ICCV, pp. 1365–1374 (2019)
34. Wen, W., Wu, C., Wang, Y., Chen, Y., Li, H.: Learning structured sparsity in deep neural networks. In: Advances in Neural Information Processing Systems, pp. 2074–2082 (2016)
35. Xie, S., Zheng, H., Liu, C., Lin, L.: SNAS: stochastic neural architecture search. In: ICLR (2019)
36. Xu, Y., et al.: PC-DARTS: partial channel connections for memory-efficient differentiable architecture search. In: ICLR (2020)
37. You, S., Xu, C., Xu, C., Tao, D.: Learning from multiple teacher networks. In: KDD, pp. 1285–1294. ACM (2017)
38. Zagoruyko, S., Komodakis, N.: Paying more attention to attention: improving the performance of convolutional neural networks via attention transfer. arXiv preprint arXiv:1612.03928 (2016)
39. Zagoruyko, S., Komodakis, N.: Wide residual networks. arXiv preprint arXiv:1605.07146 (2016)
40. Zela, A., Elsken, T., Saikia, T., Marrakchi, Y., Brox, T., Hutter, F.: Understanding and robustifying differentiable architecture search. In: ICLR (2020)
41. Zoph, B., Le, Q.V.: Neural architecture search with reinforcement learning. In: ICLR (2017)
42. Zoph, B., Vasudevan, V., Shlens, J., Le, Q.V.: Learning transferable architectures for scalable image recognition. In: CVPR, pp. 8697–8710 (2018)

Attention Guided Anomaly Localization in Images

Shashanka Venkataramanan[1]([✉]) [iD], Kuan-Chuan Peng[2] [iD],
Rajat Vikram Singh[3] [iD], and Abhijit Mahalanobis[1] [iD]

[1] Center for Research in Computer Vision, University of Central Florida,
Orlando, FL, USA
shashankv@Knights.ucf.edu, amahalan@crcv.ucf.edu
[2] Mitsubishi Electric Research Laboratories, Cambridge, MA, USA
kpeng@merl.com
[3] Siemens Corporate Technology, Princeton, NJ, USA
singh.rajat@siemens.com

Abstract. Anomaly localization is an important problem in computer vision which involves localizing anomalous regions within images with applications in industrial inspection, surveillance, and medical imaging. This task is challenging due to the small sample size and pixel coverage of the anomaly in real-world scenarios. Most prior works need to use anomalous training images to compute a class-specific threshold to localize anomalies. Without the need of anomalous training images, we propose Convolutional Adversarial Variational autoencoder with Guided Attention (CAVGA), which localizes the anomaly with a *convolutional latent variable* to preserve the spatial information. In the unsupervised setting, we propose an *attention expansion loss* where we encourage CAVGA to focus on all normal regions in the image. Furthermore, in the weakly-supervised setting we propose a *complementary guided attention loss*, where we encourage the attention map to focus on all normal regions while minimizing the attention map corresponding to anomalous regions in the image. CAVGA outperforms the state-of-the-art (SOTA) anomaly localization methods on MVTec Anomaly Detection (MVTAD), modified ShanghaiTech Campus (mSTC) and Large-scale Attention based Glaucoma (LAG) datasets in the unsupervised setting and when using only 2% anomalous images in the weakly-supervised setting. CAVGA also outperforms SOTA anomaly detection methods on the MNIST, CIFAR-10, Fashion-MNIST, MVTAD, mSTC and LAG datasets.

Keywords: Guided attention · Anomaly localization · Convolutional adversarial variational autoencoder

Electronic supplementary material The online version of this chapter (https://doi.org/10.1007/978-3-030-58520-4_29) contains supplementary material, which is available to authorized users.

A. Vedaldi et al. (Eds.): ECCV 2020, LNCS 12362, pp. 485–503, 2020.
https://doi.org/10.1007/978-3-030-58520-4_29

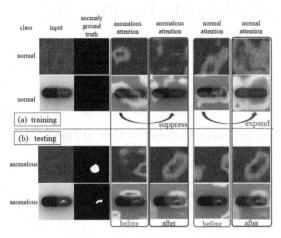

dataset	task	improvement
MVTAD [5]	l	(9/15; 4∼85%)
MVTAD [5]	d	(9/15; 2∼30%)
mSTC [31]	l	(7/12; 2∼42%)
mSTC [31]	d	(8/12; 1∼38%)
LAG [29]	l	(1/1; 16%)
LAG [29]	d	(1/1; 1.1%)
MNIST [27]	d	(8/10; 0.1∼2.5%)
CIFAR-10 [25]	d	(7/10; 3∼31%)
F-MNIST [57]	d	(8/10; 2∼24%)

l: localization; d: detection
F-MNIST: Fashion-MNIST [57]

- metric for l : IoU
- metric for d in MVTAD, mSTC, and LAG: classification accuracy
- metric for d in MNIST, CIFAR-10 and Fashion-MNIST: area under ROC curve

CAVGA main idea   improvement summary

Fig. 1. (i) CAVGA uses the proposed complementary guided attention loss to encourage the attention map to cover the entire normal regions while suppressing the attention map corresponding to anomalous class in the training image. This enables the trained network to generate the anomalous attention map to localize the anomaly better at testing (ii) CAVGA's improvement over SOTA in the form of (number of outperforming/total categories; improvement (%) in its metric)

1   Introduction

Recognizing whether an image is homogeneous with its previously observed distribution or whether it belongs to a novel or anomalous distribution has been identified as an important problem [5]. In this work, we focus on a related task, anomaly localization in images, which involves segmenting the anomalous regions within them. Anomaly localization has been applied in industrial inspection settings to segment defective product parts [5], in surveillance to locate intruders [38], in medical imaging to segment tumor in brain MRI or glaucoma in retina images [4,29], etc. There has been an increase in analysis towards segmenting potential anomalous regions in images as acknowledged in [13].

Existing state-of-the-art (SOTA) anomaly localization methods [6,47] are based on deep learning. However, developing deep learning based algorithms for this task can be challenging due to the small pixel coverage of the anomaly and lack of suitable data since images with anomalies are rarely available in real-world scenarios [5]. Existing SOTA methods tackle this challenge using autoencoders [15,47] and GAN based approaches [3,43,59], which use a thresholded pixel-wise difference between the input and reconstructed image to localize anomalies. But, their methods need to determine class-specific thresholds using anomalous training images which can be unavailable in real-world scenarios.

To tackle these drawbacks of using anomalous training images, we propose Convolutional Adversarial Variational autoencoder with Guided Attention

(CAVGA), an unsupervised anomaly localization method which requires no anomalous training images. CAVGA comprises of a *convolutional latent variable* to preserve the spatial relation between the input and latent variable. Since real-world applications may have access to only limited training data [5], we propose to localize the anomalies by using supervision on attention maps. This is motivated by the finding in [28] that attention based supervision can alleviate the need of using large amount of training data. Intuitively, without any prior knowledge of the anomaly, humans need to look at the entire image to identify the anomalous regions. Based on this idea, we propose an *attention expansion loss* where we encourage the network to generate an attention map that focuses on all normal regions of the image.

Since annotating segmentation training data can be laborious [22], in the case when the annotator provides few anomalous training images without ground truth segmented anomalous regions, we extend CAVGA to a weakly supervised setting. Here, we introduce a classifier in CAVGA and propose a *complementary guided attention loss* computed only for the normal images correctly predicted by the classifier. Using this complementary guided attention loss, we expand the normal attention but suppress the anomalous attention on the normal image, where normal/anomalous attention represents the areas affecting the classifier's normal/anomalous prediction identified by existing network visualization methods (e.g. Grad-CAM [49]). Figure 1(i)(a) illustrates our attention mechanism during training, and Fig. 1(i)(b) demonstrates that the resulting normal attention and anomalous attention on the anomalous testing images are visually complementary, which is consistent with our intuition. Furthermore, Fig. 1(ii) summarizes CAVGA's ability to outperform SOTA methods in anomaly localization on industrial inspection (MVTAD) [5], surveillance (mSTC) [31] and medical imaging (LAG) [29] datasets. We also show CAVGA's ability to outperform SOTA methods in anomaly detection on common benchmarks.

To the best of our knowledge, we are the first in anomaly localization to propose an end-to-end trainable framework with attention guidance which explicitly enforces the network to learn representations from the entire normal image. As compared to the prior works, our proposed approach CAVGA needs no anomalous training images to determine a class-specific threshold to localize the anomaly. Our contributions are:

- **An attention expansion loss (L_{ae})**, where we encourage the network to focus on the entire normal images in the unsupervised setting.
- **A complementary guided attention loss (L_{cga})**, which we use to minimize the anomalous attention and simultaneously expand the normal attention for the normal images correctly predicted by the classifier.
- **New SOTA**: In anomaly localization, CAVGA outperforms SOTA methods on the MVTAD and mSTC datasets in IoU and mean Area under ROC curve (AuROC) and also outperforms SOTA anomaly localization methods on LAG dataset in IoU. We also show CAVGA's ability to outperform SOTA methods for anomaly detection on the MVTAD, mSTC, LAG, MNIST [27], CIFAR-10 [25] and Fashion-MNIST [57] datasets in classification accuracy.

Table 1. Comparison between CAVGA and other anomaly localization methods in the unsupervised setting in terms of the working properties. Among all the listed methods, only CAVGA satisfies all the listed properties

Does the method satisfy each property?	[3,48] [6,43]	[4]	[47]	[54] [50]	[13,32] [2]	CAVGA
not using anomalous training images	N	N	Y	Y	Y	Y
localize **multiple** modes of anomalies	Y	N	N	N	Y	Y
pixel (not patch) based localization	Y	Y	N	Y	Y	Y
use **convolutional latent variable**	N	Y	N	N	N	Y

2 Related Works

Often used interchangeably, the terms anomaly localization and anomaly segmentation involve pixel-accurate segmentation of anomalous regions within an image [5]. They have been applied to industrial inspection settings to segment defective product parts [5], medical imaging to segment glaucoma in retina images [29], etc. Image based anomaly localization has not been fully studied as compared to anomaly detection, where methods such as [3,4,6,43,48] employ a thresholded pixel wise difference between the input and reconstructed image to segment the anomalous regions. [47] proposes an inpainter-detector network for patch-based localization in images. [13] proposes gradient descent on a regularized autoencoder while Liu *et al.* [32] (denoted as ADVAE) generate gradient based attention maps from the latent space of the trained model. We compare CAVGA with the existing methods relevant to anomaly localization in the unsupervised setting in Table 1 and show that among the listed methods, only CAVGA shows all the listed properties.

Anomaly detection involves determining an image as normal or anomalous [3]. One-class classification and anomaly detection are related to novelty detection [41] which has been widely studied in computer vision [3,20,35,37,53] and applied to video analysis [10], remote sensing [36], etc. With the advance in GANs [17], SOTA methods perform anomaly detection by generating realistic normal images during training [21,22,42,46,48]. [12] proposes to search the latent space of the generator for detecting anomalies. [41] introduces latent-space-sampling-based network with information-negative mining while [30] proposes normality score function based on capsule network's activation and reconstruction error. [2] proposes a deep autoencoder that learns the distribution of latent representation through autoregressive procedure. Unlike [7,11,44,55] where anomalous training images are used for anomaly detection, CAVGA does not need anomalous training images.

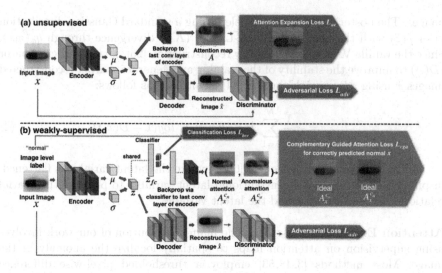

Fig. 2. (a) The framework of CAVGA$_u$ where the attention expansion loss L_{ae} guides the attention map A computed from the latent variable z to cover the entire normal image. (b) Illustration of CAVGA$_w$ with the complementary guided attention loss L_{cga} to minimize the anomalous attention $A_x^{c_a}$ and expand the normal attention $A_x^{c_n}$ for the normal images correctly predicted by the classifier

3 Proposed Approach: CAVGA

3.1 Unsupervised Approach: CAVGA$_u$

Figure 2(a) illustrates CAVGA in the unsupervised setting (denoted as CAVGA$_u$). CAVGA$_u$ comprises of a convolutional latent variable to preserve the spatial information between the input and latent variable. Since attention maps obtained from feature maps illustrate the regions of the image responsible for specific activation of neurons in the feature maps [58], we propose an attention expansion loss such that the feature representation of the latent variable encodes all the normal regions. This loss encourages the attention map generated from the latent variable to cover the entire normal training image as illustrated in Fig. 1(i)(a). During testing, we localize the anomaly from the areas of the image that the attention map does not focus on.

Convolutional Latent Variable. Variational Autoencoder (VAE) [23] is a generative model widely used for anomaly detection [24,40]. The loss function of training a vanilla VAE can be formulated as:

$$L = L_R(x, \hat{x}) + KL(q_\phi(z|x)||p_\theta(z|x)), \tag{1}$$

where $L_R(x, \hat{x}) = \frac{-1}{N}\sum_{i=1}^{N} x_i log(\hat{x}_i) + (1-x_i)log(1-\hat{x}_i)$ is the reconstruction loss between the input (x) and reconstructed images $(\hat{x})$, and N is the total number of

images. The posterior $p_\theta(z|x)$ is modeled using a standard Gaussian distribution prior $p(z)$ with the help of Kullback-Liebler (KL) divergence through $q_\phi(z|x)$. Since the vanilla VAE results in blurry reconstruction [26], we use a discriminator $(D(.))$ to improve the stability of the training and generate sharper reconstructed images $\hat{x}$ using adversarial learning [34] formulated as follows:

$$L_{adv} = -\frac{1}{N} \sum_{i=1}^{N} log(D(x_i)) + log(1 - D(\hat{x}_i)) \qquad (2)$$

Unlike traditional autoencoders [6,18] where the latent variable is flattened, inspired from [4], we use a convolutional latent variable to preserve the spatial relation between the input and the latent variable.

Attention Expansion Loss L_{ae}. The main contribution of our work involves using supervision on attention maps to spatially localize the anomaly in the image. Most methods [3,48,53] employ a thresholded pixel-wise difference between the reconstructed image and the input image to localize the anomaly where the threshold is determined by using anomalous training images. However, CAVGA$_u$ learns to localize the anomaly using an attention map reflected through an end-to-end training process without the need of any anomalous training images. We use the feature representation of the latent variable z to compute the attention map (A). A is computed using Grad-CAM [49] such that $A_{i,j} \in [0,1]$, where $A_{i,j}$ is the (i,j) element of A.

Intuitively, A obtained from feature maps focuses on the regions of the image based on the activation of neurons in the feature maps and its respective importance [58,60]. Due to the lack of prior knowledge about the anomaly, in general, humans need to look at the entire image to identify anomalous regions. We use this notion to learn the feature representation of the entire normal image by proposing an attention expansion loss, where we encourage the network to generate an attention map covering all the normal regions. This attention expansion loss for each image $L_{ae,1}$ is defined as:

$$L_{ae,1} = \frac{1}{|A|} \sum_{i,j} (1 - A_{i,j}) \qquad (3)$$

where $|A|$ is the total number of elements in A. The final attention expansion loss L_{ae} is the average of $L_{ae,1}$ over the N images. Since the idea of attention mechanisms involves locating the most salient regions in the image [29] which typically does not cover the entire image, we use L_{ae} as an additional supervision on the network, such that the trained network generates an attention map that covers all the normal regions. Figure 1(i)(a) shows that before using L_{ae} i.e. training CAVGA$_u$ only with adversarial learning $(L_{adv} + L)$ does not encode all the normal regions into the latent variable, and that the attention map fails to cover the entire image, which is overcome after using L_{ae}. Furthermore, supervising on attention maps prevents the trained model to make inference based on

incorrect areas and also alleviates the need of using large amount of training data as shown in [28], which is not explicitly enforced in existing methods [3,6,47].

We form the final objective function L_{final} below:

$$L_{final} = w_r L + w_{adv} L_{adv} + w_{ae} L_{ae}, \tag{4}$$

where w_r, w_{adv}, and w_{ae} are empirically set as $1, 1$, and 0.01 respectively.

During testing, we feed an image x_{test} into the encoder followed by the decoder, which reconstructs an image $\hat{x}_{test}$. As defined in [48], we compute the pixel-wise difference between $\hat{x}_{test}$ and x_{test} as the anomalous score s_a. Intuitively, if x_{test} is drawn from the learnt distribution of z, then s_a is small. Without using any anomalous training images in the unsupervised setting, we normalize s_a between $[0, 1]$ and empirically set 0.5 as the threshold to detect an image as anomalous. The attention map A_{test} is computed from z using Grad-CAM and is inverted ($1 - A_{test}$) to obtain an anomalous attention map which localizes the anomaly. Here, 1 refers to a matrix of all ones with the same dimensions as A_{test}. We empirically choose 0.5 as the threshold on the anomalous attention map to evaluate the localization performance.

3.2 Weakly Supervised Approach: CAVGA$_w$

CAVGA$_u$ can be further extended to a weakly supervised setting (denoted as CAVGA$_w$) where we explore the possibility of using few anomalous training images to improve the performance of anomaly localization. Given the labels of the anomalous and normal images without the pixel-wise annotation of the anomaly during training, we modify CAVGA$_u$ by introducing a binary classifier C at the output of z as shown in Fig. 2(b) and train C using the binary cross entropy loss L_{bce}. Given an image x and its ground truth label y, we define $p \in \{c_a, c_n\}$ as the prediction of C, where c_a and c_n are anomalous and normal classes respectively. From Fig. 2(b) we clone z into a new tensor, flatten it to form a fully connected layer z_{fc}, and add a 2-node output layer to form C. z and z_{fc} share parameters. Flattening z_{fc} enables a higher magnitude of gradient backpropagation from p [49].

Complementary Guided Attention Loss L_{cga}. Although, attention maps generated from a trained classifier have been used in weakly supervised semantic segmentation tasks [39,49], to the best of our knowledge, we are the first to propose supervision on attention maps for anomaly localization in the weakly supervised setting. Since the attention map depends on the performance of C [28], we propose the complementary guided attention loss L_{cga} based on C's prediction to improve anomaly localization. We use Grad-CAM to compute the attention map for the anomalous class $A_x^{c_a}$ and the attention map for the normal class $A_x^{c_n}$ on the normal image x ($y = c_n$). Using $A_x^{c_a}$ and $A_x^{c_n}$, we propose L_{cga} where we minimize the areas covered by $A_x^{c_a}$ but simultaneously enforce $A_x^{c_n}$ to cover the entire normal image. Since the attention map is computed by backpropagating the gradients from p, any incorrect p would generate an undesired attention map.

Table 2. Our experimental settings. Notations: u: unsupervised; w: weakly supervised; D_M: MNIST [27]; D_F: Fashion-MNIST [57]; D_C: CIFAR-10 [25]

Property\Dataset	MVTAD [5]		mSTC [31]		LAG [29]	D_M	D_F	D_C
Setting	u	w	u	w	u	u	u	u
# total classes	15	15	13	13	1	10	10	10
# normal training images	3629	3629	244875	244875	2632	~6k	6k	5k
# anomalous training images	0	35	0	1763	0	0	0	0
# normal testing images	467	467	21147	21147	800	~1k	1k	1k
# anomalous testing images	1223	1223	86404	86404	2392	~9k	9k	9k

This would lead to the network learning to focus on erroneous areas of the image during training, which we avoid using L_{cga}. We compute L_{cga} only for the normal images correctly classified by the classifier i.e. if $p = y = c_n$. We define $L_{cga,1}$, the complementary guided attention loss for each image, in the weakly supervised setting as:

$$L_{cga,1} = \frac{\mathbb{1}\,(p = y = c_n)}{|A_x^{c_n}|} \sum_{i,j}(1 - (A_x^{c_n})_{i,j} + (A_x^{c_a})_{i,j}), \qquad (5)$$

where $\mathbb{1}\,(\cdot)$ is an indicator function. L_{cga} is the average of $L_{cga,1}$ over the N images. Our final objective function L_{final} is defined as:

$$L_{final} = w_r L + w_{adv}L_{adv} + w_c L_{bce} + w_{cga}L_{cga}, \qquad (6)$$

where w_r, w_{adv}, w_c, and w_{cga} are empirically set as $1, 1, 0.001$, and 0.01 respectively. During testing, we use C to predict the input image x_{test} as anomalous or normal. The anomalous attention map A_{test} of x_{test} is computed when $y = c_a$. We use the same evaluation method as that in Sect. 3.1 for anomaly localization.

4 Experimental Setup

Benchmark Datasets: We evaluate CAVGA on the MVTAD [5], mSTC [31] and LAG [29] datasets for anomaly localization, and the MVTAD, mSTC, LAG, MNIST [27], CIFAR-10 [25] and Fashion-MNIST [57] datasets for anomaly detection. Since STC dataset [31] is designed for video instead of image anomaly detection, we extract every 5th frame of the video from each scene for training and testing without using any temporal information. We term the modified STC dataset as mSTC and summarize the experimental settings in Table 2.

Baseline Methods: For anomaly localization, we compare CAVGA with AVID [47], AE_{L2} [6], AE_{SSIM} [6], AnoGAN [48], CNN feature dictionary (CNNFD) [37], texture inspection (TI) [8], γ-VAE grad [13] (denoted as γ-VAE_g), LSA [2], ADVAE [32] and variation model (VM) [52] based approaches

Table 3. Performance comparison of anomaly localization in category-specific IoU, mean IoU ($\overline{\text{IoU}}$), and mean AuROC ($\overline{\text{AuROC}}$) on the MVTAD dataset. The darker cell color indicates better performance ranking in each row

Category	AVID [47]	AE$_{\text{SSIM}}$ [6]	AE$_{\text{L2}}$ [6]	AnoGAN [48]	γ-VAE$_g$ [13]	LSA [2]	ADVAE [32]	CAVGA -D$_u$	CAVGA -R$_u$	CAVGA -D$_w$	CAVGA -R$_w$
Bottle	0.28	0.15	0.22	0.05	0.27	0.27	0.27	0.30	0.34	0.36	0.39
Hazelnut	0.54	0.00	0.41	0.02	0.63	0.41	0.44	0.44	0.51	0.58	0.79
Capsule	0.21	0.09	0.11	0.04	0.24	0.22	0.11	0.25	0.31	0.38	0.41
Metal Nut	0.05	0.01	0.26	0.00	0.22	0.38	0.49	0.39	0.45	0.46	0.46
Leather	0.32	0.34	0.67	0.34	0.41	0.77	0.24	0.76	0.79	0.80	0.84
Pill	0.11	0.07	0.25	0.17	0.48	0.18	0.18	0.34	0.40	0.44	0.53
Wood	0.14	0.36	0.29	0.14	0.45	0.41	0.14	0.56	0.59	0.61	0.66
Carpet	0.25	0.69	0.38	0.34	0.79	0.76	0.10	0.71	0.73	0.70	0.81
Tile	0.09	0.04	0.23	0.08	0.38	0.32	0.23	0.31	0.38	0.47	0.81
Grid	0.51	0.88	0.83	0.04	0.36	0.20	0.02	0.32	0.38	0.42	0.55
Cable	0.27	0.01	0.05	0.01	0.26	0.36	0.18	0.37	0.44	0.49	0.51
Transistor	0.18	0.01	0.22	0.08	0.44	0.21	0.30	0.30	0.35	0.38	0.45
Toothbrush	0.43	0.08	0.51	0.07	0.37	0.48	0.14	0.54	0.57	0.60	0.63
Screw	0.22	0.03	0.34	0.01	0.38	0.38	0.17	0.42	0.48	0.51	0.66
Zipper	0.25	0.10	0.13	0.01	0.17	0.14	0.06	0.20	0.26	0.29	0.31
$\overline{\text{IoU}}$	0.26	0.19	0.33	0.09	0.39	0.37	0.20	0.41	0.47	0.50	0.59
$\overline{\text{AuROC}}$	0.78	0.87	0.82	0.74	0.86	0.79	0.86	0.85	0.89	0.92	0.93

on the MVTAD and mSTC datasets. Since [13] does not provide the code for their method, we adapt the code from [1] and report its best result using our experimental settings. We also compare CAVGA$_u$ with CAM [60], GBP [51], SmoothGrad [50] and Patho-GAN [54] on the LAG dataset. In addition, we compare CAVGA$_u$ with LSA [2], OCGAN [41], ULSLM [56], CapsNet PP-based and CapsNet RE-based [30] (denoted as CapsNet$_{\text{PP}}$ and CapsNet$_{\text{RE}}$), AnoGAN [48], ADGAN [12], and β-VAE [21] on the MNIST, CIFAR-10 and Fashion-MNIST datasets for anomaly detection.

Architecture Details: Based on the framework in Fig. 2(a), we use the convolution layers of ResNet-18 [19] as our encoder pretrained from ImageNet [45] and finetuned on each category/scene individually. Inspired from [9], we propose to use the residual generator as our residual decoder by modifying it with a convolution layer interleaved between two upsampling layers. The skip connection added from the output of the upsampling layer to the output of the convolution layer, increases mutual information between observations and latent variable and also avoids latent variable collapse [14]. We use the discriminator of DC-GAN [42] pretrained on the Celeb-A dataset [33] and finetuned on our data as our discriminator and term this network as CAVGA-R. For fair comparisons with the baseline approaches in terms of network architecture, we use the discriminator and generator of DC-GAN pretrained on the Celeb-A dataset as our encoder and decoder respectively. We keep the same discriminator as discussed previously and term this network as CAVGA-D. CAVGA-D$_u$ and CAVGA-R$_u$ are termed

as $CAVGA_u$ in the unsupervised setting, and $CAVGA\text{-}D_w$ and $CAVGA\text{-}R_w$ as $CAVGA_w$ in weakly supervised setting respectively.

Training and Evaluation: For anomaly localization and detection on the MVTAD, mSTC and LAG datasets, the network is trained only on normal images in the unsupervised setting. In the weakly supervised setting, since none of the baseline methods provide the number of anomalous training images they use to compute the threshold, we randomly choose 2% of the anomalous images along with all the normal training images for training. On the MNIST, CIFAR-10 and Fashion-MNIST datasets, we follow the same procedure as defined in [12] (training/testing uses single class as normal and the rest of the classes as anomalous. We train $CAVGA\text{-}D_u$ using this normal class). For anomaly localization, we show the AuROC [5] and the Intersection-over-Union (IoU) between the generated attention map and the ground truth. Following [5], we use the mean of accuracy of correctly classified anomalous images and normal images to evaluate the performance of anomaly detection on both the normal and anomalous images on the MVTAD, mSTC and LAG datasets. On the MNIST, CIFAR-10, and Fashion-MNIST datasets, same as [12], we use AuROC for evaluation.

5   Experimental Results

We use the cell color in the quantitative result tables to denote the performance ranking in that row, where darker cell color means better performance.

Performance on Anomaly Localization: Figure 3(a) shows the qualitative results and Table 3 shows that $CAVGA_u$ localizes the anomaly better compared to the baselines on the MVTAD dataset. $CAVGA\text{-}D_u$ outperforms the best performing baseline method ($\gamma\text{-}VAE_g$) in mean IoU by 5%. Most baselines use anomalous training images to compute class-specific threshold to localize anomalies. *Needing no anomalous training images*, $CAVGA\text{-}D_u$ still outperforms all the mentioned baselines in mean IoU. In terms of mean AuROC, $CAVGA\text{-}D_u$ outperforms CNNFD, TI and VM by 9%, 12% and 10% respectively and achieves comparable results with best baseline method. Table 3 also shows that $CAVGA\text{-}D_w$ outperforms $CAVGA\text{-}D_u$ by 22% and 8% on mean IoU and mean AuROC respectively. $CAVGA\text{-}D_w$ also outperforms the baselines in mean AuROC. Figure 4 illustrates that one challenge in anomaly localization is the low contrast between the anomalous regions and their background. In such scenarios, although still outperforming the baselines, CAVGA does not localize the anomaly well.

Figure 3(b) illustrates the qualitative results and Table 4 shows that CAVGA also outperforms the baseline methods in mean IoU and mean AuROC on the mSTC dataset. Table 5 shows that CAVGA outperforms the most competitive baseline Patho-GAN [54] by 16% in IoU on the LAG dataset. CAVGA is practically reasonable to train on a single GTX 1080Ti GPU, having comparable training and testing time with baseline methods.

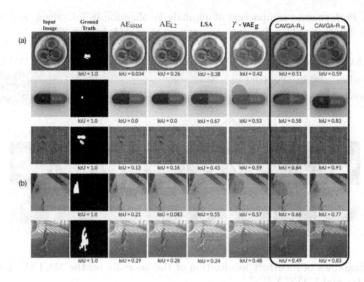

Fig. 3. Qualitative results on (a) MVTAD & (b) mSTC datasets respectively. The anomalous attention map (in red) depicts the localization of the anomaly. (Color figure online)

Table 4. Performance comparison of anomaly localization in IoU and its mean ($\overline{\text{IoU}}$) along with anomaly detection in terms of mean of accuracy of correctly classified anomalous images and normal images on the mSTC dataset for each scene ID s_i. For anomaly localization, we also list the mean AuROC ($\overline{\text{AuROC}}$)

Task\Method	s_i	γ-VAE$_g$ [13]	AVID [47]	LSA [2]	AE$_{SSIM}$ [6]	AE$_{L2}$ [6]	CAVGA-D$_u$	CAVGA-R$_u$	CAVGA-D$_w$	CAVGA-R$_w$
Localization	01	0.239	0.182	0.244	0.201	0.163	0.267	0.316	0.383	0.441
	02	0.206	0.206	0.183	0.081	0.172	0.190	0.234	0.257	0.349
	03	0.272	0.162	0.265	0.218	0.240	0.277	0.293	0.313	0.465
	04	0.290	0.263	0.271	0.118	0.125	0.283	0.349	0.360	0.381
	05	0.318	0.234	0.287	0.162	0.129	0.291	0.312	0.408	0.478
	06	0.337	0.314	0.238	0.215	0.198	0.344	0.420	0.455	0.589
	07	0.168	0.214	0.137	0.191	0.165	0.198	0.241	0.284	0.366
	08	0.220	0.168	0.233	0.069	0.056	0.219	0.254	0.295	0.371
	09	0.174	0.193	0.187	0.038	0.021	0.247	0.284	0.313	0.365
	10	0.146	0.137	0.146	0.116	0.141	0.149	0.166	0.245	0.295
	11	0.277	0.264	0.286	0.101	0.075	0.309	0.372	0.441	0.588
	12	0.162	0.180	0.108	0.203	0.164	0.098	0.141	0.207	0.263
	$\overline{\text{IoU}}$	0.234	0.210	0.215	0.143	0.137	0.239	0.281	0.330	0.412
	$\overline{\text{AuROC}}$	0.82	0.77	0.81	0.76	0.74	0.83	0.85	0.89	0.90
Detection	01	0.75	0.68	0.75	0.65	0.72	0.77	0.85	0.84	0.87
	02	0.75	0.75	0.79	0.70	0.61	0.76	0.84	0.89	0.90
	03	0.81	0.68	0.63	0.79	0.71	0.82	0.84	0.86	0.88
	04	0.83	0.71	0.79	0.81	0.66	0.80	0.80	0.81	0.83
	05	0.86	0.59	0.68	0.71	0.67	0.81	0.86	0.90	0.94
	06	0.59	0.62	0.58	0.47	0.55	0.64	0.67	0.65	0.70
	07	0.59	0.63	0.63	0.36	0.59	0.60	0.64	0.75	0.77
	08	0.77	0.73	0.75	0.69	0.70	0.74	0.74	0.76	0.80
	09	0.89	0.88	0.79	0.84	0.73	0.87	0.88	0.90	0.91
	10	0.64	0.80	0.84	0.83	0.88	0.88	0.92	0.94	0.94
	11	0.78	0.68	0.71	0.71	0.75	0.79	0.81	0.83	0.83
	12	0.71	0.66	0.63	0.65	0.52	0.76	0.79	0.81	0.83
	avg	0.75	0.70	0.71	0.68	0.67	0.77	0.80	0.83	0.85

Table 5. Performance comparison of anomaly localization in IoU along with anomaly detection in terms of classification accuracy on the LAG dataset [29]

Task\Method	CAM [60]	GBP [51]	SmoothGrad [50]	Patho-GAN [54]	CAVGA-D_u
Localization	0.13	0.09	0.14	0.37	0.43
Detection	0.68	0.84	0.79	0.89	0.90

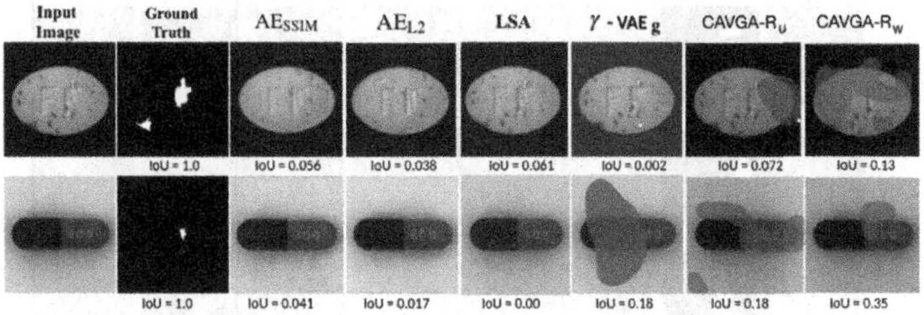

Fig. 4. Examples of incorrect localization of the anomaly on the MVTAD dataset by CAVGA-R_u and CAVGA-R_w

Table 6. The mean of accuracy of correctly classified anomalous images and normal images in anomaly detection on the MVTAD dataset

Category	AVID [47]	AE$_{SSIM}$ [6]	AE$_{L2}$ [6]	AnoGAN [48]	γ-VAE$_g$ [13]	LSA [2]	CAVGA-D_u	CAVGA-R_u	CAVGA-D_w	CAVGA-R_w
Bottle	0.88	0.88	0.80	0.69	0.86	0.86	0.89	0.91	0.93	0.96
Hazelnut	0.86	0.54	0.88	0.50	0.74	0.80	0.84	0.87	0.90	0.92
Capsule	0.85	0.61	0.62	0.58	0.86	0.71	0.83	0.87	0.89	0.93
Metal Nut	0.63	0.54	0.73	0.50	0.78	0.67	0.67	0.71	0.81	0.88
Leather	0.58	0.46	0.44	0.52	0.71	0.70	0.71	0.75	0.80	0.84
Pill	0.86	0.60	0.62	0.62	0.80	0.85	0.88	0.91	0.93	0.97
Wood	0.83	0.83	0.74	0.68	0.89	0.75	0.85	0.88	0.89	0.89
Carpet	0.70	0.67	0.50	0.49	0.67	0.74	0.73	0.78	0.80	0.82
Tile	0.66	0.52	0.77	0.51	0.81	0.70	0.70	0.72	0.81	0.86
Grid	0.59	0.69	0.78	0.51	0.83	0.54	0.75	0.78	0.79	0.81
Cable	0.64	0.61	0.56	0.53	0.56	0.61	0.63	0.67	0.86	0.97
Transistor	0.58	0.52	0.71	0.67	0.70	0.50	0.73	0.75	0.80	0.89
Toothbrush	0.73	0.74	0.98	0.57	0.89	0.89	0.91	0.97	0.96	0.99
Screw	0.66	0.51	0.69	0.35	0.71	0.75	0.77	0.78	0.79	0.79
Zipper	0.84	0.80	0.80	0.59	0.67	0.88	0.87	0.94	0.95	0.96
Mean	0.73	0.63	0.71	0.55	0.77	0.73	0.78	0.82	0.86	0.90

Performance on Anomaly Detection: Table 6 shows that CAVGA$_u$ outperforms the baselines in the mean of accuracy of correctly classified anomalous images and normal images on the MVTAD dataset. CAVGA-D_u outperforms the best performing baseline (γ-VAE$_g$) in mean of classification accuracy by 1.3%. Table 4 and Table 5 show that CAVGA outperforms the baseline methods in classification accuracy on both the mSTC and LAG datasets by 2.6% and 1.1%

respectively. Furthermore, Table 7 shows that CAVGA-D_u outperforms all the baselines in mean AuROC in the unsupervised setting on the MNIST, CIFAR-10 and Fashion-MNIST datasets. CAVGA-D_u also outperforms MemAE [16] and β-VAE [21] by 1.1% and 8% on MNIST and by 21% and 38% on CIFAR-10 datasets respectively. CAVGA-D_u also outperforms all the listed baselines in mean AuROC on the Fashion-MNIST dataset.

6 Ablation Study

All the ablation studies are performed on 15 categories on the MVTAD dataset, of which 5 are reported here. The mean of all 15 categories is shown in Table 8. We illustrate the effectiveness of the convolutional z in CAVGA, L_{ae} in the unsupervised setting, and L_{cga} in the weakly supervised setting. The qualitative results are shown in Fig. 5. The column IDs to refer to the columns in Table 8.

Effect of Convolutional Latent Variable z: To show the effectiveness of the convolutional z, we flatten the output of the encoder of CAVGA-R_u and CAVGA-R_w, and connect it to a fully connected layer as latent variable. Following [6], the dimension of latent variable is chosen as 100. We call these network as

Table 7. Performance comparison of anomaly detection in terms of AuROC and mean AuROC with the SOTA methods on MNIST (D_M) and CIFAR-10 (D_C) datasets . We also report the mean AuROC on Fashion-MNIST (D_F) dataset

Dataset	Class	γ-VAE$_g$ [13]	LSA [2]	OCGAN [41]	ULSLM [56]	CapsNet$_{PP}$ [30]	CapsNet$_{RE}$ [30]	AnoGAN [48]	ADGAN [12]	CAVGA -D_u
D_M [27]	0	0.991	0.993	0.998	0.991	0.998	0.947	0.990	0.999	0.994
	1	0.996	0.999	0.999	0.972	0.990	0.907	0.998	0.992	0.997
	2	0.983	0.959	0.942	0.919	0.984	0.970	0.888	0.968	0.989
	3	0.978	0.966	0.963	0.943	0.976	0.949	0.913	0.953	0.983
	4	0.976	0.956	0.975	0.942	0.935	0.872	0.944	0.960	0.977
	5	0.972	0.964	0.980	0.872	0.970	0.966	0.912	0.955	0.968
	6	0.993	0.994	0.991	0.988	0.942	0.909	0.925	0.980	0.988
	7	0.981	0.980	0.981	0.939	0.987	0.934	0.964	0.950	0.986
	8	0.980	0.953	0.939	0.960	0.993	0.929	0.883	0.959	0.988
	9	0.967	0.981	0.981	0.967	0.990	0.871	0.958	0.965	0.991
	Mean	0.982	0.975	0.975	0.949	0.977	0.925	0.937	0.968	0.986
D_C [25]	0	0.702	0.735	0.757	0.740	0.622	0.371	0.610	0.661	0.653
	1	0.663	0.580	0.531	0.747	0.455	0.737	0.565	0.435	0.784
	2	0.680	0.690	0.640	0.628	0.671	0.421	0.648	0.636	0.761
	3	0.713	0.542	0.620	0.572	0.675	0.588	0.528	0.488	0.747
	4	0.770	0.761	0.723	0.678	0.683	0.388	0.670	0.794	0.775
	5	0.689	0.546	0.620	0.602	0.635	0.601	0.592	0.640	0.552
	6	0.805	0.751	0.723	0.753	0.727	0.491	0.625	0.685	0.813
	7	0.588	0.535	0.575	0.685	0.673	0.631	0.576	0.559	0.745
	8	0.813	0.717	0.820	0.781	0.710	0.410	0.723	0.798	0.801
	9	0.744	0.548	0.554	0.795	0.466	0.671	0.582	0.643	0.741
	Mean	0.717	0.641	0.656	0.736	0.612	0.531	0.612	0.634	0.737
D_F [57]	Mean	0.873	0.876	–	–	0.765	0.679	–	–	0.885

Table 8. The ablation study on 5 randomly chosen categories showing anomaly localization in IoU on the MVTAD dataset. The mean of all 15 categories is reported. CAVGA-R_u^* and CAVGA-R_w^* are our base architecture with a flattened z in the unsupervised and weakly supervised settings respectively. "conv z" means using convolutional z

Method / Category	CAVGA -R_u^*	CAVGA -R_u^* + L_{ae}	CAVGA -R_u + conv z	CAVGA -R_u + conv z + L_{ae}	CAVGA -R_w^*	CAVGA -R_w^* + L_{cga}	CAVGA -R_w + conv z	CAVGA -R_w + conv z + L_{cga}
Column ID	c_1	c_2	c_3	c_4	c_5	c_6	c_7	c_8
Bottle	0.24	0.27	0.26	0.33	0.16	0.34	0.28	0.39
Hazelnut	0.16	0.26	0.31	0.47	0.51	0.76	0.67	0.79
Capsule	0.09	0.22	0.14	0.31	0.18	0.36	0.27	0.41
Metal Nut	0.28	0.38	0.34	0.45	0.25	0.38	0.28	0.46
Leather	0.55	0.71	0.64	0.79	0.72	0.79	0.75	0.84
Mean	0.24	0.34	0.33	0.47	0.39	0.52	0.48	0.60

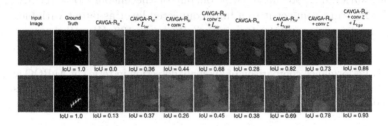

Fig. 5. Qualitative results of the ablation study to illustrate the performance of the anomaly localization on the MVTAD dataset

CAVGA-R_u^* and CAVGA-R_w^* in the unsupervised and weakly supervised settings respectively. In the unsupervised setting, we train CAVGA-R_u and CAVGA-R_u^* using $L + L_{adv}$ as our objective function and compute the anomalous attention map from the feature map of the latent variable during inference. Similarly, in the weakly supervised setting, we train CAVGA-R_w and CAVGA-R_w^* using $L + L_{adv} + L_{bce}$ as our objective function and compute the anomalous attention map from the classifier's prediction during inference. Comparing column c_1 with c_3 and c_5 with c_7 in Table 8, we observe that preserving the spatial relation of the input and latent variable through the convolutional z improves the IoU in anomaly localization without the use of L_{ae} in the unsupervised setting and L_{cga} in the weakly supervised setting. Furthermore, comparing column c_2 with c_4 and c_6 with c_8 in Table 8, we observe that using convolutional z in CAVGA-R_u and CAVGA-R_w outperforms using a flattened latent variable even with the help of L_{ae} in the unsupervised setting and L_{cga} in the weakly supervised setting.

Effect of Attention Expansion Loss L_{ae}: To test the effectiveness of using L_{ae} in the unsupervised setting, we train CAVGA-R$_u^*$ and CAVGA-R$_u$ with Eq. 4. During inference, the anomalous attention map is computed to localize the anomaly. Comparing column c_1 with c_2 and c_3 with c_4 in Table 8, we observe that L_{ae} enhances the IoU regardless of a flattened or convolutional latent variable.

Effect of Complementary Guided Attention Loss L_{cga}: We show the effectiveness of L_{cga} by training CAVGA-R$_w^*$ and CAVGA-R$_w$ using Eq. 6. Comparing column c_5 with c_6 and c_7 with c_8 in Table 8, we find that using L_{cga} enhances the IoU regardless of a flattened or convolutional latent variable.

7 Conclusion

We propose an end-to-end convolutional adversarial variational autoencoder using guided attention which is a novel use of this technique for anomaly localization. Applicable to different network architectures, our attention expansion loss and complementary guided attention loss improve the performance of anomaly localization in the unsupervised and weakly supervised (with only 2% extra anomalous images for training) settings respectively. We quantitatively and qualitatively show that CAVGA outperforms the state-of-the-art (SOTA) anomaly localization methods on the MVTAD, mSTC and LAG datasets. We also show CAVGA's ability to outperform SOTA anomaly detection methods on the MVTAD, mSTC, LAG, MNIST, Fashion-MNIST and CIFAR-10 datasets.

Acknowledgments. This work was done when Shashanka was an intern and Kuan-Chuan was a Staff Scientist at Siemens. Shashanka's effort was partially supported by DARPA under Grant D19AP00032.

References

1. Code for iterative energy-based projection on a normal data manifold for anomaly localization. https://qiita.com/kogepan102/items/122b2862ad5a51180656. Accessed 29 Feb 2020
2. Abati, D., Porrello, A., Calderara, S., Cucchiara, R.: Latent space autoregression for novelty detection. In: Proceedings of the IEEE Conference on Computer Vision and Pattern Recognition, pp. 481–490 (2019)
3. Akcay, S., Atapour-Abarghouei, A., Breckon, T.P.: GANomaly: semi-supervised anomaly detection via adversarial training. In: Jawahar, C.V., Li, H., Mori, G., Schindler, K. (eds.) ACCV 2018. LNCS, vol. 11363, pp. 622–637. Springer, Cham (2019). https://doi.org/10.1007/978-3-030-20893-6_39
4. Baur, C., Wiestler, B., Albarqouni, S., Navab, N.: Deep autoencoding models for unsupervised anomaly segmentation in brain MR images. In: Crimi, A., Bakas, S., Kuijf, H., Keyvan, F., Reyes, M., van Walsum, T. (eds.) BrainLes 2018. LNCS, vol. 11383, pp. 161–169. Springer, Cham (2019). https://doi.org/10.1007/978-3-030-11723-8_16

5. Bergmann, P., Fauser, M., Sattlegger, D., Steger, C.: MVTec AD-a comprehensive real-world dataset for unsupervised anomaly detection. In: Proceedings of the IEEE Conference on Computer Vision and Pattern Recognition, pp. 9592–9600 (2019)
6. Bergmann, P., Löwe, S., Fauser, M., Sattlegger, D., Steger, C.: Improving unsupervised defect segmentation by applying structural similarity to autoencoders. In: International Joint Conference on Computer Vision, Imaging and Computer Graphics Theory and Applications (VISIGRAPP), vol. 5 (2019)
7. Bian, J., Hui, X., Sun, S., Zhao, X., Tan, M.: A novel and efficient CVAE-GAN-based approach with informative manifold for semi-supervised anomaly detection. IEEE Access **7**, 88903–88916 (2019)
8. Böttger, T., Ulrich, M.: Real-time texture error detection on textured surfaces with compressed sensing. Pattern Recogn. Image Anal. **26**(1), 88–94 (2016)
9. Brock, A., Donahue, J., Simonyan, K.: Large scale GAN training for high fidelity natural image synthesis. In: International Conference on Learning Representations (2019)
10. Cheng, K.W., Chen, Y.T., Fang, W.H.: Abnormal crowd behavior detection and localization using maximum sub-sequence search. In: Proceedings of the 4th ACM/IEEE International Workshop on Analysis and Retrieval of Tracked Events and Motion in Imagery Stream, pp. 49–58. ACM (2013)
11. Daniel, T., Kurutach, T., Tamar, A.: Deep variational semi-supervised novelty detection. arXiv preprint arXiv:1911.04971 (2019)
12. Deecke, L., Vandermeulen, R., Ruff, L., Mandt, S., Kloft, M.: Image anomaly detection with generative adversarial networks. In: Berlingerio, M., Bonchi, F., Gärtner, T., Hurley, N., Ifrim, G. (eds.) ECML PKDD 2018. LNCS (LNAI), vol. 11051, pp. 3–17. Springer, Cham (2019). https://doi.org/10.1007/978-3-030-10925-7_1
13. Dehaene, D., Frigo, O., Combrexelle, S., Eline, P.: Iterative energy-based projection on a normal data manifold for anomaly localization. In: International Conference on Learning Representations (2020)
14. Dieng, A.B., Kim, Y., Rush, A.M., Blei, D.M.: Avoiding latent variable collapse with generative skip models. In: The 22nd International Conference on Artificial Intelligence and Statistics, pp. 2397–2405 (2019)
15. Dimokranitou, A.: Adversarial autoencoders for anomalous event detection in images. Ph.D. thesis (2017)
16. Gong, D., et al.: Memorizing normality to detect anomaly: memory-augmented deep autoencoder for unsupervised anomaly detection. In: Proceedings of the IEEE International Conference on Computer Vision, pp. 1705–1714 (2019)
17. Goodfellow, I., et al.: Generative adversarial nets. In: Advances in Neural Information Processing Systems, pp. 2672–2680 (2014)
18. Gutoski, M., Aquino, N.M.R., Ribeiro, M., Lazzaretti, E., Lopes, S.: Detection of video anomalies using convolutional autoencoders and one-class support vector machines. In: XIII Brazilian Congress on Computational Intelligence, 2017 (2017)
19. He, K., Zhang, X., Ren, S., Sun, J.: Deep residual learning for image recognition. In: Proceedings of the IEEE Conference on Computer Vision and Pattern Recognition, pp. 770–778 (2016)
20. Hendrycks, D., Mazeika, M., Dietterich, T.G.: Deep anomaly detection with outlier exposure. In: International Conference on Learning Representations (2019)
21. Higgins, I., et al.: beta-VAE: learning basic visual concepts with a constrained variational framework. In: International Conference on Learning Representations, vol. 2, no. 5, p. 6 (2017)

22. Kimura, D., Chaudhury, S., Narita, M., Munawar, A., Tachibana, R.: Adversarial discriminative attention for robust anomaly detection. In: The IEEE Winter Conference on Applications of Computer Vision (WACV), March 2020
23. Kingma, D.P., Welling, M.: Auto-encoding variational Bayes. In: International Conference on Learning Representations (2014)
24. Kiran, B., Thomas, D., Parakkal, R.: An overview of deep learning based methods for unsupervised and semi-supervised anomaly detection in videos. J. Imaging 4(2), 36 (2018)
25. Krizhevsky, A., Hinton, G., et al.: Learning multiple layers of features from tiny images. Technical report, Citeseer (2009)
26. Larsen, A.B.L., Sønderby, S.K., Larochelle, H., Winther, O.: Autoencoding beyond pixels using a learned similarity metric. In: International Conference on Machine Learning (2016)
27. LeCun, Y., Bottou, L., Bengio, Y., Haffner, P., et al.: Gradient-based learning applied to document recognition. Proc. IEEE 86(11), 2278–2324 (1998)
28. Li, K., Wu, Z., Peng, K.C., Ernst, J., Fu, Y.: Tell me where to look: guided attention inference network. In: Proceedings of the IEEE Conference on Computer Vision and Pattern Recognition, pp. 9215–9223 (2018)
29. Li, L., Xu, M., Wang, X., Jiang, L., Liu, H.: Attention based glaucoma detection: a large-scale database and CNN model. In: The IEEE Conference on Computer Vision and Pattern Recognition (CVPR), June 2019
30. Li, X., Kiringa, I., Yeap, T., Zhu, X., Li, Y.: Exploring deep anomaly detection methods based on capsule net. In: International Conference on Machine Learning 2019 Workshop on Uncertainty and Robustness in Deep Learning (2019)
31. Liu, W., Luo, W., Lian, D., Gao, S.: Future frame prediction for anomaly detection-a new baseline. In: Proceedings of the IEEE Conference on Computer Vision and Pattern Recognition, pp. 6536–6545 (2018)
32. Liu, W., et al.: Towards visually explaining variational autoencoders. In: Proceedings of the IEEE Conference on Computer Vision and Pattern Recognition (2020)
33. Liu, Z., Luo, P., Wang, X., Tang, X.: Deep learning face attributes in the wild. In: Proceedings of International Conference on Computer Vision (ICCV), December 2015
34. Makhzani, A., Shlens, J., Jaitly, N., Goodfellow, I., Frey, B.: Adversarial autoencoders. In: International Conference on Learning Representations (2016)
35. Masana, M., Ruiz, I., Serrat, J., van de Weijer, J., Lopez, A.M.: Metric learning for novelty and anomaly detection. In: British Machine Vision Conference (BMVC) (2018)
36. Matteoli, S., Diani, M., Theiler, J.: An overview of background modeling for detection of targets and anomalies in hyperspectral remotely sensed imagery. IEEE J. Sel. Top. Appl. Earth Obs. Remote Sens. 7(6), 2317–2336 (2014)
37. Napoletano, P., Piccoli, F., Schettini, R.: Anomaly detection in nanofibrous materials by CNN-based self-similarity. Sensors 18(1), 209 (2018)
38. Nguyen, P., Liu, T., Prasad, G., Han, B.: Weakly supervised action localization by sparse temporal pooling network. In: Proceedings of the IEEE Conference on Computer Vision and Pattern Recognition, pp. 6752–6761 (2018)
39. Oquab, M., Bottou, L., Laptev, I., Sivic, J.: Is object localization for free?-weakly-supervised learning with convolutional neural networks. In: Proceedings of the IEEE Conference on Computer Vision and Pattern Recognition, pp. 685–694 (2015)
40. Pawlowski, N., et al.: Unsupervised lesion detection in brain CT using bayesian convolutional autoencoders. In: Medical Imaging with Deep Learning (2018)

41. Perera, P., Nallapati, R., Xiang, B.: OCGAN: one-class novelty detection using GANs with constrained latent representations. In: Proceedings of the IEEE Conference on Computer Vision and Pattern Recognition, pp. 2898–2906 (2019)

42. Radford, A., Metz, L., Chintala, S.: Unsupervised representation learning with deep convolutional generative adversarial networks. In: International Conference on Learning Representations (2016)

43. Ravanbakhsh, M., Sangineto, E., Nabi, M., Sebe, N.: Training adversarial discriminators for cross-channel abnormal event detection in crowds. In: 2019 IEEE Winter Conference on Applications of Computer Vision (WACV), pp. 1896–1904. IEEE (2019)

44. Ruff, L., et al.: Deep semi-supervised anomaly detection. In: International Conference on Learning Representations (2020)

45. Russakovsky, O., et al.: ImageNet large scale visual recognition challenge. Int. J. Comput. Vision 115(3), 211–252 (2015)

46. Sabokrou, M., Khalooei, M., Fathy, M., Adeli, E.: Adversarially learned one-class classifier for novelty detection. In: Proceedings of the IEEE Conference on Computer Vision and Pattern Recognition, pp. 3379–3388 (2018)

47. Sabokrou, M., et al.: AVID: adversarial visual irregularity detection. In: Jawahar, C.V., Li, H., Mori, G., Schindler, K. (eds.) ACCV 2018. LNCS, vol. 11366, pp. 488–505. Springer, Cham (2019). https://doi.org/10.1007/978-3-030-20876-9_31

48. Schlegl, T., Seeböck, P., Waldstein, S.M., Schmidt-Erfurth, U., Langs, G.: Unsupervised anomaly detection with generative adversarial networks to guide marker discovery. In: Niethammer, M., et al. (eds.) IPMI 2017. LNCS, vol. 10265, pp. 146–157. Springer, Cham (2017). https://doi.org/10.1007/978-3-319-59050-9_12

49. Selvaraju, R.R., Cogswell, M., Das, A., Vedantam, R., Parikh, D., Batra, D.: Grad-CAM: visual explanations from deep networks via gradient-based localization. In: Proceedings of the IEEE International Conference on Computer Vision, pp. 618–626 (2017)

50. Smilkov, D., Thorat, N., Kim, B., Viégas, F., Wattenberg, M.: SmoothGrad: removing noise by adding noise. arXiv preprint arXiv:1706.03825 (2017)

51. Springenberg, J.T., Dosovitskiy, A., Brox, T., Riedmiller, M.: Striving for simplicity: the all convolutional net. arXiv preprint arXiv:1412.6806 (2014)

52. Steger, C.: Similarity measures for occlusion, clutter, and illumination invariant object recognition. In: Radig, B., Florczyk, S. (eds.) DAGM 2001. LNCS, vol. 2191, pp. 148–154. Springer, Heidelberg (2001). https://doi.org/10.1007/3-540-45404-7_20

53. Vu, H.S., Ueta, D., Hashimoto, K., Maeno, K., Pranata, S., Shen, S.M.: Anomaly detection with adversarial dual autoencoders. arXiv preprint arXiv:1902.06924 (2019)

54. Wang, X., Xu, M., Li, L., Wang, Z., Guan, Z.: Pathology-aware deep network visualization and its application in glaucoma image synthesis. In: Shen, D., et al. (eds.) MICCAI 2019. LNCS, vol. 11764, pp. 423–431. Springer, Cham (2019). https://doi.org/10.1007/978-3-030-32239-7_47

55. Wang, Z., Fan, M., Muknahallipatna, S., Lan, C.: Inductive multi-view semi-supervised anomaly detection via probabilistic modeling. In: 2019 IEEE International Conference on Big Knowledge (ICBK), pp. 257–264. IEEE (2019)

56. Wolf, L., Benaim, S., Galanti, T.: Unsupervised learning of the set of local maxima. In: International Conference on Learning Representations (2019)

57. Xiao, H., Rasul, K., Vollgraf, R.: Fashion-MNIST: a novel image dataset for benchmarking machine learning algorithms. arXiv preprint arXiv:1708.07747 (2017)

58. Zagoruyko, S., Komodakis, N.: Paying more attention to attention: improving the performance of convolutional neural networks via attention transfer. In: International Conference on Learning Representations (2017)

59. Zenati, H., Foo, C.S., Lecouat, B., Manek, G., Chandrasekhar, V.R.: Efficient GAN-based anomaly detection. arXiv preprint arXiv:1802.06222 (2018)

60. Zhou, B., Khosla, A., Lapedriza, A., Oliva, A., Torralba, A.: Learning deep features for discriminative localization. In: Proceedings of the IEEE Conference on Computer Vision and Pattern Recognition, pp. 2921–2929 (2016)

Self-supervised Video Representation Learning by Pace Prediction

Jiangliu Wang[1], Jianbo Jiao[2], and Yun-Hui Liu[1(✉)]

[1] The Chinese University of Hong Kong, Hong Kong, China
{jlwang,yhliu}@mae.cuhk.edu.hk
[2] University of Oxford, Oxford, UK
jianbo@robots.ox.ac.uk

Abstract. This paper addresses the problem of self-supervised video representation learning from a new perspective – by video pace prediction. It stems from the observation that human visual system is sensitive to video pace, *e.g.*, slow motion, a widely used technique in film making. Specifically, given a video played in natural pace, we randomly sample training clips in different paces and ask a neural network to identify the pace for each video clip. The assumption here is that the network can only succeed in such a pace reasoning task when it understands the underlying video content and learns representative spatio-temporal features. In addition, we further introduce contrastive learning to push the model towards discriminating different paces by maximizing the agreement on similar video content. To validate the effectiveness of the proposed method, we conduct extensive experiments on action recognition and video retrieval tasks with several alternative network architectures. Experimental evaluations show that our approach achieves state-of-the-art performance for self-supervised video representation learning across different network architectures and different benchmarks. The code and pre-trained models are available at https://github.com/laura-wang/video-pace.

Keywords: Self-supervised learning · Video representation · Pace

1 Introduction

Convolutional neural networks have witnessed absolute success in video representation learning [7,13,47] with human-annotated labels. Researchers have developed a wide range of neural networks [43,46,47] ingeniously, which extract powerful spatio-temporal representations for video understanding. Meanwhile, millions of labeled training data [26,27] and powerful training resources are also the fundamental recipes for such great success. However, obtaining a large

Electronic supplementary material The online version of this chapter (https://doi.org/10.1007/978-3-030-58520-4_30) contains supplementary material, which is available to authorized users.

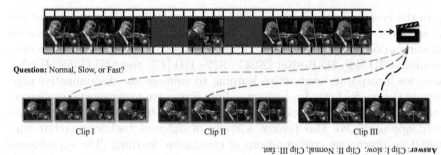

Question: Normal, Slow, or Fast?

Clip I   Clip II   Clip III

Answer: Clip I: slow; Clip II: Normal; Clip III: fast.

Fig. 1. Illustration of the proposed pace prediction task. Given a video sample, frames are randomly selected by different paces to formulate the training inputs. Here, three different clips, *Clip I, II, III*, are sampled by normal, slow and fast pace randomly. Can you ascribe the corresponding pace label to each clip? (Answer is provided below.)

number of labeled video samples requires massive human annotations, which is expensive and time-consuming. Whereas at the same time, billions of unlabeled videos are available freely on the Internet. Therefore, video representation learning from unlabeled data is crucial for video understanding and analysis.

Among all the unsupervised learning paradigms, self-supervised learning is proved to be one promising methodology [1,38]. The typical solution is to propose appropriate *pretext tasks* that generate free training labels automatically and encourage neural networks to learn transferable semantic spatio-temporal features for the *downstream tasks*. Such pretext tasks can be roughly divided into two categories: (1) generative dense prediction, such as flow fields prediction [15], future frame prediction [45,48], *etc.* (2) discriminative classification/regression, such as video order prediction [14,28,34,36,57], rotation transformation prediction [25], motion and appearance statistics regression [51], *etc.* While promising results have been achieved, some of the approaches leverage pre-computed motion channels [15,51], *e.g.*, optical flow, to generate the training labels. This could be both time and space consuming, especially when the pre-training dataset scales to millions/trillions of data. To alleviate such a problem, in this work, we propose a simple yet effective pretext task without referring to pre-computed motion. Instead, we only base on the original videos as input.

Inspired by the rhythmic montage in film making, we observe that human visual system is sensitive to motion pace and can easily distinguish different paces once understanding the covered content. Such a property has also been revealed in neuroscience studies [17,54]. To this end, we propose a simple yet effective task to perform self-supervised video representation learning: pace prediction. Specifically, given videos played in natural pace, video clips with different paces are generated according to different temporal sampling rates. A learnable model is then trained to identify which pace the input video clip corresponds to. As aforementioned, the assumption here is that if the model is able to distinguish different paces, it has to understand the underlying content. Figure 1 illustrates the basic idea of the proposed approach.

In the proposed pace prediction framework, we utilize 3D convolutional neural networks (CNNs) as our backbone network to learn video representation, following prior works [35,57]. Specifically, we investigated several architectures, including C3D [46], 3D-ResNet [20,47], R(2+1)D [47], and S3D-G [56]. Furthermore, we incorporate contrastive learning to enhance the discriminative capability of the model for video understanding. Extensive experimental evaluations with several video understanding tasks demonstrate the effectiveness of the proposed approach. We also present a study of different backbone architectures as well as alternative configurations of contrastive learning. The experimental result suggests that the proposed approach can be well integrated into different architectures and achieves state-of-the-art performance for self-supervised video representation learning.

The main contributions of this work are summarized as follows.

- We propose a simple yet effective approach for self-supervised video representation learning by pace prediction. This novel pretext task provides a solution to learn spatio-temporal features without explicitly leveraging the motion channel, e.g., optical flow.
- We further introduce contrastive learning to regularize the pace prediction objective. Two configurations are investigated by maximizing the mutual information either between same video pace or same video context.
- Extensive experimental evaluations on three network architectures and two downstream tasks across three datasets show that the proposed approach achieves state-of-the-art performance and demonstrates great potential to learn from tremendous amount of video data, in a simple manner.

2   Related Work

Video Representation Learning. Video understanding, especially action recognition, has been extensively studied for decades, where video representation learning serves as the fundamental problem of other video-related tasks, such as complex action recognition [23], action temporal localization [8,41,42], video caption [49,52], etc. Initially, various hand-crafted local spatio-temporal descriptors are proposed for video representations, such as STIP [32], HOG3D [29], etc. Wang et al. [50] proposed improved dense trajectories (iDT) descriptors, which combined the effective HOG, HOF [33] and MBH descriptors [10], and achieved the best results among all hand-crafted features. With the impressive success of CNN in image understanding problem and the availability of large-scale video datasets such as sports1M [26], ActivityNet [5], Kinetics-400 [7], studies on data-driven deep learning-based video analysis started to emerge. According to the input modality, these video representation learning methods can be roughly divided into two categories: one is to directly take RGB videos as inputs, while the other is to take both RGB videos and optical flows as inputs. Tran et al. [46] extended the 2D convolution kernels to 3D and proposed C3D network to learn spatio-temporal representations. Simonyan and Zisserman [43] proposed

a two-stream network that extracts spatial features from RGB inputs and temporal features from optical flows, followed by a fusion scheme. Recently, [13] proposed to capture the video information in a slow-fast manner, which showed that input videos with slow and fast speed help the supervised action recognition task. Although impressive results have been achieved, video representation learning with human-annotated label is both time-consuming and expensive.

Self-supervised Learning. Self-supervised learning is becoming increasingly attractive due to its great potential to leverage the large amount of unlabeled data. The key idea behind it is to propose a pretext task that generates pseudo training labels without human annotation. Various pretext tasks have been proposed for self-supervised image representation learning, such as context-based prediction [11], rotation prediction [16], colorization [60], inpainting [40], clustering [6] and contrastive learning [2,9,22,38], to name a few.

Recently, pretext tasks designed for videos are investigated to learn generic representations for downstream video tasks, such as action recognition, video retrieval, *etc.* Intuitively, a large number of studies [14,34,36] leveraged the distinct temporal information of videos and proposed to use frame sequence ordering as their pretext tasks. Büchler *et al.* [4] further used deep reinforcement learning to design the sampling permutations policy for order prediction tasks. Gan *et al.* [15] proposed to learn video representations by predicting the optical flow or disparity maps between frames. Although these methods demonstrate promising results, the learned representations are only based on one or two frames as they used 2D CNN for self-supervised learning. Consequently, some recent works [19,28,35,57] proposed to use 3D CNNs as backbone networks for spatio-temporal representations learning, among which [28,35,57] extended the 2D frame ordering pretext tasks to 3D video clip ordering, and [19] proposed a pretext task to predict future frames embedding. Some concurrent works [3,58] also investigate the speed property of video as in this work, and the reader is encouraged to review them for a broader picture. Self-supervised learning from multi-modality sources, *e.g.*, video and audio [1,30,39], also demonstrated promising results. In this paper, we focus on the video modality only and leave the potential extension to multi-modality as future research.

3   Our Approach

We address the video representation learning problem in a self-supervised manner. To achieve this goal, rather than training with human-annotated labels, we train a model with labels generated *automatically* from the video inputs X. The essential problem is how to design an appropriate transformation $g(\cdot)$, usually termed as pretext task, so as to yield transformed video inputs $\widetilde{X}$ with human-annotated free labels that encourage the network to learn powerful semantic spatio-temporal features for the downstream tasks, *e.g.*, action recognition.

In this work, we propose pace transformation $g_{pac}(\cdot)$ with a pace prediction task for self-supervised learning. Our idea is inspired by the *slow motion* which is

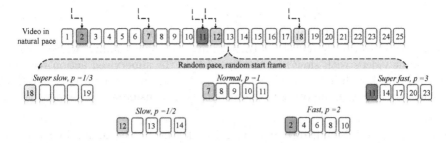

Fig. 2. Generating training samples and pace labels from the proposed pretext task. Here, we show five different sampling paces, named as *super slow, slow, normal, fast,* and *super fast.* The darker the initial frame is, the faster the entire clip plays.

widely used in film making for capturing a key moment and producing dramatic effect. Humans can easily identify it due to their sensitivity of the pace variation and a sense of normal pace. We explore whether a network could also have such ability to distinguish video play pace. Our assumption is that a network is not capable to perform such pace prediction task effectively unless it understands the video content and learns powerful spatio-temporal representations.

3.1 Pace Prediction

We aim to train a model with pace-varying video clips as inputs and ask the model to predict the video play paces. We assume that such a pace prediction task will encourage the neural network to learn generic transferable video representations and benefit downstream tasks. Figure 2 shows an example of generating the training samples and pace labels. Note that in this example, we only illustrate one training video with five distinct sampling paces. Whereas in our final implementation, the sampling pace is randomly selected from several pace candidates, not restricted to these five specific sampling paces.

As shown in Fig. 2, given a video in natural pace with 25 frames, training clips will be sampled by different paces p. Typically, we consider five pace candidates {super slow, slow, normal, fast, super fast}, where the corresponding paces p are 1/3, 1/2, 1, 2, and 3, respectively. Start frame of each video clip is randomly generated and will loop over the video sample if the desired training clip is longer than the original video sample. Methods to generate each training clip with a specific p are illustrated in the following:

– *Normal motion*, where $p = 1$, training clips are sampled consecutively from the original video. The video play speed is the same as the normal pace.
– *Fast motion*, where $p > 1$, we directly sample a video frame from the original video for every p frames, *e.g.*, super fast clip with $p = 3$ contains frames 11, 14, 17, 20 and 23. As a result, when we play the clip in nature 25 fps, it looks like the video is speed up compared to the original pace.
– *Slow motion*, where $p < 1$, we put the sampled frames into the five-frames clip for every $1/p$ frames instead, *e.g.*, slow clip with $p = 1/2$, only frames

1, 3, 5 are filled with sampled frames. Regarding the blank frames, one may consider to fill it with preceding frame, or apply interpolation algorithms [24] to estimate the intermediate frames. In practice, for simplicity, we use the preceding frame for the blank frames.

Formally, we denote the pace sampling transformation as $g(x)$. Given a video x, we apply $g(x|p)$ to obtain the training clip $\widetilde{x}$ with a training pace p. The pace prediction pretext task is formulated as a classification problem and the neural network $f(\widetilde{x})$ is trained with cross entropy loss $\mathcal{L}_{cls}$ described as:

$$\mathcal{L}_{cls} = - \sum_{i=1}^{M} y_i (\log \frac{\exp(h_i)}{\sum_{j=1}^{M} \exp(h_j)}), \quad h = f(\widetilde{x}) = f(g_{pac}(x|p)), \qquad (1)$$

where M is the number of all the pace rate candidates.

Avoid Shortcuts. As first pointed out in [11], when designing a pretext task, one must pay attention to the possibility that a network could be cheating or taking shortcuts to accomplish the pretext task by learning trivial solutions/low-level features rather than the desired high-level semantic representations. Such observations are also reported in [19, 28] for self-supervised video representation learning. In this work, we adopt color jittering augmentation to avoid such shortcuts. Empirically, we find that color jittering applied to each frame achieves much better performance than to the entire video clip. More details see Sect. 4.2.

3.2 Contrastive Learning

To further enhance the pace prediction task and regularize the learning process, we propose to leverage contrastive learning as an additional objective. Contrastive learning in a self-supervised manner has shown great potential and achieved comparable results with supervised visual representation learning recently [2, 9, 19, 22, 38, 55]. It stems from Noise-Contrastive Estimation [18] and aims to distinguish the positive samples from a group of negative samples. The fundamental problem of contrastive learning lies in the definition of *positive* and *negative* samples. For example, Chen *et al.* [22] consider the pair with different data augmentations applied to the same sample as positive, while Bachman *et al.* [2] takes different views of a shared context as positive pair. In this work, we consider two possible strategies to define positive samples: same context and same pace. In the following, we elaborate on these two strategies.

Same Context. We first consider to use clips from the same video but with different sampling paces as positive pairs, while those clips sampled from different videos as negative pair, *i.e.*, content-aware contrastive learning.

Formally, given a mini-batch of N video clips $\{x_1, \ldots, x_N\}$, for each video input x_i, we randomly sample n training clips from it by different paces, resulting in an actual training batch size $n * N$. Here, for simplicity, we consider $n = 2$,

and the corresponding positive pairs are $\{(\widetilde{x}_i, p_i), (\widetilde{x}_i', p_i')\}$, where $\widetilde{x}_i$ and $\widetilde{x}_i'$ are sampled from the same video. Video clips sampled from different video are considered as negative pairs, denoted as $\{(\widetilde{x}_i, p_i), (\widetilde{x}_{\mathcal{J}}, p_{\mathcal{J}})\}$. Each video clip is then encoded into a feature vector z_i in the latent space by the neural network $f(\cdot)$. Then the positive feature vector pair is (z_i, z_i') while the negative pairs are $\{(z_i, z_{\mathcal{J}})\}$. Denote $\mathrm{sim}(z_i, z_i')$ as the similarity between feature vector z_i and z_i' and $\mathrm{sim}(z_i, z'_{\mathcal{J}})$ as the similarity between feature vector z_i and $z'_{\mathcal{J}}$, the content-aware contrastive loss is defined as:

$$\mathcal{L}_{ctr\_sc} = -\frac{1}{2N} \sum_{i,\mathcal{J}} \log \frac{\exp(\mathrm{sim}(z_i, z_i'))}{\sum_i \exp(\mathrm{sim}(z_i, z_i')) + \sum_{i,\mathcal{J}} \exp(\mathrm{sim}(z_i, z_{\mathcal{J}}))}, \qquad (2)$$

where $\mathrm{sim}(z_i, z_i')$ is achieved by the dot product $z_i^{\top} z_i'$ between the two feature vectors and so as $\mathrm{sim}(z_i, z'_{\mathcal{J}})$.

Same Pace. Concerning the proposed pace prediction pretext task, another alternative contrastive learning strategy based on same pace is explored. Specifically, we consider video clips with the same pace as positive samples regardless of the underlying video content, *i.e.*, content-agnostic contrastive learning. In this way, the contrastive learning is investigated from a different perspective that is explicitly related to pace.

Formally, given a mini-batch of N video clips $\{x_1, \ldots, x_N\}$, we first apply the pace sampling transformation $g_{pac}(\cdot)$ described above to each video input to obtain the training clips and their pace labels, denoted as $\{(\widetilde{x}_1, p_1), \ldots, (\widetilde{x}_N, p_N)\}$. Each video clip is then encoded into a feature vector z_i in the latent space by the neural network $f(\cdot)$. Consequently, (z_i, z_j) is considered as positive pair if $p_i = p_j$ while (z_i, z_k) is considered as negative pair if $p_i \neq p_k$, where $j, k \in \{1, 2, \ldots, N\}$. Denote $\mathrm{sim}(z_i, z_j)$ as the similarity between feature vector z_i and z_j and $\mathrm{sim}(z_i, z_k)$ as the similarity between feature vector z_i and z_k, the contrastive loss is defined as:

$$\mathcal{L}_{ctr\_sp} = -\frac{1}{N} \sum_{i,j,k} \log \frac{\exp(\mathrm{sim}(z_i, z_j))}{\sum_{i,j} \exp(\mathrm{sim}(z_i, z_j)) + \sum_{i,k} \exp(\mathrm{sim}(z_i, z_k))}, \qquad (3)$$

where $\mathrm{sim}(z_i, z_j)$ is achieved by the dot product $z_i^{\top} z_j$ between the two feature vectors and so as $\mathrm{sim}(z_i, z_k)$.

3.3   Network Architecture and Training

The framework of the proposed pace prediction approach is illustrated in Fig. 3. Given a set of unlabeled videos, we firstly sample various video clips with different paces. Then these training clips are fed into a deep model (3D CNN here) for spatio-temporal representation learning. The final objective is to optimize the model to predict the pace of each video clip and maximize the agreement (mutual information) between positive pairs at the same time.

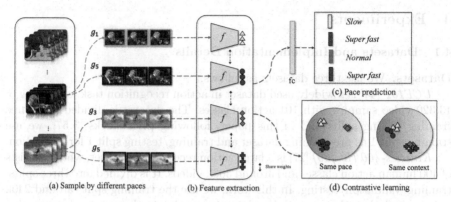

(a) Sample by different paces   (b) Feature extraction   (d) Contrastive learning

Fig. 3. Framework of the proposed approach. (a) Training clips are sampled by different paces. Here, g_1, g_3, g_5 illustrates examples of *slow*, *normal* and *super fast* pace. (b) A 3D CNN f is leveraged to extract spatio-temporal features. (c) The model is trained to predict the specific pace applied to each video clip. (d) Two possible contrastive learning strategies are considered to regularize the learning process at the latent space. The symbols at the end of the CNNs represent feature vectors extracted from different video clips, where the intensity represents different video pace.

In terms of the network architecture, we mainly consider three backbone networks, *i.e.* C3D [46], 3D-ResNet [20] and R(2+1)D [47], to study the effectiveness of the proposed approach. C3D is a classic neural network which operates on 3D video volume by extending 2D convolutional kernel to 3D. 3D-ResNet (R3D) [20] is an extension of the ResNet [21] architecture to videos. In this work, we use 3D-ResNet18 (R3D-18). R(2+1)D [47] is proposed to break the original spatio-temporal 3D convolution into a 2D spatial convolution and a 1D temporal convolution. Apart from these three networks, we also use a state-of-the-art model S3D-G [56] to further exploit the potential of the proposed approach.

By jointly optimizing the classification objective (Eq. 1) and the contrastive objective (Eq. 2 or 3), the final training loss is defined as:

$$\mathcal{L} = \lambda_{cls}\mathcal{L}_{cls} + \lambda_{ctr}\mathcal{L}_{ctr}, \tag{4}$$

where $\lambda_{cls}, \lambda_{ctr}$ are weighting parameters to balance the optimization of pace prediction and contrastive learning, respectively. The $\mathcal{L}_{ctr}$ refers to either contrastive learning with same pace $\mathcal{L}_{ctr\_sp}$ or with same context $\mathcal{L}_{ctr\_sc}$.

4 Experiments

4.1 Datasets and Implementation Details

Datasets. We use three datasets as follows:

UCF101 [44] is a widely used dataset in action recognition task, consisting of 13,320 video samples with 101 action classes. The dataset is divided into three training/testing splits and in this paper, following prior works [3,57], we use training split 1 as pre-training dataset and training/testing split 1 for evaluation.

Kinetics-400 (K-400) [27] is a large action recognition dataset, which consists of 400 human action classes and around 306k videos. It is divided into three splits: training/validation/testing. In this work, we use the training split (around 240k video samples) as the pre-training dataset, to validate the proposed approach.

HMDB51 [31] is a relatively small action recognition dataset, which contains around 7,000 videos with 51 action classes. It is divided into three training/testing splits and following prior works [3,57], we use training/testing split 1 for downstream task evaluation.

Self-supervised Pre-training Stage. When pre-training on the K-400 dataset, for each video input, we first generate a frame index randomly and then start from the index, sample a consecutive 16-frame video clip. While when pre-training on UCF101 dataset, as it only contains around 9k videos in the training split, we set epoch size to be around 90k for temporal jittering following [1]. As for data augmentation, we randomly crop the video clip to 112×112 and flip the whole video clip horizontally. The batch size is 30 and SGD is used as optimizer with an initial learning rate 1×10^{-3}. The leaning rate is divided by 10 for every 6 epochs and the training process is stopped after 18 epochs. When jointly optimizing $\mathcal{L}_{cls}$ and $\mathcal{L}_{ctr}$, λ_{cls} is set to 1 and λ_{ctr} is set to 0.1.

Supervised Fine-Tuning Stage. Regarding the action recognition task, during the fine-tuning stage, weights of convolutional layers are retained from the self-supervised learning networks while weights of fully-connected layers are randomly initialized. The whole network is then trained with cross-entropy loss. Image pre-processing method and training strategy are the same as the self-supervised pre-training stage, except that the initial learning rate is set to 0.01 for S3D-G and 3×10^{-3} for the others.

Evaluation. During inference, following the evaluation protocol in [35,57], we sample 10 clips uniformly from each video in the testing set of UCF101 and HMDB51. For each clip, center crop is applied. The predicted label of each video is generated by averaging the softmax probabilities of all clips in the video.

Table 1. Explore the best setting for pace prediction task. Sampling pace $p = [a, b]$ represents that the lowest value of pace p is a and the highest is b with an interval of 1, except $p = [\frac{1}{3}, 3]$, where p is selected from $\{\frac{1}{3}, \frac{1}{2}, 1, 2, 3\}$.

Color jittering	Method	#Classes	UCF101
×	Random	–	56.0
×	$p = [1, 3]$	3	71.4
×	$p = [1, 4]$	4	**72.0**
×	$p = [1, 5]$	5	72.0
×	$p = [1, 6]$	6	71.1
✓	$p = [1, 4]$	4	**73.9**
✓	$p = [\frac{1}{3}, 3]$	5	73.9

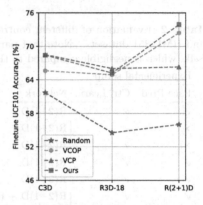

Fig. 4. Action recognition accuracy on three backbone architectures (horizontal axis) using four initialization methods.

4.2 Ablation Studies

In this section, we firstly explore the best sampling pace design for the pace prediction task. We apply it to three different backbone networks to study the effectiveness of the pretext task and the network architectures. Experimental results show that respectable performance can be achieved by only using the pace prediction task. When introducing the contrastive learning, the performance is further boosted, and the same content configuration performs much better than the same pace one. More details are illustrated in the following.

Sampling Pace. We investigate the best setting for pace prediction task with R(2+1)D backbone network [47] in Table 1. To study the relationship between the complexity of the pretext task and the effectiveness on the downstream task, we first use a *relative* pace design with only normal and fast motion. For example, regarding $p = [1, 3]$, we assume clips with $p = 2$ to be the anchor, *i.e.*, normal pace and therefore, clips with $p = 3$ are with faster pace and $p = 1$ are with slower pace. It can be seen from the table that with the increase of the maximum pace, namely the number of training classes, the accuracy of the downstream action recognition task keeps increase, until $p = [1, 4]$. When the sampling pace increases to $p = [1, 6]$, the accuracy starts to drop. We believe that this is because such a pace prediction task is becoming too difficult for the network to learn useful semantic features. This provides an insight on the pretext task design that a pretext task should not be too simple nor too ambiguous to solve, in consistent with the observations found in [14, 37].

We further validate the effectiveness of color jittering based on the best sampling pace design $p = [1, 4]$. It can be seen from Table 1 that with color jittering, the performance is further improved by 1.9%. It is also interesting to note that the *relative* pace, *i.e.*, $p = [1, 4]$, achieves comparable result with the *absolute*

Table 2. Evaluation of different contrastive learning configurations on both UCF101 and HMDB51 datasets. *Note that parameters when adding an fc layer only increase ~4k, which is negligible compared to the original 14.4M parameters.

Experimental setup					Downstream tasks	
Pace Pred.	Ctr. Learn.	Network	Configuration	Params	UCF101	HMDB51
✓	×	R(2+1)D	–	14.4M	**73.9**	**33.8**
×	✓	R(2+1)D	Same pace	14.4M	59.4	20.3
×	✓	R(2+1)D	Same context	14.4M	67.3	28.6
✓	✓	R(2+1)D	Same pace	14.4M	73.6	32.3
✓	✓	R(2+1)D	Same context	14.4M	75.8	35.0
✓	✓	R(2+1)D + fc	Same context	14.4M*	**75.9**	**35.9**

pace, $i.e.$, $p = [\frac{1}{3}, 3]$, but with less number of classes. In the following experiments, we use sampling pace $p = [1, 4]$ along with color jittering by default.

Backbone Network. We validate the proposed pace prediction task without contrastive learning using three backbone networks. Some recent works [35, 57] validate their proposed self-supervised learning approaches on modern spatio-temporal representation learning networks, such as R3D-18 [20,47], R(2+1)D [47], $etc.$ This practice could influence the direct evaluation of the pretext tasks, as the performance improvement can also come from the usage of more powerful networks. Therefore, we study the effectiveness of the pace prediction task and compare with some recent works on three backbone networks, as shown in Fig. 4. For a fair comparison, following [35,57], we use the first training split of UCF101 as the pre-training dataset and evaluate on training/testing split 1.

Some key observations are listed in the following: (1) The proposed approach achieves significant improvement over the random initialization across all three backbone networks. (2) Although in the random initialization setting, C3D achieves the best results, R(2+1)D and R3D-18 benefit more from the self-supervised pre-training and R(2+1)D finally achieves the best performance. (3) Without contrastive learning, the proposed pace prediction task already demonstrates impressive effectiveness to learn video representations, achieving comparable performance with current state-of-the-art methods VCP [35] and VCOP [57] on C3D and R3D-18 and outperforms them when using R(2+1)D.

Contrastive Learning. The performances of the two contrastive learning configurations are shown in Table 2. Some key observations are listed for a better understanding of contrastive learning: (1) The same pace configuration achieves much worse results than the same context configuration. We suspect the reason is that in the same pace configuration, as there are only four pace candidates $p = [1, 4]$, video clips are tend to belong to the same pace. Therefore, compared

with the same context configuration, much fewer negative samples are presented in the training batches, withholding the effectiveness of contrastive learning. (2) Pace prediction task achieves much better performance compared to each of the two contrastive learning settings. This demonstrates the superiority of the proposed pace prediction task.

When combining the pace prediction task with contrastive learning, similar to the observation described above, regarding the same pace configuration, performance is slightly deteriorated and regarding the same context configuration, performance is further improved both on UCF101 and HMDB51 datasets. It shows that appropriate multi-task self-supervised learning can further boost the performances, in consistent with the observation in [12]. Based on the same video content configuration, we further introduce a nonlinear layer between the embedding space and the final contrastive learning space to alleviate the direct influence on the pace prediction learning. It is shown that such a practice can further improve the performance (last row in Table 2).

4.3   Action Recognition

We compare our approach with other methods on the action recognition task in Table 3. We have the following key observations: (1) Our method achieve the state-of-the-art results on both UCF101 and HMDB51 dataset. When pre-trained on UCF101, we outperform the current best-performing method PRP [58]. When pre-trained on K-400, we outperform the current best-performing method DPC [19]. (2) Note that here the DPC method uses R3D-34 as their backbone network and the video input size is 224×224 while we only use 112×112. When the input size of DPC is at the same scale as ours, $i.e.$, 128×128, we outperform it by 8.9% on UCF101 dataset. We attribute such success to both our pace prediction task and the usage of R(2+1)D. It can be observed that with R(2+1)D and only UCF101 as pre-train dataset, VCOP [57] can achieve 72.4% on UCF101 and 30.9% on HMDB51. (3) Backbone networks, input size and clip length do play important roles in the self-supervised video representation learning. As shown in the last row, by using the S3D-G [56] architecture with 64-frame clips as inputs, pre-training only on UCF101 can already achieve remarkable performance, even superior to fully supervised pre-training on ImageNet (on UCF101).

To further validate the proposed approach, we visualize the attention maps based on the pre-trained R(2+1)D model, as shown in Fig. 5. It can be seen from the attention maps that the neural network will pay more attention to the motion areas when learning the pace prediction task. It is also interesting to note that in the last row, as attention map on $p = 4$ computes the layer information spanning 64 frames, it is activated at several motion locations.

4.4   Video Retrieval

We further validate the proposed approach on the video retrieval task. Basically, we follow the same evaluation protocol described in [35,57]. Ten 16-frames

Table 3. Comparison with the state-of-the-art self-supervised learning methods on UCF101 and HMDB51 dataset (Pre-trained on video modality only). *The input video clips contain 64 frames.

Method	Pre-training settings				Evaluation	
	Network	Input size	Params	Dataset	UCF101	HMDB51
Fully supervised	S3D-G	224 × 224*	9.6M	ImageNet	86.6	57.7
Fully supervised	S3D-G	224 × 224*	9.6M	K-400	96.8	74.5
Object Patch [53]	AlexNet	227 × 227	62.4M	UCF101	42.7	15.6
ClipOrder [36]	CaffeNet	227 × 227	58.3M	UCF101	50.9	19.8
Deep RL [4]	CaffeNet	227 × 227	–	UCF101	58.6	25.0
OPN [34]	VGG	80 × 80	8.6M	UCF101	59.8	23.8
VCP [35]	R(2+1)D	112 × 112	14.4M	UCF101	66.3	32.2
VCOP [57]	R(2+1)D	112 × 112	14.4M	UCF101	72.4	30.9
PRP [58]	R(2+1)D	112 × 112	14.4M	UCF101	72.1	35.0
Ours	R(2+1)D	112 × 112	14.4M	UCF101	**75.9**	**35.9**
MAS [51]	C3D	112 × 112	27.7M	K-400	61.2	33.4
RotNet3D [25]	R3D-18	224 × 224	33.6M	K-400	62.9	33.7
ST-puzzle [28]	R3D-18	224 × 224	33.6M	K-400	65.8	33.7
DPC [19]	R3D-18	128 × 128	14.2M	K-400	68.2	34.5
DPC [19]	R3D-34	224 × 224	32.6M	K-400	75.7	35.7
Ours	R(2+1)D	112 × 112	14.4M	K-400	**77.1**	**36.6**
SpeedNet [3]	S3D-G	224 × 224*	9.6M	K-400	81.1	48.8
Ours	S3D-G	224 × 224*	9.6M	UCF101	**87.1**	**52.6**

clips are sampled from each video and then go through a feed-forward pass to generate features from the last pooling layer (p5). For each clip in the testing split, the Top$k$ nearest neighbors are queried from the training split by computing the cosine distances between every two feature vectors. We consider k to be 1, 5, 10, 20, 50. To align the experimental results with prior works [35,57] for fair comparison, we use pre-trained models from the pace prediction task on UCF101 dataset. As shown in Table 4 and Table 5, our method outperforms the VCOP [57] and VCP [35] in most cases on the two datasets across the three backbone networks. In practice, we also find that significant improvement can be achieved by using the second last pooling layer (p4).

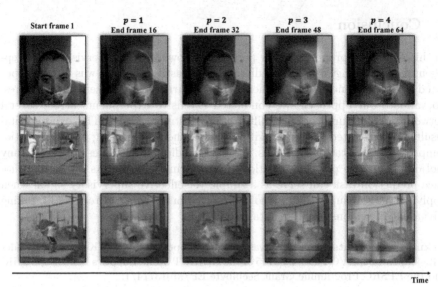

Fig. 5. Attention visualization of the conv5 layer from self-supervised pre-trained model using [59]. Attention map is generated with 16-frames clip inputs and applied to the last frame in the video clips. Each row represents a video sample while each column illustrates the end frame *w.r.t.* different sampling pace *p*.

Table 4. Comparison with state-of-the-art methods for nearest neighbour retrieval task on UCF101 dataset.

	Method	Top1	Top5	Top10	Top20	Top50
AlexNet	Jigsaw [37]	19.7	28.5	33.5	40.0	49.4
	OPN [34]	19.9	28.7	34.0	40.6	51.6
	Deep RL [4]	25.7	36.2	42.2	49.2	59.5
C3D	Random	16.7	27.5	33.7	41.4	53.0
	VCOP [57]	12.5	29.0	39.0	50.6	66.9
	VCP [35]	17.3	31.5	42.0	52.6	67.7
	Ours (p5)	20.0	37.4	46.9	58.5	73.1
	Ours(p4)	**31.9**	**49.7**	**59.2**	**68.9**	**80.2**
R3D-18	Random	9.9	18.9	26.0	35.5	51.9
	VCOP [57]	14.1	30.3	40.4	51.1	66.5
	VCP [35]	18.6	33.6	42.5	53.5	68.1
	Ours (p5)	19.9	36.2	46.1	55.6	69.2
	Ours(p4)	**23.8**	**38.1**	**46.4**	**56.6**	**69.8**
R(2+1)D	Random	10.6	20.7	27.4	37.4	53.1
	VCOP [57]	10.7	25.9	35.4	47.3	63.9
	VCP [35]	19.9	33.7	42.0	50.5	64.4
	Ours (p5)	17.9	34.3	44.6	55.5	72.0
	Ours(p4)	**25.6**	**42.7**	**51.3**	**61.3**	**74.0**

Table 5. Comparison with state-of-the-art methods for nearest neighbor retrieval task on HMDB51 dataset.

	Method	Top1	Top5	Top10	Top20	Top50
C3D	Random	7.4	20.5	31.9	44.5	66.3
	VCOP [57]	7.4	22.6	34.4	48.5	70.1
	VCP [35]	7.8	23.8	35.5	49.3	71.6
	Ours (p5)	8.0	25.2	37.8	54.4	77.5
	Ours(p4)	**12.5**	**32.2**	**45.4**	**61.0**	**80.7**
R3D-18	Random	6.7	18.3	28.3	43.1	67.9
	VCOP [57]	7.6	22.9	34.4	48.8	68.9
	VCP [35]	7.6	24.4	36.6	53.6	76.4
	Ours (p5)	8.2	24.2	37.3	53.3	74.5
	Ours(p4)	**9.6**	**26.9**	**41.1**	**56.1**	**76.5**
R(2+1)D	Random	4.5	14.8	23.4	38.9	63.0
	VCOP [57]	5.7	19.5	30.7	45.8	67.0
	VCP [35]	6.7	21.3	32.7	49.2	73.3
	Ours (p5)	10.1	24.6	37.6	54.4	77.1
	Ours(p4)	**12.9**	**31.6**	**43.2**	**58.0**	**77.1**

5   Conclusion

In this paper, we proposed a new perspective towards self-supervised video representation learning, by pace prediction. Contrastive learning was also incorporated to further encourage the networks to learn high-level semantic features. To validate our approach, we conducted extensive experiments across several network architectures on two different downstream tasks. The experimental results demonstrated the superiority of our method on learning powerful spatiotemporal representations. Besides, the pace prediction task does not rely on any motion channel as prior information/input during training. As a result, such a pace prediction task can serve as a simple yet effective supervisory signal when applying the self-supervised video representation learning in real world, taking advantage of billions of video data freely.

Acknowledgements. This work was partially supported by the HK RGC TRS under T42-409/18-R, the VC Fund 4930745 of the CUHK T Stone Robotics Institute, CUHK, and the EPSRC Programme Grant Seebibyte EP/M013774/1.

References

1. Alwassel, H., Mahajan, D., Torresani, L., Ghanem, B., Tran, D.: Self-supervised learning by cross-modal audio-video clustering. arXiv preprint arXiv:1911.12667 (2019)
2. Bachman, P., Hjelm, R.D., Buchwalter, W.: Learning representations by maximizing mutual information across views. In: NeurIPS (2019)
3. Benaim, S., et al.: SpeedNet: learning the speediness in videos. In: CVPR (2020)
4. Büchler, U., Brattoli, B., Ommer, B.: Improving spatiotemporal self-supervision by deep reinforcement learning. In: Ferrari, V., Hebert, M., Sminchisescu, C., Weiss, Y. (eds.) ECCV 2018. LNCS, vol. 11219, pp. 797–814. Springer, Cham (2018). https://doi.org/10.1007/978-3-030-01267-0_47
5. Caba Heilbron, F., Escorcia, V., Ghanem, B., Carlos Niebles, J.: ActivityNet: a large-scale video benchmark for human activity understanding. In: CVPR (2015)
6. Caron, M., Bojanowski, P., Joulin, A., Douze, M.: Deep clustering for unsupervised learning of visual features. In: ECCV (2018)
7. Carreira, J., Zisserman, A.: Quo vadis, action recognition? A new model and the kinetics dataset. In: CVPR (2017)
8. Chao, Y.W., Vijayanarasimhan, S., Seybold, B., Ross, D.A., Deng, J., Sukthankar, R.: Rethinking the faster R-CNN architecture for temporal action localization. In: CVPR (2018)
9. Chen, T., Kornblith, S., Norouzi, M., Hinton, G.: A simple framework for contrastive learning of visual representations. arXiv preprint arXiv:2002.05709 (2020)
10. Dalal, N., Triggs, B., Schmid, C.: Human detection using oriented histograms of flow and appearance. In: Leonardis, A., Bischof, H., Pinz, A. (eds.) ECCV 2006. LNCS, vol. 3952, pp. 428–441. Springer, Heidelberg (2006). https://doi.org/10.1007/11744047_33
11. Doersch, C., Gupta, A., Efros, A.A.: Unsupervised visual representation learning by context prediction. In: ICCV (2015)

12. Doersch, C., Zisserman, A.: Multi-task self-supervised visual learning. In: ICCV (2017)
13. Feichtenhofer, C., Fan, H., Malik, J., He, K.: Slowfast networks for video recognition. In: ICCV (2019)
14. Fernando, B., Bilen, H., Gavves, E., Gould, S.: Self-supervised video representation learning with odd-one-out networks. In: CVPR (2017)
15. Gan, C., Gong, B., Liu, K., Su, H., Guibas, L.J.: Geometry guided convolutional neural networks for self-supervised video representation learning. In: CVPR (2018)
16. Gidaris, S., Singh, P., Komodakis, N.: Unsupervised representation learning by predicting image rotations. In: ICLR (2018)
17. Giese, M.A., Poggio, T.: Neural mechanisms for the recognition of biological movements. Nat. Rev. Neurosci. 4(3), 179–192 (2003)
18. Gutmann, M., Hyvärinen, A.: Noise-contrastive estimation: a new estimation principle for unnormalized statistical models. In: AISTATS (2010)
19. Han, T., Xie, W., Zisserman, A.: Video representation learning by dense predictive coding. In: ICCV Workshops (2019)
20. Hara, K., Kataoka, H., Satoh, Y.: Can spatiotemporal 3D CNNs retrace the history of 2D CNNs and ImageNet? In: CVPR (2018)
21. He, K., Zhang, X., Ren, S., Sun, J.: Deep residual learning for image recognition. In: CVPR (2016)
22. Hénaff, O.J., Razavi, A., Doersch, C., Eslami, S., Oord, A.v.d.: Data-efficient image recognition with contrastive predictive coding. arXiv preprint arXiv:1905.09272 (2019)
23. Hussein, N., Gavves, E., Smeulders, A.W.: Timeception for complex action recognition. In: CVPR (2019)
24. Jiang, H., Sun, D., Jampani, V., Yang, M.H., Learned-Miller, E., Kautz, J.: Super SloMo: high quality estimation of multiple intermediate frames for video interpolation. In: CVPR (2018)
25. Jing, L., Yang, X., Liu, J., Tian, Y.: Self-supervised spatiotemporal feature learning via video rotation prediction. arXiv preprint arXiv:1811.11387 (2018)
26. Karpathy, A., Toderici, G., Shetty, S., Leung, T., Sukthankar, R., Fei-Fei, L.: Large-scale video classification with convolutional neural networks. In: CVPR (2014)
27. Kay, W., et al.: The kinetics human action video dataset. arXiv preprint arXiv:1705.06950 (2017)
28. Kim, D., Cho, D., Kweon, I.S.: Self-supervised video representation learning with space-time cubic puzzles. In: AAAI (2019)
29. Klaser, A., Marszałek, M., Schmid, C.: A spatio-temporal descriptor based on 3D-gradients. In: BMVC (2008)
30. Korbar, B., Tran, D., Torresani, L.: Cooperative learning of audio and video models from self-supervised synchronization. In: NeurIPS (2018)
31. Kuehne, H., Jhuang, H., Garrote, E., Poggio, T., Serre, T.: HMDB: a large video database for human motion recognition. In: ICCV (2011)
32. Laptev, I.: On space-time interest points. IJCV 64(2–3), 107–123 (2005)
33. Laptev, I., Marszalek, M., Schmid, C., Rozenfeld, B.: Learning realistic human actions from movies. In: CVPR (2008)
34. Lee, H.Y., Huang, J.B., Singh, M., Yang, M.H.: Unsupervised representation learning by sorting sequences. In: ICCV (2017)
35. Luo, D., et al.: Video cloze procedure for self-supervised spatio-temporal learning. arXiv preprint arXiv:2001.00294 (2020)

36. Misra, I., Zitnick, C.L., Hebert, M.: Shuffle and learn: unsupervised learning using temporal order verification. In: Leibe, B., Matas, J., Sebe, N., Welling, M. (eds.) ECCV 2016. LNCS, vol. 9905, pp. 527–544. Springer, Cham (2016). https://doi.org/10.1007/978-3-319-46448-0_32

37. Noroozi, M., Favaro, P.: Unsupervised learning of visual representations by solving jigsaw puzzles. In: Leibe, B., Matas, J., Sebe, N., Welling, M. (eds.) ECCV 2016. LNCS, vol. 9910, pp. 69–84. Springer, Cham (2016). https://doi.org/10.1007/978-3-319-46466-4_5

38. Oord, A.v.d., Li, Y., Vinyals, O.: Representation learning with contrastive predictive coding. arXiv preprint arXiv:1807.03748 (2018)

39. Owens, A., Efros, A.A.: Audio-visual scene analysis with self-supervised multisensory features. In: Ferrari, V., Hebert, M., Sminchisescu, C., Weiss, Y. (eds.) ECCV 2018. LNCS, vol. 11210, pp. 639–658. Springer, Cham (2018). https://doi.org/10.1007/978-3-030-01231-1_39

40. Pathak, D., Krahenbuhl, P., Donahue, J., Darrell, T., Efros, A.A.: Context encoders: feature learning by inpainting. In: CVPR (2016)

41. Shou, Z., Chan, J., Zareian, A., Miyazawa, K., Chang, S.F.: CDC: convolutional-de-convolutional networks for precise temporal action localization in untrimmed videos. In: CVPR (2017)

42. Shou, Z., Wang, D., Chang, S.F.: Temporal action localization in untrimmed videos via multi-stage CNNs. In: CVPR (2016)

43. Simonyan, K., Zisserman, A.: Two-stream convolutional networks for action recognition in videos. In: NeruIPS (2014)

44. Soomro, K., Zamir, A.R., Shah, M.: UCF101: a dataset of 101 human actions classes from videos in the wild. arXiv preprint arXiv:1212.0402 (2012)

45. Srivastava, N., Mansimov, E., Salakhudinov, R.: Unsupervised learning of video representations using LSTMs. In: ICML (2015)

46. Tran, D., Bourdev, L., Fergus, R., Torresani, L., Paluri, M.: Learning spatiotemporal features with 3D convolutional networks. In: ICCV (2015)

47. Tran, D., Wang, H., Torresani, L., Ray, J., LeCun, Y., Paluri, M.: A closer look at spatiotemporal convolutions for action recognition. In: CVPR (2018)

48. Vondrick, C., Pirsiavash, H., Torralba, A.: Generating videos with scene dynamics. In: NeurIPS (2016)

49. Wang, B., Ma, L., Zhang, W., Liu, W.: Reconstruction network for video captioning. In: CVPR (2018)

50. Wang, H., Schmid, C.: Action recognition with improved trajectories. In: ICCV (2013)

51. Wang, J., Jiao, J., Bao, L., He, S., Liu, Y., Liu, W.: Self-supervised spatio-temporal representation learning for videos by predicting motion and appearance statistics. In: CVPR (2019)

52. Wang, J., Jiang, W., Ma, L., Liu, W., Xu, Y.: Bidirectional attentive fusion with context gating for dense video captioning. In: CVPR (2018)

53. Wang, X., Gupta, A.: Unsupervised learning of visual representations using videos. In: ICCV (2015)

54. Watamaniuk, S.N., Duchon, A.: The human visual system averages speed information. Vision. Res. **32**(5), 931–941 (1992)

55. Wu, Z., Xiong, Y., Yu, S.X., Lin, D.: Unsupervised feature learning via non-parametric instance discrimination. In: CVPR (2018)

56. Xie, S., Sun, C., Huang, J., Tu, Z., Murphy, K.: Rethinking spatiotemporal feature learning: speed-accuracy trade-offs in video classification. In: Ferrari, V., Hebert, M., Sminchisescu, C., Weiss, Y. (eds.) ECCV 2018. LNCS, vol. 11219, pp. 318–335. Springer, Cham (2018). https://doi.org/10.1007/978-3-030-01267-0_19
57. Xu, D., Xiao, J., Zhao, Z., Shao, J., Xie, D., Zhuang, Y.: Self-supervised spatiotemporal learning via video clip order prediction. In: CVPR (2019)
58. Yao, Y., Liu, C., Luo, D., Zhou, Y., Ye, Q.: Video playback rate perception for self-supervised spatio-temporal representation learning. In: CVPR (2020)
59. Zagoruyko, S., Komodakis, N.: Paying more attention to attention: improving the performance of convolutional neural networks via attention transfer. In: ICLR (2017)
60. Zhang, R., Isola, P., Efros, A.A.: Colorful image colorization. In: Leibe, B., Matas, J., Sebe, N., Welling, M. (eds.) ECCV 2016. LNCS, vol. 9907, pp. 649–666. Springer, Cham (2016). https://doi.org/10.1007/978-3-319-46487-9_40

Full-Body Awareness from Partial Observations

Chris Rockwell$^{(\boxtimes)}$ and David F. Fouhey

University of Michigan, Ann Arbor, USA
{cnris,fouhey}@umich.edu

Abstract. There has been great progress in human 3D mesh recovery and great interest in learning about the world from consumer video data. Unfortunately current methods for 3D human mesh recovery work rather poorly on consumer video data, since on the Internet, unusual camera viewpoints and aggressive truncations are the norm rather than a rarity. We study this problem and make a number of contributions to address it: (i) we propose a simple but highly effective self-training framework that adapts human 3D mesh recovery systems to consumer videos and demonstrate its application to two recent systems; (ii) we introduce evaluation protocols and keypoint annotations 13 K frames across four consumer video datasets for studying this task, including evaluations on out-of-image keypoints; and (iii) we show that our method substantially improves PCK and human-subject judgments compared to baselines, both on test videos from the dataset it was trained on, as well as on three other datasets without further adaptation.

Keyword: Human pose estimation

1 Introduction

Consider the images in Fig. 1: what are these people doing? Are they standing or sitting? While a human can readily recognize what is going on in the images, having a similar understanding is a severe challenge to current human 3D pose estimation systems. Unfortunately, in the world of Internet video, frames like these are the rule rather than rarities since consumer videos are recorded not with the goal of providing clean demonstrations of people performing poses, but are instead meant to show something interesting to people who already know how to parse 3D poses. Accordingly, while videos from consumer sharing sites may be a useful source of data for learning how the world works [2,14,59,62], most consumer videos depict a confusing jumble of limbs and torsos flashing across the screen. The goal of this paper is to make sense of this jumble.

Electronic supplementary material The online version of this chapter (https://doi.org/10.1007/978-3-030-58520-4_31) contains supplementary material, which is available to authorized users.

© Springer Nature Switzerland AG 2020
A. Vedaldi et al. (Eds.): ECCV 2020, LNCS 12362, pp. 522–539, 2020.
https://doi.org/10.1007/978-3-030-58520-4_31

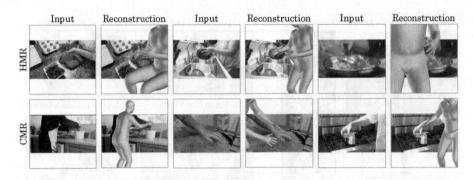

Fig. 1. We present a simple but highly effective framework for adapting human pose estimation methods to highly truncated settings that requires no additional pose annotation. We evaluate the approach on HMR [24] and CMR [26] by annotating four Internet video test sets: VLOG [14] (top-left, top-middle), Cross-Task [62] (top-right, bottom-left), YouCookII [59] (bottom-middle), and Instructions [2] (bottom-right).

Current work in human pose estimation is usually not up to the challenge of the jumble of Internet footage. Recent work in human pose estimation [3,9,24, 35,38] is typically trained and evaluated on 2D and 3D pose datasets [4,19,21, 30,37] that show full human poses from level cameras often in athletic settings Fig. 2 (left). Unfortunately, Internet footage tends to be like Fig. 2 (right), and frequently only part of the body is visible to best show off how to perform a task or highlight something of interest. For instance, on VLOG [14], all human joints are visible in only 4% of image frames. Meanwhile, all leg keypoints are *not* visible 63% of the time, and head keypoints such as eyes are *not* visible in about 45% of frames. Accordingly, when standard approaches are tested on this sort of data, they tend to fail catastrophically, which we show empirically.

We propose a simple but surprisingly effective approach in Sect. 3 that we apply to multiple forms of human mesh recovery. The key insight is to combine both cropping *and* self-training on confident video frames: cropping introduces the model to truncation, video matches context to truncations. After pre-training on a cropped version of a standard dataset, we identify reliable predictions on a large unlabeled video dataset, and promote these instances to the training set and repeat. Unlike standard self-training, we add crops, which lets confident full-body predictions (identified via [5]) provide a training signal for challenging crops. This approach requires no extra annotations and takes < 30k iterations of additional training (with total time < 8 h on a single RTX2080 Ti GPU).

We demonstrate the effectiveness of our approach on two human 3D mesh recovery techniques – HMR [24] and CMR [26] – and evaluate on four consumer-video datasets – VLOG [14], Instructions [2], YouCookII [59], and Cross-Task [62]. To lay the groundwork for future work, we annotate keypoints on 13k frames across these datasets and provide a framework for evaluation in and out of images. In addition to keypoints, we evaluate using human-study experiments. Our experiments in Sect. 4 demonstrate the effectiveness of our method

Fig. 2. Partially Visible Humans. Consumer video, seen in datasets like VLOG [14], Instructions [62], or YouCook2 [59], is considerably different from canonical human pose datasets. Most critically, only part of a person is typically visible within an image, making pose estimation challenging. In fact, all keypoints are only visible in 4% of VLOG test set images, while all leg joints are not visible 61% of the time. Four of the most common configurations of visible body parts are listed above.

compared to off-the-shelf mesh recovery and training on crops from a standard image dataset (MPII). Our approach improves PCK both *in-image* and *out-of-image* across methods and datasets: e.g., after training on VLOG, our approach leads to a 20.7% improvement on YouCookII over off-the-shelf HMR and a 10.9% improvement over HMR trained on crops (with gains of 36.4% and 19.1% on out-of-image keypoints) Perceptual judgments by annotators show similar gains: e.g., on Cross-Task, our proposed method improves the chance of a CMR output being rated as correct by 25.6% compared to off-the-shelf performance.

2   Related Work

Human Pose Estimation In the Wild: Human pose estimation has improved substantially in recent years due in part to improved methods for 2D [9,17,38, 51,56] and 3D [1,28,35,43,45,60] pose, which typically utilize deep networks as opposed to classic approaches such as deformable part models [7,10,12,58]. Performance of such pose models also relies critically on datasets [4,18,19,21, 30,34,37,48]. By utilizing annotated people *in-the-wild*, methods have moved toward understanding realistic, challenging settings, and become more robust to occlusion, setting, challenging pose, and scale variation [3,36,37,40,41,61].

However, these *in-the-wild* datasets still rarely encounter close, varied camera angles common in consumer Internet video, which can result in people being only partially within an image. Furthermore, images that do contain truncated people are sometimes filtered out [24]. As a result, the state-of-the-art on common benchmarks performs poorly in consumer videos. In this work, we utilize the unlabeled video dataset VLOG to improve in this setting.

3D Human Mesh Estimation: A 3D mesh is a rich representation of pose, which is employed for the method presented in this paper. Compared to keypoints, a mesh represents a clear understanding of a person's body invariant to global orientation and scale. A number of recent methods [6,24,27,42,52,55] build this mesh by learning to predict parametric human body models such as SMPL [31] or the closely-related Adam [23]. To increase training breadth, some of these methods train on 2D keypoints [24,42] and utilize a shape prior.

The HMR [24] model trains an adversarial prior with a variety of 2D keypoint datasets to demonstrate good performance *in-the-wild*, making it a strong candidate to extend to more challenging viewpoints. CMR [26] also produces strong results using a similar *in-the-wild* training methodology. We therefore apply our method to both models, rapidly improving performance on Internet video.

Understanding Partially-Observed People: Much of the prior work studying global understanding of partially-observed people comes from ego-centric action recognition [11,29,33,47,49]. Methods often use observations of the same human body-parts between images, typically hands [11,29,33], to classify global activity. In contrast, our goal is to predict pose, from varied viewpoints.

Some recent work explores ego-centric pose estimation. Recent setups use cameras mounted in a variety of clever ways, such as chest [20,46], bike helmet [44], VR goggles [50], and hat [57]. However, these methods rely on camera always being in the same spot relative to the human to make predictions. On the other hand, our method attains global understanding of the body by training on entire people to reason about unseen joints as it encounters less visible images.

Prior work also focuses on pose estimation specifically in cases of occlusion [15,16]. While this setting requires inference of non-visible joints, it does not face the same scale variation occurring in consumer video, which can contain people much larger than the image. Some recent work directly addresses truncation. Vosoughi and Amer predict truncated 3D keypoints on random crops of Human3.6M [54]. In concurrence with our work, Exemplar Fine-Tuning [22] uses upper-body cropping to improve performance in Internet video [34]. Nevertheless, consumer Internet video (Fig. 2) faces more extreme truncation. We show cropping alone is not sufficient for this setting; rather cropping *and* self-training on confident video frames provides the best results.

3 Approach

Our goal is the ability to reconstruct a full human-body 3D mesh from an image of part or all of a person in consumer video data. We demonstrate how to do this using a simple but effective self-training approach that we apply to two 3D human mesh recovery models, HMR [24] and CMR [26]. Both systems can predict a mesh by regressing SMPL [31] parameters from which a human mesh can be generated, but work poorly on this consumer video data.

Our method, shown in Fig. 3, adapts each method to this challenging setting of partial visibility by sequentially self-training on confident mesh and keypoint

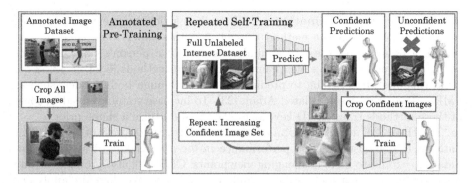

Fig. 3. Our method adapts human pose models to truncated settings by self-training on cropped images. After pre-training using an annotated pose dataset, the method applies small translations to an unlabeled video dataset and selects predictions with consistent pose predictions across translations as pseudo-ground-truth. Repeating the process increases the training set to include more truncated people.

predictions. Starting with a model trained on crops from a labeled dataset, the system makes predictions on video data. We then identify confident predictions using the equivariance technique of Bahat and Shakhnarovich [5]. Finally, using the confident examples as pseudo-ground-truth, the model is trained to map crops of the confident images to the full-body inferences, and the process of identifying confident images and folding them into a training set is continued. Our only assumption is that we can identify frames containing a single person (needed for training HMR/CMR). In this paper, we annotate this for simplicity but assume this can be automated via an off-the-shelf detection system.

3.1 Base Models

Our base models [24,26] use SMPL [31], which is a differentiable, generative model of human 3D meshes. SMPL maps parameters Θ to output a triangulated mesh $\mathbf{Y}$ with $N = 6980$ vertices. Θ consists of parameters $[\boldsymbol{\theta}, \boldsymbol{\beta}, \mathbf{R}, \mathbf{t}, \mathbf{s}]$: joint rotations $\boldsymbol{\theta} \in \mathbb{R}^{69}$, shape parameters $\boldsymbol{\beta} \in \mathbb{R}^{10}$, global rotation $\mathbf{R}$, global translation $\mathbf{t}$, and global scale $\mathbf{s}$. We abstract each base model as a function f mapping an image I to a SMPL parameter Θ. As described in [24], the SMPL parameters can be used to yield a set of 2D projected keypoints $\mathbf{x}$.

Our training process closely builds off the original methods: we minimize a sum of losses on a combination of projected 2D keypoints $\hat{\mathbf{x}}$, predicted vertices $\hat{\mathbf{Y}}$, and SMPL parameters $\hat{\Theta}$. The most important distinctions are, we assume we have access to SMPL parameters Θ for each image, and we train on all annotated keypoints, even if they are outside the image. We describe salient differences between the models and original training below.

HMR [24]: Kanazawa *et al.* use MoSh [32,53] for their ground truth SMPL loss. However, this data is not available in most images, and thus the model relies primarily on keypoint loss. Instead, we train directly on predicted SMPL rotations,

available in all images; we find L_1 loss works best. To encourage our network to adapt to poses of new datasets, we do not use a discriminator loss. We also supervise $(\mathbf{t}, \mathbf{s})$, though experiments indicated this did not impact performance (less than 1% difference on keypoint results). The loss for a single datapoint is:

$$L = \left\| [\boldsymbol{\theta}, \mathbf{R}, \boldsymbol{\beta}, \mathbf{t}, \mathbf{s}] - [\hat{\boldsymbol{\theta}}, \hat{\mathbf{R}}, \hat{\boldsymbol{\beta}}, \hat{\mathbf{t}}, \hat{\mathbf{s}}] \right\|_1 + \| \mathbf{x} - \hat{\mathbf{x}} \|_1 \tag{1}$$

CMR [26]: CMR additionally regresses predicted mesh, and has intermediate losses after the Graph CNN. We do not change their loss, other than by always using 3D supervision and out-of-image keypoints. It is distinct from our HMR loss as it uses L_2 loss on keypoints and SMPL parameters, and converts $\boldsymbol{\theta}$ and $\mathbf{R}$ to rotation matrices for training [39], although they note conversion does not change quantitative results. The loss for a single datapoint is:

$$L = \left\| [\boldsymbol{\theta}, \mathbf{R}] - [\hat{\boldsymbol{\theta}}, \hat{\mathbf{R}}] \right\|_2^2 + \lambda \left\| \boldsymbol{\beta} - \hat{\boldsymbol{\beta}} \right\|_2^2 + \| \mathbf{x} - \hat{\mathbf{x}} \|_2^2 + \left\| \mathbf{Y} - \hat{\mathbf{Y}} \right\|_1 \tag{2}$$

such that $\lambda = 0.1$, each norm is reduced by its number of elements, and keypoint and mesh losses are also applied after the Graph CNN. While Kolotouros *et al.* train the Graph CNN before the MLP, we find the pretrained model trains well with both losses simultaneously.

3.2   Iterative Adaptation to Partial Visibility

Our approach follows a standard self-training approach to semi-supervised learning. In self-training, one begins with an **initial model** $f_0 : \mathcal{X} \rightarrow \mathcal{Y}$ as well as a collection of unlabeled data $U = \{u : u \in \mathcal{X}\}$. Here, the inputs are images, outputs SMPL parameters, and model either CMR or HMR. The key idea is to use the inferences of each round's model f_i to produce labeled data for training the next round's model f_{i+1}. More specifically, at each iteration t, the model f_t is applied to each element of U, and a **confident prediction subset** $C \subseteq U$ is identified. Then, predictions of model f on elements are treated as new ground-truth for training the next round model f_{i+1}. In standard self-training, the new training set is the original unlabeled inputs and model outputs, or $\{(c, f_i(c)) : c \in C\}$. In our case, this would never learn to handle more cropped people, and the training set is thus augmented with **transformations** of the confident samples, or $\{(t(c), t(f_i(c))) : c \in C, t \in T\}$ for some set of crops T. The new model f_{i+1} is **retrained** and the process is repeated until convergence. We now describe more concretely what we mean by each bolded point.

Initial Model: We begin by training the pretrained HMR and CMR models on MPII (Fig. 3, left) such that we apply cropping transformations to images and keypoints. SMPL predictions from full images are used for supervision, and are typically very accurate considering past training on this set. This training scheme is the same as that used for self-training (Fig. 3, right), except we use MPII ground truth keypoints instead of pseudo-ground truths.

Identifying Confident Predictions: In order to apply self-training, we need to be able to find confident outputs of each of our SMPL-regressing models. Unfortunately, it is difficult to extract confidence from regression models because there is no natural and automatically-produced confidence measure unlike in classification where measures like entropy provide a starting point.

We therefore turn to an empirical result of Bahat and Shakhnarovich [5] that invariance to image transformations is often indicative of confidence in neural networks. Put simply, confident predictions of networks tend to be more invariant to small transformations (e.g., a shift) than non-confident predictions. We apply this technique in our setting by examining changes of parameters after applying small translational jitter: we apply the model f to copies of the image with the center jittered 10 and 20 pixels and look at joint rotation parameters θ. We compute the variance of each joint rotation parameter across the jittered samples, then average the variances across joints. For HMR, we define confident samples as ones with a variance below 0.005 (chosen empirically). For CMR, for simplicity, we ensure that we have the same acceptance rate as HMR of 12%; this results in a similar variance threshold of 0.004.

Applying Transformations: The set of inputs and confident pseudo-label outputs that can be used for self-training is not enough. We therefore apply a family of crops that mimic empirical frequencies found in consumer video data. Specifically, crops consist of 23% most of body visible, 29% legs not visible, 10% head not visible, and 22% only hands or arms visible. Examples of these categories are shown in Fig. 2. Although proportions were chosen empirically from VLOG, other consumer Internet video datasets considered [2,59,62] exhibit similar visibility patterns, and we empirically show that our results generalize.

Retraining: Finally, given the set of samples of crops of confident images and corresponding full bodies, we retrain each model.

3.3   Implementation Details

Our cropping procedure and architecture is detailed in supplemental for both HMR [24] and CMR [26]; we initialize both with weights pretrained on *in-the-wild* data. On MPII, we continue using the same learning rate and optimizer used by each model (1e-5 for HMR, 3e-4 for CMR, both use Adam [25]) until validation loss converges. Training converges within 20k iterations in both cases.

Next, we identify confident predictions as detailed above on VLOG. We use the subset of the hand-contact state dataset containing single humans, which consists of 132k frames in the train + validation set. We note we could have used a simple classifier to filter by visible people in a totally unlabeled setting. Our resulting confident train + validation set is 15k images. We perform the same cropping transformations as in MPII, and continue training with the same parameters. Validation loss converges within 10k iterations. We repeat this semi-supervised component one additional time, and the new train + validation set is of approximately size 40k. Training again takes less than 10k iterations.

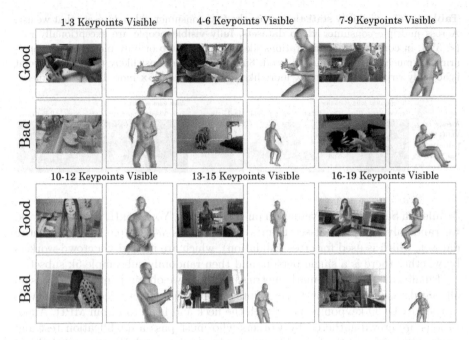

Fig. 4. Randomly sampled positive and negative predictions by number of keypoints visible, as identified by workers. Images with fewer keypoints visible are typically more difficult, and our method improves most significantly in these cases (Table 2). (Color figure online)

4 Experiments

We now describe a set of experiments done to investigate the following experimental questions: (1) how well do current 3D human mesh recovery systems work on consumer internet video? (2) can we improve the performance of these systems, both on an absolute basis and in comparison to alternate simple models that do not self-train? We answer these questions by evaluating the performance of a variety of adaptation methods applied to both HMR [24] and CMR [26] on four independent datasets of Internet videos. After introducing the datasets (Sect. 4.1) and experimental setup (Sect. 4.2), we describe experiments on VLOG (Sect. 4.3), which we use for our self-training video adaptation. To test the generality of our conclusions, we then repeat the same experiments on three other consumer datasets without any retraining (Sect. 4.4). We validate our choice of confidence against two other methods in (Sect. 4.5) (Fig. 4).

4.1 Datasets and Annotations

We rely on four datasets of consumer video from the Internet for evaluating our method: VLOG [14], Instructions [2], YouCookII [59], and Cross-Task [62]. Evaluation on VLOG takes place on a random 5k image subset of the test set

Table 1. Joint visibility statistics across the four consumer video datasets that we use. Across multiple consumer video datasets, fully visible people are exceptionally rare (< 3%), in contrast to configurations like an upper torso or only pieces of someone's arms, or much of a body but no head. Surprisingly, the most likely to be visible joint is actually wrists, more than 2× more likely than hips and 5× more likely than knees.

	Independent joint statistics							Joint joint statistics			
	Ankle	Knee	Hip	Wrist	Elbow	Neck + Should.	Head + Face	Fully Visible	Upper Torso	Only Arms	All But Head
Average	7.0	12.9	31.9	71.9	50.8	53.9	51.1	2.8	26.2	31.8	18.8
VLOG [14]	10.5	20.0	34.0	71.5	54.5	61.0	53.3	4.0	32.0	21.0	14.0
Instructions [2]	14.0	24.5	32.5	73.5	52.0	44.7	43.3	5.0	14.0	32.0	18.0
YouCook II [59]	0.0	1.0	30.0	71.0	45.5	53.7	52.7	0.0	28.0	39.0	24.0
Cross-Task [62]	3.5	6.0	31.0	71.5	51.0	56.3	55.0	2.0	31.0	32.0	19.0

detailed in Sect. 3.3. For evaluation on Instructions, YouCookII, and Cross-Task, we randomly sample test-set frames (Instructions we sample from the entire dataset, which is used for cross-validation), which are filtered via crowd-workers by whether there is a single person, and then randomly subsample 5k subset.

Finally, to enable automatic metrics like PCK, we obtain joint annotations on all four datasets. We annotate keypoints for the 19 joints reprojected from HMR, or the 17 COCO keypoints along with the neck and head top from MPII. Annotations are crowd-gathered by workers who must pass a qualification test and are monitored by sentinels, and is detailed in supplemental. We show statistics of these joints in Table 1, which show quantitatively the lack of visible keypoints. In stark contrast to canonical pose datasets, the head is often not visible. Instead, the most frequently visible joints are wrists.

4.2   Experimental Setup

We evaluate our approaches as well as a set of baselines that test concrete hypotheses using two styles of metrics: 2D keypoint metrics, specifically PCK measured on both in-image joints as well as via out-of-image joints (via evaluation on crops); and 3D Mesh Human Judgments, where crowd workers evaluate outputs of the systems on an absolute or relative basis.

2D Keypoint Metrics: Our first four metrics compare predicted keypoints with annotated ones. Our base metric is PCK @ 0.5 [4], the percent of keypoints within a threshold of 0.5 times head segment, the most commonly reported threshold on MPII. Our first metric, *Uncropped PCK*, is performance on images where the head is visible to define PCK. We choose PCK since head segment length is typically undistorted in our data, as opposed to alternates where identifying a stable threshold is difficult: PCP [13] is affected by our high variance in body 3D orientation, and PCPm [4] by high inter-image scale variation.

PCK is defined only on images where the head is visible (a shortcoming we address with human judgment experiments). In addition to being a subset, these frames are not representative of typical visibility patterns in consumer video (as shown in Fig. 2 and Table 1), so we evaluate on crops. We sample crops to closely

match the joint visibility statistics of each entire annotated test set (detailed in supplemental). We can then evaluate *In-Image PCK*, or PCK on joints in the cropped image. Because the original image contains precise annotations of joints not visible in the crop, we can also evaluate *Out-of-Image PCK*, or PCK on joints outside the crop. *Total PCK* is PCK on both. We calculate PCK on each image and then average over images. Not doing this gives significantly more weight to images with many keypoints in them, and ignores images with few.

3D Mesh Human Judgments: While useful, keypoint metrics like PCK suffer from a number of shortcomings. They can only be evaluated on a subset of images: this ranges from 37% of images from Instructions to 50% of images in Cross-Task. Moreover, these subsets are not necessarily representative, as argued before. Finally, in the case of out-of-image keypoints, PCK does not distinguish between plausible predictions that happen to be incorrect according to the fairly exacting PCK metric, and implausible guesses. We therefore turn to human judgments, measuring results in absolute and comparative terms.

Mesh Score/Absolute Judgment: We show workers an image and single mesh, and ask them to classify it as largely correct or not (precise definition in supplemental), from which we can calculate Percentage of Good Meshes: the proportion of predicted meshes workers consider good. Predictions from all methods are aggregated and randomly ordered, so are evaluated by the same pool of workers.

Relative Judgment: As a verification, we also perform A/B testing on HMR predictions. We follow a standard A/B paradigm and show human workers an image and two meshes in random order and ask which matches the image better with the option of a tie; when workers cannot agree, we report this as a tie.

Baselines: We compare our proposed model with two baselines to answer a few scientific questions.

Base Method: We compare with the base method being used, either HMR [24] or CMR [26], without any further training past their original pose dataset training sets. This both quantifies how well 3D pose estimation methods work on consumer footage and identifies when our approach improves over this model.

Crops: We also compare with a model trained on MPII Crops (including losses on out-of-image keypoints). This tests whether simply training the model on crops is sufficient compared to also self-training on Internet video.

4.3   Results on VLOG

Our first experiments are on VLOG [14], the dataset that we train on. We begin by showing qualitative results, comparing our method with a number of baselines in Fig. 5. While effective on full-body cases, the initial methods perform poorly on truncated people. Training on MPII Crops prepares the model to better identify truncated people, but self-training on Internet video provides the model

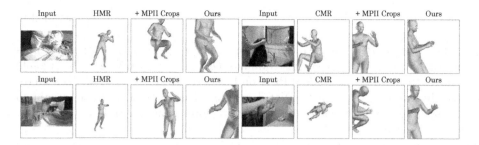

Fig. 5. Selected comparison of results on VLOG [14]. We demonstrate sequential improvement between ablations on HMR (left) and CMR (right). Training on MPII Crops prepares the model for truncation, while self-training provides context clues it can associate with full-body pose, leading to better predictions, particularly outside images.

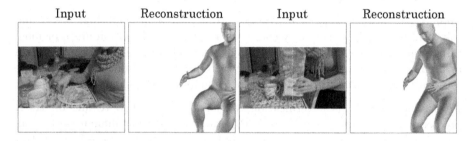

Fig. 6. Shots focused on hands occur often in consumer video. While the visible body may look similar across instances, full-body pose can vary widely, meaning keypoint detection is not sufficient for full-body reasoning. After self-training, our method learns to differentiate activity such as standing and sitting given similar visible body.

context clues it can associate with people largely outside of images—some of the largest improvements occur when key indicators such as sinks and tables (Fig. 5) are present. In Fig. 6, the model identifies distinct leg and head poses outside of images given minute difference in visible pose and appearance.

Human 3D Mesh Judgments: We then consider human 3D Mesh Judgments, which quantitatively confirm the trends observed in the qualitative results. We report the frequency that each method's predictions were rated as largely correct on the test set, broken down by the number of visible joints, in Table 2. Our approach *always* outperforms using the base method, and only is outperformed by Crops on full or near-full keypoint visibility. These performance gains are particularly strong in the less-visible cases compared to both the base method and crops. For instance, by using our technique, HMR's performance in highly truncated configurations (1–3 Keypoints Visible) is improved by 23.7 points compared to the base and 11.0 compared to using crops.

Table 2. Percentage of Good Meshes on VLOG, as judged by human workers. We report results on *All* images and examine results by number of visible keypoints.

| | HMR [24] | | | | | | | CMR [26] | | | | | | |
| | By # of visible joints | | | | | | | By # of visible joints | | | | | | |
	1–3	4–6	7–9	10–12	13–15	16–19	All	1–3	4–6	7–9	10–12	13–15	16–19	All
Base	19.2	52.7	70.1	80.1	85.2	82.1	60.6	13.6	37.9	53.4	68.0	79.0	74.8	51.1
Crops	31.9	68.7	76.9	86.8	91.0	**85.9**	69.4	33.7	65.8	75.7	82.5	88.4	**80.9**	67.5
Full	**42.9**	**72.1**	**82.8**	**89.6**	**92.3**	83.1	**73.9**	**40.9**	**71.2**	0.2	**86.0**	**89.2**	79.5	**71.2**

Table 3. PCK @ 0.5 on VLOG. We compute PCK on the 1.8k image VLOG test set, in which the head is fully visible, as *Uncr. Total*. These images are then *Cropped* to emulate the keypoint visibility statistics of the entire dataset, on which we can calculate PCK *In* and *Out* of cropped images, and their union *Total*.

| Method | HMR [24] | | | | CMR [26] | | | |
| | Cropped | | | Uncr | Cropped | | | Uncr |
	Total	In	Out	Total	Total	In	Out	Total
Base	48.6	65.2	14.7	68.5	36.1	50.2	13.2	49.5
Crops	51.6	**65.3**	24.2	**68.8**	47.3	58.1	26.2	**59.5**
Ours	**55.9**	61.6	**38.9**	68.7	**50.9**	**60.3**	**34.6**	58.1

2D Keypoints: We next evaluate keypoints, reporting results for all four variants in Table 3. On cropped evaluations that match the actual distribution of consumer video, our approach produces substantial improvement, increasing performance overall for both HMR and CMR. On the *uncropped images* where the head of the person is visible (which is closer to distributions seen on e.g., MPII), our approach remains approximately the same for HMR and actually improves by 8.6% for CMR. We note our method underperforms within cropped images on HMR. There are two reasons for this: first, supervising on out-of-image keypoints encourages predictions outside of images, sacrificing marginal in-image performance gains. Second, the cost of supervising on self-generated keypoints is reduced precision in familiar settings. Nevertheless, CMR improves enough using semi-supervision to still increase on in-image-cropped keypoints.

4.4 Generalization Evaluations

We now test generalization to other datasets. Specifically, we take the approaches evaluated in the previous section and apply them directly to Instructions [2], YouCookII [59], and Cross-Task [62] *with no further training*. This tests whether the additional learning is simply overfitting to VLOG. We show qualitative results of our system applied to these datasets in Fig. 7. Although the base models also work poorly on these consumer videos, simply training on VLOG is sufficient to produce more reasonable outputs.

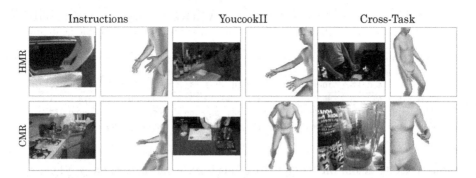

Fig. 7. Results on External Datasets. While our method trains on Internet Vlogs, performance generalizes to other Internet video consisting of a variety of activities and styles; specifically instructional videos and cooking videos.

Table 4. Percentage of Good Meshes on External Datasets, as judged by human workers. We report results on *All* images and in the case of few visible keypoints.

	Instructions [2]				YouCook II [59]				Cross-Task [62]			
	HMR		CMR		HMR		CMR		HMR		CMR	
	1–6	All	1–6	All	1–6	All	1–6	All	1–6	All	1–6	All
Base	10.7	42.2	7.4	30.9	15.9	54.6	8.5	41.8	13.6	52.6	7.7	37.9
Crops	25.5	53.8	28.8	52.5	24.9	60.8	24.3	60.2	22.3	59.0	21.5	57.7
Full	**37.3**	**60.5**	**35.2**	**57.0**	**43.4**	**71.5**	**39.9**	**68.5**	**37.0**	**68.1**	**31.0**	**63.5**

3D Mesh Judgments: This is substantiated quantitatively across the full dataset since, as shown in Table 4, HMR and CMR perform poorly out-of-the-box. Our approach, however, can systematically improve their performance without any additional pose annotations: gains over the best baseline range from 4.5% points (CMR tested on Instructions) to 10.7% points (HMR tested on YouCookII). Our outputs are systematically preferred by humans in A/B tests (Table 5): our approach is 4.6×–8.9× more likely to be picked as preferable compared to the base system than the reverse, and similarly 2.4×–7. × 8 more likely to be picked as preferable to crops than the reverse.

2D Keypoints: Finally, we evaluate PCK. Our approach produces strong performance gains on two out of the three datasets (YouCookII and Cross-Task), while its performance is more mixed on Instructions *relative to MPII Crops*. We hypothesize the relatively impressive performance of MPII Crops is due to 40% of this dataset consisting of car mechanical fixes. These videos frequently feature people bending down, for instance while replacing car tires. Similar activities such as swimming are more common in MPII than VLOG. The corresponding array of outdoor scenes also provides less context to accurately infer out-of-image body parts. Yet, strong human judgment results (Table 4 and 5) indicate training on VLOG improves coarse prediction quality, even in this setting.

Table 5. A/B testing on All Datasets, using HMR. For each entry we report how frequently (%) the row wins/ties/loses to the column. For example, row 2, column 6 shows that our full method is preferred 47% of the time over a method trained on MPII Crops, and MPII Crops is preferred over the full method just 6% of the time

Method	VLOG [14]		Instructions [2]		YouCookII [59]		Cross-Task [62]	
	Base	Crops	Base	Crops	Base	Crops	Base	Crops
Crops	53/28/19	–	56/28/16	–	49/35/16	–	46/39/15	
Full	63/23/15	45/43/12	65/21/14	40/43/17	62/32/7	47/47/6	57/36/7	41/53/7

Table 6. PCK @ 0.5 on External Datasets. We compute PCK in test set images in which the head is fully visible. These images are then cropped to emulate the keypoint visibility statistics of the entire dataset, on which we can calculate PCK on predictions outside the image.

Method	Instructions [2]				YouCookII [59]				Cross-Task [62]			
	HMR [24]		CMR [26]		HMR [24]		CMR [26]		HMR [24]		CMR [26]	
	Total	Out	Total	Out	Total	Out	Total	Out	Total	Out	Total	Out
Base	42.0	19.6	32.8	17.1	56.0	27.7	44.0	26.9	56.1	20.3	44.1	19.8
MPII Crops	**50.6**	33.7	**47.9**	**33.9**	65.8	45.0	65.0	48.6	62.9	32.5	61.9	38.2
Ours	48.7	**36.4**	44.8	33.7	**76.7**	**64.1**	**70.7**	**58.5**	**74.5**	**57.2**	**66.9**	**47.9**

4.5   Additional Comparisons

To validate our choice of confidence, we consider two alternative criteria for selecting confident images: agreement between HMR and CMR SMPL parameters, and agreement between HMR and Openpose [8] keypoints. For fair comparison, implementations closely match our confidence method; full details and tables are in supplemental. Compared to both, our system does about the same or better across datasets, but does not require running two systems. Agreement with CMR yields cropped keypoint accuracy of 1.5–2.7% lower, and uncropped accuracy of 0.6% higher – 0.6% lower. Agreement with Openpose is stronger on uncropped images: 0.3%–2.4% higher, but weaker on uncropped: 1.3%–3.5% lower.

We additionally consider performance of our model to the model after only the first iteration of VLOG training, through A/B testing (full table in supplemental). In all four datasets, the final method is 1.7×–2.8× more likely to be picked as preferable to the model after only one round than the reverse (Table 6).

5   Discussion

We presented a simple but effective approach for adapting 3D mesh recovery models to the challenging world of Internet videos. In the process, we showed that current methods appear to work poorly on Internet videos, presenting a new opportunity. Interestingly, while CMR outperforms HMR on Human3.6M, the opposite is true on this new data, suggesting that performance gains on standard pose estimation datasets do not always translate into performance gains on Internet videos. Thanks to the new annotations across the four video datasets, however, we can quantify this. These keypoint metrics are validated as a measure for prediction quality given general agreement with human judgement metrics in extensive testing. We see getting systems to work on consumer videos, including both the visible and out-of-image parts, as an interesting and impactful challenge and believe our simple method provides a strong baseline for work in this area.

Acknowledgments. This work was supported by the DARPA Machine Common Sense Program. We thank Dimitri Zhukov, Jean-Baptiste Alayrac, and Luowei Zhou, for allowing sharing of frames from their datasets, and Angjoo Kanazawa and Nikos Kolotouros for polished and easily extended code. Thanks to the members of Fouhey AI Lab and Karan Desai for the great suggestions!

References

1. Akhter, I., Black, M.J.: Pose-conditioned joint angle limits for 3D human pose reconstruction. In: CVPR (2015)
2. Alayrac, J.B., Bojanowski, P., Agrawal, N., Laptev, I., Sivic, J., Lacoste-Julien, S.: Unsupervised learning from narrated instruction videos. In: CVPR (2016)
3. Alp Güler, R., Neverova, N., Kokkinos, I.: Densepose: dense human pose estimation in the wild. In: CVPR (2018)
4. Andriluka, M., Pishchulin, L., Gehler, P., Schiele, B.: 2D human pose estimation: new benchmark and state of the art analysis. In: CVPR (2014)
5. Bahat, Y., Shakhnarovich, G.: Confidence from invariance to image transformations. arXiv preprint arXiv:1804.00657 (2018)
6. Bogo, F., Kanazawa, A., Lassner, C., Gehler, P., Romero, J., Black, M.J.: Keep it SMPL: automatic estimation of 3D human pose and shape from a single image. In: Leibe, B., Matas, J., Sebe, N., Welling, M. (eds.) ECCV 2016. LNCS, vol. 9909, pp. 561–578. Springer, Cham (2016). https://doi.org/10.1007/978-3-319-46454-1_34
7. Bourdev, L., Malik, J.: Poselets: body part detectors trained using 3D human pose annotations. In: ICCV (2009)
8. Cao, Z., Hidalgo, G., Simon, T., Wei, S.E., Sheikh, Y.: Openpose: real-time multi-person 2D pose estimation using part affinity fields. arXiv preprint arXiv:1812.08008 (2018)
9. Cao, Z., Simon, T., Wei, S.E., Sheikh, Y.: Realtime multi-person 2D pose estimation using part affinity fields. In: CVPR (2017)
10. Desai, C., Ramanan, D.: Detecting actions, poses, and objects with relational phraselets. In: Fitzgibbon, A., Lazebnik, S., Perona, P., Sato, Y., Schmid, C. (eds.) ECCV 2012. LNCS, vol. 7575, pp. 158–172. Springer, Heidelberg (2012). https://doi.org/10.1007/978-3-642-33765-9_12

11. Fathi, A., Farhadi, A., Rehg, J.M.: Understanding egocentric activities. In: ICCV, pp. 407–414 (2011)
12. Felzenszwalb, P., McAllester, D., Ramanan, D.: A discriminatively trained, multi-scale, deformable part model. In: CVPR (2008)
13. Ferrari, V., Marin-Jimenez, M., Zisserman, A.: Progressive search space reduction for human pose estimation. In: CVPR (2008)
14. Fouhey, D.F., Kuo, W., Efros, A.A., Malik, J.: From lifestyle VLOGs to everyday interactions. In: CVPR (2018)
15. Ghiasi, G., Yang, Y., Ramanan, D., Fowlkes, C.C.: Parsing occluded people. In: CVPR (2014)
16. Haque, A., Peng, B., Luo, Z., Alahi, A., Yeung, S., Fei-Fei, L.: Towards viewpoint invariant 3D human pose estimation. In: Leibe, B., Matas, J., Sebe, N., Welling, M. (eds.) ECCV 2016. LNCS, vol. 9905, pp. 160–177. Springer, Cham (2016). https://doi.org/10.1007/978-3-319-46448-0_10
17. Insafutdinov, E., Pishchulin, L., Andres, B., Andriluka, M., Schiele, B.: DeeperCut: a deeper, stronger, and faster multi-person pose estimation model. In: Leibe, B., Matas, J., Sebe, N., Welling, M. (eds.) ECCV 2016. LNCS, vol. 9910, pp. 34–50. Springer, Cham (2016). https://doi.org/10.1007/978-3-319-46466-4_3
18. Ionescu, C., Li, F., Sminchisescu, C.: Latent structured models for human pose estimation. In: ICCV (2011)
19. Ionescu, C., Papava, D., Olaru, V., Sminchisescu, C.: Human3.6m: large scale datasets and predictive methods for 3D human sensing in natural environments. TPAMI **36**, 1325–1339 (2013)
20. Jiang, H., Grauman, K.: Seeing invisible poses: estimating 3D body pose from egocentric video. In: CVPR (2017)
21. Johnson, S., Everingham, M.: Clustered pose and nonlinear appearance models for human pose estimation. In: BVMC (2010)
22. Joo, H., Neverova, N., Vedaldi, A.: Exemplar fine-tuning for 3D human pose fitting towards in-the-wild 3D human pose estimation. arXiv preprint arXiv:2004.03686 (2020)
23. Joo, H., Simon, T., Sheikh, Y.: Total capture: a 3D deformation model for tracking faces, hands, and bodies. In: CVPR (2018)
24. Kanazawa, A., Black, M.J., Jacobs, D.W., Malik, J.: End-to-end recovery of human shape and pose. In: CVPR (2018)
25. Kingma, D.P., Ba, J.: Adam: A method for stochastic optimization (2014)
26. Kolotouros, N., Pavlakos, G., Daniilidis, K.: Convolutional mesh regression for single-image human shape reconstruction. In: CVPR (2019)
27. Lassner, C., Romero, J., Kiefel, M., Bogo, F., Black, M.J., Gehler, P.V.: Unite the people: closing the loop between 3D and 2D human representations. In: CVPR (2017)
28. Lee, H.J., Chen, Z.: Determination of 3D human body postures from a single view. Comput. Vis. Graph. Image Process. **30**(2), 148–168 (1985)
29. Li, Y., Ye, Z., Rehg, J.M.: Delving into egocentric actions. In: CVPR (2015)
30. Lin, T.Y., et al.: Microsoft COCO: common objects in context. In: Fleet, D., Pajdla, T., Schiele, B., Tuytelaars, T. (eds.) ECCV 2014. LNCS, vol. 8693, pp. 740–755. Springer, Cham (2014). https://doi.org/10.1007/978-3-319-10602-1_48
31. Loper, M., Mahmood, N., Romero, J., Pons-Moll, G., Black, M.J.: SMPL: a skinned multi-person linear model. ACM Trans. Graphics (Proc. SIGGRAPH Asia) **34**(6), 1–16 (2015)
32. Loper, M., Mahmood, N., Black, M.J.: Mosh: motion and shape capture from sparse markers. ACM Trans. Graph. (TOG) **33**(6), 220 (2014)

33. Ma, M., Fan, H., Kitani, K.M.: Going deeper into first-person activity recognition. In: CVPR (2016)
34. von Marcard, T., Henschel, R., Black, M.J., Rosenhahn, B., Pons-Moll, G.: Recovering accurate 3D human pose in the wild using IMUS and a moving camera. In: Proceedings of the European Conference on Computer Vision (ECCV), pp. 601–617 (2018)
35. Martinez, J., Hossain, R., Romero, J., Little, J.J.: A simple yet effective baseline for 3D human pose estimation. In: CVPR (2017)
36. Mehta, D., et al.: Monocular 3D human pose estimation in the wild using improved cnn supervision. In: 2017 International Conference on 3D Vision (3DV), pp. 506–516. IEEE (2017)
37. Mehta, D., et al.: Vnect: real-time 3D human pose estimation with a single RGB camera. ACM Trans. Graph. (TOG) **36**(4), 44 (2017)
38. Newell, A., Yang, K., Deng, J.: Stacked hourglass networks for human pose estimation. In: Leibe, B., Matas, J., Sebe, N., Welling, M. (eds.) ECCV 2016. LNCS, vol. 9912, pp. 483–499. Springer, Cham (2016). https://doi.org/10.1007/978-3-319-46484-8_29
39. Omran, M., Lassner, C., Pons-Moll, G., Gehler, P., Schiele, B.: Neural body fitting: Unifying deep learning and model based human pose and shape estimation. In: 2018 international conference on 3D vision (3DV), pp. 484–494. IEEE (2018)
40. Papandreou, G., et al.: Towards accurate multi-person pose estimation in the wild. In: CVPR (2017)
41. Pavlakos, G., Zhou, X., Derpanis, K.G., Daniilidis, K.: Coarse-to-fine volumetric prediction for single-image 3D human pose. In: CVPR (2017)
42. Pavlakos, G., Zhu, L., Zhou, X., Daniilidis, K.: Learning to estimate 3D human pose and shape from a single color image. In: CVPR (2018)
43. Ramakrishna, V., Kanade, T., Sheikh, Y.: Reconstructing 3D human pose from 2D image landmarks. In: Fitzgibbon, A., Lazebnik, S., Perona, P., Sato, Y., Schmid, C. (eds.) ECCV 2012. LNCS, vol. 7575, pp. 573–586. Springer, Heidelberg (2012). https://doi.org/10.1007/978-3-642-33765-9_41
44. Rhodin, H., et al.: Egocap: egocentric marker-less motion capture with two fisheye cameras. ACM Trans. Graph. (TOG) **35**(6), 1–11 (2016)
45. Rogez, G., Schmid, C.: Mocap-guided data augmentation for 3D pose estimation in the wild. In: Advances in Neural Information Processing Systems (2016)
46. Rogez, G., Supancic, J.S., Ramanan, D.: First-person pose recognition using egocentric workspaces. In: CVPR (2015)
47. Ryoo, M.S., Matthies, L.: First-person activity recognition: what are they doing to me? In: CVPR (2013)
48. Sigal, L., Balan, A.O., Black, M.J.: Humaneva: synchronized video and motion capture dataset and baseline algorithm for evaluation of articulated human motion. Int. J. Comput. Vis. **87**(1–2), 4 (2010)
49. Sigurdsson, G.A., Varol, G., Wang, X., Farhadi, A., Laptev, I., Gupta, A.: Hollywood in homes: crowdsourcing data collection for activity understanding. In: Leibe, B., Matas, J., Sebe, N., Welling, M. (eds.) ECCV 2016. LNCS, vol. 9905, pp. 510–526. Springer, Cham (2016). https://doi.org/10.1007/978-3-319-46448-0_31
50. Tome, D., Peluse, P., Agapito, L., Badino, H.: xR-EgoPose: egocentric 3D human pose from an HMD camera. In: ICCV (2019)
51. Toshev, A., Szegedy, C.: Deeppose: human pose estimation via deep neural networks. In: CVPR (2014)
52. Tung, H.Y., Tung, H.W., Yumer, E., Fragkiadaki, K.: Self-supervised learning of motion capture. In: NeurIPS (2017)

53. Varol, G., et al.: Learning from synthetic humans. In: CVPR (2017)
54. Vosoughi, S., Amer, M.A.: Deep 3D human pose estimation under partial body presence. In: ICIP (2018)
55. Xiang, D., Joo, H., Sheikh, Y.: Monocular total capture: posing face, body, and hands in the wild. In: CVPR (2019)
56. Xiao, B., Wu, H., Wei, Y.: Simple baselines for human pose estimation and tracking. In: ECCV (2018)
57. Xu, W., Chatterjee, A., Zollhoefer, M., Rhodin, H., Fua, P., Seidel, H.P., Theobalt, C.: Mo 2 cap 2: real-time mobile 3D motion capture with a cap-mounted fisheye camera. IEEE Trans. Vis. Comput. Graph. **25**(5), 2093–2101 (2019)
58. Yang, Y., Ramanan, D.: Articulated pose estimation using flexible mixtures of parts. In: CVPR (2011)
59. Zhou, L., Xu, C., Corso, J.J.: Towards automatic learning of procedures from web instructional videos. In: AAAI (2018)
60. Zhou, X., Zhu, M., Leonardos, S., Derpanis, K.G., Daniilidis, K.: Sparseness meets deepness: 3D human pose estimation from monocular video. In: CVPR (2016)
61. Zhou, X., Huang, Q., Sun, X., Xue, X., Wei, Y.: Towards 3D human pose estimation in the wild: a weakly-supervised approach. In: ICCV (2017)
62. Zhukov, D., Alayrac, J.B., Cinbis, R.G., Fouhey, D., Laptev, I., Sivic, J.: Cross-task weakly supervised learning from instructional videos. In: CVPR (2019)

Reinforced Axial Refinement Network for Monocular 3D Object Detection

Lijie Liu[1], Chufan Wu[1], Jiwen Lu[1(✉)], Lingxi Xie[2], Jie Zhou[1], and Qi Tian[2]

[1] Department of Automation, State Key Lab of Intelligent Technologies and Systems, Beijing National Research Center for Information Science and Technology, Tsinghua University, Beijing, China
llj95luffy@gmail.com, chufanwu15@gmail.com, lujiwen@tsinghua.edu.cn, jzhou@tsinghua.edu.cn
[2] Huawei Inc., Shenzhen, China
198808xc@gmail.com, tian.qi1@huawei.com

Abstract. Monocular 3D object detection aims to extract the 3D position and properties of objects from a 2D input image. This is an ill-posed problem with a major difficulty lying in the information loss by depth-agnostic cameras. Conventional approaches sample 3D bounding boxes from the space and infer the relationship between the target object and each of them, however, the probability of effective samples is relatively small in the 3D space. To improve the efficiency of sampling, we propose to start with an initial prediction and refine it gradually towards the ground truth, with only one 3d parameter changed in each step. This requires designing a policy which gets a reward after several steps, and thus we adopt reinforcement learning to optimize it. The proposed framework, Reinforced Axial Refinement Network (RAR-Net), serves as a post-processing stage which can be freely integrated into existing monocular 3D detection methods, and improve the performance on the KITTI dataset with small extra computational costs.

Keywords: 3D Object Detection · Refinement · Reinforcement learning

1 Introduction

Over the past years, monocular 3D object detection has attracted increasing attentions in computer vision [6,7,19,39,42]. For many practical applications such as autonomous driving [2,8,14,15,18], augmented reality [1,37] and robotic grasping [21,27,40], high-precision 3D perception of surrounding objects is an essential prerequisite. Compared to 2D object detection, monocular 3D object detection can provide more useful information including orientation, dimension, and 3D spatial location. However, due to the increase in dimensionality, the 3D Intersection-over-Union (3D-IoU) evaluation criterion is much more strict than 2D-IoU, making monocular 3D object detection a very difficult problem.

ⓒ Springer Nature Switzerland AG 2020
A. Vedaldi et al. (Eds.): ECCV 2020, LNCS 12362, pp. 540–556, 2020.
https://doi.org/10.1007/978-3-030-58520-4_32

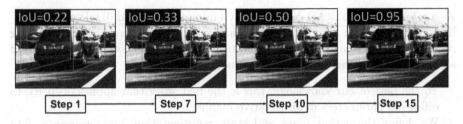

Fig. 1. Illustration of our idea that sequentially refines 3D detection using deep reinforcement learning. During the process, the 3D parameters are refined iteratively. In this example, we can see the trend that 3D-IoU gets improved as the 3D box gradually fits the object. Many intermediate steps are omitted here due to the limited space.

In some challenging scenarios, state-of-the-art methods can only achieve a 3D average precision (3D AP) of around 10% [3,26].

There have been a variety of efforts on detecting the objects in 3D space from a single image, and two popular trends are using geometry constraints [20,22,32] and depth estimation [28,35,44,47]. Due to the lack of real 3D cues, these methods often suffer from the problem of foreshortening (for distant objects, a tiny displacement on the image plane can lead to a large shift in the 3D space), and thus fail to achieve high 3D-IoU rates between detection results and ground-truth. To make up for the loss of 3D information, recently researchers propose to use a sampling-based method [25] to score the fitting degree between a sampled box and the object. However, in 3D space, the efficiency of sampling is very low and a randomly placed 3D box often has no overlap (3D-IoU is 0) to the target, which leads to inefficient learning. To this end, it is desirable to propose a method which can significantly increase the sampling efficiency.

In this paper, we ease this challenge by presenting a new framework called Reinforced Axial Refinement Network (RAR-Net), which, as illustrated in Fig. 1, iteratively refines the detected 3D object to the most probable direction. In this way, the probability of effective sampling (finding a positive example with a non-zero 3D-IoU) increases with iteration. This is a Markov Decision Process (MDP), which involves optimizing a strategy that gets a reward after multiple steps. We train the model using a Reinforcement Learning (RL) algorithm.

RAR-Net takes the current status as input, and outputs one refining action at a time. In each step, to provide the current detection information as auxiliary cues, we project it to an image of the same spatial resolution as the input image (each face of the box is painted in a specific color), concatenate this additional image to the original input, and feed the 6-channel input to the RAR-Net. This implicit way of embedding the 2D image and 3D information into the same feature space brings consistent accuracy gain. Overall, RAR-Net is optimized smoothly during training, in particular, with the help of abundant training data that are easily generated by simply jittering the ground-truth 3D box.

We conduct extensive experiments on the KITTI object orientation estimation benchmark, 3D object detection benchmark and bird's eye view benchmark.

As a refinement step, RAR-Net works well upon four popular 3D detection baselines, improving the base detection accuracy by a large margin, while requiring relatively small extra computational costs. This implies its potential in real-world scenarios. In summary, our contributions are three-fold:

- To the best of our knowledge, this is the first work that applies deep RL to refine 3D parameters in an iterative manner.
- We define the action space and state representation, and propose a data enhancement which embeds axial information and image contents.
- RAR-Net is a plug-and-play refinement module. Experimental results on the KITTI dataset demonstrate its effectiveness and efficiency.

2   Related Work

Monocular 3D Object Detection. Monocular 3D object detection aims to generate 3D bounding-boxes for objects from single RGB images. It is more challenging than 2D object detection due to the increased dimension and the absence of depth information. Early studies use handcrafted approaches trying to design efficient features for certain domain scenarios [9,13,33,34]. However, they suffer with the ability to generalize. Recently, researchers have developed deep learning based approaches aiming to solve this problem leveraging largely labeled data. One cut-in point is to use geometry constraints to make up for the lack of 3D information. Mousavian et al. [32] present MultiBin architecture for orientation regression and compute the 3D translation using tight constraint. Kundu et al. [20] propose a differentiable Render-and-Compare loss to supervise 3D parameters learning. Li et al. [22] utilize surface features to explore the 3D structure information of the object. Apart from these pure geometry-based methods, there are some other methods which turn to the depth estimation to recover 3D information. One straightforward way is to first predict the depth map using the depth estimation module and then perform 3D detection using the estimated 3D depth [26,28,44,47]. Another way is to infer instance depth instead of global depth map [35], which does not require additional training data. Recently, Liu et al. [25] propose to sample 3D bounding boxes from the space and introduce fitting degree to score the candidates. Brazil et al. [3] design a 3D region proposal network called M3D-RPN to generate 3D object proposals in the space. However, the performance of these methods is still limited because of the low efficiency of sampling in the 3D space. Our work jumps out of the limitation of trending object detection modules by iteratively refining the box to the ground-truth. It greatly solves the issue when network cannot directly regress to the goal detection and achieves better result.

Pose Refinement Methods. Our method belongs to the large category of coarse-to-fine learning [5,48,49], which refines visual recognition in an iterative manner. The approaches most relevant to ours are the iterative 3D object pose refinement approaches in [23,29]. Manhardt et al. [29] train a deep neural network to predict a translational and rotational update for 6D model tracking.

DeepIM [23] aims to iteratively refine estimated 6D pose of objects given the initial pose estimation. They also see the limitation of direct regression of images. However, these methods require the CAD model of the objects for fine correction and cannot be used in autonomous driving directly. In our case, we do not require complex CAD models and optimize the whole pose refinement process using deep RL.

Deep RL. RL aims at maximizing a reward signal instead of trying to generate a representational hidden state like traditional supervised learning problem [24, 31,43]. Deep RL is the method of incorporating RL with deep learning. Due to the distinguished feature of delayed reward and the massive power of deep learning, deep RL has been widely used on decision making in goal-oriented problems like object detection [4,30], deformable face tracking [16], interaction mining [12], object tracking [38,50] and video face recognition [36]. However, to our best knowledge, little work has been made in RL for pose refinement, especially in monocular 3D object detection. Our approach sees 3D parameter refinement problem as a multi-step decision-making problem by updating the 3D box using action from each step, which takes advantage of trial-and-error search in RL to achieve better result.

3   Approach

The monocular 3D object detection task requires solving a 9-Degree-of-Freedom (9-DoF) problem including dimension, orientation and location using a single RGB image as input. In this paper, we focus on improving the detection accuracy in the context of autonomous driving, where the object can only rotate around the Y axis, so the orientation has only 1-DoF. Although many excellent methods have been proposed so far, the monocular 3D object detection accuracy is still below satisfactory. So, we formulate the refinement problem as follows: given an initial estimation $(\hat{x}, \hat{y}, \hat{z}, \hat{h}, \hat{w}, \hat{l}, \hat{\theta})$, the refinement model predicts a set of displacement values $(\Delta x, \Delta y, \Delta z, \Delta h, \Delta w, \Delta l, \Delta \theta)$. Then, a new estimation is computed as $(\hat{x} + \Delta x, \hat{y} + \Delta y, \hat{z} + \Delta z, \hat{h} + \Delta h, \hat{w} + \Delta w, \hat{l} + \Delta l, \hat{\theta} + \Delta \theta)$ and fed into the refinement model again. After several iterations, the refinement model can generate more and more accurate estimates.

3.1   Baseline and the Curse of Sampling in 3D Space

Monocular 3D object detection is an ill-posed problem, *i.e.*, to recover 3D perception from 2D data. Although some powerful models have been proposed for 3D understanding [3,32,35], it is still difficult to build relationship between the depth-agnostic input image and the desired 3D location. To alleviate the information gap, researchers came up with an alternative idea that samples a number of 3D boxes from the space and asks the model to judge the IoU between the target object and each sampled box [25]. Such models, sometimes referred to as a fitting network, produced significant improvement under sufficient training data and the help of extra (*e.g.*, geometric) constraints.

However, we point out that the above sampling-based approaches suffer a difficulty in finding 'effective samples' (those having non-zero overlap with the target) especially in the testing stage. This is mainly caused by the increased dimensionality: the probability that a randomly placed 3D box has overlap to a pre-defined object is much lower than that in the 2D scenario. For example, if we use a Gaussian distribution with a deviation of 1 m, there is only a chance of 0.12 to place an effective sample on a car that is 5 m away from the initial detection result. This situation even deteriorates with the distance becomes larger. That being said, unless the initial detection is sufficiently accurate, the sampling efficiency can be very low.

3.2   Towards Higher Sampling Efficiency

To improve the sampling efficiency, a straightforward idea is to go towards a roughly correct direction and then perform sampling at a better place. For the same example of the car that is 5 m behind the detection result, if we move the current detection result towards the back direction for 2 m, the possibility of sampling a non-zero IoU box will increase to 0.63. Furthermore, with multi-step refinement, the 3D box can even converge to the ground-truth and sampling becomes unnecessary.

There are many moving options to choose, and we find that moving in only one direction at a time is the most efficient, because the training data collected in this way is the most concentrated (the output targets will not be scattered throughout the three-dimensional space). Most existing refinement models choose to optimize their objective function using one-step optimization, which learns to move from the initial estimate to the ground-truth directly. However, one-step optimization can barely achieve the global optimum, especially when there is more than one variable to be refined, because different variables can have an effect on each other. For example, refining the orientation first can help the model make better use of appearance information to refine to a more precise location. Two-stage cascaded refinement algorithm is another design choice, but it may bring considerable difficulties in algorithm design, especially in the way of defining different stages. Also, it is a challenging topic to prepare data for each stage, e.g. how to guarantee the training input fed into the second stage match the case in testing scenario.

Motivated by this concern, we choose to optimize the learning objective for the entire MDP instead of one step using RL-based framework which can support an arbitrary number of stages and the training procedure is elegant (few heuristic rules are required). Our approach starts from an initial estimate $(\hat{x}, \hat{y}, \hat{z}, \hat{h}, \hat{w}, \hat{l}, \hat{\theta})$, and outputs a refining operation at a time. The 3D-IoU of the predicted object is therefore improved as the refinement of the 3D parameters.

Figure 2 shows our overall pipeline, Reinforced Axial Refinement Network (RAR-Net), where we first enhance the input information using a parameter-aware module and then use a ResNet-101 [17] backbone to output the action value (Q-value). Similar to [4], we also use the history vector to encode 10 past

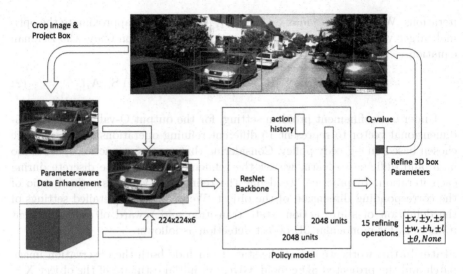

Fig. 2. The proposed framework for monocular 3D object detection. It is an iterative algorithm optimized by RL. In each iteration, an input image is enhanced by a parameter-aware mask and fed into a deep network, which produces a Q-value for each action as output and the 3D box is refined according to ϵ-greedy policy.

actions in order to stabilize search trajectories that might get stuck in repetitive cycles. We formulate the process of refining the 3D box from initial coarse estimate to the destination as an MDP and introduce an RL method for optimization. The goal is to predict a tight bounding-box with a high 3D-IoU.

3.3   Refining 3D Detection with Reinforcement Learning

In the RL setting, the optimal policy of selecting actions should maximize the sum of expected rewards $\mathbf{R}$ on a given initial estimated state $\mathbf{S}_i$. Since we do not have a priori knowledge about the optimal path to refine the initial predicted 3D bounding-box to the destination, we address the learning problem through standard DQN [31]. This approach learns an approximate action value function $Q(\mathbf{S}_i, \mathbf{A}_i)$ for each action $\mathbf{A}_i$, and selects the action with the maximum value as the next action to be done at each iteration. In order to prevent falling into local optimum, we use ϵ-greedy policy, where there is certain possibility to choose random actions. The learning process iteratively updates the action-selection policy by minimizing the following loss function:

$$\mathcal{L}(\theta) = [\mathbf{R}_i + \gamma \max_{\mathbf{A}_{i+1}} Q(\mathbf{S}_{i+1}, \mathbf{A}_{i+1}; \theta^{-1}) - Q(\mathbf{S}_i, \mathbf{A}_i; \theta)]^2, \qquad (1)$$

where γ is the discount factor, θ are the parameters of the Q-network, and θ^{-1} are the parameters of the target-Q-network, whose weights are kept frozen most of the time, but are updated with the Q-network's weights every few hundred

iterations. We use $[\mathbf{R}_i + \gamma \max_{\mathbf{A}_{i+1}} Q(\mathbf{S}_{i+1}, \mathbf{A}_{i+1}; \theta^{-1})]$ to approximate the optimal target value, because the optimal action-value function obeys the Bellman equation:

$$Q^\star(\mathbf{S}_i, \mathbf{A}_i) = \mathbb{E}_{\mathbf{S}_{i+1}}[\mathbf{R}_i + \gamma \max_{\mathbf{A}_{i+1}} Q^\star(\mathbf{S}_{i+1}, \mathbf{A}_{i+1})|\mathbf{S}_i, \mathbf{A}_i]. \tag{2}$$

Under our refinement problem setting, for the output Q-value, we use a 15-dimensional vector to represent 15 different refining operations and actions are chosen based on ϵ-greedy policy. Considering that continuous action space is too large and difficult to learn, we set the refinement value to be discrete during each iteration. In practice, we define the refinement value as a fixed ratio of the corresponding dimension of the object. We present the detailed settings of the definition of state, action, state transition and reward of our refinement framework for monocular 3D object detection as follows:

State: In this work, we define the state to include both the observation image patch and the projected 3D cuboid. Given an initial estimate of the object $\mathbf{X} = (\hat{x}, \hat{y}, \hat{z}, \hat{h}, \hat{w}, \hat{l}, \hat{\theta})$, which is often the detection results of other monocular 3D object detection methods, we use a standard camera projection to obtain the top left point and bottom right point of the crop image patch:

$$(u_{\min}, v_{\min}, u_{\max}, v_{\max}) = \mu(\mathbf{X}, \mathbf{K}), \tag{3}$$

where $\mathbf{K} \in \mathbb{R}^{3\times 4}$ is the camera intrinsic matrix and the function μ is the projection operation. To include more context information, we enlarge the patch regions by a factor of 1.2 in height and width. For the projected 3D cuboid, we crop in the same position as the image patch and use white color as the background. Therefore, our state is a 6-channal image patch:

$$\mathbf{S} = [\phi(u_{\min}, v_{\min}, u_{\max}, v_{\max}, \mathbf{I}); \mathbf{P}(\mathbf{X}, \mathbf{K})], \tag{4}$$

where $\mathbf{I}$ is the original image, $\mathbf{P}(\mathbf{X}, \mathbf{K})$ is the projected 3D cuboid and $\phi(\cdot)$ is the crop operation. Finally, $\mathbf{S}$ is resized to fit the input size of RAR-Net.

Action: Our action set $\mathcal{A}$ consists of 15 refining operations, including a none operation indicating no refinement. These operations are related to the 3D parameters of the detections. For instance, the action $+\Delta x$ will lead to a displacement along the width axis of the object with the value $(\Delta x' = \delta \times \hat{w})$, where δ is a fixed ratio. It is worth mentioning that there are two choices for the definition of our shifting actions, one is defined in the world coordinate system and the other is defined in the axial coordinate system of the object as shown in Fig. 3. If we need to move the object to the left in the world coordinate system, for the former definition, we have to predict the same moving action for cars with different orientations (appearances). But, if we use the latter definition, the shifting operation will be related to the orientation of the cars, thus turning a many-to-one mapping to one-to-one mapping and easing the training process.

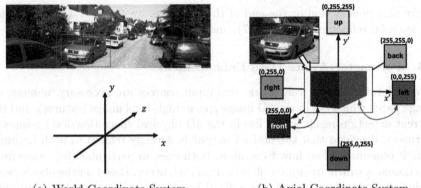

(a) World Coordinate System   (b) Axial Coordinate System

Fig. 3. (a) shows the world coordinate system, which is related to the camera pose and shared by all the objects. (b) shows the axial coordinate system for one sample object. We also illustrate how to generate the parameter-aware mask from a 3D object (best viewed in color). Each color indicates one fixed face. Only two faces are visible in this real example. (Color figure online)

State Transition: Our state transition function T refines the predicted box of the objects from $\mathbf{X}_i = (\hat{x}, \hat{y}, \hat{z}, \hat{h}, \hat{w}, \hat{l}, \hat{\theta})$ to $\mathbf{X}_{i+1} = (\hat{x} + \Delta x, \hat{y} + \Delta y, \hat{z} + \Delta z, \hat{h} + \Delta h, \hat{w} + \Delta w, \hat{l} + \Delta l, \hat{\theta} + \Delta\theta)$. However, the moving direction is defined along the coordinate axes of the object, while the $(\hat{x}, \hat{y}, \hat{z})$ is defined in the world coordinate system, so we need to transform the displacement value across two different coordinate systems. Denote the output displacement of RAR-Net as $(\Delta x', \Delta y', \Delta z')$, which is defined in the axial coordinate system, we have:

$$
\begin{cases}
\Delta x = \Delta z' \times \cos\hat{\theta} + \Delta x' \times \sin\hat{\theta} \\
\Delta y = \Delta y' \\
\Delta z = \Delta z' \times (-\sin\hat{\theta}) + \Delta x' \times \cos\hat{\theta}
\end{cases}
\tag{5}
$$

Therefore, we can translate state $\mathbf{S}_i$ to state $\mathbf{S}_{i+1}$ according to the output displacement value of RAR-Net.

Reward: The reward function R reflects the detection accuracy improvement from state $\mathbf{S}_i$ to $\mathbf{S}_{i+1}$. Considering that increasing the 3D-IoU will have positive reward and decreasing the 3D-IoU will have negative reward, we define the reward function as:

$$
\mathbf{R}_i =
\begin{cases}
+1, & \text{if } \Delta\text{IoU}_{3D} > 0 \\
-1, & \text{if } \Delta\text{IoU}_{3D} < 0 \\
\text{sgn}[(\mathbf{X}_{i+1} - \mathbf{X}_i)(\mathbf{X}^\star - \mathbf{X}_i)], & \text{if } \Delta\text{IoU}_{3D} = 0
\end{cases}
\tag{6}
$$

where $\mathbf{X}^\star$ is the ground-truth 3D parameters and ΔIoU_{3D} is the changes of 3D-IoU. When there is no overlap between the estimated and ground-truth boxes, we use the changes in 3D parameters as the reward signal. In addition, when we

arrive at a none action or the end of the sequence, we set the reward to $+3$ for a successful refinement (IoU ≥ 0.7), and -3 otherwise.

3.4 Parameter-Aware Data Enhancement

In our iteration-based framework, two input sources are necessary, namely, an image patch which lies in the 2D image space (high-level image features), and the current detection result which lies in the 3D physical space (low-level geometry features). Provided that the desired output is strongly related to both information, it remains unclear how to combine both cues, in particular they come from two domains which are quite different from each other. Based on the above motivation, we propose to attach the refined result of last iteration into the input of current iteration. There are many options to achieve this goal, and the naive case is to concatenate the 3D parameters and the image feature in a late-fusion manner, but this practice can barely provide enough appearance cues. Another way is to project the 3D bounding-box on the input image patch [25] or render the 3D object when 3D CAD models are available [20], but these methods may damage the original information since the projection result will obscure the original image.

To avoid loss of information while providing sufficient appearance cues, we propose to project the 3D bounding box on the 2D image plane, and draw different colors on each face of the projected cuboid. This idea is similar to [38]. In order to prevent loss of depth information during the projection operation, we embed the instance depth into the intensity of the color as c', where $c' = c \times \frac{128}{255}$ if $z > 50$, and $c' = c \times (1 - \frac{z}{100})$ if $z \leq 50$, c is the base RGB value shown in Fig. 3, and z is the instance depth of the object. Thus, different appearance will represent different 3D parameters of the object. For example, we paint blue for the front face, so the blue cue can guide the model to learn the refining policy along the forward-backward axis. A sample projection is shown in Fig. 3. We concatenate the painted cuboid and the original image patch to construct a 6-channel input patch as the final input of our RAR-Net.

For the painting process, we use the OpenCV function `fillConvexPoly` to color each face of the projected cuboid. We also apply black to the edges of the projected cuboid to strengthen the boundary. Since some faces are invisible from the front view, we have to determine the visibility of each face. Denote the center of i-th face as $\mathbf{C}_i$, and the center of the 3D bounding box as $\mathbf{C}$, the visibility of i-th face, V_i, is determined by whether $(\mathbf{0} - \mathbf{C})(\mathbf{C}_i - \mathbf{C})$ is greater than 0.

3.5 Implementation Details

Training: We used the ResNet-101 as backbone, and changed the input size into $224 \times 224 \times 6$, and the output size into 15. We trained the model from scratch. In order to speed up the RL process, we first performed supervised pre-training using one-step optimization where the model learns to perform the operation with the largest amount of correction. To create the training set, we added a jitter of Gaussian distribution to the 3D bounding boxes and each object leads to

300 training samples, whose projection is checked to be inside the image space. During the pre-training process, the model was trained with SGD optimizer using a start learning rate of 10^{-2} with a batch size of 64. The model was trained for 15 epochs and the learning rate was decayed by 10 every 5 epochs. During RL, The model was trained with Adam optimizer using a start learning rate of 10^{-4} with a batch size of 64 for 40000 iterations. We used memory replay [41] with buffer size of 10^4. The target Q-Network is updated for every 1000 iterations. The ϵ for greedy policy is set to 0.5 and will decay exponentially towards 0.05. The discount factor γ is set to 0.9. **Testing:** we set the total refinement steps to 20, and during each step, we chose the action based on ϵ-greedy policy, which is to take actions either randomly or with the highest action-value. For each action, the refining stride was set to $0.05\times$ corresponding dimensions. The ϵ for greedy policy is set to 0.05.

4   Experiments

4.1   Dataset and Evaluation

We evaluate our method on the real-world KITTI dataset [15], including the object orientation estimation benchmark, the 3D object detection benchmark, and the bird's eye view benchmark. There are 7481 training images and 7518 testing images in the dataset, and in each image, the object is annotated with 2D location, dimension, 3D location, and orientation. However, only the labels in the KITTI training set are released, so we mainly conduct controlled experiments in the training set. Results are evaluated based on three levels of difficulty, namely, Easy, Moderate, and Hard, which are defined according to the minimum bounding-box height, occlusion, and truncation grade. There are two commonly used train/val experimental settings: Chen *et al.* [9,10] (val 1) and Xiang *et al.* [45,46] (val 2). Both splits guarantee that images from the training set and validation set are sampled from different videos.

We evaluate 3D object detection results using the official evaluation metrics from KITTI. 3D box evaluation is conducted on both two validation splits (different models are trained with the corresponding training sets). We focus our experiments on the car category as KITTI provides enough car instances for our method. Following the KITTI setting, we perform evaluation on the three difficulty regimes individually. In our evaluation, the 3D-IoU threshold is set to be 0.5 and 0.7 for better comparison. We compute the Average Orientation Similarity (AOS) for the object orientation estimation benchmark, the Average Precision (AP) for the bird's eye view boxes (which are obtained by projecting the 3D boxes to the ground plane), and the 3D Average Precision (3D AP) metric for evaluating the full 3D bounding-boxes.

4.2   Comparison to the State-of-the-Arts

To demonstrate that our proposed refinement method's effectiveness, we use the 3D detection results from different state-of-the-art 3D object detectors including

Table 1. Comparisons of the Average Orientation Similarity (AOS, %) to baseline methods on the KITTI orientation estimation benchmark. (In each group, we also show the 2D Average Precision (2D AP) of 2D detection results, which is the upper bound of AOS).

Method	Easy		Moderate		Hard	
	Val 1	Val 2	Val 1	Val 2	Val 1	Val 2
Deep3DBox [32]	-	98.59 (98.84)	-	**96.69** (97.20)	-	80.50 (81.16)
+RAR-Net	-	**98.61** (98.84)	-	96.68 (97.20)	-	**80.51** (81.16)
MonoGRNet [35]	87.83 (88.17)	-	77.80 (78.24)	-	67.49 (68.02)	-
+RAR-Net	**87.86** (88.17)	-	77.80 (78.24)	-	**67.51** (68.02)	-
GS3D [22]	81.08 (82.02)	81.02 (81.66)	73.01 (74.47)	70.76 (71.68)	64.65 (66.21)	61.77 (62.80)
+RAR-Net	**81.32** (82.02)	**81.21** (81.66)	**73.64** (74.47)	**70.92** (71.68)	**64.89** (66.21)	**61.88** (62.80)
M3D-RPN [3]	90.71 (91.49)	-	82.50 (84.09)	-	66.44 (67.94)	-
+RAR-Net	**91.01** (91.49)	-	**82.92** (84.09)	-	**66.74** (67.94)	-

Table 2. Comparisons of 3D localization accuracy (AP, %) to state-of-the-arts methods on the KITTI bird's eye view benchmark.

Method	IoU = 0.5						IoU = 0.7					
	Easy		Moderate		Hard		Easy		Moderate		Hard	
	Val 1	Val 2	Val 1	Val 2	Val 1	Val 2	Val 1	Val 2	Val 1	Val 2	Val 1	Val 2
Deep3DBox [32]	-	30.02	-	23.77	-	18.83	-	9.99	-	7.71	-	5.30
+RAR-Net	-	**33.12**	-	**24.42**	-	**19.11**	-	**14.38**	-	**10.28**	-	**8.29**
MonoGRNet [35]	53.91	-	39.45	-	32.84	-	24.84	-	19.27	-	16.20	-
+RAR-Net	**54.01**	-	**41.29**	-	**32.89**	-	**26.34**	-	**23.15**	-	**19.12**	-
GS3D [22]	38.24	46.50	32.01	39.15	28.71	33.46	14.34	20.00	12.52	16.44	11.36	13.40
+RAR-Net	**38.31**	**48.90**	**34.01**	**39.91**	**29.70**	**35.16**	**18.47**	**24.29**	**16.21**	**19.23**	**14.10**	**15.92**
M3D-RPN [3]	56.92	-	43.03	-	35.86	-	27.56	-	21.66	-	18.01	-
+RAR-Net	**57.12**	-	**44.41**	-	**37.12**	-	**29.16**	-	**22.14**	-	**18.78**	-

Deep3DBox [32], MonoGRNet [35], GS3D [22] and M3D-RPN [3] as the initial coarse estimates. These detection results are provided by the authors, except that we reproduce M3D-RPN by ourselves.

We first compare AOS with these baseline methods, and the results are shown in Table 1. The 2D Average Precision (2D AP) is the upper bound of AOS by definition, and we can see that our refinement method can improve the baseline even if the performance is already very close to the upper bound. Then we compare 2D AP in bird's view of our method with these published methods. As can be seen in Table 2, our method improve the existing monocular 3D object detection methods for a large margin. For example, the AP of Deep3DBox in the setting of IoU = 0.7 gains a 4% improvement. We also notice that for different baselines, our improvements differ – for the lower baseline, the improvements are larger because they have more less perfect detection results. Similarly, we report a performance boost on 3D AP as shown in Table 3. In addition, our method works better in the hard scenario that requires IoU = 0.7.

Table 3. Comparisons of 3D detection accuracy (AP, %) with state-of-the-arts on the KITTI 3D object detection benchmark.

Method	IoU = 0.5						IoU = 0.7					
	Easy		Moderate		Hard		Easy		Moderate		Hard	
	Val 1	Val 2	Val 1	Val 2	Val 1	Val 2	Val 1	Val 2	Val 1	Val 2	Val 1	Val 2
Deep3DBox [32]	-	27.04	-	20.55	-	15.88	-	5.85	-	4.10	-	3.84
+RAR-Net	-	**28.92**	-	**22.13**	-	**16.12**	-	**14.25**	-	**9.90**	-	**6.14**
MonoGRNet [35]	50.27	-	36.67	-	30.53	-	13.84	-	10.11	-	7.59	-
+RAR-Net	**54.17**	-	**39.71**	-	**31.82**	-	**18.25**	-	**14.40**	-	**11.98**	-
GS3D [22]	30.60	42.15	26.40	31.98	22.89	30.91	11.63	13.46	10.51	10.97	10.51	10.38
+RAR-Net	**33.12**	**42.29**	**28.11**	**32.18**	**24.12**	**31.85**	**17.82**	**19.10**	**14.71**	**15.72**	**14.81**	**13.85**
M3D-RPN [3]	50.24	-	40.01	-	**33.48**	-	20.45	-	17.03	-	15.32	-
+RAR-Net	**51.20**	-	**44.12**	-	32.12	-	**23.12**	-	**19.82**	-	**16.19**	-

Table 4. 3D detection accuracy (AP, %) in the KITTI test set (in each group, the left accuracy is produced by M3D-RPN, and the right one by M3D-RPN+RAR-Net).

Metirc	Easy	Moderate	Hard
AOS	88.38/88.48	82.81/83.29	67.08/67.54
Bird	21.02/22.45	13.67/15.02	10.23/12.93
3D AP	14.76/16.37	9.71/11.01	7.42/9.52

Table 4 shows our results on the KITTI test set using M3D-RPN as baseline, which is consistent with the results in the validation set. We also tried to use D4LCN [11] as a baseline, which used additional depth data for training, and we can still observe accuracy gain (0.51% AP) with a smaller step size (0.02).

4.3 Diagnostic Studies

In the ablation study we want to analyze the contributions of different sub-module and different design choices of our framework. In Table 5, We use the initial detection results of MonoGRNet [35] as baseline. Discrete Output is to output a discrete refining choice instead of a continuous refining value. We also tried three different feature combining methods: Simple Fusion is the naive option which concatenates the current detection results parameters and the image feature vector, Direct Projection is to project the bounding box on the original image as [25] did, and Parameter-aware means our parameter-aware module. We refer Axial Coordinate to the option of refining the location along the axial coordinate system rather than the world coordinate system. Single Action is to output one single refinement operation at a time rather than output all refinement operations for all the 3D parameters at the same time. RL is to optimize the model using RL. Final Model is our fully model with the best design choices.

Through comparing Discrete Output with Final Model, we find that directly regressing the continuous 3D parameters can easily lead to a failure in refinement and with controlled discrete refinement stride, the results can be much better.

Table 5. Ablation experiments on KITTI dataset (val 1, Easy, IoU = 0.7). The performance difference can be seen by comparing each column with the last column.

Module	Design Choices						Final Model
Discrete Output		✓	✓	✓	✓	✓	✓
Simple Fusion		✓					
Direct Projection			✓				
Parameter-aware	✓			✓	✓	✓	✓
Axial Coordinate	✓	✓	✓		✓	✓	✓
Single Action	✓	✓	✓	✓		✓	✓
RL	✓	✓	✓	✓			✓
3D AP	1.81	0.40	10.88	5.34	2.27	13.96	18.25

Also, we can see that Simple Fusion does not work well, which verifies that our image enhancement approach captures richer information. Besides, moving along the axial coordinate system and using the single refinement operation can also improve the performance and verify our arguments. Experiment also demonstrate that RL play an important role in boosting the performance further since it optimizes the whole refinement process.

We notice that the number of steps and the refining stride have great impact to the final refinement results. So, during the test phase, we have tried different setting of steps and stride. With smaller strides and more steps, better performance can be achieved but with lager time cost. In addition, when the strides are too large, the initial 3D box of an object may jump to its neighboring object occasionally and some false positives can also be adjusted to overlap with an existing, true 3D box by accident. Since the moving stride and steps are also a part of the refinement policy, using RL to optimize them is feasible as well.

Last but not least, we visualize some refinement results in Fig. 4, where the initial 3D bounding box and the final refinement result are in shown with their 3D-IoU to ground-truth. We can see that our refinement method can refine the 3D bounding box from a coarse estimate to the destination where it can fit the object tightly. Apart from drawing the starting point and ending point of 3D detection boxes on 2D images, we also show some intermediate result for better understanding. During each iteration, our approach can output a refining operation to increase the detection performance.

4.4   Computational Costs

We also compute the latency for our model. Our method achieves about 4% improvement compared to baseline, with a computation burden of 0.3s (10 steps), which is much smaller than the detection time cost: 2s (GS3D [22]). Generally speaking, the cost is related to three aspects: (1) network backbone (2) number of steps (3) number of objects. For (1), using smaller backbone (such as ResNet-18) can further speed up the refinement process with some degraded performance.

Fig. 4. Top 2 rows: Representative examples on which the proposed refinement method achieves significant improvement beyond the baseline detection results. The rightmost example is further detailed in the bottom 2 rows.

For (2), we can increase the refining stride of each step that will cause the number of steps to drop and further accelerate the refining stage, with the price of some imperfect correction. For (3), multiple objects in one image can be fed into the GPU as a batch and processed in parallel, so the inference time does not increase significantly compared to a single object.

5 Conclusions

In this paper, we have proposed a unified refinement framework called RAR-Net. In order to use multi-step refinement to increase the sampling efficiency, we formulate the entire refinement process as an MDP and use RL to optimize the model. At each step, to fuse two information sources from the image and 3D spaces into the same input, we project the current detection into the image space, which maximally preserves information and eases model design. quantitative and qualitative results demonstrate that our approach boost the performance of the state-of-the-art monocular 3D detectors with a small time cost.

The success of our approach sheds light on applying indirect optimization to improve the data sampling efficiency in challenging vision problems. We believe that inferring 3D parameters from 2D cues will be a promising direction of a variety of challenges in the future research.

Acknowlegements. This work was supported in part by the National Key Research and Development Program of China under Grant 2017YFA0700802, in part by the National Natural Science Foundation of China under Grant 61822603, Grant U1813218, Grant U1713214, and Grant 61672306, in part by Beijing Natural Science Foundation under Grant No. L172051, in part by Beijing Academy of Artificial Intelligence

(BAAI), in part by a grant from the Institute for Guo Qiang, Tsinghua University, in part by the Shenzhen Fundamental Research Fund (Subject Arrangement) under Grant JCYJ20170412170602564, and in part by Tsinghua University Initiative Scientific Research Program.

References

1. Alhaija, H.A., Mustikovela, S.K., Mescheder, L., Geiger, A., Rother, C.: Augmented reality meets computer vision: efficient data generation for urban driving scenes. IJCV **126**(9), 961–972 (2018)
2. Bertozzi, M., Broggi, A., Fascioli, A.: Vision-based intelligent vehicles: state of the art and perspectives. Robot. Auton. Syst. **32**(1), 1–16 (2000)
3. Brazil, G., Liu, X.: M3d-rpn: monocular 3d region proposal network for object detection. In: CVPR (2019)
4. Caicedo, J.C., Lazebnik, S.: Active object localization with deep reinforcement learning. In: ICCV (2015)
5. Cao, C., et al.: Look and think twice: capturing top-down visual attention with feedback convolutional neural networks. In: ICCV (2015)
6. Chabot, F., Chaouch, M., Rabarisoa, J., Teulière, C., Chateau, T.: Deep manta: a coarse-to-fine many-task network for joint 2d and 3d vehicle analysis from monocular image. In: CVPR (2017)
7. Chang, J., Wetzstein, G.: Deep optics for monocular depth estimation and 3d object detection. In: ICCV (2019)
8. Chen, C., Seff, A., Kornhauser, A., Xiao, J.: Deepdriving: learning affordance for direct perception in autonomous driving. In: ICCV (2015)
9. Chen, X., Kundu, K., Zhang, Z., Ma, H., Fidler, S., Urtasun, R.: Monocular 3d object detection for autonomous driving. In: CVPR (2016)
10. Chen, X., et al.: 3D object proposals for accurate object class detection. In: NeurIPS (2015)
11. Ding, M., et al.: Learning depth-guided convolutions for monocular 3d object detection. In: CVPR (2020)
12. Duan, Y., Wang, Z., Lu, J., Lin, X., Zhou, J.: Graphbit: bitwise interaction mining via deep reinforcement learning. In: CVPR (2018)
13. Fidler, S., Dickinson, S., Urtasun, R.: 3D object detection and viewpoint estimation with a deformable 3d cuboid model. In: NeurIPS (2012)
14. Geiger, A., Lenz, P., Stiller, C., Urtasun, R.: Vision meets robotics: the kitti dataset. IJRR **32**(11), 1231–1237 (2013)
15. Geiger, A., Lenz, P., Urtasun, R.: Are we ready for autonomous driving the kitti vision benchmark suite. In: CVPR (2012)
16. Guo, M., Lu, J., Zhou, J.: Dual-agent deep reinforcement learning for deformable face tracking. In: ECCV (2018)
17. He, K., Zhang, X., Ren, S., Sun, J.: Deep residual learning for image recognition. In: CVPR (2016)
18. Janai, J., Güney, F., Behl, A., Geiger, A.: Computer vision for autonomous vehicles: problems, datasets and state-of-the-art. arXiv preprint arXiv:1704.05519 (2017)
19. Ku, J., Pon, A.D., Waslander, S.L.: Monocular 3d object detection leveraging accurate proposals and shape reconstruction. In: CVPR (2019)
20. Kundu, A., Li, Y., Rehg, J.M.: 3d-rcnn: instance-level 3d object reconstruction via render-and-compare. In: CVPR (2018)

21. Levine, S., Pastor, P., Krizhevsky, A., Ibarz, J., Quillen, D.: Learning hand-eye coordination for robotic grasping with deep learning and large-scale data collection. IJRR **37**(4–5), 421–436 (2018)
22. Li, B., Ouyang, W., Sheng, L., Zeng, X., Wang, X.: Gs3d: an efficient 3d object detection framework for autonomous driving. In: CVPR (2019)
23. Li, Y., Wang, G., Ji, X., Xiang, Y., Fox, D.: Deepim: deep iterative matching for 6d pose estimation. In: ECCV (2018)
24. Littman, M.L.: Reinforcement learning improves behaviour from evaluative feedback. Nature **521**(7553), 445 (2015)
25. Liu, L., Lu, J., Xu, C., Tian, Q., Zhou, J.: Deep fitting degree scoring network for monocular 3d object detection. In: CVPR (2019)
26. Ma, X., Wang, Z., Li, H., Zhang, P., Ouyang, W., Fan, X.: Accurate monocular 3d object detection via color-embedded 3d reconstruction for autonomous driving. In: CVPR (2019)
27. Mahler, J., et al.: Dex-net 2.0: deep learning to plan robust grasps with synthetic point clouds and analytic grasp metrics. In: RSS (2017)
28. Manhardt, F., Kehl, W., Gaidon, A.: Roi-10d: monocular lifting of 2d detection to 6d pose and metric shape. In: CVPR (2019)
29. Manhardt, F., Kehl, W., Navab, N., Tombari, F.: Deep model-based 6d pose refinement in rgb. In: ECCV (2018)
30. Mathe, S., Pirinen, A., Sminchisescu, C.: Reinforcement learning for visual object detection. In: CVPR (2016)
31. Mnih, V., et al.: Human-level control through deep reinforcement learning. Nature **518**(7540), 529 (2015)
32. Mousavian, A., Anguelov, D., Flynn, J., Košecká, J.: 3D bounding box estimation using deep learning and geometry. In: CVPR (2017)
33. Payet, N., Todorovic, S.: From contours to 3d object detection and pose estimation. In: ICCV (2011)
34. Pepik, B., Stark, M., Gehler, P., Schiele, B.: Multi-view and 3d deformable part models. TPAMI **37**(11), 2232–2245 (2015)
35. Qin, Z., Wang, J., Lu, Y.: Monogrnet: a geometric reasoning network for monocular 3d object localization. In: AAAI (2019)
36. Rao, Y., Lu, J., Zhou, J.: Attention-aware deep reinforcement learning for video face recognition. In: ICCV (2017)
37. Rematas, K., Kemelmacher-Shlizerman, I., Curless, B., Seitz, S.: Soccer on your tabletop. In: CVPR (2018)
38. Ren, L., Yuan, X., Lu, J., Yang, M., Zhou, J.: Deep reinforcement learning with iterative shift for visual tracking. In: ECCV (2018)
39. Roddick, T., Kendall, A., Cipolla, R.: Orthographic feature transform for monocular 3d object detection. In: BMVC (2019)
40. Saxena, A., Driemeyer, J., Ng, A.Y.: Robotic grasping of novel objects using vision. IJRR **27**(2), 157–173 (2008)
41. Schaul, T., Quan, J., Antonoglou, I., Silver, D.: Prioritized experience replay. In: ICLR (2016)
42. Simonelli, A., Bulò, S.R.R., Porzi, L., López-Antequera, M., Kontschieder, P.: Disentangling monocular 3d object detection. In: ICCV (2019)
43. Sutton, R.S., Barto, A.G.: Reinforcement Learning: An Introduction. MIT press, Cambridge (2018)
44. Wang, Y., Chao, W.L., Garg, D., Hariharan, B., Campbell, M., Weinberger, K.Q.: Pseudo-lidar from visual depth estimation: bridging the gap in 3d object detection for autonomous driving. In: CVPR (2019)

45. Xiang, Y., Choi, W., Lin, Y., Savarese, S.: Data-driven 3d voxel patterns for object category recognition. In: CVPR (2015)
46. Xiang, Y., Choi, W., Lin, Y., Savarese, S.: Subcategory-aware convolutional neural networks for object proposals and detection. In: WACV (2017)
47. Xu, B., Chen, Z.: Multi-level fusion based 3d object detection from monocular images. In: CVPR (2018)
48. Yoo, D., Park, S., Lee, J.Y., Paek, A.S., So Kweon, I.: Attentionnet: aggregating weak directions for accurate object detection. In: ICCV (2015)
49. Yu, Q., Xie, L., Wang, Y., Zhou, Y., Fishman, E.K., Yuille, A.L.: Recurrent saliency transformation network: incorporating multi-stage visual cues for small organ segmentation. In: CVPR (2018)
50. Yun, S., Choi, J., Yoo, Y., Yun, K., Young Choi, J.: Action-decision networks for visual tracking with deep reinforcement learning. In: CVPR (2017)

Self-supervised Multi-task Procedure Learning from Instructional Videos

Ehsan Elhamifar[✉][iD] and Dat Huynh[iD]

Khoury College of Computer Sciences, Northeastern University, Boston, USA
{e.elhamifar,huynh.dat}@northeastern.edu

Abstract. We address the problem of unsupervised procedure learning from instructional videos of multiple tasks using Deep Neural Networks (DNNs). Unlike existing works, we assume that training videos come from multiple tasks without key-step annotations or grammars, and the goals are to classify a test video to the underlying task and to localize its key-steps. Our DNN learns task-dependent attention features from informative regions of each frame without ground-truth bounding boxes and learns to discover and localize key-steps without key-step annotations by using an unsupervised subset selection module as a teacher. It also learns to classify an input video using the discovered key-steps using a learnable key-step feature pooling mechanism that extracts and learns to combine key-step based features for task recognition. By experiments on two instructional video datasets, we show the effectiveness of our method for unsupervised localization of procedure steps and video classification.

Keywords: Procedure learning · Instructional videos · Subset selection · Self-supervised learning · Deep Neural Networks · Attention modeling

1 Introduction

The large number of instructional and everyday activity videos has provided great resources for automatic procedure learning (APL), which is to learn the sequence and visual models of key-steps required to achieve a certain task. Procedure learning can be used to teach autonomous agents perform complex tasks [33], help humans in achieving tasks [28], or build large knowledge bases of instructions. Understanding videos at the scale necessary to build knowledge bases or assistive robots that handle a large number of tasks requires unsupervised methods that do not rely on costly to gather annotated videos.

Electronic supplementary material The online version of this chapter (https://doi.org/10.1007/978-3-030-58520-4_33) contains supplementary material, which is available to authorized users.

© Springer Nature Switzerland AG 2020
A. Vedaldi et al. (Eds.): ECCV 2020, LNCS 12362, pp. 557–573, 2020.
https://doi.org/10.1007/978-3-030-58520-4_33

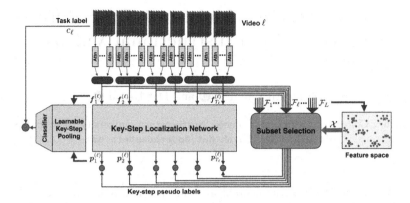

Fig. 1. We develop a self-supervised method for key-step localization and task classification using a deep network. Our framework uses unsupervised subset selection to self-supervise training of a key-step localization network (KLN), where both share attention features that focus on task-related informative regions in video frames. The attention features and output of KLN will be used in a task-classification network (TCN) that uses a learnable key-step pooling mechanism to automatically upweight discriminative key-steps.

1.1 Prior Work

Over the past few years, we have seen advances on multiple aspects of understanding instructions [1,9,12,18,20,22,27,29,31,36]. Depending on the type of supervision, existing works can be divided into three categories. The first group of works assumes that annotations of key-steps (also referred to as procedure steps) are given in videos and the goal is to learn how to segment new videos [36] or anticipate future key-steps [28]. To reduce the costly and unscalable annotation requirement, weakly supervised learning methods [3,5,13,23,37] assume that each video is accompanied with an ordered or unordered list of key-steps (subactions) appearing in it, and the goals are to localize the key-steps in videos and learn a model for each key-step. [31] further reduces the annotation cost by only marking one frame from each key-step in videos without requiring to label the selected frames. While removing the stringent requirement of annotating each frame, the weakly supervised methods still require annotators to watch each video entirely and provide its (ordered) list of key-steps.

To remove the need for annotation, unsupervised procedure learning methods have focused on exploiting the structure of videos of the same task in order to discover and localize key-steps in videos [1,9,10,16,27,29]. Several works have addressed understanding procedures from narration or text [1,6,18,29,34]. However, reliably obtaining text from spoken natural language using videos on the Internet is still challenging, often requiring manual cleaning of the automatic speech recognition results. Moreover, to learn visual models of key-steps, existing methods assume that the text and visual information are aligned [1,18,34], which could be violated in videos, e.g., human narrators first speak about one or

multiple key-steps and then perform the subactions. Thus, to learn reliable visual models of key-steps, recent works have focused on learning key-steps directly from visual data [9, 16, 27], using a Mallows model [27], joint dynamic summarization [9] or clustering and ordering of visual features [16].

Limitations. Existing works on unsupervised procedure learning are limited in three aspects. First, most methods assume videos of only one task are given, with the goal of discovering a common procedure as well as the localization of key-steps in videos [1, 9, 16, 27]. This requires running such methods on each task separately, while it is not clear how to discover the key-steps of a new video that may belong to any of the tasks.

On the other hand, despite great success of DNNs for recognition, detection, captioning, semantic segmentation and tracking, they have not been fully explored for procedure learning. This comes from the difficulty of the unsupervised problem, which often requires a multi-stage solution with each stage involving a non-convex problem, e.g., multiple sequence alignment and discriminative clustering [1], temporal embedding, clustering and decoding [16] or subset selection and multiple sequence alignment [9]. Thus, unsupervised procedure learning based on DNNs, which once learned allows fast and efficient inference on a test video belonging to one of many possible tasks, remains an important yet challenging problem to address.

Finally, the majority of existing works on unsupervised procedure learning lack the ability to learn informative features for key-step discovery, often relying on precomputed features. Recent works have focused on using narration and visual data jointly to learn features [19, 20], yet they require access to narrations and rely on weak alignment between the modalities. In this paper, we focus on *visual data only*, motivated by problems such as learning from home activity videos where users do not explain their actions while performing different tasks. We make the key observation that in instructional videos, information about a key-step is often contained in a small region of a frame (e.g., for the key-step 'unscrew the wheel' in the 'change tire' task, the information is contained in the region of a frame that contains the lug nuts). Hence, to effectively perform procedure learning, we need to successfully localize and extract features from regions in each frame where a key-step is being performed.

1.2   Paper Contributions

We develop a self-supervised procedure learning method from videos of multiple tasks using Deep Neural Network (DNNs), addressing the above challenges. Unlike existing works that assume all videos come from the same task, we consider the more challenging and practical scenario where training videos come from different tasks without key-step annotations or grammars, and the goals are to classify a test video to the underlying task and to localize its key-steps. To tackle the problem, we study a DNN-based framework (see Fig. 1) that

- learns *task-dependent attention features* from informative regions of frames using a self-attention mechanism trained without bounding box annotations;

- learns to discover and *localize key-steps without ground-truth annotations of key-steps* by using an *unsupervised subset selection* module as a teacher;
- learns to *classify a video using a learnable key-step feature pooling mechanism* that extracts and learns to combine key-step based features.

While subset selection does not allow backpropagation of gradients due to its discrete non-differentiable nature, our framework allows us to *learn attention features for both DNN and subset selection*, hence, improving the performance of both for key-step localization and task classification. In addition, the unsupervised subset selection provides pseudo labels for DNN to learn to localize key-steps in videos. Our experiments show that once learned, the DNN outperforms subset selection in key-step localization, thanks to its higher capacity.

Remark 1. Our framework can be thought as a *teacher-student* framework, with major differences with most existing works [2,11,21,25,35]: i) our teacher is a non-convex subset selection, which unlike prior work is not first learned and then fixed; ii) both the teacher (subset selection) and the student (key-step localization network) share the same attention feature learning module, where the supervision by the non-differentiable teacher and back-propagating gradient of loss via the differentiable student, allows to learn better (attention) features that subsequently *improve the performance of both.*[1]

2   Self-supervised Procedure Learning

Assume we have a training set of videos and their labels $\{(\mathcal{Y}_\ell, c_\ell)\}_{\ell=1}^L$, where $\mathcal{Y}_\ell = (\boldsymbol{y}_1^{(\ell)}, \ldots, \boldsymbol{y}_{T_\ell}^{(\ell)})$ denotes the sequence of feature vectors of the video ℓ with T_ℓ frames and $\boldsymbol{y}_t^{(\ell)}$ denotes the feature vector of the t-th frame. Also, $c_\ell \in \mathcal{A}$ is the task label of the video ℓ, where $\mathcal{A}$ is the set of labels of all tasks, e.g., $\mathcal{A} = \{$'change tire', 'jump-start car', ...$\}$. Given a desired procedure length k, which is a hyperparameter, our goal is to recover in a test video all frames that belong to each of the k key-steps and the underlying task label of the video.

2.1   Proposed Framework

We develop a DNN-based method for efficient key-step discovery and video classification by learning from training videos that do not have key-step annotations or grammars. To do so, we propose a framework in which the DNN component that predicts assignments to key-steps is self-supervised by the output of an unsupervised subset selection module on training videos, while the DNN component that predicts the task label is supervised by the ground-truth task labels of training videos. Moreover, the DNN and unsupervised subset selection use the same attention features as inputs. This allows us to backpropagate gradients for the attention module via DNN. More specifically, Our framework consist of the following components:

---

[1] A similar idea was used in [4] to train a deep classification network using kmeans.

- A *spatial attention network (SAN)* that learns to focus on informative task-related regions of each frame to extract feature from. The attention mechanism in our work does not require any ground-truth bounding boxes and is learned with self-supervision on key-steps and supervision on task labels. As we show in the experiments, the presence of this component significantly improves the performance of both DNN and subset selection.
- An *unsupervised subset selection* component whose inputs are the attention features of all videos and M latent states learned from features that ideally capture different key-steps across tasks and background subactions. It then selects a subset of the latent states as key-steps and finds assignments of video frames to them, hence localizing key-steps. We use the output of the subset selection as pseudo labels for training the DNN.
- A *key-step localization network (KLN)* that receives the attention feature of each frame in a video and outputs an M-dimensional vector for each frame that corresponds to the probability vector of the frame belonging to each of the M states. We use the output of the subset selection to provide supervisory information, i.e., pseudo labels, for key-step localization in KLN.
- A *task classification network (TCN) with learnable key-step feature pooling* that uses the attention features and key-step assignment probabilities (i.e., input and output of KLN) and predicts the video task label. Our key observation is that some key-steps (e.g., the ones common across tasks) should be less emphasized for video classification, while discriminative key-steps (e.g., the ones more specific to a particular task) should be more emphasized. Thus, we propose to build M key-step based features and a learnable pooling mechanism that learns to combine and attend to discriminative key-step based features.

2.1.1 Spatial Attention Network (SAN)

We make the observation that task-related discriminative information about each key-step is contained in specific regions of a frame, e.g., in the task of 'changing tire', for the key-step of 'loosen lug nuts', the information is contained in the region of the frame that contains the lug nuts and the wheel. Thus, we use a spatial attention module [14,15,32] that, without costly ground-truth bounding box supervision, learns to extract features from the most informative regions of a frame.

We divide the frame t of the video ℓ, denoted by $I_t^{(\ell)}$, into R equal-sized grid cells, denoted by $I_{t,1}^{(\ell)}, \ldots, I_{t,R}^{(\ell)}$. Let $\boldsymbol{y}_{t,r}^{(\ell)} = f_\Theta(I_{t,r}^{(\ell)})$ be the feature vector of the region r, extracted using a CNN parametrized by Θ (see experiments for the details). Given region features $\{\boldsymbol{y}_{t,r}^{(\ell)}\}_{r=1}^R$, the spatial attention module learns to find the most relevant regions to the underlying key-step. This is done by finding an attention feature, $\boldsymbol{f}_t^{(\ell)}$, defined as

$$\boldsymbol{f}_t^{(\ell)} = \sum_{r=1}^R \alpha_r(\boldsymbol{y}_{t,r}^{(\ell)})\boldsymbol{y}_{t,r}^{(\ell)}, \quad \alpha_r(\boldsymbol{y}_{t,r}^{(\ell)}) = \frac{\exp(m_\alpha(\boldsymbol{y}_{t,r}^{(\ell)}))}{\sum_{r'=1}^R \exp(m_\alpha(\boldsymbol{y}_{t,r'}^{(\ell)}))} \tag{1}$$

where $\alpha_r(\boldsymbol{y}_{t,r}^{(\ell)})$ denotes the weight of selecting the region r. These weights are computed by a neural network whose outputs $m_\alpha(\boldsymbol{y}_{t,r}^{(\ell)})$ for given inputs $\{\boldsymbol{y}_{t,r}^{(\ell)}\}_{r=1}^R$ are normalized by a softmax function across all image regions. The weights are unknown and the task of the attention module is to find them for an input image.

2.1.2   Subset Selection

The goal of subset selection is to find a small subset of representative points from a dataset and it has shown promising results for procedure learning [7–9,31]. Here, we use unsupervised subset selection to provide pseudo key-step labels for the DNN. More specifically, the subset selection takes attention features of all videos and M learned latent states (corresponding to key-steps and background subactions across tasks) and selects a subset of the states as key-steps and finds the assignments of the frames to them.

Given $\{\boldsymbol{f}_t^{(\ell)}\}_{t,\ell}$, we first run kmeans with M centers to find latent states $\mathcal{X} = \{\boldsymbol{x}_1, \ldots, \boldsymbol{x}_M\}$ that capture all key-steps and background subactions. Ideally, videos of the same task would share the same set of key-steps, i.e., there exists $k \ll M$ latent states that well represent videos of the same task. Notice that the set of k representative states for different tasks could have large or small/no overlap, depending on the similarity between the tasks. During training, the subset selection module takes the M states in $\mathcal{X}$ and the video features, $\{\boldsymbol{f}_t^{(\ell)}\}_{t,\ell}$, for all videos from the same task and selects k out of M centers that well represent the videos. To do so, we use a clustering-based subset selection method, where for the video of task $a \in \mathcal{A}$, we solve

$$\min_{\substack{\mathcal{S} \subseteq \{1,\ldots,M\} \\ |\mathcal{S}| \leq k}} J_a(\mathcal{S}) \triangleq \sum_{\ell:c_\ell=a} \frac{1}{T_\ell} \sum_{t=1}^{T_\ell} \min_{i \in \mathcal{S}} \|\boldsymbol{f}_t^{(\ell)} - \boldsymbol{x}_i\|_2, \tag{2}$$

whose outputs are the k selected states, corresponding to key-steps, and the assignment of each frame to each key-state. We denote by $r_t^\ell \in \{1, \ldots, M\}$, the index of the key-state (key-step) assigned to $\boldsymbol{f}_t^{(\ell)}$. This will be used for training the localization network, which we discuss in the next subsection.

To solve (2), we use a greedy algorithm, by considering an active set Γ that is incrementally grown to select at most k states. Initializing $\Gamma = \varnothing$, at each iteration, we add the state from $\mathcal{X}$ that minimizes the cost function the most compared to only using Γ. More specifically, we find $j^* \in \{1, \ldots, M\}\backslash\Gamma$ for which the gain, $\delta_\Gamma(j^*) \triangleq J_a(\Gamma) - J_a(\Gamma \cup j^*)$, is maximum. Thus, including the center j^* gives the largest decrease in the loss function. We include j^* in the active set and repeat the process k times.

Notice that subset selection allows different tasks to share some key-steps, e.g., it is expected that videos of 'making omelette' and 'making scrambled egg' share some key-steps, e.g., 'break egg', 'pour oil', etc.

2.1.3 Key-Step Localization Network (KLN)

The KLN is a student deep neural network that learns to localize key-steps using pseudo labels provided by subset selection. More importantly, it allows backpropagating gradients for attention feature learning by bypassing the non-differentiable discrete subset selection module. More specifically, for a video ℓ with T_ℓ frames, KLN receives T_ℓ attention feature vectors, $\{f_t^{(\ell)}\}_{t=1}^{T_\ell}$. The network then produces outputs $\{s_t^{(\ell)}\}_{t=1}^{T_\ell}$ corresponding to T_ℓ frames, where each output $s_t^{(\ell)} = \begin{bmatrix} s_{1,t}^{(\ell)} & s_{2,t}^{(\ell)} & \cdots & s_{M,t}^{(\ell)} \end{bmatrix}^\top$ is an M-dimensional vector specifying the score that the frame t of the video ℓ belongs to each of the M latent states in $\mathcal{X}$. We further normalize the scores using the softmax function to obtain the probability of each segment t being assigned to each latent state x_m as

$$p_{m,t}^{(\ell)} \triangleq \frac{\exp\left(s_{m,t}^{(\ell)}\right)}{\sum_{n=1}^{M} \exp\left(s_{n,t}^{(\ell)}\right)}, \quad \forall m = 1, \ldots, M. \tag{3}$$

In the experiments, we describe the exact architecture, consisting of a sequence of 1D convolutions, 1D pooling and 1D deconvolutions, used for the KLN. Given that training videos do not have key-step annotations and only contain video task labels, we use the output of the subset selection, which gives the M-dimensional one-hot encoding of each frame to each latent state (more precisely, the assignment of each frame to each of the k selected key-states) as pseudo labels to train the KLN; see the subsection for the loss function and the learning scheme.

Remark 2. While one can only use the task labels of videos as a form of weak supervision, we show in the experiments that key-step supervision from subset selection plays a pivotal role in improving the key-step localization performance.

2.1.4 Task Classification Network (TCN) with Learnable Key-Step Pooling

Our goal is to have a network that predicts the task label of a video, in addition to localization of key-steps. This also allows us to use the weak supervision, i.e., video label, for better localization of key-steps. To do so, we make two observations: i) *not all attention features should be used for video classification*: only the ones corresponding to key-steps should be used; ii) *not all attention features corresponding to key-steps are equally important* for video classification: the key-steps common across different tasks should be less emphasized, while discriminative key-steps more specific to the task should be more emphasized for video classification.

To take into account these observations, we first compute a key-step based attention feature for each of the M latent states by aggregating attention features that are assigned to each latent state by using the output of the KLN. More specifically, for each latent state m, we build a global *key-step based feature*

$$h_m^{(\ell)} \triangleq \sum_{t=1}^{T_\ell} p_{m,t}^{(\ell)} f_t^{(\ell)}, \tag{4}$$

by taking the weighted average of the frame attention features, where the weight of each frame is the probability that it belongs to the latent state m. Given M global feature, $\{h_m^{(\ell)}\}_{m=1}^M$, we propose a learnable pooling mechanism that aggregates the features with different weights, by upweighting the discriminative ones for video classification and downweighting the non-discriminative ones. More specifically, we learn weights $\beta_m(h_m^{(\ell)})$ for each key-step based attention feature and combine them to form the final video feature,

$$\bar{h}^{(\ell)} \triangleq \sum_{m=1}^M \beta_m(h_m^{(\ell)}) h_m^{(\ell)}, \quad \beta_m(h_m^{(\ell)}) = \frac{\exp(m_\beta(h_m^{(\ell)}))}{\sum_{m'=1}^M \exp(m_\beta(h_{m'}^{(\ell)}))}. \tag{5}$$

where the weights are parameterized by a neural network whose outputs $m_\beta(h_m^{(\ell)})$ for given inputs $\{h_m^{(\ell)}\}_{m=1}^M$ are normalized by a softmax function across all key-steps. This could also be seen as an *attention mechanism on the key-step based features*. Finally, we use the global video feature, $\bar{h}^{(\ell)}$, as input to a fully connected network, whose output is the probability of the video belonging to each of the $|\mathcal{A}|$ tasks.

2.2   Proposed Learning Method

In order to train the parameters of the spatial attention network (SAN), key-step localization network (KLN) and Task Classification Network (TCN), using the key-step pseudo labels provided by the unsupervised subset selection module and using the ground-truth task labels, we propose to minimize a loss function that consists of the combination of a ranking loss for the key-step supervision and the cross-entropy loss for the video classification. More specifically, we minimize

$$\mathcal{L} \triangleq \mathcal{L}_{rank} + \lambda \mathcal{L}_{ce}, \quad \mathcal{L}_{ce} \triangleq -\sum_\ell \log p_\ell^{c_\ell}, \tag{6}$$

where $\mathcal{L}_{ce}$ is the cross-entropy loss that measures the consistency between the classification network's output and the ground-truth task label (p_ℓ^a is the probability of video ℓ belonging to task a). The ranking loss, $\mathcal{L}_{rank}$, promotes consistency between the outputs of the localization network and subset selection, i.e., for the t-th frame of the video ℓ, it must produce a higher score for the state $r_t^{(\ell)}$, which is the key-state obtained by subset selection to represent the segment t. Hence, we define

$$\mathcal{L}_{rank} \triangleq \sum_\ell \frac{1}{T_\ell} \sum_t \sum_{m \neq r_t^{(\ell)}} \max\left(0, 1 - s_{r_t^{(\ell)},t}^{(\ell)} + s_{m,t}^{(\ell)}\right), \tag{7}$$

whose minimization promotes to have the score of the pseudo ground-truth state $s_{r_t^{(\ell)},t}^{(\ell)}$ in the output of KLN be larger by a margin of one (other margins could

be used as the network learns to automatically adjusts the weights accordingly) than the scores of other latent states.

We train our model by alternating between running subset selection and learning the DNN parameters. To find M states for subset selection, we use mini-batch kmeans [26], which finds cluster centers via gradient descent steps. Therefore, we refine the cluster centers while ensuring the consistency on the cluster assignments every time we rerun the kmeans (making sure the m-th center in an iteration of kmeans updates the m-th center in the previous iteration).

Remark 3. One could use a cross entropy loss instead of the ranking loss on the output of of KLN. In our experiments, however, the ranking loss performed better, as it is less restrictive, only enforcing the output of the KLN to give better score for the true key-step.

3   Experiments

3.1   Experimental Setup

Datasets. We perform experiments on ProceL [9] and CrossTask [37]. The ProceL is a medium-scale dataset of 12 diverse tasks, such as *set up Chromecast, assemble clarinet* and *replace iPhone battery*. Each task consists of about 60 videos and on average contains 8 key-steps. CrossTask is a large instructional video dataset with 18 primary tasks ranging from cooking activities such as *make kimchi fried rice* to fixing car such as *jack up car*. There are 2,750 videos for these primary tasks with 7 key-steps per task on average. In both datasets, each task has a grammar of key-steps, e.g. 'perform CPR' consists of 'call emergency', 'check pulse', 'open airway', 'give compression' and 'give breath', where each video is annotated with the key-steps. Each video may not contain all the key-steps and the order of key-steps in some videos could be different, as there are multiple ways to perform the same task.

In the multi-task experiments, for ProceL, we randomly select videos in each task such that it has at least 10 videos for testing and at most 50 training videos. For CrossTask, we randomly select 70% of the videos in each task for training and the remaining 30% of videos are used for testing.

Evaluation Metrics. We measure the performance of key-step localization and task label classification as a function of the number of key-steps. For key-step localization, we report Recall and F1 score (Precision can be computed from Recall and F1). For Recall, we compute the ratio between the number of frames having correct key-step prediction and the number of ground-truth key-step frames across all key-steps. Precision is similar to recall except the denominator is the number of frames assigned to key-steps. F1 is the harmonic mean between Recall and Precision. Thus, unlike prior work [1,9] that count 1 or 10 correct frame intersection as a true detection, we use the actual number of frames in the intersection to compute the scores, hence, the scores will be lower. For task classification, we use the standard classification accuracy over videos.

Implementation Details. We extract feature map from the last convolutional layer of VGG19 which has the size of $7 \times 7 \times 512$ as frame inputs to the model. We subsample 2 frames per second from each video to reduce the complexity of the model. In our framework, the spatial attention and the learnable key-step pooling each is parametrized by a neural network with 1 hidden layer of size equal to the input layer and the activation is set to hyperbolic tangent function. In the task classification network, once the global video feature is computed using the output of the learnable key-step pooling, we apply an additional layer to classify the task label of the given video.

To build the key-step localization network (KLN), we make connection between our goal, which is to take T_ℓ input vectors and output T_ℓ vectors each of dimension M, and semantic image segmentation whose goal is to take an input image and produce an output image where each pixel takes one of few discrete values corresponding to a category. Thus, we take the network in [17] and, given that we are working with sequential data instead of 2D images, we convert 2D convolutions, 2D pooling and 2D deconvolutions to, respectively, 1D temporal convolutions, 1D pooling and 1D deconvolutions [24].

We implement our model in PyTorch and optimize with the default setting of RMSprop [30] with the learning rate 0.001, weight decay 0.0001 and batch size of 1 video. For the task-specific setting, where we use videos of each task separately to learn one model per task, we train all variants of our model for 10 and 5 epochs on ProceL and CrossTask, respectively, and use $M = 30$. In the multi-task setting, where we use all videos across all tasks to learn a single model, we train our framework with 3 and 2 epochs for ProceL and CrossTask, respectively. To optimize our model, we set $\lambda = 0.5$ for the multi-task setting ($\lambda = 0$ for single-task) and set $M = 50$ (we use larger M compared to the single-task setting as we have more key-steps collectively). Given that ProceL comes with segmentation of videos into superframes, we use segments and aggregate attention features in each segment as the input to DNNs and subset selection. For CrossTask, we use attention features of frames directly as inputs.

3.2   Experimental Results

We perform experiments for the *task-specific setting, learning a model for each task*, and the *multi-task setting, learning one model for videos across all tasks*.

3.2.1   Task-Specific Results

Given that existing unsupervised procedure learning algorithms work with videos of one task and learn a model separately for each task, we first perform experiments in this task-specific setting to investigate the effectiveness of our approach compared to the state of the art.[2] We compare with a simplified version of JointSeqFL [9] by ignoring the dynamical model (we refer to it as JointSeqFL-ND, where ND stands for no dynamics) and with the Temporal Embedding and

---

[2] In this setting, there is no training and testing splits and all videos are used for learning and the localization performance is measured on all videos.

Table 1. Recall and F1 (%) on CrossTask for different number of key-steps, k.

	$k = 7$		$k = 10$		$k = 12$		$k = 15$	
	Recall	F1	Recall	F1	Recall	F1	Recall	F1
Random	14.8	6.5	10.8	5.8	9.2	5.6	7.5	5.3
JseqFL-ND	29.6	12.5	26.6	12.6	23.0	12.1	21.3	12.4
TEC	**34.0**	**13.9**	28.5	13.0	27.2	**13.2**	25.5	12.7
Ours	33.3	13.4	**31.6**	**13.5**	**29.8**	13.0	**32.2**	**14.1**
Ours (multi-task)	*41.7*	*16.2*	*41.7*	*16.2*	*41.7*	*16.2*	*41.6*	*16.3*

Clustering (TEC) [16], as the two state-of-the-art methods that already have been shown to outperform other algorithms, including [1, 27]. We also compare with a simple baseline, called Random, where we predict the key-step labels of each video by randomly sampling prediction from a uniform distribution with k values, independently for each segment/frame. To have a fair comparison, we run our method on videos of each task *without the task classification network*, i.e., we do not use the task labels. Thus, KLN is only self-supervised by the subset selection module.

Tables 1 shows the average Recall and F1 scores (%) of different algorithms on the CrossTask dataset, as a function of the number of key-steps in each task. Notice that both our method and TEC perform better than JointSeqFL, which shows the importance of feature learning, as our method is self-supervised by subset selection, yet allows to learn attention features. Except $k = 7$, where the scores of our method are close to TEC, for other values of k, our method generally achieves much higher localization scores than TEC, especially for $k = 15$. Notice also that for all methods, the F1 score is much lower than Recall, which shows methods do better on recall than precision.

To investigate the effect of using videos from other tasks, we also show the results of running our method in the multi-task setting where the TCN is included and the classification loss is used in addition to the self-supervision (referred to as *"Ours (multi-task)"*). In this case, the localization accuracy of our method significantly improves while being less dependent on the value of k. This comes from the fact that taking advantage of other tasks allows to better discover the commonalities within the same task, by predicting the video label as well. Another advantage of this approach is that we will learn *one model across all tasks*, which we could later apply to any new video, while for the state of the art, one learns a separate model for each task and it is not clear how to localize key-steps of a new video for which the underlying task label is unknown.

3.2.2 Multi-task Results

We consider the setting where we have videos of multiple tasks and our goal is to learn a single model that classifies the underlying task of a test video and recovers

Table 2. Localization scores (Recall, F1) and classification accuracy (Acc), in precent, of different algorithms on ProceL for different number of key-steps, k.

	$k = 7$			$k = 10$			$k = 12$			$k = 15$		
	R	F1	Acc	R	F1	Acc	R	F1	Acc	R	F1	Acc
Attention	22.0	11.3	88.3	**24.4**	**12.6**	89.6	**24.7**	**12.9**	88.3	20.9	10.4	89.2
Learn. Pool.	25.7	13.3	91.7	24.0	12.1	90.8	23.1	12.0	90.8	**24.5**	**12.5**	90.8
Both	**26.7**	**14.0**	**92.6**	23.8	12.4	**91.7**	23.8	12.8	**93.3**	22.8	11.8	**93.8**

Table 3. Localization scores (Recall, F1) and classification accuracy (Acc) of different algorithms on CrossTask for different number of key-steps, k.

	$k = 7$			$k = 10$			$k = 12$			$k = 15$		
	R	F1	Acc	R	F1	Acc	R	F1	Acc	R	F1	Acc
Attention	39.2	16.0	74.3	27.6	11.1	71.7	28.3	11.4	71.7	34.9	13.8	73.8
Learn. Pool.	34.7	13.8	70.1	24.2	10.4	66.6	29.9	12.5	72.9	22.8	10.6	72.8
Both	**41.1**	**16.2**	**79.1**	**41.2**	**16.3**	**80.4**	**41.1**	**16.2**	**79.5**	**41.0**	**16.3**	**77.9**

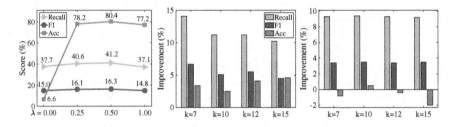

Fig. 2. Effect of the regularization parameter λ (left), effect of self-supervision for the multi-task setting on ProceL (middle) and CrossTask (right).

its segmentation according to assignments to key-steps.[3] We investigate the effect of different components of our framework as well as the effect of training using video label only versus training using both video labels and self-supervision.

Tables 2 and 3 show the Recall and F1 scores for key-step localization and task classification accuracy on ProceL and CrossTask, respectively. We show the effect of using spatial attention alone, learnable key-step pooling alone, and the combination of the two, where in all we use the supervision from both task class and subset selection. From the results, we make the following conclusions:

– The video classification accuracy on both datasets is always higher when using both spatial attention and learnable key-step pooling than using only one. For localization, the performance of different settings are close on ProceL, where there is no clear winner across all k's. We believe this is due to not having

---

[3] This is different and more challenging than weakly supervised learning from instructional videos [3,5,13,23,37], which assume knowing the list of key-steps in videos.

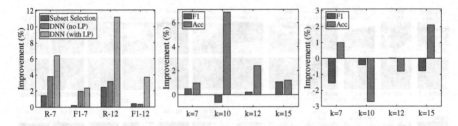

Fig. 3. Improvement obtained by learning attention features on CrossTask (left), improvement obtained by fine tuning when learning attention features on ProceL (middle) and CrossTask (right). All results are for the multi-task setting.

enough videos to effectively train the deep networks. On the other hand, on CrossTask that has a larger number of videos, the localization performance significantly improves when using both attention and learnable pooling, in particular, improving the F1 score by more than 5.7% for both $k \in \{10, 15\}$ and more than 2.4% for $k \in \{7, 12\}$. Notice that, similar to the task-specific setting, the performance of our method on CrossTask is robust for different values of k.

– Given that CrossTask has a larger number of videos per task than ProceL, the localization is generally higher on CrossTask than ProceL, as the DNN benefits from having more training videos. On the other hand, the task classification accuracy is higher on ProceL than CrossTask. This comes from the fact that the 12 tasks in ProceL are diverse with less overlap (except two about cooking and two about fixing cars), while the18 tasks in CrossTask have more overlap (e.g., several on cooking and several on making drinks).

Effect of Self-Supervision and Hyperparameter. Fig. 2 (left) shows the effect of the regularization parameter λ in (6) on the localization performance (Recall and F1) and classification accuracy (Acc) on CrossTask for $k = 10$. Notice that while all scores are maximum for $\lambda = 0.5$, achieving Recall= 41.2, F1= 16.3 and Acc=80.4, the performance does not change much for other values of λ, e.g., achieving Recall= 40.6, F1= 16.1 and Acc=78.2 for $\lambda = 0.25$. As expected, when $\lambda = 0$ (no task classification loss), Acc is low. Figure 2 (middle, right) show the improvement obtained by using both self-supervision via subset selection and task labels of videos over only using task labels on ProceL (middle) and CrossTask (right). Notice that the localization performance significantly improves on both datasets when using the self supervision. The classification accuracy always improves on ProceL with smaller number of videos, as subset selection provides more supervision to train the deep architecture, including the classification network. On the other hand, the classification accuracy on CrossTask slightly decreases. This comes from the fact that there are already enough videos for effective training of the video classifier, hence, including the localization loss puts less emphasis on the video classification performance.

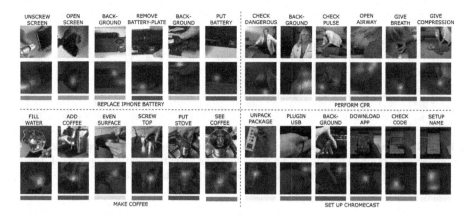

Fig. 4. Visualization of the spatial attention and strength of key-step weights (shown below spatial attention) for videos from four tasks. Notice that, in general, our method successfully focuses on the informative regions of frames and the learnable pooling gives higher weights to more informative key-steps.

3.2.3 Effect of Attention Feature Learning and Fine Tuning

We used attention features to automatically focus on informative regions (where *human and object(s) interact*) to extract feature from. These features are not only given to the DNN, but also to the subset selection that provides supervision for the localization. Figure 3 (left) shows the Recall and F1 improvement obtained by learning attention features over not using any attention for $k = 7$ and $k = 12$ for the multi-task setting on CrossTask. We show the improvement for subset selection as well as the deep network without and with learnable pooling (LP). In all cases, using attention improves the performance. In other words, using the subset selection supervision and back-propagating gradient via the differentiable network, we obtain better features that subsequently improve the performance of not only DNN but the subset selection itself. It is also worth noting that in all cases, DNN enjoys higher improvement than subset selection, thanks to the capacity and generalization power of the DNN compared to subset selection that works directly on centroids. Figure 3 (middle, right) show the effect of fine-tuning the last two layers of the VGG network on ProceL (middle) and CrossTask (right) for the multi-task setting. Notice that fine-tuning on ProceL generally improves the performance, while on CrossTask it could improve or degrade the performance. In all cases, the localization performance slightly changes, which shows attention feature learning already provides sufficient information for localization.

3.2.4 Qualitative Results

Fig. 4 shows the learned spatial attention of our network and the strength of key-steps (the product between the probability of the most probable latent state in a frame and the key-step weight corresponding to that latent state) for videos

from four tasks in ProceL. Notice that in all, our method attends to informative regions, e.g., in 'change iPhone battery', it attends to 'screen' or 'battery' in the associated key-steps. Similarly, for 'CPR', our attention learns to focus on the patient's neck for 'check pulse' or his mouth/chest for 'give breath'/'give compression'. On the other hand, to recognize the task, the learnable key-step pooling gives higher weights to actual key-steps and less weights to background frames. Most notably, it gives the largest weights to 'give breath' and 'give compression' in CPR, which are the most discriminative steps of CPR. In 'setup Chromecast' where some of the steps are visually very similar, however, it gives a high weight to the background, reducing the performance.

4 Conclusions

We developed a self-supervised multi-task procedure learning method that allows to learn a single deep neural network (DNN) for discovering key-steps and task classification using training videos from multiple tasks. By experiments on two instructional video datasets, we showed the effectiveness of our method for unsupervised discovery of procedure steps and video classification.

Acknowledgements. This work is partially supported by DARPA Young Faculty Award (D18AP00050), NSF (IIS-1657197), ONR (N000141812132) and ARO (W911NF1810300).

References

1. Alayrac, J.B., Bojanowski, P., Agrawal, N., Sivic, J., Laptev, I., Lacoste-Julien, S.: Unsupervised learning from narrated instruction videos. In: IEEE Conference on Computer Vision and Pattern Recognition (2016)
2. Ba, J., Caruana, R.: Do deep nets really need to be deep?. In: Neural Information Processing Systems (2013)
3. Bojanowski, P., et al.: Weakly supervised action labeling in videos under ordering constraints. In: European Conference on Computer Vision (2014)
4. Caron, M., Bojanowski, P., Joulin, A., Douze, M.: Deep clustering for unsupervised learning of visual features. In: European Conference on Computer Vision (2018)
5. Ding, L., Xu, C.: Weakly-supervised action segmentation with iterative soft boundary assignment. In: IEEE Conference on Computer Vision and Pattern Recognition (2018)
6. Du, X., et al.: Weakly-supervised action segmentation with iterative soft boundary assignment. In: Annual Meeting of the North American Association for Computational Linguistics (2019)
7. Elhamifar, E.: Sequential facility location: approximate submodularity and greedy algorithm. In: International Conference on Machine Learning (2019)
8. Elhamifar, E., De-Paolis-Kaluza, M.C.: Subset selection and summarization in sequential data. In: Neural Information Processing Systems (2017)
9. Elhamifar, E., Naing, Z.: Unsupervised procedure learning via joint dynamic summarization. In: International Conference on Computer Vision (2019)

10. Goel, K., Brunskill, E.: Learning procedural abstractions and evaluating discrete latent temporal structure. In: International Conference on Learning Representation (2019)
11. Hinton, G.E., Vinyals, O., Dean, J.: Distilling the knowledge in a neural network. ArXiv (2015)
12. Huang, D., Buch, S., Dery, L., Garg, A., Fei-Fei, L., Niebles, J.C.: Finding it?: Weakly-supervised reference-aware visual grounding in instructional videos. In: IEEE Conference on Computer Vision and Pattern Recognition (2018)
13. Huang, D.A., Fei-Fei, L., Niebles, J.C.: Connectionist temporal modeling for weakly supervised action labeling. In: European Conference on Computer Vision (2016)
14. Huynh, D., Elhamifar, E.: Fine-grained generalized zero-shot learning via dense attribute-based attention. In: IEEE Conference on Computer Vision and Pattern Recognition (2020)
15. Huynh, D., Elhamifar, E.: A shared multi-attention framework for multi-label zero-shot learning. In: IEEE Conference on Computer Vision and Pattern Recognition (2020)
16. Kukleva, A., Kuehne, H., Sener, F., Gall, J.: Unsupervised learning of action classes with continuous temporal embedding. In: IEEE Conference on Computer Vision and Pattern Recognition (2019)
17. Long, J., Shelhamer, E., Darrell, T.: Fully convolutional networks for semantic segmentation. In: IEEE Conference on Computer Vision and Pattern Recognition (2015)
18. Malmaud, J., Huang, J., Rathod, V., Johnston, N., Rabinovich, A., Murphy, K.: What's cookin'? Interpreting cooking videos using text, speech and vision. In: NAACL (2015)
19. Miech, A., Alayrac, J.B., Smaira, L., Laptev, I., Sivic, J., Zisserman, A.: End-to-end learning of visual representations from uncurated instructional videos. arXiv:1912.06430 (2019)
20. Miech, A., Zhukov, D., Alayrac, J.B., Tapaswi, M., Laptev, I., Sivic, J.: HowTo100M: learning a text-video embedding by watching hundred million narrated video clips. In: International Conference on Computer Vision (2019)
21. Phuong, M., Lampert, C.: Towards understanding knowledge distillation. In: International Conference on Machine learning (2019)
22. Puig, X., et al.: Simulating household activities via programs. In: IEEE Conference on computer Vision and Pattern Recognition (2018)
23. Richard, A., Kuehne, H., Gall, J.: Weakly supervised action learning with RNN based fine-to-coarse modeling. In: IEEE Conference on Computer Vision and Pattern Recognition (2017)
24. Rochan, M., Ye, L., Wang, Y.: Video summarization using fully convolutional sequence networks. In: European Conference on Computer Vision (2018)
25. Romero, A., Ballas, N., Kahou, S.E., Chassang, A., Gatta, C., Bengio, Y.: FitNets: hints for thin deep nets. In: International Conference on Learning Representations (2014)
26. Sculley, D.: Web-scale k-means clustering. WWW (2010)
27. Sener, F., Yao, A.: Unsupervised learning and segmentation of complex activities from video. In: IEEE Conference on Computer Vision and Pattern Recognition (2018)
28. Sener, F., Yao, A.: Zero-shot anticipation for instructional activities. In: International Conference on Computer Vision (2019)
29. Sener, O., Zamir, A.R., Savarese, S., Saxena, A.: Unsupervised semantic parsing of video collections. In: IEEE International Conference on Computer Vision (2015)

30. Tijmen, T., Hinton, G.: Lecture 6.5-RMSProp: divide the gradient by a running average of its recent magnitude. In: COURSERA: Neural networks for machine learning 4.2 (2012)

31. Xu, C., Elhamifar, E.: Deep supervised summarization: algorithm and application to learning instructions. In: Neural Information Processing Systems (2019)

32. Xu, K., et al.: Show, attend and tell: neural image caption generation with visual attention (2015)

33. Yang, Y., Li, Y., Fermüller, C., Aloimonos, Y.: Robot learning manipulation action plans by watching unconstrained videos from the World Wide Web. In: AAAI (2015)

34. Yu, S.I., Jiang, L., Hauptmann, A.: Instructional videos for unsupervised harvesting and learning of action examples. In: ACM International Conference on Multimedia (2014)

35. Zagoruyko, S., Komodakis, N.: Paying more attention to attention: improving the performance of convolutional neural networks via attention transfer. In: International Conference on Learning Representations (2017)

36. Zhou, L., Xu, C., Corso, J.J.: Towards automatic learning of procedures from web instructional videos. In: AAAI (2018)

37. Zhukov, D., Alayrac, J.B., Cinbis, R.G., Fouhey, D., Laptev, I., Sivic, J.: Cross-task weakly supervised learning from instructional videos. In: IEEE Conference on Computer Vision and Pattern Recognition (2019)

CosyPose: Consistent Multi-view Multi-object 6D Pose Estimation

Yann Labbé[1,2]([✉]), Justin Carpentier[1,2], Mathieu Aubry[3], and Josef Sivic[1,2,4]

[1] École normale supérieure, CNRS, PSL Research University, Paris, France
[2] INRIA, Paris, France
`yann.labbe@inria.fr`
[3] LIGM (UMR 8049), École des Ponts, UPE, Marne-la-Valle, France
[4] Czech Institute of Informatics, Robotics and Cybernetics, Czech Technical University in Prague, Prague, Czech Republic

Abstract. We introduce an approach for recovering the 6D pose of multiple known objects in a scene captured by a set of input images with unknown camera viewpoints. First, we present a single-view single-object 6D pose estimation method, which we use to generate 6D object pose hypotheses. Second, we develop a robust method for matching individual 6D object pose hypotheses across different input images in order to jointly estimate camera viewpoints and 6D poses of all objects in a *single consistent scene*. Our approach explicitly handles object symmetries, does not require depth measurements, is robust to missing or incorrect object hypotheses, and automatically recovers the number of objects in the scene. Third, we develop a method for global scene refinement given multiple object hypotheses and their correspondences across views. This is achieved by solving an *object-level bundle adjustment* problem that refines the poses of cameras and objects to minimize the reprojection error in all views. We demonstrate that the proposed method, dubbed CosyPose, outperforms current state-of-the-art results for single-view and multi-view 6D object pose estimation by a large margin on two challenging benchmarks: the YCB-Video and T-LESS datasets. Code and pre-trained models are available on the project webpage. (https://www.di.ens.fr/willow/research/cosypose/.)

1 Introduction

The goal of this work is to estimate accurate 6D poses of multiple known objects in a 3D scene captured by multiple cameras with unknown positions, as illustrated in Fig. 1. This is a challenging problem because of the texture-less nature of many objects, the presence of multiple similar objects, the unknown number and type of objects in the scene, and the unknown positions of cameras. Solving

Electronic supplementary material The online version of this chapter (https://doi.org/10.1007/978-3-030-58520-4_34) contains supplementary material, which is available to authorized users.

© Springer Nature Switzerland AG 2020
A. Vedaldi et al. (Eds.): ECCV 2020, LNCS 12362, pp. 574–591, 2020.
https://doi.org/10.1007/978-3-030-58520-4_34

(a) Input: RGB images.   (b) Output: full scene model including objects and camera poses.

Fig. 1. CosyPose: 6D object pose estimation optimizing multi-view COnSistencY. Given (a) a set of RGB images depicting a scene with known objects taken from unknown viewpoints, our method accurately reconstructs the scene, (b) recovering all objects in the scene, their 6D pose and the camera viewpoints. Objects are enlarged for the purpose of visualization.

this problem would have, however, important applications in robotics where the knowledge of accurate position and orientation of objects within the scene would allow the robot to plan, navigate and interact with the environment.

Object pose estimation is one of the oldest computer vision problems [1–3], yet it remains an active area of research [4–11]. The best performing methods that operate on RGB (no depth) images [7,8,10–12] are based on trainable convolutional neural networks and are able to deal with symmetric or textureless objects, which were challenging for earlier methods relying on local [3,13–16] or global [17] gradient-based image features. However, most of these works consider objects independently and estimate their poses using a single input (RGB) image. Yet, in practice, scenes are composed of many objects and multiple images of the scene are often available, e.g. obtained by a single moving camera, or in a multi-camera set-up. In this work, we address these limitations and develop an approach that combines information from *multiple views* and estimates jointly the pose of *multiple objects* to obtain a single consistent scene interpretation.

While the idea of jointly estimating poses of multiple objects from multiple views may seem simple, the following challenges need to be addressed. First, object pose hypotheses made in individual images cannot easily be expressed in a common reference frame when the relative transformations between the cameras are unknown. This is often the case in practical scenarios where camera calibration cannot easily be recovered using local feature registration because the scene lacks texture or the baselines are large. Second, the single-view 6D object pose hypotheses have gross errors in the form of false positive and missed detections. Third, the candidate 6D object poses estimated from input images are noisy as they suffer from depth ambiguities inherent to single view methods.

In this work, we describe an approach that addresses these challenges. We start from 6D object pose hypotheses that we estimate from each view using a new render-and-compare approach inspired by DeepIM [10]. First, we match individual object pose hypotheses across different views and use the resulting *object-level* correspondences to recover the relative positions between the cameras. Second, gross errors in object detection are addressed using a robust object-level matching procedure based on RANSAC, optimizing the overall scene consistency. Third, noisy single-view object poses are significantly improved using a global *refinement procedure* based on object-level bundle adjustment. The outcome of our approach that optimizes multi-view COnSistencY, hence dubbed CosyPose, is a single consistent reconstruction of the input scene. Our single-view single-object pose estimation method obtains state-of-the-art results on the YCB-Video [18] and T-LESS [19] datasets, achieving a significant 33.8% absolute improvement over the state-of-the-art [7] on T-LESS. Our multi-view framework clearly outperforms [20] on YCB-Video while not requiring known camera poses and not being limited to a single object of each class per scene. On both datasets, we show that our multi-view solution significantly improves pose estimation and 6D detection accuracy over our single-view baseline.

2   Related Work

Our work builds on results in single-view and multi-view object 6D pose estimation from RGB images and object-level SLAM.

Single-view Single-Object 6D Pose Estimation. The object pose estimation problem [15,16] has been approached either by estimating the pose from 2D-3D correspondences using local invariant features [3,13], or directly by estimating the object pose using template-matching [14]. However, local features do not work well for texture-less objects and global templates often fail to detect partially occluded objects. Both of these approaches (feature-based and template matching) have been revisited using deep neural networks. A convolutional neural network (CNN) can be used to detect object features in 2D [4,6,18,21,22] or to directly find 2D-to-3D correspondences [5,7,8,23]. Deep approaches have also been used to match implicit pose features, which can be learned without requiring ground truth pose annotations [12]. The estimated 6D pose of the objects can be further refined [4,10] using an iterative procedure that effectively moves the camera around the object so that the rendered image of the object best matches the input image. Such a refinement step provides important performance improvements and is becoming common practice [8,11] as a final stage of the estimation process. Our single-view single-object pose estimation described in Sect. 3.2 builds on DeepIM [10]. The performance of 6D pose estimation can be further improved using depth sensors [10,11,18], but in this work we focus on the most challenging scenario where only RGB images are available.

Multi-view Single-Object 6D Pose Estimation. Multiple views of an object can be used to resolve depth ambiguities and gain robustness with respect to occlusions. Prior work using local invariant features includes [15,16,24,25] and involves some form of feature matching to establish correspondences across views to aggregate information from multiple viewpoints. More recently, the multi-view single-object pose estimation problem has been revisited with a deep neural network that predicts an object pose candidate in each view [20] and aggregates information from multiple views assuming known camera poses. In contrast, our work does not assume the camera poses to be known. We experimentally demonstrate that our approach outperforms [20] despite requiring less information.

Multi-view Multi-object 6D Pose Estimation. Other works consider all objects in a scene together in order to jointly estimate the state of the scene in the form of a compact representation of the object and camera poses in a common coordinate system. This problem is known as object-level SLAM [26] where a depth-based object pose estimation method [27] is used to recognize objects from a database in individual images and estimate their poses. The individual objects are tracked across frames using depth measurements, assuming the motion of the sensor is continuous. Consecutive depth measurements also enable to produce hypotheses for camera poses using ICP [28] and the poses of objects and cameras are finally refined in a joint optimization procedure. Another approach [29] uses local RGBD patches to generate object hypotheses and find the best view of a scene. All of these methods, however, strongly rely on depth sensors to estimate the 3D structure of the scene while our method only exploits RGB images. In addition, they assume temporal continuity between the views, which is also not required by our approach.

Other works have considered monocular RGB only object-level SLAM [30–32]. Related is also [33] where semantic 2D keypoint correspondences across multiple views and local features are used to jointly estimate the pose of a single human and the positions of the observing cameras. All of these works rely on local images features to estimate camera poses. In contrast, our work exploits 6D pose hypotheses generated by a neural network which allows to recover camera poses in situations where feature-based registration fails, as is the case for example for the complex texture-less images of the T-LESS dataset. In addition, [31,32] do not consider full 6D pose of objects, and [20,33] only consider scenes with a single instance of each object. In contrast, our method is able to handle scenes with multiple instances of the same object.

3 Multi-view Multi-object 6D Object Pose Estimation

In this section, we present our framework for multi-view multi-object pose estimation. We begin with an overview of the approach (Sect. 3.1 and Fig. 2), and then detail the three main steps of the approach in the remaining sections.

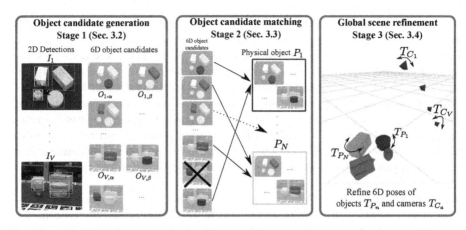

Fig. 2. Multi-view multi-object 6D pose estimation. In the first stage, we obtain initial object candidates in each view separately. In the second stage, we match these object candidates across views to recover a single consistent scene. In the third stage, we globally refine all object and camera poses to minimize multi-view reprojection error.

3.1   Approach Overview

Our goal is to reconstruct a scene composed of multiple objects given a set of RGB images. We assume that we know the 3D models of objects of interest. However, there can be multiple objects of the same type in the scene and no information on the number or type of objects in the scene is available. Furthermore, objects may not be visible in some views, and the relative poses between the cameras are unknown. Our output is a scene model, which includes the number of objects of each type, their 6D poses and the relative poses of the cameras. Our approach is composed of three main stages, summarized in Fig. 2.

In the first stage, we build on the success of recent methods for single-view RGB object detection and 6D pose estimation. Given a set of objects with known 3D models and a single image of a scene, we output a set of candidate detections for each object and for each detection the 6D pose of the object with respect to the camera associated to the image. Note that some of these detections and poses are wrong, and some are missing. We thus consider the poses obtained in this stage as a set of initial *object candidates*, i.e. objects that may be seen in the given view together with an estimate of their pose with respect to this view. This *object candidate generation* process is described in Sect. 3.2.

In the second stage, called *object candidate matching* and described in detail in Sect. 3.3, we match objects visible in multiple views to obtain a single consistent scene. This is a difficult problem since object candidates from the first stage typically include many errors due to (i) heavily occluded objects that might be mis-identified or for which the pose estimate might be completely wrong; (ii) confusion between similar objects; and (iii) unusual poses that do not appear in the training set and are not detected correctly. To tackle these challenges,

we take inspiration from robust patch matching strategies that have been used in the structure from motion (SfM) literature [34, 35]. In particular, we design a matching strategy similar in spirit to [36] but where we match entire 3D objects across views to obtain a single consistent 3D scene, rather than matching local 2D patches on a single 3D object [36].

The final stage of our approach, described in Sect. 3.4, is a global *scene refinement*. We draw inspiration from bundle adjustment [37], but the optimization is performed at the level of objects: the 6D poses of all objects and cameras are refined to minimize a global reprojection error.

3.2   Stage 1: Object Candidate Generation

Our system takes as input multiple photographs of a scene $\{I_a\}$ and a set of 3D models, each associated to an object label l. We assume the intrinsic parameters of camera C_a associated to image I_a are known as is usually the case in single-view pose estimation methods. In each view I_a, we obtain a set of object detections using an object detector (e.g. FasterRCNN [38], RetinaNet [39]), and a set of candidate pose estimates using a single-view single-object pose estimator (e.g. PoseCNN [18], DPOD [8], DeepIM [10]). While our approach is agnostic to the particular method used, we develop our own single-view single-object pose estimator, inspired by DeepIM [10], which improves significantly over state of the art and which we describe in the next paragraph. Each 2D candidate detection in view I_a is identified by an index α and corresponds to an *object candidate* $O_{a,\alpha}$, associated with a predicted object label $l_{a,\alpha}$ and a 6D pose estimate $T_{C_a O_{a,\alpha}}$ with respect to camera C_a. We model a 6D pose $T \in \mathrm{SE}(3)$ as a 4×4 homogeneous matrix composed of a 3D rotation matrix and a 3D translation vector.

Single-View 6D Pose Estimation. We introduce a method for single-view 6D object pose estimation building on the idea of DeepIM [10] with some simplifications and technical improvements. First, we use a more recent neural-network architecture based on EfficientNet-B3 [40] and do not include auxiliary signals while training. Second, we exploit the rotation parametrization recently introduced in [41], which has been shown to lead to more stable CNN training than quaternions. Third, we disentangle depth and translation prediction in the loss following [42] and handle symmetries explicitly as in [9] instead of using the point-matching loss. Fourth, instead of fixing focal lengths to 1 during training as in [10], we use focal lengths of the camera equivalent to the cropped images. Fifth, in addition to the real training images supplied with both dataset, we also render a million images for each dataset using the provided CAD models for T-LESS and the reconstructed models for YCB-Video. The CNNs are first pretrained using synthetic data only, then fine-tuned on both real and synthetic images. Finally, we use data augmentation on the RGB images while training our models, which has been demonstrated to be crucial to obtain good performance on T-LESS [12]. We also note that this approach can be used for coarse estimation simply by providing a canonical pose as the input pose estimate during both

training and testing. We rendered objects at a distance of 1 m from the camera and used this approach to perform coarse estimate on T-LESS. Additional details are provided in the supplementary material.

Object Symmetries. Handling object symmetries is a major challenge for object pose estimation since the object pose can only be estimated up to a symmetry. This is in particular true for our object candidates pose estimates. We thus need to consider symmetries explicitly together with the pose estimates. Each 3D model l is associated to a set of symmetries $S(l)$. Following the framework introduced in [43], we define the set of symmetries $S(l)$ as the set of transformations S that leave the appearance of object l unchanged:

$$S(l) = \{S \in \text{SE}(3) \text{ s.t } \forall T \in \text{SE}(3), \mathcal{R}(l,T) = \mathcal{R}(l,TS)\}, \tag{1}$$

where $\mathcal{R}(l,X)$ is the rendered image of object l captured in pose X and S is the rigid motion associated to the symmetry. Note that $S(l)$ is infinite for objects that have axes of symmetry (e.g. bowls).

Given a set of symmetries $S(l)$ for the 3D object l, we define the symmetric distance D_l which measures the distance between two 6D poses represented by transformations T_1 and T_2. Given an object l associated to a set $\mathcal{X}_l$ of $|\mathcal{X}_l|$ 3D points $\text{x} \in \mathcal{X}_l$, we define:

$$D_l(T_1,T_2) = \min_{S \in S(l)} \frac{1}{|\mathcal{X}_l|} \sum_{\text{x} \in \mathcal{X}_l} ||T_1 S\text{x} - T_2\text{x}||_2. \tag{2}$$

$D_l(T_1,T_2)$ measures the average error between the points transformed with T_1 and T_2 for the symmetry S that best aligns the (transformed) points. In practice, to compute this distance for objects with axes of symmetries, we discretize $S(l)$ using 64 rotation angles around each symmetry axis, similar to [9].

3.3   Stage 2: Object Candidate Matching

As illustrated in Fig. 2, given the object candidates for all views $\{O_{a,\alpha}\}$, our matching module aims at (i) removing the object candidates that are not consistent across views and (ii) matching object candidates that correspond to the same physical object. We solve this problem in two steps detailed below: (A) selection of candidate pairs of objects in all pairs of views, and (B) scene-level matching.

A. 2-View Candidate Pair Selection. We first focus on a single pair of views (I_a, I_b) of the scene and find all pairs of object candidates $(O_{a,\alpha}, O_{b,\beta})$, one in each view, which correspond to the same physical object in these two views. To do so, we use a RANSAC procedure where we hypothesize a relative pose between the two cameras and count the number of inliers, i.e. the number of consistent pairs of object candidates in the two views. We then select the solution with the most inliers which gives associations between the object candidates in the two views. In the rest of the section, we describe in more detail how we sample relative camera poses and how we define inlier candidate pairs.

Sampling of Relative Camera Poses. Sampling meaningful camera poses is one of the main challenges for our approach. Indeed, directly sampling at random the space of possible camera poses would be inefficient. Instead, as usual in RANSAC, we sample pairs of object candidates (associated to the same object label) in the two views, hypothesize that they correspond to the same physical object and use them to infer a relative camera pose hypothesis. However, since objects can have symmetries, a single pair of candidates is not enough to obtain a relative pose hypothesis without ambiguities and we thus sample two pairs of object candidates, which in most cases is sufficient to disambiguate symmetries.

In detail, we sample two tentative object candidate pairs with pair-wise consistent labels $(O_{a,\alpha}, O_{b,\beta})$ and $(O_{a,\gamma}, O_{b,\delta})$ and use them to build a relative camera pose hypothesis, $T_{C_aC_b}$. We obtain the relative camera pose hypothesis by (i) assuming that $(O_{a,\alpha}, O_{b,\beta})$ correspond to the same physical object and (ii) disambiguating symmetries by assuming that $(O_{a,\gamma}, O_{b,\delta})$ also correspond to the same physical object, and thus selecting the symmetry that minimize their symmetric distance

$$T_{C_aC_b} = T_{C_aO_{a,\alpha}} S^\star T_{C_bO_{b,\beta}}^{-1} \tag{3}$$

$$\text{with} \quad S^\star = \underset{S \in S(l)}{\operatorname{argmin}} D_l(T_{C_aO_{a,\gamma}}, (T_{C_aO_{a,\alpha}} S T_{C_bO_{b,\beta}}^{-1}) T_{C_bO_{b,\delta}}), \tag{4}$$

where $l = l_{a,\alpha} = l_{b,\beta}$ is the object label associated to the first pair, and $S^\star$ is the object symmetry which best aligns the point clouds associated to the second pair of objects ($O_{a,\gamma}$ and $O_{b,\delta}$). If the union of the two physical objects is symmetric, e.g. two spheres, the pose computed may be incorrect but it would not be verified by a third pair of objects, and the hypothesis would be discarded.

Counting Pairs of Inlier Candidates. Let's assume we are given a relative pose hypothesis between the cameras $T_{C_aC_b}$. For each object candidate $O_{a,\alpha}$ in the first view, we find the object candidate in the second view $O_{b,\beta}$ with the same label $l = l_{a,\alpha} = l_{b,\beta}$ that minimizes the symmetric distance $D_l(T_{C_aO_{a,\alpha}}, T_{C_aC_b} T_{C_bO_{b,\beta}})$. In other words, $O_{b,\beta}$ is the object candidate in the second view closest to $O_{a,\alpha}$ under the hypothesized relative pose between the cameras. This pair $(O_{a,\alpha}, O_{b,\beta})$ is considered an inlier if the associated symmetric distance is smaller than a given threshold C. The total number of inliers is used to score the relative camera pose $T_{C_aC_b}$. Note that we discard the hypothesis which have fewer than three inliers.

B. Scene-Level Matching. We use the result of the 2-view candidate pair selection applied to each image pair to define a graph between all candidate objects. Each vertex corresponds to an object candidate in one view and edges correspond to pairs selected from 2-view candidate pair selection, i.e. pairs that had sufficient inlier support. We first remove isolated vertices, which correspond to object candidates that have not been validated by other views. Then, we associate to each connected component in the graph a unique physical object, which corresponds to a set of initial object candidates originating from different views. We call

these physical objects $P_1, ... P_N$ with N the total number of physical objects, i.e. the number of connected components in the graph. We write $(a, \alpha) \in P_n$ to denote the fact that an object candidate $O_{a,\alpha}$ is in the connected component of object P_n. Since all the objects in a connected component share the same object label (they could not have been connected otherwise), we can associate without ambiguity an object label l_n to each physical object P_n.

3.4   Stage 3: Scene Refinement

After the previous stage, the correspondences between object candidates in the individual images are known, and the non-coherent object candidates have been removed. The final stage aims at recovering a unique and consistent scene model by performing global joint refinement of objects and camera poses.

In detail, the goal of this stage is to estimate poses of physical objects P_n, represented by transformations $T_{P_1}, \ldots, T_{P_N}$, and cameras C_v, represented by transformations $T_{C_1}, \ldots, T_{C_V}$, in a common world coordinate frame. This is similar to the standard bundle adjustment problem where the goal is to recover the 3D points of a scene together with the camera poses. This is typically addressed by minimizing a reconstruction loss that measures the 2D discrepancies between the projection of the 3D points and their measurements in the cameras. In our case, instead of working at the level of points as done in the bundle adjustment setting, we introduce a reconstruction loss that operates at the level of objects.

More formally, for each object present in the scene, we introduce an object-candidate reprojection loss accounting for symmetries. We define the loss for a candidate object $O_{a,\alpha}$ associated to a physical object P_n (i.e. $(a, \alpha) \in P_n$) and the estimated candidate object pose $T_{C_a O_{a,\alpha}}$ with respect to C_a as:

$$L\left(T_{P_n}, T_{C_a} | T_{C_a O_{a,\alpha}}\right) = \min_{S \in S(l)} \frac{1}{|\mathcal{X}_l|} \sum_{x \in \mathcal{X}_l} ||\pi_a(T_{C_a O_{a,\alpha}} S x) - \pi_a(T_{C_a}^{-1} T_{P_n} x)||, \quad (5)$$

where $||\cdot||$ is a truncated L2 loss, $l = l_n$ is the label of the physical object P_n, T_{P_n} the 6D pose of object P_n in the world coordinate frame, T_{C_a} the pose of camera C_a in the world coordinate frame, $\mathcal{X}_l$ the set of 3D points associated to the 3D model of object l, $S(l)$ the symmetries of the object model l, and the operator π_a corresponds to the 2D projection of 3D points expressed in the camera frame C_a by the intrinsic calibration matrix of camera C_a. The inner sum in Eq. (5) is the error between (i) the 3D points x of the object model l projected to the image with the single view estimate of the transformation $T_{C_a O_\alpha}$ that is associated with the physical object (i.e. $(a, \alpha) \in P_n$) (first term, the image measurement) and (ii) the 3D points $T_{P_n} x$ on the object P_n projected to the image by the global estimate of camera C_a (second term, global estimates).

Recovering the state of the unique scene which best explains the measurements consists in solving the following consensus optimization problem:

$$\min_{T_{P_1}, \ldots, T_{P_N}, T_{C_1}, \ldots, T_{C_V}} \sum_{n=1}^{N} \sum_{(a,\alpha) \in P_n} L\left(T_{P_n}, T_{C_a} | T_{C_a O_{a,\alpha}}\right), \quad (6)$$

Table 1. Single-view 6D pose estimation. Comparisons with state-of-the-art methods on the YCB-Video (a) and T-LESS datasets (b).

	AUC of ADD-S	AUC of ADD(-S)
PoseCNN [18]	–	61.3
MCN [21]	75.1	-
PVNet [5]	–	73.4
DeepIM [10]	88.1	81.9
Ours	**89.8**	**84.5**

(a) YCB-Video

	$e_{vsd} < 0.3$
Implicit [12]	26.8
Pix2pose [7]	29.5
Ours	**63.3**
w/o loss	59.5
w/o network	58.9
w/o rot.	60.5
w/o data augm.	35.5

(b) T-LESS SiSo task

where the first sum is over all the physical objects P_n and the second one over all object candidates $O_{a,\alpha}$ corresponding to the physical object P_n. In other words, we wish to find global estimates of object poses T_{P_n} and camera poses T_{C_a} to match the (inlier) object candidate poses $T_{C_a O_{a,\alpha}}$ obtained in the individual views. The optimization problem is solved using the Levenberg-Marquart algorithm. We provide more details in the supplementary.

4   Results

In this section, we experimentally evaluate our method on the YCB-Video [18] and T-LESS [19] datasets, which both provide multiple views and ground truth 6D object poses for cluttered scenes with multiple objects. In Sect. 4.1, we first validate and analyze our single-view single-object 6D pose estimator. We notably show that our single-view single-object 6D pose estimation method already improves state-of-the-art results on both datasets. In Sect. 4.2, we validate our multi-view multi-object framework by demonstrating consistent improvements over the single-view baseline.

4.1   Single-View Single-Object Experiments

Evaluation on YCB-Video. Following [5,10,18], we evaluate on a subset of 2949 keyframes from videos of the 12 testing scenes. We use the standard ADD-S and ADD(-S) metrics and their area-under-the-curves [18] (please see supplementary material for details on the metrics). We evaluate our refinement method using the same detections and coarse estimates as DeepIM [10], provided by PoseCNN [18]. We ran two iterations of pose refinement network. Results are shown in Table 1a. Our method improves over the current-state-of-the-art DeepIM [10], by approximately 2 points on the AUC of ADD-S and ADD(-S) metrics.

Evaluation on T-LESS. As explained in Sect. 3.2, we use our single-view app-roach both for coarse pose estimation and refinement. We compare our method against the two recent RGB-only methods Pix2Pose [7] and Implicit [12]. For a fair comparison, we use the detections from the same RetinaNet model as in [7]. We report results on the SiSo task [44] and use the standard visual surface discrepancy (vsd) recall metric with the same parameters as in [7,12]. Results are presented in Table 1b. On the $e_{vsd} < 0.3$ metric, our {coarse + refinement} solution achieves a significant 33.8% absolute improvement compared to existing state-of-the-art methods. Note that [10] did not report results on T-LESS. We also evaluate on this dataset the benefits of the key components of our single view approach compared to the components used in DeepIM [10]. More precisely, we evaluate the importance of the base network (our EfficientNet vs FlowNet pre-trained), loss (our symmetric and disentangled vs. point-matching loss with L_1 norm), rotation parametrization (our using [41] vs. quaternions) and data augmentation (our color augmentation, similar to [12] vs. none). Loss, network and rotation parametrization bring a small but clear improvement. Using data augmentation is crucial on the T-LESS dataset where training is performed only on synthetic data and real images of the objects on dark background.

4.2   Multi-view Experiments

As shown above, our single-view method achieves state-of-the-art results on both datasets. We now evaluate the performance of our multi-view approach to esti-mate 6D poses in scenes with multiple objects and multiples views.

Implementation Details. On both datasets, we use the same hyper-parameters. In stage 1, we only consider object detections with a score superior to 0.3 to limit the number of detections. In stage 2, we use a RANSAC 3D inlier thresh-old of $C = 2$ cm. This low threshold ensures that no outliers are considered while associating object candidates. We use a maximum number of 2000 RANSAC iter-ations for each pair of views, but this limit is only reached for the most complex scenes of the T-LESS dataset containing tens of detections. For instance, in the context of two views with six different 6D object candidates in each view, only 15 RANSAC iterations are enough to explore all relative camera pose hypotheses. For the scene refinement (stage 3), we use 100 iterations of Levenberg-Marquart (the optimization typically converges in less than 10 iterations).

Evaluation Details. In the single-view evaluation, the poses of the objects are expressed with respect to the camera frame. To fairly compare with the single-view baseline, we also evaluate the object poses in the camera frames, that we compute using the absolute object poses and camera placements estimated by our global scene refinement method. Standard metrics for 6D pose estimation strongly penalize methods with low detection recall. To avoid being penalized for removing objects that cannot be verified across several views, we thus add the initial object candidates to the set of predictions but with confidence scores strictly lower than the predictions from our full scene reconstruction.

Table 2. Multi-view multi-object results. (a) Our approach significantly outperforms [20] on the YCB-Video dataset in both the single view and multi-view scenarios while not requiring known camera poses. (b) Results on the T-LESS dataset. Using multiple views clearly improves our results.

	1 view	5 views
[21]	75.1	80.2
Ours	89.8	**93.4**

(a) YCB-Video (AUC of ADD-S)

	1 view	4 views	8 views
AUC of ADD-S	72.1	76.0	**78.9**
ADD-S < 0.1d	62.7	66.6	**70.9**
$e_{vsd} < 0.3$	57.7	61.8	**65.6**
mAP@ADD-S<0.1d	55.0	61.6	**69.0**

(b) T-LESS ViVo task (ours, 1000 images)

Table 3. Benefits of the scene refinement stage. We report pose ADD-S errors (in mm) for the inlier object candidates before and after global scene refinement. Scene-refinement improves 6D pose estimation accuracy.

	YCB dataset	T-LESS dataset
Before refinement	6.40	4.43
After refinement	**5.05**	**3.19**

Multi-view Multi-object Quantitative Results. The problem that we consider, recovering the 6D object poses of multiple known objects in a scene captured by several RGB images taken from unknown viewpoints has not, to the best of our knowledge, been addressed by prior work reporting results on the YCB-Video and T-LESS datasets. The closest work is [20], which considers multi-view scenarios on YCB-Video and uses ground truth camera poses to align the viewpoints. In [20], results are provided for prediction using 5 views. We use our approach with the same number of input images but without using ground truth calibration and report results in Table 2a. Our method significantly outperforms [20] in both single-view and multi-view scenarios.

We also perform multi-view experiments on T-LESS with a variable number of views. We follow the multi-instance BOP [44] protocol for ADD-S<0.1d and $e_{vsd} < 0.3$. We also analyze precision-recall tradeoff similar to the standard practice in object detection. We consider positive predictions that satisfy ADD-S<0.1d and report mAP@ADD-S<0.1d. Results are shown in Table 2b for the ViVo task on 1000 images. To the best of our knowledge, no other method has reported results on this task. As expected, our multi-view approach brings significant improvements compared to only single-view baseline.

Benefits of Scene Refinement. To demonstrate the benefits of global scene refinement (stage 3), we report in Table 3 the average ADD-S errors of the inlier candidates before and after solving the optimization problem of Eq.(6). We note a clear relative improvement, around 20% on both datasets..

Relative Camera Pose Estimation. A key feature of our method is that it does not require camera position to be known and instead robustly estimates it from the 6D object candidates. We investigated alternatives to our joint camera pose estimation. First, we used COLMAP [45,46], a popular feature-based SfM software, to recover camera poses. On randomly sampled groups of 5 views from the YCB-Video dataset COLMAP outputs camera poses in only 67% of cases compared to 95% for our method. On groups of 8 views from the more difficult T-LESS dataset, COLMAP outputs camera poses only in 4% of cases, compared to 74% for our method. Our method therefore demonstrates a significant interest compared to COLMAP that uses features to recover camera poses, especially for complex textureless scenes like in the T-LESS dataset. Second, instead of estimating camera poses using our approach, we investigated using ground truth camera poses available for the two datasets. We found that the improvements using ground truth camera poses over the camera poses recovered automatically by our method were only minor: within 1% for T-LESS (4 views) and YCB-Video (5 views), and within 3% for T-LESS (8 views). This demonstrates that our approach recovers accurate camera poses even for scenes containing only symmetric objects as in the T-LESS dataset.

Qualitative Results. We provide examples of recovered 6D object poses in Fig. 3 where we show both object candidates and the final estimated scenes. **Please see the supplementary material for additional results**, including detailed discussion of failure modes and examples on the YCB-Video dataset.

Computational Cost. For a common case with 4 views and 6 2D detections per view, our approach takes approximately 320 ms to predict the state of the scene. This timing includes: 190 ms for estimating the 6D poses of all candidates (stage 1, 1 iteration of the coarse and refinement networks), 40 ms for the object candidate association (stage 2) and 90 ms for the scene refinement (stage 3). Further speed-ups towards real-time performance could be achieved, for example, by exploiting temporal continuity in a video sequence.

Input images	2D detections	Objects candidates	Final scene

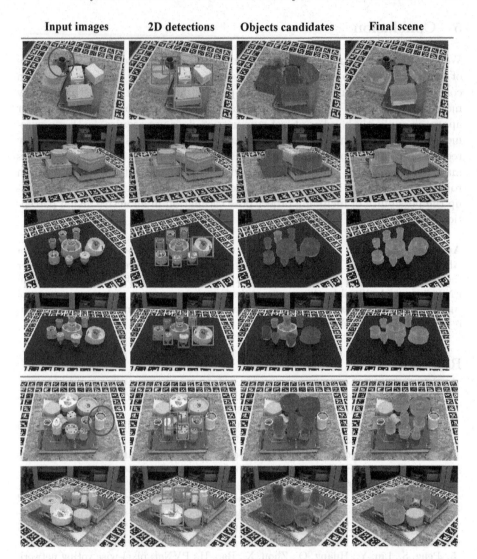

Fig. 3. Qualitative results. We present three examples of scene reconstructions. For each scene, two (out of 4) views that were used to reconstruct the scene are shown as two rows. In each row, the first column shows the input RGB image. The second column shows the 2D detections. The third column shows all object candidates with marked inliers (green) and outliers (red). The fourth column shows the final scene reconstruction. Objects marked by red circles are not in the database, but are sometimes incorrectly detected. Notice how our method estimates accurate 6D object poses for many objects in challenging scenes containing texture-less and symmetric objects, severe occlusions, and where many objects are similar to each other. **More examples are in the supplementary material.** (Color figure online)

5   Conclusion

We have developed an approach, dubbed CosyPose, for recovering the 6D pose of multiple known objects viewed by several non-calibrated cameras. Our main contribution is to combine learnable 6D pose estimation with robust multi-view matching and global refinement to reconstruct a single consistent scene. Our approach explicitly handles object symmetries, does not require depth measurements, is robust to missing and incorrect object hypothesis, and automatically recovers the camera poses and the number of objects in the scene. These results make a step towards the robustness and accuracy required for visually driven robotic manipulation in unconstrained scenarios with moving cameras, and open-up the possibility of including object pose estimation in an active visual perception loop.

Acknowledgments. This work was partially supported by the HPC resources from GENCI-IDRIS (Grant 011011181), the European Regional Development Fund under the project IMPACT (reg. no. CZ.02.1.01/0.0/0.0/15 003/0000468), Louis Vuitton ENS Chair on Artificial Intelligence, and the French government under management of Agence Nationale de la Recherche as part of the "Investissements d'avenir" program, reference ANR-19-P3IA-0001 (PRAIRIE 3IA Institute).

References

1. Roberts, L.G.: Machine perception of three-dimensional solids. Ph.D. thesis, Massachusetts Institute of Technology (1963)
2. Lowe, D.G.: Three-dimensional object recognition from single two-dimensional images. Artif. Intell. **31**(3), 355–395 (1987)
3. Lowe, D.G.: Object recognition from local scale-invariant features. In: Proceedings of the Seventh IEEE International Conference on Computer Vision, vol. 2, pp. 1150–1157, September 1999
4. Rad, M., Lepetit, V.: BB8: a scalable, accurate, robust to partial occlusion method for predicting the 3D poses of challenging objects without using depth. In: Proceedings of the IEEE International Conference on Computer Vision, pp. 3828–3836 (2017)
5. Peng, S., Liu, Y., Huang, Q., Zhou, X., Bao, H.: PVNet: pixel-wise voting network for 6DoF pose estimation. In: Proceedings of the IEEE Conference on Computer Vision and Pattern Recognition, pp. 4561–4570 (2019)
6. Tremblay, J., To, T., Sundaralingam, B., Xiang, Y., Fox, D., Birchfield, S.: Deep object pose estimation for semantic robotic grasping of household objects. In: Conference on Robot Learning (CoRL) (2018)
7. Park, K., Patten, T., Vincze, M.: Pix2Pose: pixel-wise coordinate regression of objects for 6D pose estimation. In: Proceedings of the IEEE International Conference on Computer Vision, pp. 7668–7677 (2019)
8. Zakharov, S., Shugurov, I., Ilic, S.: DPOD: 6D pose object detector and refiner. In: Proceedings of the IEEE International Conference on Computer Vision, pp. 1941–1950 (2019)

9. Wang, H., Sridhar, S., Huang, J., Valentin, J., Song, S., Guibas, L.J.: Normalized object coordinate space for category-level 6D object pose and size estimation. In: Proceedings of the IEEE Conference on Computer Vision and Pattern Recognition, pp. 2642–2651 (2019)

10. Li, Y., Wang, G., Ji, X., Xiang, Y., Fox, D.: DeepIM: deep iterative matching for 6D pose estimation. In: Proceedings of the European Conference on Computer Vision (ECCV), pp. 683–698 (2018)

11. Wang, C., et al.: DenseFusion: 6D object pose estimation by iterative dense fusion. In: Proceedings of the IEEE Conference on Computer Vision and Pattern Recognition, pp. 3343–3352 (2019)

12. Sundermeyer, M., Marton, Z.C., Durner, M., Brucker, M., Triebel, R.: Implicit 3D orientation learning for 6D object detection from RGB images. In: Proceedings of the European Conference on Computer Vision (ECCV), pp. 699–715 (2018)

13. Bay, H., Tuytelaars, T., Van Gool, L.: SURF: speeded up robust features. In: Leonardis, A., Bischof, H., Pinz, A. (eds.) ECCV 2006. LNCS, vol. 3951, pp. 404–417. Springer, Heidelberg (2006). https://doi.org/10.1007/11744023_32

14. Hinterstoisser, S., et al.: Multimodal templates for real-time detection of texture-less objects in heavily cluttered scenes. In: 2011 International Conference on Computer Vision, pp. 858–865, November 2011

15. Collet, A., Srinivasa, S.S.: Efficient multi-view object recognition and full pose estimation. In: 2010 IEEE International Conference on Robotics and Automation, pp. 2050–2055, May 2010

16. Collet, A., Martinez, M., Srinivasa, S.S.: The moped framework: object recognition and pose estimation for manipulation. Int. J. Rob. Res. **30**(10), 1284–1306 (2011)

17. Dalal, N., Triggs, B.: Histograms of oriented gradients for human detection. In: 2005 IEEE Computer Society Conference on Computer Vision and Pattern Recognition (CVPR 2005), vol. 1, pp. 886–893, June 2005

18. Xiang, Y., Schmidt, T., Narayanan, V., Fox, D.: PoseCNN: a convolutional neural network for 6D object pose estimation in cluttered scenes. In: Robotics: Science and Systems XIV (2018)

19. Hodan, T., Haluza, P., Obdržálek, Š., Matas, J., Lourakis, M., Zabulis, X.: T-LESS: an RGB-D dataset for 6D pose estimation of Texture-Less objects. In: 2017 IEEE Winter Conference on Applications of Computer Vision (WACV), pp. 880–888, March 2017

20. Li, C., Bai, J., Hager, G.D.: A unified framework for multi-view multi-class object pose estimation. In: Proceedings of the European Conference on Computer Vision (ECCV), pp. 254–269 (2018)

21. Kehl, W., Manhardt, F., Tombari, F., Ilic, S., Navab, N.: SSD-6D: making RGB-based 3D detection and 6D pose estimation great again. In: Proceedings of the IEEE International Conference on Computer Vision, pp. 1521–1529 (2017)

22. Tekin, B., Sinha, S.N., Fua, P.: Real-time seamless single shot 6D object pose prediction. In: Proceedings of the IEEE Conference on Computer Vision and Pattern Recognition, pp. 292–301 (2018)

23. Pitteri, G., Ilic, S., Lepetit, V.: CorNet: generic 3D corners for 6D pose estimation of new objects without retraining. In: Proceedings of the IEEE International Conference on Computer Vision Workshops (2019)

24. Grossberg, M.D., Nayar, S.K.: A general imaging model and a method for finding its parameters. In: Proceedings Eighth IEEE International Conference on Computer Vision. ICCV 2001, vol. 2, pp. 108–115. IEEE (2001)

25. Pless, R.: Using many cameras as one. In: 2003 IEEE Computer Society Conference on Computer Vision and Pattern Recognition, 2003 Proceedings, vol. 2, II-587, June 2003
26. Salas-Moreno, R.F., Newcombe, R.A., Strasdat, H., Kelly, P.H.J., Davison, A.J.: SLAM++: simultaneous localisation and mapping at the level of objects. In: 2013 IEEE Conference on Computer Vision and Pattern Recognition, pp. 1352–1359, June 2013
27. Drost, B., Ulrich, M., Navab, N., Ilic, S.: Model globally, match locally: efficient and robust 3D object recognition. In: 2010 IEEE Computer Society Conference on Computer Vision and Pattern Recognition, pp. 998–1005, June 2010
28. Zhang, Z.: Iterative point matching for registration of free-form curves and surfaces. Int. J. Comput. Vis. **13**(2), 119–152 (1994)
29. Doumanoglou, A., Kouskouridas, R., Malassiotis, S., Kim, T.K.: Recovering 6D object pose and predicting next-best-view in the crowd. In: Proceedings of the IEEE conference on computer vision and pattern recognition, pp. 3583–3592 (2016)
30. Bao, S.Y., Savarese, S.: Semantic structure from motion. In: CVPR 2011, pp. 2025–2032. IEEE (2011)
31. Pillai, S., Leonard, J.: Monocular SLAM supported object recognition. In: Robotics: Science and Systems XI, Robotics: Science and Systems Foundation, July 2015
32. Yang, S., Scherer, S.: CubeSLAM: monocular 3-D object slam. IEEE Trans. Rob. **35**(4), 925–938 (2019)
33. Bachmann, R., Spörri, J., Fua, P., Rhodin, H.: Motion capture from pan-tilt cameras with unknown orientation. In: 2019 International Conference on 3D Vision (3DV), pp. 308–317. IEEE (2019)
34. Szeliski, R., Kang, S.B.: Recovering 3D shape and motion from image streams using nonlinear least squares. J. Vis. Commun. Image Represent. **5**(1), 10–28 (1994)
35. Hartley, R., Zisserman, A.: Multiple View Geometry in Computer Vision. Cambridge University Press, Cambridge (2003)
36. Rothganger, F., Lazebnik, S., Schmid, C., Ponce, J.: 3D object modeling and recognition using local Affine-Invariant image descriptors and multi-view spatial constraints. Int. J. Comput. Vis. **66**(3), 231–259 (2006)
37. Triggs, B., McLauchlan, P.F., Hartley, R.I., Fitzgibbon, A.W.: Bundle adjustment — a modern synthesis. In: Triggs, B., Zisserman, A., Szeliski, R. (eds.) IWVA 1999. LNCS, vol. 1883, pp. 298–372. Springer, Heidelberg (2000). https://doi.org/10.1007/3-540-44480-7_21
38. Ren, S., He, K., Girshick, R., Sun, J.: Faster R-CNN: towards real-time object detection with region proposal networks. IEEE Trans. Pattern Anal. Mach. Intell. **39**(6), 1137–1149 (2017)
39. Lin, T.Y., Goyal, P., Girshick, R., He, K., Dollár, P.: Focal loss for dense object detection. In: Proceedings of the IEEE International Conference on Computer Vision, pp. 2980–2988 (2017)
40. Tan, M., Le, Q.V.: EfficientNet: rethinking model scaling for convolutional neural networks. In: Chaudhuri, K., Salakhutdinov, R. (eds.) Proceedings of the 36th International Conference on Machine Learning, ICML 2019, 9–15 June 2019, Long Beach, California, USA, Proceedings of Machine Learning Research, PMLR, vol. 97, pp. 6105–6114 (2019)
41. Zhou, Y., Barnes, C., Lu, J., Yang, J., Li, H.: On the continuity of rotation representations in neural networks. In: Proceedings of the IEEE Conference on Computer Vision and Pattern Recognition, pp. 5745–5753 (2019)

42. Simonelli, A., Bulo, S.R., Porzi, L., López-Antequera, M., Kontschieder, P.: Disentangling monocular 3D object detection. In: Proceedings of the IEEE International Conference on Computer Vision, pp. 1991–1999 (2019)
43. Pitteri, G., Ramamonjisoa, M., Ilic, S., Lepetit, V.: On object symmetries and 6D pose estimation from images. In: 2019 International Conference on 3D Vision (3DV), pp. 614–622. IEEE (2019)
44. Hodan, T., et al.: Bop: Benchmark for 6d object pose estimation. In: Proceedings of the European Conference on Computer Vision (ECCV), pp. 19–34 (2018)
45. Schönberger, J.L., Frahm, J.M.: Structure-from-motion revisited. In: Conference on Computer Vision and Pattern Recognition (CVPR) (2016)
46. Schönberger, J.L., Zheng, E., Pollefeys, M., Frahm, J.M.: Pixelwise view selection for unstructured multi-view stereo. In: European Conference on Computer Vision (ECCV) (2016)

In-Domain GAN Inversion for Real Image Editing

Jiapeng Zhu[1]⬤, Yujun Shen[1]⬤, Deli Zhao[2]⬤, and Bolei Zhou[1(✉)]⬤

[1] The Chinese University of Hong Kong, Hong Kong, China
{jpzhu,sy116,bzhou}@ie.cuhk.edu.hk
[2] Xiaomi AI Lab, Beijing, China
zhaodeli@gmail.com

Abstract. Recent work has shown that a variety of semantics emerge in the latent space of Generative Adversarial Networks (GANs) when being trained to synthesize images. However, it is difficult to use these learned semantics for real image editing. A common practice of feeding a real image to a trained GAN generator is to invert it back to a latent code. However, existing inversion methods typically focus on reconstructing the target image by pixel values yet fail to land the inverted code in the semantic domain of the original latent space. As a result, the reconstructed image cannot well support semantic editing through varying the inverted code. To solve this problem, we propose an *in-domain* GAN inversion approach, which not only faithfully reconstructs the input image but also ensures the inverted code to be semantically meaningful for editing. We first learn a novel *domain-guided* encoder to project a given image to the native latent space of GANs. We then propose *domain-regularized* optimization by involving the encoder as a regularizer to fine-tune the code produced by the encoder and better recover the target image. Extensive experiments suggest that our inversion method achieves satisfying real image reconstruction and more importantly facilitates various image editing tasks, significantly outperforming start-of-the-arts. (Code and models are available at https://genforce.github.io/idinvert/.)

1 Introduction

Generative Adversarial Networks (GANs) [12] are formulated as a two-player game between a generator to synthesize images and a discriminator to differentiate real data from fake data. Recent work [11,16,30] has shown that GANs spontaneously learn to encode rich semantics inside the latent space and that varying the latent code leads to the manipulation of the corresponding attributes

---

J. Zhu and Y. Shen—Equal contribution.

Electronic supplementary material The online version of this chapter (https://doi.org/10.1007/978-3-030-58520-4_35) contains supplementary material, which is available to authorized users.

A. Vedaldi et al. (Eds.): ECCV 2020, LNCS 12362, pp. 592–608, 2020.
https://doi.org/10.1007/978-3-030-58520-4_35

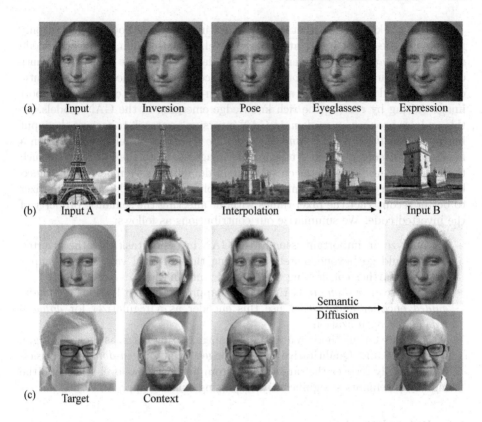

Fig. 1. Real image editing using the proposed *in-domain* GAN inversion with a *fixed* GAN generator. (a) Semantic manipulation with respect to various facial attributes. (b) Image interpolation by linearly interpolating two inverted codes. (c) Semantic diffusion which diffuses the target face to the context and makes them compatible.

occurring in the output image. However, it remains difficult to apply such manipulation capability to real images since GANs lack the ability of taking a particular image as the input to infer its latent code.

Many attempts have been made to reverse the generation process by mapping the image space back to the latent space, which is widely known as *GAN inversion*. They either learn an extra encoder beyond the GAN [4,23,36] or directly optimize the latent code for an individual image [8,22,24]. However, existing methods mainly focus on reconstructing the pixel values of the input image, leaving some important open questions about the property of the inverted code. For example, does the inverted code lie in the original latent space of GANs? Can the inverted code semantically represent the target image? Does the inverted code support image editing by reusing the knowledge learned by GANs? Can we use a well-trained GAN to invert any image? Answering these questions not only deepens our understanding of the internal mechanism of GANs, but is also able to unleash the pre-trained GAN models for the versatile image editing capability.

In this work, we show that a good GAN inversion method should not only reconstruct the target image at the *pixel* level, but also align the inverted code with the *semantic* knowledge encoded in the latent space. We call such semantically meaningful codes as *in-domain* codes since they are subject to the semantic domain learned by GANs. We also find that in-domain codes can better support image editing by reusing the rich knowledge emerging in the GAN models. To this end, we propose an *in-domain* GAN inversion approach to recover the input image at *both the pixel level and the semantic level*. Concretely, we first train a novel *domain-guided* encoder to map the image space to the latent space such that all codes produced by the encoder are in-domain. We then perform instance-level *domain-regularized* optimization by involving the encoder as a regularizer to better reconstruct the pixel values without affecting the semantic property of the inverted code. We summarize our contributions as follows:

- We analyze an important issue in the GAN inversion task that the inverted code should go beyond merely recovering the per-pixel values of the input image by further considering the semantic information.
- We propose an *in-domain* GAN inversion approach by first learning a *domain-guided* encoder and further use this encoder as a regularizer for *domain-regularized* optimization.
- We evaluate our method on a variety of image editing tasks, as shown in Fig. 1. Qualitative and Quantitative results suggest that our *in-domain* inversion can faithfully recover the target image from both the low-level pixels and the high-level semantics, significantly surpassing existing approaches.

1.1 Related Work

Generative Adversarial Networks (GANs). By learning the distribution of real images via adversarial training, GANs [12] have advanced image synthesis in recent years. Many variants of GANs are proposed to improve the synthesis quality [7,18,19,25,34] and training stability [2,6,14]. Recently, GANs are shown to spontaneously learn semantics inside the latent space, which can be further used to control the generation process. Goetschalckx *et al.* [11] explored how to make the synthesis from GANs more memorable, Jahanian *et al.* [16] achieved camera movements and color changes by shifting the latent distribution, Shen *et al.* [30] interpreted the latent space of GANs for semantic face editing, and Yang *et al.* [32] observed that hierarchical semantics emerge from the layer-wise latent codes of GANs for scene synthesis. However, due to the lack of inference capability in GANs, it remains difficult to apply the rich semantics encoded in the latent space to editing real images.

GAN Inversion. To better apply well-trained GANs to real-world applications, GAN inversion enables real image editing from the latent space [3,27,36]. Given a fixed GAN model, GAN inversion aims at finding the most accurate latent code to recover the input image. Existing inversion approaches typically fall into two types. One is learning-based, which first synthesizes a collection of images with randomly sampled latent codes and then uses the images and codes as

inputs and supervisions respectively to train a deterministic model [27,36]. The other is optimization-based, which deals with a single instance at one time by directly optimizing the latent code to minimize the pixel-wise reconstruction loss [8,22,24,29]. Some work combines these two ideas by using the encoder to generate an initialization for optimization [4,5]. There are also some models that take invertibility into account at the training stage by designing new architectures [9,10,21,35]. Some concurrent work improves GAN inversion with better reconstruction quality: Gu *et al.* [13] employs multiple latent codes to recover a single image, Pan *et al.* [26] optimizes the parameters of the generator together with the latent code, Karras *et al.* [20] and Abdal *et al.* [1] focus on inverting StyleGAN [19] models by exploiting the layer-wise noises.

Key Difference. One important issue omitted by existing inversion methods is that they merely focus on reconstructing the target image at the pixel level without considering the semantic information in the inverted code. If the code cannot align with the semantic domain of the latent space, even being able to recover the per-pixel values of the input image, it would still fail to reuse the knowledge learned by GANs for semantic editing. Therefore, in this work, we argue that only using the pixel-wise reconstruction loss as the metric to evaluate a GAN inversion approach is not proper enough. Instead, we deeply study the property of the inverted code from the *semantic* level and propose the *in-domain* GAN inversion that well supports real image editing.

2   In-Domain GAN Inversion

As discussed above, when inverting a GAN model, besides recovering the input image by pixel values, we also care about whether the inverted code is semantically meaningful. Here, the semantics refer to the emergent knowledge that GAN has learned from the observed data [11,16,30,32]. For this purpose, we propose to first train a *domain-guided* encoder and then use this encoder as a regularizer for the further *domain-regularized* optimization, as shown in Fig. 2.

Problem Statement. Before going into details, we briefly introduce the problem setting with some basic notations. A GAN model typically consists of a generator $G(\cdot) : \mathcal{Z} \to \mathcal{X}$ to synthesize high-quality images and a discriminator $D(\cdot)$ to distinguish real from synthesized data. GAN inversion studies the reverse mapping of $G(\cdot)$, which is to find the best latent code z^{inv} to recover a given real image x^{real}. We denote the semantic space learned by GANs as $\mathcal{S}$. We would like z^{inv} to also align with the prior knowledge $\mathcal{S}$ in the pre-trained GAN model.

Choice of Latent Space. Typically, GANs sample latent codes z from a predefined distributed space $\mathcal{Z}$, such as normal distribution. The recent StyleGAN model [19] proposes to first map the initial latent space $\mathcal{Z}$ to a second latent space $\mathcal{W}$ with Multi-Layer Perceptron (MLP), and then feed the codes $w \in \mathcal{W}$ to the generator for image synthesis. Such additional mapping has already been proven to learn more disentangled semantics [19,30]. As a result, the disentangled space $\mathcal{W}$ is widely used for the GAN inversion task [1,20,29,35]. Similarly, we

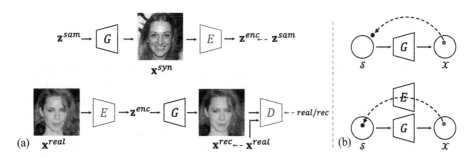

Fig. 2. (a) The comparison between the training of conventional encoder and *domain-guided* encoder for GAN inversion. Model blocks in **blue** are trainable and red dashed arrows indicate the supervisions. Instead of being trained with synthesized data to recover the latent code, our *domain-guided* encoder is trained with the objective to recover the real images. The *fixed* generator is involved to make sure the codes produced by the encoder lie in the native latent space of the generator and stay semantically meaningful. (b) The comparison between the conventional optimization and our *domain-regularized* optimization. The well-trained *domain-guided* encoder is included as a regularizer to land the latent code in the semantic domain during the optimization process. (Color figure online)

also choose $\mathcal{W}$ space as the inversion space for three reasons: (i) We focus on the semantic (*i.e., in-domain*) property of the inverted codes, making $\mathcal{W}$ space more appropriate for analysis. (ii) Inverting to $\mathcal{W}$ space achieves better performance than $\mathcal{Z}$ space [35]. (iii) It is easy to introduce the $\mathcal{W}$ space to any GAN model by simply learning an extra MLP ahead of the generator. Hence, it will not harm the generalization ability of our approach. In this work, we conduct all experiments on the $\mathcal{W}$ space, but our approach can be performed on the $\mathcal{Z}$ space as well. For simplicity, we use $\mathbf{z}$ to denote the latent code in the following sections.

2.1   Domain-Guided Encoder

Training an encoder is commonly used for GAN inversion problem [4,5,27,36] considering its fast inference speed. However, existing methods simply learn a deterministic model with no regard to whether the codes produced by the encoder align with the semantic knowledge learned by $G(\cdot)$. As shown on the top of Fig. 2(a), a collection of latent codes $\mathbf{z}^{sam}$ are randomly sampled and fed into $G(\cdot)$ to get the corresponding synthesis $\mathbf{x}^{syn}$. Then, the encoder $E(\cdot)$ takes $\mathbf{x}^{syn}$ and $\mathbf{z}^{sam}$ as inputs and supervisions respectively and is trained with

$$\min_{\Theta_E} \mathcal{L}_E = ||\mathbf{z}^{sam} - E(G(\mathbf{z}^{sam}))||_2, \tag{1}$$

where $|| \cdot ||_2$ denotes the l_2 distance and Θ_E represents the parameters of the encoder $E(\cdot)$. We argue that the supervision by only reconstructing $\mathbf{z}^{sam}$ is not powerful enough to train an accurate encoder. Also, the generator is actually omitted and cannot provide its domain knowledge to guide the training of encoder since the gradients from $G(\cdot)$ are not taken into account at all.

To solve these problems, we propose to train a *domain-guided* encoder, which is illustrated in the bottom row of Fig. 2(a). There are three main **differences** compared to the conventional encoder: (i) The output of the encoder is fed into the generator to reconstruct the input image such that the objective function comes from the image space instead of latent space. This involves semantic knowledge from the generator in training and provides more informative and accurate supervision. The output code is therefore guaranteed to align with the semantic domain of the generator. (ii) Instead of being trained with synthesized images, the *domain-guided* encoder is trained with real images, making our encoder more applicable to real applications. (iii) To make sure the reconstructed image is realistic enough, we employ the discriminator to compete with the encoder. In this way, we can acquire as much information as possible from the GAN model (*i.e.*, both two components of GAN are used). The adversarial training manner also pushes the output code to better fit the semantic knowledge of the generator. We also introduce perceptual loss [17] by using the feature extracted by VGG [31]. Hence, the training process can be formulated as

$$
\min_{\Theta_E} \mathcal{L}_E = ||\mathbf{x}^{real} - G(E(\mathbf{x}^{real}))||_2 + \lambda_{vgg}||F(\mathbf{x}^{real}) - F(G(E(\mathbf{x}^{real})))||_2
$$
$$
- \lambda_{adv} \mathop{\mathbb{E}}_{\mathbf{x}^{real} \sim P_{data}} [D(G(E(\mathbf{x}^{real})))], \tag{2}
$$

$$
\min_{\Theta_D} \mathcal{L}_D = \mathop{\mathbb{E}}_{\mathbf{x}^{real} \sim P_{data}} [D(G(E(\mathbf{x}^{real})))] - \mathop{\mathbb{E}}_{\mathbf{x}^{real} \sim P_{data}} [D(\mathbf{x}^{real})]
$$
$$
+ \frac{\gamma}{2} \mathop{\mathbb{E}}_{\mathbf{x}^{real} \sim P_{data}} [||\nabla_{\mathbf{x}} D(\mathbf{x}^{real})||_2^2], \tag{3}
$$

where P_{data} denotes the distribution of real data and γ is the hyper-parameter for the gradient regularization. λ_{vgg} and λ_{adv} are the perceptual and discriminator loss weights. $F(\cdot)$ denotes the VGG feature extraction model.

2.2   Domain-Regularized Optimization

Unlike the generation process of GANs which learns a mapping at the distribution level, *i.e.* from latent distribution to real image distribution, GAN inversion is more like an instance-level task which is to best reconstruct a given individual image. From this point of view, it is hard to learn a perfect reverse mapping with an encoder alone due to its limited representation capability. Therefore, even though the inverted code from the proposed *domain-guided* encoder can well reconstruct the input image based on the pre-trained generator and ensure the code itself to be semantically meaningful, we still need to refine the code to make it better fit the target individual image at the pixel values.

Previous methods [8,24,29] propose to gradient descent algorithm to optimize the code. The top row of Fig. 2(b) illustrates the optimization process where the latent code is optimized "freely" based on the generator only. It may very likely produce an out-of-domain inversion since there are no constraints on the

latent code at all. Relying on our *domain-guided* encoder, we design a *domain-regularized* optimization with two improvements, as shown at the bottom of Fig. 2(b): (i) We use the output of the *domain-guided* encoder as an ideal starting point which avoids the code from getting stuck at a local minimum and also significantly shortens the optimization process. (ii) We include the *domain-guided* encoder as a regularizer to preserve the latent code within the semantic domain of the generator. To summarize, the objective function for optimization is

$$\mathbf{z}^{inv} = \arg\min_{\mathbf{z}} \ ||\mathbf{x} - G(\mathbf{z})||_2 + \lambda_{vgg}||F(\mathbf{x}) - F(G(\mathbf{z}))||_2$$
$$+ \lambda_{dom}||\mathbf{z} - E(G(\mathbf{z}))||_2, \tag{4}$$

where $\mathbf{x}$ is the target image to invert. λ_{vgg} and λ_{dom} are the loss weights corresponding to the perceptual loss and the encoder regularizer respectively.

3   Experiments

In this section, we experimentally show the superiority of the proposed *in-domain* GAN inversion over existing methods in terms of semantic information preservation, inversion quality, inference speed, as well as real image editing.

3.1   Experimental Settings

We conduct experiments on FFHQ dataset [19], which contains 70,000 high-quality face images, and LSUN dataset [33], which consists of images from 10 different scene categories. Only results on the tower category are shown in the main paper. More results can be found in the **supplementary material**. The GANs to invert are pre-trained following StyleGAN [19].[1] When training the encoder, the generator is *fixed* and we only update the encoder and discriminator according to Eq. (2) and Eq. (3). As for the perceptual loss in Eq. (2), we take conv4_3 as the VGG [31] output. Loss weights are set as $\lambda_{vgg} = 5e^{-5}$, $\lambda_{adv} = 0.1$, and $\gamma = 10$. We set $\lambda_{dom} = 2$ in Eq. (4) for the *domain-regularized* optimization.

3.2   Semantic Analysis of the Inverted Codes

In this part, we evaluate how the inverted codes can semantically represent the target images. As pointed out by prior work [19,30], the latent space of GANs is linearly separable in terms of semantics. In particular, for a binary attribute (*e.g.*, male *v.s.* female), it is possible to find a latent hyperplane such that all points from the same side correspond to the same attribute. We use this property to evaluate the alignment between the inverted codes and the latent semantics.

We collect 7,000 real face images and use off-the-shelf attribute classifiers to predict age (young *v.s.* old), gender (female *v.s.* male), eyeglasses (absence *v.s.* presence), and pose (left *v.s.* right). These predictions are considered

---

[1] Different from StyleGAN, we use different latent codes for different layers.

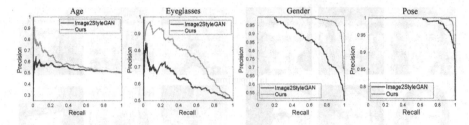

Fig. 3. Precision-recall curves by directly using the inverted codes for facial attribute classification. Our *in-domain* inversion shows much better performance than Image2StyleGAN [29], suggesting a stronger semantic preservation.

Table 1. Quantitative comparison between different inversion methods. For each model, we invert 500 images for evaluation. ↓ means lower number is better.

Method	Speed	Face			Tower		
		FID↓	SWD↓	MSE↓	FID↓	SWD↓	MSE↓
Traditional encoder [36]	**0.008 s**	88.48	100.5	0.507	73.02	69.19	0.455
MSE-based optimization [29]	290 s	58.04	29.19	**0.026**	69.16	55.35	0.068
Domain-guided encoder (ours)	0.017 s	52.85	**13.02**	0.062	46.81	27.13	0.071
In-domain inversion (ours)	8 s	**42.64**	13.44	0.030	**44.77**	**26.44**	**0.052**

as ground-truth. Then, we use the state-of-the-art GAN inversion method, Image2StyleGAN [29], and our proposed *in-domain* GAN inversion to invert these images back to the latent space of a *fixed* StyleGAN model trained on FFHQ dataset [19]. InterFaceGAN [30] is used to search the semantic boundaries for the aforementioned attributes in the latent space. Then, we use these boundaries as well as the inverted codes to evaluate the attribute classification performance. Figure 3 shows the precision-recall curves on each semantic. We can easily tell that the codes inverted by our method are more semantically meaningful. This quantitatively demonstrates the effectiveness of our proposed *in-domain* inversion for preserving the semantics property of the inverted code.

3.3   Inversion Quality and Speed

As discussed above, our method can produce *in-domain* codes for the GAN inversion task. In this part, we would like to verify that the improvement of our approach from the semantic aspect does not affect its performance on the traditional evaluation metric, *i.e.*, image reconstruction quality. Figure 4 shows the qualitative comparison between different inversion methods including training traditional encoder [36], MSE-based optimization [29], as well as our proposed *domain-guided* encoder and the *in-domain* inversion. Comparison between Fig. 4(b) and (d) shows the superiority of our *domain-guided* encoder in learning a better mapping from the image space to the latent space. Also, our full algorithm (Fig. 4(e)) shows the best reconstruction quality. Table 1 gives the

(a) Input Image

(b) Conventional Encoder

(c) Image2StyleGAN

(d) Domain-Guided Encoder (Ours)

(e) In-Domain Inversion (Ours)

Fig. 4. Qualitative comparison on image reconstruction with different GAN inversion methods. (a) Input image. (b) Conventional encoder [36]. (c) Image2StyleGAN [29]. (d) Our proposed *domain-guided* encoder. (e) Our proposed *in-domain* inversion.

quantitative comparison results, where *in-domain* inversion surpasses other competitors from all metrics, including Fréchet Inception Distance (FID) [15], Sliced Wasserstein Discrepancy (SWD) [28], and Mean-Square Error (MSE). The inference speed is also shown in Table 1. Our *domain-guided* encoder can produce much better reconstruction results compared to the traditional encoder with comparable inference time. It also provides a better initialization for further the *domain-regularized* optimization, leading to a significantly faster speed (∼35X faster) than the state-of-the-art optimization-based method [29].

3.4   Real Image Editing

In this section, we evaluate our *in-domain* GAN inversion approach on real image editing tasks, including image interpolation and semantic image manipulation. We also come up with a novel image editing task, called *semantic image diffusion*,

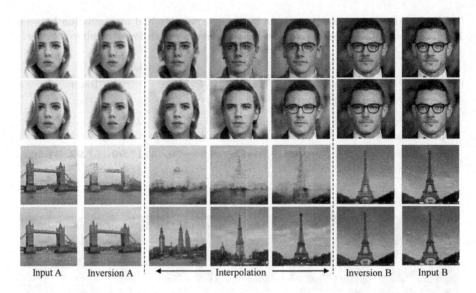

Input A   Inversion A   ◄———— Interpolation ————►   Inversion B   Input B

Fig. 5. Qualitative comparison on image interpolation between Image2StyleGAN [29] (odd rows) and our *in-domain* inversion (even rows).

to see how our approach is able to adapt the content from one image into another and keep the results semantically meaningful and seamlessly compatible.

Image Interpolation. Image interpolation aims at semantically interpolating two images, which is suitable for investigating the semantics contained in the inverted codes. In other words, for a good inversion, the semantic should vary continuously when interpolating two inverted codes. Figure 5 shows the comparison results on the image interpolation task between Image2StyleGAN [29] and our *in-domain* inversion. We do experiments on both face and tower datasets to more comprehensively analyze the semantic property. For the face dataset, our method achieves much smoother interpolated faces than Image2StyleGAN. For example, in the first two rows of Fig. 5, eyeglasses are distorted during the interpolation process with Image2StyleGAN and the change from female to male is unnatural. For tower images, which are much more diverse than faces, the interpolation results from Image2StyleGAN exhibit artifacts and blurriness. By contrast, our inverted codes lead to more satisfying interpolation. One noticeable thing is that during interpolating two towers with different types (*e.g.*, one with one spire and the other with multiple spires), the interpolated images using our approach are still high-quality towers. This demonstrates the *in-domain* property of our algorithm. Quantitative evaluation in Table 2 gives the same conclusion.

Semantic Manipulation. Image manipulation is another way to examine whether the embedded latent codes align with the semantic knowledge learned by GANs. As pointed out by prior work [30,32], GANs can learn rich semantics

Table 2. Quantitative comparison on image interpolation and manipulation between Image2StyleGAN [29] and our *in-domain* inversion. ↓ means lower number is better.

Method	Interpolation				Manipulation			
	Face		Tower		Face		Tower	
	FID↓	SWD↓	FID↓	SWD↓	FID↓	SWD↓	FID↓	SWD↓
MSE-based optimization [29]	112.09	38.20	121.38	67.75	83.69	28.48	113	52.91
In-domain inversion (ours)	**91.18**	**33.91**	**57.22**	**28.24**	**76.43**	**17.99**	**57.92**	**31.50**

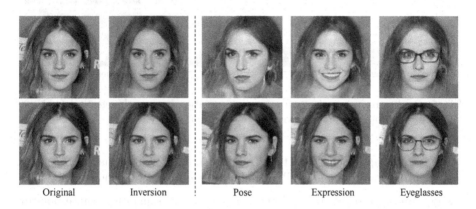

| Original | Inversion | Pose | Expression | Eyeglasses |

Fig. 6. Comparison of Image2StyleGAN [29] (top row) and our *in-domain* inversion (bottom row) on facial attribute manipulation.

| Input | Inversion | − Clouds + | − Sunny + |

Fig. 7. Comparison of Image2StyleGAN [29] (top row) and our *in-domain* inversion (bottom row) on tower image editing. For the manipulation of each attribute, we show the results by either decreasing or increasing the semantic degree.

in the latent space, enabling image manipulation by linearly transforming the latent representation. This can be formulated as

$$\mathbf{x}^{edit} = G(\mathbf{z}^{inv} + \alpha \mathbf{n}), \tag{5}$$

where $\mathbf{n}$ is the normal direction corresponding to a particular semantic in the latent space and α is the step for manipulation. In other words, if a latent code is moved towards this direction, the semantics contained in the output image should vary accordingly. We follow [30] to search the semantic direction $\mathbf{n}$.

Figure 6 and Fig. 7 show the comparison results of manipulating faces and towers using Images2StyleGAN [29] and our *in-domain* GAN inversion. We can see that our method shows more satisfying manipulation results than Image2StyleGAN. Taking face manipulation (Fig. 6) as an example, the hair of the actress becomes blurred after the pose rotation using Image2StyleGAN and the identity changes a lot when editing expression and eyeglasses with the codes from Image2StyleGAN. That is because it only focuses on the reconstruction of the per-pixel values yet omits the semantic information contained in the inverted codes. On the contrary, our *in-domain* inversion can preserve most other details when editing a particular facial attribute. As for tower manipulation, we observe from Fig. 7 that our *in-domain* approach surpasses MSE-based optimization by both decreasing and increasing the semantic level. For example, when removing or adding clouds in the sky, Image2StyleGAN will blur the tower together with the sky, since it only recovers the image at the pixel level without considering the semantic meaning of the recovered objects. Therefore, the cloud is added to the entire image regardless whether a particular region belongs to sky or tower. By contrast, our algorithm barely affects the tower itself when editing clouds, suggesting that our *in-domain* inversion can produce semantically informative latent codes for image reconstruction. We also include the quantitative evaluation on the manipulation task in Table 2. We can tell that our *in-domain* inversion outperforms Image2StyleGAN from all evaluation metrics.

Semantic Diffusion. Semantic diffusion aims at diffusing a particular part (usually the most representative part) of the target image into the context of another image. We would like the fused result to keep the characteristics of the target image (*e.g.*, identity of face) and adapt the context information at the same time. Figure 8 shows some examples where we successfully diffuse various target faces into diverse contexts using our *in-domain* GAN inversion approach. We can see that the results well preserve the identity of the target face and reasonably integrate into different surroundings. This is different from style mixing since the center region of our resulting image is kept the same as that of the target image. More detailed analysis on the semantic diffusion operation can be found in the **supplementary material**.

3.5 Ablation Study

In this part, we conduct an ablation study to analyze the proposed *in-domain* inversion. After the initial training of the encoder, we perform the *domain-regularized* optimization on each image to further improve the reconstruction

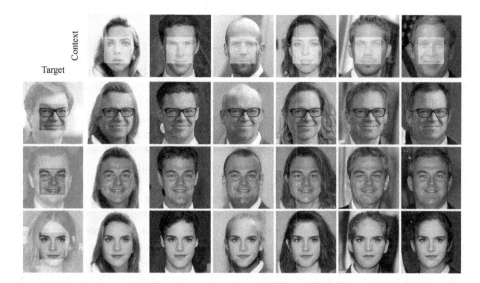

Fig. 8. Semantic diffusion result using our *in-domain* GAN inversion. Target images (first column) are seamlessly diffused into context images (first row) while the identify remains the same as the target.

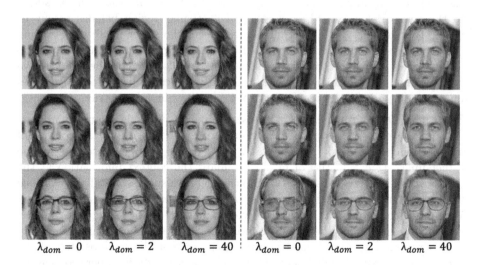

$\lambda_{dom} = 0$ $\lambda_{dom} = 2$ $\lambda_{dom} = 40$ $\lambda_{dom} = 0$ $\lambda_{dom} = 2$ $\lambda_{dom} = 40$

Fig. 9. Ablation study on the loss weight in Eq. (4) for the *domain-regularized* optimization. From top to bottom: original images, reconstructed images, and manipulation results (wearing eyeglasses). For each group of images, the weight λ_{dom} is set to be 0, 2, 40. When λ_{dom} equals to 0, it produces the best reconstructed results but relatively poor manipulation results. When λ_{dom} equals to 40, we get worse reconstruction but more satisfying manipulation.

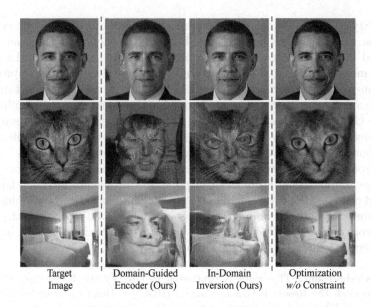

| Target Image | Domain-Guided Encoder (Ours) | In-Domain Inversion (Ours) | Optimization w/o Constraint |

Fig. 10. Results on inverting face, cat face, and bedroom using the same face synthesis model. From left to right: target images, reconstruction results with the outputs from the *domain-guided* encoder, reconstruction results with the proposed *in-domain* inversion, reconstruction results by directly optimizing the latent code *w/o* considering domain alignment [29].

quality. Different from the previous MSE-based optimization, we involve the learned *domain-guided* encoder as a regularizer to land the inverted code inside the semantic domain, as described in Eq. (4). Here, we study the role of the encoder in the optimization process by varying the weight λ_{dom} in Eq. (4). Figure 9 shows the comparison between $\lambda_{dom} = 0, 2, 40$. We observe the trade-off between the image reconstruction quality and the manipulation quality. Larger λ_{dom} will bias the optimization towards the domain constraint such that the inverted codes are more semantically meaningful. Instead, the cost is that the target image cannot be ideally recovered for per-pixel values. In practice, we set $\lambda_{dom} = 2$.

4 Discussion and Conclusion

In this work, we explore the *semantic* property of the inverted codes in the GAN inversion task and propose a novel *in-domain* inversion method. To the best of our knowledge, this is the first attempt to invert a pre-trained GAN model *explicitly* considering the semantic knowledge encoded in the latent space. We show that the code that simply recovers the pixel value of the target image is not sufficient to represent the image at the semantic level. For example, in Fig. 10, we invert different types of image instances (*i.e.*, face, cat face, and bedroom) with the face synthesis model. The last column shows the results from

Image2StyleGAN [29] which recovers a cat or a bedroom with the domain knowledge learned to synthesis human faces. By contrast, the face outline can still be observed in the reconstructions using our *in-domain* inversion (third column). This demonstrates, from a different angle, the superiority of our approach in producing semantically meaningful codes. Taking inverting bedroom (third row) as an example, the bedroom image is outside the domain of the training data and the GAN model should not be able to learn the bedroom-related semantics. Accordingly, reusing the face knowledge to represent a bedroom is ill-defined. Even though we can always use more parameters to over-fit the pixel values of the bedroom (*e.g.*, the last column), such over-fitting would fail to support semantic image manipulation. From this viewpoint, our *in-domain* inversion lands the inverted code inside the original domain to make it semantically meaningful. In other words, we aim at finding the most adequate code to recover the target image from *both the pixel level and the semantic level*. Such *in-domain* inversion significantly facilitates real image editing.

Acknowledgement. This work is supported in part by the Early Career Scheme (ECS) through the Research Grants Council (RGC) of Hong Kong under Grant No. 24206219, CUHK FoE RSFS Grant, and SenseTime Collaborative Grant.

References

1. Abdal, R., Qin, Y., Wonka, P.: Image2stylegan++: How to edit the embedded images? arXiv preprint arXiv:1911.11544 (2019)
2. Arjovsky, M., Chintala, S., Bottou, L.: Wasserstein generative adversarial networks. In: ICML (2017)
3. Bau, D., et al.: Semantic photo manipulation with a generative image prior. In: SIGGRAPH (2019)
4. Bau, D., et al.: Inverting layers of a large generator. In: ICLR Workshop (2019)
5. Bau, D., et al.: Seeing what a GAN cannot generate. In: ICCV (2019)
6. Berthelot, D., Schumm, T., Metz, L.: Began: Boundary equilibrium generative adversarial networks. arXiv preprint arXiv:1703.10717 (2017)
7. Brock, A., Donahue, J., Simonyan, K.: Large scale GAN training for high fidelity natural image synthesis. In: ICLR (2019)
8. Creswell, A., Bharath, A.A.: Inverting the generator of a generative adversarial network. TNNLS 30, 1967–1974 (2018)
9. Donahue, J., Krähenbühl, P., Darrell, T.: Adversarial feature learning. In: ICLR (2017)
10. Dumoulin, V., et al.: Adversarially learned inference. In: ICLR (2017)
11. Goetschalckx, L., Andonian, A., Oliva, A., Isola, P.: GANalyze: toward visual definitions of cognitive image properties. In: ICCV (2019)
12. Goodfellow, I., et al.: Generative adversarial nets. In: NeurIPS (2014)
13. Gu, J., Shen, Y., Zhou, B.: Image processing using multi-code GAN prior. In: CVPR (2020)
14. Gulrajani, I., Ahmed, F., Arjovsky, M., Dumoulin, V., Courville, A.C.: Improved training of Wasserstein GANs. In: NeurIPS (2017)
15. Heusel, M., Ramsauer, H., Unterthiner, T., Nessler, B., Hochreiter, S.: GANs trained by a two time-scale update rule converge to a local Nash equilibrium. In: NeurIPS (2017)

16. Jahanian, A., Chai, L., Isola, P.: On the "steerability" of generative adversarial networks. arXiv preprint arXiv:1907.07171 (2019)
17. Johnson, J., Alahi, A., Fei-Fei, L.: Perceptual losses for real-time style transfer and super-resolution. In: Leibe, B., Matas, J., Sebe, N., Welling, M. (eds.) ECCV 2016. LNCS, vol. 9906, pp. 694–711. Springer, Cham (2016). https://doi.org/10.1007/978-3-319-46475-6_43
18. Karras, T., Aila, T., Laine, S., Lehtinen, J.: Progressive growing of GANs for improved quality, stability, and variation. In: ICLR (2018)
19. Karras, T., Laine, S., Aila, T.: A style-based generator architecture for generative adversarial networks. In: CVPR (2019)
20. Karras, T., Laine, S., Aittala, M., Hellsten, J., Lehtinen, J., Aila, T.: Analyzing and improving the image quality of StyleGAN. arXiv preprint arXiv:1912.04958 (2019)
21. Kingma, D.P., Dhariwal, P.: Glow: generative flow with invertible 1x1 convolutions. In: NeurIPS (2018)
22. Lipton, Z.C., Tripathi, S.: Precise recovery of latent vectors from generative adversarial networks. In: ICLR Workshop (2017)
23. Luo, J., Xu, Y., Tang, C., Lv, J.: Learning inverse mapping by autoencoder based generative adversarial nets. In: Liu, D., Xie, S., Li, Y., Zhao, D., El-Alfy, E.S. (eds.) ICONIP 2017. LNCS, vol. 10635. Springer, Cham (2017). https://doi.org/10.1007/978-3-319-70096-0_22
24. Ma, F., Ayaz, U., Karaman, S.: Invertibility of convolutional generative networks from partial measurements. In: NeurIPS (2018)
25. Miyato, T., Kataoka, T., Koyama, M., Yoshida, Y.: Spectral normalization for generative adversarial networks. In: ICLR (2018)
26. Pan, X., Zhan, X., Dai, B., Lin, D., Loy, C.C., Luo, P.: Exploiting deep generative prior for versatile image restoration and manipulation. arXiv preprint arXiv:2003.13659 (2020)
27. Perarnau, G., Van De Weijer, J., Raducanu, B., Álvarez, J.M.: Invertible conditional GANs for image editing. In: NeurIPS Workshop (2016)
28. Rabin, J., Peyré, G., Delon, J., Bernot, M.: Wasserstein barycenter and its application to texture mixing. In: Bruckstein, A.M., ter Haar Romeny, B.M., Bronstein, A.M., Bronstein, M.M. (eds.) SSVM 2011. LNCS, vol. 6667, pp. 435–446. Springer, Heidelberg (2012). https://doi.org/10.1007/978-3-642-24785-9_37
29. Rameen, A., Yipeng, Q., Peter, W.: Image2stylegan: how to embed images into the StyleGAN latent space? In: ICCV (2019)
30. Shen, Y., Gu, J., Tang, X., Zhou, B.: Interpreting the latent space of GANs for semantic face editing. In: CVPR (2020)
31. Simonyan, K., Zisserman, A.: Very deep convolutional networks for large-scale image recognition. In: ICLR (2015)
32. Yang, C., Shen, Y., Zhou, B.: Semantic hierarchy emerges in deep generative representations for scene synthesis. arXiv preprint arXiv:1911.09267 (2019)
33. Yu, F., Seff, A., Zhang, Y., Song, S., Funkhouser, T., Xiao, J.: LSUN: construction of a large-scale image dataset using deep learning with humans in the loop. arXiv preprint arXiv:1506.03365 (2015)

34. Zhang, H., Goodfellow, I., Metaxas, D., Odena, A.: Self-attention generative adversarial networks. In: ICML (2019)
35. Zhu, J., Zhao, D., Zhang, B.: LIA: Latently invertible autoencoder with adversarial learning. arXiv preprint arXiv:1906.08090 (2019)
36. Zhu, J.-Y., Krähenbühl, P., Shechtman, E., Efros, A.A.: Generative visual manipulation on the natural image manifold. In: Leibe, B., Matas, J., Sebe, N., Welling, M. (eds.) ECCV 2016. LNCS, vol. 9909, pp. 597–613. Springer, Cham (2016). https://doi.org/10.1007/978-3-319-46454-1_36

Key Frame Proposal Network for Efficient Pose Estimation in Videos

Yuexi Zhang[1] , Yin Wang[2] , Octavia Camps[1($\boxtimes$)] , and Mario Sznaier[1]

[1] Electrical and Computer Engineering, Northeastern University,
Boston, MA 02115, USA
zhang.yuex@northeastern.edu, {camps,msznaier}@coe.neu.edu
[2] Motorola Solutions, Inc., Somerville, MA 02145, USA
yin.wang@motorolasolutions.com
http://robustsystems.coe.neu.edu/

Abstract. Human pose estimation in video relies on local information by either estimating each frame independently or tracking poses across frames. In this paper, we propose a novel method combining local approaches with global context. We introduce a light weighted, unsupervised, key frame proposal network (K-FPN) to select informative frames and a learned dictionary to recover the entire pose sequence from these frames. The K-FPN speeds up the pose estimation and provides robustness to bad frames with occlusion, motion blur, and illumination changes, while the learned dictionary provides global dynamic context. Experiments on Penn Action and sub-JHMDB datasets show that the proposed method achieves state-of-the-art accuracy, with substantial speed-up.

Keywords: Fast human pose estimation in videos · Key frame proposal network (K-FPN) · Unsupervised learning

1 Introduction

Human pose estimation [2,21,28,34,35], which seeks to estimate the locations of human body joints, has many practical applications such as smart video surveillance [8,26], human computer interaction [29], and VR/AR [16].

The most general pose estimation pipeline extracts features from the input, and then uses a classification/regression model to predict the location of the joints. Recently, [3] introduced a Pose Warper capable of using a few manually annotated frames to propagate pose information across the complete video. However, it relies on annotations of every k^{th} frame and thus it fails to fully exploit the dynamic correlation between them.

Here, we propose an alternative pose estimation pipeline based on two observations: All frames are not equally informative; and the dynamics of the body joints can be modeled using simple dynamics. The new pipeline uses a light

Electronic supplementary material The online version of this chapter (https://doi.org/10.1007/978-3-030-58520-4_36) contains supplementary material, which is available to authorized users.

A. Vedaldi et al. (Eds.): ECCV 2020, LNCS 12362, pp. 609–625, 2020.
https://doi.org/10.1007/978-3-030-58520-4_36

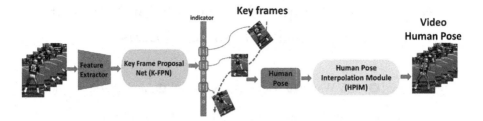

Fig. 1. Proposed pipeline for video human pose detection. The K-FPN net, which is trained unsupervised, selects a set of key frames. The Human Pose Interpolation Module (HPIM), trained to learn human pose dynamics, generates human poses for the entire input sequence from the poses in the key frames.

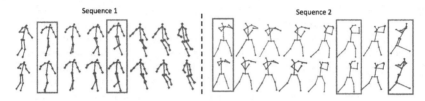

Fig. 2. Two examples of the output of our pipeline. Top: ground truth. Bottom: poses recovered from the automatically selected key frames (red boxes).(Color figure online)

weighted *key frame proposal* network (K-FPN), shown in Fig. 1, to select a small number of frames to apply a pose estimation model. One of the main contributions of this paper is a new loss function based on the *recovery error in the latent feature space* for *unsupervised training* of this network. The second module of the pipeline is an efficient Human Pose Interpolation Module (HPIM), which uses a dynamics-based dictionary to obtain the pose in the remaining frames. Figure 2 shows two sample outputs of our pipeline, where the poses shown in purple were interpolated from the automatically selected red key frames. The advantages of the proposed approach are:

- It uses a very light, unsupervised, model to select "important" frames.
- It is highly efficient, since pose is estimated only at key frames.
- It is robust to challenging conditions present in the non-key frames, such as occlusion, poor lighting conditions, motion blur, etc.
- It can be used to reduce annotation efforts for supervised approaches by selecting which frames should be manually annotated.

2   Related Work

Image Based Pose Estimation. Classical approaches use the structure and inter-connectivity among the body parts and rely on hand-crafted features. Currently, deep networks are used instead of hand-crafted features. [6] used Deep Convolutional Neural Networks (DCNNs) to learn the conditional probabilities

for the presence of parts and their spatial relationships. [40] combined in an end-to-end framework the DCNN with the expressive mixture of parts model. [7] learned the correlations among body joints using an ImageNet pre-trained VGG-16 base model. [35] implicitly modeled long-range dependencies for articulated pose estimation. [21] proposed a "hourglass" architecture to handle large pixel displacements, opening a pathway to incorporate different scaled features stacked together. [11,18,24,32,39] made several improvements on multi-scaled feature pyramids for estimating human pose. However, capturing sufficient scaled features is computationally expensive. [42] proposed a teacher-student architecture to reduce network complexity and computational time. Finally, [4,15,22] refined the location of keypoints by exploiting the human body structure.

Video Based Pose Estimation. Human pose estimation can be improved by capturing temporal and appearance information across frames. [30,31] use deep Convolutional Networks (ConvNet) with optical flow as its input motion features. [27] shows that an additional convolutional layer is able to learn a simpler model of the spatial human layout. [5] improves this work to demonstrate that the joint estimations can be propagated from poses on the first few frames by integrating optical flows. Furthermore, tracking on poses is another popular methodology such as [13,36] which can jointly refine estimations. Others adopt Recurrent Neural Networks(RNN) [9,17,20]. [9] shows that a sequence-to-sequence model can work for structured output prediction. A similar work [20] imposes sequential geometric consistency to handle image quality degradation. Despite of notable accuracy, RNN-based methods suffer from the expensive computations required. [23] proposed to address this issue by using a light-weighted distillator to online distill pose kernels by leveraging the temporal information among frames.

3 Proposed Approach

Figure 1 shows the proposed architecture. Given T consecutive frames, we aim to select a small number of frames, which can capture the global context and provide enough information to interpolate the poses in the entire video. This is challenging since annotations for this task are usually unavailable. Next, we formulate this problem as the minimization of a loss function, which allows us to provide a set of optimal proposals deterministically and without supervision.

The main intuition behind the proposed architecture is that there is a high degree of spatial and temporal correlation in the data, which can be captured by a simple dynamics-based model. Then, key frames should be selected such that they are enough (but no more than strictly needed) to learn the dynamic model and recover the non-selected frames.

3.1 Atomic Dynamics-Based Representation of Temporal Data

We will represent the dynamics of the input data by using the dynamics-based atomic (DYAN) autoencoder introduced in [19], where the atoms are the impulse

response $y(k) = cp^{k-1}$ of linear time invariant (LTI) systems with a pole[1] p, c is a constant and k indicates time. The model uses $N \gg T$ atoms, collected as columns of a dictionary matrix $\mathbf{D} \in \mathbb{R}^{T \times N}$:

$$\mathbf{D} = \begin{bmatrix} 1 & 1 & \cdots & 1 \\ p_1 & p_2 & \cdots & p_N \\ \vdots & \vdots & \vdots & \vdots \\ p_1^{T-1} & p_2^{T-1} & \cdots & p_N^{T-1} \end{bmatrix} \tag{1}$$

Let $\mathbf{Y} \in \mathbb{R}^{T \times M}$ be the input data matrix, where each column has the temporal evolution of a datapoint (i.e. one coordinate of a human joint or the value of a feature, from time 1 to time T). Then, we represent $\mathbf{Y}$ by a matrix $\mathbf{C} \in \mathbb{R}^{N \times M}$ such that $\mathbf{Y} = \mathbf{DC}$, where the element $\mathbf{C}(i,j)$ indicates how much of the output of the ith atom is used to recover the jth input data in $\mathbf{Y}$:

$$\mathbf{Y}(k,j) = \sum_{i=1}^{N} \mathbf{C}(i,j) p_i^{k-1}$$

In [19], the dictionary $\mathbf{D}$ was learned from training data to predict future frames by minimizing a loss function that penalized the reconstruction error of the input and the ℓ_1 norm of $\mathbf{C}$ to promote the sparsity of $\mathbf{C}$ (i.e. using as few atoms/pixel as possible):

$$\mathcal{L}_{dyn} = \|\mathbf{Y} - \mathbf{DC}\|_2^2 + \alpha \sum_{i,j} |\mathbf{C}(i,j)| \tag{2}$$

In this paper, we propose a different loss function to learn $\mathbf{D}$, which is better suited to the task of key frame selection. Furthermore, the learning procedure in [19] requires solving a Lasso optimization problem for each input before it can evaluate the loss (2). In contrast, the loss function we derive in Sect. 3.2 is computationally very efficient, since it does not require such optimization step.

3.2   Key Frame Selection Unsupervised Loss

Given an input video $\mathcal{V}$ with T frames, consider a tensor of its deep features $\mathcal{Y} \in \mathbb{R}^{T \times c \times w \times h}$ with c channels of width w and height h, reshaped into a matrix $\mathbf{Y} \in \mathbb{R}^{T \times M}$. That is, the element $\mathbf{Y}(k,j)$ has the value of the feature j, $j = 1, \ldots, M = cwh$, at time k. Then, our goal is to select a subset of key frames, as small as possible, that captures the content of all the frames. Thus, we propose to cast this problem as finding a *minimal subset of rows* of $\mathbf{Y}$ (the *key frames*), such that it would be possible to recover the left out frames (the other rows of $\mathbf{Y}$) by using these few frames and their atomic dynamics-based representation.

---

[1] Poles are in general complex numbers. Systems with real outputs with a non real pole p must also have its conjugate pole p^*: $y(k) = cp^{k-1} + c^*.p^{*(k-1)}$.

Problem 1. Given a matrix of features $\mathbf{Y} \in \mathbb{R}^{T \times M}$, an overcomplete dictionary $\mathbf{D} \in \mathbb{R}^{T \times N}$, $N \gg T$, for which there exist an atomic dynamics-based representation $\mathbf{C} \in \mathbb{R}^{N \times M}$ such that $\mathbf{Y} = \mathbf{DC}$, find a binary selection matrix $\mathbf{P}_r \in \mathbb{R}^{r \times T}$ with the least number of rows r, such that $\mathbf{Y} \approx \mathbf{DC}_r$, where $\mathbf{C}_r \in \mathbb{R}^{N \times M}$ is the atomic dynamics-based representation of the selected key frames $\mathbf{Y}_r = \mathbf{P}_r \mathbf{Y}$.

Problem 1 can be written as the following optimization problem:

$$\min_{r, \mathbf{P}_r \in \mathbb{R}^{r \times T}} \|\mathbf{Y} - \mathbf{DC}_r\|_F^2 + \lambda r, \tag{3}$$

subject to:

$$\mathbf{P}_r \mathbf{Y} = \mathbf{P}_r \mathbf{DC}_r \tag{4}$$

$$\mathbf{P}_r(i,j) \in \{0,1\} \quad \sum_j \mathbf{P}_r(i,j) = 1 \quad \sum_i \mathbf{P}_r(i,j) \le 1 \tag{5}$$

The first term in the objective (3) minimizes the recovery error while the second term penalizes the number of frames selected. The constraint (4) establishes that $\mathbf{C}_r$ should be the atomic dynamics-based representation of the key frames and the constraints (5) force the binary selection matrix P_r to select r distinct frames. However, this problem is hard to solve since the optimization variables are integer (r) or binary (elements of $\mathbf{P}_r$).

Next, we show how we can obtain a relaxation of this problem, which is differentiable and suitable as a unsupervised loss function to train our key frame proposal network. The derivation has three main steps. First, we use the constraint (4) to replace $\mathbf{C}_r$ with an expression that depends on $\mathbf{P}_r$, $\mathbf{D}$ and $\mathbf{Y}$. Next, we make a change of variables so we do not have to minimize with respect to a matrix of unknown dimensions. Finally, in the last step we relax the constraint on the binary variables to be real between 0 and 1.

Eliminating $\mathbf{C}_r$: Consider the atomic dynamics-based representation of $\mathbf{Y}$:

$$\mathbf{Y} = \mathbf{DC} \tag{6}$$

Multiplying both sides by $\mathbf{P}_r$, defining $\mathbf{D}_r = \mathbf{P}_r \mathbf{D}$, and using (4), we have:

$$\mathbf{P}_r \mathbf{Y} = \mathbf{D}_r \mathbf{C} = \mathbf{D}_r \mathbf{C}_r \tag{7}$$

Noting that $\mathbf{D}_r$ is an overcomplete dictionary, we select the solution for $\mathbf{C}_r$ from (7) with minimum Frobenious norm, which can be found by solving:

$$\min_{\mathbf{C}_r} \|\mathbf{C}_r\|_F^2 \quad \text{subject to: } \mathbf{P}_r \mathbf{Y} = \mathbf{D}_r \mathbf{C}_r \tag{8}$$

The solution of this problem is:

$$\mathbf{C}_r = \mathbf{D}_r^T (\mathbf{D}_r \mathbf{D}_r^T)^{-1} \mathbf{P}_r \mathbf{Y} \tag{9}$$

since the rows of $\mathbf{D}$ (see (1)) are linearly independent and hence the inverse $(\mathbf{D}_r \mathbf{D}_r^T)^{-1}$ exists. Substituting (9) in the first term in (3) we have:

$$\|\mathbf{Y} - \mathbf{DC}_r\|_F^2 = \left\|[\mathbf{I} - \mathbf{DD}_r^T (\mathbf{D}_r \mathbf{D}_r^T)^{-1} \mathbf{P}_r]\mathbf{Y}\right\|_F^2 \tag{10}$$

Using the fact that $\mathbf{D}_r = \mathbf{P}_r\mathbf{D}$ yields the following equivalent to Problem 1:

$$\min_{r,\mathbf{P}_r\in\mathbb{R}^{r\times T}} \left\|[\mathbf{I} - \mathbf{D}\mathbf{D}^T\mathbf{P}_r^T(\mathbf{P}_r\mathbf{D}\mathbf{D}^T\mathbf{P}_r^T)^{-1}\mathbf{P}_r]\mathbf{Y}\right\|_F^2 + \lambda r, \quad \text{subject to (5)} \quad (11)$$

Minimizing with Respect to a Fixed Size Matrix: Minimizing with respect to $\mathbf{P}_r$ is difficult because one of its dimensions is r, which is a variable that we also want to minimize. To avoid this issue, we introduce an approximation trick, where we add a small perturbation $\rho > 0$ to the diagonal of $\mathbf{P}_r\mathbf{D}\mathbf{D}^T\mathbf{P}_r^T$:

$$\min_{r,\mathbf{P}_r\in\mathbb{R}^{r\times T}} \left\|[\mathbf{I} - \mathbf{D}\mathbf{D}^T\mathbf{P}_r^T(\rho\mathbf{I} + \mathbf{P}_r\mathbf{D}\mathbf{D}^T\mathbf{P}_r^T)^{-1}\mathbf{P}_r]\mathbf{Y}\right\|_F^2 + \lambda r, \quad \text{subject to (5)}$$

$$(12)$$

and combine (12) with the Woodbury matrix identity

$$\mathbf{A}^{-1} - \mathbf{A}^{-1}\mathbf{U}[\mathbf{B}^{-1} + \mathbf{V}\mathbf{A}^{-1}\mathbf{U}]^{-1}\mathbf{V}\mathbf{A}^{-1} = [\mathbf{A} + \mathbf{U}\mathbf{B}\mathbf{V}]^{-1}$$

by setting $\mathbf{A} = \mathbf{I}$, $\mathbf{U} = \mathbf{D}\mathbf{D}^T\mathbf{P}_r^T$, $\mathbf{B}^{-1} = \rho\mathbf{I}$, and $\mathbf{V} = \mathbf{P}_r$, to get:

$$\min_{r,\mathbf{P}_r\in\mathbb{R}^{r\times T}} \left\|[\mathbf{I} + \rho^{-1}\mathbf{D}\mathbf{D}^T\mathbf{P}_r^T\mathbf{P}_r]^{-1}\mathbf{Y}\right\|_F^2 + \lambda r, \quad \text{subject to (5)} \quad (13)$$

Now, define $\mathbf{S} = \mathbf{P}_r^T\mathbf{P}_r$, which is a matrix of fixed size $T \times T$. Furthermore using the constraints (5), it is easy to show that $\mathbf{S}$ is diagonal and that its diagonal elements $\mathbf{s}_i$ are 1 if $\mathbf{P}_r$ selects frame i and 0 otherwise. Thus, the vector $\mathbf{s} = \text{diagonal}(\mathbf{S})$ is an indicator vector for the sought key frames and the number of key frames is given by $r = \sum_i \mathbf{s}_i$. Therefore, the objective becomes:

$$\min_{\mathbf{s}\in\mathbb{R}^{T\times 1},\mathbf{s}_i\in\{0,1\}} \left\|[\mathbf{I} + \rho^{-1}\mathbf{D}\mathbf{D}^T\mathbf{S}]^{-1}\mathbf{Y}\right\|_F^2 + \lambda\sum_i \mathbf{s}_i \quad (14)$$

Note that the fact that the inverse $(\mathbf{I} + \rho^{-1}\mathbf{D}\mathbf{D}^T\text{diagonal}(\mathbf{s}))]^{-1}$ is well defined follows from Woodbury's identity and the fact that $(\rho\mathbf{I} + \mathbf{P}_r\mathbf{D}\mathbf{D}^T\mathbf{P}_r^T)^{-1}$ exists since $\rho > 0$ and $\mathbf{P}_r\mathbf{D}\mathbf{D}^T\mathbf{P}_r^T$ is positive semi-definite.

Relaxing the Binary Constraints: Finally, we relax the binary constraints on the elements of the indicator vector $\mathbf{s}$ and let them be real numbers between 0 and 1. We now have the differentiable objective function:

$$\min_{\mathbf{s}\in\mathbb{R}^{T\times 1},0\leq\mathbf{s}_i\leq 1} \left\|[\mathbf{I} + \rho^{-1}\mathbf{D}\mathbf{D}^T\mathbf{S}]^{-1}\mathbf{Y}\right\|_F^2 + \lambda\sum_i \mathbf{s}_i \quad (15)$$

where the only unknown is $\mathbf{s} = \text{diagonal}(\mathbf{S})$. Then, we can use the loss function:

$$\boxed{\mathcal{L}_{K-FPN} = \left\|[\mathbf{I} + \rho^{-1}\mathbf{D}\mathbf{D}^T\mathbf{S}]^{-1}\mathbf{Y}\right\|_F^2 + \lambda\sum_i \mathbf{s}_i} \quad (16)$$

where the vector $\mathbf{s}$ should be the output of a sigmoid layer in order to push its elements to binary values (See Sect. 3.4 for more details).

3.3 Human Pose Interpolation

Given a video with T frames, let $\mathbf{H}_r \in \mathbb{R}^{r \times 2J}$ be the 2D coordinates of J human joints for r key frames, $\mathbf{P}_r \in \mathbb{R}^{r \times T}$ be the associated selection matrix, and $\mathbf{D}^{(h)}$ be a dynamics-based dictionary trained on skeleton sequences using a DYAN autoencoder [19]. Then, the Human Pose Interpolation Module (HPIM) finds the skeletons $\mathbf{H} \in \mathbb{R}^{T \times 2J}$ for the entire sequence, which can be efficiently computed. Its expression can be derived as follows. First, use the reduced dictionary: $\mathbf{D}_r^{(h)} = \mathbf{P}_r \mathbf{D}^{(h)}$ and (9) to compute the minimum Frobenius norm atomic dynamics-based representation for the key frame skeletons $\mathbf{H}_r$: $\mathbf{C}_r = \mathbf{D}_r^{(h)^T} (\mathbf{D}_r^{(h)} \mathbf{D}_r^{(h)^T})^{-1} \mathbf{H}_r$. Then, using the complete dictionary $\mathbf{D}^{(h)}$, the entire skeleton sequence $\mathbf{H} = \mathbf{D}^{(h)} \mathbf{C}_r$ is given by:

$$\mathbf{H} = (\mathbf{D}^{(h)} \mathbf{D}^{(h)^T}) \mathbf{P}_r^T [\mathbf{P}_r (\mathbf{D}^{(h)} \mathbf{D}^{(h)^T}) \mathbf{P}_r^T]^{-1} \mathbf{H}_r \qquad (17)$$

where $\mathbf{D}^{(h)} \mathbf{D}^{(h)^T}$ can be computed ahead of time.

3.4 Architecture, Training, and Inference

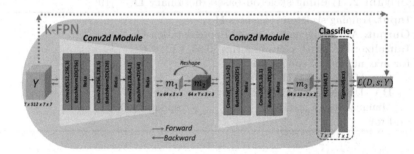

Fig. 3. K-FPN Architecture and details of its modules.

Figure 3 shows the architecture for the K-FPN, which is trained completely unsupervised, by minimizing the loss (16). It consists of two Conv2D modules (Conv + BN + Relu) followed by a Fully Connected (FC) and a Sigmoid layers. The first Conv2D downsizes the input feature tensor from $(T \times 512 \times 7 \times 7)$ to $(T \times 64 \times 3 \times 3)$ while the second one uses the temporal dimension as input channels. The $T \times 1$ output of the FC layer is forced by the Sigmoid layer into logits close to either 0 or 1, where a '1' indicates 'key frame' and its index which one. Inspired by [38], we utilized a control parameter α to form a customized classification layer, represented as $\sigma(\alpha x) = [1 + exp(-\alpha x)]^{-1}$, where α is linearly increased with the training epoch. By controlling α, the output from the K-FPN is nearly a binary indicator such that the sum of its elements is the total number of key frames. The training and inference procedures are summarized

in Algorithms 1 to 3. and code is available at https://github.com/Yuexiaoxi10/Key-Frame-Proposal-Network-for-Efficient-Pose-Estimation-in-Videos.

Algorithm 1. Training K-FPN model (Dictionary $\mathbf{D}$)

1: **Input:** Training video sequences $\mathcal{V}$ with up to T frames
2: **Output:** key frame indicator $\mathbf{s}$
3: **Initialized:** $\mathbf{D}$ with N poles $p \in \mathbb{C}$ in a ring in [0.85,1.15]
4: **for** max number of epochs **do**
5:     $\mathcal{Y} \leftarrow \text{ResNet}(\mathcal{V})$
6:     $m_1 \leftarrow \text{Conv2D}(\mathcal{Y})$ // spatial embedding
7:     $m_2 \leftarrow \text{Reshape}(m_1)$
8:     $m_3 \leftarrow \text{Conv2D}(m_2)$ // temporal embedding
9:     $\mathbf{F} \leftarrow \text{FC}(m_3)$ // mapping to 1D latent space
10:     $\mathbf{s} \leftarrow \text{Sigmoid}(\mathbf{F})$ // key frame binary indicator
11:     Minimize loss $\mathcal{L}_{K-FPN}(\mathbf{D}, \mathbf{s}; \mathcal{Y})$ // updating $\mathbf{D}$, $\mathbf{s}$
12: **end for**

Algorithm 2. Training skeleton-based dictionary $\mathbf{D}^{(h)}$ [19]

1: **Input:** Training skeleton sequences $\mathbf{H}$
2: **Output:** Atomic Dynamics-based Representation $\mathbf{C}$
3: **Initialize:** $\mathbf{D}^{(h)}$ with poles in a ring [0.85, 1.15] $\in \mathbb{C}$
4: **for** max number of epochs **do**
5:     $\mathbf{C} \leftarrow \text{DYAN}_{\text{encoder}}(\mathbf{H}, \mathbf{D}^{(h)})$
6:     $\hat{\mathbf{H}} \leftarrow \text{DYAN}_{\text{decoder}}(\mathbf{C}, \mathbf{D}^{(h)})$
7:     Minimize loss $L_{dyn}(\mathbf{H}, \hat{\mathbf{H}})$ // updating $\mathbf{D}^{(h)}$
8: **end for**

Algorithm 3. Inference K-FPN model and Human Pose Interpolation Module

---

1: **Input:** Testing video sequences $\mathcal{V}$, dictionary $\mathbf{D}^{(h)}$
2: **Output:** key frame indicator $\mathbf{s}$, reconstructed human skeletons $\mathbf{H}$
3: $\mathbf{DDT} = \mathbf{D}^{(h)}\mathbf{D}^{(h)T}$ // Precompute
4: **for** all testing sequences **do**
5:     $\mathbf{s} \leftarrow \text{K-FPN}(\mathcal{V})$ // Select Key Frames
6:     $\mathbf{P}_r \leftarrow \text{SelectionMatrix}(\mathbf{s})$
7:     $\mathbf{H}_r \leftarrow \text{PoseEstimator}(\mathbf{s}, \mathcal{V})$ // key frame skeletons
8:     $\mathbf{H} = \mathbf{DDT} \cdot \mathbf{P}_r^T \cdot [\mathbf{P}_r \cdot \mathbf{DDT} \cdot \mathbf{P}_r^T]^{-1} \cdot \mathbf{H}_r$ // Reconstructed skeletons
9: **end for**

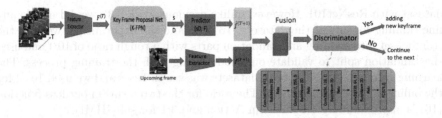

Fig. 4. Online key frame detection. The discriminator distinguishes between input features and features predicted from previous key frames to decide if a new frame should be added as a key frame.

3.5 Online Key Frame Detection

The proposed K-FPN can be modified to process incoming frames, after a minimum set of initial frames has been processed. To do this, we add a discriminator module as shown in Fig. 4, consisting of four (Conv2D + BN + Relu) blocks, which is used to decide if an incoming frame should be selected as a key frame or not. The discriminator is trained to distinguish between features of the incoming frame and features predicted from the set of key frames selected so far, which are easily generated by multiplying the atomic dynamics-based representation of the current key frames with the associated dynamics-based dictionary extended with an additional row (since the number of frames is increased by one) [19]. The reasoning behind this design is that when the features of the new frame cannot be predicted correctly, it must be because the frame brings novel information and hence it should be incorporated as a key frame.

4 Experiments

Following [20,23], we evaluated the K-FPN on two widely-used public datasets: Penn Action [43] and sub-JHMDB [14]. Penn Action is a large-scale benchmark, which depicts human daily activities in unconstrained videos. It has 2326 video clips, with 1258 reserved for training and 1068 for testing with varied frames. It provides 13 annotated joint positions on each frame as well as their visibilities. Following common convention, we only considered the visible joints to evaluate. sub-JHMDB [14] has 319 video clips in three different splits with a training and testing ratio of roughly 3:1. It provides 15 annotations on each human body. However, it only annotates visible joints. Following [20,23,31], the evaluation is reported as the average precision over all splits.

We adopted the ResNet family [10] as our feature encoder and evaluated our method, as the depth was varied from 18 to 101 (see Subsect. 4.3). During training, we froze the ResNet$X$, where $X \in [18/34/50/101]$, and then our K-FPN was trained only on the features output from the encoder. Following [23], we adopted the pre-trained model from [36] as our pose estimator. During our experiments, we applied a specific model, which was trained on the MPII [1]

dataset with ResNet101. However, unlike previous work [23], we did not do any fine-tunning for any of the datasets. To complete the experiments, we split the training set into training and validation parts with a rough ratio of 10:1 and used the validation split to validate our model along with the training process. The learning rate of K-FPN for both datasets was set as $1e-8$ and we used $1e-4$ for the online-updating experiment. The ratio for the two terms in our loss function (16) is approximately 1:2 for Penn Action and 3:1 for sub-JHMDB.

The K-FPN and HPIM dictionaries were initialized as in [19], with $T = 40$ rows for both datasets. Since videos vary in length, we added dummy frames when they had less than 40 frames. For clips longer than 40 frames, we randomly selected 40 consecutive frames as our input during training and used an sliding window of size 40 during testing, in order to evaluate the entire input sequence.

4.1 Data Preprocessing and Evaluation Metrics

We followed conventional data preprocessing strategies. Input images were resized to $3 \times 224 \times 224$ and normalized using the parameters provided by [10]. After that, in order to capture a better pose estimation from the pose model, we utilized the person bounding box to crop each image and pad to 384×384 with a varying scaling factor from 0.8 to 1.4. The Penn Action dataset provides such an annotation, while JHMDB does not. Therefore, we generated the person bounding box on each image by using the person mask described in [20].

Following [20,23,31], we evaluated our performance using the PCK score [41]: a body joint is considered to be correct only if it falls within a range of βL pixels, where L is defined by $L = \max(H, W)$, where H and W denote the height and width of the person bounding box and β controls the threshold to justify how precise the estimation is. We follow convention and set $\beta = 0.2$.

Our full framework consists of three steps: given an input video of length T, K-FPN first samples k key frames; then, pose estimation is done on these k frames; and HPIM interpolates these results for the full sequence. The reported running times are the aggregated time for these three steps. All running times were computed on NVIDIA GTX 1080ti for all methods.

4.2 Qualitative Examples

Figures 1, 2, 3, 4 and 5 show qualitative examples where it can be seen that the proposed approach can successfully recover the skeletons from a few key frames. Please see the supplemental material for more examples and videos.

4.3 Ablation Studies

In order to evaluate the effectiveness of our approach, we conducted ablation studies on the validation split for each dataset.

Backbone Selection. We tested K-FPN using different backbones from the ResNet family. Since sub-JHMDB is not a large dataset, we believe that our K-FPN would be easily overfitted by using deeper feature maps. Thus, we didn't

Fig. 5. Qualitative Examples. The yellow bounding box indicates key frames chosen by K-FPN. The red skeletons are the ground truth, and blue ones are the ones recovered by the interpolation module HPIM. (Color figure online)

Table 1. Backbone selection: PCK for sub-JHMDB and Penn Action.

Backbone	FLOPs(G)	Time(ms)	Head	Sho.	Elbow	Wrist	Hip	Knee	Ankle	Avg.	Avg. #key frames(Std.)
Study on sub-JHMDB validation split											
K-FPN (Resnet50)	5.37	6.9	98.3	98.5	97.7	95.4	98.6	98.5	98.0	97.9	17.5(1.5)
K-FPN (Resnet34)	4.68	5.7	98.0	98.3	97.3	95.4	98.2	97.8	97.2	97.5	17.1(1.0)
K-FPN (Resnet18)	2.32	4.6	98.1	98.4	96.8	93.6	98.4	98.3	97.7	97.3	15.8(1.8)
Study on Penn Action Validation split											
K-FPN (Resnet 101)	10.23	9.7	99.2	98.6	97.3	95.8	98.1	97.9	97.4	97.7	17.7(3.1)
K-FPN (Resnet 50)	5.37	6.6	98.6	98.3	96.0	94.3	98.6	98.7	98.8	97.5	16.6(4.9)
K-FPN (Resnet 34)	4.68	5.5	98.2	98.1	95.1	92.9	98.5	98.7	98.6	97.1	15.0(3.5)

apply ResNet101 on this dataset specifically. Table 1 summarizes the results of this study, where we report running time(ms) and Flops(G) along with PCK scores (higher is better) and average number of selected key frames. These results show that the smaller networks provide faster speed with minor degradation of the performance. Based on these results, for the remaining experiments we used the best model on the validation set. Specifically, we used ResNet34 for Penn Action and Resnet18 for sub-JHMDB.

Number of Key Frames Selection. To evaluate the selectivity of the K-FPN, we randomly picked $n = 100$ validation instances with T frames, ran the K-FPN (using Penn action validation set with Resnet34) and recorded the

Table 2. Number of Key frames Evaluation (PCK). K-FPN vs best out of 100 random samples and uniform sampling on the Penn Action dataset.

Key frames Selection Method			
	K-FPN	Best Sample	Uniform Sample
PCK	98.0	96.4	79.3

number of key frames selected for each of these instances: $K = [k_1, k_2, ..., k_n]$. Given the number of key frames k_i, theoretically, one could determine the best selection by evaluating the PCK score for each of the $\binom{T}{k_i}$ possibilities. Since it is infeasible to run that many combinations, we tried two alternatives: i) selected frames by uniformly sampling the sequence (Uniform Sample), and ii) randomly sampled 100 out of all possible combinations and kept the one with the best PCK score (Best Sample). Table 2 compares the average PCK score using the K-FPN against Uniform Sampling and Best Random Sampling. From [33], it follows that the best PCK score over 100 subsets has a probability >95%, with 99% confidence, of being the true score over the set of all possible combinations and hence provides a good estimate of the unknown optimum. Thus, our *unsupervised* approach indeed achieves performance very close to the theoretical optimum.

Table 3. Online vs Batch Key Frame Selection. We evaluated the performance on sub-JHMDB using $T = T_b + T_o$ frames.

$T_b = 30, T_o = 10$									
	Head	Should	Elbow	Wrist	Hip	Knee	Ankle	Mean	Avg. #Key frames(Std.)
Online	94.8	96.3	95.2	89.6	96.7	95.2	92.3	94.4	15.2(2.4)
Batch	94.7	96.3	95.2	90.2	96.4	95.5	93.2	94.5	16.3(1.8)

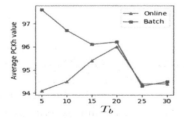 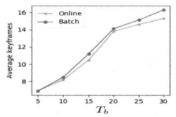

Fig. 6. Online vs Batch Key Frame Selection. We evaluated the performance on sub-JHMDB. The entire length of videos to obtain keyframes is $T_b + T_o$

Table 4. Evaluation on Penn Action and Sub-JHDMB Dataset. We achieve state-of-art performance on both datasets, using same pose model as [23], but without any fine-tuning and using a small number of the key frames.

Evaluation on Penn Action dataset

Method	FLOPs(G)	Time(ms)	Head	Sho.	Elb.	Wri.	Hip	Knee	Ank.	Avg.	Key frames(Std.)
Nie et al. [37]	-	-	64.2	55.4	33.8	22.4	56.4	54.1	48.0	48.0	N/A
Iqal et al. [12]	-	-	89.1	86.4	73.9	73.0	85.3	79.9	80.3	81.1	N/A
Gkioxari et al. [9]	-	-	95.6	93.8	90.4	90.7	91.8	90.8	91.5	91.9	N/A
Song et al. [31]	-	-	98.0	97.3	95.1	94.7	97.1	97.1	96.9	96.8	N/A
Luo et al. [20]	70.98	25.0	98.9	98.6	96.6	96.6	98.2	98.2	97.5	97.7	N/A
DKD(smallCPM) [23]	9.96	12.0	98.4	97.3	96.1	95.5	97.0	97.3	96.6	96.8	N/A
baseline [36]	11.96	11.3	98.1	98.2	96.3	96.4	98.4	97.5	97.1	97.4	N/A
DKD(Resnet50) [23]	8.65	11.0	98.8	98.7	96.8	97.0	98.2	98.1	97.2	97.8	N/A
Ours(Resnet50)	5.37	6.8	98.7	**98.7**	**97.0**	95.3	**98.8**	**98.7**	**98.6**	**98.0**	17.5(4.9)
Ours(Resnet34)	**4.68**	**5.3**	98.2	98.2	96.0	93.6	98.7	98.6	98.4	97.4	**15.2(3.3)**

Evaluation on sub-JHMDB dataset

Methods	FLOPs(G)	Time(ms)	Head	Sho.	Elbow	Wrist	Hip	Knee	Ankle	Avg.	Key frames(Std.)
Park et al. [25]	-	-	79.0	60.3	28.7	16.0	74.8	59.2	49.3	52.5	N/A
Nie et al. [37]	-	-	83.3	63.5	33.8	21.6	76.3	62.7	53.1	55.7	N/A
Iqal et al. [12]	-	-	90.3	76.9	59.3	55.0	85.9	76.4	73.0	73.8	N/A
Song et al. [31]	-	-	97.1	95.7	87.5	81.6	98.0	92.7	89.8	92.1	N/A
Luo et al. [20]	70.98	24.0	98.2	96.5	89.6	86.0	98.7	95.6	90.0	93.6	N/A
DKD(Resnet50) et al. [23]	8.65	-	98.3	96.6	90.4	87.1	99.1	96.0	92.9	94.0	N/A
baseline et al. [36]	11.96	10.0	97.5	97.8	91.1	86.0	99.6	96.8	92.6	94.4	N/A
Ours(Resnet50)	5.37	7.0	95.1	96.4	**95.3**	**91.3**	96.3	95.6	92.6	**94.7**	17.8(1.4)
Ours(Resnet18)	**4.68**	**4.7**	94.7	96.3	95.2	90.2	96.4	95.5	**93.2**	94.5	**16.3(1.8)**

Online Key Frame Selection. We compared the performance between using batch and online updating key frame selection. All evaluations were done with the sub-JHDMB dataset. In this experiment, we use a set of T_b frames to select an initial set of key frames (using "batch" mode) and process the following $To = 10$ frames using online detection. We compare the achieved PCK score and the number of selected frames against the results obtained using a batch approach on all $T_b + T_o$ frames. The results of this experiment for $T_b = 30$ and for $5 \leq T_b \leq 30$ are shown in Table 3 and Fig. 6, respectively. This experiment shows that on one hand, using batch mode, shorter videos ($T_b + T_o$ small) have better PCK score than longer ones. This is because the beginning of the action is often simple (i.e. there is little motion at the start) and is well represented with very few key frames. On the other hand, online updating performs as well as batch, as long as the initial set of frames is big enough ($T_b = 20$ frames). This can be explained by the fact that if T_b is too small, there is not enough information to predict future frames when $T_b + T_o$ is large, making it difficult to decide if a new frame should be selected.

Table 5. Robustness Evaluation

Perturbed frame ratio v.s average PCK score on sub-JHMBD							
Perturbed frames (%)	0	10	20	30	40	50	60
Illum.changes: [36]/Ours	94.4/94.5	94.0/94.2	93.2/93.7	92.3/93.0	91.6/92.7	90.9/92.3	90.2/92.1
Blurring: [36]/Ours	94.4/94.5	92.6/93.4	91.1/92.7	89.9/91.7	89.1/91.4	88.5/91.2	87.9/91.0
Occlusions: [36]/Ours	94.4/94.5	92.8/94.0	90.8/93.1	89.3/92.1	88.0/91.7	86.5/91.3	85.4/90.4

4.4   Comparison Against the State-of-Art

Comparisons against the state-of-art are reported in Table 4. We report our performance using Resnet34 for Penn Action and Resnet18 for Sub-JHMDB, and also using Resnet50, since it is the backbone used by [23]. Our approach achieves the best performance and is 1.6X faster (6.8 ms v.s 11 ms) than the previous state-of-art [23] for the Penn Action dataset, using an average of 17.5 key frames. Moreover, if we use our lightest model (Resnet34), our approach is 2X faster than [23] with a minor PCK degradation. For the sub-JHMDB dataset, [23] did not provide running time and it is not open-sourced. Thus, we compare time against the best available open sourced method [20]. Our approach performed the best of all methods, with a significant improvement on elbow (95.3%) and wrist (91.3%). For completeness, we also compared against the baseline [36], which is a frame-based method, on both datasets. We can observe that by applying our approach with the lightest model, we run more than 2X faster than [36] without any degradation in accuracy.

4.5   Robustness of Our Approach

We hypothesize that our approach can achieve better performance than previous approaches using fewer input frames because the network selects "good" input frames, which are more robust when used with the frame-based method [36]. To better quantify this, we ran an experiment where we randomly partially occluded/blurred/changed illumination at random frames in the sub-JHMBD dataset. Table 5 shows that our approach (using ResNet18) is more robust to all of these perturbations when compared to [36].

5   Conclusion

In this paper, we introduced a *key frame proposal* network (K-FPN) and a *human pose interpolation* module (HPIM) for efficient video based pose estimation. The proposed K-FPN can identify the dynamically informative frames from a video, which allows an image based pose estimation model to focus on only a few "good" frames instead of the entire video. With a suitably learned pose dynamics-based dictionary, we show that the entire pose sequence can be recovered by the HPIM, using only the pose information from the frames selected by the K-FPN. The proposed method achieves better (similar) accuracy than current state-of-art methods using 60% (50%) of the inference time.

Acknowledgements. This work was supported by NSF grants IIS–1814631 and ECCS–1808381; and the Alert DHS Center of Excellence under Award Number 2013-ST-061-ED0001. The views and conclusions contained in this document are those of the authors and should not be interpreted as necessarily representing the official policies, either expressed or implied, of the U.S. Department of Homeland Security.

References

1. Andriluka, M., Pishchulin, L., Gehler, P., Schiele, B.: 2D human pose estimation: new benchmark and state of the art analysis. In: IEEE Conference on Computer Vision and Pattern Recognition (CVPR), June 2014
2. Belagiannis, V., Zisserman, A.: Recurrent human pose estimation. In: 2017 12th IEEE International Conference on Automatic Face and Gesture Recognition (FG 2017), pp. 468–475. IEEE (2017)
3. Bertasius, G., Feichtenhofer, C., Tran, D., Shi, J., Torresani, L.: Learning temporal pose estimation from sparsely-labeled videos. In: Wallach, H., Larochelle, H., Beygelzimer, A., dÁlché-Buc, F., Fox, E., Garnett, R. (eds.) Advances in Neural Information Processing Systems 32, pp. 3027–3038. Curran Associates, Inc. (2019). http://papers.nips.cc/paper/8567-learning-temporal-pose-estimation-from-sparsely-labeled-videos.pdf
4. Cao, Z., Hidalgo, G., Simon, T., Wei, S.E., Sheikh, Y.: OpenPose: real-time multi-person 2D pose estimation using part affinity fields. arXiv preprint arXiv:1812.08008 (2018)
5. Charles, J., Pfister, T., Magee, D., Hogg, D., Zisserman, A.: Personalizing human video pose estimation. In: Proceedings of the IEEE Conference on Computer Vision and Pattern Recognition, pp. 3063–3072 (2016)
6. Chen, X., Yuille, A.L.: Articulated pose estimation by a graphical model with image dependent pairwise relations. In: Advances in Neural Information Processing Systems, pp. 1736–1744 (2014)
7. Chu, X., Ouyang, W., Li, H., Wang, X.: Structured feature learning for pose estimation. In: Proceedings of the IEEE Conference on Computer Vision and Pattern Recognition, pp. 4715–4723 (2016)
8. Cristani, M., Raghavendra, R., Del Bue, A., Murino, V.: Human behavior analysis in video surveillance: a social signal processing perspective. Neurocomputing **100**, 86–97 (2013)
9. Gkioxari, G., Toshev, A., Jaitly, N.: Chained predictions using convolutional neural networks. In: Leibe, B., Matas, J., Sebe, N., Welling, M. (eds.) ECCV 2016. LNCS, vol. 9908, pp. 728–743. Springer, Cham (2016). https://doi.org/10.1007/978-3-319-46493-0_44
10. He, K., Zhang, X., Ren, S., Sun, J.: Deep residual learning for image recognition. CoRR abs/1512.03385 http://arxiv.org/abs/1512.03385 (2015)
11. Ilg, E., Mayer, N., Saikia, T., Keuper, M., Dosovitskiy, A., Brox, T.: FlowNet 2.0: evolution of optical flow estimation with deep networks. CoRR abs/1612.01925 http://arxiv.org/abs/1612.01925 (2016)
12. Iqbal, U., Garbade, M., Gall, J.: Pose for action-action for pose. In: 2017 12th IEEE International Conference on Automatic Face and Gesture Recognition (FG 2017), pp. 438–445. IEEE (2017)
13. Iqbal, U., Milan, A., Gall, J.: Pose-track: joint multi-person pose estimation and tracking. CoRR abs/1611.07727 http://arxiv.org/abs/1611.07727 (2016)

14. Jhuang, H., Gall, J., Zuffi, S., Schmid, C., Black, M.J.: Towards understanding action recognition. In: International Conference on Computer Vision (ICCV), pp. 3192–3199, December 2013
15. Kreiss, S., Bertoni, L., Alahi, A.: PifPaf: composite fields for human pose estimation. In: The IEEE Conference on Computer Vision and Pattern Recognition (CVPR), June 2019
16. Lin, H.-Y., Chen, T.-W.: Augmented reality with human body interaction based on monocular 3D pose estimation. In: Blanc-Talon, J., Bone, D., Philips, W., Popescu, D., Scheunders, P. (eds.) ACIVS 2010. LNCS, vol. 6474, pp. 321–331. Springer, Heidelberg (2010). https://doi.org/10.1007/978-3-642-17688-3_31
17. Lin, M., Lin, L., Liang, X., Wang, K., Cheng, H.: Recurrent 3D pose sequence machines. CoRR abs/1707.09695 http://arxiv.org/abs/1707.09695 (2017)
18. Lin, T., Dollár, P., Girshick, R.B., He, K., Hariharan, B., Belongie, S.J.: Feature pyramid networks for object detection. CoRR abs/1612.03144 http://arxiv.org/abs/1612.03144 (2016)
19. Liu, W., Sharma, A., Camps, O.I., Sznaier, M.: DYAN: a dynamical atoms network for video prediction. CoRR abs/1803.07201 http://arxiv.org/abs/1803.07201 (2018)
20. Luo, Y., et al.: LSTM pose machines. In: Proceedings of the IEEE Conference on Computer Vision and Pattern Recognition, pp. 5207–5215 (2018)
21. Newell, A., Yang, K., Deng, J.: Stacked hourglass networks for human pose estimation. CoRR abs/1603.06937 http://arxiv.org/abs/1603.06937 (2016)
22. Nie, X., Feng, J., Yan, S.: Mutual learning to adapt for joint human parsing and pose estimation. In: ECCV (2018)
23. Nie, X., Li, Y., Luo, L., Zhang, N., Feng, J.: Dynamic kernel distillation for efficient pose estimation in videos. In: The IEEE International Conference on Computer Vision (ICCV), October 2019
24. Papandreou, G., et al.: Towards accurate multi-person pose estimation in the wild. CoRR abs/1701.01779 http://arxiv.org/abs/1701.01779 (2017)
25. Park, D., Ramanan, D.: N-best maximal decoders for part models. In: 2011 International Conference on Computer Vision, pp. 2627–2634. IEEE (2011)
26. Park, S., Trivedi, M.M.: Understanding human interactions with track and body synergies (TBS) captured from multiple views. Comput. Vis. Image Underst. 111(1), 2–20 (2008)
27. Pfister, T., Charles, J., Zisserman, A.: Flowing convnets for human pose estimation in videos. In: Proceedings of the IEEE International Conference on Computer Vision, pp. 1913–1921 (2015)
28. Pishchulin, L., Andriluka, M., Gehler, P., Schiele, B.: Strong appearance and expressive spatial models for human pose estimation. In: Proceedings of the IEEE International Conference on Computer Vision, pp. 3487–3494 (2013)
29. Shotton, J., et al.: Real-time human pose recognition in parts from single depth images. In: CVPR 2011, pp. 1297–1304. IEEE (2011)
30. Simonyan, K., Zisserman, A.: Two-stream convolutional networks for action recognition in videos. In: Advances in Neural Information Processing Systems, pp. 568–576 (2014)
31. Song, J., Wang, L., Van Gool, L., Hilliges, O.: Thin-slicing network: a deep structured model for pose estimation in videos. In: Proceedings of the IEEE Conference on Computer Vision and Pattern Recognition, pp. 4220–4229 (2017)
32. Tang, W., Yu, P., Wu, Y.: Deeply learned compositional models for human pose estimation. In: The European Conference on Computer Vision (ECCV), September 2018

33. Tempo, R., Bai, E.W., Dabbene, F.: Probabilistic robustness analysis: explicit bounds for the minimum number of samples. In: Proceedings of 35th IEEE Conference on Decision and Control, vol. 3, pp. 3424–3428, December 1996
34. Toshev, A., Szegedy, C.: DeepPose: human pose estimation via deep neural networks. In: 2014 IEEE Conference on Computer Vision and Pattern Recognition, pp. 1653–1660, June 2014. https://doi.org/10.1109/CVPR.2014.214
35. Wei, S.E., Ramakrishna, V., Kanade, T., Sheikh, Y.: Convolutional pose machines. In: Proceedings of the IEEE Conference on Computer Vision and Pattern Recognition, pp. 4724–4732 (2016)
36. Xiao, B., Wu, H., Wei, Y.: Simple baselines for human pose estimation and tracking. CoRR abs/1804.06208 http://arxiv.org/abs/1804.06208 (2018)
37. Xiaohan Nie, B., Xiong, C., Zhu, S.C.: Joint action recognition and pose estimation from video. In: Proceedings of the IEEE Conference on Computer Vision and Pattern Recognition, pp. 1293–1301 (2015)
38. Yang, J., et al.: Quantization networks. In: The IEEE Conference on Computer Vision and Pattern Recognition (CVPR), June 2019
39. Yang, W., Li, S., Ouyang, W., Li, H., Wang, X.: Learning feature pyramids for human pose estimation. arXiv preprint arXiv:1708.01101 (2017)
40. Yang, W., Ouyang, W., Li, H., Wang, X.: End-to-end learning of deformable mixture of parts and deep convolutional neural networks for human pose estimation. In: Proceedings of the IEEE Conference on Computer Vision and Pattern Recognition, pp. 3073–3082 (2016)
41. Yang, Y., Ramanan, D.: Articulated pose estimation with flexible mixtures-of-parts. In: CVPR 2011, pp. 1385–1392 (2011). https://doi.org/10.1109/CVPR.2011.5995741
42. Zhang, F., Zhu, X., Ye, M.: Fast human pose estimation. In: The IEEE Conference on Computer Vision and Pattern Recognition (CVPR), June 2019
43. Zhang, W., Zhu, M., Derpanis, K.G.: From actemes to action: a strongly-supervised representation for detailed action understanding. In: 2013 IEEE International Conference on Computer Vision, pp. 2248–2255, December 2013. https://doi.org/10.1109/ICCV.2013.280

Exchangeable Deep Neural Networks for Set-to-Set Matching and Learning

Yuki Saito[1,2]($\boxtimes$) (iD), Takuma Nakamura[1] (iD), Hirotaka Hachiya[3] (iD),
and Kenji Fukumizu[2,4] (iD)

[1] ZOZO Research, Jingumae, Shibuya, Tokyo, Japan
{yuki.saito,takuma.nakamura}@zozo.com
[2] The Graduate University for Advanced Studies, SOKENDAI,
Tachikawa, Tokyo, Japan
[3] Wakayama University, Wakayama, Japan
hhachiya@wakayama-u.ac.jp
[4] The Institute of Statistical Mathematics, Tachikawa, Tokyo, Japan
fukumizu@ism.ac.jp

Abstract. Matching two different sets of items, called heterogeneous set-to-set matching problem, has recently received attention as a promising problem. The difficulties are to extract features to match a correct pair of different sets and also preserve two types of exchangeability required for set-to-set matching: the pair of sets, as well as the items in each set, should be exchangeable. In this study, we propose a novel deep learning architecture to address the abovementioned difficulties and also an efficient training framework for set-to-set matching. We evaluate the methods through experiments based on two industrial applications: fashion set recommendation and group re-identification. In these experiments, we show that the proposed method provides significant improvements and results compared with the state-of-the-art methods, thereby validating our architecture for the heterogeneous set matching problem.

Keywords: Set to set matching · Deep learning · Permutation invariance

1 Introduction

Matching pairs of data is a crucial part of many machine learning tasks, including recommendation [36,56,61], person re-identification (re-id) [87], image search [74], and face recognition [54], as typical industrial applications. Over the past decade, a deep learning framework for matching up data, e.g., images, has served as the core of such systems.

Aside from these tasks, set-to-set matching, which is an extension of multiple instance matching, has recently been identified as an important element in

Electronic supplementary material The online version of this chapter (https:// doi.org/10.1007/978-3-030-58520-4_37) contains supplementary material, which is available to authorized users.

A. Vedaldi et al. (Eds.): ECCV 2020, LNCS 12362, pp. 626–646, 2020.
https://doi.org/10.1007/978-3-030-58520-4_37

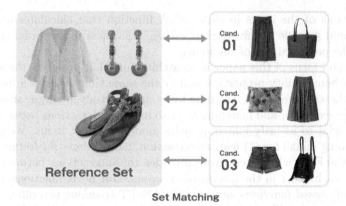

Set Matching

Fig. 1. One of the main questions that set-to-set matching attempts to answer is as follows: which candidate is more compatible than others with the reference set? Here, we consider the matching of the reference set and the respective candidate set and then selecting the best pair.

various applications required by emerging web technologies or services. A representative example in e-commerce is fashion recommendation, where a group of fashion items deemed to match the collection of fashion items already owned by a user is recommended. Regarding the group as an unordered set, we can consider this task a set-to-set matching problem, as shown in Fig. 1. Another example is group re-identification (group re-id) in surveillance systems [40, 41, 77], which has recently started implementing a function to track known groups of suspicious persons or criminals, a task that can also be simplified as a set-to-set matching problem. Other examples include image-set retrieval [9, 11], image-set classification [45], image-set reconstruction [42], person re-id [44], taxonomy matching [59], cross-lingual matching [29], relational data matching [30], and face verification [43, 78]. Earlier studies have also explored face recognition as a set-to-set matching problem [1, 6, 63, 79] and next-basket recommendation [56].

Set matching scenarios can be grouped into two classes: homogeneous set matching and heterogeneous set matching. In the former, two positive sets comprising the same instances, such as the images of the face of the same person, are to be matched. Except for variations such as differences in illumination or pose in the images, both sets contain similar instances. This scenario has been investigated in several studies [1, 6, 9, 11, 42–45, 63, 78, 79]. In the heterogeneous case, the instances within paired sets can be considerably different, as is the case in fashion recommendation and group re-id. To the best of our knowledge, there are very few studies on constructing deep learning models for heterogeneous set matching. We consider that matching heterogeneous sets is a more difficult task and requires a strong learning architecture to match different sets.

Furthermore, another fundamental difficulty in set-to-set matching, compared with ordinary data matching, lies in the two types of exchangeability required: exchangeability between the pair of sets and invariance across different

permutations of the items in each set. A function that calculates a matching score should provide an invariant response, regardless of the order of the two sets, or the permutations of the items.

The main focus of this paper is an architecture that preserves the aforementioned exchangeability properties, and at the same time, realizes a high performance in heterogeneous set matching tasks. In this study, we argue that allowing the feature extractor and matching layer to include interactions between the two sets is crucial to identify matching pairs among different items. We propose a deep learning model for (1) feature extraction, named *cross-set feature transformation* (CSeFT), which iteratively provides the interactions between the pair of sets to each other in the intermediate layers. Our novel functions, *attention-* and *affinity-based functions*, organize the CSeFT spanning two different sets in the feature spaces, thereby improving the feature representations. The proposed architecture also includes (2) a matching layer, named *cross-similarity function* (CS function), that calculates the matching score between the features of the set members across the two sets accurately. Our model guarantees both types of exchangeability in the modules. Figure 2 shows the proposed architecture.

We examine the set-to-set matching problem in a supervised setting, where examples of correctly paired sets are deployed as training data. The objective is to train the feature extractor and matching layer in an end-to-end manner such that the appropriate sets of features to be matched can be extracted. To train the model efficiently, we also propose a novel training framework, *K-pair-set loss*. Following training, the model is then used to find correct pairs of sets among a group of candidates.

The effectiveness of our approach is demonstrated in two real-world applications. First, we consider fashion set matching, where provided examples of the outfits are used as correct combinations of items (clothes). Using a large number of examples of the outfits in the form of images, we aim to match the correct pair of defined sets using the IQON dataset [51]. Since two positive sets include images of different fashion items, we regard this case as heterogeneous set matching. Next, we evaluate our methods through group re-id experiments using two datasets, a new extension of the Market-1501 dataset [87] (Market-1501 Group) and the Road Group dataset [77]. We use the Market-1501 Group dataset to analyze sensitivity to noises or outliers in set matching and the Road Group dataset as a more practical search task. Considering group membership change caused by the noises, we regard group re-id as a heterogeneous set matching problem. In the fashion set matching and group re-id experiments performed on the Market-1501 Group dataset, our methods show significant improvements compared with the results of baseline methods. Moreover, using the data augmentation method that we developed for the pair set (set-aug), our methods show competitive results without using any external datasets or spatial layout information on the Road Group dataset.

The main contributions of this paper are as follows. (i) A novel deep learning architecture is proposed to provide the two types of exchangeability required for set-to-set matching. (ii) The proposed feature extractors using the

interactions between two sets are shown to extract better features for heterogeneous set matching. (iii) A new loss function, K-pair-set loss, is proposed and provide better performances in our tasks. (iv) We introduce set-input methods into group re-id tasks (Road Group) using a new set-data augmentation, thereby showing competitive results without using external datasets or spatial relations. (v) The proposed models show state-of-the-art results for the fashion set matching and group re-id, supporting the claim that the interactions and exchangeability improve the accuracy and robustness of the set-matching procedure.

2   Preliminaries: Set-to-Set Matching

We introduce the necessary notation as follows. Let $\boldsymbol{x}_n, \boldsymbol{y}_m \in \mathfrak{X} = \mathbb{R}^d$ be feature vectors representing the features of each individual item. Let $\mathcal{X} = \{\boldsymbol{x}_1, \ldots, \boldsymbol{x}_N\}$ and $\mathcal{Y} = \{\boldsymbol{y}_1, \ldots, \boldsymbol{y}_M\}$ be *sets* of these feature vectors, where $\mathcal{X}, \mathcal{Y} \in 2^{\mathfrak{X}}$.

The function $f : 2^{\mathfrak{X}} \times 2^{\mathfrak{X}} \to \mathbb{R}$ calculates a matching score between the two sets $\mathcal{X}$ and $\mathcal{Y}$. Guaranteeing the exchangeability of the set-to-set matching requires that the matching function $f(\mathcal{X}, \mathcal{Y})$ is *symmetric* and *invariant* under any permutation of items within each set.

We consider tasks where the matching function f is used per pair of sets [92] to select a correct matching. Given candidate pairs of sets $(\mathcal{X}, \mathcal{Y}^{(k)})$, where $\mathcal{X}, \mathcal{Y}^{(k)} \in 2^{\mathfrak{X}}$ and $k \in \{1, \cdots, K\}$, we choose $\mathcal{Y}^{(k^*)}$ as a correct one so that $f(\mathcal{X}, \mathcal{Y}^{(k^*)})$ achieves the maximum score from amongst the K candidates. In this study, a supervised learning setting is considered, where the function f is trained to classify the correct pair and unmatched pairs.

2.1   Mappings of Exchangeability

We present a brief review on several notions of exchangeability, which are used in building our models.

Permutation Invariance. A set-input function f is said to be *permutation invariant* if

$$f(\mathcal{X}, \mathcal{Y}) = f(\pi_x \mathcal{X}, \pi_y \mathcal{Y}) \tag{1}$$

for permutations π_x on $\{1, \ldots, N\}$ and π_y on $\{1, \ldots, M\}$.

Permutation Equivariance. A map $f : \mathfrak{X}^N \times \mathfrak{X}^M \to \mathfrak{X}^N$ is said to be *permutation equivariant* if

$$f(\pi_x \mathcal{X}, \pi_y \mathcal{Y}) = \pi_x f(\mathcal{X}, \mathcal{Y}) \tag{2}$$

for permutations π_x and π_y, where π_x and π_y are on $\{1, \ldots, N\}$ and $\{1, \ldots, M\}$, respectively. Note that f is permutation invariant for permutations within $\mathcal{Y}$.

Symmetric Function. A map $f : 2^{\mathfrak{X}} \times 2^{\mathfrak{X}} \to \mathbb{R}$ is said to be *symmetric* if

$$f(\mathcal{X}, \mathcal{Y}) = f(\mathcal{Y}, \mathcal{X}). \tag{3}$$

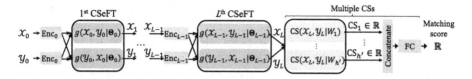

Fig. 2. Our model calculates a matching score between the paired sets. Enc_i, CSeFT, CS, and FC indicate an $(i+1)$-th (one-layered) encoder sharing weights within the same layer, cross-set feature transformation, cross-similarity function, and fully connected layer, respectively. We exclude the multihead structure in g.

Two-Set-Permutation Equivariance. Given $\mathcal{Z}^{(1)} \in \mathcal{X}^N$ and $\mathcal{Z}^{(2)} \in \mathcal{X}^M$, a map $f : \mathcal{X}^* \times \mathcal{X}^* \to \mathcal{X}^* \times \mathcal{X}^*$ is said to be *two-set-permutation equivariant* if

$$pf(\mathcal{Z}^{(1)}, \mathcal{Z}^{(2)}) = f(\mathcal{Z}^{(p(1))}, \mathcal{Z}^{(p(2))}) \tag{4}$$

for any permutation operator p exchanging the two sets, where $\mathcal{X}^* = \cup_{n=0}^{\infty} \mathcal{X}^n$ indicates a sequence of arbitrary length such as $\mathcal{X}^N$ or $\mathcal{X}^M$.

3   Matching and Learning for Sets

3.1   Cross-Set Feature Transformation

We construct the architecture of the feature extractor, which transforms sets of features using the interactions between the pair of sets, and extracts the desired features to be matched in the post-processing stages (Sect. 3.2).

Here, consider the transformation of a pair of set-feature vectors $(\mathcal{X}, \mathcal{Y})$ into new feature representations on $\mathcal{X}^N \times \mathcal{X}^M$, using two-set-permutation equivariant functions. Let i be the iteration (layer) number of the CSeFT layers. Our feature extraction then can be described as a map of $(\mathcal{X}_i, \mathcal{Y}_i) \to (\mathcal{X}_{i+1}, \mathcal{Y}_{i+1})$, where $\mathcal{X}_{i+1}, \mathcal{X}_i \in \mathcal{X}^N$, $\mathcal{Y}_{i+1}, \mathcal{Y}_i \in \mathcal{X}^M$, $\mathcal{X}_{i+1} = (\boldsymbol{x}_{(n,i+1)})_{n=1}^N$, $\mathcal{X}_i = (\boldsymbol{x}_{(n,i)})_{n=1}^N$, $\mathcal{Y}_{i+1} = (\boldsymbol{y}_{(m,i+1)})_{m=1}^M$, and $\mathcal{Y}_i = (\boldsymbol{y}_{(m,i)})_{m=1}^M$. For example, $\boldsymbol{x}_{(n,i)} \in \mathcal{X}$ denotes the feature vector extracted by the i-th layer representing the n-th item, $\boldsymbol{x}_n$, and $\boldsymbol{y}_{(m,i)}$ is defined similarly. Note that the initial feature vectors with $i = 0$ are found with a typical feature extractor, i.e., a deep convolutional neural network (CNN) for the image of each item. Then, we construct a parallel architecture of CSeFT, with an asymmetric transformation g, as follows:

$$\text{cross-set feature transformation (CSeFT)} : \begin{cases} \mathcal{X}_{i+1} = g(\mathcal{X}_i, \mathcal{Y}_i | \boldsymbol{\Theta}_i) \\ \mathcal{Y}_{i+1} = g(\mathcal{Y}_i, \mathcal{X}_i | \boldsymbol{\Theta}_i), \end{cases} \tag{5}$$

where $g : \mathcal{X}^* \times \mathcal{X}^* \to \mathcal{X}^*$ is a permutation equivariant function and $\boldsymbol{\Theta}_i$ is learnable weights shared in the same layer. Also, we introduce the respective residual paths [17] to Eq. (5). Figure 3 shows the model of our CSeFT.

We propose two possible feature extractors for g: an *attention-based function*, and an *affinity-based function*. Both are constructed to assign the *matched*

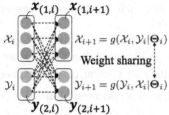
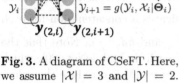
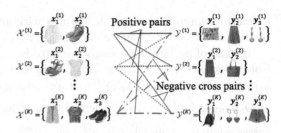

Fig. 3. A diagram of CSeFT. Here, we assume $|\mathcal{X}| = 3$ and $|\mathcal{Y}| = 2$. The colors indicate the respective set members.

Fig. 4. K-pair-set-based matching candidates. Red and blue lines indicate correct pairs ($\mathcal{X}^{(k)}$, $\mathcal{Y}^{(k)}$) and negative cross pairs ($\mathcal{X}^{(k)}$, $\mathcal{Y}^{(k')}$) : $\forall k' \neq k$, where $k, k' \in \{1, \cdots, K\}$, respectively. (Color figure online)

feature vectors to the *reference* feature vector, taking account of interactions between the two sets. For simplicity, we provide an explanation via the case of extracting the features for $\mathcal{X}$ as follows (we can easily exchange $\mathcal{X}$ and $\mathcal{Y}$ for $\mathcal{Y}$).

The attention-based function of g maps $\boldsymbol{x}_{(n,i)} \rightarrow \boldsymbol{x}_{(n,i+1)}$ as follows:

$$\boldsymbol{x}_{(n,i+1)} = \frac{1}{|\mathcal{Y}_i|} \sum_{y \in \mathcal{Y}_i} \left(\frac{l_i^{(1)}(\boldsymbol{x}_{(n,i)})^{\mathrm{T}} l_i^{(2)}(\boldsymbol{y})}{\sqrt{d_g}} \right)_+ l_i^{(3)}(\boldsymbol{y}), \tag{6}$$

where $n \in \{1, \cdots, N\}$, $\boldsymbol{\Theta}_i = \{\Theta_i^{(1)}, \Theta_i^{(2)}, \Theta_i^{(3)}\}$, $\Theta_i^{(j)} \in \mathbb{R}^{d_g \times d}$, $|\mathcal{Y}_i| = M$, $l_i^{(j)}$ denote a linear transformation, i.e., $l_i^{(j)}(\boldsymbol{x}) := \Theta_i^{(j)}\boldsymbol{x}$, and $()_+$ is a non-negative mapping, i.e., ReLU [13], which introduces nonlinear interactions between the two elements.

Note that Eq. (6) relates to other attention models [22,28,31,37,70,81], especially the dot-product attention [37,70]. The dot-product attention has been introduced to calculate the weighted average on $\mathcal{Y}$ using softmax as the coefficients. However, the softmax operation would be inconsistent with our matching objective, as through normalization it increases the coefficients even in unmatched cases of $\mathcal{X}$ and $\mathcal{Y}$. To preserve non-linearity, we use the non-negative weighted sum instead and average it.

The affinity-based function of g maps $\boldsymbol{x}_{(n,i)} \rightarrow \boldsymbol{x}_{(n,i+1)}$ as follows:

$$\boldsymbol{x}_{(n,i+1)} = \frac{1}{2} \left(\bar{\boldsymbol{x}}_{(n,i)} + \frac{1}{|\bar{\mathcal{Y}}_i|} \sum_{\bar{\boldsymbol{y}} \in \bar{\mathcal{Y}}_i} \left(\frac{\bar{\boldsymbol{x}}_{(n,i)}^{\mathrm{T}} \bar{\boldsymbol{y}}}{\sqrt{d_g}} \right)_+ \bar{\boldsymbol{y}} \right), \tag{7}$$

where $\boldsymbol{\Theta}_i = \{\Theta_i^{(1)}, \Theta_i^{(2)}\}$, $\bar{\boldsymbol{x}}_{(n,i)} = l_i^{(1)}(\boldsymbol{x}_{(n,i)})$, and $\bar{\mathcal{Y}}_i = \{l_i^{(2)}(\boldsymbol{y}_{(m,i)})\}_{m=1}^{M}$. Using the two linear transformations $l_i^{(1)}$ and $l_i^{(2)}$, the affinity-based function combines the resembling feature vectors within different sets so that the feature vectors for $\mathcal{X}$ have similar representations to the linearly transformed vectors in $\mathcal{Y}$.

Other simple permutation equivariant functions of g, e.g., $\boldsymbol{x}_{(n,i+1)} = \boldsymbol{x}_{(n,i)} + \frac{1}{|\mathcal{Y}_i|} \sum_{y \in \mathcal{Y}_i} \boldsymbol{y}$, may be utilized. However, we consider it a function incapable of

extracting appropriate enough features without any rich interactions between the two sets to yield accurate matching for two sets.

Instead of performing g singly, we introduce a multihead structure [70] to our feature extractor g, which is also a permutation equivariant function. Denoting the output of $g(\mathcal{X}_i, \mathcal{Y}_i | \Theta_i^{(j)})$ as $g_{\mathcal{X}_i}^{(j)}$, the multihead version of g is defined as $\Theta_h \text{Concat}\left(g_{\mathcal{X}_i}^{(1)}, \cdots, g_{\mathcal{X}_i}^{(h)}\right)$, where Concat indicates a concatenation for each corresponding set member in $g_{\mathcal{X}_i}^{(j)}$, $\Theta_h \in \mathbb{R}^{d \times hd_g}$, and $hd_g = d$. Note that the multihead structure is related to recent models such as MobileNet [20], which isolates and places the convolutional operations in parallel to reduce the calculation costs whilst preserving the accuracy of the recognition. We assume that the multihead structure provides various interactions between the set members, reducing the calculation costs as well.

Note that we can stack CSeFTs or combine it with other networks that operate upon the sets or items independently, which preserves the symmetric architecture. Although a function of our CSeFT does not entail interactions within a set, stacking CSeFTs takes account of higher-order interactions between multiple elements involving the intra-set, which is a similar way of overlaying convolution layers for CNNs. We discuss the overall architecture in Sect. 5.1.

3.2   Calculating Matching Score for Sets

We introduce a matching layer to calculate the matching score between two given sets, mapping $2^{\mathfrak{X}} \times 2^{\mathfrak{X}} \to [0, \infty]$. It is designed to calculate the inner product for every combination of set members across sets, so we call this *cross-similarity* (CS), defined as follows:

$$\text{CS}(\mathcal{X}, \mathcal{Y} | W) := \frac{1}{|\mathcal{X}||\mathcal{Y}|} \sum_{x \in \mathcal{X}} \sum_{y \in \mathcal{Y}} \left(\frac{l(\boldsymbol{x}|W)^{\mathrm{T}} l(\boldsymbol{y}|W)}{\sqrt{d_w}} \right)_+, \qquad (8)$$

where x and y are feature vectors in $\mathcal{X}$ and $\mathcal{Y}$, respectively, l is a linear function allowing conversions into a lower-dimensional space using learnable weights $W \in \mathbb{R}^{d_w \times d}$, i.e., $l(\boldsymbol{x}|W) := W\boldsymbol{x}$, and d_w is the number of dimensions of the lower-dimensional space. CS can be seen as a calculation of the average similarity in the linear subspaces created by the dimensionality reduction l, or the normalized and non-negative inner product if both sets contain only one set member.

While CS function is based on a simple pair relationship, considering the feature extraction provided by CSeFT layers that involves multiple elements to represent each feature, thereby higher-order relationships are included.

Instead of calculating CS singly, we utilize multiple CSs (mCS) to combine the CSs calculated with different linear mappings. The procedure runs as follows:

$$\text{mCS}(\mathcal{X}, \mathcal{Y} | \mathbf{W}) = l(\text{Concat}(\text{CS}_1, \cdots, \text{CS}_{h'}) | W_o), \qquad (9)$$

where $\mathbf{W} = \{W_1, \cdots, W_{h'}, W_o\}$, $\text{CS}_j = \text{CS}(\mathcal{X}, \mathcal{Y} | W_j) \in \mathbb{R}$, the linear function l with learnable weights W_o maps $\mathbb{R}^{h'} \to \mathbb{R}$, and $h'd_w = d$.

Since CS and mCS are symmetric and permutation invariant functions, combined with the fact that CSeFT is a two-set-permutation equivariant function, our model is symmetric and invariant under any permutation of items within each set in these properties.

3.3 Training for Pairs of Sets

Next, the task of maximizing the matching score is translated into a minimization of a loss function of set matching, allowing for comparison against the scores for other matching candidates. Although several studies have investigated loss functions for point-to-point [48,67] or point-to-set [84,90] metric learning, the loss function for set matching has not been well studied, and the efficient approach to preparing K candidates for each query set is non-trivial.

To train our model efficiently, we create matching candidates from the correct pairs, as described in Fig. 4. Let $(\mathcal{X}^{(k)}, \mathcal{Y}^{(k)})$ be a correct pair of sets, where $k \in \{1, \cdots, K\}$. From those K-pair, by extracting all $\mathcal{Y}^{(k)}$, we create the set of $\mathcal{Y}^{(k)}$ as $\mathbf{Y} = \{\mathcal{Y}^{(1)}, \cdots, \mathcal{Y}^{(K)}\}$. That is, $\mathbf{Y}$ is composed of sets exhibiting correct relations to the respective $\mathcal{X}^{(k)}$, and $\mathbf{Y}$ can be used as a set of candidates for each $\mathcal{X}^{(k)}$ in the training stage. We construct positive pairs and negative cross pairs from these candidates by assuming that one correct pair exists for the respective sets, as described in Sect. 2. Then, we train our models using these pairs with a conventional softmax cross-entropy loss. We consider the above training method as a set version of N-pair loss [67], so we call this K-pair-set loss.

4   Related Works

Set-Input Neural Networks. Deep learning architectures for set data have been well studied [37,55,72,85], and several studies have investigated its representation universality [60,62,73,82]. In the work of Lee et al. [37], the state-of-the-art set-feature model, Set Transformer, was introduced by applying a self-attention based Transformer [70] to a set data. Set Transformer is trained through supervised/unsupervised learning and transforms a set data into a vector/matrix representation to recognize set features. However, constructing a deep learning model that can manage multiple sets has not been well studied.

Set-to-Set Matching. Various studies have suggested modeling a set as a hull [6,23,80,92], hyperplanes [12,71], linear subspace [15,34,76,79], convex cone [66], covariance matrix [4,75], Gaussian model [1,63], among others, for matching sets. The methods above do not include feature learning schemes for paired sets, and most of them require specific computations involving optimization methods to measure the similarity/distance between the set models. Compared with these optimization-based methods, our models are based on a feed-forward function, thus are potentially easier to scale up.

Applications. Many fashion item recommendation studies have investigated natural combinations of fashion items, the so-called visual fashion compatibility,

to recommend fashion items or outfits [16,18,21,39,69]. In this study, the main difficulties of the fashion set matching procedures lie in satisfying the fashion compatibility requirements of the matched sets.

In the applications of group re-id [4,24,40,41,77,88,91], problems of multiple instance matching arise. One group re-id scenario has been proposed that the detection of known groups from videos [40] is required. Also, two group re-id datasets, the Road Group dataset, and the DukeMTMC Group dataset[1] have been constructed [40], which include bounding box annotations for each person. Our experiments focus on set-to-set matching using these given cropped images.

Methods for Non-exchangeable Data. Many powerful data-processing methods, such as graph matching [2,3,10,14,38,83,86], graph classification [47], entity matching [50], and sequence matching [5,64] have been proposed based on the specific data structures. In natural language processing, Devlin et al. achieved state-of-the-art results in various tasks using the bidirectional encoder representations from transformers (BERT) [8]. Furthermore, Cucurull et al. applied graph neural networks (GNNs) to predict fashion compatibility between related fashion items using graph structures [7]. Although the data in those tasks are known to be non-exchangeable, we still consider that comparing these promising models with our model is possible and necessary.

5 Experiments

5.1 Overall Architecture

In this section, we briefly describe our models. Borrowing from the encoder–decoder structure [37,52,70], we construct our architecture by combining the encoder [37], called a self-attention block, with the decoder of our CSeFT. We apply a feed-forward network comprising two fully connected layers with a leaky ReLU [46] to the first argument of each function g. We then repeat this structure L times in succession, as described in Fig. 2. We set h, h', L, and d to 8, 8, 2, and 512, respectively. To combine it with CNN features, for the fashion task, we use the Inception-v3 [68], which is pre-trained using the ILSVRC-2012 ImageNet [58], and finetune it. We extract the feature vectors on $\mathbb{R}^{2048}$ from the global average pooling layer and linearly transform it into $\mathbb{R}^{512}$. For the group re-id tasks, we utilize a simple CNN that maps $3 \rightarrow 64 \rightarrow 128 \rightarrow 256 \rightarrow 512$ channels using 3×3 kernels and train it from scratch.

5.2 Baselines for Comparisons

We validate our architecture through comparison with other set-matching models. However, to the best of our knowledge, studies using deep neural networks for matching two heterogeneous sets are non-existent. Instead, we use extensions from the state-of-the-art set-input method and the promising models in other

---

[1] Note that the DukeMTMC [57] is no longer available.

related domains to a set-to-set matching procedure as described below, and consider this acceptable for the comparison. We also present ablation studies including other ordinary set matching functions.

Set Transformer. The Set Transformer [37] transforms a set of feature vectors into a vector on $\mathbb{R}^d$. Denoting the Set Transformer model ST, we perform the extension by calculating the matching score between the two sets $\mathcal{X}$ and $\mathcal{Y}$ via the inner product $ST(\mathcal{X})^T ST(\mathcal{Y})$, sharing the weights between the two ST.

BERT. We consider a union of two sets as a set-input for the extension of BERT [8] and omit the individual token embedding, i.e., the position embedding. We use the segment embedding to designate items of $\mathcal{X}$ and $\mathcal{Y}$. We use three variants: $BERT_{BASE}$ is the same model as described in [8]; $BERT_{BASE-AP}$ uses the average pooling in the last layer; and $BERT_{SMALL}$ is a four-layered version of $BERT_{BASE}$ with eight heads, and the hidden size is 512.

GNN. We combine two sets as one input for the extension of GNN [7]. Because this model is not presented to train in an end-to-end with the feature extractor, we do not finetune the CNN in fashion set matching, where pre-trained CNNs are used, but train it in an end-to-end manner for the group re-id task. Note that we omit the context provided from the external graphs in the evaluation stage to apply this model in the same scenarios of our tasks. We set the training epoch to 256 in the group re-id to enhance the training results of the GNN.

The properties in the above models are different from ours. The extension of Set Transformer satisfies the exchangeability criteria; however, no interactions between paired sets are provided. Both extensions of BERT and GNN provide the interactions but do not facilitate the exchangeability of two sets.

Additionally, in our first experiments, we introduce a conventional CNN, trained by Hard-Aware Point-to-Set loss (HAP2S) [84] as a minimum configuration. We use the exponential weighting and the same parameter setting described in [84]. We also use the *batch all* strategy [19] to train the CNN effectively.

5.3 Training Settings

In this section, we briefly describe the training settings. We use a stochastic gradient descent method with a learning rate of 0.005, a momentum of 0.5, and a weight decay of 0.00004. We set the numbers of matching candidates and the training epochs to 4 and 32, 16 and 128, and 81 and 3500, for the tasks of fashion set matching, Market-1501 Group dataset, and Road Group dataset, respectively. We train both the CNN and set-matching model in an end-to-end manner. In each iteration, we randomly swap pairs of sets and items in each set, and randomly flip images horizontally, to learn all the methods stably.

5.4 Fashion Set Matching

Dataset. We examine the set matching task for fashion recommendation, using the *IQON dataset* [51]. The dataset consists of recently created, high-quality

outfits, including 199,792 items grouped into 88,674 outfits. We split these outfits into groups, using 70,997 for training, 8,842 for validation, and 8,835 for testing.

Our task can be considered an extended version of a standard task, Fill-In-The-Blank [7], which requires us to select an item that best extends an outfit from among four candidates. Because selecting a set corresponds to filling multiple blanks, we consider the set matching problem as Fill-In-The-N-Blank.

Preparing Set Pairs. To construct the correct pair of sets to be matched, we randomly halve the given outfit $\mathcal{O}$ into two non-empty proper subsets $\mathcal{X}$ and $\mathcal{Y}$ as follows: $\mathcal{O} \rightarrow \{\mathcal{X}, \mathcal{Y}\}$, where $\mathcal{X} \cap \mathcal{Y} = \emptyset$. Here, we extend this setting to include more general situations. We select Q outfits $\{\mathcal{O}^{(1)}, \cdots, \mathcal{O}^{(Q)}\}$ randomly and split the respective outfits in half $\mathcal{O}^{(q)} \rightarrow \{\mathcal{X}^{(q)}, \mathcal{Y}^{(q)}\}$, where $q \in \{1, \cdots, Q\}$. We regard the two sets $\{\mathcal{X}^{(1)}, \cdots, \mathcal{X}^{(Q)}\}$ and $\{\mathcal{Y}^{(1)}, \cdots, \mathcal{Y}^{(Q)}\}$ as the correct pair, which consists of Q fashion styles. In the training phase, we set $Q = 4$.

Fashion Set Matching. We discuss the experimental results of the fashion set matching. Table 1 shows significantly different results between our models and the baselines. Here, Cross Attention and Cross Affinity denote our models with the attention-based and affinity-based functions, respectively. Comparing the performance of Cross Affinity and BERT$_{\text{SMALL}}$, which is the most accurate among the baselines, the differences in their accuracy were 5.2%, on average, 8.9%, at maximum, where the differences were relatively significant in the complicated setting on Mix:4. Furthermore, Table 1 shows that the affinity-based function performed better than the attention-based one.

In this experiment, we consider that the components on which the comparative effectiveness of the proposed models depended were potentially three-fold. Compared with the extensions of BERT, (a) our model preserves the exchangeability in two sets, which may ensure that the set features to be matched are accurately represented. Furthermore, (b) our model preserves two set features explicitly, whereas BERT provides a set of features with segment embedding that may have a limitation. Compared with the results of the Set Transformer, our models and BERT yielded accurate results is made possible by (c) providing the strength of interactions between two sets. Therefore, we conclude that these results justify the fine aspects of our architecture.

5.5   Group Re-identification

We present the results of a group re-id on the Market-1501 Group dataset, a new extension of a well-known person re-id dataset, Market-1501 [87], and the Road Group dataset [77]. The task is to identify the pairs of sets that consist of individual images of the (mostly) same multiple persons under noisy situations.

Evaluation on Market-1501 Group Dataset. We constructed the training/validation data based on query/gallery splits provided in [87]. Because there are few person images provided for each camera position, we did not consider camera information. We regard sets of gallery and query data as $\mathcal{X}$ and $\mathcal{Y}$, respectively, where each set contains three persons in non-noisy cases, and each person is represented by three different images.

Table 1. Accuracy of fashion set matching (%). Cand and Mix indicate the number of matching candidates and number of mixed outfits (Q), respectively.

Method	Cand:4			Cand:8		
	Mix:1	Mix:2	Mix:4	Mix:1	Mix:2	Mix:4
Set Transformer	68.0	73.5	65.3	50.5	57.5	49.6
BERT$_{SMALL}$	82.1	87.3	69.7	69.9	77.0	53.0
BERT$_{BASE}$	81.4	86.6	66.1	69.2	76.3	50.8
BERT$_{BASE-AP}$	80.8	86.4	65.4	68.6	75.7	49.5
GNN	35.4	32.4	25.5	19.9	17.5	13.4
HAP2S	39.3	36.6	32.0	23.3	20.8	17.8
Cross Attention (ours)	80.8	88.8	74.3	68.9	80.6	58.9
Cross Affinity (ours)	**85.1**	**90.6**	**75.9**	**73.8**	**82.8**	**61.9**

We investigated noise robustness through the experiments to show that our models do not over-fit on the data; here, the *noise* means that random persons that accidentally contained into the group additionally or that the label noise [32] for paired sets generated based on the given noise fraction. Note that the noise persons and label noise have some relations, e.g., a candidate set composed of only noise persons corresponds to a set mislabelled by label noise.

Table 2 presents the comparison results. In the non-noisy case, many models showed almost perfect accuracies; we consider that *averaging feature vectors in sets* achieves high accuracy in this homogeneous case. In the case the noise person included, the noise ratio was inversely proportional to the accuracy across all the models; however, our models yielded more accurate results, e.g., the average accuracy of Cross Affinity, Set Transformer, and BERT$_{BASE-AP}$ was 87.0, 80.6, and 72.4%, respectively. Because the main differences between the architectures exist in the interactions for paired sets or the exchangeability, the results support the claim that considering these properties improves both the accuracy and robustness. Furthermore, in the case of label noise fraction is 0.8, the permutation invariance would be essential to preserve high accuracy.

Evaluation on Road Group Dataset. We conduct experiments on the Road Group dataset [40,77], which consists of 162 group pairs taken from a 2-camera-view of a crowded road scene. One image per group for each camera is provided, where most groups do not have the same person's image in common with the different group pairs. Following the experimental protocol described in [40,77], we construct training/validation datasets, splitting the 162 group pairs randomly in half into two different 81 group pairs, and reporting the accuracies calculated by the cumulative matching characteristic (CMC) metric [49].

Because group re-id is a newly emerging task, most datasets, including the Road Group dataset, contain a small number of groups and images, and training on such datasets is difficult [27]. Specifically, our set-to-set matching method extracts features that rely on input set pairs, thus, the variations in the set pairs

Table 2. Accuracy (%) for Market-1501 Group. The number of candidates is 5.

Method	Non-noisy	Ratio of *noise* persons in $\mathcal{X} \times \mathcal{Y}$						Label noise frac.		
		$(\frac{0}{3},\frac{1}{4})$	$(\frac{1}{4},\frac{1}{4})$	$(\frac{0}{3},\frac{3}{6})$	$(\frac{0}{3},\frac{5}{8})$	$(\frac{3}{6},\frac{3}{6})$	$(\frac{5}{8},\frac{5}{8})$	0.2	0.4	0.8
Set Transformer	99.5	95.1	89.9	85.7	80.4	65.7	48.1	**99.3**	98.8	95.6
BERT$_{SMALL}$	94.3	77.6	69.2	83.7	64.9	49.5	24.7	99.2	98.7	79.5
BERT$_{BASE}$	96.8	80.5	77.6	68.8	69.9	61.9	49.2	98.9	98.1	76.0
BERT$_{BASE-AP}$	97.3	84.4	74.7	70.7	69.3	62.8	47.7	**99.3**	97.5	77.9
GNN	82.0	29.3	46.0	23.7	22.1	29.3	21.1	81.7	73.0	76.7
Cross Attention (ours)	99.6	**96.9**	**94.8**	91.9	90.7	**72.9**	56.1	**99.3**	99.6	95.5
Cross Affinity (ours)	**99.7**	96.5	92.5	**94.4**	**92.4**	72.0	**61.7**	**99.3**	99.9	98.4

are crucial. Considering the difference in appearances or camera parameters, however, importing external data [26,27] is also a challenging task itself.

To relax the data limitation, we introduce our novel set-data augmentation (set-aug) method that significantly enhances the learning results of the proposed set-to-set matching modules by increasing the training data. Given positive person image pairs and several negative person images, creating set pairs randomly on each training iteration, our set-aug effectively increases the group member variations (please refer to supplementary materials for details).

Table 3 shows the experimental results. The top block in Table 3 indicates the results of our methods with three types of data augmentation: (a) the horizontal flipping [35], which is used to train the baseline model; (b) image-based data augmentation (img-aug), which includes both scale augmentation [17,65] and random erasing [89] on images; and (c) our set-aug. Using the 81 pre-defined groups, the baseline model was not very effective, even with img-aug. However, using the set-aug, our method exhibited significant improvements without applying img-aug. These results imply that generating combinations on sets is very beneficial to our models. The other parts in Table 3 show that our methods yield very competitive results, compared with the state-of-the-art methods that utilize a large transferred external dataset or auxiliary features such as spatial layout information within each group. Furthermore, compared with MGM w/o spatial layout [40], which also does not use the spatial layout information, our methods significantly improved the accuracy of CMC-1 by 13.6%.

Table 3. Evaluation results (%) for Road Group dataset.

Method (detector-based)	CMC-1	CMC-5	CMC-10	CMC-15	CMC-20
Data augmentation ablation					
Cross Affinity (our baseline)	45.2 ± 3.5	77.5 ± 2.9	87.9 ± 3.8	91.9 ± 2.4	94.1 ± 2.1
Baseline + img-aug	47.7 ± 4.2	78.3 ± 3.2	87.7 ± 2.6	91.1 ± 2.4	93.3 ± 1.8
Baseline + set-aug	**84.0** ± 3.6	93.8 ± 0.8	**96.8** ± 0.6	**97.0** ± 1.0	97.5 ± 1.1
Baseline + set-aug + img-aug	81.7 ± 1.9	**94.1** ± 1.3	96.5 ± 1.1	**97.0** ± 0.9	**97.8** ± 0.8
Baseline + set-aug (ours)	**84.0** ± 3.6	93.8 ± 0.8	**96.8** ± 0.6	97.0 ± 1.0	97.5 ± 1.1
MGM w/ spatial layout [40]	80.2	93.8	96.3	**97.5**	97.5
MGM w/o spatial layout [40]	70.4	90.1	91.3	92.6	96.3
TSCN w/ external data [27]	**84.0**	**95.1**	96.3	-	**98.8**
GNN w/ external data [26]	74.1	90.1	92.6	-	**98.8**
Method (GT-based)	CMC-1	CMC-5	CMC-10	CMC-15	CMC-20
Baseline + set-aug (ours)	**85.7** ± 3.7	**96.3** ± 0.8	**97.8** ± 0.5	**98.3** ± 0.6	**98.3** ± 0.6
MGM w/ spatial layout [40]	82.4	95.1	96.3	97.5	98.0

5.6 Ablation Study

In this section, we report the results of an ablation study performed to highlight the importance of each proposed component. The top part in Table 4 shows the two results obtained when our models are trained using triplet loss with the soft-margin and batch all strategy [19] or the proposed K-pair-set loss. Triplet loss triggered significant accuracy degradation, even though the losses converged to near zero in the training stages. On the other hand, the proposed K-pair-set loss can manage to accurately train the models by considering the loss of selecting paired sets among multiple candidates. The second topmost part in Table 4 shows the results of ablations in the feature extractor. Reducing the number of layers and number of multiheads in the CSeFT, and excluding the encoder and CSeFT, the accuracies are degraded by 1.0, 1.1, 1.3, and 4.2%. Our model without the encoder performed well (1.3% degradation) but showed a somewhat slow convergence. However, excluding the CSeFT module significantly reduced the accuracy (4.2% degradation).

These results imply that the proposed CSeFT module is a crucial part of the set-to-set matching model architecture. The second lower part of Table 4 shows the results of ablation study performed on the matching layer. Reducing mCS to a single CS and excluding ReLU from the CS functions reduced the accuracies of both models by 1.0 and 2.0%, respectively. It is interesting to observe that the ReLU was more important than the number of CS functions; this demonstrated the importance of nonlinearity in the matching layer. Furthermore, replacing our mCS with max pooling, average pooling, projection metric [25], covariance matrix [4,75], set kernel [33], and cosine similarity metric [53] all resulted in significant accuracy degradation implying the effectiveness of our mCS functions (see supplementary materials for details). The lowermost part of Table 4 shows the results of ablation study performed on the feature extractor and matching layer. The extension of Set Transformer, which does not include the proposed CSeFT module and CS

Table 4. Ablation study. Average accuracies (%) on Market-1501 Group are shown, where the non-noisy and six noise person patterns, presented in Table 2, are included.

Method	Accuracy
Training method ablation	
Cross Affinity (baseline)	**87.0**
Baseline with triplet loss	45.5
Feature extractor ablation	
Baseline with $L=1$	86.0
Baseline with $h=1$	85.9
w/o Enc	85.7
w/o CSeFT	82.8
Matching layer ablation	
Single CS	86.0
w/o ReLU in mCS	85.0
Max pooling	86.1
Average pooling	85.8
Projection metric	67.0
Covariance matrix	61.1
Set kernel	53.3
Cosine similarity metric	53.1
Feature & matching layer ablation	
Set Transformer	80.6

function, yielded significant accuracy degradation. These results show the validity of our architecture for heterogeneous set-to-set matching.

6   Conclusion

In this study, we investigated the heterogeneous set-to-set matching problem. We proposed a novel architecture comprising the (1) cross-set feature transformation (CSeFT) module and (2) cross-similarity (CS) function, in addition to a loss function and set-data augmentation for performing set-to-set matching.

We showed that our architecture preserves the two types of exchangeability for a pair of sets and also the items within them, thereby satisfying the requirements of set-to-set matching procedure.

We demonstrated that our models performed well compared with the state-of-the-art methods and baselines in the fashion set matching and group re-id experiments. Furthermore, we validated our proposed architecture through the ablation study. These results support the claim that the exchangeability and the

feature representations extracted with interactions between the two sets improve the accuracy and robustness of the heterogeneous set-to-set matching.

References

1. Arandjelovic, O., Shakhnarovich, G., Fisher, J., Cipolla, R., Darrell, T.: Face recognition with image sets using manifold density divergence. In: 2005 IEEE Computer Society Conference on Computer Vision and Pattern Recognition, CVPR 2005, vol. 1, pp. 581–588. IEEE (2005)
2. Bai, Y., Ding, H., Bian, S., Chen, T., Sun, Y., Wang, W.: SimGNN: a neural network approach to fast graph similarity computation. In: Proceedings of the 12th ACM International Conference on Web Search and Data Mining, pp. 384–392 (2019)
3. Bai, Y., Ding, H., Sun, Y., Wang, W.: Convolutional set matching for graph similarity. arXiv preprint arXiv:1810.10866 (2018)
4. Cai, Y., Takala, V., Pietikainen, M.: Matching groups of people by covariance descriptor. In: 2010 20th International Conference on Pattern Recognition, pp. 2744–2747. IEEE (2010)
5. Caspi, Y., Simakov, D., Irani, M.: Feature-based sequence-to-sequence matching. Int. J. Comput. Vis. **68**(1), 53–64 (2006)
6. Cevikalp, H., Triggs, B.: Face recognition based on image sets. In: 2010 IEEE Computer Society Conference on Computer Vision and Pattern Recognition, pp. 2567–2573. IEEE (2010)
7. Cucurull, G., Taslakian, P., Vazquez, D.: Context-aware visual compatibility prediction. In: Proceedings of the IEEE Conference on Computer Vision and Pattern Recognition, pp. 12617–12626 (2019)
8. Devlin, J., Chang, M.W., Lee, K., Toutanova, K.: BERT: Pre-training of deep bidirectional transformers for language understanding. arXiv preprint arXiv:1810.04805 (2018)
9. Feng, J., Karaman, S., Chang, S.F.: Deep image set hashing. In: 2017 IEEE Winter Conference on Applications of Computer Vision (WACV), pp. 1241–1250. IEEE (2017)
10. Fey, M., Lenssen, J.E., Morris, C., Masci, J., Kriege, N.M.: Deep graph matching consensus. arXiv preprint arXiv:2001.09621 (2020)
11. Gao, Z., Wang, D., He, X., Zhang, H.: Group-pair convolutional neural networks for multi-view based 3D object retrieval. In: 32nd AAAI Conference on Artificial Intelligence (2018)
12. Gionis, A., Indyk, P., Motwani, R., et al.: Similarity search in high dimensions via hashing. In: VLDB, vol. 99, pp. 518–529 (1999)
13. Glorot, X., Bordes, A., Bengio, Y.: Deep sparse rectifier neural networks. In: Proceedings of the 14th International Conference on Artificial Intelligence and Statistics, pp. 315–323 (2011)
14. Guo, M., Chou, E., Huang, D.-A., Song, S., Yeung, S., Fei-Fei, L.: Neural graph matching networks for fewshot 3D action recognition. In: Ferrari, V., Hebert, M., Sminchisescu, C., Weiss, Y. (eds.) ECCV 2018. LNCS, vol. 11205, pp. 673–689. Springer, Cham (2018). https://doi.org/10.1007/978-3-030-01246-5_40
15. Hamm, J., Lee, D.D.: Grassmann discriminant analysis: a unifying view on subspace-based learning. In: Proceedings of the 25th International Conference on Machine Learning, pp. 376–383 (2008)

16. Han, X., Wu, Z., Jiang, Y.G., Davis, L.S.: Learning fashion compatibility with bidirectional LSTMs. In: Proceedings of the 25th ACM International Conference on Multimedia, pp. 1078–1086. ACM (2017)
17. He, K., Zhang, X., Ren, S., Sun, J.: Deep residual learning for image recognition. In: Proceedings of the IEEE Conference on Computer Vision and Pattern Recognition, pp. 770–778 (2016)
18. He, R., Packer, C., McAuley, J.: Learning compatibility across categories for heterogeneous item recommendation. In: 2016 IEEE 16th International Conference on Data Mining (ICDM), pp. 937–942. IEEE (2016)
19. Hermans, A., Beyer, L., Leibe, B.: In defense of the triplet loss for person re-identification. CoRR abs/1703.07737 (2017). http://arxiv.org/abs/1703.07737
20. Howard, A.G., et al.: MobileNets: Efficient convolutional neural networks for mobile vision applications. CoRR abs/1704.04861 (2017). http://arxiv.org/abs/1704.04861
21. Hsiao, W.L., Grauman, K.: Creating capsule wardrobes from fashion images. In: Proceedings of the IEEE Conference on Computer Vision and Pattern Recognition, pp. 7161–7170 (2018)
22. Hu, J., Shen, L., Sun, G.: Squeeze-and-excitation networks. In: Proceedings of the IEEE Conference on Computer Vision and Pattern Recognition, pp. 7132–7141 (2018)
23. Hu, Y., Mian, A.S., Owens, R.: Sparse approximated nearest points for image set classification. In: CVPR 2011, pp. 121–128. IEEE (2011)
24. Huang, Z., Wang, Z., Hung, T., Satoh, S., Lin, C.: Group re-identification via transferred representation and adaptive fusion. In: 2019 IEEE 5th International Conference on Multimedia Big Data (BigMM), pp. 128–132 (September 2019). https://doi.org/10.1109/BigMM.2019.00-34
25. Huang, Z., Wu, J., Van Gool, L.: Building deep networks on Grassmann manifolds. In: 32nd AAAI Conference on Artificial Intelligence (2018)
26. Huang, Z., Wang, Z., Hu, W., Lin, C.W., Satoh, S.: DoT-GNN: domain-transferred graph neural network for group re-identification. In: Proceedings of the 27th ACM International Conference on Multimedia, pp. 1888–1896 (2019)
27. Huang, Z., Wang, Z., Satoh, S., Lin, C.W.: Group re-identification via transferred single and couple representation learning. arXiv preprint arXiv:1905.04854 (2019)
28. Ilse, M., Tomczak, J.M., Welling, M.: Attention-based deep multiple instance learning. arXiv preprint arXiv:1802.04712 (2018)
29. Iwata, T., Kanagawa, M., Hirao, T., Fukumizu, K.: Unsupervised group matching with application to cross-lingual topic matching without alignment information. Data Min. Knowl. Discov. **31**(2), 350–370 (2017)
30. Iwata, T., Lloyd, J.R., Ghahramani, Z.: Unsupervised many-to-many object matching for relational data. IEEE Trans. Pattern Anal. Mach. Intell. **38**(3), 607–617 (2015)
31. Jain, S., Wallace, B.C.: Attention is not explanation (2019)
32. Jiang, L., Zhou, Z., Leung, T., Li, L., Fei-Fei, L.: MentorNet: Regularizing very deep neural networks on corrupted labels. CoRR abs/1712.05055 (2017), http://arxiv.org/abs/1712.05055
33. Kim, J., McCourt, M., You, T., Kim, S., Choi, S.: Practical Bayesian optimization over sets (2019)
34. Kim, T.K., Kittler, J., Cipolla, R.: Discriminative learning and recognition of image set classes using canonical correlations. IEEE Trans. Pattern Anal. Mach. Intell. **29**(6), 1005–1018 (2007)

35. Krizhevsky, A., Sutskever, I., Hinton, G.E.: ImageNet classification with deep convolutional neural networks. In: Advances in Neural Information Processing Systems, pp. 1097–1105 (2012)

36. Le, D.T., Lauw, H.W., Fang, Y.: Correlation-sensitive next-basket recommendation. In: Proceedings of the 28th International Joint Conference on Artificial Intelligence, IJCAI-19, pp. 2808–2814. International Joint Conferences on Artificial Intelligence Organization (July 2019). https://doi.org/10.24963/ijcai.2019/389

37. Lee, J., Lee, Y., Kim, J., Kosiorek, A., Choi, S., Teh, Y.W.: Set transformer: a framework for attention-based permutation-invariant neural networks. In: International Conference on Machine Learning, pp. 3744–3753 (2019)

38. Li, Y., Gu, C., Dullien, T., Vinyals, O., Kohli, P.: Graph matching networks for learning the similarity of graph structured objects. arXiv preprint arXiv:1904.12787 (2019)

39. Li, Y., Cao, L., Zhu, J., Luo, J.: Mining fashion outfit composition using an end-to-end deep learning approach on set data. CoRR abs/1608.03016 (2016). http://arxiv.org/abs/1608.03016

40. Lin, W., et al.: Group reidentification with multigrained matching and integration. IEEE Trans. Cybern. (2019)

41. Lisanti, G., Martinel, N., Bimbo, A.D., Foresti, G.L.: Group re-identification via unsupervised transfer of sparse features encoding. CoRR abs/1707.09173 (2017). http://arxiv.org/abs/1707.09173

42. Liu, D., Liang, C., Zhang, Z., Qi, L., Lovell, B.C.: Exploring inter-instance relationships within the query set for robust image set matching. Sensors **19**(22), 5051 (2019)

43. Liu, X., et al.: Permutation-invariant feature restructuring for correlation-aware image set-based recognition. arXiv preprint arXiv:1908.01174 (2019)

44. Liu, Y., Yan, J., Ouyang, W.: Quality aware network for set to set recognition. In: Proceedings of the IEEE Conference on Computer Vision and Pattern Recognition, pp. 5790–5799 (2017)

45. Lu, J., Wang, G., Deng, W., Moulin, P., Zhou, J.: Multi-manifold deep metric learning for image set classification. In: Proceedings of the IEEE Conference on Computer Vision and Pattern Recognition, pp. 1137–1145 (2015)

46. Maas, A.L., Hannun, A.Y., Ng, A.Y.: Rectifier nonlinearities improve neural network acoustic models. In: Proceedings of the ICML, vol. 30, p. 3 (2013)

47. Maron, H., Ben-Hamu, H., Shamir, N., Lipman, Y.: Invariant and equivariant graph networks. arXiv preprint arXiv:1812.09902 (2018)

48. Mishchuk, A., Mishkin, D., Radenovic, F., Matas, J.: Working hard to know your neighbor's margins: local descriptor learning loss. In: Advances in Neural Information Processing Systems, pp. 4826–4837 (2017)

49. Moon, H., Phillips, P.J.: Computational and performance aspects of PCA-based face-recognition algorithms. Perception **30**(3), 303–321 (2001)

50. Mudgal, S., et al.: Deep learning for entity matching: a design space exploration. In: Proceedings of the 2018 International Conference on Management of Data, pp. 19–34 (2018)

51. Nakamura, T., Goto, R.: Outfit generation and style extraction via bidirectional LSTM and autoencoder. CoRR abs/1807.03133 (2018). http://arxiv.org/abs/1807.03133

52. Newell, A., Yang, K., Deng, J.: Stacked hourglass networks for human pose estimation. CoRR abs/1603.06937 (2016). http://arxiv.org/abs/1603.06937

53. Nguyen, H.V., Bai, L.: Cosine similarity metric learning for face verification. In: Kimmel, R., Klette, R., Sugimoto, A. (eds.) ACCV 2010. LNCS, vol. 6493, pp. 709–720. Springer, Heidelberg (2011). https://doi.org/10.1007/978-3-642-19309-5_55

54. Parkhi, O.M., Vedaldi, A., Zisserman, A., et al.: Deep face recognition. In: BMVC, vol. 1, p. 6 (2015)

55. Qi, C.R., Su, H., Mo, K., Guibas, L.J.: PointNet: Deep learning on point sets for 3D classification and segmentation. CoRR abs/1612.00593 (2016). http://arxiv.org/abs/1612.00593

56. Rendle, S., Freudenthaler, C., Schmidt-Thieme, L.: Factorizing personalized Markov chains for next-basket recommendation. In: Proceedings of the 19th International Conference on World Wide Web, pp. 811–820. ACM (2010)

57. Ristani, E., Solera, F., Zou, R.S., Cucchiara, R., Tomasi, C.: Performance measures and a data set for multi-target, multi-camera tracking (2016)

58. Russakovsky, O., et al.: ImageNet large scale visual recognition challenge. Int. J. Comput. Vis. **115**(3), 211–252 (2015) ·

59. Saito, Y., Hong, P.K., Niihara, T., Miyamoto, H., Fukumizu, K.: Data-driven taxonomy matching of asteroid and meteorite. Meteoritics Planetary Science **55**(1), 193–206 (2020). https://doi.org/10.1111/maps.13428. https://onlinelibrary.wiley.com/doi/abs/10.1111/maps.13428

60. Sannai, A., Takai, Y., Cordonnier, M.: Universal approximations of permutation invariant/equivariant functions by deep neural networks. arXiv preprint arXiv:1903.01939 (2019)

61. Sarwar, B.M., Karypis, G., Konstan, J.A., Riedl, J., et al.: Item-based collaborative filtering recommendation algorithms. In: WWW 2001, pp. 285–295 (2001)

62. Segol, N., Lipman, Y.: On universal equivariant set networks. arXiv preprint arXiv:1910.02421 (2019)

63. Shakhnarovich, G., Fisher, J.W., Darrell, T.: Face recognition from long-term observations. In: Heyden, A., Sparr, G., Nielsen, M., Johansen, P. (eds.) ECCV 2002. LNCS, vol. 2352, pp. 851–865. Springer, Heidelberg (2002). https://doi.org/10.1007/3-540-47977-5_56

64. Si, J., et al.: Dual attention matching network for context-aware feature sequence based person re-identification (2018)

65. Simonyan, K., Zisserman, A.: Very deep convolutional networks for large-scale image recognition. arXiv preprint arXiv:1409.1556 (2014)

66. Sogi, N., Nakayama, T., Fukui, K.: A method based on convex cone model for image-set classification with CNN features. In: 2018 International Joint Conference on Neural Networks (IJCNN), pp. 1–8. IEEE (2018)

67. Sohn, K.: Improved deep metric learning with multi-class n-pair loss objective. In: Lee, D.D., Sugiyama, M., Luxburg, U.V., Guyon, I., Garnett, R. (eds.) Advances in Neural Information Processing Systems, vol. 29, pp. 1857–1865. Curran Associates, Inc. (2016). http://papers.nips.cc/paper/6200-improved-deep-metric-learning-with-multi-class-n-pair-loss-objective.pdf

68. Szegedy, C., Vanhoucke, V., Ioffe, S., Shlens, J., Wojna, Z.: Rethinking the inception architecture for computer vision. In: Proceedings of the IEEE Conference on Computer Vision and Pattern Recognition, pp. 2818–2826 (2016)

69. Vasileva, M.I., Plummer, B.A., Dusad, K., Rajpal, S., Kumar, R., Forsyth, D.A.: Learning type-aware embeddings for fashion compatibility. CoRR abs/1803.09196 (2018). http://arxiv.org/abs/1803.09196

70. Vaswani, A., et al.: Attention is all you need. CoRR abs/1706.03762 (2017). http://arxiv.org/abs/1706.03762

71. Vincent, P., Bengio, Y.: K-local hyperplane and convex distance nearest neighbor algorithms. In: Advances in Neural Information Processing Systems, pp. 985–992 (2002)

72. Vinyals, O., Bengio, S., Kudlur, M.: Order matters: Sequence to sequence for sets. arXiv preprint arXiv:1511.06391 (2015)

73. Wagstaff, E., Fuchs, F.B., Engelcke, M., Posner, I., Osborne, M.: On the limitations of representing functions on sets. arXiv preprint arXiv:1901.09006 (2019)

74. Wang, J., et al.: Learning fine-grained image similarity with deep ranking. CoRR abs/1404.4661 (2014). http://arxiv.org/abs/1404.4661

75. Wang, R., Guo, H., Davis, L.S., Dai, Q.: Covariance discriminative learning: a natural and efficient approach to image set classification. In: 2012 IEEE Conference on Computer Vision and Pattern Recognition, pp. 2496–2503. IEEE (2012)

76. Wang, R., Shan, S., Chen, X., Gao, W.: Manifold-manifold distance with application to face recognition based on image set. In: 2008 IEEE Conference on Computer Vision and Pattern Recognition, pp. 1–8. IEEE (2008)

77. Xiao, H., et al.: Group re-identification: leveraging and integrating multi-grain information. In: Proceedings of the 26th ACM International Conference on Multimedia, MM 2018, pp. 192–200. ACM, New York (2018). https://doi.org/10.1145/3240508.3240539. http://doi.acm.org/10.1145/3240508.3240539

78. Xie, W., Shen, L., Zisserman, A.: Comparator networks. In: Ferrari, V., Hebert, M., Sminchisescu, C., Weiss, Y. (eds.) ECCV 2018. LNCS, vol. 11215, pp. 811–826. Springer, Cham (2018). https://doi.org/10.1007/978-3-030-01252-6_48

79. Yamaguchi, O., Fukui, K., Maeda, K.: Face recognition using temporal image sequence. In: Proceedings 3rd IEEE International Conference on Automatic Face and Gesture Recognition, pp. 318–323. IEEE (1998)

80. Yang, M., Zhu, P., Van Gool, L., Zhang, L.: Face recognition based on regularized nearest points between image sets. In: 2013 10th IEEE International Conference and Workshops on Automatic Face and Gesture Recognition (FG), pp. 1–7. IEEE (2013)

81. Yang, Z., Yang, D., Dyer, C., He, X., Smola, A., Hovy, E.: Hierarchical attention networks for document classification. In: Proceedings of the 2016 Conference of the North American Chapter of the Association for Computational Linguistics: Human Language Technologies, pp. 1480–1489 (2016)

82. Yarotsky, D.: Universal approximations of invariant maps by neural networks. arXiv preprint arXiv:1804.10306 (2018)

83. Yoshida, T., Takeuchi, I., Karasuyama, M.: Learning interpretable metric between graphs: convex formulation and computation with graph mining. In: Proceedings of the 25th ACM SIGKDD International Conference on Knowledge Discovery & Data Mining, KDD 2019, pp. 1026–1036. Association for Computing Machinery, New York (2019). https://doi.org/10.1145/3292500.3330845

84. Yu, R., Dou, Z., Bai, S., Zhang, Z., Xu, Y., Bai, X.: Hard-aware point-to-set deep metric for person re-identification. In: Ferrari, V., Hebert, M., Sminchisescu, C., Weiss, Y. (eds.) ECCV 2018. LNCS, vol. 11220, pp. 196–212. Springer, Cham (2018). https://doi.org/10.1007/978-3-030-01270-0_12

85. Zaheer, M., Kottur, S., Ravanbakhsh, S., Póczos, B., Salakhutdinov, R., Smola, A.J.: Deep sets. CoRR abs/1703.06114 (2017). http://arxiv.org/abs/1703.06114

86. Zanfir, A., Sminchisescu, C.: Deep learning of graph matching. In: Proceedings of the IEEE Conference on Computer Vision and Pattern Recognition, pp. 2684–2693 (2018)

87. Zheng, L., Shen, L., Tian, L., Wang, S., Wang, J., Tian, Q.: Scalable person re-identification: a benchmark. In: Proceedings of the IEEE International Conference on Computer Vision (2015)
88. Zheng, W.S., Gong, S., Xiang, T.: Associating groups of people. In: BMVC, vol. 2 (2009)
89. Zhong, Z., Zheng, L., Kang, G., Li, S., Yang, Y.: Random erasing data augmentation. arXiv preprint arXiv:1708.04896 (2017)
90. Zhou, S., Wang, J., Wang, J., Gong, Y., Zheng, N.: Point to set similarity based deep feature learning for person re-identification. In: Proceedings of the IEEE Conference on Computer Vision and Pattern Recognition, pp. 3741–3750 (2017)
91. Zhu, F., Chu, Q., Yu, N.: Consistent matching based on boosted salience channels for group re-identification. In: 2016 IEEE International Conference on Image Processing (ICIP), pp. 4279–4283. IEEE (2016)
92. Zhu, P., Zhang, L., Zuo, W., Zhang, D.: From point to set: extend the learning of distance metrics. In: Proceedings of the IEEE International Conference on Computer Vision, pp. 2664–2671 (2013)

Making Sense of CNNs: Interpreting Deep Representations and Their Invariances with INNs

Robin Rombach[⊠], Patrick Esser, and Björn Ommer

Interdisciplinary Center for Scientific Computing, HCI, Heidelberg University,
Heidelberg, Germany
robin.rombach@iwr.uni-heidelberg.de
https://hci.iwr.uni-heidelberg.de/compvis

Abstract. To tackle increasingly complex tasks, it has become an essential ability of neural networks to learn abstract representations. These task-specific representations and, particularly, the invariances they capture turn neural networks into black box models that lack interpretability. To open such a black box, it is, therefore, crucial to uncover the different semantic concepts a model has learned as well as those that it has learned to be invariant to. We present an approach based on INNs that (i) recovers the task-specific, learned invariances by disentangling the remaining factor of variation in the data and that (ii) invertibly transforms these recovered invariances combined with the model representation into an equally expressive one with accessible semantic concepts. As a consequence, neural network representations become understandable by providing the means to (i) expose their semantic meaning, (ii) semantically modify a representation, and (iii) visualize individual learned semantic concepts and invariances. Our invertible approach significantly extends the abilities to understand black box models by enabling post-hoc interpretations of state-of-the-art networks without compromising their performance.

1 Introduction

Key to the wide success of deep neural networks is end-to-end learning of powerful hidden representations that aim to *(i)* capture all task-relevant characteristics while *(ii)* being invariant to all other variability in the data [1,31]. Deep learning can yield abstract representations that are perfectly adapted feature encodings for the task at hand. However, their increasing abstraction capability and performance comes at the expense of a lack in interpretability [3]: Although the

---

R. Rombach and P. Esser—Both authors contributed equally to this work.

Electronic supplementary material The online version of this chapter (https://doi.org/10.1007/978-3-030-58520-4_38) contains supplementary material, which is available to authorized users.

© Springer Nature Switzerland AG 2020
A. Vedaldi et al. (Eds.): ECCV 2020, LNCS 12362, pp. 647–664, 2020.
https://doi.org/10.1007/978-3-030-58520-4_38

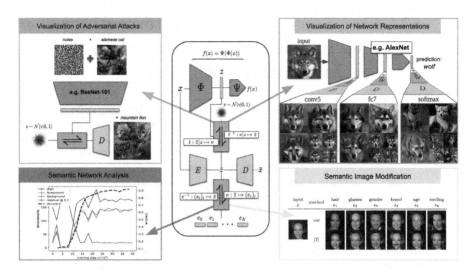

Fig. 1. Proposed architecture. We provide post-hoc interpretation for a given deep network $f = \Psi \circ \Phi$. For a deep representation $z = \Phi(x)$ a conditional INN t recovers Φ's invariances v from a representation $\bar{z}$ which contains entangled information about *both* z and v. The INN e then translates the representation $\bar{z}$ into a factorized representation with accessible semantic concepts. This approach allows for various applications, including visualizations of network representations of natural and altered inputs, semantic network analysis and semantic image modifications.

network may solve a problem, it does not convey an understanding of its predictions or their causes, oftentimes leaving the impression of a black box [39]. In particular, users are missing an explanation of semantic concepts that the model has learned to *represent* and of those it has learned to *ignore*, i.e. its invariances.

Providing such explanations and an understanding of network predictions and their causes is thus crucial for transparent AI. Not only is this relevant to discover limitations and promising directions for future improvements of the AI system itself, but also for compliance with legislation [9,20], knowledge distillation from such a system [33], and post-hoc verification of the model [49]. Consequently, research on interpretable deep models has recently gained a lot of attention, particularly methods that investigate latent representations to understand what the model has learned [4,15,16,49,57].

Challenges and Aims. Assessing these latent representations is challenging due to two fundamental issues: *(i)* to achieve robustness and generalization despite noisy inputs and data variability, hidden layers exhibit a distributed coding of semantically meaningful concepts [16]. Attributing semantics to a single neuron via backpropagation [40] or synthesis [61] is thus impossible without altering the network [41,66], which typically degrades performance. *(ii)* end-to-end learning trains deep representations towards a goal task, making them invariant to features irrelevant for this goal. Understanding these characteristics

that a representation has abstracted away is challenging, since we essentially need to portray features that have been discarded.

These challenges call for a method that can interpret existing network representations by recovering their invariances without modifying them. Given these recovered invariances, we seek an invertible mapping that translates a representation *and* the invariances onto understandable semantic concepts. The mapping disentangles the distributed encoding of the high-dimensional representation and its invariances by projecting them onto separate multi-dimensional factors that correspond to human understandable semantic concepts. Both this translation and the recovering of invariances are implemented with invertible neural networks (INNs) [12,26,46]. For the translation, this guarantees that the resulting understandable representation is equally expressive as the model representation combined with the recovered invariances (no information is lost). Its invertibility also warrants that feature modifications applied in the semantic domain correctly adjust the recovered representation.

Our contributions to a comprehensive understanding of deep representations are as follows: (i) We present an approach, which, by utilizing invertible neural networks, improves the understanding of representations produced by existing network architectures with no need for re-training or otherwise compromising their performance. (ii) Our generative approach is able to recover the invariances that result from the non-injective projection (of input onto a latent representation) which deep networks typically learn. This model then provides a probabilistic visualization of the latent representation and its invariances. (iii) We bijectively translate an arbitrarily abstract representation and its invariances via a non-linear transformation into another representation of equal expressiveness, but with accessible semantic concepts. (iv) The invertibility also enables manipulation of the original latent representations in a semantically understandable manner, thus facilitating further diagnostics of a network.

2   Background

Two main approaches to interpretable AI can be identified, those which aim to incorporate interpretability directly into the design of models, and those which aim to provide interpretability to existing models [41]. Approaches from the first category range from modifications of network architectures [66], over regularization of models encouraging interpretability [37,45], towards combinations of both [63]. However, these approaches always involve a trade-off between model performance and model interpretability. Being of the latter category, our approach allows to interpret representations of existing models without compromising their performance.

To better understand what an existing model has learned, its representations must be studied [49]. [57] shows that both random directions and coordinate axes in the feature space of networks can represent semantic properties and concludes that they are not necessarily represented by individual neurons. Different works attempt to select groups of neurons which have a certain semantic meaning,

such as based on scenes [65], objects [54] and object parts [55]. [4] studied the interpretability of neurons, and found that a rotation of the representation space spanned by the neurons decreases its interpretability. While this suggests that the neurons provide a more interpretable basis compared to a random basis, [16] shows that the choice of basis is not the only challenge for interpretability of representations. Their findings demonstrate that learned representations are distributed, *i.e.* a single semantic concept is encoded by an activation pattern involving multiple neurons, and a single neuron is involved in the encoding of multiple different semantic concepts. Instead of selecting a set of neurons directly, [15] learns an INN that transforms the original representation space to an interpretable space, where a single semantic concept is represented by a known group of neurons and a single neuron is involved in the encoding of just a single semantic concept. However, to interpret not only the representation itself but also its invariances, it is insufficient to transform only the representation itself. Our approach therefore transforms the latent representation space of an autoencoder, which has the capacity to represent its inputs faithfully, and subsequently translates a model representation and its invariances into this space for semantic interpretation and visualization.

A large body of works approach interpretability of existing networks based on visualizations. [52] uses gradients of network outputs with respect to a convolutional layer to obtain coarse localization maps. [3] proposes an approach to obtain pixel-wise relevance scores for a specific class of models which is generalized in [40]. To obtain richer visual interpretations, [38,56,61,62] reconstruct images which maximally activate certain neurons. [44] uses a generator network for this task, which was introduced in [13] for reconstructing images from their feature representation. Our key insight is that these existing approaches do not explicitly account for the invariances learned by a model. Invariances imply that feature inversion is a one-to-many mapping and thus they must be recovered to solve the task. Recently, [53] introduced a GAN-based approach that utilizes features of a pre-trained classifier as a semantic pyramid for image generation. [43] used samples from an autoregressive model of images conditioned on a feature representation to gain insights into the representation's invariances. In contrast, our approach recovers an explicit representation of the invariances, which can be recombined with modified feature representations, and thus makes the effect of modifications to representations, *e.g.* through adversarial attacks, visible.

Other works consider visual interpretations for specialized models. [50] showed that the quality of images which maximally activate certain neurons is significantly improved when activating neurons of an adversarially robust classifier. [5] explores the relationship between neurons and the images produced by a Generative Adversarial Network. For the same class of models, [18] finds directions in their input space which represent semantic concepts corresponding to certain cognitive properties. Such semantic directions have previously also been found in classifier networks [58] but requires aligned data. All of these approaches require either special training of models, are limited to a very special class of models which already provide visualizations or depend on special assump-

tions on model and data. In contrast, our approach can be applied to arbitrary models without re-training or modifying them, and provides both visualizations and semantic explanations, for both the model's representation and its learned invariances.

3 Approach

Common tasks of computer vision can be phrased as a mapping from an input image x to some output $f(x)$ such as a classification of the image, a regression (e.g. of object locations), a (semantic) segmentation map, or a re-synthesis that yields another image. Deep learning utilizes a hierarchy of intermediate network layers that gradually transform the input into increasingly more abstract representations. Let $z = \Phi(x) \in \mathbb{R}^{N_z}$ be the representation extracted by one such layer (without loss of generality we consider z to be a N_z-dim vector, flattening it if necessary) and $f(x) = \Psi(z) = \Psi(\Phi(x))$ the mapping onto the output.

An essential characteristic of a deep feature encoding z is the increasing abstractness of higher feature encoding layers and the resulting reduction of information. To explain a latent representation, we need to recover its invariances v and make z *and* v interpretable by learning a bijective mapping onto understandable semantic concepts, see Fig. 1. Section 3.1 describes our INN t to recover an encoding v of the invariances. Due to the generative nature of t, our approach can correctly sample visualizations of the model representation and its invariances without leaving the underlying data distribution and introducing artifacts. With v then available, Sect. 3.2 presents an INN e that translates t's encoding of z and v without losing information onto disentangled semantic concepts. Moreover, the invertibility allows modifications in the semantic domain to correctly project back onto the original representation or into image space.

3.1 Recovering the Invariances of Deep Models

Learning an Encoding to Help Recover Invariances. Key to a deep representation is not only the information z captures, but also what is has learned to abstract away. To learn what z misses with respect to x, we need an encoding $\bar{z}$, which, in contrast to z, includes these invariances. Without making prior assumptions about the deep model f, autoencoders provide a generic way to obtain such an encoding $\bar{z}$, since they ensure that their input x can be recovered from their learned representation $\bar{z}$, which hence also comprises the invariances.

Therefore, we learn an autoencoder with an encoder E that provides the data representation $\bar{z} = E(x)$ and a decoder D producing the data reconstruction $\bar{x} = D(\bar{z})$. Section 3.2 will utilize the decoding from $\bar{z}$ to $\bar{x}$ to visualize both z and v. The autoencoder is trained to reconstruct its inputs by minimizing a perceptual metric between input and reconstruction, $\|x - \bar{x}\|$, as in [13]. The details of the architecture and training procedure can be found in Sect. A.1. It is crucial that the autoencoder only needs to be trained once on the training data. Consequently, the same E can be used to interpret different representations z,

e.g. different models or layers within a model, thus ensuring fair comparisons between them. Moreover, the complexity of the autoencoder can be adjusted based on the computational needs, allowing us to work with much lower dimensional encodings $\bar{z}$ compared to reconstructing the invariances directly from the images x. This reduces the computational demands of our approach significantly.

Learning a Conditional INN that Recovers Invariances. Due to the reconstruction task of the autoencoder, $\bar{z}$ not only contains the invariances v, but also the representation z. Thus, we must disentangle [14,27,32] v and z using a mapping $t(\cdot|z) : \bar{z} \mapsto v = t(\bar{z}|z)$ which, depending on z, extracts v from $\bar{z}$.

Besides extracting the invariances from a given $\bar{z}$, t must also enable an inverse mapping from given model representations z to $\bar{z}$ to support a further mapping onto semantic concepts (Sect. 3.2) and visualization based on $D(\bar{z})$. There are many different x with $\Phi(x) = z$, namely all those x which differ only in properties that Φ is invariant to. Thus, there are also many different $\bar{z}$ that this mapping must recover. Consequently, the mapping from z to $\bar{z}$ is set-valued. However, to understand f we do not want to recover all possible $\bar{z}$, but only those which are likely under the training distribution of the autoencoder. In particular, this excludes unnatural images such as those obtained by DeepDream [42], or adversarial attacks [57]. In conclusion, we need to sample $\bar{z} \sim p(\bar{z}|z)$.

To avoid a costly inversion process of Φ, t must be invertible (implemented as an INN) so that a change of variables

$$p(\bar{z}|z) = \frac{p(v|z)}{|\det \nabla(t^{-1})(v|z)|} \quad \text{where } v = t(\bar{z}|z) \tag{1}$$

yields $p(\bar{z}|z)$ by means of the distribution $p(v|z)$ of invariances, given a model representation z. Here, the denominator denotes the absolute value of the determinant of Jacobian $\nabla(t^{-1})$ of $v \mapsto t^{-1}(v|z) = \bar{z}$, which is efficient to compute for common invertible network architectures. Consequently, we obtain $\bar{z}$ for given z by sampling from the invariant space v given z and then applying t^{-1},

$$\bar{z} \sim p(\bar{z}|z) \quad \Longleftrightarrow \quad v \sim p(v|z), \bar{z} = t^{-1}(v|z). \tag{2}$$

Since v is the invariant space for z, both are complementary thus implying independence $p(v|z) = p(v)$. Because a powerful transformation t^{-1} can transform between two arbitrary densities, we can assume without loss of generality a Gaussian prior $p(v) = \mathcal{N}(v|0, \mathbb{1})$. Given this prior, our task is then to learn the transformation t that maps $\mathcal{N}(v|0, \mathbb{1})$ onto $p(\bar{z}|z)$. To this end, we maximize the log-likelihood of $\bar{z}$ given z, which results in a per-example loss of

$$\ell(\bar{z}, z) = -\log p(\bar{z}|z) = -\log \mathcal{N}(t(\bar{z}|z)) - \log |\det \nabla t(\bar{z}|z)|. \tag{3}$$

Minimizing this loss over the training data distribution $p(x)$ gives t, a bijective mapping between $\bar{z}$ and (z, v),

$$\mathcal{L}(t) = \mathbb{E}_{x \sim p(x)} \left[\ell(E(x), \Phi(x)) \right] \tag{4}$$

$$= \mathbb{E}_{x \sim p(x)} \left[\frac{1}{2} \|t(E(x)|\Phi(x))\|^2 + N_{\bar{z}} \log 2\pi - \log |\det \nabla t(E(x)|\Phi(x))| \right] \tag{5}$$

Note that both E and Φ remain fixed during minimization of $\mathcal{L}$.

3.2 Interpreting Representations and Their Invariances

Visualizing Representations and Invariances. For an image representation $z = \Phi(x)$, Eq. (2) presents an efficient approach (a single forward pass through the INN t) to sample an encoding $\bar{z}$, which is a combination of z with a particular realization of its invariances v. Sampling multiple realizations of $\bar{z}$ for a given z highlights what remains constant and what changes due to different v: information preserved in the representation z remains constant over different samples and information discarded by the model ends up in the invariances v and shows changes over different samples. Visualizing the samples $\bar{z} \sim p(\bar{z}|z)$ with $\bar{x} = D(\bar{z})$ portrays this constancy and changes due to different v. To complement this visualization, in the following, we learn a transformation of $\bar{z}$ into a semantically meaningful representation which allows to uncover the semantics captured by z and v.

Learning an INN to Produce Semantic Interpretations. The autoencoder representation $\bar{z}$ is an equivalent representation of (z, v) but its feature dimensions do not necessarily correspond to semantic concepts [16]. More generally, without supervision, we cannot reliably discover semantically meaningful, explanatory factors of $\bar{z}$ [36]. In order to explain $\bar{z}$ in terms of given semantic concepts, we apply the approach of [15] and learn a bijective transformation of $\bar{z}$ to an interpretable representation $e(\bar{z})$ where different groups of components, called factors, correspond to semantic concepts.

To learn the transformation e, we parameterize e by an INN and assume that semantic concepts are defined implicitly by pairs of images, *i.e.* for each semantic concept we have access to training pairs x^a, x^b that have the respective concept in common. For example, the semantic concept 'smiling' is defined by pairs of images, where either both images show smiling persons or both images show non-smiling persons. Applying this formulation, input pairs which are similar in a certain semantic concept are similar in the corresponding factor of the interpretable representation $e(\bar{z})$.

Following [15], the loss for training the invertible network e is then given by

$$\mathcal{L}(e) = \mathbb{E}_{x^a, x^b} \left[- \log p(e(E(x^a)), e(E(x^b))) \right.$$
$$\left. - \log | \det \nabla e(E(x^a))| - \log | \det \nabla e(E(x^b))| \right] . \tag{6}$$

Further details regarding the application of this approach within our setting can be found in the supplementary, Sect. A.2.

Interpretation by Applying the Learned INNs. After training, the combination of e with t from Sect. 3.1 provides semantic interpretations given a model representation z: Eq. (2) gives realizations of the invariances v which are combined with z to produce $\bar{z} = t^{-1}(v|z)$. Then e transforms $\bar{z}$ without loss of information into a semantically accessible representation $(e_i)_i = e(\bar{z}) = e(t^{-1}(v|z))$ consisting of different semantic factors e_i. Comparing the e_i for different model

representations z and invariances v allows us to observe which semantic concepts the model representation $z = \Phi(\cdot)$ is sensitive to, and which it is invariant to.

Semantic Modifications of Latent Representations. t^{-1} and e not only interpret a representation z in terms of accessible semantic concepts $(e_i)_i$. Given $v \sim p(v)$, they also allow to modify $\bar{z} = t^{-1}(v|z)$ in a semantically meaningful manner by altering its corresponding $(e_i)_i$ and then applying the inverse translation e^{-1},

$$\bar{z} \xrightarrow{e} (e_i) \xrightarrow{\text{modification}} (e_i^*) \xrightarrow{e^{-1}} \bar{z}^* \tag{7}$$

The modified representation $\bar{z}^*$ is then readily transformed back into image space $\bar{x}^* = D(\bar{z}^*)$. Besides visual interpretation of the modification, $\bar{x}^*$ can be fed into the model $\Psi(\Phi(\bar{x}^*))$ to probe for sensitivity to certain semantic concepts.

4 Experiments

To explore the applicability of our approach, we conduct experiments on several models which we aim to understand: *SqueezeNet* [23], which provides lightweight classification, *FaceNet* [51], a baseline for face recognition and clustering, trained on the *VGGFace2 dataset* [7], and variants *ResNet* [21], a popular architecture, often used when finetuning a classifier on a specific task and dataset.

Experiments are conducted on the following datasets: *CelebA* [35], *Animal-Faces* [34], *Animals* (containing carnivorous animals, see Sect. B.3), *ImageNet* [11] and *ColorMNIST*, which is an augmented version of the *MNIST* dataset [30], where both background and foreground have random, independent colors.

4.1 Comparison to Existing Methods

A key insight of our work is that reconstructions from a given model's representation $z = \Phi(x)$ are impossible if the invariances the model has learned are not considered. In Fig. 2 we compare to existing methods that either try to reconstruct the image via gradient-based optimization [38] or by training a reconstruction network directly on the representations z [13]. By conditionally sampling images $\bar{x} = D(\bar{z})$, where we obtain $\bar{z}$ via the INN t as described in Eq. (2) based on the invariances $v \sim p(v) = \mathcal{N}(0, \mathbb{1})$, we bypass this shortcoming and obtain natural images without artifacts for any layer depth. The increased image quality is further confirmed by the FID scores reported in Table 1.

4.2 Understanding Models

Interpreting a Face Recognition Model. *FaceNet* [51] is a widely accepted baseline in the field of face recognition. This model embeds input images of human faces into a latent space where similar images have a small L_2-distance. We aim to understand the process of face recognition within this model by analyzing and visualizing learned invariances for several layers explicitly; see

reconstructions $\bar{x}$ from representations $z = \Phi(x)$ of different layers

method	input	conv5	fc6	fc7	fc8

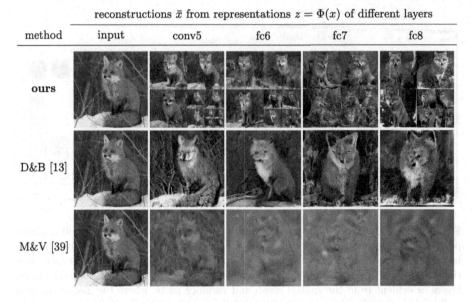

ours

D&B [13]

M&V [39]

Fig. 2. Comparison to existing network inversion methods for *AlexNet* [28]. In contrast to the methods of [13] (D&B) and [38] (M&V), our invertible method explicitly samples the invariances of Φ w.r.t. the data, which circumvents a common cause for artifacts and produces natural images independent of the depth of the layer which is reconstructed.

Table 1. FID scores for layer visualizations of *AlexNet*, obtained with our method and [13] (D&B). Scores are calculated on the *Animals* dataset.

Layer	conv5	fc6	fc7	fc8	Output
Ours	**23.6 ± 0.5**	**24.3 ± 0.7**	**24.9 ± 0.4**	**26.4 ± 0.4**	**27.4 ± 0.3**
D&B	25.2	**24.9**	27.2	36.1	352.6

Table S12 for a detailed breakdown of the various layers of *FaceNet*. For the experiment, we use a pretrained *FaceNet* and train the generative model presented in Eq. (2) by conditioning on various layers. Figure 3 depicts the amount of variance present in each selected layer when generating $n = 250$ samples for each of 100 different input images. This variance serves as a proxy for the amount of abstraction capability *FaceNet* has learned in its respective layers: More abstract representations allow for a rich variety of corresponding synthesized images, which results in a large variance in image space when being decoded. We observe an approximate exponential growth of learned invariances with increasing layer depth, suggesting that abstraction mainly happens in the deepest layers of the network. Furthermore, we are able to synthesize images that correspond to the given model representation for each selected layer.

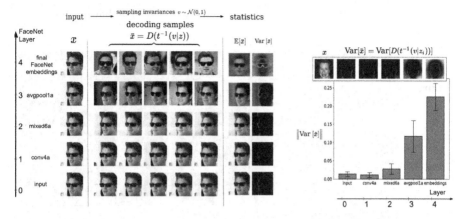

Fig. 3. *left*: Visualizing *FaceNet* representations and their invariances. Sampling multiple reconstructions $\bar{x} = D(t^{-1}(v|z))$ shows the degree of invariance learned by different layers. The invariance w.r.t. pose increases for deeper layers as expected for face identification. Surprisingly, FaceNet uses glasses as an identity feature throughout all its layers as evident from the spatial mean and variance plots, where the glasses are still visible. This reveals a bias and weakness of the model. *right*: Spatially averaged variances over multiple x for different layers.

How Does Relevance of Different Concepts Emerge During Training?
Humans tend to provide explanations of entities by describing them in terms of their semantics, e.g. size or color. In a similar fashion, we want to semantically understand how a network (here: *SqueezeNet*) learns to solve a given problem.

Intuitively, a network should for example be able to solve a given classification problem by focusing on the relevant information while discarding task-irrelevant information. To build on this intuition, we construct a toy problem: Digit classification on ColorMNIST. We expect the model to ignore both the random back- and foreground color of the input data, as it does not help making a classification decision. Thus, we apply the invertible approach presented in Sect. 3.2 and recover three distinct factors: *digit class*, *background color* and *foreground color*. To capture the semantic changes occurring over the course of training of this classifier, we couple 20 instances of the invertible interpretation model on the last convolutional layer, each representing a checkpoint between iteration 0 and iteration 40000 (equally distributed). The result is shown in Fig. 4: We see that the *digit* factor becomes increasingly more relevant, with its relevance being strongly correlated to the accuracy of the model.

4.3   Effects of Data Shifts on Models

This section investigates the effects that altering the input data has on the model we want to understand. We examine these effects by manipulating the input data explicitly through adversarial attacks or image stylization.

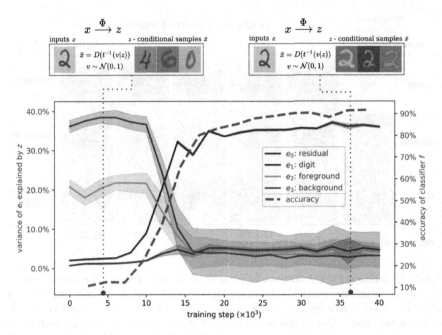

Fig. 4. Analyzing the degree to which different semantic concepts are captured by a network representation changes as training progresses. For *SqueezeNet* on *ColorMNIST* we measure how much the data varies in different semantic concepts e_i and how much of this variability is captured by z at different training iterations. Early on z is sensitive to foreground and background color, and later on it learns to focus on the digit attribute. The ability to encode this semantic concept is proportional to the classification accuracy achieved by z. At training iterations 4k and 36k we apply our method to visualize model representations and thereby illustrate how their content changes during training.

How Do Adversarial Attacks Affect Network Representations? Here, we experiment with *Fast Gradient Sign* (FGSM) attacks [19], which manipulate the input image by maximizing the objective of a given classification model. To understand how such an attack modifies representations of a given model, we first compute the image's invariances with respect to the model as $v = t(E(x)|\Phi(x))$. For an attacked image x^*, we then compute the attacked representation as $z^* = \Phi(x^*)$. Decoding this representation with the original invariance v, allows us to precisely visualize what the adversarial attack changed. This decoding, $\bar{x}^* = D(t(v|z^*))$, is shown in Fig. 5. We observe that, over layers of the network, the adversarial attack gradually changes the representation towards its target. Its ability to do so is strongly correlated with the amount of invariances, quantified as the total variance explained by v (see Sect. B.2), for a given layer as also observed in [24]. For additional examples, see Fig. S13.

How Does Training on Different Data Affect the Model? [17] proposed the hypothesis that classification networks based on convolutional blocks mainly

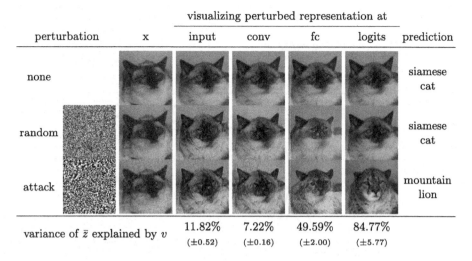

perturbation	x	visualizing perturbed representation at				prediction
		input	conv	fc	logits	
none						siamese cat
random						siamese cat
attack						mountain lion
variance of $\bar{z}$ explained by v		11.82% (±0.52)	7.22% (±0.16)	49.59% (±2.00)	84.77% (±5.77)	

Fig. 5. Visualizing FGSM adversarial attacks on *ResNet-101*. To the human eye, the original image and its attacked version are almost indistinguishable. However, the input image is correctly classified as "siamese cat", while the attacked version is classified as "mountain lion". Our approach visualizes how the attack spreads throughout the network. Reconstructions of representations of attacked images demonstrate that the attack targets the semantic content of deep layers. The variance of $\bar{z}$ explained by v combined with these visualizations show how increasing invariances cause vulnerability to adversarial attacks.

focus on texture patterns to obtain class probabilities. We further validate this hypothesis by training our invertible network t conditioned on pre-logits $z = \Phi(x)$ (*i.e.* the penultimate layer) of two ResNet-50 realizations. As shown in Fig. 6, a ResNet architecture trained on standard ImageNet is susceptible to the so-called "texture-bias", as samples generated conditioned on representation of pure texture images consistently show valid images of corresponding input classes. We furthermore visualize that this behavior can indeed be removed by training the same architecture on a stylized version of ImageNet[1]; the classifier does focus on shape. Rows 10–12 of Fig. 6 show that the proposed approach can be used to generate sketch-based content with the texture-agnostic network.

4.4   Modifying Representations

Invertible access to semantic concepts enables targeted modifications of representations $\bar{z}$. In combination with a decoder for $\bar{z}$, we obtain semantic image editing capabilities. We provide an example in Fig. 7, where we modify the factors hair color, glasses, gender, beard, age and smile. We infer $\bar{z} = E(x)$ from an input image. Our semantic INN e then translates this representation into

---

[1] We used weights available at https://github.com/rgeirhos/texture-vs-shape.

samples $\bar{x} = D(t^{-1}(v|z))$ conditioned on *ResNet* pre-logits $z = \Phi(x)$

inputs	$\Phi_{vanilla}$: ResNet-50 trained on standard ImageNet	$\Phi_{stylized}$: ResNet-50 trained on stylized ImageNet

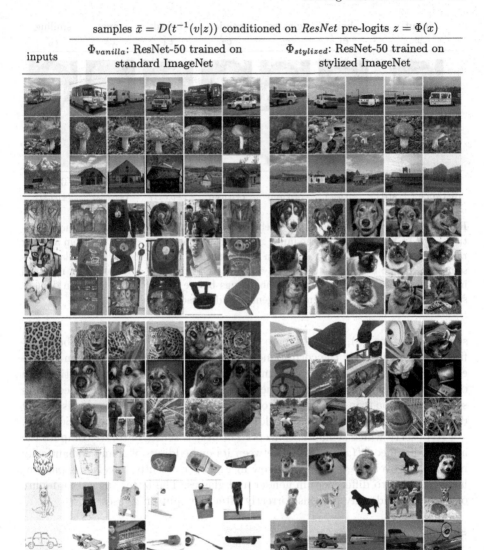

Fig. 6. Revealing texture bias in ImageNet classifiers. We compare visualizations of z from the penultimate layer of *ResNet-50* trained on standard ImageNet (left) and a stylized version of ImageNet (right). On natural images (rows 1–3) both models recognize the input, removing textures through stylization (rows 4–6) makes images unrecognizable to the standard model, however it recognizes objects from textured patches (rows 7–9). Rows 10–12 show that a model without texture bias can be used for sketch-to-image synthesis.

input x	hair e_1	glasses e_2	gender e_3	beard e_4	age e_5	smiling e_6

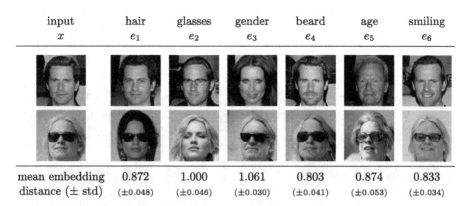

mean embedding distance ($\pm$ std)	0.872 ($\pm$0.048)	1.000 ($\pm$0.046)	1.061 ($\pm$0.030)	0.803 ($\pm$0.041)	0.874 ($\pm$0.053)	0.833 ($\pm$0.034)

Fig. 7. Semantic Modifications on CelebA. For each column, after inferring the semantic factors $(e_i)_i = e(E(x))$ of the input x, we replace one factor e_i by that from another randomly chosen image that differs in this concept. The inverse of e translates this semantic change back into a modified $\bar{z}$, which is decoded to a semantically modified image. Distances between *FaceNet* embeddings before and after modification demonstrate its sensitivity to differences in gender and glasses (see also Fig. 3).

semantic factors $(e_i)_i = e(\bar{z})$, where individual semantic concepts can be modified independently via the corresponding factor e_i. In particular, we can replace each factor with that from another image, effectively transferring semantics from one representation onto another. Due to the invertibility of e, the modified representation can be translated back into the space of the autoencoder and is readily decoded to a modified image x^*. Additional examples can be found in Sect. B.5.

To observe which semantic concepts *FaceNet* is sensitive to, we compute the average distance $\|f(x) - f(x^*)\|$ between its embeddings of x and semantically modified x^* over the test set (last row in Fig. 7). Evidently, FaceNet is particularly sensitive to differences in gender and glasses. The latter suggests a failure of FaceNet to identify persons correctly after they put on glasses.

5   Conclusion

Understanding a representation in terms of both its semantics and learned invariances is crucial for interpretation of deep networks. We presented an approach to (*i*) recover the invariances a model has learned and (*ii*) translate the representation and its invariances onto an equally expressive yet semantically accessible encoding. Our diagnostic method is applicable in a plug-and-play fashion on top of existing deep models with no need to alter or retrain them. Since our translation onto semantic factors is bijective, it loses no information and also allows for semantic modifications. Moreover, recovering invariances probabilistically guarantees that we can correctly visualize representations and sample them without leaving the underlying distribution, which is a common cause for artifacts. Altogether, our approach constitutes a powerful, widely applicable diagnostic pipeline for explaining deep representations.

Acknowledgments. This work has been supported in part by the German Research Foundation (DFG) projects 371923335, 421703927, and EXC 2181/1 - 390900948 and the German federal ministry BMWi within the project "KI Absicherung".

References

1. Achille, A., Soatto, S.: Emergence of invariance and disentanglement in deep representations. J. Mach. Learn. Res. **19**(1), 1947–1980 (2018)
2. Ardizzone, L., et al.: Analyzing inverse problems with invertible neural networks (2018)
3. Bach, S., Binder, A., Montavon, G., Klauschen, F., Müller, K.R., Samek, W.: On pixel-wise explanations for non-linear classifier decisions by layer-wise relevance propagation. PLoS ONE **10**(7), e0130140 (2015)
4. Bau, D., Zhou, B., Khosla, A., Oliva, A., Torralba, A.: Network dissection: quantifying interpretability of deep visual representations. In: 2017 IEEE Conference on Computer Vision and Pattern Recognition (CVPR) (2017). https://doi.org/10.1109/CVPR.2017.354
5. Bau, D., et al.: GAN dissection: visualizing and understanding generative adversarial networks (2018)
6. Brock, A., Donahue, J., Simonyan, K.: Large scale GAN training for high fidelity natural image synthesis. arXiv preprint arXiv:1809.11096 (2018)
7. Cao, Q., Shen, L., Xie, W., Parkhi, O.M., Zisserman, A.: VGGFace2: a dataset for recognising faces across pose and age. In: 2018 13th IEEE International Conference on Automatic Face & Gesture Recognition (FG 2018), pp. 67–74. IEEE (2018)
8. Choi, Y., Choi, M., Kim, M., Ha, J.W., Kim, S., Choo, J.: StarGAN: unified generative adversarial networks for multi-domain image-to-image translation. In: Proceedings of the IEEE Conference on Computer Vision and Pattern Recognition (2018)
9. Commission, E.: On artificial intelligence - a European approach to excellence and trust. Technical report (2020). https://eur-lex.europa.eu/legal-content/EN/TXT/?uri=COM:2020:65:FIN. Accessed Feb 2020
10. Dai, B., Wipf, D.: Diagnosing and enhancing VAE models (2019)
11. Deng, J., Dong, W., Socher, R., Li, L.J., Li, K., Fei-Fei, L.: ImageNet: a large-scale hierarchical image database. In: 2009 IEEE Conference on Computer Vision and Pattern Recognition, pp. 248–255. IEEE (2009)
12. Dinh, L., Sohl-Dickstein, J., Bengio, S.: Density estimation using real NVP (2016)
13. Dosovitskiy, A., Brox, T.: Generating images with perceptual similarity metrics based on deep networks (2016)
14. Esser, P., Haux, J., Ommer, B.: Unsupervised robust disentangling of latent characteristics for image synthesis. In: 2019 IEEE/CVF International Conference on Computer Vision (ICCV) (2019). https://doi.org/10.1109/ICCV.2019.00279
15. Esser, P., Rombach, R., Ommer, B.: A disentangling invertible interpretation network for explaining latent representations. In: Proceedings of the IEEE/CVF Conference on Computer Vision and Pattern Recognition, pp. 9223–9232 (2020)
16. Fong, R., Vedaldi, A.: Net2Vec: quantifying and explaining how concepts are encoded by filters in deep neural networks. In: 2018 IEEE/CVF Conference on Computer Vision and Pattern Recognition, pp. 8730–8738 (2018). https://doi.org/10.1109/CVPR.2018.00910

17. Geirhos, R., Rubisch, P., Michaelis, C., Bethge, M., Wichmann, F.A., Brendel, W.: ImageNet-trained CNNs are biased towards texture; increasing shape bias improves accuracy and robustness. arXiv preprint arXiv:1811.12231 (2018)
18. Goetschalckx, L., Andonian, A., Oliva, A., Isola, P.: GANalyze: toward visual definitions of cognitive image properties. arXiv preprint arXiv:1906.10112 (2019)
19. Goodfellow, I.J., Shlens, J., Szegedy, C.: Explaining and harnessing adversarial examples. arXiv preprint arXiv:1412.6572 (2014)
20. Goodman, B., Flaxman, S.: European union regulations on algorithmic decision-making and a "right to explanation". AI Mag. **38**(3), 50–57 (2017). https://doi.org/10.1609/aimag.v38i3.2741
21. He, K., Zhang, X., Ren, S., Sun, J.: Deep residual learning for image recognition. In: Proceedings of the IEEE Conference on Computer Vision and Pattern Recognition, pp. 770–778 (2016)
22. Heusel, M., Ramsauer, H., Unterthiner, T., Nessler, B., Hochreiter, S.: GANs trained by a two time-scale update rule converge to a local Nash equilibrium (2017)
23. Iandola, F.N., Han, S., Moskewicz, M.W., Ashraf, K., Dally, W.J., Keutzer, K.: SqueezeNet: AlexNet-level accuracy with 50x fewer parameters and <0.5 mb model size. arXiv preprint arXiv:1602.07360 (2016)
24. Jacobsen, J.H., Behrmann, J., Zemel, R., Bethge, M.: Excessive invariance causes adversarial vulnerability (2018)
25. Kingma, D.P., Welling, M.: Auto-encoding variational Bayes. arXiv preprint arXiv:1312.6114 (2013)
26. Kingma, D.P., Dhariwal, P.: Glow: generative flow with invertible 1x1 convolutions. In: Advances in Neural Information Processing Systems, pp. 10215–10224 (2018)
27. Kotovenko, D., Sanakoyeu, A., Lang, S., Ommer, B.: Content and style disentanglement for artistic style transfer. In: 2019 IEEE/CVF International Conference on Computer Vision (ICCV), pp. 4421–4430 (2019)
28. Krizhevsky, A., Sutskever, I., Hinton, G.E.: ImageNet classification with deep convolutional neural networks. In: Advances in Neural Information Processing Systems, pp. 1097–1105 (2012)
29. Kulkarni, T.D., Whitney, W., Kohli, P., Tenenbaum, J.B.: Deep convolutional inverse graphics network (2015)
30. LeCun, Y.: The MNIST database of handwritten digits (1998). http://yann.lecun.com/exdb/mnist/
31. LeCun, Y.: Learning invariant feature hierarchies. In: Fusiello, A., Murino, V., Cucchiara, R. (eds.) ECCV 2012. LNCS, vol. 7583, pp. 496–505. Springer, Heidelberg (2012). https://doi.org/10.1007/978-3-642-33863-2_51
32. Li, Y., Singh, K.K., Ojha, U., Lee, Y.J.: MixNMatch: multifactor disentanglement and encoding for conditional image generation (2019)
33. Lipton, Z.C.: The mythos of model interpretability (2016)
34. Liu, M.Y., et al.: Few-shot unsupervised image-to-image translation. arXiv preprint arXiv:1905.01723 (2019)
35. Liu, Z., Luo, P., Wang, X., Tang, X.: Deep learning face attributes in the wild. In: Proceedings of International Conference on Computer Vision (ICCV) (2015)
36. Locatello, F., et al.: Challenging common assumptions in the unsupervised learning of disentangled representations (2018)
37. Lorenz, D., Bereska, L., Milbich, T., Ommer, B.: Unsupervised part-based disentangling of object shape and appearance. In: 2019 IEEE/CVF Conference on Computer Vision and Pattern Recognition (CVPR), pp. 10947–10956 (2019)
38. Mahendran, A., Vedaldi, A.: Visualizing deep convolutional neural networks using natural pre-images. Int. J. Comput. Vis. **120**(3), 233–255 (2016)

39. Miller, T.: Explanation in artificial intelligence: insights from the social sciences. Artif. Intell. **267**, 1–38 (2019)
40. Montavon, G., Lapuschkin, S., Binder, A., Samek, W., Müller, K.R.: Explaining nonlinear classification decisions with deep Taylor decomposition. Pattern Recogn. **65**, 211–222 (2017)
41. Montavon, G., Samek, W., Müller, K.R.: Methods for interpreting and understanding deep neural networks. Digit. Signal Proc. **73**, 1–15 (2018)
42. Mordvintsev, A., Olah, C., Tyka, M.: Inceptionism: going deeper into neural networks (2015)
43. Nash, C., Kushman, N., Williams, C.K.: Inverting supervised representations with autoregressive neural density models. In: The 22nd International Conference on Artificial Intelligence and Statistics, pp. 1620–1629 (2019)
44. Nguyen, A., Dosovitskiy, A., Yosinski, J., Brox, T., Clune, J.: Synthesizing the preferred inputs for neurons in neural networks via deep generator networks (2016)
45. Plumb, G., Al-Shedivat, M., Xing, E., Talwalkar, A.: Regularizing black-box models for improved interpretability (2019)
46. Redlich, A.N.: Supervised factorial learning. Neural Comput. **5**(5), 750–766 (1993). https://doi.org/10.1162/neco.1993.5.5.750
47. Rezende, D.J., Mohamed, S., Wierstra, D.: Stochastic backpropagation and approximate inference in deep generative models. In: Proceedings of the 31st International Conference on International Conference on Machine Learning, vol. 32, pp. II-1278. JMLR.org (2014)
48. Rombach, R., Esser, P., Ommer, B.: Network fusion for content creation with conditional INNs (2020)
49. Samek, W., Wiegand, T., Müller, K.R.: Explainable artificial intelligence: understanding, visualizing and interpreting deep learning models. arXiv preprint arXiv:1708.08296 (2017)
50. Santurkar, S., Tsipras, D., Tran, B., Ilyas, A., Engstrom, L., Madry, A.: Image synthesis with a single (robust) classifier (2019)
51. Schroff, F., Kalenichenko, D., Philbin, J.: FaceNet: a unified embedding for face recognition and clustering. In: Proceedings of the IEEE Conference on Computer Vision and Pattern Recognition, pp. 815–823 (2015)
52. Selvaraju, R.R., Cogswell, M., Das, A., Vedantam, R., Parikh, D., Batra, D.: Grad-CAM: visual explanations from deep networks via gradient-based localization. Int. J. Comput. Vis. **128**(2), 336–359 (2019). https://doi.org/10.1007/s11263-019-01228-7
53. Shocher, A., et al.: Semantic pyramid for image generation. In: Proceedings of the IEEE/CVF Conference on Computer Vision and Pattern Recognition (CVPR) (2020)
54. Simon, M., Rodner, E.: Neural activation constellations: unsupervised part model discovery with convolutional networks. In: 2015 IEEE International Conference on Computer Vision (ICCV) (2015). https://doi.org/10.1109/ICCV.2015.136
55. Simon, M., Rodner, E., Denzler, J.: Part detector discovery in deep convolutional neural networks. ArXiv abs/1411.3159 (2014)
56. Simonyan, K., Vedaldi, A., Zisserman, A.: Deep inside convolutional networks: visualising image classification models and saliency maps. arXiv preprint arXiv:1312.6034 (2013)
57. Szegedy, C., et al.: Intriguing properties of neural networks (2013)
58. Upchurch, P., et al.: Deep feature interpolation for image content changes. In: Proceedings of the IEEE Conference on Computer Vision and Pattern Recognition, pp. 7064–7073 (2017)

59. Xian, Y., Lampert, C.H., Schiele, B., Akata, Z.: Zero-shot learning'a comprehensive evaluation of the good, the bad and the ugly. IEEE Trans. Pattern Anal. Mach. Intell. **41**(9), 2251–2265 (2018)
60. Xiao, Z., Yan, Q., Amit, Y.: Generative latent flow (2019)
61. Yosinski, J., Clune, J., Nguyen, A., Fuchs, T., Lipson, H.: Understanding neural networks through deep visualization (2015)
62. Zeiler, M.D., Fergus, R.: Visualizing and understanding convolutional networks. In: Fleet, D., Pajdla, T., Schiele, B., Tuytelaars, T. (eds.) ECCV 2014. LNCS, vol. 8689, pp. 818–833. Springer, Cham (2014). https://doi.org/10.1007/978-3-319-10590-1_53
63. Zhang, Q., Nian Wu, Y., Zhu, S.C.: Interpretable convolutional neural networks. In: Proceedings of the IEEE Conference on Computer Vision and Pattern Recognition, pp. 8827–8836 (2018)
64. Zhang, R., Isola, P., Efros, A.A., Shechtman, E., Wang, O.: The unreasonable effectiveness of deep features as a perceptual metric. In: CVPR (2018)
65. Zhou, B., Khosla, A., Lapedriza, A., Oliva, A., Torralba, A.: Object detectors emerge in deep scene CNNs (2014)
66. Zhou, B., Khosla, A., Lapedriza, A., Oliva, A., Torralba, A.: Learning deep features for discriminative localization. In: 2016 IEEE Conference on Computer Vision and Pattern Recognition (CVPR) (2016). https://doi.org/10.1109/CVPR.2016.319

Cross-Modal Weighting Network
for RGB-D Salient Object Detection

Gongyang Li[1], Zhi Liu[1]([✉]), Linwei Ye[2], Yang Wang[2,4],
and Haibin Ling[3]

[1] Shanghai University, Shanghai, China
ligongyang@shu.edu.cnm, liuzhi@staff.shu.edu.cn
[2] University of Manitoba, Winnipeg, Canada
{yel3,ywang}@cs.umanitoba.ca
[3] Stony Brook University, Stony Brook, NY, USA
hling@cs.stonybrook.edu
[4] Huawei Technologies Canada, Markham, Canada
https://github.com/MathLee/CMWNet

Abstract. Depth maps contain geometric clues for assisting Salient
Object Detection (SOD). In this paper, we propose a novel Cross-
Modal Weighting (CMW) strategy to encourage comprehensive interactions between RGB and depth channels for RGB-D SOD. Specifically,
three RGB-depth interaction modules, named CMW-L, CMW-M and
CMW-H, are developed to deal with respectively low-, middle- and high-
level cross-modal information fusion. These modules use Depth-to-RGB
Weighing (DW) and RGB-to-RGB Weighting (RW) to allow rich cross-
modal and cross-scale interactions among feature layers generated by
different network blocks. To effectively train the proposed Cross-Modal
Weighting Network (CMWNet), we design a composite loss function
that summarizes the errors between intermediate predictions and ground
truth over different scales. With all these novel components working
together, CMWNet effectively fuses information from RGB and depth
channels, and meanwhile explores object localization and details across
scales. Thorough evaluations demonstrate CMWNet consistently outperforms 15 state-of-the-art RGB-D SOD methods on seven popular benchmarks.

Keywords: RGB-D salient object detection · Cross-Modal
Weighting · Depth-to-RGB weighting · RGB-to-RGB weighting

1 Introduction

Salient object detection (SOD) aims to pick the regions/objects in an image
that are most attractive to human visual attention. It has a wide range of applications as summarized in recent surveys [1,2,39]. Most existing SOD solutions

© Springer Nature Switzerland AG 2020
A. Vedaldi et al. (Eds.): ECCV 2020, LNCS 12362, pp. 665–681, 2020.
https://doi.org/10.1007/978-3-030-58520-4_39

take as input an RGB image (or video), which is convenient in many application scenarios, but may suffer from challenges such as low contrast and disturbing background. Alternatively, one can seek help from the depth information typically provided with an RGB-D input. In fact, with the popularity of depth sensors/devices, RGB-D SOD has received extensive attention recently, and numerous approaches [4,8,13,16,20,25,28,31,36,42] have been proposed to extract salient objects from paired RGB images and depth maps.

Starting with the first stereoscopic image SOD dataset STEREO [28], traditional RGB-D SOD methods mainly apply contrast cue [14,15,35], fusion framework [19,29,36,37] and measure strategy [9,16,25] to extract the complementary information in depth maps. These well-designed hand-crafted features-based methods, which are influenced by RGB SOD solutions, have achieved remarkable results. However, salient objects in the generated saliency maps are sometimes blocky because of inappropriate over-segmentation, while salient objects may be confused by complex scenes.

Recently, with the rapid development of deep learning, convolutional neural networks (CNNs) have shown strong dominance in many computer vision problems. Many CNN-based RGB-D SOD methods have been proposed and greatly outperformed traditional ones. Early CNN-based methods [31,33] feed the superpixel-based hand-crafted features of RGB-D pairs into CNNs, but their results are still patch-based. Subsequent methods instead assign saliency values for each pixel based on the RGB image and depth map in an end-to-end manner. Among these methods, the two-stream architecture [4,6,10,20,38,44] fuses cross-modal features/saliency maps in the middle/late stage, while the single-stream architecture [13,26] directly handles RGB-D pairs. These methods, despite achieving great performance gain, do not take full advantage of rich interactive information between different modalities and scales of CNN blocks.

Motivated by the above observation, in this paper, we propose a novel *Cross-Modal Weighting Network* (CMWNet) that significantly improves RGB-depth interactions, and hence boosts RGB-D SOD performances as demonstrated in our thorough experiments. Our key idea is to jointly explore the information carried by both RGB and depth channels, and to encourage cross-modal and cross-scale RGB-depth interactions among different CNN feature blocks. This way, our algorithm can capture both microscopic details carried by shallow blocks and macroscopic object location information carried by deep blocks. CMWNet adopts a three-level representation, capturing low-, middle-, and high-level information respectively; and multiple blocks at different scales are allowed to be within a level. The cross-modal cross-scale interactions are modeled through the novel Cross-Modal Weighting (CMW) modules to highlight salient objects.

In particular, we propose three CMW modules, CMW-L, CMW-M and CMW-H. For low- and middle-level parts, CMW-L and CMW-M are used to enhance salient object details in a cross-scale manner. For high-level part, CMW-H is used to enhance salient object localization, which plays a crucial role in subsequent prediction of salient objects. The key components in these CMW modules are the proposed Depth-to-RGB Weighting (DW) and RGB-to-RGB

Weighting (RW) operations that enhance RGB features in each channel based on corresponding response maps. In addition to the encoder, a three-level decoder is designed to connect the three-level enhanced features to predict the final salient objects. In this way, the proposed CMWNet effectively exploits the properties of CNN features and strengthens the cross-modal and cross-scale interactions, resulting in excellent performance.

Our major contributions are summarized as follows:

- We explore the complex complementarity between RGB image and depth map in a three-level encoder-decoder structure, and propose a novel *Cross-Modal Weighting Network* (CMWNet) to encourage the cross-modal and cross-scale interactions, boosting the performance of RGB-D SOD.
- We propose three novel RGB-depth interaction modules to effectively enhance both salient object details (CMW-L and CMW-M) and salient object localization (CMW-H).
- Extensive experiments on seven popular public datasets under six commonly used evaluation metrics show that the proposed method achieves the best performance compared with 15 state-of-the-art RGB-D SOD methods.

2   Related Work

Traditional RGB-D SOD. Starting from the first work for saliency detection [21], the contrast-based approaches are the mainstream for saliency detection. This trend has spread to traditional RGB-D SOD. Numerous contrast-based RGB-D SOD methods have been proposed, such as disparity contrast [28], depth contrast [7,14,15,35], and multi-contextual contrast [29]. Song *et al.* [36] employed the multi-scale fusion to merge saliency maps to obtain the final RGB-D saliency map, which is similar to methods based on two-stream saliency fusion [29] and multiple-cues fusion [19,37]. By adopting the objectness measure [25], depth confidence measure [9] and salient structure measure [16], the performance gets clear improvement. Besides, other methods (*i.e.*, global prior [32], cellular automata [18], transformation strategy [8]) have been proposed for RGB-D SOD. However, these traditional methods are often based on superpixels, regions and patches, which cause saliency maps to appear blocky and saliency values to be scattered.

CNN-Based RGB-D SOD. In recent years, numerous CNN-based RGB-D SOD methods [4–6,10,13,20,26,31,33,38,42,44] have been proposed. As pioneering work based on CNNs, Qu *et al.* [31] fed the superpixel-based RGB-D saliency features into a five-layer CNN. Shigematsu *et al.* [33] sent ten superpixel-based depth features to a network. Being patch-based methods, these methods sometimes generate results that appear blocky. To overcome the limitation, Han *et al.* [20] proposed a transfer and fusion based network to predict pixel-level saliency values. The single-stream architecture [13,26] adopts a straightforward way to handle the four-channel RGB-D pair. This architecture does not effectively capture the cross-modal interactions between the RGB image and the

depth map, so the performance depends largely on the network structure rather than the cross-modal interactions. The two-stream architecture employs two separate networks to extract features [4,6,20,44] and saliency maps [10,38], and then fuse them with various strategies. Some works [10,20,38,44] only fuse saliency maps and high-level features. As a result, they do not capture more complex cross-modal interactions at other levels of the network. Some other works [4,5] consider cross-modal CNN features, but the same module is used to process cross-modal CNN features at different blocks. Consequently, these methods ignore the different properties of CNN features at different blocks and cannot provide specific enhancements to object details and object localization.

In this work, we propose a novel three-level CMWNet to encourage interactions between RGB and depth channels and propose several modules to treat differently detail features and localization features carried in CNN feature blocks at various scales. Moreover, we process CNN features in a cross-modal and cross-scale manner to effectively capture the interactions across modalities and scales. Thus, our network can accurately enhance the details and localization of salient objects in the encoder part and precisely infer salient objects in the three-level decoder.

3   Proposed Method

In this section, we start with the overview of Cross-Modal Weighting Network (CMWNet) (Sect. 3.1). In Sect. 3.2, we provide the details of low- and middle-level cross-modal weighting modules, *i.e.* CMW-L and CMW-M, and then in Sect. 3.3 we introduce the high-level cross-modal weighting module CMW-H. Finally, we describe the implementation details in Sect. 3.4.

3.1   Network Overview and Motivation

The proposed CMWNet follows a three-level Siamese encoder-decoder structure, as summarized in Fig. 1.

Three-Level Encoder. We adopt the VGG16 [34] as the backbone. The depth map branch and the RGB image branch share the same weights. In the Siamese encoder part, five CNN blocks of the depth map and the RGB image are denoted as D-E$^{(l)}$ and R-E$^{(l)}$ ($l \in \{1, 2, 3, 4, 5\}$ is the block index), respectively. Considering the unique properties of features, we divide the first and second CNN blocks into low-level part, the third and fourth CNN blocks into middle-level part, and the last CNN block into high-level part.

Low- and Middle-Level Cross-Modal Weighting Modules. The weighting mechanism [43] is an extended version of attention mechanism, and it aims to modulate features of each channel according to particular response maps. The abundant geometric knowledge of depth maps is helpful to provide object details and object localization for SOD. We novelly extend the weighting mechanism with cross-modal information (*i.e.* RGB image and depth map), and propose

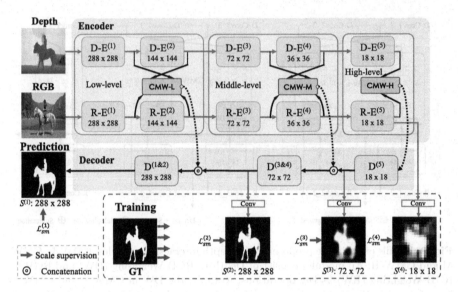

Fig. 1. Illustration of the proposed CMWNet. For both RGB and depth channel, the Siamese encoder network is employed to extract feature blocks organized in three levels. Three Cross-Modal Weighting (CMW) modules, CMW-L, CMW-M and CMW-H, are proposed to capture the interactions at corresponding level, and provide inputs for the decoder. The decoder progressively aggregates all the cross-modal cross-scale information for the final prediction. For training, multi-scale pixel-level supervision for intermediate predictions are utilized.

cross-modal RGB-depth interaction modules, which adopt weighting mechanism to reweight the RGB features based on depth response maps and RGB response maps to focus on salient objects.

Considering that the low- and middle-level parts carry abundant information about object details, we treat the features in these two levels as responsible for object details enhancement, and propose CMW-L and CMW-M. Each of the low- and middle-level contains the two adjacent CNN blocks, one contains relatively macroscopic information while the other relatively microscopic. To balance these two types of information within a level, we use the higher *depth* block to enhance the lower *RGB* block, and use the lower *depth* block to enhance the higher *RGB* block, namely *cross-scale Depth-to-RGB weighting*. It is an important component of CMW-L and CMW-M. Concretely, the higher depth response maps are in charge of modulating the lower RGB features, and the lower depth response maps are responsible to modulate the higher RGB features. Such a cross-scale way captures cross-scale complementarity of cross-modal features. Besides, the Depth-to-RGB weighting is executed between two adjacent blocks, which can capture the continuity of features.

On the other hand, RGB features have the ability to modulate themselves. For this purpose, we introduce the *RGB-to-RGB weighting* to CMW-L and CMW-M. RGB features are enhanced by RGB response maps, which are

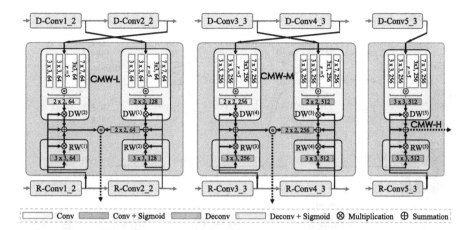

Fig. 2. Details of the three proposed RGB-depth interaction modules: CMW-L, CMW-M and CMW-H. All modules consist of Depth-to-RGB Weighting (DW) and RGB-to-RGB Weighting (RW) as key operations. Notably, the DW in CMW-L and CMW-M is performed in the cross-scale manner between two adjacent blocks, which effectively captures the feature continuity and activates cross-modal cross-scale interactions.

generated from RGB features. This allows our weighting modules to learn and adjust salient parts in an adaptive manner. Depth-to-RGB weighting and RGB-to-RGB weighting complement each other, improving the stability and robustness of our inference. Thus, for example, in CMW-M, R-E$^{(3)}$ is enhanced by D-E$^{(4)}$ and R-E$^{(3)}$, and R-E$^{(4)}$ is enhanced by D-E$^{(3)}$ and R-E$^{(4)}$. Notably, CMW-L and CMW-M perform the same cross-scale scheme, but with different resolutions. The multi-resolution enhanced object details of features benefit SOD.

High-Level Cross-Modal Weighting Module. The high-level part is distinct from the other two parts, and it contains rich global information. Thus, in the high-level part, we adopt CNN features of the highest blocks (*i.e.*, D-E$^{(5)}$ and R-E$^{(5)}$) to accurately locate salient objects. We propose the CMW-H module, which is the modified variant of CMW-L and CMW-M, to enhance the macroscopic localization of salient objects. The RGB features of R-E$^{(5)}$ are enhanced by the depth response maps generated from D-E$^{(5)}$ and the RGB response maps generated from R-E$^{(5)}$.

Three-Level Decoder. The decoder can make good use of features from the encoder with skip-connections. To fuse all the enhanced features for effective inference, the decoder part also consists of three levels, *i.e.*, D$^{(5)}$, D$^{(3\&4)}$ and D$^{(1\&2)}$ as shown in Fig. 1, corresponding to high-level, middle-level and low-level encoder parts. Between the two adjacent levels, we employ the deconvolutional layer for 4× upsampling. Specifically, to effectively train the proposed CMWNet, we adopt the deep scale supervision [40] behind each level to force features of the decoder network to focus on salient objects.

3.2   Low- and Middle-Level Cross-Modal Weighting

We perform the enhancement on RGB features at low-level and middle-level parts with the CMW-L and CMW-M, respectively. The details of **CMW-L** and **CMW-M** are shown in Fig. 2. There are two types of weighting in each module, *i.e.*, cross-scale Depth-to-RGB weighting (DW) and RGB-to-RGB weighting (RW). For each encoder block, those two types of weighting only apply to the last feature layer. So we denote the last layer of features in D-E$^{(l)}$ and R-E$^{(l)}$ as $\mathbf{f}_d^{(l)}$ and $\mathbf{f}_r^{(l)}$, respectively.

We provide a simplified version to explain the principle of DW and RW. For a feature map $\mathbf{F} \in \mathbb{R}^{C_0 \times W_0 \times H_0}$, there are two groups of weighting response maps $\mathbf{r}_1 \in [0,1]^{C_0 \times W_0 \times H_0}$ and $\mathbf{r}_2 \in [0,1]^{C_0 \times W_0 \times H_0}$ to modulate it at pixel level, and then the two types of weighting can be formulated as:

$$\mathbf{EF} = \mathbf{F} + \mathbf{r}_1 \otimes \mathbf{F} + \mathbf{r}_2 \otimes \mathbf{F}, \tag{1}$$

where $\mathbf{EF} \in \mathbb{R}^{C_0 \times W_0 \times H_0}$ is the enhanced feature, $\otimes$ is the element-wise multiplication, and $+$ is the element-wise summation. $\mathbf{r}_1 \otimes \mathbf{F}$ and $\mathbf{r}_2 \otimes \mathbf{F}$ can be regarded as the DW operation and RW operation, respectively. If $\mathbf{r}_1$ and $\mathbf{r}_2$ have good responses to salient objects (*i.e.*, the pixel value is close to 1 on salient objects and close to 0 on background), $\mathbf{F}$ will be accurately modulated to focus on the desired salient parts and $\mathbf{EF}$ will have a stronger representation for salient objects. Thus, we apply the two types of weighting to RGB features and depth features for enhancement of salient object details in the CMW-L and CMW-M modules.

Depth-to-RGB Weighting. In our network, the Depth-to-RGB weighting is the most important operation to mine the complementarity of depth maps. It works in a cross-modal and cross-scale manner. To expand the receptive field and increase the feature diversity, we design a comprehensive structure of filters to generate the local and global features $\mathbf{f}_{lg}^{(l)}$.

Concretely, we adopt two convolutional layers with 3×3 kernel as local filters. We also adopt a dilated convolution [41] with 3×3 kernel and $rate = 5$ and a convolutional layers with 7×7 kernel as global filters, as shown in DW$^{(l)}$ of Fig. 2. The global filters in the comprehensive structure expand the receptive field of convolution operations. The obtained global features can capture macro-level information of depth features, which are complementary to the local features. For each $\mathbf{f}_d^{(l)}$, $\mathbf{f}_{lg}^{(l)}$ can be computed as:

$$\mathbf{f}_{lg}^{(l)} = \text{concat}\big(C(\mathbf{f}_d^{(l)}; \mathbf{W}_{loc}^{(l_1)}), C(\mathbf{f}_d^{(l)}; \mathbf{W}_{loc}^{(l_2)}), C(\mathbf{f}_d^{(l)}; \mathbf{W}_{glo}^{(l_1)}), C(\mathbf{f}_d^{(l)}; \mathbf{W}_{glo}^{(l_2)})\big), \tag{2}$$

where concat$(\cdot)$ denotes the cross-channel concatenation, $C(*; \mathbf{W}_{loc}^{(l_i)})$ is a convolutional layer with parameters $\mathbf{W}_{loc}^{(l_i)}$ (*i.e.*, $\mathbf{W}_{loc}^{(l_1)}$ and $\mathbf{W}_{loc}^{(l_2)}$ are 3×3 kernel) for producing local features, $C(*; \mathbf{W}_{glo}^{(l_1)})$ is a convolutional layer with parameters $\mathbf{W}_{glo}^{(l_1)}$ (*i.e.*, $\mathbf{W}_{glo}^{(l_1)}$ is 7×7 kernel), and $C(*; \mathbf{W}_{glo}^{(l_2)})$ is the dilated convolution with parameters $\mathbf{W}_{glo}^{(l_2)}$ (*i.e.*, $\mathbf{W}_{glo}^{(l_2)}$ is 3×3 kernel with $rate = 5$).

Then, the multi-scale features in $\mathbf{f}_{lg}^{(l)}$ are fused to generate the depth response maps $\mathbf{r}_{dw}^{(l)}$. Specifically, to make $\mathbf{r}_{dw}^{(l)}$ have the same resolution as the corresponding cross-scale RGB features, the fusion operation is a convolutional layer with stride 2 for 2× downsampling for $\mathrm{DW}^{(1)}$ and $\mathrm{DW}^{(3)}$, while a deconvolutional layer is used for $\mathrm{DW}^{(2)}$ and $\mathrm{DW}^{(4)}$ for 2× upsampling. Thus, $\mathbf{r}_{dw}^{(l)}$ can be computed as:

$$\mathbf{r}_{dw}^{(l)} = \begin{cases} \sigma(C(\mathbf{f}_{lg}^{(l)}; \mathbf{W}_{dw}^{(l)})), \, l = 1, 3 \\ \sigma(De(\mathbf{f}_{lg}^{(l)}; \mathbf{W}_{dw}^{(l)})), \, l = 2, 4 \end{cases}, \tag{3}$$

where $\sigma(\cdot)$ is the sigmoid function, and $De(*; \mathbf{W}_{dw}^{(l)})$ is the deconvolutional layer with parameters $\mathbf{W}_{dw}^{(l)}$, which are 2×2 kernel with stride 2.

Finally, $\mathbf{r}_{dw}^{(l)}$ is used to enhance the cross-scale RGB features as follows:

$$\mathbf{f}_{dw}^{(l)} = \begin{cases} \mathbf{r}_{dw}^{(l+1)} \otimes \mathbf{f}_{r}^{(l)}, \, l = 1, 3 \\ \mathbf{r}_{dw}^{(l-1)} \otimes \mathbf{f}_{r}^{(l)}, \, l = 2, 4 \end{cases}. \tag{4}$$

RGB-to-RGB Weighting. Considering that the RGB features of low- and middle-level parts also contain rich information about details of salient objects, we propose the RGB-to-RGB weighting to adaptively enhance RGB features with the RGB response maps $\mathbf{r}_{rw}^{(l)}$, which are generated from $\mathbf{f}_{r}^{(l)}$ as follows:

$$\mathbf{r}_{rw}^{(l)} = \sigma(C(\mathbf{f}_{r}^{(l)}; \mathbf{W}_{rw}^{(l)})). \tag{5}$$

The details of filters in $\mathrm{RW}^{(l)}$ are also presented in Fig. 2. Then, similar as depth response maps, $\mathbf{r}_{rw}^{(l)}$ can enhance $\mathbf{f}_{r}^{(l)}$ as follows:

$$\mathbf{f}_{rw}^{(l)} = \mathbf{r}_{rw}^{(l)} \otimes \mathbf{f}_{r}^{(l)}. \tag{6}$$

Aggregation of Double Weighting Features. After the DW and RW operations, the RGB features are enhanced twice and can capture the details of salient objects. To preserve the original color information, we add RGB features to these two groups of enhanced features to produce the double enhanced features $\mathbf{f}_{de}^{(l)}$. The aggregation of double weighting features is defined as:

$$\mathbf{f}_{de}^{(l)} = \mathbf{f}_{r}^{(l)} + \mathbf{f}_{dw}^{(l)} + \mathbf{f}_{rw}^{(l)}. \tag{7}$$

Combining Eqs. 4, 6 and 7, we find that Eq. 7 is similar to Eq. 1. Thus, for the CMW-L and CMW-M, the output features $\mathbf{f}_{cmw}^{(k)}$ can be computed as:

$$\mathbf{f}_{cmw}^{(k)} = Cat(\mathbf{f}_{de}^{(2k-1)}, De(\mathbf{f}_{de}^{(2k)}; \mathbf{W}_{cmw}^{(2k)})), \qquad k = 1, 2. \tag{8}$$

Then, $\mathbf{f}_{cmw}^{(2)}$ and $\mathbf{f}_{cmw}^{(1)}$ boost the salient object inference in $\mathrm{D}^{(3\&4)}$ and $\mathrm{D}^{(1\&2)}$, respectively, through skip-connections (i.e., the dashed line in Fig. 1). More detailed parameters of CMW-L and CMW-M are shown in Fig. 2.

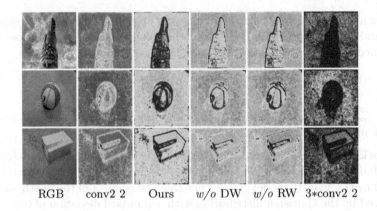

RGB   conv2 2   Ours   *w/o* DW   *w/o* RW   3*conv2 2

Fig. 3. Visualizing features of RGB conv2_2 in CMW-L. *w/o* DW: without adding DW features; *w/o* RW: without adding RW features; 3*conv2_2: features with triple linear enhancement.

In Fig. 3, we visualize features of RGB conv2_2 in **CMW-L** to verify the effectiveness of the double weighting enhancement. By comparing "conv2_2" and "Ours", salient objects are highlighted more clearly in "Ours". If we delete $\mathbf{f}_{dw}^{(l)}$ (*w/o* DW) or $\mathbf{f}_{rw}^{(l)}$ (*w/o* RW), salient objects are more indistinct than "Ours". We also show the features with triple linear enhancement ("3*conv2_2") to demonstrate that the double weighting enhancement is more effective than the conventional linear enhancement.

3.3 High-Level Cross-Modal Weighting

As for the high-level part, we modify the cross-scale CMW-L to the same-scale manner to effectively utilize the macroscopic semantic information. We propose the CMW-H for object localization enhancement. For DW operation in CMW-H, the RGB features are enhanced by depth response maps of the same layer. So, the DW operation in Eq. 4 is modified as follows:

$$\mathbf{f}_{dw}^{(l)} = \sigma(C(\mathbf{f}_{lg}^{(l)}; \mathbf{W}_{dw}^{(l)})) \otimes \mathbf{f}_r^{(l)}, \qquad l = 5. \tag{9}$$

Other operations, such as the RW and features aggregation, are the same as those in CMW-L. Notably, the output of CMW-H is $\mathbf{f}_{de}^{(5)}$, which is directly fed to the decoder part. It leads the inference process of SOD, as shown in Fig. 1. The detailed structure of CMW-H is present in Fig. 2.

3.4 Implementation Details

Loss Function. As shown in Fig. 1, we add a convolutional layer after R-E$^{(5)}$, D$^{(5)}$ and D$^{(3\&4)}$ to generate intermediate predictions $S^{(4)}$, $S^{(3)}$ and $S^{(2)}$ at the

training phase. Then, we utilize different scales of ground truth (GT) to supervise them and the final prediction $S^{(1)}$ with the softmax loss. The total loss $\mathbb{L}$ can be defined as:

$$\mathbb{L} = \sum_{t=1}^{4} \alpha_t \cdot \mathcal{L}_{sm}^{(t)}(S^{(t)}, G^{(t)}), \tag{10}$$

where $\mathcal{L}_{sm}^{(t)}(\cdot, \cdot)$ is the softmax loss, α_t is the loss weight and set to 1, and $G^{(t)}$ is a GT of the same resolution as $S^{(t)}$.

Network Training Protocol. Our CMWNet is implemented in Caffe [22] with an NVIDIA Titan X GPU. The parameters of the Siamese encoder part are initialized by the VGG16 model [34], except that the conv1_1 of the depth stream is initialized by the Gaussian distribution with a standard deviation of 0.01. Other newly added layers are initialized using the Xavier initialization [17]. Following [13,20], the training set consists of 1,400 triplets from NJU2K [23] and 650 triplets from NLPR [29]. We resize all training triplets to 288×288, and then we adopt the rotation (90°, 180° and 270°) and mirror reflection for augmentation, resulting 10.25K training triplets. We employ the SGD [3] to train the network 22.5K iterations. The learning rate, batch size, iteration size, momentum and weight decay are set to 10^{-7}, 1, 8, 0.9 and 0.0001, respectively. The learning rate will be divided by 10 12.5K iterations.

4   Experiments

4.1   Datasets and Evaluation Metrics

Datasets. We evaluate the proposed method and all compared methods on seven public benchmark datasets, including STEREO [28], NJU2K [23], LFSD [25], DES [7], NLPR [29], SSD [24] and SIP [13].

Evaluation Metrics. We evaluate the performance of our method and other methods using six widely used evaluation metrics including maximum F-measure ($\mathcal{F}_\beta$, $\beta^2 = 0.3$), weighted F-measure ($\mathcal{F}_\beta^w$, $\beta^2 = 1$) [27], mean absolute error (MAE, $\mathcal{M}$), precision-recall (PR) curve, S-measure ($\mathcal{S}_\lambda$, $\lambda = 0.5$) [11], and maximum E-measure ($\mathcal{E}_\xi$) [12].

4.2   Comparison with State-of-the-Art Methods

Comparison Methods. We compare the proposed CMWNet with 6 state-of-the-art traditional methods, which are LBE [16], DCMC [9], SE [18], CDCP [45], MDSF [36] and DTM [8], and 9 state-of-the-art CNN-based methods, which are DF [31], CTMF [20], PCF [4], AFNet [38], MMCI [6], TANet [5], CPFP [42], DMRA [30] and D3Net [13]. The saliency maps of all compared methods are provided by authors or obtained by running their released codes. Notably, we retest DMRA [30] on STEREO dataset with 1,000 images, which results in different performances from the original DMRA paper.

Table 1. Quantitative results of 15 state-of-the-art methods on 7 datasets. ↑ and ↓ stand for larger and smaller is better, respectively. The best two results are in **bold** and *italics*. The *corner note* of each method is the publication year.

Models	STEREO [28]				NJU2K-T [23]				LFSD [25]				DES [7]				NLPR-T [29]				SSD [24]				SIP [13]			
	$S_\lambda\uparrow$	$F_\beta\uparrow$	$\mathcal{E}_\xi\uparrow$	$\mathcal{M}\downarrow$	$S_\lambda\uparrow$	$F_\beta\uparrow$	$\mathcal{E}_\xi\uparrow$	$\mathcal{M}\downarrow$	$S_\lambda\uparrow$	$F_\beta\uparrow$	$\mathcal{E}_\xi\uparrow$	$\mathcal{M}\downarrow$	$S_\lambda\uparrow$	$F_\beta\uparrow$	$\mathcal{E}_\xi\uparrow$	$\mathcal{M}\downarrow$	$S_\lambda\uparrow$	$F_\beta\uparrow$	$\mathcal{E}_\xi\uparrow$	$\mathcal{M}\downarrow$	$S_\lambda\uparrow$	$F_\beta\uparrow$	$\mathcal{E}_\xi\uparrow$	$\mathcal{M}\downarrow$	$S_\lambda\uparrow$	$F_\beta\uparrow$	$\mathcal{E}_\xi\uparrow$	$\mathcal{M}\downarrow$
LBE[16] [16]	.660	.633	.787	.250	.695	.748	.803	.153	.736	.726	.804	.208	.703	.788	.890	.208	.762	.745	.855	.081	.621	.619	.736	.278	.727	.751	.853	.200
DCMC[16] [9]	.731	.740	.819	.148	.686	.715	.799	.172	.753	.817	.856	.155	.707	.666	.773	.111	.724	.648	.793	.117	.704	.711	.786	.169	.683	.518	.743	.186
SE[16] [18]	.708	.755	.846	.143	.664	.748	.813	.169	.698	.791	.840	.167	.741	.741	.856	.090	.756	.713	.847	.091	.675	.710	.800	.165	.628	.661	.771	.164
CDCP[17] [45]	.713	.664	.786	.149	.669	.621	.741	.180	.717	.703	.786	.167	.709	.631	.811	.115	.727	.645	.820	.112	.603	.535	.700	.214	.595	.505	.721	.224
MDSF[17] [36]	.728	.719	.809	.176	.748	.775	.838	.157	.700	.783	.826	.190	.741	.746	.851	.122	.805	.793	.885	.095	.673	.703	.779	.192	.717	.698	.798	.167
DTM[19] [8]	.747	.743	.837	.168	.706	.716	.799	.190	.783	.825	.853	.160	.752	.697	.858	.123	.733	.677	.833	.145	.677	.651	.773	.199	.690	.659	.778	.203
DF[17] [31]	.757	.757	.847	.141	.763	.804	.864	.141	.791	.817	.865	.138	.752	.766	.870	.093	.802	.778	.880	.085	.747	.735	.828	.142	.653	.657	.759	.185
CTMF[18] [20]	.848	.831	.912	.086	.849	.845	.913	.085	.796	.791	.865	.119	.863	.844	.932	.055	.860	.825	.929	.056	.776	.729	.865	.099	.716	.694	.829	.139
PCF[18] [4]	.875	.860	.925	.064	.877	.872	.924	.059	.794	.779	.835	.112	.842	.804	.893	.049	.874	.841	.925	.044	.841	.807	.894	.062	.842	.838	.901	.071
AFNet[19] [38]	.825	.823	.887	.075	.772	.775	.853	.100	.738	.744	.815	.133	.770	.728	.881	.068	.799	.771	.879	.058	.714	.687	.807	.118	.720	.712	.819	.118
MMCI[19] [6]	.873	.863	.927	.068	.858	.852	.915	.079	.787	.771	.839	.132	.848	.822	.928	.065	.856	.815	.913	.059	.813	.781	.882	.082	.833	.818	.897	.086
TANet[19] [5]	.871	.861	.923	.060	.878	.874	.925	.060	.801	.796	.847	.111	.858	.827	.910	.046	.886	.863	.941	.041	.839	.810	.897	.063	.835	.830	.895	.075
CPFP[19] [42]	.879	.874	.925	*.051*	.878	.877	.923	.053	.828	.826	.872	.088	.872	.846	.923	.038	.888	.867	.932	.036	.807	.766	.852	.082	.850	.851	*.903*	.064
DMRA[19] [30]	.835	.847	.911	.066	.886	.886	.927	*.051*	*.847*	*.856*	*.900*	.075	.900	.888	.943	.030	.899	.879	*.947*	*.031*	.857	.844	.906	.058	.806	.821	.875	.085
D3Net[19] [13]	*.891*	*.881*	*.930*	.054	*.895*	*.889*	*.932*	*.051*	.832	.819	.864	.099	*.904*	*.885*	*.946*	.030	*.906*	*.885*	.946	.034	*.866*	*.847*	*.910*	.058	**.864**	*.862*	*.903*	*.063*
Ours	**.905**	**.901**	**.944**	**.043**	**.903**	**.902**	**.936**	**.046**	**.876**	**.883**	**.912**	.066	**.934**	**.930**	**.969**	**.022**	**.917**	**.903**	**.951**	**.029**	**.875**	**.871**	**.930**	.051	*.867*	**.874**	**.913**	.062

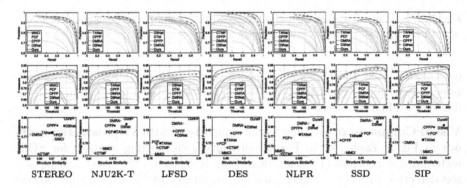

STEREO	NJU2K-T	LFSD	DES	NLPR	SSD	SIP

Fig. 4. Quantitative comparisons on PR curve, F-measure curve and S_λ-$\mathcal{F}_\beta^w$ coordinates. The top 5 methods on PR and F-measure curves are shown in color. For S_λ-$\mathcal{F}_\beta^w$ coordinates, we only compare with several representative methods. (Color figure online)

Quantitative Comparison. We evaluate our method and the other 15 state-of-the-art methods under four quantitative metrics, including S-measure S_λ, max F-measure $\mathcal{F}_\beta$, max E-measure $\mathcal{E}_\xi$ and MAE $\mathcal{M}$. As shown in Table 1, our method favorably outperforms all compared methods under these four metrics, and the recently proposed CNN-based methods [5,13,30,42] and our method are superior to traditional methods by a large margin. Comparing to the second best results in Table 1, the performance of our method on the largest and challenging dataset STEREO [28] is improved by 1.6% and 2.0% in S_λ and $\mathcal{F}_\beta$, respectively. The improvement on the relatively small dataset DES [7] is remarkable, with an increase of 3.0% and 4.2% in S_λ and $\mathcal{F}_\beta$, respectively. For the salient person detection, our method improves the performance by 1.2% in $\mathcal{F}_\beta$ on SIP [13].

In addition, we also present the PR curves, F-measure curves and S_λ (X-axis) - $\mathcal{F}_\beta^w$ (Y-axis) coordinates in Fig. 4. The performance under these metrics is consistent with that in Table 1. The superiority of our method is more visible

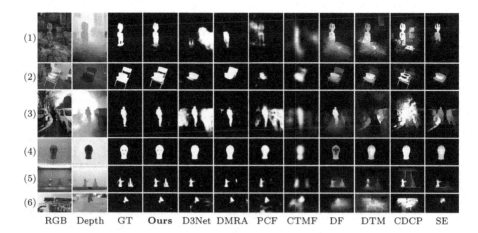

RGB   Depth   GT   **Ours**   D3Net   DMRA   PCF   CTMF   DF   DTM   CDCP   SE

Fig. 5. Visual comparisons with eight representative methods, including five CNN-based methods and three traditional methods.

on STEREO [28], LFSD [25] and DES [7]. Both Table 1 and Fig. 4 demonstrate that our method is consistently better than all compared methods in terms of different evaluation metrics.

Visual Comparison. We show visual comparisons with 8 representative methods in Fig. 5. Each row in Fig. 5 represents a challenging scenario for SOD, including low contrast (1st row), disturbing background (2nd row), salient person detection (3rd row), object with fine structures (4th row), multiple objects (5th row) and small object (6th row). Regardless of different scene, our method can accurately highlight salient objects with fine details. Notably, in the 4th row, the mask has a fine structure with three holes on it. Thanks to the DW and RW operations in our method, our method successfully highlights the mask with three holes, while other methods fail.

4.3   Ablation Studies

We conduct detailed ablation studies of our CMWNet on a big dataset, NJU2K [23], and a small but challenging dataset, SSD [24]. Specifically, we assess (1) the rationality of enhancing RGB features with depth features; (2) the individual contributions of CMW-L&M and CMW-H; (3) the importance of weighting; (4) the rationality of cross-scale weighting of CMW-L&M; and (5) the necessity of deep scale supervision of decoder part. We change one component at a time to evaluate individual contributions.

Rationality of Enhancing RGB Features with Depth Features. In our method, we use depth features to enhance RGB features ("DeR"). To study the rationality of this enhancement manner, we explore another baseline variant: adopting RGB features to enhance depth features ("ReD"). From Table 2, we

Table 2. Ablation studies on *NJU2K* [23] and *SSD* [24]. The best result of each column is **bold**. Details are introduced in Sect. 4.3.

Models	NJU2K-T [23]				SSD [24]			
	$S_\lambda \uparrow$	$\mathcal{F}_\beta \uparrow$	$\mathcal{E}_\xi \uparrow$	$\mathcal{M} \downarrow$	$S_\lambda \uparrow$	$\mathcal{F}_\beta \uparrow$	$\mathcal{E}_\xi \uparrow$	$\mathcal{M} \downarrow$
Ours (DeR)	**.903**	**.902**	**.936**	**.046**	**.875**	**.871**	**.930**	**.051**
ReD	.889	.887	.927	.056	.864	.850	.909	.063
w/o depth (*w/o* DW)	.886	.886	.924	.056	.855	.842	.915	.064
w/o CMW-L&M	.891	.886	.932	.053	.849	.839	.909	.066
w/o CMW-H	.896	.894	.929	.051	.853	.845	.908	.063
w/o RW	.901	.899	.933	.046	.868	.861	.919	.056
w/o Wei	.900	.898	.933	.048	.858	.839	.899	.061
DW *w/o* GF	.900	.898	.933	.048	.868	.858	.923	.054
RW *w/* GF	.901	.900	.934	.046	.870	.867	.924	.052
w/o CS	.901	.898	.932	.047	.864	.861	.922	.060
C2S	.900	.899	.933	.049	.864	.847	.906	.060
w/o DS	.898	.898	.933	.049	.866	.862	.923	.055

observe that the performance on both datasets has dropped (*e.g.* $\mathcal{M}$: 0.046 → 0.056 on NJU2K and 0.051 → 0.063 on SSD). This confirms that using depth features to enhance RGB features is more reasonable than the other direction for extracting the cross-modal complementarity.

In addition, we remove the depth map input in our network to evaluate the power of depth map (*w/o* depth). This variant is for RGB SOD. The performance of *w/o* depth drops sharply (*e.g.* $\mathcal{M}$: 0.046 → 0.056 on NJU2K). This confirms that the way of exploring complementary distance information of depth map in our network is effective.

Individual Contributions of CMW-L&M and CMW-H. The proposed three RGB-depth interaction modules can be divided into two types. CMW-L and CMW-M (CMW-L&M) are responsible for object details enhancement, and CMW-H for object localization enhancement. Thus, we provide two variants of our network: removing the CMW-L&M (*w/o* CMW-L&M) and removing the CMW-H (*w/o* CMW-H). From Table 2, we observe a significant performance degradation (*e.g.* S_λ: 0.903 → 0.891 on NJU2K and 0.875 → 0.849 on SSD) of *w/o* CMW-L&M. This confirms that the proposed CMW-L&M are momentous to our network, and they enhance the details of salient object in low- and middle-level features clearly. Some enhanced features in **CMW-L** are shown in the third column of Fig. 3. The performance drop (*e.g.* $\mathcal{F}_\beta$: 0.902 → 0.894 on NJU2K and 0.871 → 0.845 on SSD) of *w/o* CMW-H means that the proposed CMW-H is also important to our network and it enhances the salient object localization in high-level features accurately.

Importance of Weighting. To study the importance of two types of weighting, we derive three variants: removing the Depth-to-RGB weighting (w/o DW), removing the RGB-to-RGB weighting (w/o RW), and using concatenation of depth features and RGB features instead of two types of weighting (w/o Wei). Specifically, w/o DW is the same as w/o depth, *i.e.*, the depth map does not participate in SOD. The depth map is still utilized in w/o Wei, which is not equal to w/o (DW + RW). It focuses on evaluating the impact of weighting mechanism. According to the statistics in Table 2, we observe the performance of these three variants is worse than our complete CMWNet. This demonstrates that the two types of weighting can help our CMWNet to better highlight salient objects with effective feature enhancement. We also provide two variants, *i.e.* DW w/o GF and RW $w/$ GF, to confirm the rationality of specific global filters (GF) in DW.

In addition, the visualization of features w/o DW and w/o RW is shown in Fig. 3, in which the boundaries of salient objects w/o RW are much clearer than w/o DW. This demonstrates that the depth map does assist the RGB-D SOD, and the enhancement effect of DW is more effective than RW.

Rationality of Cross-Scale Weighting in CMW-L&M. To study the rationality of cross-scale weighting in CMW-L&M, we modify the cross-scale DW to the same-scale manner (w/o CS), which is the same as CMW-H. The double enhanced features of each scale in CMW-L&M are concatenated for inference. By comparing w/o CS and Ours in Table 2, we find that the performance of w/o CS decreases on both NJU2K and SSD. This demonstrates that the DW of CMW-L&M in the cross-scale manner is rational, and this manner can enhance interactions between different scales to further boost performance.

Besides, to study the rationality of performing cross-scale weighting between adjacent CNN blocks, we provide a variant which performs cross-scale weighting between nonadjacent CNN blocks, *i.e.*, R-E$^{(1)}$ is enhanced by D-E$^{(3)}$, R-E$^{(2)}$ is enhanced by D-E$^{(4)}$, R-E$^{(3)}$ is enhanced by D-E$^{(1)}$ and R-E$^{(4)}$ is enhanced by D-E$^{(2)}$ (C2S). As the results presented in Table 2, we observe that the results of C2S are worse than Ours. The reason behind this is that the weighting performed across two scales (*i.e.* C2S) may lose the continuity of features, causing the depth response maps to fail to highlight the salient objects of RGB features. In contrast, the weighting performed between two adjacent CNN blocks (*i.e.* Ours) can capture the continuity of features and precisely increase cross-scale interactions.

Necessity of Deep Scale Supervision in Decoder. To study the necessity of deep scale supervision, we provide a baseline with only one supervision of the final prediction $S^{(1)}$ (w/o DS). As shown in Table 2, we observe that network training with additional supervision is better than the single supervision. This verifies that the multiple scale supervision during network training can improve the testing performance. Besides, the intermediate predictions $S^{(4)}$, $S^{(3)}$ and $S^{(2)}$ are also shown in Fig. 1. We can observe that the refinement process of prediction from coarse ($S^{(4)}$) to fine ($S^{(1)}$) benefits from the deep scale supervision in decoder part, which visually confirms the necessity of deep scale supervision.

5 Conclusion

In this paper, we propose a novel Cross-Modal Weighting Network (CMWNet) for RGB-D SOD. In particular, three novel cross-modal cross-scale weighting modules (CWM-L, CMW-M and CMW-H) are designed to encourage feature interactions for improving SOD performance. Based on these improvements, a three-level decoder progressively refines salient objects. Extensive experiments are conducted to validate our CMWNet, which achieves the best performance on seven public RGB-D SOD benchmarks in comparison with 15 state-of-the-arts.

Acknowledgments. This work was supported by the National Natural Science Foundation of China under Grant 61771301. Linwei Ye and Yang Wang were supported by NSERC.

References

1. Borji, A., Cheng, M.-M., Hou, Q., Jiang, H., Li, J.: Salient object detection: a survey. Comput. Vis. Media **5**(2), 117–150 (2019)
2. Borji, A., Cheng, M.M., Jiang, H., Li, J.: Salient object detection: a benchmark. IEEE TIP **24**(12), 5706–5722 (2015)
3. Bottou, L.: Large-scale machine learning with stochastic gradient descent. In: COMPSTAT (2010)
4. Chen, H., Li, Y.: Progressively complementarity-aware fusion network for RGB-D salient object detection. In: IEEE CVPR (2018)
5. Chen, H., Li, Y.: Three-stream attention-aware network for RGB-D salient object detection. IEEE TIP **28**(6), 2825–2835 (2019)
6. Chen, H., Li, Y., Su, D.: Multi-modal fusion network with multi-scale multi-path and cross-modal interactions for RGB-D salient object detection. Pattern Recogn. **86**, 376–385 (2019)
7. Cheng, Y., Fu, H., Wei, X., Xiao, J., Cao, X.: Depth enhanced saliency detection method. In: ACM ICIMCS (2014)
8. Cong, R., Lei, J., Fu, H., Hou, J., Huang, Q., Kwong, S.: Going from RGB to RGBD saliency: a depth-guided transformation model. IEEE TCYB **50**, 3627–3639 (2019). https://doi.org/10.1109/TCYB.2019.2932005
9. Cong, R., Lei, J., Zhang, C., Huang, Q., Cao, X., Hou, C.: Saliency detection for stereoscopic images based on depth confidence analysis and multiple cues fusion. IEEE SPL **23**(6), 819–823 (2016)
10. Ding, Y., Liu, Z., Huang, M., Shi, R., Wang, X.: Depth-aware saliency detection using convolutional neural networks. J. Vis. Commun. Image Represent. **61**, 1–9 (2019)
11. Fan, D.P., Cheng, M.M., Liu, Y., Li, T., Borji, A.: Structure-measure: a new way to evaluate foreground maps. In: IEEE ICCV (2017)
12. Fan, D.P., Gong, C., Cao, Y., Ren, B., Cheng, M.M., Borji, A.: Enhanced-alignment measure for binary foreground map evaluation. In: IJCAI (2018)
13. Fan, D.P., et al.: Rethinking RGB-D salient object detection: models, datasets, and large-scale benchmarks. arXiv preprint arXiv:1907.06781 (2019)
14. Fan, X., Liu, Z., Sun, G.: Salient region detection for stereoscopic images. In: IEEE DSP (2014)

15. Fang, Y., Wang, J., Narwaria, M., Callet, P.L., Lin, W.: Saliency detection for stereoscopic images. IEEE TIP **23**(6), 2625–2636 (2014)
16. Feng, D., Barnes, N., You, S., McCarthy, C.: Local background enclosure for RGB-D salient object detection. In: IEEE CVPR (2016)
17. Glorot, X., Bengio, Y.: Understanding the difficulty of training deep feedforward neural networks. In: AISTATS (2010)
18. Guo, J., Ren, T., Bei, J.: Salient object detection for RGB-D image via saliency evolution. In: IEEE ICME (2016)
19. Guo, J., Ren, T., Jia, B., Zhu, Y.: Salient object detection in RGB-D image based on saliency fusion and propagation. In: ACM ICIMCS (2015)
20. Han, J., Chen, H., Liu, N., Yan, C., Li, X.: CNNs-based RGB-D saliency detection via cross-view transfer and multiview fusion. IEEE TCYB **48**(11), 3171–3183 (2018)
21. Itti, L., Koch, C., Niebur, E.: A model of saliency-based visual attention for rapid scene analysis. IEEE TPAMI **20**(11), 1254–1259 (1998)
22. Jia, Y., et al.: Caffe: convolutional architecture for fast feature embedding. In: ACM MM (2014)
23. Ju, R., Ge, L., Geng, W., Ren, T., Wu, G.: Depth saliency based on anisotropic center-surround difference. In: IEEE ICIP (2014)
24. Li, G., Zhu, C.: A three-pathway psychobiological framework of salient object detection using stereoscopic technology. In: IEEE ICCVW (2017)
25. Li, N., Ye, J., Ji, Y., Ling, H., Yu, J.: Saliency detection on light field. In: IEEE CVPR (2014)
26. Liu, Z., Shi, S., Duan, Q., Zhang, W., Zhao, P.: Salient object detection for RGB-D image by single stream recurrent convolution neural network. Neurocomputing **363**, 46–57 (2019)
27. Margolin, R., Zelnik-Manor, L., Tal, A.: How to evaluate foreground maps. In: IEEE CVPR (2014)
28. Niu, Y., Geng, Y., Li, X., Liu, F.: Leveraging stereopsis for saliency analysis. In: IEEE CVPR (2012)
29. Peng, H., Li, B., Xiong, W., Hu, W., Ji, R.: RGBD salient object detection: a benchmark and algorithms. In: Fleet, D., Pajdla, T., Schiele, B., Tuytelaars, T. (eds.) ECCV 2014. LNCS, vol. 8691, pp. 92–109. Springer, Cham (2014). https://doi.org/10.1007/978-3-319-10578-9_7
30. Piao, Y., Ji, W., Li, J., Zhang, M., Lu, H.: Depth-induced multi-scale recurrent attention network for saliency detection. In: IEEE ICCV (2019)
31. Qu, L., He, S., Zhang, J., Tian, J., Tang, Y., Yang, Q.: RGBD salient object detection via deep fusion. IEEE TIP **26**(5), 2274–2285 (2017)
32. Ren, J., Gong, X., Yu, L., Zhou, W., Yang, M.Y.: Exploiting global priors for RGB-D saliency detection. In: IEEE CVPRW (2015)
33. Shigematsu, R., Feng, D., You, S., Barnes, N.: Learning RGB-D salient object detection using background enclosure, depth contrast, and top-down features. In: IEEE ICCVW (2017)
34. Simonyan, K., Zisserman, A.: Very deep convolutional networks for large-scale image recognition. In: ICLR (2015)
35. Song, H., Liu, Z., Du, H., Sun, G., Bai, C.: Saliency detection for RGBD images. In: ACM ICIMCS (2015)
36. Song, H., Liu, Z., Du, H., Sun, G., Olivier, L.M., Ren, T.: Depth-aware salient object detection and segmentation via multiscale discriminative saliency fusion and bootstrap learning. IEEE TIP **26**(9), 4204–4216 (2017)

37. Wang, A., Wang, M.: RGB-D salient object detection via minimum barrier distance transform and saliency fusion. IEEE SPL **24**(5), 663–667 (2017)
38. Wang, N., Gong, X.: Adaptive fusion for RGB-D salient object detection. IEEE Access **7**, 55277–55284 (2019)
39. Wang, W., Lai, Q., Fu, H., Shen, J., Ling, H.: Salient object detection in the deep learning era: an in-depth survey. arXiv preprint arXiv:1904.09146 (2019)
40. Xie, S., Tu, Z.: Holistically-nested edge detection. In: IEEE ICCV (2015)
41. Yu, F., Koltun, V.: Multi-scale context aggregation by dilated convolutions. In: ICLR (2016)
42. Zhao, J.X., Cao, Y., Fan, D.P., Cheng, M.M., Li, X.Y., Zhang, L.: Contrast prior and fluid pyramid integration for RGBD salient object detection. In: IEEE CVPR (2019)
43. Zhou, Z., Wang, Z., Lu, H., Wang, S., Sun, M.: Global and local sensitivity guided key salient object re-augmentation for video saliency detection. arXiv preprint arXiv:1811.07480 (2018)
44. Zhu, C., Cai, X., Huang, K., Li, T.H., Li, G.: PDNet: prior-model guided depth-enhanced network for salient object detection. In: IEEE ICME (2019)
45. Zhu, C., Li, G., Wang, W., Wang, R.: An innovative salient object detection using center-dark channel prior. In: IEEE ICCVW (2017)

Open-Set Adversarial Defense

Rui Shao[1][(✉)] , Pramuditha Perera[2] , Pong C. Yuen[1] ,
and Vishal M. Patel[3]

[1] Department of Computer Science, Hong Kong Baptist University,
Kowloon Toon, Hong Kong
{ruishao,pcyuen}@comp.hkbu.edu.hk
[2] AWS AI Labs, New York, USA
pramudi@amazon.com
[3] Department of Electrical and Computer Engineering,
Johns Hopkins University, Baltimore, USA
vpatel36@jhu.edu

Abstract. Open-set recognition and adversarial defense study two key
aspects of deep learning that are vital for real-world deployment. The
objective of open-set recognition is to identify samples from open-set
classes during testing, while adversarial defense aims to defend the network against images with imperceptible adversarial perturbations. In
this paper, we show that open-set recognition systems are vulnerable
to adversarial attacks. Furthermore, we show that adversarial defense
mechanisms trained on known classes do not generalize well to open-set
samples. Motivated by this observation, we emphasize the need of an
Open-Set Adversarial Defense (OSAD) mechanism. This paper proposes
an Open-Set Defense Network (OSDN) as a solution to the OSAD problem. The proposed network uses an encoder with feature-denoising layers
coupled with a classifier to learn a noise-free latent feature representation. Two techniques are employed to obtain an informative latent feature space with the objective of improving open-set performance. First,
a decoder is used to ensure that clean images can be reconstructed from
the obtained latent features. Then, self-supervision is used to ensure that
the latent features are informative enough to carry out an auxiliary task.
We introduce a testing protocol to evaluate OSAD performance and show
the effectiveness of the proposed method in multiple object classification
datasets. The implementation code of the proposed method is available
at: https://github.com/rshaojimmy/ECCV2020-OSAD.

Keywords: Adversarial defense · Open-set recognition

P. Perera—This work was conducted prior to joining AWS AI Labs when the author
was affiliated with Johns Hopkins University.

Electronic supplementary material The online version of this chapter (https://
doi.org/10.1007/978-3-030-58520-4_40) contains supplementary material, which is
available to authorized users.

A. Vedaldi et al. (Eds.): ECCV 2020, LNCS 12362, pp. 682–698, 2020.
https://doi.org/10.1007/978-3-030-58520-4_40

1 Introduction

A significant improvement has been achieved in the image classification task since the advent of deep convolutional neural networks (CNNs) [14]. The promising performance in classification has contributed to many real-world computer vision applications [2,20,36–42,45–47]. However, there exist several limitations of conventional CNNs that have an impact in real-world applications. In particular, open-set recognition [3,10,25,30–33,48,50] and adversarial attacks [5,12,19,24,44] have received a lot of interest in the computer vision community in the last few years.

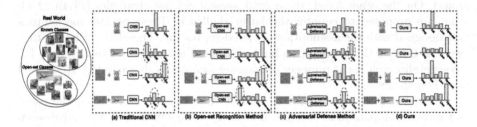

Fig. 1. Challenges in classification. (a) Conventional CNN classifiers fail in the presence of both open-set and adversarial images. (b) Open-set recognition methods can successfully identify open-set samples, but fail on adversarial samples. (c) Adversarial defense methods are unable to identify open-set samples. (d) Proposed method can identify open-set images and it is robust to adversarial images.

Table 1. Importance of an Open-set Adversarial Defense (OSAD) mechanism.

	Clean Images	Adversarial Images	
	Original Network	Original Network	Proposed Method
Closed Set Accuracy	96.0	31.8	88.2
Open-set Detection (AUC-ROC)	81.2	51.5	79.1

A classifier is conventionally trained assuming that classes encountered during testing will be identical to classes observed during training. But in a real-world scenario, a trained classifier is likely to encounter open-set samples from classes unseen during training. When this is the case, the classifier will erroneously associate a known-set class identity to an open-set sample. Consider a CNN trained on animals classes. Given an input that is from an animal class (such as a cat), the network is able to produce the correct prediction as shown in Fig. 1(a-First Row). However, when the network is presented with a non-animal image, such as an Airplane image, the classifier wrongly classifies it as one of the known classes as shown in Fig. 1(a-Second Row). On the other hand, it is a well known fact that adding carefully designed imperceptible perturbations to clean

images can alter model prediction in a classifier [12]. These types of *adversarial attacks* are easy to deploy and may be encountered in real-world applications [9]. In Fig. 1(a-Third Row) and Fig. 1(a-Fourth Row), we show how such adversarial attacks can affect model prediction for known and open-set images, respectively.

Computer vision community has developed several open-set recognition algorithms [3,10,25,30,48] to combat against the former challenge. These algorithms convert the c-class classification problem into a $c+1$ class problem by considering open-set classes as an additional class. These algorithms provide correct classification decisions for both known and open-set classes as shown in Fig. 1(b-First and Second rows). However, in the presence of adversarial attacks, these models fail to produce correct predictions as illustrated in Fig. 1(b-Third and Fourth rows). On the other hand, there exist several defense strategies [17,19,22,44] that are proposed to counter the latter challenge. These defense mechanisms are designed with the assumption of closed-set testing. Therefore, although they work well when this assumption holds (Fig. 1(c-First and third rows)), they fail to generalize well in the presence of open-set samples as shown in Fig. 1(c-Second and Fourth rows).

Based on this discussion, it is evident that existing solutions in the open-set recognition paradigm does not necessarily complement well with adversarial defense and vise versa. This observation motivates us to introduce a new research problem – Open-Set Adversarial Defense (OSAD), where the objective is to simultaneously detect open-set samples and classify known classes in the presence of adversarial noise. In order to demonstrate the significance of the proposed problem, we conducted an experiment on the CIFAR10 dataset by considering only 6 classes to be known to the classifier. In Table 1 we tabulate both open-set detection performance (expressed in terms of area under the curve of the ROC curve) and closed-set classification accuracy for this experiment. When the network is presented with clean images, it produces a performance better than 0.8 in both open-set detection and closed set classification. However, as evident from Table 1, when images are attacked, open-set detection performance drops along with the closed set accuracy by a significant margin. It should be noted that, open-set detection performance in this case is close to random guessing (0.5).

This paper proposes an Open-Set Defense Network (OSDN) that learns a noise-free, informative latent feature space with the aim of detecting open-set samples while being robust to adversarial images. We use an autoencoder network with a classifier branch attached to its latent space as the backbone of our solution. The encoder network is equipped with feature-denoising layers [44] with the aim of removing adversarial noise. We use self-supervision and decoder reconstruction processes to make sure that the learned feature space is informative enough to detect open-set samples. The reconstruction process uses the decoder to generate noise-free images based on the obtained latent features. Self-supervision is carried out by forcing the network to perform an auxiliary classification task based on the obtained features. The proposed method is able to provide robustness against adversarial attacks in terms of classification as well

as open-set detection as shown in Table 1. Main contributions of our paper can be summarized as follows:

1. This paper proposes a new research problem named Open-Set Adversarial Defense (OSAD) where adversarial attacks are studied under an open-set setting.
2. We propose an Open-Set Defense Network (OSDN) that learns a latent feature space that is robust to adversarial attacks and informative to identify open-set samples.
3. A test protocol is defined to the OSAD problem. Extensive experiments are conducted on three publicly available image classification datasets to demonstrate the effectiveness of the proposed method.

2 Related Work

Adversarial Attack and Defense Methods. Szegedy *et al.* [43] reported that carefully crafted imperceptible perturbations can be used to fool a CNN to make incorrect predictions. Since then, various adversarial attacks have been proposed in the literature. Fast Gradient Sign Method (FGSM) [12] was proposed to consider the sign of a gradient update from the classifier to generate adversarial images. Basic Iteration Method (BIM) [19] and Projected Gradient Descent (PGD) [24] extended FGSM to stronger attacks using iterative gradient descent. Different from the above gradient-based adversarial attacks, Carlini and Wagner [5] proposed the C &W attack to generate adversarial samples by taking a direct optimization approach. Adversarial training [24] is one of the most widely-used adversarial defense mechanisms. It provides defense against adversarial attacks by training the network on adversarially perturbed images generated on-the-fly based on model's current parameters. Several recent works have proposed denoising-based operations to further improve adversarial training. Pixel denoising [22] was proposed to exploit the high-level features to guide the denoising process. The most influential local parts to conduct the pixel-level denoising is found in [13] based on class activation map responses. Adversarial noise removal is carried out in the feature-level using denoising filters in [44]. Effectiveness of this process is demonstrated using a selection of different filters.

Open-Set Recognition. Possibility for open-set samples to generate very high probability scores in a closed-set classifier was first brought to attention in [35]. It was later shown that deep learning models are also affected by the same phenomena [3]. Authors in [3] proposed a statistical solution, called OpenMax, for this problem. They converted the c-class classification problem into a $c + 1$ problem by considering the extra class to be the open-set class. They apportioned logits of known classes to the open-set class considering spatial positioning of a query sample in an intermediate feature space. This formulation was later adopted by [10] and [25] by using a generative model to produce logits of the open-set class. Authors in [48] argued that a generative feature contain information that

can benefit open-set recognition. On these grounds they considered a concatenation of a generative feature and a classifier feature when building the OpenMax layer. A generative approach was used in [30] where a class conditioned decoder was used to detect open-set samples. Works of both [30] and [48] show that incorporating generative features can benefit open-set recognition. Note that open-set recognition is more challenging than the novelty detection [27–29,31,34] which only aims to determine whether an observed image during inference belongs to one of the known classes.

Self-supervision. Self-supervision is an unsupervised machine learning technique where the data itself is used to provide supervision. Recent works in self-supervision introduced several techniques to improve the performance in classification and detection tasks. For example, in [7], given an anchor image patch, self-supervision was carried out by asking the network to predict the relative position of a second image patch. In [8], a multi-task prediction framework extended this formulation, forcing the network to predict a combination of relative order and pixel color. In [11], the image was randomly rotated by a factor of 90° and the network was forced to predict the angle of the transformed image.

3   Background

Adversarial Attacks. Consider a trained network parameterized by parameters θ. Given a data and label pair $(\mathbf{x}, \mathbf{y})$, an adversarial image $\mathbf{x}_{adv}$, can be produced using $\mathbf{x}_{adv} = \mathbf{x} + \delta$, where δ can be determined by a given white-box attack based on the models parameters. In this paper, we consider two types of adversarial attacks.

The first attack considered is the Fast Gradient Signed Method (FGSM) [12] where the adversarial images are formed as follows,

$$\mathbf{x}_{adv} = \text{Proj}_\chi(\mathbf{x} + \epsilon sign(\bigtriangledown_\mathbf{x} \mathcal{L}(\mathbf{x}, \mathbf{y}; \theta))), \tag{1}$$

where $\mathcal{L}(\cdot)$ is a classification loss. Proj_χ denotes the projection of its element to a valid pixel value range, and ϵ denotes the size of l_∞-ball. The second attack considered is Projective Gradient Descent (PGD) attacks [24]. Adversarial images are generated in this method as follows,

$$\mathbf{x}_{adv}^{(t+1)} = \text{Proj}_{\zeta \cap \chi}(\mathbf{x}_{adv}^{(t)} + \epsilon_{step} sign(\bigtriangledown_\mathbf{x} \mathcal{L}(\mathbf{x}_{adv}^{(t)}, \mathbf{y}; \theta))), \tag{2}$$

where $\text{Proj}_{\zeta \cap \chi}(\cdot)$ denotes the projection of its element to l_∞-ball ζ and a valid pixel value range, and ϵ_{step} denotes a step size smaller than ϵ. We use the adversarial samples of the final step T: $\mathbf{x}_{adv} = \mathbf{x}_{adv}^{(T)}$.

OpenMax Classifier. A SoftMax classifier trained for a c-class problem typically has c probability predictions. OpenMax is an extension where the probability scores of $c + 1$ classes are produced. The probability of the final class corresponds to the open-set class. Given c known classes $\mathcal{K} = \{C_1, C_2, ..., C_c\}$,

OpenMax is designed to identify open-set samples by calibrating the final hidden layer of a classifier as follows:

$$\hat{l}_i = \begin{cases} l_i \boldsymbol{w}_i & (i \leq c) \\ \sum_{i=1}^{c} l_i(1 - \boldsymbol{w}_i) & (i = c + 1) \end{cases}, \text{OpenMax}_i(\mathbf{x}) = \text{SoftMax}_i(\hat{l}) \quad (3)$$

where l denotes the logit vector obtained prior to the SoftMax operation in a classifier, $\boldsymbol{w}_i$ represents the belief that $\mathbf{x}_{adv}$ belongs to the known class C_i. Here, the class C_{N+1} corresponds to the open-set class. Belief $\boldsymbol{w}_i$ is calculated considering the distance of a given sample to it's class mean μ in an intermediate feature space. During training, distance of all training image samples from a given class to its corresponding class mean μ is evaluated to form a matched score distribution. Then, a Weibull distribution is fitted to the tail of the matched distribution. If the feature representation of the input in the same feature space is $v(\boldsymbol{x})$, $\boldsymbol{w}_i$ is calculated as

$$\boldsymbol{w}_i = 1 - \max \left(0, \frac{\sigma - \text{rank}(i)}{\sigma}\right) e^{\left(-\left(\frac{|v(\boldsymbol{x}) - \mu_i|_2}{\eta_i}\right)^{m_i}\right)}, \quad (4)$$

where m_i, η_i are parameters of the Weibull distribution that corresponding to class C_i. σ is hyperparameter and rank(i) is the index in the logits sorted in the descending order.

4 Proposed Method

The proposed network consists of four CNNs: encoder, decoder, open-set classifier and transformation classifier. In Fig. 2, we illustrate the network structure of the proposed method and denote computation flow. The encoder network consists of several feature-denoising layers [44] between the convolutional layers. Open-set classifier has no structural difference from a regular classifier. However, an OpenMax layer is added to the end of the classifier during inference. We denote this by indicating an OpenMax layer in Fig. 2.

Given an input image, first the network generates an adversarial image based on the current network parameters. This image is passed through the encoder network to obtain the latent feature. This feature is passed through the open-set classifier via path (1) to evaluate the cross entropy loss $\mathcal{L}_{cls}$. Then, the image corresponding to the obtained latent feature is generated by passing the feature through the decoder following path (2). The decoded image is used to calculate its difference to the corresponding clean image based on the reconstruction loss $\mathcal{L}_{rec}$. Finally, the input image is subjected to a geometric transform. An adversarial image corresponding to the transformed image is obtained. This image is passed through path (3) to arrive at the transformation classifier. Output of the classifier is used to calculate the cross entropy loss $\mathcal{L}_{ssd}$ considering the transform applied to the image. The network is trained end-to-end using the following loss function

$$\mathcal{L}_{OSDN} = \mathcal{L}_{cls} + \mathcal{L}_{rec} + \mathcal{L}_{ssd}. \quad (5)$$

In the following subsections, we describe various components and computation involved in all three paths in detail.

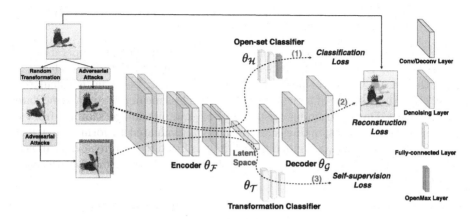

Fig. 2. Network structure of the proposed Open-Set Defense Network (OSDN). It consists of four components: encoder, decoder, open-set classifier and transformation classifier.

Noise-Free Feature Encoding. The proposed network uses an encoder network to produce noise-free features. Then, the open-set classifier operating on the learned feature is used to perform classification. During training, there is no structural difference in the open-set classifier from a standard classifier. Inspired by [44], we embed denoising layers after the convolutional layer blocks in the encoder so that feature denoising can be explicitly carried out on adversarial samples. We adopt the Gaussian (softmax) based non-local means filter [4] as the denoising layer. Given an input feature map m, non-local means [4] takes a weighted mean of features in the spatial region $\mathcal{R}$ to compute a denoised feature map g as follows

$$g_i = \frac{1}{\mathcal{N}(m)} \sum_{\forall j \sim \mathcal{R}} f(m_i, m_j) \cdot m_j, \tag{6}$$

where $f(m_i, m_j)$ is a feature-dependent weighting function. For the Gaussian (softmax) based version, $f(m_i, m_j) = e^{\alpha(m_i)^T \beta(m_j)/\sqrt{d}}$. α and β are two 1×1 convolutional layers as embedding functions and d corresponds to the number of channels. $\mathcal{N}(m)$ is a normalization function and $\mathcal{N}(m) = \sum_{\forall j \sim \mathcal{R}} f(m_i, m_j)$.

Formally, we denote the encoder embedded with denoising layers as $\mathcal{F}$ parameterized by $\theta_{\mathcal{F}}$, and the classifier as $\mathcal{H}$ parameterized by $\theta_{\mathcal{H}}$. Given the labeled clean data $(\mathbf{x}, \mathbf{y}) \sim \mathcal{I}$ from the data distribution of known classes, we can generate the corresponding adversarial images $\mathbf{x}_{adv}$ on-the-fly using either FGSM or PGD attacks based on the current parameters $\theta_{\mathcal{F}}$, $\theta_{\mathcal{H}}$ using the true label $\mathbf{y}$. Obtained adversarial image $\mathbf{x}_{adv}$ is passed through encoder and classifier (via

path (1)) to arrive at the cross-entropy loss defined as

$$\mathcal{L}_{cls} = \min_{\theta_{\mathcal{F}}, \theta_{\mathcal{H}}} \mathbb{E}_{(\mathbf{x}_{adv}, \mathbf{y}) \sim \mathcal{I}} \mathcal{L}_{CE}(\mathbf{x}_{adv}, \mathbf{y}; \theta_{\mathcal{F}}, \theta_{\mathcal{H}}). \tag{7}$$

By minimizing the above adversarial training loss, the trained encoder embedded with the denoising layers is able to learn a noise-free latent feature space. During inference, an OpenMax layer is added on top of the classifier. With this formulation, open-set classifier operating on the noise-free latent feature learns to predict the correct class, for both known and open-set samples, even when the input is contaminated with adversarial noise.

Clean Image Generation. In this section, we introduce the image generation branch proposed in our method. The objective of the image generation branch is to generate noise-free images from adversarial images by taking advantage of the decoder network. This is motivated by two factors.

First, autoencoders are widely used in the literature for image denoising applications. By forcing the autoencoder network to produce noise-free images, we are providing additional supervision to remove noise in the latent feature space. Secondly, it is a well known fact that open-set recognition becomes more effective in the presence of more descriptive features [48]. When a classifier is trained, it models the boundary of each class. Therefore, a feature produced by a classification network only contains information that is necessary to model class boundaries. However, when the network is asked to generate noise-free images based on the latent representations, it ends up with learning generative features. As a result, features become more descriptive than in the case of a pure classifier. In fact, such generative features are used in [48] and [30] to boost the open-set recognition performance. Therefore, we argue that adding the decoder as an image generation branch can mutually benefit both open-set recognition and adversarial defense.

We pass adversarial images through path (2) as illustrated in Fig. 2 to generate the decoded images. The decoder network denoted as $\mathcal{G}$ parameterized by $\theta_{\mathcal{G}}$ and the encoder network $\mathcal{F}$ are jointly optimized to minimize the distance between the decoded images and the corresponding clean images using the following loss

$$\mathcal{L}_{rec} = \min_{\theta_{\mathcal{F}}, \theta_{\mathcal{G}}} \mathbb{E}_{(\mathbf{x}, \mathbf{x}_{adv}) \sim \mathcal{I}} \|\mathbf{x} - \mathcal{G}(\mathcal{F}(\mathbf{x}_{adv}))\|_2^2. \tag{8}$$

Self-supervised Denoising. Finally, we propose to use self-supervision as a means to further increase the informativeness and robustness of the latent feature space. Self-supervision is a machine learning technique that is used to learn representations in the absence of labeled data. In our work we adopt rotation-based self-supervision proposed in [11]. In [11], first, a random rotation from a finite set of possible rotations is applied to an image. Then, a classifier is trained on top of a latent feature vector to automatically recognize the applied rotation.

In our approach, similar to [11], we first generate a random number $r \in \{0, 1, 2, 3\}$ as the rotation ground-truth and transform the input clean image $\mathbf{x}$ by rotating it with $90°r$ degrees. Then, based on the rotated clean image,

we generate a rotated adversarial image $\mathbf{x}_{adv}^{T}$ on-the-fly using either FGSM or PGD attack based on the current network parameters and rotation ground-truth r, which is passed through the transformation classifier to generate the cross-entropy loss with respect to the ground-truth r. We denote the transformation classifier as $\mathcal{T}$ parameterized by $\theta_{\mathcal{T}}$ and formulate the adversarial training loss function for self-supervised denoising as follows

$$\mathcal{L}_{ssd} = \min_{\theta_{\mathcal{F}}, \theta_{\mathcal{T}}} \mathbb{E}_{\mathbf{x}_{adv}^{T} \sim \mathcal{I}} \mathcal{L}_{CE}(\mathbf{x}_{adv}^{T}, r; \theta_{\mathcal{F}}, \theta_{\mathcal{T}}). \qquad (9)$$

There are multiple reasons why we use self-supervision in our method. When a classifier learns to differentiate between different rotations, it learns to pay attention to object structures and orientations of known classes. As a result, when self-supervision is carried out in addition to classification, the underlying feature space learns to represent additional information that was not considered in the case of a pure classifier. Therefore, self-supervision enhances the informativeness of the latent feature space which would directly benefit the open-set recognition process. On the other hand, since we use adversarial images for self-supervision, this operation directly contributes towards learning the denoising operator in the encoder. It should also be noted that recent work [16] has found that self-supervised learning contributes towards robustness against adversarial samples. Therefore, we believe that addition of self-supervision benefits both open-set detection and adversarial defense processes.

Implementation Details. We adopt the structure of Resnet-18 [14], which has four main blocks, for the encoder network. Denoising layers are embedded after each main blocks in the encoder. For the decoder, we use the decoder network proposed in [25] with three transpose-convolution layers for conducting experiments with the SVHN and CIFAR10 dataset. Four transpose-convolution layers are used for conducting experiments with the TinyImageNet dataset. For both open-set classifier and transformation classifier, we use a single fully connected layers. We use the Adam optimizer [18] for the optimization with a learning rate of 1e−3. We carried out model selection considering the trained model that has produced the best closed-set accuracy on the validation set. We use the iteration = 5 for the PGD attacks and $\epsilon = 0.3$ for the FGSM attacks in both adversarial training and testing.

5   Experimental Results

In order to assess the effectiveness of the proposed method, we carry out experiments on three multiple-class classification datasets. In this section, we first describe datasets, baseline methods and the protocol used in our experiments. We evaluate our method and baselines in the task of open-set recognition under adversarial attacks. To further validate the effectiveness of our method, additional experiments in the task of out-of-distribution detection under adversarial attacks are conducted. We conclude the section by presenting an ablation study and various visualizations with a brief analysis of the results.

5.1 Datasets

The evaluation of our method and other state-of-the-arts are conducted on three standard images classification datasets for open-set recognition:

SVHN and CIFAR10. Both CIFAR10 [1] and SVHN [26] are classification datasets with 10 classes with images of size 32×32. Street-View House Number dataset (SVHN) contains house number signs extracted from Google Street View. CIFAR10 contains images from four vehicle classes and six animal classes. We randomly split 10 classes into 6 known classes and 4 open-set classes to simulate open-set recognition scenario. We consider three randomly selected splits for testing[1].

TinyImageNet. TinyImageNet contains a sub-set of 200 classes selected from the ImageNet dataset [6] with image size of 64×64. 20 classes are randomly selected to be known and the remaining 180 classes are chosen to be open-set classes. We consider three randomly chosen splits for evaluation.

5.2 Baseline Methods

We consider the following two recently proposed adversarial defense methods as baselines: **Adversarial Training** [24] and **Feature Denoising** [44]. We add an OpenMax layer in the last hidden layer during testing for both baselines to facilitate a fair comparison in open-set recognition. Moreover, to evaluate the performance of a classifier without a defense mechanism, we train a Resnet-18 network on clean images obtained from known classes and add an OpenMax layer during testing. We test this network using clean images for inference and we denote this test case by **clean**. Furthermore, we test this model with adversarial images, which is denoted as **adv on clean**.

5.3 Quantitative Results

Open-set Recognition. In conventional open-set recognition, the model is required to perform two tasks. First, it should be able to detect open-set samples effectively. Secondly, it should be able to perform correct classification on closed set samples. In order to evaluate the open-set defense performance, we take these two factors into account. In particular, following previous open-set works [25], we use area under the ROC curve (AUC-ROC) to evaluate the performance on identifying open-set samples under adversarial attacks. In order to evaluate the closed-set accuracy, we calculate prediction accuracy by only considering known-set samples in the test set. In our experiments, both known and open-set samples were subjected to adversarial attacks prior to testing. During our experiments we consider FGSM and PGD attacks to attack the model. We generated adversarial samples from known classes using the ground-truth labels, while we generated the adversarial samples from open-set classes based on model's prediction.

---

[1] Details about known classes present in each split can be found in supplementary materials.

Table 2. Adversarial Defense: Closed-set accuracy.

Method	SVHN		CIFAR-10		TinyImageNet	
	FGSM	PGD	FGSM	PGD	FGSM	PGD
Clean	96.0 ± 0.6	96.0 ± 0.6	93.1 ± 1.8	93.1 ± 1.8	56.8 ± 3.6	56.8 ± 3.6
Adv on clean	41.6 ± 3.2	39.3 ± 1.8	31.8 ± 4.5	13.0 ± 4.0	11.2 ± 2.6	4.4 ± 0.8
Adversarial training	88.5 ± 2.7	75.8 ± 2.5	87.3 ± 1.1	72.4 ± 4.6	66.6 ± 1.2	40.3 ± 2.3
Feature denoising	86.9 ± 3.7	75.5 ± 2.6	87.4 ± 2.3	72.5 ± 4.5	64.5 ± 1.3	39.3 ± 3.0
Ours	$\mathbf{89.3 \pm 0.7}$	$\mathbf{77.9 \pm 1.6}$	$\mathbf{88.2 \pm 2.9}$	$\mathbf{74.2 \pm 4.3}$	$\mathbf{75.1 \pm 7.9}$	41.6 ± 2.2

We tabulate the obtained performance for closed-set accuracy and open-set detection in Tables 2 and 3, respectively. We note that, networks trained on clean images produce very high recognition performance for clean images under both scenarios. However, when the adversarial noise is present, both open-set detection and closed-set classification performance drops significantly. This validates that current adversarial attacks can easily fool an open-set recognition method such as OpenMax, and thus OSAD is a critical research problem. Both baseline defense mechanisms considered are able to improve the recognition on both known and open-set samples. It can be observed from Tables 2 and 3, that the proposed method obtains the best open-set detection performance and closed-set accuracy compared to all considered baselines across all three datasets. In particular, the proposed method has achieved about 7% improvement in open-set detection on the SVHN dataset compared to the other baselines. On other datasets, this improvement varies between 1–5%. The proposed method is also able to perform better in terms of closed-set accuracy compared to the baselines consistently across datasets.

It is interesting to note that methods involving adversarial training perform better than the baseline of clean image classification under FGSM attacks on the TinyImageNet dataset. This is because only 20 classes from the TinyImageNet dataset are selected for training and each class has only 500 images. When a small dataset is used to train a model with large number of parameters, it is easier for the network to overfit to the training set. Such network observes variety of data in the presence of adversarial training. Therefore model reaches a more generalizable optimization solution during training.

Table 3. Open Set Classification: Area under the ROC curve.

Method	**SVHN**		**CIFAR-10**		**TinyImageNet**	
	FGSM	PGD	FGSM	PGD	FGSM	PGD
Clean	91.3 ± 2.4	91.3 ± 2.4	81.2 ± 2.9	81.2 ± 2.9	59.5 ± 0.8	59.5 ± 0.8
Adv on clean	56.4 ± 1.2	54.1 ± 2.9	51.5 ± 2.8	45.5 ± 0.5	47.9 ± 2.7	48.6 ± 1.3
Adversarial training	61.4 ± 8.0	65.2 ± 4.0	75.2 ± 1.2	68.7 ± 3.2	65.1 ± 8.1	56.5 ± 0.9
Feature denoising	64.5 ± 14.7	64.9 ± 4.2	76.9 ± 3.7	69.8 ± 2.4	65.3 ± 5.1	56.1 ± 1.6
Ours	$\mathbf{71.4 \pm 4.2}$	$\mathbf{71.6 \pm 2.6}$	$\mathbf{79.1 \pm 1.0}$	$\mathbf{70.6 \pm 1.7}$	$\mathbf{70.8 \pm 5.1}$	$\mathbf{58.2 \pm 1.9}$

Out-of-Distribution Detection. In this sub-section, we evaluate the performance of the proposed method on the out-of-distribution detection (OOD) [15] problem on CIFAR10 using the protocol described in [48]. We considered all classes in CIFAR10 as known-classes and consider test images from ImageNet and LSUN dataset [49] (both cropped and resized) as out-of-distribution images [21]. We tested the performance of adversarial images by creating adversarial images using the PGD attacks for both known and OOD data. We generated adversarial samples from the known classes using the ground-truth labels, while we generated adversarial samples from the OOD class based on model's prediction. We evaluated the performance of the model on adversarial samples based on macro-averaged F1 score. We used OpenMax layer with threshold 0.95 when assigning open-set labels to the query images, In Table 4, we tabulate the OOD detection performance across all four cases considered for both baselines as well as the proposed method. As evident from Table 4, the proposed method outperforms baseline methods in all test cases in the ODD task. This experiment further verifies the effectiveness of our method to identify samples from open-set classes even under the adversarial attacks.

Table 4. Performance of out-of-distribution object detection on the CIFAR10 dataset.

Detector	ImageNet-Crop	ImageNet-Resize	LSUN-Crop	LSUN-Resize
Clean	78.9	76.2	82.1	78.7
Adv on clean	4.7	4.4	7.3	3.8
Adversarial training	35.2	34.5	35.0	34.7
Feature denoising	43.2	41.0	43.5	41.2
Ours	**46.5**	**44.8**	**47.1**	**44.2**

5.4 Ablation Study

The proposed network consists of four CNN components. In this sub-section we investigate the impact of each network component to the overall performance of the system. To validate the effectiveness of various parts integrated in our proposed network, this section conducts the ablation study in our network using the CIFAR10 dataset for the task of open-set recognition. Considered cases and the corresponding results obtained for each case are tabulated Table 5 (C-accuracy means closed-set accuracy). From Table 5, it can be seen that compared to normal adversarial training with an encoder, embedding the denoising layers helps to improve the open-set classification performance. Moreover, as evident from Table 5, adding a denoising layer to perform feature denoising and adding self-supervision both have resulted in improved performance. The proposed method that integrates all these components has the best performance, which shows that added components complement each other to produce better performance for both adversarial defense and open-set recognition.

Table 5. Results corresponding to the ablation study.

Method	CIFAR-10	
	AUC-ROC	C-accuracy
clean	83.7	92.7
adv on clean	45.9	8.6
Encoder	66.1	69.9
Encoder+Denoising Layer	68.5	70.4
Encoder+Decoder	67.3	68.8
Encoder+Decoder+Denoising Layer	68.2	70.6
Encoder+Decoder+self-supervised Denoising	68.5	71.9
ours	**69.6**	**72.8**

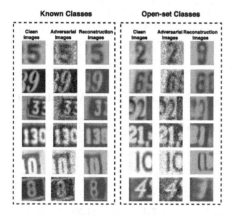

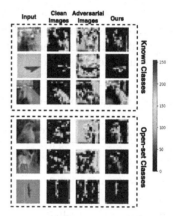

Fig. 3. Visualization of input clean images, corresponding adversarial images, and the reconstructed images from the decoder.

Fig. 4. Feature map visualization in the res$_2$ block of Resnet-18 and the encoder of proposed network.

5.5 Qualitative Results

In this section, we visualize the results of the denoising operation and obtained features in a 2D plane to qualitatively analyze the performance of the proposed method. For this purpose, we first consider the SVHN dataset. Figure 3 shows a set of clean images, corresponding PGD attacks adversarial images and images obtained when the latent feature is decoded under the proposed method. We have indicated known and open-set sample visualizations in two columns. From the image samples shown in Fig. 3, it can be observed that image noise has been removed in both open-set and known-class images. However, the reconstruction quality is superior for the known-class samples compared to the open-set images. Reconstructions of open-set samples look blurry and structurally different. For example, the image of digit 2 shown in the first row, looks similar to the digit 9 once reconstructed.

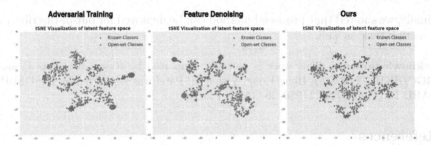

Fig. 5. tSNE visualization of the latent feature space corresponding to our method and two baselines.

In Fig. 5 we visualize latent features obtained in the proposed method along with two other baselines using tSNE visualization [23]. As shown in Fig. 5, most of open-set features lie away from the known-set feature distribution based on our method. This is why the proposed method is able to obtain good open-set detection performance. On the other hand, it can be observed from Fig. 5 that there is more overlap between the two types of features in all baseline methods. When open-set features lie away from the data manifold of known set classes, the reconstruction obtained through the decoder network tends to be poor. Therefore, the tSNE plot justifies why the reconstruction of our method was poor for open-set samples in Fig. 3. As such, Fig. 3 and Fig. 5 mutually verify the effectiveness of our method for defending adversarial samples and identifying open-set samples simultaneously.

Moreover, we visualize randomly selected feature maps of the second residual block from the trained Resnet-18 [14] and the encoder of the proposed OSDN network applied on clean images and on its adversarially perturbed counterpart in the CIFAR10 dataset. From Fig. 4, it can be observed that compared to Resnet-18, the proposed network is able to reduce adversarial noise significantly in feature maps of adversarial images in both known and open-set classes. This further demonstrates that the proposed network indeed carries out the feature denoising through the embedded feature denoising layers.

6   Conclusion

In this paper, we studied a novel research problem – Open-set Adversarial Defense (OSAD). We first showed that existing adversarial defense mechanisms do not generalize well to open-set samples. Furthermore, we showed that even open-set classifiers can be easily attacked using the existing attack mechanisms. We proposed an Open-Set Defense Network (OSDN) with the objective of producing a model that can detect open-set samples while being robust against adversarial attacks. The proposed network consisted of feature denoising operation, self-supervision operation and a denoised image generation function. We demonstrated the effectiveness of the proposed method under both open-set and adversarial attack settings on three publicly available classification datasets.

Finally, we showed that proposed method can be deployed for out-of-distribution detection task as well.

Acknowledgments. This work is partially supported by Research Grants Council (RGC/HKBU12200518), Hong Kong. Vishal M. Patel was supported by the DARPA GARD Program HR001119S0026-GARD-FP-052.

References

1. Alex Krizhevsky, V.N., Hinton, G.: CIFAR-10 (Canadian Institute For Advanced Research)
2. Baweja, Y., Oza, P., Perera, P., Patel, V.M.: Anomaly detection-based unknown face presentation attack detection. In: IJCB (2020)
3. Bendale, A., Boult, T.E.: Towards open set deep networks. In: CVPR (2016)
4. Buades, A., Coll, B., Morel, J.M.: A non-local algorithm for image denoising. In: CVPR (2005)
5. Carlini, N., Wagner, D.: Towards evaluating the robustness of neural networks. In: SP (2017)
6. Deng, J., Dong, W., Socher, R., Li, L.J., Li, K., Fei-Fei, L.: ImageNet: a large-scale hierarchical image database. In: CVPR (2009)
7. Doersch, C., Gupta, A., Efros, A.A.: Unsupervised visual representation learning by context prediction. In: ICCV (2015)
8. Doersch, C., Zisserman, A.: Multi-task self-supervised visual learning. In: ICCV (2017)
9. Evtimov, I., et al.: Robust physical-world attacks on deep learning models. In: CVPR (2018)
10. Ge, Z., Demyanov, S., Chen, Z., Garnavi, R.: Generative openmax for multi-class open set classification. In: BMVC (2017)
11. Gidaris, S., Singh, P., Komodakis, N.: Unsupervised representation learning by predicting image rotations. In: ICLR (2018)
12. Goodfellow, I.J., Shlens, J., Szegedy, C.: Explaining and harnessing adversarial examples. In: ICLR (2014)
13. Gupta, P., Rahtu, E.: CIIDefence: defeating adversarial attacks by fusing class-specific image inpainting and image denoising. In: CVPR (2019)
14. He, K., Zhang, X., Ren, S., Sun, J.: Deep residual learning for image recognition. In: CVPR (2016)
15. Hendrycks, D., Gimpel, K.: A baseline for detecting misclassified and out-of-distribution examples in neural networks. In: ICLR (2017)
16. Hendrycks, D., Mazeika, M., Kadavath, S., Song, D.: Using self-supervised learning can improve model robustness and uncertainty. In: NIPS (2019)
17. Jang, Y., Zhao, T., Hong, S., Lee, H.: Adversarial defense via learning to generate diverse attacks. In: ICCV (2019)
18. Kingma, D.P., Ba, J.: Adam: a method for stochastic optimization. arXiv preprint arXiv:1412.6980 (2014)
19. Kurakin, A., Goodfellow, I., Bengio, S.: Adversarial machine learning at scale. In: ICLR (2017)
20. Lan, X., Ye, M., Shao, R., Zhong, B., Yuen, P.C., Zhou, H.: Learning modality-consistency feature templates: a robust RGB-infrared tracking system. IEEE Trans. Ind. Electron. **66**(12), 9887–9897 (2019)

21. Liang, S., Li, Y., Srikant, R.: Enhancing the reliability of out-of-distribution image detection in neural networks. In: ICLR (2018)
22. Liao, F., Liang, M., Dong, Y., Pang, T., Hu, X., Zhu, J.: Defense against adversarial attacks using high-level representation guided denoiser. In: CVPR (2018)
23. Maaten, L.V.D., Hinton, G.: Visualizing data using t-SNE. J. Mach. Learn. Res. **9**(Nov), 2579–2605 (2008)
24. Madry, A., Makelov, A., Schmidt, L., Tsipras, D., Vladu, A.: Towards deep learning models resistant to adversarial attacks. In: ICLR (2018)
25. Neal, L., Olson, M., Fern, X., Wong, W.K., Li, F.: Open set learning with counterfactual images. In: ECCV (2018)
26. Netzer, Y., Wang, T., Coates, A., Bissacco, A., Wu, B., Ng, A.Y.: Reading digits in natural images with unsupervised feature learning (2011)
27. Oza, P., Nguyen, H.V., Patel, V.M.: Multiple class novelty detection under data distribution shift. In: ECCV (2020)
28. Oza, P., Patel, V.M.: Utilizing patch-level activity patterns for multiple class novelty detection. In: ECCV (2020)
29. Oza, P., Patel, V.M.: One-class convolutional neural network. IEEE Signal Process. Lett. **26**(2), 277–281 (2018)
30. Oza, P., Patel, V.M.: C2AE: Class conditioned auto-encoder for open-set recognition. In: CVPR (2019)
31. Perera, P., Patel, V.M.: Deep transfer learning for multiple class novelty detection. In: CVPR (2019)
32. Perera, P., et al.: Generative-discriminative feature representations for open-set recognition. In: CVPR (2020)
33. Perera, P., Nallapati, R., Xiang, B.: OCGAN: One-class novelty detection using GANs with constrained latent representations. In: CVPR (2019)
34. Perera, P., Patel, V.M.: Learning deep features for one-class classification. IEEE Trans. Image Process. **28**(11), 5450–5463 (2019)
35. Scheirer, W.J., Rocha, A., Sapkota, A., Boult, T.E.: Towards open set recognition. IEEE Trans. Pattern Anal. Mach. Intell. (T-PAMI) **35**, 1757–1772 (2013)
36. Shao, R., Lan, X.: Adversarial auto-encoder for unsupervised deep domain adaptation. In: IET Image Processing (2019)
37. Shao, R., Lan, X., Li, J., Yuen, P.C.: Multi-adversarial discriminative deep domain generalization for face presentation attack detection. In: CVPR (2019)
38. Shao, R., Lan, X., Yuen, P.C.: Deep convolutional dynamic texture learning with adaptive channel-discriminability for 3D mask face anti-spoofing. In: IJCB (2017)
39. Shao, R., Lan, X., Yuen, P.C.: Feature constrained by pixel: hierarchical adversarial deep domain adaptation. In: ACM MM (2018)
40. Shao, R., Lan, X., Yuen, P.C.: Joint discriminative learning of deep dynamic textures for 3D mask face anti-spoofing. IEEE Trans. Inf. Forensics Secur. **14**(4), 923–938 (2019)
41. Shao, R., Lan, X., Yuen, P.C.: Regularized fine-grained meta face anti-spoofing. In: AAAI (2020)
42. Shao, R., Perera, P., Yuen, P.C., Patel, V.M.: Federated face anti-spoofing. arXiv preprint arXiv:2005.14638 (2020)
43. Szegedy, C., et al.: Intriguing properties of neural networks. In: ICLR (2014)
44. Xie, C., Wu, Y., Maaten, L.v.d., Yuille, A.L., He, K.: Feature denoising for improving adversarial robustness. In: CVPR (2019)
45. Ye, M., Shen, J., Lin, G., Xiang, T., Shao, L., Hoi, S.C.H.: Deep learning for person re-identification: a survey and outlook. arXiv preprint arXiv:2001.04193 (2020)

46. Ye, M., Shen, J., Zhang, X., Yuen, P.C., Chang, S.F.: Augmentation invariant and instance spreading feature for softmax embedding. IEEE Trans. Pattern Anal. Mach. Intell. (2020)
47. Ye, M., Zhang, X., Yuen, P.C., Chang, S.F.: Unsupervised embedding learning via invariant and spreading instance feature. In: CVPR (2019)
48. Yoshihashi, R., Shao, W., Kawakami, R., You, S., Iida, M., Naemura, T.: Classification-reconstruction learning for open-set recognition. In: CVPR (2019)
49. Yu, F., Seff, A., Zhang, Y., Song, S., Funkhouser, T., Xiao, J.: LSUN: construction of a large-scale image dataset using deep learning with humans in the loop. arXiv preprint arXiv:1506.03365 (2015)
50. Zhang, H., Patel, V.M.: Sparse representation-based open set recognition. IEEE Trans. Pattern Anal. Mach. Intell. **39**(8), 1690–1696 (2016)

Deep Image Compression Using Decoder Side Information

Sharon Ayzik$^{(\boxtimes)}$ and Shai Avidan$^{(\boxtimes)}$

Department of Electrical Engineering, Tel Aviv University, Tel Aviv-Yafo, Israel
ayziksha@mail.tau.ac.il, avidan@eng.tau.ac.il

Abstract. We present a Deep Image Compression neural network that relies on side information, which is only available to the decoder. We base our algorithm on the assumption that the image available to the encoder and the image available to the decoder are correlated, and we let the network learn these correlations in the training phase.

Then, at run time, the encoder side encodes the input image without knowing anything about the decoder side image and sends it to the decoder. The decoder then uses the encoded input image and the side information image to reconstruct the original image.

This problem is known as Distributed Source Coding (DSC) in Information Theory, and we discuss several use cases for this technology. We compare our algorithm to several image compression algorithms and show that adding decoder-only side information does indeed improve results. Our code is publicly available Our code is available at: https://github.com/ayziksha/DSIN.

Keywords: Deep Distributed Source Coding · Deep Neural Networks · Deep Learning · Image reconstruction

1 Introduction

Deep Image Compression uses Deep Neural Networks (DNN) for image compression. Instead of relying on handcrafted representations to capture natural image statistics, DNN methods learn this representation directly from the data. Recent results show that indeed they perform better than traditional methods.

Ultimately, there is a limit to the compression rate of all methods, that is governed by the rate-distortion curve. This curve determines, for any given rate, what is the minimal amount of distortion that we must pay. We can break this barrier by introducing side information that can assist the network in compressing the target image even further.

Figure 1 gives an example of results obtained by our system. The left image shows the results of a state-of-the-art deep image compression algorithm. The right image shows the results of our method that relies on side information. As can be seen, our method does a better job of restoring the details.

Electronic supplementary material The online version of this chapter (https://doi.org/10.1007/978-3-030-58520-4_41) contains supplementary material, which is available to authorized users.

Without SI 0.03199 bpp

With SI (ours) 0.03019 bpp

Fig. 1. Reconstruction from very low bits per pixel (bpp). Our method that use an additional Side Information (SI) image in the decoders' side can restore fine details as well as colors and textures that vanished as a result of the aggressive compression rate. Note the small red car, the crosswalk, the building to the back right side with the blue vehicle, and even the trees textures.(Color figure online)

One can catalogue image compression schemes into three classes (see Fig. 2). The first (top row) is a standard image compression scheme. Such a network makes no use of side information, and the trade-off is governed by the rate-distortion curve of the image.

Deep Video Compression (second row in Fig. 2) goes one step further and, in addition to natural image statistics, also relies on previous frames as side information that is available to both the encoder and the decoder. The availability of this side information improves the compression ratio of video compared to images. The limit of this scheme is bounded by the conditional probability of the current frame given previous frames. This works well when the two frames are correlated, as is often the case in video.

We consider a different scenario in which the side information is only available at the decoder side (third row of Fig. 2). This is different from deep video compression, where side information is available both to the decoder and the encoder. It turns out that even in this case, the compression scheme can benefit from side information. That is, DSC can, in theory, achieve the same compression ratios as deep video compression, even though the side information is *not* available to the encoder. But when does this scenario occur in practice?

It turns out that this DSC scenario occurs quite frequently, and here are a couple of examples. Consider the case of a camera array. For simplicity, we focus on a stereo camera, which is the simplest of camera arrays. The left and right cameras of the stereo pair are each equipped with a micro-controller that captures the image from the camera, compresses it, and sends it to the host computer. Since both cameras capture the same scene at the same time, their content is highly correlated with each other. But since the left and right cameras do not communicate, they only communicate with the host computer and can not use the fact that they capture highly correlated images to improve the compression ratio. This puts a heavy burden on the host computer, which must capture two images in the case of stereo camera and many more in the case of a camera array.

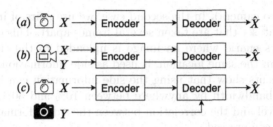

Fig. 2. Different compression schemes. (*a*) Single image encoding-decoding. (*b*) Video coding: joint encoding-decoding. The successive frame Y is used as side information. (*c*) Distributed source coding - image X is encoded and then decoded using correlated side information image Y.

Now suppose that the left camera transmitted its image to the host computer and the right camera as well. Then the right camera can encode its image conditioned on the left image and transmit fewer bits to the host computer. This reduces the burden on the host computer at the cost of sending the left image to the right camera. Distributed Source Coding theory tells us that we do not have to transmit the image from the left camera to the right camera at all, and still achieve the same compression ratio. When considering a camera array with multiple cameras, the savings can be substantial.

Camera arrays are assumed to be calibrated and synchronized, but we can take a much more general approach. For example, a group of people taking pictures of some event is a common occurrence nowadays. We can treat that as a distributed, uncalibrated, and unsynchronized camera array. Instead of each person uploading his images to the cloud, we can pick, at random, a reference person to upload his images to the cloud and let the rest of the people upload their images conditioned on the reference images.

Taking this idea one step further, we envision a scenario in which before uploading an image to the cloud, we will first transmit the camera's position and orientation (information that is already collected by smartphones). As a result, the cloud will be able to select existing images that are only stored in the cloud to use as side information.

Our approach is using recent advances in deep image compression, where we add side information to the decoder side. During training, we provide the network with pairs of real-world, correlated images. The network learns to compress the input image, and then add the side information image to help restore the original image. At inference time, the encoder is used for compressing the image before transmitting it. The rest of the network, which lies at the receiver side, is used by the decoder to decode the original image, using the compressed image and the side information image. To the best of our knowledge, this is the first time Deep Learning is used for DSC in the context of image compression.

We evaluate our system on two versions of the KITTI dataset that are designed to simulate some of the scenarios described earlier. In the first, we use the KITTI Stereo dataset to simulate the scenario of a camera array (in

this case, a stereo camera). In the second case, we use pairs of images from the KITTI Stereo dataset that are taken several frames apart. This case is designed to simulate the scenario where an image is uploaded to the cloud, and some other image, from the same location, is used as side information.

Our experiments show that using the side information can help reduce the communication bandwidth by anywhere between 10% and 50%, depending on the distortion level and the correlation between the side information image and the image to be compressed.

2   Related Work

Deep Compression: Using DNN in many applications has gained much popularity in recent years, the same goes for the task of image compression. Common usage of DNN for the task of compression are RNNs [28,29] and auto-encoders [4,19,36]. The networks are usually designed in an end-to-end manner, aiming to minimize the final loss on the decompressed image.

Toderici *et al.* [28,29] used progressive image compression techniques and tested various types of recurrent neural networks to create a hybrid network that extracts a binary representation code using an entropy coder. Ballé *et al.* [4] used quantization rather than binarization. Theis *et al.* [27] use a simple approximation to replace the rounding-based quantization, in addition to bounding the discrete entropy loss. And Mentzer *et al.* [19] use an auto-encoder and a context model that learns to asses the distribution of the bitstream in addition to an importance map to improve performance.

Recent work by Agustsson *et al.* [3] suggests using GAN based architecture to break the rate-distortion bounds. They encode the image with fewer bits than what is dictated by the rate-distortion curve. Then they use a GAN, on the decoder side, to synthesize a similar image that is visually pleasant.

Building on the success of Deep image compression schemes, we witnessed the emergence of Deep video compression schemes. Early work replaced various steps in the video compression scheme with a DNN counterpart. For example, Lu *et al.* [18] use a deep network to remove compression artifacts in the postprocessing step. Tsai *et al.* [30] use an auto-encoder to compress the residuals of an H.264 encoder. Wu *et al.* [34] treat video compression as a repeated image interpolation and build a full network for that. Recently, Lu *et al.* [18] proposed a network that replaces all the components of a video encoder with a single end-to-end architecture.

Distributed Source Coding: Distributed Source Coding (DSC) started with the groundbreaking result of Slepian-Wolf [10,25] who proved that it is possible to encode a source X given a correlated source Y even if Y is only available to the decoder side. This result applied to the lossless case and was later extended by Wyner-Ziv [35] to the lossy case by first quantizing the continuous signal and then applying the Slepian-Wolf theorem.

Although the theory of DSC dates back to the '70s, it was only 30 years later that its first practical implementation was presented. One of the most

important works was done by Pradhan and Ramchandran - Distributed Source Coding Using Syndromes (DISCUS) [23]. They presented a practical framework for the asymmetric case of source coding with side information at the decoder, based on sending the syndrome of the code-word coset for statistically dependent binary and Gaussian sources.

Much of the work on DSC was in the context of light-weight video compression. That is, instead of running a standard video compression scheme (i.e., MPEG) that requires motion estimation on the encoder side [17], DSC offers the possibility of shifting the computational load from the encoder to the decoder. This scheme is useful, for example, in the case of a smartphone that needs to send a video to the cloud. For example, Girod *et al.* [1,2,12] focused on Distributed Video Coding (DVC). The video sequence was split to odd and even frames, the odd frames were used as side information at the decoder while Wyner-Ziv coding was applied to the even frames.

In [8,31] the authors apply DSC to stereo images, in which one encoded image is decoded with reference to side information derived from disparity-compensated versions of the other image with the additional use of gray code.

3   Deep Distributed Source Coding for Images

Toy Example: To gain some intuition into the DSC problem, consider the following toy example. Suppose X and Y are two 8-bit gray-scale images that are known to be aligned such that pixel $X(i)$ corresponds to pixel $Y(i)$. Assume image X is available to the encoder on the smartphone, and image Y is available to the decoder in the cloud. Transmitting X to the cloud requires 8-bits per pixel. But what if the corresponding pixels, $X(i), Y(i)$ are correlated? For example, they satisfy the following correlation: $|X(i) - Y(i)| \leq 3$. How can we take advantage of this correlation? A moment of thought shows that given $Y(i)$, $X(i)$ can only take seven different values, so we should hope to encode $X(i)$ using only 3 bits and not 8.

How can we do this in practice? Here is a numerical example. Let $X(i) = 110$ and $Y(i) = 113$. Consider the following DSC scheme: the encoder computes $6 = \mod(X(i), 8)$ and sends the number 6 to the cloud using only 3 bits. The modulo operation created a *coset* $\{6, 14, 22, ..., 102, 110, 118, ..., 254\}$ of pixel values. Every element x of this coset satisfy the constraint that $\mod(x, 8) = 6$. And, by construction, the minimal distance between any pair of elements in the coset is at least 8. Given these facts, the decoder knows that the unknown $X(i)$ must be one of the elements in the coset. It also knows that $|X(i) - Y(i)| \leq 3$. Given that $Y(i) = 113$, the decoder can deduce that $X(i)$ must be 110. We have encoded X using only 3 bits per pixel, instead of 8. Observe that the encoder did not know the value of pixel $Y(i)$ that is only available to the decoder. The prior information on the correlation between the two images is sufficient.

DSC for Images: DSC was applied to video compression, where successive frames are almost aligned. This near alignment was enough to assume that patches in successive frames that are in the same location in the image plane

are correlated. Applying DSC to video compression did not get traction because the side information (i.e., previous frame in the case of video) is known to the encoder as well as the decoder.

Here, we consider the case where the two images are taken by two *different* cameras at slightly different time steps. We assume that one camera uploads its image to the cloud and then let the other camera upload its image conditioned on the other image *without* ever having access to that image. The shift in space and time is enough to render the alignment assumption useless. We can no longer assume that the two images are aligned, nor that the layout of the images is similar. For example, we would like two images containing a house next to a tree to be correlated even if the tree is to the right of the house in one image, and is to the left in the other.

One way to address this challenge is to break the two images into patches and use patches to measure the correlation between the images. But this raises a new problem- instead of having one (image) X and one (image) Y, we now have multiple (patches) X and multiple (patches) Y. Now, if we use the coset trick, then we don't know which patch in Y to use since the images are not aligned.

We have conflicting demands. On the one hand, we need to transmit sufficient information about a patch in X, to allow the decoder to pick the correlated patch in Y. On the other hand, we only wish to transmit a code for the coset and let the decoder use that, together with the corresponding patch in Y, to recover the correct patch in X. We solve the DSC problem for images using DNN.

3.1 Architecture

The overall architecture of the network is given in Fig. 3. The encoder has access to the input image X, and the decoder has access to a correlated image Y. Our architecture consists of two sub-networks, the first is an auto-encoder designed for image compression and based on the model of Mentzer *et al.* [19]. It takes the input image X and produces the decoded image X_{dec}. The second network takes the decoded image X_{dec} along with image Y and uses it to construct a synthetic side information image Y_{syn}. The decoded image X_{dec} and synthetic side information Y_{syn} are then concatenated and used to produce the final output image $\hat{X}$. The entire network, consisting of both sub-networks, is trained jointly. Then, at inference time, the encoder uses the encoder part of the auto-encoder sub-network, while the decoder uses the rest of the network.

It should be noted that the quantized latent vector $\bar{Z}$ of our auto-encoder network is not designed to reconstruct the original image X, nor is it designed to create a coset from which the decoder can recover the correct X. Its goal is to provide sufficient information to construct a good synthetic image Y that, together with the decoded image X_{dec}, can be used to recover the final result $\hat{X}$. This means it should reconstruct an image X_{dec} that has sufficient details to search for good patches in Y that are as correlated, as much as possible, with their corresponding patches in X.

Formally, image compression algorithms encode an input image X to some quantized latent representation $\bar{Z}$ from which they can decode a reconstructed

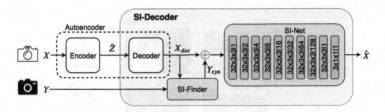

Fig. 3. Our network's architecture. The image X is encoded to $\bar{Z}$ and decoded to the image X_{dec} using the auto-encoder model based on [19]. X_{dec} is used to create Y_{syn} using the SI-Finder block that finds for each patch in X_{dec}, the closest patch in Y. X_{dec} and Y_{syn} are concatenated (marked as $\oplus$) and forwarded to the SI-Net block that outputs the final reconstruction - $\hat{X}$. The SI-Net block is based on [9] and uses convolution layers with increasing dilation rates that approximate enlarged convolutions receptive field. $C \times K \times K$ notation in the SI-Net block refers to $K \times K$ convolutions with C filters. The number following the pipe indicates the rate of kernel dilation.

image X_{dec}. The goal of the compression is to minimize a distortion function. The trade-off between compression rate and distortion is defined by:

$$d(X, \hat{X}) + \beta H(\bar{Z}) \qquad (1)$$

where $H(\bar{Z})$ is the entropy of $\bar{Z}$ (i.e., the bit cost of encoding $\bar{Z}$), $d(X, \hat{X})$ is the distortion function and β is a scalar that sets the trade-off between the two.

3.2 Using Side Information

We wish to minimize (1) given a correlated image Y that is only available to the decoder. To do that, we wish to create an image Y_{syn} from Y that is aligned with X. Let f encode the offset of every patch in X_{dec} to its corresponding patch in Y_{dec}, where Y_{dec} is the result of passing Y through the auto-encoder:

$$f(i) = \underset{j}{\operatorname{argmax}} \operatorname{corr}(\pi(X_{dec}(i)), \pi(Y_{dec}(j))) \qquad (2)$$

where $\operatorname{corr}(\cdot)$ is a correlation metric, $\pi(X_{dec}(i))$ is the patch around pixel $X_{dec}(i)$. Then the synthetic image Y_{syn} is given by:

$$Y_{syn}(i) = Y(f(i)) \qquad (3)$$

That is, Y_{syn} is a reconstruction of X from Y. We perform this reconstruction step in the SI-Finder block, which is illustrated in Fig. 4. It receives the images X_{dec} and Y. We then pass Y through the auto-encoder to produce Y_{dec} (this is only done at inference mode, so the encoder does not learn anything about Y). We do this since we found that matching Y_{dec} with X_{dec} works better than matching Y with X_{dec}. Then, the SI-Finder compares each non-overlapping patch in X_{dec} to all possible patches in Y_{dec}. This creates a (sparse) function

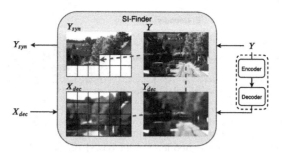

Fig. 4. SI-Finder block illustration. This block receives X_{dec} and Y images, projects Y to the same plane as X_{dec} by passing Y through the auto-encoder in inference mode to receive Y_{dec}. Each non-overlapping patch in image X_{dec} is compared to all possible patches in Y_{dec}. The location of the maximum correlation patch in Y_{dec} is chosen, and the corresponding patch is taken from Y image. Finally, the patch is placed in Y_{syn} in the corresponding X_{dec} patch location.

f that is used to create Y_{syn} from Y. It should be noted that the SI-Finder is implemented as part of the network graph using CNN layers but is non-trainable since the CNN kernels are the image X_{dec}.

Eventually we feed X_{dec} and Y_{syn} to the SI-Net block and let it try to reconstruct X. Since we use concatenation of X_{dec} to the side information image Y_{syn} during training, we must maintain a reconstruction loss over X_{dec}. Therefore, the total rate-distortion trade-off from (1) is set to be:

$$(1 - \alpha) \cdot d(X, X_{dec}) + \alpha d(X, \hat{X}) + \beta H(\bar{Z}) \qquad (4)$$

where α denotes the weight for the final system's output $\hat{X}$, and the total distortion weight sums to 1 in order to maintain the balance between the distortion and the rate.

4   Experiments

In the following section, we discuss the datasets we use and the training procedure in Sect. 4.1, and then present the results of our experiments in Sect. 4.2. A detailed example regarding our chosen prior, images from our constructed dataset, and additional visual results appear in the supplementary material.

4.1   Implementation Details

Datasets: We constructed our datasets from the KITTI 2012 [11] and KITTI 2015 [20,21] datasets to approximate the two settings discussed in Sect. refsec:intro.

The first termed *KITTI Stereo*, consists of 1578 stereo pairs taken from the calibrated stereo cameras in the KITTI stereo datasets (*i.e.* a pair of two images

each taken at the same time from a different camera). It is designed to illustrate the calibrated and synchronized camera array use case.

The second termed *KITTI General*, consists of 789 scenes with 21 stereo pairs per scene taken sequentially. We constructed the dataset from pairs of images where one image is taken from the left camera and the second image from the right camera, but now, the images are taken from different time steps, in our case, 1 to 3 time steps apart. In this dataset, the images are taken up to $\sim 9\,\text{m}$ apart. As a result, objects between the two images can change scale, position, or even not appear at all. This dataset is designed to simulate a much more general case where images are only loosely co-located in space or time.

Evaluation Criteria: Following [15,19,24,28] we evaluated our results by an averaged rate-distortion curve using MS-SSIM [33], which is reported to correlate better with human perception of distortion than mean squared error (MSE) and variants such as PSNR especially in cases where distortion is large [14,22].

Training: We implemented our model in *TensorFlow*. For each dataset and bit rate in the range of 0.02 to 0.2 bpp, we trained the baseline model (*i.e.*, auto-encoder only) according to the training details in [19], using L_1 reconstruction loss (we found that training using the MS-SSIM loss for the low bit rates, suffers from instabilities and failed to reach the desired bit rates. In contrast, the L_1 loss led to shorter training time and better stability of the algorithm). Then we trained the full model with image size of 320×960 for $300K$ iterations (which took 24 h per model on a single GPU), using the pre-trained auto-encoder weights as initialization and L_1 loss on both the auto-encoder and the final output - $\hat{X}$ with the trade-off weight $\alpha = 0.7$ from (4). We used Adam [16] optimizer with an initial learning rate of $1 \cdot 10^{-4}$ and a batch size of 1 (i.e., each iteration included a pair of images X, Y). When training the full model, the original image size was used to enable the SI-Finder module full freedom of choice for locating the best patch possible for any given patch of X_{dec}. As for the SI-Finder block, we used a patch size of 20×24, and the similarity measure between patches was chosen to be the Pearson correlation on color transformed images according to [7]. We tested our models on 790 images for *KITTI Stereo* and 556 for *KITTI General* with size of 320×1224.

4.2 Results

We compared our baseline model without side information (i.e., auto-encoder only) to the model trained with side information. In addition, we compare ourselves to JPEG 2000 [26] and to BPG [6] (HEVC based image codec that surpassed all other codecs in the past). For BPG, we used the non-default 4:4:4 chroma format following [24]. We also compared our results to JPEG [32] and WebP [13], but they failed to reach our low bit rates and therefore are not shown here. We focus on low bit rates because they demonstrate the power of DSC to leverage the side information.

Following [19], and to perform a fair comparison, for each image in the test set, we extracted the sets of matching bpps and MS-SSIM measurements. Since

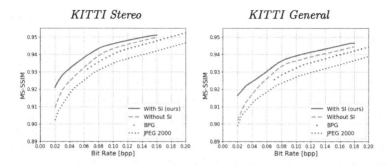

Fig. 5. Rate-Distortion curve - MS-SSIM as a function of bit rate on both datasets. We outperform the baseline model (without side information) as well as BPG and JPEG 2000. Note the substantial amount of bits that can be 'saved' by our method. For example, in *KITTI Stereo*, looking at the same value of 0.93 MS-SSIM, it can be seen that instead of sending 0.05 bpp (using the baseline model), one can send 0.03 bpp, meaning 40% reduction.

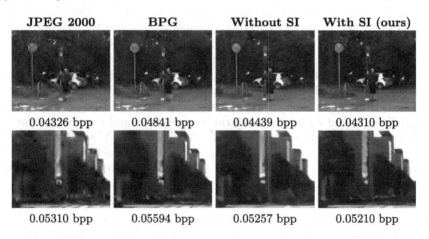

Fig. 6. Examples for images compressed using the different codecs. Top row: *KITTI Stereo*, bottom row: *KITTI General*.

each image has a different rate-distortion curve, we created for each image an interpolated curve and averaged the curves for all test images using a dense bpp grid. We did the same for the baseline model, BPG and JPEG 2000.

We report the results in Fig. 5. As can be seen, our method (using side information) outperformed all compared methods. The gains are quite substantial. For example, In the *KITTI Stereo* dataset at MS-SSIM score of 0.94, the bpp rate drops from about 0.08 bpp using no side information to about 0.065 bpp using side information, a drop of nearly 20%. The drop is even larger compared to other methods.

In addition, when comparing the two datasets, *KITTI Stereo* achieved greater improvement than *KITTI General* when using side information. This is aligned

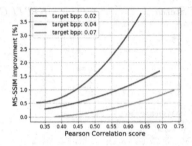

Fig. 7. Correlation vs. Side-Information contribution on the *KITTI General* dataset. x-axis is the Pearson score between X and Y_{syn}. y-axis is the improvement percentage of MS-SSIM between with and without side information models. Each curve represents a model trained to a different target bpp. As can be seen, higher correlation leads to better reconstruction results.

with the theory stating that the more correlated X and Y, a more significant improvement can be achieved.

In Fig. 6, we visually compare reconstructed images compressed using our approach to the model without side information as well as to JPEG 2000 and BPG. It can be seen that using side information improves the reconstruction - new details that were lost due to the compression are recovered as well as the color that was lost in the quantization process.

Correlation Test: The DSC theorem implies that as the correlation between X and Y increase, so does the contribution of Y in reconstructing X. We have seen this indirectly when analyzing the results of *KITTI Stereo* and *KITTI General*.

To measure this connection directly, we examined the relationship between the correlation of (X, Y_{syn}) and the improvement in MS-SSIM, between the model with and model without side-information. For each test image, we calculated the average Pearson correlation between non-overlapping patches of size (20×24) in X and their corresponding patches in Y_{syn}. We then computed the ratio of the MS-SSIM score of the reconstructed image $\hat{X}$ using the model with side-information to that without. We followed this procedure for three tested bpp rates and report the results in Fig. 7. As expected, there is a direct link between correlation and reconstruction improvement. A higher correlation leads to better reconstruction results. While all curves show positive relation, each curve (*i.e.*, different bpp) has a different exponential growth. Therefore, providing Y_{syn} with a similar Pearson score results in a more significant improvement for the lower bpp models. We argue that this behavior relates to the fact that Pearson score is biased towards structures, *i.e.*, the higher frequencies, which effected the most at low bpps. By using this metric to create Y_{syn}, we provide the structural information that is more beneficial in the lower bpps.

Guided Search: A major challenge in our technique is the matching step in which we attempt to find the correct patch in Y for every patch in X. The results so far are based on pure visual search. However, in some cases, we might have

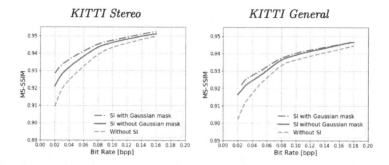

Fig. 8. Comparison between models trained with and without a 2D Gaussian mask. It can be seen that the results of *KITTI Stereo* were improved the most, as expected when using the mask.

additional information that can be used. In particular, we assume that given a patch in X, its corresponding patch in Y should be roughly in the same location in the image plane. We enforce this assumption using a 2D Gaussian mask that helps weight patch similarity in the SI-Finder block. The mean of the mask is taken to be the position of the patch in the image plane, and the variance of the mask is roughly half image size in both axis. This encourages the SI-Finder block to pick patches in Y from roughly the same location, in the image plane, as the patch in X.

Fig. 9. Different approaches to creating Y_{syn}. Left to right: original X, PathMatch based side information, Y_{syn} without and with a 2D Gaussian mask. As can be seen, using the 2D Gaussian mask as a prior improved the creation of Y_{syn}.

To verify the impact of the mask on our system, we trained the full model using the SI-Finder block with and without the use of the mask. See Fig. 8. The use of the mask improved results for most bpp (except for a single point). In Fig. 9, we present an example of creating Y_{syn} with and without a 2D Gaussian mask. As can be seen, the mask helps the algorithm pick better patches, especially in smooth regions where the Pearson correlation score fails. For comparison, we tested PatchMatch [5] to recover side information by comparing X_{dec} to Y_{dec} and taking the patches from Y. This scenario is not practical because PatchMatch does not run in the network, but it serves as a possible upper bound. As

Without SI

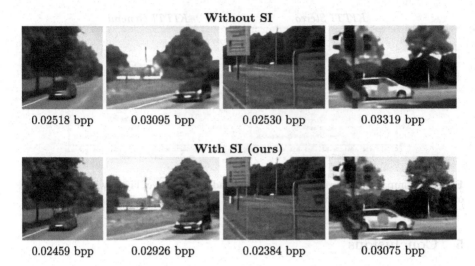

| 0.02518 bpp | 0.03095 bpp | 0.02530 bpp | 0.03319 bpp |

With SI (ours)

| 0.02459 bpp | 0.02926 bpp | 0.02384 bpp | 0.03075 bpp |

Fig. 10. Reconstruction examples from *KITTI Stereo* compressed using very low bpp with and without the use of side information. Complete objects, fine details and color are restored.

can be seen, the recovered side information using PatchMatch, in this case, looks much better. But upon close inspection, it can be seen that the high-frequency details are distorted. We tested using PatchMatch based side information and got results worst than the once reported here. Nevertheless, we leave the integration of PatchMatch into our network as a possible future research direction. In Fig. 10 we share additional reconstruction examples trained using the Gaussian mask and compressed to very low bit rates (that BPG failed to reach) on *KITTI Stereo*.

4.3 Ablation Study

Impact of SI-Net Layers: In order to prove that the improved reconstruction quality is a result of the side information and not an effect of the additional learnable layers, we train our network with the additional layers, *i.e.* the SI-Net layers, but without any use of side information Y. As can be seen in Fig. 11, adding layers (SI-Net block) has no effect on the reconstruction abilities of the model. Therefore, it is clear that the model gain in performance results from exploiting the additional information of the side information image.

Y Instead of Y_{syn}: To demonstrate the benefit of Y_{syn}, we trained new models (for all the bit rates) using the image Y 'as is'. That is, we concatenated the image Y directly with X_{dec} and skipped the entire block of the SI-Finder. As can be seen in Fig. 11, when comparing the results to the model trained with Y_{syn}, using Y as side information yields inferior results.

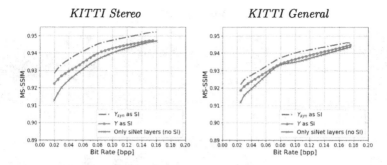

Fig. 11. Comparsion between models that use additional siNet layers without SI image, original Y image as side information and Y_{syn} (with the Gaussian mask).

5   Conclusions

We proposed a novel Deep Image Compression neural network with decoder-only side information. The proposed algorithm relies on the fact that it is possible to improve the compression of an image at the encoder, given that there is a correlated image available only at the decoder. To the best of our knowledge, we are the first to apply Deep Learning techniques to the problem of Distributed Source Coding for image compression. This scenario is quite common in practice, and we considered two such cases. The first is the case of a camera array, and the second is the case of uploading an image to the cloud, where similar images from the same location are already stored. Experiments that were designed to mimic these scenarios show that we can reduce communication bandwidth anywhere between 10% to 50%. This demonstrates the advantages of our approach.

Acknowledgments. This work was partly funded by ISF grant number 1549/19.

References

1. Aaron, A., Rane, S., Zhang, R., Girod, B.: Wyner-Ziv coding for video: applications to compression and error resilience. In: Data Compression Conference, pp. 93–102 (2003)
2. Aaron, A., Zhang, R., Girod, B.: Wyner-Ziv coding of motion video. In: Asilomar Conference on Signals, Systems and Computers, vol. 1, pp. 240–244 (2002)
3. Agustsson, E., Tschannen, M., Mentzer, F., Luc Van Gool, R.T.: Generative adversarial networks for extreme learned image compression. In: International Conference on Computer Vision (2019)
4. Ballé, J., Laparra, V., Simoncelli, E.P.: End-to-end optimized image compression. In: International Conference on Learning Representations (2017)
5. Barnes, C., Shechtman, E., Finkelstein, A., Goldman, D.B.: PatchMatch: a randomized correspondence algorithm for structural image editing. ACM Trans. Graph. **28**(3), 24 (2009)
6. Bellard, F.: BPG image format (2014). https://bellard.org/bpg/

7. Chambon, S., Crouzil, A.: Colour correlation-based matching. Int. J. Robot. Autom. **20**, 78–85 (2005)
8. Chen, D., Varodayan, D., Flierl, M., Girod, B.: Wyner-Ziv coding of multiview images with unsupervised learning of disparity and gray code. In: IEEE International Conference on Image Processing, pp. 1112–1115 (2008)
9. Chen, Q., Xu, J., Koltun, V.: Fast image processing with fully-convolutional networks. In: International Conference on Computer Vision, pp. 2516–2525 (2017)
10. Cover, T.M.: A proof of the data compression theorem of Slepian and Wolf for ergodic sources. IEEE Trans. Inf. Theory **21**(2), 226–228 (1975)
11. Geiger, A., Lenz, P., Urtasun, R.: Are we ready for autonomous driving? The Kitti vision benchmark suite. In: Computer Vision and Pattern Recognition (2012)
12. Girod, B., Aaron, A.M., Rane, S., Rebollo-Moneddero, D.: Distributed video coding. Proc. IEEE **93**(1), 71–83 (2005)
13. Google: WebP image format. https://developers.google.com/speed/webp/
14. Goyal, M., Lather, Y., Lather, V.: Analytical relation & comparison of PSNR and SSIM on babbon image and human eye perception using matlab. Int. J. Adv. Res. Eng. Appl. Sci. **4**(5), 108–119 (2015)
15. Johnston, N., et al.: Improved lossy image compression with priming and spatially adaptive bit rates for recurrent networks. In: Computer Vision and Pattern Recognition (2018)
16. Kingma, D.P., Ba, J.: Adam: a method for stochastic optimization. arXiv abs/1412.6980 (2014)
17. Le Gall, D.: MPEG: a video compression standard for multimedia applications. Commun. ACM **34**(4), 46–58 (1991)
18. Lu, G., Ouyang, W., Xu, D., Zhang, X., Gao, Z., Sun, M.: Deep Kalman filtering network for video compression artifact reduction. In: European Conference on Computer Vision, pp. 591–608 (2018)
19. Mentzer, F., Agustsson, E., Tschannen, M., Timofte, R., Gool, L.V.: Conditional probability models for deep image compression. In: Computer Vision and Pattern Recognition, pp. 4394–4402 (2018)
20. Menze, M., Heipke, C., Geiger, A.: Joint 3D estimation of vehicles and scene flow. ISPRS-Image Seq. Anal. (2015)
21. Menze, M., Heipke, C., Geiger, A.: Object scene flow. ISPRS - Photogram. Remote Sens. **140**, 60–76 (2018)
22. Ndajah, P., Kikuchi, H., Yukawa, M., Watanabe, H., Muramatsu, S.: SSIM image quality metric for denoised images. In: International Conference on Visualization, Imaging and Simulation, pp. 53–58 (2010)
23. Pradhan, S.S., Ramchandran, K.: Distributed source coding using syndromes (DISCUS): design and construction. IEEE Trans. Inf. Theory **49**(3), 626–643 (2003)
24. Rippel, O., Bourdev, L.: Real-time adaptive image compression. In: International Conference on Machine Learning, vol. 70, pp. 2922–2930 (2017)
25. Slepian, D., Wolf, J.K.: Noiseless coding of correlated information sources. IEEE Trans. Inf. Theory **19**(4), 471–480 (1973)
26. Taubman, D.S., Marcellin, M.W.: JPEG 2000: Image Compression Fundamentals, Standards and Practice. Kluwer Academic Publishers, Dordrecht (2001)
27. Theis, L., Shi, W., Cunningham, A., Huszár, F.: Lossy image compression with compressive autoencoders. In: International Conference on Learning Representations (2017)
28. Toderici, G., et al.: Variable rate image compression with recurrent neural networks. In: International Conference on Learning Representations (2016)

29. Toderici, G., et al.: Full resolution image compression with recurrent neural networks. In: Computer Vision and Pattern Recognition (2017)
30. Tsai, Y., Liu, M., Sun, D., Yang, M., Kautz, J.: Learning binary residual representations for domain-specific video streaming. In: Conference on Artificial Intelligence, pp. 7363–7370 (2018)
31. Varodayan, D., Lin, Y.C., Mavlankar, A., Flierl, M., Girod, B.: Wyner-Ziv coding of stereo images with unsupervised learning of disparity. In: Proceedings of Picture Coding Symposium, pp. 1–4 (2007)
32. Wallace, G.K.: The JPEG still picture compression standard. Commun. ACM **38**, 30–44 (1991)
33. Wang, Z., Simoncelli, E.P., Bovik, A.C.: Multiscale structural similarity for image quality assessment. In: Asilomar Conference on Signals, Systems Computers, vol. 2, pp. 1398–1402 (2003)
34. Wu, C., Singhal, N., Krähenbühl, P.: Video compression through image interpolation. In: European Conference on Computer Vision, pp. 425–440 (2018)
35. Wyner, A.D., Ziv, J.: The rate-distortion function for source coding with side information at the decoder. IEEE Trans. Inf. Theory **22**(1), 1–10 (1976)
36. Xiong, Z., Liveri, A.D., Cheng, S.: Distributed source coding for sensor networks. IEEE Signal Process. Mag. **21**(5), 80–94 (2004)

Meta-Sim2: Unsupervised Learning of Scene Structure for Synthetic Data Generation

Jeevan Devaranjan[1,3], Amlan Kar[1,2,4(✉)], and Sanja Fidler[1,2,4]

[1] NVIDIA, Waterloo, Canada
amlan@cs.toronto.edu
[2] University of Toronto, Toronto, Canada
[3] University of Waterloo, Waterloo, Canada
[4] Vector Institute, Toronto, Canada

Abstract. Procedural models are being widely used to synthesize scenes for graphics, gaming, and to create (labeled) synthetic datasets for ML. In order to produce realistic and diverse scenes, a number of parameters governing the procedural models have to be carefully tuned by experts. These parameters control both the *structure* of scenes being generated (*e.g.* how many cars in the scene), as well as *parameters* which place objects in valid configurations. Meta-Sim aimed at automatically tuning parameters given a target collection of real images in an unsupervised way. In Meta-Sim2, we aim to learn the scene *structure* in addition to parameters, which is a challenging problem due to its discrete nature. Meta-Sim2 proceeds by learning to sequentially sample rule expansions from a given probabilistic scene grammar. Due to the discrete nature of the problem, we use Reinforcement Learning to train our model, and design a feature space divergence between our synthesized and target images that is key to successful training. Experiments on a real driving dataset show that, without any supervision, we can successfully learn to generate data that captures discrete structural statistics of objects, such as their frequency, in real images. We also show that this leads to downstream improvement in the performance of an object detector trained on our generated dataset as opposed to other baseline simulation methods. Project page: https://nv-tlabs.github.io/meta-sim-structure/.

1 Introduction

Synthetic datasets are creating an appealing opportunity for training machine learning models *e.g.* for perception and planning in driving [18,53,55], indoor

---

J. Devaranjan and A. Kar—Contributed equally, work done during JD's internship at NVIDIA.

Electronic supplementary material The online version of this chapter (https://doi.org/10.1007/978-3-030-58520-4_42) contains supplementary material, which is available to authorized users.

© Springer Nature Switzerland AG 2020
A. Vedaldi et al. (Eds.): ECCV 2020, LNCS 12362, pp. 715–733, 2020.
https://doi.org/10.1007/978-3-030-58520-4_42

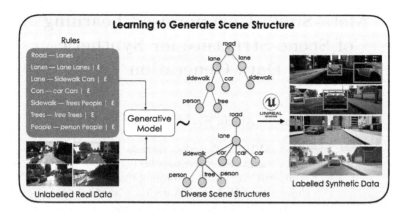

Fig. 1. We present a method that learns to generate synthetic scenes from real imagery in an unsupervised fashion. It does so by learning a generative model of scene structure, samples from which (with additional scene parameters) can be rendered to create synthetic images and labels.

scene perception [46,57], and robotic control [61]. Via graphics engines, synthetic datasets come with perfect ground-truth for tasks in which labels are expensive or even impossible to obtain, such as segmentation, depth or material information. Adding a new type of label to synthetic datasets is as simple as calling a renderer, rather than embarking on a time consuming annotation endeavor that requires new tooling and hiring, training and overseeing annotators.

Creating synthetic datasets comes with its own hurdles. While content, such as 3D CAD models that make up a scene are available on online asset stores, artists write complex procedural models that synthesize scenes by placing these assets in realistic layouts. This often requires browsing through massive amounts of real imagery to carefully tune a procedural model – a time consuming task. For scenarios such as street scenes, creating synthetic scenes relevant for one city may require tuning a procedural model made for another city from scratch. In this paper, we propose an automatic method to carry out this task (Fig. 1).

Recently, Meta-Sim [30] proposed to optimize scene parameters in a synthetically generated scene by exploiting the visual similarity of (rendered) generated synthetic data with real data. They represent scene structure and parameters in a *scene graph*, and generate data by sampling a random scene structure (and parameters) from a given *probabilistic grammar* of scenes, and then modifying the scene parameters using a learnt model. Since they only learn scene parameters, a sim-to-real gap in the scene structure remains. For example, one would likely find more cars, people and buildings in Manhattan over a quaint village in Italy. Other work on generative models of structural data such as graphs and grammar strings [12,17,37,42] require large amounts of ground truth data for training to generate realistic samples. However, scene structures are extremely cumbersome to annotate and thus not available in most real datasets.

In this paper, we propose a procedural generative model of synthetic scenes that is learned unsupervised from real imagery. We generate *scene graphs* object-by-object by learning to sample rule expansions from a given probabilistic scene grammar and generate scene parameters using [30]. Learning without supervision here is a challenging problem due to the discrete nature of the scene structures we aim to generate and the presence of a non-differentiable renderer in the generative process. To this end, we propose a feature space divergence to compare (rendered) generated scenes with real scenes, which can be computed per scene and is key to allowing credit assignment for training with reinforcement learning.

We evaluate our method on two synthetic datasets and a real driving dataset and find that our approach significantly reduces the distribution gap between scene structures in our generated and target data, improving over human priors on scene structure by learning to closely align with target structure distributions. On the real driving dataset, starting from minimal human priors, we show that we can almost exactly recover the structural distribution in the real target scenes (measured using GT annotations available for cars) – an exciting result given that the model is trained without any labels. We show that an object detector trained on our generated data outperforms those trained on data generated with human priors or by [30], and show improvements in distribution similarity measures of our generated rendered images with real data.

2 Related Work

2.1 Synthetic Content Creation

Synthetic content creation has been receiving significant interest as a promising alternative to dataset collection and annotation. Various works have proposed generating synthetic data for tasks such as perception and planning in driving [2,14,18,48,53,55,68], indoor scene perception [4,24,46,57,59,70,75], game playing [6,28], robotic control [6,56,61,63], optical flow estimation [7,58], home robotics [20,34,49] amongst many others, utilizing procedural modeling, existing simulators or human generated scenarios.

Learnt Scene Generation brings a data-driven nature to scene generation. [64,74] propose learning hierarchical spatial priors between furniture, that is integrated into a hand-crafted cost used to generate optimized indoor scene layouts. [50] similarly learn to synthesize indoor scenes using a probabilistic scene grammar and human-centric learning by leveraging affordances. [64] learn to generate intermediate object relationship graphs and instantiate scenes conditioned on them. [76] use a scene graph representation and learn adding objects into existing scenes. [40,54,65] propose methods for learning deep priors from data for indoor scene synthesis. [16] introduce a generative model that sequentially adds objects into scenes, while [29] propose a generative model for object layouts in 2D given a label set. [60] generate batches of data using a neural network that is used to train a task model, and learn by differentiating through the learning process of the task model. [30] propose learning to generate scenes by modifying the parameters of objects in scenes that are sampled from a probabilistic scene

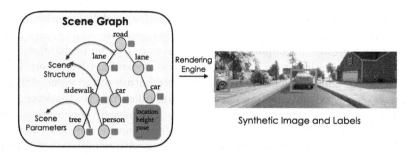

Fig. 2. Example scene graph (structure and parameters) and depiction of its rendering

grammar. We argue that this ignores learning structural aspects of the scene, which we focus on in our work. Similar to [16,30], and contrary to other works, we learn this in an unsupervised manner *i.e.* given only target images as input. **Learning with Simulators:** Methods in Approximate Bayesian Inference have looked into inferring the parameters of a simulator that generate a particular data point [35,45]. [11] provide a great overview of advances in simulator based inference. Instead of running inference per scene [35,69], we aim to generate new data that resembles a target distribution. [44] learn to optimize non-differentiable simulators using a variational upper bound of a GAN-like objective. [8] learn to optimize simulator parameters for robotic control tasks by directly comparing trajectories between a real and a simulated robot. [19,47] train an agent to paint images using brush strokes in an adversarial setting with Reinforcement Learning. We learn to generate discrete scene structures constrained to a grammar, while optimizing a distribution matching objective (with Reinforcement Learning) instead of training adversarially. Compared to [47], we generate large and complex scenes, as opposed to images of single objects or faces.

2.2 Graph Generation

Generative models of graphs and trees [3,10,17,42,43,73] generally produce graphs with richer structure with more flexibility over grammar based models, but often fail to produce syntactically correct graphs for cases with a defined syntax such as programs and scene graphs. **Grammar based methods** have been used for a variety of tasks such as program translation [9], conditional program generation [71,72], grammar induction [32] and generative modelling on structures with syntax [12,37], such as molecules. These methods, however, assume access to ground-truth graph structures for learning. We take inspiration from these methods, but show how to learn our model unsupervised *i.e.* without any ground truth scene graph annotations.

3 Methodology

We aim to learn a generative model of synthetic scenes. In particular, given a dataset of real imagery X_R, the problem is to create synthetic data $D(\theta) = (X(\theta), Y(\theta))$ of images $X(\theta)$ and labels $Y(\theta)$ that is representative of X_R, where θ represents the parameters of the generative model. We exploit advances in graphics engines and rendering, by stipulating that the synthetic data D is the output of creating an abstract scene representation and rendering it with a graphics engine. Rendering ensures that low level pixel information in $X(\theta)$ (and its corresponding annotation $Y(\theta)$) does not need to be modelled, which has been the focus of recent research in generative modeling of images [31,51]. Ensuring the semantic *validity* of sampled scenes requires imposing constraints on their structure. Scene grammars use a set of rules to greatly reduce the space of scenes that can be sampled, making learning a more structured and tractable problem. For example, it could explicitly enforce that a car can only be on a road which then need not be implicitly learned, thus leading us to use probabilistic scene grammars. Meta-Sim [30] sampled *scene graph* structures (see Fig. 2) from a prior imposed on a Probabilistic Context-Free Grammar (PCFG), which we call the *structure prior*. They sampled parameters for every node in the scene graph from a *parameter prior* and learned to predict new parameters for each node, keeping the structure intact. Their generated scenes therefore come from a structure prior (which is context-free) and the learnt parameter distribution, resulting in an untackled sim-to-real gap in the scene structures. In our work, we aim to alleviate this by learning a context-dependent structure distribution *unsupervised* of synthetic scenes from images.

We utilize *scene graphs* as our abstract scene representation, that are rendered into a corresponding image with labels (Sect. 3.1). Our generative model sequentially samples expansion rules from a given probabilistic scene grammar (Sect. 3.2) to generate a scene graph which is rendered. We train the model *unsupervised* and with reinforcement learning, using a feature-matching based distribution divergence specifically designed to be amenable to our setting (Sect. 3.3).

3.1 Representing Synthetic Scenes

In Computer Graphics and Vision, **Scene Graphs** are commonly used to describe scenes in a concise hierarchical manner, where each node describes an object in the scene along with its parameters such as the 3D asset, pose etc. Parent-child relationships define the child's parameters relative to its parent, enabling easy scene editing and manipulation. Additionally, camera, lighting, weather etc. are also encoded into the scene graph. Generating corresponding pixels and annotations amounts to placing objects into the scene in a graphics engine and rendering with the defined parameters (see Fig. 2).

Notation: A context-free grammar G is defined as a list of symbols (terminal and non-terminal) and expansion rules. Non-terminal symbols have at least one expansion rule into a new set of symbols. Sampling from a grammar involves

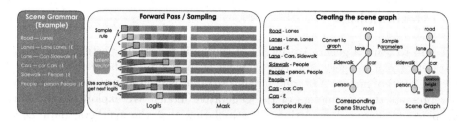

Fig. 3. Representation of our generative process for a scene graph. The logits and mask are of shape $T_{max} \times K$. Green represents a higher value and red is lower. At every time step, we autoregressively sample a rule and predict the logits for the next rule conditioned on the sample (capturing context dependencies). The figure on the right shows how sampled rules from the grammar are converted into a graph structure (only objects that are renderable are kept from the full grammar string). Parameters for every node can be sampled from a prior or optionally learnt with the method of [30]. A generated scene graph can be rendered as shown in Fig. 2. (Color figure online)

expanding a start symbol till only non-terminal symbols remain. We denote the total number of expansion rules in a grammar G as K. We define scene grammars and represent strings sampled from the grammar as scene graphs following [30,48] (see Fig. 3). For each scene graph, a structure T is sampled from the grammar G followed by sampling corresponding parameters α for every node in the graph.

3.2 Generative Model

We take inspiration from previous work on learning generative models of graphs that are constrained by a grammar [37] for our architecture. Specifically, we map a latent vector z to unnormalized probabilities over all possible grammar rules in an autoregressive manner, using a recurrent neural network till a maximum of T_{max} steps. Deviating from [37], we sample one rule r_t at every time step and use it to predict the logits for the next rule f_{t+1}. This allows our model to capture context-dependent relationships easily, as opposed to the context-free nature of scene graphs in [30]. Given a list of at most T_{max} sampled rules, the corresponding scene graph is generated by treating each rule expansion as a node expansion in the graph (see Fig. 3).

Sampling Correct Rules: To ensure the validity of sampled rules in each time step t, we follow [37] and maintain a last-in-first-out (LIFO) stack of unexpanded non-terminal nodes. Nodes are popped from the stack, expanded according to the sampled rule-expansion, and the resulting new non-terminal nodes are pushed to the stack. When a non-terminal is popped, we create a mask m_t of size K which is 1 for valid rules from that non-terminal and 0 otherwise. Given the logits for the next expansion f_t, the probability of a rule $r_{t,k}$ is represented as,

$$p(r_t = k | f_t) = \frac{m_{t,k} exp(f_{t,k})}{\sum_{j=1}^{K} m_{t,j} exp(f_{t,j})}$$

Sampling from this masked multinomial distribution ensures that only valid rules are sampled as r_t. Given the logits and sampled rules, $(f_t, r_t) \forall t \in 1 \ldots T_{max}$, the probability of the corresponding scene structure T given z is simply,

$$q_\theta(T|z) = \sum_{t=1}^{T_{max}} p(r_t | f_t)$$

Putting it together, images are generated by sampling a scene structure $T \sim q_\theta(\cdot|z)$ from the model, followed by sampling parameters for every node in the scene $\alpha \sim q(\cdot|T)$ and rendering an image $v' = R(T, \alpha) \sim q_I$. For some $v' \sim q_I$, with parameters α and structure T, we assume[1],

$$q_I(v'|z) = q(\alpha|T) q_\theta(T|z)$$

3.3   Training

Training such a generative model is commonly done using *variational inference* [33,52] or by optimizing a measure of *distribution similarity* [22,30,39,41]. Variational Inference allows using reconstruction based objectives by introducing an approximate learnt posterior. Our attempts at using variational inference to train this model failed due to the complexity coming from discrete sampling and having a renderer in the generative process. Moreover, the recognition network here would amount to doing inverse graphics – an extremely challenging problem [36] in itself. Hence, we optimize a measure of distribution similarity of the generated and target data. We do not explore using a *trained critic* due to the clear visual discrepancy between rendered and real images that a critic can exploit. Moreover, adversarial training is known to be notoriously difficult for discrete data. We note that recent work [19,47] has succeeded in adversarial training of a generative model of discrete brush strokes with reinforcement learning (RL), by carefully limiting the critic's capacity. We similarly employ RL to train our discrete generative model of scene graphs. While *two sample tests*, such as MMD [23] have been used in previous work to estimate and minimize the distance between two empirical distributions [15,30,39,41], training with MMD and RL resulted in credit-assignment issues as it is a single score for the similarity of two full sets(batches) of data. Instead, our metric can be computed for every sample, which greatly helps training as shown empirically in Sect. 4.

Distribution Matching: We train the generative model to match the distribution of features of the real data in the latent space of some feature extractor φ. We define the real feature distribution p_f s.t $F \sim p_f \iff F = \varphi(v)$ for some $v \sim p_I$. Similarly we define the generated feature distribution q_f s.t

---

[1] This equality does not hold in general for rendering, but it worked well in practice.

$F \sim q_f \iff F = \varphi(v)$ for some $v \sim q_I$. We accomplish distribution matching by approximately computing p_f, q_f from samples and minimizing the KL divergence from p_f to q_f. Our training objective is

$$\min_\theta \quad KL(q_f\|p_f)$$

$$\min_\theta \quad \mathbb{E}_{F\sim q_f}[\log q_f(F) - \log p_f(F)]$$

Using the feature distribution definition above, we have the equivalent objective

$$\min_\theta \mathbb{E}_{v\sim q_I}[\log q_f(\varphi(v)) - \log p_f(\varphi(v))] \tag{1}$$

The true underlying feature distributions q_f and p_f are usually intractable to compute. We use approximations $\tilde{q}_f(F)$ and $\tilde{p}_f(F)$, computed using kernel density estimation (KDE). Let $V = \{v_1, \ldots, v_l\}$ and $B = \{v'_1, \ldots, v'_m\}$ be a batch of real and generated images. KDE with B, V to estimate q_f, p_f yield

$$\tilde{q}_f(F) = \frac{1}{m}\sum_{j=1}^m K_H(F - \varphi(v'_j))$$

$$\tilde{p}_f(F) = \frac{1}{l}\sum_{j=1}^l K_H(F - \varphi(v_j))$$

where K_H is the standard multivariate normal kernel with bandwidth matrix H. We use $H = dI$ where d is the dimensionality of the feature space.

Our generative model involves making a discrete (non-differentiable) choice at each step, leading us to optimize our objective using reinforcement learning techniques[2]. Specifically, using the REINFORCE [67] score function estimator along with a moving average baseline, we approximate the gradients of Eq. 1 as

$$\nabla_\theta \mathcal{L} \approx \frac{1}{M}\sum_{j=1}^m (\log \tilde{q}_f(\varphi(v'_j)) - \log \tilde{p}_f(\varphi(v'_j)))\nabla_\theta \log q_I(v'_j) \tag{2}$$

where M is the batch size, $\tilde{q}_f(F)$ and $\tilde{p}_f(F)$ are density estimates defined above.

Notice that the gradient above requires computing the marginal probability $q_I(v')$ of a generated image v', instead of the conditional $q_I(v'|z)$. Computing the **marginal probability of a generated image** requires an intractable marginalization over the latent variable z. To circumvent this, we use a fixed finite number of latent vectors from a set Z sampled uniformly, enabling easy marginalization. This translates to,

$$q_\theta(T) = \frac{1}{|Z|}\sum_{z\in Z} q_\theta(T|z)$$

$$q_I(v') = q(\alpha|T)q_\theta(T)$$

---

[2] We did not explore sampling from a continuous relaxation of the discrete variable here.

We find that this still has enough modeling capacity, since there are only finitely many scene graphs of a maximum length T_{max} that can be sampled from the grammar. Empirically, we find using one latent vector to be enough in our experiments. Essentially, stochasticity in the rule sampling makes up for lost stochasticity in the latent space.

Pretraining is an essential step for our method. In every experiment, we define a simple handcrafted prior on scene structure. For example, a simple prior could be to put one car on one road in a driving scene. We pre-train the model by sampling strings (scene graphs) from the grammar prior, and training the model to maximize the log-likelihood of these scene graphs. We provide specific details about the priors used in Sect. 4.

Feature Extraction for distribution matching is a crucial step since the features need to capture structural scene information such as the number of objects and their contextual spatial relationships for effective training. We describe the feature extractor used and its training for each experiment in Sect. 4.

Ensuring Termination: During training, sampling can result in incomplete strings generated with at most T_{max} steps. Thus, we repeatedly sample a scene graph T until its length is at most T_{max}. To ensure that we do not require too many attempts, we record the rejection rate $r_{reject}(F)$ of a sampled feature F as the average failed sampling attempts when sampling the single scene graph used to generate F. We set a threshold ϵ on $r_{reject}(F)$ (representing the maximum allowable rejections) and weight λ and add it to our original loss as,

$$\mathcal{L}' = \mathbb{E}_{F \sim q_F}[\log q_f(F) - \log p_f(F) + \lambda \mathbf{1}_{(\epsilon,\infty)}(r_{reject}(F))]$$

We found that $\lambda = 10^{-2}$ and $\epsilon = 1$ worked well for all of our experiments.

4   Experiments

We show two controlled experiments, on the MNIST dataset [38] (Sect. 4.1) and on synthetic aerial imagery [30] (Sect. 4.2), where we showcase the ability of our model to learn synthetic structure distributions **unsupervised**. Finally, we show an experiment on generating 3D driving scenes (Sect. 4.3), mimicking structure distributions on the KITTI [21] driving dataset and showing the performance of an object detector trained on our generated data. The renderers used in each experiment are adapted from [30]. For each experiment, we first discuss the corresponding scene grammar. Then, we discuss the feature extractor and its training. Finally, we describe the structure prior used to pre-train the model, the target data, and show results on learning to mimic structures in the target data without any access to ground-truth structures. Additionally, we show comparisons with learning with MMD [23] (Sect. 4.1) and show how our model can learn to generate context-dependent scene graphs from the grammar (Sect. 4.2).

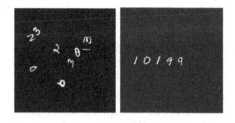

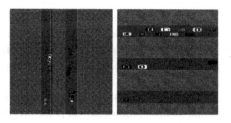

Fig. 4. Prior (Left) and Validation (Right) example for MultiMNIST experiments

Fig. 5. Prior (Left) and Validation (Right) example for Aerial 2D experiments

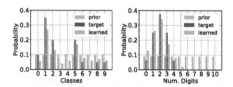

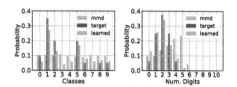

Fig. 6. Distributions of classes and number of digits, in the prior, learned and target scene structures

Fig. 7. Distributions of classes and number of digits, comparing learning with MMD, ours and the target

4.1 Multi MNIST

We first evaluate our approach on a toy example of learning to generate scenes with multiple digits. The grammar defining the scene structure is:

$$\text{Scene} \rightarrow bg\ \text{Digits}, \quad \text{Digits} \rightarrow \text{Digit Digits} \mid \epsilon, \quad \text{Digit} \rightarrow 0 \mid 1 \mid 2 \mid \cdots \mid 9$$

Sampled digits are placed onto a black canvas of size 256×256.

Feature Extraction Network: We train a network to determine the binary presence of a digit class in the scene. We use a Resnet [26] made up of three residual blocks each containing two 3×3 convolutional layers to produce an image embedding and three fully connected layers from the image embedding to make the prediction. We use the Resnet embeddings as our image features. We train the network on synthetic data generated by our simple prior for both structure and continuous parameters. Training is done with a simple binary cross-entropy criterion for each class. The exact prior and target data used is explained below.

Prior and Target Data: We sample the number of digits in the scene n_d uniformly from 0 to 10, and sample n_d digits uniformly to place on the scene. The digits are placed (parameters) uniformly on the canvas. The target data has digits upright in a straight line in the middle of the canvas. Figure 4 shows example prior samples, and target data. We show we can learn scene structures with a gap remaining in the parameters by using the parameter prior during training.

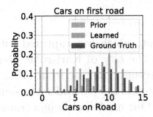 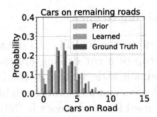

Fig. 8. #cars distribution learned in the Aerial 2D experiment. We can learn *context dependent* relationships, placing different number of cars on different roads

We attempt **learning a random distribution of number of digits** with random classes in the scene. Figure 6 shows the prior, target and learnt distribution of the number of digits and their class distribution. We see that our model can faithfully approximate the target, even while learning it unsupervised. We also **train with MMD** [23], computed using two batches of real and generated images and used as the reward for every generated scene. Figure 7 shows that using MMD results in the model learning a smoothed approximation of the target distribution, which comes from the lack of credit assignment in the score, that we get with our objective.

4.2 Aerial 2D

Next, we evaluate our approach on a harder synthetic scenario of aerial views of driving scenes. The grammar and the corresponding rendered scenes offer additional complexity to test the model. The grammar here is as follows:

$$\text{Scene} \rightarrow \text{Roads}, \qquad\qquad \text{Roads} \rightarrow \text{Road Roads} \mid \epsilon$$
$$\text{Road} \rightarrow \text{Cars}, \qquad\qquad\qquad \text{Cars} \rightarrow car\text{ Cars} \mid \epsilon$$

Feature Extraction Network: We use the same Resnet [26] architecture from the MNIST experiment with the FC layers outputting the number of cars, roads, houses and trees in the scene as 1-hot labels. We train by minimizing the cross entropies these labels, trained on samples generated from the prior.

Prior: We sample the number of roads $n_r \in [0, 4]$ uniformly. On each road, we sample $c \in [0, 8]$ cars uniformly. Roads are placed sequentially by sampling a random distance d and placing the road d pixels in front of the previous one. Cars are placed on the road with uniform random position and rotation (Fig. 5).

Learning Context-Dependent Relationships: For the target dataset, we sample the number of roads $n_r \in [0, 4]$ with probabilities (0.05, 0.15, 0.4, 0.4). On the first road we sample $n_1 \sim \text{Poisson}(9)$ cars and $n_i \sim \text{Poisson}(3)$ cars for each of the remaining roads. All cars are placed well spaced on their respective road. Unlike the Multi-MNIST experiment, these structures cannot be modelled by a Probabilistic-CFG, and thus by [30,37]. We see that our model can learn this context-dependent distribution faithfully as well in Fig. 8.

4.3 3D Driving Scenes

We experiment on the KITTI [21] dataset, which was captured with a camera mounted on top of a car driving around the city of Karlsruhe, Germany. The dataset contains a wide variety of road scenes, ranging from urban traffic scenarios to highways and more rural neighborhoods. We utilize the same grammar and renderer used for road scenes in [30]. Our model, although trained unsupervised, can learn to get closer to the underlying structure distribution, improve measures of image generation, and the performance of a downstream task model (Fig. 9).

Fig. 9. Generated images (good prior expt.). (Left) Using both the structure and parameter prior, (Middle) Using our learnt structure and parameters from [30], (Right) Real KITTI samples. Our model (middle), although unsupervised, adds diverse scene elements like vegetation, pedestrians, signs etc. to better resemble the real dataset.

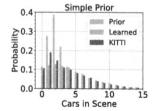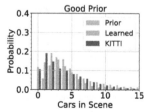

Fig. 10. #cars/scene learned from a simple prior (left) and good prior (right) on KITTI

Prior and Training: Following SDR [48], we define three different priors to capture three different modes in the KITTI dataset. They are the 'Rural', 'Suburban' and 'Urban' scenarios, as defined in [48]. We train three different versions of our model, one for each of the structural priors, and sample from each of them uniformly. We use the scene parameter prior and learnt scene parameter model

Fig. 11. Generated images (simple prior expt.). (Left) Using both the structure and parameter prior, (Middle) Using our learnt structure and parameters from [30], (Right) Real samples from KITTI. Our model, although trained unsupervised, learns to add an appropriate frequency and diversity of scene elements to resemble the real data, even when trained from a very weak prior.

from [30] to produce parameters for our generated scene structures to get the final scene graphs, which are rendered and used for our distribution matching.

Feature Extraction Network: We use the pool-3 layer of an Inception-V3 network, pre-trained on the ImageNet [13] dataset as our feature extractor. Interestingly, we found this to work as well as using features from Mask-RCNN [25] trained on driving scenes.

Distribution Similarity Metrics: In generative modeling of images, the Frechet Inception Distance [27], and the Kernel Inception Distance [5] have been used to measure progress. We report FID and KID in Table 1 and 2 between our generated synthetic dataset and the KITTI-train set. We do so by generating 10K synthetic samples and using the full KITTI-train set, computed using the pool-3 features of an Inception-v3 network. Figure 10 (left) shows the distribution of the number of cars generated by the prior, learnt model and in the KITTI dataset (since we have GT for cars). We do not have ground truth for which KITTI scenes could be classified into rural/suburban/urban, so we compare against the global distribution of the whole dataset. We notice that the model bridges the gap between this particular distribution well after training.

Task Performance: We report average precision for detection at 0.5 IoU *i.e.* AP@0.5 (following [30]) of an object detector trained to convergence on our synthetic data and tested on the KITTI validation set. We use the detection head from Mask-RCNN [25] with a Resnet-50-FPN backbone initialized with pre-trained ImageNet weights as our object detector. The task network in each result row of Table 1 is finetuned from the snapshot of the previous row. [30] show results with adding Image-to-Image translation to the generated images to reduce the *appearance gap* and results with training on a small amount of real

Table 1. AP@0.5 on KITTI-val and distribution similarity metrics between generated synthetic data and KITTI-train. Learnt parameters are used from [30]. *Results from [30] are our reproduced numbers, and we show learning the structure additionally helps close the distribution gap and improves downstream task performance.

Method	Structure	Parameters	Easy	Medium	Hard	KID [5]	FID [27]
Prob. grammar	Prior	Prior	63.7	63.7	62.2	0.066	106.6
Meta-Sim* [30]	Prior	Learnt	66.5	66.3	65.8	0.072	111.6
Ours	Learnt	Learnt	**67.0**	**67.0**	**66.2**	**0.054**	**99.7**

Table 2. Repeat of experiments in Table 1 with a *simple prior on the scene structure. Parameters are learnt using [30]. We observe a significant boost in both task performance and distribution similarity metrics, by learning the structure and parameters.

Method	Structure	Parameters	Easy	Medium	Hard	KID [5]	FID [27]
Prob. grammar	Prior*	Prior	61.3	59.8	58.0	0.101	130.3
Ours	Learnt	Prior	63.2	62.5	61.2	**0.059**	**100.0**
Ours	Learnt	Learnt	**65.2**	**64.7**	**63.4**	0.060	101.7

data. We omit those experiments here and refer the reader to their paper for a sketch of expected results in these settings. Training this model directly on the full KITTI training set obtains AP@0.5 of 81.52(easy), 83.58(medium) and 84.48(hard), denoting a large sim-to-real performance gap left to bridge.

Using a Simple Prior: The priors on the structure in the previous experiments were taken from [48]. These priors already involved some human intervention, which we aim to minimize. Therefore, we repeat the experiments above with a very simple and quick to create prior on the scene structure, where a few instances of each kind of object (car, house etc.) is placed in the scene (see Fig. 11 (Left)). [30] requires a decently crafted structure prior to train the parameter network. Thus, we use the prior parameters while training our structure generator in this experiment (showing the robustness of training with randomized prior parameters), and learn the parameter network later (Table 2). Figure 10 (right) shows that the method learned the distribution of the number of cars well (unsupervised), even when initialized from a bad prior. Notice that the FID/KID of the learnt model from the simple prior in Table 2 is comparable to that trained from a tuned prior in Table 1, which we believe is an exciting result.

Discussion: We noticed that our method worked better when initialized with more spread out priors than more localized priors (Table 1 and 2, Fig. 10) We hypothesize this is due to the distribution matching metric we use being the the reverse-KL divergence between the generated and real data (feature) distributions, which is mode-seeking instead of being mode-covering. Therefore, an initialization with a narrow distribution around one of the modes has low incentive to move away from it, hampering learning. Even then, we see a signif-

icant improvement in performance when starting from a peaky prior as shown in Table 2. We also note the importance of pre-training the task network. Rows in Table 1 and Table 2 were finetuned from the checkpoint of the previous row. The first row (Prob. Grammar) is a form of Domain Randomization [48,62], which has been shown to be crucial for sim-to-real adaptation. Our method, in essence, reduces the randomization in the generated scenes (by learning to generate scenes similar to the target data), and we observe that progressively training the task network with our (more specialized) generated data improves its performance. [1,66] show the opposite behavior, where increasing randomization (or environment difficulty) through task training results in improved performance. A detailed analysis of this phenomenon is beyond the current scope and is left for future work.

5   Conclusion

We introduced an approach to unsupervised learning of a generative model of synthetic scene structures by optimizing for visual similarity to the real data. Inferring scene structures is known to be notoriously hard even when annotations are provided. Our method is able to perform the generative side of it without any ground truth information. Experiments on two toy and one real dataset showcase the ability of our model to learn a plausible posterior over scene structures, significantly improving over manually designed priors. Our current method needs to optimize for both the scene structure and parameters of a synthetic scene generator in order to produce good results. This process has many moving parts and is generally cumbersome to make work in a new application scenario. Doing so, such as learning the grammar itself, requires further investigation, and opens an exciting direction for future work.

References

1. Akkaya, I., et al.: Solving Rubik's cube with a robot hand. arXiv preprint arXiv:1910.07113 (2019)
2. Alhaija, H.A., Mustikovela, S.K., Mescheder, L., Geiger, A., Rother, C.: Augmented reality meets computer vision: efficient data generation for urban driving scenes. Int. J. Comput. Vis. **126**(9), 961–972 (2018)
3. Alvarez-Melis, D., Jaakkola, T.S.: Tree-structured decoding with doubly-recurrent neural networks (2016)
4. Armeni, I., et al.: 3D scene graph: a structure for unified semantics, 3D space, and camera. In: Proceedings of the IEEE International Conference on Computer Vision (2019)
5. Bińkowski, M., Sutherland, D.J., Arbel, M., Gretton, A.: Demystifying MMD GANs. In: ICLR (2018)
6. Brockman, G., et al.: OpenAI Gym. arXiv arXiv:1606.01540 (2016)
7. Butler, D.J., Wulff, J., Stanley, G.B., Black, M.J.: A naturalistic open source movie for optical flow evaluation. In: Fitzgibbon, A., Lazebnik, S., Perona, P., Sato, Y., Schmid, C. (eds.) ECCV 2012. LNCS, vol. 7577, pp. 611–625. Springer, Heidelberg (2012). https://doi.org/10.1007/978-3-642-33783-3_44

8. Chebotar, Y., et al.: Closing the sim-to-real loop: Adapting simulation randomization with real world experience. arXiv preprint arXiv:1810.05687 (2018)
9. Chen, X., Liu, C., Song, D.: Tree-to-tree neural networks for program translation. In: Bengio, S., Wallach, H., Larochelle, H., Grauman, K., Cesa-Bianchi, N., Garnett, R. (eds.) Advances in Neural Information Processing Systems, vol. 31, pp. 2547–2557. Curran Associates, Inc. (2018). http://papers.nips.cc/paper/7521-tree-to-tree-neural-networks-for-program-translation.pdf
10. Chu, H., et al.: Neural turtle graphics for modeling city road layouts. In: Proceedings of the IEEE International Conference on Computer Vision, pp. 4522–4530 (2019)
11. Cranmer, K., Brehmer, J., Louppe, G.: The frontier of simulation-based inference. arXiv preprint arXiv:1911.01429 (2019)
12. Dai, H., Tian, Y., Dai, B., Skiena, S., Song, L.: Syntax-directed variational autoencoder for structured data. arXiv preprint arXiv:1802.08786 (2018)
13. Deng, J., Dong, W., Socher, R., Li, L.J., Li, K., Fei-Fei, L.: ImageNet: a large-scale hierarchical image database. In: 2009 IEEE Conference on Computer Vision and Pattern Recognition, pp. 248–255. IEEE (2009)
14. Dosovitskiy, A., Ros, G., Codevilla, F., Lopez, A., Koltun, V.: CARLA: an open urban driving simulator. In: CORL, pp. 1–16 (2017)
15. Dziugaite, G.K., Roy, D.M., Ghahramani, Z.: Training generative neural networks via maximum mean discrepancy optimization. In: UAI (2015)
16. Eslami, S.A., Heess, N., Weber, T., Tassa, Y., Szepesvari, D., Hinton, G.E., et al.: Attend, infer, repeat: fast scene understanding with generative models. In: Advances in Neural Information Processing Systems, pp. 3225–3233 (2016)
17. Fan, S., Huang, B.: Labeled graph generative adversarial networks. CoRR abs/1906.03220 (2019). http://arxiv.org/abs/1906.03220
18. Gaidon, A., Wang, Q., Cabon, Y., Vig, E.: Virtual worlds as proxy for multi-object tracking analysis. In: CVPR (2016)
19. Ganin, Y., Kulkarni, T., Babuschkin, I., Eslami, S., Vinyals, O.: Synthesizing programs for images using reinforced adversarial learning. arXiv preprint arXiv:1804.01118 (2018)
20. Gao, X., Gong, R., Shu, T., Xie, X., Wang, S., Zhu, S.: VRKitchen: an interactive 3D virtual environment for task-oriented learning. arXiv arXiv:1903.05757 (2019)
21. Geiger, A., Lenz, P., Urtasun, R.: Are we ready for autonomous driving? The KITTI vision benchmark suite. In: CVPR (2012)
22. Goodfellow, I., et al.: Generative adversarial nets. In: NIPS (2014)
23. Gretton, A., Borgwardt, K.M., Rasch, M.J., Schölkopf, B., Smola, A.: A kernel two-sample test. JMLR **13**, 723–773 (2012)
24. Handa, A., Patraucean, V., Badrinarayanan, V., Stent, S., Cipolla, R.: Understanding real world indoor scenes with synthetic data. In: Proceedings of the IEEE Conference on Computer Vision and Pattern Recognition, pp. 4077–4085 (2016)
25. He, K., Gkioxari, G., Dollár, P., Girshick, R.: Mask R-CNN. In: Proceedings of the IEEE International Conference on Computer Vision, pp. 2961–2969 (2017)
26. He, K., Zhang, X., Ren, S., Sun, J.: Deep residual learning for image recognition. CoRR abs/1512.03385 (2015). http://arxiv.org/abs/1512.03385
27. Heusel, M., Ramsauer, H., Unterthiner, T., Nessler, B., Hochreiter, S.: GANs trained by a two time-scale update rule converge to a local Nash equilibrium. In: Advances in Neural Information Processing Systems, pp. 6626–6637 (2017)
28. Juliani, A., et al.: Unity: A general platform for intelligent agents. arXiv preprint arXiv:1809.02627 (2018)

29. Jyothi, A.A., Durand, T., He, J., Sigal, L., Mori, G.: LayoutVAE: stochastic scene layout generation from a label set. In: The IEEE International Conference on Computer Vision (ICCV) (October 2019)
30. Kar, A., et al.: Meta-Sim: learning to generate synthetic datasets. In: ICCV (2019)
31. Karras, T., Laine, S., Aila, T.: A style-based generator architecture for generative adversarial networks. arXiv preprint arXiv:1812.04948 (2018)
32. Kim, Y., Dyer, C., Rush, A.M.: Compound probabilistic context-free grammars for grammar induction. CoRR abs/1906.10225 (2019). http://arxiv.org/abs/1906.10225
33. Kingma, D.P., Welling, M.: Auto-encoding variational Bayes. arXiv preprint arXiv:1312.6114 (2013)
34. Kolve, E., Mottaghi, R., Gordon, D., Zhu, Y., Gupta, A., Farhadi, A.: AI2-THOR: An interactive 3D environment for visual AI. arXiv:1712.05474 (2017)
35. Kulkarni, T.D., Kohli, P., Tenenbaum, J.B., Mansinghka, V.: Picture: a probabilistic programming language for scene perception. In: Proceedings of the IEEE Conference on Computer Vision and Pattern Recognition, pp. 4390–4399 (2015)
36. Kulkarni, T.D., Whitney, W.F., Kohli, P., Tenenbaum, J.: Deep convolutional inverse graphics network. In: NIPS, pp. 2539–2547 (2015)
37. Kusner, M.J., Paige, B., Hernández-Lobato, J.M.: Grammar variational autoencoder. In: Proceedings of the 34th International Conference on Machine Learning, ICML 2017, vol. 70, pp. 1945–1954. JMLR.org (2017). http://dl.acm.org/citation.cfm?id=3305381.3305582
38. LeCun, Y.: The MNIST database of handwritten digits. http://yann.lecun.com/exdb/mnist/
39. Li, C.L., Chang, W.C., Cheng, Y., Yang, Y., Póczos, B.: MMD GAN: towards deeper understanding of moment matching network. In: NIPS (2017)
40. Li, M., et al.: Grains: generative recursive autoencoders for indoor scenes. ACM Trans. Graph. (TOG) **38**(2), 12 (2019)
41. Li, Y., Swersky, K., Zemel, R.: Generative moment matching networks. In: ICML (2015)
42. Li, Y., Vinyals, O., Dyer, C., Pascanu, R., Battaglia, P.: Learning deep generative models of graphs. arXiv preprint arXiv:1803.03324 (2018)
43. Liao, R., et al.: Efficient graph generation with graph recurrent attention networks. arXiv preprint arXiv:1910.00760 (2019)
44. Louppe, G., Cranmer, K.: Adversarial variational optimization of non-differentiable simulators. arXiv preprint arXiv:1707.07113 (2017)
45. Mansinghka, V.K., Kulkarni, T.D., Perov, Y.N., Tenenbaum, J.: Approximate Bayesian image interpretation using generative probabilistic graphics programs. In: Advances in Neural Information Processing Systems, pp. 1520–1528 (2013)
46. McCormac, J., Handa, A., Leutenegger, S., Davison, A.J.: SceneNet RGB-D: 5M photorealistic images of synthetic indoor trajectories with ground truth. arXiv preprint arXiv:1612.05079 (2016)
47. Mellor, J.F.J., et al.: Unsupervised doodling and painting with improved spiral (2019)
48. Prakash, A., et al.: Structured domain randomization: Bridging the reality gap by context-aware synthetic data. arXiv:1810.10093 (2018)
49. Puig, X., et al.: VirtualHome: simulating household activities via programs. In: CVPR (2018)
50. Qi, S., Zhu, Y., Huang, S., Jiang, C., Zhu, S.C.: Human-centric indoor scene synthesis using stochastic grammar. In: Proceedings of the IEEE Conference on Computer Vision and Pattern Recognition, pp. 5899–5908 (2018)

51. Razavi, A., van den Oord, A., Vinyals, O.: Generating diverse high-fidelity images with VQ-VAE-2. arXiv preprint arXiv:1906.00446 (2019)
52. Rezende, D.J., Mohamed, S., Wierstra, D.: Stochastic backpropagation and approximate inference in deep generative models. arXiv preprint arXiv:1401.4082 (2014)
53. Richter, S.R., Vineet, V., Roth, S., Koltun, V.: Playing for data: ground truth from computer games. In: Leibe, B., Matas, J., Sebe, N., Welling, M. (eds.) ECCV 2016. LNCS, vol. 9906, pp. 102–118. Springer, Cham (2016). https://doi.org/10.1007/978-3-319-46475-6_7
54. Ritchie, D., Wang, K., Lin, Y.A.: Fast and flexible indoor scene synthesis via deep convolutional generative models. In: The IEEE Conference on Computer Vision and Pattern Recognition (CVPR) (June 2019)
55. Ros, G., Sellart, L., Materzynska, J., Vazquez, D., Lopez, A.: The SYNTHIA dataset: a large collection of synthetic images for semantic segmentation of urban scenes. In: CVPR (2016)
56. Sadeghi, F., Levine, S.: CAD2RL: Real single-image flight without a single real image. arXiv preprint arXiv:1611.04201 (2016)
57. Savva, M., et al.: Habitat: A platform for embodied AI research. arXiv preprint arXiv:1904.01201 (2019)
58. Shugrina, M., et al.: Creative flow+ dataset. In: Proceedings of the IEEE Conference on Computer Vision and Pattern Recognition, pp. 5384–5393 (2019)
59. Song, S., Yu, F., Zeng, A., Chang, A.X., Savva, M., Funkhouser, T.: Semantic scene completion from a single depth image. In: Proceedings of 30th IEEE Conference on Computer Vision and Pattern Recognition (2017)
60. Such, F.P., Rawal, A., Lehman, J., Stanley, K.O., Clune, J.: Generative teaching networks: Accelerating neural architecture search by learning to generate synthetic training data. arXiv preprint arXiv:1912.07768 (2019)
61. Tassa, Y., et al.: DeepMind control suite. Technical report, DeepMind (January 2018). https://arxiv.org/abs/1801.00690
62. Tobin, J., Fong, R., Ray, A., Schneider, J., Zaremba, W., Abbeel, P.: Domain randomization for transferring deep neural networks from simulation to the real world. In: IROS (2017)
63. Todorov, E., Erez, T., Tassa, Y.: MuJoCo: a physics engine for model-based control. In: International Conference on Intelligent Robots and Systems (2012)
64. Wang, K., Lin, Y.A., Weissmann, B., Savva, M., Chang, A.X., Ritchie, D.: PlanIT: planning and instantiating indoor scenes with relation graph and spatial prior networks. ACM Trans. Graph. (TOG) **38**(4), 132 (2019)
65. Wang, K., Savva, M., Chang, A.X., Ritchie, D.: Deep convolutional priors for indoor scene synthesis. ACM Trans. Graph. (TOG) **37**(4), 70 (2018)
66. Wang, R., Lehman, J., Clune, J., Stanley, K.O.: Poet: open-ended coevolution of environments and their optimized solutions. In: Proceedings of the Genetic and Evolutionary Computation Conference, pp. 142–151 (2019)
67. Williams, R.J.: Simple statistical gradient-following algorithms for connectionist reinforcement learning. Mach. Learn. **8**, 229–256 (1992). https://doi.org/10.1007/BF00992696
68. Wrenninge, M., Unger, J.: SynScapes: A photorealistic synthetic dataset for street scene parsing. arXiv:1810.08705 (2018)
69. Wu, J., Tenenbaum, J.B., Kohli, P.: Neural scene de-rendering. In: IEEE Conference on Computer Vision and Pattern Recognition (CVPR) (2017)
70. Wu, Y., Wu, Y., Gkioxari, G., Tiani, Y.: Building generalizable agents with a realistic and rich 3D environment. arXiv arXiv:1801.02209 (2018)

71. Yin, P., Neubig, G.: A syntactic neural model for general-purpose code generation. CoRR abs/1704.01696 (2017). http://arxiv.org/abs/1704.01696
72. Yin, P., Zhou, C., He, J., Neubig, G.: StructVAE: Tree-structured latent variable models for semi-supervised semantic parsing. CoRR abs/1806.07832 (2018). http://arxiv.org/abs/1806.07832
73. You, J., Ying, R., Ren, X., Hamilton, W., Leskovec, J.: GraphRNN: generating realistic graphs with deep auto-regressive models. In: International Conference on Machine Learning, pp. 5694–5703 (2018)
74. Yu, L.F., Yeung, S.K., Tang, C.K., Terzopoulos, D., Chan, T.F., Osher, S.: Make it home: automatic optimization of furniture arrangement. ACM Trans. Graph. **30**(4), 86 (2011)
75. Zhang, Y., et al.: Physically-based rendering for indoor scene understanding using convolutional neural networks. In: The IEEE Conference on Computer Vision and Pattern Recognition (CVPR) (July 2017)
76. Zhou, Y., While, Z., Kalogerakis, E.: SceneGraphNet: neural message passing for 3D indoor scene augmentation. In: The IEEE International Conference on Computer Vision (ICCV) (October 2019)

A Generic Visualization Approach
for Convolutional Neural Networks

Ahmed Taha$^{(\boxtimes)}$, Xitong Yang, Abhinav Shrivastava, and Larry Davis

University of Maryland, College Park, USA
ahmdtaha@umd.edu

Abstract. Retrieval networks are essential for searching and indexing. Compared to classification networks, attention visualization for retrieval networks is hardly studied. We formulate attention visualization as a constrained optimization problem. We leverage the unit L2-Norm constraint as an attention filter (L2-CAF) to localize attention in both classification and retrieval networks. Unlike recent literature, our approach requires neither architectural changes nor fine-tuning. Thus, a pre-trained network's performance is never undermined.

L2-CAF is quantitatively evaluated using weakly supervised object localization. State-of-the-art results are achieved on classification networks. For retrieval networks, significant improvement margins are achieved over a Grad-CAM baseline. Qualitative evaluation demonstrates how the L2-CAF visualizes attention per frame for a recurrent retrieval network. Further ablation studies highlight the computational cost of our approach and compare L2-CAF with other feasible alternatives. Code available at https://bit.ly/3iDBLFv.

1 Introduction

Both classification and retrieval neural networks need attention visualization tools. These tools are important in medical and autonomous navigation to understand and interpret networks' decisions. Moreover, attention visualization enables weakly supervised object localization (WSOL) which reduces the cost of data annotation. WSOL avoids bounding-box labeling required by fully supervised approaches. Attention visualization and WSOL have been intensively studied for classification architectures [7,32,34,44,45,48]. However, these approaches do not address retrieval networks. In this paper, we leverage the unit L2-Norm constraint as an attention filter (L2-CAF) that works for both classification and retrieval neural networks, as shown in Figure 1.

For classification networks, Zhou *et al.* [48] propose class activation maps (CAM) for attention visualization and WSOL. Further research [7,34,45,46] improved WSOL by augmenting the most discriminative region with other less

Electronic supplementary material The online version of this chapter (https://doi.org/10.1007/978-3-030-58520-4_43) contains supplementary material, which is available to authorized users.

A. Vedaldi et al. (Eds.): ECCV 2020, LNCS 12362, pp. 734–750, 2020.
https://doi.org/10.1007/978-3-030-58520-4_43

Class-oblivious   Class-specific   Class-oblivious   Class-specific

Fig. 1. L2-CAF enables both class-oblivious and class-specific visualizations. This separates our work from dominant literature that targets classification networks only. The supplementary video shows more vivid and challenging visualizations.

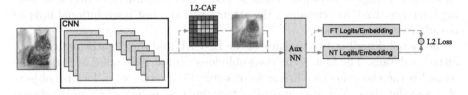

Fig. 2. An overview of the proposed unit L2-Norm constrained attention filter (L2-CAF). Given a pre-trained CNN with an auxiliary head (Aux NN), feed an input frame through a normal feed-forward pass (green solid path) to generate the network output logits/embedding $NT(x)$. Then, feed the same input again but multiply the last convolutional feature map by a constrained attention filter f (orange dashed path) to generate a new filtered output $FT(x, f)$. Optimize the filter's weights through gradient descent to minimize the difference between $NT(x)$ and $FT(x, f)$. In standard CNN architectures, the L2-CAF is typically 7×7, *i.e.*, a cheap optimization problem $\in R^{49}$. (Color figure online)

discriminative parts, *e.g.*, augment a cat's head with its legs. This improvement comes at the cost of few drawbacks: (1) They impose architectural constraints, *e.g.*, global average pooling (GAP) layer; (2) While fine-tuning boosts localization efficiency, it degrades classification accuracy. Grad-CAM [32] avoids these limitations, but it is originally formulated for classification networks.

Retrieval networks are essential for visual search [19,25], zero-shot learning [3,43,47], and fine-grained retrieval [26,36]. The large metric learning [6,26,40] and product quantization [4,9,23] literature reflect their importance. Despite that, attention visualization for retrieval networks has not been evaluated quantitatively. It is more challenging compared to classification due to the network's output – a class-oblivious embedding.

The <u>main contribution</u> of this paper is to leverage the L2-CAF as a visualization filter to identify key features of both classification and retrieval networks' output. Figure 2 illustrates the approach. Given a pre-trained CNN, feeding the same input x through the network (green solid path) will always generate the same output $NT(x)$. If the final convolutional feature map is multiplied by a constrained attention filter f in an element-wise manner (orange dashed path), the network generates a filtered output $FT(x, f)$. Through gradient descent, we optimize f to minimize the L2 loss $L = ||NT(x) - FT(x, f)||^2$. The optimized

filter f reveals key spatial regions, *e.g.*, the cat's head. The filter size (f_w, f_h) depends on the convolution layer size, *e.g.*, the last convolution layer in standard CNNs $\in R^{7 \times 7}$.

This approach imposes no constraints on the network architecture besides having a convolution layer. The input can be a regular image or a pre-extracted convolutional feature. The network output can be logits trained with softmax or a feature embedding trained with a ranking loss. Furthermore, this approach neither changes the original network weights nor requires fine-tuning. Thus, network performance remains intact. The visualization filter is applied only when an attention map is required. Thus, it poses no computational overhead during inference. L2-CAF visualizes the attention of the last convolutional layer of GoogLeNet within 0.3 s.

Section 3 describes two variants of the L2-CAF and their mathematical optimization details. The first is the class-oblivious variant illustrated in Fig. 2. The second is the class-specific variant for classification networks to localize objects of a specific class. We also present a technique to reduce the computational cost of the L2-CAF's optimization formulation. We benchmark our approach quantitatively using WSOL for both classification and retrieval architectures.

In summary, the key contributions of this paper are:

1. A novel attention visualization approach for *both* classification and retrieval networks (Sect. 3). This approach achieves state-of-the-art WSOL results using classification architectures (Sect. 4.1).
2. A modified Grad-CAM to better support WSOL on retrieval networks (Sect. 4.2); L2-CAF achieves significant localization improvement margins, up to an absolute 36%, compared to the vanilla Grad-CAM.
3. A method to visualize attention for video frames that are temporally fused using a recurrent network (Sect. 4.3).

2   Related Work

This section briefly reviews weakly supervised object localization (WSOL) for classification networks. Grad-CAM is reviewed in the WSOL retrieval evaluation Sect. 4.2. The supplementary material reviews different ranking losses (*e.g.*, N-pair). Figure 3 presents a high-level categorization of WSOL approaches in terms of (1) supported architectures; (2) whether fine-tuning is required or not? The experiment section provides further one-to-one comparisons.

Classification networks' attention visualization increases interpretability and enables WSOL. CAM [48] and Grad-CAM [32] identify the most discriminative spatial region. To boost WSOL performance, [7,34,45,46] propose architectural modifications to augment the most discriminative region with less-discriminative object regions. This is achieved by fine-tuning a pre-trained network while hiding the most discriminative region stochastically. This forces the network to recognize other informative regions and thus improve WSOL. To detect and hide the most discriminative region while fine-tuning, a network is assumed to use

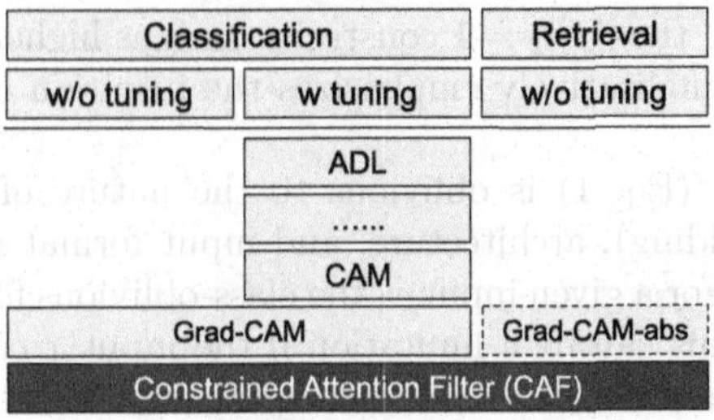

Fig. 3. An overview of weakly supervised object localization (WSOL) approaches for classification and retrieval networks. Some approaches impose architectural constraints and require fine-tuning, *e.g.*, CAM and ADL.

global average pooling (GAP) [7,34,48] or an equivalent 1×1 feature reduction convolution layer [45]. This fine-tuning paradigm tends to degrade classification performance.

3   Constrained Attention Filter (CAF)

This section presents two variants for optimizing the proposed L2-CAF. The first variant, *class-oblivious*, works for both classification and retrieval CNNs. It generates a single heatmap per frame. The second variant, *class-specific*, works for classification CNNs and generates class-specific heatmaps per frame. Both variants impose no architectural constraints in terms of spatial pooling (GAP, FCN) or temporal fusing components (RNN, LSTM).

3.1   Class-Oblivious Variant

Given a pre-trained network and an input $x \in R^{W \times H \times 3}$, the last convolution layer provides a feature map $A \in R^{w \times h \times k}$, with size $w \times h$ and k channels. The network's output $NT(x)$, logits or embedding, depends on discriminative features in A. We optimize an L2 normalized filter f to identify the discriminative features to the network's output $NT(x)$. After multiplying A by the filter f $\left(A \odot f = A' \in R^{w \times h \times k}\right)$, the network generates a filtered output $FT(x, f)$. While fixing the network's weights and input, we optimize f to minimize

$$L = ||NT(x) - FT(x, f)||^2, \quad \text{subject to} \quad ||f||_2 = 1, \tag{1}$$

$FT(x, f)$ equals $NT(x)$ if and only if $f = f_I = \{1\}^{w \times h}$ which is infeasible due to the unit L2-Norm constraint.

Intuition: An ideal heatmap can be regarded as a filter that approximates $NT(x)$ by blocking irrelevant features in A. Accordingly, we seek a filter f that *spatially* prioritizes convolutional features and *flexibly* captures irregular (*e.g.*, discontinuous) shapes or multiple different agents in a frame. The L2-Norm, a simple *multi-mode* differentiable filter, satisfies these requirements. On account

of irrelevant features, the $||f||_2 = 1$ constraint assigns higher weights to relevant features. Figure 11 qualitatively emphasizes the intuition behind the L2-Norm constraint.

This formulation (Eq. 1) is oblivious to the nature of the network's output (logits or embedding), architecture, and input format (RGB image or pre-extracted features). For a given input x, the class-oblivious formulation generates a single heatmap. This can be a limitation if the input x contains objects from different classes. The next subsection tackles this limitation by offering an alternative class-specific optimization formulation.

3.2 Class-Specific Variant

To support class-specific heatmaps per input, we first assume a classification CNN architecture with class-specific logits. We learn the attention for class c by optimizing the L2-CAF f using the following loss function

$$L_c = -FT_c(x, f) + \sum_{i=0,\ i \neq c}^{N} FT_i(x, f), \quad \text{subject to} \quad ||f||_2 = 1, \qquad (2)$$

where $FT_c(x, f)$ is the filtered output's logit for class c and N is the total number of classes. This loss maximizes the output logit for the intended class c while minimizing the output logits for all other classes.

Figure 1 presents a qualitative comparison between the class-oblivious and class-specific variants. For example, the first example shows an image of a butterfly standing on a mastiff's nose. The first image shows the resulting heatmap from optimizing Eq. 1. The following two images show the result heatmaps from optimizing Eq. 2 for the mastiff and butterfly classes, respectively. In these examples, the L2-CAF is applied to the last convolutional layer.

Technical Details: To compute the class-oblivious heatmap for an input x, we utilize gradient descent for l iterations. At iteration i, L^i is computed using the filter $\frac{f^i}{||f^i||_2}$. The filter f is initialized randomly, i.e., $f^1 \in [0, 1]^{w \times h}$. Gradient descent iteratively updates f to minimize L. We terminate when L converges and remains approximately the same for d iterations. Concretely, we terminate the gradient descent at $i = l$ when $\left| L^l - L^{l-d} \right| < \epsilon$ where $\epsilon = 10^{-5}$ and $d = 50$. This constrained minimization formulation is non-convex, so we also impose a maximum number of iterations L_{max} to avoid oscillating between local minima. After termination, the heatmap is generated by resizing $\frac{|f|^l}{||f^i||_2}$ to the input's size. The same procedure is used for class-specific heatmaps with L_c (Eq. 2). For more details, please refer to our released code.

Timing: To optimize the small (e.g., 7×7) L2-CAF using gradient descent, the vanilla L2-CAF requires multiple feed-forward and backpropagation passes through the network. This is affordable for lightweight networks like MobileNet [16] and GoogLeNet (InceptionV1) [37] but computationally expensive for bulky networks like VGG [33] and DenseNet [17]. We propose a technique

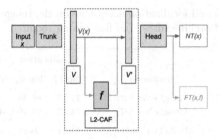

Fig. 4. Reduce the computational optimization cost of the L2-CAF f by solving an equivalent sub-problem (blue-dashed). Instead of using the network's endpoints (x, $NT(x)$), use ($V(x)$, $V'(x)$) to optimize f.

to reduce this cost through (1) making a single feed-forward pass through the whole network to compute the network's output at every layer, (2) optimizing the L2-CAF f using a small subset of layers.

Figure 4 illustrates this technique. Instead of optimizing the filter f through the network's endpoints (x, $NT(x)$), it is equivalent to use the outputs of the direct pre and post layers (V, V') to the attention filter. For a given input x, these layers' outputs ($V(x)$, $V'(x)$) require a single feedforward pass through the whole network. Once computed, the loss function from Eq. 1 becomes

$$L = ||V'(x) - FT(V(x), f)||^2, \quad \text{subject to} \quad ||f||_2 = 1. \tag{3}$$

To generate class-specific heatmaps for a classification network, $V'(x)$ must be the network's logits $NT(x)$. Since it is typical to visualize the attention of the last convolution layer, this formulation skips the overhead of a network's trunk and significantly reduces the computational cost. The speed-up of this technique is quantified through an ablation study.

The fast L2-CAF approach is a computationally cheaper alternative to sampling [27,35] and masking [10,11] approaches. In addition, the L2-CAF has a smaller set of hyper-parameters. For instance, while both L2-CAF and masking [10,11] approaches require a stopping criterion for an optimization problem, Fong *et al.* [10] evaluate multiple mask-sizes per image. Furthermore, the fast L2-CAF works on a small subset of network layers, *i.e.*, independent of the network backbone. Thus, it compares favorably for video processing. For $3D$ volumes (*e.g.*, medical images), our optimization problem remains independent of the network size, *i.e.*, $\in R^{7 \times 7 \times 7}$.

4 Experiments

The next two subsections present L2-CAF's quantitative evaluation using classification and retrieval networks, respectively. Then, a recurrent retrieval network qualitatively illustrates L2-CAF's potential for video applications. Finally, we present our ablation studies.

Table 1. Classification and localization accuracies on the ImageNet (ILSVRC) validation set using standard architectures – no fine-tuning required.

		Classification		Localization	
Method	Backbone	Top 1↑	Top 5↑	Top 1↑	Top 5↑
Grad-CAM	GoogLeNet [37]	71.17	86.39	44.43	57.50
L2-CAF (ours)	GoogLeNet [37]	71.17	86.39	**45.48**	**59.32**
Grad-CAM	ResNetV2-50 [14]	71.51	86.56	46.57	59.96
L2-CAF (ours)	ResNetV2-50 [14]	71.51	86.56	**48.18**	**62.38**
Grad-CAM	DenseNet-161 [17]	78.20	91.39	49.28	**66.57**
L2-CAF (ours)	DenseNet-161 [17]	78.20	91.39	**49.68**	65.28

4.1   WSOL Using Classification Networks

The L2-CAF is quantitatively evaluated using WSOL on both *standard* and *fine-tuned* classification architectures. We leverage the ImageNet validation set [8] for evaluation on standard architectures. For fined-tuned architectures, we follow ADL [7] evaluation procedure and utilize both ImageNet [8] and CUB-200-2011 [39] datasets. In all experiments, we use the fast L2-CAF technique. The loss in Eq. 2 is minimized using the last convolution layer and the network's logits (before softmax) as endpoints.

Evaluation Using Standard Architectures is performed using both the top-1 and top-5 predictions. Similar to [32], we obtain the top predictions for every image, then, optimize our filter f to learn the corresponding heatmap for every prediction. Following Zhou *et al.* [48], we segment the heatmap using a simple thresholding technique. This generates connected segments of pixels; we draw a bounding box around the largest segment. Localization is correct if the predicted class is correct and the intersection over union (IoU) between the ground truth and estimated bounding boxes is ≥50%. Table 1 compares L2-CAF and Grad-CAM using three architectures. Both approaches are applied to the last 7×7 convolution layer. We fix the architecture and evaluate different localization approaches – same classification but different localization performance.

L2-CAF Versus Grad-CAM: Grad-CAM is 5 times faster than L2-CAF on DenseNet-161 (7 times on GoogLeNet). Both approaches support a large variety of architectures. In terms of localization accuracy, L2-CAF compares favorably to Grad-CAM. Fong and Vedaldi [11] explain why gradient-based approaches like Grad-CAM are not optimal for visualization. They show that neural networks' gradients $\frac{\partial y}{\partial x}$ are independent of the input image x for linear classifiers ($y = wx + b$; $\frac{\partial y}{\partial x} = w$). For non-linear architectures, this problem is reduced but not eliminated. They also show qualitatively that gradient saliency maps contain strong responses in irrelevant image regions. We hypothesize that DenseNet-

Table 2. Classification and localization accuracies on the CUB-200-2011 test and ImageNet validation split using fine-tuned architectures. The accuracy with an asterisk* indicates that the score is from the original paper.

			CUB-200-2011		ImageNet	
Method	Backbone	Tuning	CLS ↑	LOC ↑	CLS ↑	LOC ↑
CAM	VGG-GAP	GAP	68.53	45.66	69.96	43.46
L2-CAF (ours)	VGG-GAP	GAP	68.53	46.01	69.96	44.09
Fuse 2 CAMs	VGG-GAP	ACoL [45]	71.90	45.90*	67.50	**45.83***
CAM	VGG-GAP	ADL	64.16	48.27	69.58	42.93
L2-CAF (ours)	VGG-GAP	ADL	64.16	**48.55**	69.58	43.27
CAM	ResNet50-SE	ADL	78.94	**61.71**	76.218	49.90
L2-CAF (ours)	ResNet50-SE	ADL	78.94	61.16	76.218	**50.49**

161's better classification accuracy and, accordingly, better gradient closes the localization performance gap.

Evaluation Using Fine-Tuned Architectures is performed using the top-1 accuracy on fine-tuned architectures (*e.g.*, VGG-GAP [48]); this follows the evaluation procedure in attention-based dropout layer (ADL) [7]. ADL is the current state-of-the-art method for WSOL. During fine-tuning, ADL applies dropout at multiple network stages. It is not straightforward to determine where to plug these extra dropout layers – it is network dependent. Therefore, we leverage their publicly released VGG-GAP and ResNet50-SE implementations to evaluate our approach. The ACoL performance is reported from the original paper.

Table 2 presents a quantitative evaluation using CUB-200-2011 and ImageNet datasets. The first column denotes the object localization approach, *e.g.*, CAM versus L2-CAF. Grad-CAM is dropped because it is equivalent to CAM when a GAP layer is utilized [32]. In the second column (backbone), all the architectures utilize a global average pooling or an equivalent surrogate [45]. The third column denotes the fine-tuning approaches considered: GAP [48], ACol [45], ADL [7]. We fine-tune the VGG-GAP architecture with both GAP and ADL. L2-CAF consistently outperforms CAM's localization on the ImageNet validation set.

Relation with WSOL Approaches (*e.g.*, **ADL**): To generate class activation maps (CAMs), WSOL approaches employ a global average pooling layer (GAP) [7,34,46,48], or equivalent [45]. L2-CAF relaxes this architectural requirement. Thus, while supporting previous WSOL approaches, L2-CAF introduces a new degree of freedom. This flexibility is vital to explore attention visualization and WSOL beyond standard supervised classification networks.

4.2 WSOL Using Retrieval Networks

Weakly supervised object localization provides a quantitative evaluation metric for attention visualization approaches. The ability to localize attention for

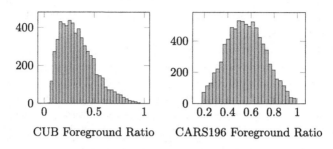

CUB Foreground Ratio   CARS196 Foreground Ratio

Fig. 5. Histogram of the foreground objects' bounding box size relative to the whole image in CUB and CARS196 datasets. CUB birds tend to occupy less than 50% of the whole image (left-skewed), while the Stanford cars are normally distributed.

various architectures is a core advantage of L2-CAF. In this subsection, we quantitatively evaluate L2-CAF against Grad-CAM. We employ the class oblivious formulation (Eq. 1) using the last convolution layer and the raw embedding (before unit-circle normalized) as endpoints.

Datasets: We employ CUB-200-2011 birds [39] and Stanford CARS196 [21] retrieval datasets, *i.e.*, standard retrieval datasets [6,26,40,41]. Both datasets provide the ground truth bounding box annotation. They pose several challenges for foreground objects' localization. Birds are not naturally rectangular; discriminative parts (*e.g.*, head [5]) occupy a small part of the body. Cars pose a similar challenge in terms of relatively smaller discriminative parts (*e.g.*, wheel) relative to the whole body. Figure 5 depicts the ratio of the ground truth bounding box to the whole image size for both datasets.

Evaluation Metrics: For retrieval, we utilize both Recall@1 (R@1) and the Normalized Mutual Information (NMI) metrics. For localization, we follow the same evaluation procedure in [32,48] for classification networks. We replace the top-1 by R@1 metric to decide if the network's output is correct or not. The same IoU > 50% criterion is used to evaluate localization.

Vanilla Grad-CAM Baseline: To evaluate L2-CAF quantitatively, we extend the classification Grad-CAM to deal with retrieval networks. The Grad-CAM class-discriminative localization map M^c has been proposed as follows

Table 3. Triplet (TL) and N-pair (NP) losses' quantitative retrieval evaluation using NMI and Recall@1 on CUB-200-2011 and CARS196. Quantitative localization accuracy evaluation using the 0.5 intersection over union (IoU) criterion. $\triangle$ column indicates the absolute localization improvement margin relative to the vanilla Grad-CAM.

| | | | CUB-200-2011 | | | | CARS196 | | | |
| | | | Retrieval | | Localization | | Retrieval | | Localization | |
Method	Backbone	Loss	NMI↑	R@1↑	LOC↑	$\triangle$	NMI↑	R@1↑	LOC↑	$\triangle$
Grad-CAM	GoogLeNet	TL	0.582	47.75	20.63	-	0.532	54.55	32.38	-
Grad-CAM-abs	GoogLeNet	TL	0.582	47.75	22.96	+2.33	0.532	54.55	46.21	+13.82
L2-CAF (ours)	GoogLeNet	TL	0.582	47.75	**29.63**	+9.00	0.532	54.55	**54.10**	+21.72
Grad-CAM	ResNet	TL	0.601	50.06	16.15	-	0.565	61.55	31.77	-
Grad-CAM-abs	ResNet	TL	0.601	50.06	29.49	+13.34	0.565	61.55	56.32	+24.55
L2-CAF (ours)	ResNet	TL	0.601	50.06	**39.28**	+23.13	0.565	61.55	**61.27**	+29.50
Grad-CAM	GoogLeNet	NP	0.583	48.95	14.13	-	0.597	65.23	28.29	-
Grad-CAM-abs	GoogLeNet	NP	0.583	48.95	19.87	+5.74	0.597	65.23	55.01	+26.72
L2-CAF (ours)	GoogLeNet	NP	0.583	48.95	**30.50**	+16.37	0.593	65.23	**64.85**	+36.56
Grad-CAM	ResNet	NP	0.580	47.92	11.92	-	0.609	67.61	32.42	-
Grad-CAM-abs	ResNet	NP	0.580	47.92	26.67	+14.75	0.609	67.61	61.62	+29.20
L2-CAF (ours)	ResNet	NP	0.580	47.92	**38.69**	+26.77	0.609	67.61	**67.35**	+34.93

Image   Grad-CAM   Grad-CAM-abs   L2-CAF

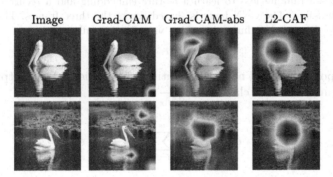

Fig. 6. Qualitative attention evaluation for different visualization approaches on retrieval networks. Both Grad-CAM variants suffer near images' corners.

$$M^c = RELU\left(\sum_k \alpha_k^c A^k\right) \tag{4}$$

$$\alpha_k^c = \frac{1}{w \times h} \sum_{i=0}^{w} \sum_{j=0}^{h} \frac{\partial y^c}{\partial A_{i,j}^k}, \tag{5}$$

where $M^c \in R^{w \times h}$ for any class c, $A \in R^{w \times h \times k}$ is a convolutional feature map with k channels. $\alpha^c \in R^k$ quantifies the kth channel's importance for a target class c. Basically, $\sum_k \alpha_k^c A^k$ provides a weighted sum of the feature maps (A) for class c. α_k^c is computed using the gradient of the score for class y^c with respect to the feature maps A^k.

Fig. 7. Qualitative localization evaluation on CUB-200-2011 and CARS196 using a retrieval network trained with a triplet loss. The green and blue bounding boxes indicate the ground truth and the L2-CAF bounding boxes, respectively. (Color figure online)

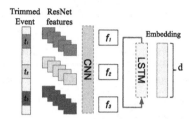

Fig. 8. A convolution architecture to embed autonomous navigation videos. This network employs a ranking loss to learn a feature embedding and a recurrent layer for temporal modeling. The CNN layer is shared across the three frames. The attention filters (f_1, f_2, f_3) are used during attention visualization only.

To support a retrieval network, we utilize the gradient of the output embedding $\frac{\partial y}{\partial A_{i,j}^k}$ instead of the class score $\frac{\partial y^c}{\partial A_{i,j}^k}$ as follows

$$\alpha_k^y = \frac{1}{w \times h} \sum_{i=0}^{w} \sum_{j=0}^{h} \frac{\partial y}{\partial A_{i,j}^k}, \tag{6}$$

we denote this formulation as *vanilla Grad-CAM* for retrieval. We compute $\frac{\partial y}{\partial A_{i,j}^k}$ using tf.gradients [1].

Grad-CAM-abs Baseline: The Vanilla Grad-CAM is largely inferior for retrieval networks because of the *RELU* in Eq. 4. *RELU* is introduced for classification networks to emphasize feature maps that have a positive influence on the class of interest y^c, assuming pixels with negative gradient belong to other classes. This assumption is valid for classification but invalid for retrieval. Therefore, we further modify the Grad-CAM formulation by replacing the *RELU* with the absolute function *abs*. This Grad-CAM-abs baseline is defined as follows

$$M_{abs}^y = abs\left(\sum_k \alpha_k^y A^k\right). \tag{7}$$

Implementation Details are reported in the supplementary material.

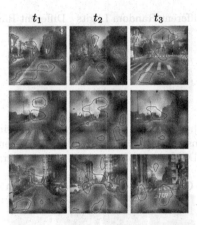

Fig. 9. The recurrent network's attention visualization at different time steps using heatmaps. Each row depicts three frames sampled from an action video. Contours highlight regions with higher attention. The network attends to the spatial locations of traffic lights and road signs. This figure is best viewed on a screen (color and zoom).

Results: Table 3 presents a quantitative evaluation for both retrieval and localization performance. ResNet-50 has more parameters than GoogLeNet; and is marginally better in terms of retrieval. Generally, N-pair loss outperforms triplet loss. Cars are rectangular and thus simpler than CUB birds for bounding box localization. The localization error is highly correlated and upper-bounded by the retrieval performance (R@1). Grad-CAM-abs outperforms the vanilla Grad-CAM for retrieval. L2-CAF brings further localization improvement.

Figure 6 qualitatively compares different localization approaches. We found that feature maps at the images' corners can have a high positive gradient, while the feature maps at the foreground object can have a high negative gradient. It is a common practice to embed images into the unit-circle, *i.e.*, some images are embedded in the negative space. When this happens, the vanilla Grad-CAM ignores the foreground objects. Grad-CAM-abs handles negative gradient better but still suffers around the corners. Grad-CAM inferior behavior around the corner is qualitatively reported in [10]. This undesirable behavior degrades Grad-CAM's WSOL performance. Figure 7 shows a qualitative localization evaluation on both datasets. For CUB-200-2011, our estimated bounding box (blue) tends to be centered around the birds' heads.

4.3   Recurrent Networks' Attention

This subsection illustrates how to visualize attention for temporally fused video frames through the Honda driving dataset (HDD) [29]. HDD is a video dataset for reasoning about drivers' actions (events) like crossing intersections, making left and right turns. A key objective is modeling the subtle intra-action (events) variations without explicit fine-grained labeling. For instance, an autonomous

Pretrained   Different Random Logits   Different Random Weights

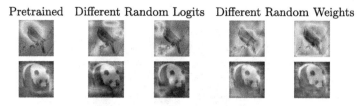

Fig. 10. Sanity checks [2]. First column visualizes attention using a pretrained network–nothing random. Columns two to five visualize attention when logits and weights (all-layers) are randomized. Different random initializations generate different heatmaps.

Original L2-CAF Softmax Gaussian

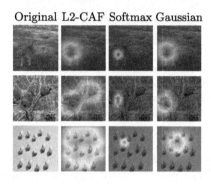

Fig. 11. Qualitative evaluation for alternative constraints. Softmax offers a sparse result while the Gaussian filter assumes a single mode. L2-CAF supports multi-mode. The supplementary material shows more vivid visualizations for the L2-CAF, randomly initialized, converging in slow motion.

navigation application with a left-turn query video should differentiate smooth left-turns maneuvers from those interrupted by crossing pedestrians. A retrieval network models these intra-action variations through a feature embedding.

Figure 8 presents a recurrent retrieval network for video embedding. Given a trimmed video event, three frames are sampled at t_1, t_2, and t_3. To enable a large training mini-batch for triplet loss, a pre-trained ResNet is employed to extract convolutional features for every frame. The extracted ResNet features are fed into a trainable shallow CNN. The resulting convolutional features are temporally fused using an LSTM [12,15].

After training, we employ three L2-CAF filters (f_1, f_2, and f_3) to visualize attention, *i.e.*, one filter per frame. These filters are inserted between the shallow CNN and the LSTM layers *during inference only*. To ground attention in each frame, we optimize each filter independently. Concretely, we pass the first frame's features through f_1 and optimize f_1 while feeding the second and third frames' features normally, *i.e.*, f_2 and f_3 are inactive. After f_1 converges, we deactivate it and optimize the next filter f_2 and so on. After optimizing all filters, each filter provides an attention map for the corresponding frame.

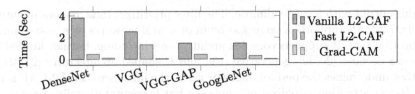

Fig. 12. Time analysis for the L2-CAF. The fast L2-CAF brings a significant speed-up while solving the same optimization problem.

Figure 9 presents our qualitative evaluation. In the first row at t_3, the network attention is drawn to the traffic lights and double yellow lane marks. Similarly, the second row shows attention drawn toward the traffic light at $t_{1,2}$. The final row shows an interesting case at t_3 where the attention is drawn to the stop sign and also to the frame's top center, which is the typical location for a traffic light. Through visualization, we can see that the network uses traffic lights, signs, and road signs as discriminative features. We found that a Mast Arm (L-shaped) traffic light is easier to detect by a neural network compared to a straight pole traffic light. The variable height of a straight pole traffic light poses a challenge for neural networks. For instance, the network attends to the right side of the frame multiple times at different heights in the second row at $t_{1,2}$.

4.4   Ablation Study

This subsection provides sanity checks for saliency maps [2], then evaluates alternative attention constraints, and finally presents a timing analysis.

Sanity Checks: Figure 10 shows how L2-CAF is affected by randomly initialized logits-layer or weights (all layers). Sanity checks [2] emphasize a high dependency between the optimized L2-CAF (heatmap) and the network's weights.

Alternative Attention Constraints: We qualitatively compare the L2-CAF with both softmax and Gaussian constraints. These are selected for their differentiability, simplicity, and usability in recent literature. Other filtering alternatives (*e.g.*, L1-Norm) are also feasible. Softmax is a typical attention mechanism for image captioning [18,42] and machine translation [38]. In these problems, the softmax attention module is employed *recurrently* on a single image frame or an input sentence for every output word. This fits the softmax's sparse nature. Gaussian filters have been utilized for temporal action localization [24,28]. They are denser (more relaxed) compared to softmax but also assume a single mode (elliptical shape). To localize objects in images using a Gaussian constraint, we optimize the filter's mean $\mu \in R^2$ while fixing the covariance matrix $\sigma \in R^{2\times 2}$ to the identity matrix. σ must be constrained to avoid a degenerate solution where the Gaussian becomes a uniform distribution, *i.e.*, $\sigma \to \infty$. All filters are optimized using the class-oblivious formulation (Sect. 3.1).

Figure 11 provides a qualitative evaluation using GoogLeNet architecture and three attention constraints. The L2-CAF identifies key region(s) for a net-

work's output with a single glimpse. The filter prioritizes these regions quantitatively. L2-CAF supports a large spectrum of neural networks as a post-training inspection tool. It supports complex architectures including, but not limited to, encoder-decoder [20,30], generative [13], and U-shaped architectures [22,31]. It neither undermines the performance nor raises the inference cost. L2-CAF is not the fastest attention visualization approach but is computationally cheap.

Timing Analysis: Speed is the main limitation of our iterative formulation. Figure 12 presents a timing analysis for L2-CAF. The y-axis denotes the processing time per frame in seconds. The vanilla L2-CAF uses the default endpoints $(x, NT(x))$, while the fast L2-CAF uses the output of the last convolution layer and the logits $NT(x)$ as endpoints. The vanilla and fast L2-CAF are equivalent optimization problems but the fast L2-CAF provides a significant speed-up. The three fully connected layers in VGG, between the last convolution layer and the logits, limit the fast optimization technique. VGG-GAP replaces these fully connected layers with an average pooling layer, so its speed is similar to GoogLeNet. Fast L2-CAF takes $\approx$ 0.4 and 0.3 s per frame on VGG-GAP and GoogLeNet, respectively. The DenseNet-161's speed-up is maximum because the fast L2-CAF skips all dense blocks before the last convolution layer.

5   Conclusion

We have introduced the unit L2-Norm constrained attention filter (L2-CAF) as a visualization tool that works for a large spectrum of neural networks. L2-CAF neither requires fine-tuning nor imposes architectural constraints. Weakly supervised object localization is utilized for quantitative evaluation. State-of-the-art results are achieved on both standard and fine-tuned classification architectures. For retrieval networks, L2-CAF significantly outperforms Grad-CAM baselines. Ablation studies highlight L2-CAF's superiority to alternative constraints and analyze L2-CAF's computational cost.

Acknowledgments:. This work was partially funded by independent grants from Office of Naval Research (N000141612713) and Facebook AI.

References

1. tf.gradients. https://www.tensorflow.org/api_docs/python/tf/gradients
2. Adebayo, J., Gilmer, J., Muelly, M., Goodfellow, I., Hardt, M., Kim, B.: Sanity checks for saliency maps. In: NIPS (2018)
3. Bucher, M., Herbin, S., Jurie, F.: Improving semantic embedding consistency by metric learning for zero-shot classification. In: Leibe, B., Matas, J., Sebe, N., Welling, M. (eds.) Computer Vision – ECCV 2016. Lecture Notes in Computer Science, vol. 9909, pp. 730–746. Springer, Cham (2016). https://doi.org/10.1007/978-3-319-46454-1_44
4. Cao, Y., Long, M., Wang, J., Zhu, H., Wen, Q.: Deep quantization network for efficient image retrieval. In: AAAI (2016)

5. Chen, C., Li, O., Tao, C., Barnett, A.J., Su, J., Rudin, C.: This looks like that: deep learning for interpretable image recognition. In: NeurIPS (2018)

6. Chen, W., Chen, X., Zhang, J., Huang, K.: Beyond triplet loss: a deep quadruplet network for person re-identification. In: CVPR (2017)

7. Choe, J., Shim, H.: Attention-based dropout layer for weakly supervised object localization. In: CVPR (2019)

8. Deng, J., Dong, W., Socher, R., Li, L.J., Li, K., Fei-Fei, L.: ImageNet: a large-scale hierarchical image database. In: CVPR (2009)

9. Eghbali, S., Tahvildari, L.: Deep spherical quantization for image search. In: CVPR (2019)

10. Fong, R., Patrick, M., Vedaldi, A.: Understanding deep networks via extremal perturbations and smooth masks. In: ICCV (2019)

11. Fong, R.C., Vedaldi, A.: Interpretable explanations of black boxes by meaningful perturbation. In: ICCV (2017)

12. Funahashi, K.i., Nakamura, Y.: Approximation of dynamical systems by continuous time recurrent neural networks. Neural Netw. **16**, 801–806 (1993)

13. Goodfellow, I., et al.: Generative adversarial nets. In: NIPS (2014)

14. He, K., Zhang, X., Ren, S., Sun, J.: Identity mappings in deep residual networks. In: Leibe, B., Matas, J., Sebe, N., Welling, M. (eds.) ECCV 2016. LNCS, vol. 9908, pp. 630–645. Springer, Cham (2016). https://doi.org/10.1007/978-3-319-46493-0_38

15. Hochreiter, S., Schmidhuber, J.: Long short-term memory. Neural Comput. **9**, 1735–1780 (1997)

16. Howard, A.G., et al.: MobileNets: efficient convolutional neural networks for mobile vision applications. arXiv preprint arXiv:1704.04861 (2017)

17. Huang, G., Liu, Z., Van Der Maaten, L., Weinberger, K.Q.: Densely connected convolutional networks. In: CVPR (2017)

18. Kazemi, V., Elqursh, A.: Show, ask, attend, and answer: a strong baseline for visual question answering. arXiv preprint arXiv:1704.03162 (2017)

19. Kim, S., Seo, M., Laptev, I., Cho, M., Kwak, S.: Deep metric learning beyond binary supervision. In: CVPR (2019)

20. Kingma, D.P., Welling, M.: Auto-encoding variational Bayes. arXiv preprint arXiv:1312.6114 (2013)

21. Krause, J., Stark, M., Deng, J., Fei-Fei, L.: 3D object representations for fine-grained categorization. In: ICCVW (2013)

22. Li, J., Lo, P., Taha, A., Wu, H., Zhao, T.: Segmentation of renal structures for image-guided surgery. In: Frangi, A.F., Schnabel, J.A., Davatzikos, C., Alberola-López, C., Fichtinger, G. (eds.) MICCAI 2018. LNCS, vol. 11073, pp. 454–462. Springer, Cham (2018). https://doi.org/10.1007/978-3-030-00937-3_52

23. Li, Q., Sun, Z., He, R., Tan, T.: Deep supervised discrete hashing. In: NIPS (2017)

24. Long, F., Yao, T., Qiu, Z., Tian, X., Luo, J., Mei, T.: Gaussian temporal awareness networks for action localization. In: CVPR (2019)

25. Oh Song, H., Jegelka, S., Rathod, V., Murphy, K.: Deep metric learning via facility location. In: CVPR (2017)

26. Oh Song, H., Xiang, Y., Jegelka, S., Savarese, S.: Deep metric learning via lifted structured feature embedding. In: CVPR (2016)

27. Petsiuk, V., Das, A., Saenko, K.: Rise: randomized input sampling for explanation of black-box models. arXiv preprint arXiv:1806.07421 (2018)

28. Piergiovanni, A., Ryoo, M.S.: Learning latent super-events to detect multiple activities in videos. In: CVPR (2018)

29. Ramanishka, V., Chen, Y.T., Misu, T., Saenko, K.: Toward driving scene understanding: a dataset for learning driver behavior and causal reasoning. In: CVPR (2018)
30. Rezende, D.J., Mohamed, S., Wierstra, D.: Stochastic backpropagation and approximate inference in deep generative models. PMLR (2014)
31. Ronneberger, O., Fischer, P., Brox, T.: U-Net: convolutional networks for biomedical image segmentation. In: Navab, N., Hornegger, J., Wells, W.M., Frangi, A.F. (eds.) MICCAI 2015. LNCS, vol. 9351, pp. 234–241. Springer, Cham (2015). https://doi.org/10.1007/978-3-319-24574-4_28
32. Selvaraju, R.R., Cogswell, M., Das, A., Vedantam, R., Parikh, D., Batra, D.: Grad-CAM: visual explanations from deep networks via gradient-based localization. In: ICCV (2017)
33. Simonyan, K., Zisserman, A.: Very deep convolutional networks for large-scale image recognition. arXiv preprint arXiv:1409.1556 (2014)
34. Singh, K.K., Lee, Y.J.: Hide-and-seek: forcing a network to be meticulous for weakly-supervised object and action localization. In: ICCV (2017)
35. Smilkov, D., Thorat, N., Kim, B., Viégas, F., Wattenberg, M.: SmoothGrad: removing noise by adding noise. arXiv preprint arXiv:1706.03825 (2017)
36. Sohn, K.: Improved deep metric learning with multi-class n-pair loss objective. In: NIPS (2016)
37. Szegedy, C., et al.: Going deeper with convolutions. In: CVPR (2015)
38. Vaswani, A., et al.: Attention is all you need. In: NIPS (2017)
39. Wah, C., Branson, S., Welinder, P., Perona, P., Belongie, S.: The caltech-UCSD birds-200-2011 dataset (2011)
40. Wang, J., Zhou, F., Wen, S., Liu, X., Lin, Y.: Deep metric learning with angular loss. In: ICCV (2017)
41. Wu, C.Y., Manmatha, R., Smola, A.J., Krahenbuhl, P.: Sampling matters in deep embedding learning. In: CVPR (2017)
42. Xu, K., et al.: Show, attend and tell: neural image caption generation with visual attention. arXiv preprint arXiv:1502.03044 (2015)
43. Yuan, Y., Yang, K., Zhang, C.: Hard-aware deeply cascaded embedding. In: ICCV (2017)
44. Zeiler, M.D., Fergus, R.: Visualizing and understanding convolutional networks. In: Fleet, D., Pajdla, T., Schiele, B., Tuytelaars, T. (eds.) ECCV 2014. LNCS, vol. 8689, pp. 818–833. Springer, Cham (2014). https://doi.org/10.1007/978-3-319-10590-1_53
45. Zhang, X., Wei, Y., Feng, J., Yang, Y., Huang, T.: Adversarial complementary learning for weakly supervised object localization. In: CVPR (2018)
46. Zhang, X., Wei, Y., Kang, G., Yang, Y., Huang, T.: Self-produced guidance for weakly-supervised object localization. In: Ferrari, V., Hebert, M., Sminchisescu, C., Weiss, Y. (eds.) ECCV 2018. LNCS, vol. 11216, pp. 610–625. Springer, Cham (2018). https://doi.org/10.1007/978-3-030-01258-8_37
47. Zhang, Z., Saligrama, V.: Zero-shot learning via joint latent similarity embedding. In: CVPR (2016)
48. Zhou, B., Khosla, A., Lapedriza, A., Oliva, A., Torralba, A.: Learning deep features for discriminative localization. In: CVPR (2016)

Interactive Annotation of 3D Object Geometry Using 2D Scribbles

Tianchang Shen[1,2]($\boxtimes$), Jun Gao[1,2,3], Amlan Kar[1,2,3], and Sanja Fidler[1,2,3]

[1] University of Toronto, Toronto, Canada
{shenti11,jungao,amlan,fidler}@cs.toronto.edu
[2] Vector Institute, Toronto, Canada
[3] Nvidia, Santa Clara, USA

Abstract. Inferring detailed 3D geometry of the scene is crucial for robotics applications, simulation, and 3D content creation. However, such information is hard to obtain, and thus very few datasets support it. In this paper, we propose an interactive framework for annotating 3D object geometry from both point cloud data and RGB imagery. The key idea behind our approach is to exploit strong priors that humans have about the 3D world in order to interactively annotate complete 3D shapes. Our framework targets naive users without artistic or graphics expertise. We introduce two simple-to-use interaction modules. First, we make an automatic guess of the 3D shape and allow the user to provide feedback about large errors by drawing scribbles in desired 2D views. Next, we aim to correct minor errors, in which users drag and drop mesh vertices, assisted by a neural interactive module implemented as a Graph Convolutional Network. Experimentally, we show that only a few user interactions are needed to produce good quality 3D shapes on popular benchmarks such as ShapeNet, Pix3D and ScanNet. We implement our framework as a web service and conduct a user study, where we show that user annotated data using our method effectively facilitates real-world learning tasks. Web service: http://www.cs.toronto.edu/~shenti11/scribble3d.

1 Introduction

3D scene understanding is a crucial component of numerous robotic applications such as autonomous driving, household robots, and delivery drones. In order to successfully plan its next move, an agent needs to infer 3D geometry of both the scene and relevant objects. Furthermore, the inferred 3D geometry should be sufficiently detailed to afford fine-grained interaction such as manipulation and grasping. We stress that reasoning about the visible scene alone is insufficient: objects occupy physical space in the world, extending beyond what is visible, which needs to be taken into account for downstream tasks. Reconstructing

---

T. Shen and J. Gao—Equal contribution.

Electronic supplementary material The online version of this chapter (https://doi.org/10.1007/978-3-030-58520-4_44) contains supplementary material, which is available to authorized users.

© Springer Nature Switzerland AG 2020
A. Vedaldi et al. (Eds.): ECCV 2020, LNCS 12362, pp. 751–767, 2020.
https://doi.org/10.1007/978-3-030-58520-4_44

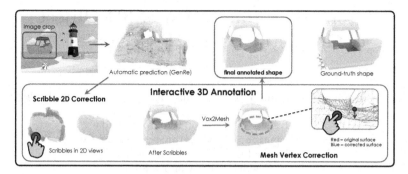

Fig. 1. Interactive 3D Annotation Framework: Our framework has two interaction modules: **1) large errors**: user provides feedback by drawing scribbles in desired 2D views – we exploit this to predict a better shape, **2) small errors**: user drags & drops mesh vertices, and we repredict the mesh locally. Invisible object regions are up to user's priors/imagination.

detailed and complete geometry of each object is also important for simulation, where the goal is to convert scanned point cloud scenes into interactive virtual environments to train artificial agents in, prior to real world deployment.

We need datasets in order to infer complete 3D object geometry from partial observations (point clouds or imagery), which have been collected with two dominant approaches. In [6], the authors exhaustively scan each individual object, followed by a point-registration method. However, detailed scanning is time consuming and limited to static scenes and objects that can be scanned from all possible views – which may require lifting the object from its support surface. The second approach employs fitting CAD models to segmented point clouds [8,16,17] or RGB images [21,32]. This is an undesirable alternative as it requires a large and diverse collection of CAD models to faithfully match input shapes. Such collections are not always available for any object class.

In this paper, we propose an interactive framework for annotating 3D object geometry from both point clouds and RGB images (Fig. 1). At its core, we exploit the extensive prior knowledge in humans to complete (annotate) objects. Since 3D CAD model creation typically requires artistic expertise, our key contribution lies in an interactive learning-based approach that enables a graphics layman to produce good quality 3D meshes that fit (partial) 3D observations.

Our annotation framework is composed of two stages. First, we employ existing methods to produce an initial guess of the 3D shape. To leverage the fact that 2D interactions are easier on existing digital media than 3D, we introduce a simple interface to correct large 3D errors by scribbling corrections in one or several desired 2D views. We propose a neural architecture that uses these scribbles to produce an improved prediction of the 3D shape. Next, for final fine-grained corrections, the annotator makes edits directly to 3D vertices of the object mesh using a drag-and-drop interface. Our 3D Graph Convolutional Network takes this correction into account and aims to re-predict refined local geometry, while ensuring that the majority of the object geometry remains intact.

We demonstrate that our interactive approach, **1)** is able to generate high-quality meshes from single images on the ShapeNet [3] and Pix3D [29] datasets, even on unseen object categories with very few interactions from an user. The annotated shapes can facilitates real-world learning tasks, **2)** comparing favourably to existing annotation strategies such as those employing CAD model retrieval and **3)** can be used for full-scene annotation on the popular ScanNet dataset [6].

2 Related Work

3D Reconstruction: The problem of recovering 3D shape from RGB-D or RGB images is challenging due to the inherent ambiguity in going from a lower to a higher dimensional space. Existing learning-based works can be categorized into four different categories based on output representation [19]: voxel [7,28], point cloud [10], mesh [5,14,30] and signed distance field [25,34]. In practice, by design, these approaches memorize the classes seen during training and exhibit limited generalization ability to unseen classes. Recently, GenRe [35] proposed to exploit spherical maps in order to perform depth completion which has been shown to achieve better generalization to unseen classes. Our framework employs GenRe for its generalization ability, but is not limited to it, *i.e.* other methods can be used. Our key contribution is in making these methods interactive.

Interactive 3D Modeling is a long studied topic in computer graphics [4,9,13, 27]. Image-based methods assist the user to snap parametric primitives (*e.g.* generalized cylinders, ellipsoids) to image contours [4,12,27]. A combination of such primitives forms the final shape. [13] further allows users to indicate higher-level semantic information, *e.g.* equal length/angles, symmetries. The major drawback of these methods is that they require the user to mentally imagine how to decompose 3D shape into primitives and perform their composition. This is not an easy task for a naive user. In our paper, we propose a learning-based interactive approach that assists a graphics layman to annotate complex shapes.

Data-driven approaches have also been proposed to create 3D models. Early works mainly perform retrieval from a database, by either retrieving a whole 3D shape [11], or procedurally obtain predefined assemblies [20,33]. [23] proposed to learn the correlation between 2D sketches and 3D shape. Recently, [9] utilized a deep network to learn this correlation, and users are able to modify the 3D shape via 2D sketches. However, drawing detailed sketches requires some level of artistic expertise. [24] extend the idea of [36] into 3D by utilizing a GAN to learn a latent representation of 3D shapes. User's edits are mapped to this latent space and the network regenerates a shape. This approach loses control over the generation and the network easily neglects user's corrections.

3 Interactive 3D Annotation

We now describe our framework for annotating 3D object. Key desired properties include: **1)** naturally incorporate user interactions, **2)** generalize to unseen object classes and **3)** produce high-quality shapes. We emphasize that generalization

beyond training shapes is crucial to scale to the diversity in the real-world. Since our goal is to produce annotated data to power applications required to predict high quality 3D shapes (*e.g.* VR/AR, simulation, manipulation in robotics), we want our framework to support annotation of detailed geometry. Furthermore, we want our interactive tool to be seamlessly usable by anyone, without assuming expertise in 3D modeling, which is key in undertaking large-scale annotation endeavours in the future.

Our method supports annotating 3D geometry from RGB images and point clouds. It is designed to reconstruct a complete 3D object shape in a coarse-to-fine manner, incorporating annotator corrections at all stages. In particular, it consists of two modules. The *Scribble Interaction Module* (SIM), allows the user to make dramatic changes to the annotated shape by drawing coarse scribbles. The user inspects the 3D shape by rotating it to any viewpoint, and makes corrections to the projected silhouette by drawing scribbles in 2D, which is used to re-predict the shape. The user iterates until the desired quality is achieved. Next, the *Point Interaction Module* (PIM) allows the user to make fine corrections directly in 3D by moving vertices of the object's mesh to obtain fine-grained geometric details. We use this feedback to re-predict the local mesh geometry in order to minimize human effort in editing the final mesh.

In Sect. 3.1, we describe our annotation setup, including the initial automatic prediction of the 3D shape. In Sect. 3.2, we introduce our Scribble Interaction Module. Finally, we describe our Point Interaction Module in Sect. 3.3.

3.1   Annotation Setup

We envision a human user annotating 3D shapes for possibly multiple objects in an image (or a point cloud scene). The user is expected to indicate which object to annotate by drawing a 2D mask overlaying the object. Note that this can be done very quickly by using existing interactive techniques [22,31]. Given the selected object, we aim to predict and assist in the interactive annotation of an accurate 3D shape. Our framework can incorporate any existing 3D prediction network, and our main contribution is in making annotation interactive.

Automatic 3D Shape Prediction: We choose GenRe [35] as our automatic prediction network, for its ability to generalize to beyond training shapes. We briefly summarize it here and refer readers to the original paper for details. GenRe uses three steps: 1) predicting a depth map from an RGB image (cropped to contain a single object), 2) converting the depth map into a spherical map and inpainting the missing depth information with a 2D CNN and 3) refining the 3D shape. The first module is optional and is used when the input is a monocular image. With access to a depth map or a point cloud, this step can be omitted. In the third module, the completed spherical depth map from the second module is back-projected into a 3D occupancy grid, which is further refined to a volume of size 128^3 using a 3D-UResNet (visualization is provided in the Appendix).

We note that the resulting shape is viewer-centric, allowing us to easily overlay it onto sensor inputs (*e.g.* RGB image, point cloud), which is useful for the user tasked to provide corrections to the predicted shape. When depth is available, we can place the object in camera coordinates, *i.e.* into the world scene.

3.2   Scribble Interaction Module

The Scribble Interaction Module (SIM) helps correct major errors in the initial 3D shape prediction. It is purposefully designed to be 2D view-based, targeting an average 3D illiterate user. Unless specially trained to craft 3D content such as artists or graphics experts, a naive user is known to be better at 2D editing. SIM then learns to propagate 2D corrections to 3D in order to refine the shape.

Annotation Setup: To make edits to a shape (automatic prediction initially), the user views it in 3D and rotates it to any desired viewpoint. If a view with a major flaw is discovered, the user can indicate errors by drawing scribbles onto the (2D) projection (Fig. 2 provides an illustration). Following existing work on scribble-based image annotation [26], we support "additive" scribbles to indicate false negative areas and "deletion" scribbles to indicate false positive areas. A scribble contains pixels obtained by dilating the trace of the mouse cursor with a kernel of a user-specified bandwidth, called the scribble width. When the user wants to add (or remove) fine details to the 3D shape, a small scribble width can be used. Nonetheless, this interaction is coarse in the sense that a scribble typically does not accurately trace high frequency regions.

Scribble-Based Neural Module: Since the scribble is marked in 2D, there is an inherent ambiguity in 3D associated with 2D correction. We design a neural architecture that makes a best guess of which voxels in the 3D volume should be corrected based on 2D scribbles. The annotation module allows the user to iteratively rotate the refined shapes and indicate errors, until a satisfactory quality is achieved. Our architecture (Fig. 3) is based on the intuition that predicting 2D projections of a shape is likely an easier task compared to predicting a 3D occupancy grid. The network needs to infer how the refined silhouette of the shape would look in the view in which the scribbles were drawn, and other related views (*e.g.* two orthogonal views), while exploiting depth information and user scribbles. The shape can then be obtained by 3D carving using the predicted silhouettes, and refining the "carved" shape with a simple architecture.

Overview of Architecture: The model takes as input a 3D feature map (from GenRe) and rotates it to align with the user-specified view. We perform maxpooling along the z axis to obtain a *2D-view feature representation* of the input projected into user's view. Scribbles are encoded along with the projected feature map to obtain a new representation of the corrected viewpoint using a *2D-scribble encoder*. In order to propagate this information to the orthogonal

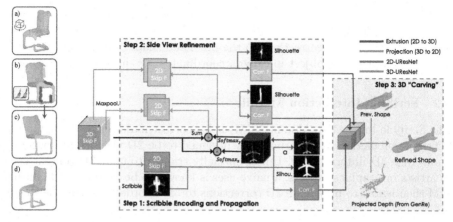

Fig. 2. 2D scribble annotation.

Fig. 3. Our Scribble Interaction Module: We first get 3D skip features from GenRe (left cube), which we rotate and project to the user's view and its orthogonal views. User draws scribbles in the 2D view to indicate errors in the predicted shape. Our network encodes and propagates scribbles to orthogonal views. Lastly, we concatenate refined features from all three orthogonal views, along with the shape from the previous step and the projected depth, to predict a new refined shape.

views, we similarly project GenRe's feature map onto the two other views, and concatenate information propagated from the user-specified view to each of the projected feature maps, using the *scribble propagation module*. We decode these concatenated maps into the final view representations using a 2D-UResNet. To predict the final 3D shape, the *3D carving module* performs an operation mimicking carving in the feature space to obtain a 3D volumetric representation which is decoded into a 3D occupancy grid. We provide details next.

2D-view Feature Representation: Let R denote the rotation that rotates the object into the user's viewpoint. We extract skip feature maps, $F \in \mathbb{R}^{C \times 64 \times 64 \times 64}$, from the first and last 3D convolutional layers of GenRe's 3D-UResNet and rotate it to the user's 3D viewpoint via R. The feature map is upscaled by a factor of 2 using bilinear interpolation, denoted by $F_v \in \mathbb{R}^{C \times 128 \times 128 \times 128}$. F_v is passed through a single FC layer and is projected to three orthogonal views by max-pooling along x, y, and z axes, *i.e.* $F_v^{xy} = \mathrm{maxpool}_z(F_v)$ (similar for F_v^{yz} and F_v^{xz}). Pooling along z mimics an orthographic projection into the user's view, while pooling along x and y projects into its orthogonal views. While more elaborate pooling operations could be performed mimicking perspective projection, we found the simpler approach to work well in practice.

Iterative Correction: Note that our interactive approach runs iteratively, allowing the user to draw scribbles in a different viewpoint each time. In the

first correction round, we use 3D features from GenRe, while in all subsequent rounds we use features from SIM. However, since GenRe's and SIM's outputs differ, we choose to use 2 different weight matrices for the first vs other steps. The 3D refinement network weights are shared across all correction rounds.

Scribble Encoder: We encode positive/negative scribbles by concatenating them along with the initial (binary) silhouette into $S \in \mathbb{R}^{3 \times 128 \times 128}$. To process scribbles, we use a 2D-UResNet, that takes a concatenation of the projected 2D feature F_v^{xy} and S as input and predicts a refined silhouette M^{xy} as well as refined features F_c^{xy} in the user's view:

$$F_s = \text{concat}\{F_v^{xy},\ S\}, \tag{1}$$

$$M^{xy}, F_c^{xy} = \text{2D-UResNet}(F_s) \tag{2}$$

F_c^{xy} is used in the 3D carving module, while the mask prediction is used for an auxilliary loss function during training.

Scribble Propagation Module aims to propagate scribble information from the user's view into orthogonal views. We utilize a 2D-UResNet to predict an attention map $\mathbf{A}^{xy} = \text{2D-UResNet}(F_s) \in \mathbb{R}^{128 \times 128}$, which functions as a gate to silence or amplify features of the entire tube. We then extrude the attention map along z-axis: $\hat{\mathbf{A}}^{xy} \in \mathbb{R}^{128 \times 128 \times 128}$, and perform softmax along different axes when propagating to the orthogonal views:

$$\hat{\mathbf{A}}^{yz}_{i,j,k} = \frac{\exp(\hat{\mathbf{A}}^{xy}_{i,j,k})}{\sum_i \exp(\hat{\mathbf{A}}^{xy}_{i,j,k})},\ \hat{\mathbf{A}}^{xz}_{i,j,k} = \frac{\exp(\hat{\mathbf{A}}^{xy}_{i,j,k})}{\sum_j \exp(\hat{\mathbf{A}}^{xy}_{i,j,k})} \tag{3}$$

where i, j, k denote 3D tensor indices. We compute the weighted feature map:

$$\hat{F}_v^{yz} = F_v \circ \hat{\mathbf{A}}^{yz}, \hat{F}_v^{xz} = F_v \circ \hat{\mathbf{A}}^{xz}, \tag{4}$$

where $\circ$ denotes the Hadamard product. $M^{yz}, F_c^{yz}, M^{xz}, F_c^{xz}$ are predicted in a similar manner as in the user's view, but taking projected features from both F_v and the weighted feature map. For the yz-plane features (similar for xz),

$$M^{yz}, F_c^{yz} = \text{2D-UResNet}(\text{concat}\{\sum_x (\hat{F}_v^{yz}), F_v^{yz}\}) \tag{5}$$

3D Carving Module: The refined view features are backprojected to 3D by extruding F_c^{xy}, F_c^{yz} and F_c^{xz} along their orthogonal axes. A simple refinement network takes the concatenation of the three extruded feature maps, previous occupancy grid and the projected depth map as input, and outputs a new volume as the final prediction. The projected depth map is included to preserve consistency with sensor observations. Note that we do not explicitly use the predicted silhouettes, but instead use the predicted feature maps. We argue that the feature maps preserve more information and thus are better for 3D refinement, while predicting and supervising silhouettes helps learn better features.

3.3 Point Interaction Module

A voxelgrid with limited resolution lacks fine geometric details. We thus convert the predicted occupancy grid to a triangular mesh and allow the annotator to drag-and-drop vertices, one at a time, and employ the point interaction module to locally refine the mesh based on user feedback. To convert the occupancy grid to a mesh, a Vox2Mesh method similar to [14,30] is used, with minor but important modifications that yield visibly better meshes (details in suppl.).

Point-Based Neural Module takes the user's vertex correction and employs a GCN to repredict its neighboring vertices. As shown in the Fig. 4, we use a similar network architecture to [22], which is designed for interactive 2D curve correction. In particular, it performs:

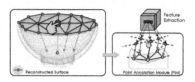

Fig. 4. PIM allows users to interactively edit a mesh.

$$f_i = \text{concat}(F(p_i); p_i; q_i - p_i), \tag{6}$$
$$\Delta p_j = \text{GCN}(f_1, f_2, \cdots, f_N; G), \tag{7}$$

where $F(p_i)$ represents the feature tilinearly sampled from 3D feature map with position p_i, which is corrected to q_i, N is the number mesh vertices, and G is the topology of the mesh. Δp_j represents the predicted offset for each local point p_j. We restrict movement to only neighbours along paths of length l from the edited vertex. It is trained using similar loss as MeshRCNN [14] (see appendix).

4 Experiments

In this section, we provide extensive evaluation of our model. To demonstrate the model's capability as an annotation tool, we report interactive single image shape reconstruction results on ShapeNet for both seen and unseen classes in Sect. 4.2. We further evaluate our full pipeline on the challenging Pix3D [29], ScanNet [8] and Scan2CAD [2] dataset to show the generalizability of our method to real-world sensor inputs in Sect. 4.3. In addition, we provide quantitative analysis comparing our method to CAD Retrieval using ShapeNet models to annotate Pix3D instances in Sect. 4.3. We show ablation studies comparing SIM with other network architectures in Sect. 4.4. Finally, we annotate real data in a user study and show results of models trained on this data in Sect. 4.5.

4.1 Experimental Settings

For all experiments, we train our model on Car, Chair and Airplane, which are the three largest categories in ShapeNet [3]. We use the same subset split and rendered images as in [35]. For evaluation on real-world data, we use the Pix3D [29] and ScanNet [8]. ScanNet is a richly annotated indoor dataset that

Table 1. Reconstruction results of the training classes and 9 unseen classes from ShapeNet. With our interactive method, we consistently improve and significantly improve over the automatic 3D reconstruction approach.

		Seen classes	Unseen classes									
			Bch	Vsl	Rfl	Sfa	Tbl	Phn	Dsp	Spk	Lmp	Avg
Chamfer Dist.	GenRe	0.1093	0.1158	0.1477	0.1570	0.1140	0.1572	0.1522	0.1921	0.1738	0.2667	0.1640
	+ Scribble Annot.	0.0503	0.0435	0.0517	**0.0289**	0.0465	0.0565	**0.0315**	**0.0461**	**0.0630**	0.1190	**0.0541**
	+ Vox2Mesh	**0.0474**	**0.0412**	**0.0474**	0.0301	**0.0452**	**0.0545**	0.0345	0.0499	0.0681	**0.1178**	0.0543
F1 Score	GenRe	0.8392	0.8211	0.7270	0.6837	0.8368	0.7221	0.6993	0.6014	0.6832	0.4927	0.6963
	+ Scribble Annot.	0.9743	0.9806	**0.9787**	0.9916	0.9629	0.9629	0.9871	**0.9774**	**0.9490**	0.8307	0.9578
	+ Vox2Mesh	**0.9757**	**0.9849**	0.9780	**0.9854**	**0.9858**	**0.9642**	**0.9885**	0.9714	0.9387	**0.8320**	**0.9587**
Normal Consist.	GenRe	0.6353	0.6131	0.5640	0.4945	0.6266	0.6202	0.6029	0.5632	0.6030	0.5004	0.5764
	+ Scribble Annot.	0.7954	0.7633	0.7522	**0.7454**	0.8429	0.8171	0.8907	0.8506	0.8371	**0.7031**	0.8002
	+ Vox2Mesh	**0.8128**	**0.7905**	**0.7563**	0.7257	**0.8477**	**0.8360**	**0.8946**	**0.8692**	**0.8386**	0.7002	**0.8065**

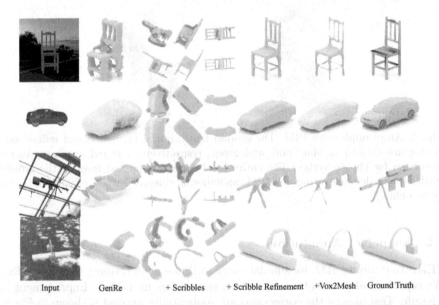

Input   GenRe   + Scribbles   + Scribble Refinement   +Vox2Mesh   Ground Truth

Fig. 5. Examples of ShapeNet objects annotated using our framework. First two rows are from seen classes while others are from unseen classes. Output shape from each intermediate step is shown from left to right, followed by GT mesh. Additive/deletion scribbles are shown in green/red. Although the additive scribbles are drawn in 2D, SIM accurately infers the depth of added shape (e.g. bipods in the third example). With a few scribbles, our model predicts shape close to GT. Vox2Mesh further converts a discrete voxel grid to a fine mesh.

provides RGB-D sequences, cameras, surface reconstructions, and instance-level semantic segmentation. It further provides CAD models aligned to the objects on Scan2CAD [2]. During inference, we use 5 correction steps for both interaction methods unless otherwise mentioned. More details are in appendix.

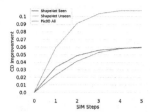 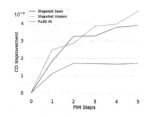 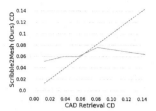

Fig. 6. Improvements in Chamfer Dist vs num of scribble refin. steps.

Fig. 7. Improvements in Chamfer Dist vs. # of point annotation steps.

Fig. 8. Chamfer Dist of the best-aligned CAD model vs. result obtained by our method.

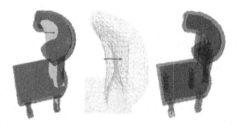

Fig. 9. An example with PIM. The ground truth, initial prediction and refined prediction are colored in blue, pink and green, respectively. The red arrow represents correction for chosen vertex. The entire local surface is pushed towards the ground truth surface, demonstrating that PIM can annotate concave surfaces effectively. (Color figure online)

4.2 ShapeNet Annotation

SIM: To evaluate SIM, we simulate user scribbles as in training (see appendix). We report results on both seen and unseen classes in Table 1. Improvement in Chamfer Distance as the corrections are sequentially applied is shown in Fig. 6. With only coarse annotation, SIM significantly improves raw predictions under all metrics, and across all object categories with higher improvement in unseen classes. This demonstrates that our method generalizes to novel objects, making it suitable for the annotation task. We provide qualitative examples in Fig. 5, demonstrating that with a few scribbles, our proposed module can significantly improve the initial prediction, bringing it very close to the ground-truth shape.

PIM: PIM is used to further refine the mesh (from Vox2Mesh). Following [1,22], we use the same method to simulate the annotator to correct vertices in training. We report improvements in Chamfer Distance in Fig. 7. As a local correction method, applying point annotation gradually improves the quality of 3D shape. Qualitative result in Fig. 9 shows that with 1 correction, PIM can effectively push the prediction to a concave surface, which cannot be annotated by scribbles.

Table 2. Reconstruction results on the Pix3D Objects dataset.

		Chair	Bed	Bookcase	Desk	Sofa	Table	Wardrobe
Chamfer Distance	GenRe	0.1161	0.1427	0.1167	0.1526	0.0939	0.1735	0.1128
	+ Scribble Annotation	0.0609	**0.0696**	**0.0546**	0.0748	0.0596	0.0968	**0.0413**
	+ Vox2Mesh	**0.0588**	0.0703	0.0575	**0.0705**	**0.0579**	**0.0915**	0.0458
F1 Score	GenRe	0.8251	0.7483	0.8126	0.7145	0.8957	0.6667	0.8302
	+ Scribble Annotation	0.9549	**0.9362**	**0.9660**	0.9306	0.9720	0.8775	**0.9851**
	+ Vox2Mesh	**0.9591**	0.9358	0.9614	**0.9345**	**0.9779**	**0.8808**	0.9819
Normal Consistency	GenRe	0.6217	0.6479	0.5673	0.6110	0.6541	0.6347	0.6462
	+ Scribble Annotation	0.7358	0.7935	0.7022	0.7807	**0.8160**	0.7784	**0.8776**
	+ Vox2Mesh	**0.7587**	**0.8000**	**0.7037**	**0.7990**	0.8147	**0.7969**	0.8628

4.3 Annotating Real Scans

Pix3D Annotation: We now evaluate our trained model on Pix3D [29]. We do not fine-tune the model, and only run inference on this dataset. We test on un-occluded and un-truncated shapes and use ground-truth 3D shape to simulate scribbles. Quantitative results are shown in Table 2. Our model achieves the same level of improvement across all Pix3D categories despite the domain gap between synthetic images rendered from ShapeNet models and real imagery.

We compare with a common alternative approach for 3D annotation of retrieving and aligning CAD models from a large database [2,29]. For fair comparison, we use our training and validation sets as the retrieval database. For retrieval, we pick the object with the minimum Chamfer Distance to the ground-truth CAD model (or scanned surface). Comparison on all 200 chair models in Pix3D is shown in Fig. 8. CAD retrieval is promising if the database contains similar objects, but it fails for unseen objects, which is crucial in practice. Our model overcomes this limitation and performs consistently regardless of the similarity to the training objects (Fig. 10). Our method achieves more faithful reconstruction to unseen objects, and can be used alongside CAD retrieval in a real application.

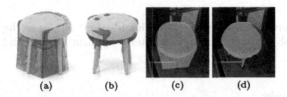

(a)   (b)   (c)   (d)

Fig. 10. Example of CAD alignment (a) vs. our approach (b). Light blue shape is the ground truth. We render both shapes on the input image at c) and d). Our method is more consistent with both ground-truth shape and input. (Color figure online)

4.4 Analysis

Ablation Study: We explore two alternatives for scribble propagation. We could directly extrude 2D scribbles to 3D, or learn to encode the 2D scribbles in the correction view and extrude the learned feature directly to 3D (avoiding prediction of 2D side views in our model). The second approach is a generalization

of the updater network in [9], combined with volumetric aggregation in [18] to avoid repeated rotation of the feature space. We train these with the same training scheme and 3D U-ResNet architecture. The result is summarized in Table 3. Our proposed multi-view correction module outperforms both alternatives in all metrics, and the reconstruction is more plausible and complete (see Fig. 11).

Fig. 11. (From left to right) The same chair annotated by 3D-scribble, single-view and multi-view SIM respectively.

Table 3. Comparison of different SIM architectures.

	Seen			Unseen		
	CD	F1	Normal	CD	F1	Normal
3D-Scribble	0.0628	0.9539	0.7729	0.0804	0.9109	0.7574
1-View	0.0555	0.9652	0.7795	0.0609	0.9499	0.7791
Multi-View	**0.0535**	**0.9694**	**0.7899**	**0.0589**	**0.9538**	**0.7838**

Shape Creation with Scribbles: Our model is capable of creating a plausible shape purely from scribble inputs, as shown in Fig. 12. This mimics the scenario where the user wants to create 3D shapes by simply drawing scribbles on a blank screen. As before, we allow the user to iteratively add scribbles from multiple views in order to obtain the desired shape. In the example, the user is able to create a plausible full chair with only 3 drawing steps.

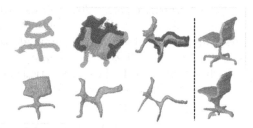

Fig. 12. Shape creation from only scribble inputs. (top) Images on the left show scribbles, (bottom) object in correction view after refinement. The ground truth is shown on top right.

4.5   User Study

To evaluate our method with real human annotators, we built a web tool visualized in Fig. 13, and conducted a user study on two real-world datasets: Pix3D [29] and ScanNet [6]. The annotator engaged in the user study had no prior experience in 3D modeling and did not have access to ground truth shapes. The tool only uses scribble corrections with SIM. Details can be found in appendix.

Fig. 13. Screenshot.

Table 4. Statistics on Pix3D.

	Bed	Bookcase	Desk	Sofa	Table	Wardrobe	Avg
Avg. # Scrib	15	18	10	10	19	9	14
Avg. Time(sec)	141	109	116	71	184	55	113
CD Before	0.1555	0.1048	0.1330	0.0893	0.1637	0.1043	0.1251
CD After	0.0859	0.0517	0.0778	0.0746	0.0989	0.0513	0.0733

Table 5. Reconstruction results of OccNet on Pix3D before and after fine-tuning.

	Bed	Bookcase	Desk	Sofa	Table	Wardrobe	Avg.
Pretrained	0.1728	0.1603	0.2581	0.0998	0.1659	0.1863	0.1738
Tuning on Ours	0.1094	0.1017	0.1642	0.0870	0.1279	0.0898	0.1133
Tuning on GT	0.0712	0.0776	0.1168	0.0800	0.1023	0.0555	0.0839

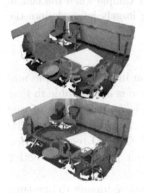

Fig. 14. Full scene annotation (top) vs. CAD alignment (bottom) on ScanNet.

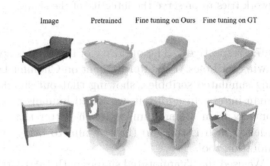

Image   Pretrained   Fine tuning on Ours   Fine tuning on GT

Fig. 15. Examples showing fine-tuning OccNet with shapes annotated by our tool can effectively improve the quality of reconstruction on target task. Note that the *bed* category (top) is unseen in the pre-trained OccNet model.

Full Scene Annotation: We show full scene annotation capability of our approach on ScanNet [6]. We compare with CAD alignment in Fig. 14 (Scan2CAD provides human-annotated CAD alignment as ground truth). Annotators took 2.48 min on avg. to find the appropriate CAD model and align it in the scene. We report an avg. time of 1.88 min in Table 4. Our model faithfully reconstructs the surface of all objects in the scene, aligning better with the partial surface from the scan than CAD retrieval.

Real Dataset Creation: To validate if our annotated data is useful for learning, we create a dataset from Pix3D images and use it to fine-tune a 3D reconstruction model pretrained on synthetic data. In this study, we chose to annotate all unseen categories in Pix3D, which has 2817 images containing un-occluded and un-truncated objects, corresponding to 147 different CAD shapes. The annotator was asked to annotate 95 randomly-selected shapes from random views and the remaining shapes were used for testing. Annotation results are shown in Table 4. We found that the large errors in the initial prediction were effectively fixed by user corrections, but the surface is often jagged due to human error. Qualitative examples and screen recordings of the annotation process are available in the appendix. Note that runtimes of SIM and Vox2Mesh are 0.49s and

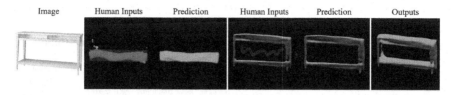

Fig. 16. (Left): Example of user annotating with a polygon, which traces the boundary instead of the skeleton of the negative region. (Right): Example when the human provides wrong scribbles. Notice that this scribble is being largely ignored since the network tries to preserve the integrity of the shape.

0.007s, respectively. The majority of the time is spent on inspecting shapes and drawing scribbles. The improvement on Chamfer Distance is comparable to that using simulated scribbles, showing that our simulation is representative of real human inputs. In addition, we found humans can infer invisible (occluded) 3D geometry from a single image much better than the SOTA 3D reconstruction models, which is the gap that we aim to bridge with our proposed interactive annotation tool.

We used the 95 annotated shapes with 1880 corresponding images to fine-tune OccNet [25] (instead of GenRe, to avoid model bias) pre-trained on ShapeNet, and report performance in Table 5 with qualitative examples in Fig. 15. Despite the remaining artifacts due to annotation errors, the integrity of the reconstructed shape is largely improved, which demonstrates that our annotation tool is a step towards facilitating real-world 3D annotation for learning. Note that although SIM is trained with simulated scribbles, our model shows **robustness to human input** *i.e.* to human annotation errors or noise (see Fig. 16).

Limitation and Future Work: During our user study, we found it was difficult to annotate 1) complex shapes from bad initial predictions and 2) small but fine details. The *addition* signal from the user is sometimes falsely ignored, causing repeated scribbles at the same location. Vox2Mesh sometimes creates artifacts along thin edges (*e.g.*,chair leg, airfoil), which is commonly observed in deformation-based mesh generation methods [14,15,30]. We include examples of these failure cases in the appendix. To further improve our model, a possible direction is to apply the interaction in other form of representations, such as implicit function, instead of volumetric space to improve the quality of the generated shape, and avoid the additional step of converting voxels to a mesh.

5   Conclusion

In this paper, we provide a 3D annotation framework with two simple-to-use interaction methods, where user can correct 3D shape with scribbles and drag-and-drop clicks, and our model takes these feedback and refines 3D prediction. Experiments on both synthetic images and real sensory data demonstrate the

effectiveness of our method. Our tool is available as a webservice to facilitate the progress of 3D dataset collection for 3D reasoning.

Acknowledgments. We thank Louis Clergue for assistance with developing the web tool and extended discussion. This work was supported by NSERC. SF acknowledges the Canada CIFAR AI Chair award at the Vector Institute.

References

1. Acuna, D., Ling, H., Kar, A., Fidler, S.: Efficient interactive annotation of segmentation datasets with Polygon-RNN++. In: CVPR, pp. 859–868 (2018)
2. Avetisyan, A., Dahnert, M., Dai, A., Savva, M., Chang, A.X., Niessner, M.: Scan2CAD: learning CAD model alignment in RGB-D scans. In: The IEEE Conference on Computer Vision and Pattern Recognition (CVPR) (2019)
3. Chang, A.X., et al.: ShapeNet: an information-rich 3D model repository. arXiv preprint arXiv:1512.03012 (2015)
4. Chen, T., Zhu, Z., Shamir, A., Hu, S.M., Cohen-Or, D.: 3-Sweep: extracting editable objects from a single photo. ACM Trans. Graph. (TOG) **32**(6), 195 (2013)
5. Chen, W., et al.: Learning to predict 3d objects with an interpolation-based differentiable renderer. In: Advances In Neural Information Processing Systems (2019)
6. Choi, S., Zhou, Q.Y., Miller, S., Koltun, V.: A large dataset of object scans. arXiv:1602.02481 (2016)
7. Choy, C.B., Xu, D., Gwak, J.Y., Chen, K., Savarese, S.: 3D-R2N2: a unified approach for single and multi-view 3D object reconstruction. In: Leibe, B., Matas, J., Sebe, N., Welling, M. (eds.) ECCV 2016. LNCS, vol. 9912, pp. 628–644. Springer, Cham (2016). https://doi.org/10.1007/978-3-319-46484-8_38
8. Dai, A., Chang, A.X., Savva, M., Halber, M., Funkhouser, T., Nießner, M.: ScanNet: richly-annotated 3D reconstructions of indoor scenes. In: CVPR (2017)
9. Delanoy, J., Aubry, M., Isola, P., Efros, A.A., Bousseau, A.: 3D sketching using multi-view deep volumetric prediction. Proc. ACM Comput. Graph. Interact. Tech. **1**(1), 21 (2018)
10. Fan, H., Su, H., Guibas, L.J.: A point set generation network for 3D object reconstruction from a single image. In: Proceedings of the IEEE Conference on Computer Vision and Pattern Recognition, pp. 605–613 (2017)
11. Funkhouser, T., et al.: A search engine for 3D models. ACM Trans. Graph. (TOG) **22**(1), 83–105 (2003)
12. Gao, J., Tang, C., Ganapathi-Subramanian, V., Huang, J., Su, H., Guibas, L.J.: DeepSpline: data-driven reconstruction of parametric curves and surfaces. arXiv preprint arXiv:1901.03781 (2019)
13. Gingold, Y., Igarashi, T., Zorin, D.: Structured annotations for 2D-to-3D modeling. ACM Trans. Graph. (TOG) **28**, 148 (2009)
14. Gkioxari, G., Malik, J., Johnson, J.: Mesh R-CNN. arXiv preprint arXiv:1906.02739 (2019)
15. Groueix, T., Fisher, M., Kim, V.G., Russell, B., Aubry, M.: AtlasNet: a Papier-Mâché approach to learning 3D surface generation. In: Proceedings IEEE Conference on Computer Vision and Pattern Recognition (CVPR) (2018)
16. Guo, R., Hoiem, D.: Support surface prediction in indoor scenes. In: ICCV, pp. 2144–2151 (2013)

17. Huang, X., Wang, P., Cheng, X., Zhou, D., Geng, Q., Yang, R.: The apolloscape open dataset for autonomous driving and its application. arXiv:1803.06184 (2018)
18. Iskakov, K., Burkov, E., Lempitsky, V., Malkov, Y.: Learnable triangulation of human pose. In: International Conference on Computer Vision (ICCV) (2019)
19. Jatavallabhula, K.M., et al.: Kaolin: a pytorch library for accelerating 3D deep learning research. arXiv:1911.05063 (2019)
20. Lee, J., Funkhouser, T.A.: Sketch-based search and composition of 3D models. In: SBM, pp. 97–104 (2008)
21. Lim, J.J., Pirsiavash, H., Torralba, A.: Parsing IKEA objects: fine pose estimation. In: ICCV (2013)
22. Ling, H., Gao, J., Kar, A., Chen, W., Fidler, S.: Fast interactive object annotation with Curve-GCN. In: CVPR, pp. 5257–5266 (2019)
23. Lipson, H., Shpitalni, M.: Conceptual design and analysis by sketching. AI EDAM 14(5), 391–401 (2000)
24. Liu, J., Yu, F., Funkhouser, T.: Interactive 3D modeling with a generative adversarial network. In: 2017 International Conference on 3D Vision (3DV), pp. 126–134. IEEE (2017)
25. Mescheder, L., Oechsle, M., Niemeyer, M., Nowozin, S., Geiger, A.: Occupancy networks: learning 3D reconstruction in function space. In: Proceedings of the IEEE Conference on Computer Vision and Pattern Recognition, pp. 4460–4470 (2019)
26. Oh, S.W., Lee, J., Xu, N., Kim, S.J.: Fast user-guided video object segmentation by interaction-and-propagation networks. CoRR abs/1904.09791 (2019). http://arxiv.org/abs/1904.09791
27. Shtof, A., Agathos, A., Gingold, Y., Shamir, A., Cohen-Or, D.: Geosemantic snapping for sketch-based modeling. Comput. Graph. Forum 32, 245–253 (2013)
28. Smith, E., Fujimoto, S., Meger, D.: Multi-view silhouette and depth decomposition for high resolution 3D object representation. In: Bengio, S., Wallach, H., Larochelle, H., Grauman, K., Cesa-Bianchi, N., Garnett, R. (eds.) Advances in Neural Information Processing Systems 31, pp. 6479–6489. Curran Associates, Inc., Red Hook (2018)
29. Sun, X., et al.: Pix3D: dataset and methods for single-image 3D shape modeling. In: IEEE Conference on Computer Vision and Pattern Recognition (CVPR) (2018)
30. Wang, N., Zhang, Y., Li, Z., Fu, Y., Liu, W., Jiang, Y.-G.: Pixel2Mesh: generating 3D mesh models from single RGB images. In: Ferrari, V., Hebert, M., Sminchisescu, C., Weiss, Y. (eds.) ECCV 2018. LNCS, vol. 11215, pp. 55–71. Springer, Cham (2018). https://doi.org/10.1007/978-3-030-01252-6_4
31. Wang, Z., Acuna, D., Ling, H., Kar, A., Fidler, S.: Object instance annotation with deep extreme level set evolution. In: CVPR (2019)
32. Xiang, Y., et al.: ObjectNet3D: a large scale database for 3D object recognition. In: Leibe, B., Matas, J., Sebe, N., Welling, M. (eds.) ECCV 2016. LNCS, vol. 9912, pp. 160–176. Springer, Cham (2016). https://doi.org/10.1007/978-3-319-46484-8_10
33. Xie, X., et al.: Sketch-to-design: context-based part assembly. Comput. Graph. Forum 32, 233–245 (2013)
34. Xu, Q., Wang, W., Ceylan, D., Mech, R., Neumann, U.: DISN: deep implicit surface network for high-quality single-view 3D reconstruction. arXiv preprint arXiv:1905.10711 (2019)

35. Zhang, X., Zhang, Z., Zhang, C., Tenenbaum, J.B., Freeman, W.T., Wu, J.: Learning to reconstruct shapes from unseen classes. In: NeurIPS (2018)
36. Zhu, J.-Y., Krähenbühl, P., Shechtman, E., Efros, A.A.: Generative visual manipulation on the natural image manifold. In: Leibe, B., Matas, J., Sebe, N., Welling, M. (eds.) ECCV 2016. LNCS, vol. 9909, pp. 597–613. Springer, Cham (2016). https://doi.org/10.1007/978-3-319-46454-1_36

Hierarchical Kinematic Human Mesh Recovery

Georgios Georgakis[1,2], Ren Li[1], Srikrishna Karanam[1(✉)], Terrence Chen[1], Jana Košecká[2], and Ziyan Wu[1]

[1] United Imaging Intelligence, Cambridge, MA, USA
{georgios.georgakis,ren.li,srikrishna.karanam,terrence.chen,
ziyan.wu}@united-imaging.com
[2] George Mason University, Fairfax, VA, USA
kosecka@cs.gmu.edu

Abstract. We consider the problem of estimating a parametric model of 3D human mesh from a single image. While there has been substantial recent progress in this area with direct regression of model parameters, these methods only implicitly exploit the human body kinematic structure, leading to sub-optimal use of the model prior. In this work, we address this gap by proposing a new technique for regression of human parametric model that is explicitly informed by the known hierarchical structure, including joint interdependencies of the model. This results in a strong prior-informed design of the regressor architecture and an associated hierarchical optimization that is flexible to be used in conjunction with the current standard frameworks for 3D human mesh recovery. We demonstrate these aspects by means of extensive experiments on standard benchmark datasets, showing how our proposed new design outperforms several existing and popular methods, establishing new state-of-the-art results. By considering joint interdependencies, our method is equipped to infer joints even under data corruptions, which we demonstrate by conducting experiments under varying degrees of occlusion.

1 Introduction

We consider 3D human mesh recovery, *i.e.*, fitting a parametric model to an image of a person that best explains the body pose and shape. With a variety of applications [1,2], there has been notable recent interest in this field [3–6].

The dominant paradigm for this problem involves an *encoder-regressor* architecture [5]; the deep CNN encoder takes the input image and produces the feature representation which the regressor processes to produce the model parameters.

G. Georgakis and R. Li—Joint first authors and contributed equally to this work done during their internships with United Imaging Intelligence, Cambridge MA, USA.

Electronic supplementary material The online version of this chapter (https:// doi.org/10.1007/978-3-030-58520-4_45) contains supplementary material, which is available to authorized users.

© Springer Nature Switzerland AG 2020
A. Vedaldi et al. (Eds.): ECCV 2020, LNCS 12362, pp. 768–784, 2020.
https://doi.org/10.1007/978-3-030-58520-4_45

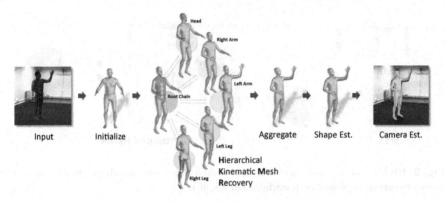

Fig. 1. We present HKMR, a new structure-informed design that hierarchically regresses the pose and shape parameters of the human body mesh.

A recent method [6] extends this to the *encoder-regressor-optimizer* framework by introducing an in-the-loop optimization step [3] which uses the output of the regressor as the starting point to iteratively optimize and generate more accurate model estimates. The regressor forms the core of both of these approaches and is typically realized with a block of fully-connected layers with non-linear activation units, taking feature vectors as input and producing the shape and rotation/pose parameter vectors as output.

However, it has been shown [7] that direct regression of rotation parameters is a very challenging task. The difficulty is exacerbated in our case of human joints due to multiple rotations and their dependencies, as noted in prior work [5,8]. Kendall *et al.* [7] further notes such regression tasks can be made more amenable, with significant performance improvements, by grounding regressor design considerations in geometry which in our context is the underlying structure of the model we are attempting to fit. However, existing *encoder-regressor* methods do not include such structural information in their design, leaving much room for performance improvement. This is even more pronounced in situations involving data corruptions (*e.g.*, occlusions), where intuitively structural information (*e.g.*, one joint dependent on or connected to another joint) can readily help infer these model parameters even when one or more joints are occluded.

To this end, we present a new architecture, called **HKMR**, and an associated hierarchical optimization technique, for 3D human mesh recovery. While Kolotouros *et al.* [8] avoids direct regression of model parameters and instead estimates the 3D mesh vertices, we investigate a more model-structure-informed design that exploits the strengths of such a representation. We use the popular SMPL model [9], which is based on the standard skeletal rig with a well-known hierarchical structure of chains with interdependent joints. Note however that HKMR can be used with other hierarchical human model instantiations as well.

HKMR defines six chains following the standard skeletal rig (a root chain and five dependent child chains: head, left/right arms, left/right legs). Each chain is

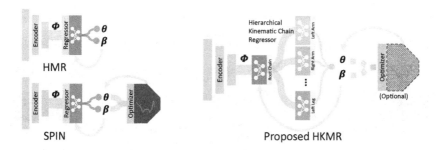

Fig. 2. HKMR can be used in either the *encoder-regressor* paradigm (HMR [5]) or the *encoder-regressor-optimizer* paradigm (SPIN [6]).

designed following the skeletal rig's kinematic model, with explicit interdependencies of joints. We repeat this for all the chains, with each non-root chain's predictions conditioned on the root chain's output, thus modeling HKMR with a set of hierarchically-nested operations (see Fig. 1). As one can note, this is in stark contrast to the existing paradigm [5] that simply operates in a *features-in-parameters-out* fashion without explicitly exploiting the underlying structure of the model. Furthermore, such a design for the regressor is particularly beneficial for parameter inference under data corruptions. By modeling hierarchical joint interdependencies, HKMR facilitates the inference of the current joint even if the previous joint is unreliable or unobserved due to occlusions or other reasons. We show HKMR leads to a new architecture for 3D human mesh estimation that substantially outperforms currently dominant baseline architectures for this problem [5,8]. Our method is flexible to be used in both the *encoder-regressor* and *encoder-regressor-optimizer* paradigms (see Fig. 2, where we show how the *optimizer* can be optionally added to our pipeline), and we demonstrate substantial performance improvements in both these cases.

To summarize, our key contributions include:

– We present HKMR, a new parameter regressor that is flexible to be used in either of the two existing *encoder-regressor* or *encoder-regressor-optimizer* paradigms for 3D human mesh recovery.
– Our key insight is the design of the parameter regressor in a way that explicitly exploits structural constraints of the human body model, resulting in a strong model-design-informed architecture.
– We empirically show HKMR improves the performance of both *encoder-regressor* and *encoder-regressor-optimizer* methods and establishes new state-of-the-art results on several human mesh recovery benchmark datasets.
– HKMR is robust to occlusions, as evidenced by substantial relative performance improvements on data under a wide variety of occlusion conditions.

2   Related Work

There is a large body of work on human pose estimation, formulating the problem as one of predicting 2D keypoints [10–12], estimating 3D joints [13–15], or model-based parametric human body estimation [16–21]. Here, we discuss most relevant methods with particular focus on their structure-related design choices.

Flat-Regression Methods. A common paradigm has been the direct CNN-based regression of the body model parameters with focus on capturing multi-scale information [22,23] or encoding spatial relationships between keypoints [24–26]. With the increasing adoption of parametric human models such as SMPL [9], several methods shifted focus to regressing the model parameters [5,27–32]. The most representative in this line of work is of Kanazawa *et al.* [5] that learned an end-to-end image-to-SMPL-parameter regressor. Kolotouros *et al.* [6] extended this work by combining the initial regressor estimates with an in-the-loop SMPLify [3] optimization step, reporting the most competitive performance on benchmark datasets to date. However, these methods tend to ignore the inherent structure of the body model in their regressor design.

Structure-Aware Methods. Several methods have sought to include structural priors in their design. Earlier works considered pictorial structures [33,34] where the human body was modeled as a set of rigid templates with pairwise potentials. More recently, Cai *et al.* [35] and Kolotouros *et al.* [8] exploited variants of graph CNNs to encode the 2D keypoint or mesh structure. Ci *et al.* [36] went a step further and proposed a generic framework for graph CNNs, introducing a specific formulation focusing on local joint neighborhoods. Aksan *et al.* [37] explicitly modeled the joint dependencies by means of a structured prediction layer. Tang *et al.* [38] investigated the relationship between different parts of the human body to learn part-specific features for 2D keypoint prediction. Fang *et al.* [39] encoded human body dependencies by employing Bi-directional RNNs during 3D joint prediction, while Isack *et al.* [40] attempted to learn priors between keypoints by following a pre-specified prediction order and connectivity. In contrast to these approaches, our method explicitly encodes both the hierarchical structure as well as joint interdependencies through a kinematics model. Zhou *et al.* [41] also proposed kinematic modeling but is substantially different from our method. First, it does not model joint interdependencies in each chain, thus failing to take full advantage of the kinematic formulation. Next, it models all joints as part of one large chain, therefore not exploiting the skeletal rig's hierarchical nature. Finally, it only generates 3D joints and not the full mesh.

3   Approach

As noted in Sects. 1 and 2, existing mesh recovery methods formulate the problem as purely one of regressing the real-valued parameter vectors. While the network (during training) is regularized by priors learned from data (mixture models as in [3]) or even discriminator models [5], we contend this does not

fully exploit the knowledge we have about the structure of the SMPL model. From SMPL's design principles, we know it is motivated by the standard skeletal rig, and that this rig has an associated hierarchy. We argue that a parameter estimation procedure that is explicitly informed by this hierarchy constitutes a stronger integration of the structure of the SMPL model as opposed to HMR-like [5] methods that generate the parameter vectors by means of a structure-agnostic set of fully-connected units (see HMR in Fig. 2). Motivated by this intuition, we propose **HKMR**, a new architecture for the parameter regressor. As we demonstrate in Sect. 4, this leads to a new convolutional neural network architecture that substantially outperforms the currently dominant paradigm of *encoder-regressor* architectures [5,8], while also lending itself favorably applicable to *encoder-regressor-optimizer* approaches like SPIN [6].

3.1 3D Body Representation

We use the SMPL model of Loper *et al.* [9] to parameterize the 3D human mesh. SMPL is a differentiable model defined in the real-valued space of pose $\Theta \in \mathbb{R}^{72}$ and shape $\beta \in \mathbb{R}^{10}$ parameters. While Θ models the relative 3D rotation of $K = 24$ joints in the axis-angle representation, β models the shape of the body as captured by the first 10 coefficients of a PCA projection of the shape space. SMPL defines a function $\mathcal{M}(\Theta, \beta) \in \mathbb{R}^{N \times 3}$ that produces the $N = 6890$ 3D vertices representing the human mesh. Starting from a template mesh, the desired body mesh is obtained by applying forward kinematics based on the joint rotations Θ and by applying shape deformations conditioned on both Θ and β. Finally, the joint locations are defined as a linear combination of the mesh vertices, obtained by a linear regression function $\mathcal{X}(\mathcal{M}(\Theta, \beta)) \in \mathbb{R}^{K \times 3}$.

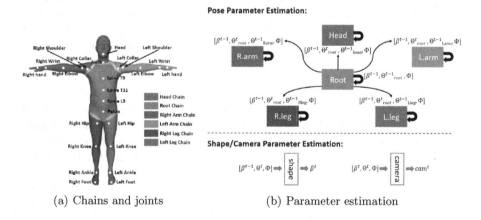

(a) Chains and joints   (b) Parameter estimation

Fig. 3. The kinematic chains and our hierarchical optimization workflow.

3.2   Hierarchical Kinematic Pose and Shape Estimation

Our architecture comprises an encoder to generate features (the same ResNet50 [42] to existing models [5,8]), followed by our proposed regressor that explicitly models the hierarchy between various body parts and the interdependency of the body joints within these parts. We define each body part by a standalone kinematic chain with joints at the same locations as the SMPL model (see Fig. 3(a)). As in the standard skeletal rig, we consider the chain representing the torso of the body as root, with all other chains (arms, leg, and head) hierarchically dependent on this root chain. We estimate Θ and β in the same spirit as the iterative feedback of HMR [5] but is realized substantially differently. Given six chains corresponding to different parts of the body, we express Θ as a concatenation of all the individual chain pose parameters: $\Theta = [\theta_{\text{root}}, \theta_{\text{head}}, \theta_{\text{R.arm}}, \theta_{\text{L.arm}}, \theta_{\text{R.leg}}, \theta_{\text{L.leg}}]$, where each θ represents chains' angle-axis pose parameters. For example root chain is comprised by 4 joints, θ_{root} is of dimensionality 12. Starting from the mean pose and shape Θ^0 and β^0, our method first estimates the next Θ^t, which is then used to update the next β^t. This process is repeated for $t = T$ iterations resulting in final estimates $\hat{\Theta} = [\hat{\theta}_{\text{root}}, \hat{\theta}_{\text{head}}, \hat{\theta}_{\text{R.arm}}, \hat{\theta}_{\text{L.arm}}, \hat{\theta}_{\text{R.leg}}, \hat{\theta}_{\text{L.leg}}]$ and $\hat{\beta}$. This constitutes what we call the **outer iterative** process involving all the chains. Each chain c also has an **inner iterative** process estimating its pose $\hat{\theta}_c^t$ at each outer iterative step t, i.e., $\hat{\theta}_c^t$ itself is updated for multiple iterations at the outer step t. In the following, we first describe the inner iterative process of each chain c, followed interaction between inner and outer iterative steps, leading up to the overall hierarchical process for parameter optimization.

Iterative Kinematic Chain Parameter Estimation. For simplicity of exposition, we focus on one chain here. As noted above, at each outer iterative step t, the chain c has an inner-iterative process to estimate its pose parameters θ^t. Specifically, the chain c takes as input its previous estimates at $t - 1$, $\theta^{t-1} = \theta^I$ and $\beta^{t-1} = \beta^I$ and iteratively refines it yielding θ^t at the current outer step t. In the following section we drop the superscripts $t - 1$ and t for clarity.

We take inspiration from inverse kinematics, more specifically from iterative solvers for the problem. The 3D location of the chain's end-effector $e = [e_x, e_y, e_z]^T$ is related to the pose of the rigid bodies in the chain by a nonlinear function characterizing forward kinematics $e = g(\theta)$. For inverse kinematics, we seek θ (system configuration) that will realize it: $\theta = g^{-1}(e)$. Considering the Taylor series expansion of g, we can characterize changes in the end-effector's current position e relative to changes in θ in terms of the Jacobian matrix $J(\theta)$ of partial derivatives of the system as $\Delta e = J \Delta \theta$. Since we are interested in the inverse estimation (i.e., how θ changes with respect to e), the pseudo-inverse of the Jacobian J^+ is used to estimate the residual $\Delta \theta = J^+ \Delta e$, followed by the update $\theta \leftarrow \theta + \alpha \Delta \theta$, where α is a small scalar. This update is repeated in the inner-iterative process until a proximity to the goal end-effector position criterion is reached. This is the essence of iterative solvers for inverse kinematics problems frequently used for kinematic chains in robotics. With the forward kinematics model being a continuous function of θ [41], we can incorporate this solution framework into an end-to-end learning paradigm. In other words, we

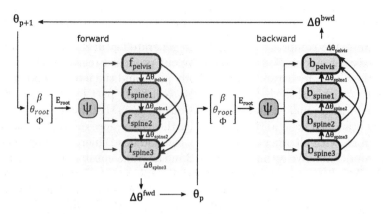

Fig. 4. The forward-backward cycle in Q_{root} that corresponds to the inner iterative procedure of each chain (here we use the root chain as example). E_{root} produces a common embedding ψ between the model parameters θ, β and image features Φ. Note θ_{root} is replaced by θ_p/θ_{p+1} at the end of the forward/backward process respectively.

design a learnable function for the chain c that predicts the residuals $\Delta\theta$ and updates θ iteratively with the available 3D joint annotations as supervision.

Specifically, we estimate the θ for each kinematic chain c with a trainable neural network Q_c that takes as input values β^I, θ^I, and image features Φ extracted from the encoder. Given Φ, β^I and the chain-specific θ^I, we first learn a low-dimensional embedding $\psi \in \mathbb{R}^d$ with Q_c's embedding module E_c. Our key insight is that the predicted angle of a certain joint affects the predictions of all the following joint angles in the chain. Any predicted angle in the chain changes the system configuration, consequently requiring the adjustment of the following angle predictions, which we do iteratively. To this end, we predict the $\Delta\theta_{i,p}$ of the ith joint ($i = 0, 1, \cdots, K_c - 1$, K_c: number of joints in c) starting from $i = 0$ at the inner iteration step p through a *forward* pass of the kinematic chain. In this process, we concatenate ψ and the estimated residuals of all previous joints in the following chain sequence:

$$\Delta\theta_{i,p}^{\mathrm{fwd}} = f_i([\psi, \Delta\theta_{i-1,p}, \Delta\theta_{i-2,p}, \cdots, \Delta\theta_{0,p}]). \tag{1}$$

where the function f_i is realized as one fully-connected layer for the joint i that outputs three real-valued numbers. See Fig. 4 for a visual summary. For the first joint $i = 0$ (`pelvis`) in the chain, we use $[\psi, 0]$ as input to f_i. In other words, the second joint's prediction is dependent on the first (`spine1` depends on `pelvis`), the third is dependent on both first and second (`spine2` depends on both `spine1` and `pelvis`), and so on. When all residuals are predicted, the current estimate (at inner iteration step p) for the pose of the chain $\theta_p = [\theta_{0,p}, \cdots, \theta_{K_c-1,p}]$ is updated as $\theta_{i,p} = \theta_{i,p-1} + \Delta\theta_{i,p}^{\mathrm{fwd}}$; the embedding ψ is then updated using E_c based on this new θ_p. Specifically, as above, this step takes Φ, β^I and the updated θ_p as input, producing an updated ψ. Since these joint angles can be affected by both the next and previous joints, after the forward update as above,

we additionally perform a *backward* pass:

$$\Delta\theta^{\text{bwd}}_{i,p+1} = b_i([\psi, \Delta\theta_{i-1,p+1}, \Delta\theta_{i-2,p+1}, \cdots, \Delta\theta_{0,p+1}]) \tag{2}$$

where b_i is defined similarly to f_i above. Note that the notation p is used to differentiate between the forward and backward pass (i.e. θ_p referred to the estimated pose parameters after the forward pass, and θ_{p+1} to the corresponding backward). The backward update takes the updated embedding ψ from the forward update as the input and starts from the last joint $i = K_c - 1$ in the forward update (spine3, see backward in Fig. 4). Specifically, in predicting the $\Delta\theta$ for spine3, the input to its corresponding b_i is $[\psi, 0]$, as with the initial step in the forward update as above. Subsequently, every other joint prediction depends on all the preceding predictions (*e.g.*, spine2 depends on spine3, spine1 depends on both spine2 and spine3, and so on; see backward in Fig. 4). Once the backward residuals are computed, the current estimate for the pose of the chain $\theta_{p+1} = [\theta_{0,p+1}, \cdots, \theta_{K_c-1,p+1}]$ at inner iteration step $p + 1$ (the forward pass above is step p) is updated as $\theta_{i,p+1} = \theta_{i,p} + \Delta\theta^{\text{bwd}}_{i,p+1}$. Again, as above, given this updated θ_{p+1}, we update ψ using E_c. This forward-backward cycle (forward is inner iterative step p, backward is inner iterative step $p+1$) is repeated for multiple iterations. Following the inverse kinematics formulation, we seek to optimize the prediction of θ so we can reach the position of the chain's end-effector e given the desired pose. This constitutes defining an e in the chain and using an L_1-like distance function to minimize the distance between e and its ground truth. In practice, since inverse kinematics can produce multiple solutions, we apply this loss on all joints in the chain, as we show next.

Hierarchical Optimization. As noted above, we denote the torso kinematic chain as root, and the others as its n_c dependent/children chains. The purpose of having this hierarchy is to allow the pose predicted by the root chain to affect how the rest of the chains operate. This is achieved by using the prediction of the root chain's θ as part of the input to all other chains' neural networks. Specifically, while the root chain network takes β^{t-1}, $\theta^{t-1}_{\text{root}}$, and Φ as input in predicting the next θ^t_{root}, all other chains' networks take the previous β^{t-1}, θ^{t-1}_c, Φ, and the current θ^t_{root} as input in predicting the next θ^t_c. This is also visually summarized in Fig. 3(b). Since the kinematic chains operate only on the pose parameters, the shape parameters β remain constant during this process. We re-estimate β after every Θ prediction cycle ends (*i.e.*, after each of the six chains have completed their inner-iterative estimation process). To this end, we define a shape-estimation neural network that takes the previous outer iteration step's shape prediction $\hat{\beta}^{t-1}$, the current outer iteration's pose prediction $\hat{\Theta}^t$, and the features Φ as input and produces the current outer iteration step's shape estimate $\hat{\beta}^t$. This updated $\hat{\beta}^t$ (along with $\hat{\Theta}^t$) will then be used to initialize the next (outer iteration step $t + 1$) Θ prediction cycle. We supervise the prediction of both pose and shape parameters by applying an L_1 loss between the predicted 3D joint locations $\hat{X}^t = \mathcal{X}(\mathcal{M}(\hat{\Theta}^t, \hat{\beta}^t))$ of the chain and their respective ground-truth: $L^t_{\text{3D}} = \sum_{i=1}^{N_{\text{3d}}} ||\hat{X}^t_i - X_i||_1$, where the subscript i represents the ith joint and N_{3d} is the number of available annotated 3D joints. Note that if SMPL

parameter ground-truth is available, we can also use this to directly supervise the pose and shape parameters: $L_{\text{smpl}}^t = ||[\hat{\boldsymbol{\Theta}}^t, \hat{\beta}^t] - [\boldsymbol{\Theta}, \beta]||_2^2$.

Camera Parameter Estimation. In order to fully utilize the 2D joints annotations available in most datasets, we define a camera-estimation network that takes the predicted parameters $\hat{\boldsymbol{\Theta}}^t$, $\hat{\beta}^t$ at the outer step t, and image features $\boldsymbol{\Phi}$ to estimate the camera parameters that model a weak-perspective projection as in HMR [5], giving translation $\rho^t \in \mathbb{R}^2$ and scale $s^t \in \mathbb{R}$. Consequently, 2D joints $\hat{\boldsymbol{x}}$ can be derived from the 3D joints $\hat{\boldsymbol{X}}^t$ as $\hat{\boldsymbol{x}}^t = s\Pi(\hat{\boldsymbol{X}}^t) + \rho^t$, where Π is an orthographic projection. We then supervise the estimated 2D joints with an L1 loss: $L_{\text{2D}}^t = \sum_{i=1}^{N_{\text{2d}}} ||\hat{\boldsymbol{x}}_i^t - \boldsymbol{x}_i||_1$, where the subscript i represents the ith joint and N_{2d} is the number of available annotated 2D joints.

Pose Prior. To ensure realism, we follow Pavlakos *et al.* [43] and train a VAE to learn a distribution over plausible human poses. The VAE encodes the 69-D $\boldsymbol{\Theta}$ (corresponding to 23 joints excluding the global orientation) to the latent vector $\boldsymbol{Z}_{\boldsymbol{\Theta}}$, which is then used, via re-parameterization [44], by the decoder to reconstruct $\boldsymbol{\Theta}$. We use the MoSh dataset [45], comprising about 6 million synthetic human poses and shapes, to train our VAE with the standard learning objective. Once trained, we discard the decoder and only use the encoder to ensure the pose predicted by our regressor is physically plausible. To this end, we use this encoder to compute the latent representation $\boldsymbol{Z}_{\hat{\boldsymbol{\Theta}}^t}$ of the predicted $\hat{\boldsymbol{\Theta}}^t$ at the current outer iteration step t. We then enforce $\boldsymbol{Z}_{\hat{\boldsymbol{\Theta}}^t}$ to follow the same unit normal distribution used to train the encoder, which is realized with the KL divergence loss at outer iteration step t: $L_{\text{KL}}^t = KL(\boldsymbol{Z}_{\hat{\boldsymbol{\Theta}}^t}||\mathcal{N}(\boldsymbol{0}, \mathcal{I}))$.

3.3 Overall Learning Objective

During training, we add up all the losses over the T outer iterations (λs are the corresponding loss weights):

$$L = \sum_{t=1}^{T} \lambda_{\text{smpl}} L_{\text{smpl}}^t + \lambda_{\text{3D}} L_{\text{3D}}^t + \lambda_{\text{2D}} L_{\text{2D}}^t + \lambda_{\text{KL}} L_{\text{KL}}^t, \tag{3}$$

With Eq. 3, we perform a single backward pass during which the individual chain models, the shape model, and the camera model are optimized jointly.

3.4 In-the-Loop Optimization

SPIN [6] introduced the *encoder-regressor-optimizer* paradigm with an in-the-loop SMPLify [3] optimization step. Like *encoder-regressor* above, our method can be used in this framework as well. Since SPIN [6] used an HMR-inspired [5] regressor, our proposed regressor can be used as a direct drop-in replacement, and we show in Sect. 4 this results in performance improvements.

4   Experiments and Results

Datasets. Following HMR [5], we use the training splits of LSP [46], LSP-extended [47], MPII [48], MS COCO [49], Human3.6M [50] and MPI-INF-3DHP [51] for network training. We use the same encoder as HMR [5] (ResNet50) and exactly follow their experimental setup, reporting results for both protocols P1 and P2 of Human3.6M (P1 uses videos of all cameras whereas P2 uses only the frontal one - camera 3). We use the mean per joint position error (MPJPE) without any Procrustes post-processing as our evaluation metric. Additional implementation information results/discussion are in the supplementary material.

Occlusions. In order to demonstrate robustness to occlusions, given an image, we generate multiple synthetically occluded images. Specifically, following Sarandi *et al.* [52], we use three occlusion patterns (oriented bars, circles, rectangles) and generate three sets of data, one under each such occlusion pattern (see Fig. 5 for an illustration). Note that these synthetic occlusions are used only at test time, not during model training.

(a) Original   (b) Oriented bar   (c) Circle   (d) Rectangle

Fig. 5. Examples of occlusion patterns.

Baseline Architecture Evaluation. We first evaluate the efficacy of our proposed regressor design. In Table 1, we compare HKMR's to the currently dominant methods in the encoder-regressor paradigm- HMR [5] and CMR [8]. Note that we use exactly the same encoder (ResNet50) as these methods, so we essentially compare our proposed regressor with their regressors. Here, "Standard" refers to the standard/existing Human3.6M test set (same as in HMR [5]), whereas each of the last three columns refers to the Human3.6M test set with the corresponding synthetically generated occlusion pattern. We make several observations from these results. First, on the standard Human3.6M test set, our proposed method outperforms both HMR [5] and CMR [8] for both P1 and P2 protocols. For example, the MPJPE of our method for P1 is 71.08 mm, almost 17 mm lower than that of HMR. Similarly, our MPJPE is almost 4 mm lower than CMR in both P1 and P2. Next, these trends hold even under all the three types of occlusions. For example, for "Bar", our MPJPE is approximately 21 mm and 24 mm lower than HMR for P1 and P2. Finally, our method takes about

Table 1. MPJPE (lower the better) baseline architecture evaluation on Human3.6M.

	#Param	Standard		Bar		Circle		Rectangle	
		P1	P2	P1	P2	P1	P2	P1	P2
HMR [5]	26.8M	87.97	88.00	98.74	98.54	95.28	91.71	100.23	99.61
CMR [8]	42.7M	74.70	71.90	82.99	78.85	83.50	79.24	89.01	84.73
HKMR	26.2M	**71.08**	**67.74**	**78.34**	**74.91**	**77.60**	**71.38**	**81.33**	**76.79**

0.044 s per image, whereas the corresponding numbers for CMR and HMR are 0.062 s and 0.009 s on a Tesla V100 GPU.

Robustness to Degree of Occlusions. We next evaluate the robustness of our regressor as we vary the degree of occlusion in the data. For "Bar", we do this by increasing the width of the bar uniformly from 10 pixels (degree of occlusion or DoC of 1) to 50 pixels (degree of occlusion or DoC of 5). For "Circle", we increase the radius of the circle from 10 pixels (DoC 1) to 50 pixels (DoC 5). Finally, for "Rectangle", we increase the area of the rectangle from 3,000 pixels (DoC 1) to 15,000 pixels (DoC 5). In each case, we perform the occlusion on one joint at a time and compute the average MPJPE over all the joints. The results of this experiment are shown in Fig. 6, where the first row shows the average MPJPE for protocol P1, whereas the second row shows this number for P2. As expected, as the DoC increases, the average MPJPE increases for all three methods. However, this increase is lower for our proposed method, resulting in generally lower average MPJPE values when compared to both HMR and CMR.

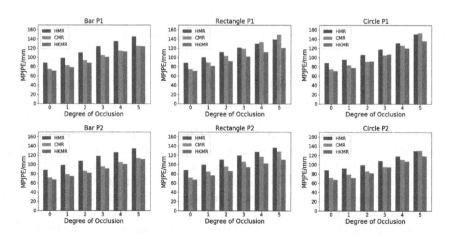

Fig. 6. Robustness to occlusions: HMR, CMR, and our proposed method.

Ablation Study. We next conduct an ablation study to understand the impact of various design considerations in our proposed regressor. The results are shown

Table 2. MPJPE (lower the better) ablation results on Human3.6M.

	No joint hierarchy	Forward only	Discriminator	Full model
P1	77.10	75.99	74.21	**71.08**
P2	74.28	72.10	71.72	**67.74**

in Table 2. "No joint hierarchy" indicates the scenario in our regressor design where each joint prediction is dependent on just the immediately preceding joint, not all the previous joints. "Forward only" corresponds to conducting only the *forward* pass in the inner-iterative process, not the full forward-backward cycle. "Discriminator" indicates our full model but using a discriminator [5] instead of our VAE for the pose prior. "Full model" indicates our proposed HKMR. As can be seen from the MPJPE values for both P1 and P2, modeling all the joint interdependencies hierarchically as in HKMR is important, with an MPJPE gain of almost 6 mm for both protocols. Similarly, there is a 5 mm gain when modeling both forward and backward joint dependence, and finally, our full HKMR model with the VAE performs better than the discriminator, resulting in a 3–4 mm MPJPE gain across both protocols. Finally, we also conduct experiments with a varying number of inner and outer iterations (see Table 3). One can note that while increasing the number of outer or inner iterations reduces MPJPE, too many iterations actually leads to diminishing returns. In our experiments, we found 3 outer and 4 inner iterations worked best.

Table 3. MPJPE (lower the better) ablation results with varying numbers of outer (left) and inner (right) iterations on Human3.6M.

#Outer Iter	1	2	3	4	#Inner Iter	2	4	6
P1	93.79	80.96	**71.08**	73.16	P1	83.34	**71.08**	73.61
P2	88.61	76.41	**67.74**	69.40	P2	82.94	**67.74**	69.55

In-the-Loop Optimization Evaluation. As discussed in Sect. 3.4, the in-the-loop optimization techniques follow the encoder-regressor-optimizer paradigm, with SPIN [6] the first method to be proposed under this framework. SPIN used the same regressor design as HMR [5] for predicting the model parameters. Clearly, our proposed method is applicable to this scheme as a simple drop-in replacement of the HMR regressor with our proposed regressor (HKMR$_{MF}$). We present the results of this experiment in Table 4. As can be noted from the results, our proposed regressor gives lower MPJPE compared to SPIN [6] for both P1 and P2. In fact, our MPJPE result of 64.02 mm and 59.62 mm establishes a new state-of-the-art on Human3.6M. Furthermore, we observe similar trends under the three different kinds of occlusions as well. Qualitative results in Fig. 7

Table 4. Model fitting in-the-loop evaluation on Human3.6M and MPII invisible joints.

Human3.6M	Standard		Bar		Circle		Rectangle		MPII	MPJPE	PCK
MPJPE (mm)↓	P1	P2	P1	P2	P1	P2	P1	P2	Invisible	(pixel)↓	(%)↑
SPIN [6]	65.60	62.23	74.40	68.61	74.06	67.03	77.21	70.35	SPIN [6]	59.52	62.16
HKMR$_{MF}$	**64.02**	**59.62**	**70.10**	**64.91**	**69.60**	**63.22**	**70.10**	**64.91**	**HKMR**$_{MF}$	**55.56**	**66.24**

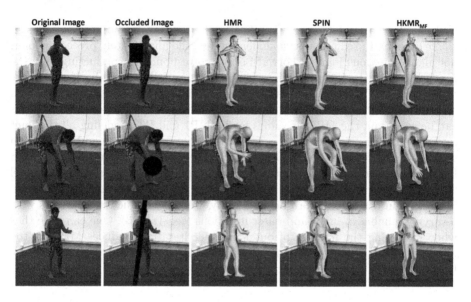

Fig. 7. Our proposed method results in more accurate fits: right hand in first row, left leg in second row, and root orientation in third row.

reinforce this point. For instance, our method results in a better fit in the right hand region (first row) and left leg region (second row) even under occlusions. To further demonstrate the efficacy of our method under occlusions, we also report results on the MPII invisible joints validation dataset [48] in Table 4 (right), where we see substantial gains compared to SPIN for both MPJPE and PCK. Figure 8 shows some qualitative results on this data where we see obvious differences - our method results in substantially better model fits even in challenging cases such as those in columns 1–3.

Comparison with the State of the Art. Finally, we compare the results of our method with competing state-of-the-art methods on the Human3.6M and LSP test set (see Table 5). Note that we follow the same protocol as Kolotouros [6] in the evaluation on the LSP dataset. From Table 5, our proposed method gives the highest accuracy and F1-score on the LSP dataset and the lowest MPJPE for both protocols on the Human3.6M dataset, thereby establishing new state-of-the-art results on both these datasets. To further put these numbers in perspective, our method substantially outperforms even competing

Fig. 8. Qualitative results on the invisible parts in the MPII validation set.

Table 5. Segmentation (% ↑) and MPJPE (mm ↓) on LSP and Human3.6M ("-" indicates result is not reported/unavailable in original papers).

LSP	FB Seg.		Part Seg.		Human3.6M	P1	P2
	acc.	f1	acc.	f1	HMR [5]	87.97	88.00
Oracle [3]	92.17	**0.88**	88.82	0.67	Arnab *et al.* [20]	-	77.80
SMPLify [3]	91.89	**0.88**	87.71	0.64	HoloPose [16]	-	64.28
SMPLify+[28]	92.17	**0.88**	88.24	0.64	CMR [8]	74.70	71.90
HMR [5]	91.67	0.87	87.12	0.60	DaNet [17]	-	61.50
CMR [8]	91.46	0.87	88.69	0.66	DenseRaC [18]	76.80	-
TexturePose [21]	91.82	0.87	89.00	0.67	VIBE [19]	-	65.60
SPIN [6]	91.83	0.87	89.41	0.68	SPIN [6]	65.60	62.23
HKMR$_{MF}$	**92.23**	**0.88**	**89.59**	**0.69**	**HKMR**$_{MF}$	**64.02**	**59.62**

methods that use extra information, *e.g.*, Arnab *et al.* [20] that uses temporal image sequences as opposed to just one single frame, or DenseRaC [18] that uses UV maps as an additional source of supervision. Finally, even compared to the recently published work of Kocabas *et al.* [19], our proposed method gives almost 6 mm lower MPJPE. In fact, even Kocabas *et al.* [19] uses extra temporal information as opposed to just one single frame in our case. The strong performance of our method despite these seemingly disadvantageous factors further substantiates the motivation and competitiveness of our technique. As discussed previously, note that all numbers in Table 5 are standard MPJPE values without any Procrustes (rigid transformation) post-processing.

5   Summary

We presented a new architecture for regressing the pose and shape parameters of a parametric human mesh model that is explicitly informed by the structural knowledge of the model being fit. The proposed new design is quite flexible, which we demonstrated by means of applicability to both the popular encoder-regressor and encoder-regressor-optimizer paradigms for 3D human mesh estimation. By means of extensive experiments on standard benchmark datasets, we

demonstrated the efficacy of our proposed new design, establishing new state-of-the-art performance and improved robustness under a wide variety of data occlusions.

References

1. Singh, V., et al.: DARWIN: deformable patient avatar representation with deep image network. In: Descoteaux, M., Maier-Hein, L., Franz, A., Jannin, P., Collins, D.L., Duchesne, S. (eds.) MICCAI 2017. LNCS, vol. 10434, pp. 497–504. Springer, Cham (2017). https://doi.org/10.1007/978-3-319-66185-8_56
2. Martínez-González, A., Villamizar, M., Canévet, O., Odobez, J.-M.: Real-time convolutional networks for depth-based human pose estimation. In: IROS. IEEE (2018)
3. Bogo, F., Kanazawa, A., Lassner, C., Gehler, P., Romero, J., Black, M.J.: Keep it SMPL: automatic estimation of 3D human pose and shape from a single image. In: Leibe, B., Matas, J., Sebe, N., Welling, M. (eds.) Computer Vision - ECCV 2016. LNCS, vol. 9905. Springer, Cham (2016)
4. Tung, H.-Y., Tung, H.-W., Yumer, E., Fragkiadaki, K.: Self-supervised learning of motion capture. In: NIPS. Curran Associates Inc. (2017)
5. Kanazawa, A., Black, M.J., Jacobs, D.W., Malik, J.: End-to-end recovery of human shape and pose. In: CVPR. IEEE (2018)
6. Kolotouros, N., Pavlakos, G., Black, M.J., Daniilidis, K.: Learning to reconstruct 3D human pose and shape via model-fitting in the loop. In: ICCV. IEEE (2019)
7. Kendall, A., Cipolla, R.: Geometric loss functions for camera pose regression with deep learning. In: CVPR. IEEE (2017)
8. Kolotouros, N., Pavlakos, G., Daniilidis, K.: Convolutional mesh regression for single-image human shape reconstruction. In: CVPR. IEEE (2019)
9. Loper, M., Mahmood, N., Romero, J., Pons-Moll, G., Black, M.J.: SMPL: a skinned multi-person linear model. ACM TOG 34(6), 1–16 (2015)
10. Cao, Z., Hidalgo, G., Simon, T., Wei, S.-E., Sheikh, Y.: OpenPose: real-time multi-person 2D pose estimation using part affinity fields. arXiv preprint arXiv:1812.08008, 2018
11. Carreira, J., Agrawal, P., Fragkiadaki, K., Malik, J.: Human pose estimation with iterative error feedback. In: CVPR. IEEE (2016)
12. Güler, R.A., Neverova, N., Kokkinos, I.: Dense human pose estimation in the wild. In: CVPR. IEEE, Densepose (2018)
13. Mehta, D., et al.: VNect: real-time 3D human pose estimation with a single RGB camera. ACM TOG 36(4), 1–14 (2017)
14. Moreno-Noguer, F.: 3D human pose estimation from a single image via distance matrix regression. In: CVPR. IEEE (2017)
15. Pavlakos, G., Zhou, X., Daniilidis, K.: Ordinal depth supervision for 3D human pose estimation. In: CVPR. IEEE (2018)
16. Guler, R.A., Kokkinos, I.: HoloPose: holistic 3D human reconstruction in-the-wild. In: CVPR. IEEE (2019)
17. Zhang, H., Cao, J., Guo, L., Ouyang, W., Sun, Z.: DaNet: decompose-and-aggregate network for 3D human shape and pose estimation. In: ACM MM. ACM (2019)
18. Xu, Y., Zhu, S.-C., Tung, T.: DenseRaC: joint 3D pose and shape estimation by dense render-and-compare. In: ICCV. IEEE (2019)

19. Kocabas, M., Athanasiou, N., Black, M.J.: VIBE: video inference for human body pose and shape estimation. In: CVPR. IEEE (2020)
20. Arnab, A., Doersch, C., Zisserman, A.: Exploiting temporal context for 3D human pose estimation in the wild. In: CVPR. IEEE (2019)
21. Pavlakos, G., Kolotouros, N., Daniilidis, K.: TexturePose: supervising human mesh estimation with texture consistency. In: ICCV. IEEE (2019)
22. Newell, A., Yang, K., Deng, J.: Stacked hourglass networks for human pose estimation. In: Leibe, B., Matas, J., Sebe, N., Welling, M. (eds.) ECCV 2016. LNCS, vol. 9912, pp. 483–499. Springer, Cham (2016). https://doi.org/10.1007/978-3-319-46484-8_29
23. Pavlakos, G., Zhou, X., Derpanis, K.G., Daniilidis, K.: Coarse-to-fine volumetric prediction for single-image 3d human pose. In: CVPR. IEEE (2017)
24. Wei, S.-E., Ramakrishna, V., Kanade, T., Sheikh, Y.: Convolutional pose machines. In: CVPR. IEEE (2016)
25. Toshev, A., Szegedy, C.: DeepPose: human pose estimation via deep neural networks. In: CVPR. IEEE (2014)
26. Martinez, J., Hossain, R., Romero, J., Little, J.J.: A simple yet effective baseline for 3D human pose estimation. In: ICCV. IEEE (2017)
27. Tan, V., Budvytis, I., Cipolla, R.: Indirect deep structured learning for 3D human body shape and pose prediction. In: BMVC. BMVA Press (2017)
28. Pavlakos, G., Zhu, L., Zhou, X., Daniilidis, K.: Learning to estimate 3D human pose and shape from a single color image. In: CVPR. IEEE (2018)
29. Omran, M., Lassner, C., Pons-Moll, G., Gehler, P., Schiele, B.: Neural body fitting: unifying deep learning and model based human pose and shape estimation. In: 3DV. IEEE (2018)
30. Yao, P., Fang, Z., Wu, F., Feng, Y., Li., J.: DenseBody: directly regressing dense 3D human pose and shape from a single color image. arXiv preprint arXiv:1903.10153 (2019)
31. Varol, G., et al.: BodyNet: volumetric inference of 3D human body shapes. In: Ferrari, V., Hebert, M., Sminchisescu, C., Weiss, Y. (eds.) ECCV 2018. LNCS, vol. 11211, pp. 20–38. Springer, Cham (2018). https://doi.org/10.1007/978-3-030-01234-2_2
32. Lassner, C., Romero, J., Kiefel, M., Bogo, F., Black, M.J., Gehler, P.V.: Unite the people: closing the loop between 3D and 2D human representations. In: CVPR. IEEE (2017)
33. Felzenszwalb, P.F., Huttenlocher, D.P.: Pictorial structures for object recognition. IJCV 61(1), 55–79 (2005)
34. Yang, Y., Ramanan, D.: Articulated human detection with flexible mixtures of parts. IEEE T-PAMI 35(12), 2878–2890 (2012)
35. Cai, Y., et al.: Exploiting spatial-temporal relationships for 3D pose estimation via graph convolutional networks. In: ICCV. IEEE (2019)
36. Ci, H., Wang, C., Ma, X., Wang, Y.: Optimizing network structure for 3D human pose estimation. In: ICCV. IEEE (2019)
37. Aksan, E., Kaufmann, M., Hilliges, O.: Structured prediction helps 3D human motion modelling. In: ICCV, pp. 7144–7153. IEEE (2019)
38. Tang, W., Ying, W.: Does learning specific features for related parts help human pose estimation? In: CVPR. IEEE (2019)
39. Fang, H.-S., Xu, Y.,Wang, W., Liu, X., Zhu, S.-C.: Learning pose grammar to encode human body configuration for 3D pose estimation. In: AAAI. AAAI (2018)
40. Isack, H., et al.: RePose: learning deep kinematic priors for fast human pose estimation. arXiv preprint arXiv:2002.03933 (2020)

41. Zhou, X., Sun, X., Zhang, W., Liang, S., Wei, Y.: Deep kinematic pose regression. In: Hua, G., Jégou, H. (eds.) ECCV 2016. LNCS, vol. 9915, pp. 186–201. Springer, Cham (2016). https://doi.org/10.1007/978-3-319-49409-8_17

42. He, K., Zhang, X., Ren, S., Sun, J.: Deep residual learning for image recognition. In: CVPR. IEEE (2016)

43. Pavlakos, G., et al.: Expressive body capture: 3D hands, face, and body from a single image. In: CVPR. IEEE (2019)

44. Kingma, D.P., Welling. M.: Auto-encoding variational Bayes. In: ICLR (2014)

45. Loper, M., Mahmood, N., Black, M.J.: MoSh: motion and shape capture from sparse markers. ACM TOG **33**(6), 1–13 (2014)

46. Johnson, S., Everingham, M.: Clustered pose and nonlinear appearance models for human pose estimation. In: BMVC. BMVA Press (2010)

47. Johnson, S., Everingham, M.: Learning effective human pose estimation from inaccurate annotation. In: CVPR. IEEE (2011)

48. Andriluka, M., Pishchulin, L., Gehler, P., Schiele, B.: 2D human pose estimation: new benchmark and state of the art analysis. In: CVPR. IEEE (2014)

49. Lin, T.-Y., et al.: Microsoft COCO: common objects in context. In: Fleet, D., Pajdla, T., Schiele, B., Tuytelaars, T. (eds.) ECCV 2014. LNCS, vol. 8693, pp. 740–755. Springer, Cham (2014). https://doi.org/10.1007/978-3-319-10602-1_48

50. Ionescu, C., Papava, D., Olaru, V., Sminchisescu, C.: Human3.6M: large scale datasets and predictive methods for 3D human sensing in natural environments. IEEE T-PAMI **36**(7), 1325–1339 (2013)

51. Mehta, D., et al.: Monocular 3D human pose estimation in the wild using improved CNN supervision. In: 3DV. IEEE (2017)

52. Sárándi, I., Linder, T., Arras, K.O., Leibe, B.: How robust is 3D human pose estimation to occlusion? arXiv preprint arXiv:1808.09316 (2018)

Multi-loss Rebalancing Algorithm for Monocular Depth Estimation

Jae-Han Lee[ID] and Chang-Su Kim[(✉)][ID]

School of Electrical Engineering, Korea University, Seoul, Korea
jaehanlee@mcl.korea.ac.kr , changsukim@korea.ac.kr

Abstract. An algorithm to combine multiple loss terms adaptively for training a monocular depth estimator is proposed in this work. We construct a loss function space containing tens of losses. Using more losses can improve inference capability without any additional complexity in the test phase. However, when many losses are used, some of them may be neglected during training. Also, since each loss decreases at a different speed, adaptive weighting is required to balance the contributions of the losses. To address these issues, we propose the loss rebalancing algorithm that initializes and rebalances the weight for each loss function adaptively in the course of training. Experimental results show that the proposed algorithm provides state-of-the-art depth estimation results on various datasets. Codes are available at https://github.com/jaehanlee-mcl/multi-loss-rebalancing-depth.

Keywords: Monocular depth estimation · Multi-loss rebalancing

1 Introduction

Monocular depth estimation is the task to estimate depth information of a scene from a single image. It is applicable to various higher-level vision tasks, since the depth information is essential for understanding 3D scene geometry. It is more challenging than the depth estimation using stereo images [38] or video frames [44] due to the lack of reliable cues. Early algorithms [7,13,26,39] made assumptions, such as 'blocks world,' to make it easier. They yield unreliable results when the assumptions are invalid. After Eigen *et al.* [9] introduced a convolutional neural network (CNN) for monocular depth estimation, various CNN-based algorithms have been developed.

Recent advances in monocular depth estimation are due to better backbone networks [14,17,18,42], huge RGBD datasets [4,5,11,39,41,43,45], richer labels for training [22,37,48], or sophisticated loss functions [5,8–10,16,25]. Among them, the loss function design has two advantages. First, using a sophisticated

---

Electronic supplementary material The online version of this chapter (https://doi.org/10.1007/978-3-030-58520-4_46) contains supplementary material, which is available to authorized users.

loss can improve inference capability without requiring additional memory complexity for more complicated networks. Second, it may increase the computation time for training but does not affect the time complexity for testing. Existing algorithms adopt various loss functions, including scale-invariant loss [9], gradient loss [8], and normal loss [16]. They also formulate a loss function as a combination of several losses for more effective training.

However, there is no systematic analysis of these loss functions, and there is a lack of understanding how these losses improve the performance. In this paper, we attempt to address this issue. We construct a loss function space, containing many loss terms: some are from existing algorithms, and the others are newly designed. Through extensive experiments and analysis, we find that, as more loss terms are used to train a depth estimator, the performance gets better. However, to exploit a large loss function space in training, two weighting issues should be addressed. First, each loss has a different order of magnitudes. Thus, some losses may be neglected, if the losses are simply summed up. Second, in the course of training, each loss decreases at a different speed. Hence, the contributions of the losses should be balanced periodically. Therefore, we propose the loss rebalancing algorithm that initializes and adjusts the weights for multiple losses adaptively, so that each loss contributes properly to the training of a depth estimator and thus improves the estimation performance. Figure 1 shows an overview of the proposed loss rebalancing algorithm.

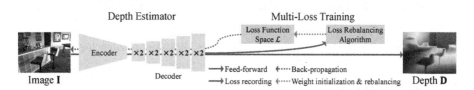

Fig. 1. Overview of the loss rebalancing algorithm: A depth estimator estimates a depth map **D** from an image **I**. Throughout its training, losses are recorded and their weights are initialized and adjusted by the loss rebalancing algorithm.

Extensive experimental results and ablation studies show that the proposed loss rebalancing algorithm improves the performances of monocular depth estimators meaningfully.

This paper has the following main contributions:

- For monocular depth estimation, we construct a loss function space of several tens of losses, and propose the loss rebalancing algorithm to utilize the loss function space effectively.
- The proposed algorithm improves depth estimation performance significantly, without requiring additional network parameters or inference time.
- The proposed depth estimators yield excellent results on the NYUv2 [41] and Make3D [39] datasets.

2   Related Work

Loss Functions: To train monocular depth estimators based on deep learning, many loss functions have been proposed. *Depth losses* directly measure the differences between ground-truth depths and their estimates. Several depth losses are based on the L2-norm [2,8,9,15,31,49], but there are different types of depth losses, such as the L1-norm [35], multinomial logistic loss [10,28,30,36] and berHu loss [25].

Eigen *et al.* [9] pointed out that, in monocular depth estimation, it is ill-posed to estimate a global depth scale, and a significant amount of depth errors are caused by the mismatch between true and predicted scales. They hence proposed a *scale-invariant loss* to eliminate the impacts of global scales, which has been also adopted in [8,36].

Gradient losses and *normal losses* are also often used. A gradient loss penalizes errors, especially near object boundaries in a scene. It is measured from the differences between the derivatives of ground-truth and predicted depth maps. Some algorithms [8,12,16,22] use gradient losses jointly with depth losses. Chakrabarti *et al.* [3] generalized the gradient losses using higher-order derivatives. A normal loss imposes a penalty on mismatches between ground-truth and predicted normal vectors. It can be computed using normal vector labels of training data [37]. When they are unavailable, normal vectors can be approximated from depth maps [16]. In addition, the semantic loss [19], the pairwise loss [50], the SSIM loss [12] have been developed.

Even though various losses have been proposed to yield successful results, to the best of our knowledge, no paper analyzes the effectiveness of different losses systematically. Moreover, in most algorithms, the overall loss is defined as a weighted sum of only a few loss terms, and the weights are determined heuristically. In this work, we define a loss function space consisting of 78 losses. Then, we propose an effective algorithm to use all those losses and to initialize and adjust their weights.

Loss Function Balancing: Balancing between various loss functions has been considered in the multi-task learning field [6,21,40]. During the training of models, the weights of loss functions for various tasks, such as depth estimation, semantic segmentation, and surface normal estimation, are dynamically adjusted. Kendall *et al.* [21] proposed a weighting scheme based on the uncertainty of each loss function. They assumed that the tasks are independent of one another in their maximum likelihood formulation. Chen *et al.* [6] designed another weighting scheme, which balances the gradient magnitude for each task. Sener and Koltun [40] attempted to achieve a Pareto optimum between loss functions. Note that, in both [6] and [40], it was assumed that the objectives of multiple loss functions conflict with one another. All these algorithms are for multi-task learning, so they are fundamentally different from the proposed rebalancing algorithm of loss functions for a monocular depth estimator. Their assumptions are invalid in the proposed loss function space, because we derive all losses from the same depth map.

3 Proposed Algorithm

Figure 1 is an overview of the proposed algorithm. The proposed depth estimator has the encoder-decoder architecture [1,47] similarly to most deep-learning-based depth estimators. The architecture is described in detail in Sect. 4.1. During the training, losses are recorded by the loss rebalancing algorithm, which initializes and adjusts the weights of loss functions.

Let f denote the depth estimator network and θ be its parameters. Given an image $\mathbf{I}$, f estimates a depth map $\widehat{\mathbf{D}} = f(\mathbf{I}; \theta)$. The objective is to determine the optimal parameters to minimize the overall loss function ℓ_{all},

$$\theta^* = \arg\min_{\theta} \sum_{k:\mathbf{I}_k \in \mathcal{I}} \ell_{\text{all}}\left(f(\mathbf{I}_k; \theta), \mathbf{D}_k\right) \tag{1}$$

where $\mathcal{I}$ is the set of training images, and $\mathbf{D}_k$ is the ground-truth depth map for the kth training image $\mathbf{I}_k$.

3.1 Loss Function Space

The overall loss function ℓ_{all} is defined as a weighted sum of multiple loss functions in the loss function space $\mathcal{L}$,

$$\ell_{\text{all}} = \sum_{i:\ell_i \in \mathcal{L}} w_i \ell_i \tag{2}$$

where ℓ_i denotes the ith loss function in $\mathcal{L}$ and w_i is the corresponding weight. Table 1 lists all 78 ($= 6 \times 13$) losses in $\mathcal{L}$. Given a depth map $\mathbf{D}^0$, we repeatedly halve its spatial resolution in both horizontal and vertical directions to yield downsampled depth maps $\mathbf{D}^1, \mathbf{D}^2, \mathbf{D}^3, \mathbf{D}^4, \mathbf{D}^5$. Here, superscripts denote spatial scales. Then, we compute 13 kinds of losses at each spatial scale. Let us describe each loss subsequently. For notational convenience, we omit the superscripts representing spatial scales.

Let $\mathbf{D}$ be a ground-truth depth map and $\widehat{\mathbf{D}}$ be its estimate. The common depth loss ℓ_{D} is given by the entrywise L1-norm for a matrix,

$$\ell_{\text{D}} = \frac{1}{HW} \left\| \widehat{\mathbf{D}} - \mathbf{D} \right\|_1 \tag{3}$$

where W and H are the width and height of the depth maps. We use the L1-norm for most losses, which is known to facilitate more efficient training than the L2-norm [35].

A mean-removed loss measures a difference between depth maps after removing depth scales. This loss function is similar to the scale-invariant term in [9]. First, the global-mean-removed loss ℓ_{M} is defined as

$$\ell_{\text{M}} = \frac{1}{HW} \left\| (\widehat{\mathbf{D}} - \hat{\mu}) - (\mathbf{D} - \mu) \right\|_1 \tag{4}$$

Table 1. Loss functions, which compose the loss function space $\mathcal{L}$.

	Spatial scale					
	0	1	2	3	4	5
Depth losses	ℓ_D^0	ℓ_D^1	ℓ_D^2	ℓ_D^3	ℓ_D^4	ℓ_D^5
Mean-removed losses	ℓ_M^0	ℓ_M^1	ℓ_M^2	ℓ_M^3	ℓ_M^4	ℓ_M^5
	ℓ_{M5}^0	ℓ_{M5}^1	ℓ_{M5}^2	ℓ_{M5}^3	ℓ_{M5}^4	ℓ_{M5}^5
	ℓ_{M17}^0	ℓ_{M17}^1	ℓ_{M17}^2	ℓ_{M17}^3	ℓ_{M17}^4	ℓ_{M17}^5
	ℓ_{M65}^0	ℓ_{M65}^1	ℓ_{M65}^2	ℓ_{M65}^3	ℓ_{M65}^4	ℓ_{M65}^5
Gradient losses	ℓ_r^0	ℓ_r^1	ℓ_r^2	ℓ_r^3	ℓ_r^4	ℓ_r^5
	ℓ_c^0	ℓ_c^1	ℓ_c^2	ℓ_c^3	ℓ_c^4	ℓ_c^5
	ℓ_{rr}^0	ℓ_{rr}^1	ℓ_{rr}^2	ℓ_{rr}^3	ℓ_{rr}^4	ℓ_{rr}^5
	ℓ_{rc}^0	ℓ_{rc}^1	ℓ_{rc}^2	ℓ_{rc}^3	ℓ_{rc}^4	ℓ_{rc}^5
	ℓ_{cc}^0	ℓ_{cc}^1	ℓ_{cc}^2	ℓ_{cc}^3	ℓ_{cc}^4	ℓ_{cc}^5
Normal losses	ℓ_N^0	ℓ_N^1	ℓ_N^2	ℓ_N^3	ℓ_N^4	ℓ_N^5
	ℓ_{Nr}^0	ℓ_{Nr}^1	ℓ_{Nr}^2	ℓ_{Nr}^3	ℓ_{Nr}^4	ℓ_{Nr}^5
	ℓ_{Nc}^0	ℓ_{Nc}^1	ℓ_{Nc}^2	ℓ_{Nc}^3	ℓ_{Nc}^4	ℓ_{Nc}^5

where $\hat{\mu}$ and μ are the average depths in $\hat{\mathbf{D}}$ and $\mathbf{D}$, respectively. This loss is based on the observation that, although it is ambiguous to estimate the global depth scale (*i.e.* average depth) from an image, the relative depth of each pixel with respect to the average depth can be predicted more reliably. Note that relative estimation is easier than absolute estimation in other applications as well, such as age estimation [32]. Similarly, a depth estimator should be capable of predicting whether a pixel within a region is farther or nearer than the average depth of the region. Thus, we introduce a local-mean-removed loss ℓ_{Mn}, which penalizes the relative depth errors with respect to local $n \times n$ square regions,

$$\ell_{Mn} = \frac{1}{HW} \left\| \left(\hat{\mathbf{D}} - \hat{\mathbf{D}} \circledast \frac{\mathbf{J}_n}{n^2} \right) - \left(\mathbf{D} - \mathbf{D} \circledast \frac{\mathbf{J}_n}{n^2} \right) \right\|_1 \tag{5}$$

where $\circledast$ denotes the convolution, and $\mathbf{J}_n$ is the $n \times n$ matrix composed of all ones. As listed in Table 1, we consider three square sizes ($n = 5, 17, 65$).

Next, we use gradient losses [3,8,12,22]. The gradient loss ℓ_r in the row direction is defined as

$$\ell_r = \frac{1}{HW} \left\| \nabla_r \hat{\mathbf{D}} - \nabla_r \mathbf{D} \right\|_1 \tag{6}$$

where the partial derivative ∇_r is implemented as the difference between horizontally adjacent pixels. Similarly, the gradient loss ℓ_c in the column direction and the 2nd-order derivatives ℓ_{rr}, ℓ_{rc}, and ℓ_{cc} are also defined.

We also use the normal loss ℓ_N. This loss may be computed using ground-truth normal vectors [8,37]. However, we train a depth estimator using only depth labels. Thus, as in [16], we approximate the normal vector $\mathbf{n}_{ij}$ at (i,j)

from the depth gradient by

$$\mathbf{n}_{ij} = [-\nabla_\mathrm{r}\mathbf{D}(i,j), -\nabla_\mathrm{c}\mathbf{D}(i,j), 1]^T. \tag{7}$$

Then, ℓ_N is defined using the cosine similarity by

$$\ell_\mathrm{N} = \frac{1}{HW} \sum_{i=1}^{H}\sum_{j=1}^{W} \left(1 - \frac{\widehat{\mathbf{n}}_{ij}^T \mathbf{n}_{ij}}{\|\widehat{\mathbf{n}}_{ij}\|_2 \|\mathbf{n}_{ij}\|_2}\right) \tag{8}$$

We further introduce the 2nd-order normal losses ℓ_{Nr} and ℓ_{Nc}, by measuring the normal vectors of the partial derivative maps $\nabla_\mathrm{r}\mathbf{D}$ and $\nabla_\mathrm{c}\mathbf{D}$. Specifically, to compute ℓ_{Nr}, the second-order normal vector $[-\nabla_\mathrm{r}\nabla_\mathrm{r}\mathbf{D}, -\nabla_\mathrm{c}\nabla_\mathrm{r}\mathbf{D}, 1]^T$ is used instead of (7). Similarly, ℓ_{Nc} is computed.

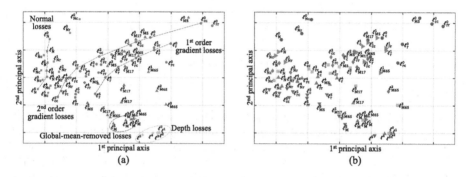

Fig. 2. Projection of the losses in $\mathcal{L}$ onto the plane, determined by the two principal axes. The losses are represented by different colors and marks according to (a) loss types and (b) spatial scales. Also, in (a), to facilitate observation, some losses in the same types are connected by dashed lines or enclosed by dashed ellipses.

Some loss functions in $\mathcal{L}$ exhibit similar tendencies during the training. To analyze the similarity or dissimilarity among the loss functions, we train a preliminary depth estimator and record the output values of each loss function ℓ_i in a vector $\mathbf{t}_i$. Then, we project these vectors $\mathbf{t}_i$ for $\ell_i \in \mathcal{L}$ onto the 2D plane, by performing the principal component analysis (PCA). Figure 2 shows the projection results. In Fig. 2(a), losses are represented in different colors and marks according to their types. The depth losses ℓ_D and the global-mean-removed losses ℓ_M, respectively, are tightly located regardless of the spatial scales. In contrast, the gradient losses, especially the 2nd-order ones ℓ_{rr} and ℓ_{cc}, exhibit different characteristics according to the spatial scales and are located far from one another in the function space. In Fig. 2(b), we also classify the losses by their spatial scales. Except for the depth losses ℓ_D and the global-mean-removed losses ℓ_M, each type of losses are widely distributed in the space according to the scales.

3.2 Loss Rebalancing Algorithm

We use the loss functions in $\mathcal{L}$ to train a monocular depth estimator. Those functions address different aspects of depth structures. Combining these diverse loss functions improves the inference capability of the trained estimator. As compared to using a single loss function, the proposed approach increases the training time but does not require any additional complexity in the test phase; after training, it demands the same time or memory complexity to estimate the depth map of a test image.

There are two weighting issues to be addressed.

- How to initialize the weight w_i for each $\ell_i \in \mathcal{L}$ in (2)?
- In the course of training, how to adjust w_i for ℓ_i, whose output values decrease at a different speed from the other loss functions? For example, if ℓ_i is a relatively easy optimization function and decreases much faster than the others, should we increase or decrease w_i?

To solve these issues, we propose weight initialization and rebalancing schemes.

Weight Initialization: Each loss function ℓ_i yields output values, which may have different orders of magnitudes from those of the other loss functions. This is because ℓ_i is computed at a different spatial scale, or it deals with a different feature. Thus, to balance the contribution of each ℓ_i to the overall loss function ℓ_{all}, we train the network preliminarily after setting each weight equally to $\frac{1}{|\mathcal{L}|}$ and record the average output $\bar{\ell}_i$ of ℓ_i. Then, we initialize the weight w_i so that the contribution $w_i\bar{\ell}_i$ to the overall loss $\bar{\ell}_{\text{all}}$ is identical for every i. In other words, we initially set

$$w_i^{(0)} = \frac{\bar{\ell}_{\text{all}}}{\bar{\ell}_i} \qquad \text{for each } \ell_i \in \mathcal{L}, \tag{9}$$

where the superscripts (0) mean that it is the initial weight.

Weight Rebalancing: During the training, we adjust the weights periodically. Suppose that a period consists of N training images. Let $L_i^{(t)}$ denote the sum of the N losses, generated by ℓ_i in period t. Also, let $w_i^{(t-1)}$ be the weight for $L_i^{(t)}$, which is determined after the previous period $t-1$ and used for the current period t. Then, the overall loss $L_{\text{all}}^{(t)}$ in period t is given by

$$L_{\text{all}}^{(t)} = \sum_i w_i^{(t-1)} L_i^{(t)}. \tag{10}$$

After period t, we update weight $w_i^{(t)}$ by comparing $L_i^{(t)}$ with $L_i^{(t-1)}$. Let $P_i^{(t)} = L_i^{(t)}/L_{\text{all}}^{(t)}$ be the ratio of the ith loss $L_i^{(t)}$ to the overall loss $L_{\text{all}}^{(t)}$. We

compute the change in the ratio by $\Delta P_i^{(t)} = P_i^{(t)} - P_i^{(t-1)}$. Then, we adjust the weight $w_i^{(t)}$ via

$$w_i^{(t)} = w_i^{(t-1)} \left(1 - \lambda \times \frac{\Delta P_i^{(t)}}{P_i^{(t)}}\right) \tag{11}$$

where λ is called the rebalancing parameter. This rebalancing equation has the following properties:

- If $\lambda = 0$, then $w_i^{(t)} = w_i^{(t-1)}$. Thus, the initial weights remain unchanged without rebalancing.
- If $\lambda = 1$, (11) can be rewritten as

$$w_i^{(t)} P_i^{(t)} = w_i^{(t-1)} P_i^{(t-1)}, \tag{12}$$

  which means that the weight is updated to maintain the contribution of ith loss to the overall loss at the same level between the two periods $t - 1$ and t.
- In general, if $\lambda > 0$, the weight for an 'easy' loss function increases. Suppose that a certain loss function ℓ_i is easier to train than the others. Then, its current percentage $P_i^{(t)}$ is lower than the previous $P_i^{(t-1)}$, resulting in a negative $\Delta P_i^{(t)}$. Then, $w_i^{(t)} > w_i^{(t-1)}$ from (11). Therefore, ℓ_i is multiplied with a bigger weight in the next period. Hence, a positive λ encourages the training algorithm to focus on easy loss terms.
- On the contrary, if $\lambda < 0$, the training focuses on 'difficult' loss terms.
- It can be shown that $\sum_i w_i^{(t-1)} L_i^{(t)} = \sum_i w_i^{(t)} L_i^{(t)}$ for all t. Thus, rebalancing in (11) is done so that the overall loss $L_{\text{all}}^{(t)}$ in (10) is maintained when $w_i^{(t-1)}$ is replaced with $w_i^{(t)}$. This makes the monitoring of overall losses over periods easier, since the scale of an overall loss is not affected by the rebalancing.

We can start with a positive λ to reduce easy losses more quickly and teach the network to learn uncomplicated depth structures in scenes first. Then, we can gradually reduce λ to teach the network hard-to-learn structures. In the default mode, we start with $\lambda = 3$ and monotonically decrease it to -3.

Figure 3 visualizes the contributions of losses according to the scheduling of λ. The radius of each circle indicates the magnitude of $w_i^{(t)} P_i^{(t)}$ for the corresponding loss, and its color represents the increase or decrease of the magnitude. Losses with increased contributions (*i.e.* magnitudes), as compared to the previous epoch, are in red, while those with decreased contributions are in blue. The following observations can be made from Fig. 3.

- ($\lambda = 0$) The loss rebalancing is not applied. Difficult loss terms, such as ℓ_{rr}^0 and ℓ_{cc}^0, occupy more portions of contributions as the training goes on.
- ($\lambda = 1$) The contribution of each loss is maintained at the same level.
- ($\lambda = 3$) Easy losses are emphasized as the training goes on. We see that ℓ_{D} and ℓ_{M} at all scales and all types of coarse scale losses are on the easier side.
- ($\lambda = -3$) Difficult losses are emphasized. Most fine-scale losses are difficult.
- ($\lambda : 3 \to -3$) By decreasing λ from 3 to -3, the training focuses on easy loss terms first and on difficult ones later.

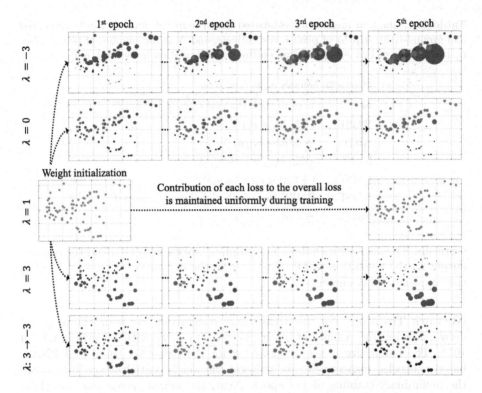

Fig. 3. Visualizing the contributions of losses according to the scheduling of λ: The radius of each circle represents the magnitude of $w_i^{(t)} P_i^{(t)}$ for the corresponding loss. If the magnitude decreases as compared to the previous epoch, the circle is in blue. If it increases, the circle is in red. Green means no change. Please refer to Fig. 2 to see which loss is indicated by each circle. (Color figure online)

In Sect. 4, it is shown experimentally that the default mode ($\lambda : 3 \rightarrow -3$) provides the best depth estimation results.

4 Experimental Results

4.1 Implementation Details

Encoder-Decoder Architecture: We adopt the encoder-decoder architecture [1,47] for the monocular depth estimator. We design the network structure of the depth estimator in the simplest way, so that the proposed multi-loss rebalancing algorithm can be applied to other existing or future backbone networks with minimal modifications.

For the encoder, we test two backbones, DenseNet161 [18] and PNASNet [33], after removing their classification layers. The spatial resolution of an input image to the encoder is 288×384, while that of the encoder output is 9×12. Thus, the encoder reduces the spatial resolution by a factor of $\frac{1}{2^5}$ both horizontally and

Table 2. Evaluation metrics for estimated depth maps: $\hat{d}_i$ and d_i denote estimated and ground-truth depths of pixel i, respectively, and N is the number of pixels. Also, l_{ij} has a value of 1 or -1 depending on the relative relation between d_i and d_j.

Metrics for ordinary depth estimation	
δ_n	% of d_i such that $\max\{\frac{\hat{d}_i}{d_i}, \frac{d_i}{\hat{d}_i}\} < 1.25^n$
RMSE_{lin}	$(\frac{1}{N}\Sigma_i(\hat{d}_i - d_i)^2)^{0.5}$
ARD	$\frac{1}{N}\Sigma_i|\hat{d}_i - d_i|/d_i$
log10	$\frac{1}{N}\Sigma_i|\log_{10}\hat{d}_i - \log_{10}d_i|$
RMSE_{log}	$(\frac{1}{N}\Sigma_i(\log\hat{d}_i - \log d_i)^2)^{0.5}$
RMSE_{si}	RMSE (log) with global scale removed
SRD	$\frac{1}{N}\Sigma_i|\hat{d}_i - d_i|^2/d_i$

vertically. The decoder includes 5 up-sampling blocks, which expand the encoder output to the resolution of $\mathbf{D}^0$. We describe the decoder structure in detail in the supplemental document.

Network Training: For the performance comparison, we train the proposed networks using the Adam optimizer [23] for 20 epochs with a learning rate of 10^{-4}. The batch size is set to 12 and 8 for the DenseNet-based and PNAS-based networks, respectively. We perform the weight initialization in (9) after the preliminary training of 1/4 epoch. Next, the weight rebalancing in (11) is performed periodically every 1/4 epoch. In the default mode, the rebalancing parameter λ is initialized to 3 at the first epoch and gradually decreased to -3 until the fifth epoch. Also, we adopt the augmentation policy of [16].

Relative Depth Perception: We apply the proposed algorithm to relative depth perception [5, 45, 52] as well. By fusing relative depth maps with ordinary ones, we can improve the depth estimation performance further. We include the training details and experiment results for the relative depth estimator in the supplemental document.

4.2   Datasets and Evaluation Metrics

We use two depth datasets: NYUv2 [41] for indoor scene and Make3D [39] for outdoor scene. Ground-truth depth maps have blank areas with missing depth. For training, we fill in the incomplete depth maps using the colorization scheme [29], as done in [41].

For experiments on NYUv2, we develop two depth estimators: 'Proposed (Dense)' and 'Proposed (PNAS)'. Both estimators are trained using the sequences of the training split in [41]. The two estimators differ only in the encoder backbones, and their training details are the same. For experiments on Make3D, we train 'Proposed (PNAS)' using the Make3D training data.

Table 2 lists the evaluation metrics. We follow the evaluation protocol of [10].

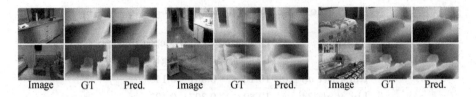

Image   GT   Pred.   Image   GT   Pred.   Image   GT   Pred.

Fig. 4. Qualitative results. Farther depths are in red, while closer ones in blue. (Color figure online)

Table 3. Performance comparison on NYUv2 [41]. The best results are boldfaced.

	The higher, the better			The lower, the better					
	δ_1	δ_2	δ_3	$RMSE_{lin}$	ARD	log10	$RMSE_{log}$	$RMSE_{si}$	SRD
Eigen et al. [9]	61.1%	88.7%	97.1%	0.907	0.215	–	0.285	0.219	0.212
Li et al. [31]	62.1%	88.6%	96.8%	0.821	0.232	0.094	–	–	–
Eigen and Fergus [8]	76.9%	95.0%	98.8%	0.641	0.158	–	0.214	0.171	0.121
Chakrabarti et al. [3]	80.6%	95.8%	98.7%	0.620	0.149	–	0.205	–	0.118
Laina et al. [25]	81.1%	95.3%	98.8%	0.573	0.127	0.055	0.195	–	–
Xu et al. [46]	81.1%	95.4%	98.7%	0.586	0.121	0.052	–	–	–
Lee et al. [27]	81.5%	96.3%	99.1%	0.572	0.139	–	0.193	–	0.096
Fu et al. [10]	82.8%	96.5%	99.2%	0.509	0.115	0.051	–	–	–
Kundu et al. [24]	85.6%	96.6%	99.1%	0.506	0.114	0.046	–	–	–
Zhang et al. [51]	81.5%	96.2%	99.2%	0.501	0.144	–	0.181	–	–
Lee and Kim [28]	83.7%	97.1%	**99.4%**	0.538	0.131	–	0.180	0.148	0.087
Zhang et al. [50]	84.6%	96.8%	**99.4%**	0.497	0.121	–	0.175	–	–
Hu et al. [16]	86.6%	**97.5%**	99.3%	0.530	**0.115**	0.050	–	–	–
Proposed (Dense)	85.0%	96.9%	99.2%	0.457	0.127	0.053	0.160	0.128	0.088
Proposed (PNAS)	**87.0%**	97.4%	99.3%	**0.430**	0.119	**0.050**	**0.151**	**0.123**	**0.078**

4.3 Comparison with Conventional Algorithms

Table 3 compares the performances on NYUv2. Even 'Proposed (Dense)' outperforms all conventional algorithms by a large margin in terms of $RMSE_{lin}$ and $RMSE_{log}$, and provides comparable or better results in terms of other metrics. In particular, [28] adopts the same DenseNet as the backbone, but its decoder structure and post-processing scheme are much more complicated that those of 'Proposed (Dense)'. Nevertheless, 'Proposed (Dense)' outperforms [28] in most metrics, which means that the proposed loss rebalancing algorithm improves the depth estimation performance effectively. Moreover, 'Proposed (PNAS)' outperforms all algorithms in most metrics. Figure 4 shows examples of depths maps, predicted by 'Proposed (PNAS)'.

Table 4 shows that the proposed algorithm also provides excellent performance on the outdoor dataset Make3D. We see that the proposed algorithm outperforms the existing algorithms in terms of $RMSE_{lin}$. The supplemental document shows that the proposed algorithm yields competitive results on the KITTI dataset [11] as well.

Table 4. Comparison on Make3D [39].

	Evaluated in 0–70 depth range		
	$RMSE_{lin}$	ARD	log10
Karsch et al. [20]	15.10	0.361	0.148
Liu et al. [34]	12.89	0.307	0.125
Kundu et al. [24]	9.56	0.452	–
Xu et al. [46]	8.56	0.198	–
Fu et al. [10]	7.32	**0.162**	**0.067**
Proposed	**5.87**	0.231	0.082

4.4   Ablation Studies

We analyze the depth estimation performance of the proposed algorithm on the NYUv2 test split in Table 5. Here, $\mathcal{L}_D$. $\mathcal{L}_M$, $\mathcal{L}_G$, and $\mathcal{L}_N$ denote the sets of depth, mean-removed, gradient, and normal losses in Table 1, respectively. Also, $\mathcal{L}^k$ denotes the set of losses at spatial scale k. Each model is trained for 5 epochs using three training datasets [4, 41, 43]. Since the network training has stochastic properties, we show the average performance of the three models for each setting for more reliable comparison.

Loss Function Space: From Part (a), the following observations are made.

- $\{\ell_D^0, \ell_M^0, \ell_r^0, \ell_c^0\}$ and $\{\ell_D^0, \ell_r^0, \ell_c^0, \ell_N^0\}$ correspond to the loss sets of [8] and [16], respectively. They make small improvements as compared with the baseline using only ℓ_D^0.
- By employing multi-scale losses, greater performance gains are achieved. It is most effective to combine gradient losses with depth losses ($\mathcal{L}_D \cup \mathcal{L}_G$). This is presumably because gradient losses are more widely distributed in the loss function space in Fig. 2 than mean-removed or normal losses are.
- Coarse-scale losses ($\mathcal{L}^3 \cup \mathcal{L}^4 \cup \mathcal{L}^5$) are more effective than fine-scale ones ($\mathcal{L}^0 \cup \mathcal{L}^1 \cup \mathcal{L}^2$). Using the finest-scale set $\mathcal{L}^0$ only is the least reliable.

Loss Rebalancing: Part (b) demonstrates the effectiveness of the proposed loss rebalancing algorithm. Compared with the corresponding settings in Part (a) using the same loss functions, the improved scores are in red, while the worsened ones in blue. As mentioned above, coarse-scale losses are more important for reliable depth estimation. Also, as shown in the bottom row in Fig. 3, the loss rebalancing algorithm emphasizes these important losses at the beginning of training. Therefore, in all cases including coarse-scale losses, the loss rebalancing algorithm improves the depth estimation performances. On the other hand, if only fine-scale losses are used ($\mathcal{L}^0$ or $\mathcal{L}^0 \cup \mathcal{L}^1 \cup \mathcal{L}^2$), the loss rebalancing algorithm becomes ineffective. However, by comparing the results of the entire loss function space $\mathcal{L}$ to those of $\mathcal{L}^3 \cup \mathcal{L}^4 \cup \mathcal{L}^5$, we see that these fine-scale losses also contribute to the performance improvement.

Table 5. Ablation studies using various settings: 'I' means the weight initialization and 'R' means the weight rebalancing. The best results are boldfaced. In Part (b), the improved results (compared to Part (a)) are in red, while the degraded ones in blue.

	# Losses	I	R	λ	δ_1	RMSE$_{\text{lin}}$	RMSE$_{\text{log}}$	ARD
(a) Combination of loss functions								
$\{\ell_D^0\}$	1	-	-	0	84.8%	0.474	0.164	0.128
$\{\ell_D^0, \ell_M^0, \ell_r^0, \ell_c^0\}$	4	-	-	0	85.6%	0.456	0.159	0.124
$\{\ell_D^0, \ell_r^0, \ell_c^0, \ell_N^0\}$	4	-	-	0	84.8%	0.472	0.164	0.127
$\mathcal{L}_D \cup \mathcal{L}_N$	24	-	-	0	86.3%	0.448	0.155	0.121
$\mathcal{L}_D \cup \mathcal{L}_M$	30	-	-	0	85.9%	0.455	0.157	0.124
$\mathcal{L}_D \cup \mathcal{L}_G$	36	-	-	0	86.5%	0.445	0.153	**0.117**
$\mathcal{L}^0$	13	-	-	0	85.3%	0.462	0.160	0.132
$\mathcal{L}^0 \cup \mathcal{L}^1 \cup \mathcal{L}^2$	39	-	-	0	85.7%	0.454	0.157	0.122
$\mathcal{L}^3 \cup \mathcal{L}^4 \cup \mathcal{L}^5$	39	-	-	0	**86.6%**	0.444	**0.153**	0.119
$\mathcal{L}$	78	-	-	0	86.4%	**0.440**	**0.153**	0.122
(b) Effectiveness of loss rebalancing algorithm								
$\mathcal{L}_D \cup \mathcal{L}_N$	24	✓	✓	$3 \rightarrow -3$	86.3%	0.440	0.153	0.119
$\mathcal{L}_D \cup \mathcal{L}_M$	30	✓	✓	$3 \rightarrow -3$	86.3%	0.446	0.154	0.119
$\mathcal{L}_D \cup \mathcal{L}_G$	36	✓	✓	$3 \rightarrow -3$	86.9%	0.437	0.151	0.118
$\mathcal{L}^0$	13	✓	✓	$3 \rightarrow -3$	84.8%	0.466	0.161	0.126
$\mathcal{L}^0 \cup \mathcal{L}^1 \cup \mathcal{L}^2$	39	✓	✓	$3 \rightarrow -3$	85.5%	0.456	0.158	0.123
$\mathcal{L}^3 \cup \mathcal{L}^4 \cup \mathcal{L}^5$	39	✓	✓	$3 \rightarrow -3$	86.7%	0.443	0.152	0.116
$\mathcal{L}$	78	✓	✓	$3 \rightarrow -3$	87.0%	0.434	0.150	0.117
(c) Scheduling of λ								
		✓	✓	-3	84.7%	0.459	0.161	0.130
		✓	-	0	86.5%	0.443	0.154	0.118
		✓	✓	1	86.5%	0.442	0.154	0.123
$\mathcal{L}$	78	✓	✓	3	86.6%	0.445	0.153	0.117
		✓	✓	$2 \rightarrow -2$	86.8%	0.439	0.151	**0.116**
		✓	✓	$3 \rightarrow -3$	**87.0%**	**0.434**	**0.150**	0.117
		✓	✓	$5 \rightarrow -5$	86.4%	0.445	0.153	0.121
(d) Necessity of weight initialization								
		-	-	0	86.4%	0.440	0.153	0.122
$\mathcal{L}$	78	✓	-	0	86.5%	0.443	0.154	0.118
		-	✓	$3 \rightarrow -3$	85.6%	0.459	0.157	0.127
		✓	✓	$3 \rightarrow -3$	**87.0%**	**0.434**	**0.150**	**0.117**
(e) Another weighting algorithm [21]								
$\mathcal{L}$	78	-			85.6%	0.455	0.160	0.125

Table 6. Performance comparison of the proposed depth estimators using different backbones on NYUv2 [41].

	The higher, the better			The lower, the better					
	δ_1	δ_2	δ_3	$RMSE_{lin}$	ARD	log10	$RMSE_{log}$	$RMSE_{si}$	SRD
VGG16	77.2%	95.0%	99.0%	0.544	0.160	0.067	0.196	0.160	0.117
ResNet50	82.4%	96.3%	99.1%	0.482	0.138	0.058	0.174	0.142	0.094
SENet154	87.1%	97.5%	99.4%	0.426	0.116	0.049	0.149	0.123	0.074

Scheduling of λ: Part (c) compares the performance according to the scheduling of λ in (11). As discussed in Sect. 3.2, a bigger λ focuses more on easy losses, such as depth, global-mean-removed, and other coarse-scale ones. Note that $\lambda = 3$ provides better results than $\lambda = -3$. However, the settings using decreasing λ provide better results. This implies that focusing on easy losses first and on difficult ones later is an effective strategy. Among all settings, the default setting $\lambda : 3 \rightarrow -3$ provides the best results.

Weight Initialization: The first two rows in Part (d) show that the weight initialization in itself does not contribute to the training. However, prior to the weight rebalancing, it is essential to equalize the contribution of losses. If each loss has a different magnitudes, the ratio $P_i^{(t)}$ and its change $\Delta P_i^{(t)}$ in (11) are not meaningful, invalidating the rebalancing algorithm. Thus, the rebalancing without the initialization yields unreliable results in the third row of Part (d).

Weighting Algorithm [21]: Part (e) replaces the proposed loss rebalancing algorithm with the weighting scheme in [21]. Their maximum likelihood formulation assumes the tasks are independent of one another. This assumption is invalid in $\mathcal{L}$ because all losses are derived from the same depth map. Hence, their scheme performs worse than the proposed algorithm. Similarly to the first row of Fig. 3, [21] emphasizes difficult losses.

4.5   Different Backbone Networks

We verify that the proposed algorithm is effective regardless of a backbone network. In Table 6, We replace the encoder backbone with widely-used networks: VGG16 [42], ResNet50 [14], and SENet154 [17]. By comparing Table 6 to Table 3, we see that, for each backbone, the proposed algorithm outperforms the conventional algorithms using the same backbone. For instance, [8], [25], and [16] use VGG16, ResNet50, and SENet154 as their backbones, respectively.

Table 7. Training and testing times of the proposed algorithm on NYUv2 [41].

Training	$\{\ell_D^0\}$	$\mathcal{L}^3 \cup \mathcal{L}^4 \cup \mathcal{L}^5$	$\mathcal{L}$	Testing	
s/iter	1.63	1.70	1.97	s/scene	0.047

4.6 Time Complexity

Table 7 analyzes the complexity of the proposed algorithm in training and testing. The experiments are done with a TITAN X GPU. For training, using more losses increases the training time. However, compared to the use of ℓ_D^0 alone, the training time increases only 4% and 21% for $\mathcal{L}^3 \cup \mathcal{L}^4 \cup \mathcal{L}^5$ and $\mathcal{L}$, respectively, even though the number of losses increases from 1 to 39 and 78. Regardless of the loss setting, proposed algorithm requires the same inference time.

5 Conclusions

For monocular depth estimation, we constructed a loss function space of diverse loss terms and showed that the proposed space improves the depth estimation accuracy without increasing the network complexity or inference time. Also, we proposed the loss rebalancing algorithm to make each loss term contribute to the training in a balanced manner. Experimental results showed that the proposed depth estimators achieve excellent performances on various datasets.

Acknowledgment. This work was conducted by Center for Applied Research in Artificial Intelligence (CARAI) grant funded by Defense Acquisition Program Administration (DAPA) and Agency for Defense Development (ADD) (UD190031RD).

References

1. Badrinarayanan, V., Kendall, A., Cipolla, R.: SegNet: a deep convolutional encoder-decoder architecture for image segmentation. IEEE Trans. Pattern Anal. Mach. Intell. **39**(12), 2481–2495 (2017)
2. Gan, Y., Xu, X., Sun, W., Lin, L.: Monocular depth estimation with affinity, vertical pooling, and label enhancement. In: Ferrari, V., Hebert, M., Sminchisescu, C., Weiss, Y. (eds.) ECCV 2018. LNCS, vol. 11207, pp. 232–247. Springer, Cham (2018). https://doi.org/10.1007/978-3-030-01219-9_14
3. Chakrabarti, A., Shao, J., Shakhnarovich, G.: Depth from a single image by harmonizing overcomplete local network predictions. In: NIPS (2016)
4. Chang, A., et al.: Matterport3D: Learning from RGB-D data in indoor environments. In: 3DV (2018)
5. Chen, W., Fu, Z., Yang, D., Deng, J.: Single-image depth perception in the wild. In: NIPS (2016)
6. Chen, Z., Badrinarayanan, V., Lee, C.Y., Rabinovich, A.: GradNorm: gradient normalization for adaptive loss balancing in deep multitask networks. In: ICML (2018)
7. Delage, E., Lee, H., Ng, A.Y.: A dynamic Bayesian network model for autonomous 3D reconstruction from a single indoor image. In: CVPR (2006)
8. Eigen, D., Fergus, R.: Predicting depth, surface normals and semantic labels with a common multi-scale convolutional architecture. In: ICCV (2015)
9. Eigen, D., Puhrsch, C., Fergus, R.: Depth map prediction from a single image using a multi-scale deep network. In: NIPS (2014)
10. Fu, H., Gong, M., Wang, C., Batmanghelich, K., Tao, D.: Deep ordinal regression network for monocular depth estimation. In: CVPR (2018)

11. Geiger, A., Lenz, P., Stiller, C., Urtasun, R.: Vision meets robotics: the KITTI dataset. Int. J. Robot. Res. **32**(11), 1231–1237 (2013)
12. Godard, C., Aodha, O.M., Brostow, G.J.: Unsupervised monocular depth estimation with left-right consistency. In: CVPR (2017)
13. Gupta, A., Efros, A.A., Hebert, M.: Blocks world revisited: image understanding using qualitative geometry and mechanics. In: Daniilidis, K., Maragos, P., Paragios, N. (eds.) ECCV 2010. LNCS, vol. 6314, pp. 482–496. Springer, Heidelberg (2010). https://doi.org/10.1007/978-3-642-15561-1_35
14. He, K., Zhang, X., Ren, S., Sun, J.: Deep residual learning for image recognition. In: CVPR (2016)
15. Heo, M., Lee, J., Kim, K.-R., Kim, H.-U., Kim, C.-S.: Monocular depth estimation using whole strip masking and reliability-based refinement. In: Ferrari, V., Hebert, M., Sminchisescu, C., Weiss, Y. (eds.) ECCV 2018. LNCS, vol. 11208, pp. 39–55. Springer, Cham (2018). https://doi.org/10.1007/978-3-030-01225-0_3
16. Hu, J., Ozay, M., Zhang, Y., Okatani, T.: Revisiting single image depth estimation: toward higher resolution maps with accurate object boundaries. In: WACV (2019)
17. Hu, J., Shen, L., Sun, G.: Squeeze-and-excitation networks. In: CVPR (2018)
18. Huang, G., Liu, Z., van der Maaten, L.: Densely connected convolutional networks. In: CVPR (2017)
19. Jiao, J., Cao, Y., Song, Y., Lau, R.: Look deeper into depth: monocular depth estimation with semantic booster and attention-driven loss. In: Ferrari, V., Hebert, M., Sminchisescu, C., Weiss, Y. (eds.) ECCV 2018. LNCS, vol. 11219, pp. 55–71. Springer, Cham (2018). https://doi.org/10.1007/978-3-030-01267-0_4
20. Karsch, K., Liu, C., Kang, S.B.: Depth transfer: depth extraction from video using non-parametric sampling. IEEE Trans. Pattern Anal. Mach. Intell. **36**(11), 2144–2158 (2014)
21. Kendall, A., Gal, Y., Cipolla, R.: Multi-task learning using uncertainty to weigh losses for scene geometry and semantics. In: CVPR (2018)
22. Kim, S., Park, K., Sohn, K., Lin, S.: Unified depth prediction and intrinsic image decomposition from a single image via joint convolutional neural fields. In: Leibe, B., Matas, J., Sebe, N., Welling, M. (eds.) ECCV 2016. LNCS, vol. 9912, pp. 143–159. Springer, Cham (2016). https://doi.org/10.1007/978-3-319-46484-8_9
23. Kingma, D.P., Ba, J.: Adam: a method for stochastic optimization. In: ICLR (2015)
24. Kundu, J.N., Uppala, P.K., Pahuja, A., Babu, R.V.: AdaDepth: unsupervised content congruent adaptation for depth estimation. In: CVPR (2018)
25. Laina, I., Rupprecht, C., Belagiannis, V., Tombari, F., Navab, N.: Deeper depth prediction with fully convolutional residual networks. In: 3DV (2016)
26. Lee, D.C., Gupta, A., Hebert, M., Kanade, T.: Estimating spatial layout of rooms using volumetric reasoning about objects and surfaces. In: NIPS (2010)
27. Lee, J.H., Heo, M., Kim, K.R., Kim, C.S.: Single-image depth estimation based on Fourier domain analysis. In: CVPR (2018)
28. Lee, J.H., Kim, C.S.: Monocular depth estimation using relative depth maps. In: CVPR (2019)
29. Levin, A., Lischinski, D., Weiss, Y.: Colorization using optimization. ACM Trans. Graph. **23**(3), 689–694 (2004)
30. li, B., Dai, Y., He, M.: Monocular depth estimation with hierarchical fusion of dilated CNNs and soft-weighted-sum inference. Pattern Recognit. **83**, 328–339 (2018)
31. Li, B., Shen, C., Dai, Y., van den Hengel, A., He, M.: Depth and surface normal estimation from monocular images using regression on deep features and hierarchical CRFs. In: CVPR (2015)

32. Lim, K., Shin, N.H., Lee, Y.Y., Kim, C.S.: Order learning and its application to age estimation. In: ICLR (2020)
33. Liu, C., et al.: Progressive neural architecture search. In: Ferrari, V., Hebert, M., Sminchisescu, C., Weiss, Y. (eds.) ECCV 2018. LNCS, vol. 11205, pp. 19–35. Springer, Cham (2018). https://doi.org/10.1007/978-3-030-01246-5_2
34. Liu, F., Shen, C., Lin, G., Reid, I.: Learning depth from single monocular images using deep convolutional neural fields. IEEE Trans. Pattern Anal. Mach. Intell. **38**(10), 2024–2039 (2016)
35. Ma, F., Karaman, S.: Sparse-to-Dense: depth prediction from sparse depth samples and a single image. In: ICRA (2018)
36. Mousavian, A., Pirsiavash, H.: Joint semantic segmentation and depth estimation with deep convolutional networks. In: 3DV (2016)
37. Qi, X., Liao, R., Liu, Z., Urtasun, R., Jia, J.: GeoNet: geometric neural network for joint depth and surface normal estimation. In: CVPR (2018)
38. Rajagopalan, A., Chaudhuri, S., Mudenagudi, U.: Depth estimation and image restoration using defocused stereo pairs. IEEE Trans. Pattern Anal. Mach. Intell. **26**(11), 1521–1525 (2004)
39. Saxena, A., Sun, M., Ng, A.Y.: Make3D: learning 3-D scene structure from a single still image. IEEE Trans. Pattern Anal. Mach. Intell. **31**(5), 824–840 (2009)
40. Sener, O., Koltun, V.: Multi-task learning as multi-objective optimization. In: NIPS (2018)
41. Silberman, N., Hoiem, D., Kohli, P., Fergus, R.: Indoor segmentation and support inference from RGBD images. In: Fitzgibbon, A., Lazebnik, S., Perona, P., Sato, Y., Schmid, C. (eds.) ECCV 2012. LNCS, vol. 7576, pp. 746–760. Springer, Heidelberg (2012). https://doi.org/10.1007/978-3-642-33715-4_54
42. Simonyan, K., Zisserman, A.: Very deep convolutional networks for large-scale image recognition. In: ICLR (2015)
43. Song, S., Lichtenberg, S.P., Xiao, J.: SUN RGB-D: a RGB-D scene understanding benchmark suite. In: CVPR (2015)
44. Wedel, A., Franke, U., Klappstein, J., Brox, T., Cremers, D.: Realtime depth estimation and obstacle detection from monocular video. In: Franke, K., Müller, K.-R., Nickolay, B., Schäfer, R. (eds.) DAGM 2006. LNCS, vol. 4174, pp. 475–484. Springer, Heidelberg (2006). https://doi.org/10.1007/11861898_48
45. Xian, K., Shen, C., Cao, Z., Lu, H., Xiao, Y.: Monocular relative depth perception with web stereo data supervision. In: CVPR (2018)
46. Xu, D., Ricci, E., Ouyang, W., Wang, X., Sebe, N.: Multi-scale continuous CRFs as sequential deep networks for monocular depth estimation. In: CVPR (2017)
47. Yang, J., Price, B., Cohen, S.: Object contour detection with a fully convolutional encoder-decoder network. In: CVPR (2016)
48. Yin, Z., Shi, J.: GeoNet: unsupervised learning of dense depth, optical flow and camera pose. In: CVPR (2018)
49. Zhang, Y., Funkhouser, T.: Deep depth completion of a single RGB-D image. In: CVPR (2018)
50. Zhang, Z., Cui, Z., Xu, C.: Pattern-affinitive propagation across depth, surface normal and semantic segmentation. In: CVPR (2019)
51. Zhang, Z., Cui, Z., Xu, C., Jie, Z., Li, X., Yang, J.: Joint task-recursive learning for semantic segmentation and depth estimation. In: Ferrari, V., Hebert, M., Sminchisescu, C., Weiss, Y. (eds.) ECCV 2018. LNCS, vol. 11214, pp. 238–255. Springer, Cham (2018). https://doi.org/10.1007/978-3-030-01249-6_15
52. Zoran, D., Isola, P., Krishnan, D., Freeman, W.T.: Learning ordinal relationships for mid-level vision. In: ICCV (2015)

Author Index

Aldea, Emanuel   105
Arora, Chetan   399
Aubry, Mathieu   574
Avidan, Shai   699
Ayzik, Sharon   699

Bai, Shuai   1
Barnes, Connelly   156
Barnes, Nick   349
Bhattacharya, Nilavra   417
Bian, Kaigui   469
Bloch, Isabelle   105
Bursuc, Andrei   105

Camps, Octavia   609
Carpentier, Justin   574
Chen, Hung-Jen   18
Chen, Terrence   768
Chen, Wanli   52
Chen, Xinyun   122
Cheng, Guangliang   435
Cheng, Xi   265
Cholakkal, Hisham   88
Costain, Theo W.   383

Davis, Larry   734
Devaranjan, Jeevan   715
Dhawan, Pranaab   453
Dubuisson, Séverine   105

Eboli, Thomas   314
Efros, Alexei A.   156
Elhamifar, Ehsan   557
Esser, Patrick   647

Fan, Junsong   332
Fidler, Sanja   715, 751
Fouhey, David F.   522
Franchi, Gianni   105
Fu, Zhenyong   265
Fukumizu, Kenji   626

Gan, Weihao   1
Gao, Jun   751

Gennari do Nascimento, Marcelo   383
Georgakis, Georgios   768
Guan, Yushuo   469
Guo, Guodong   34
Gurari, Danna   417

Hachiya, Hirotaka   626
He, Junjun   52
Heo, Yuk   297
Hilliges, Otmar   211
Hu, Hanzhe   1
Hu, Rui   453
Huang, Huaiyi   139
Huang, Qingqiu   139
Huang, Tairan   122
Huynh, Dat   557

Iqbal, Umar   211

J. Crandall, David   229
Ji, Deyi   1
Jiao, Jianbo   504
Jun Koh, Yeong   297

Kahr, Patrick   281
Kar, Amlan   715, 751
Karanam, Srikrishna   768
Kautz, Jan   211
Kim, Chang-Su   297, 785
Košecká, Jana   768

Labbé, Yann   574
Lee, Jae-Han   785
Li, Gongyang   665
Li, Ren   768
Li, Ruiyu   52
Li, Xia   435
Li, Xiangtai   435
Li, Xilai   70
Lin, Dahua   139
Lin, Zhe   156
Lin, Zhouchen   435
Ling, Haibin   665

Liu, Aishan 122
Liu, Jerry 453
Liu, Lijie 540
Liu, Xianglong 122
Liu, Yun-Hui 504
Liu, Zhi 665
Lu, Huiao-Han 18
Lu, Jingwan 156
Lu, Jiwen 540
Lu, Yu 34
Luo, Jiebo 229
Lüthi, Marcel 281

Ma, Chao 367
Ma, Liqian 156
Ma, Wei-Chiu 453
Ma, Yuqing 122
Ma, Zhanyu 34
Madsen, Dennis 281
Mahalanobis, Abhijit 485
Marlet, Renaud 192
Maybank, Stephen J. 122
Molchanov, Pavlo 211
Morel-Forster, Andreas 281
Muhammad Anwer, Rao 88

Nakamura, Takuma 626
Nigam, Aditya 399

Ommer, Björn 647

Pang, Yanwei 88
Patel, Vishal M. 682
Peng, Kuan-Chuan 485
Perera, Pramuditha 682
Ponce, Jean 314
Prisacariu, Victor Adrian 383

Rahbani, Dana 281
Rockwell, Chris 522
Rombach, Robin 647
Rui Tam, Zhi 18

Saito, Yuki 626
Shah, Meet 453
Shah, Mubarak 88
Shahbaz Khan, Fahad 88
Shao, Ling 88, 229
Shao, Rui 682

Shen, Jianbing 229
Shen, Tianchang 751
Shen, Xiaoyong 52
Shen, Yujun 592
Shi, Jianping 435
Shrivastava, Abhinav 734
Shuai, Hong-Han 18
Singh, Rajat Vikram 485
Sivic, Josef 574
Song, Yibing 367
Song, Yun-Zhu 18
Spurr, Adrian 211
Sun, Jian 314
Sun, Ruoqi 52
Sun, Wei 70
Sznaier, Mario 609

Taha, Ahmed 734
Tan, Shaohua 435
Tan, Tieniu 332
Tang, Jian 469
Tao, Dacheng 122
Thapar, Daksh 399
Tian, Qi 540
Tong, Yunhai 435

Urtasun, Raquel 453

Venkataramanan, Shashanka 485
Vetter, Thomas 281

Wang, Bingxuan 469
Wang, Hai 248
Wang, Jiangliu 504
Wang, Shenlong 453
Wang, Yang 665
Wang, Yin 609
Wang, Yinglong 367
Wei, Fangyun 174
Wu, Chufan 540
Wu, Ming 34
Wu, Tianfu 70
Wu, Tianyi 34
Wu, Tong 139
Wu, Wei 1
Wu, Ziyan 768

Xiao, Yang 192
Xie, Jianwen 349
Xie, Jin 88

Xie, Lingxi   540
Xu, Yitao   122

Yan, Junjie   1
Yang, Jian   265
Yang, Lei   139
Yang, Xiao   174
Yang, Xitong   734
Yao, Cong   469
Ye, Linwei   665
Ye, Mang   229
Yingbiao, Ling   248
Yu, Bei   52
Yuen, Pong C.   682

Zeng, Bing   367
Zhang, Chuang   34

Zhang, Hongyang   174
Zhang, Jing   349
Zhang, Li   435
Zhang, Meng   417
Zhang, Yuanxing   469
Zhang, Yuexi   609
Zhang, Zhaoxiang   332
Zhao, Deli   592
Zhao, Pengyu   469
Zhao, Yinan   417
Zheng, Wei-shi   248
Zhou, Bolei   592
Zhou, Jie   540
Zhu, Jiapeng   592
Zhu, Jun   174
Zhu, Xinge   52
Zhu, Yu   34

T0189330

Printed in the United States
By Bookmasters